June 13–15, 2015
Portland, OR, USA

I0047356

Association for Computing Machinery

Advancing Computing as a Science & Profession

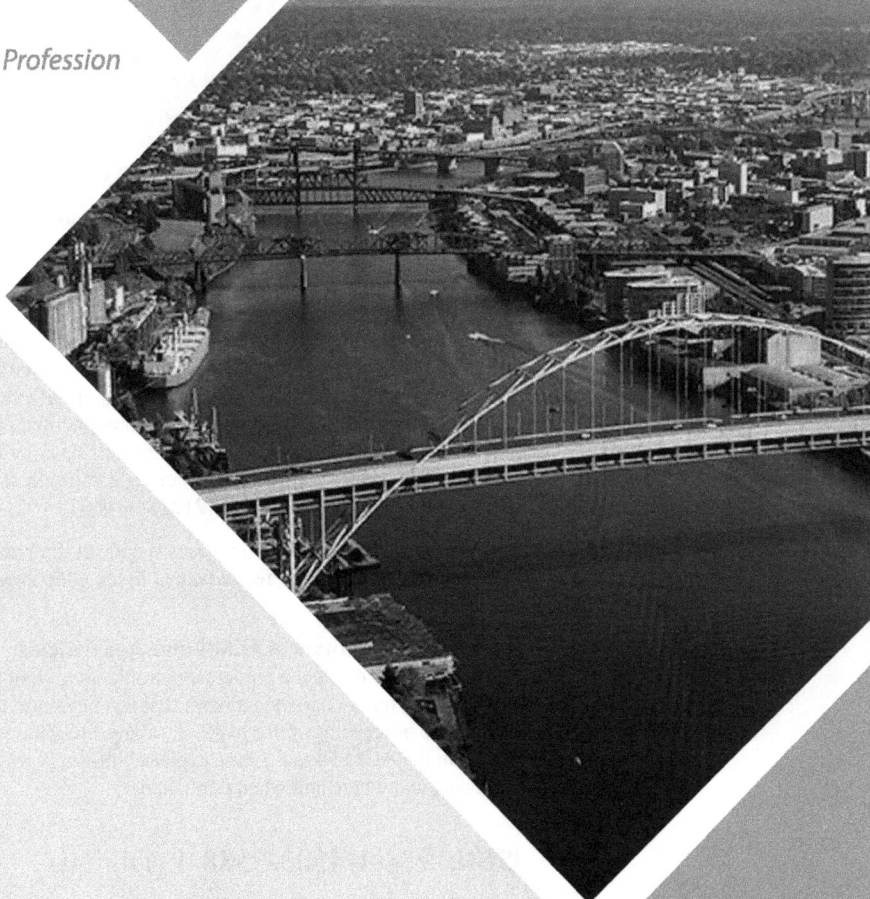

SPAA'15

Proceedings of the 27th ACM
Symposium on Parallelism in Algorithms and Architectures

Sponsored by:
ACM SIGACT and ACM SIGARCH

Supported by:
Akamai, Oracle Labs, and Intel Labs

**Association for
Computing Machinery**

Advancing Computing as a Science & Profession

ISBN: 978-1-4503-3588-1 (Digital)

ISBN: 978-1-4503-3875-2 (Print)

Additional copies may be ordered prepaid from:

ACM Order Department
PO Box 30777
New York, NY 10087-0777, USA

Phone: 1-800-342-6626 (USA and Canada)
+1-212-626-0500 (Global)
Fax: +1-212-944-1318
E-mail: acmhelp@acm.org
Hours of Operation: 8:30 am – 4:30 pm ET

Printed in the USA

Foreword

This volume consists of papers that were presented at the 27th ACM Symposium on Parallelism in Algorithms and Architectures (SPAA 2015) held on 13–15 June 2015, in Portland, Oregon, USA, as part of Federated Computing Research Conference (FCRC 2015). SPAA 2015 was sponsored by the ACM Special Interest Groups on Algorithms and Computation Theory (SIGACT) and Computer Architecture (SIGARCH) and organized in cooperation with the European Association for Theoretical Computer Science (EATCS). Financial support was provided by Akamai, Oracle Labs, and Intel Labs.

We received a total of 131 submissions and the program committee selected 31 papers for full presentation. Of these papers, "Speed Scaling in the Non-clairvoyant Model" by Yossi Azar, Nikhil Devanur, Zhiyi Huang, and Debmalya Panigrahi was selected to receive the Best Paper Award. In addition, the PC selected 11 papers to be presented as brief announcements. Finally, this year's program also included two invited talks: "Myths and Misconceptions about Threads" by Hans-J Boehm and "The Revolution in Graph Theoretic Optimization Problems" by Gary Miller.

The mix of selected papers reflects the unique nature of SPAA in bringing together the theory and practice of parallel computing. SPAA defines parallelism broadly to encompass any computational device or scheme that can perform multiple operations or tasks simultaneously or concurrently. The technical papers in this volume are to be considered preliminary versions, and authors are generally expected to publish polished and complete versions in archival scientific journals. The committee's decisions in accepting brief announcements were based on the perceived interest of these contributions, with the goal that they serve as bases for further significant advances in parallel computing. Extended versions of the SPAA brief announcements may be published later in other conferences or journals.

The reviewing process consisted of multiple steps. Each paper received a minimum of 3 reviews in the initial phase. After this phase, the authors were given a chance to reply to the reviews during a 2-day rebuttal period. After all the rebuttals were received, there was extensive online discussion of the papers over a period of a week and additional reviews were solicited for some papers. The final decisions were made during a phone meeting on March 10.

We would like to thank the program committee as well as the external reviewers for their help during the review and paper selection process. Last, but not least, we want to thank all the authors who submitted papers. The authors, the external reviewers, and the program committee together made it possible to select a great collection of papers for the conference.

Kunal Agrawal
Washington University in St. Louis
SPAA 2015 Program Chair

Guy Blelloch
Carnegie Mellon University
SPAA 2015 General Chair

Table of Contents

Session 4: Tools
Session Chair: Michael Spear *(Lehigh University)*

Session 5: Scheduling
Session Chair: Tao Schardl *(Massachusetts Institute of Technology)*

SPAA 2015 Symposium Organization

General Chair: Guy Blelloch (Carnegie Mellon University, USA)

Program Chair: Kunal Agrawal (Washington University in St. Louis, USA)

Program Committee: Umut Acar (Carnegie Mellon University, USA)
Grey Ballard (Sandia National Labs, USA)
Petra Berenbrink (Simon Fraser University, Canada)
Dave Dice (Oracle Labs, USA)
Jeremy Fineman (Georgetown University, USA)
Pierre Fraigniaud (University of Paris-Sud, France)
Seth Gilbert (National University of Singapore, Singapore)
Rachid Guerraoui (EPFL, Switzerland)
MohammadTaghi HajiAghayi (University of Maryland, USA)
Maurice Herlihy (Brown University, USA)
Martin Hoefer (MPI Saarbrücken, Germany)
Peter Kling (University of Pittsburgh, USA)
Bradley Kuzsmaul (Massachusetts Institute of Technology, USA)
Angelina Lee (Washington University in St. Louis, USA)
Ryan Newton (Indiana University, USA)
Gopal Pandurangan (University of Houston, USA)
Michael Spear (Lehigh University, USA)
Cliff Stein (Columbia University, USA)
Kanat Tangwongsan (Mahidol University, Thailand)
Sivan Toledo (Tel Aviv University, Israel)
Uzi Vishkin (University of Maryland, USA)

Publicity Chair: Jeremy Fineman (Georgetown University, USA)

Treasurer: David Bunde (Knox College, USA)

Secretary: Christian Scheideler (University of Paderborn, Germany)

Steering Committee: Guy Blelloch (Carnegie Mellon University, USA)
David Culler (University of California, Berkeley, USA)
Frank Dehne (Carleton University, Canada)
Pierre Fraigniaud (University of Paris-Sud, France)
Phil Gibbons (Intel Research, USA)
Maurice Herlihy (Brown University, USA)
Tom Leighton (MIT and Akamai Technologies, USA)
Charles Leiserson (Massachusetts Institute of Technology, USA)
Fabrizio Luccio (University of Pisa, Italy)
Friedhelm Meyer auf der Heide (University of Paderborn, Germany)
Gary Miller (Carnegie Mellon University, USA)
Burkhard Monien (University of Paderborn, Germany)
Franco Preparata (Brown University, USA)

Steering Committee (continued): Vijaya Ramachandran (University of Texas, Austin, USA)
Arnold Rosenberg (University of Massachusetts, Amherst, USA)
Paul Spirakis (CTI, Greece)
Uzi Vishkin (University of Maryland, USA)

Additional Reviewers:

Fidaa Abed
Michael Anderson
Antonios Antoniadis
John Augustine
Rachata Ausavarungnirun
Oana Balmau
Scott Beamer
Michael Bender
Austin Benson
Aaron Bernstein
Mohammad Slim Bouguerra
Rezaul Chowdhury
Andrew Davidson
Sina Dehghani
Pawel Dlotko
Soheil Ehsani
Yousef El-Kurdi
Leah Epstein
Hossein Esfandiari
David Moises Fernandez
Dimitris Fotakis
Tom Friedetzky
Nick Harvey
Derek Juba
Tim Kaler
Shahin Kamali
Maleq Khan
Rohit Khandekar
Reza Khani
Nicholas Knight
Bojana Kodric
Justin Kopinsky
Guy Kortsarz
Ravi Kumar
Silvio Lattanzi
William Leiserson
Christoph Lenzen
Peng Li
Frederik Mallmann
Euripides Markou
Russell Martin
Kevin Matulef

Morteza Monemizadeh
Ehab Morsy
Benjamin Moseley
Viswanath Nagarajan
Lars Nagel
Danupon Nanongkai
Rupesh Nasre.
Calvin Newport
Krzysztof Onak
Dominik Pajak
Debmalya Panigrahi
Ali Pinar
Bogdan Prisacari
Kirk Pruhs
Manish Purohit
Harald Räcke
Vijay Reddi
Peter Robinson
Barna Saha
Kanthi Sarpatwar
Thomas Sauerwald
Anshul Sawant
Tao Schardl
Christian Scheideler
Scott Schneider
Oded Schwartz
Michele Scquizzato
Saeed Seddighin
Hadas Shachnai
Don Sheehy
Harsha Vardhan Simhadri
Edgar Solomonik
Hsin-Hao Su
Tim Suess
Amitabh Trehan
David Wagner
Joel Wolf
Maxwell Young
Igor Zablotchi
Morteza Zadimoghaddam
Uri Zwick

SPAA 2015 Sponsors & Supporters

Sponsors:

Supporters:

Oracle Labs

Sorting with Asymmetric Read and Write Costs

Guy E. Blelloch
Carnegie Mellon University
guyb@cs.cmu.edu

Jeremy T. Fineman
Georgetown University
jfineman@cs.georgetown.edu

Phillip B. Gibbons
Intel Labs & CMU
gibbons@cs.cmu.edu

Yan Gu
Carnegie Mellon University
yan.gu@cs.cmu.edu

Julian Shun
Carnegie Mellon University
jshun@cs.cmu.edu

ABSTRACT

Emerging memory technologies have a significant gap between the cost, both in time and in energy, of writing to memory versus reading from memory. In this paper we present models and algorithms that account for this difference, with a focus on write-efficient sorting algorithms. First, we consider the PRAM model with asymmetric write cost, and show that sorting can be performed in $O(n)$ writes, $O(n \log n)$ reads, and logarithmic depth (parallel time). Next, we consider a variant of the External Memory (EM) model that charges $k > 1$ for writing a block of size B to the secondary memory, and present variants of three EM sorting algorithms (multi-way merge-sort, sample sort, and heapsort using buffer trees) that asymptotically reduce the number of writes over the original algorithms, and perform roughly k block reads for every block write. Finally, we define a variant of the Ideal-Cache model with asymmetric write costs, and present write-efficient, cache-oblivious parallel algorithms for sorting, FFTs, and matrix multiplication. Adapting prior bounds for work-stealing and parallel-depth-first schedulers to the asymmetric setting, these yield parallel cache complexity bounds for machines with private caches or with a shared cache, respectively.

Categories and Subject Descriptors

F.2.2 [**Analysis of Algorithms and Problem Complexity**]: Non-numerical Algorithms and Problems—*Sorting and searching*

Keywords

Sorting, asymmetric read-write costs, non-volatile memory, persistent memory, write-efficient, write-avoiding, parallel algorithms, cache-oblivious algorithms, external memory model, mergesort, sample sort, I/O buffer tree, FFT, matrix multiplication.

1. INTRODUCTION

Emerging nonvolatile/persistent memory (NVM) technologies such as Phase-Change Memory (PCM), Spin-Torque Transfer Magnetic RAM (STT-RAM), and Memristor-based Resistive RAM (ReRAM) offer the promise of significantly lower energy and higher density (bits per area) than DRAM. With byte-addressability and

read latencies approaching or improving on DRAM speeds, these NVM technologies are projected to become the dominant memory within the decade [27, 40], as manufacturing improves and costs decrease.

Although these NVMs could be viewed as just a layer in the memory hierarchy that provides persistence, there is one important distinction: *Writes are significantly more costly than reads,* suffering from higher latency, lower per-chip bandwidth, higher energy costs, and endurance problems (a cell wears out after 10^8–10^{12} writes [27]). Thus, unlike DRAM, there is a significant (often an order of magnitude or more) asymmetry between read and write costs [3, 6, 16, 17, 23, 25, 31, 38], motivating the study of *write-efficient* (*write-limited*, *write-avoiding*) algorithms, which reduce the number of writes relative to existing algorithms.

Related Work. While read-write asymmetry in NVMs has been the focus of many systems efforts [13, 26, 39, 41, 42], there have been very few papers addressing this from the algorithmic perspective. Reducing the number of writes has long been a goal in disk arrays, distributed systems, cache-coherent multiprocessors, and the like, but that work has not focused on NVMs and the solutions are not suitable for their properties. Several papers [7, 18, 21, 28, 30, 36] have looked at read-write asymmetries in the context of NAND flash memory. This work has focused on (i) the fact that in NAND flash chips, bits can only be cleared by incurring the overhead of erasing a large block of memory, and/or (ii) avoiding individual cell wear out. Eppstein et al. [18], for example, presented a novel cuckoo hashing algorithm that chooses where to insert/reinsert each item based on the number of writes to date for the cells it hashes to. Emerging NVMs, in contrast, do not suffer from (i) because they can write arbitrary bytes in-place. As for (ii), we choose not to focus on wear out (beyond reducing the total number of writes to all of memory) because system software (e.g., the garbage collector, virtual memory manager, or virtual machine hypervisor) can readily balance application writes across the physical memory over the long time horizons (many orders of magnitude longer than NAND Flash) before an individual cell would wear out from too many writes to it.

A few prior works [12, 36, 37] have looked at algorithms for asymmetric read-write costs in emerging NVMs, in the context of databases. Chen et al. [12] presented analytical formulas for PCM latency and energy, as well as algorithms for B-trees and hash joins that are tuned for PCM. For example, their B-tree variant does not sort the keys in a leaf node nor repack a leaf after a deleted key, thereby avoiding the write cost of sorting and repacking, at the expense of additional reads when searching. Similarly, Viglas [37] traded off fewer writes for additional reads by rebalancing a B^+-tree only if the cost of rebalancing has been amortized. Viglas [36] presented several "write-limited" sorting and join algorithms within the context of database query processing.

Our Results. In this paper, we seek to systematically study algorithms under asymmetric read and write costs. We consider natural extensions to the RAM/PRAM models, to the External Memory model, and to the Ideal-Cache model to incorporate an integer cost, $k > 1$, for writes relative to reads. We focus primarily on sorting algorithms, given their fundamental role in computing and as building blocks for other problems, especially in the External Memory and Parallel settings—but we also consider additional problems.

We first observe that in the RAM model, it is well known that sorting by inserting each key into a balanced search tree requires only $O(n)$ writes with no increase in reads ($O(n \log n)$). Applying this idea to a carefully-tuned sort for the asymmetric CRCW PRAM yields a parallel sort with $O(n)$ writes, $O(n \log n)$ reads and $O(k \log n)$ depth (with high probability[1]).

Next, we consider an Asymmetric External Memory (AEM) model, which has a small primary memory (cache) of size M and transfers data in blocks of size B to (at a cost of k) and from (at unit cost) an unbounded external memory. We show that three asymptotically-optimal EM sorting algorithms can each be adapted to the AEM with reduced write costs. First, following [30, 36], we adapt multi-way mergesort by merging kM/B sorted runs at a time (instead of M/B as in the original EM version). This change saves writes by reducing the depth of the recursion. Each merge makes k passes over the runs, using an in-memory heap to extract values for the output run for the pass. Our algorithm and analysis is somewhat simpler than [30, 36]. Second, we present an AEM sample sort algorithm that uses kM/B splitters at each level of recursion (instead of M/B in the original EM version). Again, the challenge is to both find the splitters and partition using them while incurring only $O(N/B)$ writes across each level of recursion. We also show how this algorithm can be parallelized to run with linear speedup on the Asymmetric Private-Cache model (Section 2) with $p = n/M$ processors. Finally, our third sorting algorithm is an AEM heapsort using a buffer-tree-based priority queue. Compared to the original EM algorithm, both our buffer-tree nodes and the number of elements stored outside the buffer tree are larger by a factor of k, which adds nontrivial changes to the data structure. All three sorting algorithms have the same asymptotic complexity on the AEM.

Finally, we define an Asymmetric Ideal-Cache model, which is similar to the AEM model in terms of M and B and having asymmetric read/write costs, but uses an asymmetric ideal replacement policy instead of algorithm-specified transfers. We extend important results for the Ideal-Cache model and thread schedulers to the asymmetric case—namely, the Asymmetric Ideal-Cache can be (constant factor) approximated by an asymmetric-LRU cache, and it can be used in conjunction with a work-stealing (parallel-depth-first) scheduler to obtain good parallel cache complexity bounds for machines with private caches (a shared cache, respectively). We use this model to design write-efficient cache-oblivious algorithms for sorting, Fast Fourier Transform, and matrix multiplication. Our sorting algorithm is adapted from [9], and again deals with the challenges of reducing the number of writes. All three algorithms use $\Theta(k)$ times more reads than writes and have good parallelism.

2. PRELIMINARIES AND MODELS

This section presents background material on NVMs and models, as well as new (asymmetric cost) models and results relating models. We first consider models whose parallelism is in the parallel transfer of the data in a larger block, then consider models with parallel processors.

Emerging NVMs. While DRAM stores data in capacitors that typically require refreshing every few milliseconds, and hence must be continuously powered, emerging NVM technologies store data as "states" of the given material that require no external power to retain. Energy is required only to read the cell or change its value (i.e., its state). While there is no significant cost difference between reading and writing DRAM (each DRAM read of a location not currently buffered requires a write of the DRAM row being evicted, and hence is also a write), emerging NVMs such as Phase-Change Memory (PCM), Spin-Torque Transfer Magnetic RAM (STT-RAM), and Memristor-based Resistive RAM (ReRAM) each incur significantly higher cost for writing than reading. This large gap seems fundamental to the technologies themselves: to change the physical state of a material requires relatively significant energy for a sufficient duration, whereas reading the current state can be done quickly and, to ensure the state is left unchanged, with low energy. An STT-RAM cell, for example, can be read in $0.14\ ns$ but uses a $10\ ns$ writing pulse duration, using roughly 10^{-15} joules to read versus 10^{-12} joules to write [17] (these are the raw numbers at the materials level). A Memristor ReRAM cell uses a $100\ ns$ write pulse duration, and an 8MB Memrister ReRAM chip is projected to have reads with $1.7\ ns$ latency and $0.2\ nJ$ energy versus writes with $200\ ns$ latency and $25\ nJ$ energy [38]—over two orders of magnitude differences in latency and energy. PCM is the most mature of the three technologies, and early generations are already available as I/O devices. A recent paper [25] reported $6.7\ \mu s$ latency for a 4KB read and 128 μs latency for a 4KB write. Another reported that the sector I/O latency and bandwidth for random 512B writes was a factor of 15 worse than for reads [23]. As a future memory/cache replacement, a 512Mb PCM memory chip is projected to have $16\ ns$ byte reads versus $416\ ns$ byte writes, and writes to a 16MB PCM L3 cache are projected to be up to 40 times slower and use 17 times more energy than reads [16]. While these numbers are speculative and subject to change as the new technologies emerge over time, there seems to be sufficient evidence that writes will be considerably more costly than reads in these NVMs.

Sorting. The sorting problem we consider is the standard comparison based sorting with n records each containing a key. We assume the input is in an unsorted array, and the output needs to be placed into a sorted array. Without loss of generality, we assume the keys are unique (a position index can always be added to make them unique).

The Asymmetric RAM model. This is the standard RAM model but with a cost $k > 1$ for writes, while reads are still unit cost.

The (Asymmetric) External Memory model. The widely studied External Memory (EM) model [2] (also called I/O model, Disk Model and Disk Access Model) assumes a two level memory hierarchy with a fixed size primary memory (cache) of size M and a secondary memory of unbounded size. Both are partitioned into blocks of size B. Standard RAM instructions can be used within the primary memory, and in addition the model has two special *memory transfer* instructions: a *read* transfers (alternatively, copies) an arbitrary block from secondary memory to primary memory, and a *write* transfers an arbitrary block from primary to secondary memory. The I/O complexity of an algorithm is the total number of memory transfers. Sorting n records can be performed in the EM model with I/O complexity

$$\Theta\left(\frac{n}{B} \log_{\frac{M}{B}} \frac{n}{B}\right) \tag{1}$$

---

[1] *With high probability (w.h.p.)* means with probability $1 - n^{-c}$, for a constant c.

This is both an upper and lower bound [2]. The upper bound can be achieved with at least three different algorithms, a multi-way mergesort [2], a distribution sort [2], and a priority-queue (heap) sort based on buffer trees [4].

The *Asymmetric External Memory* (AEM) model simply adds a parameter k to the EM model, and charges this for each write of a block. Reading a block still has unit cost.

Throughout the paper, we assume that M and B are measured in terms of the number of data objects. If we are sorting, for example, it is the number records. We assume that the memory has an extra $O(\log M)$ locations just for storing a stack to compute with.

The (Asymmetric) Ideal-Cache model. The Ideal-Cache model [20] is a variant of the EM model. The machine model is still organized in the same way with two memories each partitioned into blocks, but there are no explicit memory transfer instructions. Instead all addressable memory is in the secondary memory, but any subset of up to M/B of the blocks can have a copy resident in the primary memory (cache). Any reference to a resident block is a *cache hit* and is free. Any reference to a word in a block that is not resident is a *cache miss* and requires a memory transfer from the secondary memory. The cache miss can replace a block in the cache with the loaded block, which might require *evicting* a cache block. The model makes the *tall cache assumption* where $M = \Omega(B^2)$, which is easily met in practice. The I/O or *cache complexity* of an algorithm is the number of cache misses. An optimal (offline) cache eviction policy is assumed—i.e., one that minimizes the I/O complexity. It is well known that the optimal policy can be approximated using the online least recently used (LRU) policy at a cost of at most doubling the number of misses, and doubling the cache size [35].

The main purpose of the Ideal-Cache model is for the design of *cache-oblivious algorithms*. These are algorithms that do not use the parameters M and B in their design, but for which one can still derive effective bounds on I/O complexity. This has the advantage that the algorithms work well for any cache sizes on any cache hierarchies. The I/O complexity of cache-oblivious sorting is asymptotically the same as for the EM model.

We define the *Asymmetric Ideal-Cache* model by distinguishing reads from writes, as follows. A cache block is *dirty* if the version in the cache has been modified since it was brought into the cache, and *clean* otherwise. When a cache miss evicts a clean block the cost is 1, but when evicting a dirty block the cost is $1 + k$, 1 for the read and k for the write. Again, we assume an ideal offline cache replacement policy—i.e., minimizing the total I/O cost. Under this model we note that the LRU policy is no longer 2-competitive. However, the following variant is competitive within a constant factor. The idea is to separately maintain two equal-sized pools of blocks in the cache (primary memory), a read pool and a write pool. When reading a location, (i) if its block is in the read pool we just read the value, (ii) if it is in the write pool we copy the block to the read pool, or (iii) if it is in neither, we read the block from secondary memory into the read pool. In the latter two cases we evict the LRU block from the read pool if it is full, with cost 1. The rules for the write pool are symmetric when writing to a memory location, but the eviction has cost $k + 1$ because the block is dirty. We call this the read-write LRU policy. This policy is competitive with the optimal offline policy:

LEMMA 2.1. *For any sequence S of instructions, if it has cost $Q_I(S)$ on the Asymmetric Ideal-Cache model with cache size M_I, then it will have cost*

$$Q_L(S) \le \frac{M_L}{(M_L - M_I)} Q_I(S) + (1+k)M_I/B$$

on an asymmetric cache with read-write LRU policy and cache sizes (read and write pools) M_L.

PROOF. Partition the sequence of instructions into regions that contain memory reads to exactly M_L/B distinct memory blocks each (except perhaps the last). Each region will require at most M_L/B misses under LRU. Each will also require at least $(M_L - M_I)/B$ cache misses on the ideal cache since at most M_I/B blocks can be in the cache at the start of the region. The same argument can be made for writes, but in this case each operation involves evicting a dirty block. The $(1 + k)M_I/B$ is for the last region. To account for the last region, in the worst case at the start of the last write region the ideal cache starts with M_I/B blocks which get written to, while the LRU starts with none of those blocks. The LRU therefore invokes an addition M_I/B write misses each costing $1 + k$ (1 for the load and k for the eviction). Note that if the cache starts empty then we do not have to add this term since an equal amount will be saved in the first round. $\square$

The Asymmetric PRAM model. In the *Asymmetric PRAM*, the standard PRAM is augmented such that each write costs k and all other instructions cost 1. In this paper we analyze algorithms in terms of work (total cost of the operations) and depth (parallel time using an unbounded number of processors). If we have depth $d(n)$ and separate the work into $w(n)$ writes and $r(n)$ other instructions, then the time on p processors is bounded by:

$$T(n,p) = O\left(\frac{kw(n) + r(n)}{p} + d(n)\right)$$

using Brent's theorem [24]. This bound assumes that work can be allocated to processors efficiently. We allow for concurrent reads and writes (CRCW), and for concurrent writes we assume an arbitrary write takes effect. Note that a parallel algorithm that require $O(D)$ depth in the PRAM model requires $O(kD)$ depth in the asymmetric PRAM model to account for the fact that writes are k times more expensive than reads.

The Asymmetric Private-Cache model. In the *Asymmetric Private-Cache* model (a variant of the Private-Cache model [1, 5]), each processor has its own primary memory of size M, and all processors share a secondary memory. We allow concurrent reads but do not use concurrent writes. As in the AEM model, transfers are in blocks of size B and transfers to the shared memory cost k.

The (Asymmetric) Low-depth Cache-Oblivious Paradigm. The final model that we consider is based on developing low-depth cache-oblivious algorithms [9]. In the model algorithms are defined as nested parallel computations based on parallel loops, possibly nested (this is a generalization of a PRAM). The depth of the computation is the longest chain of dependences—i.e., the depth of a sequential strand of computation is its sequential cost, and the depth of a parallel loop is the maximum of the depths of its iterates. The computation has a natural sequential order by converting each parallel loop to a sequential loop. The cache complexity can be analyzed on the Ideal-Cache model under this sequential order.

Using known scheduling results the depth and sequential cache complexity of a computation are sufficient for deriving bounds on parallel cache complexity. In particular, let D be the depth and Q_1 be the sequential cache complexity. Then for a p-processor shared-memory machine with private caches (each processor has its own cache) using a work-stealing scheduler, the total number of misses Q_p across all processors is at most $Q_1 + O(pDM/B)$ with high probability [1]. For a p-processor shared-memory machine with a shared cache of size $M + pBD$ using a parallel-depth-first (PDF) scheduler, $Q_p \le Q_1$ [8]. These bounds can be extended to multi-

---

Algorithm 1 ASYMMETRIC-PRAM SORT

Input: An array of records A of length n

1: Select a sample S from A independently at random with per-record probability $1/\log n$, and sort the sample.
2: Use every $(\log n)$-th element in the sorted S as splitters, and for each of the about $n/\log^2 n$ buckets defined by the splitters allocate an array of size $c\log^2 n$.
3: In parallel locate each record's bucket using a binary search on the splitters.
4: In parallel insert the records into their buckets by repeatedly trying a random position within the associated array and attempting to insert if empty.
5: Pack out all empty cells in the arrays and concatenate all arrays.
   // Step 6 is an optional step used to obtain $O(k\log n)$ depth
6: **For** round $r \leftarrow 1$ to 2 **do**
       for each array A' generated in previous round
           Deterministically select $|A'|^{1/3} - 1$ samples as splitters and apply integer sort on the bucket number to partition A' into $|A'|^{1/3}$ sub-arrays.
7: **For each** subarray apply the asymmetric RAM sort.
8: Return the sorted array.

---

level hierarchies of private or shared caches, respectively [9]. Thus, algorithms with low depth have good parallel cache complexity.

Our asymmetric variant of the low-depth cache-oblivious paradigm simply accounts for k in the depth and uses the Asymmetric Ideal-Cache model for sequential cache complexity. We observe that the above scheduler bounds readily extend to this asymmetric setting. The $O(pDM/B)$ bound on the additional cache misses under work-stealing arises from an $O(pD)$ bound on the number of steals and the observation that each steal requires the stealer to incur $O(M/B)$ misses to "warm up" its cache. Pessimistically, we will charge $2M/B$ writes (and reads) for each steal, because each line may be dirty and need writing back before the stealer can read it into its cache and, once the stealer has completed the stolen work (reached the join corresponding to the fork that spawned the stolen work), the contents of its cache may need to be written back. Therefore for private caches we have $Q_P \leq Q_1 + O(pkDM/B)$. The PDF bounds extend because there are no additional cache misses and hence no additional reads or writes.

3. SORTING ON RAM/PRAM

The number of writes on an asymmetric RAM can be bound for a variety of algorithms and data structures using known techniques. For example, there has been significant research on maintaining balanced search trees such that every insertion and deletion only requires a constant number of rotations (see e.g., [29] and references within). While the motivation for that work is that for certain data structures rotations can be asymptotically more expensive than visiting a node (e.g., if each node of a tree maintains a secondary set of keys), the results apply directly to improving bounds on the asymmetric RAM. Sorting can be done by inserting n records into a balanced search tree data structure, and then reading them off in order. This requires $O(n\log n)$ reads and $O(n)$ writes, for total cost $O(n(k+\log n))$. Similarly, we can maintain priority queues (insert and delete-min) and comparison-based dictionaries (insert, delete and search) in $O(1)$ writes per operation.

We now consider how to sort on an asymmetric CRCW PRAM (arbitrary write). Algorithm 1 outlines a sample sort (with oversampling) that does $O(n\log n)$ reads and $O(n)$ writes and has depth $O(k\log n)$. It is similar to other sample sorts [10, 19, 24]. We consider each step in more detail and analyze its cost.

Step 1 can use Cole's parallel mergesort [14] requiring $O(n)$ reads and writes w.h.p. (because the sample is size $\Theta(n/\log n)$ w.h.p.), and $O(k\log n)$ depth. In step 2 for sufficiently large c, w.h.p. all arrays will have at least twice as many slots as there are records belonging to the associated bucket [10]. The cost of step 2 is a lower-order term. Step 3 requires $O(n\log n)$ reads, $O(n)$ writes and $O(k + \log n)$ depth for the binary searches and writing the resulting bucket numbers. Step 4 is an instance of the so-called placement problem (see [32, 33]). This can be implementing by having each record select a random location within the array associated with its bucket and if empty, attempting to insert the record at that location. This is repeated if unsuccessful. Since multiple records might try the same location at the same time, each record needs to check if it was successfully inserted. The expected number of tries per record is constant. Also, if the records are partitioned into groups of size $\log n$ and processed sequentially within the group and in parallel across groups, then w.h.p. no group will require more than $O(\log n)$ tries across all of its records [32]. Therefore, w.h.p., the number of reads and writes for this step are $O(n)$ and the depth is $O(k\log n)$. Step 5 can be done with a prefix sum, requiring a linear number of reads and writes, and $O(k\log n)$ depth. At this point we could apply the asymmetric RAM sort to each bucket giving a total of $O(n\log n)$ reads, $O(n)$ writes and a depth of $O(k\log^2 n + \log^2 n \log\log n)$ w.h.p. (the first term for the writes and second term for the reads).

We can reduce the depth to $O(k\log n)$ by further deterministically sampling inside each bucket (step 6) using the following lemma:

LEMMA 3.1. *We can partition m records into $m^{1/3}$ buckets $M_1, \ldots, M_{m^{1/3}}$ such that for any i and j where $i < j$ all records in M_i are less than all records in M_j, and for all i, $|M_i| < m^{2/3}\log m$. The process requires $O(m\log m)$ reads, $O(m)$ writes, and $O(k\sqrt{m})$ depth.*

PROOF. We first split the m records into groups of size $m^{1/3}$ and sort each group with the RAM sort. This takes $O(m\log m)$ reads, $O(m)$ writes and $O(km^{1/3}\log m)$ depth. Then for each sorted group, we place every $\log m$'th record into a sample. Now we sort the sample of size $m/\log m$ using Cole's mergesort, and use the result as splitters to partition the remaining records into buckets. Finally, we place the records into their respective buckets by integer sorting the records based on their bucket number. This can be done with a parallel radix sort in a linear number of reads/writes and $O(k\sqrt{m})$ depth [32].

To show that the largest bucket has size at most $m^{2/3}\log m$, note that in each bucket, we can pick at most $\log m$ consecutive records from each of the $m^{2/3}$ groups without picking a splitter. Otherwise there will be a splitter in the bucket, which is a contradiction. $\square$

Step 6 applies two iterations of Lemma 3.1 to each bucket to partition it into sub-buckets. For an initial bucket of size m, this process will create sub-buckets of at most size $O\left(m^{4/9}\log^{5/3} m\right)$. Plugging in $m = O\left(\log^2 n\right)$ gives us that the largest sub-bucket is of size $O\left(\log^{8/9} n(\log\log n)^{5/3}\right)$. We can now apply the RAM sort to each bucket in $O(k\log n)$ depth. This gives us the following theorem.

THEOREM 3.2. *Sorting n records can be performed using $O(n\log n)$ reads, $O(n)$ writes, and in $O(k\log n)$ depth w.h.p. on the Asymmetric CRCW PRAM.*

This implies

$$T(n) = O\left(\frac{n \log n + kn}{p} + k \log n \right)$$

time. Allocating work to processors is outlined above or described in the cited references. In the standard PRAM model, the depth of our algorithm matches that of the best PRAM sorting algorithm [14], although ours is randomized and requires the CRCW model. We leave it open whether the same bounds can be met deterministically and on a PRAM without concurrent writes.

4. EXTERNAL MEMORY SORTING

In this section, we present sorting algorithms for the Asymmetric External Memory model. We show how the three approaches for EM sorting—mergesort, sample sort, and heapsort (using buffer trees)—can each be adapted to the asymmetric case.

In each case we trade off a factor of k additional reads for a larger branching factor (kM/B instead of M/B), hence reducing the number of rounds. It is interesting that the same general approach works for all three types of sorting. The first algorithm, the mergesort, has been described elsewhere [30] although in a different model (their model is specific to NAND flash memory and has different sized blocks for reading and writing, among other differences). Our parameters are therefore different, and our analysis is new. To the best of our knowledge, our other two algorithms are new.

4.1 Mergesort

We use an l-way mergesort—i.e., a balanced tree of merges with each merge taking in l sorted arrays and outputting one sorted array consisting of all records from the input. We assume that once the input is small enough a different sort (the *base case*) is applied. For $l = M/B$ and a base case of $n \leq M$ (using any sort since it fits in memory), we have the standard EM mergesort. With these settings there are $\log_{M/B}(n/M)$ levels of recursion, plus the base case, each costing $O(n/B)$ memory operations. This gives the well-known overall bound from Equation 1 [2].

To modify the algorithm for the asymmetric case, we increase the branching factor and the base case by a factor of k, i.e. $l = kM/B$ and a base case of $n \leq kM$. This means that it is no longer possible to keep the base case in the primary memory, nor one block for each of the input arrays during a merge. The modified algorithm is described in Algorithm 2.

Each merge proceeds in a sequence of rounds, where a round is one iteration of the **while** loop starting on line 5. During each round we maintain a priority queue within the primary memory. Because operations within the primary memory are free in the model, this can just be kept as a sorted array of records, or even unsorted, although a balanced search tree can be a feasible solution in practice. Each round consists of two phases. The first phase (the **for** loop on line 6) considers each of the l input subarrays in turn, loading the current block for the subarray into the load buffer, and then inserting each record e from the block into the priority queue if not already written to the output (i.e. $e.key > lastV$), and if smaller than the maximum in the queue (i.e. $e.key < Q.max$). This might bump an existing element out of the queue. Also, if a record is the last in its block then it is marked and tagged with its subarray number.

The second phase (the **while** loop starting on line 8) starts writing the priority queue to the output one block at a time. Whenever reaching a record that is marked as the last in its block, the algorithm increments the pointer to the corresponding subarray and processes the next block in the subarray. We repeat the rounds until all records from all subarrays have been processed.

Algorithm 2 AEM-MERGESORT

Input: An array A of records of length n
1: **if** $|A| \leq kM$ **then**   // base case
2:      Sort A using $k|A|/B$ reads and $|A|/B$ writes, and return.
3: Evenly partition A into $l = kM/B$ subarrays $A_1, \ldots, A_l$ (at the granularity of blocks) and recursively apply AEM-MERGESORT to each.
4: **Initialize Merge.** Initialize an empty output array O, a load buffer and an empty store buffer each of size B, an empty priority queue Q of size M, an array of pointers $I_1, \ldots, I_l$ that point to the start of each sorted subarray, $c = 0$, and $lastV = -\infty$. Associated with Q is $Q.max$, which holds the maximum element in Q if Q is full, and $+\infty$ otherwise.
5: **while** $c < |A|$ **do**
6:      **for** $i \leftarrow 1$ to l **do**
7:          PROCESS-BLOCK(i).
8:      **while** Q is not empty **do**
9:          $e \leftarrow Q.deleteMin$.
10:         Write e to the store buffer, $c \leftarrow c + 1$.
11:         If the store buffer is full, flush it to O and update $lastV$.
12:         **if** e is marked as last record in its subarray block **then**
13:             $i = e.subarray$.
14:             Increment I_i to point to next block in subarray i.
15:             PROCESS-BLOCK(i).
16: $A \leftarrow O$. // Logically, don't actually copy

17: **function** PROCESS-BLOCK(subarray i)
18:     **If** I_i points to the end of the subarray **then** return.
19:     Read the block I_i into the load buffer.
20:     **for all** records e in the block **do**
21:         **if** $e.key$ is in the range $(lastV, Q.max)$ **then**
22:             If Q is full, eject $Q.max$.
23:             Insert e into Q, and mark if last record in block.

To account for the space for the pointers $I = I_1, \ldots, I_l$, let $\alpha = (\log n)/s$, where s is the size of a record in bits, and n is the total number of records being merged. The cost of the merge is bounded as follows:

LEMMA 4.1. $l = kM/B$ *sorted sequences with total size* n *(stored in $\lceil n/B \rceil$ blocks, and block aligned) can be merged using at most $(k+1)\lceil n/B \rceil$ reads and $\lceil n/B \rceil$ writes, on the AEM model with primary memory size $(M + 2B + 2\alpha kM/B)$.*

PROOF. Each round (except perhaps the last) outputs at least M records, and hence the total number of rounds is at most $\lceil n/M \rceil$. The first phase of each round requires at most kM/B reads, so the total number of reads across all the first phases is at most $k\lceil n/B \rceil$ (the last round can be included in this since it only loads as many blocks as are output). For the second phase, a block is only read when incrementing its pointer, therefore every block is only read once in the second phase. Also every record is only written once. This gives the stated bounds on the number of reads and writes. The space includes the space for the in-memory heap (M), the load and store buffers, the pointers I ($\alpha kM/B$), and pointers to maintain the last-record in block information ($\alpha kM/B$). □

We note that it is also possible to keep I in secondary memory. This will double the number of writes because every time the algorithm moves to a new block in an input array i, it would need to write out the updated I_i. The increase in reads is small. Also, if one uses a balanced search tree to implement the priority queue Q then the size increases by $< M(\log M)/s$ in order to store the pointers in the tree.

For the base case when $n \leq kM$ we use the following lemma.

LEMMA 4.2. $n \leq kM$ *records stored in* $\lceil n/B \rceil$ *blocks can be sorted using at most* $k \lceil n/B \rceil$ *reads and* $\lceil n/B \rceil$ *writes, on the AEM model with primary memory size* $M + B$.

PROOF. We sort the elements using a variant of selection sort, scanning the input list a total of at most k times. In the first scan, store in memory the M smallest elements seen so far, performing no writes and $\lceil n/B \rceil$ reads. After completing the scan, output all the $\min(M, n)$ elements in sorted order using $\lceil \min(M, n)/B \rceil$ writes. Record the maximum element written so far. In each subsequent phase (if not finished), store in memory the M smallest records larger than the maximum written so far, then output as before. The cost is $\lceil n/B \rceil$ reads and M/B writes per phase (except perhaps the last phase). We need one extra block to hold the input. The largest output can be stored in the $O(\log M)$ locations we have allowed for in the model. This gives the stated bounds because every element is written out once and the input is scanned at most k times. $\square$

Together we have:

THEOREM 4.3. *Algorithm 2 sorts* n *records using*

$$R(n) \leq (k+1) \left\lceil \frac{n}{B} \right\rceil \left\lceil \log_{\frac{kM}{B}} \left(\frac{n}{B} \right) \right\rceil$$

reads, and

$$W(n) \leq \left\lceil \frac{n}{B} \right\rceil \left\lceil \log_{\frac{kM}{B}} \left(\frac{n}{B} \right) \right\rceil$$

writes on an AEM with primary memory size $(M + 2B + 2\alpha kM/B)$.

PROOF. The number of recursive levels of merging is bounded by $\left\lceil \log_{\frac{kM}{B}} \left(\frac{n}{kM} \right) \right\rceil$, and when we add the additional base round we have $1 + \left\lceil \log_{\frac{kM}{B}} \left(\frac{n}{kM} \right) \right\rceil = \left\lceil \log_{\frac{kM}{B}} \left(\frac{n}{kM} \frac{kM}{B} \right) \right\rceil = \left\lceil \log_{\frac{kM}{B}} \left(\frac{n}{B} \right) \right\rceil$. The cost for each level is at most $(k+1) \lceil n/B \rceil$ reads and $\lceil n/B \rceil$ writes (only one block on each level might not be full). $\square$

4.2 Sample Sort

We now describe an l-way randomized sample sort [10, 19] (also called distribution sort), which asymptotically matches the I/O bounds of the mergesort. The idea of sample sort is to partition n records into l approximately equally sized buckets based on a sample of the keys within the records, and then recurse on each bucket until an appropriately-sized base case is reached. As with the mergesort, here we will use a branching factor $l = kM/B$. Again this branching factor will reduce the number of levels of recursion relative to the standard EM sample sort which uses $l = M/B$ [2]. We describe how to process each partition and the base case.

The partitioning starts by selecting a set of splitters. This can be done using standard techniques, which we review later. The splitters partition the input into buckets that w.h.p. are within a constant factor of the average size n/l. The algorithm now needs to bucket the input based on the splitters. The algorithm processes the splitters in k rounds of size M/B each, starting with the first M/B splitters. For each round the algorithm scans the whole input array, partitioning each value into the one of M/B buckets associated with the splitters, or skipping a record if its key does not belong in the current buckets. One block for each bucket is kept in memory. Whenever a block for one of the buckets is full, it is written out to memory and the next block is started for that bucket. Each k rounds reads all of the input and writes out only the elements associated with these buckets (roughly a $1/k$ fraction of the input).

The base case occurs when $n \leq kM$, at which point we apply the selection sort from Lemma 4.2.

Let n_0 be the original input size. The splitters can be chosen by randomly picking a sample of keys of size $m = \Theta(l \log n_0)$, sorting them, and then sub-selecting the keys at positions $m/l, 2m/l, \ldots, (l-1)m/l$. By selecting the constant in the Θ sufficiently large, this process ensures that, w.h.p., every bucket is within a constant factor of the average size [10]. To sort the samples apply a RAM mergesort, which requires at most $O(((l \log n_0)/B) \log(l \log n_0/M))$ reads and writes. This is a lower-order term when $l = O(n/\log^2 n)$, but unfortunately this bound on l may not hold for small subproblems. There is a simple solution—when $n \leq k^2 M^2/B$, instead use $l = n/(kM)$. With this modification, we always have $l \leq \sqrt{n/B}$.

It is likely that the splitters could also be selected deterministically using an approach used in the original I/O-efficient distribution sort [2].

THEOREM 4.4. *The* kM/B*-way sample sort sorts* n *records using, w.h.p.,*

$$R(n) = O\left(\frac{kn}{B} \left\lceil \log_{\frac{kM}{B}} \left(\frac{n}{B} \right) \right\rceil \right)$$

reads, and

$$W(n) = O\left(\frac{n}{B} \left\lceil \log_{\frac{kM}{B}} \left(\frac{n}{B} \right) \right\rceil \right)$$

writes on an AEM with primary memory size $(M + B + M/B)$.

PROOF. (Sketch) The primary-memory size allows one block from each bucket as well as the M/B splitters to remain in memory. Each partitioning step thus requires $\lceil n/B \rceil + kM/B$ writes, where the second term arises from the fact that each bucket may use a partial block. Since $n \geq kM$ (this is not a base case), the cost of each partitioning step becomes $O(n/B)$ writes and $O(kn/B)$ reads. Because the number of splitters is at most $\sqrt{n} = O(n/\log^2 n)$, choosing and sorting the splitters takes $O(n/B)$ reads and writes. Observe that the recursive structure matches that of a sample sort with an effective memory of size kM, and that there will be at most two rounds at the end where $l = n/(kM)$. As in standard sample sort, the number of writes is linear with the size of the subproblem, but here the number of reads is multiplied by a factor of k. The standard samplesort analysis thus applies, implying the bound stated.

It remains only to consider the base case. Because all buckets are approximately the same size, the total number of leaves is $O(n/B)$—during the recursion, a size $n > kM$ problem is split into subproblems whose sizes are $\Omega(B)$. Applying Lemma 4.2 to all leaves, we get a cost of $O(kn/B)$ reads and $O(n/B)$ writes for all base cases. $\square$

Extensions for the Private-Cache Model. The above can be readily parallelized. Here we outline the approach. We assume that there are $p = n/M$ processors. We use parallelism both within each partition, and across the recursive partitions. Within a partition we first find the l splitters in parallel. (As above, $l = kM/B$ except for the at most two rounds prior to the base case where $l = n/(kM)$.) This can be done on a sample that is a logarithmic factor smaller than the partition size, using a less efficient sorting algorithm such as parallel mergesort, and then sub-selecting l splitters from the sorted order. This requires $O(k(M/B + \log^2 n))$ time, where the second term ($O(k \log^2 n)$) is the depth of the parallel mergesort, and the first term is the work term $O((k/B)((n/\log n) \log n)/P) = O(kM/B)$.

The algorithm groups the input into $n/(kM)$ chunks of size kM each. As before we also group the splitters into k rounds of size

M/B each. Now in parallel across all chunks and across all rounds, partition the chunk based on the round. We have $n/(kM) \times k = n/M$ processors so we can do them all in parallel. Each will require kM reads and M writes. To ensure that the chunks write their buckets to adjacent locations (so that the output of each bucket is contiguous) we will need to do a pass over the input to count the size of each bucket for each chunk, followed by a prefix sum. This can be done before processing the chunks and is a lower-order term. The time for the computation is $O(kM/B)$.

The processors are then divided among the sub-problems proportional to the size of the sub-problem, and we repeat. The work at each level of recursion remains the same, so the time at each level remains the same. For the base case of size $\leq kM$, instead of using a selection sort across all keys, which is sequential, we find k splitters and divide the work among k processors to sub-select their part of the input, each by reading the whole input, and then sorting their part of size $O(M)$ using a selection sort on those keys. This again takes $O(kM/B)$ time. The total time for the algorithm is therefore:

$$O\left(k\left(\frac{M}{B} + \log^2 n\right)\left\lceil 1 + \log_{\frac{kM}{B}}\left(\frac{n}{kM}\right)\right\rceil\right)$$

with high probability. This is linear speedup assuming $\frac{M}{B} \geq \log^2 n$. Otherwise the number of processors can be reduced to maintain linear speedup.

4.3 I/O Buffer Trees

This section describes how to augment the basic buffer tree [4] to build a priority queue that supports n INSERT and DELETE-MIN operations with an amortized cost of $O((k/B)(1 + \log_{kM/B} n))$ reads and $O((1/B)(1 + \log_{kM/B} n))$ writes per operation. Using the priority queue to implement a sorting algorithm trivially results in a sort costing a total of $O((kn/B)(1 + \log_{kM/B} n))$ reads and $O((n/B)(1 + \log_{kM/B} n))$ writes. These bounds asymptotically match the preceding sorting algorithms, but some additional constant factors are introduced because a buffer tree is a dynamic data structure.

Our buffer tree-based priority queue for the AEM contains a few differences from the regular EM buffer tree [4]: (1) the buffer tree nodes are larger by a factor k, (2) consequently, the "buffer-emptying" process uses an efficient sort on kM elements instead of an in-memory sort on M elements, and (3) to support the priority queue, $O(kM)$ elements are stored outside the buffer tree instead of $O(M)$, which adds nontrivial changes to the data structure.

4.3.1 Overview of a buffer tree

A buffer tree [4] is an augmented version of an (a, b)-tree [22], where $a = l/4$ and $b = l$ for large branching factor l. In the original buffer tree $l = M/B$, but to reduce the number of writes we instead set $l = kM/B$. As an (a, b) tree, all leaves are at the same depth in the tree, and all internal nodes have between $l/4$ and l children (except the root, which may have fewer). Thus the height of the tree is $O(1 + \log_l n)$. An internal node with c children contains $c - 1$ keys, stored in sorted order, that partition the elements in the subtrees. The structure of a buffer tree differs from that of an (a, b) tree in two ways. Firstly, each leaf of the buffer tree contains between $lB/4$ and lB elements stored in l blocks.[2] Secondly, each

node in the buffer tree also contains a dense unsorted list, called a **buffer**, of partially inserted elements that belong in that subtree.

We next summarize the basic buffer tree insertion process [4]. Supporting general deletions is not much harder, but to implement a priority queue we only need to support deleting an entire leaf. The insertion algorithm proceeds in two phases: the first phase moves elements down the tree through buffers, and the second phase performs the (a, b)-tree rebalance operations (i.e., splitting nodes that are too big). The first phase begins by appending the new element to the end of the root's buffer. We say that a node is **full** if its buffer contains at least lB elements. If the insert causes the root to become full, then a **buffer-emptying process** commences, whereby all of the elements in the node's buffer are sorted then distributed to the children (appended to the ends of their buffers). This distribution process may cause children to become full, in which case they must also be emptied. More precisely, the algorithm maintains a list of internal nodes with full buffers (initially the root) and a separate list of leaves with full buffers. The first phase operates by repeatedly extracting a full internal node from the list, emptying its buffer, and adding any full children to the list of full internal or leaf nodes, until there are no full internal nodes.

Note that during the first phase, the buffers of full nodes may far exceed lB, e.g., if all of the ancestors' buffer elements are distributed to a single descendant. Sorting the buffer from scratch would therefore be too expensive. Fortunately, each distribution process writes elements to the child buffers in sorted order, so all elements after the lB'th element (i.e., those written in the most recent emptying of the parent) are sorted. It thus suffices to split the buffer at the lB'th element and sort the first lB elements, resulting in a buffer that consists of two sorted lists. These two lists can trivially be merged as they are being distributed to the sorted list of children in a linear number of I/O's.

When the first phase completes, there may be full leaves but no full internal nodes. Moreover, all ancestors of each full leaf have empty buffers. The second phase operates on each full leaf one at a time. First, the buffer is sorted as above and then merged with the elements stored in the leaf. If the leaf contains $X > lB$ elements, then a sequence of (a, b)-tree rebalance operations occur whereby the leaf may be split into $\Theta(X/(lB))$ new nodes. These splits cascade up the tree as in a typical (a, b)-tree insert.

4.3.2 Buffer tree with fewer writes

To reduce the number of writes, we set the branching factor of the buffer tree to $l = kM/B$ instead of $l = M/B$. The consequence of this increase is that the buffer emptying process needs to sort $lB = kM$ elements, which cannot be done with an in-memory sort. The advantage is that the height of the tree reduces to $O(1 + \log_{kM/B} n)$.

LEMMA 4.5. *It costs $O(kX/B)$ reads and $O(X/B)$ writes to empty a full buffer containing X elements using $\Theta(M)$ memory.*

PROOF. By Lemma 4.2, the cost of sorting the first kM elements is $O(k^2M/B)$ reads and $O(kM/B)$ writes. The distribute step can be performed by simultaneously scanning the sorted list of children along with the two sorted pieces of the buffer, and outputting to the end of the appropriate child buffer. A write occurs only when either finishing with a child or closing out a block. The distribute step thus uses $O(kM/B + X/B)$ reads and writes, giving a total of $O(k^2M/B + X/B)$ reads and $O(kM/B + X/B)$ writes including the sort step. Observing that full means $X > kM$ completes the proof. $\square$

---

[2] Arge [4] defines the "leaves" of a buffer tree to contain $\Theta(B)$ elements instead of $\Theta(lB)$ elements. Since the algorithm only operates on the parents of those "leaves", we find the terminology more convenient when flattening the bottom two levels of the tree. Our leaves thus correspond to what Arge terms "leaf nodes" [4] (not

to be confused with leaves) or equivalently what Sitchinava and Zeh call "fringe nodes" [34].

THEOREM 4.6. *Suppose that the partially empty block belonging to the root's buffer is kept in memory. Then the amortized cost of each insert into an n-element buffer tree is $O((k/B)(1 + \log_{kM/B} n))$ reads and $O((1/B)(1 + \log_{kM/B} n))$ writes.*

PROOF. This proof follows from Arge's buffer tree performance proofs [4], augmented with the above lemma. We first consider the cost of reading and writing the buffers. The last block of the root buffer need only be written when it becomes full, at which point the next block must be read, giving $O(1/B)$ reads and writes per insert. Each element moves through buffers on a root-to-leaf path, so it may belong to $O(1 + \log_{kM/B} n)$ emptying processes. According to Lemma 4.5, emptying a full buffer costs $O(k/B)$ reads and $O(1/B)$ writes per element. Multiplying these two gives an amortized cost per element matching the theorem.

We next consider the cost of rebalancing operations. Given the choice of (a, b)-tree parameters, the total number of node splits is $O(n/(lB))$ [4, Theorem 1] which is $O(n/(kM))$. Each split is performed by scanning a constant number of nodes, yielding a cost of $O(kM/B)$ reads and write per split, or $O(n/(kM) \cdot kM/B) = O(n/B)$ reads and writes in total or $O(1/B)$ per insert. $\square$

4.3.3 An efficient priority queue with fewer writes

The main idea of Arge's buffer tree-based priority queue [4] is to store a working set of the $O(lB)$ smallest elements resident in memory. When inserting an element, first add it to the working set, then evict the largest element from the working set (perhaps the one just inserted) and insert it into the buffer tree. To extract the minimum, find it in the working set. If the working set is empty, remove the $\Theta(lB)$ smallest elements from the buffer tree and add them to the working set. In the standard buffer tree, $l = M/B$ and hence operating on the working set is free because it fits entirely in memory. In our case, however, extra care is necessary to maintain a working set that has size roughly k times larger.

Our AEM priority queue follows the same idea except the working set is partitioned into two pieces, the alpha working set and beta working set. The *alpha working set*, which is always resident in memory, contains at most $M/4$ of the smallest elements in the priority queue. The *beta working set* contains at most $2kM$ of the next smallest elements in the data structure, stored in $O(kM/B)$ blocks. The motivation for having a beta working set is that during DELETE-MIN operations, emptying elements directly from the buffer tree whenever the alpha working set is empty would be too expensive—having a beta working set to stage larger batches of such elements leads to better amortized bounds. Coping with the interaction between the alpha working set, the beta working set, and the buffer tree, is the main complexity of our priority queue. The beta working set does not fit in memory, but we keep a constant number of blocks from the beta working set and the buffer tree (specifically, the last block of the root buffer) in memory.

We begin with a high-level description of the priority-queue operations, with details of the beta working set deferred until later. For now, it suffices to know that we keep the maximum key in the beta working set in memory. To insert a new element, first compare its key against the maximums in the alpha and beta working set. Then insert it into either the alpha working set, the beta working set, or the buffer tree depending on the key comparisons. If the alpha working set exceeds maximum capacity of $M/4$ elements, move the largest element to the beta working set. If the beta working set hits its maximum capacity of $2kM$ elements, remove the largest kM elements and insert them into the buffer tree.

To delete the minimum from the priority queue, remove the smallest element from the alpha working set. If the alpha working set is empty, extract the $M/4$ smallest elements from the beta working

set (details to follow) and move them to the alpha working set. If the beta working set is empty, perform a buffer emptying process on the root-to-leftmost-leaf path in the buffer tree. Then delete the leftmost leaf and move its contents to the beta working set.

The beta working set. The main challenge is in implementing the beta working set. An unsorted list or buffer allows for efficient inserts by appending to the last block. The challenge, however, is to extract the $\Theta(M)$ smallest elements with $O(M/B)$ writes—if $k > B$, each element may reside in a separate block, and we thus cannot afford to update those blocks when extracting the elements. Instead, we perform the deletions implicitly.

To facilitate implicit deletions, we maintain a list of ordered pairs $(i_1, x_1), (i_2, x_2), (i_3, x_3), \ldots$, where (i, x) indicates that all elements with index at most i and key at most x are invalid. Our algorithm maintains the invariant that for consecutive list elements (i_j, x_j) and (i_{j+1}, x_{j+1}), we have $i_j < i_{j+1}$ and $x_j > x_{j+1}$ (recall that all keys are distinct).

To insert an element to the beta working set, simply append it to the end. The invariant is maintained because its index is larger than any pair in the list.

To extract the minimum $M/4$ elements, scan from index 0 to i_1 in the beta working set, ignoring any elements with key at most x_1. Then scan from $i_1 + 1$ to i_2, ignoring any element with key at most x_2. And so on. While scanning, record in memory the $M/4$ smallest valid elements seen so far. When finished, let x be the largest key and let i be the length of the beta working set. All elements with key at most x have been removed from the full beta working set, so they should be implicitly marked as invalid. To restore the invariant, truncate the list until the last pair (i_j, x_j) has $x_j > x$, then append (i, x) to the list. Because the size of the beta working set is growing, $i_j < i$. It should be clear that truncation does not discard any information as (i, x) subsumes any of the truncated pairs.

Whenever the beta working set grows too large ($2kM$ valid elements) or becomes too sparse (k extractions of $M/4$ elements each have occurred), we first rebuild it. Rebuilding scans the elements in order, removing the invalid elements by packing the valid ones densely into blocks. Testing for validity is done as above. When done, the list of ordered pairs to test invalidity is cleared.

Finally, when the beta working set grows too large, we extract the largest kM elements by sorting it (using the selection sort of Lemma 4.2).

Analyzing the priority queue. We begin with some lemmas about the beta working set.

LEMMA 4.7. *Extracting the $M/4$ smallest valid elements from the beta working set and storing them in memory costs $O(kM/B)$ reads and amortized $O(1)$ writes.*

PROOF. The extraction involves first performing read-only passes over the beta working set and list of pairs, keeping one block from the working set and one pair in memory at a time. Because the working set is rebuilt after k extractions, the list of pairs can have at most k entries. Even if the list is not I/O efficient, the cost of scanning both is $O(kM/B + k) = O(kM/B)$ reads. Next the list of pairs indicating invalid elements is updated. Appending one new entry requires $O(1)$ writes. Truncating and deleting any old entries can be charged against their insertions. $\square$

The proof of the following lemma is similar to the preceding one, with the only difference being that the valid elements must be moved and written as they are read.

LEMMA 4.8. *Rebuilding the beta working set costs $O(kM/B)$ reads and writes.* $\square$

THEOREM 4.9. *Our priority queue, if initially empty, supports* n INSERT *and* DELETE-MIN *operations with an amortized cost of* $O((k/B)(1 + \log_{kM/B} n))$ *reads and* $O((1/B)(1 + \log_{kM/B} n))$ *writes per operation.*

PROOF. Inserts are the easier case. Inserting into the alpha working set is free. The amortized cost of inserting directly into the beta working set (a simple append) is $O(1/B)$ reads and writes, assuming the last block stays in memory. The cost of inserting directly into the buffer tree matches the theorem. Occasionally, the beta working set overflows, in which case we rebuild it, sort it, and insert elements into the buffer tree. The rebuild costs $O(kM/B)$ reads and writes (Lemma 4.8), the sort costs $O(k^2 M/B)$ reads and $O(kM/B)$ writes (by Lemma 4.2), and the kM buffer tree inserts cost $O((k^2 M/B)(1 + \log_{kM/B} n))$ reads and $O((kM/B)(1 + \log_{kM/B} n))$ writes (by Theorem 4.6). The latter dominates. Amortizing against the kM inserts that occur between overflows, the amortized cost per insert matches the theorem statement.

Deleting the minimum element from the alpha working set is free. When the alpha working set becomes empty, we extract $M/4$ elements from the beta working set, with a cost of $O(kM/B)$ reads and $O(1)$ writes (Lemma 4.7). This cost may be amortized against the $M/4$ deletes that occur between extractions, for an amortized cost of $O(k/B)$ reads and $O(1/M)$ writes per delete-min. Every k extractions of $M/4$ elements, the beta working set is rebuilt, with a cost of $O(kM/B)$ reads and writes (Lemma 4.8) or amortized $O(1/B)$ reads and writes per delete-min. Adding these together, we so far have $O(k/B)$ reads and $O(1/B)$ writes per delete-min.

It remains to analyze the cost of refilling the beta working set when it becomes empty. The cost of removing a leaf from the buffer tree is dominated by the cost of emptying buffers on a length-$O(\log_{kM/B} n)$ path. Note that the buffers are not full, so we cannot apply Lemma 4.5. But a similar analysis applies. The cost per node is $O(k^2 M/B + X/B)$ reads and $O(kM/B + X/B)$ writes for an X-element buffer. As with Arge's version of the priority queue [4], the $O(X/B)$ terms can be charged to the insertion of the X elements, so we are left with a cost of $O(k^2 M/B)$ read and $O(kM/B)$ writes per buffer. Multiplying by $O(1 + \log_{kM/B} n)$ levels gives a cost of $O((k^2 M/B)(1 + \log_{kM/B} n))$ reads and $O((kM/B)(1 + \log_{kM/B} n))$ writes. Because each leaf contains at least $kM/4$ elements, we can amortize this cost against at least $kM/4$ deletions, giving a cost that matches the theorem. □

With this priority queue, sorting can be trivially implemented in $O((kn/B)(1 + \log_{kM/B} n))$ reads and $O((n/B)(1 + \log_{kM/B} n))$ writes, matching the bounds of the previous sorting algorithms.

5. CACHE-OBLIVIOUS PARALLEL ALGORITHMS

In this section we present low-depth cache-oblivious parallel algorithms for sorting and Fast Fourier Transform, with asymmetric read and write costs. Both algorithms (i) have only polylogarithmic depth, (ii) are processor-oblivious (i.e., no explicit mention of processors), (iii) can be cache-oblivious or cache-aware, and (iv) map to low cache complexity on parallel machines with hierarchies of shared caches as well as private caches using the results of Section 2. We also present a linear-depth, cache-oblivious parallel algorithm for matrix multiplication. All three algorithms use $\Theta(k)$ fewer writes than reads.

5.1 Sorting

We show how the low-depth, cache-oblivious sorting algorithm from [9] can be adapted to the asymmetric case. The original algorithm is based on viewing the input as a $\sqrt{n} \times \sqrt{n}$ array, sorting the rows, partitioning them based on splitters, transposing the partitions, and then sorting the buckets. The original algorithm incurs $O((n/B) \log_M(n))$ reads and writes. To reduce the number of writes, our revised version partitions slightly differently and does extra reads to reduce the number of levels of recursion. The algorithm does $O((n/B) \log_{kM}(kn))$ writes, $O((kn/B) \log_{kM}(kn))$ reads, and has depth $O(k \log^2(n/k))$ w.h.p.

The algorithm uses matrix transpose, prefix sums and mergesort as subroutines. Efficient parallel and cache-oblivious versions of these algorithm are described in [9]. For an input of size n, prefix sums has depth $O(k \log n)$ and requires $O(n/B)$ reads and writes, merging two arrays of lengths n and m has depth $O(k \log(n + m))$ and requires $O((n + m)/B)$ reads and writes, and mergesort has depth $O(k \log^2 n)$ and requires $O((n/B) \log_2(n/M))$ reads and writes. Transposing an $n \times m$ matrix has depth $O(k \log(n + m))$ and requires $O(nm/B)$ reads and writes.

Our cache-oblivious sorting algorithm works recursively, with a base case of $n \leq M$, at which point any parallel sorting algorithm with $O(n \log n)$ reads/writes and $O(k \log n)$ depth can be applied (e.g. [14]).

Figure 1 illustrates the steps of the algorithm. Given an input array of size n, the algorithm first splits it into $\sqrt{nk}$ subarrays of size $\sqrt{n/k}$ and recursively sorts each of the subarrays. This step corresponds to step (a) in Figure 1.

Then the algorithm determines the splitters by sampling. After the subarrays are sorted, every $(\log n)$'th element from each row is sampled, and these $n/\log n$ samples are sorted using a cache-oblivious mergesort. Then $\sqrt{n/k} - 1$ evenly-distributed splitters are picked from the sorted samples to create $\sqrt{n/k}$ buckets. The algorithm then determines the boundaries of the buckets in each subarray, which can be implemented by merging the splitters with each row, requiring $O(k \log n)$ depth and $O(n/B)$ writes overall. This step is shown as step (b) in Figure 1. Notice that on average the size of each bucket is $O\left(\sqrt{nk}\right)$, and the largest bucket has no more than $2\sqrt{nk} \log n$ elements.

After the subarrays are split into $\sqrt{n/k}$ buckets, prefix sums and a matrix transpose can be used to place all keys destined for the same bucket together in contiguous arrays. This process is illustrated as step (c) in Figure 1. This process requires $O(n/B)$ reads and writes, and $O(k \log n)$ depth.

The next step is new to the asymmetric algorithm and is the part that requires extra reads. As illustrated in Figure 1 (d), $k - 1$ pivots are chosen from each bucket to generate k sub-buckets. We sample $\max\{k, \sqrt{kn}/\log n\}$ samples, apply a mergesort, and evenly pick $k - 1$ pivots in the sample. Then the size of each sub-bucket can be shown to be $O\left(\sqrt{n/k} \log n\right)$ w.h.p. using Chernoff bounds. We then scan each bucket for k rounds to partition all elements into k sub-buckets, and sort each sub-bucket recursively.

THEOREM 5.1. *Our cache-oblivious sorting algorithm requires* $O((kn/B) \log_{kM}(kn))$ *reads,* $O((n/B) \log_{kM}(kn))$ *writes, and* $O(k \log^2(n/k))$ *depth w.h.p.*

PROOF. All the subroutines except for the recursive calls do $O(n/B)$ writes. The last partitioning process to put elements into sub-buckets takes $O(kn/B)$ reads and the other subroutines require fewer reads. The overall depth is dominated by the mergesort to find the first $\sqrt{n/k}$ pivots, requiring $O(k \log^2(n/k))$ depth per level of recursion. Hence, the recurrence relations (w.h.p.) for read I/O's (R), write I/O's (W), and depth (D) are:

$$R(n) = O\left(\frac{kn}{B}\right) + \sqrt{kn} \cdot R\left(\sqrt{\frac{n}{k}}\right) + \sum_{i=1}^{\sqrt{kn}} R(n_i)$$

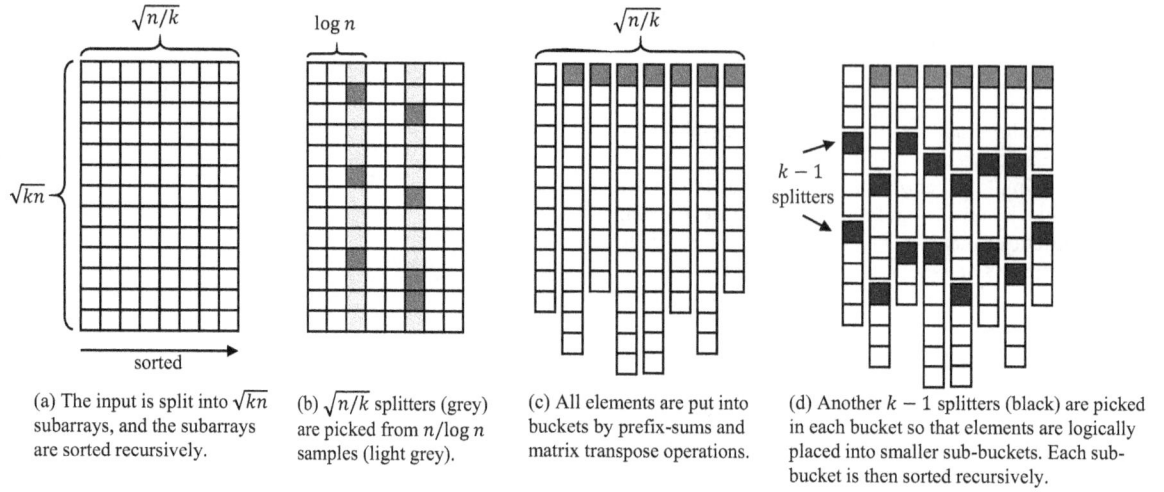

(a) The input is split into $\sqrt{kn}$ subarrays, and the subarrays are sorted recursively.

(b) $\sqrt{n/k}$ splitters (grey) are picked from $n/\log n$ samples (light grey).

(c) All elements are put into buckets by prefix-sums and matrix transpose operations.

(d) Another $k-1$ splitters (black) are picked in each bucket so that elements are logically placed into smaller sub-buckets. Each sub-bucket is then sorted recursively.

Figure 1: The low-depth cache-oblivious algorithm on asymmetric read and write costs to sort an input array of size n.

$$W(n) = O\left(\frac{n}{B}\right) + \sqrt{kn} \cdot W\left(\sqrt{\frac{n}{k}}\right) + \sum_{i=1}^{\sqrt{kn}} W(n_i)$$

$$D(n) = O\left(k \log^2 \frac{n}{k}\right) + \max_{i=1,\cdots,\sqrt{kn}}\{D(n_i)\}$$

where n_i is the size of the i'th sub-bucket, and $n_i = O\left(\sqrt{n/k}\log n\right)$ and $\sum n_i = n$. The base case for the I/O complexity is $R(M) = W(M) = O(M/B)$. Solving these recurrences proves the theorem. □

5.2 Fast Fourier Transform

We now consider a parallel cache-oblivious algorithm for computing the Discrete Fourier Transform (DFT). The algorithm we consider is based on the Cooley-Tukey FFT algorithm [15], and our description follows that of [20]. We assume that n at each level of recursion and k are powers of 2. The standard cache-oblivious divide-and-conquer algorithm [20] views the input matrix as an $\sqrt{n} \times \sqrt{n}$ matrix, and incurs $O((n/B)\log_M(n))$ reads and writes. To reduce the number of writes, we modify the algorithm to the following:

1. View input of size n as a $k\sqrt{n/k} \times \sqrt{n/k}$ matrix in row-major order. Transpose the matrix.

2. Compute a DFT on each row of the matrix as follows

   (a) View the row as a $k \times \sqrt{n/k}$ matrix

   (b) For each row i

      i. Calculate the values of column DFTs for row i using the brute-force method. This will require k reads (each row) and 1 write (row i) per value.

      ii. Recursively compute the FFT for the row.

   (c) Incorporate twiddle factors

   (d) Transpose $k \times \sqrt{n/k}$ matrix

3. Transpose matrix

4. Recursively compute an FFT on each length $\sqrt{n/k}$ row.

5. Transpose to final order.

The difference from the standard cache-oblivious algorithms is the extra level of nesting in step 2, and the use of a work-inefficient DFT over k elements in step 2(b). The transposes in steps 1, 2(d) and 3 can be done with $O(n/B)$ reads/writes and $O(k \log n)$ depth. The brute-force calculations in step 2(b)i require a total of kn reads (and arithmetic operations) and n writes. This is where we waste a k factor in reads in order to reduce the recursion depth. The twiddle factors can all be calculated with $O(n)$ reads and writes. There are a total of $2k\sqrt{n/k}$ recursive calls on problems of size $\sqrt{n/k}$.

Our base case is of size M, which uses M/B reads and writes. The number of reads therefore satisfies the following recurrence:

$$R(n) = \begin{cases} O(n/B) & \text{if } n \leq M \\ 2k\sqrt{n/k}\, R\left(\sqrt{n/k}\right) + O(kn/B) & \text{otherwise} \end{cases}$$

which solves to $R(n) = O((kn/B)\log_{kM}(kn))$, and the number of writes is

$$W(n) = \begin{cases} O(n/B) & \text{if } n \leq M \\ 2k\sqrt{n/k}\, W\left(\sqrt{n/k}\right) + O(n/B) & \text{otherwise} \end{cases}$$

which solves to $W(n) = O((n/B)\log_{kM}(kn))$.

Since we can do all the rows in parallel for each step, and the brute-force calculation in parallel, the only important dependence is that we have to do step 2 before step 5. This gives a recurrence $D(n) = 2D\left(\sqrt{n/k}\right) + O(k \log n)$ for the depth, which solves to $O(k \log n \log \log n)$.

We note that the algorithm as described requires an extra transpose and an extra write in step 2(b)i relative to the standard version. This might negate any advantage from reducing the number of levels, however we note that these can likely be removed. In particular the transpose in steps 2(d) and 3 can be merged by viewing the results as a three dimensional array and transposing the first and last dimensions (this is what the pair of transposes does). The write in step 2(b)i can be merged with the transpose in step 1 by combining the columnwise FFT with the transpose, and applying it k times.

5.3 Matrix Multiplication

In this section, we consider matrix multiplication in the asymmetric read/write setting. The standard cubic-work sequential algorithm trivially uses $O(n^3)$ reads and $\Theta(n^2)$ writes, one for each entry in the output matrix. For the EM model, the blocked algorithm that divides the matrix into sub-matrices of size $\sqrt{M} \times \sqrt{M}$ uses $O\left(n^3/(B\sqrt{M})\right)$ reads [11, 20]. Because we can keep each $\sqrt{M} \times \sqrt{M}$ sub-matrix of the output matrix in memory until it is completely computed, the number of writes is proportional to the number of blocks in the output, which is $O\left(n^2/B\right)$. This gives the following simple result:

THEOREM 5.2. *External-memory matrix multiplication can be done in* $O\left(n^3/(B\sqrt{M})\right)$ *reads and* $O\left(n^2/B\right)$ *writes.*

We now turn to a divide-and-conquer algorithm for matrix multiplication, which is parallel and cache-oblivious. We assume that we can fit $3M$ elements in cache instead of M, which only affects our bounds by constant factors. Note that the standard cache-oblivious divide-and-conquer algorithm [11, 20] recurses on four parallel subproblems of size $n/2 \times n/2$, resulting in $\Theta\left(n^3/(B\sqrt{M})\right)$ reads and writes. To reduce the writes by a factor of $\Theta(k)$, we instead recurse on k^2 parallel subproblems (blocks) of size $n/k \times n/k$. On each level of recursion, computing each output block of size $n/k \times n/k$ requires summing over the k products of $n/k \times n/k$ size input matrices. We assume the recursive calls writing to the same target block are processed sequentially so that all writes (and reads) can be made at the leaves of the recursion to their final locations.

For the purpose of analysis we consider a base case when the problem is of size $k\sqrt{M} \times k\sqrt{M}$. At this point each of its subproblems of size $\sqrt{M} \times \sqrt{M}$ is writing into an output block of size M, which fits in cache. Therefore since we do the products for the output blocks sequentially, the result can stay in cache and only be written when all k are done. The number of writes is therefore M/B per output block and $k^2 M/B$ total. For reads all of the k^3 subproblems might require reading both inputs so there are $2k^3 M/B$ reads. The non-base recursive calls do not contribute any significant reads or writes since all reading and writing to the arrays is done at the leaves. This gives us the following recurrence for the number of writes for an $n \times n$ matrix:

$$
W(n) = \begin{cases} k^2 M/B & \text{if } n < k\sqrt{M} \\ k^3 W(n/k) + O(1) & \text{otherwise} \end{cases}
$$

This solves to $W(n) = O\left(n^3/(kB\sqrt{M})\right)$, which is a factor of k less than for the standard EM or cache-oblivious matrix multiply.[3] The number of reads satisfies:

$$
R(n) = \begin{cases} 2k^3 M/B & \text{if } n < k\sqrt{M} \\ k^3 R(n/k) + O(1) & \text{otherwise} \end{cases}
$$

This solves to $R(n) = O\left(n^3/(B\sqrt{M})\right)$, which is the same as for the standard EM or cache-oblivious matrix multiply.

Because the products contributing to a block are done sequentially, the depth of the algorithm satisfies the recurrence $D(n) = kD(n/k) + O(1)$ with base case $D(1) = k$, which solves to $O(kn)$. This gives the following theorem:

THEOREM 5.3. *Our cache-oblivious matrix multiplication algorithm requires* $O\left(n^3/(B\sqrt{M})\right)$ *reads,* $O\left(n^3/(kB\sqrt{M})\right)$ *writes, and* $O(kn)$ *depth.*

---

[3]Note that for this analysis we assume the initial problem is of size $n = k^i \sqrt{M}$ for some integer i.

6. CONCLUSION

Motivated by the high cost of writing relative to reading in emerging non-volatile memory technologies, we have considered a variety of models for accounting for read-write asymmetry, and proposed and analyzed a variety of sorting algorithms in these models. For the asymmetric RAM and PRAM models, we have shown how to reduce the number of writes from $O(n \log n)$ to $O(n)$ without asymptotically increasing the other costs (reads, parallel depth). For the asymmetric external memory models (including the cache-oblivious model) the reductions in writes are mostly more modest, often increasing the base of a logarithm, and at the cost of asymptotically more reads. However, these algorithms might still have practical benefit. We also presented a cache-oblivious matrix-multiply that asymptotically reduces the writes by a factor of k while not asymptotically increasing reads. Future work includes proving lower bounds for the asymmetric external memory models, devising write-efficient algorithms for additional problems, and performing experimental studies.

Acknowledgments

This research was supported in part by NSF grants CCF-1218188, CCF-1314633, and CCF-1314590, and by the Intel Science and Technology Center for Cloud Computing.

7. REFERENCES

[1] U. A. Acar, G. E. Blelloch, and R. D. Blumofe. The data locality of work stealing. *Theory Comput. Sys.*, 35(3), 2002.

[2] A. Aggarwal and J. S. Vitter. The input/output complexity of sorting and related problems. *CACM*, 31(9), 1988.

[3] A. Akel, A. M. Caulfield, T. I. Mollov, R. K. Gupta, and S. Swanson. Onyx: A prototype phase change memory storage array. In *HotStorage*, 2011.

[4] L. Arge. The buffer tree: A technique for designing batched external data structures. *Algorithmica*, 37(1), 2003.

[5] L. Arge, M. T. Goodrich, M. Nelson, and N. Sitchinava. Fundamental parallel algorithms for private-cache chip multiprocessors. In *SPAA*, 2008.

[6] M. Athanassoulis, B. Bhattacharjee, M. Canim, and K. A. Ross. Path processing using solid state storage. In *ADMS*, 2012.

[7] A. Ben-Aroya and S. Toledo. Competitive analysis of flash-memory algorithms. In *ESA*, 2006.

[8] G. E. Blelloch and P. B. Gibbons. Effectively sharing a cache among threads. In *SPAA*, 2004.

[9] G. E. Blelloch, P. B. Gibbons, and H. V. Simhadri. Low-depth cache oblivious algorithms. In *SPAA*, 2010.

[10] G. E. Blelloch, C. E. Leiserson, B. M. Maggs, C. G. Plaxton, S. J. Smith, and M. Zagha. A comparison of sorting algorithms for the Connection Machine CM-2. In *SPAA*, 1991.

[11] R. D. Blumofe, M. Frigo, C. F. Joerg, C. E. Leiserson, and K. H. Randall. An analysis of dag-consistent distributed shared-memory algorithms. In *SPAA*, 1996.

[12] S. Chen, P. B. Gibbons, and S. Nath. Rethinking database algorithms for phase change memory. In *CIDR*, 2011.

[13] S. Cho and H. Lee. Flip-N-Write: A simple deterministic technique to improve PRAM write performance, energy and endurance. In *MICRO*, 2009.

[14] R. Cole. Parallel merge sort. *SIAM J. Comput.*, 17(4), 1988.

[15] J. W. Cooley and J. W. Tukey. An algorithm for the machine calculation of complex fourier series. *Mathematics of Computation*, 19, 1965.

[16] X. Dong, N. P. Jouupi, and Y. Xie. PCRAMsim: System-level performance, energy, and area modeling for phase-change RAM. In *ICCAD*, 2009.

[17] X. Dong, X. Wu, G. Sun, Y. Xie, H. Li, and Y. Chen. Circuit and microarchitecture evaluation of 3D stacking magnetic RAM (MRAM) as a universal memory replacement. In *DAC*, 2008.

[18] D. Eppstein, M. T. Goodrich, M. Mitzenmacher, and P. Pszona. Wear minimization for cuckoo hashing: How not to throw a lot of eggs into one basket. In *SEA*, 2014.

[19] W. D. Frazer and A. C. McKellar. Samplesort: A sampling approach to minimal storage tree sorting. *J. ACM*, 17(3), 1970.

[20] M. Frigo, C. E. Leiserson, H. Prokop, and S. Ramachandran. Cache-oblivious algorithms. In *FOCS*, 1999.

[21] E. Gal and S. Toledo. Algorithms and data structures for flash memories. *ACM Computing Surveys*, 37(2), 2005.

[22] S. Huddleston and K. Mehlhorn. A new data structure for representing sorted lists. *Acta Informatica*, 17, 1982.

[23] www.slideshare.net/IBMZRL/theseus-pss-nvmw2014, 2014.

[24] J. Jaja. *Introduction to Parallel Algorithms*. Addison-Wesley Professional, 1992.

[25] H. Kim, S. Seshadri, C. L. Dickey, and L. Chu. Evaluating phase change memory for enterprise storage systems: A study of caching and tiering approaches. In *FAST*, 2014.

[26] B. C. Lee, E. Ipek, O. Mutlu, and D. Burger. Architecting phase change memory as a scalable DRAM alternative. In *ISCA*, 2009.

[27] J. S. Meena, S. M. Sze, U. Chand, and T.-Y. Tseng. Overview of emerging nonvolatile memory technologies. *Nanoscale Research Letters*, 2014.

[28] S. Nath and P. B. Gibbons. Online maintenance of very large random samples on flash storage. *VLDB J.*, 19(1), 2010.

[29] T. Ottmann and D. Wood. How to update a balanced binary tree with a constant number of rotations. In *SWAT*, 1990.

[30] H. Park and K. Shim. FAST: flash-aware external sorting for mobile database systems. *Journal of Systems and Software*, 82(8), 2009.

[31] M. K. Qureshi, S. Gurumurthi, and B. Rajendran. *Phase Change Memory: From Devices to Systems*. Morgan & Claypool, 2012.

[32] S. Rajasekaran and J. H. Reif. Optimal and sublogarithmic time randomized parallel sorting algorithms. *SIAM J. Comput.*, 18(3), 1989.

[33] J. H. Reif and S. Sen. Parallel computational geometry: An approach using randomization. In J. Sack and J. Urrutia, editors, *Handbook of Computational Geometry*, chapter 18. Elsevier Science, 1999.

[34] N. Sitchinava and N. Zeh. A parallel buffer tree. In *SPAA*, 2012.

[35] D. D. Sleator and R. E. Tarjan. Amortized efficiency of list update and paging rules. *Commun. ACM*, 28(2), 1985.

[36] S. Viglas. Write-limited sorts and joins for persistent memory. *PVLDB*, 7(5), 2014.

[37] S. D. Viglas. Adapting the B$^+$-tree for asymmetric I/O. In *ADBIS*, 2012.

[38] C. Xu, X. Dong, N. P. Jouppi, and Y. Xie. Design implications of memristor-based RRAM cross-point structures. In *DATE*, 2011.

[39] B.-D. Yang, J.-E. Lee, J.-S. Kim, J. Cho, S.-Y. Lee, and B.-G. Yu. A low power phase-change random access memory using a data-comparison write scheme. In *ISCAS*, 2007.

[40] Yole Developpement. Emerging non-volatile memory technologies, 2013.

[41] P. Zhou, B. Zhao, J. Yang, and Y. Zhang. A durable and energy efficient main memory using phase change memory technology. In *ISCA*, 2009.

[42] O. Zilberberg, S. Weiss, and S. Toledo. Phase-change memory: An architectural perspective. *ACM Computing Surveys*, 45(3), 2013.

Practical Massively Parallel Sorting

Michael Axtmann
Karlsruhe Inst. of Technology
Karlsruhe, Germany
michael.axtmann@kit.edu

Timo Bingmann
Karlsruhe Inst. of Technology
Karlsruhe, Germany
bingmann@kit.edu

Peter Sanders
Karlsruhe Inst. of Technology
Karlsruhe, Germany
sanders@kit.edu

Christian Schulz
Karlsruhe Inst. of Technology
Karlsruhe, Germany
christian.schulz@kit.edu

ABSTRACT

Previous parallel sorting algorithms do not scale to the largest available machines, since they either have prohibitive communication volume or prohibitive critical path length. We describe algorithms that are a viable compromise and overcome this gap both in theory and practice. The algorithms are multi-level generalizations of the known algorithms sample sort and multiway mergesort. In particular, our sample sort variant turns out to be very scalable both in theory and practice where it scales up to 2^{15} MPI processes with outstanding performance in particular for medium sized inputs. Some tools we develop may be of independent interest – a simple, practical, and flexible sorting algorithm for very small inputs, a near linear time optimal algorithm for solving a constrained bin packing problem, and an algorithm for data delivery, that guarantees a small number of message startups on each processor.

Categories and Subject Descriptors

F.2.2 [**Nonnumerical Algorithms and Problems**]: Sorting and searching; D.1.3 [**PROGRAMMING TECHNIQUES**]: Parallel programming

General Terms

Algorithms; Experimentation; Performance; Theory

Keywords

parallel sorting; multiway mergesort; sample sort

1. INTRODUCTION

Sorting is one of the most fundamental non-numeric algorithms which is needed in a multitude of applications. For example, load balancing in supercomputers often uses space-filling curves. This boils down to sorting data by their position on the curve. Note that in this case most of the work is done for the application and the inputs are relatively small. For these cases, we need sorting algorithms that are not only asymptotically efficient for huge inputs but as fast as possible down to the range where near linear speedup is out of the question.

We study the problem of sorting n elements evenly distributed over p processing elements (PEs) numbered $1..p$.[1] The output requirement is that the PEs store a permutation of the input elements such that the elements on each PE are sorted and such that no element on PE i is larger than any elements on PE $i + 1$.

There is a gap between the theory and practice of parallel sorting algorithms. Between the 1960s and the early 1990s there has been intensive work on achieving asymptotically fast and efficient parallel sorting algorithms. The "best" of these algorithms, e.g., Cole's celebrated $\mathcal{O}(\log p)$ algorithm [9], have prohibitively large constant factors. Some simpler algorithms with running time $\mathcal{O}(\log^2 p)$, however, contain interesting techniques that are in principle practical. These include parallelizations of well known sequential algorithms like mergesort and quicksort [18]. However, when scaling these algorithms to the largest machines, these algorithms cannot be directly used since all data elements are moved a logarithmic number of times which is prohibitive except for very small inputs.

For sorting large inputs, there are algorithms which have to move the data only once. Parallel sample sort [6], is a generalization of quicksort to $p - 1$ splitters (or pivots) which are chosen based on a sufficiently large sample of the input. Each PE partitions its local data into p pieces using the splitters and sends piece i to PE i. After the resulting all-to-all exchange, each PE sorts its received pieces locally. Since every PE at least has to receive the $p - 1$ splitters, sample sort can only by efficient for $n = \Omega(p^2/\log p)$, i.e., it has isoefficiency function $\Omega(p^2/\log p)$ (see also [20]). Indeed, the involved constant factors may be fairly large since the all-to-all exchange implies $p - 1$ message startups if data exchange is done directly. Our generalization of sample sort has isoefficiency function $\mathcal{O}(p^{1+1/k}/\log p)$ when data is allowed to be moved k times.

In parallel p-way multiway mergesort [33, 30], each PE first sorts its local data. Then, as in sample sort, the data is partitioned into p pieces on each PE which are exchanged using an all-to-all exchange. Since the local data is sorted, it becomes feasible to partition the data *perfectly* so that every PE gets the same amount of data.[2] Each PE receives p pieces which have to be merged together. Multiway mergesort has isoefficiency function $\mathcal{O}(p^{1+1/k}\log p)$. This is a factor $\log^2 p$ worse than for sample sort.

---

[1] We use the notation $a..b$ as a shorthand for $\{a, \ldots, b\}$.

[2] Of course this is only possible up to rounding n/p up or down. To simplify the notation and discussion we will often neglect these issues if they are easy to fix.

SPAA'15, June 13–15, 2015, Portland, OR, USA.
Copyright is held by the owner/author(s). Publication rights licensed to ACM.
ACM 978-1-4503-3588-1/15/06 ...$15.00.
DOI: http://dx.doi.org/10.1145/2755573.2755595.

Compromises between these two extremes – high asymptotic scalability but logarithmically many data exchanges versus low scalability but only a single communication – have been considered in the BSP model [32]. Gerbessiotis and Valiant [12] develop a multi-level BSP variant of sample sort. Goodrich [13] gives communication efficient sorting algorithms in the BSP model based on multiway merging. However, these algorithms need a significant constant factor more communications per element than our algorithms. Moreover, the BSP model allows arbitrarily fine-grained communication at no additional cost. In particular, an implementation of the global data exchange primitive of BSP that delivers messages directly has a bottleneck of p message startups for every global message exchange. Also see Section 4.2 for a discussion why it is not trivial to adapt the BSP algorithms to a more realistic model of computation – it turns out that for worst case inputs, one PE may have to receive a large number of small messages.

In Section 4 we give building blocks that may also be of independent interest. We give a simple and fast sorting algorithm for very small inputs. This algorithm is very useful when speed is more important than efficiency, e.g., for sorting samples in sample sort. Furthermore, we present an algorithm for distributing data destined for r groups of PEs in such a way that all PEs in a group get the same amount of *data and* a similar number of *messages*.

Sections 5 and 6 develop multi-level variants of multiway mergesort and sample sort respectively. The basic tuning parameter of these two algorithms is the number of (recursion) levels. With k levels, we basically trade moving the data k times for reducing the startup overheads to $\mathcal{O}(k\sqrt[k]{p})$. Recurse last multiway mergesort (RLM-sort) described in Section 5 has the advantage of achieving perfect load balance. The adaptive multi-level sample sort (AMS-sort) introduced in Section 6 accepts a slight imbalance in the output but is up to a factor $\log^2 p$ faster for small inputs. A feature of AMS-sort that is also interesting for single-level algorithms is that it uses overpartitioning. This reduces the dependence of the required sample size for achieving imbalance ε from $\mathcal{O}(1/\varepsilon^2)$ to $\mathcal{O}(1/\varepsilon)$.

In Section 7 we report results of an experimental implementation of both algorithms. In particular AMS-sort scales up to 2^{15} cores even for moderate input sizes. Multiple levels have a clear advantage over the single-level variants.

2. PRELIMINARIES

For simplicity, we will assume all elements to have unique keys. This is without loss of generality in the sense that we can enforce this assumption by an appropriate tie-breaking scheme. For example, replace a key x with a triple (x, y, z) where y is the PE number where this element is input and z the position in the input array. With some care, this can be implemented in such a way that y and z do not have to be stored or communicated explicitly (see Appendix B).

2.1 Model of Computation

A successful realistic model is (symmetric) single-ported message passing: Sending a message of size ℓ machine words takes time $\alpha + \ell\beta$. The parameter α models startup overhead and β the time to communicate a machine word. For simplicity of exposition, we equate the machine word size with the size of a data element to be sorted. We use this model whenever possible. In particular, it yields good and realistic bounds for collective communication operations. For example, broadcast, reduction, and prefix sums can be implemented to run in time $\mathcal{O}(\beta\ell + \alpha \log p)$ for vectors of length ℓ [2, 27]. However, for moving the bulk of the data, we get very

complex communication patterns where it is difficult to enforce the single-ported requirement.

Our algorithms are bulk synchronous. Such algorithms are often described in the framework of the BSP model [32]. Let BSP(h) denote the time needed to execute a data exchange step where no PE receives or sends more than h words in total. Unfortunately, it is not clear how to implement the data exchange step of BSP efficiently on a realistic parallel machine. In particular, actual implementations of the BSP model deliver the messages directly using up to p startups. For massively parallel machines this is not scalable enough. The BSP* model [4] takes this into account by imposing a minimal message size. However, it also charges the cost for the maximal message size occurring in a data exchange for all its messages and this would be too expensive for our sorting algorithms. We therefore use our own generalization of the BSP model: We consider a black box data exchange function Exch(P, h, r) telling us how long it takes to exchange data on a compact subnetwork of P PEs in such a way that no PE receives or sends more than h words in total and at most r messages in total. Note that all three parameters of the function Exch(P, h, r) may be essential, as they model locality of communication, bottleneck communication volume (see also [8, 26]), and startups respectively. Sometimes we also write $\widetilde{\text{Exch}}(P, h, r)$ as a shorthand for $(1 + o(1))\text{Exch}(P, h, r)$ in order to summarize a sum of Exch($\cdot$) terms by the dominant one. We will also use that to absorb terms of the form $\mathcal{O}(\alpha \log p)$ and $\mathcal{O}(\beta r)$.

When comparing algorithms in different models, we can exploit that Exch(P, h, r) $\leq$ BSP(h) and BSP(h) $\geq$ Exch(p, h, p). Comparing to the single ported model we get Exch(P, h, r) $\geq h\beta + r\alpha$ when data is delivered directly. There are reasons to believe that we can come close to this but we are not aware of actual matching upper bounds. There are offline scheduling algorithms which can deliver the data using time $h\beta$ when startup overheads are ignored (using edge coloring of bipartite multi-graphs). However, this chops messages into many blocks and also requires us to run a parallel edge-coloring algorithm.

2.2 Multiway Merging and Partitioning

Sequential multiway merging of r sequences with total length N can be done in time $\mathcal{O}(N \log r)$. An efficient practical implementation may use tournament trees [19, 24, 30]. If r is small enough, this is even cache efficient, i.e., it incurs only $\mathcal{O}(N/B)$ cache faults where B is the cache block size. If r is too large, i.e., $r > M/B$ for cache size M, then a multi-pass merging algorithm may be advantageous.

The dual operation for sample sort is partitioning the data according to $r - 1$ splitters. This can be done with the same number of comparisons and similarly cache efficiently as r-way merging but has the additional advantage that it can be implemented without causing branch mispredictions [29].

2.3 Multisequence Selection

In its simplest form, given sorted sequences $d_1, \ldots, d_p$ (not necessarily of equal legth) and a rank k, multisequence selection asks for finding an element x with rank k in the union of these sequences. If all elements are different, x also defines positions in the sequences such that there is a total number of k elements to the left of these positions.

There are several algorithms for multisequence selection, e.g. [33, 30]. Here we use a particularly simple and intuitive method based on an adaptation of the well-known quick-select algorithm [15, 22]. This algorithm may be folklore. See also [16]. The algorithm has also been on the publicly available slides of

$$\left(\begin{array}{cccc} [c] & [\,] & [\,] & [f] \\ [\,] & [a] & [e] & [\,] \\ [\,] & [g] & [\,] & [b,d] \end{array}\right) \xrightarrow[\text{rank}]{\text{gossip}} \left(\begin{array}{cccc} [c,f]/\overset{0}{[c]} & [c,f]/\overset{0\ 2}{[a,g]} & [c,f]/\overset{1}{[e]} & [c,f]/\overset{0\ 1\ 1}{[b,d,f]} \\ [a,e]/\overset{1}{[c]} & [a,e]/\overset{0\ 2}{[a,g]} & [a,e]/\overset{1}{[e]} & [a,e]/\overset{1\ 1\ 2}{[b,d,f]} \\ [b,d,g]/\overset{1}{[c]} & [b,d,g]/\overset{0\ 2}{[a,g]} & [b,d,g]/\overset{2}{[e]} & [b,d,g]/\overset{0\ 1\ 2}{[b,d,f]} \end{array}\right) \Bigg\downarrow$$

$$[\text{row}]/\overset{}{[\text{col}]}$$

$$r[c]=2 \qquad \begin{array}{l} r[a]=0, \\ r[g]=6 \end{array} \qquad r[e]=4 \qquad \begin{array}{l} r[b]=1,\, r[d]=3, \\ r[f]=5 \end{array}$$

sum ranks

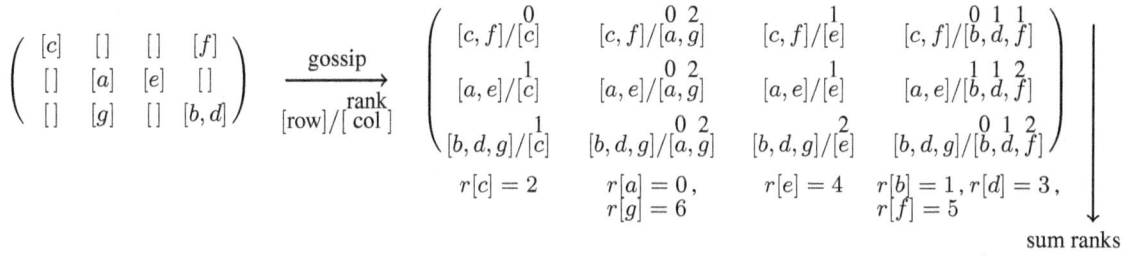

Figure 1: Example calculations done during fast work inefficient sorting algorithm on a 3×4 array of processors. The entries in the matrix on the right show elements received from the particular row and column during the allGather, and the corresponding calculated ranks.

Sanders' lecture on parallel algorithms since 2008 [25]. The base case occurs if there is only a single element (and $k = 1$). Otherwise, a random element is selected as a pivot. This can be done in parallel by choosing the same pseudorandom number between 1 and $\sum_i |d_i|$ on all PEs. Using a prefix sum over the sizes of the sequences, this element can be located easily in time $\mathcal{O}(\alpha \log p)$. Where ordinary quickselect has to partition the input doing linear work, we can exploit the sortedness of the sequences to obtain the same information in time $\mathcal{O}(\log D)$ with $D := \max_i |d_i|$ by doing binary search in parallel on each PE. If items are evenly distributed, we have $D = \Theta(\frac{n}{p})$, and thus only time $\mathcal{O}(\log \frac{n}{p})$ for the search, which partitions all the sequences into two parts. Deciding whether we have to continue searching in the left or the right parts needs a global reduction operation taking time $\mathcal{O}(\alpha \log p)$. The expected depth of the recursion is $\mathcal{O}(\log \sum_i |d_i|) = \mathcal{O}(\log n)$ as in ordinary quickselect. Thus, the overall expected running time is $\mathcal{O}((\alpha \log p + \log \frac{n}{p}) \log n)$.

In our application, we have to perform r simultaneous executions of multisequence selection on the same input sequences but on r different rank values. The involved collective communication operations will then get a vector of length r as input and their running time using an asymptotically optimal implementation is $\mathcal{O}(r\beta + \alpha \log p)$ [2, 27]. Hence, the overall expected running time of multisequence selection becomes

$$\mathcal{O}((\alpha \log p + r\beta + r \log \tfrac{n}{p}) \log n) \ . \tag{1}$$

3. MORE RELATED WORK

We refer to the extended paper [1] for more details and data.

Cole and Ramachandran [10] and Blelloch et al. [7] give multi-level sorting algorithms for cache oblivious shared memory models. Translating them to a distributed memory model looks nontrivial and is likely to result in worse bounds.

Li and Sevcik [21] describe the idea of overpartitioning. However, they use centralized sorting of the sample and a master-worker load balancer dealing out buckets for sorting in order of decreasing bucket size. This leads to very good load balance but is not scalable enough for our purposes and heuristically disperses buckets over all PEs. Achieving the more strict output format that our algorithm uses would require an additional complete data exchange. Our AMS-sort from Section 6 is fully parallelized without sequential bottlenecks and optimally partitions consecutive ranges of buckets.

A state of the art practical parallel sorting algorithm is described by Solomonik and Kale [31]. This single level algorithm can be viewed as a hybrid between multiway mergesort and (deterministic) sample sort. Sophisticated measures are taken for overlapping internal work and communication. TritonSort [23] is a very successful sorting algorithm from the database community. TritonSort is a version of single-level sample-sort with centralized generation of splitters.

There has been a lot of work on making sorting fast on small systems exploiting SIMD, GPU, and shared memory parallelism. We view these results as largely orthogonal to ours. We use the sequential sorting from the STL as our base case for simplicity and portability. However, it should be noted that large performance gains due to exploiting low level hardware properties are mostly observed when sorting unrealistically small objects like 32-bit numbers. Also, since the communication inevitably becomes the bottleneck for very large machines, other optimizations become less and less important.

4. BUILDING BLOCKS

4.1 Fast Work Inefficient Sorting

We generalize an algorithm from [17] which may also be considered folklore. In its most simple form, the algorithm arranges n^2 PEs as a square matrix using PE indices from $1..n \times 1..n$. Input element i is assumed to be present at PE (i, i) initially. The elements are first broadcast along rows and columns. Then, PE (i, j) computes the result of comparing elements i and j (0 or 1). Summing these comparison results over row i yields the rank of element i.

Our generalization works for a rectangular $a \times b$ array of processors where $a = \mathcal{O}(\sqrt{p})$ and $b = \mathcal{O}(\sqrt{p})$. In particular, when $p = 2^P$ is a power of two, then $a = 2^{\lceil P/2 \rceil}$ and $b = 2^{\lfloor P/2 \rfloor}$. Initially, there are n elements uniformly distributed over the PEs, i.e. each PE has at most $\lceil n/p \rceil$ elements as inputs. These are first sorted locally in time $\mathcal{O}(\frac{n}{p} \log \frac{n}{p})$.

Then the locally sorted elements are gossiped (allGather) along both rows and columns (see Figure 1), making sure that the received elements are sorted. This can be achieved in time $\mathcal{O}(\alpha \log p + \beta \frac{n}{\sqrt{p}})$. For example, if the number of participating PEs is a power of two, we can use the well known hypercube algorithm for gossiping (e.g., [20]). The only modification is that received sorted sequences are not simply concatenated but merged.[3]

Elements received from column i are then ranked with respect to the elements received from row j. This can be done in time $\mathcal{O}(\frac{n}{\sqrt{p}})$ by merging these two sequences. Summing these local ranks along rows then yields the global rank of each element. If desired, this information can then be used for routing the input elements in such a way that a globally sorted output is achieved. In our application this is not necessary because we want to extract elements with certain specified ranks as a sample. Either way, we get overall execution time

$$\mathcal{O}\left(\alpha \log p + \beta \frac{n}{\sqrt{p}} + \frac{n}{p} \log \frac{n}{p}\right) \ . \tag{2}$$

---

[3]For general p, we can also use a gather algorithm along a binary tree and finally broadcast the result.

15

Simple Exchange:

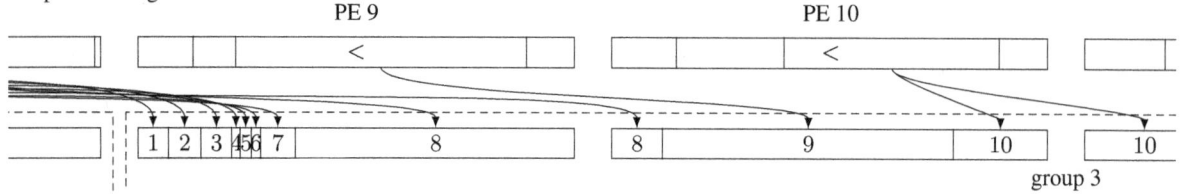

Only first stage, randomly permute PEs during prefix sum:

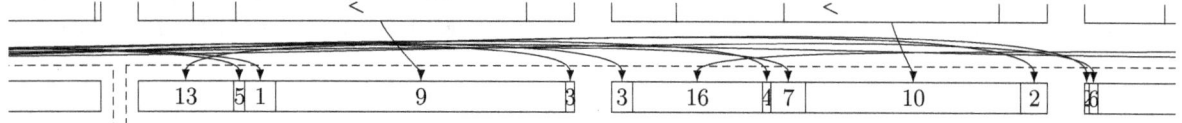

Figure 2: Exchange schema without and with first stage: permutation of PEs

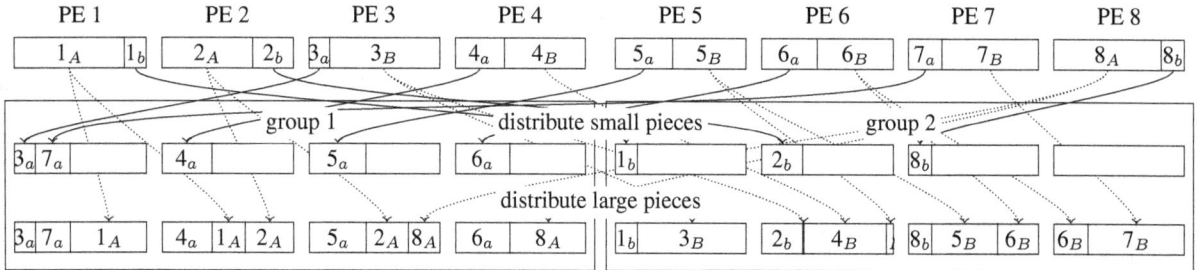

Figure 3: Deterministic data delivery schema

Note that for n polynomial in p this bound is $\mathcal{O}(\alpha \log p + \beta \frac{n}{\sqrt{p}})$. This restrictions is fulfilled for all reasonable applications of this sorting algorithm.

4.2 Delivering Data to the Right Place

In the sorting algorithms considered here we face the following data redistribution problem: Each PE has partitioned its locally present data into r pieces. The pieces with number i have to be moved to PE group i which consists of PEs $(i-1)r + 1..ir$. Each PE in a group should receive the same amount of data except for rounding issues. To simplify the discussion, we describe the algorithm for the case that every PE sends and receives exactly n/p elements. For applicatons with slightly imbalanced data like AMS-sort, we get additional $(1 + \epsilon)$-factors.

We begin with a simple approach and then refine it in order to handle bad cases. The basic idea is to compute a prefix sum over the piece sizes – this is a vector-valued prefix sum with vector length r. As a result, each piece is labeled with a range of positions within the group it belongs to. Positions are numbers between 1 and n/r. An element with number j in group i is sent to PE $(i - 1)\frac{p}{r} + \lceil \frac{jp}{n} \rceil$. This way, each PE sends and receives exactly n/p elements. Moreover, each piece is sent to one or two target PEs responsible for handling it in the recursion. Thereby, each PE *sends* at most $2r$ messages for the data exchange. Unfortunately, the number of *received messages*, although the same on average, may vary widely in the worst case. There are inputs where some PEs have to *receive* $\Omega(p)$ very small pieces. This happens when many consecutively numbered PEs send only very small pieces of data (see PE 9 in the top of Figure 2).

One way to limit the number of received pieces is to use randomization (see [1]). Here we describe a deterministic solution. The basic idea is to distribute small and large pieces separately. In Figure 3 we illustrate the process. First, small pieces of size at most

$n/2pr$ are enumerated using a prefix sum. Small piece i of group j is assigned to PE $\lfloor i/r \rfloor$ of group j. This way, all small pieces are assigned without having to split them and no receiving PE gets more than half its final load.

In the second phase, the remaining (large) pieces are assigned taking the residual capacity of the PEs into account. PE i sends the description of its piece for group j to PE $\lfloor i/r \rfloor$ of group j. This can be done in time $\text{Exch}(p, \mathcal{O}(r), r)$. Now, each group produces an assignment of its large pieces independently, i.e., each group of p/r PEs assigns up to p pieces $- r$ on each PE. In the following, we describe the assignment process for a single group.

Conceptually, we enumerate the unassigned elements on the one hand and the unassigned slots able to take them on the other hand and then map element i to slot i.[4] To implement this, we compute a prefix sum of the residual capacities of the receiving PEs on the one hand and the sizes of the unassigned pieces of the other hand. This yields two sorted sequences X and Y respectively which are merged in order to locate the destination PEs of each large piece. Assume that ties in values of X and Y are broken such that elements from X are considered smaller. In the merged sequence, a subsequence of the form $\langle x_i, y_j, \ldots, y_{j+k}, x_{i+1}, z \rangle$ indicates that pieces $j, \ldots, j + k$ have to moved to PE i. Piece $j + k$ may also wrap over to PE $i + 1$, and possibly to PE $i + 2$ if $z = x_{i+2}$. The assumptions on the input guarantee that no further wrapping over is possible since no piece can be larger than n/p and since every PE has residual capacity at least $\frac{n}{2p}$. Similarly, since large pieces have size at least $n/2pr$ and each PE gets assigned at most n/p elements, no PE gets more than $\frac{n}{p} / \frac{n}{2pr} = 2r$ large pieces.

---

[4]A similar approach to data redistribution is described in [16]. However, here we can exploit special properties of the input to obtain a simpler solution that avoids segmented gather and scatter operations.

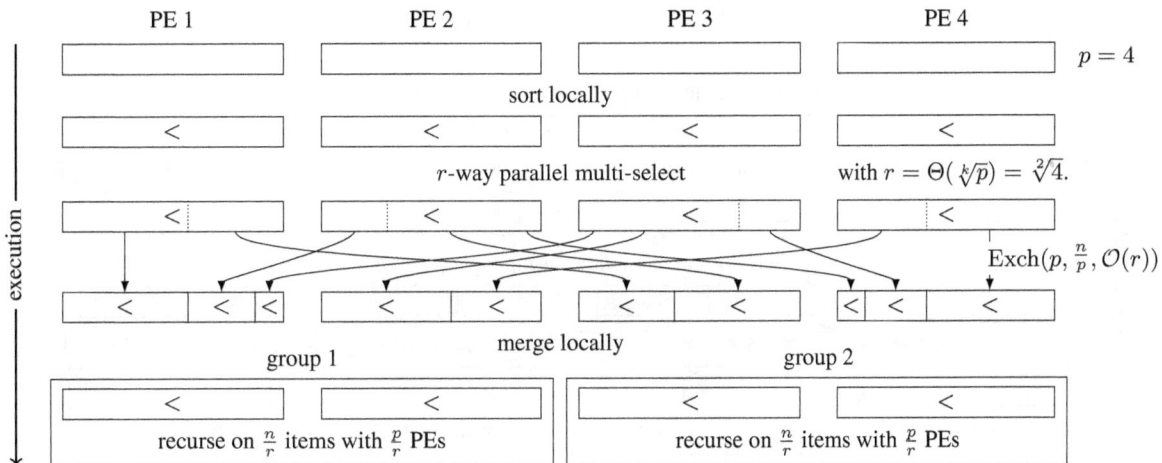

Figure 4: Algorithm schema of Recurse Last Parallel Multiway Mergesort

The difficult part is merging the two sorted sequences X and Y. Here one can adapt and simplify the work efficient parallel merging algorithm for EREW PRAMs from [14]. Essentially, one first merges the p/r elements of X with a deterministic sample of Y – we include the prefix sum for the first large piece on each PE into Y. This merging operation can be done in time $\mathcal{O}(\alpha \log(p/r))$ using Batcher's merging network [3]. Then each element of X has to be located within the $\leq r$ local elements of Y on one particular PE. Since it is impossible that these pieces (of total size $\leq rn/p$) fill more than $2r$ PEs (of residual capacity $> n/2p$), each PE will have to locate only $\mathcal{O}(r)$ elements. This can be done using local merging in time $\mathcal{O}(r)$. In other words, the special properties of the considered sequence make it unnecessary to perform the contention resolution measures making [14] somewhat complicated. Overall, we get the following deterministic result (recall from Section 2.1 that $\widetilde{\mathrm{Exch}}(\cdot)$ also absorbs terms of the form $\mathcal{O}(\alpha \log p + \beta r)$).

THEOREM 1. *Data delivery of $r \times p$ pieces to r parts can be implemented to run in time*

$$\widetilde{\mathrm{Exch}}(p, \tfrac{n}{p}, \mathcal{O}(r)) \ .$$

5. GENERALIZING MULTI-LEVEL MERGESORT (RLM-SORT)

We subdivide the PEs into "natural" groups of size p' on which we want to recurse. Asymptotically, $r := p/p'$ around $\sqrt[k]{p}$ is a good choice if we want to make k levels of recursion. However, we may also fix p' based on architectural properties. For example, in a cluster of many-core machines, we might choose p' as the number of cores in one node. Similarly, if the network has a natural hierarchy, we will adapt p' to that situation. For example, if PEs within a rack are more tightly connected than inter-rack connections, we may choose p' to be the number of PEs within a rack. Other networks, e.g., meshes or tori have less pronounced cutting points. However, it still makes sense to map groups to subnetworks with nice properties, e.g., nearly cubic subnetworks. For simplicity, we will assume that p is divisible by p', and that $r = \Theta(\sqrt[k]{p})$.

There are several ways to define multi-level multiway mergesort. We describe a method we call "recurse last" (see Figure 4) that needs to communicate the data only k times and avoids problems with many small messages. Every PE sorts locally first. Then each of these p sorted sequences is partitioned into r pieces in such a way that the sum of these piece sizes is n/r for each of these

r resulting *parts*. In contrast to the single level algorithm, we run only r multisequence selections in parallel and thus reduce the bottleneck due to multisequence selection by a factor of p'.

Now we have to move the data to the responsible groups. We defer to Section 4.2 which shows how this is possible using time $\widetilde{\mathrm{Exch}}(p, \tfrac{n}{p}, \mathcal{O}(\sqrt[k]{p}))$.

Afterwards, group i stores elements which are no larger than any element in group $i + 1$ and it suffices to recurse within each group. However, we do not want to ignore the information already available – each PE stores not an entirely unsorted array but a number of sorted sequences. This information is easy to use though – we merge these sequences locally first and obtain locally sorted data which can then be subjected to the next round of splitting.

THEOREM 2. *RLM-sort with $k = \mathcal{O}(1)$ levels of recursion can be implemented to run in time*

$$\mathcal{O}\left(\left(\alpha \log p + \sqrt[k]{p}\,\beta + \sqrt[k]{p} \log \tfrac{n}{p} + \tfrac{n}{p}\right) \log n\right) +$$
$$\sum_{i=1}^{k} \widetilde{\mathrm{Exch}}\left(p^{\frac{i}{k}}, \tfrac{n}{p}, \mathcal{O}(\sqrt[k]{p})\right) \ . \tag{3}$$

PROOF. (Outline) Local sorting takes time $\mathcal{O}(\tfrac{n}{p} \log n)$. For $k = \mathcal{O}(1)$ multiselections we get the bound from Equation (1), $\mathcal{O}((\alpha \log p + r\beta + r \log \tfrac{n}{p}) \log n)$. Summing the latter two contributions, we get the first term of Equation (3).

In level i of the recursion we have r^i independent groups containing $p/r^i = p/p^{i/k} = p^{1-i/k}$ PEs each. An exchange within the group in level i costs $\widetilde{\mathrm{Exch}}(p^{1-i/k}, \tfrac{n}{p}, \mathcal{O}(\tfrac{r}{r^i}))$ time. Since all independent exchanges are performed simultaneously, we only need to sum over the k recursive levels, which yields the second term of Equation (3). □

Equation (3) is a fairly complicated expression but using some reasonable assumptions we can simplify it. If all communications are equally expensive, the sum becomes $k\widetilde{\mathrm{Exch}}(p, \tfrac{n}{p}, \mathcal{O}(\sqrt[k]{p}))$ – we have k message exchanges involving all the data but we limit the number of startups to $\mathcal{O}(\sqrt[k]{p})$. On the other hand, on mesh or torus networks, the first (global) exchange will dominate the cost and we get $\widetilde{\mathrm{Exch}}(p, \tfrac{n}{p}, \mathcal{O}(\sqrt[k]{p}))$ for the sum. If we also assume that data is delivered directly, $\Omega(\sqrt[k]{p})$ startups hidden in the $\widetilde{\mathrm{Exch}}()$ term will dominate the $\mathcal{O}(\log^2 p)$ startups in the remaining algorithm. We can assume that n is bounded by a polynomial in p – otherwise, a traditional single-phase multi-way mergesort would be a

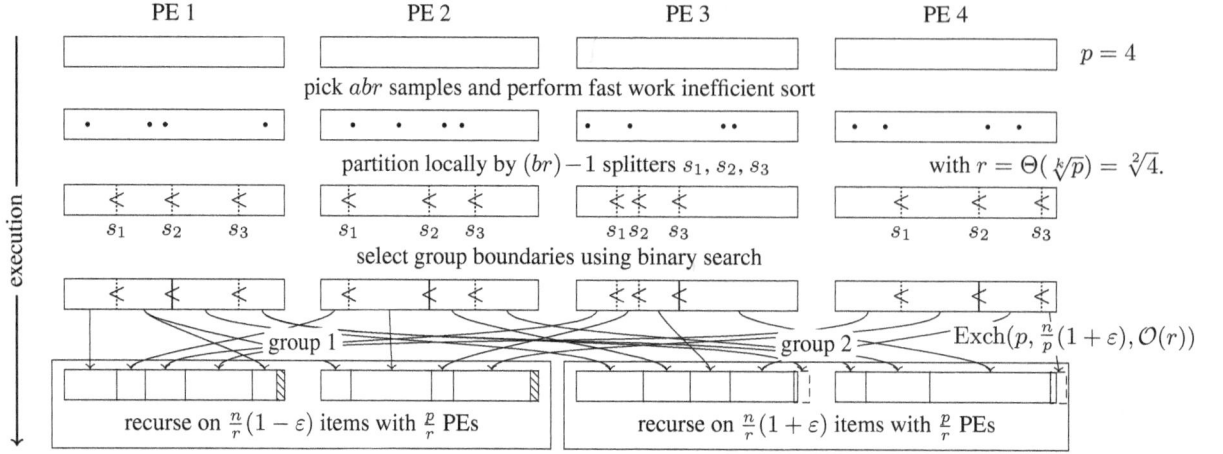

Figure 5: Algorithm schema of AMS-sort

better algorithm. This implies that $\log n = \Theta(\log p)$. Furthermore, if $n = \omega(p^{1+1/k} \log p)$ then $n/p = \omega(p^{\frac{1}{k}} \log p)$, and the term $\Omega(\beta \frac{n}{p})$ hidden in the data exchange term dominates the term $\mathcal{O}(\beta p^{\frac{1}{k}} \log n)$. Thus Equation (3) simplifies to $\mathcal{O}(\frac{n}{p} \log n)$ (essentially the time for internal sorting) plus the data exchange term.

If we also assume α and β to be constants and estimate $\widehat{\text{Exch}}$-term as $\mathcal{O}(\frac{n}{p})$, we get execution time

$$\mathcal{O}(\sqrt[k]{p} \log^2 p + \frac{n}{p} \log n) \ .$$

From this, we can infer a $\mathcal{O}(p^{1+1/k} \log p)$ as isoefficiency function.

6. ADAPTIVE MULTI-LEVEL SAMPLE SORT (AMS-SORT)

A good starting point is the multi-level sample sort algorithm by Gerbessiotis and Valiant [12]. However, they use centralized sorting of the sample and their data redistribution may lead to some processors receiving $\Omega(p)$ messages (see also Section 4.2). We improve on this algorithm in several ways to achieve a truly scalable algorithm. First, we sort the sample using fast parallel sorting. Second, we use the advanced data delivery algorithms described in Section 4.2, and third, we give a scalable parallel adaptation of the idea of overpartitioning [21] in order to reduce the sample size needed for good load balance.

But back to our version of multi-level sample sort (see Figure 5). As in RLM-sort, our intention is to split the PEs into r groups of size $p' = p/r$ each, such that each group processes elements with consecutive ranks. To achieve this, we choose a random sample of size abr where the *oversampling factor* a and the *overpartitioning factor* b are tuning parameters. The sample is sorted using a fast sorting algorithm. We assume the fast inefficient algorithm from Section 4.1. Its execution time is $\mathcal{O}(\frac{abr}{p} \log \frac{abr}{p} + \beta \frac{abr}{\sqrt{p}} + \alpha \log p)$.

From the sorted sample, we choose $br - 1$ splitter elements with equidistant rank. These splitters are broadcast to all PEs. This is possible in time $\mathcal{O}(\beta br + \alpha \log p)$.

Then every PE partitions its local data into br buckets corresponding to these splitters. This takes time $\mathcal{O}(\frac{n}{p} \log(br))$.

Using a global (all-)reduction, we then determine global bucket sizes in time $\mathcal{O}(\beta br + \alpha \log p)$. These can be used to assign buckets to PE-groups in a load balanced way: Given an upper bound L on the number of elements per PE-group, we can scan through

the array of bucket sizes and skip to the next PE-group when the total load would exceed L. Using binary search on L, this finds an optimal value for L in time $\mathcal{O}(br \log n)$ using a sequential algorithm. In Appendix A we explain how this can be improved to $\mathcal{O}(br \log br)$ and, using parallelization, even to $\mathcal{O}(br + \alpha \log p)$.

LEMMA 1. *The above binary search scanning algorithm indeed finds the optimal L.*

PROOF. We first show that binary search suffices to find the optimal L for which the scanning algorithm succeeds. Let L^* denote this value. For this to be true, it suffices to show that for any $L \geq L^*$, the scanning algorithm finds a feasible partition into groups with load at most L. This works because the scanning algorithm maintains the invariant that after defining i groups, the algorithm with bound L has scanned at least as many buckets as the algorithm with bound L^*. Hence, when the scanning algorithm with bound L^* has defined all groups, the one with bound L has scanned at least as many buckets as the algorithm with bound L^*. Applying this invariant to the final group yields the desired result.

Now we prove that no other algorithm can find a better solution. Let L^* denote the maximum group size of an optimal partitioning algorithm. We argue that the scanning algorithm with bound L^* will succeed. We now compare any optimal algorithm with the scanning algorithm. Consider the first i buckets defined by both algorithms. It follows by induction on i that the total size s_i^s of these buckets for the scanning algorithm is at least as large as the corresponding value s_i^* for the optimal algorithm: This is certainly true for $i = 0$ ($s_0^s = s_0^* = 0$). For the induction step, suppose that the optimal algorithm chooses a bucket of size y, i.e., $s_{x+1}^* = s_x^* + y$. By the induction hypothesis, we know that $s_i^s \geq s_i^*$. Now suppose, the induction invariant would be violated for $i + 1$, i.e., $s_{i+1}^s < s_{i+1}^*$. Overall, we get $s_i^* \leq s_i^s < s_{i+1}^s < s_{i+1}^*$. This implies that $s_{i+1}^s - s_i^s$ – the size of group $i + 1$ for the scanning algorithm – is smaller than y. Moreover, this group contains a proper subset of the buckets included by the optimal algorithm. This is a impossible since there is no reason why the scanning algorithm should not at least achieve a bucket size $s_{i+1}^s - s_i^s \leq y \leq L^*$. □

LEMMA 2. *We can achieve $L = (1+\varepsilon)\frac{n}{r}$ with high probability choosing appropriate $b = \Omega(1/\varepsilon)$ and $ab = \Omega(\log r)$.*

PROOF. We only give the basic idea of a proof. We argue that the scanning algorithm is likely to succeed with $L = (1+\varepsilon)\frac{n}{r}$ as a group size limit. Using Chernoff bounds it can be shown that $ab = \Omega(\log r)$ ensures that no bucket has size larger than $\frac{n}{r}$ with

18

high probability. Hence, the scanning algorithm can always build feasible PE groups from one or multiple buckets.

Choosing $b \geq 2/\varepsilon$ means that the expected bucket size is $\leq \frac{\varepsilon}{2} \cdot \frac{n}{r}$. Indeed, most elements will be in buckets of size less than $\varepsilon \frac{n}{r}$. Hence, when the scanning algorithm adds a bucket to a PE-group such that the average group size $\frac{n}{r}$ is passed for the first time, most of the time this additional group will also fit below the limit of $(1+\varepsilon)\frac{n}{r}$. Overall, the scanning algorithm will mostly form groups of size exceeding $\frac{n}{r}$ and thus r groups will suffice to cover all buckets of total size n. $\quad\square$

The data splitting defined by the bucket group is then the input for the data delivery algorithm described in Section 4.2. This takes time $\mathrm{E\widehat{xc}h}\,(p, (1+o(1))L, (2+o(1))r))$.

We recurse on the PE-groups similar to Section 5. Within the recursion it can be exploited that the elements are already partitioned into br buckets.

We get the following overall execution time for one level:

LEMMA 3. *One level of AMS-sort works in time*

$$\mathcal{O}\left(\frac{n}{p}\log\frac{r}{\varepsilon} + \beta\frac{r}{\varepsilon}\right) + \mathrm{E\widehat{xc}h}(p, (1+\varepsilon)\frac{n}{p}, \mathcal{O}(r)) \quad. \quad (4)$$

PROOF. (Outline) This follows from Lemma 2 and the individual running times described above using $ab = \Theta(\max(\log r, 1/\varepsilon))$, $b = \Theta(1/\varepsilon)$, and fast inefficient sorting for sorting the sample. The sample sorting term then reads $\mathcal{O}(\frac{abr}{p}\log\frac{abr}{p} + \beta\frac{abr}{\sqrt{p}} + \alpha\log p)$ which is $o(\frac{n}{p}\log\frac{r}{\varepsilon} + \frac{\beta}{\varepsilon}) + \alpha\log p$. Note that the term $\alpha\log p$ is absorbed into the $\mathrm{E\widehat{xc}h}$-term. $\quad\square$

Compared to previous implementations of sample sort, including the one from Gerbessiotis and Valiant [12], AMS-sort improves the sample size from $\mathcal{O}(p\log p/\varepsilon^2)$ to $\mathcal{O}(p(\log r + 1/\varepsilon))$ and the number of startup overheads in the Exch-term from $\mathcal{O}(p)$ to $\mathcal{O}(r)$.

In the base case of AMS-sort, when the recursion reaches a single PE, the local data is sorted sequentially.

THEOREM 3. *Adaptive multi-level sample sort (AMS-sort) with k levels of recursion and a factor $(1 + \varepsilon)$ imbalance in the output can be implemented to run in time*

$$\mathcal{O}\left(\frac{n}{p}\log n + \beta\frac{k^2\sqrt[k]{p}}{\varepsilon}\right) + \sum_{i=1}^{k}\mathrm{E\widehat{xc}h}\left(p^{\frac{i}{k}}, (1+\varepsilon)\frac{n}{p}, \mathcal{O}(\sqrt[k]{p})\right)$$

if $k = \mathcal{O}(\log p/\log\log p)$ and $\frac{1}{\varepsilon} = \mathcal{O}(\sqrt[k]{n})$.

PROOF. We choose $r = \sqrt[k]{p}$. Since errors multiply, we choose $\varepsilon' = \sqrt[k]{1+\varepsilon} - 1 = \Theta(\frac{\varepsilon}{k})$ as the balance parameter for each level. Using Lemma 3 we get the following terms.
For internal computation: $\mathcal{O}(\frac{n}{p})\log n$ for the final internal sorting. (We do not exploit that overpartitioning presorts the data to some extent.) For partitioning, we apply Lemma 3 and get time

$$\mathcal{O}\left(k\log\frac{r}{\epsilon'}\right) = \mathcal{O}\left(k\frac{n}{p}\log\frac{k\sqrt[k]{p}}{\varepsilon}\right)$$
$$= \frac{n}{p}\mathcal{O}\left(\log p + k\log k + k\log\frac{1}{\varepsilon}\right) \quad (5)$$
$$= \frac{n}{p}\mathcal{O}(\log p + \log n) \quad.$$

The last estimate uses the preconditions $k = \mathcal{O}(\log p/\log\log p)$ and $\frac{1}{\varepsilon} = \mathcal{O}(\sqrt[k]{n})$ in order to simplify the theorem.

For communication volume we get $k \cdot \beta\frac{r}{\varepsilon'} = \mathcal{O}(\beta\frac{k^2\sqrt[k]{p}}{\varepsilon})$. For startup latencies we get $\mathcal{O}(\alpha k\log p)$ which can be absorbed into the $\mathrm{E\widehat{xc}h}()$-terms.

The data exchange term is the same as for RLM-sort except that we have a slight imbalance in the communication volume. $\quad\square$

Using a similar argument as for RLM-sort, for constant k and ε, we get an isoefficiency function of $p^{1+1/k}/\log p$ for $r = \sqrt[k]{p}$. This is a factor $\log^2 p$ better than for RLM-sort and is an indication that AMS-sort might be the better algorithm – in particular if some imbalance in the output is acceptable and if the inputs are rather small.

Another indicator for the good scalability of AMS-sort is that we can view it as a generalization of parallel quicksort that also works efficiently for very small inputs. For example, suppose $n = \mathcal{O}(p\log p)$ and $1/\varepsilon = \mathcal{O}(1)$. We run $k = \mathcal{O}(\log p)$ levels of AMS-sort with $r = \mathcal{O}(1)$ and $\varepsilon' = \mathcal{O}(k/\varepsilon)$. This yields running time $\mathcal{O}(\log^2 p\log\log p + \alpha\log^2 p)$ using the bound from Equation (5) for the local work. This does a factor $\mathcal{O}(\log\log p)$ more local work than an asymptotically optimal algorithm. However, this is likely to be irrelevant in practice since it is likely that $\alpha \gg \log\log p$. Also the factor $\log\log p$ would disappear in an implementation that exploits the information gained during bucket partitioning.

7. EXPERIMENTAL RESULTS

We now present the results of our AMS-sort and RLM-sort experiments. In our experiments we run a *weak scaling* benchmark, which shows how the wall-time varies for an increasing number of processors for a fixed number of elements per processor. The test covers the AMS-sort and RLM-sort algorithms executed with 10^5, 10^6, and 10^7 64-bit integers. We ran our experiments at the thin node cluster of the SuperMUC (www.lrz.de/supermuc), an island-based distributed system consisting of 18 islands, each with 512 computation nodes. However, the maximum number of islands available to us was four. Each computation node has two Sandy Bridge-EP Intel Xeon E5-2680 8-core processors with a nominal frequency of 2.7 GHz and 32 GByte of memory. However, jobs will run at the standard frequency of 2.3 GHz as the LoadLeveler does not classify the implementation as accelerative based on the algorithm's energy consumption and runtime. A non-blocking topology tree connects the nodes within an island using the Infiniband FDR10 network technology. Computation nodes are connected to the non-blocking tree by Mellanox FDR ConnectX-3 InfiniBand mezzanine adapters. A pruned tree connects the islands among each other with a bidirectional bisection bandwidth ratio of $4 : 1$. The interconnect has a theoretical bisection bandwidth of up to 35.6 TB/s.

7.1 Implementation Details

We implemented AMS-sort and RLM sort in C++ with the main objective to demonstrate that multi-level algorithms can be useful for large p and moderate n. We use naive prefix-sum based data delivery since we currently only use random inputs anyway – for these, the naive algorithm coincides with the deterministic algorithm since all pieces are large with high probability.

AMS-sort implements overpartitioning, however it uses the simple sequential algorithm for bucket grouping which incurs an avoidable factor $\mathcal{O}(\log n)$. Also, information stemming from overpartitioning is not yet exploited for the recursive subproblems. This means that overpartitioning is not yet as effective as it would be in a full-fledged implementation.

We divide each level of the algorithms into four distinct phases: splitter selection, bucket processing (multiway merging or distribution), data delivery, and local sorting. To measure the time of each phase, we place an MPI barrier before each phase. Timings for these phases are accumulated over all recursion levels.

k	level	p			
		512	2 048	8 192	32 768
1	1	16	16	16	16
2	1	32	128	512	2 048
	2	16	16	16	16
3	1	8	16	32	64
	2	4	8	16	32
	3	16	16	16	16

Table 1: Selection of r for weak scaling experiments

n/p	p			
	512	2 048	8 192	32 768
10^5	0.0228	0.0277	0.0359	0.0707
10^6	0.2212	0.2589	0.2687	0.9171
10^7	2.6523	2.9797	4.0625	6.0932

Table 2: AMS-sort median wall-times of weak scaling experiments in seconds

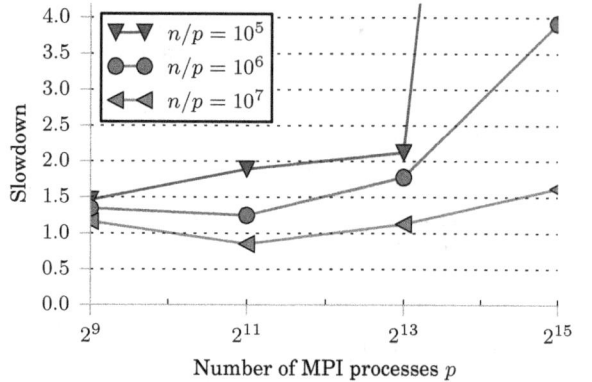

Figure 6: Slowdown of RLM-sort compared to AMS-sort based on optimal level choice

The time for building MPI communicators (which can be considerable) is not included in the running time since this can be viewed as a precomputation that can be reused over arbitrary inputs.

The algorithms are written in C++11 and compiled with version 15.0 of the Intel icpc compiler, using the full optimization flag *-O3* and the instruction set specified with *-march=corei7-avx*. For inter-process communication, we use version 1.3 of the IBM mpich2 library.

During the bucket processing phase of RLM-sort, we use the sequential_multiway_merge implementation of the GNU Standard C++ Library to merge buckets [30]. We used our own implementation of multisplitter partitioning in the bucket processing phase, borrowed from super scalar sample sort [29].

For the data delivery phase, we use our own implementation of a 1-factor algorithm [28] and compare it against the all-to-allv implementation of the IBM mpich2 library. The 1-factor implementation performs up to p pairwise MPI_Isend and MPI_Irecv operations to distribute the buckets to their target groups. In contrast to the mpich2 implementation, our 1-factor implementation omits the exchange of empty messages. We found that the 1-factor implementation is more stable and exchanges data with a higher throughput on the average. Local sorting uses std::sort.

7.2 Weak Scaling Analysis

The experimental setting of the weak scaling test is as follows: We benchmarked AMS-sort at 32, 128, 512, and 2 048 nodes. Each node executed 16 MPI processes. This results in 512, 2 048, 8 192, and 32 768 MPI processes. The benchmark configuration for 2 048 nodes has been executed on four exclusively allocated islands. Table 1 shows the level configurations of our algorithm. AMS-sort, configured with more than one level, splits the remaining processes into groups with a size of 16 MPI processes at the second to last level. Thereby, the last level communicates just node-internally. For the 3-level AMS-sort, we split the MPI processes at the first level into $2^{\lceil \log(p)/2 \rceil}$ groups. AMS-sort configured the splitter selection phase with an overpartitioning factor of $b = 16$ and an oversampling factor of $ab = 1.6 \log_{10} n$.

Figure 7 details the wall-time of AMS-sort up to three levels. For each wall-time, we show the proportion of time taken by each phase. The depicted wall-time is the median of five measurements. Observe that AMS-sort is not limited by the splitter selection phase in all test cases. In most cases, AMS-sort with more than one level

decreases the wall-time up to 8 192 MPI processes. Also, there is a speedup in the data delivery phase and no significant slowdown in the bucket processing phase due to cache effects. In these cases, the cost for partitioning the data and distributing more than once is compensated by the decreased number of startups. For the smaller volume of 10^5 elements per MPI process, note that 3-level AMS-sort is much faster than 2-level AMS-sort in our experimental setup; the effect is reversed for more elements. Note that there is inter-island data delivery at the first and second level of 3-level AMS-sort. The slowdown of sorting 10^6 elements per MPI process with 3-level AMS-sort compared to 2-level AMS-sort is small. So we assume that the three level version becomes faster than the two level version executed at more than four islands. In that case, it is more reasonable to set the number of groups in the first level equal the number of islands. This results in inter-island communication just within the first level.

Table 2 depicts the median wall-time of our weak scaling experiments of AMS-sort. Each entry is selected based on the level which performed best. For a fixed p, the wall-time increases almost linearly with the number of elements per MPI process. One exception is the wall-time for 8 192 nodes and 10^7 elements. We were not able to measure the 2-level AMS-sort as the MPI-implementation failed during this experiment. The wall-time increases by a small factor up to 8 192 MPI processes for increasing p. Executed with 32 768 MPI processes, AMS-sort is up to 3.5 times slower compared to intra-island sorting, allocated at one whole island. The slowdown can be feasibly explained by the interconnect which connects islands among each other. The interconnect has an bandwidth ratio of $4 : 1$ compared to the intra-island interconnect.

Generally, for large p, the execution time fluctuates a lot (see [1]). This fluctuation is almost exclusively within the all-to-all exchange. Further research has to show to what extent this is caused by interference due to network traffic of other applications or by a suboptimal implementation of the all-to-all data exchange. Both effects seem to be independent of the sorting algorithm however.

Figure 6 illustrates the slowdown of RLM-sort compared to AMS-sort. For each algorithm, we selected the number of levels with the best wall-time. Note that the slowdown of RLM-sort is higher than one in almost all test cases. The slowdown is significantly increased for small n and large p. This observation matches with the isoefficiency function of RLM-sort which is a $\log^2 p$ factor worse than the isoefficiency function of AMS-sort.

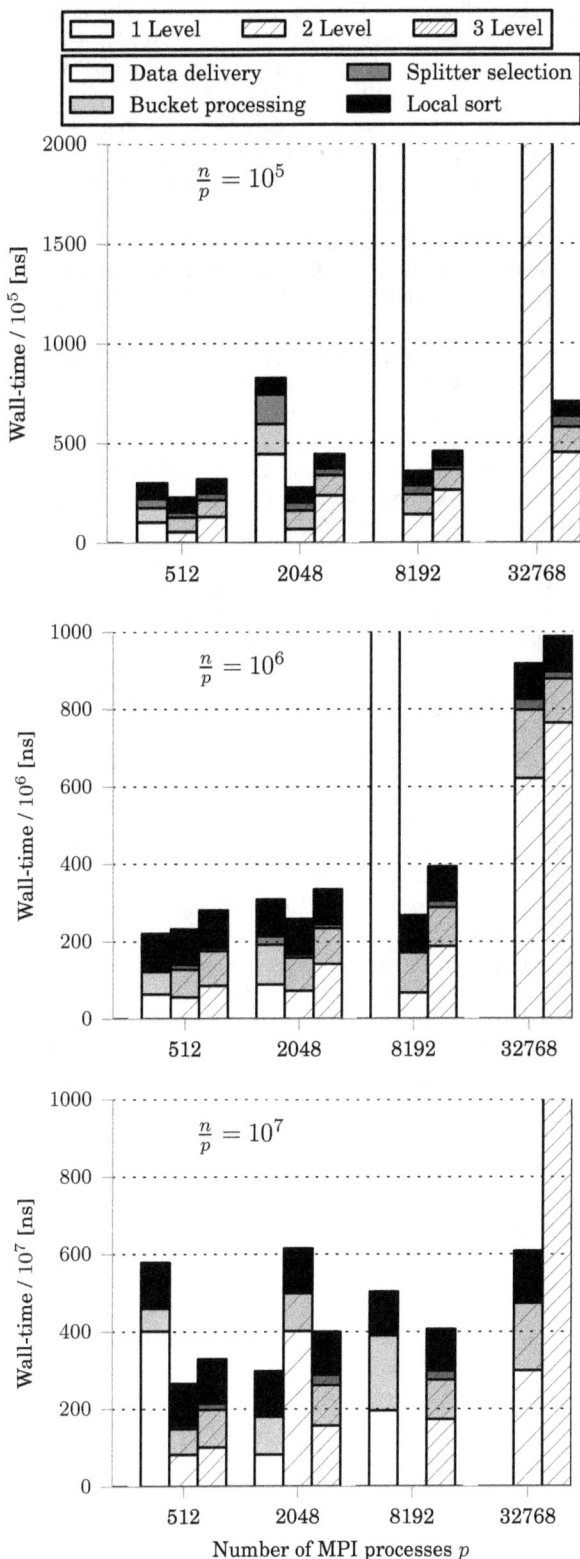

Figure 7: Weak scaling with 10^5, 10^6, and 10^7 elements per MPI process of AMS-sort

7.3 Speedup Analysis

| n/p | \multicolumn{4}{c}{p} | | | |
	512	2 048	8 192	32 768
10^5	273	956	3 208	6 929
10^6	321	1 146	4 747	6 164
10^7	295	1 124	–	–

Table 3: Speedup of AMS-sort compared to sequential sorting

The total amount of data sorted during the larger weak scaling experiments is much larger than the memory of a single SuperMUC node. In order to obtain some information on speedup over the sequential case, we therefore make comparisons with a system that has a similar processor (Sandy Bridge-EP Intel Xeon E5-4640 2.4 GHz, Turbo Boost disabled) but 512 GB RAM and thus allows us to measure sequential execution times for all the instances except for the two largest ones. Table 3 shows the speedups obtained over sequential std::sort which is also used for the sequential base case of our parallel sorters.[5] In most cases, the efficiency of AMS-sort executed on a single island ($p \leq 8\,192$) is higher than 0.5. The efficiency of sorting on four islands drops to approximately 0.2. One possible reason is that the bisection bandwidth between islands is four times less than the bandwidth between nodes within the same island.

7.4 Comparison with Other Implementations

Comparisons to other systems are difficult, since it is not easy to simply download other people's software and to get it to run on a large machine. Hence, we have to compare to the literature and the web. Our absolute running times for $n = 10^7 p$ are similar to those of observed in Solomonik and Kale [31] for $n = 8 \cdot 10^6 \cdot p$ on a CrayXT 4 with up to 2^{15} PEs. This machine has somewhat slower PEs (2.1 GHz AMD Barcelona) but higher communication bandwidth per PE. No running times for smaller inputs are given. It is likely that there the advantage of multi-level algorithms such as ours becomes more visible. Still, adapting their techniques for overlapping communication and sorting might be useful for our codes too.

A more recent experiment running on even more PEs is MP-sort [11]. MP-sort is a single-level multiway mergesort that implements local multiway merging by sorting from scratch. They run the same weak scaling test as we do using up to 160 000 cores of a Cray XE6 (16 AMD Opteron cores × 2 processors × 5 000 nodes). This code is much slower than ours. For $n = 10^5 \cdot p$, and $p = 2^{14}$ the code needs 20.45 seconds – 289 times more than ours for $p = 2^{15}$. When going to $p = 80\,000$ the running time of MP-sort goes up by another order of magnitude. At large p, MP-sort is hardly slower for larger inputs (however still about six times slower than AMS-sort). This is a clear indication that a single level algorithm does not scale for small inputs.

Different but also interesting is the Sort Benchmark which is quite established in the data base community (sortbenchmark.org). The closest category is Minute-Sort. The 2014 winner, Baidu-Sort (which uses the same algorithm as TritonSort [23]), sorts 7 TB of data (100 byte elements with 10 byte random keys) in 56.7s using 993 nodes with two 8-core processors (Intel Xeon E5-2450, 2.2 GHz) each ($p = 15\,888$). Compared to our experiment at $n = 10^7 \cdot 2^{15}$, they use about half as many cores as we do, and sort about 2.7 times more data. On the other hand, Baidu-Sort

---
[5]There may be faster sequential sorters. But if we only consider codes with comparable robustsness, generality, and space consumption, we may be close to measuring absolute speedup here.

takes about 9.3 times longer than our 2-level algorithm. Even disregarding that we also sort about 5 times more (8-byte) elements, this leaves us being about two times more efficient. This comparison is unfair to some extent since Minute-Sort requires the input to be read from disk and the result to be written to disk. However, the machine used by Baidu-Sort has 993×8 hard disks. At a typical transfer rate of 150 MB/s this means that, in principle, it is possible to read and write more than 30 TB of data within the execution time. Hence, it seems that also for Baidu-Sort, the network was the major performance bottleneck.

8. CONCLUSION

We have shown how practical parallel sorting algorithms like multi-way mergesort and sample sort can be generalized so that they scale on massively parallel machines without incurring a large additional amount of communication volume. Already our prototypical implementation of AMS-sort shows very competitive performance that is probably the best by orders of magnitude for large p and moderate n. For large n it can compete with the best single-level algorithms.

Future work should include experiments on more PEs, a native shared-memory implementation of the node-local level, a full implementation of data delivery, faster implementation of overpartitioning, and, at least for large n, more overlapping of communication and computation. However, the major open problem seems to be better data exchange algorithms, possibly independently of the sorting algorithm.

Acknowledgments:. The authors gratefully acknowledge the Gauss Centre for Supercomputing e.V. (www.gauss-centre.eu) for funding this project by providing computing time on the GCS Supercomputer SuperMUC at Leibniz Supercomputing Centre (LRZ, www.lrz.de). Special thanks go to SAP AG, Ingo Mueller, and Sebastian Schlag for making their 1-factor algorithm [26] available. Additionally, we would like to thank Christian Siebert for valuable discussions. This research was partially supported by DFG project SA 933/11-1.

9. REFERENCES

[1] M. Axtmann, T. Bingmann, P. Sanders, and C. Schulz. Practical massively parallel sorting. *CoRR*, abs/1410.6754v2, 2015.

[2] V. Bala, J. Bruck, R. Cypher, P. Elustondo, A. Ho, C. Ho, S. Kipnis, and M. Snir. CCL: A portable and tunable collective communication library for scalable parallel computers. *IEEE Transactions on Parallel and Distributed Systems*, 6(2):154–164, 1995.

[3] K. E. Batcher. Sorting networks and their applications. In *AFIPS Spring Joint Computing Conference*, pages 307–314, 1968.

[4] A. Bäumker, W. Dittrich, and F. Meyer auf der Heide. Truly efficient parallel algorithms: c-optimal multisearch for an extension of the BSP model. In *3rd European Symposium on Algorithms (ESA)*, volume 979 of *LNCS*, pages 17–30. Springer, 1995.

[5] T. Bingmann, A. Eberle, and P. Sanders. Engineering parallel string sorting. *Preprint arXiv:1403.2056*, 2014.

[6] G. E. Blelloch et al. A comparison of sorting algorithms for the connection machine CM-2. In *3rd ACM Symposium on Parallel Algorithms and Architectures (SPAA)*, pages 3–16, 1991.

[7] G. E. Blelloch, P. B. Gibbons, and H. V. Simhadri. Low depth cache-oblivious algorithms. In *22nd ACM Symposium on Parallelism in Algorithms and Architectures (SPAA)*, pages 189–199, 2010.

[8] S. Borkar. Exascale computing – a fact or a fiction? Keynote presentation at IPDPS 2013, Boston, May 2013.

[9] R. Cole. Parallel merge sort. *SIAM Journal on Computing*, 17(4):770–785, 1988.

[10] R. Cole and V. Ramachandran. Resource oblivious sorting on multicores. In *Automata, Languages and Programming (ICALP)*, volume 6198 of *LNCS*, pages 226–237. Springer, 2010.

[11] Y. Feng, M. Straka, T. di Matteo, and R. Croft. MP-sort: Sorting at scale on blue waters. https://www.writelatex.com/read/sttmdgqthvyv accessed Jan 17, 2015, 2014.

[12] A. Gerbessiotis and L. Valiant. Direct bulk-synchronous parallel algorithms. *Journal of Parallel and Distributed Computing*, 22(2):251–267, 1994.

[13] M. T. Goodrich. Communication-efficient parallel sorting. *SIAM Journal on Computing*, 29(2):416–432, 1999.

[14] T. Hagerup and C. Rüb. Optimal merging and sorting on the EREW-PRAM. *Information Processing Letters*, 33:181–185, 1989.

[15] C. A. R. Hoare. Algorithm 65 (find). *Communication of the ACM*, 4(7):321–322, 1961.

[16] L. Hübschle-Schneider, P. Sanders, and I. Müller. Communication efficient algorithms for top-k selection problems. *CoRR*, abs/1502.03942, 2015.

[17] M. Ikkert, T. Kieritz, and P. Sanders. Parallele Algorithmen. course notes, October 2009.

[18] J. Jájá. *An Introduction to Parallel Algorithms*. Addison Wesley, 1992.

[19] D. E. Knuth. *The Art of Computer Programming—Sorting and Searching*. Addison Wesley, 1998.

[20] V. Kumar, A. Grama, A. Gupta, and G. Karypis. *Introduction to Parallel Computing. Design and Analysis of Algorithms*. Benjamin/Cummings, 1994.

[21] H. Li and K. C. Sevcik. Parallel sorting by overpartitioning. In *6th ACM Symposium on Parallel Algorithms and Architectures (SPAA)*, pages 46–56, Cape May, New Jersey, 1994.

[22] K. Mehlhorn and P. Sanders. *Algorithms and Data Structures — The Basic Toolbox*. Springer, 2008.

[23] A. Rasmussen, G. Porter, M. Conley, H. V. Madhyastha, R. N. Mysore, A. Pucher, and A. Vahdat. Tritonsort: A balanced large-scale sorting system. In *NSDI*, 2011.

[24] P. Sanders. Fast priority queues for cached memory. *ACM Journal of Experimental Algorithmics*, 5, 2000.

[25] P. Sanders. Course on Parallel Algorithms, lecture notes, 2008. http://algo2.iti.kit.edu/sanders/courses/paralg08/.

[26] P. Sanders, S. Schlag, and I. Müller. Communication efficient algorithms for fundamental big data problems. In *IEEE Int. Conf. on Big Data*, 2013.

[27] P. Sanders, J. Speck, and J. L. Träff. Two-tree algorithms for full bandwidth broadcast, reduction and scan. *Parallel Computing*, 35(12):581–594, 2009.

[28] P. Sanders and J. L. Träff. The factor algorithm for regular all-to-all communication on clusters of SMP nodes. In *8th Euro-Par*, number 2400, pages 799–803. Springer ©, 2002.

[29] P. Sanders and S. Winkel. Super scalar sample sort. In *12th European Symposium on Algorithms (ESA)*, volume 3221 of *LNCS*, pages 784–796. Springer, 2004.

[30] J. Singler, P. Sanders, and F. Putze. MCSTL: The multi-core standard template library. In *13th Euro-Par*, volume 4641 of *LNCS*, pages 682–694. Springer, 2007.

[31] E. Solomonik and L. Kale. Highly scalable parallel sorting. In *IEEE International Symposium on Parallel Distributed Processing (IPDPS)*, pages 1–12, April 2010.

[32] L. Valiant. A bridging model for parallel computation. *Communications of the ACM*, 33(8):103–111, 1994.

[33] P. J. Varman et al. Merging multiple lists on hierarchical-memory multiprocessors. *J. Par. & Distr. Comp.*, 12(2):171–177, 1991.

APPENDIX

A. FAST BUCKET GROUPING

The first observation for improving the binary search algorithm from Section 6 is that a PE-group size can take only $\mathcal{O}((br)^2)$ different values since it is defined by a range of buckets. We can modify the binary search in such a way that it operates not over all conceivable group sizes but only over those corresponding to ranges of buckets. When a scanning step succeeds, we can safely reduce the upper bound for the binary search to the largest PE-group actually used. On the other hand, when a scanning step fails, we can increase the lower bound: during the scan, whenever we finish a PE-group of size x because the next bucket of size y does not fit (i.e., $x + y > L$), we compute $z = x + y$. The minimum over all observed z-values is the new lower bound. This is safe, since a value of the scanning bound L less then z will reproduce the same failed partition. This already yields an algorithm running in time $\mathcal{O}(br \log(br)^2) = \mathcal{O}(br \log(br))$.

The second observation is only values for L in the range $\lceil n/r - 1 \rceil ..(1 + \mathcal{O}(1/b))n/r$ are relevant (see Lemma 2). Only $\mathcal{O}(br)$ bucket ranges will have a total size in this range. To see this, consider any particular starting bucket for a bucket range. Searching from there to the right for range end points, we can skip all end buckets where the total size is below n/r. We can stop as soon as the total size leaves the relevant range. Since buckets have average size $\mathcal{O}(n/b)$, only a constant number of end points will be in the relevant range on the average. Overall, we get $\mathcal{O}(br) \cdot \mathcal{O}(1) = \mathcal{O}(br)$ relevant bucket ranges. Using this for initializing the binary search speeds up the sequential algorithm by a factor of about two.

Using all p available PEs, we can do even better: in each iteration, we split the remaining range for L evenly into $p+1$ subranges. Each PE tries one subrange end point for scanning and uses the first observation to round up or down to an actually occurring size of a bucket range. Using a reduction we find the largest L-value $L_{\min}$ for a failed scan and the smallest L value $L_{\max}$ for a successful scan. When $L_{\max} = L_{\min}$ we have found the optimal value for L. Otherwise, we continue with the range $L_{\max}..L_{\min}$. Since the bucket range sizes in the feasible region are fairly uniformly distributed, the number of iterations will be $\log_{p+1} \mathcal{O}(br)$. Since $p \geq r$, this is $\mathcal{O}(1)$ if b is polynomial in r. Indeed, one or two iterations are likely to succeed in all reasonable cases.

B. TIE-BREAKING FOR COMPARISONS

Conceptually, we assign the key (x, i, j) to an element with key x, stored on PE i at position j of the input array. Using lexicographic ordering makes the keys unique. For a practical implementation, it is important not to do this explicitly for every element. We explain how this can be done for AMS-sort. First note, that in AMS-sort there is no need to do tie breaking across levels or for the final local sorting. Sample sorting and splitter determination can afford to do tie breaking explicitly, since these steps are more latency bound. For partitioning, we can use a version of super scalar sample sort, that also produces a bucket for elements equal to the splitter (equality bucket). This takes only one additional comparison [5] per element. Only if an input element x ends up in an equality bucket we need to perform the lexicographic comparison. Note that at this point, the PE number for x and its input position are already present in registers anyway.

C. PSEUDOCODES

Algorithm 1: AMS-Sort

Input: data elements $a[1..n/p]$, p PEs, r PE-groups, oversampling factor a, overpartitioning factor b

1   **if** $p = 1$ **then**
2     $a' = \text{sort}(a)$
3   **return** a'

4   choose random sample S with $|S| = abr$
5   $S' = \text{FastWorkInefficientSorting}(S)$
6   choose $br - 1$ equidistant splitters $\mathcal{E}$ from S'
7   replicate $\mathcal{E}$ # gossiping
8   locally partition elements into br buckets
9   determine global bucket sizes using (all-)reduction
10   assign buckets to PE-groups
11   $a'' = $ deliver elements a' using data delivery algorithm
12   AMS-Sort $(a'', p/r, r, a, b)$ # recurse on PE-groups

Algorithm 2: RLM-Sort

Input: data elements $a[1..n/p]$, p PEs, r PE-groups

1   $a' = \text{sort } a$
2   **return** RLM-Algo (a', p, r)
3
4   **Procedure** RLM-Algo(a, p, r)
    Input: data elements $a[1..n/p]$, p PEs, r PE-groups
5   **if** $p = 1$ **then**
6   **return** a
7   **for** $i \in \{1..r - 1\}$ **do in parallel**
8     $S[i] = $ multisequence selection of splitter at rank $n/r \cdot i$
9   deliver elements using data delivery algorithm
10   $a' = $ merge received elements
11   RLM-Algo $(a', p/r, \sqrt{r})$ # recurse on PE-groups

A Top-Down Parallel Semisort

Yan Gu
Carnegie Mellon University
yan.gu@cs.cmu.edu

Julian Shun
Carnegie Mellon University
jshun@cs.cmu.edu

Yihan Sun
Carnegie Mellon University
yihans@cs.cmu.edu

Guy E. Blelloch
Carnegie Mellon University
guyb@cs.cmu.edu

ABSTRACT

Semisorting is the problem of reordering an input array of keys such that equal keys are contiguous but different keys are not necessarily in sorted order. Semisorting is important for collecting equal values and is widely used in practice. For example, it is the core of the MapReduce paradigm, is a key component of the database join operation, and has many other applications.

We describe a (randomized) parallel algorithm for the problem that is theoretically efficient (linear work and logarithmic depth), but is designed to be more practically efficient than previous algorithms. We use ideas from the parallel integer sorting algorithm of Rajasekaran and Reif, but instead of processing bits of a integers in a reduced range in a bottom-up fashion, we process the hashed values of keys directly top-down. We implement the algorithm and experimentally show on a variety of input distributions that it outperforms a similarly-optimized radix sort on a modern 40-core machine with hyper-threading by about a factor of 1.7–1.9, and achieves a parallel speedup of up to 38x. We discuss the various optimizations used in our implementation and present an extensive experimental analysis of its performance.

Categories and Subject Descriptors

F.2.2 [**Analysis of Algorithms and Problem Complexity**]: Nonnumerical Algorithms and Problems—*Sorting and searching*

Keywords

Parallel Algorithms, Semisorting, Integer Sorting

1. INTRODUCTION

The semisorting problem [22] is defined to take as input an array of records with associated keys, and return a reordered array such that records with identical keys are contiguous. Unlike sorting, it does not require that records with distinct keys are ordered. The problem has many applications. In

the popular MapReduce paradigm [9], for example, the most expensive step is typically the so-called shuffle step, which collects the tuples with equal keys returned from the map stage together so the reducer can be applied to each group. Also in the relational join operation common in database processing [6], equal values of a field of a relation have to be put together with equal values of a field of another. Indeed in practice, the most recent work on analyzing the performance of in-memory database joins has focused on hash and sorting based methods for semisorting [1]. Most database languages also have a direct `groupBy` operation that groups together records by a given key.

Theoretically, semisorting also has many applications. The term was coined by Valiant in developing techniques for simulating various parallel machine models with other machine models [22]. In such simulations, memory operations to the same location are collected so they can be combined. Semisorting can also be used in many divide-and-conquer algorithms to collect together the parts that go to each recursive call [18], and to collect values associated with vertices in a graph [12]. Bast and Hagerup cite many other applications of semisorting [2].

As with sorting, there are several variants on semisorting depending on the type of keys and the operations allowed. The semisorting problem we consider here is defined as follows: given an array of n records each containing a key from a universe U, along with a family of hash functions $h : U \to [1, \ldots, n^k]$, for some constant k, and an equality test $f : U \times U \to Boolean$, return an array of the same records such that the only records between two equal records are other equal records. Other authors have considered semisorting applied to a bounded set of integer keys in the range $[1, \ldots, n]$ [2, 18]. From a theoretical perspective, this is equivalent to our definition since a hash table can be used to first assign unique labels in the range $[1, \ldots, n]$ to each key (assuming the hash table is asymptotically as fast as the semisort). Here we consider the more general definition since it allows for more practical implementations than first assigning unique labels and then performing integer sorting.

Sequential semisorting can be performed by maintaining a hash table in which each entry is a list of records with equal valued keys. The records can then be inserted one at a time. Whenever a key is first encountered a new list is added to the table, and when a key is encountered again, the record is added to the existing list for that key. This simple randomized technique takes linear expected work. Semisorting can also be implemented in linear work by hashing into range

$[1, \ldots, n^k]$ and then sorting the keys using an integer sort. For sufficiently large k (i.e. $k > 2$), it is unlikely there are collisions.

Parallel semisorting is not as simple. Although parallel hash tables that insert each distinct key once are simple and efficient in parallel [19], what makes semisorting hard is the need to insert all the duplicate entries, which need to be collected together. Given that there are many efficient parallel sorting algorithms, one might instead consider an approach based on integer sorting. Interestingly, however, it is not known how to sort integer keys in the range $[1, \ldots, n^k]$, $k > 1$ in linear work and polylogarithmic depth.[1] This problem has been open for almost 30 years with many researchers working on it. What is known is how to sort (but not stably) integers in the range $[1, \ldots, n \log^k n]$ in $O(kn)$ work and $O(k \log n)$ depth [16] with high probability.[2] As mentioned above, this can be used to solve the semisorting problem after a preprocessing step that reduces the integer range. In practice, however, this is not a competitive approach since just the initial preprocessing using a hash table requires about as much work as the whole sequential algorithm that simply inserts the keys into a hash table. Furthermore the integer sort is itself quite complicated.

In this paper, our goal is to develop a theoretically efficient parallel semisorting algorithm (linear work and polylogarithmic depth) that also performs well in practice, ideally closely matching the work done by the sequential algorithm. Our algorithm uses many of the ideas from the Rajasekaran and Reif integer sort [16] but instead of working bottom-up (i.e. least-significant bits first) on the bits generated from a reduced integer range, it works top-down (most-significant bits first) directly on the hash values. It significantly improves on constant factors while matching the theoretical bounds.

Our algorithm works as follows. We first hash the keys of the records into enough bits so that collisions are unlikely. We then take a sample of these hashed keys and sort them. The sorted hashes are used to predict the number of keys in each range of the hash, as well as to detect keys with many duplicates, which we refer to as *heavy keys*. The remaining keys are referred to as *light keys*. Next, appropriately-sized arrays are allocated for each of the heavy keys and for ranges of the light keys. Then, the records are all written to random locations within their appropriate array, retrying at the next location when there is a collision. Finally, a counting sort is used on each array of records associated with light keys, which are reasonably small. Each step takes at most linear work and logarithmic depth.

In practice the algorithm is quite efficient since much of the work is in the single write to memory for each key (when writing to the allocated arrays). The other memory operations performed by the algorithm are computations on a smaller sample (the sample sort), reads from a much smaller sample (determining the array for writing), adjacent writes typically on the same cache line (when colliding on a write, and using an optimization that we describe), linear scans of the data (to read the records, and to compact the arrays),

or reads and writes within a polylogarithmic-sized block of keys (for the final sorts).

We implement algorithm and describe the results of a variety of experiments to measure its performance and compare it to other methods. Our experiments are performed on a 40-core machine with two-way hyper-threading. On all 40 cores (with hyper-threading enabled), our code achieves up to a factor of 38 speedup over its performance on a single thread. Also even on one thread, our algorithm is 20% faster than a simple sequential version using a hash table. This is because the sequential version requires using linked lists to link the elements going to the same bucket, which is not as efficient as estimating sizes and writing directly to an array.

We measure our algorithm on a variety of different distributions and show that it is robust across the distributions, only differing in running time by about 20% between the best and worst distribution. Our experiments are done on a variety of sizes ranging from 10 million records to one billion records. The per-record performance improves for larger inputs. We also present a breakdown of the running time into the components of the algorithm, and show that the time is dominated by the single loop that writes the records into their respective arrays. In addition, we compare our algorithm to a radix sort from an existing library and show that it is about twice as fast. We finally compare our algorithm to comparison sorting algorithms from existing libraries, and our results show that our algorithm outperforms them on large inputs.

2. PRELIMINARIES

We use the work-depth model [13] allowing for concurrent reads and writes, where **work** W is equal to the number of operations required (equivalently, the product of the time and the number of processors) and **depth (span)** D is equal to the number of time steps required. The parallelism of an algorithm is therefore W/D. For our algorithms, the same bounds can be obtained on the arbitrary CRCW PRAM model. Using Brent's scheduling theorem [5], we can obtain a running time of $W/P + D$ when using P processors.

We use the notation $[n]$ to indicate the range $[1, \ldots, n]$. We make use of a variety of standard problems as building blocks. The **prefix-sum (scan)** problem takes an array of n integers and returns an equal length array in which each element is the sum of the previous elements, as well as the overall sum. The **packing** problem takes an array of values and an equal length array of flags, and packs the elements at positions with true flags down into a contiguous output array. It can be implemented in parallel with a prefix sum on the flags (treated as 0s and 1s) followed by a write to the resulting positions. The **naming** problem takes a set of n keys with m distinct values, and a hash function h on the keys, and output a unique label for each distinct key with a value in the range $[O(m)]$. The problem can be solved easily with a parallel hash table. The **placement** problem [18] (also called the assignment problem [16], or multiple compaction problem [10]) takes an input array A of records each with an integer key in the range $[m]$, and also for each key value i an array B_i of size $n_i \geq \sum_{j=1}^{n} [A_j = i]$.[3] It places each record of A somewhere in the array associated with its key.

---

[1]This statement assumes the standard word length of $O(\log n)$. Linear work and logarithmic depth can be achieved if a non-standard polynomial word length is assumed [17].

[2]We use "with high probability" (w.h.p.) to mean with probability at least $1 - 1/n^c$ for any constant $c > 0$, and with the constant in the big-O linear in c.

[3]$[\cdot]$ is the Iverson bracket.

All of these problems have simple linear work algorithms with $O(\log n)$ depth (using randomization and high probability bounds for naming and placement). See, for example [13]. Furthermore the algorithms are quite efficient in practice. The problems also have significantly more complicated sublogarithmic depth algorithms, at least for approximate versions [16, 11, 2]. In this paper, however, we are satisfied with the more practical logarithmic depth algorithms. We also use comparison-based sorting, which can be implemented using Cole's mergesort in $O(n \log n)$ work and $O(\log n)$ depth [7] or with slightly more depth with a variety of algorithms.

We say that a sorting algorithm is **stable** if the output preserves the relative order among equal keys from the input order, and otherwise we say that the algorithm is **unstable**.

We review the Rajasekaran and Reif integer sorting algorithm [16]—both because it is relevant to the discussion and also because our algorithm uses some of the ideas. The algorithm consists of two components. The first is a unstable randomized sort for integers in the range $[n / \log^2 n]$ and takes $O(n)$ work and $O(\log n)$ span (w.h.p.). The second is a stable counting sort for integers in the range $[m]$, $m \leq n$ and requires $O(n)$ work and $O(m + \log n)$ span. Using these sorts, integers in the range $[n \log^k n]$ can be sorted in $O(kn)$ work and $O(k \log n)$ span (w.h.p.). In particular, one round of the unstable randomized sort is applied on the $\log(n / \log^2 n)$ low-order bits, followed by $k + 2$ rounds of the stable counting sort on integers in the range $[\log n]$ on the high-order bits of the keys. Since the counting sort is stable, it maintains the relative order of the randomized sort on the low-order bits.

The stable counting sort is a simple parallel version of sequential counting sort. It partitions the sequence into n/m blocks each of size m, and works in three phases. In the first phase it counts how many keys of each value are in each block. This can be run in parallel across the blocks and sequentially within each block. Then a prefix sum is used to calculate an offset for each key within each block where the keys will be written. Finally each block goes over its elements again and writes them to their final location. The first and last steps take $O(n)$ work and $O(m)$ span. The middle step takes $O(n)$ work and $O(\log n)$ span. The sort is fully deterministic and gives the stated bounds.

The unstable randomized sort consists of four steps: generating an upper bound on the cardinality of each key, allocating a sufficiently sized array for each key value, writing each key into a random location of its array, and packing the result into a contiguous sorted array. The upper bound on the cardinality for each key is determined by taking a randomly selected sample of size $\Theta(n / \log n)$ and sorting it using a parallel comparison sort, giving a count for each key $c(i)$. Using Chernoff bounds, one can show that with high probability the values $u(i) = c' \max(\log^2 n, c(i) \log n)$ give an upper bound on the cardinality of key i (for some constant c'). Furthermore the estimate ensures that $\sum_{i=1}^{m} u(i) = O(n)$ in expectation. Arrays of size $u(i)$ are then allocated using a prefix sum on the $u(i)$ values, giving an offset for each subarray within an array of length $O(n)$. Now each key is written in parallel into some position in its subarray using an algorithm for the placement problem. The final step does a packing operation to remove the empty spots in the resulting array. All steps take $O(n)$ work and $O(\log n)$ depth (w.h.p.), and follow from the the building blocks listed above.

Algorithm 1 Parallel Semisort

Input: An array A with n records each containing a key.
Output: An array A' storing the records of A in semisorted order.

1: Hash each key into the range $[n^k]$ $(k > 2)$
2: Select a sample S of the hashed keys, independently with probability $p = \Theta(1/\log n)$.
3: Sort S.
4: Partition S into two sets H and L, where H contains the records with keys that appear at least $\delta = \Theta(\log n)$ times in S (heavy keys), and L contains the remaining records (light keys).
5: Create a hash table T which maps each heavy key to its associated array.
6: **Heavy keys:**

  (a) For each distinct hashed key in H allocate an appropriately-sized array for it.

  (b) Insert the records in A associated with heavy keys (which can be checked by hash table lookup in T) into their associated array.

7: **Light keys:**

  (a) Evenly partition the hash range into $\Theta(n / \log^2 n)$ buckets, and create an appropriately-sized array for each bucket by counting light keys in S.

  (b) Insert the records in A associated with light keys (which again can be checked by hash table lookup in T) into a random location in the array of its associated bucket.

  (c) Semisort each bucket.

8: Pack all of the arrays into a contiguous output array A'.

---

3. OUR ALGORITHM

In this section, we describe and analyze our algorithm for semisorting. In the next section, we will describe various implementation decisions we made to improve the performance. The input to our algorithm is an array of n records. Each record contains a key. We assume a uniform random hash function that maps keys to integers in the range $[n^k]$ in constant time. The outline of our parallel semisorting algorithm is given in Algorithm 1. We prove the following theorem regarding the complexity of our algorithm.

THEOREM 3.1. *Algorithm 1 for parallel semisorting can be implemented in $O(n)$ expected work and space, and $O(\log n)$ depth w.h.p.*

The algorithm first hashes the keys into a sufficient large range $[n^k]$ and $k > 2$ so that collisions are unlikely (i.e. there is a one-to-one correspondence between keys and hashed keys). The remainder of the algorithm semisorts these *hashed keys*. Step 2 generates a sample S of the hashed keys, where each hashed key is included in S with probability $p = \Theta(1/\log n)$. This can be done with a parallel pack operation in $O(n)$ work and $O(\log n)$ depth. The expected size of S is $\Theta(n / \log n)$. Step 3 sorts S using Cole's parallel mergesort [7] in $O(n)$ expected work and $O(\log n)$ depth. With S in sorted order we can now compute the multiplicity of each sampled hashed key in S.

We define a hashed key to be a **heavy key** if records with that key appear at least $\delta = \Theta(\log n)$ times in the sample S, and a **light key** otherwise. A **heavy record** is a record associated with a heavy key, and a **light record** is a record associated with a light key. Heavy records appear many times in the input, and are handled differently than light records for both theoretical and practical reasons. Step 4 partitions S into heavy keys H and light keys L. This can be done with prefix sums in linear work and logarithmic depth.

Steps 5 and 6 collect all heavy records with the same hashed key into its own bucket. In Step 5, we create a hash table T which maps the hash value of each heavy key to an appropriate array. The arrays for the heavy keys are allocated in Step 6a. For a heavy key appearing s times in S (we know s from previous steps), it will appear $O(s/p)$ times in A w.h.p. In Section 3.1, we provide a precise high probability upper bound on the number of times a key will appear in A, which we denote by $f(s)$. The step allocates an array of size $\alpha f(s)$ ($\alpha > 1$) for each heavy key in the sample. The expected work and space for allocating the arrays is $O(n)$, as we show in Section 3.1 that the sum of all $f(s)$'s is $O(n)$ in expectation. T can be created and filled in $O(n/\log n)$ work and $O(\log n)$ depth w.h.p., and supports $O(1)$ work lookups [11].

Step 6b uses the placement problem (described in Section 2) to place the heavy records into their appropriate array. The placement problem can be implemented by partitioning the input into blocks of size $\log n$ and inserting records in rounds. In each round, we take an uninserted record from each block in parallel, select a random location in its associated array, check if the location is empty, and if so write the record into the location. Each such record then checks to see if it was successfully written (since another block could have also written to the location). If unsuccessful it will continue to the next round, otherwise we move to the next record in the block. Each record has at least a $1 - 1/\alpha$ probability of succeeding in each round since each array is at least α times the size of the number of records destined for it. This means the expected number of rounds is $(\alpha/(\alpha - 1))\log n$. Since the rounds are independent, after $O(\log n)$ rounds w.h.p. all blocks finish (using Chernoff bounds). Each round has constant depth. The total work is $(n/\log n) \times O(\log n) = O(n)$.

Step 7 collects all light keys within ranges of the hash space into their own bucket. First, we evenly partition the hash range into $\Theta(n/\log^2 n)$ buckets, and create appropriately-sized arrays for each bucket (Step 7a). This is done by counting the number of records with light keys in S that fall into each bucket using a prefix sum. If s fall into a bucket, we allocate an array of size $\alpha f(s)$ for the bucket. We can again use the placement problem to insert the records into their appropriate arrays (Step 7b). Unlike the heavy keys, each bucket can contain records with different hashed keys. We therefore now need to semisort within the buckets (Step 7c). To do this work-efficiently we note that w.h.p. there are at most $O(\log^2 n)$ distinct keys per bucket—we are throwing at most n balls (distinct keys) into $\Theta(n/\log^2 n)$ buckets assuming the hash function is uniform [8]. For each bucket, we use the naming problem to give new labels to the keys in the range $[O(\log^2 n)]$ by inserting and then looking up in a hash table. This has expected linear work and $O(\log n)$ depth w.h.p. For each bucket we then use two passes of the stable counting sort on the newly labeled records, each pass sorting $O(\log \log n)$ bits. The work and space summed over all the light key buckets is $O(n)$ and the depth is $O(\log n)$.

Finally, Step 8 uses a parallel pack over all the arrays. Since the expected total size of the arrays is $O(n)$ (see Section 3.1), the expected work and space is $O(n)$, and depth is $O(\log n)$.

Combining the complexity of each step gives Theorem 3.1.

The algorithm's correctness (assuming no collisions in the initial hashing) is easily verified by noting that each heavy key array contains records with the same key, and the light key arrays are sorted so records with the same key appear next to each other. Concatenating the arrays together gives a semisorted output. Because of the initial hashing, this is a Monte Carlo algorithm, but can be converted into a Las Vegas algorithm by checking for correctness of the initial hashing with a parallel hash table and restarting the algorithm if there are collisions. Lastly, although unlikely to happen (Corollary 3.4), it is possible that a bucket can overflow. This can be checked by keeping a counter of the number of trials, and if it exceeds a threshold, the algorithm can be restarted.

3.1 Lemmas for size estimation

Consider some set of keys K. We are interested in estimating the number of records in A that have a key in K, given that there are s such records in S. We define the following function:

$$f(s) = \left(s + c\ln n + \sqrt{c^2 \ln^2 n + 2sc\ln n}\right)/p$$

where $p = \Theta(1/\log n)$ is the sampling probability and c is a constant. We will prove that the function f gives a high probability upper bound on the number of records with a key in K in the input array A, given that there are s such records in the sample S. Our motivation for providing a precise upper bound is because in our implementation we must obtain accurate estimates for efficiency.

LEMMA 3.2. *For a sample S in which an element in A is included with probability p, if there are s records in S with a key in K, then the probability that the number of such records in A is greater than $f(s)$ is at most n^{-c}.*

To prove Lemma 3.2, we first prove a lemma stating that for records with a key in K appearing $f(s)$ times in A, the probability that there are at most s such records in S is at most n^{-c}. This can be shown by applying a Chernoff bound with the mean of s being $pf(s)$ in the following lemma. Let σ be the number of such records in S, and ν be the number of such records in A.

LEMMA 3.3. $\Pr[\sigma \leq s \,|\, \nu = \lceil f(s) \rceil] \leq n^{-c}$.
PROOF.

$$\Pr[\sigma \leq s \,|\, \nu = \lceil f(s) \rceil]$$

$$\leq \exp\left[-\left(1 - \frac{s}{pf(s)}\right)^2 \cdot pf(s)/2\right]$$

$$= \exp\left[s - \frac{1}{2} \cdot \left(pf(s) + \frac{s^2}{pf(s)}\right)\right]$$

$$= \exp\left[s - \frac{1}{2}\left(pf(s) + \frac{s^2\left(s + c\ln n - \sqrt{\Delta}\right)}{(s + c\ln n)^2 - \Delta}\right)\right] (*)$$

$$= \exp\left[s - \frac{1}{2}(2s + 2c\ln n)\right]$$

$$= \exp[-c\ln n] = n^{-c}$$

27

where $\Delta = \left(c^2 \ln^2 n + 2sc \ln n\right)$ on the line marked $(*)$. $\square$

With Lemma 3.3, we now prove Lemma 3.2.

PROOF OF LEMMA 3.2. Applying the law of total probability, we have:

$$\Pr[f(\sigma) \le \nu]$$
$$= \sum_{\nu'} \Pr\big[f(\sigma) \le \nu' \,|\, \nu = \nu'\big] \Pr\big[\nu = \nu'\big] \qquad (1)$$

We first rearrange the terms so that we can apply Lemma 3.3. We use the fact that $f(s)$ is a monotonically increasing function.

$$\Pr\big[f(\sigma) \le \nu' \,|\, \nu = \nu'\big]$$
$$= \Pr\big[f(\sigma) \le f\big(f^{-1}(\nu')\big) \,|\, \nu = f\big(f^{-1}(\nu')\big)\big]$$
$$= \Pr\big[\sigma \le f^{-1}(\nu') \,|\, \nu = f\big(f^{-1}(\nu')\big)\big] \qquad (2)$$
$$\le n^{-c} \qquad (3)$$

We obtain (3) from (2) by plugging in $s = f^{-1}(\nu')$ into Lemma 3.3. Plugging this into (1), we have

$$\Pr[f(\sigma) \le \nu]$$
$$= \sum_{\nu'} \Pr\big[f(\sigma) \le \nu' \,|\, \nu = \nu'\big] \Pr\big[\nu = \nu'\big]$$
$$\le \sum_{\nu'} n^{-c} \Pr\big[\nu = \nu'\big]$$
$$= n^{-c} \sum_{\nu'} \Pr\big[\nu = \nu'\big]$$
$$= n^{-c}$$

which gives the high probability bound. $\square$

We now apply Lemma 3.2 for each bucket in Algorithm 1. For heavy key buckets K is a single key, whereas for light key buckets K is the set of keys falling in the range of the bucket. Over all buckets, $f(s)$ is an upper bound on the number of records appearing in the bucket with probability at least $1 - \Theta(n^{-c+1}/\log^2 n)$ by applying a union bound with Lemma 3.2 (there are at most $\Theta(n/\log^2 n)$ buckets). This gives us the following corollary:

COROLLARY 3.4. *The probability that f gives an upper bound on the number of records in each bucket is at least* $1 - \Theta(n^{-c+1}/\log^2 n)$.

Picking $c > 1$ gives a high probability bound as required in the proof of Theorem 3.1. The constant hidden by $\Theta(\cdot)$ can be arbitrarily small since it is decided by the default constants p, δ, and the number of buckets for light keys.

We will now prove that using the function f, the sum of estimates over all buckets is $O(n)$ in expectation. Recall that the n input records are partitioned into $\Theta(n/\log^2 n)$ buckets for the light keys and $O(n/\log^2 n)$ buckets (expected) for the heavy keys (the sample size is $\Theta(n/\log n)$ and heavy keys appear $\delta = \Omega(\log n)$ times in the sample). Therefore there are a total of $\Theta(n/\log^2 n)$ buckets in expectation. Let R denote the number of buckets, and let s_i denote the number of times records belonging to bucket i appear in the sample S.

LEMMA 3.5. $\sum_{i=1}^{R} f(s_i) = \Theta(n)$ *holds in expectation.*

PROOF. Note that $E\big[\sum_{i=1}^{R} s_i\big] = E[|S|] = \Theta(n/\log n)$. Therefore,

$$E\left[\sum_{i=1}^{R} f(s_i)\right] = \sum_{i=1}^{R} E[f(s_i)]$$
$$= \sum_{i=1}^{R} E\left[\left(s_i + c\ln n + \sqrt{c^2 \ln^2 n + 2s_i c \ln n}\right)/p\right]$$
$$\le \frac{1}{p} \sum_{i=1}^{R} E[s_i] + \frac{2c}{p} R \ln n + \frac{1}{p} \sum_{i=1}^{R} E\left[\sqrt{2s_i c \ln n}\right]$$
$$\le \Theta(\log n) \cdot \Theta(n/\log n)$$
$$\quad + 2c \cdot \Theta(\log n) \cdot \Theta(n/\log^2 n) \ln n$$
$$\quad + \frac{1}{p} \cdot \sqrt{2c \ln n} \cdot E\left[\sqrt{R \sum_{i=1}^{R} s_i}\right] \qquad (4)$$
$$= \Theta(n) + \Theta(n) + \sqrt{2c \ln n} \cdot \ln n \cdot \Theta\left(\sqrt{\frac{n^2}{\log^3 n}}\right)$$
$$= \Theta(n)$$

where we apply the Cauchy-Schwarz inequality at (4). $\square$

Since we allocate arrays of size $\alpha f(s)$ for each bucket, Lemma 3.5 implies that the total work and space required for allocating and packing the the arrays is linear in expectation, as required by Theorem 3.1.

3.2 Comparison to integer sorting

Our semisorting algorithm uses various ideas from Rajasekaran and Reif's (RR) integer sorting algorithm [16]. Also as mentioned the RR algorithm can be used for the semisorting problem by first using the naming problem (with a hash table) to reduce the range of the hash values to $[n]$ and then integer sorting (recall that RR is limited to keys in the range $[n \log^k n]$). Here we discuss the differences between the two approaches and why we made the various choices, with the view of developing a more practical algorithm in mind. Firstly, we do not need to reduce the range of the hash values and instead can work directly with hashed keys in the range $[n^k]$, with k picked so collisions are unlikely. This avoids an extra hashing step across all keys. This is possible since the hashed keys are uniformly distributed. This played a critical role in bounding the number of distinct keys in each light bucket.

Secondly, we separate light keys from heavy keys. This has the advantage that the heavy records can immediately be placed in their correct bucket without the need for a secondary sort. This is important in practice because there can be many (perhaps all) equal valued keys meaning that buckets with heavy keys can be very large making sorting more expensive. The remaining light buckets have at most $O(\log^3 n)$ keys (w.h.p.) and have expected size $O(\log^2 n)$. Therefore sorting them is very cache-friendly. Also, from a practical standpoint, the hash table of heavy keys can be made small enough to fit in cache, as can the array of pointers to the light buckets.

Thirdly, the RR algorithm for keys in the range $[n]$ uses two rounds of the stable counting sort to start with after applying the randomized unstable sort. These are expensive since they create global movement. Instead our algorithm applies the stable counting sort separately on buckets that are always small (polylogarithmic size). More discussion of practical aspects of our particular implementation are described in the next section.

4. IMPLEMENTATION DETAILS

In this section, we discuss some of the details of our implementation. To start with, we introduce the default constants in the algorithm. We set the sampling probability p to be $1/16$, and δ to be 16, which we found to give the best overall performance in our experiments for our range of input sizes (10^7 to 10^9 records). The number of light key buckets is set to be 2^{16}. Our implementation heavily based on the Problem Based Benchmark Suite (PBBS) [20] which contains simple and efficient parallel code to a number of problems and parallel primitives, including prefix sum, filter/pack, radix sort, and concurrent hash tables based on linear probing [19].

The implementation of this algorithm is broken down into five phases, and this is also the breakdown that we use in the detailed experimental analysis in Section 5.

Phase 1: Sampling and sorting. This phase corresponds to Steps 2 and 3 in Algorithm 1. When sampling, the i'th sample is randomly picked from the $(\lceil (i-1)/p \rceil + 1)$'th to the $\lceil i/p \rceil$-th record. Theoretically, for each key, the average number of samples using this sampling scheme is the same as the method that picks every sample independently.

To sort the samples in S, we use the parallel radix sort in the PBBS. The radix sort is a top-down sort, which processes 8 bits of the key at a time to place the records into buckets, and recurses on each bucket. This parallel radix sort is also the baseline algorithm we compare against in Section 5.

Phase 2: Bucket allocation. In this phase we perform Steps 4, 5, 6a and 7a in Algorithm 1. Since this phase is inexpensive relative to the whole algorithm (about 1% of the overall running time), we use a straightforward implementation. To filter out heavy keys and get their counts, we first compute the offsets corresponding to the start of each key in the sorted array, which can be done with a simple comparison with the preceding key. We then gather these offsets using a parallel filter, and finally compute the counts by using the difference between consecutive offsets. If the count for a key is greater than $\delta = 16$, we insert the key into a hash table. This hash table stores pointers to the arrays associated with heavy keys, and the arrays are allocated using the size computed from the f function in Section 3.1. All of these steps run in parallel.

We also use the f function to compute the size of the light key arrays, but use a minor optimization where we combine small (adjacent) buckets into a single bucket corresponding to at least δ light key records in S. This optimization reduces the overall running time by at most 10%. This is because the estimation function f is more accurate with a larger number of samples, and therefore the overall used memory space is reduced. Then the following steps (local sort and packing phases) will touch less memory, and this improves the running time.

We sequentially create the associated arrays for the heavy key and light key buckets since it is a very small fraction of the running time. To allow for efficient packing later, we use a single large array for all of the buckets, and each bucket simply stores an offset into this array to indicate the start of its associated array. The heavy key buckets are all before the light key buckets in the array. Each bucket with s samples allocates an array of size $1.1f(s)$ with $c = 1.25$, and rounded up to the nearest power of 2. In our experiments, this size was sufficient to prevent overflow on all of our inputs.

Phase 3: Scattering. This phase corresponds to Steps 6b and 7b in Algorithm 1, where every record is scattered to a random location in the array of its bucket. In contrast to the discussion in Section 3, we perform the insertions using a compare-and-swap, which is supported on most modern multicore machines. A compare-and-swap returns *true* if a record was successfully inserted into an initially empty location and *false* otherwise. On a failure, instead of picking another random location, a record tries the next location (linear probing). This gives better cache performance. Bounds for linear probing show that the expected cost per insertion is $O(1)$, leading to linear work. Furthermore, the largest cluster in the array is $O(\log n)$ w.h.p., which gives a depth bound of $O(\log n)$ w.h.p. [8].

Phase 4: Local sort. This phase corresponds to Step 7c in Algorithm 1. After all the records are inserted into the buckets, a pack followed by a local sort is executed on each bucket. In our implementation, the local sort in each array is sequential since sorting a single array is fast, and usually there are many more arrays than processors, so this step has good parallelism. We tried several versions including a bucket sort, some comparison-based hybrid sort algorithms, and the sort in the C++ Standard Library (STL). The running times for the various algorithms were similar. In our final implementation, we choose to use the sort in the C++ Standard Library, which is implemented using a hybrid of quicksort, heap sort and insertion sort, since it provided consistent performance on all of our input distributions.

Phase 5: Packing. This phase corresponds to Step 8 in Algorithm 1. The algorithm that we use to pack the portion of the array for the heavy key buckets consists of 3 steps (recall that we use a single array A' to represent all the buckets): first, the array A' is divided into 1000 intervals and each interval is packed individually and sequentially by just scanning the interval; second, we apply a sequential prefix sum on the counts for the intervals to compute the boundaries in A' for each interval; finally, we write the records into their appropriate indices in A' in parallel. The portion of the array for the light key buckets is already packed from Phase 4 so we simply copy the records into A' in parallel.

5. EXPERIMENTS

We measure the performance of the implementation of our parallel semisorting algorithm using various parameters. We also compare the performance of our semisorting algorithm to the parallel integer sorting algorithm from the Problem Based Benchmark Suite (PBBS) [20], which can be used to perform semisorting. Finally, we compare with a sequential implementation of semisorting.

We run our experiments on a 40-core (with two-way hyper-threading) machine with 4×2.4GHz Intel 10-core E7-8870 Xeon processors (with a 1066MHz bus and 30MB L3 cache) and 256GB of main memory. We run all parallel experiments with hyper-threading enabled, for a total of 80 hyper-threads. We compile our code with **g++** version 4.8.0 with the **-O2** flag. The parallel codes use Cilk Plus [14] to express parallelism, which is supported by the **g++** compiler that we use. In particular, the parallel for-loops are written using the `cilk_for` construct. Divide-and-conquer parallelism, which is required by the parallel integer sort, is written using the `cilk_spawn` construct. For an algorithm with work W and depth D, Cilk's randomized work-stealing scheduler [4] with P available threads gives an expected running time of $W/P + O(D)$. When running in parallel, we use the command `numactl -i all` to evenly distribute the allocated memory among the processors.

5.1 Input data

All of our experiments use an 8-byte (64-bit) hash value along with 8-byte payload (16 bytes total per record). We assume that the keys have been pre-hashed, since the cost for hashing itself would depend on the particular type of value being semisorted and the cost is common across any of the hash-based techniques (including radix sort). Furthermore, the cost for hashing is typically small. With an 8-byte hash the probability of a collision is small, and checking for collisions is easy once the sort is done.

Although the values are hashed, the distribution of duplicates can vary significantly. We use a variety input distributions, including uniform distributions, exponential distributions, and Zipfian distributions. Each class of distribution has a parameter. For uniform distributions, the parameter N indicates the range from which the integers are chosen from. More precisely, each key will be chosen uniformly from the range $[N]$. Hence, a smaller N will create more equal keys. The parameter λ for exponential distributions represents the mean of the distribution, and accordingly, the variance of the distribution is λ^2. The parameter M of Zipfian distributions denotes the range $[M]$ that the keys can be chosen from. The i-th number in this range has a probability $1/(i\bar{M})$ of being chosen, where $\bar{M} = \sum_{i=1}^{M} 1/i$ is the normalizing factor.

In Section 5.2, we use all three classes of distributions with various parameters to show the stability of our algorithm. In Sections 5.3–5.5 we present a detailed performance analysis using two representative distributions, the uniform distribution with parameter $N = n$ (input size), and the exponential distribution with parameter $\lambda = n/10^3$. These two distributions were chosen because the first one contains only light keys, and the second distribution contains about 30% light keys and 70% heavy keys while not containing too many (as many as a constant fraction of) duplicates. Hence, the performance of both the heavy-key arrays and light-key arrays can be analyzed.

For most of the experiments the input is 100 million 64-bit key-value pairs. However, in Section 5.4 we analyze the performance with various input sizes. All our experiments use 16 byte records in which 8 bytes are the hash of the keys, and the other 8 bytes are the payload.

5.2 Consistency of performance

To show the stability of the parallel semisorting algorithm with different input distributions, we tested the performance on three different classes of distributions with 17 distributions in total. The distributions include different percentages of heavy keys, and span the entire range of 0% to 100%. The average number of duplicates for each key also varies significantly among distributions.

A detailed running time and speedup for each experimental run is reported in Table 1 with different thread counts.

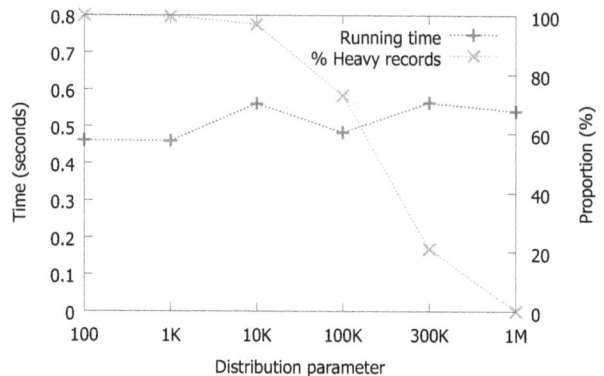

(a) Exponential distributions.

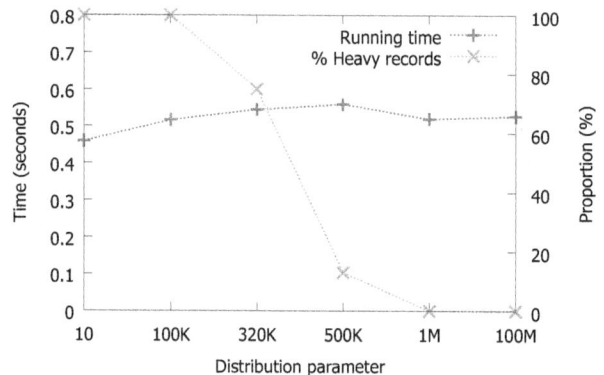

(b) Uniform distributions.

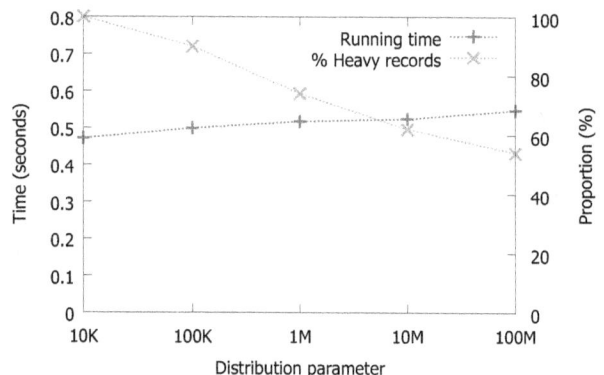

(c) Zipfian distributions.

Figure 1: Running time (seconds) using 40 cores with hyper-threading and the proportion (%) of heavy keys of three different classes of distributions with various parameters. The input size is 10^8.

We also plot the 40-core (with hyper-threading) running time for each class of distributions versus the distribution parameter on 10^8 records in Figure 1.

From the figure, we can see that the lowest running time (0.46s) appears in three test cases, and in all three of these cases, more than 99% records have heavy keys. The algorithm is particularly efficient in this case because no local sort for the light keys is required. Meanwhile, the highest running time is 0.56s, and the common situation in these cases is that most of the keys are close to the threshold between heavy and light key but the majority of keys are

	Sequential		40h		Speedup
	time (s)	%	time (s)	%	
sample and sort	1.03	7.41	0.06	13.29	16.03
construct buckets	0.11	0.77	0.02	3.32	6.65
scatter	9.81	70.60	0.25	51.95	39.08
local sort	0.18	1.30	0.01	1.22	30.51
pack	2.77	19.93	0.15	30.22	18.97

Table 2: Breakdown of running time and percentage for sequential and 40 cores with hyper-threading versions. The input has 10^8 records and the keys follow the exponential distribution with parameter $\lambda = 10^5$. (40h) indicates 40 cores with two-way hyper-threading.

	Sequential		40h		Speedup
	time (s)	%	time (s)	%	
sample and sort	1.55	8.52	0.08	15.18	19.42
construct buckets	0.18	1.00	0.02	3.68	9.40
scatter	9.15	50.25	0.24	45.98	37.81
local sort	6.56	36.02	0.13	23.75	52.48
pack	0.77	4.21	0.06	11.42	12.75

Table 3: Breakdown of running time and percentage for sequential and 40 cores with hyper-threading versions. The input has 10^8 records and the keys follow the uniform distribution with parameter $N = 10^8$. (40h) indicates 40 cores with two-way hyper-threading.

light. Therefore, the size of light key arrays can easily exceed $\Theta(\log^2 n)$, which increases the workload in the local sorting phase.

However, the difference between the extreme cases is only 0.1s, which is about only 20% of the overall running time. This shows that the parallel semisorting algorithm has a reasonably consistent performance on various input distributions.

5.3 Performance, speedup, and breakdown

The parallel speedup of the semisorting algorithm is shown in Table 1. The speedup lines for the two representative distributions are also shown in Figure 2 to demonstrate that the algorithm has good parallel speedup. For example, an average speedup of 14.3x is obtained using 16 threads. Moreover, the speedups for 40 cores with hyper-threading are 31.7 and 34.6 on the two input distributions, respectively. Given that some subroutines in the algorithm are memory-bandwidth bound, this speedup is quite good.

To further analyze the performance of the algorithm, we show the breakdown of running time among the different phases in Tables 2 and 3, and Figure 3. The array construction is inexpensive, and hence a lower speedup is tolerable. The speedup of the sampling/sorting phase is determined by the radix sort and is between 16 and 20. The packing phase is memory-bandwidth bound, and gets 12–19x speedup. The scatter process achieves 37–39x speedup. The highest speedup comes from the local sort (30–52x). Since all the light-key arrays fit into caches, this phase is dominated by the computation and not the memory access. The overall cost is dominated by the scatter.

5.4 Scalability with varying input sizes

In this section we analyze the performance of our algorithm as a function of input size. We use inputs with 7

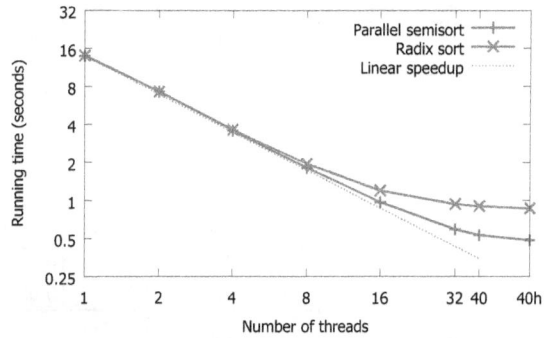

(a) Exponential distribution ($\lambda = 10^5$).

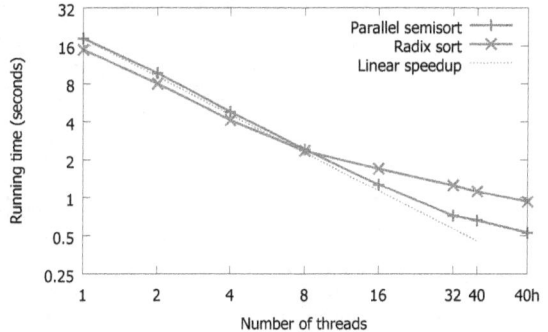

(b) Uniform distribution ($N = 10^8$).

Figure 2: Running times (seconds) of parallel semisort and radix sort with varying number of threads on an input size of 10^8. (40h) corresponds to 40-cores with two-way hyper-threading. The linear speedup line is plotted for reference.

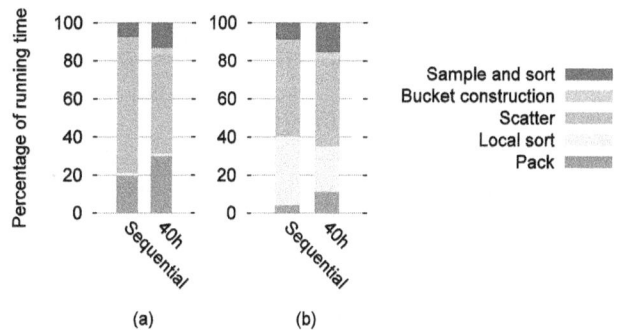

Figure 3: Breakdown of the different phases in terms of percentage of the total running time for running sequentially and on 40 cores with hyper-threading (40h). The input has 10^8 records and the keys follow: (a) exponential distribution with parameter $\lambda = 10^5$, (b) uniform distribution with parameter $N = 10^8$. The data for this figure is taken from Table 2 and 3.

different sizes from 10^7 to 10^9. The running times and speedups for the two representative distributions for these sizes are shown in Table 4. The speedups for the algorithm using 40 cores with hyper-threading are also plotted in Figure 4(a)–(b) and the corresponding speed (records per second) is shown in Figure 4(c)–(d). From the figure we can see that the speedup improves from 23 to 35.2 for the exponential distribution with increasing input size. Similarly for the uniform distribution the speedup improves from 25.2 to 38.2. The speedup for both distributions is high, and higher

Indicator		#threads	Exponential distribution						Uniform distribution						Zipfian distribution				
Parameter			100	1K	10K	100K	300K	1M	10	100K	320K	500K	1M	100M	10K	100K	1M	10M	100M
% Heavy key records			99.97	99.7	97	73	21	0	100	100	75	13	0	0	100	90	74	62	54
Parallel semisort	Time	1	13.46	13.48	17.82	13.90	17.24	18.56	12.43	14.73	15.77	18.54	17.50	18.21	13.01	14.51	15.47	16.28	17.83
		2	6.95	7.00	9.34	7.22	8.79	10.00	6.54	7.63	8.10	9.73	9.36	9.67	6.81	7.52	8.22	8.69	9.43
		4	3.46	3.47	4.65	3.56	4.27	4.92	3.26	3.73	3.94	4.82	4.60	4.78	3.39	3.71	4.09	4.26	4.66
		8	1.75	1.76	2.34	1.80	2.17	2.48	1.67	1.89	1.98	2.45	2.33	2.40	1.72	1.88	2.04	2.14	2.38
		16	0.94	0.94	1.25	0.96	1.16	1.30	0.90	1.01	1.06	1.27	1.22	1.26	0.93	1.01	1.09	1.14	1.25
		32	0.57	0.58	0.73	0.59	0.71	0.74	0.56	0.62	0.67	0.79	0.70	0.72	0.57	0.64	0.66	0.69	0.73
		40	0.54	0.53	0.66	0.53	0.65	0.72	0.52	0.59	0.60	0.67	0.64	0.66	0.54	0.56	0.61	0.62	0.66
		40h	0.46	0.46	0.56	0.48	0.56	0.54	0.46	0.52	0.54	0.56	0.52	0.53	0.47	0.50	0.52	0.52	0.55
	Speedup	2	1.94	1.93	1.91	1.92	1.96	1.86	1.90	1.93	1.95	1.90	1.87	1.88	1.91	1.93	1.88	1.87	1.89
		4	3.89	3.89	3.83	3.90	4.04	3.77	3.81	3.95	4.00	3.84	3.80	3.81	3.84	3.91	3.78	3.82	3.83
		8	7.68	7.67	7.61	7.71	7.94	7.50	7.46	7.79	7.98	7.58	7.52	7.58	7.56	7.73	7.56	7.59	7.49
		16	14.38	14.39	14.23	14.43	14.87	14.25	13.77	14.53	14.85	14.57	14.36	14.41	14.07	14.41	14.18	14.29	14.31
		32	23.55	23.30	24.43	23.50	24.19	25.15	22.24	23.59	23.58	23.54	24.83	25.37	22.68	22.69	23.58	23.57	24.53
		40	25.07	25.64	27.21	26.11	26.45	25.89	23.84	25.01	26.11	27.63	27.55	27.55	24.32	25.98	25.31	26.39	26.87
		40h	29.15	29.31	31.74	28.76	30.62	34.37	27.07	28.54	28.98	33.20	33.71	34.60	27.61	29.11	29.91	31.06	32.57
Radix sort	Time	1	12.00	10.33	14.00	13.70	13.90	14.50	14.10	13.80	13.80	13.80	13.90	14.80	13.10	13.60	13.80	14.20	14.00
		40h	0.88	0.88	0.90	0.88	0.90	0.92	0.91	0.89	0.89	0.90	0.90	0.93	0.93	0.94	0.92	0.96	0.90
	Speedup	40h	13.59	11.79	15.56	15.57	15.43	15.83	15.48	15.45	15.47	15.37	15.51	15.90	14.10	14.55	14.95	14.85	15.50

Table 1: **Running times (seconds) and speedup of parallel semisort and radix sort on various distributions using a 40-core machine. (40h) indicates 40 cores with two-way hyper-threading. The input size is 10^8.**

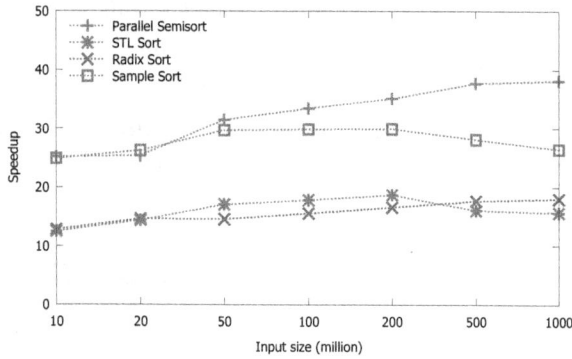

(a) Parallel speedup versus input size on the exponential distribution ($\lambda = n/10^3$).

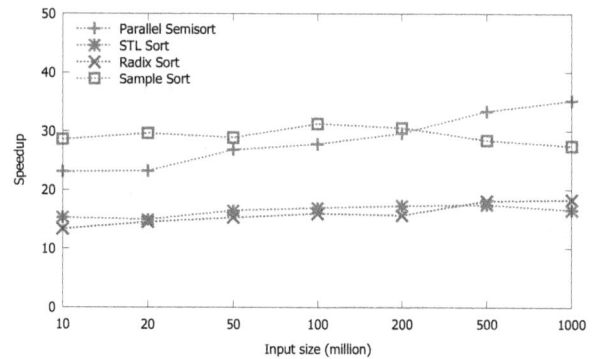

(b) Parallel speedup versus input size on the uniform distribution ($N = n$).

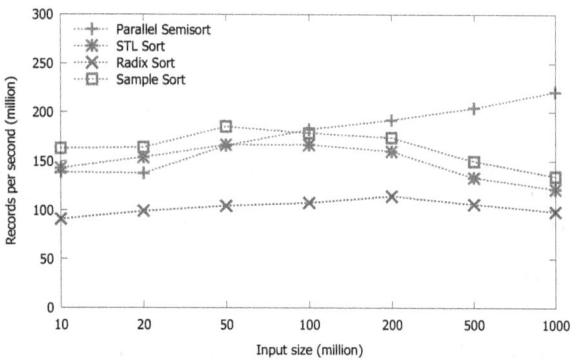

(c) Million records/second processed versus input size on the exponential distribution ($\lambda = n/10^3$).

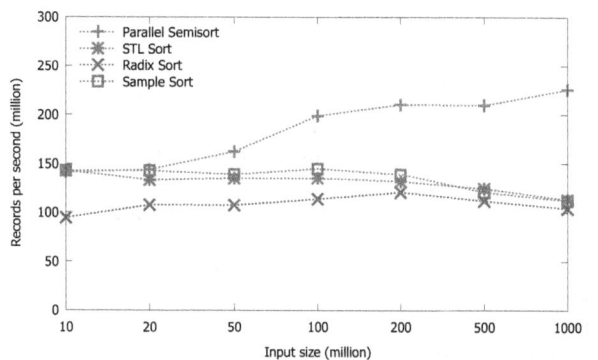

(d) Million records/second processed versus input size on the uniform distribution ($N = n$).

Figure 4: **Parallel speedup and records per second (million) for four different algorithms on two distributions with varying input size from $n = 10^7$ to $n = 10^9$, using 40 cores with hyper-threading.**

on the uniform distribution since the local sort has very high parallelism across the different buckets. The lower speedup for smaller input sizes is likely due to overhead of parallelism on smaller data.

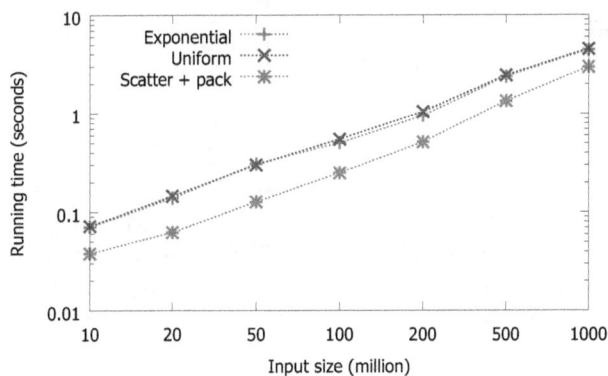

Figure 5: Parallel running times (seconds) with varying input size from $n = 10^7$ to $n = 10^9$, and the comparison to a scatter and pack operation.

As a baseline, we compare the performance of our semisorting algorithm to just a scatter and pack (the minimal work one would need to do to perform semisorting) and show that our algorithm is not much more expensive. In particular, Table 4 and Figure 5 show that on both the uniform and exponential distributions, our semisorting algorithm is just 1.5–2 times slower in parallel than a scatter followed by a pack on an array of size n, with better relative performance as we increase the input size.

We also compared with a simple sequential chained hash table-based algorithm for semisorting and found our algorithm to be 20% faster on a single thread. This is because the sequential implementation requires linked lists to link the elements going to the same bucket, which is not as efficient as estimating sizes and writing directly to an array. In addition, we tried other sequential implementations (e.g. STL vectors, hash tables using open addressing on keys and separate chaining on records with the same key, and a two-phase approach where we simply count the multiplicity of each key, allocate enough space for each key, and write the records into the appropriate locations) but found them to be even less efficient.

5.5 Comparison with other sorting implementations

In this section we compare the performance of our parallel semisorting algorithm with other optimized parallel sorting algorithms: radix sort, STL sort, and sample sort.

We compare the performance of our algorithm to the parallel radix sort in PBBS, which is a top-down recursive approach. The code for the radix sort is equally-optimized and is also a subroutine in our parallel semisorting code. The sequential and parallel running time of the radix sort is provided in Table 1 and Figure 2. The results show that the sequential running times for both algorithms are similar, but the parallel semisort gets about twice the parallel speedup compared to the radix sort. This is because the radix sort works by executing many rounds over the data, thus involving more reads and writes to memory, which limits the speedup as memory bandwidth is the bottleneck.

We also looked at the highly-optimized radix sort of [15], which is the fastest radix sort that we are aware of. Their code is highly-optimized with over 15,000 lines of code. It makes heavy use of AVX vector instructions, which are not supported on our 40-core Intel Nehalem test machine, so we

are unable to directly compare with our reported numbers. Based on our experiments on another machine supporting AVX instructions, their code is faster than our code on the uniform random distribution (a particularly easy case), but did not work on more skewed distributions. We believe that their code is designed to only handle well-balanced distributions, and so it is not surprising that it outperforms our code. Furthermore, their code is much more complicated than ours.

In addition, we compare our algorithm with two optimized comparison sorts: GNU libstdc++ (STL) parallel sort [21] implemented with OpenMP and sample sort [3] implemented with Cilk Plus in PBBS [20]. The experiment is run on inputs of varying sizes, ranging from 10^7 to 10^9, and two representative distributions: exponential and uniform distributions. The sequential and parallel running times are shown in Table 5, and the speedup and records per second comparing to parallel semisort are provided in Figure 4.

Although the work complexity of these two algorithms is $O(n \log n)$, they are more cache-friendly, and so their performance is competitive with our parallel semisort. In parallel, the comparison sorts are faster than our semisort on the uniform distribution with an input size of no more than 20 million, and exponential distribution with an input size of no more than 50 million. The STL sort is efficient sequentially (faster than all other algorithms on all inputs), but only has moderate speedup of at most 20 on all cases. The sample sort is designed as a cache-efficient algorithm so it gets consistent speedup of about 30 on all inputs. However, since the work of the comparison sorts is super-linear, their performance (records per second) decreases as the input size grows past 100 million. In contrast, the semisort algorithm scales better since it does linear work.

In our experiments, radix sort is the least efficient in almost all cases. This is because the radix sort is designed for sorting keys from a small range, and the 64-bit keys used in our experiments require too many rounds to sort.

6. CONCLUSION

We have described a parallel algorithm for semisorting that requires linear work and space and logarithmic depth. The algorithm is both theoretically efficient and also practical. We show experimentally that it achieves good parallel speedup on various input distributions and input sizes, and outperforms similarly-optimized comparison and radix sorts for large inputs.

Acknowledgments

This work is partially supported by the National Science Foundation under grant CCF-1218188, and by the Intel Science and Technology Center for Cloud Computing.

7. REFERENCES

[1] C. Balkesen, G. Alonso, J. Teubner, and M. T. Ozsu. Main-memory hash joins on modern processor architectures. In *IEEE Transactions on Knowledge and Data Engineering (TKDE)*, 2014.

[2] H. Bast and T. Hagerup. Fast parallel space allocation, estimation and integer sorting. *Information and Computation*, 123(1):72–110, 1995.

[3] G. E. Blelloch, P. B. Gibbons, and H. V. Simhadri. Low depth cache-oblivious algorithms. In *Proc. ACM*

#records (million)	Exponential distribution				Uniform distribution				40h Running time (sec.)		
	Running time (sec.)		Speedup	Records / sec. (million)	Running time (sec.)		Speedup	Records / sec. (million)	Scatter	Pack	Scatter + Pack
	Sequential	40h			Sequential	40h					
10	1.64	0.07	23.09	141.20	1.82	0.07	25.17	138.56	0.02	0.02	0.04
20	3.23	0.14	23.24	143.92	3.69	0.15	25.36	137.54	0.03	0.03	0.06
50	8.25	0.31	26.80	162.36	9.49	0.30	31.45	165.70	0.07	0.06	0.13
100	13.99	0.50	27.81	198.79	18.34	0.55	33.43	182.29	0.14	0.11	0.25
200	28.18	0.95	29.64	210.33	36.64	1.04	35.14	191.85	0.28	0.23	0.51
500	79.53	2.38	33.38	209.85	92.47	2.45	37.75	204.11	0.70	0.64	1.35
1000	155.90	4.43	35.19	225.69	173.03	4.53	38.19	220.69	1.62	1.35	2.97

Table 4: **Running time (seconds), speedup, and records per second (million) for input with varying sizes from 10^7 to 10^9, and the running time for a scatter, a pack and both operations. (40h) indicates 40 cores with two-way hyper-threading.**

#records (million)	GNU STL Sort				Sample Sort				Radix Sort			
	Exponential		Uniform		Exponential		Uniform		Exponential		Uniform	
	Seq.	40h	Seq.	40h	Seq.	40h	Seq.	40h	Seq.	40h	Seq.	40h
10	0.88	0.07	1.07	0.07	1.53	0.06	2.00	0.07	1.46	0.11	1.36	0.11
20	1.87	0.13	2.24	0.15	3.20	0.12	4.15	0.14	2.93	0.20	2.72	0.19
50	5.12	0.30	6.08	0.37	8.02	0.27	10.41	0.36	7.30	0.48	6.79	0.47
100	10.70	0.60	12.50	0.74	16.70	0.56	21.56	0.69	14.80	0.93	13.70	0.88
200	23.40	1.25	26.20	1.52	34.40	1.15	44.00	1.44	27.30	1.75	27.60	1.66
500	60.50	3.76	70.00	4.02	93.90	3.34	118.00	4.14	85.30	4.72	79.00	4.47
1000	129.00	8.23	146.00	8.84	197.00	7.44	245.00	8.93	186.00	10.20	173.00	9.60

Table 5: **Sequential and parallel running time (seconds) for input with varying sizes from 10^7 to 10^9. (40h) indicates 40 cores with two-way hyper-threading.**

Symp. on Parallelism in Algorithms and Architectures (SPAA), pages 189–199, 2010.

[4] R. D. Blumofe and C. E. Leiserson. Scheduling multithreaded computations by work stealing. *J. ACM (JACM)*, 46(5), Sept. 1999.

[5] R. P. Brent. The parallel evaluation of general arithmetic expressions. *J. ACM (JACM)*, 21(2):201–206, 1974.

[6] E. F. Codd. A relational model of data for large shared data banks. *Commun. ACM (CACM)*, 13(6):377–387, June 1970.

[7] R. Cole. Parallel merge sort. *SIAM J. Comput.*, 17(4):770–785, 1988.

[8] T. H. Cormen, C. E. Leiserson, R. L. Rivest, and C. Stein. *Introduction to Algorithms (3. ed.)*. MIT Press, 2009.

[9] J. Dean and S. Ghemawat. MapReduce: Simplified data processing on large clusters. *Commun. ACM (CACM)*, 51(1):107–113, Jan. 2008.

[10] P. B. Gibbons, Y. Matias, and V. Ramachandran. Efficient low-contention parallel algorithms. *Journal of Computer and System Sciences*, 53(3):417–442, 1996.

[11] J. Gil, Y. Matias, and U. Vishkin. Towards a theory of nearly constant time parallel algorithms. In *Foundations of Computer Science (FOCS)*, pages 698–710, 1991.

[12] W. Hasenplaugh, T. Kaler, T. B. Schardl, and C. E. Leiserson. Ordering heuristics for parallel graph coloring. In *Proc. ACM Symp. on Parallelism in Algorithms and Architectures (SPAA)*, pages 166–177, 2014.

[13] J. Jaja. *Introduction to Parallel Algorithms*. Addison-Wesley Professional, 1992.

[14] C. E. Leiserson. The Cilk++ concurrency platform. *The Journal of Supercomputing*, 51(3):244–257, 2010.

[15] O. Polychroniou and K. A. Ross. A comprehensive study of main-memory partitioning and its application to large-scale comparison- and radix-sort. In *Proc. ACM SIGMOD International Conference on Management of Data*, pages 755–766, 2014.

[16] S. Rajasekaran and J. H. Reif. Optimal and sublogarithmic time randomized parallel sorting algorithms. *SIAM J. Comput.*, 18(3):594–607, 1989.

[17] S. Rajasekaran and S. Sen. On parallel integer sorting. *Acta Informatica*, 29(1):1–15, 1992.

[18] J. H. Reif and S. Sen. Parallel computational geometry: An approach using randomization. In J. Sack and J. Urrutia, editors, *Handbook of Computational Geometry*, chapter 18, pages 765–828. 1999.

[19] J. Shun and G. E. Blelloch. Phase-concurrent hash tables for determinism. In *Proc. ACM Symp. on Parallelism in Algorithms and Architectures (SPAA)*, pages 96–107, 2014.

[20] J. Shun, G. E. Blelloch, J. T. Fineman, P. B. Gibbons, A. Kyrola, H. V. Simhadri, and K. Tangwongsan. Brief announcement: the Problem Based Benchmark Suite. In *Proc. ACM Symp. on Parallelism in Algorithms and Architectures (SPAA)*, pages 68–70, 2012.

[21] J. Singler, P. Sanders, and F. Putze. Mcstl: The multi-core standard template library. In *Euro-Par*, pages 682–694. 2007.

[22] L. G. Valiant. Handbook of theoretical computer science (vol. a). chapter General Purpose Parallel Architectures, pages 943–973. MIT Press, 1990.

Matrix Multiplication I/O-Complexity by Path Routing

Jacob Scott
University of California at
Berkeley
jnscott@math.berkeley.edu

Olga Holtz
University of California at
Berkeley
holtz@math.berkeley.edu

Oded Schwartz
The Hebrew University of
Jerusalem
odedsc@cs.huji.ac.il

ABSTRACT

We apply a novel technique based on path routings to obtain optimal I/O-complexity lower bounds for all Strassen-like fast matrix multiplication algorithms computed in serial or in parallel, assuming no reuse of nontrivial intermediate linear combinations. Given fast memory of size M, we prove an I/O-complexity lower bound of $\Omega\left(\left(\frac{n}{\sqrt{M}}\right)^{\omega_0} \cdot M\right)$ for any Strassen-like matrix multiplication algorithm applied to $n \times n$ matrices of arithmetic complexity $\Theta(n^{\omega_0})$ with $\omega_0 < 3$ under this assumption. This generalizes an approach by Ballard, Demmel, Holtz, and Schwartz that provides a tight lower bound for Strassen's matrix multiplication algorithm but which does not apply to algorithms with disconnected encoding or decoding components of the underlying computation graph or algorithms with multiply copied values. We overcome these challenges via a new graph-theoretical approach for proving I/O-complexity lower bounds without the use of edge expansions.

Categories and Subject Descriptors

F.2.1 [**Analysis of Algorithms and Problem Complexity**]: Numerical Algorithms and Problems; Computations on matrices

General Terms

Algorithms, Design, Performance

Keywords

Communication-avoiding algorithms; Fast matrix multiplication; I/O-complexity

SPAA'15, June 13–15, 2015, Portland, OR, USA.
Copyright is held by the owner/author(s). Publication rights licensed to ACM.
ACM 978-1-4503-3588-1/15/06 ...$15.00.
http://dx.doi.org/10.1145/2755573.2755594 .

1. INTRODUCTION

In practice, most of the runtime of an algorithm is often due to the communication of data within memory hierarchy and between multiple processors, rather than the arithmetic computations. The amount of communication performed during an algorithm depends on the order in which intermediate values are computed and kept in/discarded from cache. While much work has gone into constructing implementations of algorithms that reduce communication, in this paper we show lower bounds on the communication of any implementation of a common class of fast (but not classical; see Lemma 1) matrix multiplication algorithms.

The I/O-complexity of an algorithm is defined as the minimum possible number of cache operations required to compute all outputs of the algorithm using a fixed cache size M. In 2011, Ballard, Demmel, Holtz, and Schwartz showed a tight lower bound on the I/O-complexity of Strassen's fast matrix multiplication algorithm [6]. We prove an analogous I/O-complexity bound via a more general technique for any fast square matrix multiplication algorithm based on a uniform recursive step that does not recompute any intermediate values, subject to the assumption that every intermediate linear combination is used in only one multiplication. We also claim, without proof, that this assumption can be lifted. Because algorithms achieving our I/O-complexity bounds have been found [3], our bounds are optimal.

Machine model

In this paper, we assume a 2-layer memory hierarchy for sequential computations consisting of slow memory and fast memory. The slow memory is of unlimited size and represents the hard drive of a computer, while the fast memory, called cache, is of limited size M and may represent RAM. We model the I/O communication of an algorithm as follows: initially, all data resides in slow memory and the cache is empty. A single value may be input into cache from slow memory or output to slow memory from cache for the cost of one I/O. A computation in the algorithm may only be performed if all input values to that computation already reside in cache; when computed, the result is also put in cache. The algorithm halts when all outputs of the algorithm are stored in slow memory. In this model we assume that no arithmetic computation is ever performed more than once. See [10] for the formalization of this model as a pebble game played on the computation graph.

The number of cache I/Os (henceforth simply called I/Os) required may depend on the order in which intermediate values of the algorithm are computed. The algorithm's *I/O-*

complexity is thus defined as the minimum number of I/Os over all sequences of computations and I/Os that computes the algorithm's outputs.

For parallel computations we consider P processors, each having independent local memory of size M. As in [6] and [16], we define the bandwidth cost of an algorithm executed in parallel to be the number of values communicated between processors along the critical path. In other words, we count the total number of words (single values) sent between processors, except that words sent between processors simultaneously count as only one I/O. We call this the *bandwidth cost* of the algorithm.

Previous Work

In 1981 Hong and Kung [10] proved a tight lower bound on the I/O-complexity of the classical $\Theta(n^3)$ matrix multiplication algorithm (achieved by blocked multiplication) using S-partitions. A different proof of this result was given in [12] and later generalized in [5] via the Loomis-Whitney inequality [13]; this approach was also shown to apply to several other problems in numerical linear algebra. See [1] and [9] for further generalizations using other geometric bounds. However, these proofs apply only to direct numerical linear algebra algorithms, but not to algorithms that use distributivity for cancellation, such as Strassen's algorithm.

The edge expansion approach detailed in [6] relates the I/O-complexity of an algorithm to the edge expansion properties of the underlying computation graph. This technique provides an I/O-complexity lower bound for Strassen's fast matrix multiplication algorithm, but fails for algorithms with base graphs (the computation graph representing one recursive step; see Section 3) containing disconnected encoding or decoding graphs and those involving multiple copying. In [4], this approach is extended to fast recursive matrix multiplication algorithms for rectangular matrices whose base graphs consist of multiple equal-size connected components. This is sufficient to yield lower bounds for some common fast matrix multiplication algorithms, such as Bini's algorithm [8] and the Hopcroft-Kerr algorithm [11], but still does not address algorithms with general base graphs.

In this paper we present the first approach for proving I/O-complexity lower bounds for recursive fast matrix multiplication algorithms involving arbitrary base graphs, as long as the same base graph is used at each recursive step.

2. NEW APPROACH

Most previous lower bounds in this field are based on the Loomis-Whitney inequality (as in [12]), dominator sets/S-partitions (as in [10], [14], and [7]), or edge expansions (as in [6] and [4]). In this paper we apply a new technique, based on the existence of a routing of paths within the underlying computation graph. In particular, we show the existence of a set of paths between all the inputs and all the outputs of sufficiently large matrix multiplication subcomputations such that each vertex is hit relatively few times. We then show that if some, but not all, of these input and output vertices are to be computed in one computation segment, then there must exist many other vertices that contribute cache I/Os as a result. This new approach may generalize to other problems that have sufficient symmetry to guarantee the existence of an efficient routing.

3. PRELIMINARIES

As in [6], we define the computation directed acyclic graph (CDAG) of an algorithm to be the directed graph that contains a vertex for every value in the computation (input, output, or intermediate value) and an edge whenever one value depends directly on another.

Strassen's matrix multiplication algorithm works as follows: to multiply 2×2 matrices A and B, compute specific linear combinations of the entries of A and linear combinations of the entries of B, perform 7 multiplications of these linear combinations, and then take linear combinations of the results to get the entries of $C = AB$. For larger square input matrices, divide each input matrix in half horizontally and vertically and apply the above procedure, recursively computing the necessary products of submatrices.

A *Strassen-like* algorithm is a square matrix multiplication algorithm that takes a similar form: to multiply matrices of dimensions $n_0 \times n_0$, take linear combinations of the input matrices, compute products, and take linear combinations of the results to yield the entries of the output matrix. For larger matrices, divide into blocks and recurse.

Let G_r be the CDAG of a Strassen-like algorithm for $n_0^r \times n_0^r$ square matrix multiplication $C = AB$, necessarily consisting of r recursive levels. We call G_1 the *base graph*. G_1 consists of two *encoding graphs*, which compute linear combinations of entries of A and of B, a *multiplication layer* with b *multiplication vertices*, which compute products of these linear combinations, and then a *decoding graph*, which takes linear combinations of these products to yield the entries of C. Note that G_1 has $2n_0^2$ inputs, n_0^2 from each input matrix. Further note that the same linear combination of input elements may be used as inputs in multiple product vertices. In this paper all figures show computations that proceed from bottom to top; we therefore omit the directions of edges. See Figure 1.

Figure 1: The base graph G_1 of Strassen's algorithm for multiplying two 2×2 matrices A and B. Here $b = 7$.

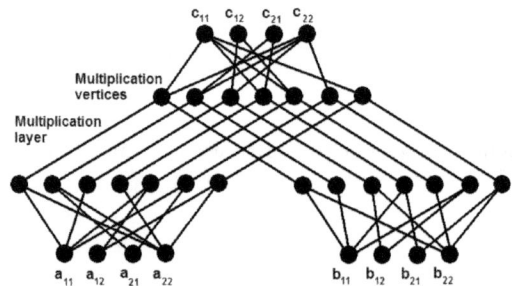

Note that G_r is a ranked graph, with inputs on rank 0 and outputs on rank $2r$. Ranks 0 through r lie in the encoding graphs and ranks $r+1$ through $2r$ lie in the decoding graph; the multiplication layer occurs between ranks r and $r+1$.

An intermediate vertex in G_r may have a single input vertex and, in this case, may have the same value as its one input. We call this *copying*; if the same value is copied to more than one child vertex, we call it *multiple copying*. We could consider this an artifact of our drawing of G_r and choose to identify these vertices. However, doing so would break the simple ranked, recursive structure of G_r. Instead, we group all vertices that represent the same value into a single *meta-vertex*. The vertices corresponding to each meta-vertex form a chain in the case of single copying and an upwards-branching subtree of the CDAG in the case of multiple copying, where each vertex of the subtree apart from the root has no other edges entering it from below. See Figure 2 for a depiction of a meta-vertex in the case of multiple copying. For most of this paper we consider only vertices, not meta-vertices, and then show that our technique still applies when copying or multiple copying occurs.

Figure 2: The meta-vertex corresponding to copies of the vertex v. Edges whose endpoints are not shown denote edges to vertices not in the shown meta-vertex. If this meta-vertex is in the CDAG for Strassen-like matrix multiplication, the structure of the meta-vertex is actually more regular than depicted due to the simple recursion.

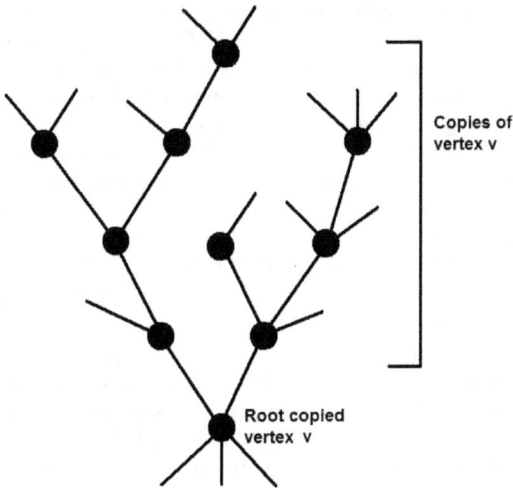

The approach in [6] fails when the decoding graph of the base graph G_1 has a disconnected encoding or decoding graph. Note that the entire CDAG G_r (and similarly G_1) must be connected simply because it computes matrix multiplication (this will be shown in greater detail in the process of proving Lemma 4), but the decoding graph and/or encoding graph may not be connected individually.

In this paper, we first demonstrate a technique to derive the I/O-complexity bound for Strassen's algorithm presented in [6] more easily. We then show how to extend the technique, via use of Theorem 2, to the case of disconnected decoding and/or encoding graphs, allowing us to derive strong lower bounds for all Strassen-like matrix multiplication algorithms in which each linear combination is used in only one multiplication. This will prove Theorem 1, our main result. Finally, we present a proof of Theorem 2.

THEOREM 1 (MAIN THEOREM). *Let a and b be small constants. Consider a Strassen-like matrix multiplication algorithm for $n \times n$ matrices with arithmetic complexity $o(n^3)$ using cache size $M \leq o(n^2)$ in which the base graph has $2a$ inputs and b outputs. If in the base graph every nontrivial linear combination of elements of the input matrices*

is used in only one multiplication, then the algorithm has I/O-complexity

$$\Omega\left(\left(\frac{n}{\sqrt{M}}\right)^{2\log_a b} \cdot M\right).$$

If run on P processors each of local cache size M, then the bandwidth cost is

$$\Omega\left(\left(\frac{n}{\sqrt{M}}\right)^{2\log_a b} \cdot \frac{M}{P}\right).$$

In other words, if a Strassen-like matrix multiplication algorithm performs $\Theta(n^{\omega_0})$ arithmetic operations with $\omega_0 < 3$, then its I/O-complexity is

$$\Omega\left(\left(\frac{n}{\sqrt{M}}\right)^{\omega_0} \cdot M\right).$$

If run on P processors, the bandwidth cost is

$$\Omega\left(\left(\frac{n}{\sqrt{M}}\right)^{\omega_0} \cdot \frac{M}{P}\right).$$

Furthermore, regardless of the cache size the bandwidth cost is

$$\Omega\left(\frac{n^2}{P^{2/\omega_0}}\right)$$

as long as computation is load balanced per rank of the computation graph.

In [3] an explicit algorithm is given that attains the bounds in Theorem 1. The sequential-to-parallel argument from [2] (as well as [6], [12], and [5]) allows us to take $P = 1$ – that is, work entirely in the serial model – and get the factor of $\frac{1}{P}$ in the parallel case with no additional work. Therefore, the remainder of this paper is devoted to proving a lower bound of $\Omega\left(\left(\frac{n}{\sqrt{M}}\right)^{2\log_a b} \cdot M\right)$ in the sequential case, from which Theorem 1 follows. By [3], the lower bounds in Theorem 1 are optimal.

4. DEFINITIONS

The proof presented in [6] relies on the notion of edge expansion; it shows a lower bound for the edge expansion of small subsets of vertices of the CDAG for Strassen's algorithm and then applies a lemma to yield a better edge expansion bound that relies on the fact that G_r contains as subgraphs many edge-disjoint copies of G_k for $k < r$. In our proof we bypass edge expansions entirely by explicitly cutting G_r into many copies of G_k for $k < r$. Both methods rely on the following fact, which is a consequence of the recursive definition of Strassen-like algorithms:

FACT 1. *For $0 \leq k \leq r$, let $G_{r,k}$ be the induced subgraph of G_r formed by the middle $2(k+1)$ levels of vertices (i.e. ranks $r - k$ through r of the encoding graphs and rank 0 through k of the decoding graph). Then $G_{r,k}$ consists of b^{r-k} vertex-disjoint copies of the graph G_k.*

In other words, the middle $2(k+1)$ layers of G_r are responsible for computing b^{r-k} independent matrix multiplications of square matrices of size $n_0^k \times n_0^k$.

DEFINITION 1. *For any subset S of vertices of a computation graph G with directed edges E, define the following:*

1. $R(S) = \{v \in G - S \mid$ for some $w \in S$, $(v, w) \in E\}$

2. $W(S) = \{v \in S \mid$ for some $w \in G - S$, $(v, w) \in E\}$

3. $\delta(S) = R(S) \bigcup W(S)$

Note that $R(S)$ and $W(S)$ are disjoint, so $|\delta(S)| = |R(S)| + |W(S)|$. If S denotes a set of consecutively-computed vertices of G, then $R(S)$ denotes the set of vertices of G that must be read into cache, if not already present, during the computation of the vertices of S, and $W(S)$ the set of vertices of G that must be written to cache, if not to remain in cache after the computation of S. We assume that no vertex in G is ever computed more than once, meaning that if a vertex is used in the computations of multiple other vertices, it must either remain in cache until all the computations of vertices depending on it have finished or else be written to and read from cache.

We also assume that every linear combination of inputs in the base graph – except for the inputs themselves – is used in at most one multiplication in the base graph; this implies that every meta-vertex in the base graph is either a single vertex or else is rooted at one of the input vertices.

If S' is a subset of meta-vertices of G, we similarly define
$\delta'(S') = \{$meta-vertex v' of G not in $S' \mid$
for some $w' \in S'$, v' and w' are adjacent$\}$,
where two meta-vertices v' and w' are considered to be adjacent if for some vertex $v \in v'$ and vertex $w \in w'$, $(v, w) \in E$ or $(w, v) \in E$. In other words, $\delta'(S')$ is the set of meta-vertices adjacent to any of those in S'.

The main proof in this paper is based on finding routings of paths between sets of vertices in subgraphs of the CDAG that avoid using any vertex too many times. To this end we make the following definition:

DEFINITION 2. *If X and Y are subsets of the vertices $V(G)$ of a directed graph G, define an m-routing between X and Y to be a collection R of $|X||Y|$ paths such that for any $x \in X$ and $y \in Y$ there exists a path, ignoring the directedness of edges, in G between x and y and such that every vertex of G is used collectively amongst all the paths in R at most m times. Similarly, if F is a subset of $V(G) \times V(G)$, define an m-routing for F to be a collection of paths, one for every $(v, w) \in F$, such that every vertex of G is hit at most m times.*

We will consider only the case where X and Y are disjoint. Note that m-routings need not be unique, and in fact part of the challenge of our proof is constructing a canonical m-routing with sufficiently small m.

DEFINITION 3. *Let $G = (V, E)$ and $S \subseteq V$. If p is a path in G that contains at least one vertex in S and at least one vertex in $G - S$, then we call p boundary-crossing with respect to S in G.*

Note that any boundary-crossing path contains a pair of adjacent vertices such that one is in S and the other is not. Our basic strategy will be to show the existence of m-routings for relatively small m, and then show that such a routing must contain many boundary-crossing paths, implying the existence of many vertices in $\delta(S)$ and thus many meta-vertices in $\delta'(S')$.

5. SIMPLE PROOF FOR STRASSEN'S ALGORITHM

First we use our technique to rederive the lower bound on the I/O-complexity for Strassen's algorithm presented in [6], $\Omega\left(\left(\frac{n}{\sqrt{M}}\right)^{\log_2 7} \cdot M\right)$. As in [6], we consider the sequence of computations of vertices performed by the algorithm. In [6], this sequence is divided up into segments of sufficient length such that the I/O due to each segment is guaranteed to be at least M, the cache size. To do this, the smallest segment length s is found such that for any segment S of size s we are guaranteed that $|\delta(S)| \geq 3M$. All vertices present in $\delta(S)$ contribute to the I/Os due to S, except for vertices in $R(S)$ already present in cache (at most M) and vertices in $W(S)$ that need not be written to cache (at most M). Because [6] considers only the decoding graph of G_r, there are no concerns about vertex copying.

We use the same basic argument, but instead divide the sequence of vertex computations of the CDAG G_r into the smallest segments possible such that each segment S (except perhaps the last segment) contains $66M$ vertices from rank k of the decoding graph (rank $r + k$ of G_r) [1]. When a vertex v is in S we consider every vertex in the same meta-vertex as v to also be in S; however, because there is no copying in the decoding graph every meta-vertex can contain only one vertex from the decoding graph. Note that the size of each segment may be different; we care only about the number of vertices on this specific rank. We let $k = \lceil \log_4(132M) \rceil$, the smallest integer k such that $4^k \geq 2 \cdot 66M$. Because rank k of the decoding graph contains $4^k 7^{r-k}$ vertices, there are $\lfloor \frac{4^k 7^{r-k}}{66M} \rfloor$ such complete segments. Let S be one such complete segment and let $\bar{S}$ denote the vertices in S on rank k of the decoding graph of G_r. Thus we pick S as small as possible such that $|\bar{S}| = 66M$. If G_r is the CDAG for Strassen's algorithm for multiplying $n_0^r \times n_0^r$ matrices, recall that $G_{r,k}$ contains 7^{r-k} copies of the graph G_k. For $1 \leq i \leq 7^{r-k}$, let G_k^i be the ith such copy, S_i be the subset of S in G_k^i, and $\bar{S}_i$ be the subset of vertices of S_i on rank k of G_r.

Intuitively, we "count" S by the number of vertices of S on this particular rank. It is these vertices that will contribute, perhaps indirectly, to I/Os performed during the computation of S, regardless of what vertices on other ranks lie in S.

Let D_k be the decoding graph of G_k. We now claim that there exists a routing of paths between all the input vertices and output vertices of D_k such that no vertex of D_k is hit too often:

CLAIM 1. *There exists an $(11 \cdot 7^k)$-routing in D_k between the set of inputs of D_k and the set of outputs of D_k.*

PROOF. If D_1 were simply the complete graph $K_{7,4}$, there would exist a very natural routing of paths between inputs and outputs of D_k: for any input and output, there is a unique chain of vertices between them defined by the sequence of subcomputations the input lies in. A vertex on rank i of D_k is then hit $7^i 4^{k-i} \leq 7^k$ times in this routing, once for every pair of input vertex beneath it and output vertex above it.

Unfortunately, D_1 is not a complete graph. However, because D_1 is connected there still exists a path within each copy of D_1 from any input vertex to any output vertex.

---

[1] We did not optimize for the constant factor.

Where each path previously went directly from an input vertex v to an output vertex w of each D_1, it will now take any path (that doesn't repeat vertices) through the same D_1 component from v to w. This idea is depicted in Figure 3. This multiplies the number of times a vertex is hit in the routing by at most the number of vertices in D_1, 11. $\square$

Figure 3: One of the encoding graphs in G_1 for Strassen's algorithm. Because there is no edge from v to w, a chain must instead take a more indirect path, shown in red, through the encoding graph.

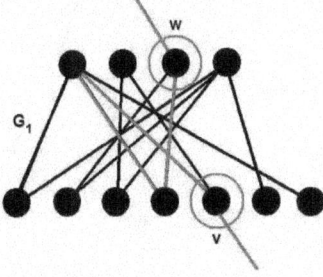

Each G_k^i contains a copy of D_k – for this proof we consider only the decoding piece D_k of G_k, but in the full proof we must consider G_k in its entirety in order to account for base graphs with disconnected encoding/decoding portions. Let D_k^i be the copy of D_k lying in G_k^i and note that $|\bar{S}_i| \leq \frac{1}{2} 4^k$, so at most half of the vertices on the top rank of D_k^i are in S. For each $1 \leq i \leq 7^{r-k}$, fix an $(11 \cdot 7^k)$-routing in D_k^i between the 7^k inputs and 4^k outputs. See Figure 4. There are now two cases:

1. Fewer than half of the 7^k vertices on the bottom rank of D_k^i are in S. In this case, there exist at least $|\bar{S}_i| \frac{1}{2} 7^k$ paths in the routing going from an input to D_k^i not in S to an output in S.

2. At least half of the vertices on the bottom rank of D_k^i are in S. In this case, there exist at least $\left(4^k - |\bar{S}_i| \right) \frac{1}{2} 7^k$ paths in the routing going from an input in S to an output not in S.

In either case, there are at least $\frac{1}{2} |\bar{S}_i| 7^k$ boundary-crossing (between S_i and $D_k^i - S_i$) paths in the routing. Associate to each boundary-crossing path an edge in the path that crosses between S_i and $D_k^i - S_i$. The vertex of this edge that is not in S lies in $\delta(S_i)$. By the definition of m-routing,

$$|\delta(S_i)| \geq \frac{\frac{1}{2} |\bar{S}_i| 7^k}{11 \cdot 7^k} = \frac{1}{22} |\bar{S}_i|$$

Adding this up over all the $\bar{S}_i$ yields

$$|\delta(S)| \geq \sum_{i=1}^{7^{r-k}} \frac{1}{22} |\bar{S}_i| = \frac{1}{22} |\bar{S}| \qquad (1)$$

This step relies on the D_k being disjoint and the lack of copying in the decoding graph of Strassen's (or any Strassen-like) matrix multiplication algorithm. If multiple copying did occur, vertices in the different D_k^i need not correspond to distinct computations. This will add an additional layer of complexity to the upcoming proof.

Since $|\bar{S}|$ was chosen to be $66M$, this yields $\delta(S) \geq 3M$. Therefore the computation of S contributes at least M I/Os. Thus the total I/O is at least

$$\left\lfloor \frac{4^k 7^{r-k}}{66M} \right\rfloor \cdot M = \Omega \left(7^r \left(\frac{4}{7} \right)^k \right) = \Omega \left(|V(G_r)| \frac{M}{M^{\log_4 7}} \right)$$

$$= \Omega \left(\left(\frac{n_0}{\sqrt{M}} \right)^{\log_2 7} \cdot M \right)$$

as long as $M \leq o\left(n_0^2 \right)$ (which guarantees that $66M \leq 4^k 7^{r-k}$). $\square$

Figure 4: An example of a path considered in the $\left(11 \cdot 7^k \right)$-routing between an input vertex (to D_k^1) that is not in S and an output vertex that is in S. The submultiplications are shown in red, S_1 is shown in blue, and $\bar{S}_1$ is circled. Note that the path zags up and down, as explained in Figure 3. For simplicity, only one encoding graph is shown and only 3 submultiplications are drawn.

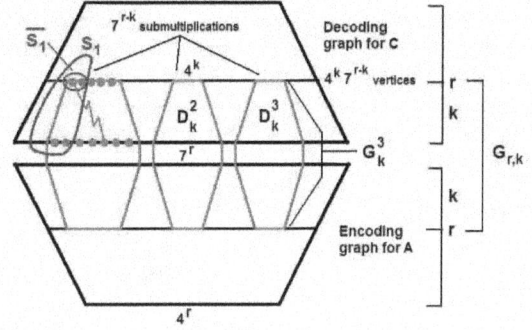

6. STRASSEN-LIKE ALGORITHMS

We now turn our attention to Strassen-like square matrix multiplication algorithms. Several nuances prevent our above proof from working as-is:

1. G_1 may have disconnected encoding or decoding graphs. This prevents us from finding an m-routing in the decoding graph D_k because D_k itself may no longer be connected. We will solve this problem by considering G_k, consisting of the decoding graph as well as the two encoding graphs. The paths in our m-routing will no longer be chains or even chains with length 1 "zags," but may need to bounce between inputs and outputs of G_k several times. See Figure 5.

2. Multiple copying may occur in the encoding graphs. This means a collection of m-routings for the G_k^i could potentially hit a meta-vertex more than m times. We will show via Theorem 2 that m-routings will only hit a meta-vertex entirely within G_k at most m times and then change the overall counting argument slightly to prevent meta-vertices between multiple G_k^is from being hit too often.

39

As before, we divide the sequence of vertex computations of G_r into segments such that each segment S contains enough vertices of a certain type. Again let G_k^i be the ith subcomputation of $G_{r,k}$ for $1 \leq i \leq b^{r-k}$. Let a *duplicated* vertex be a vertex of the CDAG G_r with at least one other copy (called a *duplicate*) in G_r, that is one whose meta-vertex contains more than one vertex. We call two subcomputations *input-disjoint* if none of their inputs lie in the same meta-vertex.

Let S be a segment of the sequence of vertex computations. Recall that when $v \in S$ we consider every vertex w in the same meta-vertex as v to also be in S. For this argument we count only the vertices on rank k of the decoding graph of G_r and rank $r-k$ of either encoding graph that are in mutually input-disjoint subcomputations $G_{r,k}$. We choose $k = \lceil \log_a 72M \rceil$, the smallest integer k such that $a^k \geq 2 \cdot 36M$.

First we show that counting only vertices lying in subcomputations that do not share inputs reduces the number of vertices on the relevant ranks by only a constant factor.

LEMMA 1. *Let $k \leq r - 2$. If not every vertex in the encoding graph for A of G_1 is a duplicated vertex and similarly for the encoding graph for B of G_1, then a fraction $\frac{1}{b^2}$ of the subcomputations G_k^i are mutually input-disjoint.*

PROOF. Consider the recursion tree of subcomputations computed by G_r. Let P_1 be the "grandparent" subcomputation of G_k^i – the subcomputation in the recursion tree two levels above G_k^i – and suppose P_1 multiplies matrices A_1 by B_1. Then at least one child subcomputation P_2 of P_1 multiplies matrices A_2 by B_2 such that A_2 shares no meta-vertices with A_1. Similarly, at least one child subcomputation of P_2 multiplies matrices A_3 by B_3 such that B_3 shares no meta-vertices with B_2, and hence with B_1. Thus at least one subsubcomputation of P_1 is input-disjoint from it. P_1 has b^2 subcomputations two levels down from it, so at least a fraction $\frac{1}{b^2}$ of all the subcomputations G_k^i are mutually input-disjoint. $\square$

Fix a collection C of b^{r-k-2} mutually input-disjoint subcomputations G_k^i. Let $\bar{S}$ be the set of vertices of S on the aforementioned ranks in these subcomputations. Formally, for $v \in S$ we let $v \in \bar{S}$ if both conditions below are met:

1. v lies on one of the following ranks: rank k of the decoding graph of G_r, rank $r-k$ of the encoding graph of G_r that encodes A, or rank $r-k$ of the encoding graph of G_r that encodes B.

2. The subcomputation G_k^i that v lies in (necessarily as an input or output of) is in C.

Divide the sequence of vertex computations into the smallest segments such that for each segment S we have $|\bar{S}| \geq 36M$. Let S_i be the subset of S in G_k^i and $\bar{S}_i$ be the subset of $\bar{S}$ in G_k^i. Note that if G_k^i is not one of the chosen input-disjoint subcomputations then $\bar{S}_i = \emptyset$. Intuitively, only the vertices in $\bar{S}$ "count" towards our I/O lower bound, regardless of how many other vertices lie in S, and we choose our segment divisions such that each segment has enough counted vertices. See Figure 5.

Note that if the condition of Lemma 1 is not met, then the algorithm never computes linear combinations of one of the input matrices. It is well known that any matrix

Figure 5: The overall idea of the main proof. For simplicity only one encoding graph is explicitly drawn. The set S is shown in blue. Note that only the elements on rank k of the decoding graph and rank $r - k$ of the encoding graphs in input-disjoint G_k^is lie in $\bar{S}$. A typical boundary-crossing path in G_k^3 is shown. (Not shown) The two vertices of the path on the bottom rank of G_k^3 lie in different encoding graphs.

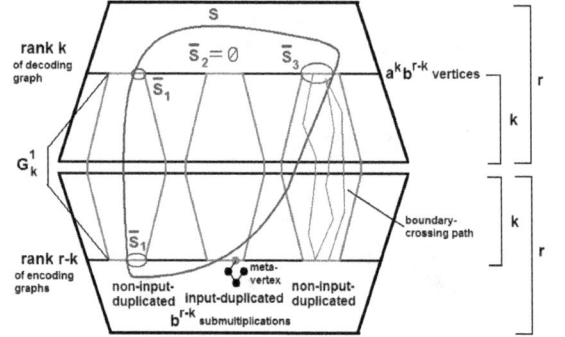

multiplication algorithm that computes linear combinations of only one of the input matrices performs no better than naive matrix multiplication and so does not have $o(n^3)$ arithmetic complexity (i.e., is not a fast matrix multiplication algorithm). Thus from now on we assume the condition of Lemma 1 is met.

Second, we show that our choice of partitioning the sequence of vertex computations into segments S exists. If meta-vertices contained multiple input and/or output vertices counted in $\bar{S}$, then including into S the next vertex v in the sequence of vertex computations – which by definition also includes into S every vertex in the same meta-vertex as v – could increase this count by more than one.

LEMMA 2. *If G_k^i and G_k^j are input-disjoint, then the meta-vertices corresponding to the inputs and outputs of G_k^i and G_k^j are all distinct.*

PROOF. Note that the decoding graph of G_1 cannot contain copying. If it did, then in the base case of $n_0 \times n_0$ matrix multiplication $C_1 = A_1 B_1$ some outputs would be identically equal, which is not the case. Hence the decoding graph of G_r contains no copying, and so every output vertex of G_k^i and G_k^j is non-duplicated. By definition, the input vertices of G_k^i and G_k^j are in distinct meta-vertices, proving the lemma. $\square$

For the remainder of this proof we will consider, for each i, the entire subcomputation graph G_k^i (as opposed to just the decoding portion D_k^i). We must consider the decoding graph and both encoding graphs of G_k^i together because the decoding graph by itself, or even the decoding graph plus one encoding graph, may be disconnected. We now state the main theorem used in our proof, whose proof we defer until Section 7. Compare to the routing found in Section 5 between the input and output vertices of each D_k^i.

THEOREM 2 (ROUTING THEOREM). *Let G_k be the CDAG for $n_0^k \times n_0^k$ matrix multiplication, $a = n_0^2$, and let the encoding graph of the base graph G_1 have $2a$ inputs and b outputs. Then there exists a $6a^k$-routing between the set of inputs of G_k and the set of outputs of G_k. Furthermore, every meta-vertex in G_k is also hit by the routing at most $6a^k$ times.*

For each of the mutually input-disjoint G_k^i in C, fix a $6a^k$-routing guaranteed by the Routing Theorem between the inputs and outputs of G_k^i. Because the size of the top rank of G_k^i is a^k and the size of the bottom rank is $2a^k$ and $|\bar{S}_i| \leq |\bar{S}| \leq \frac{1}{2}a^k$, for every vertex v in $\bar{S}_i$ there exist at least $\frac{1}{2}a^k$ paths in the routing that go either:

1. between a vertex in S on the bottom rank of G_k^i and a vertex not in S on the top rank of G_k^i (if v is on the bottom rank)

2. between a vertex not in S on the bottom rank of G_k^i and a vertex in S on the top rank of G_k^i (if v is on the top rank).

Thus the routing in G_k^i contains at least $\frac{1}{2}a^k|\bar{S}_i|$ boundary-crossing paths; call the set of such paths P_i and let $P = \bigcup_i P_i$ be all these boundary-crossing paths in the above routings for all input-disjoint G_k^i. Then $|P| \geq \sum_i \frac{1}{2}a^k|\bar{S}_i| = \frac{1}{2}a^k|\bar{S}|$.

By the Routing Theorem every meta-vertex contained entirely within G_k^i is hit by the routing at most $6a^k$ times. No meta-vertex in G_k^i extends beneath the bottom rank of G_k^i, and so every meta-vertex in G_r intersects at most one of the mutually input-disjoint G_k^i. Therefore every meta-vertex in G_r is hit at most $6a^k$ times by the paths in P.

Let S' be the set of meta-vertices represented by S, and recall that $\delta'(S')$ denotes all meta-vertices adjacent to S' that are not in S' itself. Then

$$|\delta'(S')| \geq \frac{\frac{1}{2}a^k|\bar{S}|}{6a^k} = \frac{1}{12}|\bar{S}| \qquad (2)$$

This is a more general analogue of Equation 1.

Every meta-vertex adjacent to S necessarily contributes one to the I/Os due to computing S, except possibly for those meta-vertices already in memory (at most M) and those that need not be written to cache (at most M). Because $|\bar{S}| = 36M$, we have $|\delta'(S')| \geq 3M$, and so computing S requires at least M I/Os.

As indicated above, because G_r has $o(n^3)$ multiplications we may apply Lemma 1. Because rank k of the decoding graph of G_r and rank $r - k$ of the encoding graphs of G_r together have size $3a^k b^{r-k}$ and $\frac{1}{b^2}$ of these vertices are in mutually input-disjoint subcomputations G_k^i, the total I/O from computing G_r is at least

$$\left\lfloor \frac{\frac{1}{b^2}3a^k b^{r-k}}{36M} \right\rfloor \cdot M = \Omega\left(b^r \left(\frac{a}{b}\right)^k \right) = \Omega\left(|V(G_r)| \frac{M}{M^{\log_a b}} \right)$$

$$= \Omega\left(\left(\frac{n}{\sqrt{M}}\right)^{2\log_a b} \cdot M \right)$$

as long as $M \leq o\left(n^2\right)$ (which guarantees that $36M \leq \frac{1}{b^2}3a^k b^{r-k}$ and $k \leq r - 2$).

In the parallel case, we apply the above argument to a processor that computes an above-average number of vertices

of $\bar{S}$, yielding a factor of $\frac{1}{P}$ as in [2]. The cache-independent result comes from instead picking $k = \Theta\left(\log_b \frac{n^{\omega_0}}{P}\right)$ and letting S represent the computations performed by just one processor. This proves Theorem 1. $\square$

7. PROOF OF THE ROUTING THEOREM

In this section we prove Theorem 2. Let G_k be the CDAG for a square Strassen-like matrix multiplication algorithm for $C = AB$, let Out be the set of outputs of G_k (corresponding to entries of C), In be the set of inputs, In_A be the set of inputs to the encoding graph for A within G_k, and In_B be the inputs to the encoding graph for B. Then $|Out| = |In_A| = |In_B| = a^k = n_0^{2k}$. For $v \in In$ and $w \in Out$, we say that the input-output pair (v, w) is a *guaranteed dependence* if in any correct matrix multiplication algorithm there exists a chain from v to w, or equivalently if the output element corresponding to w explicitly depends on the input element corresponding to v. It is clear that if $v \in In_A$ represents the input a_{ij} and w represents the output $c_{i'j'}$ then there is a guaranteed dependence between v and w if and only if $i = i'$, and similarly if $v \in In_B$ represents the input b_{ij}, then there is a guaranteed dependence between v and w if and only if $j = j'$.

To prove the Routing Theorem we will combine the following two lemmas, whose proofs follow in the succeeding sections:

LEMMA 3. *Let $F \subseteq V(G_k) \times V(G_k)$ be the set of all guaranteed dependencies (v, w) of G_k with $v \in In$ and $w \in Out$. Then there exists a $2n_0^k$-routing for F in G_k consisting only of chains.*

Intuitively, we can route chains between all pairs of input and output vertices where a chain is guaranteed to exist while using no vertex more than $2\sqrt{a^k}$ times. That every path of the routing is a chain is not necessary to complete the proof of the Routing Theorem.

LEMMA 4. *Fix a routing for F, where F is as defined in Lemma 3. Then there exists a routing between In and Out such that every path in the routing consists of the concatenation of chains in F – some reversed in direction – such that each chain in F is used $3n_0^k$ times.*

In other words, given any way of routing chains between all guaranteed dependencies, we can combine those chains, backwards and forwards, to give a path between every input and every output vertex while not using any such chain more than $3\sqrt{a^k}$ times.

Given these lemmas, the proof is simple:

PROOF OF THE ROUTING THEOREM. By Lemma 3, fix a $2n_0^k$-routing R_0 for the set of guaranteed dependencies F. By Lemma 4, there exists a routing R between the inputs and outputs of G_r composed of concatenations of chains (some reversed) in R_0 such that every chain in R_0 is used at most $3n_0^k$ times. Thus in the routing R every vertex of G is used at most $2n_0^k \cdot 3n_0^k = 6a^k$ times, and so R is a $6a^k$-routing, as desired.

Because every meta-vertex is an upward-facing subtree (see Figure 2), any path hitting a meta-vertex also hits the root vertex of the meta-vertex. Hence every meta-vertex is also hit at most $6a^k$ times. $\square$

7.1 Proof of Lemma 4

In this section we prove the second, significantly easier, lemma. The proof of this lemma is constructive, yielding an explicit scheme for routing chains between all inputs and outputs given a routing for all guaranteed dependencies. This lemma holds for any correct matrix multiplication algorithm based only on the definition of matrix multiplication.

PROOF OF LEMMA 4. For an input vertex v of G_k and output vertex w corresponding to element $c_{i'j'}$ of C, suppose first that $v \in In_A$. Let v then represent element a_{ij} of A. We form the following sequence of guaranteed dependencies:

$$a_{ij} \to c_{ij'} \to b_{jj'} \to c_{i'j'}$$

That is, $(a_{ij}, c_{ij'})$ is a guaranteed dependence, $(b_{jj'}, c_{ij'})$ is a guaranteed dependence, and $(b_{jj'}, c_{i'j'})$ is a guaranteed dependence. Note that every guaranteed dependence in this chain involves 3 out of the 4 variables i, i', j, and j'. Hence as i, j, i', and j' vary between 1 and n_0^k, each guaranteed dependence above is used n_0^k times, once for each value of the missing variable (for each time it appears in the above sequence). For example, for any i, j, and j', the guaranteed dependence between a_{ij} and $c_{ij'}$ is used exactly once for every $1 \leq i' \leq n_0^k$. See Figure 6 for another interpretation of this pattern.

Similarly, if $v \in In_B$ let v correspond to element b_{ij} of B. The following sequence of guaranteed dependencies has the same properties:

$$b_{ij} \to c_{i'j} \to a_{i'i} \to c_{i'j'}$$

Amongst both these sequences, each guaranteed dependence between an element of A and one of C is used exactly $3 \cdot n_0^k$ times and similarly for every guaranteed dependence between B and C. This proves Lemma 4. □

Note that these sequences are not unique. When routing a_{ij} to $c_{i'j'}$, any sequence of the form

$$a_{ij} \to c_{ij'} \to b_{\_j'} \to c_{i'j'}$$

where the blank is any value forms a set of sequences of guaranteed dependencies. However, unless the values that the blank takes are well-distributed over j for all choices of i, i', and j', this sequence will not have the desired property. This explains the odd use of j as a row index, and similarly the use of i as a column index when routing b_{ij} to $c_{i'j'}$.

Figure 6: The sequence of guaranteed dependencies between a_{ij} and $c_{i'j'}$ shown as elements in the matrices A, B, and C. Note the use of j as a row index.

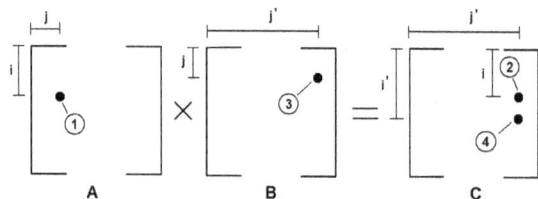

7.2 Proof of Lemma 3

This lemma is significantly harder to prove. We use the following overall strategy: In order to prove there exists a $2n_0^k$-routing between all guaranteed dependencies, we show there exists a n_0-routing of guaranteed dependencies in the subgraph of G_1 formed by the decoding graph together with the encoding graph for A; by the recursive structure of G_k, this is sufficient to prove it in general. Define a *middle-rank* vertex of G_1 to be a vertex on the top rank of the encoding graph of A. To show the lemma for this $\frac{2}{3}$ of G_1, we show a (several-to-one) matching between guaranteed dependencies and middle-rank vertices on some chain satisfying the dependence. By assumption, every vertex representing a linear combination of elements of A is adjacent to exactly one multiplication vertex; thus a routing of guaranteed dependencies that uses each middle-rank vertex at most n_0 times also uses each multiplication vertex at most n_0 times.

We will prove the existence of this matching via a version of Hall's Matching Theorem. In order to apply this theorem, we will need to show that for every set of d guaranteed dependencies, there exist chains between those dependencies collectively hitting at least $\frac{d}{n_0}$ middle-rank vertices. We demonstrate that if this is not the case, then setting some entries of the $n_0 \times n_0$ input matrix A to be identically 0 results in an algorithm that correctly computes many of the guaranteed dependencies between C and A using relatively few multiplications. Finally, we show that this implies the existence of an algorithm for multiplying a $n_0 \times n_0$ matrix by a length n_0 vector in fewer than n_0^2 operations, which is known to be impossible [15]. This will conclude the proof.

Let G_k' be the induced subgraph of G_k containing the vertices from the decoding graph of G_k and the encoding graph of G_k for A (excluding only the encoding graph for B). Let F' be the subset of F with both vertices lying in G_k', that is the set of guaranteed dependencies (v, w) between inputs v of A and outputs w of C. For simplicity, we simply call F' the *guaranteed dependencies of G_k'*. We now consider m-routings for the set of guaranteed dependencies (that is, F') of G_k'. It then suffices to find an a^k-routing of guaranteed dependencies in G_k'.

CLAIM 2. *If there exists an m-routing for the guaranteed dependencies of G_1', then there exists an m^k-routing for the guaranteed dependencies of G_k'.*

PROOF. This lemma follows from the recursive structure of G_k'. Intuitively, the graph G_k' is formed by placing b copies of G_{k-1}' in parallel, connecting up their inputs with a^{k-1} copies of the encoding graph for A, and connecting up their outputs with a^{k-1} copies of the decoding graph for C. See Figure 7. In other words, take a^{k-1} copies of G_1' and replace their middle two ranks with copies of G_{k-1}'. Any number of copies of G_1' in parallel still have an m-routing for guaranteed dependencies, and replacing their middle ranks effectively replaces a pair of adjacent vertices on the middle ranks with a guaranteed dependence in G_{k-1}'. Thus if there exists an m^{k-1}-routing for G_{k-1} then there exists an m^k routing for G_k. The claim then follows by induction. □

Therefore it will suffice to prove the existence of an n_0-routing for the guaranteed dependencies of G_1'. We now apply a version of Hall's Matching Theorem:

Figure 7: The construction of G'_k from b copies of G'_{k-1}. A pair of adjacent vertices on the middle two ranks is replaced with a guaranteed dependence in one of the G'_{k-1}.

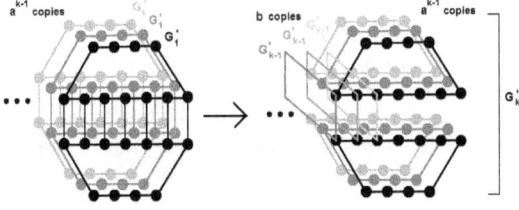

THEOREM 3 (HALL'S MATCHING THEOREM). *(Many-to-one version) Let $G = (X, Y)$ be a bipartite graph and for $D \subseteq V(G)$ let $N(D)$ denote the set of neighbors of D in G. If for every $D \subseteq X$ we have $|N(D)| \geq \frac{|D|}{p}$, then there exists a many-to-one matching between X and Y such that every vertex in X is used exactly once and every vertex in Y is used at most p times.*

This theorem follows from the standard form of Hall's Matching Theorem by simply duplicating all vertices in Y p times.

We now construct a graph $H = (X, Y)$ to which to apply Theorem 3. For every guaranteed dependence (v, w) in G'_1 (with v an input representing an element of A and w an output representing an element of C), define a corresponding vertex in X. Let Y be the set of middle-rank vertices of G_1: all vertices on the top rank of the encoding graph for A. It suffices to assign to each guaranteed dependence in X a middle-rank vertex from Y through which its chain may pass. To this end, if $x \in X$ corresponds to the guaranteed dependence (v, w) and $y \in Y$ corresponds to the middle-rank vertex t, let there be an edge between x and y if there exists some chain between v and w passing through t. See Figure 8.

Figure 8: The vertices shown in red are those adjacent to the vertex in H corresponding to the guaranteed dependence (v, w), where v corresponds to the input a_{12} of A and w corresponds to the output c_{11} of C. The graph shown is the G'_1 for Strassen's algorithm.

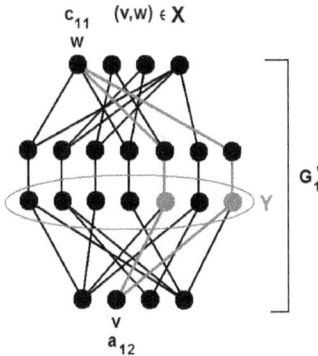

LEMMA 5. *For any set $D \subseteq X$, we have $|N(D)| \geq \frac{|D|}{n_0}$.*

From Lemma 5, the proof of Lemma 3 follows, and thus our main result:

PROOF OF LEMMA 3. By Hall's Matching Theorem (Theorem 3), there exists a many-to-one matching from X to Y using every vertex in Y at most n_0 times. Fix such a matching. For every guaranteed dependence (v, w) of G'_1, simply route a chain through the vertex of Y that (v, w) is matched with. Every vertex on the middle two ranks of G'_1 is thus hit at most n_0 times. Every vertex on the top and bottom ranks of G'_1 is hit exactly n_0 times by any routing for guaranteed dependencies that uses only chains, because in $n_0 \times n_0$ matrix multiplication every element of A influences n_0 elements of C, and every element of C depends on n_0 elements of A. Thus there exists a n_0-routing for the guaranteed dependencies in G'_1, and so by Claim 2 there exists a n_0^k-routing for the guaranteed dependencies of G'_k. The same holds for the induced subgraph of G_1 consisting of the decoding graph together with the encoding graph for B, yielding a $2n_0^k$-routing for the guaranteed dependencies of G_k. □

7.3 Proof of Lemma 5

Finally, we prove Lemma 5 to complete the proof of the Routing Theorem and thus our main result, Theorem 1:

PROOF OF LEMMA 5. Suppose by way of contradiction that for some subset $D \subseteq X$ of guaranteed dependencies in G'_1 we have $|N(D)| < \frac{|D|}{n_0}$. Recall that a guaranteed dependence occurs between the vertex representing a_{ij} and the vertex representing $c_{i'j'}$ exactly when $i = i'$. We may thus partition D by the choice of i: let D_i be the subset of D consisting of guaranteed dependencies between a_{ij} and $c_{ij'}$ for some j and j'. Because $1 \leq i \leq n_0$, for some i we have $|D_i| \geq \frac{|D|}{n_0}$. Since $N(D_i) \subseteq N(D)$, we have $|N(D_i)| < \frac{|D|}{n_0} \leq |D_i|$. In other words, the set of guaranteed dependencies D_i is computed using fewer than $|D_i|$ multiplication vertices.

We now demonstrate that this is impossible by using this structure to create a matrix-vector multiplication algorithm that requires fewer than n_0^2 multiplications. For fixed D_i, define the computation graph G_1° as follows: G_1° is the induced subgraph of G_1 containing as inputs vertices corresponding to all the elements of B and their linear combinations, the elements a_{ij} of A for all j, and the elements $c_{ij'}$ of C for all j'. G_i° additionally contains all the middle-rank vertices in $N(D_i)$ and all vertices on the bottom rank of the decoding graph. G_1° may now contain "useless" vertices – we draw G_1° with these vertices additionally removed, but it does not matter for the bounds in this proof.

By the structure of G_1, every multiplication vertex multiplies a linear combination $\sum_{i,j} \lambda_{ij}^A a_{ij}$ by a linear combination $\sum_{i,j} \lambda_{ij}^B b_{ij}$ for some coefficients λ_{ij}^A and λ_{ij}^B in the ground field F ($\mathbb{R}$ or $\mathbb{C}$). We consider linear combinations of the a_{ij}s with coefficients in $F[b_{11}, b_{12}, \ldots, b_{n_0 n_0}]$. In other words, consider b_{ij}s to be coefficients and a_{ij}s to be variables. For $1 \leq j \leq n_0$, let a_{ij} and c_{ij} be the inputs and outputs of G_1° respectively. Note that for all $1 \leq j, j' \leq n_0$, c_{ij} depends on $a_{ij'}$. We now define a boolean-valued function f that represents whether the coefficient of each input is correct in each output: For $1 \leq j, j' \leq n_0$, define $f(j, j')$ to be 1

Figure 9: G_1° for Strassen's algorithm when $i = 2$ and $D_2 = \{(a_{21}, c_{21}), (a_{21}, c_{22}), (a_{22}, c_{22})\}$. The crossed-out vertices are those removed from G_1 to construct this reduced computation graph G_1°. Because the guaranteed dependence (a_{22}, c_{21}) is not included in D_2, the vertex crossed out in blue is removed, and so G_1° does not quite compute vector-matrix multiplication; the coefficient of a_{22} in the computation of c_{21} may not be correct.

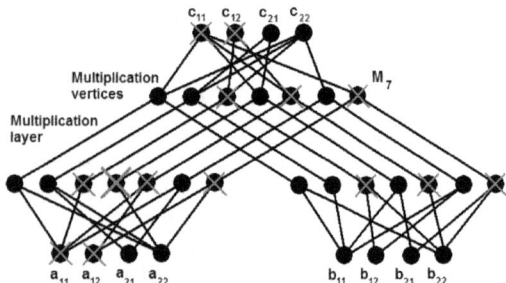

exactly when the coefficient of $a_{ij'}$ in c_{ij} is its correct value for matrix multiplication, namely $b_{j'j}$, and otherwise 0.

Let n_f denote the number of pairs (j, j') with $1 \leq j, j' \leq n_0$ at which f takes the value 1 – that is, the number of coefficients correctly set by G_1°. By the definition of G_1° relative to the matching graph H, we have $n_f \geq |D_i|$: If the guaranteed dependence of c_{ij} on $a_{ij'}$ is represented in D_i, then the coefficient of $a_{ij'}$ in c_{ij} must be "correct" for matrix multiplication, since, by definition of G_1°, there exists no chain between the vertices corresponding to c_{ij} and $a_{ij'}$ contained in G_1 (which correctly computes matrix multiplication) but not in G_1°.

Finally, we use G_1° to construct a new, correct, vector-matrix multiplication algorithm. Define $\bar{G}_1^\circ$ to be the CDAG formed as follows: to the CDAG G_1° add $n_0^2 - n_f$ multiplication vertices, one for each pair (j, j') for which $f(j, j') = 0$. For $1 \leq j, j' \leq n_0$ let the coefficient of $a_{ij'}$ in c_{ij} computed by G_1° be $x_{j'j} \in F[b_{11}, b_{12}, \ldots, b_{n_0 n_0}]$ – a linear combination of the "coefficients" b_{ij}. For each such j and j' at which $f(j, j') = 0$, use a multiplication vertex to compute $a_{ij'}(b_{j'j} - x_{j'j})$ and add it to the output vertex representing c_{ij}. In other words, for every incorrect dependence of c_{ij} on $a_{ij'}$ we may use a single multiplication vertex to "fix" the dependence. Now $\bar{G}_1^\circ$ correctly computes $n_0 \times n_0$ vector-matrix multiplication. G_1° contained fewer than $|D_i|$ multiplication vertices and we added at most $n_0^2 - n_f$, so $\bar{G}_1^\circ$ has $< |D_i| + n_0^2 - n_f \leq |D_i| + n_0^2 - |D_i| = n_0^2$ multiplication vertices. Thus we have constructed a correct algorithm for computing $n_0 \times n_0$ vector-matrix multiplication using fewer than n_0^2 multiplications, which is known to be impossible [15]. This concludes the proof of Lemma 5 and hence of our main result Theorem 1. $\square$

We state the result we obtained in the proof of Lemma 5 as its own Lemma:

LEMMA 6. *Let G_1° be a CDAG with inputs a_{ij} and b_{ij} and outputs c_{ij} for $1 \leq i, j \leq n_0$ where each c_{ij} is computed as a product of linear combinations of the a_{ij} and b_{ij}. If for d pairs (j, j'), $1 \leq j, j' \leq n_0$, the coefficient of $a_{ij'}$ in c_{ij} is $b_{j'j}$, then G_1° uses at least d multiplications.*

8. CONCLUSION

We have proven optimal lower bounds for the I/O-complexity of any Strassen-like square matrix multiplication algorithm in which every linear combination in the base graph is used in only one multiplication by proving the existence of a routing between the inputs and outputs of such an algorithm that uses every intermediate computation vertex relatively few times. The proof generalizes easily to algorithms composed of different base graphs, as long as each base graph performs square matrix multiplication with $2a$ inputs and b subcomputations and satisfies the conditions of Lemma 1. This bound holds regardless of the form of the base graph(s), including those that have disconnected encoding or decoding pieces and those that perform multiple copying. Our technique provides a novel alternative to the edge expansion argument in [6] that applies to less straightforward recursive computation graphs.

We believe that the assumption that every linear combination is used in only one multiplication can also be lifted. Without this assumption Lemma 5 no longer holds; vertices representing linear combinations used in multiple multiplications may require too many paths routed through them. Thus a more general approach to routing guaranteed dependencies is required. This difficulty can be overcome by routing paths in response to the choice of S, where paths are now allowed to "jump" to other vertices on the same rank of G_k that have the same membership in S. We believe it can be shown that this optimization does not decrease the number of boundary-crossing edges and still results in every vertex lying on at most $6a^k$ "generalized" paths, thus extending our result to all fast Strassen-like matrix multiplication algorithms.

9. ACKNOWLEDGMENTS

Research is supported by grants 1878/14, and 1901/14 from the Israel Science Foundation (founded by the Israel Academy of Sciences and Humanities) and grant 3-10891 from the Ministry of Science and Technology, Israel. Research is also supported by the Einstein Foundation and the Minerva Foundation.

10. REFERENCES

[1] G. Ballard, E. Carson, J. Demmel, M. Hoemmen, N. Knight, and O. Schwartz. Communication lower bounds and optimal algorithms for numerical linear algebra. *Acta Numerica*, 23:1–155, 5 2014.

[2] G. Ballard, J. Demmel, O. Holtz, B. Lipshitz, and O. Schwartz. Brief announcement: strong scaling of matrix multiplication algorithms and memory-independent communication lower bounds. In *Proc. 24th ACM Symposium on Parallelism in Algorithms and Architectures (SPAA)*, SPAA '12, pages 77–79, New York, NY, USA, 2012. ACM.

[3] G. Ballard, J. Demmel, O. Holtz, B. Lipshitz, and O. Schwartz. Communication-optimal parallel algorithm for Strassen's matrix multiplication. *Proceedings of the 24th ACM Symposium on Parallelism in Algorithms and Architectures, SPAA 2012*, 2012.

[4] G. Ballard, J. Demmel, O. Holtz, B. Lipshitz, and O. Schwartz. Graph expansion analysis for communication costs of fast rectangular matrix

multiplication. *Design and Analysis of Algorithms*, 7659:13–36, 2012.

[5] G. Ballard, J. Demmel, O. Holtz, and O. Schwartz. Minimizing communication in numerical linear algebra. *SIAM J. Matrix Anal. & Appl.*, 32(3):866–901, 2011.

[6] G. Ballard, J. Demmel, O. Holtz, and O. Schwartz. Graph expansion and communication costs of fast matrix multiplication. *Journal of the ACM*, 59(6), 2012.

[7] G. Bilardi, A. Pietracaprina, and P. D'Alberto. On the space and access complexity of computation dags. *Proceedings of the 26th International Workshop on Graph-Theoretic Concepts in Computer Science, London, UK*, pages 47–58, 2000.

[8] D. Bini, M. Capovani, F. Romani, and G. Lotti. $o(n^{2.7799})$ complexity for $n \times n$ approximate matrix multiplication. *Information processing letters*, 8(5):234–235, 1979.

[9] M. Christ, J. Demmel, N. Knight, T. Scanlon, and K. A. Yelick. Communication lower bounds and optimal algorithms for programs that reference arrays - part 1. Technical Report UCB/EECS-2013-61, EECS Department, University of California, Berkeley, May 2013.

[10] J. W. Hong and H. T. Kung. The red-blue pebble game. *STOC 1981: Proceedings of the thirteenth annual ACM symposium on theory of computing*, pages 326–333, 1981.

[11] J. Hopcroft and L. Kerr. On minimizing the number of multiplications necessary for matrix multiplication. *SIAM Journal on Applied Mathematics*, 20(1):30–36, 1971.

[12] D. Irony, S. Toledo, and A. Tiskin. Communication lower bounds for distributed-memory matrix multiplication. *J. Parallel Distrib. Comput.*, 64(9):1017–1026, 2004.

[13] L. H. Loomis and H. Whitney. An inequality related to the isoperimetric inequality. *Bulletin of the American Mathematical Society*, 55(10), 1949.

[14] J. Savage. Space-time tradeoffs in memory hierarchies. *Technical report, Brown University, Providence, RI, USA*, 1994.

[15] S. Winograd. On the number of multiplications required to compute certain functions. *Proceedings of the National Academy of Science*, 58(5), 1967.

[16] C.-Q. Yang and B. Miller. Critical path analysis for the execution of parallel and distributed programs. *Proceedings of the 8th International Conference on Distributed Computing Systems*, pages 366–373, 1988.

Online Caching with Convex Costs

[Extended Abstract]

Ishai Menache
Microsoft Research
Redmond, WA
ishai@microsoft.com

Mohit Singh
Microsoft Research
Redmond, WA
mohits@microsoft.com

ABSTRACT

Modern software applications and services operate nowadays on top of large clusters and datacenters. To reduce the underlying infrastructure cost and increase utilization, different services share the same physical resources (e.g., CPU, bandwidth, I/O, memory). Consequently, the cluster provider often has to decide in real-time how to allocate resources in overbooked systems, taking into account the different characteristics and requirements of users. In this paper, we consider an important problem within this space – how to share *memory* between users, whose memory access patterns are unknown in advance. We assume that the overall performance (or cost) of each user is a non-linear function of the total number of misses over a given period of time. We develop an online caching algorithm for arbitrary cost functions. We further provide theoretical guarantees for *convex* functions (which capture plausible practical scenarios). In particular, our algorithm is $\alpha^\alpha k^\alpha$-competitive, where k is the memory (cache) size, and α is a constant which depends on the curvature of the cost functions. We also obtain a bi-criteria result which trades-off the performance and the memory size. Finally, we give a lower bound on the performance of any online deterministic algorithm which nearly matches the upper bound of our algorithm.

Categories and Subject Descriptors

F.2.2 [**Analysis of Algorithms and Problem Complexity**]: Non-numerical Algorithms and Problems—*sequencing and scheduling*; D.4.2 [**Operating Systems**]: Storage Management—*Main memory*

General Terms

Algorithms

Keywords

online caching; resource management; cloud computing; competitive analysis

1. INTRODUCTION

1.1 Background and Motivation

The cloud computing paradigm builds upon the economy of scale, where customers utilize compute resources contained in large datacenters. The potential economic gains rely on *multi-tenancy* – assigning different users and services into the same physical hardware. Multi-tenancy allows for cost reduction and increased utilization of the infrastructure, as the cloud provider can often exploit statistical multiplexing for overbooking of physical resources.

Memory is inarguably a crucial resource for many applications and services operating on the cloud, such as dynamic web applications and Databases as a Service (DaaS). In some of these systems, the physical memory is shared between different users, e.g., in Microsoft Azure SQL Database [13]. In addition, distributed memory systems have been designed and deployed in order to accelerate the performance of cloud applications. Examples include Memcached [10], an open-source in-memory key-value store, and commercial offerings such as Microsoft Azure Cache [12] and Amazon ElastiCache [2].

An important issue in such shared memory systems is how to allocate the physical memory between different users and applications. Static memory allocation are inherently both wasteful (i.e., users holding to memory which that do not utilize) and might fail to meet user requirements (e.g., a performance-sensitive user needs more memory than expected). Instead, when oversubscription is in place, the memory allocation problem can be treated as a dynamic, *online caching* problem: the "cache" here is the total available physical memory, and the provider needs to determine in real-time which pages of which users should be stored in memory, and which ones need to be evicted. Variants of the LRU algorithm, such as LRU-K[16] have been employed for many shared-memory systems, however they treat all users equally. Weighted caching [20, 3] generalizes LRU to settings where users may have different weights (priorities). Under the weighted caching model, each miss of user i has a fixed cost w_i. Unfortunately, this model is not general enough, since the costs associated with misses could be *non-linear*, i.e., each additional miss need not cost the same as previous misses of the user.

In this paper, we develop a cost-aware, online caching algorithm for the case where the cost of each user is non-linear in the number of misses. The objective of the algorithm is to minimize the sum of tenants' costs. We further provide performance guarantees when the costs are *convex*. The convexity assumption is natural in practical settings, since each additional miss has often times an increasingly greater impact on tenant performance. For example, a user can tolerate up to around M misses in a time window of T, and any number of misses greater than that will result in substantial degradation in performance. Such scenarios can be captured through, e.g., piecewise-linear, convex cost functions.

Based on the algorithm developed in this paper, we have recently designed and prototyped a memory replacement mechanism for SQLVM [15], a multi-tenant DaaS system. In the SQLVM context, the shared memory is the so-called *buffer pool* memory, which serves as a cache of database pages and is crucial for the performance of user workloads. The Service Level Agreements (SLAs) between the provider and users is captured via non-linear cost functions, which could correspond, for example, to the refund paid by a service provider as a function of the total number of misses or related measures thereof; see [14] for more examples. Experiments with real workloads demonstrate the merits of our cost-aware approach [14].

1.2 Our Model and Results

We consider the problem of having multiple tenants sharing a single cache[1] and propose the following model. We have a single cache of size k which is shared among set of users U. We let $n = |U|$ denote the number of users. Each user $i \in U$, owns a set of pages P_i and we receive a sequence of T page requests $(p_1, p_2, \ldots, p_T)$ where each page p_t belongs to a unique user $i \in U$. We assume that the number of requests in unknown to the algorithm designer. At each time $1 \leq t \leq T$, the page p_t is requested and the algorithm must ensure that page p_t must either be in the cache or be fetched into the cache. If the cache is full, i.e., exactly k pages are already in the cache, we must evict one of the pages from the cache to make space for the requested page p_t. The algorithm designer does not know the whole sequence of page requests in advance, but it is rather revealed over time. When deciding the action for page p_t, only the request sequence till page p_t is known to the algorithm and not the page requests which come after page p_t. Each user $i \in U$ is also associated with a cost function $f_i : \mathbb{R} \to \mathbb{R}$ where $f_i(x)$ denotes the cost paid if user i has x misses. For our analysis, we assume each f_i is differentiable, convex, increasing and non-negative function with $f_i(0) = 0$. The objective is to minimize the sum total cost paid for all users.

Since the problem is online in nature, we appeal to *competitive analysis* to study the performance of our algorithm, see [6] for an introduction on online algorithms and competitive analysis. We compare the performance of our online algorithm to the performance of the optimal *offline* algorithm that knows the sequence of page requests σ in advance. We prove the following theorem.

THEOREM 1.1. *There exists an online deterministic algorithm for the multiple tenant caching problem which given any request sequence σ has $a_i(\sigma)$ misses for each user $i \in U$ such that*

$$\sum_{i \in U} f_i(a_i(\sigma)) \leq \sum_{i \in U} f_i(\alpha k b_i(\sigma)) \qquad (1)$$

where $b_i(\sigma)$ are the number of misses by the optimal offline algorithm, and $\alpha = \sup_{x,i} \frac{x f_i'(x)}{f(x)}$.

Our algorithm is a primal-dual algorithm for a convex programming relaxation for the multiple tenant caching problem. Observe that when each f_i is a linear function, i.e., each miss costs the same, then $\alpha = 1$ and we obtain the standard k-competitive algorithm which is the best possible competitive ratio for any algorithm [19]. The following corollary is useful to illustrate our results when the convex functions are monomial functions.

---

[1]Throughout the paper, we use the terms "cache" and "memory" interchangeably.

COROLLARY 1.2. *Suppose that the cost function f_i for each user i is given by $f_i(x) = x^\beta$ for some $\beta \geq 1$. There exists an online algorithm which is $(\beta^\beta k^\beta)$-competitive. Thus given any request sequence σ, the algorithm has $a_i(\sigma)$ misses for each user $i \in U$ such that*

$$\sum_{i \in U} f_i(a_i(\sigma)) \leq \beta^\beta k^\beta \sum_{i \in U} f_i(b_i(\sigma)), \qquad (2)$$

where $b_i(\sigma)$ are the number of misses by the optimal offline algorithm.

We also give a bi-criteria result which trades off the performance of the algorithm with the cache size. In particular, we compare the performance of our algorithm with the optimal offline algorithm where the offline algorithm must work with a cache size of $h \leq k$. In such a setting, we give an improved result in Theorem 1.3. Observe that the algorithm proving the guarantee of Theorem 1.3 is the same as the algorithm of Theorem 1.1 and is also independent of h.

THEOREM 1.3. *There exists an online deterministic algorithm for the multiple tenant caching problem which given any request sequence σ has $a_i(\sigma)$ misses for each user $i \in U$ such that*

$$\sum_{i \in U} f_i(a_i(\sigma)) \leq \sum_{i \in U} f_i(\alpha \frac{k}{k - h + 1} b_i(\sigma)), \qquad (3)$$

where $b_i(\sigma)$ are the number of misses by the optimal offline algorithm which is given a cache of size $h \leq k$ and $\alpha = \sup_{x,i} \frac{x f_i'(x)}{f(x)}$.

We also obtain nearly matching lower bounds for our algorithm in the following theorem.

THEOREM 1.4. *For any n and integer β, there exists an instance of the multi-tenancy caching problem with n users and cost functions $f_i(x) = x^\beta$ for each user $i \in U$, such that any online deterministic algorithm must pay a cost of at least $(\Omega(k))^\beta$ times the cost of the optimal offline solution.*

To compare the result in Theorem 1.4 with the upper bound in Corollary 1.2, we observe that lower bound and upper bounds match up to a factor of β^β.

1.3 Related Work

Competitive analysis of the caching problem was introduced by Sleator and Tarjan [19] who gave a k-competitive algorithm and also showed that the classical algorithm LRU is k-competitive. In our setting, the basic caching problem corresponds to the special case of our problem with a single user. Sleator and Tarjan [19] also showed that this is the best possible competitive ratio for any deterministic algorithm. Young [20] generalized this result to the weighted caching problem, which in our setting corresponds to the case where each of the functions f_i is linear. The algorithm in [20] uses a primal-dual framework over the corresponding linear program. While we also provide a primal-dual algorithm, our convex program builds on a different linear program which was given by Bansal, Buchbinder and Naor [3] for the weighted caching problem; [3] obtains improved competitive algorithms using randomization. We also mention that their results also generalize to the bi-criteria setting; we refer the reader to the survey by Buchbinder and Naor [8] for more details.

Caching algorithms have been widely applied for over half a century to divide memory in various computer systems, including operating systems (e.g., [9]), multi-core processors (e.g., [11]) and databases (e.g., [21] and references therein). Accordingly, much

$$\text{(ICP)} \quad \min \sum_{i=1}^m f_i \left(\sum_{p \in P_i} \sum_{j=1}^{r(p,T)} x(p,j) \right)$$

s.t.

$$\forall 1 \le t \le T \quad \sum_{p \in B(t) \setminus \{p_t\}} x(p, j(p,t)) \ge |B(t)| - k$$
$$\forall p \in P, \forall j \quad x(p,j) \in \{0,1\}$$

$$\text{(CP)} \quad \min \sum_{i=1}^m f_i \left(\sum_{p \in P_i} \sum_{j=1}^{r(p,T)} x(p,j) \right)$$

s.t.

$$\forall 1 \le t \le T \quad \sum_{p \in B(t) \setminus \{p_t\}} x(p, j(p,t)) \ge |B(t)| - k$$
$$\forall p \in P, \forall j \quad x(p,j) \le 1$$
$$\forall p \in P, \forall j \quad x(p,j) \ge 0$$

Figure 1: Integer Convex Program and its Convex Programming Relaxation

research has been devoted to understand and analyze caching algorithms that work well in practice [4, 1, 17]. Recently, there has been some interest in developing caching algorithms for cloud computing scenarios [18, 5]. The latter references consider scenarios where the memory available to an algorithm can vary over time. Our work is different in the sense that we consider systems with fixed memory size with more complicated user cost models.

The rest of the paper is organized as follows. In Section 2 we give our online algorithm and prove Theorem 1.1. In Section 3, we prove the bi-criteria result (Theorem 1.3). The lower bound in Theorem 1.4 is proven in Section 4.

2. ALGORITHM

Before we describe the algorithm, we first give a convex programming formulation for the multiple tenant caching problem. We remark that the algorithm does not solve this convex program but uses it as a tool to guide the algorithm, in the spirit of primal-dual algorithms. As mentioned above, the algorithm can actually be used for general non-linear cost functions (see Section 2.5 for details), yet our performance guarantees require convexity.

We begin with some notation. We let $P = \cup_i P_i$ denote the set of all pages. For any page p, we let $i(p) \in U$ denote the user owning that page. Given any sequence σ of requests of pages which comes online, we index the sequence with time. Hence at time t, we obtain the tth request in sequence σ and let p_t be the page requested at time t. We let $r(p,t)$ denote the number of requests of page p till time t. We also denote T to be length of σ. Let $B(t)$ denote the number of distinct pages requested up to time t. For any page p, the time between its two consecutive requests is an interval. We let $j(p,t)$ denotes the interval index corresponding to page p at time t (notice that $j(p,t)$ does not depend on the algorithm but only on the sequence σ).

2.1 Convex Programming Formulation

We now formulate the following integer convex programming formulation for our problem assuming that we have knowledge of the sequence of requests σ. Relaxing the integer constraints, we obtain a convex programming relaxation for our problem. We have a variable $x(p,j)$ for each page p and each $1 \le j \le r(p,T)$ where $x(p,j)$ will be set to 1 if the page p is evicted between its jth and $(j+1)^{th}$ request. We assume that the cost paid by the algorithm is for evicting a page and not when bringing it in. We remedy this by assuming that the algorithm needs to return an empty cache, therefore each page is evicted exactly equal number of times it is brought in the cache. This is implemented by a dummy user who owns k pages and all these k pages are appended at the end of sequence σ. The cost of evicting any page for this dummy user is assumed to be infinite. Then the overall cost for user i is given by $f_i(\sum_{p \in P_i} \sum_{j=1}^{r(p,T)} x(p,j))$.

The integer convex program (ICP) is formalized in Figure 1. The constraints for the convex program are indexed by time t. For each time t, we must have all but k pages outside the cache. Moreover, page p_t which is requested at time t must not be counted in the ex-

cluded pages. We first observe that every algorithm must imply a feasible solution to (ICP) by simply setting $x(p,j) = 1$ if page p is evicted between its jth and $(j+1)^{th}$-request. Moreover, the cost of the objective function is also the same as the cost of the solution given by the algorithm. Our aim will be to construct a feasible solution to (ICP) in an online fashion as the sequence σ is revealed. We emphasize that we do not solve the convex program in the algorithm. Nonetheless, as the sequence σ is revealed, we extend the convex program to include the relevant set of variables and constraints. We will use convex duality to guide the algorithm as well as for the analysis which we describe in the following sections.

2.2 Optimality Conditions

Our algorithm will aim to maintain an approximately optimal primal solution along with a Lagrangian dual solution certifying the approximate optimality. First, we describe the Lagrangian dual of the convex program (CP) and the optimality conditions. We then also list the approximate optimality conditions that will be maintained by our algorithm.

Let y_t, $z(p,j)$ and $\mu(p,j)$ denote the Lagrange multipliers corresponding to first, second and third set of constraints in the convex program (CP), respectively. Then the Lagrangian $L(x, y, z, \mu)$ is given by

$$\min \sum_{i=1}^m f_i \left(\sum_{p \in P_i} \sum_{j=1}^{r(p,T)} x(p,j) \right) + \sum_{p,j} z(p,j)\,(x(p,j) - 1) +$$
$$+ \sum_t y_t \left(|B(t)| - k - \sum_{p \in B(t) \setminus \{p_t\}} x(p, j(p,t)) \right) - \sum_{p,j} \mu(p,j) x(p,$$

Now, the KKT optimality conditions [7] imply that (x, y, z, μ) will be optimal if we satisfy the following conditions.

1. Primal and Dual Feasibility

   (a) $\sum_{p \in B(t) \setminus \{p_t\}} x(p, j(p,t)) \ge |B(t)| - k \quad \forall t$

   (b) $0 \le x(p,j) \le 1$ for all p, j

   (c) $0 \le y, z, \mu$

2. Complementary Slackness

   (a) $y_t \left(\sum_{p \in B(t) \setminus \{p_t\}} x(p, j(p,t)) - |B(t)| + k \right) = 0 \quad \forall t$

   (b) $z(p,j)\,(x(p,j) - 1) = 0 \quad \forall p, j$

   (c) $\mu(p,j) x(p,j) = 0 \quad \forall p, j$

3. Gradient conditions.

   (a) $f'_{i(p)} \left(\sum_{p' \in P_{i(p)}} \sum_{r=1}^{r(p,T)} x(p', r) \right) - \sum_{t=t(p,j)+1}^{t(p,j+1)-1} y_t + z(p,j) - \mu(p,j) = 0$ for all p, j

48

where $t(p, j)$ is the time when the j-th request to page p. The primal and dual feasibility conditions are natural. The complementary conditions ensure the dual variable is non-zero only if the primal constraints are tight. Moreover, the partial derivative of the Lagrangian objective must be non-negative for all primal variables, and if the primal variable is strictly positive then the gradient must be zero. Of course all these conditions will not be satisfied exactly by our algorithm as that would imply solving the problem exactly but we would aim to satisfy most of them. The exact invariants of the algorithm are described later.

Eliminating the dual variables μ, we obtain the following optimality conditions.

1. Primal and Dual Feasibility

    (a) $\sum_{p \in B(t) \setminus \{p_t\}} x(p, j(p, t)) \geq |B(t)| - k \ \ \forall t$

    (b) $0 \leq x(p, j) \leq 1$ for all p, j

    (c) $0 \leq y, z$

2. Complementary Slackness

    (a) $z(p, j)\,(x(p, j) - 1) = 0 \quad \forall p, j,$

    (b) $y_t \left(\sum_{p \in B(t) \setminus \{p_t\}} x(p, j(p, t)) - |B(t)| + k \right) = 0 \quad \forall t,$

    (c) $f'_{i(p)} \left(\sum_{p' \in P_{i(p)}} \sum_{r=1}^{r(p,T)} x(p', r) \right) - \sum_{t=t(p,j)+1}^{t=t(p,j+1)-1} y_t + z(p, j) = 0$ if $x(p, j) > 0$

3. Gradient conditions.

    (a) $f'_{i(p)} \left(\sum_{p' \in P_{i(p)}} \sum_{r=1}^{r(p,T)} x(p', r) \right) - \sum_{t=t(p,j)+1}^{t=t(p,j+1)-1} y_t + z(p, j) \geq 0$ for all p, j

2.3 Primal-Dual Online Algorithm

We describe the continuous version of the algorithm in Figure 2. A discrete version of the algorithm can be simply implemented by observing that all continuous changes boil down to discrete amounts. We shall present the discrete version and discuss some implementation details in Section 2.5.

For every time $1 \leq t \leq T$, let p_t be the requested page. Do

- Initialize $x^\circ(p_t, j_t) \leftarrow 0$, $z^\circ(p_t, j_t) \leftarrow 0$, $y_t^\circ \leftarrow 0$

- If (CP) remains feasible, do nothing.
  We do need to remove any page from the cache. Either the requested page p_t is already in the cache or we have space for the new page in the cache.

- Else

    - Increase y_t° continuously.

    - For each page p outside cache (i.e., $x^\circ(p, j(p, t)) = 1$), increase $z^\circ(p, j(t))$ at same rate of y_t°

    - Let p' be the first page in the cache for which

      $$f'_{i(p')} \left(m(i(p'), t-1) + 1 \right) - \sum_{t=t(p',j)+1}^{t(p',j+1)-1} y_t^\circ + z^\circ(p', j) = 0$$

      is satisfied; set $x^\circ(p', j(p', t)) \leftarrow 1$
      We remove page p' from the cache and bring in page p_t.

Figure 2: Algorithm ALG-CONT

Invariant of Algorithm ALG-CONT. Our algorithm will maintain primal solution x° and dual solution (y°, z°) such that we satisfy primal and dual feasibility, i.e. conditions (1a)-(1c). While the algorithm can be described in terms of the primal solution alone, we need the dual solution to guide the algorithm and prove the guarantee as claimed in Theorem 1.1. For ease of notation, for any user $i \in U$ and $1 \leq t \leq T$, we let $m(i, t)$ be the total number of evictions of pages owned by user i till time t by our algorithm, i.e., $m(i, t) = \sum_{p \in P_i} \sum_{j=1}^{r(p,t)} x^\circ(p, j)$. We let $m(i, T)$ to be the total misses for pages owned by user i. We maintain the following invariants:

1. Primal and Dual Feasibility

    (a) $\sum_{p \in B(t) \setminus \{p_t\}} x^\circ(p, j(p, t)) \geq |B(t)| - k \ \ \forall t$

    (b) $0 \leq x^\circ(p, j) \leq 1$ for all p, j

    (c) $0 \leq y^\circ, z^\circ$

2. Complementary Slackness

    (a) $z^\circ(p, j)\,(x^\circ(p, j) - 1) = 0 \quad \forall p, j,$

    (b) $f'_{i(p)} \left(\sum_{p' \in P_{i(p)}} \sum_{r=1}^{r(p,\hat{t})} x^\circ(p', r) \right) - \sum_{t=t(p,j)+1}^{t=t(p,j+1)-1} y_t^\circ + z^\circ(p, j) = 0$ if $x^\circ(p, j)$ is set to 1 at time $\hat{t}$.

3. Gradient conditions.

    (a) $f'_{i(p)} \left(\sum_{p' \in P_{i(p)}} \sum_{r=1}^{r(p,T)} x^\circ(p', r) \right) - \sum_{t=t(p,j)+1}^{t=t(p,j+1)-1} y_t^\circ + z^\circ(p, j) \geq 0$ for all p, j

The main difference from the optimality conditions (after eliminating the dual variables μ) is the complemenatry slackness condition (2b) in the invariant as compared to condition (2c) in the optimality conditions. The algorithm tries to maintain condition (2c) as if the derivative of the lagrangian is evaluated at the current primal and dual solution and not at the final solution. At a later time t, $\sum_{r=1}^{r(p,t)} x^\circ(p', r) \geq \sum_{r=1}^{r(p,\hat{t})} x^\circ(p', r)$ and therefore, the gradient of f at the former sum might be larger than the gradient at the latter term due to convexity of f. While this does not affect feasibility of primal and dual solutions, we will violate the complementary slackness conditions. The technical heart of the analysis will be to show that we can still bound the violation in terms of the degree of f.

2.4 Proof of Theorem 1.1

The proof of Theorem 1.1 follows from the following two lemmas which we prove in this section. Lemma 2.1 states that the algorithm ALG-CONT satisfies the invariants as stated above. Then in Lemma 2.2, we show that any algorithm which satisfies the invariant conditions must satisfy the claimed guarantee in Theorem 1.1.

LEMMA 2.1. *At all times t, ALG-CONT satisfies the invariant conditions as claimed.*

PROOF. We check each of the invariants.

Primal and Dual Feasibility. Clearly conditions (1b) and dual feasibility (1c) are satisfied by construction. Variable $x^\circ(p, j)$ takes values from $\{0, 1\}$ and $y^\circ(t)$ and $z^\circ(p, j)$ are initialized to 0 and only increase as the algorithm progresses. To see that we satisfy the condition (1a), a simple induction suffices. At $t = 0$, we have $|B(t)| = 0$ and therefore, $x^\circ(p, j)$ and $(y^\circ(t), z^\circ(t))$ are feasible. In any other step, as we go from time $t - 1$ to time t, one of the following happens. If after setting $x^\circ(p_t, j_t) = 0$, $z^\circ(p_t, j_t) = 0$ and $y^\circ(t) = 0$, we obtain a feasible solution then induction holds. Else,

49

this initialization of $x^\circ(p_t, j_t) = 0$, $z^\circ(p_t, j_t) = 0$ and $y^\circ(t) = 0$ must violate the primal feasibility constraint for time t. Observe that this can only happen in the following two scenarios. In the first case, we see the page p_t for the first time and we increase $B(t)$ by one and therefore the RHS of constraint (1a) increases by one. Otherwise, it must be the case that $x^\circ(p_t, j_t - 1) = 1$ and the term $\sum_{p \in B(t) \setminus \{p_t\}} x^\circ(p, j(p, t))$ in the feasibility constraint reduces by one since we set $x^\circ(p_t, j_t) = 0$. In either of the cases, the page p_t was not in the cache and the cache already had k pages. Thus bringing in page p_t violates the cache size constraint. But observe that the algorithm finds a page p' in the cache and sets its $x^\circ(p', j(p', t))$ to one, hence the LHS increases by one again giving us feasibility.

Complementary Slackness. To observe that we maintain condition (2a), observe that we increase $z^\circ(p, j)$ only if $x^\circ(p, j) = 1$. Since we never decrease the x° for any variable, we maintain the complementary slackness till the end.

Now consider the condition (2b). Again consider any page p and request j. If $x^\circ(p, j)$ remains zero, there is nothing to prove. Suppose $x^\circ(p, j)$ is set to one say at time $\hat{t}$. Then at time $\hat{t}$, we must have

$$f'_{i(p)}\left(m(i(p), \hat{t} - 1) + 1\right) - \sum_{t=t(p,j)+1}^{\hat{t}} y^\circ_t + z^\circ(p, j) = 0$$

which implies that

$$f'_{i(p)}\left(m(i(p), \hat{t})\right) - \sum_{t=t(p,j)+1}^{\hat{t}} y^\circ_t + z^\circ(p, j) = 0$$

since $m(i(p), \hat{t} - 1) + 1 = m(i(p), \hat{t})$.

At any later time $t \in (\hat{t}, t(p, j + 1))$, if we increase y_t we increase z° at the same rate maintaining equality. After time $t > t(p, j + 1)$ none of the variables in the term change proving the lemma. Thus we obtain that

$$f'_{i(p)}\left(m(i(p), \hat{t})\right) - \sum_{t=t(p,j)+1}^{t(p,j+1)-1} y^\circ_t + z^\circ(p, j) = 0,$$

as required.

Gradient Conditions. We show condition (3a). Consider any page p and its jth request. Suppose the variable $x^\circ(p, j)$ is set to one at $t \in (t(p, j), t(p, j + 1))$. Then the primal and dual solution at that time must satisfy

$$f'_{i(p)}\left(m(i(p), t - 1) + 1\right) - \sum_{t=t(p,j)+1}^{t(p,j+1)-1} y^\circ_t + z^\circ(p, j) = 0$$

Now consider how the LHS changes as the algorithm proceeds, if we increase y°_t for any $\hat{t} < t < t(p, j + 1)$, then we also increase $z^\circ(p, j)$ at the same rate and we maintain equality. Now, we must have

$$m(i(p), T) \geq m(i(p), t - 1) + 1$$

since the LHS at least counts the eviction of page p at time t and is not counted in RHS. Using the fact that f' is an increasing function, we obtain that

$$f'_{i(p)}\left(m(i(p), T)\right) - \sum_{t=t(p,j)+1}^{t(p,j+1)-1} y^\circ_t + z^\circ(p, j) \geq 0.$$

Now, consider the case when page p is not evicted between its jth and $(j + 1)^{th}$ request. Thus $x^\circ(p, j)$ remains zero till the end. Firstly, this implies that page j is not the last request since we evict every page in the last request. Then, consider the expression

$$f'_{i(p)}\left(m(i(p), t') + 1\right) - \sum_{t=t(p,j)+1}^{t(p,j+1)-1} y^\circ_t + z^\circ(p, j)$$

evaluated with values of primal and dual variables at time $t' = t(p, j)$. Since only the first term is non-zero, the expression is non-negative. As we proceed with the algorithm and increase t' from $t(p, j)$ to $t(p, j + 1) - 1$, the expression will never go below zero, otherwise, we would have set $x^\circ(p, j)$ to one. Since there is another request of page p where it is evicted (in particular the last one), we have $m(i(p), T) \geq m(i(p), t(p, j + 1) - 1) + 1$ and therefore

$$f'_{i(p)}\left(m(i(p), T)\right) - \sum_{t=t(p,j)+1}^{t(p,j+1)-1} y^\circ_t + z^\circ(p, j) \geq 0$$

and we obtain feasibility of condition (3a).

$\square$

We now prove the following lemma which will complete the proof of Theorem 1.1.

LEMMA 2.2. *Let $x^\star$ be an optimal solution to the convex program and x° denote any solution satisfying the invariant conditions. Then we must have*

$$\sum_{i \in U} f_i\left(m(i, T)\right) \leq \sum_{i \in U} f_i\left(\alpha k \bar{m}(i, T)\right)$$

where $\alpha = \sup_{x,i} \frac{x f'_i(x)}{f(x)}$ and $\bar{m}(i, T)$ is the number misses for user i by the optimal solution $x^\star$.

PROOF. The following auxiliary claim will be required in the sequel. This claim will help us bridge the gap introduced by violation of the complementary slackness conditions by the algorithm.

CLAIM 2.3. *Let f be a convex increasing function with $f(0) = 0$. Then*

$$f'\left(\sum_{j=1}^{n} x_j\right) \sum_{j=1}^{n} x_j \leq \alpha \sum_{j=1}^{n} x_j f'\left(\sum_{i=1}^{j} x_i\right), \tag{4}$$

where

$$\alpha = \max_x \frac{f'(x) x}{f(x)}. \tag{5}$$

As special case, note that when f is a polynomial with positive coefficients and degree β, we have $\alpha = \beta$.

PROOF. Note that it suffices to show that

$$\sum_{j=1}^{n} x_j f'\left(\sum_{i=1}^{j} x_i\right) \geq f\left(\sum_{j=1}^{n} x_j\right). \tag{6}$$

Indeed if (6) holds, then we have that the RHS of (4) satisfies

$$RHS \geq \alpha f(\sum_{j=1}^{n} x_j) \geq \frac{\sum_{j=1}^{n} x_j f'(\sum_{j=1}^{n} x_j)}{f(\sum_{j=1}^{n} x_j)} f(\sum_{j=1}^{n} x_j) = LHS.$$

To prove (6), we use the first order condition for convex functions, which implies the following set of inequalities: $f(0) - f(x_1) \geq -x_1 f'(x_1), f(x_1) - f(x_1 + x_2) \geq -x_2 f'(x_1 + x_2), \ldots, f(x_1 + \ldots x_{n-1}) - f(\sum_{j=1}^{n} x_j) \geq -x_n f(\sum_{j=1}^{n} x_j)$. Summing this set and recalling that $f(0) = 0$ immediately yields (6). $\square$

By definition, we have $m(i, T) = \sum_{p \in P_i} \sum_{j=1}^{r(p,T)} x^\circ(p, j)$ and $\bar{m}(i, T) = \sum_{p \in P_i} \sum_{j=1}^{r(p,T)} x^\star(p, j)$. For any convex function f, we have $f(y) - f(x) \geq f'(x)(y - x)$ and therefore we obtain that

$$\sum_{i \in U} f_i \left(\alpha k \bar{m}(i, T) \right) - \sum_{i \in U} f_i \left(m(i, T) \right)$$

$$= \sum_{i \in U} f_i \left(\alpha k \sum_{p \in P_i} \sum_{j=1}^{r(p,T)} x^\star(p, j) \right) - \sum_{i \in U} f_i \left(\sum_{p \in P_i} \sum_{j=1}^{r(p,T)} x^\circ(p, j) \right)$$

$$\geq \sum_{i \in U} f_i' \left(m(i, T) \right) \cdot \left(\alpha k \bar{m}(i, T) - m(i, T) \right)$$

$$= \sum_{i \in U} \sum_{p \in P_i} \sum_{j=1}^{r(p,T)} f_i' \left(m(i, T) \right) \cdot \left(\alpha k \cdot x^\star(p, j) - x^\circ(p, j) \right)$$

$$= \sum_{p \in P} \sum_{j=1}^{r(p,T)} \alpha k \cdot x^\star(p, j) \cdot f_{i(p)}' \left(m(i(p), T) \right) -$$

$$\sum_{i \in U} \sum_{p \in P_i} \sum_{j=1}^{r(p,T)} x^\circ(p, j) \cdot f_i' \left(\sum_{p' \in P_i} \sum_{j=1}^{r(p,T)} x^\circ(p', j) \right)$$

We now have the following claim.

CLAIM 2.4. *For any i,*

$$\sum_{p \in P_i} \sum_{j=1}^{r(p,T)} x^\circ(p, j) \cdot f_i' \left(\sum_{p' \in P_i} \sum_{j=1}^{r(p',T)} x^\circ(p', j) \right)$$

$$\leq \alpha \sum_{p \in P_i} \sum_{j=1}^{r(p,T)} x^\circ(p, j) \cdot f_i' \left(m(i, s(p, j)) \right)$$

where $s(p, j)$ is the time at which $x^\circ(p, j)$ is set to 1 and T if $x^\circ(p, j)$ remains 0.

PROOF. Order the variables $x^\circ(p, j)$ for all $p \in P_i$ and all j in increasing order of $s(p, j)$ and apply Claim 2.3 on this order. Observe that

$$\sum_{(p', j') : s(p,j) \geq s(p', j')} x(p', j') = m(i, s(p, j)).$$

Thus we obtain the inequality. $\square$

Thus we obtain that

$$\sum_{i \in U} f_i \left(\alpha k \bar{m}(i, T) \right) - \sum_{i \in U} f_i \left(m(i, T) \right)$$

$$\geq \sum_{p \in P} \sum_{j=1}^{r(p,T)} \alpha k \cdot x^\star(p, j) \cdot f_{i(p)}' \left(m(i(p), T) \right)$$

$$- \sum_{i \in U} \alpha \sum_{p \in P_i} \sum_{j=1}^{r(p,T)} x^\circ(p, j) \cdot f_i' \left(m(i, s(p, j)) \right)$$

$$\geq \sum_{p \in P} \sum_{j=1}^{r(p,T)} \alpha k \cdot x^\star(p, j) \cdot \left(\sum_{t=t(p,j)+1}^{t=t(p,j+1)-1} y_t^\circ - z^\circ(p, j) \right)$$

$$- \sum_{i \in U} \alpha \sum_{p \in P_i} \sum_{j=1}^{r(p,T)} x^\circ(p, j) \cdot \left(\sum_{t=t(p,j)+1}^{t=t(p,j+1)-1} y_t^\circ - z^\circ(p, j) \right)$$

where we have used condition (3a) in the first term and condition (2b) in the second term.

Thus we have

$$\sum_{i \in U} f_i \left(\alpha k \bar{m}(i, T) \right) - \sum_{i \in U} f_i \left(m(i, T) \right)$$

$$\geq \alpha \left(k \sum_{t=1} y_t^\circ \sum_{p \in B(t) \backslash p_t} x^\star(p, j(p, t)) - k \sum_{p,j} x^\star(p, j) z^\circ(p, j) \right)$$

$$- \alpha \left(\sum_{t=1} y_t^\circ \sum_{p \in B(t) \backslash p_t} x^\circ(p, j(p, t)) - \sum_{p,j} x^\circ(p, j) z^\circ(p, j) \right)$$

We now claim that the RHS is non-negative. Fix $x^\star$ and x° to their final values. We now see how the RHS changes as the algorithm changes the dual solution (y°, z°). We show that every change only increases the RHS. Initially $y^\circ = 0$ and $z^\circ = 0$ and therefore the RHS is 0. Now consider any step of the algorithm where we increase y_t° by ϵ for some t. Simultaneously, we would have increased $z^\circ(p, j)$ by ϵ for all pages outside the cache except for page p_t, page requested at time t. Let Q be the of pages not in the cache at this time. Thus $z^\circ(p, j(p, t))$ increases for exactly $|B(t)| - k - 1$ pages, all pages in Q except p_t.

$$\Delta \left(\alpha \left(k \sum_{t=1} y_t^\circ \sum_{p \in B(t) \backslash p_t} x^\star(p, j(p, t)) - k \sum_{p,j} x^\star(p, j) z^\circ(p, j) \right) \right)$$

$$= \alpha k \epsilon \left(\sum_{p \in B(t) \backslash p_t} x^\star(p, j(p, t)) - \sum_{Q \backslash p_t} x^\star(p, j(p, t)) \right)$$

$$\geq \alpha k \epsilon \left(|B(t)| - k - 1 \cdot (|Q| - 1) \right)$$

$$= \alpha k \epsilon$$

Thus the first term increases by at least $\alpha k \epsilon$. Now consider the change in the second term.

$$\Delta \left(\alpha \left(\sum_{t=1} y_t^\circ \sum_{p \in B(t) \backslash p_t} x^\circ(p, j(p, t)) - \sum_{p,j} x^\circ(p, j) z^\circ(p, j) \right) \right)$$

$$= \alpha \epsilon \left(\sum_{p \in B(t) \backslash p_t} x^\circ(p, j(p, t)) - \sum_{Q \backslash p_t} x^\circ(p, j(p, t)) \right)$$

$$\leq \alpha \epsilon \left(\sum_{p \in B(t) \backslash \{Q \cup \{p_t\}\}} 1 \right)$$

$$= \alpha k \epsilon$$

For every time t, let p_t be the required page at time t. Do

- If the cache is not full or page p_t is already in cache then bring in page p_t in cache and update

$$B(p_t) \leftarrow f'_{i(p_t)}\left(m(i(p_t), t-1) + 1\right).$$

- Else

    - Let p be the page in the cache with smallest $B(p)$. Remove page p from the cache and bring in p_t.
    - Set $B(p_t) \leftarrow f'_{i(p_t)}\left(m(i(p_t), t-1) + 1\right)$.
    - For each $p' \notin \{p, p_t\}$ in the cache, let $B(p') \leftarrow B(p') - B(p)$.
    - For each page p' in the cache such that $i(p') = i(p)$, set

$$B(p') \leftarrow B(p') + f'_{i(p')}\left(m(i(p'), t-1) + 2\right) \\ - f'_{i(p')}\left(m(i(p'), t-1) + 1\right)$$

Figure 3: Algorithm ALG-DISCRETE

where we use the fact that $|B(t) \setminus \{Q \cup \{p_t\}\}| \leq k$ since $|Q| \geq |B(t)| - k - 1$. Thus we must have that

$$\sum_{i \in U} f_i\left(\alpha k \bar{m}(i, T)\right) - \sum_{i \in U} f_i\left(m(i, T)\right) \geq 0$$

proving the lemma and Theorem 1.1.

2.5 Implementation of Algorithm ALG-CONT

We now give an implementation of ALG-CONT that does discrete updates. The algorithm, termed ALG-DISCRETE is summarized in Figure 3. The algorithm maintains a budget $B(p)$ for each page p in the cache and updates them in each iteration. A simple check shows that the ALG-CONT will be the same algorithm by observing that y_t increases in iteration t by the current value of $B(p)$ when page p is evicted.

We note that while the guarantee in Theorem 1.1 relies on the assumption that each of the cost functions f_i are convex, the algorithm ALG-CONT or its discrete implementation ALG-DISCRETE do not require the convexity assumption, and can in fact be applied for arbitrary cost functions. In fact, the cost functions f_i need not even be continuous; the derivatives in the algorithms can be replaced by their discrete versions. We indeed demonstrate in [14] that variants of our algorithms perform well in settings where the assumptions of Theorem 1.1 do not necessarily hold.

3. BI-CRITERIA APPROXIMATION

In this section, we prove Theorem 1.3. As mentioned above, we again analyze ALG-CONT. To compare the performance of our algorithm with the offline algorithm with a smaller cache size of h, we consider the convex program where the cache size is h.

We prove the following lemma which generalizes Lemma 2.2 and will prove Theorem 1.3. Observe that $x^\star$ is an optimal solution to (CP-h) (cf. Figure 4) while x° is feasible for (CP) and might not feasible for (CP-h) due to stronger constraints for smaller cache size.

LEMMA 3.1. *Let $x^\star$ be an optimal solution to the convex program (CP-h) and x° denote any solution satisfying the invariant conditions. Then we must have*

$$\sum_{i \in U} f_i\left(m(i, T)\right) \leq \sum_{i \in U} f_i\left(\alpha \frac{k}{k-h+1} \bar{m}(i, T)\right)$$

where $\alpha = \sup_{x,i} \frac{x f'_i(x)}{f(x)}$ and $\bar{m}(i, T)$ is the number misses for user i by the optimal solution $x^\star$.

PROOF. The proof follows along the same lines as proof of Lemma 2.2 and we highlight the differences. First, following the same argument as in proof of Lemma 2.2, we obtain that

$$\sum_{i \in U} f_i\left(\alpha \frac{k}{k-h+1} \bar{m}(i, T)\right) - \sum_{i \in U} f_i\left(m(i, T)\right)$$

$$\geq \sum_{i \in U} \sum_{p \in P_i} \sum_{j=1}^{r(p,T)} f'_i\left(m(i, T)\right) \cdot \left(\alpha \frac{k}{k-h+1} \cdot x^\star(p, j) - x^\circ(p, j)\right)$$

$$= \sum_{p \in P} \sum_{j=1}^{r(p,T)} \alpha \frac{k}{k-h+1} \cdot x^\star(p, j) \cdot f'_{i(p)}\left(m(i(p), T)\right) -$$

$$\sum_{i \in U} \sum_{p \in P_i} \sum_{j=1}^{r(p,T)} x^\circ(p, j) \cdot f'_i\left(\sum_{p' \in P_i} \sum_{j=1}^{r(p,T)} x^\circ(p', j)\right)$$

where we have again used that a convex function f satisfies $f(y) - f(x) \geq f'(x)(y - x)$ for all x, y. Now applying Claim 2.3, we obtain that

$$\sum_{i \in U} f_i\left(\alpha \frac{k}{k-h+1} \bar{m}(i, T)\right) - \sum_{i \in U} f_i\left(m(i, T)\right)$$

$$\geq \sum_{p \in P} \sum_{j=1}^{r(p,T)} \alpha \frac{k}{k-h+1} \cdot x^\star(p, j) \cdot f'_{i(p)}\left(m(i(p), T)\right) -$$

$$\sum_{i \in U} \alpha \sum_{p \in P_i} \sum_{j=1}^{r(p,T)} x^\circ(p, j) \cdot f'_i\left(m(i, s(p, j))\right)$$

$$\geq \sum_{p \in P} \sum_{j=1}^{r(p,T)} \alpha \frac{k}{k-h+1} \cdot x^\star(p, j) \cdot \left(\sum_{t=t(p,j)+1}^{t=t(p,j+1)-1} y_t^\circ - z^\circ(p, j)\right)$$

$$- \sum_{i \in U} \alpha \sum_{p \in P_i} \sum_{j=1}^{r(p,T)} x^\circ(p, j) \cdot \left(\sum_{t=t(p,j)+1}^{t(p,j+1)-1} y_t^\circ - z^\circ(p, j)\right)$$

where we have used condition (3a) in the first term and condition (2b) in the second term. Rearranging, we obtain that

$$\sum_{i \in U} f_i\left(\alpha \frac{k}{k-h+1} \bar{m}(i, T)\right) - \sum_{i \in U} f_i\left(m(i, T)\right)$$

$$\geq \alpha \left(\frac{k}{k-h+1} \sum_{t=1} y_t^\circ \sum_{p \in B(t) \setminus p_t} x^\star(p, j(p, t))\right)$$

$$- \left(\alpha \frac{k}{k-h+1} \sum_{p,j} x^\star(p, j) z^\circ(p, j)\right)$$

$$- \alpha \left(\sum_{t=1} y_t^\circ \sum_{p \in B(t) \setminus p_t} x^\circ(p, j(p, t)) - \sum_{p,j} x^\circ(p, j) z^\circ(p, j)\right)$$

We now claim that the RHS is non-negative. Fix $x^\star$ and x° to their final values. We now see how the RHS changes as the algorithm changes the dual solution (y°, z°). We show that every

(ICP-h) $\min \sum_{i=1}^{m} f_i \left(\sum_{p \in P_i} \sum_{j=1}^{r(p,T)} x(p,j) \right)$

s.t.

$\forall 1 \leq t \leq T \quad \sum_{p \in B(t) \setminus \{p_t\}} x(p, j(p,t)) \geq |B(t)| - h$

$\forall p \in P, \forall j \quad x(p,j) \in \{0,1\}$

(CP-h) $\min \sum_{i=1}^{m} f_i \left(\sum_{p \in P_i} \sum_{j=1}^{r(p,T)} x(p,j) \right)$

s.t.

$\forall 1 \leq t \leq T \quad \sum_{p \in B(t) \setminus \{p_t\}} x(p, j(p,t)) \geq |B(t)| - h$

$\forall p \in P, \forall j \quad x(p,j) \leq 1$

$\forall p \in P, \forall j \quad x(p,j) \geq 0$

Figure 4: Integer Convex Program and its Convex Programming Relaxation for Cache Size h

change only increases the RHS. Initially $y^\circ = 0$ and $z^\circ = 0$ and therefore the RHS is 0. Now consider any step of the algorithm where we increase y_t° by ϵ for some t. Simultaneously, we would have increased $z^\circ(p, j)$ by ϵ for all pages outside the cache except for page p_t, page requested at time t. Let Q be the of pages not in the cache at this time. Thus $z^\circ(p, j(p,t))$ increases for exactly $|B(t)| - k - 1$ pages, all pages in Q except p_t.

$$\Delta \left(\alpha \left(\frac{k}{k-h+1} \sum_{t=1} y_t^\circ \sum_{p \in B(t) \setminus p_t} x^\star(p, j(p,t)) \right) \right)$$

$$- \Delta \left(\left(\frac{k}{k-h+1} \sum_{p,j} x^\star(p,j) z^\circ(p,j) \right) \right)$$

$$= \alpha \frac{k}{k-h+1} \epsilon \left(\sum_{p \in B(t) \setminus p_t} x^\star(p, j(p,t)) - \sum_{Q \setminus p_t} x^\star(p, j(p,t)) \right)$$

$$\geq \alpha \frac{k}{k-h+1} \epsilon \left(|B(t)| - h - 1 \cdot (|Q| - 1) \right)$$

$$= \alpha \frac{k}{k-h+1} \epsilon \cdot (k - h + 1)$$

$$= \alpha k \epsilon$$

where we have the used the fact $x^\star$ satisfies the stronger constraints $\sum_{p \in B(t) \setminus p_t} x^\star(p, j(p,t)) \geq |B(t)| - h$.

Thus the first term increases by at least $\alpha k \epsilon$. Now consider the change in the second term.

$$\Delta \left(\alpha \left(\sum_{t=1} y_t^\circ \sum_{p \in B(t) \setminus p_t} x^\circ(p, j(p,t)) - \sum_{p,j} x^\circ(p,j) z^\circ(p,j) \right) \right)$$

$$= \alpha \epsilon \left(\sum_{p \in B(t) \setminus p_t} x^\circ(p, j(p,t)) - \sum_{Q \setminus p_t} x^\circ(p, j(p,t)) \right)$$

$$\leq \alpha \epsilon \left(\sum_{p \in B(t) \setminus \{Q \cup \{p_t\}\}} 1 \right)$$

$$= \alpha k \epsilon$$

where we use the fact that $|B(t) \setminus \{Q \cup \{p_t\}\}| \leq k$ since $|Q| \geq |B(t)| - k - 1$. Thus we must have that

$$\sum_{i \in U} f_i \left(\alpha \frac{k}{k-h+1} \bar{m}(i, T) \right) - \sum_{i \in U} f_i (m(i, T)) \geq 0$$

proving Lemma 3.1 and Theorem 1.3. $\square$

4. LOWER BOUND

In this section, we prove Theorem 1.4 by giving a worst case instance. For any n and β, we construct an instance with n users,

each with cost function given by $f_i(x) = x^\beta$. Each user will own a single page and the cache size will be $n-1$. Let $\mathbb{A}$ be any algorithm. We now describe the input sequence σ which will depend on the algorithm. At any time $t \geq n - 1$, the cache of the algorithm will contain exactly $n - 1$ pages and therefore one of the page out of n must be missing. In sequence σ, we request exactly this missing page. Observe that this implies that the algorithm must evict a page on each request except for the first $n - 1$ requests. We run this sequence for large time T and ignore the error due to the first $n - 1$ page requests. Let there be r_i requests for page owned by user i. Then we have $\sum_{i=1}^{n} r_i \geq T$ and the cost of the algorithm $\mathbb{A}$ is at least $\sum_{i=1}^{n} r_i^\beta$. Now we show that the optimal solution is much smaller by giving an offline algorithm that costs much less. Of course, the cost of the optimal solution must be smaller than the cost achieved by this offline algorithm. First we divide the sequence of requests in batches of length $\frac{n-1}{2}$. At the start of the each batch, there are $n - 1$ pages in the cache. We choose one page to evict making sure that it is not one of the pages in the next $\frac{n-1}{2}$ page requests. This ensures that we do not have any other eviction in the next $\frac{n-1}{2}$ page requests. Observe that there are $\frac{n+1}{2}$ different choices for which page to evict. We choose the one which has had fewest number of evictions so far. We now make two observations. First that the number of total evictions is no more than $\frac{T}{\frac{n-1}{2}}$ since we make at most one eviction per batch. Second observation is that the maximum eviction for any page is bounded by $\frac{1}{\frac{n+1}{2}} \frac{T}{\frac{n-1}{2}} + 1$.

The last bound follows since there must be at least $\frac{n+1}{2}$ other pages which have nearly the same number, up to an additive factor of one, as the page with maximum number of evictions due to the rule for choosing the evictions. Thus the cost of the algorithm is bounded by $(\frac{4T}{n^2})^\beta n$. While the cost of the algorithm $\mathbb{A}$ is at least $\sum_{i=1}^{n} r_i^\beta \geq (\frac{T}{n})^\beta n$ where the last inequality follows since $\beta \geq 1$ and the sum $\sum_{i=1}^{n} r_i^\beta$ is minimized when each of r_i is equal to $\frac{T}{n}$. Thus we obtain that cost of the algorithm $\mathbb{A}$ is at least $(\frac{n}{4})^\beta$ times the cost of the optimal solution on request σ proving Theorem 1.4 since we have $k = n - 1$.

5. CONCLUSION

Multi-tenancy poses substantial challenges for modern compute systems, and sharing physical memory stands out as an important problem in this space. Modeling the user performance as a non-linear (cost) function of the total number of memory misses allows to capture practical considerations of the provider, and automate memory allocation via cost-aware algorithms. In this paper, we design algorithms to solve the respective online optimization problem. We provide performance guarantees under convexity assumptions – we prove that our algorithm is $\alpha^\alpha k^\alpha$-competitive, where k is the memory (cache) size, and α is a constant which depends on the curvature of the cost functions. We also obtain a bi-criteria result which trades the performance to the memory size, and give a nearly matching lower bound on performance. Based on the algorithm developed in this paper, we have recently designed and prototyped a memory replacement mechanism for SQLVM, a multi-tenant DaaS system, see [14].

In this paper, we assume that a single pool of memory has to be shared between tenants. An interesting direction for future work is to consider the case of multiple memory pools (e.g., each pool corresponds to a single physical server), where each user has to be assigned to a single pool, with potentially switching cost incurred for migrating users between servers.

Acknowledgements

We thank the reviewers for their thoughtful comments. We also thank Vivek Narasayya for helpful discussions.

6. REFERENCES

[1] S. Albers. *Competitive online algorithms*. Lecture Notes, Aarhus University, 1996.

[2] Amazon ElastiCache. http://aws.amazon.com/elasticache/.

[3] N. Bansal, N. Buchbinder, and J. Naor. A primal-dual randomized algorithm for weighted paging. *J. ACM*, 59(4):19, 2012.

[4] L. A. Belady. A study of replacement algorithms for a virtual-storage computer. *IBM Systems journal*, 5(2):78–101, 1966.

[5] M. A. Bender, R. Ebrahimi, J. T. Fineman, G. Ghasemiesfeh, R. Johnson, and S. McCauley. Cache-adaptive algorithms. In *SODA*, pages 958–971. SIAM, 2014.

[6] A. Borodin and R. El-Yaniv. *Online computation and competitive analysis*. Cambridge University Press, 1998.

[7] S. Boyd and L. Vandenberghe. *Convex optimization*. Cambridge university press, 2004.

[8] N. Buchbinder and J. Naor. The design of competitive online algorithms via a primal: dual approach. *Foundations and Trends® in Theoretical Computer Science*, 3(2–3):93–263, 2009.

[9] F. J. Corbato. A paging experiment with the Multics system. Technical report, DTIC Document, 1968.

[10] B. Fitzpatrick. Distributed caching with memcached. *Linux journal*, 2004(124):5, 2004.

[11] A. Hassidim. Cache replacement policies for multicore processors. In *ICS*, pages 501–509, 2010.

[12] Microsoft Azure Cache. http://azure.microsoft.com/en-us/services/cache/.

[13] Microsoft Azure SQL Database (formerly SQL Azure). http://www.windowsazure.com/en-us/services/sql-database/.

[14] V. Narasayya, I. Menache, M. Singh, F. Li, M. Syamala, and S. Chaudhuri. Sharing Buffer Pool Memory in Multi-Tenant Relational Database-as-a-Service. *Proceedings of the VLDB Endowment*, 8(7), 2015. Available from http://www.vldb.org/pvldb/vol8/p726-narasayya.pdf.

[15] V. R. Narasayya, S. Das, M. Syamala, B. Chandramouli, and S. Chaudhuri. SQLVM: Performance Isolation in Multi-Tenant Relational Database-as-a-Service. In *CIDR*, 2013.

[16] E. J. O'Neil, P. E. O'Neil, and G. Weikum. The LRU-K page replacement algorithm for database disk buffering. In *ACM SIGMOD Record*, volume 22, pages 297–306. ACM, 1993.

[17] E. J. O'Neil, P. E. O'Neil, and G. Weikum. An optimality proof of the LRU-K page replacement algorithm. *Journal of the ACM (JACM)*, 46(1):92–112, 1999.

[18] E. Peserico. Elastic paging. In *Proceedings of the ACM SIGMETRICS/international conference on Measurement and modeling of computer systems*, pages 349–350. ACM, 2013.

[19] D. D. Sleator and R. E. Tarjan. Amortized efficiency of list update and paging rules. *Communications of the ACM*, 28(2):202–208, 1985.

[20] N. Young. The k-server dual and loose competitiveness for paging. *Algorithmica*, 11(6):525–541, 1994.

[21] W. Zhang and P.-A. Larson. Dynamic memory adjustment for external mergesort. In *VLDB*, volume 97, pages 25–29, 1997.

Myths and Misconceptions about Threads

Hans-J. Boehm
Google
hboehm@google.com

ABSTRACT

The semantics of variables shared across threads, usually called "memory models", have evolved significantly over the last decade, but open problems and some controversy remains. I'll briefly review where we are, and argue that a number of assumptions that still appear common in large parts of the research and programming communities are wrong, or at least questionable, especially for programming languages like C and C++. In particular, I will argue that:

- Full, unrestricted sequential consistency is not a particularly desirable or useful programming model, in that it depends on access granularity, a property often, and for excellent reasons, hidden by both programming language and library specifications.

- Hardware level violations of sequential consistency are often not an indication of bugs. For example, correctly synchronized programs based on spin-locks can be expected to violate sequential consistency at the hardware level, while appearing sequentially consistent at the source level.

- There are no benign data races in C and C++, certainly not in theory, but also not in practice. Any data race gives license to the compiler to mis-compile your program. A future compiler is likely to use that license, even if your current one does not.

- Condition variable wait and notify, as provided by mainstream programming languages, do not impact program partial correctness beyond the fact that waiting temporarily releases a mutex. They do not, in any other way, ensure "happens-before" ordering. For partial correctness purposes, notify is a no-op.

- Relaxed memory ordering, as currently defined by Java, C, or C++, is not well-defined at the programming language, as opposed to machine architecture, level. We're working on that, but stronger ordering is much easier to define than really weak ordering.

This is based on joint work with many other people, including Sarita Adve and Brian Demsky.

Categories and Subject Descriptors

D.3.3 [Language Constructs and Features]: Concurrent Programming Structures; D.1.3 [Programming Techniques]: Concurrent Programming—*Parallel Programming*

Keywords

Threads; shared variables; sequential consistency; condition variables; data races; weak memory ordering

BIO

Hans Boehm is a member of Google's Android team, which he joined after spending most of his career in academia and industrial research labs.

In recent years he has been involved with several efforts to better specify shared variable semantics in mainstream programming languages. He participated in the Java memory model effort a decade ago, and subsequently led the corresponding effort for C++, where he continues to chair the Concurrency Study Group of the ISO C++ committee.

He is an ACM Fellow and long ago chaired ACM SIGPLAN. Even further back, he earned B.S. degrees from the University of Washington, and M.S. and Ph.D. degrees from Cornell University.

SPAA'15, June 13–15, 2015, Portland, OR, USA.
ACM 978-1-4503-3588-1/15/06.
http://dx.doi.org/10.1145/2755573.2764966

Brief Announcement: New Streaming Algorithms for Parameterized Maximal Matching & Beyond [*]

Rajesh Chitnis
Dept. of Computer Science &
Applied Mathematics
Weizmann Institute of
Science, Israel
rajesh.chitnis@weizmann.ac.il

Graham Cormode
Dept. of Computer Science.
University of Warwick, UK
g.cormode@warwick.ac.uk

Hossein Esfandiari
Dept. of Computer Science
University of Maryland,
College Park, USA
hossein@cs.umd.edu

MohammadTaghi Hajiaghayi
Dept. of Computer Science
University of Maryland,
College Park, USA
hajiagha@cs.umd.edu

Morteza Monemizadeh
Dept. of Computer Science.
Charles University, Prague,
Frankfurt, Czech Republic
monemi@iuuk.mff.cuni.cz

ABSTRACT

Very recently at SODA'15 [2], we studied maximal matching via the framework of *parameterized streaming*, where we sought solutions under the promise that no maximal matching exceeds k in size. In this paper, we revisit this problem and provide a much simpler algorithm for this problem. We are also able to apply the same technique to the *Point Line Cover* problem [3].

1. INTRODUCTION

The streaming model for processing graphs is an attractive one: we keep a compact data structure that summarizes all data seen to date, and incrementally update it as new edges are observed. However, for many problems it is known that any such data structure must be large, in the worst case proportional to the total size of the graph. An ongoing line of research asks what can be computed using resources much less than simply storing the data in full. In our recent work [2], we studied graph streaming problems in the parameterized setting: we seek solutions provided that

---

[*]R.C. was supported by a postdoctoral fellowship from I-CORE ALGO. G.C. was supported by the Yahoo Faculty Research and Engagement Program and a Royal Society Wolfson Research Merit Award. H.E. and M.H. were supported in part by NSF CAREER award 1053605, NSF Grant CCF-1161626, ONR YIP award N000141110662, DARPA/AFOSR grant FA9550-12-1-0423, and a Google Faculty Research award. M.M. was supported by the project 14-10003S of GA ČR. Part of this work was done when M.M>. was at Goethe-Universität Frankfurt, Germany and supported in part by MO 2200/1-1

SPAA'15, June 13–15, 2015, Portland, OR, USA.
ACM 978-1-4503-3588-1/15/06.
http://dx.doi.org/10.1145/2755573.2755618.

the size of the solution is bounded by a parameter k. Of particular interest is finding a matching in a graph, a fundamental question in graph algorithms. Under the promise that no maximal matching exceeds k in size, we gave an intricate algorithm to process a dynamic stream (one with both edge insertions and deletions) that required $O(k^2 \text{polylog } n)$ space, and showed that any algorithm for this problem needs $\Omega(k^2)$ space.

In this paper, we revisit this problem and provide a much simpler algorithm for this problem, which meets the same bounds. We further apply the same technique to the Point Line Cover problem [3] where we are given n points on the plane and a parameter k, and the goal is to see if we can cover all points using k lines. Our belief is that the insights gained from this algorithm could apply to other problems in this area, and that the reduced complexity of the description also makes the algorithm easier to understand and apply.

2. MAXIMAL MATCHING

DEFINITION 1. (*k-sparse recovery algorithm*) A k-sparse recovery algorithm *is a data structure which accepts insertions and deletions of elements so that, if the current number of elements stored in it is at most k, then these can be recovered in full.*

Such algorithms have been designed to operate deterministically, and require $O(k \text{polylog } n)$ space [1].

DEFINITION 2. (*k-sample algorithm*) A k-sample algorithm *is a data structure which accepts insertions and deletions of elements so that at any moment it can provide a sample of size k from the elements stored in it, provided there are at least k such elements.*

Randomized constructions of k-sample algorithms are known (which use k-sparse recovery algorithms within them), and require $O(k \text{polylog } n)$ space [1].

ASSUMPTION 3. (*promise*) We assume that, at every point during the execution of the algorithm, the maximal matching of the graph has size at most k.

Our algorithm for finding a maximal matching works as follows. It keeps information about edges in two forms. A data structure L keeps a set of edges exactly. We also maintain up to $2k + 1$ data structures S_i ($1 \leq i \leq 2k + 1$) which are capable of sampling up to $2k + 1$ edges from a set (i.e. instances of $(2k + 1)$-sample recovery algorithms). Each S_i is associated with a timestamp t_i (index of an update in the stream), which represents when the structure was created.

We partition the nodes into two classes: low-degree, meaning that they have at most $2k$ incident edges, and high-degree, meaning that they have more than $2k$ incident edges. We maintain a (sub)set H of high degree nodes, corresponding to the set of nodes which are represented with the sketches S_i. Initially, L and H are empty, the S_i are empty, and all nodes are considered low-degree.

Edge Insertion: For each edge that is inserted, we ensure that it is reflected in one of the data structures. If the edge is incident on two nodes in H, then we store the edge in the sketch S_i associated with the oldest summary, i.e. the one with the oldest timestamp. If the edge is incident on one node $v \notin H$, and another $w \in H$, then we store it in the sketch associated with w. If the edge is incident on two nodes neither of which is in H, then we store the edge explicitly in L. If this insertion causes one of the low degree nodes v to have more than $2k$ edges in L incident on it, then we create a sketch for v, and assign it the current timestamp. We extract all edges in L that are incident on v, and insert them into the sketch of v. We update H to include v.

Edge Deletion: For each edge that is deleted, we identify where it is represented in the data structures, and remove it. If the edge is present in L, then we remove it. Else, at least one of its endpoints must have a sketch. If only one has a sketch, then we remove the edge from this sketch. Else, we remove the edge from the sketch with the oldest timestamp. If removing an edge from a sketch causes the node, v to become low degree, then we interrogate the sketch to find all the edges incident on v. For each extracted edge, if it is also incident on a high degree node w, then it is placed in the sketch for w, else it is placed in L. The sketch can then be removed, and further v is removed from H.

Invariants: The update procedures above ensure that a number of invariants hold over the course of the stream.

1. (Unique representation) Each edge is represented in exactly one place within the data structures L, S_i.

2. (Old sketch) If an edge is incident on two sketches, then it is always represented in the older of these two.

These invariants can be checked easily. The property of unique representation follows from the description of the insertion and deletion procedures: when a new edge is inserted, it is stored in only one data structure; when an edge is deleted, it is removed. The operations which move edges from L into sketches, from one sketch into another sketch, or from a sketch into L also preserve this property.

The property of an edge being associated with the older of its two sketched nodes similarly follows by consideration of the update operations. The only cases which require some care are when an edge is currently associated with two sketched nodes, and the older of these sketches is removed. The deletion process makes it clear that this edge is then moved to the sketch of the other node.

Note that the algorithm does not explicitly maintain the degree of nodes that are not high degree, only those in H.

It is consequently possible that a node may reach a degree of greater than k and remain outside of H (for example, if several of its edges are incident on nodes that are in H). That is, every node in H is a high degree node, but not every high degree node necessarily has a sketch and is in H. This does not affect the correctness of the algorithm.

We now make some observations about the algorithm.

LEMMA 4. *Under Assumption 3, we have*

- *The number of high degree nodes is at most $2k + 1$*

- *The number of edges in L is bounded by $4k^2$.*

PROOF. We prove the two statements in the lemma as follows:

- If there are more than $2k + 1$ high degree nodes, then there must be a matching of size more than k. Such a matching can be found by picking a high degree node and an arbitrary neighbor. This still leaves at least $2k - 1$ nodes whose degree is at least $2k - 1$, and so the procedure can be iterated. This will result in a matching of size $k + 1$.

- This follows similarly, since we could otherwise greedily find a large matching within L. Each matched edge removes at most $4k$ other edges from L that are incident on the matched nodes, since we ensure that all nodes in L have at most $2k$ edges from L incident on them from. If we match $2k$ nodes, then we remove at most $4k^2$ edges; hence if there are more than $4k^2$ edges in L, then these can participate in the matching, violating the promise.

□

From Lemma 4 we can conclude the following theorem

THEOREM 5. *The space cost of this algorithm is $\tilde{O}(k^2)$.*

PROOF. From Assumption 3, we have that $|L|$ is $O(k^2)$, and the number of sketches stored is always $O(k)$, the size of which is bounded by $O(k \operatorname{polylog} n)$ (see Definitions 1 and 2). Hence, the total space cost is $O(k^2 \operatorname{polylog} n)$. □

Algorithm to find a matching: Given these data structures, the algorithm to find a matching is straightforward: it recovers a graph G' which is a subgraph of the graph G described by the stream. We then find a maximal matching on G', and argue that this is also maximal for G.

Graph G' is formed by extracting as many edges from the data structures as possible. That is, for each sketch S_i we extract up to $(2k + 1)$ edges incident on the corresponding node, and set G' to be the union of all these edges plus those stored in L. We now argue that this information is sufficient to find a maximal matching for G.

THEOREM 6. *The above procedure indeed finds a maximal matching for G*

PROOF. The proof hinges on the fact that high degree nodes have sufficiently high degree that it does not matter which edges we remember for them beyond a point. Specifically, suppose we have found a maximal matching of size at most k on G'. Assume that there is a node in H (of degree more than $2k$) that is unmatched. At most $2k$ of its neighbors are matched, due to the promise that the matching is size at most k. Then, it must have an unmatched neighbor which was can find from the (k sample recovery) sketch, since the sketch recovers up to $2k+1$ neighbors of the node. This contradicts the claim that the matching was maximal.

Then, all nodes in H are matched. Thus, any edge which is incident on a node in H cannot extend the matching. L consists of the set of all remaining edges, hence this represents sufficient information to ensure that the whole matching is maximal. Consequently, the matching we find on G' is also maximal on G. $\square$

Note: Note that the operation of the algorithm as updates are processed depends only on deterministic algorithms (such as the k-sparse recovery algorithms - see Definition 1). The only time a randomized data structure is made use of is in the algorithm to find a matching, where we probe the k-sample algorithms. This greatly simplifies the analysis as compared to that in [2]

3. POINT LINE COVER

In the *Point Line Cover* problem, we are given a set P of n points and the question is to find minimum number of lines which can cover all the given n points. In the parametereized version of the problem, we are given an integer k and the question is whether there exists a set of k lines which can cover all the n points. There is an (known) easy kernel of size $O(k^2)$ (see next paragraph), which was shown to be essentially tight by Kratsch et al. [3]

$O(k^2)$ **kernel for Point Line Cover**: We perform the following procedure iteratively:

- **Step 1**: Check if there exists a line ℓ which contains at least $k+1$ points

- **Step 2**: If YES then include this line in the solution, delete all the points which lie on this line and decrease k by 1. If $k > 0$, then go to Step 1. If $k = 0$ and there are still some points remaining then the given instance is a NO instance.

- **Step 3**: Otherwise if $n > k^2$ then the given instance is a NO instance.

We can check if a given line contains at least $k+1$ points in time $O(n)$: for each of the n points we just check individually if they lie on the line or not. There are $\binom{n}{2} = O(n^2)$ lines: one determined by each pair of points. So each execution of Step 1 takes $O(n^3)$ time. Since we execute Step 1 at most k times (note the parameter decreases each time we get a YES answer for Step 1, which is the only time we run Step 1 again). Hence the total running time is $O(n^3 \cdot k)$.

Now we show correctness of the kernelization algorithm. If there is a line which contains at least $k+1$ points, then we must include it in our solution; since otherwise we will need at lest $k+1$ different lines to cover each of these points. We continue this process until Step 1 answers NO or k becomes 0. If $k = 0$ and we have any points remaining to cover then the instance is obviously a NO instance. Otherwise if Step 1 answers NO, then this means that any line can cover at most k points. Hence an instance which can be covered with at most k lines can have at most k^2 points. This justifies Step 3, and shows the correctness of the kernelization algorithm.

Algorithm for Point Line Cover under Promise: We now show how to obtain an $\tilde{O}(k^2)$ algorithm for finding minimum Point Line Cover under the following promise:

ASSUMPTION 7. (promise) *We assume that, at every point during the execution of the algorithm, the number of lines needed to cover all the points is at most k.*

Given a stream of insertions and deletions of points, we maintain a kernel as follows. Let L be a set of lines such that any line in L contains at most k points. We denote set of lines containing more than k points each by H. For a line in L we just keep all the points which lie on it, and for each line in H we sample $k+1$ points using a $(k+1)$-sparse recovery algorithm. The maintenance of sets L and H, and commuting of lines in sets S and H upon point insertions and deletions is similar to the algorithm in Section 2.

4. REFERENCES

[1] N. Barkay, E. Porat, and B. Shalem. Efficient sampling of non-strict turnstile data streams. In *FCT 2013*, pages 48–59.

[2] R. H. Chitnis, G. Cormode, M. T. Hajiaghayi, and M. Monemizadeh. Parameterized streaming: Maximal matching and vertex cover. In *SODA 2015*, pages 1234–1251.

[3] S. Kratsch, G. Philip, and S. Ray. Point line cover: The easy kernel is essentially tight. In *SODA 2014*, pages 1596–1606.

Brief Announcement: Local Computation Algorithms for Graphs of Non-Constant Degrees *

Reut Levi
Ècole Normale Supèrieure
and Universitè Paris Diderot,
France.
reuti.levi@gmail.com

Ronitt Rubinfeld
CSAIL, MIT, Cambridge
MA 02139, USA and the
Blavatnik School of Computer
Science, Tel Aviv University
Tel Aviv 69978, Israel
ronitt@csail.mit.edu

Anak Yodpinyanee
CSAIL, MIT
Cambridge, MA 02139, USA
anak@csail.mit.edu

ABSTRACT

In the model of *local computation algorithms* (LCAs), we aim to compute the queried part of the output by examining only a small (sublinear) portion of the input. This key aspect of LCAs generalizes various other models such as parallel algorithms, local filters and reconstructors. For graph problems, design techniques for LCAs and distributed algorithms are closely related and have been proven useful in each other's context.

Many recently developed LCAs on graph problems achieve time and space complexities with very low dependence on n, the number of vertices. Nonetheless, these complexities are generally at least exponential in d, the upper bound on the degree of the input graph. We consider the case where the parameter d can be moderately dependent on n, and aim for complexities with subexponential dependence on d, while maintaining polylogarithmic dependence on n. We present:

- a randomized LCA for computing maximal independent sets whose time and space complexities are quasipolynomial in d and polylogarithmic in n;

- for constant $\epsilon > 0$, a randomized LCA that provides a $(1 - \epsilon)$-approximation to maximum matching with high probability, whose time and space complexities are polynomial in d and polylogarithmic in n.

Categories and Subject Descriptors

F.2.2 [**Analysis of Algorithms and Problem Complexity**]: Nonnumerical Algorithms and Problems—*computations on discrete structures*; G.2.2 [**Discrete Mathematics**]: Graph Theory—*graph algorithms*

General Terms

Algorithms, Theory

---

*A full version of this paper is available at arxiv.org/abs/ 1502.04022

SPAA'15, June 13–15, 2015, Portland, OR, USA.
ACM 978-1-4503-3588-1/15/06.
http://dx.doi.org/10.1145/2755573.2755615.

Keywords

Local Computation Algorithms, Maximal Independent Set, Maximum Matching

1. INTRODUCTION

In the face of massive data sets, classical algorithmic models, where the algorithm reads the entire input, performs a full computation, then reports the entire output, are rendered infeasible. To handle these data sets, the model of *local computation algorithms* (LCAs) has been proposed in [14]. LCAs compute the queried part of the output by examining only a small (sublinear) portion of the input. For example, the algorithm $\mathcal{A}$ for computing a maximal independent set (MIS) is given access to the graph G and asked: "is vertex v in the MIS?" $\mathcal{A}$ then explores only a small portion of G, and answers "yes" or "no." The set $\{v : \mathcal{A}$ answers "yes" on $v\}$ must indeed form a valid MIS of G. LCAs have been constructed for many problems, including MIS, maximal matching, approximate maximum matching, vertex coloring, and hypergraph coloring.

The LCA framework is motivated by the circumstances where we focus on computing a small, specified portion of the output, which generalizes many other models from various contexts. For example, LCAs can be parallelized so that, after an initial communication phase, they may answer queries in a consistent manner with no additional communication. Important applications include locally decodable codes, local decompression, local filters, reconstructors, and locally computable decisions for online algorithms and mechanism design.

Many recently developed LCAs on graph problems achieve time and space complexities with very low dependence on n, the number of vertices. Nonetheless, these complexities are at least exponential in d, the upper bound on the degree of the input graph. While these papers often consider d to be a constant, the large dependence on d may forbid practical uses of these algorithms. In this work we consider the case where the parameter d can be moderately dependent on n.

1.1 Our Contribution

This paper addresses the maximal independent set problem[1] and the approximate maximum matching problem.[2]

---

[1] An *independent set* I is a set of vertices such that no two vertices in I are adjacent.

[2] A *matching* M is a set of edges such that no two distinct edges in M share a common endpoint.

Problem	Work	Time	Space
MIS	[14]	$2^{O(d \log^2 d)} \log n$	$O(n)$
	[1]	$2^{O(d \log^2 d)} \log^3 n$	$2^{O(d \log^2 d)} \log^2 n$
	[5]	$2^{O(d^2 \log^2 d)} \log^* n^\dagger$	none
	[13]	$2^{O(d)} \log^2 n$	$2^{O(d)} \log n \log \log n$
		$2^{O(d)} \log n \log \log n$	$2^{O(d)} \log^2 n$
	here	$2^{O(\log^3 d)} \log^3 n$	$2^{O(\log^3 d)} \log^2 n$
Approx. Maximum Matching	[9]	$O(\log^4 n)^\ddagger$	$O(\log^3 n)^\ddagger$
	[5]	$2^{\text{poly}(d)} \text{poly}(\log^* n)^\dagger$	none
	here	$\text{poly}\{d, \log n\}$	$\text{poly}\{d, \log n\}$

Table 1: The summary of complexities of various LCAs. For the approximate maximum matching problem, ϵ is assumed to be constant. $\dagger$ indicates query complexity, when time complexity is not explicitly given in the paper. $\ddagger$ indicates hidden dependence on d, which is at least $2^{O(d)}$ but not explicitly known.

The comparison between our results and other approaches is given in table 1. We provide the first LCAs whose complexities are quasi-polynomial and polynomial in d for these respective problems, while maintaining polylogarithmic dependence on n. When d is non-constant, previously known LCAs have complexities with polylogarithmic dependence on n only when $d = O(\log \log n)$. Our LCAs maintain this dependence even when $d = \exp(\Theta((\log \log n)^{1/3}))$ for the MIS problem and $d = \text{poly}(\log n)$ for the approximate maximum matching problem. Our LCA for the MIS problem may be extended to handle other problems with reductions to MIS, such as maximal matching or $(d+1)$-coloring, while maintaining similar asymptotic complexities.

1.2 Related Work

We build on the Parnas-Ron reduction, proposed in their paper on approximating the size of a minimum vertex cover (VC) [12]. This reduction turns a k-round distributed algorithm into an LCA by examining all vertices at distance up to k from the queried vertex, then simulating the computation of the distributed algorithm, invoking $d^{O(k)}$ queries to the input graph. They apply this technique to compute a 2-approximation (with additive error) for the size of a minimum VC with query complexity $d^{O(\log d)}$. Distributed algorithms for the MIS problem require more rounds, and consequently, a similar reduction only yields an LCA with query and time complexities $d^{O(d \log d)} \log n$ in [14].

Many useful techniques for designing LCAs originate from algorithms for approximating the solution size in sublinear time via random sampling. A powerful technique for bounding the expected query and time complexities is the query tree method from the Nguyen-Onak algorithm [10]. This method converts *global* algorithms that operate on the entire input into *local* algorithms that adaptively make queries only when necessary. The structure of the recursive calls forms an *query tree* in the input graph. They apply this approach by constructing query trees based on a random order of vertices so that the size of the query tree can be probabilistically bounded. While the expected query tree size is still exponential in d, for certain problems, a slight modification of the their algorithm reduces the expected query tree size to $O(\bar{d})$, the average degree [15, 11].

Recently, a new method for deterministically bounding the query tree sizes using graph orientation is given in [5] based on graph coloring, which improves upon LCAs for several graph problems. They reduce the query complexity of their algorithm for the MIS problem to $d^{O(d^2 \log d)} \log^* n$, giving the lowest dependence on n currently known. This approach can also be extended back to improve distributed algorithms for certain cases [6].

While all of these LCAs have complexities with exponential dependence on d for the problems studied in this paper, the only lower bound is of $\Omega(\bar{d})$, which can be derived from the lower bound for approximation algorithms for the minimum VC problem from [12].

2. PRELIMINARIES

2.1 Graphs Oracles

We assume that the input graph G, assumed to be simple and undirected, is given through an adjacency list oracle $\mathcal{O}^G$ which answers neighbor queries: given a vertex $v \in V$ and an index $i \in [d]$, the ith neighbor of v is returned if $i \leq \deg(v)$; otherwise, $\perp$ is returned.

2.2 Local Computation Algorithms

We adopt the definition of local computation algorithms from [14], in the context of graph computation problems given an access to the adjacency list oracle $\mathcal{O}^G$.

DEFINITION 1. *A local computation algorithm $\mathcal{A}$ for a computation problem is a (randomized) algorithm with the following properties. $\mathcal{A}$ is given access to the adjacency list oracle $\mathcal{O}^G$ for the input graph G, a tape of random bits, and local read-write computation memory. When given an input (query) x, $\mathcal{A}$ must compute an answer for x. This answer must only depend on x, G, and the random bits. The answers given by $\mathcal{A}$ to all possible queries must be consistent; namely, all answers must constitute some valid solution to the computation problem.*

The complexities of an LCA $\mathcal{A}$ can be measured as follows. The *query complexity* of an LCA is the maximum number of queries that $\mathcal{A}$ makes to $\mathcal{O}^G$ to compute an answer (to the computation problem) for any single query. Similarly, the *time complexity* is the maximum amount of time that $\mathcal{A}$ requires to compute an answer. Lastly, the *space complexity* is the total size of the random tape and local computation memory used by $\mathcal{A}$.

Here we refer to the time and query complexities rather exchangeably as they are roughly a factor of $O(\log n)$ larger than the query complexities for our LCAs. The space complexity of our LCAs are dominated by the size of the random tape, so we refer to the space complexity as *seed length*. We give randomized LCAs that succeed *with high probability*.[3]

3. MAXIMAL INDEPENDENT SET

We provide an LCA for computing a MIS whose time and query complexities are quasi-polynomial in d:

THEOREM 1. *There exists a randomized local computation algorithm that computes a maximal independent set of*

---

[3] The success probability can be amplified to reach $1 - n^{-c}$ for any positive constant c without asymptotically increasing other complexities.

G with time complexity $2^{O(\log^3 d)} \log n$ and space complexity $O(n \log^2 d)$.

Our approach combines many techniques across previous works on LCAs and distributed computing. We construct a two-phase LCA similar to that of [14], which is based on Beck's algorithmic approach to Lovász local lemma [3]. In this first phase, we apply a distributed algorithm that computes an independent set which breaks the original graph into small connected components. We improve upon the distributed algorithm used by [14] by occupying new insights from [2] to reduce its running time to $O(\log^2 d)$ rounds. Our algorithm is a variation of Luby's randomized distributed algorithm [8] similar to the WEAK-MIS algorithm from [4], but requires a stronger lemma to make such guarantee on component sizes. Applying the Parnas-Ron reduction [12], the time and query complexities of this phase remain subexponential in d. Then, in the second phase, we explore each component and solve our problems deterministically; the complexities of this phase are bounded by the component sizes. Finally, by employing a technique from [1], we reduce the amount of space of our LCA so that it has roughly the same asymptotic bound as its time and query complexities.

4. APPROXIMATE MAXIMUM MATCHING

We provide an LCA that computes an approximation maximum matching whose time and query complexities are polynomial in d:

THEOREM 2. *There exists a randomized $(1-\epsilon)$-approximation local computation algorithm for maximal independent set with random seed of length $O((d^2/\epsilon^2) \log^2 n \log \log n)$ and query complexity $O((d^4/\epsilon^2) \log^2 n \log \log n)$.*

Our approach is based on a local simulation of the approximate maximum matching algorithm which iteratively augments the maintained matching with a maximal set of disjoint augmenting paths of increasing lengths [7]. We compute such augmenting paths by modifying Nguyen-Onak algorithm [10] for greedily computing MIS based on random vertex ordering which, according to the modification and analysis by Yoshida et al., yields query trees whose expected sizes are poly(d) [15]. Since complexities of LCAs are based on the maximum query tree size, we resolve this problem by constructing the following two-phase LCA. In the first phase we computes a sufficiently good vertex ordering that rarely induces large query trees. Then we use this good ordering to compute our answer, ignoring vertices with large query trees. We show that the ignored vertices only constitute to a sufficiently small fraction of error. We then reduce the amount of space by first reducing the required dependence of random orderings, then employing the construction from [1] to generate our random orderings.

5. ACKNOWLEDGMENTS

This research is supported by NSF grants CCF-1217423, CCF-1065125 and CCF-1420692, ISF grant numbers 246/08 and 1536/14, and the DPST scholarship, Royal Thai Government. We thank Dana Ron for her valuable contribution to this paper.

6. REFERENCES

[1] N. Alon, R. Rubinfeld, S. Vardi, and N. Xie. Space-efficient local computation algorithms. In *Proceedings of the Twenty-Third Annual ACM-SIAM Symposium on Discrete Algorithms*, pages 1132–1139. SIAM, 2012.

[2] L. Barenboim, M. Elkin, S. Pettie, and J. Schneider. The locality of distributed symmetry breaking. In *Foundations of Computer Science (FOCS), 2012 IEEE 53rd Annual Symposium on*, pages 321–330. IEEE, 2012.

[3] J. Beck. An algorithmic approach to the Lovász local lemma. I. *Random Structures & Algorithms*, 2(4):343–365, 1991.

[4] K.-M. Chung, S. Pettie, and H.-H. Su. Distributed algorithms for the lovász local lemma and graph coloring. In *Proceedings of the 2014 ACM symposium on Principles of distributed computing*, pages 134–143. ACM, 2014.

[5] G. Even, M. Medina, and D. Ron. Deterministic stateless centralized local algorithms for bounded degree graphs. In *Algorithms-ESA 2014*, pages 394–405. Springer, 2014.

[6] G. Even, M. Medina, and D. Ron. Distributed maximum matching in bounded degree graphs. *arXiv preprint arXiv:1407.7882*, 2014.

[7] J. E. Hopcroft and R. M. Karp. An $n^{5/2}$ algorithm for maximum matchings in bipartite graphs. *SIAM Journal on computing*, 2(4):225–231, 1973.

[8] M. Luby. A simple parallel algorithm for the maximal independent set problem. *SIAM journal on computing*, 15(4):1036–1053, 1986.

[9] Y. Mansour and S. Vardi. A local computation approximation scheme to maximum matching. In *Approximation, Randomization, and Combinatorial Optimization. Algorithms and Techniques*, pages 260–273. Springer, 2013.

[10] H. N. Nguyen and K. Onak. Constant-time approximation algorithms via local improvements. In *Foundations of Computer Science, 2008. FOCS'08. IEEE 49th Annual IEEE Symposium on*, pages 327–336. IEEE, 2008.

[11] K. Onak, D. Ron, M. Rosen, and R. Rubinfeld. A near-optimal sublinear-time algorithm for approximating the minimum vertex cover size. In *Proceedings of the Twenty-Third Annual ACM-SIAM Symposium on Discrete Algorithms*, pages 1123–1131. SIAM, 2012.

[12] M. Parnas and D. Ron. Approximating the minimum vertex cover in sublinear time and a connection to distributed algorithms. *Theoretical Computer Science*, 381(1):183–196, 2007.

[13] O. Reingold and S. Vardi. New techniques and tighter bounds for local computation algorithms. *arXiv preprint arXiv:1404.5398*, 2014.

[14] R. Rubinfeld, G. Tamir, S. Vardi, and N. Xie. Fast local computation algorithms. In *Innovations in Computer Science - ICS 2010, Tsinghua University, Beijing, China, January 7-9, 2011. Proceedings*, pages 223–238, 2011.

[15] Y. Yoshida, M. Yamamoto, and H. Ito. Improved constant-time approximation algorithms for maximum matchings and other optimization problems. *SIAM Journal on Computing*, 41(4):1074–1093, 2012.

Brief Announcement: Efficient Approximation Algorithms for Computing k Disjoint Restricted Shortest Paths *

Longkun Guo
School of Mathematics and Computer Science
Fuzhou University, China
lkguo@fzu.edu.cn

Kewen Liao
Dept. of Computing and Information Systems
University of Melbourne, Australia
kewen.liao@unimelb.edu.au

Hong Shen
School of Computer Science
University of Adelaide, Australia
hong.shen@cs.adelaide.edu.au

Peng Li
Dept. of Computer Science and Engineering
Washington University in St. Louis, United States
pengli@wustl.edu

ABSTRACT

Let $G = (V, E)$ be a digraph with nonnegative integral *cost* and *delay* on each edge, s and t be two vertices, and $D \in \mathbb{Z}_0^+$ be a delay bound, the k *disjoint Restricted Shortest Path* (*kRSP*) problem is to compute k disjoint paths between s and t with the total cost minimized and the total delay bounded by D. In this paper, we first present a pseudo-polynomial-time algorithm with a bifactor approximation ratio of $(1, 2)$, then improve the algorithm to polynomial time with a bifactor ratio of $(1 + \epsilon, 2 + \epsilon)$ for any fixed $\epsilon > 0$, which is better than the current best approximation ratio $(O(1 + \gamma), O(1 + \ln \frac{1}{\gamma}))$ for any fixed $\gamma > 0$ [3, 5]. To the best of our knowledge, this is the first constant-factor algorithm that almost strictly obeys kRSP constraint.

Keywords

k Disjoint Restricted Shortest Path, Bifactor Approximation Algorithm, Auxiliary Graph, Cycle Cancellation.

1. INTRODUCTION

1.1 Background

The disjoint quality of service (QoS) path problem is a generalization of the shortest QoS path problem and has broad applications in networking, data transmission, etc., where multiple disjoint QoS paths might be necessary. Given cost and delay as QoS constraints, k *disjoint Restricted Shortest Path* (*kRSP*) problem arises as below:

*This research was partially supported by Natural Science Foundation of China under its Grant No. #61300025, Doctoral Funds of Ministry of Education of China for Young Scholars (#20123514120013), and Natural Science Foundation of Fujian Province (#2012J05115).

DEFINITION 1. (The k disjoint Restricted Shortest Path problem, *kRSP*) *Given a digraph* $G = (V, E)$, *a pair of distinct vertices* s, $t \in V$, *a cost function* $c : E \to \mathbb{Z}_0^+$, *a delay function* $d : E \to \mathbb{Z}_0^+$, *and a delay bound* $D \in \mathbb{Z}_0^+$, *the* k *(edge) disjoint Restricted Shortest Paths (kRSP) problem is to compute* k *disjoint st-paths* $P_1, \ldots, P_k$, *such that* $E(P_i) \cap E(P_j) = \emptyset$ *for any* $i \neq j \in \{1, \ldots, k\}$, $\sum_{i=1,\ldots,k} d(P_i) \leq D$, *and the total cost of the* k *paths is minimized.*

Previous works on the kRSP problem are mainly *bifactor approximation* algorithms. An algorithm $\mathcal{A}$ is a bifactor (α, β)-approximation for the kRSP problem if and only if for every instance, $\mathcal{A}$ runs in polynomial time and outputs k disjoint st-paths with the total delay and the total cost of the k disjoint paths bounded by αD and βC_{OPT}, respectively, where C_{OPT} is the cost of an optimal solution to kRSP, and α and β are positive constants.

1.2 Related Work

A closely related problem, the k disjoint bi-constrained path problem (kBCP), targets k disjoint st-paths that satisfy the *total* cost constraint and the *total* delay constraint. For the kBCP problem, approximation algorithms with a bifactor of $(1 + \beta, 1 + \ln \frac{1}{\beta})$ or a single factor ratio of $O(\ln n)$ (i.e. bifactor approximation ratio $(1, O(\ln n))$) have been developed for general k in [5], where $\beta > 0$ is any fixed positive real number. For the kRSP problem, Peng et al. [7] and Orda et al. [6] have achieved bifactor ratios of $(1 + \frac{1}{r}, r(1 + \frac{2(\log r + 1)}{r})(1 + \epsilon))$ and $(1 + \frac{1}{r}, 1 + r)$ for $k = 2$, respectively. Based on LP-rounding technology, an approximation with bifactor ratio $(2, 2)$ has been developed in [3], which can be further improved to ratio $(1 + \beta, 1 + \ln \frac{1}{\beta})$ by following a similar idea of [5]. To the best of our knowledge, however, no algorithm has achieved a constant single factor approximation ratio.

1.3 Our Results

The results of this paper are summarized in this section. Due to space constraint, the proofs are omitted in this paper. Interested readers please refer to [4] for the proofs.

LEMMA 2. *The kRSP problem admits an approximation algorithm with an approximation ratio of* $(1, 2)$ *and runtime* $O((\sum c(e))^2 \sum d(e)(n^{4.5} C_{OPT}^{4.5} DL))$, *where* C *is the cost of an optimal solution and* L *is the maximum input length.*

The algorithm has pseudo-polynomial time complexity. By applying the technique for polynomial time approximation scheme design in [1], we can obtain a polynomial time algorithm with a bifactor of $(1 + \epsilon_1, 2 + \epsilon_2)$.

THEOREM 3. *For any constants $\epsilon_1, \epsilon_2 > 0$, the kRSP problem admits a polynomial time algorithm with an approximation ratio $(1 + \epsilon_1, 2 + \epsilon_2)$.*

Our pseudo polynomial time approximation algorithm of Lemma 2 consists of two phases. The first phase is computing a not-too-bad solution for the kRSP problem by a simple LP-rounding algorithm as in [3], whose performance guarantee has been shown as in the following:

LEMMA 4. *The kRSP problem admits an algorithm, such that for any of its output solutions, there exists a real number $0 \leq \alpha \leq 2$ such that the delay-sum and the cost-sum of the solution are bounded by αD and $(2-\alpha) * C_{OPT}$, respectively.*

Note that α differs for different instances, so the bifactor of the algorithm is actually $(2, 2)$.

The second phase of our algorithm, which is the main task of this paper, is to improve the approximation ratio $(2, 2)$ to $(1 + \epsilon, 2 + \epsilon)$ in pseudo polynomial time. The techniques involved cycle cancellation, LP-rounding, and some graph transformations. This paper not only gives an approximation algorithm for the kRSP problem, but also improves cycle cancellation methods by proposing an algorithm of computing bicameral cycle, which is a *good-enough* cycle in a graph where both negative-cost edges and negative-delay edges are allowed. As a result, our algorithm can potentially improve approximation ratios of other bicriteria optimization problems (or budgeted optimization problems) where cycle cancellation methods can be applied.

2. CYCLE CANCELLATION

This section introduces the key idea of the improved approximation for kRSP based on the cycle cancellation method. We will first describe our version of the cycle cancellation method and point out the difference compared to previous versions, then give details of the improved algorithm.

2.1 The Cycle Cancellation Method

Let E_1 and E_2 be two set of edges, and $E_1 \oplus E_2$ denote the edge set $E_1 \cup E_2 \setminus \{e(u, v) | \{e(u, v), e(v, u)\} \subseteq E_1 \cup E_2\}$, i.e., $E_1 \cup E_2$ except pairs of parallel edges in opposite direction therein. Let P be an st-path and $\overline{P} = \{e'(v, u) | e(u, v) \in P\}$, i.e., $\overline{P}$ is P but with the direction of each edge reversed. Moreover, the cost and delay of the edges of $\overline{P}$ are negated, i.e., $c(e'(v, u)) = -c(e(u, v))$ and $d(e'(v, u)) = -d(e(u, v))$ for every edge $e'(v, u) \in \overline{P}$.

DEFINITION 5. *(Residual graph) A residual graph $\widetilde{G} = G_{res}(P_1, \ldots, P_k)$, with respect to G and $P_1, \ldots, P_k \subset G$, is graph $G \cup \left(\bigcup_{i=1,\ldots,k} E(\overline{P_i}) \right) \setminus \bigcup_{i=1,\ldots,k} E(P_i)$, i.e., graph G with the direction of edges of $P_1, \ldots, P_k$ reversed, and their cost and delay negated.* [1]

For notation briefness, we use $\widetilde{G}$ instead of $G_{res}(P_1, \ldots, P_k)$. Note that [5] and [6] also employed cycle cancellation methods, but they do not allow negative cost in residual graphs.

---

[1] $\widetilde{G}$ can contain parallel edges in the same direction with different costs and delays. Thus, $\widetilde{G}$ might be a multigraph.

Our cycle cancellation method is based on the following proposition which can be derived from the flow theory:

PROPOSITION 6. *Let $P_1, \ldots, P_k$ be k disjoint st-paths in G and $O_1, \ldots, O_h$ be a set of edge-disjoint cycles in residual graph $\widetilde{G}$. Then $\{P_1, \ldots, P_k\} \oplus \{O_1, \ldots, O_h\}$ contains k disjoint st-paths in G.*

Intuitively, $\{P_1, \ldots, P_k\} \oplus \{O_1, \ldots, O_h\}$ is to replace the edges of $P_1, \ldots, P_k$, which have parallel opposite counterpart in $\{O_1, \ldots, O_h\}$, with the edges of $\{O_1, \ldots, O_h\} \setminus \{\overline{P_1}, \ldots, \overline{P_k}\}$. Such edge replacement is called *cycle cancellation*.

2.2 Cycle Cancellation with Bicameral Cycles

Let $P_1, \ldots, P_k$ be a solution resulting from the first phase with large delay, say $\sum_{i=1}^{k} d(P_i) > D$. According to Proposition 6, if we could find a set of edge-disjoint negative delay cycles $O_1, \ldots, O_h$, then we can decrease the delay of the solution to kRSP by using $\{P_1, \ldots, P_k\} \oplus \{O_1, \ldots, O_h\}$ as the k disjoint paths.

PROPOSITION 7. *Let $P_1^*, \ldots, P_k^*$ be a minimum cost solution to the kRSP problem that satisfies the delay constraint, and $P_1, \ldots, P_k$ be k disjoint st-paths, then $\{P_1^*, \ldots, P_k^*\} \oplus \{\overline{P_1}, \ldots, \overline{P_k}\}$ is exactly a set of edge-disjoint cycles.*

LEMMA 8. *If $\sum_{i=1}^{k} d(P_i) > D$, there exists at least one cycle with negative delay in $\widetilde{G}$.*

Based on Proposition 6 and Proposition 7, an idea for the improved algorithm is to find the set of cycles $\{O_1, \ldots, O_h\}$ and use them to improve the k disjoint paths $P_1, \ldots, P_k$ to an optimal solution $P_1^*, \ldots, P_k^*$. However, it is hard to identify all the cycles $\{O_1, \ldots, O_h\}$ exactly. We use a greedy approach in the improved algorithm, which repeatedly computes a "best" cycle (i.e. cycle O with optimum $\frac{d(O)}{c(O)}$) and uses it to improve the current k disjoint paths towards an optimal solution until a desired one is obtained. However, a "best" cycle is probably NP-hard to compute, so our algorithm uses *bicameral cycles* instead. Let $P_1, \ldots, P_k$ be the current solution to the kRSP problem, here are the main steps of our algorithm:

> **While** $\sum_{i=1}^{k} d(P_i) > D$ **do**
> *Compute a* bicameral *cycle O;*
> *Set* $\{P_1, \ldots, P_k\} \leftarrow \{P_1, \ldots, P_k\} \oplus O$.

3. COMPUTING BICAMERAL CYCLE

We construct two auxiliary graphs $H_v^+(B)$ and $H_v^-(B)$, such that every cycle containing v with total cost between 0 and B in $\widetilde{G}$ corresponds to a cycle in $H_v^+(B)$ while every cycle containing v with cost between $-B$ and 0 corresponds to a cycle in $H_v^-(B)$, where B is a given bound on cost and v is a vertex of $\widetilde{G}$. Then, by computing the cycles in $H_v^+(B)$ and $H_v^-(B)$ for every $v \in \widetilde{G}$ and every necessary B, we can find in $\widetilde{G}$ bicameral cycles if there exists any.

3.1 Construction of Auxiliary Graph

The algorithm of constructing auxiliary graphs $H_v^+(B)$ and $H_v^-(B)$ is inspired by the modeling of a shallow-light spanning tree path subject to multiple constraints [2]. The detail of constructing $H_v^+(B)$ is shown in Algorithm 1.

Algorithm 1 Construction of auxiliary graph $H_v^+(B)$.

Input: Residual graph $\widetilde{G}$ with edge cost $c : e \to \mathbb{Z}_0^+$ and edge delay $d : e \to \mathbb{Z}_0^+$, a specified vertex $v \in V$, a given cost constraint $B \in \mathbb{Z}^+$;
Output: Auxiliary graph $H_v^+(B)$.

1. **For** every vertex v_l of V **do**

   Add $B + 1$ vertices $v_l^0, \dots, v_l^B$ to $H_v^+(B)$;

2. **For** every edge $e = \langle v_j, v_l \rangle \in E$ **do**

   (a) if $c(e) \geq 0$, add to $H_v^+(B)$ the edges $\left\langle v_j^0, v_l^{c(e)} \right\rangle, \dots, \left\langle v_j^{B-c(e)}, v_l^B \right\rangle$, each of which is with delay $d(e)$;

   (b) if $c(e) < 0$, add to $H_v^+(B)$ the edges $\left\langle v_j^B, v_l^{B-|c(e)|} \right\rangle, \dots, \left\langle v_j^{|c(e)|}, v_l^0 \right\rangle$, each of which is with delay $d(e)$.

3. **For** each vertex v^i of $H_v^+(B)$ that corresponding to the specified vertex $v \in G$ **do**

   Add edge $e(v^i, v^0)$ to $H_v^+(B)$ with delay zero.

3.2 Computation of Bicameral Cycle

Now we show how to use LP-rounding method to compute cycles in $H_v^+(B)$ and $H_v^-(B)$, and obtain a bicameral cycle in $\widetilde{G}$. We begin with the following linear programming formula:

$$\min \sum_{e \in H} c(e)x(e) \qquad (1)$$

subject to

$$\sum_{e \in \delta^+(v)} x_e - \sum_{e \in \delta^-(v)} x_e = 0, \ \forall v \in V(H_v^+(B) \text{ or } H_v^-(B))$$

$$\sum_{e \in H} d(e)x(e) \leq \Delta D$$

$$0 \leq x(e) \leq 1, \ \forall e \in G$$

Below we only discuss $H_v^+(B)$ since $H_v^-(B)$ is similar.

LEMMA 9. *A solution to LP (1) exactly corresponds to a set of cycles with cost between B and $-B$ in $\widetilde{G}$.*

A solution to LP (1) apparently corresponds to a set of fractional cycles of $H_v^+(B)$ (or $H_v^-(B)$). So we only need to show that a cycle in $H_v^+(B)$ corresponds to a set of cycles in $\widetilde{G}$. In fact, according to the construction of $H_v^+(B)$, we have the following lemma, from which the correctness of Lemma 9 can be immediately obtained.

LEMMA 10. *A cycle in $H_v^+(B)$ corresponds to a set of cycles in $\widetilde{G}$, each of which is with cost between B and $-B$. Conversely, a cycle in $\widetilde{G}$, containing v and with cost between 0 and B, corresponds to a cycle in $H_v^+(B)$.*

THEOREM 11. *Let cycles $O_1, \dots, O_z$ be the cycles in $\widetilde{G}$ corresponding to $\chi(v, B^*)$ for every $v \in \widetilde{G}$, where $B^* =$* $\sum_{i=1}^k c(P_i^*)$ *and* $P_1^*, \dots, P_k^*$ *is an optimal solution to the kRSP problem, then there must be a bicameral cycle in $O_1, \dots, O_z$ if the kRSP problem is feasible.*

Following Theorem 11, here are the steps of our algorithm:

1. Construct $H_v^+(B)$ and $H_v^-(B)$ for all $v \in \widetilde{G}$ and every integer $0 \leq B \leq \sum_{e \in G} c(e)$;

2. Solve LP (1) against every $H_v^+(B)$ and $H_v^-(B)$, and collect optimal solutions;

3. Compute a bicameral cycle among all the cycles of G released from all the solutions.

In general, it is an LP-rounding algorithm. The algorithm solves LP formulas and rounds x_e to 1 for every edge e belonging to a computed bicameral cycle. Then the key of analysis is to show that the cycles corresponding to the solution of LP (1) always contains a bicameral cycle iff the kRSP problem is feasible. This task has actually been done in Theorem 11 (See [4] for the detailed algorithms.).

THEOREM 12. *The above algorithm correctly computes a bicameral cycle in time $t_{bc} = O(n^{4.5}C_{OPT}^{4.5} \sum c(e)L)$.*

4. CONCLUSION

The kRSP problem is known to be NP-hard. In this paper, we presented a new method for computing a bicameral cycle by constructing an auxiliary graph and employing LP-rounding. Then, based on a cycle-cancellation method that uses bicameral cycles, we designed a polynomial-time approximation algorithm for kRSP with bifactor approximation ratio $(1 + \epsilon, 2 + \epsilon)$ for any constant $\epsilon > 0$. To the best of our knowledge, our algorithm is the first constant factor approximation algorithm that computes a solution almost strictly obeying the delay constraint. In future, we plan to investigate the inapproximability of the kRSP problem.

5. REFERENCES

[1] M.R. Garey and D.S. Johnson. *Computers and intractability*. Freeman San Francisco, 1979.

[2] L. Gouveia, L. Simonetti, and E. Uchoa. Modeling hop-constrained and diameter-constrained minimum spanning tree problems as steiner tree problems over layered graphs. *Mathematical Programming*, 2011.

[3] L. Guo. Improved lp-rounding approximations for the k-disjoint restricted shortest paths problem. In *Frontiers in Algorithmics 2014*, pages 94–104, 2014.

[4] L. Guo, K. Liao, H. Shen, and P. Li. Efficient approximation algorithms for computing k disjoint restricted shortest paths. *http://arxiv.org/abs/1504.05519*.

[5] L. Guo, H. Shen, and K. Liao. Improved approximation algorithms for computing k disjoint paths subject to two constraints. *Journal of Combinatorial Optimization*, 29(1):153–164, 2015.

[6] A. Orda and A. Sprintson. Efficient algorithms for computing disjoint QoS paths. In *IEEE INFOCOM*, volume 1, pages 727–738, 2004.

[7] C. Peng and H. Shen. A new approximation algorithm for computing 2-restricted disjoint paths. *IEICE Transactions on Information and Systems*, (2), 2007.

Brief Announcement: Fast and Better Distributed MapReduce Algorithms for k-Center Clustering

Sungjin Im
University of California, Merced
Merced, CA 95343
sim3@ucmerced.edu

Benjamin Moseley
Washington University in St. Louis.
St. Louis, MO 63130
bmoseley@wustl.edu

ABSTRACT

We revisit the k-center clustering problem in MapReduce. Previously, a 10-approximation algorithm that runs in $O(1)$ rounds was known. In this work, we present two 2-approximate MapReduce algorithms that run in 3 or 4 rounds. These algorithms are essentially the best one can hope for in terms of both approximation factor and round complexity. We then consider the k-center problem with outliers for the first time in the MapReduce setting. For this problem, we introduce a 4-approximate 3-round MapReduce algorithm.

Categories and Subject Descriptors

F.2.2 [**Nonnumerical Algorithms and Problem**]: Computations on discrete structures

General Terms

Algorithms, Theory

Keywords

MapReduce, Clustering, k-center, Outliers.

1. INTRODUCTION

Clustering is a fundamental problem faced in a variety of fields and, due to this, there is a vast literature on the topic. See [14] for a survey on the literature on clustering. Generally, in a clustering problem, the goal is to partition, or cluster, a given set of points such that the points belonging to the same cluster are similar. Clustering provides a useful summary of large data sets and often serves as a key component in numerous applications arising in data mining, information retrieval, bioinformatics, and social network analysis.

One of the most basic and well-understood clustering problems is the k-center problem. In the k-center problem, the input consists of an integer k, a set U of n points along with pairwise distance $d(u, v)$ between any two points $u, v \in U$. This distance represents the dissimilarity between the points – similar points are close together while dissimilar points are farther away from each other. It is generally assumed that the data points lie in a metric space. The points in U are to be partitioned into k clusters. The partitioning of points into the clusters can be done explicitly, but alternatively can be done by choosing a set of k points. That is, to define the clustering, one chooses a set $C \subseteq U$ of k points from U which are called *centers*. For a subset $S \subseteq U$ let $d(v, S) = \min_{u \in S} d(u, v)$ be the minimum distance of a point $v \in U$ to a point in S. Choosing the set $C = \{c_1, c_2, \ldots c_k\}$ of k centers naturally defines a partitioning of U into k sets $P_1, P_2, \ldots P_k$ by setting P_i to contain each point $v \in U$ where $d(v, C) = d(v, c_i)$. Here ties are broken arbitrarily in the assignment of points to clusters. The goal is to choose the set C of k centers such that $\max_{u \in U} d(u, C)$ is minimized.

The complexity of the metric k-center problem is well-understood. The problem is NP-Hard and further for any $\epsilon > 0$, no $2-\epsilon$-approximation is possible unless P = NP [6,8]. There are 2-approximate algorithms known, giving the best worst case analysis result one could hope for [6, 8]. Besides these results, previous work has considered generalizations of the problem. One of the most popular generalizations is the k-center with *outliers* problem [4]. In this problem, the setting is the same, but additionally an algorithm is allowed to discard up to $z \geq 0$ points from U without penalty. The set of discarded points needs not be included in the partitioning and do not contributed to the objective function. Here z is a parameter input to the problem. In this problem, it is assumed that the data is noisy, which occurs frequently in practice. Unfortunately the quality of clustering solutions can dramatically change based on a small number of outliers data points and, due to this, the k-center with outliers problem has been considered. For this generalization of the k-center problem a 3-approximation algorithm is known [4].

Clustering Large Data: Today, a fundamental application of clustering is for analyzing large data sets. Unfortunately, once data sets become large enough, most sequential algorithms are rendered ineffective. This is due to the time constraints when running a sequential algorithm on the large data sets and also due to the memory constraints; a single machine may not have enough memory to fit the entire data set for a problem. For these reasons, when datasets become large, practitioners turn to alternative computational frameworks for data processing, such as distributed computing.

The MapReduce [13] paradigm has emerged as the de facto standard distributed computing framework for pro-

SPAA'15, June 13–15, 2015, Portland, OR, USA.
ACM 978-1-4503-3588-1/15/06.
http://dx.doi.org/10.1145/2755573.2755607.

cessing large data sets. A MapReduce computation begins with data being randomly (or arbitrarily) assigned to a set of machines. The data is processed in successive rounds. During a round, the dataset is processed in parallel across the machines without inter-machine communication. Communication occurs between the machines only during successive rounds. Along with being widely used in practice, MapReduce has recently been of interest to the theoretical and machine learning communities [1–3, 5, 7, 9–12]. A formal computational model of the MapReduce framework was given in [9]. The main parameters of the model are that the number of machines and memory on the machines are sublinear in the input size to the problem; a natural constraint for problems where the data is assumed to be large. The computation performed during a round is assumed to take a polynomial time and the goal is to minimize the number of rounds, the main time bottleneck in MapReduce computations. See [10] for details of the formal model. Ideally, an algorithm runs in a small constant number of rounds. Notice that by forcing the machine to have sublinear memory renders the adaptation of sequential algorithms to the MapReduce setting challenging. Further, the formal parameters of the model enforce the constraint that no machine ever sees the entire input to the problem over the entire computation, forcing the algorithm designer to use a highly parallelized algorithm.

The MapReduce framework is widely used by practitioners for clustering large data sets [5, 10, 15]. Unfortunately, known sequential algorithm techniques for the k-center problem cannot be efficiently implemented in the MapReduce setting. For example, one well known k-center algorithm starts with a set $C = \emptyset$. The algorithm begins by adding an arbitrary point form U to C. Then, the algorithm iteratively adds the point u from U to C such that $d(u, C)$ is maximized until $|C| = k$. Any naive implementation of the this algorithm in the MapReduce setting would be quite inefficient, running in $\Theta(k)$ rounds. This is because in each step of the algorithm, the point chosen is dependent on the previous points chosen to be in C. Due to this, an adaptation of the algorithm to MapReduce would only add a single point to C in one round.

To have an fast efficient MapReduce algorithm for the k-center problem, it is required that many points can be added to the solution set in one round. However, to do this, new algorithmic techniques are required beyond known sequential techniques. Previously, [5] considered the k-center clustering in MapReduce for the first time. This work showed an $O(1)$-round algorithm by iteratively sampling from the universe U to construct a sublinear sized set S that is a sketch of the original universe U. After constructing S in a distributed fashion, the algorithm then clusters S on a single machine using a known sequential k-center algorithm, resulting in a 10-approximation for the k-center problem in MapReduce in $O(1)$ rounds.

The work of [5] was the first to address the k-center problem in MapReduce theoretically. However, the work left several open questions. In particular, is there an algorithm that returns the best possible 2-approximate clustering in $O(1)$-rounds? Further, the k-center with outliers problem has not been previously considered in MapReduce. Can one design an efficient approximation algorithm for k-center with outliers in MapReduce?

Results: In this work, we consider the k-center problem in the MapReduce setting and its generalization with outliers. Throughout this work, we assume that the distance between points is given by oracle access to the function d and that the oracle can be stored on the machines without using additional memory. This is typically the case, for instance, if the points are in Euclidean space. Our work begins by showing a computationally simple MapReduce algorithm that gives the best possible 2-approximation to the k-center problem in MapReduce if the value of the of the optimal solution, OPT, is known in advance. This algorithm deviates from previous work [5] by not constructing a sketch of the universe U, but rather using a sampling technique to effectively simulate a known sequential greedy algorithm the k-center problem.

For all of our algorithms, we state the minimum memory the algorithm requires on the machines, which is sublinear. All of our algorithms only require that the total number of machines is such that the entire dataset can be stored across all the machines. We note that the memory requirement implicitly assumes that k, the number of clusters, is small. For problems where the number of clusters is pre-specified, it is almost always the case that the number of clusters is assumed to be small [5, 10]. This is because, otherwise, one typically considers a clustering problem where the algorithm determines the clusters, since when the number of clusters is large one usually is not aware of the 'right' number of clusters a priori.

THEOREM 1. *There exists a 3-round MapReduce algorithm for k-center that when knowing OPT returns a 2-approximate solution. The algorithm uses $O(kn^{1/2}\log n)$ memory on each machine w.h.p. Further, the total communication required is at most $O(kn^{1/2}\log n)$ w.h.p. assuming that the data is initially stored on the machines.*

This result does require knowledge of the value of the optimal solution, OPT. However, the algorithm can guess the value of the optimal solution and run the algorithm for each guess of the optimal solution in parallel. Let Δ be the maximum distance between two points of U and the minimum distance be 1. Notice that value of Δ is an upper bound on the optimal solution's cost. The algorithm can geometrically guess the value of the optimal solution by powers of $(1+\epsilon)$ for some $\epsilon > 0$, $(1+\epsilon)^0, (1+\epsilon)^1, ..., (1+\epsilon)^{\log_{1+\epsilon}\Delta}$, and run the algorithm for each possible guess. By increasing the communication by a $O(\log_{1+\epsilon}\Delta)$ factor and the approximation $(1+\epsilon)$ factor, the algorithm can simulate the knowledge of OPT thereby yielding a $2(1+\epsilon)$-approximate solution.

Unfortunately, this result could be seen as unsatisfactory if the maximum distance between points, Δ is very large since one cannot preform the $O(\log_{1+\epsilon}\Delta)$ guesses of OPT in parallel. Due to this, we extend the previous algorithm to not require information about the value of the optimal solution. Here we show an intricate way to circumvent the actual knowledge of OPT by using an additional round.

THEOREM 2. *There exists a 4-round MapReduce algorithm for k-center that returns a 2-approximate solution and uses memory at most $O(kn^{1/2}\log n)$ on each machine w.h.p. Further, the total communication required is at most $O(k^2 n^{1/2}\log n)$ w.h.p. assuming that the data is initially stored on the machines.*

Finally, we consider the k-center problem with outliers for the first time in the MapReduce setting. Here we give a result assuming that the algorithm guesses the value of the optimal solution in parallel. As before, we can simulate the knowledge of OPT by guessing the value of OPT and running the algorithm in parallel for each guess. Here the algorithm requires an additional z factor in memory. Recall that z is the number of outliers. Although it could be the case that the number of outliers is large in practice, our work shows that if z is smaller than $O(n^{1/2-\epsilon})$ then there is an efficient MapReduce algorithm that uses at most $\tilde{O}(n^{1-\epsilon})$ memory for any $\epsilon > 0$.

THEOREM 3. *There exists a 3-round MapReduce algorithm for k-center with outliers that when knowing* OPT *returns a 4-approximate solution and uses memory at most* $O(kzn^{1/2}\log n)$ *on each machine w.h.p. Further, the total communication required is at most* $O(kzn^{1/2}\log n)$ *w.h.p. assuming that the data is initially stored on the machines.*

2. K-CENTER KNOWING OPT

In this section, to give a taste of our results, we present an algorithm, along with a sketch of the analyisis, that produces a 2-approximate solution for the k-center problem in 2-rounds assuming it knows the value, OPT, of the optimal solution. If the maximum distance between any two points is polynomially bounded then by guessing $\Theta(\log_{1+\epsilon}\Delta)$ values for OPT and running this algorithm for each guess of OPT in parallel the algorithm will produce a $(2+\epsilon)$-approximation in $O(1)$-rounds for any $\epsilon > 0$.

Algorithm: Set $S = S_1 = S_2 = \emptyset$. The algorithm samples each point in U independently with probability $1/n^{1/2}$ and maps them to a single machine. Let X_1 be the set of sampled points. The sampling can be done in the first map phase. In the reduce phase, the machine with the sampled points runs the following greedy algorithm. It starts with a solution set S and first adds an arbitrary point from X_1 to S. Then it iteratively adds any point $i \in X_1$ to S if $d(S,i) > 2\mathrm{OPT}$ and $|S| < k$. Let S_1 be the set S the algorithm has computed when no point in X_1 could be added to S. If $|S_1| = k$, then the algorithm output S_1. Otherwise, in the next round, the algorithm checks for each points i if $d(S_1,i) > 2\mathrm{OPT}$. Let $X_2 := \{i \in U \mid d(S_1,i) > 2\mathrm{OPT}\}$ be this set of points. One can determine X_2 by sending S_1 to each machine and if the condition $d(S_1,i) > 2\mathrm{OPT}$ holds for each point i in U on this machine. Then the algorithm maps all the points in X_2 and S_1 to a single machine. Let $S_2 = S_1$. The points in X_2 are iteratively added to S_2 where, at any time, a point $i \in X_2$ is added if $d(i,S_2) > 2\mathrm{OPT}$ and $|S_2| < k$. Let S_2 be the resulting set. The algorithm outputs S_2.

Sketch of Analysis: We first show that X_1 includes $O(n^{1/2}\log n)$ points w.h.p. This is an easy consequence of standard Chernoff bounds. Then, we bound the size of the set X_2: If $|S_1| < k$ after the first phase of the algorithm, then set X_2 includes at most $O(kn^{1/2}\log n)$ points w.h.p. Intuitively, there cannot be many points that are 'far' from the points in X_1 w.h.p. This is because the algorithm then would have sampled some of these points. Then, the memory usage and communication cost claimed in Theorem 1 easily follow.

Now it remains to show our algorithm gives a 2-approximation. Let S^* be the set output by the algorithm, which is output as S_1 at the end of the first phase if $|S_1| = k$ and otherwise $S^* = S_2$ at the end of the algorithm. Notice that whenever the algorithm adds a point to the set S_1 it

never gets removed. The same holds for S_2 and $S_1 \cup S_2 = S^*$. Further, notice after the first iteration of the algorithm, any point i such that $d(S_1,i) > 2\mathrm{OPT}$ is in the set X_2. Thus, the only points discarded after the first phase are close to the set S_1. Say that there is some point $i \in U$ such that $d(S^*,i) > 2\mathrm{OPT}$. Since i would have been in the set X_2, it must be the case that $|S^*| = k$. Further, knowing that a point is only added to the solution if its distance is greater than $2\mathrm{OPT}$ from the points already in the solution set, there must be $k + 1$ points of distance greater than $2\mathrm{OPT}$ from each other. Two of these points must be served by the same center in the optimal solution, but, by the triangle inequality, this contradicts the definition of OPT.

Acknowledgements. The first author's research was supported in part by NSF grant CCF-1409130.

3. REFERENCES

[1] A. Andoni, A. Nikolov, K. Onak, and G. Yaroslavtsev. Parallel algorithms for geometric graph problems. In *STOC*, pages 574–583, 2014.

[2] B. Bahmani, B. Moseley, A. Vattani, R. Kumar, and S. Vassilvitskii. Scalable k-means++. *PVLDB*, 5(7):622–633, 2012.

[3] M. Balcan, S. Ehrlich, and Y. Liang. Distributed k-means and k-median clustering on general communication topologies. In *NIPS*, pages 1995–2003, 2013.

[4] M. Charikar, S. Khuller, D. M. Mount, and G. Narasimhan. Algorithms for facility location problems with outliers. In *SODA*, pages 642–651, 2001.

[5] A. Ene, S. Im, and B. Moseley. Fast clustering using MapReduce. In *KDD*, pages 681–689, 2011.

[6] T. F. Gonzalez. Clustering to minimize the maximum intercluster distance. *Theoretical Computer Science*, 38(0):293 – 306, 1985.

[7] M. T. Goodrich, N. Sitchinava, and Q. Zhang. Sorting, searching, and simulation in the mapreduce framework. In *ISAAC*, pages 374–383, 2011.

[8] D. S. Hochbaum and D. B. Shmoys. A best possible heuristic for the k-center problem. *Mathematics of Operations Research*, 10(2):180–184, 1985.

[9] H. J. Karloff, S. Suri, and S. Vassilvitskii. A model of computation for MapReduce. In *SODA*, pages 938–948, 2010.

[10] R. Kumar, B. Moseley, S. Vassilvitskii, and A. Vattani. Fast greedy algorithms in mapreduce and streaming. In *SPAA*, pages 1–10, 2013.

[11] S. Lattanzi, B. Moseley, S. Suri, and S. Vassilvitskii. Filtering: A method for solving graph problems in MapReduce. In *SPAA*, pages 85–94, 2011.

[12] B. Mirzasoleiman, A. Karbasi, R. Sarkar, and A. Krause. Distributed submodular maximization: Identifying representative elements in massive data. In *NIPS*, pages 2049–2057, 2013.

[13] T. White. *Hadoop: The Definitive Guide*. O'Reilly Media, 2009.

[14] R. Xu and D. Wunsch. Survey of Clustering Algorithms. *IEEE Trans Neural Netw*, 16(3):645–678, 2005.

[15] W. Zhao, H. Ma, and Q. He. In M. G. Jaatun, G. Zhao, and C. Rong, editors, *CloudCom*.

Brief Announcement: Fair Adaptive Parallelism for Concurrent Transactional Memory Applications

Amin Mohtasham
amohtasham@gsd.inesc-id.pt

João Barreto
joao.barreto@tecnico.ulisboa.pt

INESC-ID Lisboa/ Instituto Superior Técnico, Universidade de Lisboa, Portugal

ABSTRACT

Modern parallel machines are likely to run multiple parallel processes together. However, collocating parallel processes in a single machine can easily result in cross-process and cross-thread interferences that can dramatically degrade the system's performance. Such interferences can be mitigated by dynamically adjusting each process' parallelism towards a fair and efficient configuration.

We propose a decentralized method for adaptive parallelism for collocated transactional multi-threaded processes. Inspired by well-known results from flow/congestion control mechanisms in communication networks, our technique adopts a hill-climbing strategy that was previously unexplored in the context of adaptive parallelism.

Categories and Subject Descriptors

D.1.3 [**Software**]: Programming Techniques—*Concurrent Programming*

Keywords

concurrency control; feedback-driven systems; resource allocation; software transactional memory

1. INTRODUCTION

The processor industry is converging to an important technology shift: to go for more, yet simpler, cores per chip. Multi-core architectures are already the norm for most of the commodity computing devices. In a near future, many-core chips with hundreds or thousands of simple cores are expected to be an affordable reality [3].

Effectively harnessing such increasingly-parallel machines calls for parallel workloads. As recent studies observe, there are trends that suggest that modern multi/many-core machines will most likely run multiple parallel processes together, rather than a single parallel process alone at a time. Firstly, many parallel applications do not scale to the parallelism levels that will be the affordable norm in a near future [8, 14]. Hence, making effective use of a multi/many-core machine will imply running multiple parallel processes together [9]. Secondly, since many workloads exhibit fluctuating parallelism levels, collocating multiple workloads in the same machine leads to a more efficient use of hardware resources. Cloud computing is, perhaps, the strongest example of this trend, where many providers follow successful resource overbooking practices [17].

However, collocating parallel processes in a single machine can lead to interferences caused by different factors: (*i*) Higher contention in hardware resources, such as memory and input/output, increase execution overheads [13]; (*ii*) When concurrent shared objects exist, synchronization overheads increase with the number of threads sharing such locations [6, 1]; (*iii*) Frequent context switches [12] and unfair resource allocation between heterogeneous workloads [9], when there are more threads than hardware cores.

A number of studies have shown that the above interferences can substantially impact performance and scalability for many workloads [9, 4].

Recently proposed techniques try to prevent the above factors by dynamically adapt the parallelism level of parallel processes [6, 1, 9]. Conceptually, a monitoring component tries to determine the optimal parallelism level for a process and enforces that level by ordering the process to bound the number of active threads to such a level. The ultimate goal is to lead the parallel system to reduce the some of above sources of interference, thus using hardware resources more efficiently and achieving better performance.

However, finding the optimal parallelism level for each process in a system is not trivial, for a number of reasons. First, workloads can change dynamically, thereby calling for constant adaptation in parallelism levels. Furthermore, information about each process' behavior (e.g., throughput and contention within the process' threads) and the system's load (e.g., number of software threads and available resources) is not available at the same place: the kernel has the information about all threads and processes; while each process knows about the throughput of its tasks. Finally, even if the above information is obtained at the same place, this information is not complete enough to precisely determine the optimal parallelism levels in a system. Hence, hill-climbing approaches that, by gradually increasing or decreasing the actual parallelism level of each process, try to reach close to optimal parallelism levels, are usually employed.

We advocate that an adequate adaptive parallelism solution that is both precise and scalable to highly-parallel sys-

SPAA '15 , June 13-15, 2015, Portland, OR, USA.
ACM 978-1-4503-3588-1/15/06.
http://dx.doi.org/10.1145/2755573.2755609.

tems should ideally: (*i*) allow processes to dynamically and quickly adapt their parallelism level to the changes in the system's workloads or available system resources; (*ii*) converge to an efficient state, which optimizes global system throughput by avoiding system overload; (*iii*) be fair, in the sense that processes receive an even share of hardware contexts unless their workload demand for a lower parallelism level; (*iv*) achieve the above goals even if a subset of the processes in the system does not cooperate, i.e. does not adopt the adaptive parallelism scheme; and (*v*) not rely on a centralized component (such as a centralized kernel) in order to avoid introducing a new scalability bottleneck.

Herein we focus on adaptive parallelism on a prominent class of parallel applications: those based on *transactional memory* (TM) [11]. TM has proven itself as a promising paradigm for parallel programming, combining ease of programming with scalability [10].

A number of recent papers propose solutions for adaptive parallelism in transactional memory systems [6, 1, 16]. A decisive element in their effectiveness is the hill-climbing strategy. However, it is perhaps surprising to observe that, among such papers, the proposed solutions are evaluated only in single-process scenarios, thus neglecting cross-process interference in multi-process scenarios.

Inspired by results from the well-studied problem of flow/-congestion control in data communication networks, we devise a new adaptive parallelism scheme. Our solution is fully decentralized, as it relies on unilateral taken at each cooperating process, based on that process' observations. It aims at converging the set of cooperating processes to an efficient and fair configuration, even under dynamic and heterogeneous workloads. This holds even if a subset of processes in the system does not adopt our solution.

2. ADAPTIVE PARALLELISM WITH AIMD

Our method is inspired by congestion control mechanisms designed for data transmission in communication networks. The next section starts by a brief overview on the concepts and solutions used that context, establishing the analogy to the problem of adaptive parallelism. The following section then proposes our solution to adaptive parallelism.

2.1 From Flow/Congestion Control in Data Networks to Adaptive Parallelism

In data networks, congestion occurs when a link or a receiver node is carrying so much data that it can not afford handling more data and as a result its quality of service drops. Among other mechanisms, the adaptive sliding window used by the TCP protocol is proven to be a practical and efficient way to deal with the congestion problem [15].

In TCP, each sender node maintains a sliding window. The size of such window determines the maximum number of packets that a node can send before receiving their acknowledgment [15].

To avoid network congestion, the sender continually adjusts its sliding window size according to feedback it gets from the network, such as by timeouts and packet losses.

The basic window management scheme employed by TCP is known as *additive-increase/multiplicative-decrease (AIMD)*. AIMD combines linear growth of the sliding window with an exponential reduction when congestion occurs. With basic AIMD, the sender node increases the window size by 1 (i.e., AD) once each sent message is acknowledged by the receiver.

In contrast, the sender node halves the window size (i.e., MD) when it learns about a lost packet.

It has been shown that, using AIMD, multiple data flows (from multiple senders) eventually converge to a fair and efficient allocation of the bandwidth of a contended link [5].

Interestingly, the natural alternatives to AIMD such as *multiplicative-increase/multiplicative-decrease* and *additive-increase/additive-decrease* do not converge [5].

There is actually an interesting analogy between the problems of flow/congestion control in data networks and adaptive parallelism in multi/many-core systems.

Whereas the transmission rate in a physical network is physically limited by the network's bandwidth, the processing power in a multi/many-core processor is limited by the available hardware resources (e.g., CPU cores). In the former, connections at different nodes contend for the available bandwidth; in the latter, processes (and their threads) fight for the available hardware resources. In a data network, nodes wish to transmit data packets at a high data transmission rate; in a parallel system, processes aim at executing and committing computation tasks (e.g., a transaction in a transactional program) with the highest performance. In both contexts, over-utilization of the physical resources can lead to system overload, which can substantially degrade its throughput or even cause the system to collapse.

Hence, it is natural to transpose the AIMD strategy to the context of systems running collocated parallel processes. We propose a scheme to employ AIMD in such a context next.

2.2 Adaptive Parallelism Algorithm

There is a major difference between congestion control and adaptive parallelism problems, which makes it non-trivial to directly employ TCP schemes. In TCP, the congestion control mechanism is invoked upon a packet-loss event, which is a very accurate source of information about the network congestion. Such an event does not exist in parallel systems, so choosing the suitable metrics and determining when and how to take decisions based on them is needed to be able to employ TCP schemes.

In this section we present our adaptive parallelism scheme. We consider a multi/many-core system running collocated processes. Among such processes, some may not be collaborating with our adaptive parallelism scheme. Hereafter, we only focus on the collaborating processes. We assume each process runs a multi-threaded program adopting the thread pool pattern [7]. In a thread pool pattern, each process wishes to execute a number of tasks. In its simplest form, a shared queue maintains the tasks awaiting execution; more intricate variants exist, though [2]. Initially, the process spawns a number of worker threads to execute the tasks pending in the queue. As soon as a worker thread completes its current task, it will request the next task from the queue until all tasks have been completed. The worker thread can then terminate, or block until there are new tasks available. Since tasks may work on shared data, tasks may include transactions that ensure safe synchronization of concurrent accesses to shared data.

Each collaborating process runs a monitoring thread that is responsible for running the adaptive parallelism algorithm. It periodically measures the process' commit rate. After each measurement, it compares the new rate with the previous one. If there is no slowdown, the worker thread increases the number of parallel active threads by 1 (i.e., additive increase, AI), but in case of slowdown, it divides the number of active threads by a constant factor (i.e., multiplicative decrease, MD). The monitoring thread is created with higher priority than other threads inside the thread pool. This ensures that, in case of system over-subscription, the monitoring thread gets to do its duty.

To measure the commit rate, each worker thread maintains a counter variable, initialized to 0. At each commit, the thread increases its counter by one. At each periodic round, the monitoring thread reads all the thread-specific counters from the threads of the monitored process, adds them up and subtracts with the aggregated commit count it had observed in the previous round. This determines the average commit rate in the period that is just completing.

It is worth noting that, for each thread's counter, only that thread can update such a counter; the monitoring thread only reads from such counters, and the exploratory nature of the scheme tolerates occasional stale reads due to cache incoherencies. Therefore, maintaining the commit counters is very lightweight - no atomic instructions are necessary.

3. CONCLUDING REMARKS

Inspired by well-known flow/congestion control techniques in data networks, we propose a decentralized method for adaptive parallelism for collocated transactional multi-threaded processes. In the proposed method, co-existing parallel processes adjust their parallelism level in order to maximize their throughput, while preserving the fairness.

Our preliminary evaluation shows that our method achieves speed-up of over state-of-the-art adaptive parallelism techniques in multi-process environments, while exhibiting higher adaptivity and fairness, in the presence of collaborative or non-collaborative processes.

Although we focus on the specific case of programs based on the transactional memory paradigm, our method is easily extensible to any parallel programming paradigm. The key insight is that, as long as there are meaningful and precise ways of measuring the throughput of each thread, it can serve as the input to our hill-climbing method.

4. ACKNOWLEDGMENTS

This work was supported by national funds through Fundação para a Ciência e a Tecnologia (FCT), under projects UID/CEC/50021/2013 and GreenTM (EXPL/EEI-ESS/-0361/2013).

5. REFERENCES

[1] M. Ansari, M. Luján, C. Kotselidis, K. Jarvis, C. Kirkham, and I. Watson. Robust adaptation to available parallelism in transactional memory applications. In *Transactions on High-Performance Embedded Architectures and Compilers III*, volume 6590 of *Lecture Notes in Computer Science*, pages 236–255. Springer Berlin Heidelberg, 2011.

[2] R. D. Blumofe, C. F. Joerg, B. C. Kuszmaul, C. E. Leiserson, K. H. Randall, and Y. Zhou. Cilk: An efficient multithreaded runtime system. pages 207–216, 1995.

[3] S. Borkar. Thousand core chips: A technology perspective. In *Proceedings of the 44th Annual Design Automation Conference*, pages 746–749. ACM, 2007.

[4] D. Chandra, F. Guo, S. Kim, and Y. Solihin. Predicting inter-thread cache contention on a chip multi-processor architecture. In *Proceedings of the 11th International Symposium on High-Performance Computer Architecture*, pages 340–351. IEEE Computer Society, 2005.

[5] D.-M. Chiu and R. Jain. Analysis of the increase and decrease algorithms for congestion avoidance in computer networks. *Computer Networks and ISDN systems*, 17(1):1–14, 1989.

[6] D. Didona, P. Felber, D. Harmanci, P. Romano, and J. Schenker. Identifying the optimal level of parallelism in transactional memory applications. In *Networked Systems*, volume 7853 of *Lecture Notes in Computer Science*, pages 233–247. Springer Berlin Heidelberg, 2013.

[7] R. P. Garg and I. Sharapov. *Techniques for Optimizing Applications: High Performance Computing*. Prentice Hall PTR, 2001.

[8] R. Guerraoui, M. Kapalka, and J. Vitek. STMBench7: A benchmark for software transactional memory. In *Proceedings of the 2nd ACM SIGOPS/EuroSys European Conference on Computer Systems*, pages 315–324. ACM, 2007.

[9] T. Harris, M. Maas, and V. J. Marathe. Callisto: Co-scheduling parallel runtime systems. In *Proceedings of the 9th European Conference on Computer Systems*, pages 1–24. ACM, 2014.

[10] M. Herlihy, V. Luchangco, M. Moir, and W. N. Scherer, III. Software transactional memory for dynamic-sized data structures. In *Proceedings of the 22nd Annual Symposium on Principles of Distributed Computing*, pages 92–101. ACM, 2003.

[11] M. Herlihy and J. E. B. Moss. Transactional memory: Architectural support for lock-free data structures. In *Proceedings of the 20th Annual International Symposium on Computer Architecture*, pages 289–300. ACM, 1993.

[12] C. Li, C. Ding, and K. Shen. Quantifying the cost of context switch. In *Proceedings of the 2007 Workshop on Experimental Computer Science*. ACM, 2007.

[13] M. A. Marsan, G. Balbo, G. Conte, and F. Gregoretti. Modeling bus contention and memory interference in a multiprocessor system. *IEEE Transactions on Computers*, 32(1):60–72, 1983.

[14] C. C. Minh, J. Chung, C. Kozyrakis, and K. Olukotun. STAMP: Stanford transactional applications for multi-processing. In *Proceedings of the 2008 IEEE International Symposium on Workload Characterization*, pages 35–46. IEEE Computer Society, 2008.

[15] L. L. Peterson and B. S. Davie. *Computer Networks: A Systems Approach*. Elsevier, 2007.

[16] K. Ravichandran and S. Pande. F2C2-STM: Flux-based feedback-driven concurrency control for STMs. In *Proceedings of the 28th International Parallel and Distributed Processing Symposium*, pages 927–938. IEEE Computer Society, 2014.

[17] L. Tomás and J. Tordsson. Improving cloud infrastructure utilization through overbooking. In *Proceedings of the ACM Cloud and Autonomic Computing Conference*, pages 1–5. ACM, 2013.

Brief Announcement: Managing Resource Limitation of Best-Effort HTM

Mohamed Mohamedin, Roberto Palmieri, Ahmed Hassan, Binoy Ravindran
Virginia Tech
Blacksburg, VA
{mohamedin,robertop,hassan84,binoy}@vt.edu

ABSTRACT

The first release of hardware transactional memory (HTM) as commodity processor posed the question of how to efficiently handle its best-effort nature. In this paper we present Part-HTM, the first hybrid transactional memory protocol that solves the problem of transactions aborted due to the resource limitations (space/time) of current best-effort HTM. The basic idea of Part-HTM is to partition those transactions into multiple sub-transactions, which can likely be committed in hardware. Due to the eager nature of HTM, we designed a low-overhead software framework to preserve transaction's correctness (with and without opacity).

Categories and Subject Descriptors

D.1.3 [**Programming Techniques**]: Concurrent Programming; D.3.3 [**Programming Languages**]: Language Constructs and Features

Keywords

Transactional Memory, Hardware Transactions, Concurrency

1. INTRODUCTION

Transactional Memory (TM) [4] is one of the most attractive recent innovations in the area of concurrent and transactional applications. TM is a support that programmers can exploit while developing parallel applications so that the hard problem of synchronizing different threads, which operate on shared objects, is solved.

Very recently two events confirmed TM as a practical alternative to the manual implementation of thread synchronization: first, *GCC* – the famous GNU compiler, embedded interfaces for executing atomic blocks since its version 4.7; second, Intel released to the customer market the *Haswell* processor equipped with *Transactional Synchronization Extensions* (TSX) [7], which allow the execution of transactions directly on the hardware through an enriched hardware cache-coherence protocol.

Hardware transactions (or HTM transactions) are much faster than their software version because the conflict resolution is inherently provided by the hardware cache-coherence protocol; however, their downside is that they do not have commit guarantees, therefore they may fail repeatedly, and for this reason they are categorized as *best-effort*. The eventual commit of an HTM transaction is guaranteed through a software execution defined by the programmer (called *fallback path*). The default fallback path consists of executing the transaction protected by a single global lock (called GL-software path). In addition, there are other proposals that fall back to a hybrid-HTM scheme [5, 1].

Leveraging the experience learnt from recent papers on HTM [2, 1], three reasons that force a transaction to abort have been identified: *conflict*, *capacity*, and *other*. Conflict failure occurs when two transactions access the same object and at least one of them wants to write it; a transaction is aborted for capacity if the number of cache-lines accessed is higher than the maximum allowed; and any extra hardware intervention, including interrupts, is also a cause of abort.

Many recent papers propose solutions to handle aborts due to conflict efficiently (e.g., [1, 5]), and to tune the number of retries a transaction running in hardware has to accomplish before falling back to the software path [2]. Despite this body of work, one of the main unsolved problems of best-effort HTM is that there are transactions that, by nature and due to the characteristics of the underlying architecture, are impossible to be committed as hardware transactions. Examples include transactions that require non-trivial execution time even accessing few objects and thus they are aborted due to a timer interrupt (which triggers the actions of the OS scheduler); or those transactions accessing several objects, such that the problem of exceeding the cache size arises (*capacity* failure). We group these two types of failures into one superset, where, in general, a hardware transaction is aborted if the amount of resources, in terms of space and/or time required to commit, are not available. We name this superset as *resource* failures.

None of the past works target this class of aborted transactions and we turn this observation into our core motivation: solving the problem of resource failures in HTM. To pursue this goal, we propose PART-HTM, an innovative transaction processing scheme, which prevents those transactions that cannot be executed as HTM due to space and/or time limitation to fall back to the GL-software path, and commit them still exploiting the advantages of HTM.

PART-HTM's core idea is to first run transactions as HTM and, for those that abort due to resource limitations, a partitioning scheme is adopted to divide the original transaction into multiple, thus smaller, HTM transactions (called sub-HTM), which can be easily committed. However, when a sub-HTM transaction commits, its objects are immediately made visible to others and this inevitably jeopardizes the isolation guarantees of the original transaction. We solve this problem by means of a software framework that prevents other transactions from accessing (or from committing after having accessed) those committed (but still locked) objects.

This framework is designed to be low overhead: a heavy instrumentation would annul the advantages of HTM, falling back into the drawbacks of adopting a pure STM implementation. PART-HTM uses locks, to isolate new objects written by sub-HTM transactions from others, and a slight instrumentation of read/write operations using cache-aligned signature-based structures, to keep track of any accessed object. In addition, a software validation is performed to serialize all sub-HTM transactions at a single point in time.

With this limited overhead, PART-HTM gives performance close to pure HTM transactions, in scenarios where HTM transactions are likely to commit without falling back to the software path, and better than pure STM transactions, where HTM transactions repeatedly fail. This latter goal is reached exploiting sub-HTM transactions, which are indeed faster than any instrumented software transactions. In other words, PART-HTM's performance gains from HTM's advantages even for those transactions that are not originally suited for HTM due to resource failures.

Opacity [3] is the reference correctness criterion for TM implementations because it avoids any inconsistency during the execution, independently from the final transaction outcome (either commit or abort). However, ensuring opacity in PART-HTM is challenging because its overhead could nullify the achieved benefits. While acknowledging the importance of an opaque hybrid-TM protocol, in this paper we briefly introduce two versions of PART-HTM. One aims at obtaining the best performance by relaxing opacity in favor of serializability, the well-known consistency criterion for online transaction processing, and by relying on the HTM protection mechanism (i.e., sandboxing), which protects from faulty computations (e.g., division by zero). In the second version, we enriched PART-HTM for ensuring opacity but, at the same time, we present a set of innovations (e.g., *address-embedded* write locks) for reducing the transaction's memory footprint so that the overhead is kept limited (less than the achievable gain).

2. PROBLEM STATEMENT

In this section we briefly overview the principles of Intel's HTM transactions in order to highlight their limitations and motivate our proposal. The current Intel HTM implementation of the Haswell processor, also called Intel Haswell Restricted Transactional Memory (RTM) [7], is a best-effort HTM, namely no transaction is guaranteed to eventually commit. In particular, it enforces space and time limitations. Haswell's RTM uses L1 cache (32KB) as a transactional buffer for read and write operations. Accessed cache-lines are marked as "monitored" whenever accessed. This way, the cache-line size is indeed the granularity used for detecting conflicts. When two transactions need the same cache-line and at least one wants to write it, an abort occurs. When this happens, the application is notified and

the transaction can restart as HTM or can fall back to a software path.

In addition to those aborts due to data conflicts, HTM transactions can be aborted for other reasons. Any cache-line eviction (e.g., due to cache-associativity) of written memory locations causes the transaction to abort (however there is a specialized buffer for handling the eviction of a memory location previously read, but not written). This means that write operations of hardware transactions are limited in space by the size of the L1 cache. However, read operations can go beyond the L1 cache capacity by exploiting the L2 cache. Also, any hardware interrupt, including the interrupts from timers, forces HTM transactions to abort. We name the union of these two causes as *resource* limitation and in this paper we propose a solution for that.

3. ALGORITHM DESIGN

Despite the simple main idea of partitioning a transaction into smaller hardware sub-transactions, executing them efficiently in a way such that the global transaction's isolation and consistency is preserved poses a challenging research problem. In this section we describe the design principles that compose the base of PART-HTM, as well as the high level transaction execution flow. Hereafter, we refer to the original (single block) transaction as a *global* transaction and the smaller sub-transactions as *sub-HTM transactions*.

A memory transaction is a sequence of read and write operations on shared data that should appear as atomically executed at a point in time between its beginning and its completion, and in isolation from other transactions. This also entails that changes on the shared objects performed by a transaction should not be accessible (visible) to other transactions until that transaction is allowed to commit. The latter point clashes with the above idea: when a sub-HTM transaction T_{S1} of a global transaction T commits, its written objects are applied directly to the shared memory, by nature. This allows other transactions to potentially access these values, thus breaking the isolation of T. Moreover, once T_{S1} is committed, there is no record of its read/written objects during the rest of T's execution, therefore also T's correctness becomes hard to enforce.

All these problems can be trivially solved by instrumenting HTM operations for populating the same meta-data commonly used by STM protocols for tracking accesses and handling conflicts. However, applying existing STM solutions can easily lead to HTM losing its effectiveness and, consequently, lead to poor performance. In the following we point out some of these reasons:

- STM meta-data are not designed for minimizing the impact on memory capacity. Adopting them for solving our problem would stretch both the transaction execution time and the number of cache-lines needed, thus consuming precious HTM resources.
- HTM already provides a conflict detection mechanism faster than any software-based contention manager.
- HTM monitors any memory access within the transaction, including those on the meta-data or local variables, which takes the flexibility for implementing smart contention policies away from the programmer.

PART-HTM faces the challenge of how to exploit the efficiency of sub-HTM transactions, which write in-place to the shared memory, by minimizing the overhead of the instrumentation needed for maintaining the isolation and correctness of global transactions, and taking into account the above points. Given that HTM transactions commit directly to the shared memory and PART-HTM always executes transactions using HTM (except when the GL-software path is invoked), we opt for using an *eager* approach. PART-HTM first executes incoming transactions as HTM with few instrumentations (called *first-trial* HTM transactions). In case they experience a resource failure, then our software framework "kicks in" by splitting them.

Let T^x be a transaction aborted for resource limitations, and let $T_1^x, T_2^x, \ldots, T_n^x$ be the sub-HTM transactions obtained by partitioning T^x. Let T_y^x be a generic sub-HTM transaction. At the core of PART-HTM there is a software component that manages the execution of T^x's sub-HTM transactions. Specifically, it is in charge of: *1)* detecting accesses that are conflicting with any T_y^x already committed; *2)* preventing any other transaction T^k from reading and committing or overwriting values created by T_y^x before T^x is committed; and *3)* executing T^x in a way the transaction observes a consistent state of the memory.

The software framework does not handle conflicts that happen on T_y^x's accessed objects when T_y^x is still running; the HTM's hardware contention management protocol solves them efficiently. This is the main benefit of our approach over a pure STM fallback implementation.

For the achievement of the above goals, the software framework needs a hint about objects accessed by sub-HTM transactions. In order to do that, we do not use the classical address/value-based read-set or write-set as commonly adopted by STM implementations; rather we rely only on cache-aligned Bloom-filter-based meta-data (just Bloom-filter hereafter) to keep track of read/write accesses. Just before committing, a sub-HTM transaction updates a shared Bloom-filter for notifying its written objects, so that no other transaction can access them.

Two Bloom-filters per global transaction are used for recording the objects read and written by its sub-HTM transactions. In fact, these Bloom-filters are passed by the framework from one sub-HTM transaction to another. Therefore, they are not globally visible outside the transaction. The purpose of these Bloom-filters is to let read/written objects survive even after the commit of a sub-HTM transaction, allowing the framework to check the validity of the global transaction at any time. A value-based undo-log is kept for handling the abort of a transaction having sub-HTM transactions already committed.

As mentioned before, in this paper we provide also a version of PART-HTM (called PART-HTM-O) that guarantees opacity by introducing some (but limited) overheads. Specifically, any sub-HTM transaction of PART-HTM-O performs the following two additional checks. First, once an object is accessed by a sub-HTM transaction, the existence of a write lock is immediately detected. In order to minimize the impact on the memory footprint, we introduce the *address-embedded* write locks, which are locks that do not use additional memory location, whereas they are implemented by "stealing" the last bits from the accessed address. This prevents any false conflicts on the shared write locks set. Second, a sub-HTM transaction is immediately aborted once a global transaction commits. This is achieved leveraging the HTM conflict resolution itself by monitoring a shared timestamp, incremented anytime a global transaction commits, inside sub-HTM transactions.

4. PRELIMINARY EVALUATION

Figure 1 plots the results of PART-HTM using the Labyrinth application of the STAMP benchmark [6]. We selected this application because more than half of the generated transactions in Labyrinth are large and long, thus their original version cannot complete using HTM.

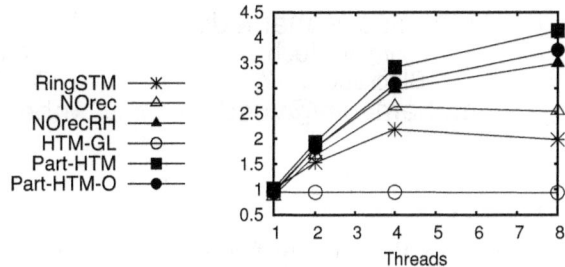

Figure 1: Speed-up over sequential (non-transactional) execution using Labyrinth of STAMP.

Table 1 reports the breakdown of the reason transactions are aborted in Labyrinth using HTM and PART-HTM. Here we can see how the percentage of HTM transactions aborted for both *capacity* and *other* forms more than 91% of all aborts, forcing HTM to often execute its GL-software path. PART-HTM solves this issue.

	Conflict	Capacity	Explicit	Other
HTM-GL	10.11%	70.76%	0.04%	19.09%
PART-HTM	93.95%	1.09%	1.14%	3.82%

Table 1: Decomposition of aborted transactions using Labyrinth and 4 threads.

5. ACKNOWLEDGMENTS

Authors would like to thank Alexander Matveev for the important feedback. This work is supported in part by US National Science Foundation under grant CNS 1217385.

6. REFERENCES

[1] I. Calciu, J. Gottschlich, T. Shpeisman, G. Pokam, and M. Herlihy. Invyswell: A hybrid transactional memory for haswell's restricted transactional memory. In *PACT*, pages 187–200, 2014.

[2] N. Diegues and P. Romano. Self-tuning intel transactional synchronization extensions. In *ICAC*, pages 209–219, 2014.

[3] R. Guerraoui and M. Kapalka. On the correctness of transactional memory. In *PPoPP*, pages 175–184, 2008.

[4] T. Harris, J. Larus, and R. Rajwar. Transactional memory, 2nd edition. *Synthesis Lectures on Computer Architecture*, 5(1), 2010.

[5] A. Matveev and N. Shavit. Reduced hardware transactions: A new approach to hybrid transactional memory. In *SPAA*, pages 11–22, 2013.

[6] C. C. Minh, J. Chung, C. Kozyrakis, and K. Olukotun. STAMP: Stanford transactional applications for multi-processing. In *IISWC*, pages 35–46, 2008.

[7] J. Reinders. Transactional synchronization in haswell. *Intel Software Network.*, 2012.

Brief Announcement: On Scheduling Best-Effort HTM Transactions

Mohamed Mohamedin
Virginia Tech
Blacksburg, VA
mohamedin@vt.edu

Roberto Palmieri
Virginia Tech
Blacksburg, VA
robertop@vt.edu

Binoy Ravindran
Virginia Tech
Blacksburg, VA
binoy@vt.edu

ABSTRACT

This paper shows the issues to face while designing contention management policies that involve best-effort hardware transactions. Also, in this paper we present Octonauts, a solution for scheduling HTM transactions without relying on on-the-fly information. Octonauts learns the objects accessed by a hardware transaction while running and it uses them in case of conflict. It also proposes an innovative scheme for optimizing the communication between transactions running in hardware and software.

Categories and Subject Descriptors

D.1.3 [**Programming Techniques**]: Concurrent Programming; D.3.3 [**Programming Languages**]: Language Constructs and Features

Keywords

Scheduling, Hardware Transactional Memory, Synchronization

1. INTRODUCTION

Transactional Memory (TM) [8] is increasingly becoming a promising technology for designing and implementing concurrent applications. Recently, TM gained more traction because hardware vendors released the first commodity processors with transactional support (i.e., hardware transactional memory or HTM): Intel *Haswell* [11], and the IBM *Power 8* [3]. The common issue of all those processors is their *best effort* nature, namely transactions are not guaranteed to progress in HTM, thus a software fallback path is a mandatory requirement, which leads to hybrid TM.

Most TM implementations achieve high concurrency when the actual contention level is low (i.e., few transactions conflict with each other). At higher contention levels, transactions abort each other more frequently and a contention manager (CM) is often required to manage concurrency. A CM is an encounter-time technique: when a transaction

conflicts with another one, the CM is consulted to decide which of the two transactions can proceed. A CM collects information about each transaction (e.g., start time, number of reads/writes, number of retries) and, according to the implemented policy, it decides priorities among conflicting transactions. This management guarantees more fairness and progress. A CM can work either during the transaction execution by using live (on the fly) information, or work prior the transaction execution. Schedulers in the latter category use information about transaction's potential working-set (reads and writes) defined a priori in order to avoid the need of solving conflicts while transactions are executing. Examples include [7, 5, 2, 13, 10, 6, 1].

The problem of defining a CM for handling HTM transactions is still not investigated because current HTM implementations embed the conflict resolution strategy entirely into the cache-coherence protocol. Roughly, *i)* the L1 cache of each CPU-core is used as a buffer for the transactional write and read operations; *ii)* the granularity used for tracking accesses is the cache line; and *iii)* the eviction and invalidation of cache lines defines when a transaction is aborted (it reproduces the idea of read-set and write-set invalidation of STM). In addition, the Intel Haswell documentation says "*Data conflicts are detected through the cache-coherence protocol. Data conflicts cause transactional aborts. In the initial implementation, the thread that detects the data conflict will transactionally abort.*". From the specification, it is impossible to unequivocally define which thread will detect the conflict as the details of the hardware cache-coherence protocol are not publicly available.

Since there is no way to change the provided HTM conflict resolution policies without modifying the hardware itself, classical CMs policies cannot be trivially ported for scheduling HTM transaction. In fact, when the hardware detects a conflict between threads (executing transactions) accessing the same cache line, the progress made by one of them is immediately aborted without giving the programmer a chance to either manage the conflict differently, or extract any runtime information (i.e., any written object is automatically discarded after an abort). As a consequence of this process, when the programmer receives the notification that a transaction is aborted, it is already too late for avoiding it or deciding which transaction is more convenient to abort.

HTM treats all reads and writes executed within the boundaries of a transaction as transactional, even if the accessed object is not shared or there is no need to guarantee atomicity on it. Non-transactional accesses inside a transaction cannot be performed in current architectures providing

HTM support. Customizing the conflict resolution policy and controlling which transaction aborts necessitates detecting the conflict before it happens. However, this fact means redoing what HTM already efficiently provides (i.e., the conflict detection). In addition, every access (read or write) to shared data should be monitored for a potential conflict. Also, per-object runtime information should also be kept (i.e., meta-data) and this leads to one of the major problems of CM in HTM: accessing shared meta-data for each object introduces more conflicts and reduces available cache-lines.

As an example of this claim, let us consider the case of adding a read/write lock for each shared object, which indicates that a transaction is currently reading/writing the object. In order to preserve the semantics of the lock, each transaction should read the value of the lock before accessing the related object. Let us now consider the case of two transactions both reading the object. In this case each transaction checks the availability of the read-lock, then it registers itself as another read-lock holder and proceeds by accomplishing the read operation. However, at the memory level, the acquisition of the lock means writing to the lock variable. Due to the HTM implementation, the lock is just an object enclosed in a cache line. Reading the lock status will add it to the transaction read-set, and acquiring (updating) the lock will add it to the write-set. Since all memory accesses in an HTM transaction are considered as transactional, once a transaction acquires the lock, it will conflict with all other transactions that read/wrote to the same lock. The issue described in the previous example can be applied to any meta-data used by the CM.

2. HTM-AWARE SCHEDULER

To circumvent the aforementioned problem, we propose a CM that operates on "static" information about incoming transactions (i.e., not collected during the transactional execution, but rather before or after it). According to these information, only those transactions that are non conflicting with each other can be concurrently scheduled. One would say that, given such a CM, transactions are not needed anymore because no conflicting executions can happen at-a-time. However the previous case is ideal because, due to the "static" nature of the runtime information, the CM could erroneously activate two conflicting transactions, concurrently. In such a case, correctness is still preserved through the conflict resolution of HTM.

We propose OCTONAUTS, an HTM-aware scheduler that deploys the idea illustrated above by using queues (called *scheduling-queues*) that guard shared objects. A transaction is associated with the objects that will be potentially accessed during the execution (called *working-set*). Then, the working-set is used for deciding which scheduling-queue(s) the transaction should be subscribed to. The subscription process is atomic. If a transaction needs to subscribe to more than one scheduling-queue, it locks the required queues in a deterministic order to avoid deadlocks, and then it proceeds with the actual enqueuing process. When the transaction reaches the top of all subscribed queues, it can execute.

The working-set could be either statically declared by the programmer or dynamically built as follow. Once submitted, HTM transactions are firstly activated as hardware transactions without waiting any decision from OCTONAUTS. While executing, the accessed objects are collected and, in case the transaction is committed, the just-composed working-set is used for classifying the next incoming transactions of the same profile (e.g., the New Order transaction profile of the TPC-C benchmark [4]). This way, after a period of application execution time, accesses can be predicted and the respective transaction will be enqueued in the appropriate scheduling-queues. This approach to populate the working-set is not deterministic and it depends on the actual runtime execution, therefore it should be refined as a result of subsequent commits.

In practice, in order to efficiently implement OCTONAUTS's scheduling scheme, we use a system inspired by the synchronization mechanism where tickets are leveraged. We associate two integers (i.e., enq_counter, deq_counter) and a lock with each scheduling-queue. The subscription process of a thread T to a scheduling-queue Q_s consists of the following steps. T increments the enq_counter of Q_s (in other words T obtains a ticket on Q_s). After that, T waits until the deq_counter reaches the value of the acquired ticket. To prevent deadlocks, T must subscribe to all required scheduling-queues atomically. To accomplish this task, T acquires all locks associated with the required scheduling-queues before incrementing all enq_counter. After executing a transaction, T increments the deq_counter of all subscribed scheduling-queues, thus allowing next (conflicting) transactions to proceed.

Using the described technique, two read-only transactions accessing the same object are not allowed to execute concurrently, although such transactions cannot conflict with each other because they just read. Serializing those read-only transactions could significantly limit the overall concurrency, especially in read dominated workloads. To overcome this drawback, we modified the aforementioned ticketing technique to accommodate reader and writer tickets. Threads owning reader tickets can proceed concurrently if there is no active writer. Rather, conflicting writers are serialized.

2.1 Handling HTM's Software Fallback

Transactions that cannot be committed in HTM (even if they run alone), need a software fallback path to ensure the application's progress. However, the communication between the STM and HTM paths should have minimal overhead, otherwise the OCTONAUTS's goal of increasing concurrency is nullified.

To minimize the aforementioned communication overhead, we use a phasing approach inspired by [9]. We execute HTM transactions in two ways: *plain* HTM and *instrumented* HTM. When the whole transactional workload runs in HTM, then the plain mode is adopted. Once an STM transaction is activated, it makes a notification so that all new HTM transactions after this point start in the instrumented HTM mode. In such a case, the STM transaction waits until all the plain HTM transactions finish, and then starts its execution. When all STM transactions are committed, the execution returns to the plain HTM mode.

When the instrumented HTM mode is active, we propose to use a circular buffer (called the *ring* [12]), which contains the write-set signatures (i.e., Bloom filters) of each committed HTM transaction. An HTM transaction gets an empty entry from the ring before starting the transaction (i.e., non-transactionally using a CAS operation). During the HTM transaction, every write operation to a shared object is logged into a local write-set signature (e.g., a Bloom filter). Before committing the HTM transaction, the local write-set signature is stored into a preemptively reserved entry of the ring. This design eliminates false conflicts due to shared HTM-STM meta-data (in our case, the ring). The ring entry is reserved before starting the HTM transaction and each HTM transaction writes to its own private ring entry. For STM transactions, they read only the ring entries so that they cannot conflict (at memory level) with any HTM transaction.

An STM transaction proceeds speculatively until its commit phase. Before committing, it validates its read objects against the concurrent HTM transactions (via the write-set signatures in the ring). If it is valid, the commit can take place. The proposed technique seems to favor HTM transactions, but since both HTM and STM transactions subscribe to the same object queues, HTM and STM transactions can only conflict due to an inaccurate definition of the working-set or due to Bloom filters' false conflicts. Thus, STM transactions cannot suffer from starvation.

3. PRELIMINARY EVALUATION

In order to show the practicality of our proposal, we built a preliminary version of OCTONAUTS using the TPC-C benchmark [4] configured with medium and high contention. The former has been enforced by selecting a total number of warehouses (the most contended object of TPC-C) as 20; whereas for the high contention case, we used 10 warehouses. We compared the throughput of OCTONAUTS against the pure HTM with the global locking as fallback. As testbed we used the Intel Haswell processor (i7-4770), which is equipped with 4 physical cores and 8 threads (given the hyper threading). Each hardware transaction retries 5 times before falling back to the software path. In this preliminary implementation, the working-set is defined by the programmer.

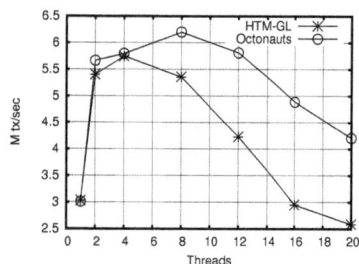

(a) Medium-contention.

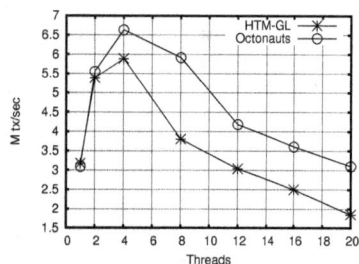

(b) High-contention.

Figure 1: Throughput using TPC-C benchmark.

Figure 1 shows the results. When the contention level in TPC-C is high, OCTONAUTS is particularly effective, be-

ing able to reduce the number of conflicts significantly. In addition, when the number of threads is larger than cores, OCTONAUTS is still able to scale because scheduling transactions properly leads to more concurrency than just leaving transactions to contend (and abort) each other. As an evidence of that, in our experiments when the number of threads is larger than 8 (which is the maximum number of hardware threads supported in the Haswell processor), both HTM-GL and OCTONAUTS can run only 8 transactions at a time and schedule the others. However, HTM-GL selects those 8 transactions according to the policy of the operating system's scheduler, whereas OCTONAUTS gives more guarantees that the selected ones are not conflicting.

4. ACKNOWLEDGMENTS

Authors would like to thank Ahmed Hassan and the anonymous reviewers for their important comments. This work is supported in part by US National Science Foundation under grant CNS 1217385 and AFOSR Grant FA9550-14-1-0187.

5. REFERENCES

[1] M. Ansari, M. Luján, C. Kotselidis, K. Jarvis, C. C. Kirkham, and I. Watson. Steal-on-abort: Improving transactional memory performance through dynamic transaction reordering. In *HiPEAC*, pages 4–18, 2009.

[2] H. Attiya and A. Milani. Transactional scheduling for read-dominated workloads. *Journal of Parallel and Distributed Computing*, 72(10):1386 – 1396, 2012.

[3] H. W. Cain, M. M. Michael, B. Frey, C. May, D. Williams, and H. Le. Robust architectural support for transactional memory in the power architecture. In *ISCA*, pages 225–236, 2013.

[4] T. Council. TPC-C benchmark. 2010.

[5] S. Dolev, D. Hendler, and A. Suissa. CAR-STM: Scheduling-based Collision Avoidance and Resolution for Software Transactional Memory. PODC, pages 125–134, 2008.

[6] A. Dragojević, R. Guerraoui, A. V. Singh, and V. Singh. Preventing versus curing: Avoiding conflicts in transactional memories. PODC, pages 7–16, 2009.

[7] R. Guerraoui, M. Herlihy, and B. Pochon. Polymorphic contention management. In *Distributed Computing*, volume 3724, pages 303–323. Springer, 2005.

[8] T. Harris, J. Larus, and R. Rajwar. Transactional memory, 2nd edition. *Synthesis Lectures on Computer Architecture*, 5(1), 2010.

[9] Y. Lev, M. Moir, and D. Nussbaum. PhTM: Phased transactional memory. In *TRANSACT*, 2007.

[10] W. Maldonado, P. Marlier, P. Felber, A. Suissa, D. Hendler, A. Fedorova, J. L. Lawall, and G. Muller. Scheduling support for transactional memory contention management. PPoPP, pages 79–90, 2010.

[11] J. Reinders. Transactional synchronization in haswell. *Intel Software Network.*, 2012.

[12] M. F. Spear, M. M. Michael, and C. von Praun. RingSTM: Scalable transactions with a single atomic instruction. In *SPAA*, 2008.

[13] R. M. Yoo and H.-H. S. Lee. Adaptive transaction scheduling for transactional memory systems. SPAA '08, pages 169–178, 2008.

Brief Announcement: Towards a Universal Approach for the Finite Departure Problem in Overlay Networks[*]

Andreas Koutsopoulos
University of Paderborn,
Germany
koutsopo@mail.upb.de

Christian Scheideler
University of Paderborn,
Germany
scheideler@.upb.de

Thim Strothmann
University of Paderborn,
Germany
thim@mail.upb.de

ABSTRACT

A fundamental problem for overlay networks is to *safely* exclude leaving nodes, i.e., the nodes requesting to leave the overlay network are excluded from it without affecting its connectivity. There are a number of studies for safe node exclusion if the overlay is in a well-defined state, but almost no formal results are known for the case in which the overlay network is in an arbitrary initial state, i.e., when looking for a *self-stabilizing* solution for excluding leaving nodes. We study this problem in two variants: the *Finite Departure Problem (FDP)* and the *Finite Sleep Problem (FSP)*. In the $\mathcal{FDP}$ the leaving nodes have to irrevocably decide when it is safe to leave the network, whereas in the $\mathcal{FSP}$, this leaving decision does not have to be final: the nodes may resume computation when woken up by an incoming message. We are the first to present a self-stabilizing protocol for the $\mathcal{FDP}$ and the $\mathcal{FSP}$ that can be combined with a large class of overlay maintenance protocols so that these are then guaranteed to safely exclude leaving nodes from the system from any initial state while operating as specified for the staying nodes. In order to formally define the properties these overlay maintenance protocols have to satisfy, we identify four basic primitives for manipulating edges in an overlay network that might be of independent interest.

Categories and Subject Descriptors

C.2.4 [**Computer-Communication Networks**]: Distributed Systems; C.2.2 [**Computer-Communication Networks**]: Network Protocols

Keywords

Distributed Systems; Self-Stabilization; Overlay Networks; Process Departures

[*]This work was partially supported by the German Research Foundation (DFG) within the Collaborative Research Center "On-The-Fly Computing" (SFB 901)

SPAA '15, June 13-15, 2015, Portland, OR, USA
ACM 978-1-4503-3588-1/15/06.
http://dx.doi.org/10.1145/2755573.2755614.

1. INTRODUCTION

Any distributed system must be based on some overlay network which specifies which nodes can directly send messages to which other nodes in the system. For distributed systems across the Internet, this is achieved by the nodes storing IP addresses of other nodes in that system, and in this case a node is said to be able to directly send a message to another node whenever it knows its IP address. A basic prerequisite for an overlay network which allows all pairs of nodes to exchange information is that it is connected, and a fundamental problem for overlay networks is to *preserve* connectivity while nodes are leaving, i.e., the nodes requesting to leave the overlay network are eventually excluded from it without disconnecting any staying nodes. If the overlay is in a well-defined state, scenarios in which the rate of node departures and arrivals is limited have already been studied [1, 5, 7]. However, due to permanent or transient failures a distributed system may rarely be in an ideal state, so it would be desirable to find *self-stabilizing* protocols for the exclusion of leaving nodes, i.e., from *any* initial state connectivity is preserved. While this seems to be a fundamental problem, only recently first solutions were found.

Foreback et al. [4] proposed to study this problem in two variants: the *Finite Departure Problem (FDP)* and the *Finite Sleep Problem (FSP)*. In the $\mathcal{FDP}$ the leaving nodes have to irrevocably decide when it is safe to leave the network, whereas in the $\mathcal{FSP}$, this leaving decision does not have to be final: the nodes may resume computation when woken up by an incoming message. On the negative side, Foreback et al. showed that there is no self-stabilizing local-control protocol for the $\mathcal{FDP}$. But if an oracle is available an appropriate local-control protocol can be constructed. Moreover, a variant of that protocol can solve the $\mathcal{FSP}$ without using an oracle. However, these protocols require that there is a fixed total order on the nodes (e.g., their names or IP addresses do not change), and they only work for a specific overlay maintenance protocol that aims at organizing the nodes in a sorted list.

In this paper, we present a self-stabilizing protocol for the $\mathcal{FDP}$ that can extend a large class of overlay maintenance protocols so that they are then guaranteed to eventually exclude the leaving nodes without risking disconnectivity and while the overlay maintenance protocol is operating as specified for the staying nodes. As a by-product, we present a set of four basic primitives for the manipulation of edges in overlay networks that are safe and universal in a sense that connectivity is preserved and that, in principle, one can get from any weakly connected graph to any other weakly connected graph. This might be of independent interest as we expect our insights to simplify the design and analysis of overlay maintenance protocols in the future.

2. MODEL & PROBLEM STATEMENT

We consider a distributed system consisting of a fixed set of processes in which each process has a unique reference (like its IP address). The system is controlled by a protocol that specifies the variables and actions that are available in each process. In addition to the protocol-based variables there is a system-based variable for each process called *channel* whose values are sets of messages. We denote the channel of process u as $u.Ch$, and it contains all incoming messages to u. Its message capacity is unbounded and messages never get lost. Messages are delivered according to the standard asynchronous message passing model, so every message is eventually delivered, but the delivery might happen in any order. A process u has a variable $mode(u) \in \{\text{leaving}, \text{staying}\}$ that is read-only. If this variable is set to **leaving**, the process is *leaving*; the process is *staying* if the variable is set to **staying**.

There are two special commands that are important for the study of our finite departure problem: **exit** and **sleep**. If a process executes **exit** it enters a designated *exit state*. We call such a process *gone*. If a process executes **sleep**, it enters a *sleep state*. Such a process is *asleep*. If a process never wakes up again, it is called *permanently asleep*. A process that is neither gone nor asleep is called *awake*. We call a process p *hibernating* if p is asleep, $p.Ch$ is empty and all processes q that have a directed path to p are also asleep and have an empty $q.Ch$.

In the following, a process is called *relevant* if it is neither gone nor hibernating. Otherwise we call it *irrelevant*. Since hibernating and gone processes will never execute any action, we only consider initial states in which all processes are relevant for the self-stabilization. We also restrict the initial state to contain only messages that can trigger actions, since other messages are ignored by the processes. Finally, we do not allow the presence of references that do not belong to a process in the system.

A system state is *legitimate* if (i) every staying process is awake, (ii) every leaving process is either hibernating or gone, and (iii) for each weakly connected component of the initial process graph, the staying processes in that component still form a weakly connected component. Now we are ready to formally state the following two problems.

Finite Departure Problem (*FDP*) : eventually reach a legitimate state for the case that the **sleep** command (and therefore the sleep state) is *not* available (but only **exit**).

Finite Sleep Problem (*FSP*) : eventually reach a legitimate state for the case that the **exit** command (and therefore the gone state) is *not* available (but only **sleep**).

A self-stabilizing solution for these problems must be able to solve these from any initial state and also satisfy the closure property afterwards. Notice that (i) and (ii) can trivially be maintained in a legitimate state, so for the closure property one just needs to ensure that (iii) is also maintained. A process p can *safely* leave a system if the removal of p and its incident edges does not disconnect any relevant

processes. As shown in [4], there is no distributed algorithm within our model that can decide when it is safe for a process p to leave the system. Hence, we need oracles.

An *oracle* $\mathcal{O}$ is a predicate that depends on the system state and the process calling it. In the context of the *FDP*, an oracle is supposed to advise a leaving process when it is safe to execute **exit**, thus we restrict our attention to protocols that *only* allow a leaving process to do so if the given oracle is **true** for it. Such a protocol is also said to *rely* on the oracle. Moreover, we restrict our attention to oracles that *only* depend on the current process graph of relevant processes and the calling process, i.e., oracles are of the form $\mathcal{O}: \mathcal{PG} \times P \to \{\text{true}, \text{false}\}$ where $\mathcal{PG}$ is the set of process graphs and P is the set of processes. We define the following oracle that we will use throughout the paper: Oracle $\mathcal{SINGLE}$ evaluates to **true** for a process u if u has edges with at most one other relevant process.

3. OUR RESULTS

Our main result is a self-stabilizing local-control protocol that can solve the *FDP* when relying on the $\mathcal{SINGLE}$ oracle. The only interfaces that it needs to an underlying communication layer is that it can send a message to a process identified by some reference and that it can check whether two references v and w point to the same or different processes. This has the advantage that the underlying layer is given full flexibility concerning the management of referencing information and that it does not have to pass any of that information (apart from whether two references point to the same process) to the process layer, which might be useful for anonymous networks. This flexibility is a major enhancement, since the previously known protocols to solve the *FDP* [4] requires that there is a fixed order on the processes. Also, the protocols in [4] were designed with a fixed topology in mind while this is not the case for our new protocol, which allows for an easy integration into existing overlay maintenance protocols, as we can also demonstrate. In order to simplify the analysis and formally specify the class of overlay maintenance protocols that can be used in conjunction with our departure protocol, we introduce four basic primitives for manipulating edges in the process graph. The four primitives are:

Introduction If a process u has a reference to two processes v and w, u *introduces* w to v if it sends a message to v containing a reference to w while keeping the reference to w.

Delegation If a process u has a reference to two processes v and w, then u *delegates* w's reference to v if it sends a message to v containing a reference to w and deletes the reference to w.

Fusion If a process u has two references v and w with $v = w$, then it *fuses* them if it only keeps one of these references.

Reversal If a process u has a reference to some other process v, then it *reverses* the connection if it sends a reference of itself to v and deletes the reference to v.

We can show some fundamental results about these primitives, i.e. they are safe (they always preserve weak connectivity) and universal (*in principle* it is possible to get from any weakly connected graph to any other weakly connected graph). Furthermore, these four primitives are not only sufficient for universality but also necessary, i.e., by removing one primitive, universality is lost. With $\mathcal{P}$ we denote the set of all distributed protocols where all interactions between processes can be decomposed into the four primitives. Not surprisingly, all of the self-stabilizing topology maintenance protocols proposed so far (e.g., [2, 3, 6, 8]) are in $\mathcal{P}$(as otherwise they would risk disconnection of their topology).

3.1 Process Departures

Our new self-stabilizing protocol that solves the $\mathcal{FDP}$ only needs to compare references for equality as needed for the four primitives. Since the protocol is self-stabilizing it is possible that information is *invalid* in an initial state, i.e., a process u assumes that another process v is leaving, even though v is staying.

Our solution makes use of a special variable called *anchor* which will only be used by the leaving nodes, so in a legitimate state, the *anchor* of a staying process is empty. The anchor is a reference of a process which a leaving process v assumes to be staying. Therefore, each time v gets a message from a third process w, v forwards w to its anchor by using the delegation primitive in the hope of eliminating all references to itself. In a nutshell, our protocol works as follows. Each process has a periodically executed *timeout* action. In case a process u is leaving, it introduces itself to its anchor in the *timeout* action (in order to verify it has a staying anchor). If it is staying, it introduces itself to all neighbors (to make other processes aware of it). This so-called *self-introduction*, which is is a special case of the introduction primitive, ensures that invalid information vanishes. Additionally, a leaving processes consults $\mathcal{SINGLE}$ in *timeout*, and if it evaluates to true, the process is safe to perform **exit**. Moreover, processes have to react to incoming introduction and delegation messages. A staying process saves references of other staying processes and reverses references to leaving processes. A leaving process will never save any references, except if it needs an anchor. In case the leaving process has an anchor it forwards all incoming messages to that anchor. Otherwise it makes use of the reversal primitive, i.e., it sends its own reference to the process whose reference was contained in the received message. To show that our proposed protocol is a self-stabilizing solution to the $\mathcal{FDP}$, it remains to show two properties.

Safety: The protocol never disconnects any relevant processes.

Liveness: All leaving processes are eventually gone.

It turns out that safety is easy to prove, since we only use the primitives to realize our protocol. In order to show liveness we first prove that all invalid information that is present in an initial state of the system eventually vanishes by a potential argument. Once all information is valid, we can prove Theorem 3.1 by induction, i.e., as long as there is a leaving process that is not gone yet, one leaving process executes **exit** eventually.

THEOREM 3.1. *Every leaving process eventually executes the* **exit** *command, thereby preserving liveness.*

Our developed protocol can be combined with a large class of distributed overlay protocols, i.e., with most protocols from $\mathcal{P}$ (see Theorem 3.2). In fact a protocol has to fulfill only two additional algorithmic requirements. First, P

conducts periodic *self-introduction*, i.e., it has a periodically executed (*timeout*) action, in which the executing process introduces itself to all processes in its neighborhood (among other activities). Second, P has a *postprocess* action, which is able to handle messages that should not be delivered, i.e., if we do not want to deliver a message, *postprocess* integrate the information contained in that message back into the sending process. This is important, since we want to avoid that P spreads information about leaving processes. In order to do so our enhanced protocol makes sure that a message is only delivered once the mode of all processes referenced in that message has been checked. If one single process is leaving, the message is not delivered and *postprocess* reintegrates the information. Note that all self-stabilizing overlay protocols proposed so far can easily be adapted to satisfy these two requirements. Moreover, we can adapt our protocol in order to solve the $\mathcal{FSP}$, so that an oracle is not required anymore. Therefore, our protocol achieves the same feasibility result as the protocol of [4] with lesser assumptions and an enhanced adaptability and flexibility.

THEOREM 3.2. *Let* $P \in \mathcal{P}$ *be a distributed overlay protocol which solves some distributed problem* $\mathcal{DP}$ *with the already mentioned requirements. Then there we can construct another protocol* P', *such that* P' *eventually solves the* $\mathcal{FDP}$. *In addition, if* P *is self-stabilizing, then* P' *also solves* $\mathcal{DP}$.

We note that our algorithms assume that there is at least one staying process. For the degenerate case in which all processes want to leave the network, we need a more intricate protocol that declares some leaving process as *pseudo-anchors* in order to solve the departure problem.

4. REFERENCES

[1] Keno Albrecht, Fabian Kuhn, and Roger Wattenhofer. Dependable peer-to-peer systems withstanding dynamic adversarial churn. In *Dependable Systems*, pages 275–294, 2006.

[2] Thomas Clouser, Mikhail Nesterenko, and Christian Scheideler. Tiara: A self-stabilizing deterministic skip list and skip graph. *Theor. Comput. Sci.*, 428:18–35, 2012.

[3] Danny Dolev, Ezra Hoch, and Robbert van Renesse. Self-stabilizing and byzantine-tolerant overlay network. In *PODC*, volume 4878, 2007.

[4] Dianne Foreback, Andreas Koutsopoulos, Mikhail Nesterenko, Christian Scheideler, and Thim Strothmann. On stabilizing departures in overlay networks. In *SSS*, pages 48–62, 2014.

[5] Thomas P. Hayes, Jared Saia, and Amitabh Trehan. The forgiving graph: a distributed data structure for low stretch under adversarial attack. *Distributed Computing*, 25(4):261–278, 2012.

[6] Riko Jacob, Andréa W. Richa, Christian Scheideler, Stefan Schmid, and Hanjo Täubig. A distributed polylogarithmic time algorithm for self-stabilizing skip graphs. In *PODC*, pages 131–140, 2009.

[7] Fabian Kuhn, Stefan Schmid, and Roger Wattenhofer. Towards worst-case churn resistant peer-to-peer systems. *Distributed Computing*, 22(4):249–267, 2010.

[8] Rizal Mohd Nor, Mikhail Nesterenko, and Christian Scheideler. Corona: A stabilizing deterministic message-passing skip list. In *SSS*, pages 356–370, October 2011.

MultiQueues: Simple Relaxed Concurrent Priority Queues

Hamza Rihani
Université Grenoble Alpes
Grenoble, France
hamza.rihani@imag.fr

Peter Sanders
Karlsruhe Inst. of Technology
Karlsruhe, Germany
sanders@kit.edu

Roman Dementiev
Intel GmbH
Munich, Germany
roman.dementiev@intel.com

ABSTRACT

We present a simple, concurrent data structure that approximates the behavior of a priority queue and that gives very good performance guarantees. We also discuss models for the semantics of relaxed priority queues and introduce a technique for "waitfree locking" that allows to convert sequential data structures to relaxed concurrent data structures.

Categories and Subject Descriptors

E.1 [**DATA STRUCTURES**]: Lists Stacks and Queues; D.1.3 [**PROGRAMMING TECHNIQUES**]: Concurrent programming

General Terms

Algorithms, Experimentation, Performance, Theory

Keywords

priority queues; concurrent data structure

1. INTRODUCTION

Priority queues (PQs) are a fundamental data structure with many applications. They manage a set of elements and support operations for inserting elements and deleting the smallest element (deleteMin). Whenever we have to dynamically reorder operations performed by an algorithm, PQs can turn out to be useful. Examples include job scheduling, graph algorithms for shortest paths and minimum spanning trees, discrete event simulation, best first branch-and-bound, and other best first heuristics.

On modern parallel hardware, we often have the situation that p parallel threads (or PEs for *processing elements*) want to access the PQ concurrently. This is problematic for several reasons. First of all, even the semantics of a parallel PQ is unclear. The classical notion of serializability is not only expensive to achieve but also not very useful from an application point of view. For example, in a branch-and-bound

SPAA'15, June 13–15, 2015, Portland, OR, USA.
ACM 978-1-4503-3588-1/15/06.
http://dx.doi.org/10.1145/2755573.2755616.

application, a serializable parallel PQ could arbitrarily postpone insertion and corresponding deletion of a search tree node on the path leading to the eventual solution. This makes the application arbitrarily slower than the sequential one. The *ideal* semantics of a parallel PQ would be that any element for which an insertion has started becomes visible instantaneously for deletion from any other PE. This is unattainable for fundamental physical reasons but can serve as a basis of reference for defining the quality of relaxed priority queues. One such measure inspired by the quality experiments in [1] is the distribution of *rank errors* of deleted elements – how many elements in the queue are smaller. A complementary measure for future work could be the *delay* of an inserted element x – how many deletions of larger elements are performed before x is deleted.

2. RELATED WORK

For a preliminary version of the full paper refer to [10]. A simple model for parallel PQs with clear semantics and performance guarantees are *bulk parallel priority queues* [4, 9, 11, 3, 7] where the PEs work in globally synchronized phases and are allowed to insert and delete sets of elements. Deleted elements are the globally smallest ones remaining from previous phases. MultiQueues can be viewed as a simplified asynchronous implementation of a bulk parallel PQ [11] or as a way to improve the quality of the approach of Karp and Zhang [8] where elements are deleted locally. Alistrah et al. [1] give a relaxed PQ (SprayLists) based on skip lists which guarantees rank error of $\mathcal{O}(p \log^3 p)$ with high probability for read only access. However, in the worst case, insertions can cause heavy contention which not only affect performance but can also increase the rank errors. Wimmer et al. propose the k-LSM relaxed PQ [12] which approximates serializability. They also give an extensive review of work on parallel PQs. Henzinger et al. [6] propose a semantics of relaxed PQs that approximates a serialization.

3. MULTIQUEUES

Our MultiQueue data structure is an array Q of cp sequential PQs where c is a tuning parameter and p is the number of parallel threads (our current implementation uses 8-ary heaps). Access to each queue is protected by a lock flag. Insert samples random queues $Q[i]$ until it manages to lock an unlocked one and then inserts the element into $Q[i]$, see Figure 1. Since at most p queues can be locked at any time, for $c > 1$ we will have constant success probability. Hence, the expected time for locking a queue is constant. Together with the time for insertion we get expected inser-

Procedure insert(e)
  repeat
      $i :=$ uniformRandom$(1..p)$
      try to lock $Q[i]$ −− e.g. a CAS instruction
  until lock was successful
  $Q[i]$.insert(e)

Procedure deleteMin
  repeat
      $i :=$ uniformRandom$(1..p)$
      $j :=$ uniformRandom$(1..p)$
      if $Q[i]$.min $> Q[j]$.min **then** swap i, j
      try to lock $Q[i]$ −− e.g. a CAS instruction
  until lock was successful
  $e :=$ $Q[i]$.deleteMin
  $Q[i]$.lock$:= 0$ −− unlock
  return e

Figure 1: Insert and DeleteMin **in MultiQueues.**

tion time $\mathcal{O}(\log n)$. Insert is wait-free in the sense that all threads make progress (in a probabilistic sense) independent of other, possibly blocked, threads.[1]

A simple implementation of deleteMin could simply lock a random unlocked queue and return its minimal element. However, it turns out that this can lead to severe quality deterioration over the execution of the algorithm. Therefore we invest slightly more effort into a deleteMin by looking at *two* random queues and deleting from the one with smaller minimum, see Figure 1. Our intuition why considering two choices may be useful, stems from previous work on randomized load balancing, where it is known that placing a ball on the least loaded of two randomly chosen machines gives a maximum load that is very close to the average load independent of the number of allocated balls [2]. The effect of an additional choice on execution time is modest – we still need only constant expected time to lock the queue we want to access and then spend logarithmic time for the local deleteMin. Once more, we get logarithmic expected execution time.

Quality Analysis. Unfortunately, we do not have a closed form analysis of the quality of the MultiQueue. However, with simplifying assumptions, we can get a reasonable approximation of what to expect. So let us assume for now that all remaining m elements have been allocated uniformly at random to the local queues. This is true when there have been no deleteMin operations so far (and the open question is whether the deleteMin operations steer the system state away from this situation and whether this is good or bad for quality). Furthermore, let us assume that no queue is locked. With these assumptions, the probability to delete an element of rank i is

$$\mathbf{P}\left[\text{rank} = i\right] = \left(1 - \frac{2}{cp}\right)^{i-1} \cdot \frac{2}{cp}$$

The first factor expresses that the $i-1$ elements with smaller ranks are not present at the two chosen queues and the sec-

ond factor is the probability that the element with rank i *is present*. Therefore, the expected rank error in the described situation is

$$\sum_{i=1}^{m} i\mathbf{P}\left[\text{rank} = i\right] \leq \sum_{i \geq 1} i \left(1 - \frac{2}{cp}\right)^{i-1} \cdot \frac{2}{cp} = \frac{c}{2}p \quad (1)$$

i.e., linear in p. We can also compute the the cumulative probability that the rank of the deleted element is larger than k. This happens when none of the k elements with rank $\leq k$ are present on the two chosen queues.

$$\mathbf{P}\left[\text{rank} > k\right] = \left(1 - \frac{2}{cp}\right)^{k} . \quad (2)$$

$\mathbf{P}\left[\text{rank} > k\right]$ drops to p^{-a} for $k = \frac{ca}{2}p \ln p$, i.e., with probability polynomially large in p, we have rank error $\mathcal{O}(p \log p)$. We can also give qualitative arguments how the performed operations change the distribution of the elements. Insertions are random and hence move the system towards a random distribution of elements. DeleteMins are more complicated. However, they tend to remove more elements from queues with small keys than from queues with large keys, thus stabilizing the system.

4. EXPERIMENTS

Experiments were performed on a dual socket system with Intel® Xeon® CPU E5-2697 v3, 2.60 GHz processors (Haswell-EP). Each socket has 14 cores with two hardware threads, i.e., 56 overall. We use GCC 4.8.2 with optimization level -O3, Boost version 1.56, and Posix threads for parallelization. Queue elements are key-value-pairs consisting of two 32 bit integers. Initially, the queues are filled with $n_0 = 10^6$ elements with keys uniformly distributed in $\{0, \dots, 10^8\}$. Our measurements use threads alternating between insert and deleteMin operations.

Figure 2 compares the overall throughput of MultiQueues to a sequential 8-ary heap (Boost) protected by a lock and other concurrent PQs which are all based on SkipLists. We see that none of the serializable queues achieves any absolute speedup. Multiqueues scale well on a single socket (≤ 14 threads). Interestingly, when using all hardware threads of a single socket (curve MultiQ HT), we are almost twice as

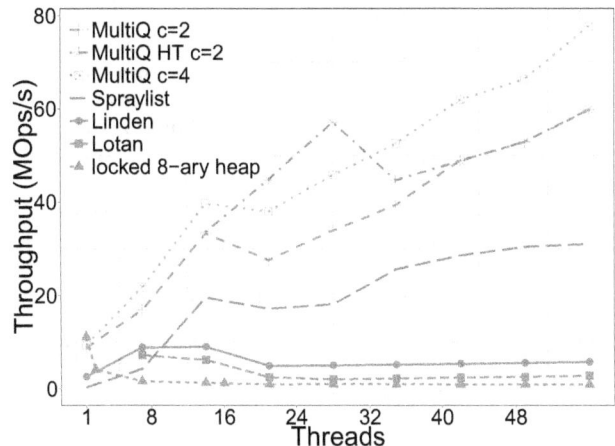

Figure 2: Throughput of 50% insert 50% deleteMin.

[1]However, it is possible that blocked threads make data inaccessible.

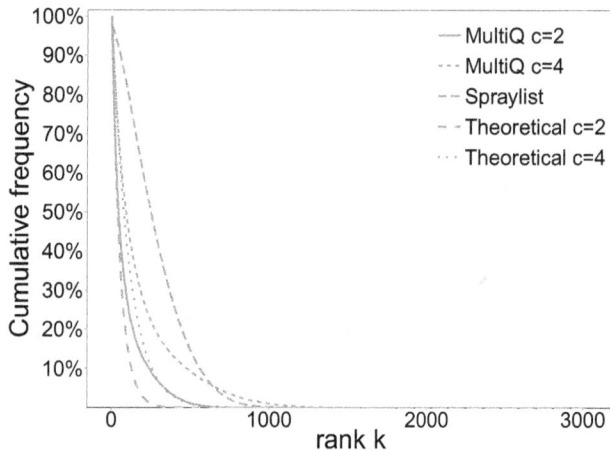

Figure 3: Tail distribution of rank error P [rank > k]. 10^7 operations and 56 threads

fast as with one hardware thread per core. This is outstanding effectiveness for hardware threads. Such speedup is expected if the workload is very latency sensitive. Going to two sockets leads to significant performance deterioration due to the high additional latency of the socket interconnect. Doubling the number of queues from $2p$ to $4p$ leads to further performance improvements. Both variants are about a factor two faster than the best competitor [1] (probably significantly more, if a complete implementation of SprayLists were available that performs memory management).

In [10] we also make measurements with a monotonic development of key values. MultiQueues are unaffected whereas SprayLists do not scale at all due to a severe bottleneck for insertions.

Wimmer et al. [12] compare MultiQueues (with $c = 2$) to k-LSM PQs. For parameter value $k = 4$ which roughly corresponds to our parameter $c = 2$ with respect to expected rank error, MultiQueues are faster. However, for large k (≥ 256), k-LSM PQs scale much better than MultiQueues.

We now measure the distribution of rank errors of MultiQueues and SprayLists. Unfortunately, it is difficult to directly measure this in a running parallel program. We therefore adapt the approach from [1] to our situation. We run a sequential thread performing the operations which keeps a sorted sequence S containing the current queue elements on the side. After each deleteMin returning x, the position of x in S gives the rank error. Figure 3 shows the result for $p = 56$ and 10^7 operations (alternating between insertions and deletions). For the "typically seen" ranks, MultiQueues with $2p = 112$ queues ($c = 2$) are much better than SprayLists and actually, the measured distribution closely follows our simplified theoretical analysis. The largest observed ranks were 1 522 for MultiQueues and 1 740 for SprayLists. For $c = 4$ the situation is similar, with the exception that the tails of the distribution are worse than for SprayLists.

5. CONCLUSIONS AND FUTURE WORK

MultiQueues are a simple way to reduce contention in relaxed PQs leading to high throughput and good quality. However, there is a need for further research. Provable quality guarantees, worst case quality guarantees and higher locality of access seem to be the main issue.

Our technique for wait-free locking may also be applicable in other situations, e.g. for other relaxed data structures. For example, when we apply our technique to relaxed FIFOs, we get a data structure similar to the DQs by Haas et al. [5] but we can use any sequential FIFO-queue for the individual queues.

Acknowledgements. We would like to thank the SAP HANA group for bringing the three authors together, and Jean-François Méhaut for providing a testing platform.

6. REFERENCES

[1] D. Alistarh, J. Kopinsky, J. Li, and N. Shavit. The SprayList: A scalable relaxed priority queue. In *20th ACM SIGPLAN Symposium on Principles and Practice of Parallel Programming (PPoPP)*, pages 11–20. ACM, September 2015.

[2] P. Berenbrink, A. Czumaj, A. Steger, and B. Vöcking. Balanced allocations: The heavily loaded case. In *32th Annual ACM Symposium on Theory of Computing*, pages 745–754, 2000.

[3] T. Bingmann, T. Keh, and P. Sanders. A bulk-parallel priority queue in external memory with STXXL. In *14th Symposium on Experimental Algorithms (SEA)*, LNCS. Springer, 2015.

[4] N. Deo and S. Prasad. Parallel heap: An optimal parallel priority queue. *The Journal of Supercomputing*, 6(1):87–98, Mar. 1992.

[5] A. Haas, M. Lippautz, T. A. Henzinger, H. Payer, A. Sokolova, C. M. Kirsch, and A. Sezgin. Distributed queues in shared memory: multicore performance and scalability through quantitative relaxation. In *Proceedings of the ACM International Conference on Computing Frontiers*, page 17. ACM, 2013.

[6] T. A. Henzinger, C. M. Kirsch, H. Payer, A. Sezgin, and A. Sokolova. Quantitative relaxation of concurrent data structures. In *ACM SIGPLAN Notices*, volume 48, pages 317–328. ACM, 2013.

[7] L. Hübschle-Schneider, P. Sanders, and I. Müller. Communication efficient algorithms for top-k selection problems. *CoRR*, abs/1502.03942, 2015.

[8] R. M. Karp and Y. Zhang. Parallel algorithms for backtrack search and branch-and-bound. *Journal of the ACM*, 40(3):765–789, 1993.

[9] A. Ranade, S. Cheng, E. Deprit, J. Jones, and S. Shih. Parallelism and locality in priority queues. In *Sixth IEEE Symposium on Parallel and Distributed Processing*, pages 97–103, October 1994.

[10] H. Rihani, P. Sanders, and R. Dementiev. Multiqueues: Simpler, faster, and better relaxed concurrent priority queues. *CoRR*, abs/1411.1209, 2014.

[11] P. Sanders. Randomized priority queues for fast parallel access. *Journal Parallel and Distributed Computing, Special Issue on Parallel and Distributed Data Structures*, 1998. extended version: http://www.mpi-sb.mpg.de/~sanders/papers/1997-7.ps.gz.

[12] M. Wimmer, J. Gruber, P. Tsigas, and J. L. Träff. The lock-free k-LSM relaxed priority queue. *CoRR*, abs/1503.05698, 2015.

Brief Announcement: A Compiler-Runtime Application Binary Interface for Pipe-While Loops

Jim Sukha
Intel Corporation
Hudson, MA 01749
jim.sukha@intel.com

ABSTRACT

Pipe-while loops have been proposed as a language construct for expressing pipeline parallelism in task-parallel languages. However, this loop construct has only been prototyped in research systems that lack compiler support. We demonstrate how to extend Intel® Cilk™ Plus, a production-quality task-parallel language, to implement pipe-while loops. We propose an extension to the compiler-runtime application binary interface (ABI) of Cilk Plus to support pipe-while loops. This extension maintains compatibility with existing language constructs and existing Cilk Plus binaries. We validate this ABI by prototyping the required runtime modifications and simulating the required front-end compiler transformations using preprocessor macros and C++ lambda functions.

1. INTRODUCTION

Pipe-while loops have been proposed by Lee et al. [5] as a new language construct for expressing pipeline parallelism. A pipe-while loop is a while loop where the iterations may execute in parallel, except where the programmer has explicitly specified dependencies between consecutive loop iterations. Figure 1 illustrates the three keywords needed to support this new construct.[1] The _Cilk_pipe_while keyword specifies a pipe-while loop. Each loop iteration is divided into *stages* by the use of the _Cilk_stage and _Cilk_stage_wait keywords. In an iteration, a statement _Cilk_stage(s) begins execution of stage s immediately. In contrast, a statement _Cilk_stage_wait(s) allows execution of stage s only after stage s in the previous iteration (if it exists) has completed. See [5] for more complex pipe-while examples and details about language semantics.

Although Lee et al. prototype runtime support for pipe-while loops, that implementation lacks compiler support and is built on a runtime that requires special OS support, significantly hindering the ability of application developers to experiment with pipe-while loops. Moreover, it is not immediately obvious if one might translate that design to Intel® Cilk™ Plus [4], a commercial production-quality instantiation of Cilk, without also breaking backwards compatibility or introducing significant implementation complexity.

---

[1]To be more consistent with Intel® Cilk™ Plus syntax, we have changed the original syntax of [5] to use the _Cilk prefix.

SPAA'15, June 13–15, 2015, Portland, OR, USA.
ACM 978-1-4503-3588-1/15/06.
http://dx.doi.org/10.1145/2755573.2755610.

```
1    bool done = false;
2    int P = __cilkrts_get_nworkers();
3    int icount = 0;
4    #pragma throttle_limit = 4*P
5    _Cilk_pipe_while(!done) {
6        int i = icount++;
7        done = exec_stage(i, 0);
8        for (int s = 1; s < 5; ++s) {
9            // Advance stage.
10           if (s % 2 != 0)
11               _Cilk_stage(s);
12           else
13               _Cilk_stage_wait(s);
14           exec_stage(i, s);
15       }
16   }
```

Figure 1: An example pipe-while loop for a simple 5-stage pipeline, where stages 0, 2, and 4 are serial, while stages 1 and 3 are parallel. The _Cilk_pipe_while keyword encloses the loop body. The _Cilk_stage or _Cilk_stage_wait keywords in the loop body indicate the beginning of a new pipeline stage in an iteration. The pragma throttle_limit tunes the maximum number of pipeline iterations that can be active at once. The function exec_stage(i, s) represents user code for stage s in iteration i.

This work proposes an extension to the Cilk Plus application binary interface (ABI) [2] to support pipe-while loops. To validate the proposed ABI, we have implemented a C++ header file that simulates the required front-end compiler transformations using preprocessor macros and C++ lambdas, and implemented the necessary modifications to the Cilk Plus runtime. An early prototype is available for download from http://www.cilkplus.org [6]. We have also simulated compilation of several of the benchmarks tested by [5]. The remainder of this brief announcement focuses on describing the compiler-runtime interface. Section 2 describes the compiler support required for pipe-while loops, and Section 3 summarizes the required runtime modifications.

2. COMPILING PIPE-WHILE LOOPS

The proposed extension to the Cilk Plus ABI for pipe-while loops is based on two analogies, namely that (1) the runtime models a pipe-while loop after a while loop that repeatedly spawns iterations, and (2) the compiler models a _Cilk_pipe_while after a _Cilk_for loop in terms of its required transformations. It turns out that these two analogies, plus some relatively straightforward extensions to handle stage boundaries, are sufficient to handle pipe-while loops without breaking binary compatibility with previously compiled Cilk Plus code.

To understand the extended ABI, it is first useful to review how Cilk Plus compiles and executes a *spawning function*, i.e., a function f that spawns another function g. For a spawn of g from a spawning function f, the compiler generates a *spawn helper* function for g to perform the spawn. During execution, Cilk Plus allocates a *stack frame* — a __cilkrts_stack_frame object — on

```
1   struct __cilkrts_pipe_control_frame {
2       __cilkrts_stack_frame sf_data;
3       control_data_t* rts_data;
4   };
5   struct __cilkrts_iter_data {
6       __cilkrts_stack_frame* hsf;
7       int64_t cached_prev_stage;
8       __cilkrts_iter_data *prev;
9       int64_t stage;
10      iter_data_t* rts_data;
11  };

13  void iter_body_lambda(
14      __cilkrts_pipe_control_frame* pcf,
15      __cilkrts_iter_data* iter_data);
16  __cilkrts_pipe_while(iter_body_lambda,
17                       pcf,
18                       throttle_limit);
19  cilk_stage(target_s, iter_data):
20      _Cilk_sync;
21      assert(target_s > iter_data->stage);
22      iter_data->stage = target_s;
23      __cilkrts_stack_frame* hsf = iter_data->hsf;
24      if (!(CILK_FRAME_DETACHED & hsf->flags)) {
25          if (CILK_FRAME_STOLEN & hsf->flags)
26              __cilkrts_pipe_iter_demotion(iter_data);
27          CILK_PIPE_DETACH_ITER(hsf);
28      }
29  cilk_stage_wait(target_s):
30      cilk_stage(target_s);
31      do {
32          int64_t prev_s = iter_data->
                cached_prev_stage;
33          if (prev_s > iter_data->stage)
34              break;
35          prev_s = iter_data->prev->stage;
36          iter_data->cached_prev_stage = prev_s;
37          if (prev_s > iter_data->stage)
38              break;
39          __cilkrts_pipe_stage_wait(iter_data);
40      } while (1);
```

Figure 2: Compiler-visible definitions for proposed pipe-while loop ABI. Four major elements are shown: (1) compiler-visible data structures for frames (lines 1–11), (2) prototype of compiler-generated lambda function for executing a pipe-while loop iteration (lines 13–15), (3) call to Cilk Plus runtime function to invoke a pipe-while loop (lines 16–18), and (4) the compiler expansion of _Cilk_stage and _Cilk_stage_wait keywords within the lambda function (lines 19–28 and lines 29–40, respectively).

the stack for both the spawning function f and each spawn helper. The stack frame contains several compiler-visible fields, including a reduced setjmp buffer that saves state for f on a spawn so that the continuation in f can be resumed on a steal.

In terms of stack frames, the extended ABI, which is summarized in Figure 2, models a pipe-while loop after a while loop that repeatedly spawns iterations. A **control frame** is allocated on the stack when the loop begins, and a separate **iteration helper (stack) frame** is allocated on the stack for each loop iteration. An iteration helper frame is exactly an ordinary stack frame, while a control frame (lines 1–4) is an ordinary stack frame (sf_data) plus an extra opaque pointer (rts_data) to runtime data structures. Both frame types utilize the setjmp buffer in their underlying __cilkrts_stack_frame for suspending/resuming execution at pipeline stage boundaries or when the loop is throttled. The extended ABI consumes only one extra flag bit in a __cilkrts_stack_frame to distinguish control frames from ordinary stack frames, so that the runtime steal loop can detect a steal of a pipe-while loop iteration. Because the current ABI has extra unused flag bits and the layout of a __cilkrts_stack_frame is unchanged, this extended ABI is binary compatible, i.e., it does not require recompilation of any old code (without pipe-while loops).

The metadata for a pipeline iteration is split between the iteration helper frame stored on the execution stack, and an **iteration data block** (defined in lines 5–11) stored in a buffer of data blocks associated with the control frame. The iteration data block is separate from the iteration helper frame because its data may need to persist after an iteration has finished executing (e.g., because the next iteration may check for a dependency only after the current iteration completes). Its only compiler-visible fields are a pointer to the corresponding iteration helper frame (hsf), a cached value of the stage counter of the previous iteration (cached_prev_stage), a pointer to the data block for the previous iteration (prev), and the stage counter (stage). All other fields are encapsulated via the opaque pointer rts_data.

Figure 2 also summarizes the required compiler transformations for a _Cilk_pipe_while loop. In a fashion analogous to a _Cilk_for loop, a compiler needs to lift the loop body into a lambda function (with prototype shown in lines 13–15) that captures variables from the function enclosing the pipe-while loop. For invoking a pipe-while loop, the compiler generates code to allocate a control frame pcf on the stack, compute the value of the throttling limit, and call a runtime function __cilkrts_pipe_while (lines 16–18). Finally, a compiler needs to transform the _Cilk_stage and _Cilk_stage_wait keywords occurring within the loop body.

The core transformation for a _Cilk_stage is the update of the stage counter to the user-specified stage (line 22). After updating the stage counter, a _Cilk_stage also tries to "detach" the iteration helper frame hsf from its parent control frame (line 27) if it has not been done already (as checked in line 24). Similar to a _Cilk_spawn as described in the Cilk Plus ABI [2], *detaching* hsf corresponds to pushing a frame onto the current worker's deque so that the continuation in the control frame (i.e., the next pipeline iteration) can be stolen. If a pipe-while loop behaved exactly as a while loop that spawns every iteration, this detach would happen before the iteration begins executing. Because the semantics of [5] impose serial dependencies between stage 0 of consecutive iterations however, the detach actually occurs at the first stage transition in each iteration (if one exists), guaranteeing that the next iteration can not be stolen until stage 0 of the previous iteration completes.

If the body of a pipe-while loop is itself a spawning function, compiling _Cilk_stage requires two extra steps. First, since every stage is supposed to end with an implicit sync, a _Cilk_sync (line 20) may be needed before computing the value of the argument to _Cilk_stage. Second, because of the different protocol for detaching the iteration helper frame, a corner case occurs if stage 0 of an iteration i has nested parallelism that has been stolen. This case requires additional runtime support (via the __cilkrts_pipe_iter_demotion call in line 26) to patch runtime invariants, as discussed in Section 3.

Finally, the transformation of _Cilk_stage_wait (lines 29–40) first executes a _Cilk_stage, and then checks and waits for the dependency on the previous iteration to be satisfied. The __cilkrts_pipe_stage_wait function in line 39 is a runtime call which suspends execution on the current stack, saves necessary runtime state (e.g., maps for supporting reducers), and then directs the current worker thread to try to steal and execute other work. Eventually, this call will return and execution will resume on the original stack, but possibly on a different worker thread.

3. CILK PLUS RUNTIME EXTENSIONS

This section briefly summarizes the main runtime modifications made to the Cilk Plus runtime to support pipe-while loops. Most of the required runtime changes are relatively straightforward translations of the approach of Lee et al. [5], with only a few minor extensions for supporting reducers [1]. We first describe how the runtime data structures are extended for pipe-while loops. Then, we explain how the runtime schedules pipe-while loop iterations. More details can be found in the runtime source documentation [6].

Data Structures

We first review some of the fundamental data structures in Cilk Plus. As described in Section 2, the basic unit that a Cilk Plus compiler works with is a stack frame, represented as a `__cilkrts_stack_frame` object. The basic unit for a Cilk Plus runtime, however, is a *full frame* — a heap-allocated object which in most cases corresponds to a particular stack frame. Cilk Plus uses essentially the protocol of Frigo et al. [1] for managing stack frames and full frames. When one worker successfully steals work from another, it steals a chain of stack frames, corresponding to functions in a call chain. On a successful steal, each stack frame in the stolen chain is *promoted* into a full frame. As steals occurs, full frames are created and linked together in a tree. When a spawning function returns, its corresponding full frame is spliced out of this tree after combining reducer maps using a similar protocol as [1].

For pipe-while loops, the Cilk Plus runtime also keeps a similar distinction between stack frames and full frames. For each pipeline iteration that is stolen, we allocate a special *pipeline full frame*, which is a standard full frame plus a few extra fields specifically for pipeline synchronization. Most notably, a pipeline full frame contains a lock and status field for its corresponding iteration data block. As an optimization, instead of dynamically allocating space for pipeline full frames lazily on each successful steal of a pipeline iteration, we instead preallocate a circular buffer of pipeline full frames on the first steal of a pipeline iteration from the loop, i.e., when the control stack frame is promoted into a full frame. This buffer, like the buffer of iteration data blocks associated with the control frame, contains enough space to handle K concurrent iterations, where K is the throttling limit specified by the user.

Runtime Scheduling

The function `__cilkrts_pipe_while`, which is called by compiler-generated code, is the core runtime function for executing pipe-while loops. As discussed in Section 2, the runtime models a pipe-while loop as though it was a while loop that spawns its iterations. Thus, the runtime implementation of `__cilkrts_pipe_while` closely resembles a hand-compiled implementation of a parent while loop that spawns iterations as children, with only minor differences for detaching iterations and suspending the parent due to throttling. Hand-compilation of `__cilkrts_pipe_while` is practical because only one instance (coded into the runtime) is sufficient for all pipe-while loops.

For pipe-while loops, there are two interesting runtime events, namely the completion of a pipeline iteration and the steal of an iteration. When a pipeline iteration finishes, three runtime actions occur. First, the runtime handles reducers. Second, the runtime determines which frame to execute next. Finally, the runtime executes a cleanup protocol to determine when an iteration data block can be reused for future iterations. For a steal of a pipeline iteration, the runtime takes a different control path as compared to normal steals. The remainder of this section describes some of the implementation details.

First, for reducers, the protocol for merging reducer maps for a pipeline full frame remains essentially the same as for a normal full frame for a spawning function that is returning.

Second, the runtime must determine which frame to execute next after a pipeline iteration finishes. If a pipe-while behaved exactly as a while loop that spawned its iterations, the runtime would either resume the parent control frame (the while loop), or stall at a sync and go look for work to steal. For a pipe-while loop, however, the runtime may also need to resume the next iteration (because of the conceptual tail-swap operation [5]), or resume a parent control frame which is stalled because of throttling of the loop.

Finally, completing a pipeline iteration also requires executing a cleanup protocol to determine when iteration data blocks in the control frame's circular buffer can be reused for future pipeline iterations. Intuitively, each iteration that finishes updates the status of both its data block and the previous iteration's data block to signal completion. This status is checked by the runtime function `__cilkrts_pipe_while` to determine whether the runtime should throttle execution of the loop because there are no more free data blocks in the buffer. A lock protects this status field for an iteration data block. Fortunately, lock contention is low since at most 3 threads can be concurrently trying to acquire a given lock.

For a steal of a pipeline iteration, the Cilk Plus runtime also takes a different control path as compared to the normal steal of a continuation of a spawn. The steal loop is modified to check for the pipeline flag bit in the `__cilkrts_stack_frame`. The implementation requires only one flag bit, to distinguish control stack frames from other ordinary stack frames. There is no need to use any extra bits to distinguish an iteration helper frame from an ordinary stack frame, since iteration helper frames are usually already promoted to pipeline full frames when the runtime works with them.

Finally, pipe-while loops introduce an interesting corner case, when we have a successful steal from stage 0 of a pipeline iteration i with nested parallelism. In this case, at the time of the steal, the normal runtime steal protocol sees the iteration helper as being called from the parent control frame. Thus, the steal promotes the iteration helper frame for i and its parent control frame to ordinary full frames, as though they were ordinary Cilk Plus functions, instead of promoting the iteration helper frame to a pipeline full frame. For this corner case, the function `__cilkrts_pipe_iter_demotion` effectively patches the desired runtime invariants when stage 0 ends by "returning" from the iteration helper frame to free its ordinary full frame, and then starting again with the appropriate pipeline iteration frame from the control frame's buffer.

4. CONCLUSION

This work proposes an extension to the Cilk Plus application binary interface (ABI) [2] to support pipe-while loops that is compatible with existing language constructs and Cilk Plus binaries. Future work is to extend the Cilk Plus/LLVM branch [3] to provide the desired compiler support.

5. REFERENCES

[1] M. Frigo, P. Halpern, C. E. Leiserson, and S. Lewin-Berlin. Reducers and other Cilk++ hyperobjects. In *Proceedings of the Twenty-first Annual Symposium on Parallelism in Algorithms and Architectures*, SPAA '09, pages 79–90, 2009.

[2] Intel Corporation. *Intel® Cilk™ Plus Application Binary Interface Specification*, 2011. Document Number: 324512-002US. Available from https://www.cilkplus.org/sites/default/files/open_specifications/CilkPlusABI_1.1.pdf.

[3] Intel Corporation. *Cilk Plus/LLVM*, 2013. Available from http://cilkplus.github.io/.

[4] Intel Corporation. *Intel® Cilk™ Plus Language Extension Specification, Version 1.2*, 2013. Document 324396-003US. Available from https://www.cilkplus.org/sites/default/files/open_specifications/Intel_Cilk_plus_lang_spec_1.2.htm.

[5] I. A. Lee, C. E. Leiserson, T. B. Schardl, J. Sukha, and Z. Zhang. On-the-fly pipeline parallelism. In *Proceedings of the Twenty-fifth Annual ACM Symposium on Parallelism in Algorithms and Architectures*, SPAA '13, pages 140–151, 2013. Also submitted for journal publication.

[6] J. Sukha. *Piper: Experimental Language Support for Pipeline Parallelism in Intel® Cilk™ Plus*. Intel Corporation, 2013. Available from https://www.cilkplus.org/sites/default/files/experimental-software/PiperReferenceGuideV1.0_0.pdf.

Brief Announcement: Hypergraph Partitioning for Parallel Sparse Matrix-Matrix Multiplication

Grey Ballard
Sandia National Laboratories
gmballa@sandia.gov

Alex Druinsky
Lawrence Berkeley National Laboratory
adruinsky@lbl.gov

Nicholas Knight
University of California, Berkeley
knight@cs.berkeley.edu

Oded Schwartz
Hebrew University, Jerusalem, Israel
odedsc@cs.huji.ac.il

ABSTRACT

The performance of parallel algorithms for sparse matrix-matrix multiplication is typically determined by the amount of interprocessor communication performed, which in turn depends on the nonzero structure of the input matrices. In this paper, we characterize the communication cost of a sparse matrix-matrix multiplication algorithm in terms of the size of a cut of an associated hypergraph that encodes the computation for a given input nonzero structure. Obtaining an optimal algorithm corresponds to solving a hypergraph partitioning problem. Our hypergraph model generalizes several existing models for sparse matrix-vector multiplication, and we can leverage hypergraph partitioners developed for that computation to improve application-specific algorithms for multiplying sparse matrices.

1. INTRODUCTION

Sparse matrix-matrix multiplication (SpGEMM) is a fundamental computation in applications ranging from linear solvers to graph algorithms and data analysis (see [5] and references therein). SpGEMM algorithms are typically communication bound, spending much more of their time moving data than performing additions and multiplications. Furthermore, the computation is usually irregular and depends on the nonzero structures of the input matrices.

Hypergraphs are used to model and optimize parallel algorithms for sparse matrix-dense vector multiplication (SpMV); see, e.g., [7, 8]. More recently, hypergraph models have been proposed for the outer-product algorithm for SpGEMM [1]. In this work, we present a hypergraph model that generalizes the "fine-grain" SpMV model [7] and considers a more general class of SpGEMM algorithms than [1] to minimize communication. Hypergraphs have been used to model more general computations than SpGEMM [10]: we differ

from this work by optimizing interprocessor communication rather than disk I/O.

In particular, in this work we consider the *critical-path communication cost* of a parallel algorithm, which is the number of words communicated between processors along a critical path of the algorithm. This cost is usually correlated with (but can exceed) the maximum number of words communicated by any processor during the algorithm, and it differs from the communication volume, which is the total number of words communicated by all processors.

The main contributions of this work are (1) showing that SpGEMM can be modeled by a hypergraph so that its communication cost corresponds to the size of a cut induced by a partition of the vertices and (2) demonstrating that hypergraph partitioners can be used to determine efficient SpGEMM algorithms for an algebraic multigrid application.

2. THEORETICAL MODEL

Let $\mathbf{A}$ and $\mathbf{B}$ be I-by-K and K-by-J matrices over X, a set closed under two binary operations denoted by addition (commutative and associative with identity element 0) and multiplication (with absorbing element 0). SpGEMM is $(\mathbf{A}, \mathbf{B}) \mapsto \mathbf{C}$, where $\mathbf{C}$ is an I-by-J matrix over X defined entrywise by $c_{ij} = \sum_{k \in [K]} a_{ik} b_{kj}$ ([K] denotes the set $\{1, \ldots, K\}$). We let $S_{\mathbf{A}} \subseteq [I] \times [K]$, $S_{\mathbf{B}} \subseteq [K] \times [J]$, and $S_{\mathbf{C}} \subseteq [I] \times [J]$ denote the nonzero structures of $\mathbf{A}$, $\mathbf{B}$, and $\mathbf{C}$. Here we consider algorithms that evaluate and sum all *nontrivial* multiplications $a_{ik} b_{kj}$, where a_{ik} and $b_{kj} \neq 0$, and thus depend only on $S_{\mathbf{A}}$ and $S_{\mathbf{B}}$. We do not consider algorithms that exploit additional structure on X or more general relations on the entries of $\mathbf{A}$ and $\mathbf{B}$: in particular, we ignore numerical cancellation, so $S_{\mathbf{A}}$ and $S_{\mathbf{B}}$ induce $S_{\mathbf{C}}$.

DEFINITION 1. *Given input matrices $\mathbf{A}$ and $\mathbf{B}$, let the SpGEMM hypergraph be $\mathcal{H}(\mathbf{A}, \mathbf{B}) = (\mathcal{V}, \mathcal{N})$, with vertices*

$$\mathcal{V} = \{ v_{ikj} : (i, k) \in S_{\mathbf{A}} \wedge (k, j) \in S_{\mathbf{B}} \}$$

and nets $\mathcal{N} = \mathcal{N}^{\mathbf{A}} \cup \mathcal{N}^{\mathbf{B}} \cup \mathcal{N}^{\mathbf{C}}$, where

$$\mathcal{N}^{\mathbf{A}} = \{ n_{ik}^{\mathbf{A}} : (i, k) \in S_{\mathbf{A}} \} \text{ with } n_{ik}^{\mathbf{A}} = \{ v_{ikj} : j \in [J] \},$$
$$\mathcal{N}^{\mathbf{B}} = \{ n_{kj}^{\mathbf{B}} : (k, j) \in S_{\mathbf{B}} \} \text{ with } n_{kj}^{\mathbf{B}} = \{ v_{ikj} : i \in [I] \},$$
$$\mathcal{N}^{\mathbf{C}} = \{ n_{ij}^{\mathbf{C}} : (i, j) \in S_{\mathbf{C}} \} \text{ with } n_{ij}^{\mathbf{C}} = \{ v_{ikj} : k \in [K] \}.$$

In $\mathcal{H}(\mathbf{A}, \mathbf{B})$, each vertex corresponds to a nontrivial multiplication, and each net $n_{ik}^{\mathbf{A}}$, $n_{kj}^{\mathbf{B}}$, and $n_{ij}^{\mathbf{C}}$ corresponds to a nonzero of $\mathbf{A}$, $\mathbf{B}$, and $\mathbf{C}$, and contains all nontrivial multiplications in which that nonzero participates.

We now consider performing SpGEMM with input matrices $\mathbf{A}$ and $\mathbf{B}$ on a parallel machine with p processors with disjoint memories. A *parallelization* is a p-way partition of $\mathcal{V}$ (assigning multiplications to processors) and a *data distribution* is a triple of p-way partitions of $S_{\mathbf{A}}$, $S_{\mathbf{B}}$, and $S_{\mathbf{C}}$ (assigning nonzeros to processors). The communication proceeds in two phases: the *expand* phase, where the processors exchange nonzero entries of $\mathbf{A}$ and $\mathbf{B}$ (initially distributed according to the partitions of $S_{\mathbf{A}}$ and $S_{\mathbf{B}}$) in order to perform their multiplications (assigned according to the partition of $\mathcal{V}$), and the *fold* phase, where the processors communicate to reduce partial sums for nonzero entries of $\mathbf{C}$ (finally distributed according to the partition of $S_{\mathbf{C}}$).

The model proposed in Definition 1 is a generalization of the fine-grain SpMV model [7], but it also has an important intuitive distinction. In the fine-grain SpMV model, nets correspond to rows and columns of the matrix and vertices correspond to entries of the matrix. In $\mathcal{H}(\mathbf{A}, \mathbf{B})$, if $\mathbf{B}$ is a dense vector, then all of the nets in $\mathcal{N}^{\mathbf{A}}$ collapse to singletons, the K nets of $\mathcal{N}^{\mathbf{B}}$ correspond to columns of the matrix $\mathbf{A}$, and the I nets of $\mathcal{N}^{\mathbf{C}}$ correspond to rows of the matrix $\mathbf{A}$. The vertices of $\mathcal{H}(\mathbf{A}, \mathbf{B})$ correspond to scalar multiplications, which in this case coincide with entries of $\mathbf{A}$. Thus, $\mathcal{H}(\mathbf{A}, \mathbf{B})$ reproduces the SpMV model.

However, we emphasize that the vertices of $\mathcal{H}(\mathbf{A}, \mathbf{B})$ correspond to computation rather than data, which in the case of general SpGEMM do not coincide (as they do for SpMV). Therefore, the principal partitioning problem is that of assigning work to processors. Data distribution, or partitioning the entries of $\mathbf{A}$, $\mathbf{B}$, and $\mathbf{C}$ among processors, is our secondary concern, much like the partitioning of the input and output vectors in the case of SpMV.

The model proposed in Definition 1 is also distinct from the ones proposed in [1]. The approach in [1] considers a restricted class of parallelizations, known as outer-product algorithms, which leads to hypergraphs with fewer vertices and nets, while our model encompasses 1D (which include outer-product), 2D, and 3D parallelizations as defined in [2]. Another difference in the models is that the approach in [1] simultaneously partitions scalar multiplications and output matrix data, while we partition only the multiplications, as described above.

DEFINITION 2. *Given a partition $\{\mathcal{V}_1, \ldots, \mathcal{V}_p\}$ of $\mathcal{V}$, for each $i \in [p]$, we define Q_i, the ith cut of $\mathcal{H}$, to be the subset of $\mathcal{N}$ having nonempty intersections with both $\mathcal{V}_i$ and $\mathcal{V} \setminus \mathcal{V}_i$.*

LEMMA 1. *Given an SpGEMM computation with parallelization $\{\mathcal{V}_1, \ldots, \mathcal{V}_p\}$ and any data distribution, the number of words each processor i sends or receives is at least $|Q_i|$, and the critical-path cost is at least $\max_{i \in [p]} |Q_i|$.*

PROOF. For each processor i, for each net in Q_i, processor i must either receive or send the corresponding nonzero, since at most one processor owns each nonzero at the start and end of the computation. (While singleton nets may not uniquely correspond to a nonzero in $\mathbf{A}$, $\mathbf{B}$, or $\mathbf{C}$, they are never cut.) The bound on the critical-path communication cost is obtained by maximizing over processors. $\square$

Lemma 1 yields a lower bound over all parallelizations, subject to a computational load balance constraint.

DEFINITION 3. *For any $\epsilon \in [0, p - 1]$, let Π_ϵ be the set of all partitions $\{\mathcal{V}_1, \ldots, \mathcal{V}_p\}$ of $\mathcal{V}$ where $|\mathcal{V}_i| \leq (1 + \epsilon)|\mathcal{V}|/p$ for each $i \in [p]$. We say an SpGEMM computation with parallelization $\{\mathcal{V}_1, \ldots, \mathcal{V}_p\} \in \Pi_\epsilon$ is ϵ-load balanced.*

Note that the sets Π_ϵ are nested: Π_0 contains only perfectly balanced partitions while Π_{p-1} contains every partition, including trivial parallelizations with no interprocessor communication where one processor performs the whole computation.

THEOREM 1. *For any ϵ-load balanced SpGEMM computation, its critical-path communication cost is at least*

$$\min_{\{\mathcal{V}_1, \ldots, \mathcal{V}_p\} \in \Pi_\epsilon} \max_{i \in [p]} |Q_i|.$$

The next result shows that this critical-path lower bound is tight up to a logarithmic factor.

THEOREM 2. *For an SpGEMM computation with parallelization $\{\mathcal{V}_1, \ldots, \mathcal{V}_p\}$, there exists a data distribution such that the number of words processor i sends/receives is $O(|Q_i|)$ and the critical-path communication cost is $O(\log p \cdot \max |Q_i|)$.*

PROOF. We construct a data distribution by assigning the nonzero corresponding to each net in $\mathcal{N}^{\mathbf{A}}$, $\mathcal{N}^{\mathbf{B}}$, and $\mathcal{N}^{\mathbf{C}}$ to one of the processors owning a vertex in that net. The expand phase proceeds in at most $O(\log p)$ steps. Each nonzero of $\mathbf{A}$ and $\mathbf{B}$ is associated with a binary-tree broadcast among the processors whose parts $\mathcal{V}_i$ intersect the corresponding nets. Processor i receives each of its nonzeros at most once and sends each at most twice, for a total cost of $O(|Q_i|)$. Further, at each step j, processor i performs its assigned sends or receives from all the broadcast trees in which it is involved at level j (at most $|Q_i|$), and so each step involves at most $O(\max_{i \in [p]} |Q_i|)$ sends/receives along the critical path. The fold phase is similar, using binary-tree reductions. $\square$

3. EXPERIMENTAL RESULTS

Theorems 1 and 2 together reduce the problem of obtaining an optimal (to within a logarithmic factor) algorithm for the multiplication for a particular pair of sparse matrices to the problem of hypergraph partitioning. Unfortunately, this would need to be solved for every instance of SpGEMM (or at least for every pair of sparsity patterns), and it is an NP-hard problem [11]. However, we propose considering representative matrices for specific application areas in order to gain intuition for algorithmic design. In addition, efficient software, such as the PaToH [6] and Zoltan [4] libraries, exists for solving the problem approximately. The main limitations of the software are that (1) there are no guarantees for the quality of approximation and (2) the typical objective function is communication volume rather than critical-path communication cost. In this section, we focus on two SpGEMM computations arising from the setup phase of algebraic multigrid.

We experimentally study the communication costs of computing the product $\mathbf{P}^T \mathbf{A} \mathbf{P}$, formed to produce the grid hierarchy of an algebraic multigrid PDE solver. Here, $\mathbf{A}$ is the adjacency matrix of a graph $G_{\mathbf{A}}$ of $N = n^3$ vertices arranged as a 3D lattice, where every non-boundary vertex is adjacent to itself and its 26 closest neighbors. The matrix $\mathbf{P}$ corresponds to a bipartite graph $G_{\mathbf{P}} = (U, V, E)$, where U is the vertex set of $G_{\mathbf{A}}$ and V is the set of $(n/3)^3$ disjoint

Table 1: Maximum per-processor communication cost of forming $\mathbf{P}^T\mathbf{AP}$.

N	p	AP		$\mathbf{P^T(AP)}$	
		row	fine	row	fine
19,683	27	5,528	4,649	10,712	964
91,125	125	5,528	5,823	10,712	1,324
250,047	343	5,528	6,160	10,712	1,444
531,441	729	5,528	6,914	10,712	1,491
970,299	1,331	5,528	6,679	10,712	1,548

3-by-3-by-3 subcubes of U. Every subcube $v \in V$ is adjacent to each vertex $u \in U$ that belongs to v or is one of v's neighbors.

We consider two approaches for multiplying these matrices. In the *fine-grained* approach, we use our hypergraph model: we populate data structures that represent $\mathcal{H}(\mathbf{A}, \mathbf{P})$ and $\mathcal{H}(\mathbf{P}^T, \mathbf{AP})$ as given in Definition 1, and use the PaToH library to obtain a good partition, i.e., one with a small cut. Theorems 1 and 2 indicate that parallelizing the computation according to this partition can minimize communication.

The other approach we consider is the *row-wise* approach that corresponds to the way multigrid matrices are usually multiplied in practice [9]. In this approach we partition the output matrix rows among the processors manually, exploiting the multigrid matrices' correspondences with 3D lattices. Consider the rows of $\mathbf{A}$ as the n^3 points of a 3D lattice, partition them into p equal subcubes, and assign the rows that belong to each subcube to a distinct processor. We use each processor to compute the corresponding rows of $\mathbf{AP}$, and then similarly partition the rows of $\mathbf{P}^T$ and compute $\mathbf{P}^T(\mathbf{AP})$. This approach corresponds to choosing one specific partition among those considered by the hypergraph partitioner and therefore it can yield a suboptimal cut.

We compare the two approaches by computing the maximum number of words sent or received by any one processor, or $\max_i |Q_i|$, using the notation of the previous section. The results are shown in Table 1, where we follow a weak-scaling scheme that increases N and p proportionally. The table shows that in the $\mathbf{AP}$ step, the cost of the row-wise approach is comparable to or less than that of the fine-grained approach. We believe the slight advantage to the row-wise approach is due to the fact that PaToH minimizes communication volume rather than maximum per-processor cost. In the $\mathbf{P}^T(\mathbf{AP})$ step, the cost of the row-wise approach is 7 to 11 times greater than that of the fine-grained approach. Although this gap slightly narrows as we scale, likely because of the mismatch in cost functions, the fine-grained approach's advantage is dramatic. Our intuitive explanation of this result is based on the observation that the row-wise approach communicates the rows of the second input matrix. When we multiply $\mathbf{AP}$, the matrix $\mathbf{P}$ is quite sparse. However, $\mathbf{AP}$ is less sparse and so for $\mathbf{P}^T(\mathbf{AP})$, another algorithm derived from the fine-grained approach is a better choice.

The results demonstrate that better algorithms for $\mathbf{P}^T\mathbf{AP}$ should be developed; improvements are described in a separate paper [3].

Acknowledgments

This research is supported by an appointment to the Sandia National Laboratories Truman Fellowship in National Security Science and Engineering, sponsored by Sandia Corporation (a wholly owned subsidiary of Lockheed Martin Corporation) as Operator of Sandia National Laboratories under its U.S. Department of Energy Contract No. DE-AC04-94AL85000; the U.S. Department of Energy, Office of Science, Office of Advanced Scientific Computing Research (ASCR), Applied Mathematics program under contract number DE-AC02-05CH11231; Department of Energy grant DE-SC0008700; grants 1878/14 and 1901/14 from the Israel Science Foundation (founded by the Israel Academy of Sciences and Humanities); grant 3-10891 from the Ministry of Science and Technology, Israel; the Einstein Foundation; and the Minerva Foundation.

4. REFERENCES

[1] K. Akbudak and C. Aykanat. Simultaneous input and output matrix partitioning for outer-product–parallel sparse matrix-matrix multiplication. *SISC*, 36(5):C568–C590, 2014.

[2] G. Ballard, A. Buluç, J. Demmel, L. Grigori, B. Lipshitz, O. Schwartz, and S. Toledo. Communication optimal parallel multiplication of sparse random matrices. In *SPAA '13*, pages 222–231. ACM, 2013.

[3] G. Ballard, J. Hu, and C. Siefert. Reducing communication costs for sparse matrix multiplication within algebraic multigrid. Technical Report SAND2015-3275, Sandia Natl. Labs., 2015.

[4] E. Boman, K. Devine, L. Fisk, R. Heaphy, B. Hendrickson, C. Vaughan, Ü. Çatalyürek, D. Bozdag, W. Mitchell, and J. Teresco. Zoltan 3.0: parallel partitioning, boad-balancing, and data management services; user's guide. Technical Report SAND2007-4748W, Sandia Natl. Labs., 2007.

[5] A. Buluç and J. R. Gilbert. Parallel sparse matrix-matrix multiplication and indexing: implementation and experiments. *SISC*, 34(4):C170–C191, 2012.

[6] Ü. Çatalyürek and C. Aykanat. PaToH: a multilevel hypergraph partitioning tool, version 3.0. Technical report, Dept. of Computer Engineering, Bilkent Univ., 1999.

[7] Ü. Çatalyürek and C. Aykanat. A fine-grain hypergraph model for 2D decomposition of sparse matrices. In *IPDPS '01*, pages 118–123, 2001.

[8] Ü. Çatalyürek, C. Aykanat, and B. Uçar. On two-dimensional sparse matrix partitioning: models, methods, and a recipe. *SISC*, 32(2):656–683, 2010.

[9] M. Gee, C. Siefert, J. Hu, R. Tuminaro, and M. Sala. ML 5.0 Smoothed Aggregation User's Guide. Technical Report SAND2006-2649, Sandia Natl. Labs., 2006.

[10] S. Krishnamoorthy, Ü. Çatalyürek, J. Nieplocha, A. Rountev, and P. Sadayappan. Hypergraph partitioning for automatic memory hierarchy management. In *SC '06*, pages 34–46, 2006.

[11] T. Lengauer. *Combinatorial Algorithms for Integrated Circuit Layout*. Wiley, 1990.

The Cilkprof Scalability Profiler

Tao B. Schardl*   Bradley C. Kuszmaul*   I-Ting Angelina Lee[†]

William M. Leiserson*   Charles E. Leiserson*

*MIT CSAIL
32 Vassar Street
Cambridge, MA 02139

[†]Washington University in St. Louis
One Brookings Drive
St. Louis, MO 63130

ABSTRACT

Cilkprof is a scalability profiler for multithreaded Cilk computations. Unlike its predecessor Cilkview, which analyzes only the whole-program scalability of a Cilk computation, Cilkprof collects work (serial running time) and span (critical-path length) data for each call site in the computation to assess how much each call site contributes to the overall work and span. Profiling work and span in this way enables a programmer to quickly diagnose scalability bottlenecks in a Cilk program. Despite the detail and quantity of information required to collect these measurements, Cilkprof runs with only constant asymptotic slowdown over the serial running time of the parallel computation.

As an example of Cilkprof's usefulness, we used Cilkprof to diagnose a scalability bottleneck in an 1800-line parallel breadth-first search (PBFS) code. By examining Cilkprof's output in tandem with the source code, we were able to zero in on a call site within the PBFS routine that imposed a scalability bottleneck. A minor code modification then improved the parallelism of PBFS by a factor of 5. Using Cilkprof, it took us less than two hours to find and fix a scalability bug which had, until then, eluded us for months.

This paper describes the Cilkprof algorithm and proves theoretically using an amortization argument that Cilkprof incurs only constant overhead compared with the application's native serial running time. Cilkprof was implemented by compiler instrumentation, that is, by modifying the LLVM compiler to insert instrumentation into user programs. On a suite of 16 application benchmarks, Cilkprof incurs a geometric-mean multiplicative overhead of only 1.9 and a maximum multiplicative overhead of only 7.4 compared with running the benchmarks without instrumentation.

Categories and Subject Descriptors

D.2.2 [**Software Engineering**]: Design Tools and Techniques; D.1.3 [**Programming Techniques**]: Concurrent Programming—*parallel programming*; I.6.6 [**Simulation and Modeling**]: Simulation Output Analysis

This research was supported in part by Foxconn, in part by Oracle, and in part by NSF Grants 1314547, 1409238, and 1447786. Tao B. Schardl was supported in part by an MIT Akamai Fellowship and an NSF Graduate Research Fellowship.

SPAA'15, June 13–15, 2015, Portland, OR, USA.
Copyright © 2015 ACM 978-1-4503-3588-1/15/06 ... $15.00.
DOI: http://dx.doi.org/10.1145/2755573.2755603.

Keywords

Cilk; Cilkprof; compiler instrumentation; LLVM; multithreading; parallelism; performance; profiling; scalability; serial bottleneck; span; work.

1. INTRODUCTION

When a Cilk [10,16,27] multithreaded program fails to attain linear speedup when scaling up to large numbers of processors, there are four common reasons [14]:

Insufficient parallelism: The program contains serial bottlenecks that inhibit its scalability.

Scheduling overhead: The work that can be done in parallel is too fine grained to be worth distributing to other processors.

Insufficient memory bandwidth: The processors simultaneously access memory (or a level of cache) at too great a rate for the bandwidth of the machine's memory network to sustain.

Contention: A processor is slowed down by simultaneous interfering accesses to synchronization primitives, such as mutex locks, or by the true or false sharing of cache lines.

Performance engineers can benefit from profiling tools that identify where in their program code these problems might be at issue, as well as eliminate consideration of code that does not have issues so that the detective work can be properly focused elsewhere. This paper introduces a scalability profiler, called Cilkprof, which can help identify the causes of insufficient parallelism and scheduling overhead in a Cilk multithreaded program.

Cilkprof builds on the approach taken by Cilkview [14], which quantifies the parallelism of a program under test using work-span analysis [8, Ch. 27]. The **work** is the total time of all instructions executed by a computation. We denote the work by T_1, because it corresponds to the time to execute the computation on a single processor. The **span** is the length of a ***critical path*** — a longest (in time) path of dependencies — in the computation. We denote the span by T_∞, because it conceptually corresponds to the time to execute the computation on an infinite number of processors. The ***parallelism***, denoted T_1/T_∞, is the ratio of a computation's work to its span. Parallelism bounds the maximum possible speedup that a computation can obtain on any number of processors. To achieve linear speedup and minimize the overhead of Cilk's randomized work-stealing scheduler [5], a Cilk computation should exhibit ample parallelism, that is, the parallelism of the computation should exceed the number of processors by a sufficient margin [10], typically a factor of 10. Cilkview measures the work and span of a Cilk computation and reports on its parallelism.

To help programmers diagnose scalability bottlenecks, Cilkview provides an API to control which portions of a Cilk program should be analyzed. This API allows a programmer to restrict Cilkview's analysis by designating "start" and "stop" points in the code, similarly to the how the programmer can measure the execution time of various portions of a C program by inserting `gettimeofday` calls. Using this API, however, requires the programmer to manually probe portions of the code, which can be cumbersome and error prone for large and complex code bases, such as code bases that contain recursive functions.

In contrast, Cilkprof profiles the parallelism, much as gprof [13] profiles execution time. Unlike gprof, however, which uses asynchronous sampling, and Cilkview, which uses dynamic binary instrumentation using Pin [29], Cilkprof uses compiler instrumentation (see, for example, [31,32]) to gather detailed information about a Cilk computation. Conceptually, during a serial run of an instrumented Cilk program, Cilkprof analyzes every *call site* — every location in the code where a function is either called or spawned. It determines how much of the work and span of the overall computation is attributable to the subcomputation that begins when the function invoked at that call site is called or spawned and that ends when that function returns. Cilkprof calculates work and span in terms of processor cycles, but it can also use other measures such as execution time, instruction count, cache misses, etc. Cilkprof's analysis allows a programmer to evaluate the scalability of that call site — the scalability of the computation attributable to that call site — and how it affects the overall computation's scalability.

Although we implemented Cilkprof to analyze Cilk Plus [16] programs, in principle, the same tool could be implemented for any of the variants of Cilk, including MIT Cilk [10] or Cilk Arts Cilk++ [27]. More generally, the Cilkprof algorithm could be adapted to profile any parallel program whose span can be computed during a serial execution. Because Cilkprof runs on a serial execution of the program under test, it does not capture variations in work and span that may occur in a nondeterministic program.

Cilkprof can help Cilk programmers quickly identify scalability bottlenecks within their programs. We used Cilkprof to analyze an 1800-line parallel breadth-first search code, called PBFS [28]. After about two hours of poring over Cilkprof data, we were able to identify a serial bottleneck within PBFS, fix it, and confirm that our modification improved parallelism by a factor of 5. Cilkprof allowed us to eliminate insufficient parallelism as the code's scalability bottleneck and, thereby, to focus on the real bottleneck, which is memory bandwidth. Section 8 describes this case study.

Efficiently computing the work and span of every call site is harder than it may appear. Suppose that we measure the execution time of every *strand* — sequence of serially executed instructions that contain no parallel control. Although smaller than the total number of executed instructions, these data would be huge for many parallel applications, with space rivaling T_1, the normal serial running time of the program being analyzed. The data thus cannot reasonably be stored for later analysis, and the computation must be performed on the fly. Because a strand's execution affects all the call sites on the call stack, a naive strategy could potentially blow up the running time to as much as $\Theta(DT_1)$, where D is the maximum depth of the call stack. Of course, if a function f calls another function g, then the profile for f must include the profile for g. We could therefore compute local profiles for each function and update the parent with the profile of the child whenever a child returns, but this strategy could be just as bad or worse than updating each function on the call stack. If the profile contains S call sites, each function return could involve $\Theta(S)$ work, blowing up the running time to as much as $\Theta(ST_1)$. Furthermore, even if one computed the work with these methods, computing the span, which is similar to computing the longest path in a directed acyclic graph, would add considerable complexity to the computation.

By using an amortized `prof` data structure to represent profiles and a carefully constructed algorithm, Cilkprof computes work and span profiles with remarkable alacrity. Theoretically, Cilkprof computes the profiles in $O(T_1)$ time and $O(DS)$ space, where T_1 is the work of the original Cilk program, D is the maximum call-stack depth, and S is the number of call sites in the program. In practice, the overheads are strikingly small. We implemented Cilkprof by instrumenting a branch of the LLVM compiler that contains the Cilk linguistic extensions [19]. On a set of 16 application benchmarks, Cilkprof incurred a geometric-mean multiplicative slowdown of 1.9 and a maximum slowdown of 7.4, compared to the uninstrumented serial running times of these benchmarks.

Cilkprof's measurements seem ample for debugging scalability bottlenecks. Naturally, the Cilkprof instrumentation introduces some error into measurements of the program under test. Cilkprof compensates by subtracting estimates of its own overhead from the work and span measurements it gathers in order to reduce the effects of compiler instrumentation. Generally, it suffices to measure the parallelism of a program to within a binary order of magnitude in order to diagnose whether the program suffers from insufficient parallelism [14]. The overhead introduced by Cilkprof instrumentation appears to deliver work and span numbers within this range. Moreover, if one considers the errors in work and span to be similarly biased, the computation of their ratio, the parallelism, should largely cancel them.

Cilkprof as described herein does not have a sophisticated user interface. The current Cilkprof "engine" simply dumps the computed profile to a file in comma-separated-value format suitable for inputting to a spreadsheet. We view the development of a compelling user interface for Cilkprof as an open research question.

This paper makes the following contributions:

- The Cilkprof algorithm for computing the work and span attributable to each call site in a program, which provably operates with only constant overhead.

- The `prof` data structure for supporting amortized $\Theta(1)$-time updates to profiles.

- An implementation of Cilkprof which runs with little slowdown compared to the uninstrumented program under test.

- Two case studies — parallel quicksort and parallel breadth-first search of a graph — demonstrating how Cilkprof can be used to diagnose scalability bottlenecks.

This remainder of this paper is organized as follows. Section 2 illustrates how the profile data computed by Cilkprof can help to analyze the scalability of a simple parallel quicksort program. Sections 3 and 4 describe how the Cilkprof algorithm works and proves that Cilkprof incurs $\Theta(1)$ amortized overhead per program instruction. Section 5 presents an implementation of the `prof` data structure and shows that profile statistics can be updated in $\Theta(1)$ amortized time. Section 6 describes the profile of work and span measurements that Cilkprof computes for a Cilk program. Section 7 overviews the implementation of Cilkprof and analyzes its empirical performance. Section 8 describes how Cilkprof was used to diagnose a scalability bottleneck in PBFS. Section 9 discusses Cilkprof's relationship to related work, and Section 10 provides some concluding remarks.

2. PARALLEL QUICKSORT

This section illustrates the usefulness of Cilkprof by means of a case study of a simple parallel quicksort program coded in Cilk. Although the behavior of parallel quicksort is well understood theoretically, the profile data computed by Cilkprof allows a programmer to diagnose quicksort's partitioning subroutine as serial bottleneck without understanding the theoretical analysis.

```
1   int partition(long array[], int low, int high) {
2     long pivot = array[low + rand(high - low)];
3     int l = low - 1;
4     int r = high;
5     while (true) {
6       do { ++l; } while (array[l] < pivot);
7       do { --r; } while (array[r] > pivot);
8       if (l < r) {
9         long tmp = array[l];
10        array[l] = array[r];
11        array[r] = tmp;
12      } else {
13        return (l == low ? l + 1 : l);
14  } } }

16  void pqsort(long array[], int low, int high) {
17    if (high - low < COARSENING) {
18      // base case: sort using insertion sort
19    } else {
20      int part = partition(array, low, high);
21      cilk_spawn pqsort(array, low, part);
22      pqsort(array, part, high);
23      cilk_sync;
24  } }

26  int main(int argc, char *argv[]) {
27    int n;
28    long *A;
29    // parse arguments
30    // initialize array A of size n
31    pqsort(A, 0, n);
32    // do something with A
33    return 0;
34  }
```

Figure 1: Cilk code for a parallel quicksort that sorts an array of 64-bit integers. The variable COARSENING is a constant defining the maximum number of integers to sort in the base case. We used COARSENING=32.

Cilk multithreaded programming

Figure 1 shows the Cilk code for a quicksort [15] program that has been parallelized using the Cilk parallel keywords cilk_spawn and cilk_sync. The cilk_spawn keyword on line 21 *spawns* the recursive pqsort instantiation following it, allowing it to execute in parallel with its *continuation*, that is, with the statements after the spawn. Spawning pqsort on line 21 allows this pqsort instantiation to execute in parallel with the recursive call to pqsort on line 22. In principle, the call to pqsort on line 22 could also have been spawned, but since the continuation of that call does nothing but synchronize the children, spawning the call would not increase the parallelism and would increase the overhead. When the program control encounters a cilk_sync statement — the function *syncs* — all spawned children must finish before the execution can proceed. The cilk_sync on line 23 ensures that the computation performed by the spawn on line 21 finishes before pqsort returns.

Parallel quicksort's scalability profile

Quicksort provides a good example to illustrate what Cilkprof does, because quicksort's behavior is well understood theoretically. With high probability, pqsort performs $\Theta(n \log n)$ work to sort an array of n elements. The call to partition in line 20 performs $\Theta(n)$ work to partition an array of n elements and is a major contributor to the critical path of the computation, precluding pqsort from exhibiting more than $O(\log n)$ parallelism. (For a similar analysis of merge sort, see [8, Ch. 27.3].) A more careful analysis — one that pays attention to the constants hidden inside the big-Oh — indicates that on an array of 10 million elements, pqsort exhibits a parallelism of approximately $\ln 10^6 = 16$. To achieve linear speedup, however, a program should exhibit substantially more parallelism than there are processors on the machine [10]. This quicksort program has too little parallelism to keep more than a few processors busy.

Suppose that we did not already know where the serial bottleneck in the code in Figure 1 lies, however. Let us see how we can use Cilkprof to discover that partition is the main culprit.

Figure 2 presents an excerpt of the data Cilkprof reports from running pqsort on an array of 10 million 64-bit integers, cleaned up for didactic clarity. (We have not yet implemented a user interface for Cilkprof, which we view as an interesting research problem.) Cilkprof computes two "profiles" for the computation: an "on-work profile" and an "on-span profile." Each *profile* contains a record of work and span data for each call site in the computation. A record in the *on-work* profile accumulates work and span data for every invocation of a particular call site in the computation. A record in the *on-span* profile accumulates work and span data only for the invocations of a particular call site that appear on the critical path of the computation. Section 6 describes precisely what work and span values each record stores and how Cilkprof accommodates recursive functions.

Let us explore the data in Figure 2 to see what these data tell us about the scalability of this quicksort code. The on-work profile shows us that the work and span of the computation is dominated by line 31, the instantiation of pqsort from main. The "T_1/T_∞ on work" value for this line tells us that this call to pqsort exhibits a parallelism of only 5.6, even less than the 16-fold parallelism that our analysis predicted. To see why this call to pqsort exhibits poor parallelism, we can examine what different call sites contribute to the span of the computation.

Let us start by examining Cilkprof's "local T_∞ on span" data. Conceptually, the "local T_∞ on span" for a call site s that calls or spawns a function f specifies how much of the span comes from instructions executed under s, not including instructions executed under f's call sites. For the quicksort code in Figure 1, we can observe two properties of these "local T_∞ on span" data. First, the sum of the "local T_∞ on span" values for the three call sites in pqsort (lines 20, 21, and 22) and the call to pqsort from main (line 31) equals the "T_∞ on work" value for the call to pqsort from main. These four call sites therefore account for the entire span of line 31. Second, the "local T_∞ on span" of line 20 accounts for practically all of the span of line 31, indicating that line 20 is the parallelism bottleneck for the instantiation of pqsort from main.

What else does Cilkprof tell us about line 20? The "T_1/T_∞ on span" for line 20 shows that all instances of this call site on the critical path are serial. Consequently, parallelizing this call site is key to improving the parallelism of the computation. From examining the code, we therefore conclude that we must parallelize partition to improve the scalability of pqsort, as we expect from our understanding of quicksort's theoretical performance. Cilkprof's data allows the serial bottleneck in quicksort to be identified without prior knowledge of its analysis.

3. COMPUTING WORK AND SPAN

This section describes how Cilkprof computes the work and span of a Cilk computation. Cilkprof's algorithm for work and span is based on a similar algorithm from [14]. After defining some useful concepts, we describe the "work-span" variables used to perform the computation. We give the algorithm and describe the invariants it maintains. We show that on a Cilk program under test that executes in T_1 time and has stack depth D, Cilkprof's work-span algorithm runs in $O(T_1)$ time using $O(D)$ extra storage. Section 4 will extend this work-span algorithm to compute profiles.

Definitions

Let us first define some terms. The program under test is a Cilk binary executable containing a set I of *instructions*. Some of the instructions in I are *functions* — they can be called or spawned

Line	On work			On span				
	T_1	T_∞	T_1/T_∞	T_1	T_∞	T_1/T_∞	Local T_1	Local T_∞
20	408,150,528	408,150,528	1.0	141,891,291	141,891,291	1.0	141,891,291	141,891,291
21	741,312,781	116,591,841	6.4	597,298,216	98,119,730	6.1	4,340	3,823
22	761,041,165	125,360,000	6.1	691,808,220	118,447,199	5.8	7,068	6,682
31	790,518,060	141,902,681	5.6	790,518,060	141,902,681	5.6	885	885

Figure 2: A subset of the data that Cilkprof reports for running the quicksort code in Figure 1 to sort an array of 10 million random 64-bit integers. The "on work" columns come from Cilkprof's on-work profile, which considers all instantiations in the computation, and the "on span" columns come from Cilkprof's on-span profile, which only considers instantiations that fall on the critical path. For each call site, the "T_1 on work" column gives the sum of the work of all invocations of that call site, and the "T_∞ on work" column gives the sum of the spans of those invocations. The "T_1/T_∞ on work" column gives the parallelism of each call site, as computed from the "T_1 on work" and "T_∞ on work" values for that call site. The "T_1 on span," "T_∞ on span," and "T_1/T_∞ on span" columns are similar to their on-work counterparts, but consider only invocations on the critical path of the computation. The "local T_1 on span" column contains, for each call site, the cumulative work of all invocations of that call site on the critical path, excluding all work in children of the instantiated function. The "Local T_∞ on span" column is similar, except that it presents the cumulative span. All times are measured in nanoseconds.

— and some are **call sites** — they call or spawn a function. The (mathematical) function φ maps a call site to the function in which the call site resides.

When the program is executed serially, it produces a sequence *XI* of **executed instructions**. The function $\sigma : XI \to I$ indicates which instruction $i \in I$ was executed to produce a given executed instruction $xi \in XI$. A contiguous subsequence of instructions in *XI* is called a **trace**. For a given executed call site $xi \in XI$, the **trace** of xi, denoted $\text{Trace}(xi)$, is the contiguous subsequence of *XI* starting with xi's successor — the first instruction of the executed function that was called or spawned — and ending with the corresponding return from the executed function.

For simplicity, assume that work and span are measured by counting instructions. It is straightforward to adapt the Cilkprof algorithm to measure work and span in terms of processor cycles, execution time, or even cache misses and other measures. The **work** of a trace T, denoted $\text{Work}(T)$, is the number of instructions in T. The **span** of a trace T, denoted $\text{Span}(T)$, is the maximum number of instructions along any path of dependencies from the first instruction in T to the last instruction in T.

Work-span variables

Cilkprof measures the work and span of a Cilk computation in a manner similar to the Cilkview algorithm [14]. As Cilkprof serially executes the Cilk program under test, it computes the work and span of each instantiated function.

For each instantiated function F, four **work-span variables** are maintained in a frame for F on a **shadow stack** which is pushed and popped in synchrony with the function-call stack. The **work** variable $F.w$ corresponds to the work on the trace of F executed so far. The remaining three **span variables** are used to compute the span of F. Conceptually, Cilkprof maintains a location u in F which is initially set to the beginning of F, but as the execution of F proceeds, is set to the cilk_spawn instruction that spawned whichever child of F realizes the largest span of any child encountered so far since the last cilk_sync. The location u is not explicitly maintained, however, but the values of the three variables reflect its position in F. Specifically, the three span variables are defined as follows:

- The **prefix** $F.p$ stores the span of the trace starting from the first instruction of F and ending with u. The path that realizes $F.p$ is guaranteed to be on the critical path of F.

- The **longest-child** $F.\ell$ stores the span of the trace from the start of F through the return of the child that F spawns at u.

- The **continuation** $F.c$ stores the span of the trace from the continuation of u through the most recently executed instruction in F.

F spawns or calls G:	Called G returns to F:
1 $G.w = 0$	5 $G.p \mathrel{+}= G.c$
2 $G.p = 0$	6 $F.w \mathrel{+}= G.w$
3 $G.\ell = 0$	7 $F.c \mathrel{+}= G.p$
4 $G.c = 0$	

Spawned G returns to F:	F syncs:
8 $G.p \mathrel{+}= G.c$	14 **if** $F.c > F.\ell$
9 $F.w \mathrel{+}= G.w$	15 $F.p \mathrel{+}= F.c$
10 **if** $F.c + G.p > F.\ell$	16 **else**
11 $F.\ell = G.p$	17 $F.p \mathrel{+}= F.\ell$
12 $F.p \mathrel{+}= F.c$	18 $F.c = 0$
13 $F.c = 0$	19 $F.\ell = 0$

F executes an instruction:
20   $F.w \mathrel{+}= 1$
21   $F.c \mathrel{+}= 1$

Figure 3: Pseudocode for Cilkprof's work-span algorithm. For simplicity, this pseudocode computes work and span by incrementing the work and continuation at each instruction, rather than by any of several more efficient methods to compute instruction counts.

The work-span algorithm

Figure 3 gives the pseudocode for the basic Cilkprof algorithm for computing work and span. At any given moment during Cilkprof's serial execution of the program under test, each nonzero work-span variable z holds a value corresponding to a trace, which we define as the **trace** of the value and denote by $\text{Trace}(z)$. The pseudocode maintains three invariants:

INVARIANT 1. *The trace of the value in a variable is well defined, that is, it is a contiguous subsequence of XI.*

INVARIANT 2. *If z is a work variable, then $z = \text{Work}(\text{Trace}(z))$.*

INVARIANT 3. *If z is a span variable, then $z = \text{Span}(\text{Trace}(z))$.*

These invariants can be verified by induction on instruction count by inspecting the pseudocode in Figure 3. For example, just before G returns from a spawn, we can assume inductively that $G.p$ and $G.c$ hold the spans of their traces. At this point, the trace of $G.p$ starts at the first instruction of G and ends with u, traversing all called and spawned children in between. The trace of $G.c$ starts at the continuation of u and continues to the current instruction, also traversing all called and spawned children in between. Thus, they have explored the entire trace of G between them. Consequently, when line 8 executes, the trace of $G.p$ becomes the entire trace of G, and $G.p$ becomes $\text{Span}((\,)G.p$, maintaining the invariants. Other code sequences succumb to similar reasoning.

Performance

The next theorem bounds the running time and space usage of Cilkprof's algorithm for computing work and span.

LEMMA 4. *Cilkprof computes the work and span of a Cilk computation in $O(T_1)$ time using $O(D)$ space, where T_1 is the work of the Cilk computation and D is the maximum call-stack depth of the computation.*

PROOF. Inspection of the pseudocode from Figure 3 reveals that a constant number of operations on work-span variables occur at each function call or spawn, each sync, and each function return in the computation. Consequently, the running time is $O(T_1)$. Since there are 4 work-span variables in each frame of the shadow stack, the space is $O(D)$. □

4. THE BASIC PROFILE ALGORITHM

This section describes the basic algorithm that Cilkprof uses to compute profiles for a Cilk computation. We first introduce the abstract interface for the prof data structure, whose implementation is detailed in Section 5. We show how to augment the work-span algorithm to additionally compute profiles for the computation. We analyze Cilkprof under the assumption, borne out in Section 5, that the prof data structure supports all of its methods in $\Theta(1)$ amortized time. We show that Cilkprof executes a Cilk computation in $O(T_1)$ time, where T_1 is the work of the original Cilk computation.

The prof data structure

As it computes the work and span of a Cilk computation, Cilkprof updates profiles in a prof data structure, which records work and span data for each call site in the computation. Let us see how Cilkprof computes these profiles, in terms of the abstract interface to the prof data structure. Section 5 describes how a prof can be implemented efficiently.

The prof data structure is a key-value store R that maintains a set of *key-value pairs* $\langle s, v \rangle$ as elements, where the key s is a call site and the value v is a record containing a *work field* $v.work$ and a *span field* $v.span$. The following methods operate on prof's:

- INIT(R): Initialize prof R to be an empty profile, deleting any key-value pairs stored in R.
- UPDATE($R, \langle s, v \rangle$): If no element $\langle s, v' \rangle$ already exists in R, store $\langle s, v \rangle$ into R. If such an element exists, store $\langle s, v' + v \rangle$, where corresponding fields of v' and v are summed.
- ASSIGN(R, R'): Move the contents of prof R' into R, deleting any old values in R, and then initialize R'.
- UNION(R, R'): Update the prof R with all the elements in the prof R', and then initialize R'.
- PRINT(R): List all the key-value pairs in the prof R, and initialize R.

We shall show in Section 5 that each of these methods can be implemented to execute in $\Theta(1)$ amortized time.

Profiles

What profiling data does Cilkprof compute? Consider a call site s. During a serial execution of the program, the function $\varphi(s)$ containing s may call or spawn a function (or functions, if the target of the call or spawn is a function pointer) at s. Let OW be the set of executed call sites for which $xi \in OW$ implies that $\sigma(xi) = s$. For each $xi \in OW$, recall that Trace(xi) is the set of instructions executed after the call or spawn at the call site until the corresponding return. Intuitively, the work-on-work for s is the total work of all of these calls, which is to say

$$\sum_{xi \in OW} \text{Work}(\text{Trace}(xi)),$$

and the span-on-work for s is

$$\sum_{xi \in OW} \text{Span}(\text{Trace}(xi)).$$

The work-on-span and span-on-span for s are similar, where the sum is taken over OS, the set of instructions along the span of the computation for which $xi \in OS$ implies that $\varphi(xi) = s$. These definitions are inadequate, however, for recursive codes, because two instantiations of s on the call stack cause double counting. Rather than complicate the explanation of the algorithm at this point, let us defer the issue of recursion until Section 6 and assume for the remainder of this section that no recursive calls occur in the execution, in which case these profile values for s are accurate.

Cilkprof computes these profile values for all call sites in the program by associating a prof data structure with each work-span variable in Figure 3. For a variable z, let $z.prof$ denote z's prof, let $z.prof[s].work$ denote the value of the *work* field for a call site $s \in I$ in the profile data for z, and let $z.prof[s].span$ denote the value of $z.prof$'s *span* field for s.

The Cilkprof algorithm

As Cilkprof performs the algorithm in Figure 3, in addition to computing the work and span, it also updates the prof associated with each work-span variable. First, just before each of lines 6 and 9, Cilkprof executes

$$\text{UPDATE}(G.w.prof, \langle s, [work: G.w, span: G.p] \rangle)$$
$$\text{UPDATE}(G.p.prof, \langle s, [work: G.w, span: G.p] \rangle).$$

In addition, Cilkprof performs the following calculations, where y and z denote two distinct variables in the pseudocode:

- Whenever the pseudocode assigns $y = 0$, Cilkprof also executes INIT($y.prof$).
- Whenever the pseudocode assigns $y = z$, Cilkprof also executes ASSIGN($y.prof, z.prof$).
- Whenever the pseudocode executes $y \mathrel{+}= z$, Cilkprof also executes UNION($y.prof, z.prof$).

As a point of clarification, executing lines 20–21 causes no additional calculations to be performed on prof data structures, because 1 is not a variable.

Correctness

Recall that each work-span variable z in Figure 3 defines a trace Trace(z). For each variable z and call site $s \in I$, Cilkprof maintains the invariant

$$z.prof[s].work = \sum_{xi \in \text{Trace}(z):\sigma(xi)=s} \text{Work}(\text{Trace}(xi))$$

and a similar invariant for $z.prof[s].span$. One can verify by induction on instruction count that the Cilkprof algorithm maintains these invariants.

Analysis of performance

The next theorem bounds the running time and space usage of Cilkprof. This analysis assumes that all prof methods execute in $\Theta(1)$ amortized time and that a single prof occupies $O(S)$ space, where S is the number of call sites in the Cilk computation. Section 5 shows how prof can achieve these bounds.

THEOREM 5. *Cilkprof executes a Cilk computation in $O(T_1)$ time using $O(DS)$ space, where T_1 is the work of the Cilk computation, D is the maximum stack depth of the computation, and S is the number of call sites in the computation.*

PROOF. By Lemma 4, the work-span algorithm contributes negligibly to either time or space, and so it suffice to analyze the contributions due to method calls on the prof data structure. Inspection of the pseudocode from Figure 3, together with the modifications to make it handle profiles, reveals that a constant number of operations on work-span variables occur at each function call or spawn, each sync, and each function return in the computation. Returning from a function causes a constant number of method calls on the prof to be performed, and each operation on a variable induces at most a constant number of method calls on its associated prof, each of which takes $\Theta(1)$ amortized time, as Theorem 6 in Section 5 will show. Consequently, each operation performed by Cilkprof to compute the work and span incurs at most constant overhead, yielding $O(T_1)$ for the total running time of Cilkprof.

The space bound is the product of the maximum depth D of function nesting and the maximum size of a frame on the shadow stack. Each frame of the shadow stack contains 4 work-span variables and their associated prof data structures, each of which has size at most S. Thus, since the size of a frame on the shadow stack is $O(S)$, the total space is $O(DS)$. □

5. THE PROF DATA STRUCTURE

This section describes how the the prof data structure employed by Cilkprof is implemented. We first assume that the number of call sites is known *a priori*. We investigate the problems that arise when implementing a prof as an array or linked list, and then we see how a hybrid implementation can achieve $\Theta(1)$ amortized time for all its methods. We then remove the assumption and extend prof to the situation when call sites are discovered dynamically on the fly while still maintaining a $\Theta(1)$ amortized time[1] for each of its methods.

The basic data structure

To simplify the description of the implementation of the prof data structure, assume for the moment that Cilkprof magically knows *a priori* the number S of call sites in the computation. The compiler sets up a global hash table h mapping each call site s to a distinct index $h(s) \in \{0, 1, \ldots, S-1\}$.

The prof data structure is a hybrid of two straightforward implementations: an array and a list. Separately, each implementation would use too much time or space, but in combination they yield the desired space and time.

The **array implementation** represents a prof R as a size-S array $R.arr[0..S-1]$. In this implementation, the INIT method allocates a new size-S array $R.arr$ and zeroes it, costing $\Theta(S)$ time. The call UPDATE$(R, \langle s,v \rangle)$ updates the entry with $R.arr[h(s)] + v$ (where $+$ performs fieldwise addition on the *work* and *span* fields of the records), taking only $\Theta(1)$ time. UNION(R, R') iterates through the entries of R' and updates the corresponding entries in R, zeroing R' as it goes, costing $\Theta(S)$ time. Finally, ASSIGN(R, R') iterates through the arrays copying the elements of R' to R, zeroing R' as it goes, also costing $\Theta(S)$ time. The inefficiency in the array implementation is due to the $\Theta(S)$-time methods.

The **list implementation** represents a prof R as a linked list $R.\ell\ell$ that logs updates to the elements stored in R. The linked list $R.\ell\ell$ is a singly linked list with a head and a tail pointer to support $\Theta(1)$-time concatenation. The INIT, UPDATE, and UNION functions are implemented using straightforward $\Theta(1)$-time linked list operations. The INIT method first deallocates any previous linked list, freeing the entries of $R.\ell\ell$ in $\Theta(1)$ amortized time, because each entry it frees must have been previously appended by UPDATE. Then INIT allocates an empty linked list with NULL head and tail pointers. Calling UPDATE$(R, \langle s,v \rangle)$ appends a new linked-list element to $R.\ell\ell$ containing $\langle s,v \rangle$. Performing UNION(R, R') concatenates the linked lists $R.\ell\ell$ and $R'.\ell\ell$, and sets $R'.\ell\ell$ to an empty linked list.

[1]Technically, the bound is $\Theta(1)$ expected time, because the implementation uses a hash table, but except for this one nit, the amortized bound better characterizes the performance of the data structure.

INIT(R)	ASSIGN(R,R')
1 Free $R.arr$	5 INIT(R)
2 Free $R.\ell\ell$	6 $R.\ell\ell = R'.\ell\ell$
3 $R.\ell\ell = \emptyset$	7 $R.arr = R.arr$
4 $R.arr = \emptyset$	8 $R'.\ell\ell = \emptyset$
	9 $R'.arr = \emptyset$

_FLUSHLIST(R)	UPDATE($R, \langle s, v \rangle$)
10 **if** $R.arr == \emptyset$	15 **if** $R.arr \neq \emptyset$
11 $R.arr =$ **new** Array(S)	16 $R.arr[h(s)] \mathrel{+}= v$
12 **for** $\langle s,v \rangle \in R.\ell\ell$	17 **else** APPEND($R.\ell\ell, \langle s,v \rangle$)
13 $R.arr[h(s)] \mathrel{+}= v$	18 **if** $|R.\ell\ell| == S$
14 Free $R.\ell\ell$	19 _FLUSHLIST(R)

UNION(R,R')	PRINT(R)
20 **if** $R.arr \neq \emptyset$	31 _FLUSHLIST(R)
21 **if** $R'.arr \neq \emptyset$	32 **for** $i = 0$ **to** $S-1$
22 **for** $i = 0$ **to** $S-1$	33 Output $R.arr[i]$
23 $R.arr[i] \mathrel{+}= R'.arr[i]$	34 INIT(R)
24 Free $R'.arr$	
25 **else** $R.arr = R'.arr$	
26 CONCATENATE($R.\ell\ell, R'.\ell\ell$)	
27 **if** $|R.\ell\ell| \geq S$	
28 _FLUSHLIST(R)	
29 $R'.arr = \emptyset$	
30 $R'.ll = \emptyset$	

Figure 4: Pseudocode for the methods of the prof data structure, including a helper routine _FLUSHLIST. A prof R consists of a linked-list component $R.\ell\ell$ and an array component $R.arr$. The linked list $R.\ell\ell$ is a singly linked list with a cardinality field to keep track of the number of elements in the list and a head and tail pointer to enable $\Theta(1)$-time list concatenation.

Similarly, PRINT operates in $\Theta(1)$ amortized time. The inefficiency in this implementation is space. Because every call to UPDATE allocates space for an update, the linked list uses space proportional to the total number of updates, which, for a Cilk computation with work T_1, is $\Theta(T_1)$ space.

The **hybrid implementation** that Cilkprof actually uses represents a prof R using both an array $R.arr$ and a linked list $R.\ell\ell$. Figure 4 gives the pseudocode for the prof methods. Conceptually, UPDATE and UNION use the linked list $R.\ell\ell$ to handle elements until $R.\ell\ell$ contains at least S updates. At this point, the elements in $R.\ell\ell$ are updated into the array $R.arr$, the linked list $R.\ell\ell$ is emptied, and UPDATE and UNION use the array $R.arr$ to handle future operations.

Intuitively, by combining the linked-list and array implementations, the prof data structure R enjoys the time efficiency of the linked list implementation with the space efficiency of the array implementation. Because UPDATE and UNION move elements from $R.\ell\ell$ into $R.arr$ when $R.\ell\ell$ contains at least S elements, R occupies $O(S)$ space. By initially storing elements in a linked list, the prof data structure can avoid performing an expensive UNION operation until it can amortize that expense against the elements that have been inserted. The following theorem formalizes this intuition.

THEOREM 6. *The* prof *data structure uses at most* $\Theta(S)$ *space and supports each of* INIT, ASSIGN, UPDATE, UNION, *and* PRINT *in* $\Theta(1)$ *amortized time.*

PROOF. The time bound follows from an amortized analysis carried out using the accounting method [8, Ch. 17]. The amortization maintains the following invariants.

INVARIANT 7. *Each linked-list element carries 2 tokens of amortized time.*

INVARIANT 8. *Each array A carries $|A|$ tokens of amortized time.*

We analyze each of the prof methods in turn.

A call to INIT(R) takes $\Theta(1)$ time to free $R.arr$ and spends 1 token on each element in $R.\ell\ell$ to cover the cost of freeing that element. Then INIT performs $\Theta(1)$ operations in $\Theta(1)$ time to reinitialize the data structure, for a total of $\Theta(1)$ amortized time.

A call to ASSIGN is $\Theta(1)$ time plus a call to INIT, for a total amortized time of $\Theta(1)$.

The helper routine _FLUSHLIST(R) is called only when its linked list $R.\ell\ell$ attains at least S elements. The routine may spend $\Theta(S)$ time to create a new array of size S, the entries of which are initialized to 0. This routine can use 1 token from each element in $R.\ell\ell$ to transfer that element's update to $R.arr$, free that element, transfer the element's other token to $R.arr$, and cover the $\Theta(1)$ real cost to initialize one entry of $R.arr$. Consequently, _FLUSHLIST takes $\Theta(1)$ amortized time and produces an array $R.arr$ with $|R.\ell\ell| \geq S = |R.arr|$ tokens, maintaining Invariant 8.

A call to UPDATE($R, \langle s, v \rangle$) exhibits one of three behaviors. First, if the call executes line 16, then it takes $\Theta(1)$ real time. Otherwise, the call executes line 17, which is charged $\Theta(1)$ real time plus 2 amortized time units to append a new linked-list element with 2 tokens onto $R.\ell\ell$ while maintaining Invariant 7. At this point, if $|R.\ell\ell| = S$, then line 19 calls _FLUSHLIST, which costs $\Theta(1)$ amortized time. Thus, UPDATE takes $\Theta(1)$ amortized time in every case.

A call to UNION(R, R') uses the tokens on $R'.arr$ to achieve a $\Theta(1)$ amortized running time. If the call executes lines 22–24, then each iteration charges 1 token from $R'.arr$ to cover the $\Theta(1)$ real cost to update an entry in $R.arr$ with an entry in $R'.arr$. Lines 22–24 therefore take $\Theta(1)$ amortized time. Line 26 takes $\Theta(1)$ time to concatenate two linked lists, and the analysis of lines 27–30 corresponds to that for lines 18–19 of UPDATE. The amortized cost of UNION is therefore $\Theta(1)$.

A call to PRINT(R) executes _FLUSHLIST in line 31 in $\Theta(1)$ amortized time, and spend the S available tokens in $R.arr$ to pay for sequencing through all the elements of R. Adding in the cost to call INIT in line 34 gives $\Theta(1)$ total amortized cost of printing.

The space bound on a prof data structure R follows from observing that the array $R.arr$ occupies $\Theta(S)$ space, and only line 17 in UPDATE and line 26 in UNION increase the size of the linked-list $R.\ell$. Because lines 18–19 in UPDATE and lines 27–30 in UNION move the elements of $R.\ell\ell$ into $R.arr$ once the size of $R.\ell\ell$ is at least S, the linked list $R.\ell\ell$ never contains more than $2S$ elements, and R therefore occupies $O(S)$ total space. $\square$

Discovering call sites dynamically

Let us now remove the assumption that the number S of call sites is known *a priori*. To handle call sites discovered dynamically as the execution unfolds, Cilkprof tracks the number S of unique call sites encountered so far. Cilkprof maintains the global hash table h using table doubling [8, Sec. 17.4], which can resize the table as it grows while still providing amortized $\Theta(1)$ operations. When Cilkprof encounters a new call site s, it increments S and stores $h(s) = S - 1$, thereby mapping the new call site to the new value of $S - 1$.

We must also modify the helper function _FLUSHLIST. First, line 15 must check whether the size of the existing array matches the current value of S, rather than simply checking if it exists. If a new array is allocated, in addition to the linked-list elements being transferred to the new array, the old array elements must also be transferred. At the end, the old array must be destroyed.

We must also modify the UPDATE and UNION methods to ensure that both UPDATE and UNION maintain the same invariants in their amortization as stated in the proof of Theorem 6. Thus, the changes do not affect the asymptotic complexity of the prof data structure. Specifically, line 15 in the pseudocode for UPDATE must be modified as in _FLUSHLIST to check whether the size of the

```
1   int fib(int n) {
2       if (n < 2) return n;
3       int x, y;
4       x = cilk_spawn fib(n-1);
5       y = fib(n-2);
6       cilk_sync;
7       return (x + y);
8   }

10  int main(int argc, char *argv[]) {
11      int n, result;
12      // parse arguments
13      result = fib(n);
14      return 0;
15  }
```

Figure 5: Cilk pseudocode for a recursive program to compute Fibonacci numbers.

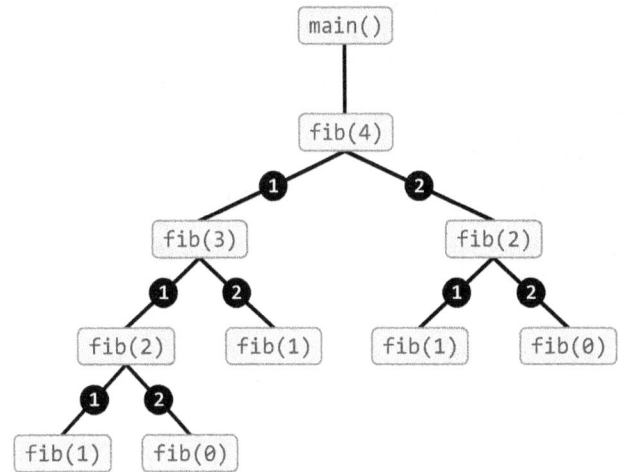

Figure 6: An invocation tree for the recursive Fibonacci program in Figure 5. Each rounded rectangle denotes a function instantiation, and an edge between tow rounded rectangles denotes the upper instantiation invoking the lower. The circled labels 1 and 2 on edges identify the call sites on lines 4 and 5, respectively, in the code in Figure 5.

existing array matches the current value of S. With this change, a call to UPDATE adds a record to the linked list whenever the array is too small, even if the array already stores some records. Lines 20–25 in the pseudocode for UNION must also be modified to copy the elements of the smaller array into the larger.

6. THE PROFILE

This section describes the profile that Cilkprof computes. Although Section 4 describes how Cilkprof can measure the work and span of each call site assuming the program contains no recursive functions, in fact, Cilkprof must handle recursive functions with care to avoid overcounting their work and span. We define the "top-call-site," "top-caller," and "local" measurements that Cilkprof accumulates for each call site, each of which we found to be easy to compute and useful for analyzing the contribution of that call site to the work and span of the overall program. We describe how to compute these measures.

A Cilkprof *measurement* for a call site s consists of the following values for a set of invocations of s:

- an *execution count* — the number of invocations of s accumulated in the profile;

- the *call-site work* — the sum of the work of those invocations;

- the *call-site span* — the sum of the spans of those invocations.

Cilkprof additionally computes the parallelism of s as the ratio of s's call-site work and call-site span.

Line	Top-call-site			Top-caller			Local		
	T_1	T_∞	T_1/T_∞	T_1	T_∞	T_1/T_∞	T_1	T_∞	T_1/T_∞
4	450,321,639	113,267	3,975.8	279,094,680	39,643	7,040.2	150,281,850	150,281,850	1.0
5	450,307,915	250,302	1,799.1	171,229,726	14,688	11,657.8	121,330,045	86,699,953	1.4
13	450,325,186	40,331	11,165.7	450,325,186	40,331	11,165.7	780	688	1.1

Figure 7: Work and span values in the on-work profile Cilkprof collects for running the recursive Fibonacci program in Figure 5 to compute `fib(30)`. All times are measured in nanoseconds.

If programs contained no recursive functions, Cilkprof could simply aggregate all executions of each call site, but generally, it must avoid overcounting the call-site work and call-site span of recursive functions. Of the many ways that Cilkprof might accommodate recursive functions, we have found three sets of measurements of a call site, called the "top-call-site," "top-caller," and "local" measurements, to be particularly useful for analyzing the parallelism of Cilk computations. These measurements maintain the basic algorithm's performance bounds given in Theorems 5 and 6 while also handling recursion.

Top-call-site measurements

Conceptually, the "top-call-site" measurement for a call site s aggregates the work and span of every execution of s that is not a recursive execution of s. Formally, an executed call site $xs \in I$ is a **top-call-site invocation** if no executed call site $xi \in I$ exists such that

$$xs \in \text{Trace}(xi) \wedge \sigma(xs) = \sigma(xi) .$$

Cilkprof's **top-call-site measurement** for s aggregates all top-call-site invocations of s.

An executed call site can be identified as a top-call-site invocation from the computation's invocation tree. Consider the parallel recursive Cilk program in Figure 5 and the example invocation tree for it in Figure 6. Each edge in this tree corresponds to an **invocation** — an executed call site that either calls or spawns a child — and the labels on edges denote the corresponding call site. From Figure 6, we see that the executed call site spawning `fib(3)` is a top-call-site invocation, because no other execution of line 4 appears above `fib(3)` in the invocation tree. The spawning of `fib(2)` by `fib(3)` is not a top-call-site invocation, however, because `fib(3)` appears above `fib(2)` in the tree.

Cilkprof's top-call-site measurements are useful for assessing the parallelism of each call site. The ratio of the call-site work over the call-site span from a call site's top-call-site data gives the parallelism of all nonrecursive executions of that call site in the computation, as if the computation performed each such call site execution in series. This parallelism value can be particularly helpful for measuring the parallelism of executed call sites that occur on the critical path of the computation.

In a function containing multiple recursive calls, however, such as the `fib` routine in Figure 5, the top-call-site measurements are less useful for comparing different call sites' relative contributions. For example, consider the top-call-site work and span values in Figure 7, which Cilkprof collected from running the code in Figure 5. As Figure 7 shows, the top-call-site work values for the recursive `fib` invocations on line 4 and line 5 are similar to that of the call to `fib` on line 13, and the top-call-site span values of these recursive invocations exceed that of line 13.

These large top-call-site measurements occur because the measurement aggregates multiple top-call-site executions of a call site under the same top-level call to `fib`. For example, as the invocation tree in Figure 6 shows, the invocations of `fib(1)` from `fib(3)`, `fib(2)` from `fib(4)`, and `fib(0)` from `fib(2)` under `fib(3)` are all top-call-site invocations for line 5. Similarly, the invocations of

```
1   void mm(double *C, double *A, double *B,
2           size_t dim, size_t n) {
3     if (n < COARSENING) {
4       return base(C, A, B, dim, n);
5     }
6   #define X(M,r,c) (M + (r * dim + c)*(n/2))
7     cilk_spawn mm(X(C,0,0), X(A,0,0), X(B,0,0),
8                   dim, n/2);
9     cilk_spawn mm(X(C,0,1), X(A,0,0), X(B,0,1),
10                  dim, n/2);
11    cilk_spawn mm(X(C,1,0), X(A,1,0), X(B,0,0),
12                  dim, n/2);
13               mm(X(C,1,1), X(A,1,0), X(B,0,1),
14                  dim, n/2);
15    cilk_sync;
16    // spawn remaining recursive mm calls
17  }
18
19  int main(int argc, char *argv[]) {
20    double *C, *A, *B;
21    int n;
22    // parse arguments
23    // initialize C, A, and B
24    mm(C, A, B, n, n);
25    return 0;
26  }
```

Figure 8: Cilk pseudocode for a divide-and-conquer parallel matrix-multiplication program. The recursive `mm` routine in this program calls the function `base` in its base case. The variable `COARSENING` is a fixed constant defining the maximum size of matrices to multiply in the base case.

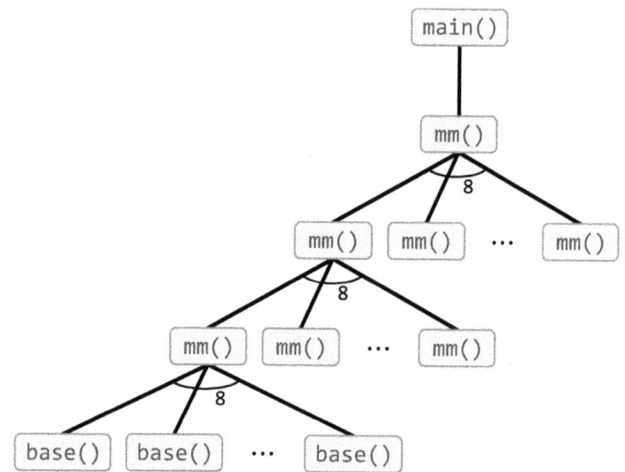

Figure 9: An invocation tree for the matrix-multiplication program in Figure 8. Each rectangle denotes a function instantiation, and an edge from one rectangle to a rectangle below it denotes the upper invocation calling the lower.

`fib(3)` from `fib(4)` and of `fib(1)` from `fib(2)` under `fib(4)` are both top-call-site invocations for line 4.

Top-caller measurements

In contrast to top-call-site measurements, the "top-caller" measurement for a call site s conceptually aggregates the work and span of every execution of s from a nonrecursive invocation of its caller. Formally, an executed call site $xs \in I$ is a **top-caller invocation** if

	Top-call-site			Top-caller			Local		
Line	T_1	T_∞	T_1/T_∞	T_1	T_∞	T_1/T_∞	T_1	T_∞	T_1/T_∞
4	185,830,187	185,830,187	1.0	0	0	—	185,830,187	185,830,187	1.0
7	77,417,401	22,010,873	3.5	23,473,633	405,947	57.8	195,079	177,786	1.1
9	77,475,639	21,983,150	3.5	23,384,174	411,099	56.9	183,232	168,249	1.1
11	77,440,990	21,988,390	3.5	23,403,194	402,281	58.2	187,472	169,541	1.1
13	77,262,499	21,853,710	3.5	23,378,967	387,880	60.3	110,374	97,656	1.1
24	187,150,784	803,122	233.0	187,150,784	803,122	233.0	1,563	957	1.6

Figure 10: Work and span values in the on-work profile Cilkprof produces for running the divide-and-conquer matrix multiplication code in Figure 8 to multiply two 512×512 matrices of doubles. All times are measured in nanoseconds.

no executed call site $xi \in I$ exists such that

$$xs \in \text{Trace}(xi) \land \varphi(\sigma(xs)) = \varphi(\sigma(xi)) .$$

Cilkprof's ***top-caller measurement*** for a call site s aggregates all top-caller invocations of s.

Like top-call-site invocations, top-caller invocations can be identified from the computation's invocation tree. Once again, consider the code in Figure 5 and its example invocation tree in Figure 6. The invocation producing fib(3) is a top-caller invocation, because no instantiation of fib exists above fib(4), the function instantiation containing this invocation, in the tree. The invocation producing fib(1) under the right child of fib(4) is not a top-caller invocation, however, because fib(4) is an instantiation of fib above the instantiation fib(2) that contains this invocation. The top-caller invocations that occur in the invocation tree in Figure 6, therefore, are from main() to fib(4) and from fib(4) to each of its children.

Top-caller measurements can be useful for comparing call sites in the same function. The top-caller measurements in Figure 7, for example, show that the ratio of the aggregate work of the top-caller invocations of lines 4 and 5 is $279,094,680/171,229,726 \approx 1.63$, which is approximately the golden ratio $\phi = (1 + \sqrt{5})/2 \approx 1.61$. This relationship makes sense, because fib(n) theoretically incurs $\Theta(\phi^n)$ work.

The top-caller measurements provide no information for call sites that are never reached from a top-level instantiation of a function, however. Consider the divide-and-conquer matrix-multiplication program in Figure 8 and its invocation tree illustrated in Figure 9. As Figure 9 shows, the function base called in the base case of mm is never called by the top-caller invocation of mm from main. Consequently, as the top-caller measurements in Figure 10 for this program show, Cilkprof measures the top-caller call-site work and span values for base to be 0. From these top-caller values, one cannot conclude that most of the computation of mm, in fact, occurs under calls to base.

Local measurements

The ***local*** measurement for a call site aggregates a "local work" and a "local span" for every execution of that call site. The ***local work*** of an executed call site $xs \in I$ is the work in Trace(xs) minus the work in the traces of the functions that xs invokes. By ignoring the contributions of its children, the local work and local span values for all executions of a call site can be aggregated without overcounting executed instructions in recursive calls.

The local measurements call sites are often useful for examining functions invoked in the base case of a recursive routine. The local measurements for mm in Figure 10, for example, make it clear that most of the total work of the call to mm from main occurs in calls to base. Furthermore, as we observed in the quicksort example in Section 2, these local work and span values can effectively identify which functions contribute directly to the span of the computation.

The local parallelism of a call site s — the ratio of the local work and local span of s — does not accurately reflect the parallelism of s, however. As Figure 10 shows, by excluding the work and span contributions of each executed call site's children, most local-parallelism values are close to 1, even for call sites such as line 24 which exhibit ample parallelism.

The top-call-site, top-caller, and local measurements for a call site s each measure qualitatively different things about s. Each of these measurements seems to be useful for analyzing a parallel program in different ways. An interesting open question is whether there are other measurements that are as useful as these three for diagnosing scalability bottlenecks.

7. EMPIRICAL EVALUATION

To implement Cilkprof, we modified a branch [19] of the LLVM [26] compiler that supports Cilk Plus [16] to instrument function entries and exits, as well as calls into the Cilk runtime from the program to handle cilk_spawn and cilk_sync statements. A Cilk program is compiled with the modified compiler produces a binary executable that executes the Cilkprof algorithm as a shadow computation. On a suite of 16 benchmark programs, we compared the Cilkprof running time of each benchmark with the benchmark's serial running time compiled with the unmodified compiler, both executions using optimization level -O3. Compared with this "native" serial execution, Cilkprof incurs a geometric-mean multiplicative slowdown of 1.9 and a maximum slowdown of 7.4.

Results

We compared the running time of Cilkprof on each benchmark to the native serial running time of the benchmark, that is, the running time of the benchmark when compiled with no instrumentation. We ran our experiments on a dual-socket Intel Xeon E5-2665 system 2.4 GHz 8-core CPU's having a total of 32 GiB of memory. Each processor core has a 32 KiB private L1-data-cache and a 256 KiB private L2-cache. The 8 cores on each chip share the same 20 MiB L3-cache. The machine was running Fedora 16, using a custom Linux kernel 3.6.11, with hyperthreading turned off.

To study the empirical overhead of Cilkprof, we compiled a suite of 16 application benchmarks, as Figure 11 describes. The mm, quicksort, and fib benchmarks correspond to the Cilk pseudocode in Figures 8, 1, and 5, respectively. The pbfs benchmark is a parallel breadth-first search code that implements the PBFS algorithm of [28]. We converted the dedup and ferret benchmarks from the PARSEC benchmark [3, 4] to use Cilk linguistics and a reducer_ostream (which is part of Cilk Plus) for writing output. The leiserchess program performs a parallel speculative game-tree search using Cilk. The hevc benchmark is a 30,000-line implementation of the H265 video encoder and decoder [22] that we parallelized using Cilk. The remaining benchmarks are the same benchmarks included in the Cilk-5 distribution [10].

Figure 11 presents our empirical results. As the figure shows, the Cilkprof implementation incurs a geometric mean slowdown of

Benchmark	Input size	Description	Overhead
mm	2048×2048 matrix	Square matrix multiplication	0.99
dedup	large	Compression program	1.03
lu	2048×2048 matrix	LU matrix decomposition	1.04
strassen	2048×2048 matrix	Strassen matrix multiplication	1.06
heat	$4096 \times 1024 \times 40$ spacetime	Heat diffusion stencil	1.07
cilksort	$10,000,000$ elements	Parallel mergesort	1.08
pbfs	$|V| = 8M, |E| = 55.8M$	Parallel breadth-first search	1.10
fft	$8,388,608$	Fast Fourier transform	1.15
quicksort	$100,000,000$ elements	Parallel quicksort	1.20
nqueens	12×12 board	n-Queens problem	1.27
ferret	large	Image similarity search	2.04
leiserchess	5.8M nodes	Speculative game-tree search	3.72
collision	$528,032$ faces	Collision detection in $3D$	4.37
cholesky	2000×2000 matrix, 16000 nonzeros	Cholesky decomposition	4.54
hevc	5 frames	H265 video encoding and decoding	6.25
fib	35	Recursive Fibonacci	7.36

Figure 11: Application benchmarks demonstrating the performance overhead of the Cilkprof prototype tool. The benchmarks are sorted in order of increasing overhead. For each benchmark, the *Overhead* column gives the ratio of its running time with when compiled with the Cilkprof implementation over its running time without instrumentation. Each ratio is computed as the geometric mean ratio of 5 runs with Cilkprof and 5 runs without Cilkprof. We used a modified version of the Cilk Plus/LLVM compiler to compile each benchmark with Cilkprof, and we used the original version of the Cilk Plus/LLVM compiler to compile the benchmarks with no instrumentation. The Cilkprof implementation and benchmark codes were compiled using the -O3 optimization level.

$1.9\times$ on these benchmarks compared to the uninstrumented version of the benchmark. Furthermore, the maximum multiplicative overhead we observed on any benchmark was 7.4.

Optimizations

The implementation contains several optimizations:

- For basic timing measurements, we chose to use a cycle counter to measure blocks of instructions, rather than naively incrementing a counter for every instruction executed, as in the basic pseudocode from Figure 3. (We also adjust the measured numbers to compensate for the time it takes Cilkprof to execute the instrumentation.)

- For a function F with no cilk_spawn's, the implementation maintains only the prefix span variable $F.p$ to store the span of F, rather than all 3 span variables.

- If a function G calls F, then the implementation sets the prof data structure for $F.p$ to be the prof data structure for either $G.p$, if G has no outstanding spawned children when it calls F, or $G.c$, otherwise.

- When the span variable associated with a prof data structure R is set to 0, the implementation simply clears the nonempty entries of the array $R.arr$, rather than freeing its memory.

- The implementation maintains the set of nonempty entries in each prof data structure array in order to optimize the processes of combining and clearing those entries.

These optimizations reduced Cilkprof's overhead on the fib benchmark by a factor of 5 and its overhead on the leiserchess benchmark dropped by a factor of 9.

At the risk of losing some information, Cilkprof declines to instrument inlined functions, which, in Intel Cilk Plus, cannot spawn. To do so, we modified LLVM such that, when it inlines a function, it removes the instrumentation for the inlined version of that function. When this program runs with Cilkprof, therefore, the work of the inlined function influences the work and span of its parent, but it will not create a separate entry in the profile Cilkprof produces.

We feel that this optimization is reasonable because inlined functions are typically unlikely to be scalability bottlenecks on their own. For example, the compiler often inlines C++ object methods to extract or set fields of that object, which the programmer wrote to provide a convenient abstraction in the program code, but which the compiler can often implement with a handful of data movement instructions in the caller. If Cilkprof instruments such a function, then

Cilkprof incurs overheads to measure and record *very* few instructions. The cost of instrumenting such functions therefore seems to outweigh the benefits to scalability analysis.

We examined Cilkprof's overhead when inlined functions are instrumented on the application benchmarks. For all benchmarks except lu, leiserchess, collision, and hevc, Cilkprof incurred less than 2 times the overhead it incurred when inlined functions in that benchmark were not instrumented. On the leiserchess and collision benchmarks, however, instrumenting inlined functions increased Cilkprof's overhead by a factor of 8–10. Both of these benchmarks make extensive use of small functions that simply get or set fields of an object, which are particularly light weight when inlined. Although this optimization does not affect every benchmark, it can dramatically improve Cilkprof's performance on the benchmarks it does affect.

8. CASE STUDY: PBFS

One of our first successes with Cilkprof[2] came when diagnosing a parallelism bottleneck in PBFS, an 1800-line parallel breadth-first search Cilk program [28]. After just 2 hours of work using Cilkprof, we were able to identify a parallelism bottleneck in the PBFS code. Fixing this bottleneck enhanced the parallelism of the code by a factor of about 5. This section presents our experience diagnosing a scalability bottleneck in the PBFS code. You should not need to understand either the PBFS algorithm or its implementation to follow this case study.

After designing and building PBFS, we observed that the code failed to achieve linear speedup on 8 processors. For example, PBFS was achieving a parallel speedup of $4-5$ on our Grid3D200 benchmark graph, a 7-point finite-difference mesh generated using the Matlab Mesh Partitioning and Graph Separator Toolbox [12], on which PBFS explored 8M vertices and 55.8M edges during a search of depth 598. A back-of-the-envelope calculation suggested that the measured parallelism of PBFS should be around $200-400$, ample for 8 processors, if one follows the rule of thumb that a program should have at least 10 times more parallelism than the number of processors for scheduling overhead to be negligible.

---

[2] Actually, the original case study used the (much slower) Cilkprof Pintool [18] we built in collaboration with Intel. Since the data from this early experiment have since been lost, we recreated the experiment with our LLVM-based Cilkprof implementation.

We suspected that the scalability of this PBFS code suffered from insufficient memory bandwidth on the machine. For example, when we artificially inflated the amount of computation that the code performed in the base case of its recursive helper functions, then the code did exhibit linear speedup. The problem with this test, however, is that it also increased the parallelism of the code. We ran Cilkview on the original PBFS code to ensure that insufficient parallelism was not the issue. Cilkview, however, reported that the parallelism of this PBFS code was merely 12, which is not ample parallelism for 8 processors.

We ran the PBFS code with Cilkprof and examined Cilkprof's profiles. The on-work profile showed us that the call to pbfs — our parallel BFS routine — from main accounted for most of the work of the program, and that the parallelism of pbfs was small, just as Cilkview had found. To discover what methods contributed most to the span, we sorted Cilkprof's data by decreasing local T_∞ on span. Viewing the data from this perspective showed us that the following three methods contributed the most to the span of the program overall:

1. First was a call to parseBinaryFile, a serial function that parses the input graph.
2. Second was a call to the serial Graph constructor to create the internal data structure storing the graph from the input.
3. Third was a call to pbfs_proc_Node, a function that processes a constant-sized array of graph vertices.

Although the top two entries were not called from pbfs, the third entry for pbfs_proc_Node was called in the base case of the recursive helper methods of pbfs. Comparing the local T_∞ on span of pbfs_proc_Node to the top-caller T_∞ of bfs showed us that this method accounted for 66% of the span of bfs. Furthermore, the top-call-site parallelism values from Cilkprof showed us that all invocations pbfs_proc_Node were serial.

These data led us to look more closely at pbfs_proc_Node. We discovered that this method evaluates a constant-sized array of vertices in the graph. Because the input array has constant size, this method evaluated the contents of this array serially. In the code, however, the size of this array was tuned to optimize the insertion of vertices into the array. The constant size of this array was therefore too large for pbfs_proc_Node, causing the serial execution of pbfs_proc_Node to become a scalability bottleneck.

We parallelized the pbfs_proc_Node function to process its input array in parallel with an appropriate base-case size. We then ran our modified PBFS code through Cilkprof and sorted the new data by local T_∞ on span to examine the effect of our efforts. We found that, although pbfs_proc_Node was still the third-largest contributor to the span of the program, the local T_∞ on span is a factor of 6 larger. Furthermore, the parallelism of pbfs is now 60, a factor of 5 larger than its previous value. Finally, pbfs_proc_Node accounts for 48% of this span. We also confirmed that reducing the new base-case size of pbfs_proc_Node can increase the parallelism of pbfs to 100, at the cost of scheduling overhead.

9. RELATED WORK

This section reviews related work on performance tools for parallel programming.

We chose to implement Cilkprof using compiler instrumentation (e.g., [31, 32]), but there are other strategies we could have used to examine the behavior of a computation, such as asynchronous sampling (e.g., [13]) and *binary instrumentation* (e.g., [6, 9, 29, 30]). Although asynchronous sampling provides low-overhead solutions for some analytical tools, we do not know of a way to measure the span of a multithreaded Cilk computation by sampling. Cilkview [14] is implemented using the Pin binary-instrumentation

framework [29] augmented by support in the Intel Cilk Plus compiler [20] for low-overhead annotations [17], and we collaborated with Intel to build a prototype Cilkprof as a Pintool. Because we found that this prototype Cilkprof ran slowly, we chose to implement Cilkprof using compiler instrumentation in order to improve its performance. In fact, because it uses compiler instrumentation, the Cilkprof implementation outperforms the existing Cilkview implementation, which only computes work and span for the entire computation and does not produce profiles of work and span for every call site as Cilkprof does.

Many parallel performance tools examine a parallel computation and report performance characteristics specific to that architecture and execution. Tools like HPCToolkit [1], Intel VTune Amplifier [21], and others [7, 25, 33] measure system counters and events, and provide reports based on a program execution. HPCToolkit, in particular, is an integrated suite of tools to measure and analyze program performance that sets a high standard for capability and usability. HPCToolkit uses statistical sampling of timers and hardware performance counters to measure a program's resource consumption, and attributes measurements to full calling contexts.

Other approaches for identifying scalability bottlenecks include normalized processor time [2] or the more precise parallel idleness metric [34]. The idea is that, in a work-stealing concurrency platform, if at some particular point in time some worker threads are idle, then we can assign blame to the function that is running on the other workers: if that function were more parallel, then the idle threads would be doing something useful. These are helpful metrics for identifying bottlenecks on the current architecture, and answer the question as to whether the program, run on a P-processor machine has at least P-fold parallelism. But they don't provide scalability analysis beyond P processors.

In contrast to all of these applications and approaches, Cilkprof's analysis applies to the measured work and span. Work and span are good metrics for inferring bounds on parallel speedup on architectures with any number of processors. A program compiled for Cilkprof will generate profile information that is generally applicable, rather than just for the architecture on which it was run. Additionally, Cilkprof is distinguished in that it uses direct instrumentation rather than statistical sampling.

Whereas Cilkprof computes the parallelism of call sites in a parallel program, the Kremlin [11, 24] and Kismet [23] tools analyze serial programs to suggest parallelism opportunities and to predict the impact of parallelization. Kremlin can suggest which parts of a serial program might benefit from parallelization. It estimates the parallelism of a serial program using "hierarchical critical-path analysis" and connects to a "parallelism planner" to evaluate many possible parallelizations of the program. Based on its determination of which regions (loops and functions) of the program should be parallelized, it computes a work/span profile of the program, computing a "self-parallelism" metric for each region, which estimates the parallelism that can be obtained from parallelizing that region separate from other regions. The analysis produces a textual report as output suggesting which regions should be parallelized. Kismet, which is a product of the same research group, attempts to predict the actual speedup after parallelization, given a target machine and runtime system.

10. CONCLUSION

Our work on Cilkprof has left us with some interesting research questions. We conclude by addressing issues of Cilkprof's user interface, parallelizing Cilkprof, and making Cilkprof functionally more "complete."

Chief among the open issues is user interface. How should the profiles produced by Cilkprof be communicated to a Cilk programmer? Although we ourselves used just a spreadsheet to divine important scalability properties of PBFS, for example, we do not recommend this method to others. A good UI integrated with the development environment would make diagnosing scalability issues much easier for average programmers.

Even though Cilkprof analyzes parallel programs, it still runs them serially. As the number of processors grows, it becomes less and less acceptable to resort to a serial execution. In principle, nothing precludes Cilkprof from running in parallel, but we have thus far been unable to create a provably good algorithm. One problem is that amortization plays havoc with the critical path of a parallel program. At some cost in programming complexity, we could deamortize the prof data structures, but it is also tricky to parallelize the strategies for handling recursion.

Cilkprof offers many opportunities for functional enhancements. The on-work and on-span profiles seem natural enough, but maybe there are better alternatives to top call site, top caller, and local profile data. In addition, Cilkprof computes on-span profiles only for call sites that lie on the global critical path. Sometimes, the critical path of a computation can be qualitatively different depending on the size of the program input. For example, two computations A and B are run in parallel, where the span of A is smaller than the span of B for small inputs, but the reverse is true for large inputs. Rather than run at scale, it could be more productive if Cilkprof were to report span-on-span profiles not just for the global critical path, but for all critical paths within all functions. Although the space required might be quadratic in call sites, such a profile would greatly speed detective work, and the cross-product of sites might be considerably sparse for many programs. Unfortunately, we do not yet see a way to calculate such a profile without also blowing up the overheads significantly.

11. ACKNOWLEDGMENTS

We thank Kerry Xing of MIT, now at Dropbox, and James Thomas of MIT for their help developing early versions of Cilkprof. We thank Michael Taylor of UCSD for his input on related work. We thank Barry Tannenbaum, Pablo Halpern, and Jim Sukha of Intel for helpful discussions. We thank the reviewers for their excellent feedback.

12. REFERENCES

[1] L. Adhianto, S. Banerjee, M. Fagan, M. Krentel, G. Marin, J. Mellor-Crummey, and N. R. Tallent. HPCToolkit: tools for performance analysis of optimized parallel programs. *Concurrency and Computation: Practice and Experience*, 22(6):685–701, 2010.

[2] T. E. Anderson and E. D. Lazowska. Quartz: A tool for tuning parallel program performance. In *SIGMETRICS*, pp. 115–125, 1990.

[3] C. Bienia, S. Kumar, J. P. Singh, and K. Li. The PARSEC benchmark suite: Characterization and architectural implications. In *PACT*, pp. 72–81, 2008.

[4] C. Bienia and K. Li. Characteristics of workloads using the pipeline programming model. In *EAMA ISCA-10 Workshop*, pp. 161–171, 2010.

[5] R. D. Blumofe and C. E. Leiserson. Scheduling multithreaded computations by work stealing. *JACM*, 46(5):720–748, 1999.

[6] D. Bruening, E. Duesterwald, and S. Amarasinghe. Design and implementation of a dynamic optimization framework for Windows. In *FDDO-4*, 2001.

[7] H. Brunst, M. Winkler, W. E. Nagel, and H.-C. Hoppe. Performance optimization for large scale computing: The scalable VAMPIR approach. In *ICCS*, pp. 751–760, 2001.

[8] T. H. Cormen, C. E. Leiserson, R. L. Rivest, and C. Stein. *Introduction to Algorithms*. The MIT Press, third edition, 2009.

[9] A. E. Eichenberger, J. Mellor-Crummey, M. Schulz, M. Wong, N. Copty, R. Dietrich, X. Liu, E. Loh, and D. Lorenz. OMPT: An OpenMP tools application programming interface for performance analysis. In *IWOMP*, pp. 171–185, 2013.

[10] M. Frigo, C. E. Leiserson, and K. H. Randall. The implementation of the Cilk-5 multithreaded language. In *PLDI*, pp. 212–223, 1998.

[11] S. Garcia, D. Jeon, C. M. Louie, and M. B. Taylor. Kremlin: Rethinking and rebooting gprof for the multicore age. In *PLDI*, pp. 458–469, 2011.

[12] J. R. Gilbert, G. L. Miller, and S.-H. Teng. Geometric mesh partitioning: Implementation and experiments. *SIAM J. Sci. Comput.*, 19(6):2091–2110, 1998.

[13] S. L. Graham, P. B. Kessler, and M. K. McKusick. gprof: A call graph execution profiler. In *SIGPLAN Symposium on Compiler Construction*, pp. 120–126, 1982.

[14] Y. He, C. E. Leiserson, and W. M. Leiserson. The Cilkview scalability analyzer. In *SPAA*, pp. 145–156, 2010.

[15] C. A. R. Hoare. Algorithm 63: Partition; Algorithm 64: Quicksort; and Algorithm 65: Find. *CACM*, 4(7):321–322, 1961.

[16] Intel Corporation. Intel Cilk Plus language specification. Document Number 324396-001US. Available from http://software.intel.com/sites/products/cilk-plus/ cilk_plus_language_specification.pdf, 2010.

[17] Intel Corporation. Intrinsics for low overhead tool annotations. Document Number 326357-001US. Available from https://www.cilkplus.org/open_specification/ intrinsics-low-overhead-tool-annotations-v10, 2011.

[18] Intel Corporation. Download Intel Cilk Plus software development kit. https://software.intel.com/en-us/articles/ download-intel-cilk-plus-software-development-kit/, 2012.

[19] Intel Corporation. CilkPlus/LLVM. http://cilkplus.github.io/, 2013.

[20] Intel Corporation. Intel Cilk Plus. https://software.intel.com/en-us/intel-cilk-plus, 2015.

[21] Intel Corporation. Intel VTune Amplifier XE 2015. http://software.intel.com/en-us/intel-vtune-amplifier-xe, 2015.

[22] High efficiency video coding. Standard H.265, ITU, 2014.

[23] D. Jeon, S. Garcia, C. Louie, and M. B. Taylor. Kismet: Parallel speedup estimates for serial programs. In *OOPSLA*, 2011.

[24] D. Jeon, S. Garcia, C. Louie, S. K. Venkata, and M. B. Taylor. Kremlin: Like gprof, but for parallelization. In *PPoPP*, pp. 293–294, 2011.

[25] A. Knüpfer, H. Brunst, J. Doleschal, M. Jurenz, M. Lieber, H. Mickler, M. S. Müller, and W. E. Nagel. The Vampir performance analysis tool-set. In *Tools for High Performance Computing*, pp. 139–155, 2008.

[26] C. Lattner and V. Adve. LLVM: A compilation framework for lifelong program analysis & transformation. In *CGO*, p. 75, 2004.

[27] C. E. Leiserson. The Cilk++ concurrency platform. *J. Supercomputing*, 51(3):244–257, 2010.

[28] C. E. Leiserson and T. B. Schardl. A work-efficient parallel breadth-first search algorithm (or how to cope with the nondeterminism of reducers). In *SPAA*, pp. 303–314, 2010.

[29] C.-K. Luk, R. Cohn, R. Muth, H. Patil, A. Klauser, G. Lowney, S. Wallace, V. J. Reddi, and K. Hazelwood. Pin: building customized program analysis tools with dynamic instrumentation. In *PLDI*, pp. 190–200, 2005.

[30] N. Nethercote and J. Seward. Valgrind: a framework for heavyweight dynamic binary instrumentation. In *PLDI*, pp. 89–100, 2007.

[31] K. Serebryany, D. Bruening, A. Potapenko, and D. Vyukov. AddressSanitizer: A fast address sanity checker. In *USENIX ATC*, pp. 309–318, 2012.

[32] K. Serebryany and T. Iskhodzhanov. ThreadSanitizer — data race detection in practice. In *WBIA*, pp. 62–71, 2009.

[33] S. S. Shende and A. D. Malony. The Tau parallel performance system. *Int. J. High Perform. Comput. Appl.*, 20(2):287–311, 2006.

[34] N. R. Tallent and J. M. Mellor-Crummey. Effective performance measurement and analysis of multithreaded applications. In *PPoPP*, pp. 229–240, 2009.

Race Detection in Two Dimensions

Dimitar Dimitrov
Department of Computer
Science, ETH Zürich
Universitätstrasse 6
8092 Zürich, Switzerland
dimitar.dimitrov@inf.ethz.ch

Martin Vechev
Department of Computer
Science, ETH Zürich
Universitätstrasse 6
8092 Zürich, Switzerland
martin.vechev@inf.ethz.ch

Vivek Sarkar
Department of Computer
Science, Rice University
6100 Main St.,
Houston, TX, USA
vsarkar@rice.edu

ABSTRACT

Dynamic data race detection is a program analysis technique for detecting errors provoked by undesired interleavings of concurrent threads. A primary challenge when designing efficient race detection algorithms is to achieve manageable space requirements.

State of the art algorithms for unstructured parallelism require $\Theta(n)$ space per monitored memory location, where n is the total number of tasks. This is a serious drawback when analyzing programs with many tasks. In contrast, algorithms for programs with a series-parallel (SP) structure require only $\Theta(1)$ space. Unfortunately, it is currently poorly understood if there are classes of parallelism beyond SP that can also benefit from and be analyzed with $\Theta(1)$ space complexity.

In the present work, we show that structures richer than SP graphs, namely that of two-dimensional (2D) lattices, can be analyzed in $\Theta(1)$ space: a) we extend Tarjan's algorithm for finding lowest common ancestors to handle 2D lattices; b) from that extension we derive a serial algorithm for race detection that can analyze arbitrary task graphs having a 2D lattice structure; c) we present a restriction to fork-join that admits precisely the 2D lattices as task graphs (e.g., it can express pipeline parallelism).

Our work generalizes prior work on race detection, and aims to provide a deeper understanding of the interplay between structured parallelism and program analysis efficiency.

1. INTRODUCTION

Ensuring correctness of parallel programs is a notoriously difficult matter. A primary reason for this is the potential for harmful interference between concurrent threads (or tasks). In particular, a root cause for interference is the presence of data races: two conflicting accesses to the same memory location, done by two concurrent tasks. The interference caused by data races increases the number of schedules that have to be considered in ensuring program correctness. That is the case because the outcome of a data race might depend on the execution order of the two conflicting accesses.

Race detection challenges.

Automatic data race detection techniques are extremely valuable in detecting potentially harmful sources of concurrent interference, and therefore in ensuring that a parallel program behaves as expected. Designing precise race detection algorithms (i.e., not reporting false positives) which scale to realistic parallel programs is a very challenging problem. In particular, it is important that a race detection algorithm continues to perform well as the number of concurrently executing threads increases.

Unfortunately, state of the art race detection techniques [13] that handle arbitrary parallelism suffer from scalability issues: their memory usage is $\Theta(n)$ per monitored memory location, where n is the number of threads in the program. As n gets larger the analyzer can quickly run out of memory, or at the very least incur prohibitive slowdowns due to overwhelming memory consumption.

A principled approach to address this problem is to design race detectors which leverage the parallel structure of a program. Languages like Cilk [5], X10 [8] or Habanero [7] provide structured-parallel constructs which express task graphs of restricted shape, namely that of series-parallel (SP) graphs. Several race detection algorithms [12, 3, 18, 17] target these specific structured-parallel constructs and are able to achieve $\Theta(1)$ memory consumption per monitored location.

Key question.

The success of race detectors which achieve $\Theta(1)$ space overhead per memory location for series-parallel graphs leads to the following fundamental question:

> Are there structures richer than SP graphs which can be analyzed in a sound and precise manner with $\Theta(1)$ space overhead per memory location?

This work.

In this work we show that structures richer than SP graphs are in fact analyzable in $\Theta(1)$ space per monitored location. We present an online race detection algorithm for programs that have the parallel structure of a *two-dimensional lattice* (2D lattice) [10]. Unlike prior work, we formulate our algorithm directly in terms of the graph structure and *not* on the programming language. Decoupling structure from language constructs leads to a clearer and deeper understanding of how the algorithm works, and also of the assumptions that it rests upon. To close the loop, we introduce a restriction of the classic fork-join constructs which expresses only those

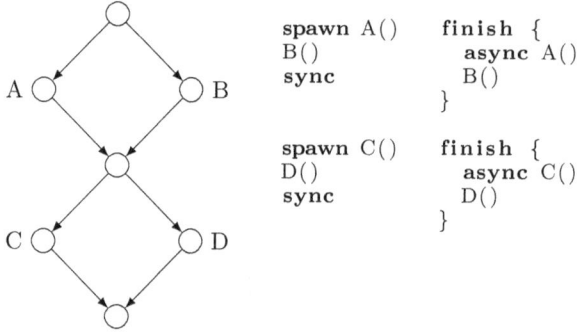

Figure 1: Two different programs having the same series-parallel task graph, one using spawn-sync while the other using async-finish.

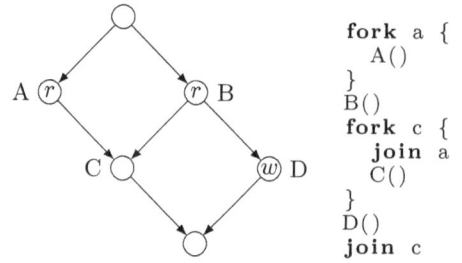

Figure 2: A fork-join program having a task graph with a two-dimensional lattice structure. Routines A and B read from the same location that D writes to. Accordingly, there is a race between A and D as they execute concurrently.

task graphs that have a 2D lattice structure. This restriction easily captures useful forms of pipeline parallelism [15], and so our race detector can be directly applied to analyze such pipelined programs. Our work can be seen as a generalization of existing race detectors for SP graphs to richer classes of graphs and language constructs.

Contributions.

The main contributions of this work are:

- an extension of Tarjan's algorithm for finding lowest common ancestors in trees, to finding suprema in 2D lattices (Tarjan's algorithm is the foundation behind prior works for SP graphs as well);

- a race detector, based on the suprema finding algorithm, that works on any task graph with a 2D lattice structure (i.e., independent of any language constructs), and has $\Theta(1)$ space overhead per tracked memory location;

- a restriction of the classic fork-join constructs which captures precisely the task graphs with a 2D lattice structure (e.g., applicable to pipeline parallelism).

Our work is a step in understanding the inherent trade-offs between parallelism structure and the resource requirements of race detection over that structure.

2. OVERVIEW

In this section we discuss several graph structures (SP graphs, 2D lattices) as well as how these are obtained from programs. We then provide an intuitive explanation of the concepts behind our online race detector for 2D lattices.

Task graphs.

Task graphs capture the ordering between operations in a particular execution of a parallel program. Operations are represented by graph vertices, and arcs (x, y) indicate that one operation y is ordered after another operation x. Thus, a task graph is a directed acyclic graph. Figures 1 and 2 show task graphs over the operations A, B, C and D, as well as some other, unnamed ones. Each of these graphs belongs to a particular class: the first is a series-parallel (SP) graph, while the second one is not SP but has the structure of a two-dimensional (2D) lattice.

2.1 SP graphs and language constructs

We now turn our attention to SP graphs, and well-known structured parallel constructs that produce such graphs. In short, an SP graph is a single-source, single-sink, directed graph which is either a series or a parallel composition of two smaller SP graphs G_1 and G_2. The serial composition $S(G_1, G_2)$ simply glues the sink of G_1 to the source of G_2, ordering the vertices in G_1 before the vertices in G_2. The parallel composition $P(G_1, G_2)$ glues the two graphs source-to-source and sink-to-sink, without imposing additional ordering on the vertices. The graph in Figure 1 can be readily constructed in this way.

Cilk's spawn-sync.

The spawn-sync parallel constructs were introduced by the Cilk [5] programming language. The **spawn** $f()$ statement activates a new parallel task to execute the given routine, while the **sync** statement suspends the currently executing task until all of its spawned children terminate. Each task has an implicit **sync** at its end. The first program in Figure 1 illustrates these two constructs. The informal semantics of spawn and sync are as follows: "**spawn** G_1; G_2" means $P(G_1, G_2)$, while "G_1; **sync**; G_2" means $S(G_1, G_2)$.

X10's async-finish.

The async-finish parallel constructs were introduced by the X10 [8] programming language, and are inherited by its descendant Habanero [7]. Here, the **async** *block* construct activates a new parallel task to execute the given block. Synchronization is done via the **finish** *block* construct, which executes the given block of code, ensuring that tasks created inside the block finish their execution together with the block. The second program in Figure 1 illustrates these constructs. An informal semantics would be: "**async** G_1; G_2" means $P(G_1, G_2)$, while "**finish** G_1; G_2" means $S(G_1, G_2)$. Note that the shown async-finish program has exactly the same task graph as the spawn-sync program to its left.

2.2 Two-dimensional lattices

In our work, we focus on task graphs which have two-dimensional (2D) lattice structure. This class of graphs is more general and extends the class of SP graphs. Two-dimensional lattices can be thought of as directed graphs that have a single source, single sink, and a monotonic planar drawing: no arcs intersect, and tracing any directed path on the drawing will always advance in the same direction, e.g., downwards. Figure 2 shows an example of a 2D lattice task graph. The monotone-planar structure is what enables us to detect races much more efficiently.

Structured fork-join.

To express programs with a 2D lattice parallel structure, we will introduce a restricted version of the fork-join constructs. We chose **fork** and **join** because they are general enough, and with them we can naturally capture variety of other constructs such as futures. As usual, a **fork** x *block* activates a new task to execute the given block, and stores the identifier of the new task into the variable x. The **join** x statement simply suspends the current thread until the task identified by x terminates.

Figure 2 demonstrates a fork-join program with a 2D lattice task graph. In contrast with the previous two programs, here A and D execute in parallel, and thus the computation does not proceed in phases. In order to ensure two-dimensionality, we shall restrict with whom a thread may join with: if a thread y executes **join** x, then x must appear immediately on the left of y in a planar diagram of the task graph. Details are discussed in Section 5.

2.3 Online race detection

We now describe the core ideas behind our online race detection algorithm (details follow in Sections 3 and 4):

1. formulating race detection as computing suprema in an execution's task graph;

2. computing suprema efficiently by traversing a 2D lattice in a particular order;

3. showing how to obtain such traversal orders from our structured fork-join constructs.

An example of a race.

Recall that a race in a particular execution occurs when two concurrent operations access the same memory and at least one of the two is a write. An online race detector runs the program, searching for races between the current operation being executed and any of the previously executed operations. The soundness guarantee that state of the art online race detectors provide is that if the program terminates with no reported races, then indeed, the program is deterministic (from the particular input state). In addition, the detector is guaranteed to be precise up to the first reported race (later ones might be false positives).

Now, consider the program in Figure 2 together with the execution of A B C D in that order. Operations A and B read and operation D writes to the same memory location, while C is a nop. A race exists between operations A and D, which an online race detector must flag when seeing D. The race occurs because operation D conflicts with A, and the two are not ordered in the task graph. Performing the same check for B and D, we observe that a directed path connects them, so the two are ordered, and not racing.

A naive algorithm.

These observations lead to a direct method for detecting races. For every location l we track the set R of prior operations that read from l, and the set W of prior operations

that wrote to l. If the current operation t reads from l, then it potentially races with an operation from $K = W$; if it writes to l, then it potentially races with an operation from $K = R \cup W$. In our case, $t = \text{D}$ and $K = R \cup W = \{\text{A}, \text{B}\}$. When executing the current operation we simply need to check whether all potentially racing operations are ordered before it, as indicated by the task graph. Denoting with $x \sqsubseteq y$ that y is reachable from x, we have:

$$\text{no race between } K \text{ and } t \iff K \sqsubseteq t.$$

Race detection via suprema.

This naive algorithm, however, is prohibitively expensive both in space and time, as it suggests tracking and checking against $O(|R \cup W|)$ operations. Efficient methods for online detection represent the sets R and W indirectly, in a way guaranteeing that a race is detected if and only if a race exists. Inspired by [12, 18], we shall represent each of R and W with a single vertex in the task graph. Recall that the supremum of a set K is the unique vertex $\sup K$ such that

$$K \sqsubseteq t \iff \sup K \sqsubseteq t.$$

For the graph in Figure 2 we have that $\sup\{\text{A}, \text{B}\}$ equals the vertex C. From the defining property of suprema, we make the following key observation:

To detect races it is sufficient to track $\sup R$ and $\sup W$ for every location x.

If the current operation t writes to x, then we can simply check whether both $\sup R \sqsubseteq t$ and $\sup W \sqsubseteq t$ hold, and flag a race if this is not the case. Similarly, for a read we compare against $\sup W$ only. This way we can keep track only of two vertices per location, and perform at most two reachability checks per memory access. We discuss this approach to race detection in more details in Section 4.

Finding suprema efficiently.

However, applying suprema to race detection requires the ability to compute them efficiently, or otherwise we will not benefit over the naive algorithm. This is where we leverage the structure of 2D lattices. We extend Tarjan's efficient algorithm for finding lowest common ancestors in trees to finding suprema in 2D lattices, as discussed in Section 3. This way we obtain a detector that runs in constant space per location and nearly constant time per memory access. Our extension was inspired by the SP-bags race detection algorithm [12] which implicitly applies Tarjan's algorithm to the decomposition trees of SP task graphs. The key insight of Tarjan's algorithm, and consequently of SP-bags and our extension, is to traverse the input graph in an order that is simultaneously topological, depth-first and left-to-right.

As an example, our algorithm would traverse the graph in Figure 2 in the order A B C D, but not A B D C, which is not left-to-right (nor right-to-left). To obtain an online race detection algorithm, the program execution order must match the required traversal order. A central insight from SP-bags is that for Cilk programs this can be achieved by executing the program in a serial, fork-first fashion. Similarly, this is also the case for our structured fork-join discussed in Section 5. This requirement makes the algorithm serial, but that is the price we pay for efficiency.

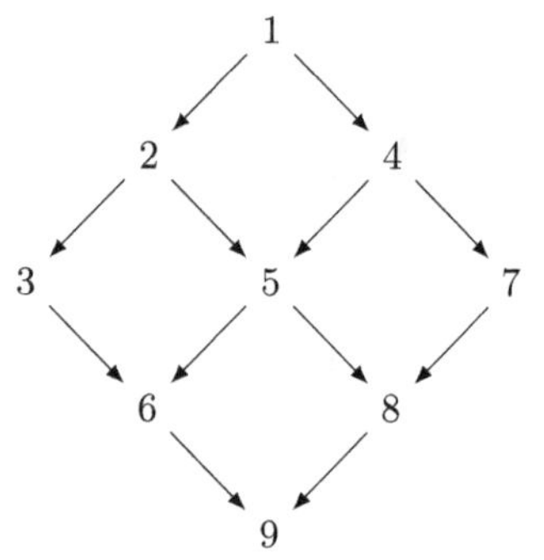

Figure 3: A planar diagram of a two-dimensional lattice. If we trace any directed path, then we always advance downwards. Arcs "intersect" only at their endpoints.

3. SUPREMA IN TWO DIMENSIONS

We continue with an efficient algorithm for computing the suprema in two-dimensional lattices, a key building block for our online race detector (discussed in the next section). The algorithm takes as input a lattice diagram, and answers supremum queries on the fly while it traverses the diagram.

Lattices.

Recall that a *lattice* is a partially ordered set $(P, \sqsubset)$ such that every pair of elements $x, y \in P$ has a greatest lower bound $\inf\{x, y\}$ and a smallest upper bound $\sup\{x, y\}$, also called the *infimum* and the *supremum*. The *closure* of any subset $U \subseteq P$ is the smallest superset of U closed under infima and suprema of pairs of elements.

We represent a lattice by an acyclic digraph $G = (V, E)$ whose reachability relation is identical to $\sqsubset$. A *diagram* is a monotonic drawing of such a representation in the Euclidean plane, as shown in Figure 3. By *monotonic* we mean that tracing a directed path on the diagram will always advance in the same direction, e.g., downwards. Further, if arcs intersect at most at their endpoints, then the diagram is called *planar* and the lattice is called *two-dimensional* (Figure 3).

Non-separating traversals.

We shall traverse *both* the arcs and the vertices of the given planar diagram in a way that reveals its lattice structure, and provides us with a direct way to answer suprema queries. We formally equate a *traversal* T of the digraph $G = (V, E)$ with a permutation of $E \cup \{(x, x) \mid x \in V\}$, where each loop (x, x) represents the vertex $x \in V$.

Definition 1. A *non-separating traversal*[1] is one which is obtained by traversing a planar diagram in a topological, depth-first and left-to-right order.

Let us denote with $<_T$ the linear order in which T visits all the arcs and vertices of G. By a *topological* traversal we mean that $(a, x) \leq_T (y, b)$ whenever y is reachable from x. This implies that incoming arcs, loops, and outgoing arcs are visited in the order $(x, y) \leq_T (y, y) \leq_T (y, z)$.

A non-separating traversal of the diagram in Figure 3 is shown in Figure 4. The black part of the picture corresponds

---

[1]The name comes from the non-separating linear extensions of lattice orders, defined by Dushnik and Miller [10].

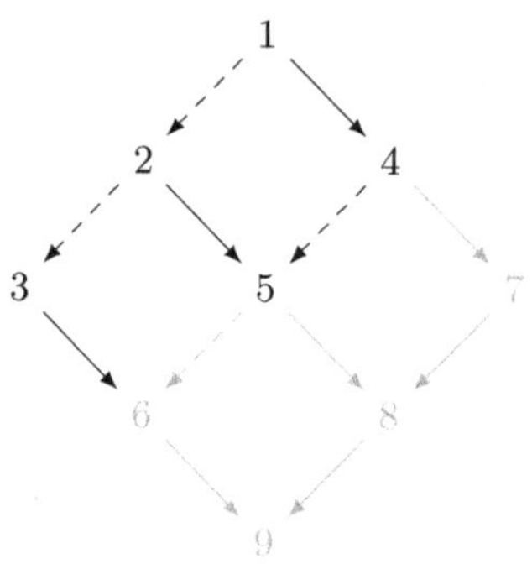

$$(1,1)(1,2)(2,2)(2,3)(3,3)(3,6)(2,5)(1,4)(4,4)(4,5)(5,5) \cdots$$
$$\cdots (5,6)(6,6)(6,9)(5,8)(4,7)(7,7)(7,8)(8,8)(8,9)(9,9)$$

Figure 4: A non-separating traversal of the arcs and the vertices of a diagram. The current point of the traversal is $(5,5)$. The black part has been "visited", while the gray part remains to be. The last-arcs are drawn solid and the rest are dashed.

to the prefix ending in $(5,5)$. Because the traversal has to be topological, $(6,6)$ cannot be visited immediately after $(3,6)$ because we must visit $(5,6)$ before $(6,6)$.

The problem.

We are given a planar diagram of a digraph $G = (V, E)$ representing a two-dimensional lattice $(P, \sqsubset)$. We wish to traverse this diagram, and for each visited vertex $t \in V$, answer supremum queries of the form $\text{SUP}(x, t)$. We shall impose the following *precondition* on all queries $\text{SUP}(x, t)$

x is in the closure of the traversal prefix ending in t. (1)

For example, given the traversal in Figure 4 the query $\text{SUP}(6, 5)$ is valid, while $\text{SUP}(7, 5)$ is not.

For a fixed vertex t, let us collect all queries of the form $\text{SUP}(x, t)$ into the set $Q(t)$. Then, our task is to process the sequence of such query sets, one per every visited vertex:

$$Q(t_1), \ldots, Q(t_n) \qquad (2)$$

This setting is adequate when the i-th query set $Q(t_i)$ is not given in advance to the traversal, but is determined on the fly from the prefix ending in t_i (as is the case in race detection).

Connection via forests.

We connect a non-separating traversal T to suprema via certain forests associated with the prefixes of T. Consider a fixed vertex $x \in V$ and the last visited arc[2] $(x, y) \in T$ that exits x. We refer to it as the *last arc* of x, or just as a *last-arc*. Taken together, the last-arcs form a tree directed towards its root (Figure 4). Thus, the last-arcs that belong to any given prefix of T form a forest:

Definition 2. For any traversal T and arc $(s, t) \in T$, define the *last-arc forest* $T/(s, t)$ to be the collection of all last-arcs $(x, y) \leq_T (s, t)$ belonging to the prefix ending in (s, t). The forest vertices are those incident to some arc in the forest.

---

[2]Equivalently, a last-arc (x, y) is the right-most arc exiting the vertex x.

```
WALK(T, Q)                          SUP(x, t)
1   for (s, t) ∈ T                   1   r ← FIND(x)
2       if (s, t) is a loop          2   if r. visited
3           t. visited ← TRUE        3       return t
4           answer Q(t)              4   else
5       if (s, t) is a last-arc      5       return r
6           UNION(t, s)
```

Figure 5: An algorithm for finding suprema in two-dimensional lattices. The input lattice is encoded by a non-separating traversal T. The algorithm answers queries $\text{SUP}(x, t) \in Q(t)$. In practice, Q can be thought of as a callback invoking SUP.

We think of (s, t) as the "current" point in the traversal, splitting it into visited prefix and unvisited suffix. For the traversal in Figure 4, the current point is $(5, 5)$, and the forest $T/(5, 5)$ is the union of the trees $\{(3, 6)\}$, $\{(2, 5)\}$ and $\{(1, 4)\}$. Note that vertex 6 belongs both to the closure of the visited prefix and also to the forest $T/(5, 5)$. In general, the closure of the prefix ending in (t, t) always equals the vertices of the forest $T/(t, t)$.

The connection between a non-separating traversal T and suprema goes through the roots of the forest $T/(t, t)$ as described by the following

THEOREM 1. *Given a non-separating traversal T and a pair of vertices x and t, where x belongs to the closure of prefix ending in (t, t), let r be the root of the tree in $T/(t, t)$ that contains x. Then $\sup\{x, t\}$ attains the form:*

$$\sup\{x, t\} = \begin{cases} t & \text{if } r \leq_T t \\ r & \text{if } t \leq_T r. \end{cases}$$

If on Figure 4 we let $x = 3$ and $t = 5$, then $r = 6$. Vertex 6 is traversed after 5, and so $\sup\{x, t\}$ equals vertex 6. On the other hand, if $x = 1$ and $t = 5$, then $r = 4$ and $\sup\{x, t\}$ equals vertex 5. We shall prove Theorem 1 in Section 6.

Suprema finding algorithm.

Theorem 1 leads directly to an algorithm for answering supremum queries. Perform a non-separating traversal T, and maintain the forest $T/(s, t)$ at every point $(s, t) \in T$. When at a vertex t, answer all queries of the form $\text{SUP}(x, t)$:

Find the root r of the tree containing x; if the root has been visited, then answer t; otherwise answer r.

Figure 5 lists a pseudo-code for this algorithm. The main routine WALK performs the traversal and maintains the last-arc forest, while the subroutine SUP answers individual queries. The main routine accepts the traversal T directly, and also a description Q of all queries. The subroutine then answers each query $\text{SUP}(x, t) \in Q(t)$. The algorithm uses an union-find data structure to maintain the mapping from each visited vertex to its root in the last-arc forest: the vertices of each tree are kept in a disjoint set labeled by the root of the tree. The FIND(x) operation returns the label of the set containing x. The UNION(y, x) operation merges the sets containing y and x under the label of the set containing y. Initially, every vertex x is alone in a set $\{x\}$ labeled by x.

THEOREM 2. *The algorithm in Figure 5 is correct.*

PROOF. By Theorem 1 it is sufficient to argue that we maintain the vertices of each tree in their own set labeled by the tree root. Assume this holds for the step $(x, y) \in T$ before we visit a last-arc $(s, t) \in T$. Because T is topological both s and t are roots in $T/(x, y)$. The new forest $T/(s, t)$ differs by having s attached as a child of t. This is exactly what lines 5–6 of the main routine WALK accomplish. □

We now elaborate on the algorithm's resource requirements. An union-find data structure can be implemented very efficiently, guaranteeing nearly constant amortized time per operation. The precise asymptotics is given in terms of Tarjan's functional inverse α of the Ackermann function.

THEOREM 3. *The algorithm in Figure 5 needs at worst $\Theta\big((m + n)\alpha(m + n, n)\big)$ time and $\Theta(n)$ space to answer m supremum queries on a lattice with n elements.*

PROOF. In total at most $m + n$ union-find operations are executed over n elements: one FIND per query and at most one UNION per element. With a fast union-find implementation they shall take at most $\Theta\big((m + n)\alpha(m + n, n)\big)$ time, as analyzed by Tarjan [19, 20], and $\Theta(n)$ space. Additionally, by Euler's formula at most $3n - 6 = \Theta(n)$ arcs are traversed, as the input diagram is planar. □

Remark 1. We assumed that a planar diagram or a non-separating traversal are directly given as input. Therefore, there stands the question of whether we can obtain them efficiently in the context of online race detection. In Section 5 we discuss a restriction to fork-join for which this is the case.

In a more general context, it is worth recalling how to obtain a planar diagram or a non-separating traversal given the input digraph alone. Without loss of generality, we can consider graphs with a single source s, a single sink t, and an arc (s, t) connecting the two. For such digraphs, we can obtain a *monotonic* planar drawing (or a non-separating traversal) from a *any* planar drawing where the arc (s, t) lies on the external face [2, 14]. Planar drawings can be constructed efficiently in linear time, e.g., by [6, 9].

Remark 2. The algorithm we presented can be seen as an extension of Tarjan's offline algorithm for finding lowest common ancestors in trees. A lowest common ancestor is just another name for infimum, and by reversing the arcs in a directed graph (poset) we switch infima and suprema. Thus, we can see Tarjan's algorithm as finding suprema in a semilattice with the shape of a tree. In this case, a simpler version of Theorem 1 holds:

For the root r of the tree in $T/(t, t)$ containing x, it is always the case that $t \leq_T r$, and therefore:

$$\sup\{x, t\} = r.$$

That is, in this case we do not need to track whether the root has already been visited or not.

Our extension to Tarjan's algorithm is inspired by the SP-bags algorithm due to Feng and Leiserson [12]. SP-bags basically applies Tarjan's algorithm to the decomposition tree of a series-parallel graph, which can be shown to be equivalent to applying Theorem 1 to the series-parallel graph directly.

Next, we show how our algorithm can be used as a building block in an online race detector.

4. ONLINE RACE DETECTION

In this section we consider the problem of detecting races in programs whose task graphs have a two-dimensional lattice structure. In particular, we apply the algorithm for finding suprema from Section 3 in an efficient race detection algorithm. Interestingly, as we discuss below, non-separating traversals are not always obtainable in the context of online race detection (as these traversals may consist of events that have not yet occurred in an execution). Thus, we show how to slightly adapt the class of traversals we consider in order to achieve a fully online algorithm for 2D lattices.

Races.

Recall that given a program execution, a *race* between a pair of conflicting memory operations exists if these operations are not synchronized to occur in a fixed order. Two operations conflict whenever they access the same memory location, and at least one of them writes to that location. The presence of racing operations indicates potentially non-deterministic behavior, as executing them in different orders might lead to different results.

We reason about operation order by querying the task graph $G = (V, E)$ of the particular execution that we are analyzing. An operation x is ordered before y, if from x we can reach y via a directed path in G. The execution itself corresponds to a traversal of the graph in topological order. A race manifests as two vertices not connected by a directed path and whose corresponding operations do conflict. To keep the graph-theoretic terminology we shall refer to operations as vertices.

The problem.

We are given a program such that the task graph of any of its executions has a two-dimensional (2D) lattice structure, i.e., a planar diagram. Our goal is to detect races online as we execute the program. In abstract terms, the execution produces a task graph G and a traversal T that we follow. For each visited vertex t, we wish to detect whether t races with another visited vertex $x <_T t$. We shall assume that T has a certain structure, namely, be non-separating. Finding an execution order which ensures that structure depends on the class of programs under consideration. In Section 5 we discuss a structured use of fork-join for which an appropriate execution order can be easily determined.

Suprema based race detector.

We arrive at a race detector by applying the algorithm for answering supremum queries from Section 3 to the lattice $(P, \sqsubset)$ determined by the task graph (recall that $\sqsubset$ equals the reachability relation of the task graph G). Of course, the traversal T dictated by the program execution must be non-separating. While traversing the task graph along T, we consider the set K of visited vertices that conflict with the current vertex t. Unless every vertex in K is ordered before t we have a race:

$$\text{no } K\text{-}t \text{ race} \iff K \sqsubseteq t \iff \sup K \sqsubseteq t. \qquad (3)$$

We can therefore reduce race detection to tracking suprema in the lattice $(P, \sqsubset)$. Note that $\sup K$ need not even access the same memory location as K and t (cf. Figure 2).

The overall approach is summarized in Figure 6. Two routines ON-READ and ON-WRITE handle respectively read

ON-READ(t)
1   **if** $\textsc{Sup}(R[t.loc], t) \neq t$
2   report a race on $t.loc$
3   $R[t.loc] \leftarrow \textsc{Sup}(R[t.loc], t)$

ON-WRITE(t)
1   **if** $\textsc{Sup}(R[t.loc], t) \neq t$ or $\textsc{Sup}(W[t.loc], t) \neq t$
2   report a race on $t.loc$
3   $W[t.loc] \leftarrow \textsc{Sup}(W[t.loc], t)$

Figure 6: Online race detection via suprema. For every memory operation t in an program execution a corresponding routine is performed. The maps $R[loc]$ and $W[loc]$ accumulate the suprema of respectively all reads and writes per location loc.

and write operations. For every memory location loc they accumulate into $R[loc]$ the supremum of those visited vertices that read from loc, and accumulate into $W[loc]$ the supremum of those visited vertices that write to loc. To check for races on the location $t.loc$ accessed by the current vertex t, the routines compare $R[t.loc]$ or $W[t.loc]$ with t in the lattice order $\sqsubset$. Such comparison $x \sqsubseteq t$ is implemented with the query $\textsc{Sup}(x, t) = t$. The suprema $R[t.loc]$ and $W[t.loc]$ are always in the closure of the vertices visited up to t as required by the problem definition in Section 3.

Obstacles to online race detection.

In general, a program may not have an execution that corresponds to a non-separating traversal, even though its task graphs have a two-dimensional lattice structure. That is because a non-separating traversal might require us to visit an arc (s, t) at a moment where t is *not yet* determined by the execution so far. For example, suppose that (s, t) is the only arc exiting s, the vertex s is the last operation of some thread, and t is a **join** operation joining that thread. Then, the presence of the arc (s, t) is determined only upon the execution of t, while a non-separating traversal requires that (s, t) is visited right after (s, s). A similar difficulty arises in answering supremum queries: when visiting a vertex t the supremum $\sup\{x, t\}$ might be indeterminate as well. These cases are demonstrated by Figure 2 in Section 2.

In order to obtain an online race detector, we shall do two things: 1) employ a slightly different class of traversals that have no obstacle to being executable; 2) relax the problem of finding suprema, such that it can be solved over the new class of traversals, and moreover still facilitate race detection.

Delayed traversals.

We shall now define *delayed* non-separating traversals. First, let us characterize the arcs (s, t) that can potentially prevent a traversal T from being executable. Assume that T visits (s, t) before it visits a vertex x on which the vertex t depends on, i.e., assume that

$$(s, t) <_T (x, x) \text{ and } x \sqsubset t. \qquad (4)$$

Whether the arc (s, t) is present in the task graph is usually determined right before the execution of t, and therefore only after the execution of x. In this case no execution corresponds to T. An example of (4) is given by $(3, 6) <_T 5 \sqsubset 6$ in Figure 4, Section 3.

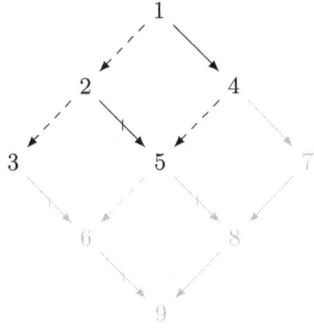

$$(1,1) \cdots (3,3)(3,\times)(2,\times)(1,4)(4,4)(2,5)(4,5)(5,5) \cdots$$

Figure 7: A delayed non-separating traversal. The traversal of the crossed arcs has been delayed so they are visited together with their target vertices. The stop-arcs $(3,\times)$, $(2,\times)$, etc. (not drawn) mark the original places of the delayed arcs.

To remove this obstacle, we shall *delay* the traversal of all arcs (4) until immediately before t. Hence, in the old place of (s,t) we leave the special marker $(s,\times)$ that we call a *stop-arc*. We obtain the transformation $T \mapsto T'$:

$$T: \quad \cdots \quad (s_i,t) \quad \cdots \quad (s_j,t) \quad \cdots \quad (s_n,t)(t,t)$$
$$\downarrow \qquad\qquad \downarrow \qquad\qquad\qquad \downarrow$$
$$T': \quad \cdots \quad \underbrace{(s_i,\times)}_{\text{stop-arc}} \quad \cdots \quad \underbrace{(s_j,\times)}_{\text{stop-arc}} \quad \cdots \quad \underbrace{..(s_i,t)..(s_j,t)..}_{\text{delayed arcs}}(s_n,t)(t,t)$$

Definition 3. A *delayed non-separating traversal* is one which is obtained in the same way as a non-separating traversal except that the arcs (4) have been delayed and stop-arcs mark their original places (Figure 7).

In Section 5 we discuss a restriction to fork-join for which delayed traversals can easily be obtained.

Relaxed query problem.

As $\sup\{x,t\}$ might be indeterminate at the moment of execution of t, we shall relax the original query problem (2) from Section 3. Observe that the race detection algorithm in Figure 6 uses the result of a query only to compare it with the current vertex. Therefore, we may answer queries differently as long as any such sequence of comparisons leads to the same outcome. Recall that the defining property of suprema is given by

$$\sup\{x,y\} \sqsubseteq t \iff x \sqsubseteq t, y \sqsubseteq t, \tag{5}$$

for all x, y and t. It is therefore sufficient to come up with a routine $\text{Sup}(x,t)$ that answers the relaxed query problem

$$\text{Sup}(x,t) = t \iff x \sqsubseteq t \tag{6}$$
$$\text{Sup}(\text{Sup}(x,y),t) = t \iff \text{Sup}(x,t) = t, \text{Sup}(y,t) = t \tag{7}$$

for all vertices x, y and t that satisfy the precondition (1) to Sup from Section 3. For example, if we execute the program in Figure 2, Section 2 in the order A B C D, then $\text{Sup}(A, B)$ is allowed return A instead of the true supremum C.

The condition (5) and the conditions (6)-(7) are of course not equivalent, for otherwise $\text{Sup}(x,y)$ must always equal $\sup\{x,y\}$. The difference is that for (6)-(7) the possible combinations of x, y and t are restricted by the Sup precondition (1), while for (5) they are unrestricted.

```
WALK(T, Q)                          SUP(x, t)
1   for (s, t) ∈ T                  1   r ← FIND(x)
2       if (s, t) is a loop         2   if r.visited
3           t.visited ← TRUE        3       return t
4           answer Q(t)             4   else
5       if (s, t) is a last-arc     5       return r
6           UNION(t, s)
7       if (s, t) is a stop-arc
8           s.visited ← FALSE
```

Figure 8: An algorithm for answering relaxed supremum queries (6)-(7) along delayed non-separating traversals. The only difference with the algorithm in Figure 5 is that this one handles stop-arcs $(s, \times)$ by marking the vertex s as unvisited.

Modified algorithm.

We shall adapt the algorithm in Figure 5, Section 3 to solve the relaxed query problem (6)-(7) along delayed non-separating traversals. In answering queries $\text{Sup}(x,t)$, we need to decide what to do when the supremum $s = \sup\{x,t\}$ has *not* been visited yet. Recall that along a normal non-separating traversal T, we can simply find the root of x in the forest $T/(t,t)$. Because s is not visited, by Theorem 1 this root must equal s. However, in the corresponding delayed traversal T' the root r of tree in $T'/(t,t)$ that contains x does not equal s, but merely has the last-arc (r,s) pointing to s. Because the last-arc (r,s) has been delayed after t, at this point we do not know what the true supremum is.

To deal with this situation, we shall answer such queries with $\text{Sup}(x,t) = r$, pretending that r is the supremum s. We need to make sure that r is marked as unvisited, so in future queries it behaves the same way as s does. When we later visit the arc (r,s) we have the chance to correct this deception by attaching r as a child of s, so that no one will notice. The moment when r should start acting like s, is when we visit the stop-arc $(r,\times)$. Then, we mark r as unvisited. Recall that the stop-arc stands in the original place of the last-arc (r,s) in the traversal T.

In essence, by marking the root r as unvisited, we make it observationally equivalent to the supremum s with respect to (6)-(7). This approach is summarized in Figure 8.

THEOREM 4. *The algorithm in Figure 8 is correct with respect to the relaxed conditions (6)-(7).*

PROOF. We begin with condition (6). Recall that along a non-separating traversal T the forest $T/(s,t)$ changes with every visited last-arc (s,t) by attaching the root s as a child of the root t. In the corresponding delayed traversal T' exactly the same changes occur but at the point right before t is visited. Consider the state of the algorithm along T' and compare the two forests $T/(t,t)$ and $T'/(t,t)$. The trees in $T/(t,t)$ having roots visited before t are precisely the trees in $T'/(t,t)$ having roots marked as visited. Therefore, by Theorem 1 we obtain (6). As for condition (7), compare the answer $r = \text{Sup}(x,y)$ over T' and $s = \sup\{x,y\}$. By the definition of a delayed traversal, (r,s) must be a last-arc. Moreover, this arc is visited before t, and so r must be attached as a child of s before t is visited. Then, assuming either side of the equivalence (7), the vertices x, y and t all belong to the same tree in $T'/(t,t)$, with t being its root. Therefore, the other side of (7) follows. $\square$

We now turn to the question of resource requirements. As currently formulated, the algorithm requires storing every visited vertex, i.e., requires at minimum space proportional to the number of executed operations. This can be too expensive in practice, and we now discuss how to reduce this number significantly. The idea is to decompose the vertices of the task graph into "threads" and identify each vertex with the thread that it belongs to, while ensuring that the race detection algorithm is sound and precise. This way we need to store only the threads and not the vertices themselves.

For a given delayed traversal T' of the graph $G = (V, E)$, we define a *thread* as the set of vertices of a maximal path of non-delayed last-arcs. For example, the threads in Figure 7 are $\{2\}$, $\{3\}$, $\{5\}$, $\{6\}$, and $\{1, 4, 7, 8, 9\}$. We assume that each thread is assigned an unique identifier, and let $tid(x)$ denote the identifier of the thread containing x. Instead of feeding the delayed traversal T' to the race detector, we transform it $T' \mapsto T''$ by replacing every arc[3] according to

$$(x, y) \mapsto (tid(x), tid(y)). \qquad (8)$$

This way the race detector operates on threads instead of vertices, and does bookkeeping proportional to the number of threads. Moreover, the transformation preserves every comparison made by the race detection:

$$\text{Sup}(x, t) = t \iff \text{Sup}(tid(x), tid(t)) = tid(t). \qquad (9)$$

This follows from the fact that a thread intersects at most one tree in $T'/(s, t)$ for every $(s, t) \in T'$.

From the already calculated resource bounds of the algorithm in Section 3 (i.e., Theorem 3), we directly obtain:

THEOREM 5. *The race detection algorithm in Figure 6 needs $\Theta(\alpha(m + n), n)$ amortized time per executed operation, where m is the number of operations, and n is the number of threads. Also, it needs $\Theta(1)$ space per thread and per tracked memory location.*

For the structured fork-join program constructs, discussed in the next section, the threads defined here correspond to actual program threads (i.e., tasks).

5. STRUCTURED FORK-JOIN

In this section we restrict the fork-join parallel constructs, such that they produce the task graphs with a two-dimensional lattice structure. For the sake of presentation we will deal with task graphs in which every vertex has at most two incoming arcs, and at most two outgoing arcs. The general case is easily obtainable from this one.

Structured fork-join.

We shall structure the use of fork and join constructs by restricting with which tasks a given task is allowed to join. The basic idea is to maintain all running tasks *as points in a line*. Each task may join only its left neighbor, removing it along the way. Similarly, a newly forked child becomes the left neighbor of the parent. This way each task x splits the line into a left part L and a right part R, or more graphically into $L \cdot x \cdot R$. The restrictions mean that task x may add and remove tasks only at the right end of L (treat it like a LIFO stack), but cannot touch R at all.

[3] We assume that the information about what operation corresponds to a vertex is preserved somewhere else.

$$L \cdot \{x \mid \textbf{fork } y \ \beta; \alpha\} \cdot R \longrightarrow L \cdot \{y \mid \beta\} \cdot \{x \mid \alpha\} \cdot R$$
$$L \cdot \{y \mid\} \cdot \{x \mid \textbf{join } y; \alpha\} \cdot R \longrightarrow L \cdot \{x \mid \alpha\} \cdot R$$

Figure 9: Fork-join rules that capture task graphs with a 2D lattice structure. Each task is represented by a pair $\{x \mid \alpha\}$, where x is the task identifier and α is a list of statements. All tasks are organized as points in a line. A forked task goes on the left of its parent, and a task may only join the one on its left.

We state these rules more formally in Figure 9. Each task is represented as a pair $\{x \mid \alpha\}$, where x is an unique identifier, and α is the sequence of statements that the task executes. The program in Figure 2, Section 2 follows the rules. Figure 10 shows a 2D task graph along with lines of task points at various moments in the execution.

Vertices in a task graph correspond to transitions taken by the program, e.g., **fork** y or **join** y. Edges signify immediate dependencies of one transition upon another, e.g., a **join** y transition depends on the previous transition by the same thread and also on the final transition by the joined thread. (This is essentially Lamport's happened-before relation.)

THEOREM 6. *The rules in Figure 9 generate task graphs with a two-dimensional lattice structure.*

PROOF. From an execution that follows the rules we can easily construct a planar diagram of the task graph. Recall that a diagram is required to be monotonic, i.e., that directed paths always advance in a fixed direction. Let us choose this direction to be downwards. Now, each program transition transforms $T_i \mapsto T_{i+1}$ the current line T_i of task points, and so we have a history of line snapshots $T_1, \ldots, T_n$.

Let us lay out the lines such that each T_i is horizontal and placed above T_{i+1} (Figure 10). Observe that every task x intersects each line T_i at exactly zero or one points $x_i \in T_i$. To build the task graph, for each $T_i \mapsto T_{i+1}$ add arcs between:

1. x_i and x_{i+1},

2. x_i and y_{i+1} if x forks y

3. y_i and x_{i+1} if x joins y

and then collapse all task points that represent the same task state. The resulting diagram is monotonic as T_i is above T_{i+1}. It is also planar, because when forking or joining the two involved points $x_i, y_i \in T_i$ are always next to each other. The resulting diagram is a diagram of a lattice by a well-know result [1, 11] in poset dimension theory. $\square$

An extension of the rules with forking and joining any number of tasks would capture all possible 2D lattices.

Obtaining delayed traversals.

The proof of Theorem 6 indicates a direct way to obtain a delayed non-separating traversal from an execution. On the resulting diagram (Figure 10) a newly forked task stays on the left of its parent task. Therefore, to traverse the diagram from left to right, we can simply execute the program *serially, fork-first*, and emit arcs on the way. Here, x and y designate task identifiers, according to (8), Section 4:

$$T \xmapsto{x \textbf{ forks } y} T \cdot (x, y), \qquad T \xmapsto{x \textbf{ steps}} T \cdot (x, x),$$
$$T \xmapsto{x \textbf{ joins } y} T \cdot (y, x), \qquad T \xmapsto{x \textbf{ halts}} T \cdot (x, \times),$$

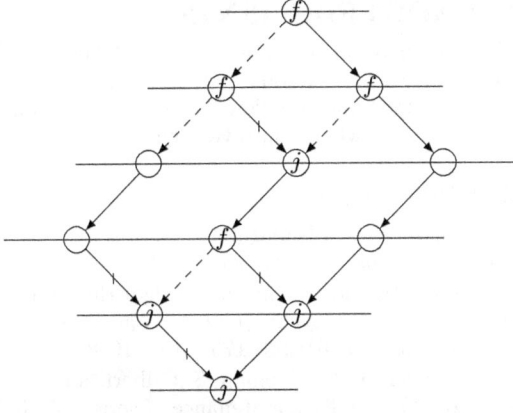

Figure 10: A fork-join task graph with a 2D lattice structure. Fork edges are dashed, step edges are solid, and join edges are crossed. A serial fork-first execution corresponds to a delayed non-separating traversal of the task graph. Lines of task points from the fork-join rules are drawn horizontally.

To motivate this construction, observe that a last-arc in the task graph connects either two consecutive operations on the same task, or a final operation on one task and a join operation from another. The one between a final operation and a join must be delayed, which is done by emitting a stop-arc when a task halts, and a last-arc when one task joins another.

To instantiate our race detection algorithm, we simply need to stream the constructed traversal T on the fly to the WALK routine in Figure 8, with the race detector in Figure 6 passed as the callback Q.

Generalization of series-parallel constructs.

It is instructive to understand how the structured fork and join presented here generalize constructs that produce series-parallel graphs, such as Cilk's spawn-sync or X10's async-finish. Consider a stylized version of the rules in Figure 9, where for clarity, program statements are omitted and only the task identifiers are kept:

$$L \cdot x \cdot R \xrightleftharpoons[x \text{ joins } y]{x \text{ forks } y} L \cdot y \cdot x \cdot R. \tag{10}$$

A situation that produces non-SP graphs can arise here. Consider which task could have forked y. As a newly forked task is placed on the left of its parent, the task that have forked y must be either x or some task in R. For example, we can have the passage

$$t \xrightarrow{t \text{ forks } y} y \cdot t \xrightarrow{t \text{ forks } x} y \cdot x \cdot t \xrightarrow{x \text{ joins } y} x \cdot t.$$

This results in a non-SP task graph (cf. Figure 2, Section 2). One way to ensure that the produced task graph is SP, is to require y to be a descendant of x. This is achieved by bracketing x in (10) together with its descendants S:

$$L \cdot [S \cdot x] \cdot R \xrightleftharpoons[x \text{ joins } y]{x \text{ forks } y} L \cdot [S \cdot [y] \cdot x] \cdot R. \tag{11}$$

This way x cannot join a task outside S. It is easy to establish that (11) indeed produces series-parallel task graphs, e.g, we recover the semantics of **sync** by automatically joining with the whole set S in addition to y.

Handling pipeline parallelism.

Before we conclude this section, we discuss another setting which can benefit from our race detector. Many applications exhibit parallel structure in the form of a linear pipeline as described in [16]: they take as input a sequence of data items $x_1, \ldots, x_n$, and feed each item x_j through a sequence of computation stages $S_1(x_j), \ldots, S_m(x_j)$.

A task $S_i(x_j)$ is allowed to depend on any $S_k(x_l)$ where $k < i$ or $l < i$, but otherwise tasks are run in parallel. Thus, the task graph of a linear pipeline can be embedded into a two-dimensional grid, i.e., it forms a two-dimensional lattice. This pattern can be directly captured in our structured fork-join and can also be analyzed with the race detection algorithm presented in this paper.

Blelloch and Reid-Miller [4] made the observation that many pipelined programs are more naturally expressed in a fork-join fashion. However, their model is more relaxed than ours as it allows non-linear pipelines, therefore leaving open the question for efficient race detection in their case. Linear pipelines are the focus of the work of Lee et al. [15] which extends Cilk with support for this setting. Interestingly, their language constructs are easily expressible in our restricted fork-join, but not the other way around, even though both models can express exactly the same task graphs, i.e., the ones having a two-dimensional lattice structure.

6. PROOFS

In this section we prove Theorem 1 in a series of four lemmas, which are basically weaker versions of it.

Let $(P, \sqsubseteq)$ be a two-dimensional lattice represented by a given planar diagram with digraph $G = (V, E)$, and let T be a non-separating traversal of the diagram. Without loss of generality we assume that $P = V$, and that the diagram is monotonic in the downwards direction, and that the traversal is from left to right. Recall that x and y are comparable if either $x \sqsubseteq y$ or $y \sqsubseteq x$, i.e., they lie on a directed path in G.

LEMMA 1. *Let x and t be two incomparable vertices such that x belongs to $T/(t,t)$. Then, $\sup\{x,t\}$ is reachable from x via a directed path consisting of last-arcs only.*

PROOF. Because the traversal is depth-first left-to-right, we can choose the planar diagram such that the vertical line crossing $\sup\{x,t\}$ has x on its left and t on its right. The diagram is planar and monotonic, hence we can select the rightmost path exiting x and the leftmost path exiting t. Then, $\sup\{x,t\}$ must lie on the intersection of the two paths, or it would not be the least upper bound of $\{x,t\}$. Any rightmost path by definition consists of last-arcs only. $\square$

LEMMA 2. *For all vertices x and t such that x belongs to $T/(t,t)$ we have that $\sup\{x,t\}$ also belongs to $T/(t,t)$.*

PROOF. If x and t are comparable then the statement is trivial, so let us assume that x and t are incomparable, and let $s = \sup\{x,t\}$. Select the last-arc (p, s) lying on the path from Lemma 1 that connects x and s. The two vertices p and t must be incomparable, and therefore (p, s) must be visited before t, for otherwise the traversal would not be depth-first left-to-right. We conclude that the last-arc (p, s) belongs to the forest $T/(t,t)$ and so does s. $\square$

LEMMA 3. *For all vertices x and t such that x belongs to $T/(t,t)$ we have that $\sup\{x,t\}$ is a root of $T/(t,t)$.*

PROOF. From Lemma 2 we known that $s = \sup\{x, t\}$ belongs to $T/(t, t)$. Because $T/(t, t)$ consists of last-arcs only, if s is not a root, then its last-arc must also belong to $T/(t, t)$, and therefore be visited before t. This contradicts the assumption that the traversal is topological as by the definition of supremum $t \sqsubseteq s$. □

LEMMA 4. *For every vertex t and root r in $T/(t, t)$ we have that r is comparable with t.*

PROOF. Assume r and t are incomparable. By Lemma 1 we conclude that $s = \sup\{r, t\}$ must be reachable from either r or t via a directed path of last-arcs. But by Lemma 3 we know that s is a root of the last-arc forest $T/(t, t)$, and therefore r and t cannot both be roots, a contradiction. □

THEOREM 1. *Given a non-separating traversal T and a pair of vertices x and t, where x belongs to the closure of prefix ending in (t, t), let r be the root of the tree in $T/(t, t)$ that contains x. Then $\sup\{x, t\}$ attains the form:*

$$\sup\{x, t\} = \begin{cases} t & \text{if } r \leq_T t \\ r & \text{if } t \leq_T r. \end{cases}$$

PROOF. It is not difficult to see that the set of vertices of $T/(t, t)$ equals the closure of the prefix ending in t. Now, by Lemma 4 and because the traversal is topological, the following equivalences hold (recall that $<_T$ is a linear order):

$$r \leq_T t \iff r \sqsubseteq t \tag{12}$$
$$t <_T r \iff t \sqsubset r. \tag{13}$$

If $r \leq_T t$, then the theorem follows directly, and so let us consider the case when $t <_T r$ and $t \sqsubset r$. Then, x and t are incomparable, and by Lemma 1 we have that $s = \sup\{x, t\}$ is reachable from x by a path of last-arcs. But by Lemma 3 s is a root in $T/(t, t)$, and therefore must equal r. □

Remark 3. Introducing two dimensional lattices as those having planar diagrams is intuitive. However, the original (and more flexible) definition due to Dushnik and Miller [10] describes them as those being the intersection of two linear orders. The fact that this is equivalent to having a planar diagram was proved by Baker et al. [1].

7. CONCLUSION

We presented an online algorithm for race detection in task graphs with a two-dimensional (2D) lattice structure. These 2D lattices are richer than SP-graphs and thus our algorithm generalizes race detectors for SP-graphs. Our algorithm is founded in reducing race detection to finding suprema in program task graphs. Building on prior work [12, 18], we extended Tarjan's algorithm for finding lowest common ancestors in trees, to finding suprema in 2D lattices. Efficient computation of suprema is based on performing a *non-separating* traversal of the lattice graph. However, such a traversal need not correspond to any program execution, thus precluding an online algorithm. To overcome this obstacle, we observed that a race detector can pose suprema queries with a relaxed semantics. We adopted our suprema finding algorithm to answer the relaxed queries over a wider class of traversals, and obtained a fully online race detector. Finally, we introduced restricted fork-join constructs which permit only task graphs with a 2D lattice structure, resulting in programs directly analyzable by our online algorithm.

8. ACKNOWLEDGMENTS

We thank Raghavan Raman and Boris Peltekov for helpful discussions on earlier versions of this work. We are also grateful to the anonymous reviewers for their questions and well-placed remarks which improved the paper.

9. REFERENCES

[1] K. A. Baker, P. C. Fishburn, and F. S. Roberts. Partial orders of dimension 2. *Networks*, 2(1):11–28, 1972.

[2] G. D. Battista and R. Tamassia. Algorithms for plane representations of acyclic digraphs. *Theoretical Computer Science*, 61(2-3):175 – 198, 1988.

[3] M. A. Bender, J. T. Fineman, S. Gilbert, and C. E. Leiserson. On-the-fly maintenance of series-parallel relationships in fork-join multithreaded programs. SPAA, pages 133–144. ACM, 2004.

[4] G. E. Blelloch and M. Reid-Miller. Pipelining with futures. SPAA, New York, NY, USA, 1997. ACM.

[5] R. D. Blumofe, C. F. Joerg, B. C. Kuszmaul, C. E. Leiserson, K. H. Randall, and Y. Zhou. Cilk: An efficient multithreaded runtime system. PPOPP, 1995.

[6] J. Boyer, P. Cortese, M. Patrignani, and G. Di Battista. Stop minding your P's and Q's: Implementing a fast and simple DFS-based planarity testing and embedding algorithm. Graph Drawing '04. Springer, 2004.

[7] V. Cavé, J. Zhao, J. Shirako, and V. Sarkar. Habanero-Java: The new adventures of old X10. PPPJ, 2011.

[8] P. Charles, C. Grothoff, V. Saraswat, C. Donawa, A. Kielstra, K. Ebcioglu, C. von Praun, and V. Sarkar. X10: An object-oriented approach to non-uniform cluster computing. OOPSLA, 2005.

[9] H. de Fraysseix and P. O. de Mendez. Trémaux trees and planarity. *E. J. Comb.*, 33(3):279 – 293, 2012.

[10] B. Dushnik and E. W. Miller. Partially ordered sets. *American Journal of Mathematics*, 63(3):600–610, 1941.

[11] S. Felsner, W. T. Trotter, and V. Wiechert. The dimension of posets with planar cover graphs. *Graphs and Combinatorics*, pages 1–13, 2014.

[12] M. Feng and C. E. Leiserson. Efficient detection of determinacy races in Cilk programs. SPAA, 1997.

[13] C. Flanagan and S. N. Freund. FastTrack: Efficient and precise dynamic race detection. PLDI, 2009.

[14] D. Kelly. Fundamentals of planar ordered sets. *Discrete Mathematics*, 63(2-3):197 – 216, 1987.

[15] I.-T. A. Lee, C. E. Leiserson, T. B. Schardl, J. Sukha, and Z. Zhang. On-the-fly pipeline parallelism. SPAA. ACM, 2013.

[16] M. McCool, J. Reinders, and A. Robison. *Structured Parallel Programming: Patterns for Efficient Computation*. Elsevier Science, 2012.

[17] R. Raman, J. Zhao, V. Sarkar, M. Vechev, and E. Yahav. Scalable and precise dynamic datarace detection for structured parallelism. PLDI, 2012.

[18] R. Raman, J. Zhao, V. Sarkar, M. T. Vechev, and E. Yahav. Efficient data race detection for async-finish parallelism. RV, 2010.

[19] R. E. Tarjan. Efficiency of a good but not linear set union algorithm. *J. ACM*, 22(2):215–225, Apr. 1975.

[20] R. E. Tarjan and J. van Leeuwen. Worst-case analysis of set union algorithms. *J. ACM*, 31(2):245–281, 1984.

Efficiently Detecting Races in Cilk Programs That Use Reducer Hyperobjects

I-Ting Angelina Lee

Washington University in St. Louis
One Brookings Drive
St. Louis, MO 63130

Tao B. Schardl

MIT CSAIL
32 Vassar Street
Cambridge, MA 02139

ABSTRACT

A multithreaded Cilk program that is ostensibly deterministic may nevertheless behave nondeterministically due to programming errors in the code. For a Cilk program that uses reducers, a general reduction mechanism supported in various Cilk dialects, such programming errors are especially challenging to debug, because the errors can expose the nondeterminism in how the Cilk runtime system manages a reducer.

We identify two unique types of races that arise from incorrect use of reducers in a Cilk program and present two algorithms to catch them. The first algorithm, called the Peer-Set algorithm, detects view-read races, which occur when the program attempts to retrieve a value out of a reducer when the read may result a nondeterministic value, such as before all previously spawned subcomputations that might update the reducer have necessarily returned. The second algorithm, called the SP+ algorithm, detects determinacy races, instances where a write to a memory location occurs logically in parallel with another access to that location, even when the raced-on memory locations relate to reducers. Both algorithms are provably correct, asymptotically efficient, and can be implemented efficiently in practice. We have implemented both algorithms in our prototype race detector, Rader. When running Peer-Set, Rader incurs a geometric-mean multiplicative overhead of 2.32 over running the benchmark without instrumentation. When running SP+, Rader incurs a geometric-mean multiplicative overhead of 16.76.

Categories and Subject Descriptors

D.1.3 [**Programming Techniques**]: Concurrent Programming—*parallel programming*; D.2.5 [**Software Engineering**]: Testing and Debugging; D.3.3 [**Programming Languages**]: Language Constructs and Features—*concurrent programming structures*

Keywords

Cilk; determinacy race; nondeterminism; reducers; view-read race

This research was supported in part by NSF Grant 1314547. Tao B. Schardl was supported in part by an MIT Akamai Fellowship and an NSF Graduate Research Fellowship.

1. INTRODUCTION

A multithreaded Cilk program that is "ostensibly deterministic" may nevertheless behave nondeterministically due to programming errors in the code. Typically these errors, also called *races*, occur when the program fails to coordinate parallel operations on a shared variable, causing accesses and updates to be performed on the variable in a nondeterministic order based on scheduling happenstance. Although provably efficient and correct race detection algorithms exist for Cilk computations[1] [3,15,23], they do not provide the same guarantees when the program under test employs a "reducer hyperobject" [18], an advanced linguistic feature supported in various Cilk dialects. Races involving the use of a reducer are particularly challenging to debug, because such races can expose the nondeterminism in how the Cilk runtime system manages a reducer. This paper addresses the question of how to efficiently and correctly detect races in Cilk programs that use reducers.

Many modern concurrency platforms provide some form of *reduction mechanism* [18,22,25,28,34,39,42,45] to support safe parallel updates to shared variables. A reduction mechanism coordinates parallel updates to a shared variable by applying the parallel updates to distinct *views* of the variable. When the parallel subcomputations that update the variable complete, these views are combined together, or *reduced*, using a binary *reduce operator*. A reduction mechanism typically encapsulates the nondeterministic behavior induced by parallel updates as long as the update and reduce operations satisfy associativity and commutativity.

Reducer hyperobjects (or *reducers* for short) [18], which are supported by Cilk dialects including Intel Cilk Plus [22], Cilk++ [26], and Cilk-M [24], provide a general reduction mechanism for Cilk programs and exhibit several useful properties.

- Reducers operate on arbitrary Cilk code. They are not tied to any particular linguistic construct.
- Reducers can operate on any abstract data type, including a set, a linked list, or even a *user-defined data type*, so long as the user supplies an appropriate reduce operator.
- To produce a deterministic result, a reducer's update and reduce operations do not need to be commutative; associativity suffices.

In contrast, other reduction mechanisms, such as OpenMP's reduction clause [34] or Microsoft's PPL's combinable objects [28], tie the reduction mechanism to a particular construct, such as a parallel loop, or require reductions to be commutative.

Although these properties make reducers a powerful general-purpose reduction mechanism, they leave open opportunities for programming errors that can produce races involving reducers. Such errors can, in particular, expose the nondeterminism in the

---

[1]Henceforth, when we say a Cilk program, we mean a Cilk program with a specific given input. On the other hand, when we say a Cilk computation, we mean an instance of an execution of a Cilk program with a given input.

Cilk runtime system's efficient management of reducers, which includes two significant optimizations [18]. First, a new reducer view is created only when a **worker** thread **steals** some parallel subcomputation. Second, views are reduced together in an opportunistic fashion, causing reductions to occur in a nondeterministic order. Consequently, the state of a reducer's view at a particular program point, the number of views created throughout the execution, and when the views are reduced together are all nondeterministic, depending on how the scheduling plays out. This nondeterminism is typically encapsulated by the reducers when used and programmed correctly, but it can become observable due to programming errors.

The incorrect use of a reducer gives rise to two unique types of races. The first type of race, called a **view-read race**, occurs when a Cilk computation reads the value of a reducer at a program point where the read might produce a nondeterministic value, such as before all previously spawned subcomputations that might update the reducer have necessarily returned. Because the Cilk runtime system creates and reduces views based on scheduling, such a read can cause multiple runs of the same Cilk program to produce different results. A second type of race, called a **determinacy race** (also called a **general race** [31]), occurs when two logically parallel instructions operate on the same memory location, and at least one of them is a write. Although ordinary Cilk programs can contain determinacy races, a Cilk program that uses a reducer can contain a determinacy race involving an **view-aware** instruction executed in updating or reducing views of a reducer. (In contrast, we refer to all other instructions that do not operate on views as **view oblivious**.) Such a determinacy race is particularly challenging to debug, because a view-aware instruction involved in a race might not execute at all if the Cilk runtime system schedules the computation differently and thus manages the views differently.

Existing algorithms for detecting determinacy races in Cilk computations, including the SP-bags algorithm [15], the SP-order algorithm [3], and the SP-hybrid algorithm [3], do not support detecting races involving reducers. Extending these race detection algorithms to handle reducers while providing provable guarantees is non-trivial for two reasons. First, the use a reducer generates parallel control dependencies that violate the structural assumptions that these algorithms depend on. Specifically, the computation can no longer be modeled as a "series-parallel dag" [15], which is a property that existing algorithms rely on. Second, different runs of a Cilk program that uses a reducer can cause different view-aware instructions to be executed, depending how the scheduling plays out. Providing complete coverage could potentially require executing exponentially many different schedules to elicit all possible view-aware instructions. Consequently, existing tools that embody the SP-bags algorithm,[2] such as the Nondeterminator [15] and Cilk Screen [23], cannot guarantee correctness when one of the instructions involved in a race is executed to operate on a reducer view.

Contributions

In this paper, we show how to efficiently and correctly detect these two types of races in a Cilk computation that uses reducers. Specifically, we make the following contributions.

The Peer-Set algorithm. We present the Peer-Set algorithm, which executes a Cilk computation serially and analyzes its logical parallelism to detect view-read races. The algorithm is provably correct, meaning it reports a view-read race if and only if the Cilk computation contains one. For a Cilk computation that runs in time T on one processor, the Peer-Set algorithm executes in time $O(T\alpha(v, v))$, where α is Tarjan's functional inverse of Ackermann's

function, a very slowly growing function which, for all practical purposes, is bounded above by 4.

The SP+ algorithm. We present the SP+ algorithm, which detects determinacy races in Cilk computations that use reducers. The SP+ algorithm extends Feng and Leiserson's SP-bags algorithm [15] for detecting determinacy races in ordinary Cilk programs that do not employ reducers. The SP+ algorithm takes as input a Cilk program, its input, and a **steal specification** that effectively fixes the schedule. That is, a steal specification specifies the program points at which steals occur and which reduce operations execute. Like the Peer-Set algorithm, SP+ executes the computation serially albeit simulates the steals according to the steal specification to detect determinacy races. The SP+ algorithm is provably correct, meaning it reports a determinacy race in the computation if and only if one exists, regardless of whether that determinacy race occurs due to an operation on a reducer. Furthermore, the SP+ algorithm executes efficiently in time $O((T + M\tau)\alpha(v, v))$, where T is the running time of the Cilk program on the given input on 1 processor, M is the number of steals in the steal specification, and τ is the worst-case running time of a reduce operation. The SP+ algorithm thus incurs overhead over the SP-bags algorithm only to execute reduce operations and simulate necessary steals.

Implementation and empirical evaluation of the algorithms. We have developed a prototype tool, called **Rader**, that implements both the Peer-Set and SP+ algorithms to debug Cilk computations that use reducers. Rader implements the Peer-Set and SP+ algorithms by using compiler instrumentation to track memory accesses and parallel control dependencies. Using Rader, we empirically demonstrate the efficiency of both algorithms in practice. We ran Rader on 6 application benchmarks that use reducers. Compared to running each benchmark without instrumentation, Rader incurred geometric-mean multiplicative overheads of 2.32 and 16.76 to run the Peer-Set and SP+ algorithms, respectively.

Analysis of SP+'s coverage guarantees. We show how the SP+ algorithm can be used to efficiently check all executions of an "ostensibly deterministic" Cilk program for determinacy races that involve at least one view-oblivious instruction. A single run of the SP+ algorithm detects determinacy races in one possible schedule and thus has limited coverage; it elicits only a subset of all possible view-aware instructions. Although an exponential number of steal specifications exist for a given Cilk program, one can do better for most Cilk programs. Most Cilk programs are written to be **ostensibly deterministic**, meaning that, in the absence of a race, its view-oblivious instructions are fixed across all executions regardless of scheduling, and that it employs only reducers with semantically associative reduce operations. For such Cilk programs, we show how to construct a polynomial number of steal specifications to elicit all possible view-aware instructions. The SP+ algorithm can use these steal specifications to exhaustively check for determinacy races between view-oblivious and view-aware instructions.

The remainder of the paper is organized as follows. Section 2 discusses the relevant background and provides an example of a program that contains races involving reducers. Sections 3 and 4 present the Peer-Set algorithm and the intuition for its correctness. Sections 5 and 6 present the SP+ algorithm and some intuition for its correctness. Section 7 shows that executing SP+ with polynomial number of different steal specifications is necessary and sufficient to elicit all possible view-aware instructions in a ostensibly deterministic Cilk program, thereby providing the stated coverage guarantees. Section 8 describes our prototype implementation of Rader and empirically evaluates its performance. Section 9 discusses related work and Section 10 provides concluding remarks.

---

[2]To the best of our knowledge, no implementation of the SP-order and SP-hybrid algorithms exists.

2. EXAMPLES OF RACES THAT INVOLVE A REDUCER

This section provides an motivational example to illustrate how races that involve operations on a reducer can occur. We review Cilk linguistics and semantics, including that of reducer hyperobjects. We walk through the example to illustrate how a subtle programming error can trigger a race between user code and a reduce operation on a reducer.

Cilk-style dynamic multithreading. Cilk extends C/C++ with the keywords `cilk_spawn`, `cilk_sync`, and `cilk_for`, of which `cilk_spawn` and `cilk_sync` are more primitive. Parallelism is created using the keyword `cilk_spawn`. When a function f invokes another function g by preceding the invocation with `cilk_spawn`, g is *spawned*, and the scheduler may continue to execute the *continuation* of f — the statement after the spawning of g — in parallel with g, without waiting for g to return. The complement of `cilk_spawn` is `cilk_sync`, which acts as a local barrier and joins together, or *sync*, the parallelism specified by `cilk_spawn`. When a function f reaches a `cilk_sync`, the Cilk runtime ensures that control in f does not pass the `cilk_sync` until all functions spawned previously in f have completed and returned. The `cilk_for` keyword defines a parallel loop — all loop iterations may run in parallel with each other — which may be understood in terms of `cilk_spawn` and `cilk_sync`.

Note that these keywords denote the *logical parallelism* of the computation, rather than the actual parallel execution. During execution, Cilk's work-stealing scheduler [5,19] dynamically load balances a parallel computation across available **worker** threads while respecting the dependencies specified by these keywords. Typically, a worker executes a Cilk computation in its *serial order* — at a `cilk_spawn`, the worker executes the spawned function before its continuation. When a worker runs out of work, it becomes a *thief* and chooses a *victim* worker at random to *steal* from. If the victim worker has excess work, the thief may steal some of this work by resuming the continuation of some function. Notably, a worker's behavior mirrors precisely the behavior of a serial execution between successful steals, and Cilk's support for reducers implements significant optimizations based on this fact.

Cilk reducer hyperobjects. A reducer is defined semantically in terms of an algebraic **monoid**: a triple $(T, \otimes, e)$, where T is a set and $\otimes$ is an associative binary operation over T with identity e. From an object-oriented programming perspective, the set T forms the base type of a reducer's views, and the reducer provides a member function REDUCE that implements the binary operator $\otimes$ and a member function CREATE-IDENTITY that constructs an identity element of type T. The reducer also provides one or more UPDATE functions, which modify an object of type T. From the programmer's perspective, the reducer library provides a list of commonly used monoids; the programmer can also declare a reducer with a user-defined view type, so long as the view type implements an identity function (invoked by the CREATE-IDENTITY function) and a binary associative operator (invoked by the REDUCE function).

During parallel execution, the Cilk runtime supports parallel updates to a reducer by generating and maintaining multiple views for that reducer, thereby allowing each parallel subcomputation to operate on its own local view. In particular, when a worker first executes a UPDATE call to a reducer after a successful steal, it automatically calls CREATE-IDENTITY to create a new identity view of the reducer. Because a worker executes a Cilk computation in its serial order between successful steals, the worker can safely apply the call to UPDATE, as well as all subsequent calls to UPDATE, to this view, until it steals again. As stolen subcomputations return,

```
1   void update_list(int n, MyList<int>& list) {
2       cilk::reducer< list_monoid<int> >
            list_reducer;
3       list_reducer.set_value(list);
4       int x = cilk_spawn foo(n, list_reducer);
5       cilk_for(int i = 0; i < n; ++i) {
6           list_reducer.view().insert(i);
7       }
8       cilk_sync;
9       list = list_reducer.get_value();
10  }

12  void race(int n, MyList<int>& list) {
13      int length = 0;
14      MyList<int> copy(list);
15      length = cilk_spawn scan_list(list);
16      update_list(n, copy);
17      cilk_sync;
18      return;
19  }
```

Figure 1: Example Cilk program that contains a determinacy race on the reduce operation of a linked-list reducer.

the runtime automatically combines their corresponding views using the REDUCE operation, in the same order as how these updates would be applied in a serial execution. In the absence of a race, as long as the REDUCE operation is semantically associative, the resulting view is the same as if the program were run serially.

How a view-read race can occur. To illustrate how a view-read race can occur, let us first consider the code for the `update_list` routine shown in Figure 1. The function `update_list` takes in as parameters an integer n and a user-defined `list` of type `MyList` that implements a singly linked list with a head and a tail pointer to enable fast list concatenation. The `update_list` routine spawns `foo` with n and `list_reducer` to perform some computation, which may execute in parallel with the continuation on lines 5–7, a parallel loop that inserts n elements into the linked list. To coordinate parallel accesses to the list, `update_list` wraps the given linked list in a reducer on line 2. Since the reducer has a user-defined view type, the programmer must also supply the functions for implementing the reducer's CREATE-IDENTITY and REDUCE operations, which are defined via the `list_monoid` type (actual implementation not shown in the pseudocode).

Assuming that `list_monoid` implements these functions correctly, `update_list` as written does not contain a determinacy race, since the runtime coordinates parallel updates to the linked list via the use of a reducer. The routine does not contain a view-read race, either, since the value of `reducer_list` is initialized at line 3 before anything is spawned, and the value of `reducer_list` is retrieved at line 9 after all spawned subcomputations that may use the reducer have returned. The code would have been a view-read race, however, if `get_value` is invoked, say, before `cilk_sync`, since at that point `foo` might be accessing the reducer in parallel.

How a determinacy race involving a reducer can occur. The code in Figure 1 can exhibit a determinacy race between the `race` and `update_list` routines, however. In this code, the `race` routine invokes `scan_list`, which iterates through the elements of `list` until one is found with a NULL pointer to the next element. This spawned `scan_list` invocation can run in parallel with its continuation, the call to `update_list` on line 16. Since `update_list` might actually insert into the list, the `race` routine makes a copy of the list first at line 14 and passes the copy to `update_list`, so as to allow the `scan_list` to scan the snapshot of the list without the new inserts performed by `update_list`. Unfortunately, this code contains a bug because the copy constructor on line 14 only performs a shallow copy. That means, even though copy is a new `MyList` object, created with its own distinct head and tail pointers, the two `list` and `copy` lists still point to the same set of linked-list elements, leading to a determinacy race in the code. In particular,

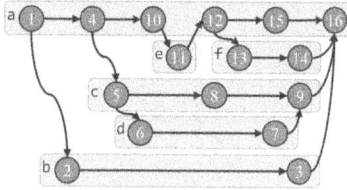

Figure 2: Example Cilk computation dag. Dark rectangles represent strands, edges represent parallel control dependencies between strands. The strands are labeled in their serial execution order. Light rectangles are labeled with the function instantiation and encompass the strands that execute within that instantiation.

whenever `scan_list` reaches the last linked-list node reading the `null` next pointer, some parallel subcomputation in `update_list` might be writing to that same next pointer to insert an element. This determinacy race means that the `scan_list` may scan a non-deterministic number of elements in the list.

Furthermore, where the determinacy race occurs is subtle. Because `update_list` employs a reducer to coordinate parallel inserts, any insert into the list can occur on a distinct view local to the subcomputation performing the insertion. What eventually writes to the `next` pointer and constitutes the race occurs is a REDUCE operation that eventually appends to the original view of `list_reducer`, as initialized in line 3. A tool such as Cilk Screen will not catch this particular race, because the determinacy race involves a view-aware instruction executed in a REDUCE operation.

3. THE PEER-SET ALGORITHM

This section presents the Peer-Set algorithm for detecting view-read races. View-read races are defined formally in terms of the "peer-set semantics" that reducers obey. We review the dag model of dynamic multithreading. We describe the "peer-set semantics" in terms of this dag computation model, and we formally define the view-read races based on these semantics. We describe the Peer-Set algorithm and how it checks for the "peer-set semantics."

The dag model for dynamic multithreading. We adopt the dag model for dynamic multithreading similar to the one introduced by Blumofe and Leiserson [5], which models a Cilk computation — the execution of a Cilk program — as a *dag (directed acyclic graph)* $A = (V, E)$, whose vertices are *strands* — sequences of one or more instructions containing no parallel control — and whose edges denote parallel control dependencies between strands. Figure 2 illustrates a Cilk computation dag that we shall use as a running example. The strands in Figure 2 are numbered in their *serial execution order* — the depth-first traversal of the dag in which every spawned child is visited before its continuation. We shall assume that strands respect boundaries of *Cilk functions* — functions that can spawn. That means, calling or spawning a Cilk function terminates a strand, as does returning from a Cilk function. Each strand thus belongs to exactly one Cilk function invocation. For now we shall not worry about modeling the executing of view-aware strands in the computation dag.

For any two strands u and v, we say that u *precedes* v, denoted as $u \prec v$, if there exists a path from u to v in the dag. Two strands u and v are logically in *series* if either $u \prec v$ or $v \prec u$; otherwise they are logically *parallel*, denoted as $u \parallel v$. In Figure 2, for example, strands 4 and 9 are logically in series, because strand 4 precedes strand 9, while strands 9 and 10 are logically in parallel.

Peer-set semantics. "Peer-set semantics" dictate which updates are guaranteed to be reflected in the view of a reducer h observed at strand u in terms of the *peers* of u — the set of strands in parallel with u, denoted by $peers(u) = \{w \in V : w \parallel u\}$. Conceptually,

"peer-set semantics" dictate that the view visible to a strand v is guaranteed to reflect the updates since a previous strand u if u and v have the same peers. In Figure 2, for example, these semantics dictate that the view of a reducer at strand 9 is guaranteed to reflect the updates since strand 5, because strands 5 and 9 have the same peers. The view at strand 14, meanwhile, is not guaranteed to reflect the updates since strand 10, because strands 10 and 14 do not share the same peers — strands 12 and 13 are in the peer set of strand 14, but not that of strand 10. The following definition formally defines *peer-set semantics*:

DEFINITION 1 (PEER-SET SEMANTICS). *Let h be a reducer with an associative operator $\otimes$. Consider a serial walk of G, and let $a_1, a_2, \ldots, a_k$ denote the updates to h after the start of instruction u and before the start of instruction v. Let $h(u)$ and $h(v)$ denote the views of h at strands u and v respectively. If $peers(u) = peers(v)$, then $h(v) = h(u) \otimes a_1 \otimes a_2 \otimes \ldots \otimes a_k$.*

View-read races. Formally, a *view-read race* occurs when two accesses to reducers, called *reducer-reads*, occur at strands with different sets of peers. Here, we broadly define a *reducer-read* as creating a reducer, resetting a reducer's value, or querying the reducer to retrieve its value. On the other hand, invoking CREATE-IDENTITY, UPDATE, or REDUCE on a reducer does not count as a reducer-read, because those functions operate on a reducer's underlying view instead of on the reducer itself. For example, consider the computation dag in Figure 2 and suppose that strands 1 and 9 read the value of the reducer. Because strands 1 and 9 do not share the same peer set, a view-read race exists between strands 1 and 9.

Given this definition of a view-read race, a Cilk program with a view-read race might nevertheless behave deterministically. For instance, in the code example shown in Figure 1, suppose that the programmer moves the call to `list_reducer.set_value(list)` to after `cilk_spawn` at line 4, thereby creating a view-read race. If `foo` does not modify `list`, however, then the `update_list` routine could behave deterministically, rendering the view-read race *benign*. We nevertheless declare this to be a race because the reducer-reads violate their peer-set semantics.

The Peer-Set algorithm. The Peer-Set algorithm executes a Cilk computation serially and evaluates its strands in their serial execution order to check for view-read races. The Peer-Set algorithm employs several data structures to track which strands read the reducer and which strands have the same peer set.

During the execution, the Peer-Set algorithm assigns a unique ID to every Cilk function instantiation and maintains, for each instantiation F on the call stack, two scalars, $F.ls$ and $F.as$, and three bags, $F.SS$, $F.SP$, and $F.P$. Each bag stores a set of ID's for completed instantiations in a fast disjoint-set data structure [10, Ch. 21].

- The $F.as$ scalar stores the *ancestor-spawn count* — the total number of spawns that each ancestor F' of F has performed since F' last synced.
- The $F.ls$ scalar stores the *local-spawn count* — the number of spawns F has executed since F last synced.
- The $F.SS$ bag contains the ID's of all completed descendants of F with the same peer set as the first strand of F.
- The $F.SP$ bag contains the ID's of all completed descendants of F with the same peer set as the last continuation strand executed in F. If F has not spawned since it last executed a sync, then $F.SP$ is empty.
- The $F.P$ bag contains the ID's of all completed descendants of F not in $F.SS$ or $F.SP$.

For each Cilk frame F, we refer to the sum of the ancestor-spawn and local-spawn counts, $F.as + F.ls$, as the *spawn count* of F, which

F calls or spawns G:	G returns to F:
1 **if** F spawns G 2 $F.ls$ += 1 3 $F.P$ ∪= $F.SP$ 4 $F.SP$ = ∅ 5 $G.as$ = $F.as + F.ls$ 6 $G.ls$ = 0 7 $G.SS$ = MakeBag(G) 8 $G.SP$ = MakeBag(∅) 9 $G.P$ = MakeBag(∅)	1 $F.P$ ∪= $G.P$ 2 **if** F spawned G 3 $F.P$ ∪= $G.SS$ 4 **elseif** $F.ls$ = 0 5 $F.SS$ ∪= $G.SS$ 6 **else** 7 $F.SP$ ∪= $G.SS$
F syncs:	F reads reducer h:
1 $F.ls$ = 0 2 $F.P$ ∪= $F.SP$ 3 $F.SP$ = MakeBag(∅)	1 **if** FindBag($reader(h)$) is a P bag **or** $reader(h).s \neq F.as + F.ls$ 2 a view-read race exists 3 $reader(h)$ = F 4 $reader(h).s$ = $F.as + F.ls$

Figure 3: Pseudocode for the Peer-Set algorithm. The MakeBag routine creates a new bag with a specified initial contents and a view ID. When passed ∅, MakeBag produces an empty bag. The FindBag routine finds the bag containing the specified element by finding the corresponding set in the disjoint-set data structure.

corresponds to the number of spawn statements executed by F and F's ancestors that have not been synced yet.

The Peer-Set algorithm also maintains a ***shadow space*** of shared memory, called *reader*, which maps each reducer to its last reader and the access context. That is, for each reducer h, $reader(h)$ stores the ID of the Cilk function F that last read h, and the associated field $reader(h).s$ stores the spawn count of F when it last read h.

Figure 3 gives the pseudocode of the Peer-Set algorithm, which maintains the bags and scalars for each function frame F as follows. When created, frame F inherits its ancestor-spawn count from the spawn count of its parent, and it initializes its local-spawn count $F.ls$ to 0. As F executes, it increments $F.ls$ when F spawns, and resets $F.l$ to 0 when F syncs. Frame F's bags are updated when a child frame G returns to F, based on whether F has spawned since it last synced. Although the bag $G.P$ is always combined with $F.P$, the bag $G.SS$ is combined with $F.SS$ only if F has not spawned since it last synced; otherwise $G.SS$ is combined with $F.SP$. The bag $G.SP$ is guaranteed to be empty when G returns to F because functions implicitly sync before they return in Cilk.

Given this algorithm, we can see that the Peer-Set algorithm has runs in the following time.

Theorem 1. *Consider a Cilk program that executes in time T on one processor and references x reducer variables. The Peer-Set algorithm checks this program execution for a view-read race in $O(T\alpha(x,x))$ time, where α is Tarjan's functiona, l inverse of Acker- mann's function.*

Proof. Given the size of the shadow memory for the Peer-Set algorithm, the theorem follows from the analyses in [15]. □

4. CORRECTNESS OF THE PEER-SET ALGORITHM

This section provides discusses why the Peer-Set algorithm is correct. We provide intuition for how the Peer-Set algorithm properly detects view-read races. We argue mathematically for its correctness.

Intuition for the Peer-Set algorithm. To understand how the Peer-Set algorithm works, let us first consider the contents of the bags of a function F when F returns, considering the execution of the Peer-Set algorithm on the dag in Figure 2 as a running example. The bag $F.SP$ is empty, because in Cilk, a function F always syncs before it returns. Consequently, the bag $F.SS$ identifies descendants of F with the same peer set as the first instruction in F, and the bag $F.P$ contains all other descendants of F. In the example dag in

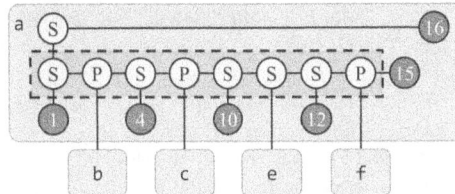

Figure 4: The canonical SP parse tree for the function instantiation a in the computation dag in Figure 2. The internal nodes of a sync block are indicated by the darkened rectangle outlined by a dashed line.

Figure 2, then when c returns, bag $c.SS$ contains the ID for c, and bag $c.P$ contains the ID for d.

What happens to these bags when a function G returns to its parent F? The functions identified in $G.P$ must have a different peer set from that of any strand in F, and therefore, $G.P$ is always unioned with $F.P$. In the example dag in Figure 2, when c returns to a, unioning bag $c.P$ with bag $a.P$ correctly identifies that d has a distinct peer set from every strand in a.

As for $G.SS$, we must consider a few cases. Suppose that F spawned G. By definition of a spawn, all descendants of G must therefore have a different peer set from any strand in F. The bag $G.SS$ is thus unioned with the bag $F.P$ when G returns. In the example dag in Figure 2, because a spawned c at strand 4, every strand in c is in parallel with strand 10, implying that c has a distinct peer set from all strands in a.

If F called G when F had no outstanding spawned children, then the first strand in G has the same peer set as the first strand in F, and the bag $G.SS$ is therefore unioned with $F.SS$. Otherwise, F called G when F's local-spawn count was nonzero, meaning that F had at least one outstanding spawned child. The first strand in G therefore has a distinct peer set from that of the first strand in F, but the same peer set as the last continuation strand F executed. The $G.SS$ bag is therefore unioned with $F.SP$, where it remains until F either spawns again or syncs. In the example dag in Figure 2, strand 11 has a distinct peer set from strand 1, but the same peer set as strand 10, the caller of e. When e returns to a, therefore, unioning the bag $e.SS$ with $a.SP$ correctly identifies that the peer set of strand 11 matches that of strand 10.

Now let us consider detecting a view-read race. If a strand reads a reducer h, and $reader(h)$ is in some ancestor's P bag $F.P$, then it certainly has a different peer set. If $reader(h)$ is in $F.SS$ or $F.SP$ for some ancestor F, however, then $reader(h)$ has the same peer set as a strand u that is either F's first strand or the last continuation strand that F executed, and the currently executing strand v might have a distinct peer set from u. To handle this case, the Peer-Set algorithm compares the spawn count of v against the spawn count of $reader(h)$, stored in $reader(h).s$, which must match the spawn count as u. As long as v has this same spawn count, then no ancestor of v below F added a peer to v that is not a peer of u, meaning that u and v have the same peer set.

Correctness of the Peer-Set algorithm. To show why the Peer-Set algorithm works correctly, we model the computation dag using an "SP parse tree" as introduced by Feng and Leiserson [15]. As Feng and Leiserson show, the dag modeling a Cilk computation (that does not use reducers) is a ***series-parallel dag***, which has a distinguished ***source*** vertex s and a distinguished ***sink*** vertex t and can be constructed recursively with series and parallel compositions. This recursive construction can be represented by a binary tree, called an ***SP parse tree***.

Figure 4 illustrates the SP parse tree corresponding to function a in the dag in Figure 2. The leaves of the SP parse tree are strands in the dag, and each internal node is either an S node or a P node, denoting either a series or parallel composition, respectively, of its two children. The SP parse tree in Figure 4 is a *canonical* parse tree [15], meaning that its internal nodes are laid out as follows. The sync strands in a Cilk function F partition the strands in F into *sync blocks*. The canonical SP parse subtree for a sync block is a chain of S and P nodes, where the left child of each node is either a strand in F or the root of the canonical parse tree for a subcomputation spawned or called in F, and the right child is the next S or P node at the root of the SP parse subtree for the vertices following the left subchild in the serial order. A chain of S nodes, called the *spine*, links the sync blocks exist within F.

To show that the Peer-Set algorithm is correct, we first show that two strands have the same peer set if and only if they are connected by S nodes in the SP parse tree.

LEMMA 2. *Two strands u and v have the same peer set, $peers(u) = peers(v)$, if and only if the path connecting u to v in the SP parse tree consists entirely of S nodes.*

PROOF. Let $LCA(u, v)$ denote the least-common ancestor of u and v in the SP parse tree. We first show that $LCA(u, v)$ must be an S node. If $LCA(u, v)$ is a P node, then $u \parallel v$, and therefore $u \in peers(v)$. Because $u \notin peers(u)$, we have that $peers(u) \neq peers(v)$.

Suppose that the path in the SP parse tree from $LCA(u, v)$ to u contains a P node. Then there must exist a strand w such that $LCA(u, w)$ is this P node, which implies that $u \parallel w$ and, therefore, that $w \in peers(u)$. Because this P node is on the path from $LCA(u, v)$ to u, we have that $LCA(w, v) = LCA(u, v)$, which is an S node. Therefore, $w \nparallel v$, and thus $w \notin peers(v)$. This P node therefore implies that $peers(u) \neq peers(v)$, so if $peers(u) = peers(v)$, then no such P node can exist. A symmetric argument shows that no P node can exist on the path from $LCA(u, v)$ to v.

Now suppose that $peers(u) \neq peers(v)$. Without loss of generality, suppose that u executes before v in the serial order. If $v \in peers(u)$, then $u \parallel v$ and $LCA(u, v)$ is a P node. Otherwise, we have $u \prec v$ and there exists some strand w in exactly one of $peers(u)$ or $peers(v)$. Suppose that $w \in peers(u)$ and $w \notin peers(v)$. Then $w \parallel u$, implying that $LCA(w, u)$ is a P node [15, Lemma 4], and $w \nparallel v$, implying that $LCA(w, v)$ is an S node. The nodes $LCA(w, u)$ and $LCA(w, v)$ therefore differ, and one can show that either $LCA(u, v)$ is one of these two. Either way, the P node $LCA(w, u)$ appears on the path from u to v in the SP parse tree. The case where $w \notin peers(u)$ and $w \in peers(v)$ is similar. □

Next, we argue that the Peer-Set algorithm identifies pairs of strands that are connected via S nodes in the SP parse tree. As in [15], we define the *procedurification* function F as the map from strands and nodes in the SP parse tree to Cilk function invocations.

LEMMA 3. *Consider an execution of the Peer-Set algorithm on a Cilk computation. Suppose that strand u executes before strand v, and let F be the procedurification function mapping the SP parse tree to Cilk function invocations. Let $a = LCA(u, v)$ be the least common ancestor of u and v in the SP parse tree. Then the both of the following conditions hold if and only if the path from u to v in the SP parse tree consists entirely of S nodes.*

- *The ID for $F(u)$ belongs to either the SS bag or the SP bag of $F(a)$ when v executes.*
- *The spawn count for $F(a)$ when u executes equals the spawn count for $F(v)$ when v executes.*

PROOF SKETCH. Bags $F(a).SS$ and $F(a).SP$ contain the set of descendants reachable from $F(a)$'s first strand and $F(a)$'s last-executed continuation strand, respectively, via S nodes in the parse tree. Either $F(a).SS$ or $F(a).SP$ contains u if and only if there is no

P node along the path from u to a. Spawn counts allow us to check whether there is any P node along the path from a to v, because the spawn count of $F(u)$ when u executes matches that of $F(v)$ when v executes if and only if the path from a to v contains no P node. □

With Lemmas 2 and 3, we show that the Peer-Set algorithm detects a view-read race if only if one exists.

THEOREM 4. *The Peer-Set algorithm detects a view-read race in a Cilk computation if and only if a view-read race exists.*

PROOF. Let F be the procedurification function mapping the SP parse tree to Cilk function invocations.

We first see that, if the Peer-Set algorithm detects a view-read race, then one exists. If the Peer-Set algorithm detects a view-read race on a reducer h when executing strand e_2, then Figure 3 shows that either $reader(h)$ belongs to a P bag or the spawn count $reader(h).s$ does not match $F(e_2).as + F(e_2).ls$. Lemma 3 therefore implies that a P node exists on the path from e_1 to e_2 in the SP parse tree, meaning that $peers(e_1) \neq peers(e_2)$ by Lemma 2. Consequently, a view-read race exists.

We now see that, if a view-read race exists on a reducer h, then the Peer-Set algorithm detects it. Let e_1 and e_2 be two strands involved in a view-read race on reducer h, where e_1 executes before e_2 in the serial order and, if several such races exist, we choose the race for which e_2 executes earliest in the serial order. The definition of a view-read race implies that $peers(e_1) \neq peers(e_2)$.

When e_2 executes, suppose that $reader(h) = F(e)$ for some strand e. If $e = e_1$, then because $peers(e_1) \neq peers(e_2)$, Lemmas 2 and 3 imply that a view-read race is reported. If $e \neq e_1$, then e must have executed after e_1, in order to overwrite $reader(h)$. We must also have that $peers(e) = peers(e_1)$; otherwise Lemmas 2 and 3 imply that a view-read race exists between e and e_1, and that fact that both e and e_1 execute before e_2 contradicts strand e_2 being the earliest strand in the serial order for which a view-read race exists on h. Because $peers(e_1) \neq peers(e_2)$, we have that $peers(e) \neq peers(e_2)$, and by Lemmas 2 and 3, a view-read race is detected. □

5. THE SP+ ALGORITHM

This section presents the SP+ algorithm for detecting determinacy races in a Cilk computation that uses a reducer. For a Cilk program that uses reducers, its parallel execution contains view-aware strands and runtime-invoked REDUCE operations that generate additional *reduce strands* and corresponding dependencies. The SP+ algorithm extends the SP-bags algorithm [15] to handle these additional complexity in execution due to the use of reducers. We describe more precisely how the Cilk runtime manages views and how one can model these additional strands and dependencies using a "performance dag." We identify the circumstances in which a determinacy race can exist in a computation that uses reducers. We describe how the SP+ algorithm detects such determinacy races.

The SP+ algorithm makes the following assumptions. First, the SP+ algorithm takes a steal specification as input, which dictates which continuations to steal, when to create new views, and how to reduce views. The steal specification removes all nondeterminism in how the Cilk runtime manages the reducers, allowing the SP+ algorithm to consider a single execution of the Cilk program. Second, it assumes that the REDUCE, CREATE-IDENTITY, and UPDATE functions execute only serial code, which is typically the case in real programs, and thus the execution of one of these functions can be modeled with a single strand. Following the same terminology as in types of instructions, we refer to a strand that arises from executing one of these functions as a *view-aware* strand, and other strands in the computation are *view-oblivious* strands.

116

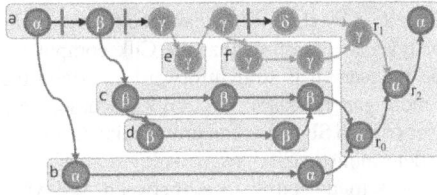

Figure 5: An example of performance dag, which corresponds to augmenting the user dag in Figure 2 in Section 2 with reduce strands r_0, r_1, and r_2. A vertical bar across an edge indicates that the following continuation strand is stolen. Each strand is labeled with its associated view ID. Strands with the same view ID are highlighted with the same color.

How the Cilk runtime manages views. To see how view-aware strands complicate determinacy race detection, let us first review how the Cilk runtime manages views in more detail. Let $h(u)$ denote the view of a reducer h seen by strand u in a dag $A = (V, E)$. The runtime system maintains the following *view invariants*:

1. If u has out-degree 1 and $(u, v) \in E$, then $h(v) = h(u)$.

2. Suppose that u is a spawn strand with outgoing edges $(u, v), (u, w) \in E$, where u spawns v and leads to continuation strand w. Then, we have $h(u) = h(v)$ and either $h(w) = h(u)$ if w was not stolen, or $h(w)$ is a new view otherwise.

3. If $u \in V$ is a sync strand, then $h(u) = h(s)$, where s is the first strand of the Cilk function containing u.

When a new view $h(w)$ is created according to Invariant 2, we the new view $h(w)$ is a *parallel view* to $h(u)$. We say that the old view $h(u)$ *dominates* $h(w)$, which we denote by $h(u) > h(w)$. For a set H of views, we say that two views $h_1, h_2 \in H$ are *adjacent* if there does not exist $h_3 \in H$ such that $h_1 > h_3 > h_2$. Each parallel view created according to Invariant 2 is eventually destroyed by a call to REDUCE. In particular, the runtime system always reduces adjacent pairs of views together, destroying the dominated view in the pair.

To maintain Invariant 3, the runtime ensures that all parallel views created within a sync block are reduced before the sync strand executes. One can show inductively that the views of the first and last strands of a function must be identical. This property holds because the first spawned child always inherits the view of the first strand, and a REDUCE operation always reduces two adjacent views and destroys the dominated view. Moreover, the runtime always performs an implicit sync before a Cilk function returns.

The performance dag. A Cilk computation that uses a reducer can be modeled as a *performance dag* [27], which augments the ordinary computation dag with additional reduce strands from executing REDUCE operations. The performance dag also modifies the dependencies going into a sync strand in order to incorporate the reduce strands and model the necessary dependencies among them. These dependencies among the reduce strands form a *reduce tree* before each sync node, with an additional dependency going from the root of the reduce tree into the corresponding sync node.

Figure 5 shows an example of a performance dag, which corresponds to augmenting the computation dag shown in Figure 2 with reduce strands. In this dag, three different continuation points are stolen, each causing a new view to be generated, leading to a total of 4 views in a. For each newly created view, there is a corresponding reduce strand produced from executing the REDUCE operation that destroys the view, reducing its value into an adjacent view that dominates it. The reduce strand r_0, for example, reduces the views α and β, destroying β and inheriting the view ID α. Figure 5 also shows how these reduce strands form a reduce tree before the final strand, which is the sync strand in a. The reduce strands and the structure of the reduce trees are both functions of the execution schedule, which is fixed by the input steal specification.

Detecting determinacy races involving view-aware strands. View-aware strands complicate the circumstances under which a determinacy race occurs. For example, in the performance dag shown in Figure 5, let e_1 be the first strand in function d, and let e_2 be the second strand in function c. Suppose that e_1 and e_2 access the same memory location ℓ with one being a write, and suppose that e_2 is a view-aware strand generated from executing an UPDATE. Because e_2 is a continuation that is not stolen in this execution, the same worker executes e_2 immediately after returning from d, and both e_1 and e_2 observe the same view β of the reducer, as Figure 5 shows. Because e_2 is view-aware, in a different execution in which e_2 is stolen, e_2 will observe a different view and might therefore write to a different memory locations. If location ℓ is part of view β, for example, then in this alternative scenario, e_2 might not write to ℓ, precluding a determinacy race with e_1. Because e_2 is view-aware, its logical parallelism with e_1 is not sufficient for it to definitively race with e_1; it must also operate on a parallel view.

We can summarize the conditions under which a determinacy race exists between two strands e_1 and e_2 in a Cilk computation that uses a reducer. Suppose that e_2 follows e_1 in the in serial execution order, both e_1 and e_2 access the same location ℓ, and at least one of them writes to ℓ.

- If e_2 is a view-oblivious strand, then a determinacy race exists between e_1 and e_2 if and only if e_1 and e_2 are logically in parallel.

- If e_2 is a view-aware strand, then a determinacy race exists between e_1 and e_2 if and only if e_1 and e_2 are logically in parallel and are associated with parallel views of a reducer.

The SP+ algorithm. Like the Peer-Set and SP-bags algorithms, the SP+ algorithm is a serial algorithm that evaluates the strands of a Cilk computation in their serial order. As it executes, SP+ employs several data structures to keep tracks of parallel views created according to the steal specification and determine the series-parallel relationships between strands, including reduce strands.

Like the SP-bags algorithm, SP+ maintains 2 shadow spaces of shared memory, called *reader* and *writer*. Each shadow space contains an entry for each memory location that the computation accesses. During the execution, each Cilk function instantiation is given a unique ID. Each location ℓ in *reader* stores the ID of the instantiation that last read ℓ, while each location ℓ in *writer* stores the ID for the instantiation that last wrote ℓ.

The SP+ algorithm also maintains a set of bags for each Cilk function F on the call stack. Each bag stores a set of ID's for completed procedures in a fast disjoint-set data structure. In particular, when executing a strand u, the bags associated with a function F on the call stack have the following contents:

- The *S bag* $F.S$ contains the ID's of F's completed descendants that precede u, as well as the ID for F itself.

- The *P stack* $F.P$ contains a stack of P bags. Together, the P bags in $F.P$ contain the set of ID's of F's completed descendants that are logically in parallel with u. The P bags $p \in F.P$ partition this set into subsets whose views are in series with the last ID to be added to the P bag p.

Figure 6 gives the pseudocode of the SP+ algorithm. Like the SP-bags algorithm, the SP+ algorithm pushes new S and P bags onto the call stack when is executes a function call or spawn, and it pops these bags off of the call stack when the function returns.

Unlike in the SP-bags algorithm, the SP+ algorithm also maintains P stacks. Conceptually, each P stack in SP+ replaces a P bag in the SP-bags algorithm in order to keep track of views. Each P bag p has an associated *view ID*, denoted $p.vid$, which is a unique ID associated with the P bag on its creation. Executing a stolen continuation pushes a new P bag with a new view ID onto the top

117

F spawns or calls G:	F syncs:
1 $G.S = \textsc{MakeBag}(G, \textsc{Top}(G).\mathit{vid})$ 2 $p = \textsc{MakeBag}(\emptyset, \textsc{Top}(G).\mathit{vid})$ 3 $G.P = \langle p \rangle$	1 $F.S \mathrel{\cup}= \textsc{Top}(F.P)$ 2 $p = \textsc{MakeBag}(\emptyset, F.S.\mathit{vid})$ 3 $\textsc{Top}(F.P) = p$

Spawned G returns to F:	Called G returns to F:
1 $\textsc{Top}(F.P) \mathrel{\cup}= G.S$	1 $F.S \mathrel{\cup}= G.S$

F executes a stolen continuation:	F executes \textsc{Reduce}:
1 $p = \textsc{MakeBag}(\emptyset, \textbf{new} \text{ view ID})$ 2 $\textsc{Push}(F.P, p)$	1 $p = \textsc{Pop}(F.P)$ 2 $\textsc{Top}(F.P) \mathrel{\cup}= p$

read a shared location ℓ by a view-oblivious strand in F:

1   **if** $\textsc{FindBag}(\mathit{writer}(\ell))$ is a P bag
2   a determinacy race exists
3   **if** $\textsc{FindBag}(\mathit{reader}(\ell))$ is an S bag
4      $\mathit{reader}(\ell) = F$

write a shared location ℓ by a view-oblivious strand in F:

1   **if** $\textsc{FindBag}(\mathit{reader}(\ell))$ is a P bag **or** $\textsc{FindBag}(\mathit{writer}(\ell))$ is a P bag
2   a determinacy race exists
3   **if** $\textsc{FindBag}(\mathit{writer}(\ell))$ is an S bag
4      $\mathit{writer}(\ell) = F$

read a shared location ℓ by a view-aware strand in F:

1   **if** $\textsc{FindBag}(\mathit{writer}(\ell))$ is a P bag **and** $\textsc{FindBag}(\mathit{writer}(\ell)).\mathit{vid} \neq \textsc{Top}(F.P).\mathit{vid}$
2   a determinacy race exists
3   **if** $\textsc{FindBag}(\mathit{reader}(\ell))$ is an S bag **or**
      (F is an invocation of \textsc{Reduce} **and** $\textsc{FindBag}(\mathit{reader}(\ell)).\mathit{vid} == \textsc{Top}(F.P).\mathit{vid}$)
4      $\mathit{reader}(\ell) = F$

write a shared location ℓ by a view-aware strand in F:

1   **if** $\textsc{FindBag}(\mathit{reader}(\ell))$ is a P bag **and** $\textsc{FindBag}(\mathit{reader}(\ell)).\mathit{vid} \neq \textsc{Top}(F.P).\mathit{vid}$
2   a determinacy race exists
3   **if** $\textsc{FindBag}(\mathit{writer}(\ell))$ is a P bag **and** $\textsc{FindBag}(\mathit{writer}(\ell)).\mathit{vid} \neq \textsc{Top}(F.P).\mathit{vid}$
4   a determinacy race exists
5   **if** $\textsc{FindBag}(\mathit{writer}(\ell))$ is an S bag **or**
      (F is an invocation of \textsc{Reduce} **and** $\textsc{FindBag}(\mathit{writer}(\ell)).\mathit{vid} == \textsc{Top}(F.P).\mathit{vid}$)
6      $\mathit{writer}(\ell) = F$

Figure 6: Pseudocode for the SP+ algorithm. Each P bag is a disjoint set with an additional *vid* field, which tracks the view ID associated with that P bag. This *vid* field is set when the P bag is first created and remains invariant as the P bag's set is modified. In particular, when a P bag is unioned into another P bag, the bags are unioned, and the view ID of the destination P bag is preserved. PUSH pushes an element on top of the specified stack, and POP pops the specified stack. TOP accesses the topmost element of the stack without modifying the stack. MAKEBAG creates a new bag with a specified initial contents and a view ID. MAKEBAG produces an empty bag when called with $\emptyset$. The FINDBAG routine finds the bag containing the specified element by finding the corresponding set in the disjoint-set data structure.

of the P stack. Executing a REDUCE operation in F combines the top two P bags in the P stack $F.P$, unioning the newer P bag into the older one. Determinacy races are detected by the code for `write` and `read`, and separate codes are used when the second strand is view-oblivious versus view-aware.

The following theorem analyzes the running time of SP+.

THEOREM 5. *Consider a Cilk program that executes in time T on one processor and references v shared memory locations. Suppose that the SP+ algorithm executes this program with M specified steals, and let τ be the worst-case running time of any REDUCE operation. The SP+ algorithm checks this program execution for a determinacy race in $O((T + M\tau)\alpha(v, v))$ time.*

PROOF. The theorem follows from the analyses in [27] and [15]. $\square$

6. CORRECTNESS OF THE SP+ ALGORITHM

This section provides intuition as to why a single run of the SP+ algorithm correctly detects determinacy races in a particular Cilk computation. Throughout this section, we analyze the correctness of the SP+ algorithm with respect to the fixed execution of a Cilk

program specified by the given steal specification.[3] For simplicity, our analysis shall assume that the Cilk computation operates on a single reducer. It is straightforward to extend the argument to handle more general cases. Section 7 discusses how a polynomial number of such SP+ runs can provide the desired coverage for ostensibly deterministic Cilk programs.

With respect to detecting races between two view-oblivious strands, it is straightforward to see that SP+ provides the same correctness guarantee as the SP-bags algorithm [15]. Like the SP-bags algorithm, as it executes, SP+ maintains, for every active Cilk function F, two sets of IDs corresponding to F's completed descendants: one set (in the S bag $F.S$) for those that are logically in series with the currently executing strand, and one set (in a stack of P bags $F.P$) for those that are logically in parallel with that strand. Both SP-bags and SP+ maintain these sets and use them to detect determinacy races between view-oblivious strands in effectively the same way. SP+ differs only in that it partitions the strands that are logically in parallel across multiple P bags.

With respect to detecting races between a view-oblivious strand and a view-aware strand, SP+ needs to manage multiple P bags per Cilk function to handle two complications arising from the use of reducers. First, when a view-aware strand is involved, a race between two strands exists only if both the strands are logically in parallel, and their views are in parallel. Consequently, the SP+ algorithm must keep track of the views that strands might operate on. Second, the SP+ algorithm must also keep track of different sets of strands within the a Cilk function F that may end up serialized with some reduce strand executed in F.

SP+ maintains P bags and their concomitant view IDs in a manner that imitates the Cilk runtime's management of views. Each P bag has a view ID. When a function F is first spawned or called, it inherits the same view ID as its parent's top P bag. Whenever SP+ executes a stolen continuation in F, as specified by the input steal specification, it pushes a new P bag onto the top of $F.P$ with a brand new view ID. For a currently executing function F, its top P bag thus has the view ID corresponding to the view of its currently executing strand. Whenever a REDUCE operation occurs, also as specified by the steal specification, the SP+ algorithm pops the top P bag off of $F.P$ and unions it into the next P bag on top, imitating how the REDUCE combines views and destroys the dominated view. Because a necessary set of REDUCE operations must occur to destroy all parallel views before a sync, when F executes a sync, SP+ maintains the invariant that only a single P bag is left in $F.P$, which is the same P bag (with the same view ID) that F had when it started. The view ID effectively simulates how the views get managed by the runtime, the view invariants in Section 5 summarize.

In addition to keeping track of parallel views via view IDs, the multiple P bags differentiate the sets of strands that can serialize with different REDUCE operations. Specifically, whenever a spawned function G returns to F, the IDs corresponding to G's descendant, including G itself, get unioned into F's top P bag. Each P bag in $F.P$ thus contains a set of IDs corresponding to F's descendants whose initial strands share the same view. Whenever a REDUCE operation occurs, the top two P bags have view IDs corresponding to views that are about to be reduced together, and the set of IDs they contain correspond to the set of F's descendants that serialize with the reduce operation. Since everything that comes after this reduce strand, including this reduce strand, is in series with the descendants corresponding to the IDs in the top two P bags, SP+ can safely union them together.

---

[3]We shall see how a steal specification can be specified inexpensively in Section 8.

To detect a potential race with a view-aware strand, SP+ checks that not only the two strands are in parallel, but that they also operate on parallel views, as verified by comparing the view IDs of the last access and currently executing strand. Note that the union of the top two P bags occurs *before* the invocation of the corresponding REDUCE operation, and thus any memory access performed by the reduce strand will have the same view IDs as the descendants in those P bags, achieving the desired effect — the reduce strand is in series with descendants in these two P bags.

There is one subtlety in how SP+ handles the shadow memory. SP+ replaces the last reader and writer only if the last access is in an S bag *or* if the current access is performed by a reduce strand and that it shares the same view as the last access. Call the last access in the shadow memory e_1, and the currently executing strand e_2. By "pseudotransitivity of $\parallel$" [15], we know that there is no need to replace e_1 in the shadow memory with e_2 if the e_2 is logically in parallel with e_1, because any strand that comes later in serial execution order that races with e_2 will race with e_1 as well. We need only to update the last reader / writer if e_2 is in series with e_1. In the case where e_2 is a reduce strand, however, e_2 is in series with e_1 even if e_1 belongs to a P bag but has the same view ID.

To illustrate how SP+ operates, consider it unfolding the performance dag shown in Figure 5 in Section 5. When it executes the fifth strand e in function a, the stolen continuation labeled with δ, it pushes a new empty P bag corresponding to view δ. The P stack a.P contains two other P bags: {b, c, d}, associated with view α, and {e, f}, associated with view γ. The first P bag resulted from unioning the P bags corresponding to views α and β before executing r_0. After SP+ executes e and encounters r_1, the steal specification dictates that the top two P bags — the empty one representing strand δ and the one containing {e, f} — are unioned before executing r_1. If r_1, a view-aware strand, happens to write to location ℓ last accessed by the first strand in f labeled with γ, SP+ will not report a race, since they now share the same view after the union. If the last access of ℓ before r_1 is performed by a strand in c, however, a race will be reported, since c is in a different P bag of a.

7. ANALYSIS OF THE SP+ ALGORITHM

This section discusses how the SP+ algorithm can be used to check if any execution on a given input of an ostensibly deterministic Cilk program that uses reducers contains a determinacy race involving a view-oblivious strand. If D is the Cilk depth and K is the maximum sync-block size (defined in Section 4), then we show that $\Omega(\max\{KD, K^3\})$ steal specifications are needed to elicit every possible view-aware strand, and $O(KD + K^3)$ steal specifications suffice. The proofs in this section can be adapted to construct these $O(KD + K^3)$ steal specifications.

The following theorem bounds the number of steal specifications needed to elicit all possible update strands to M, the maximum number of continuations in any sync block in a Cilk function. In a Cilk computation, if D is the Cilk depth and K is the maximum number of continuations in any sync block, then M can be as large as KD. The following theorem considers the Cilk computation's ordinary dag, not its performance dag.

THEOREM 6. *In a Cilk computation, all possible update strands can be elicited in $\Theta(M)$ steal specifications, where M is the maximum number of continuations not followed by a sync strand in the same Cilk function along any path in the computation dag.*

PROOF. Consider the canonical SP parse tree for the computation dag. Let a denote an internal node in this tree whose left child is l and whose right child is r. If a is an S node, then the subcomputation under r inherits the value of the view $h(l)$. Because the reducer

is a monoid, the value of $h(l)$ is the same, regardless of how the subcomputation under l was scheduled. The same situation holds if a is a P node unless the subcomputation under r is stolen, in which case the subcomputation under r executes on a new, identity view. In this case, because the reducer is a monoid, the value of $h(e)$ does not depend on the computation executed before e.

Consider the root-to-e path p in the SP parse tree. From the argument above, the value of $h(e)$ depends only on the closest P node $a \in p$ such that the right child of a inherits an identity view. The number of different values of $h(e)$ is therefore the number of P nodes a in p for which e is in the right subtree of a.

A root-to-e path in the canonical SP parse tree passes through at most one sync block in each Cilk function F, and each P node in F on that path corresponds to a continuation on the path to e in that sync block. Consequently, $\Omega(M)$ steal specifications are needed to elicit all possible update strands at the location of e. Because there exists a unique path in the SP parse tree from the root to each strand e, continuations to steal can be chosen in a breadth-first manner, where two continuations e_1 and e_2 are stolen in the same specification if the same number of P nodes occur on the root-to-e_1 and root-to-e_2 paths in the tree. Consequently, $O(M)$ steal specifications suffice to elicit all possible update strands. $\square$

We now consider the number of steal and reduce specifications needed to elicit all possible reduce strands. Every REDUCE operation on a sequence $\kappa = \langle k_1, k_2, \ldots, k_K \rangle$ of K elements combines two adjacent subsequences of κ. There are therefore $\binom{K}{3}$ distinct REDUCE operations on K, and therefore $O(K^3)$ specifications can elicit all possible reduce strands. The following theorem shows that, $\Omega(K^3)$ specifications are necessary to elicit every reduce strand.

THEOREM 7. *Let $\kappa = \langle k_1, k_2, \ldots, k_K \rangle$ be an ordered set of K elements. Any collection R of reduce trees on κ that contains each REDUCE operation at least once has size $|R| = \Omega(K^3)$.*

PROOF. To bound the number of reduce trees in R, let us characterize a REDUCE operation by the size of its larger input view. Each view h of a reducer corresponds to some subsequence of κ, and the *size* of h is the length of the subsequence corresponding to h. For example, a reduce strand that reduces the views represented by the subsequences $\langle k_a, k_{a+1}, \ldots, k_{b-1} \rangle$ and $\langle k_b, k_{b+1}, \ldots, k_{c-1} \rangle$ of κ reduces a view of size $b - a$ with one of size $c - b$. Let us consider reduce strands for which the size of its larger input is at least $n/2+1$.

To count the number of reduce trees containing such reduce strands, we imagine iteratively constructing the collection R of reduce trees by considering different view sizes in increasing order. For each size s, each view h of size s can be an input to multiple distinct possible reduce strands. Because $s \geq n/2 + 1$, each reduce tree in R can contain at most one view h of size s and at most one reduce strand r on such a view. A reduce tree in R that produces h might already contain r already; otherwise a new reduce tree must be added to R that contains r.

We can lower bound the number of reduce trees added to R for each size s using the following observations:

- There are $n - s + 1$ distinct views of size s.
- For each view h of size s, there are $n - s$ distinct reduce strands that take h as an input.
- For each view h of size s, at most 2 reduce trees in R can produce h from a smaller view of a particular size s', where $n/2 + 1 \leq s' < s$. Consequently, there are at most $2(s - n/2 - 1)$ reduce trees already in R that contain distinct reduce strands on h.

These observations show that, for a particular size $s \geq n/2 + 1$, there are $(n - s + 1)(n - s)$ different reduce strands on views of size s, and at most $(n - s + 1)2(s - n/2 - 1)$ of these reduce strands can be exist in reduce trees already in R. For each size s, we must therefore add at least $(n - s + 1)(2n - 3s + 2)$ new reduce trees to R. This bound holds as long as $2n - 3s + 2 > 0$, implying that $s < 2(n + 1)/3$. Summing over the applicable sizes s, we have that $|R| \geq \sum_{s=n/2+1}^{2(n+1)/3-1} (n - s + 1)(2n - 3s + 2) = \Omega(n^3)$. $\square$

8. RADER

This section presents Rader, our prototype implementation of Peer-Set and SP+. We evaluated Rader on 6 benchmarks. When running the Peer-Set algorithm, Rader incurs a geometric-mean multiplicative overhead of 2.32 (with a range of $1.03 - 5.95$) over running the benchmarks without instrumentation. When running the SP+ algorithm, Rader incurs an overhead of 16.76 (with a range of $3.94 - 75.60$). To get a sense of how much of the overhead comes from the instrumentation versus algorithm implementation, we measured the overhead of Rader over an empty tool (i.e., same instrumentation which leads to an empty call). When running the Peer-Set algorithm, Rader incurs a geometric-mean multiplicative overhead of 1.84 (with a range of $1 - 3.89$) over running the benchmarks with an empty tool. When running the SP+ algorithm, Rader incurs an overhead of 7.27 (with a range of $3.04 - 15.68$). This average is without considering ferret, an outlier that has very little overhead, which we explain later in the section.

Implementation. Rader uses compiler instrumentation to detect races in Cilk programs. We modified GCC 4.9 to insert instrumentation to identify parallel control constructs in the execution, akin to the Low Overhead Annotations [21] for Intel's Cilk Plus compiler.

For the SP+ algorithm, we also need to instrument reads and writes and simulate parallel executions. Rader instruments reads and writes by piggybacking on the ThreadSanitizer instrumentation [41], supported since GCC 4.8 [20]. When running SP+, Rader triggers operations in the runtime system to simulate steals at program points specified in a given steal specification. To accomplish this, Rader appropriately "promotes" various runtime data structures that would be modified if, after a worker executes the corresponding spawn, the parent of that spawn had been stolen [18]. When the worker resumes the parent later, it acts as if it stole the parent, and appropriately creates a new reducer view for the continuation. These promoted data structures also prompt the worker to check if it should execute any reduction.

Since Rader needs to check particular reductions according to the steal specification, the worker may need to hold off on a reduction instead of reducing eagerly, which is how Cilk runtime normally operates. We modified the runtime so that the worker, when simulating steals, calls back to Rader to see if it should execute a reduction. Although the modified runtime no longer always performs reduction eagerly, we optimized the steal specifications that Rader uses as follows to use only constant space per steal.

Steal specifications. Although constructing the steal specification naively can cause the input to be as large as the computation dag, one can do better. Because Section 7 showed that $\Omega(\max\{KD, K^3\})$ executions are necessary to guarantee completeness and that $O(DK + K^3)$ suffice, no time is saved asymptotically if the system checks for more than one particular reduction or update per sync block. We therefore only need to make sure that Rader checks at least one reduction or update per sync block in a given execution. Consequently, the steal specification can be as simple as specifying which three continuations to steal in a sync block (for checking reduce operations) or which continuations at a particular depth to steal (for checking updates). We can steal the same continuations for every sync block, and the completeness guarantee still stands, as long as we run Rader with $O(K^3)$ different specifications. In practice, Rader takes as an input either three values specifying

the continuations to be stolen, or a random seed and the maximum sync block size, in which case three different points are chosen randomly for each sync block. If a race is detected, Rader reports the labels corresponding to the stolen continuations that triggered the race, making it easy to repeat the run for regression tests.

Experimental evaluation. We empirically evaluated Rader on 6 benchmark applications, which Figure 7 lists. We converted the pipeline programs dedup and ferret from the PARSEC benchmark suite [4] to use Cilk linguistics and a reducer_ostream (part of Cilk Plus) to write its output. The synthetic fib benchmark uses a reducer_opadd, which is also part of Cilk Plus. All other benchmarks use user-defined reducers, including a "Bag" data structure (pbfs [27]), a "hypervector" (collision), and a user-defined struct (knapsack [17]). All experiments ran serially on an Intel Xeon E5-2665 system with 2.4 GHz CPU's and 32 GB of main memory. Each core has a 32-KB private L1-data-cache and a 256 KB private L2-cache, and shares a 20 MB L3-cache with 7 other cores.

Figure 7 shows the overhead of Rader over running each benchmark without instrumentation. As Figure 7 shows, the Peer-Set algorithm (column *Check view-read race*) incurs little overhead. The SP+ algorithm has a somewhat high overhead for fib and knapsack, but otherwise exhibits reasonable overheads. The high overheads on these two benchmarks stems from the fact that they perform very little work per strand, making the overall running time dominated by instrumentation. We have also compared Rader's overhead over running each benchmark with an empty tool to gauge how much overhead comes from instrumentation versus algorithm implementation. As can be seen in Figure 8, the overhead due to algorithm implementation is minimal. The overhead dropped from as high as 75.60 down to 13.85 on fib, for example.

In terms of the additional bookkeeping for checking reducers (i.e., comparing columns Check reductions and No steals), most applications exhibit negligible overhead; fib exhibits the highest overhead in this regard (2.25 times overhead), because fib is a synthetic benchmark we devised to stress test Rader— each function call does almost no work except for updating reducers and reducing views. The overhead is thus evident — there is not much work to amortize it against. One interesting outlier is ferret, which has virtually no overhead. It turns out that, when we instrument all the library code that came with PARSEC, lots of races get reported. We separately confirmed with this Cilk Screen using Intel compiler, and indeed there were races. Since the reporting of races (I/O) throws off timing, we opt to instrument only the main ferret code without the rest of the library, meaning that only a small fraction of memory accesses within the computation are instrumented.

9. RELATED WORK

Race detection is a rich area actively being worked on. Roughly speaking, approaches to race detection can be categorized as either static [1, 2, 6, 13, 30, 36, 44] or dynamic [8, 9, 11, 14, 16, 33, 35, 40, 43, 46]. We focus our discussion on the dynamic approach, the category our work falls under. In particular, we shall focus on related work that supports a similar language model, namely work on detecting determinacy races in programs with nested parallelism.

Nudler and Rudolph [32] proposed a ***English-Hebrew labeling*** scheme that labels "parallel tasks" in a computation based on two different traversal orders, such that comparing the labels suffice to tell whether the two tasks are logically in parallel. This scheme uses static labels, meaning that, once assigned, the labels do not change, and the label size can grow proportionally to the maximum number of fork points in the program (i.e., execution points where parallel branches are spawned off).

Benchmark	Input size	Description	Overhead over no instrumentation			
			Check view-read race	No steals	Check updates	Check reductions
collision	20	Collision detection in 3D	1.03	17.25	17.11	17.10
dedup	*medium*	Compression program	1.21	6.72	6.71	6.67
ferret	*large*	Image similarity search	1.00	2.25	2.25	2.25
fib	28	Recursive Fibonacci	5.95	33.58	36.90	75.60
knapsack	26	Recursive knapsack	2.70	49.24	56.41	66.79
pbfs	$|V| = 0.3M, |E| = 1.9M$	Parallel breadth-first search	3.34	3.94	3.94	5.65

Figure 7: Rader's overhead over running 6 benchmarks without instrumentation. Both Rader and the benchmarks are compiled with -O3. We ran Rader with different configurations. *Check view-read race* shows the overhead when running the Peer-set algorithm for checking view-read races only. *No steals* shows the overhead of checking races without eliciting any reductions. *Check reductions* shows the overhead with randomly chosen steal points to eilcit subset of possible reductions. *Check updates* shows the overhead with steals at continuation depth that's half of the maximum sync block size.

Benchmark	Input size	Description	Overhead over an empty tool			
			Check view-read race	No steals	Check updates	Check reductions
collision	20	Collision detection in 3D	1.00	8.19	8.13	8.12
dedup	*medium*	Compression program	1.22	6.53	6.52	6.48
ferret	*large*	Image similarity search	1.00	1.04	1.04	1.04
fib	28	Recursive Fibonacci	3.89	6.15	6.76	13.85
knapsack	26	Recursive knapsack	2.44	11.56	13.24	15.68
pbfs	$|V| = 0.3M, |E| = 1.9M$	Parallel breadth-first search	1.79	3.04	3.04	4.6

Figure 8: Rader's overhead over running 6 benchmarks with an empty tool, i.e., instrumentation leads to empty calls. Both Rader and the benchmarks are compiled with -O3. We ran Rader with different configurations as described in Figure 7.

Dinning and Schonberg [12] proposed ***task-recycling scheme*** that improves upon the English-Hebrew labeling scheme by recycling labels for tasks, at the expense of failing to detect some races. They empirically demonstrated that the task-recycling scheme can be implemented efficiently.

Mellor-Crummey [29] proposed a different labeling scheme called ***offset-span labeling***, where the label sizes grow proportionally to the nesting depth, improving on the bound of the English-Hebrew labeling scheme. He also observed that, for parallel determinacy race detection, it suffices to keep only two readers in shared memory, namely, the "left-most" and "right-most" parallel readers, which are the least and most recent reads in the serial execution order of the computation.

Feng and Leiserson proposed the SP-bags algorithm [15], which employs a disjoint-set data structure to maintain series-parallel relationships. SP-bags executes the computation serially and incurs near-constant overhead per check. They also observed that, the parallel relationship is pseudotransitive, and thus it suffices to store only a single reader in the shadow memory.

Bender et. al proposed the SP-hybrid algorithm [3] that employs a scheme similar to English-Hebrew labeling, but manages the labels in a concurrent order-maintenance data structure, which allows dynamic labels and supports checks with constant overhead.

Raman et. al proposed ESP-bags [37] algorithm, which is similar to the SP-bags algorithm but extended to handle async and finish in Habanero-Java [7]. They subsequently proposed SPD3 detectors [38], also for Habanero-Java that maintains series-parallel relationships by keeping track of the entire computation tree, which has a simple implementation and executes in parallel.

Since our algorithms extend upon the SP-bags algorithm and similarly use a disjoint-set data structure, they enjoy similar time and space bounds; the SP+ has the additional overhead for simulating steals and reductions. Like SP-bags, however, they execute the computation serially. One distinct difference between our work and these algorithms is that SP+ handles race detection on computations with reducers, which correspond to non-series-parallel dags. As far as we know, the SP+ algorithm is the first determinacy race detector that provides provable guarantees for computations that are not series-parallel. Nevertheless, the SP+ algorithm, albeit sound for a given execution, requires polynomial number of execu-

tions to guarantee complete coverage, due to the inherent nondeterminism in how the runtime manages reducers.

10. CONCLUSION

We have presented two algorithms for catching two unique types of races that arise from incorrect use of reducer hyperobjects. Both algorithms are provably efficient and correct with respect to a given execution, and incur modest overhead in practice. We have also shown that for an ostensibly deterministic Cilk program, polynomially many SP+ executions with different steal specifications suffice to elicit all possible view-aware strands, thereby providing the desired coverage.

Both algorithms execute the computation serially, however, and a natural question is whether they can be parallelized to execute Cilk computations in parallel, so as to achieve better execution time for race detection. In particular, the Peer-Set algorithm has demonstrated negligible overhead when running serially; an efficient parallel algorithm can lead to a light-weight always-on view-read race detection tool. Here, we lay out some of the challenges that we foresee in parallelizing these algorithms.

To parallelize the Peer-Set algorithm, one challenge is figure out what minimal information needs to be stored in the shadow memory to correctly detect view-read races. The Peer-Set algorithm maintains the shadow memory to keep track of last readers in order to properly check whether two reads to a given reducer have the same peer set. If the algorithm executes the computation in parallel, there is no longer a clear notion of the last reader. For detecting determinacy races in parallel, Mellor-Crummey has demonstrated that, it is sufficient to store only two "left-most" and "right-most" parallel readers [29]. Such a scheme works for detecting accesses that are logically in parallel, but it is unfortunately insufficient for checking for peer-set equivalence. Storing all parallel reads encountered, meanwhile, incurs non-constant space usage per reducer and time overhead per check.

The main challenge to an efficient parallel SP+ algorithm, on the other hand, is to achieve the desired time bound so that one can get speedup during parallel execution. Recall that the SP+ algorithm executes the computation according to the steal specification, which dictates what continuations to steal and what reduce operations to execute in what order. The constraints imposed by the steal specification mean that some worker threads may need to be blocked at certain execution points, which may have adversarial effects on load balancing. Conforming to the steal specification while maintaining good load balance seems to be an obstacle.

Acknowledgments

We thank Charles Leiserson of MIT for his help developing the peer-set semantics of reducers and for helpful discussions concerning determinacy races involving reducers. We thank William Leiserson of MIT for helpful discussions concerning types of determinacy races involving reducers. We thank Jeremy Fineman of Georgetown University and the Supertech group at MIT CSAIL for helpful discussions. We thank the reviewers for their excellent feedback.

11. REFERENCES

[1] M. Abadi, C. Flanagan, and S. N. Freund. Types for safe locking: Static race detection for Java. *ACM TOPLAS*, 28(2):207–255, Mar. 2006.

[2] R. Agrawal and S. D. Stoller. Type inference for parameterized race-free java. In B. Steffen and G. Levi, editors, *Verification, Model Checking, and Abstract Interpretation*, volume 2937 of *LNCS*, pp. 149–160. Springer Berlin Heidelberg, 2004.

[3] M. A. Bender, J. T. Fineman, S. Gilbert, and C. E. Leiserson. On-the-fly maintenance of series-parallel relationships in fork-join multithreaded programs. In *SPAA '04*, pp. 133–144, 2004.

[4] C. Bienia, S. Kumar, J. P. Singh, and K. Li. The PARSEC benchmark suite: Characterization and architectural implications. In *PACT '08*, October 2008.

[5] R. D. Blumofe and C. E. Leiserson. Scheduling multithreaded computations by work stealing. *Journal of the ACM*, 1999.

[6] C. Boyapati and M. Rinard. A parameterized type system for race-free Java programs. In *OOPSLA '01*, pp. 56–69. ACM, 2001.

[7] V. Cavé, J. Zhao, J. Shirako, and V. Sarkar. Habanero-Java: the new adventures of old X10. In *PPPJ '11*, pp. 51–61, 2011.

[8] G.-I. Cheng, M. Feng, C. E. Leiserson, K. H. Randall, and A. F. Stark. Detecting data races in Cilk programs that use locks. In *SPAA '98*, 1998.

[9] J.-D. Choi, K. Lee, A. Loginov, R. O'Callahan, V. Sarkar, and M. Sridharan. Efficient and precise datarace detection for multithreaded object-oriented programs. In *PLDI '02*, pp. 258–269. ACM, 2002.

[10] T. H. Cormen, C. E. Leiserson, R. L. Rivest, and C. Stein. *Introduction to Algorithms*. The MIT Press, third edition, 2009.

[11] J. Devietti, B. P. Wood, K. Strauss, L. Ceze, D. Grossman, and S. Qadeer. RADISH: Always-on sound and complete race detection in software and hardware. In *ISCA '12*, pp. 201–212. IEEE Computer Society, 2012.

[12] A. Dinning and E. Schonberg. An empirical comparison of monitoring algorithms for access anomaly detection. In *PPoPP '90*, pp. 1–10, 1990.

[13] D. Engler and K. Ashcraft. RacerX: Effective, static detection of race conditions and deadlocks. In *SOSP '03*, pp. 237–252. ACM, 2003.

[14] J. Erickson, M. Musuvathi, S. Burckhardt, and K. Olynyk. Effective data-race detection for the kernel. In *OSDI '10*, 2010.

[15] M. Feng and C. E. Leiserson. Efficient detection of determinacy races in Cilk programs. *TOCS*, 1999.

[16] C. Flanagan and S. N. Freund. Fasttrack: efficient and precise dynamic race detection. In *PLDI '09*, pp. 121–133, Dublin, Ireland, 2009. ACM.

[17] M. Frigo. A Cilk++ program for the knapsack challenge. https://software.intel.com/en-us/courseware/249567, 2009.

[18] M. Frigo, P. Halpern, C. E. Leiserson, and S. Lewin-Berlin. Reducers and other Cilk++ hyperobjects. In *SPAA '09*, pp. 79–90, 2009.

[19] M. Frigo, C. E. Leiserson, and K. H. Randall. The implementation of the Cilk-5 multithreaded language. In *PLDI '98*, 1998.

[20] GCC 4.8. GCC 4.8 release series changes, new features, and fixes. https://gcc.gnu.org/gcc-4.8/changes.html, 2014.

[21] Intel Corporation. Intrinsics for low overhead tool annotations. https://www.cilkplus.org/open_specification/intrinsics-low-overhead-tool-annotations-v10, Nov. 2011.

[22] Intel Corporation. *Intel® Cilk™ Plus Language Extension Specification, Version 1.1*. Intel Corporation, 2013. Document 324396-002US.

[23] Intel Corporation. An introduction to the Cilk Screen race detector. https://software.intel.com/en-us/articles/an-introduction-to-the-cilk-screen-race-detector, Apr. 2013.

[24] I.-T. A. Lee, S. Boyd-Wickizer, Z. Huang, and C. E. Leiserson. Using memory mapping to support cactus stacks in work-stealing runtime systems. In *PACT '10*, pp. 411–420. ACM, 2010.

[25] I.-T. A. Lee, A. Shafi, and C. E. Leiserson. Memory-mapping support for reducer hyperobjects. In *SPAA '12*, pp. 287–297, 2012.

[26] C. E. Leiserson. The Cilk++ concurrency platform. *Journal of Supercomputing*, 51(3):244–257, March 2010.

[27] C. E. Leiserson and T. B. Schardl. A work-efficient parallel breadth-first search algorithm (or how to cope with the nondeterminism of reducers). In *SPAA '10*, June 2010.

[28] D. McCrady. Avoiding contention using combinable objects. Microsoft Developer Network blog post, Sept. 2008.

[29] J. Mellor-Crummey. On-the-fly detection of data races for programs with nested fork-join parallelism. In *Proceedings of Supercomputing'91*, pp. 24–33, 1991.

[30] M. Naik, A. Aiken, and J. Whaley. Effective static race detection for Java. In *PLDI '06*, pp. 308–319. ACM, 2006.

[31] R. H. B. Netzer and B. P. Miller. What are race conditions? *ACM LOPLAS*, 1(1):74–88, March 1992.

[32] I. Nudler and L. Rudolph. Tools for the efficient development of efficient parallel programs. In *ICCSE*, 1986.

[33] R. O'Callahan and J.-D. Choi. Hybrid dynamic data race detection. In *PPoPP '03*, pp. 167–178. ACM, 2003.

[34] OpenMP Architecture Review Board. OpenMP application program interface, version 4.0. http://www.openmp.org/mp-documents/OpenMP4.0.0.pdf, 2013.

[35] E. Pozniansky and A. Schuster. MultiRace: Efficient on-the-fly data race detection in multithreaded c++ programs: Research articles. *Journal of CCPE*, 19(3):327–340, Mar. 2007.

[36] P. Pratikakis, J. S. Foster, and M. Hicks. LOCKSMITH: Practical static race detection for c. *ACM TOPLAS*, 33(1):3:1–3:55, Jan. 2011.

[37] R. Raman, J. Zhao, V. Sarkar, M. Vechev, and E. Yahav. Efficient data race detection for async-finish parallelism. In *Runtime Verification*, volume 6418 of *LNCS*, pp. 368–383. 2010.

[38] R. Raman, J. Zhao, V. Sarkar, M. Vechev, and E. Yahav. Scalable and precise dynamic datarace detection for structured parallelism. In *PLDI '12*, pp. 531–542, 2012.

[39] J. Reinders. *Intel Threading Building Blocks: Outfitting C++ for Multi-core Processor Parallelism*. O'Reilly Media, Inc., 2007.

[40] S. Savage, M. Burrows, G. Nelson, P. Sobalvarro, and T. Anderson. Eraser: A dynamic race detector for multi-threaded programs. In *SOSP '97*, Oct. 1997.

[41] K. Serebryany and T. Iskhodzhanov. Threadsanitizer: Data race detection in practice. In *WBIA '09*, pp. 62–71. ACM, 2009.

[42] J. Shirako, D. M. Peixotto, V. Sarkar, and W. N. Scherer. Phaser accumulators: a new reduction construct for dynamic parallelism. In *IPDPS '09*, 2009.

[43] C. von Praun and T. R. Gross. Object race detection. In *OOPSLA '01*, pp. 70–82. ACM, 2001.

[44] J. W. Voung, R. Jhala, and S. Lerner. Relay: Static race detection on millions of lines of code. In *ESEC-FSE '07*, pp. 205–214, Dubrovnik, Croatia, 2007. ACM.

[45] M. Wimmer. Wait-free hyperobjects for task-parallel programming systems. In *IPDPS '13*, pp. 803–812, 2013.

[46] Y. Yu, T. Rodeheffer, and W. Chen. Racetrack: Efficient detection of data race conditions via adaptive tracking. In *SOSP '05*, pp. 221–234. ACM, 2005.

ThreadScan: Automatic and Scalable Memory Reclamation

Dan Alistarh
Microsoft Research
dan.alistarh@microsoft.com

William M. Leiserson
MIT
willtor@mit.edu

Alexander Matveev
MIT
amatveev@csail.mit.edu

Nir Shavit
MIT and TAU
shanir@mit.edu

ABSTRACT

The concurrent memory reclamation problem is that of devising a way for a deallocating thread to verify that no other concurrent threads hold references to a memory block being deallocated. To date, in the absence of automatic garbage collection, there is no satisfactory solution to this problem; existing tracking methods like hazard pointers, reference counters, or epoch-based techniques like RCU, are either prohibitively expensive or require significant programming expertise, to the extent that implementing them efficiently can be worthy of a publication. None of the existing techniques are automatic or even semi-automated.

In this paper, we take a new approach to concurrent memory reclamation: instead of manually tracking access to memory locations as done in techniques like hazard pointers, or restricting shared accesses to specific epoch boundaries as in RCU, our algorithm, called ThreadScan, leverages operating system signaling to automatically detect which memory locations are being accessed by concurrent threads.

Initial empirical evidence shows that ThreadScan scales surprisingly well and requires negligible programming effort beyond the standard use of Malloc and Free.

Categories and Subject Descriptors

D.1.3 [**Programming Techniques**]: Concurrent Programming

General Terms

Data Structures, Design, Performance

Keywords

Synchronization, Memory Management

1. INTRODUCTION

An important principle for data structure scalability is having *traversals that execute without any synchronization*:

sequences of reads with no memory updates (hence no memory fences, contention or cache pollution [25]) that work correctly by utilizing the semantics of the given data structure. The gain from such unsynchronized traversals is significant because traversals account for a large fraction of data structure operations, whether these search for a given item, or lead to updates, insertions or deletions of a small set of elements.

As a simple example, consider the lazy-list algorithm [22]. This is a concurrent linked list algorithm in which modifications to the list are done by acquiring fine-grained locks on the two nodes adjacent to where an insert or remove of a node is to take place. Because chances are typically low that there will be concurrent modifications to adjacent nodes, acquiring locks for these modifications introduces virtually no overhead. However, the frequent search operations traversing the list to reach the insertion or deletion point or to check if it contains a given item, are executed by reading along the sequence of pointers from the list head, ignoring the locks, and thus incurring no synchronization overhead. These unsynchronized traversals are key to the scalability of the data structure.

Not surprisingly, the unsynchronized traversal approach is increasing in popularity: it is at the base of the widely used read-copy-update (RCU) framework for designing concurrent data structures [36], as well as high performance structures such as hash-tables [26, 30, 42], search trees [1, 4, 13, 19, 23, 31], and priority queues [3, 43]. The unsynchronized traversals are in many cases *wait-free*, that is, they complete in a finite number of operations independently of ongoing data structure modifications. They can be used both for data structures that use locks for modifications and ones that do not (see for example [23, 31]), and deliver improved performance in both cases. A detailed survey of such structures can be found in [25, 38].

These high performance, unsynchronized traversals, although a boon to languages like Java (in the form of Java's Concurrency Package [29]), are more difficult to use in languages like C and C++ which have no garbage collection. Because they use no locks, memory fences, or shared memory writes, traversing threads leave no indication for other threads to detect what they are reading at any given time. To C and C++, the unsynchronized traversals are thus *invisible*. This invisibility makes memory reclamation a nightmare, because a thread wishing to reclaim a memory block has no way of knowing how many threads are concurrently traversing that block.

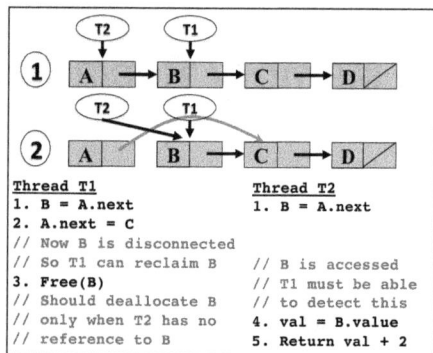

Figure 1: Concurrent memory reclamation for a linked-list: thread T1 deletes node B while thread T2 concurrently accesses the same node. Before calling free(B), thread T1 first "disconnects" B, by removing any heap (or shared) pointers that may lead to B, and only then it calls free(B) that is responsible to detect if some other thread has a reference to B. In memory reclamation, the programmer is responsible to disconnect the node, and the memory reclamation protocol is responsible to implement the free() function.

1.1 Concurrent Memory Reclamation

The *concurrent memory reclamation problem* is thus to devise techniques that will allow a deallocating thread to verify that no other thread has a reference to that block. More precisely, a programmer first makes this block "unreachable," by removing any shared reference that may lead to this block, and then uses the free(..) method of the memory reclamation scheme to safely deallocate this block. Any concurrent data-structure to be used in practice, in particular high performance ones that have invisible traversals, must include a solution to this problem. Otherwise, after a shared object gets deallocated, threads that still have a private reference (or a *dangling pointer*) to this object may access "garbage" memory and execute on an inconsistent memory state. As an example, consider the execution shown in Figure 1 on a concurrent linked-list: thread T1 deletes node B while thread T2 concurrently accesses the same node. Notice that, before calling free(B), thread T1 first "disconnects" B, by removing the shared reference from A to B (that may lead to B), and only then it calls free(B) that initiates the memory reclamation protocol.

This makes concurrent memory reclamation a simpler problem than garbage collection [5, 34, 8, 28], as we are not interested in shared references that are used to construct a data-structure on the global heap, or any shared references that are used to transfer or communicate nodes between threads. It is the responsibility of the programmer to eliminate those shared references before actually calling free(..). Providing a scalable and easy-to-use solution to the memory reclamation problem is important because historically, many high performance applications are written in unmanaged languages like C and C++ that have no built-in garbage collector support, and because of the large existing code base, these languages are likely to remain in high demand for decades to come.

As it turns out, despite being simpler than garbage collection, to date, there is no satisfactory solution to the problem: existing tracking methods are either prohibitively expensive or require significant programming expertise. Known techniques roughly fall into three categories:

Reference counting. These techniques originated in the realm of garbage collection. Algorithms such as [11, 17, 44], smart pointers [39, 41] and more recent improvements using hardware transactions [12], assign shared counters to objects, and use them to count the number of references to an object at any given time. Reference counting schemes are automatic: counters and counter modifications can be added to code at compile time. However, in all these schemes, the counting process is expensive, requiring a shared memory read-modify-write operation for each shared memory read, making them prohibitively expensive and eliminating the scalability advantages of using invisible read-based traversals.

Pointer-based. Hazard pointers [37] and *pass-the-buck* [24], or the more recent Drop-the-Anchor technique [7] require the programmer to explicitly declare the currently accessed locations, and then track them dynamically. This is a complex task even for simple data structures such as linked lists. In practice, using hazard pointers also requires modifications to the data structures to make them "hazard pointer friendly." The tracking process itself introduces a significant performance overhead, as all threads must synchronize with the reclaiming thread by executing a memory fence for each new hazard pointer. Thus, the performance advantages of having invisible readers are partly lost.

Epoch-based. Quiescence-based techniques [20, 14, 21] such as RCU [36] have threads accessing the data structure register the start and end of methods, and have the reclaiming thread wait a sufficiently long period of time until it can be ensured that no registered thread holds a reference to a deleted object. These techniques are efficient since here is no per-read tracking, making them compatible with invisible traversals. However, a delayed thread may prevent the reclamation process. Also, there are still significant programming complexities: for example, in the RCU technique, references that move outside methods must be tracked manually in ways similar to hazard pointers. This makes the design of complex data structures using such techniques a matter for concurrent programming experts [9] and does not allow for automation.

Recent work [12, 2] has explored the potential of Hardware Transactional Memory (HTM) to simplify memory reclamation. Dragojevic et al. [12] showed that HTM can be used to speed up and significantly simplify prior reclamation schemes, while Alistarh et al. [2] devised a technique which streamlines the tracking of node references, by ensuring that each data structure operation appears as having executed inside a single hardware transaction. While these techniques are promising, their performance fundamentally relies on HTM, whose availability is currently limited.

Summing up, there is currently no concurrent memory reclamation scheme that is widely-applicable, has low overhead, and works without careful programmer involvement.

1.2 Our Contribution

In this work, we take a new approach to concurrent memory reclamation: instead of manually tracking accesses to memory locations as done in techniques like hazard pointers, or limiting reclamation to specific code boundaries as done in RCU, we use the operating system signaling and thread control to automatically detect which memory locations are being accessed.

Our protocol, called ThreadScan, is designed as a memory reclamation library: the programmer provides a data structure implementation with correct *free* calls, and ThreadScan will implement it automatically ensuring efficient memory reclamation. Our main technical contribution is the protocol for tracking memory references both automatically and efficiently.

At a high level, ThreadScan works as follows: when a thread deletes a node, it adds it to a shared delete buffer. When the buffer becomes full, the thread inserting the last node initiates a Collect procedure, which examines memory for references to nodes in the delete buffer, and marks nodes which still have outstanding references. The reclaiming thread frees nodes which are no longer referenced.

The key challenge in ThreadScan is to provide an automatic and efficient implementation of Collect.

Figure 2 illustrates the key idea of ThreadScan: when initiating a Collect, the reclaiming thread sends signals to all threads accessing the data structure, asking them to scan their own stacks and registers for references to nodes in the delete buffer, and to mark nodes in the delete buffer which might still be referenced. Threads execute this procedure as part of their signal handlers. At the end of this process, each thread replies with an acknowledgment, and resumes its execution. Once all acknowledgments have been received, the thread reclaims all unmarked nodes and returns.

There are two main advantages to this design. First, ThreadScan is shielded from errors in data structure code, such as infinite loops: these will not prevent the protocol from progressing, since the operating system signal handler code always has precedence over the application [27].

Second, ThreadScan offers strong progress guarantees as long as the operating system does not starve threads. In particular, notice that since the reclaiming thread waits for acknowledgments, the reclamation mechanism could in theory be *blocking*. This is not an issue in a standard programming environment, since each participant must finish executing ThreadScan in the signal handler before returning to its code. Therefore, the only way a thread may become unresponsive is if it is starved for steps *by the operating system*. This phenomenon is highly unlikely in modern operating systems, which schedule threads fairly: for instance, the Linux kernel avoids thread starvation by using dynamic priorities [35, 40]. At the same time, we emphasize that all other data structure operations preserve their progress properties, as ThreadScan adds a bounded number of steps to their execution.

The cost of the memory scan is amortized among threads by having each thread scan its own stack and registers, marking referenced nodes in the delete buffer. The scan is performed word-by-word, checking each chunk against pointers in the delete buffer. ThreadScan does assume that the programmer will not actively "hide" pointers to live nodes.[1]

We implemented ThreadScan in C to provide memory reclamation for a set of classic data structures: Harris' lock-free linked list [20], a lock-based skip-list, and a concur-

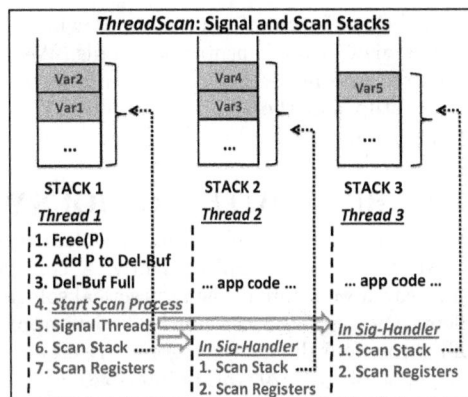

Figure 2: ThreadScan protocol illustration. Thread 1 calls Free(P) and this makes the delete buffer full. As a result, Thread 1 initiates a reclamation process that sends a signal to other threads and makes each thread scan its own stack and registers. After all threads are done, Thread 1 traverses the delete buffer and deallocates nodes that have no outstanding reference to them.

rent hash-table algorithm [25]. We ran tests on an Intel Xeon chip with 40 cores, each multiplexing two hardware threads. We compared ThreadScan against Hazard Pointers [37], epoch-based reclamation [20], and StackTrack [2], as well as an un-instrumented implementation which leaked memory. ThreadScan matches or outperforms all prior techniques, improving performance over Hazard Pointers by 2x on average, and provides similar performance to the leaky implementation. These findings hold even when the system is oversubscribed. Stack scans are the main source of overhead for ThreadScan, although the empirical results show that the overhead is well amortized across threads and against reclaimed nodes.

Besides its low footprint, the key advantage of ThreadScan is that it is automatic: the programmer just needs to pass nodes to its interface, which handles reclamation. We believe this ease-of-use can make ThreadScan a useful tool for designing scalable data structures.

ThreadScan works under the following assumptions on the application code. First, we assume that nodes in the delete buffer have already been correctly unlinked from the data structure, as is standard for memory reclamation [24]. Second, pointers to live objects should be visible to the scan, which precludes the use of pointer masking techniques. Finally, we assume a bound on the number of reclamation events that may occur during the execution of a method call, which is enforced by batching deletes.

The ThreadScan library "hooks" into the signaling mechanism of the operating system, so it is independent of bugs or infinite loops that may occur inside the application. As a result, the ThreadScan library guarantees that each operation completes within bounded time as long as all threads continue to be scheduled by the operating system. In particular, it is sufficient that signal handler code is scheduled fairly by the operating system.

The source code is available from Github [33]. It is released to the public under the MIT license, which permits copying, modifying, and redistribution with attribution.

Roadmap. We give an overview of related techniques in Section 2, and give a formal definition of the problem in Sec-

---

[1] This assumption is similar to assumptions made in conservative garbage collectors [6], and is necessary for *automatic* reclamation.

tion 3. We describe ThreadScan in Section 4, where we also provide an overview of implementation details. We provide a proof of correctness in Section 5. Section 6 describes the experimental setup and the empirical results. We discuss the results in Section 7.

2. COMPARISON WITH PREVIOUS WORK

The concurrent memory reclamation problem was first formally described in [24]. Subsequently, a considerable amount of research went into devising practical solutions for this problem. As described previously, known approaches can be split across four different categories: reference counting [10, 17], epoch-based [20, 15], pointer-based [37, 24, 7], and HTM-based [12, 2].

Our scheme could be seen as a generalization of epoch-based reclamation, where we *enforce* quiescent states through signaling: the reclaiming thread signals all other threads, which scan their memory, isolating the subset of nodes which can be safely freed. The signal-based implementation avoids some of the main shortcomings of quiescence: references that cannot be used outside epoch boundaries, and thread delays inside application code that may delay the reclamation indefinitely. ThreadScan can be seen as enforcing quiescent periods via the signaling mechanism. The idea of producing a consistent view of memory for the reclaiming thread and scanning this view for references was also used in [2]. The key difference is that their technique guarantees view atomicity by wrapping all data structure operations inside hardware transactions; here, we avoid HTM by using an inter-thread signaling protocol.

The key departure from pointer-based techniques, such as hazard pointers, is the fact that we do not ask the programmer to explicitly mark live references through hazards, guards, or anchors. References are checked by the protocol, and therefore the interaction with the application code is limited to the signal handlers. However, our technique assumes that node references are not obfuscated by the programmer.

ThreadScan has a roughly similar structure to on-the-fly garbage collectors with deferred reference counting, e.g., [5, 34]. Such garbage collectors are typically structured in phases, separated by handshakes. Regular threads are usually aware of the collector state, as they may execute barrier operations, and co-operate with the collector in scanning their stacks. In particular, some collectors require threads to provide them with a view that is equivalent to an atomic snapshot of the stack [8, 28]. We exploit a weaker property in ThreadScan, by performing a non-atomic scan of the threads' memory, which we use to identify references to reclaimed nodes. Memory reclamation is fundamentally simpler than garbage collection, and as such we focus on minimizing the performance overhead of reclamation for the original data structure operations, while working within the confines of an un-managed programming language.

3. MEMORY RECLAMATION

3.1 Problem Definition

In the following, we consider a set of n threads, communicating through shared memory via primitive memory access operations. These operations are applied to *shared objects*, where each object occupies a set of (shared) memory lo-

cations. A *node* is a set of memory locations that can be viewed as a single logical entity by a thread. A node can be in one of several states [37]:

1. *Allocated.* The node has been allocated, but not yet inserted in the object.

2. *Reachable.* The node is reachable by following valid pointers from shared objects.

3. *Removed.* The node is no longer *reachable*, but may still be accessed by some thread.

4. *Retired.* The node is removed, and cannot be accessed by any thread, but it has not yet been freed.

5. *Free.* The node's memory is available for allocation.

Memory Reclamation. The *concurrent memory reclamation* problem is defined as follows [24, 37]. We are given a node (or a set of nodes) which are *removed*, and we are asked to move them first to state *retired*, then to state *free*. Notice that, in state *retired*, nodes are no longer accessible by any thread besides the reclaiming thread, and therefore cannot lead to access violations. The key step in the problem is deciding when a node can be *retired*, i.e., when it is no longer accessible by concurrent threads. Since we wish to perform memory reclamation automatically, it is important to describe which code patterns are disallowed by the above problem definition.

3.2 Mapping to Code

Reference Types. We split node references into two types, depending on the possible thread access patterns.

1. *Shared References:* A reference that can be accessed by more than one thread.

2. *Private References:* A reference that is local to a thread, and can be used only by a particular thread.

Data structure pointers are a standard example of *shared* references. Such references are usually located on the heap, and may be accessed concurrently by multiple threads. Local pointers, such as the ones a thread uses to traverse a list, are an example of *private* reference. Such references are usually stored in the threads' stack or registers.

Code Assumptions. In developing ThreadScan, we make the following assumptions, discussed below.

ASSUMPTION 1. *We assume the following hold.*

1. Shared References. *Nodes in the delete buffer have already been* removed*, and cannot be accessed through shared references, or through references present on the heap.*

2. Reclamation Rate. *There exists a fixed finite bound on the number of distinct reclamation events that may occur during any method's execution.*

3. Matching References. *Node references are word-aligned, and they can be matched to node pointers via comparison. Arbitrary memory words do not match to node addresses.*

Discussion. Assumption 1.1 follows from the definition of concurrent memory reclamation [24, 37], and in fact is one of the main distinctions from concurrent garbage collection. Assumption 1.2 is justified by the fact that reclamation is usually batched, freeing several nodes at once. Assumption 1.3 prevents the programmer from hiding references through arithmetic operations such as XOR. It is standard for similar tasks such as conservative garbage collection, and is intuitively necessary to allow automatic reclamation.

4. THREADSCAN

Generic Structure. Our algorithm is based on the following blueprint: once a thread wishes to reclaim a node, it adds a pointer to this node to a delete buffer, whose size is fixed by the application. Whenever the buffer is full, the thread which inserted the last node into the buffer becomes the *reclaimer*. For simplicity, we assume that there can only be a single reclaimer at a given point in time. (In practice, this is enforced by a lock and choosing a delete buffer of appropriate size.)

The chosen thread starts a ThreadScan Collect operation by signaling all other threads to help with examining references to nodes in the buffer. Thus, the ThreadScan algorithm consists of the implementation of the collect procedure on the reclaimer side, and of the implementation of the scan signal handler for all other threads accessing the data structure.

In the following, we describe the implementation of Collect which works under Assumption 1. The implementation ensures that, at the end of the Collect, each node in the buffer is either *marked* or *unmarked*. Marked nodes may still have outstanding references, and cannot yet be reclaimed. Unmarked nodes are safe for reclamation, and are freed by the thread as soon as the collect procedure completes.

4.1 ThreadScan Collect

Reclamation is organized in a series of *reclamation phases*, illustrated in Figure 2. In each phase, we are given a set of *unreachable* data structure nodes, and must reclaim a subset of them ensuring that this process does not cause any access violations.

The TS-Collect procedure, whose pseudocode is given in Figure 1, works as follows. The reclaiming thread first sorts the delete buffer, to speed up the scan process. Next, the reclaimer signals all other participating threads to start a TS-Scan procedure, and executes this procedure itself. This procedure will mark all nodes with outstanding references. The reclaimer then waits for an acknowledgment from all other threads. Once it receives all thread acknowledgments, it scans the delete buffer for unmarked nodes to free.

The TS-Scan procedure is called by the signal handler for all participating threads. Each thread scans its stack and registers word-by-word,[2] and looks for each in the delete buffer. If a possible reference is found, the node is marked in the delete buffer, which prevents it from being deleted in this reclamation phase. At the end of the scan, the thread sends an acknowledgment to the reclaimer, and returns to the execution of its application code.

4.2 Implementation Details and Limitations

The previous section provides a detailed overview of our technique, but omits several important implementation de-

---

[2]The details of this procedure are given in Section 4.2.

Algorithm 1 ThreadScan Pseudocode.

```
 1: function TS-COLLECT( delete_buffer )
 2:     sort(delete_buffer)
 3:     for each thread t do
 4:         signal(t, scan)
 5:     end for
 6:
 7:     TS-Scan(delete_buffer)
 8:
 9:     wait for ACK from all other threads
10:
11:     for each pointer p in delete_buffer do
12:         if delete_buffer[p].marked == false then
13:             free(p)
14:         end if
15:     end for
16: end function
17:
18: function TS-SCAN( delete_buffer )
19:     for each word chunk in thread's stack and registers do
20:         index = binary-search(delete_buffer, chunk)
21:         if index ≠ -1 then
22:             delete_buffer[index].marked = true
23:         end if
24:     end for
25:     signal(reclaimer, ACK)
26: end function
```

---

tails, for simplicity of presentation. We provide these details below.

Signaling. We use POSIX Signals [45] for inter-thread communication. A thread that receives a signal is interrupted by the OS and begins running the signal handler immediately [27]. If another signal arrives during the execution of ThreadScan's signal handler, then a second handler will be pushed onto the thread's stack.

If the thread is blocked in a system call, the signal interrupts the system call and executes the signal handler. In this case, a system call implicitly restarts or returns the *EINTR* error code to the caller, that passes the restart responsibility to the programmer [3].

In general, if a thread is stalled due to any reason (for example, a context-switch), the OS resumes the thread immediately, and invokes the signal handler on the resume. Notice that this behavior is a standard OS feature that is used to kill or terminate threads that are stalled or stuck, and the idea of ThreadScan is to use this feature to ensure a prompt response from all of the participating threads.

Progress. The ThreadScan library uses the OS signaling system to scan the stacks. As a result, the only way to introduce delays into ThreadScan is by delaying the OS signals. This means that the progress guarantees of ThreadScan depend on the specific progress guarantees of the OS implementation. In modern systems, such as Linux, the system scheduler has a fair execution policy that is guaranteed not to starve threads, and therefore, in such systems the ThreadScan has a non-blocking progress guarantee.

Stack Boundaries. Our current implementation hooks the pthread's library *pthread_create* function call to detect the boundaries of thread stacks. In most practical cases, using this method is enough to identify the stacks, however, sometimes the stacks may have a more complex structure,

---

[3]A system call that returns EINTR documents this behavior and requires the programmer to handle these case

like the "Cactus" stacks in the Cilk programming language runtime [32]. Providing support for more complex stack structures is an interesting topic for future work.

Reclamation. For simplicity, our presentation assumed a single shared buffer to which pointers to reclaimed nodes are added. We implement a more complex, distributed version of this buffer to avoid false sharing on the buffer and contention on the index. Specifically, each thread has its own local buffer to which it adds pointers. When an individual buffer becomes full, that thread becomes the reclaimer and aggregates the pointers from all of the threads' buffers into a master buffer that is used for scanning. Individual buffers are circular arrays that are guaranteed to be single-reader, single-writer, so concurrent accesses are simple and inexpensive.

Further, we ensure that there is always at most a single active reclaimer in the system via a lock. In general, large delete buffer sizes ensure that this lock is not contended. Also, the above buffer construction has the consequence that a thread waiting to become a reclaimer will probably discover that its buffer has been drained into the master buffer, and that it can go back to work.

Pointer Operations. We assume that the underlying code does not employ pointer obfuscation. The scanning process masks off the low-order bits of memory it reads on a stack chunk, but if the pointer is obfuscated in some other way, for instance by XOR-ing, or if it is not word-aligned, the reference will not be detected by TS-Scan. We also assume that arbitrary memory chunks can not be interpreted as addresses to existing nodes in the delete buffer. While breaking this assumption does not affect the correctness of our protocol, it could prevent the reclamation of the target nodes. We consider this phenomenon unlikely.

4.3   ThreadScan Extension

Our ThreadScan algorithm, as described in Section 4, is able to detect private references that reside inside the stacks and registers of threads. However, a programmer may decide to pre-allocate a heap block and use this block to store private references on the heap (which violates code Assumption 1). For such specific scenarios, we extend the API of ThreadScan in a way that allows it to detect private references that reside on the heap.

Our extension is based on a simple observation: a heap block that holds private references is private to each thread. As a result, our extension introduces two additional methods:

1. $TS\_add\_heap\_block(start\_addr, len)$

2. $TS\_remove\_heap\_block(start\_addr, len)$

The add method allows the programmer to declare a pre-allocated heap block that the thread uses to hold private references, so that the ThreadScan signal handler can add those heap blocks to the scan process of this thread (in addition to the scan of the stack and registers). The remove method unregisters the region.

This extension makes the ThreadScan semi-automatic: the programmer must declare the per-thread heap blocks that may hold private references. However, ThreadScan still handles the scanning and reclamation process automatically.

5.   CORRECTNESS PROPERTIES

5.1   Shared Memory Model

We assume a group of n threads which cooperate to implement a general abstraction O, providing a set of methods M. The implementation of each method $m \in M$ consists of a sequence of *steps*.

The interleaving of the threads' steps is decided by an abstraction called the *scheduler*. A scheduler is *fair* if it guarantees that each thread is scheduled to perform an infinite number of shared-memory steps. This implies a finite bound on the number of steps between the invocation of an operation by a thread and its application to shared memory.

5.2   Safety Properties

In the following, we prove correctness for the basic version of ThreadScan. These properties can be easily generalized for the extended variant presented in Section 4.3.

We first prove that, if all nodes in the delete buffer are in *removed* state, then ThreadScan will not reclaim any node that is not *retired*. Thus, reclamation cannot lead to any memory access violation.

LEMMA 1. *Under Assumption 1, any node* reclaimed *by* ThreadScan *has already been* retired.

PROOF. Assume for the sake of contradiction that there exists a memory node d reclaimed by the algorithm at time τ, but is not retired at this time. In particular, the node can be reached by a thread as part of the execution after τ.

We now take cases on the location of references to node d at time τ. Since the node was reclaimed, it must have been part of the delete buffer, and therefore it must have been removed (unreachable) after the beginning of the current reclamation phase, which we denote by t_0. Therefore, by Assumption 1.1, we have that 1) no such reference could have been present in the heap after time t_0 and that 2) no such reference can be accessed by more than one thread after time t_0.

It therefore follows that the reference must have been present in the stack or registers of some thread after t_0. Further, the reference is not *shared*, therefore it cannot travel between thread stacks. Hence, in order to be able to access the node after time τ, the thread must possess a reference to this node in its stack or registers throughout the time interval $[t_0, \tau]$. However, the algorithm ensures that the thread will scan its stack and registers during this time interval, and we are guaranteed to identify the reference by Assumption 1.3. This contradicts the assumption that the node d is reclaimed by the algorithm, completing the proof.   □

5.3   Liveness Properties

Termination. We focus on the termination properties of operations under ThreadScan. First notice that, under Assumption 1.2, ThreadScan does not influence the termination of method calls that do not invoke free. This follows since ThreadScan may only add a bounded number of steps to any method invocation that does not invoke free.

LEMMA 2. *Under Assumption 1.2, any method implementation m that does not call* free *preserves its progress properties under* ThreadScan.

PROOF. Consider a method m consisting of a finite number of shared-memory steps, executing in the context of

ThreadScan. Since m does not call free, its corresponding thread may not initiate a reclamation phase. However, each time it receives a reclamation request, the thread must perform a bounded number of additional steps, scanning its stack and registers. Let B be a bound on this number of extra steps. Moreover, by Assumption 1.2 there exists a finite bound k on the number of times that the method invocation may receive scan requests. Therefore, ThreadScan adds a total of at most kB steps to any method invocation. Further, by the structure of the algorithm, if m does not call free, no such step is a busy-wait. This implies that the method preserves its progress properties, as claimed. □

We then prove termination for the free implementation. We assume a *fair* scheduler, and show that TS-Collect completes within a finite number of steps. We note that this property holds irrespective of the structure (lock-free, lock-based) of the original data structure.

LEMMA 3. *Under Assumption 1.2 and any fair scheduler, the* TS-Collect *call completes within a finite number of steps, irrespective of the progress conditions of the original implementation.*

PROOF. Recall that we assume that a single reclaimer exists at any one time. Assume such a reclaimer p, calling TS-Collect. Thread p has a finite number of steps to perform before busy-waiting for the replies to its reclamation signal. Since the scheduler is fair, these steps will be completed within finite time. Further, under Assumption 1.2, each non-reclaiming thread involved in the invocation of TS-Collect has a bounded number of steps B to perform before sending the acknowledgment to the reclaimer. Since the scheduler is fair, all threads will complete these steps within a finite number of steps, and send back an acknowledgment. Once these signals are received by the reclaimer, it returns within a finite additional number of steps. This implies that the reclaimer returns within a finite number of scheduled steps. □

Eventual Reclamation. Finally, we prove the following claim about the set of nodes freed in a reclamation phase. The proof follows from the fact that stack scans do not generate false positives. Hence, any node in the delete buffer which is not referenced by any thread will not match the result of a scan, and will hence be reclaimed.

LEMMA 4. *Under Assumption 1.3, for any reclamation phase, all nodes which can not be accessed through references in stacks or registers at the beginning of the phase will be retired by* ThreadScan.

6. EXPERIMENTAL RESULTS

Experimental Setup. Tests were performed on an 80-way Intel Xeon 2.4 GHz processor with 40-cores, where each core can multiplex 2 hardware threads. The ThreadScan library was configured to store up to 1024 pointers per thread. Threads tended to have relatively full buffers, so the total number of pointers any reclaimer worked with was roughly 1,000 times the number of threads in the process. For all tests, we used the highly scalable TCMalloc [16] allocator.

Data Structures. Tests were run on three data structures:

1. **Lock-free Linked List:** Code was adapted for C from the Java provided in [25]. Each node was padded to 172 bytes to avoid false sharing.

2. **Lock-free Hash Table:** The Synchrobench suite [18] provided a hash table that used its own lock-free linked list for its buckets. This implementation was replaced with the [25] list.

3. **Lock-based Skip List:** StackTrack [2] provided an implementation with 104 byte nodes (representing the maximum size due to height). No padding was added to these nodes.

Techniques. We tested the data structures using the following reclamation techniques.

1. **Leaky:** The original memory leaking data-structure implementation without any memory reclamation.

2. **Hazard Pointers:** As introduced by Michael et al. [37]. The programmer manually declares and constantly updates the hazard pointer tracking information for shared memory accesses, and the reclaiming thread scans this information to determine nodes that can be deallocated. This was simulated in the linked list and hash table by introducing barriers after each read while advancing along the list. Actual hazard pointers were already provided in the skip list implementation [2].

3. **Epoch:** As introduced by Harris et al. [20] and McKenney et al. [36]. The programmer delimits the epoch-start and epoch-end points in the code, and the reclaimer waits for the epoch to pass, at which point it is safe to deallocate nodes. This was simulated in all three data structures by adding thread-specific counters to be updated before and after each operation. A thread that had removed 1024 nodes would read all epoch counters before continuing.

4. **Slow Epoch:** Represents the sensitivity of Epoch to application code that has thread delays: simulated by a 40ms busy-wait by the affected thread during its cleanup phase.

5. **ThreadScan:** Our new fully automatic technique as described in Section 4.

Methodology. Each data point in the graphs represents the average number of operations over five executions of 10 seconds. The update ratio was set at 20%, so about 10% of all operations were node removals.

Linked lists were 1024 nodes long, and the range of values was 2048. Hash tables contained 131,072 nodes with a range of 262,144. The expected bucket size was 32 nodes. Skip lists contained 128,000 nodes with a range of values of 256,000.

Results. Figure 3 shows the results for the three data structures under the various memory reclamation schemes. Up to the full 80 hardware threads, ThreadScan and Epoch scale along with the Leaky implementation. ThreadScan amortizes the cost of its reclamation phase over the operations being performed by the user application. Even with 10% removals, the cost of signaling and reclaiming nodes is distributed over the cheap operations performed on the hash table. Epoch likewise scales because the burden it imposes

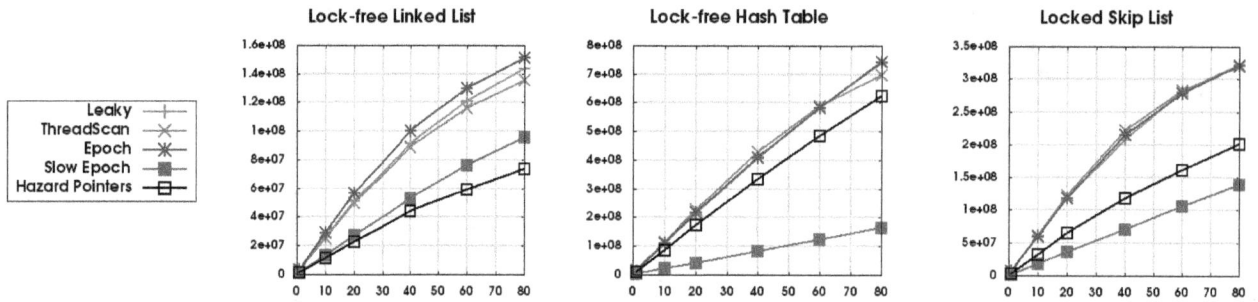

Figure 3: Throughput results for the lock-free linked list, lock-free hash table, and locked skip list: X-axis shows the number of threads, and Y-axis the total number of completed operations.

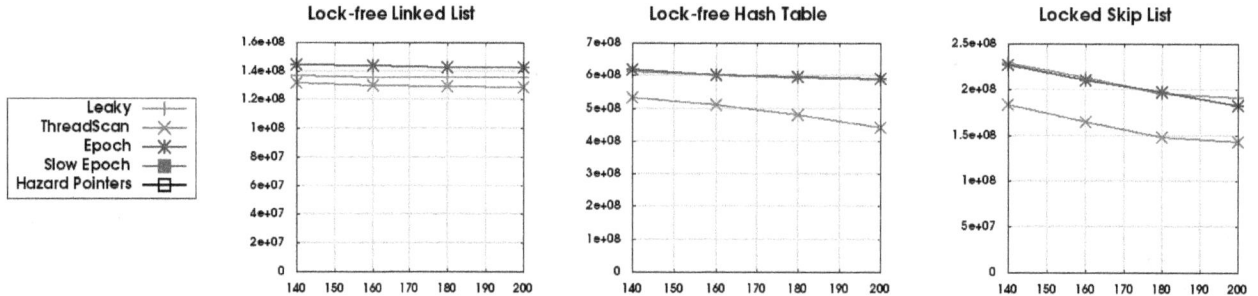

Figure 4: Throughput results for the oversubscribed system.

on the operations is low: two writes per method, except during reclamation where it must read every thread's epoch counter. But when all threads are completing their operations in a timely way, this overhead is low.

Slow Epoch, with an errant thread, shows significant burden because a thread that wants to free its pointers cannot do so until the errant thread updates its epoch counter. The reclaiming thread must wait until it has seen a change in the epoch counter of every thread that was in the midst of an operation. In this case, the thread that does not complete its operation for whatever reason holds up the reclaiming thread.

Hazard pointers scale well in the lock-free hash table because bucket traversals are short and so there are few memory barriers per operation. More overhead is visible in the other two data structures, however, as the number of hazard pointer updates increases. In the list and skip list data structures, the expected number of steps in a traversal is $O(n)$ and $O(\log(n))$, respectively. Since each step requires a barrier, even in a non-mutating operation, the overhead becomes significant.

The results of oversubscription tests, run on the same machine, are presented in Figure 4. Slow Epoch and Hazard Pointers were not included in the oversubscription experiment since they were shown not to scale well in normal circumstances. Oversubscription does not help their performance.

ThreadScan begins to show overhead versus the leaky implementation because not all threads can run simultaneously and the reclaimer must wait for all of them to complete. Additionally, overheads are higher because more signals are sent and the list of pointers to collect is larger, leading to more cache misses. Increasing the size of the delete buffer,

and thereby reducing the frequency of reclamation iterations, is a useful way of amortizing the cost of signals and of waiting. However, it also increases the size of the list of pointers. The limitations of amortizing reclamation are clearly correlated with the costs of operations on the various data structures: The linked list overhead is negligible, the skip list is about 25% at 200 threads.

ThreadScan was tuned for the hash table to improve performance. The ThreadScan line presented in the hash table graph shows the results of increasing the length of the per-thread delete buffer length to 4096. Although this led to an improvement in performance, 25% overhead at 200 threads, comparable to the skip list, the overhead is still significant. Solving the oversubscription problem in a general way is an important avenue of future work.

7. CONCLUSION AND FUTURE WORK

Discussion. The memory reclamation problem has limited the adoption of high-performance non-blocking data structures in non-garbage-collected languages like C and C++. Since a thread may access a node without notifying other threads, a thread that wants to free the node must be defensive when reclaiming memory. Existing techniques for detection typically complicate the algorithm and/or render it inefficient.

In this paper, we have presented ThreadScan, an efficient method for detecting otherwise invisible reads. The user simply hands nodes to ThreadScan, which buffers them until there are enough to start a reclamation phase. It then leverages OS signals to force all threads to make their invisible reads visible. Because a thread need only make its reads visible during a scan, that cost can be amortized over the cost of freeing the pointers being tracked.

Our empirical results show that ThreadScan matches or outperforms the performance of previous memory reclamation techniques, taking advantage of the fact that its code runs as part of signal handlers, and is thus isolated from application code. Besides good performance, ThreadScan has the advantage of being completely automatic, as the programmer simply needs to link its data structure to use the TC-Collect calls implemented by ThreadScan.

We believe ThreadScan can be a useful general tool for the design and prototyping of non-blocking concurrent data structures. It makes implementation of these structures practical in C and C++ because of the low overhead and because it encapsulates all of the complexity of tracking down references.

Available at: https://github.com/Willtor/ThreadScan

Future Work. The main usability limitation of ThreadScan is in responsiveness of the reclaimer. The reclaiming thread must wait on the other threads and perform all the free calls, itself. The number of these calls is expected to scale linearly with the number of threads on the system, and therefore the reclaimer may become unresponsive at large thread counts.

In future work, we plan to investigate whether the latter problem may be solved by sharing the reclamation overhead, requiring scanning threads to call free for some subset of retired nodes in the subsequent TS-Scan call. TS-Scan would then check to see whether there are any pending nodes to free (from a previous iteration) after it has scanned its stack for the new set of nodes. This creates a trade-off between the latency improvement for the reclaiming thread versus the added overhead for the other operations. Another direction of future work is to apply ThreadScan to large legacy systems, such as concurrent databases or the kernel reference counted data-structures (for example, the VMA), to test both its interface and its potential to improve performance in a complex practical system.

8. ACKNOWLEDGEMENTS

Support is gratefully acknowledged from the National Science Foundation under grants CCF-1217921, CCF-1301926, and IIS-1447786, the Department of Energy under grant ER26116/DE-SC0008923, and the Oracle corporation. In particular, we would like to thank Dave Dice, Alex Kogan, and Mark Moir from the Oracle Scalable Synchronization Research Group for very useful feedback on earlier drafts of this paper.

9. REFERENCES

[1] Yehuda Afek, Haim Kaplan, Boris Korenfeld, Adam Morrison, and Robert E. Tarjan. Cbtree: A practical concurrent self-adjusting search tree. In *Proceedings of the 26th International Conference on Distributed Computing*, DISC'12, pages 1–15, Berlin, Heidelberg, 2012. Springer-Verlag.

[2] Dan Alistarh, Patrick Eugster, Maurice Herlihy, Alexander Matveev, and Nir Shavit. Stacktrack: An automated transactional approach to concurrent memory reclamation. In *Proceedings of the Ninth European Conference on Computer Systems*, EuroSys '14, pages 25:1–25:14, New York, NY, USA, 2014. ACM.

[3] Dan Alistarh, Justin Kopinsky, Jerry Li, and Nir Shavit. The spraylist: A scalable relaxed priority queue. In *20th ACM SIGPLAN Symposium on Principles and Practice of Parallel Programming*, PPoPP 2015, San Francisco, CA, USA, 2015. ACM.

[4] Hillel Avni, Nir Shavit, and Adi Suissa. Leaplist: Lessons learned in designing tm-supported range queries. In *Proceedings of the 2013 ACM Symposium on Principles of Distributed Computing*, PODC '13, pages 299–308, New York, NY, USA, 2013. ACM.

[5] Stephen M. Blackburn and Kathryn S. McKinley. Ulterior reference counting: Fast garbage collection without a long wait. In *Proceedings of the 18th Annual ACM SIGPLAN Conference on Object-oriented Programing, Systems, Languages, and Applications*, OOPSLA '03, pages 344–358, New York, NY, USA, 2003. ACM.

[6] Hans-Juergen Boehm. Space efficient conservative garbage collection. In *Proceedings of the ACM SIGPLAN 1993 Conference on Programming Language Design and Implementation*, PLDI '93, pages 197–206, New York, NY, USA, 1993. ACM.

[7] Anastasia Braginsky, Alex Kogan, and Erez Petrank. Drop the anchor: lightweight memory management for non-blocking data structures. In *Proceedings of the 25th ACM symposium on Parallelism in algorithms and architectures*, SPAA '13, pages 33–42, New York, NY, USA, 2013. ACM.

[8] Perry Cheng and Guy E. Blelloch. A parallel, real-time garbage collector. In *Proceedings of the ACM SIGPLAN 2001 Conference on Programming Language Design and Implementation*, PLDI '01, pages 125–136, New York, NY, USA, 2001. ACM.

[9] Austin T. Clements, M. Frans Kaashoek, and Nickolai Zeldovich. Scalable address spaces using rcu balanced trees. *SIGPLAN Not.*, 47(4):199–210, March 2012.

[10] David Detlefs, Paul A. Martin, Mark Moir, and Guy L. Steele Jr. Lock-free reference counting. *Distributed Computing*, 15(4):255–271, 2002.

[11] David L. Detlefs, Paul A. Martin, Mark Moir, and Guy L. Steele, Jr. Lock-free reference counting. In *Proceedings of the twentieth annual ACM symposium on Principles of distributed computing*, PODC '01, pages 190–199, New York, NY, USA, 2001. ACM. http://doi.acm.org/10.1145/383962.384016.

[12] Aleksandar Dragojevic, Maurice Herlihy, Yossi Lev, and Mark Moir. On the power of hardware transactional memory to simplify memory management. In *Proceedings of the 30th Annual ACM Symposium on Principles of Distributed Computing (PODC)*, pages 99–108, 2011.

[13] Mikhail Fomitchev and Eric Ruppert. Lock-free linked lists and skip lists. In *Proceedings of the 23rd annual ACM symposium on Principles of Distributed Computing (PODC' 04)*, pages 50–59, New York, NY, USA, 2004. ACM Press. http://doi.acm.org/10.1145/1011767.1011776.

[14] Keir Fraser. Practical lock-freedom. Technical Report UCAM-CL-TR-579, University of Cambridge, Computer Laboratory, February 2004.

[15] Keir Fraser and Timothy L. Harris. Concurrent programming without locks. *ACM Trans. Comput. Syst.*, 25(2), 2007.

[16] Sanjay Ghemawat and Paul Menage. Tcmalloc, Retrieved 2015. Available at http://googperftools.sourceforge.net/doc/tcmalloc.html.

[17] Anders Gidenstam, Marina Papatriantafilou, Håkan Sundell, and Philippas Tsigas. Efficient and reliable lock-free memory reclamation based on reference counting. *IEEE Trans. Parallel Distrib. Syst.*, 20(8):1173–1187, 2009.

[18] V. Gramoli. More than you ever wanted to know about synchronization: Synchrobench. In *Proceedings of the 20th Annual ACM SIGPLAN Symposium on Principles and Practice of Parallel Programming (PPoPP)*, 2015.

[19] Sabine Hanke. The performance of concurrent red-black tree algorithms. In Jeffrey Vitter and Christos Zaroliagis, editors, *Algorithm Engineering*, volume 1668 of *Lecture Notes in Computer Science*, pages 286–300. Springer Berlin / Heidelberg, 1999. http://citeseer.ist.psu.edu/viewdoc/summary?doi=10.1.1.25.6504.

[20] Tim L. Harris. A pragmatic implementation of non-blocking linked-lists. In *Proceedings of the International Conference on Distributed Computing (DISC)*, pages 300–314, 2001.

[21] Thomas E. Hart, Paul E. McKenney, Angela Demke Brown, and Jonathan Walpole. Performance of memory reclamation for lockless synchronization. *J. Parallel Distrib. Comput.*, 67(12):1270–1285, 2007.

[22] Steve Heller, Maurice Herlihy, Victor Luchangco, Mark Moir, William N. Scherer III, and Nir Shavit. A lazy concurrent list-based set algorithm. In James H. Anderson, Giuseppe Prencipe, and Roger Wattenhofer, editors, *Proceedings of the 9th International Conference on Principles of Distributed Systems (OPODIS 2005), Revised Selected Papers*, volume 3974 of *Lecture Notes in Computer Science*, pages 3–16. Springer, 2006. http://dx.doi.org/10.1007/11795490_3.

[23] Maurice Herlihy, Yossi Lev, Victor Luchangco, and Nir Shavit. A simple optimistic skiplist algorithm. In *Proceedings of the 14th international conference on Structural information and communication complexity*, SIROCCO'07, pages 124–138, Berlin, Heidelberg, 2007. Springer-Verlag. http://dl.acm.org/citation.cfm?id=1760631.1760646.

[24] Maurice Herlihy, Victor Luchangco, Paul Martin, and Mark Moir. Nonblocking memory management support for dynamic-sized data structures. *ACM Trans. Comput. Syst.*, 23(2):146–196, May 2005.

[25] Maurice Herlihy and Nir Shavit. *The Art of Multiprocessor Programming*. Morgan Kaufmann Publishers Inc., San Francisco, CA, USA, 2008.

[26] Maurice Herlihy, Nir Shavit, and Moran Tzafrir. Hopscotch hashing. In *Proceedings of the 22nd international symposium on Distributed Computing*, DISC '08, pages 350–364, Berlin, Heidelberg, 2008. Springer-Verlag. http://dl.acm.org/citation.cfm?id=1432316.

[27] Michael Kerrisk. *The Linux Programming Interface*. No Starch Press, Inc., San Francisco, CA 94103, 2010.

[28] Gabriel Kliot, Erez Petrank, and Bjarne Steensgaard. A lock-free, concurrent, and incremental stack scanning mechanism for garbage collectors. *SIGOPS Oper. Syst. Rev.*, 43(3):3–13, July 2009.

[29] Doug Lea. Java concurrency package, 2005. Available at http://docs.oracle.com/javase/6/docs/api/java/util/concurre

[30] Doug Lea, 2007. http://g.oswego.edu/dl/jsr166/dist/docs/java/util/concurrent/ConcurrentHashMap.html.

[31] Doug Lea, 2007. http://java.sun.com/javase/6/docs/api/java/util/concurrent/ConcurrentSkipListMap.html.

[32] I-Ting Angelina Lee, Silas Boyd-Wickizer, Zhiyi Huang, and Charles E. Leiserson. Using memory mapping to support cactus stacks in work-stealing runtime systems. In Valentina Salapura, Michael Gschwind, and Jens Knoop, editors, *19th International Conference on Parallel Architecture and Compilation Techniques (PACT 2010), Vienna, Austria, September 11-15, 2010*, pages 411–420. ACM, 2010.

[33] William M. Leiserson. Threadscan git repository, 2015. Available at https://github.com/Willtor/ThreadScan.

[34] Yossi Levanoni and Erez Petrank. An on-the-fly reference-counting garbage collector for java. *ACM Trans. Program. Lang. Syst.*, 28(1):1–69, January 2006.

[35] Robert Love. *Linux System Programming, 2nd Edition*. O'Reilly Media, Sebastopol, CA 95472, 2013.

[36] P. E. McKenney, J. Appavoo, A. Kleen, O. Krieger, R. Russell, D. Sarma, , and M. Soni. Read-copy update. In *In Proc. of the Ottawa Linux Symposium*, page 338?367, 2001.

[37] Maged M. Michael. Hazard pointers: Safe memory reclamation for lock-free objects. *IEEE Trans. Parallel Distrib. Syst.*, 15(6):491–504, 2004.

[38] Mark Moir and Nir Shavit. Concurrent data structures. *Handbook of Data Structures and Applications*, pages 47–14, 2007.

[39] Objective-C, 2014. http://en.wikipedia.org/wiki/Automatic_Reference_Counting.

[40] Mark Russinovich and David A. Solomon. *Windows Internals: Including Windows Server 2008 and Windows Vista, Fifth Edition*. Microsoft Press, 5th edition, 2009.

[41] Anthony Savidis. The implementation of generic smart pointers for advanced defensive programming. *Softw., Pract. Exper.*, 34(10):977–1009, 2004.

[42] Ori Shalev and Nir Shavit. Split-ordered lists: Lock-free extensible hash tables. *J. ACM*, 53:379–405, May 2006. http://doi.acm.org/10.1145/1147954.1147958.

[43] Nir Shavit and Itay Lotan. Skiplist-based concurrent priority queues. In *Parallel and Distributed Processing Symposium, 2000. IPDPS 2000. Proceedings. 14th International*, pages 263–268. IEEE, 2000.

[44] John D. Valois. Lock-free linked lists using compare-and-swap. In *Proceedings of the 14th Annual ACM Symposium on Principles of Distributed Computing (PODC)*, pages 214–222, 1995.

[45] WIKI. http://en.wikipedia.org/wiki/Unix_signal.

Speed Scaling in the Non-clairvoyant Model

[Extended Abstract]

Yossi Azar
Tel Aviv University
Tel Aviv, Israel
azar@tau.ac.il

Nikhil R. Devanur
Microsoft Research
Redmond, WA
nikdev@microsoft.com

Zhiyi Huang
University of Hong Kong
Hong Kong
zhiyi@cs.hku.hk

Debmalya Panigrahi
Duke University
Durham, NC
debmalya@cs.duke.edu

ABSTRACT

In recent years, there has been a growing interest in speed scaling algorithms, where a set of jobs need to be scheduled on a machine with variable speed so as to optimize the flow-times of the jobs and the energy consumed by the machine. A series of results have culminated in constant-competitive algorithms for this problem in the clairvoyant model, i.e., when job parameters are revealed on releasing a job (Bansal, Pruhs, and Stein, SODA 2007; Bansal, Chan, and Pruhs, SODA 2009). Our main contribution in this paper is the first constant-competitive speed scaling algorithm in the non-clairvoyant model, which is typically used in the scheduling literature to model practical settings where job volume is revealed only after the job has been completely processed. Unlike in the clairvoyant model, the speed scaling problem in the non-clairvoyant model is non-trivial *even for a single job*. Our non-clairvoyant algorithm is defined by using the existing clairvoyant algorithm in a novel inductive way, which then leads to an inductive analytical tool that may be of independent interest for other online optimization problems. We also give additional algorithmic results and lower bounds for speed scaling on multiple identical parallel machines.

Categories and Subject Descriptors

F.2.2 [**Nonnumerical Algorithms and Problems**]: [Sequencing and scheduling]

General Terms

Theory

Keywords

Scheduling; Energy efficiency; Online algorithms

1. INTRODUCTION

Scheduling jobs released over time on one or more machines is one of the most fundamental optimization problems. A standard objective has been to minimize the average *response time* for a given set of jobs, while the devices ran at their fastest possible speed. (The technical term used for response time is *flow-time*, which for a job is the duration of time between its release and completion.) However, over the years, the *energy* consumed by the processors has become an important consideration. It was observed by Barroso [1] that in data centers, the raw performance and the performance per price of a server have been steadily growing but the performance per power consumption has remained flat. This increasing energy consumption coupled with rising prices of energy has made the cost of energy an important consideration in the design of computing infrastructure such as data centers.

One of the main algorithmic approaches to energy management is via *dynamic speed scaling*,[1] where a processor can be run at different speeds. Higher speeds finish jobs faster (improving response time) but consume more energy. The instantaneous power (which is the rate of energy consumed) is a given function of the speed, typically the cube of the speed, or more generally, speed$^\alpha$ for some fixed constant $\alpha \geq 2$. The typical objective used in the literature (introduced by Albers and Fujiwara [2]) is to minimize a linear combination of energy and weighted flow-time.[2] Jobs are released over time, each job comes with a volume and a weight, and the algorithm does not know which jobs will be released in the future. The algorithmic question posed by this problem has two components: which job to schedule next, and what speed to run the machine at. We call this the speed scaling problem. After a considerable amount of research [2, 5, 6, 7, 8, 9], it is now known that the answer to the first question is to schedule the job with the highest density first (HDF, density = weight/volume) and the answer to the second question is to pick a speed so that the power consumption equals the remaining weight of the jobs.

However, most of the results for this problem are in the *clairvoyant* setting where the algorithm knows the volume of a job when it is released. A more difficult, but in many cases more realistic, problem is one where the volume is known only when the job is

---

[1]Other approaches have been considered, for example a power down model where a machine transitions to a low power state when idle, etc.

[2]Other problems such as minimizing energy while finishing jobs within given deadlines [3] and minimizing flow-time with a hard energy budget [4] have also been considered.

completed — this is called the *non-clairvoyant* setting (introduced by Motwani, Phillips, and Torng [10] in classical scheduling). Our main contribution in this paper is to consider the speed scaling problem in the non-clairvoyant setting.

A particular application that motivated this study comes from cloud computing. Typically, a customer pays at a rate $(\lambda - \rho t_{\text{delay}})$ for each unit volume of a submitted job to the cloud service provider, where λ and ρ are predetermined payment and penalty rates for the job, and t_{delay} is the delay in processing the job, i.e., the difference between the actual and expected duration of the job. Note that the only term in the total payment for a job that is affected by the scheduling algorithm is $\rho F_{int}[j]V[j]$, where $F_{int}[j]$ is the flow-time of the job and $V[j]$ is volume. This can be interpreted as a *weighted flowtime*, where the weight is $\rho V[j]$. (Since the penalty rate ρ = weight/volume, we call it the *density*.) Since $V[j]$ is unknown to the algorithm when a job is released, but ρ is known, this is the case of known density and unknown weight. We consider two scenarios: one where all jobs have the same density and a more general one where the density is job-dependent and revealed when a job is released.

1.1 Our Results

Before describing our results, let us formally define the notion of flow-time. The *integral* (weighted) flow-time of a job is the difference of its completion and release times multiplied by its weight. The integral flow-time of a processing schedule is the sum of the integral flow-times of the individual jobs in the schedule. In defining the *fractional* flow-time of a job, we imagine breaking up the job into infinitesimal pieces each of which suffers a different flow-time based on when it is completed. We consider both fractional flow-time plus energy, henceforth called *fractional objective*, and integral flow-time plus energy, henceforth called *integral objective*.

Our main results are the first constant-competitive algorithms for non-clairvoyant scheduling with known densities on a single machine. We consider any power function of the form $P(s) = s^\alpha$ and give deterministic algorithms. These results are also summarized in Table 1.

- In the case of *uniform job densities*, we present a $(3 + \frac{1}{\alpha-1})$-competitive algorithm for the integral objective and a $(2 + \frac{1}{\alpha-1})$-competitive deterministic algorithm for the fractional objective.

  Contrast this with a competitive ratio of $\frac{2\alpha^2}{\log\alpha}$ for the integral objective in the non-clairvoyant model with known *weights*, for uniform (unit) weight jobs by Chan *et al* [11]. The best known results for the *clairvoyant* model with uniform density achieve competitive ratios of 4 and 2 respectively for integral and fractional flow-time [5, 8].[3]

- We show an $O(1)$-competitive algorithm for the general problem with non-uniform densities for both the fractional and integral objectives. The constant depends exponentially on α.

  In the non-clairvoyant model with known weights, no results are known for arbitrary weights, except in the special case where all jobs are released at time 0, for which a $(2 - \frac{1}{\alpha})^2$ competitive algorithm is given by Lam *et al* [7]. The best known results for the clairvoyant model for arbitrary weighted flow-time achieve a competitive ratio of 2 for the fractional objective (due to Bansal, Chan, and Pruhs [8]) and

$O(\frac{\alpha}{\log\alpha})$ for the integral objective (due to Bansal, Pruhs, and Stein [5] and Bansal, Chan, and Pruhs [8]).[4]

We also consider the problem of scheduling jobs on identical parallel machines. In the literature, two models for dispatching jobs to machines have been considered depending on whether the algorithm is required to do *immediate dispatch*, i.e., a job has to be assigned to a machine immediately on release. In either model, once a job has started processing on a machine, it cannot be *migrated to* any other machine in the future.

- We give an $O(\alpha)$-competitive deterministic algorithm for both the integral and fractional objectives in the case of uniform densities without immediate dispatch.

  No results are known for multiple machines in the non-clairvoyant model with known weights, even for unit weight jobs. Our results almost match the best known competitive ratios for the clairvoyant model (with immediate dispatch), which are $O(\alpha)$ and $O(\alpha^2)$ respectively for the fractional and the integral objective obtained by Anand, Garg, and Kumar [12].[5]

- We give a superconstant lower bound on the competitive ratio of any deterministic algorithm even for fractional flow-time in the case of uniform densities with immediate dispatch.

An interesting open problem is whether our results can be extended to the case of non-uniform density and multiple machines. Both the algorithm for the uniform density case and the lower bound for the immediate dispatch case do not extend readily to this case.

1.2 Techniques and Intuition

The non-clairvoyant problem with known densities is non trivial even in the case of a *single* job. The optimal speed could vary greatly with the processing volume of the job; therefore, the algorithm has to continuously adapt as it learns more about the volume of the job. Furthermore, in the case of multiple jobs, the choice of the job to process affects the information that the algorithm obtains, which in turn affects the speed of the machine. The natural choice for information gathering turns out to be first-in first-out (FIFO) but the clairvoyant algorithms suggest the HDF rule; most of the difficulty we encounter is due to the conflict between the FIFO and the HDF rules. A more detailed discussion of this conflict and how we deal with it is presented later.

In order to give a glimpse of the techniques used, we describe the simplest scenario of a single job here. On any instance I, we denote the optimal objective by $\text{opt}(I)$, and that produced by our algorithm by $\text{algo}^{(NC)}(I)$. The online problem is a game between the adversary and the algorithm with strategies that are functions of (continuous) time, where at every moment of time the adversary must declare whether the job has been completely processed or not and the algorithm responds to this declaration by setting the current speed of the machine. (The instance ends when the adversary declares that the job is completely processed.) Therefore, the algorithm must *continuously* ensure that the objective value of its schedule, $\text{algo}^{(NC)}(I(t))$, is competitive against the optimal solution, $\text{opt}(I(t))$, for the *current instance* $I(t)$ defined by the volume

---

[3]Our competitive ratio of $3 + \frac{1}{\alpha-1}$ for the integral objective in the non-clairvoyant model improves the best-known clairvoyant competitive ratio of 4 in uniform density case for $\alpha > 2$.

[4]To achieve the $O(\frac{\alpha}{\log\alpha})$ competitive ratio, one needs to combine the 2-competitive algorithm of [8] for the fractional objective with the reduction from the integral objective to the fractional objective in [5]. See, e.g., [12] for the relevant discussions.

[5]This has been improved to $O(\frac{\alpha}{\log\alpha})$ for both objectives in [13]. Otherwise, we seem to be improving [12] for integral flow-time, although the results of [12] are in a much stronger model, with unrelated machines, arbitrary weights and immediate dispatch.

Table 1: Summary of Results

	Clairvoyant	Non-clairvoyant known weight	Non-clairvoyant know density (this paper)
Integral unit density/weight	4 (unit density) [5] 3 (unit weight) [8]	$\frac{2\alpha^2}{\ln \alpha}$ [11] (unit weight)	$3 + \frac{1}{\alpha-1}$ (unit density)
Fractional unit density/weight	2 [8]		$2 + \frac{1}{\alpha-1}$ (unit density)
Integral arbitrary density/weight	$O\left(\frac{\alpha}{\log \alpha}\right)$ [8, 5]	$\left(2 - \frac{1}{\alpha}\right)^2$ [7] (jobs at time 0)	$2^{O(\alpha)}$
Fractional arbitrary density/weight	2 [8]		$2^{O(\alpha)}$

processed till the current time t. This naturally leads to an inductive analytical framework where we bound the rate of change (w.r.t. time) of the algorithmic solution against the rate of change of the optimal solution. If we can show that for any time t,

$$\frac{d\mathsf{algo}^{(NC)}(I(t))}{dt} \leq \Gamma \cdot \frac{d\mathsf{opt}(I(t))}{dt}, \tag{1}$$

then we have a competitive ratio of Γ. Unfortunately we do not have a good handle on how the optimal solution evolves with time (in the general case). We therefore use a *surrogate* of the optimal solution, the solution produced by the clairvoyant algorithm $\mathsf{algo}^{(C)}$ defined by the speed setting rule instantaneous power = remaining weight, or $P = \overline{W}$, *on the current instance*. Since this algorithm is known to be 2-competitive [8], we show that for any time t,

$$\frac{d\mathsf{algo}^{(NC)}(I(t))}{dt} \leq \Gamma' \cdot \frac{d\mathsf{algo}^{(C)}(I(t))}{dt}, \tag{2}$$

and obtain a competitive ratio of $2\Gamma'$.

Let us now take a closer look at Eqn. (1). If $s(t)$ is the speed of the machine at time t, then the incremental volume of the job processed in the interval $[t, t + dt]$ is $s(t)dt$.[6] The corresponding change in the algorithmic objective, $d\mathsf{algo}^{(NC)}(I(t))$ comprises two parts: the additional energy $P(s(t))dt$ consumed in the interval $[t, t+dt]$, and the flow-time $t \cdot s(t)dt$ of the infinitesimal part of the job processed in this interval. The sum of these quantities must be bounded in terms of the increase in the clairvoyant objective.

In order to understand how the clairvoyant schedule changes in response to an increase in weight of the job, say from W to $W + dW$, consider the "power curve" of $\mathsf{algo}^{(C)}$, i.e., the power consumed by the algorithm as a function of time. Since the algorithm sets instantaneous speed s such that power = remaining weight, this curve also gives the remaining weight $\overline{W}$ as a function of time. The remaining weight and speed satisfy $s = -d\overline{W}/dt$; therefore the power curve is defined by the differential equation $P(-d\overline{W}/dt) = \overline{W}$. The "shape" of the power curve is independent of the actual weight of the job in the current instance; the weight simply determines the point on this curve where we start from. This means that in response to an increase in weight of the job, the starting point shifts higher and the entire power curve shifts to the right (as illustrated in Fig. 1a). Let dt' denote the increase in the total processing time of the job by $\mathsf{algo}^{(C)}$ due to the increase in weight; this is how much the power curve shifts to the right by. It is now easy to see that dt' and dW are related by $dW = P^{-1}(W)dt'$. The corresponding increase in energy is $W dt' = \frac{W dW}{P^{-1}(W)}$.

We design the non-clairvoyant algorithm such that it matches the clairvoyant algorithm in terms of the increase in energy. In other words, we want $P(s(t))dt = \frac{W dW}{P^{-1}(W)}$, i.e.,

$$P^{-1}(W)P(s(t))dt = W dW = W s(t)dt. \tag{3}$$

This is achieved by setting $P(s(t)) = W$, i.e., the instantaneous power in the non-clairvoyant algorithm equals the *processed weight* of the job. This ensures that the energy consumption of $\mathsf{algo}^{(NC)}$ and $\mathsf{algo}^{(C)}$ match exactly. It is interesting to note that the power curve of $\mathsf{algo}^{(NC)}$ is exactly identical to the power curve of $\mathsf{algo}^{(C)}$ in reverse (illustrated in Fig. 1b).

But what about the flow-times? The clairvoyant algorithm, by virtue of the $P = \overline{W}$ rule, has the property that its (fractional) flow-time and energy are exactly equal. However, this is not true for the non-clairvoyant algorithm. In fact, the flow-time of the $\mathsf{algo}^{(NC)}$ is given by the area *above* the power curve since remaining weight at any instant is the total weight minus the processed weight, the latter being equal to the instantaneous power. This is illustrated in Fig. 1b. Our crucial observation, which makes this analysis work for a single job, is that if the power function is $P = s^\alpha$, then the ratio of the two areas corresponding to flow-time and energy depends only on the value of α and is independent of the actual weight of the job.

1.3 Related Work

In the last few years, there has been tremendous interest in the design of energy efficient algorithms. In the dynamic speed scaling approach, the problem of minimizing the sum of energy and flow-time was introduced by Albers and Fujiwara [2]. They also proposed what has been the thematic approach for this problem (in the clairvoyant setting): to run at a speed such that the power consumed is equal to the number of remaining jobs. This was later generalized to weighted flow-time. This approach has been analyzed in many papers (e.g., [5, 6, 7]) and the best result for this problem is by Bansal et. al. [8] who gave a $2 + \epsilon$ competitive algorithm for fractional weighted flow-time and $3 + \epsilon$ competitive algorithm for unweighted integral flow-time. For unweighted integral flow-time, Andrew et al. [9] improved the competitive ratio to 2. For weighted integral flow-time the combined results of [8] and [5] imply an $O\left(\frac{\alpha}{\log \alpha}\right)$ competitive ratio. Note that the problem we consider is harder since the volumes are not known in advance. We relate the performance of our algorithm to the algorithm of Bansal et al. [8] for fractional weighted flow-time. For scheduling on multiple machines, Gupta et al. [14] gave an $O(\alpha^2)$-competitive algorithm for the related machines case[7] which was extended to unrelated machines (with the same competitive ratio) by Anand et al. [12].

---

[6]Since we are in the single job case, we assume w.l.o.g. (without loss of generality) that the density of the job is 1.

[7]and an $O(\alpha)$-competitive algorithm for the unweighted version

(a) The clairvoyant power curve

(b) The non-clairvoyant power curve

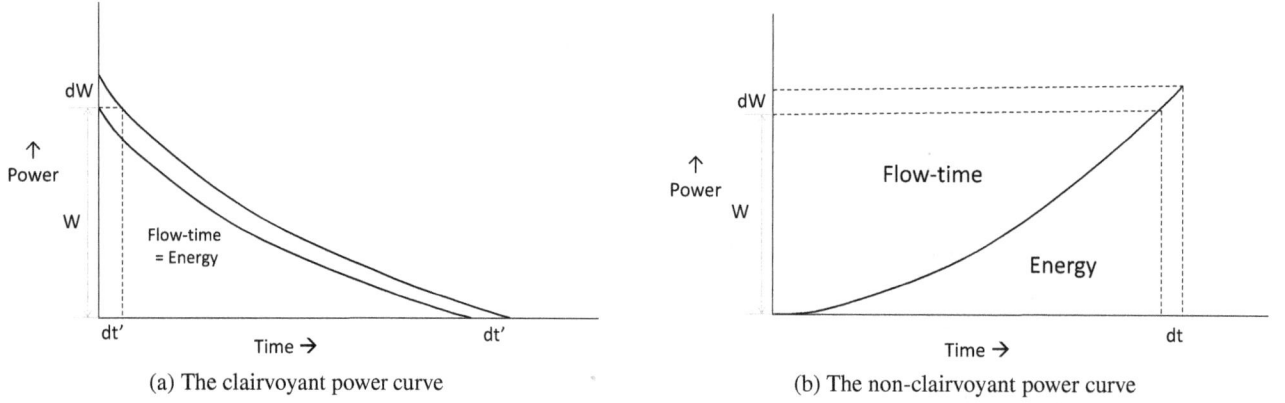

Figure 1: Analysis of a single job

The non-clairvoyant version where the weight is known at the time of release has also been considered [7, 11]. Lam *et al* [7] gave a $(2 - \frac{1}{\alpha})^2$-competitive algorithm for weighted flow-time plus energy when all jobs are released together, in the non-clairvoyant setting with known weights. Chan et al. [11] gave a $\frac{2\alpha^2}{\log \alpha}$-competitive algorithm for unweighted flow-time plus energy, once again for the non-clairvoyant setting with known (unit) weights. We consider the non-clairvoyant problem where the densities are known instead of the weights. As discussed, the two problems are very different. Moreover our most general result is for the weighted case of (integral/fractional) flow-time plus energy. Many other variants of these problems have been considered, such as when the maximum speed is bounded [6], minimizing energy for jobs with given deadlines (offline and online) [15, 3], and minimizing flow-time under an energy budget [4]. The issues tackled in these papers are quite different from the ones in this paper. The reader is referred to a survey by Albers [16] of the different approaches to energy management and corresponding results.

Roadmap. We establish preliminary notation and terminology that we use throughout the paper in section 2. In section 3, we present the algorithm for the uniform case and give its detailed analysis for both fractional and integral flow-times. Our analysis for the case of non-uniform densities on a single machine is substantially more complicated. In section 4, we give a description of the algorithm and an overview of the analytical tools that we use, but defer a detailed analysis to the full version of the paper. We give a black box extension for non-uniform densities from fractional to integral flow-times in section 5. In section 6, we give the algorithm for scheduling on identical parallel machines without immediate dispatch and the lower bound with immediate dispatch. We discuss open problems in Section 7.

2. PRELIMINARIES

The (offline) problem of scheduling to minimize flow-time plus energy is as follows. There is a single machine that can run at any non-negative speed. Running the machine at a higher speed processes jobs faster but consumes higher energy, as given by a *power function* $P : \mathbb{R}_+ \to \mathbb{R}_+$ that is monotonically non-decreasing and convex. $P(0) = 0$. There are jobs that need certain amounts of processing power. The problem is to process all the jobs in a way that minimizes the sum of the total energy consumed and the total weighted *flow-time* of all the jobs. We think of the power func-

tion as something pre-defined and not as part of an *instance* of the problem.

Input: A set of jobs J. For each job $j \in J$, its release time $r[j]$, volume $V[j]$ and density $\rho[j]$. Let the *weight* of job j be $W[j] = \rho[j] \cdot V[j]$.

Output: For each time $t \in [0, \infty)$ the job to be scheduled at time t, denoted by $j(t)$, and the speed of the machine, denoted by $s(t)$. We write just s when the dependence on t is clear from the context.

Constraints: A job can only be scheduled after its release time. For each job j, the total computational power allocated to the job must be equal to its volume, that is,

$$\int_{t \in [r[j], \infty) : j(t) = j} s(t)\, dt = V[j].$$

Objectives: The total energy consumed is the integral of the power function over time: $E = \int_{t=0}^{\infty} P(s(t))\, dt$. The integral flow-time of a given job j is

$$F_{int}[j] = W[j] \cdot (c[j] - r[j]),$$

where $c[j]$ denotes the completion time of j. The fractional flow-time of j is

$$
\begin{aligned}
F[j] &= \rho[j] \cdot \int_{t \in [r[j], \infty] : j(t) = j} (t - r[j]) s(t) dt \\
&= \rho[j] \cdot \int_{t = r[j]}^{\infty} \overline{V}(t)[j]\, dt,
\end{aligned}
$$

where $\overline{V}(t)[j]$ is the remaining volume of job j at time t, i.e.,

$$\overline{V}(t)[j] = V[j] - \int_{t' \in [r[j], t] : j(t') = j} s(t')\, dt'.$$

The problem is to minimize the sum of the flow-times of all jobs plus energy, which is (the integral objective) $G_{int} = E + \sum_j F_{int}[j]$, or (the fractional objective) $G_{frac} = E + \sum_j F[j]$.

The *online clairvoyant* problem is when the details of job j (density, volume) are given at time $r[j]$. The algorithm makes its decisions at any time without knowing which jobs will be released in the future. In the *online non-clairvoyant* problem, only the density $\rho[j]$ is given upon the release of job j at time $r[j]$. The volume $V[j]$ is not given. At any future point of time, the algorithm only knows if $\overline{V}(t)[j] > 0$ or not. If a job j is such that $\overline{V}(t)[j] > 0$,

136

we say the job is *active*, otherwise it is *inactive* (i.e., completed or not released yet).

We now describe a 2-competitive algorithm for the online clairvoyant problem. We call it **Algorithm** C. The job to be scheduled is determined by highest density first (HDF): schedule the active job with the highest density. The speed at time t is set based on the total remaining weight of active jobs at time t, denoted by $\overline{W}(t) = \sum_j \rho[j] \cdot \overline{V}(t)[j]$. The speed at time t is such that $P(s(t)) = \overline{W}(t)$. For Algorithm C, the total energy always equals the total flow-time. This is because the total flow time is

$$\sum_j F[j] = \int_{t=0}^{\infty} \sum_j \rho[j] \cdot \overline{V}(t)[j] \, dt = \int_{t=0}^{\infty} \overline{W}(t) \, dt.$$

THEOREM 1 ([8]). **Algorithm** C *is 2-competitive.*

We need the following properties of Algorithm C that follow from elementary calculus.

LEMMA 2. *Consider a run of* **Algorithm** C *on a single job of weight W and density ρ, which takes time t to complete. Then they satisfy the following relations:*

1. $\frac{dW}{dt} = \rho W^{\frac{1}{\alpha}}$,

2. $\rho(1 - \frac{1}{\alpha})t = W^{1 - \frac{1}{\alpha}}$, *and*

3. $\frac{W}{t} = (1 - \frac{1}{\alpha})\frac{dW}{dt}$.

3. UNIFORM DENSITY

In this section we consider the uniform density case, i.e., $\rho[j] = 1$ for all j. First, we give an algorithm for the online non-clairvoyant version of the problem for minimizing fractional flow-time plus energy on a single machine, which we call **Algorithm** NC. Assume w.l.o.g that the release times are all distinct. The job to be scheduled is determined according to the first-in first-out (FIFO) rule: schedule active job j, if one exists, with the smallest $r[j]$. The speed is set by considering a run of algorithm C on the same instance. Notice that by the time Algorithm NC schedules a job j, it knows the volumes/weights of all the jobs that are released earlier than $r[j]$. Thus one can simulate Algorithm C upto time $r[j]$. Let $\overline{W}^{(C)}(r[j]^-) = \lim_{t \to r[j]^-} \overline{W}^{(C)}(t)$ be the remaining weight of the active jobs in algorithm C at time $r[j]$ (not including the weight of job j). Further, let $\check{W}(t)[j]$ be the weight of job j processed by Algorithm NC till time t. At time t, Algorithm NC sets a speed s such that $P(s) = \overline{W}^{(C)}(r[j]^-) + \check{W}(t)[j]$.

We now restrict our attention to power functions of the form $P(s) = s^{\alpha}$ for some $\alpha > 1$. We obtain a competitive ratio for Algorithm NC by showing that it is almost as good as Algorithm C, which is surprising since the former is in the non-clairvoyant setting. In particular we show that the energy consumed in the two algorithms is the same (Lemma 3) and that the flow-times are within a factor of $1 - \frac{1}{\alpha}$ (Lemma 4).

LEMMA 3. *Algorithms* C *and* NC *consume the same amount of energy.*

LEMMA 4. *For all $\alpha > 1$ and power functions $P(s) = s^{\alpha}$, the total flow-time of algorithm* NC = *the total flow-time of Algorithm* C $/(1 - \frac{1}{\alpha})$.

The competitive ratio of Algorithm NC follows immediately from Lemmas 3 and 4 since we noted earlier that Algorithm C is 2-competitive (Theorem 1) and that the flow-time equals the total energy for Algorithm C. Therefore we get the following theorem.

THEOREM 5. *For all $\alpha > 1$ and power functions $P(s) = s^{\alpha}$, Algorithm* NC *is $1 + 1/(1 - \frac{1}{\alpha}) = 2 + \frac{1}{\alpha - 1}$-competitive for the objective of fractional flow-time plus energy.*

In the remainder of this section we give the proofs of Lemma 3. and Lemma 4, and the extension to the integral objective.

3.1 Energy Comparison (Proof of Lemma 3)

We show a very close structural similarity between the two algorithms, by showing that their "speed profiles" are essentially the same, upto a re-mapping of time (Lemma 6). This almost immediately implies Lemma 3. In fact, Lemmas 6 and 3 are actually true for all power functions, not just ones of the form s^{α}. The form of the power function is needed for flow-time comparison (Lemma 4).

LEMMA 6. *There exists a measure preserving 1-1 mapping $t \to t'$ from $\mathbb{R}_+$ to itself such that for all time t, the speed in Algorithm* NC *at time t is equal to the speed in Algorithm* C *at time t'.*

This lemma is proved by induction on time, with a stronger inductive hypothesis, which is stated in Lemma 7. First, we define the notion of an instantaneous instance. The stronger inductive hypothesis constructs a mapping between the two algorithms for every such instance and shows how to modify this mapping over time. The instance at time ∞ is just the original instance and hence we obtain a mapping for it as well.

For any time T, let the *clairvoyant instance at time T*, denoted by $I(T)$, be an instance where the job release times are as in the original instance, with weight of job j being $\check{W}(t)[j]$, which is the weight of job j processed by Algorithm NC till time T. This would be the instance if for algorithm NC, the instance ended at time T. (Clearly $I(T)$ depends on Algorithm NC).

For any two times $T_1 < T_2$, the run of Algorithm NC for instance $I(T_1)$ is a prefix of its run for instance $I(T_2)$. However, the run of Algorithm C is different for each instance. The proofs use how the run of Algorithm C evolves with these changing instances. We need to consider various quantities of Algorithm C that correspond to different instances. Therefore, we will denote a quantity w.r.t a particular instance by representing the time of that instance in the subscript. For example, the remaining weight at time t in instance $I(T)$ is denoted $\overline{W}_T(t)$.

We denote the speed of Algorithm C by $s^{(C)}$ and that of Algorithm NC by $s^{(NC)}$.

LEMMA 7. $\forall T \in \mathbb{R}_+$, *there exists a measure preserving $1 - 1$ mapping $t \to t'$ from $[0, T]$ to itself such that for all $t \in [0, T]$, the speed of algorithm* NC *at time t, which is $s^{(NC)}(t)$, equals the speed of algorithm* C *at time t' on instance $I(T)$, which is $s_T^{(C)}(t')$.*

PROOF. The proof is by induction on T (refer to Figure 2 for a pictorial depiction). The statement is vacuously true at time $T = 0$. Suppose the statement is true for T. We will argue that it is also true for $T + dT$, for an infinitesimal dT.

Clearly, as one goes from T to $T + dT$, the speed of algorithm NC only changes in the interval $[T, T + dT]$. Suppose Algorithm NC schedules job j during time $[T, T + dT]$. The speed $s^{(NC)}(T)$ is such that $P(s^{(NC)}(T)) = \overline{W}^{(C)}(r[j]^-) + \check{W}[j](T)$. Since dT is infinitesimal, we may assume that the speed does not change during this interval. The increase in the completed weight of job j during this interval is

$$dW = \check{W}[j](T + dT) - \check{W}[j](T) = s^{(NC)}(T)dT.$$

The change in Algorithm C due to the change in the instance from $I(T)$ to $I(T + dT)$ is more complicated. This change does

137

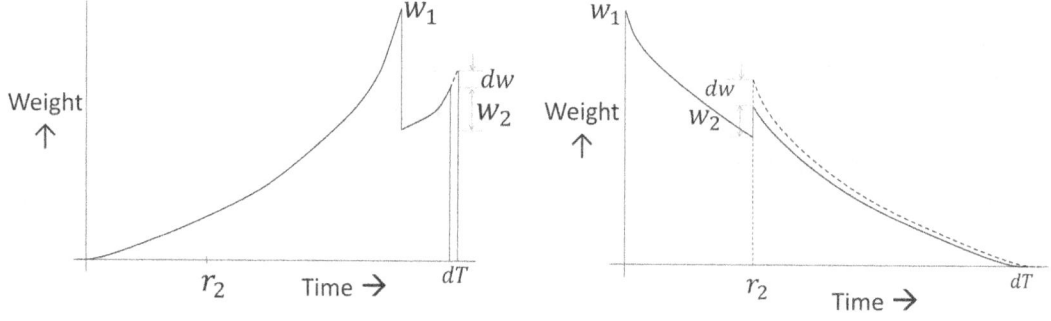

(a) The change in the non-clairvoyant algorithm upon processing an extra dw weight of job 2 which takes an extra time of dT. Job 2 is released at r_2 and has weight w_2 currently. Job 1 is released at time 0 and has weight w_1, all of which has been processed.

(b) The change in the run of the clairvoyant algorithm due to an extra dw weight of job 2. Here the speed of the algorithm changes all the way from time r_2 to the end. The extra time taken dT is however the same as in the non-clairvoyant case.

Figure 2: Analysis for the uniform density case

not affect Algorithm C before time $r[j]$. At $r[j]$, the remaining weight increases by dW, i.e.,

$$\overline{W}_{T+dT}^{(C)}(r[j]) = \overline{W}_{T}^{(C)}(r[j]) + dW,$$

which increases the speed of Algorithm C at time $r[j]$. Then as we move forward in time from $r[j]$ the remaining weight decreases.

$$\overline{W}_{T+dT}^{(C)}(r[j] + dT) = \overline{W}_{T+dT}^{(C)}(r[j]) - s^{(C)}(r[j])dT$$
$$= \overline{W}_{T}^{(C)}(r[j]) + (s^{(NC)}(T) - s^{(C)}(r[j]))dT.$$

In fact, the drop in remaining weight after time dT is the same as the initial increase since $s^{(NC)}(T) = s^{(C)}(r[j])$, which follows from

$$\overline{W}^{(C)}(r[j]) = \overline{W}^{(C)}(r[j]^-) + \check{W}[j](T), \text{ and}$$
$$P(s^{(C)}(r[j])) = \overline{W}^{(C)}(r[j]).$$

Therefore, the remaining weight at time $r[j] + dT$ in the instance $I(T + dT)$ is the same as the remaining weight at time $r[j]$ in the instance $I(T)$. This continues for all $t \geq r[j]$, i.e.,

$$\overline{W}_{T+dT}^{(C)}(t + dT) = \overline{W}_{T}^{(C)}(t).$$

We now specify the measure preserving $1-1$ mapping for $T + dT$. We map $T + dT \to r[j]$. Recall that $s^{(NC)}(T + dT) = s^{(C)}(r[j])$. For $t \leq T$, we map $t \to t' + dT$, where $t \to t'$ in $I(T)$. The speed $s^{(NC)}$ does not change for $t \leq T$, due to the change in T. The speed $s^{(C)}$ does not change for $t < r[j]$. For $t \geq r[j]$, the above argument shows that

$$s_{T+dT}^{(C)}(t' + dT) = s_{T}^{(C)}(t') = s^{(NC)}(t).$$

$\square$

3.2 Flow-time Comparison (Proof of Lemma 4)

We prove Lemma 4 by once again considering the evolution of Algorithm C with $I(T)$. We show that the rate of change of flow-time of Algorithm C on instance $I(T)$, w.r.t. T, is $1 - \frac{1}{\alpha}$ times the rate of change of flow-time of Algorithm NC w.r.t. T. The rest of this section assumes $P(s) = s^\alpha$ for some $\alpha > 1$.

As in the proof of Lemma 7, when we go from T to $T + dT$, Algorithm C processes an extra dW amount of weight at time $r[j]$ at speed $s^{(C)}(r[j])$, which takes time dT. This incurs an extra $P(s^{(C)}(r[j])) \, dT$ units of energy consumption. Therefore, the rate of change of flow-time/energy[8] of Algorithm C on instance $I(T)$ w.r.t. T is

$$\frac{dE^{(C)}(I(T))}{dT} = P(s^{(C)}(r[j])) = \overline{W}^{(C)}(r[j]^-) + \check{W}[j]. \quad (4)$$

At the same time, Algorithm NC incurs an extra flow-time due to the extra dW weight which is processed in the interval $[T, T+dT]$. This weight dW waits for time $T - r[j]$, giving an extra flow-time of $(T - r[j])dW$. Therefore the rate of change of flow-time of Algorithm NC w.r.t. time T is

$$\frac{dF^{(NC)}}{dT} = (T - r[j])\frac{d\check{W}[j]}{dT}. \quad (5)$$

Let $W' = \overline{W}^{(C)}(r[j]^-) + \check{W}[j]$ and $T' = T - r[j]$. W' is the total weight processed by Algorithm C in time T' and hence

$$W' = (1 - \tfrac{1}{\alpha})T'\frac{dW'}{dT'}, \quad \text{by Lemma 2}$$

$$\Rightarrow \frac{dE^{(C)}(I(T))}{dT} = (1 - \tfrac{1}{\alpha})\frac{dF^{(NC)}}{dT}, \quad \text{by Eqns. 4 and 5.}$$

3.3 Integral Objective

We will now show that the integral flow-time of any schedule produced by Algorithm NC can be bounded in terms of its fractional flow-time.

LEMMA 8. *The integral flow-time of any schedule produced by Algorithm NC is at most $2 - \frac{1}{\alpha-1}$ times its fractional flow-time.*

PROOF. When we go from T to $T + dT$, Algorithm NC incurs an extra fractional flow-time of $(T - r[j])dW$, i.e.,

$$\frac{dF^{(NC)}}{dT} = (T - r[j])dW. \quad (6)$$

[8]Recall that the total flow-time and energy are equal for Algorithm C.

At the same time, Algorithm NC incurs an extra integral flow-time both due to the extra dW weight which is processed between T and $T + dT$ and due to the processed weight $\check{W}[j]$ of job j that now contributes for the extra duration dt. The first part corresponds exactly to the increase in fractional flow-time, i.e., $(T - r[j])dW$. So, we bound the second part, i.e., $\check{W}[j]dt$. Let $W' = \overline{W}^{(C)}(r[j]^-) + \check{W}[j]$ and $T' = T - r[j]$. W' is the total weight processed by Algorithm C in time T', and hence by Lemma 2,

$$W' = (1 - \tfrac{1}{\alpha})T' \frac{dW'}{dT'}$$

$$\Rightarrow \check{W}[j]dt \leq (1 - \tfrac{1}{\alpha})(T - r[j])dW$$

$$\Rightarrow \check{W}[j]dt \leq (1 - \tfrac{1}{\alpha})\frac{dF^{(NC)}}{dT},$$

where the first step follows from $W' \geq \check{W}[j]$ and the second step follows from Eqn. 6. Therefore,

$$\frac{dF_{int}^{(NC)}}{dT} \leq (1 + (1 - \tfrac{1}{\alpha}))\frac{dF^{(NC)}}{dT}.$$

$\square$

The competitive ratio of Algorithm NC follows immediately from Lemmas 3, 8 and 4 since we noted earlier that Algorithm C is 2-competitive (Theorem 1) and that the total flow-time is equal to the total energy for Algorithm C. Therefore we get the following theorem.

THEOREM 9. *For all $\alpha > 1$ and power functions $P(s) = s^\alpha$, Algorithm NC is $2 + 1/(1 - \tfrac{1}{\alpha}) = 3 + \tfrac{1}{\alpha - 1}$-competitive for the objective of integral flow-time plus energy.*

4. NON-UNIFORM DENSITY

In this section, we will significantly generalize the results in the previous section, and give a non-clairvoyant algorithm for jobs of non-uniform density. First, we consider the fractional objective in this section, and then extend it to the integral objective in the next section.

To define an algorithm for our problem, we need to specify, for every time t, the job selected for processing at time t, and the speed at which the selected job is processed. Recall that in the non-clairvoyant version, the algorithm only has the following information at its disposal: the densities of all the jobs that have been released till time t, the volume/weight of all jobs that have been completed till time t, the set of active jobs, and a lower bound on the volume/weight of every active job given by the volume/weight of the job processed by the non-clairvoyant algorithm till time t. As in the case of uniform densities, the non-clairvoyant algorithm is closely related to the clairvoyant algorithm (algorithm C) for the current instance $I(t)$. Recall that algorithm C uses the HDF rule to determine the processing order among jobs of different densities that are waiting at any given time. If there are multiple jobs of the highest density, then the algorithm is agnostic to which of these jobs is chosen, but for the purpose of our analysis, it will be convenient to assume that algorithm C uses the FIFO rule, i.e. it selects the job with the highest density that was released the earliest.

As mentioned earlier, a key step in algorithm NC is to round all densities down to powers of some constant β. Similar to algorithm C, algorithm NC also processes the job with the highest density among the active jobs at any given time, and uses the FIFO rule to decide the processing order of jobs of the same density. (Note that, in effect, jobs in the same density bracket are processed in FIFO rather than HDF order since their densities are rounded to the

same value.) The speed of algorithm NC at time t is η times the speed of algorithm C for the instance $I(t)$ (we call $I(t)$ the *current instance*), i.e. $s^{(NC)}(t) = \eta \cdot s_t^{(C)}(t)$, where η is a constant that we will determine later. (Again, the rounding of densities affects the speed of algorithm NC via algorithm C since $I(t)$ is now defined to be the rounded instance at time t.)

Our analysis depends crucially on the fact that the current instance will eventually evolve to the real problem instance. But this need not be the case if algorithm NC always runs at zero speed. Indeed, initially all jobs in the current instance have zero weight; so the speed given by the above definition will be zero. We fix this issue by setting the speed of algorithm NC to be ϵ more than that given by the above definition, for some arbitrarily small but fixed ϵ. We will ignore this excess speed in the analysis.

In analyzing algorithm NC, we will compare its energy and flow-time to the energy and flow-time (which are equal) of algorithm C respectively. The energy comparison is relatively straightforward and is deferred to the full version of the paper. Intuitively, Algorithm NC uses η^α times the energy of Algorithm C. In terms of flow-times, we will show the following lemma.

LEMMA 10. *For any instance $I(t)$, the total flow-time in algorithm NC is at most a constant times that in algorithm C, where the constant depends only on α.*

4.1 Flow-time Comparison (Sketch of Proof of Lemma 10)

As in the case of uniform densities, we will establish Lemma 10 by induction over the evolving instances. The main objective of using the multiplicative factor of η in setting the speed of algorithm NC is to ensure that for every active job j, a constant fraction of j is waiting at time t in algorithm C in the current instance. Recall that in contrast, the entire weight of job j in the current instance has already been processed by algorithm NC before time t.

LEMMA 11 (PROPERTY (A)). *For any active job j,*

$$\overline{W}_t^{(C)}(t)[j] \geq \zeta \cdot W_t[j] \text{ for some constant } \zeta.$$

Another consequence of the higher speed of algorithm NC compared to algorithm C is that the total volume of jobs processed by algorithm NC dominates that processed by algorithm C for any time interval ending at the current time t.

LEMMA 12 (PROPERTY (B)). *For any time $t_1 < t$,*

$$V^{(NC)}(t_1, t) \geq \gamma \cdot V_t^{(C)}(t_1, t) \text{ for some constant } \gamma.$$

We prove the above two properties jointly using induction over the evolving instances. Once these properties have been established, we use them to show that for any active job j, the completion time of j in algorithm C is significantly greater than its completion time in algorithm NC if the job get completed right now. Let $c_t^{(C)}[j]$ denote the completion time of job j in Algorithm C in instance $I(t)$.

LEMMA 13. *For any active job j,*

$$c_t^{(C)}[j] - t \geq \psi \cdot (t - r[j]) \text{ for some constant } \psi.$$

The proofs of Lemma 11, Lemma 12, and Lemma 13 are deferred to the full version of the paper.

We now explain the difficulties of proving Lemma 10 via Lemma 13, and sketch the key ideas. Note that when we transform the instance from $I(t)$ to $I(t+dt)$ by adding a weight of $dW = dW_t[j^*]$

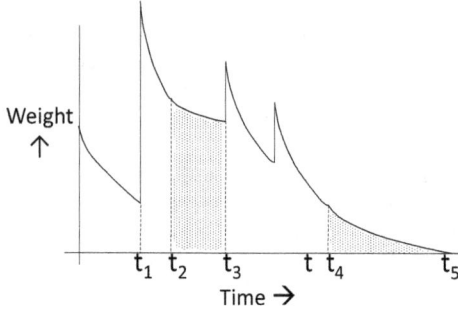

Figure 3: The structure of preemption intervals in algorithm C for the current instance. Job j^* is released at time t_1, i.e., $r_{j^*} = t_1$ and is processed in the dotted intervals. There are two preemption intervals $[t_1, t_2]$ and $[t_3, t_4]$, i.e., $\widehat{R}_1 = t_1$ and $\widehat{R}_2 = t_3$. Therefore, $i^* = 2$. The last preemption interval completes after the current time t.

to job j^*, the increase in flow-time of algorithm NC is

$$dF^{(\text{NC})} = (t - r[j^*]) \, dW \leq \frac{1}{\psi} \cdot \left(c_t^{(C)}[j] - t \right) dW, \quad \text{by Lemma 13.}$$
(7)

We can show that if the increase in the remaining weight at time t for algorithm C, i.e., $d\overline{W}_t^{(C)}(t)$, is at least a constant factor of dW, then Eqn. (7) is sufficient to prove Lemma 10. However, while this property holds in the case $j_t^{(C)}(t) = j^*$, it may not hold in general. This necessitates a more complicated proof, the first step of which is to show a somewhat weaker property that we describe below.

To describe this property, we first need to describe and establish some notation about the structure of the time interval $[r[j^*], t]$ in algorithm C for the current instance. This time interval alternates between intervals where j^* is being processed by algorithm C and intervals where jobs of densities higher than $\rho[j^*]$ are being processed (see Figure 3 for an example). We call the latter *preemption intervals*, and the jobs that are processed by algorithm C in the preemption intervals are called *preempting jobs*. We index the preemption intervals in chronological order. Let $\widehat{R}_i$ and $\widehat{V}_i$ denote the starting time and the volume of all preempting jobs in the i-th preemption interval respectively. Also, let $\overline{W}_i = \overline{W}_t^{(C)}(\widehat{R}_i^-)$. (Note that $\overline{W}_i$ does not include the weight of jobs released at time $\widehat{R}_i$.) Let i^* be the index of the last preemption interval.

The next lemma states that the increment in the remaining weight at time $\widehat{R}_{i^*}$ is a constant fraction of the added weight dW, if 1) the ratio of remaining weight at $\widehat{R}_{i^*}$ is a constant fraction of that at $\widehat{R}_1$, and 2) the total preempting volume except the last preemption interval is a constant fraction of the volume of the current job. Note that properties (A) and (B) informally correspond to these two conditions, though a formal proof will need to use induction over the properties since the following lemma is used to prove the properties themselves. Also, note that the property established by the lemma is weaker than what we would have ideally liked: the increment in the remaining weight at time t (instead of time $\widehat{R}_{i^*}$ as given by the lemma) is at least a constant factor of dW. (The proof of this lemma is deferred to the full version of the paper.)

LEMMA 14. *If* $\overline{W}_{i^*} \geq \zeta \cdot W_t[j^*]$, *then*

$$\frac{d\overline{W}_t^{(C)}(\widehat{R}_{i^*})[j^*]}{dW} \geq \left(1 - \frac{1}{4\zeta} \frac{\sum_{k=1}^{i^*-1} \widehat{V}_k}{V_t[j^*]} \right) \left(\frac{\overline{W}_{i^*}}{\overline{W}_1} \right)^{\frac{1}{\alpha}}.$$

Recall that the increase in the flow-time of Algorithm C equals the integral of $d\overline{W}_t^{(C)}(t')$ as over time t' starting from $r[j^*]$. Up to the last preemption interval, $d\overline{W}_t^{(C)}(t')$ is at least some constant factor of $dW_t[j^*]$ by Lemma 14. Therefore if the last preemption interval is short enough, i.e., if it is at most a constant factor of $(t - r[j^*])$, then we will be done. However, in general, the last preemption interval could be long. Therefore a local charging argument will not work and we resort to an amortized analysis.

The intuition for why an amortized analysis works is as follows. If a preempting job in the last preemption interval is small, then we can ignore it since the time taken by this job is small compared to the total time. On the other hand if the preempting job is large, then we can charge some of $dF^{(\text{NC})}(t)$ to $dF^{(C)}(t)$ at *an earlier time when we were processing this large preempting job*. The amortized analysis uses a potential function to accomplish this. When we have an extra amount in the $dF^{(C)}(t)$ in the charging argument, we will store this in the potential function. Later we may need help in the charging argument in which case we will draw from the stored potential function to pay for $dF^{(\text{NC})}(t)$.

More precisely, we will have one bin for each pair of density levels $k > k'$, into which we will store the extra clairvoyant flow-time when we are processing jobs with density β^k and from which we will draw when we are processing jobs with density $\beta^{k'}$. In particular, consider a bin (k, k'). Suppose $j^* = j$ with density β^k. We will show that $dF^{(C)}(t)$ is at least a constant fraction of the change in processing time of the current job times its weight. We will store $2^{k'-k}$ fraction of $dF^{(C)}(t)$ in the bin for (k, k'). By doing so, the total amount that we store in all bins is a constant factor of $dF^{(C)}(t)$. Further, when Algorithm NC finishes processing job j, the total potential stored in bin (k, k') due to j is at least the processing time of j times a $2^{k'-k}$ fraction of its weight. Later, when Algorithm NC is processing dW weight of a job j' with density $\beta^{k'}$, we can withdraw potential equal to the processing time of job j times dW from the bin (k, k'). We can keep doing this until the weight of the job j' become at least a $2^{k'-k}$ fraction of the weight of job j. Now recall that the density of the jobs are rounded to be powers of β. Choosing $\beta > 4$, we get that if the weight of the job j' becomes at least a $2^{k'-k}$ fraction of the weight of job j, then the volume of job j' is at least $(2/\beta)^{k'-k} = (\beta/2)^{k-k'} > 2^{k-k'}$ times the volume of j. So the processing time of job j is now negligible compared to that of j'. The details of the amortized analysis, which ultimately yields Lemma 10, is deferred to the full version of the paper.

5. INTEGRAL OBJECTIVE

In this section, we will give a black box reduction of any schedule optimizing fractional flow-time plus energy to one optimizing integral flow-time plus energy. Our goal is to show the following lemma.

LEMMA 15. *If a non-clairvoyant algorithm $\mathcal{A}_{frac}$ has the guarantee that the fractional flow-time plus energy of any schedule produced by the algorithm is at most Γ_{frac} times the optimum, where Γ_{frac} is a constant that depends only on α, then there is a non-clairvoyant algorithm $\mathcal{A}_{int}$ with the guarantee that the integral flow-time plus energy of any schedule produced by the algorithm is at most Γ_{int} times the optimum, where Γ_f is some constant that also depends only on α.*

PROOF. Let $j(t)$ be the job processed by algorithm $\mathcal{A}_{frac}$ at time t, and let $s(t)$ be the corresponding speed of the machine. Then, algorithm $\mathcal{A}_{int}$ is defined as follows: if job $j(t)$ is active

140

at time t (i.e., it has not been completed yet), then algorithm $\mathcal{A}_{int}$ processed job $j(t)$ at speed $(1 + \epsilon)s(t)$ for some constant $\epsilon > 0$; otherwise, if job $j(t)$ has already been completed by algorithm $\mathcal{A}_{int}$ before time t, then it keeps the machine idle at time t. Note that for every job j and every time t, the weight of job j processed by algorithm $\mathcal{A}_{int}$ till time t is exactly $1 + \epsilon$ times the weight of job j processed by algorithm $\mathcal{A}_{frac}$ till time t. In other words, when $\mathcal{A}_{int}$ finishes job j, $\frac{1}{1+\epsilon}$ fraction of the job is left in algorithm $\mathcal{A}_{frac}$. Let $T[j]$ be the difference between the completion time of job j in algorithm $\mathcal{A}_{int}$ and its release time $r[j]$. Then, the integral flow-time due to job j in algorithm $\mathcal{A}_{int}$ is exactly $W[j] \cdot T$, whereas the fractional flow-time of job j in algorithm $\mathcal{A}_{frac}$ is at least

$$(1 - \frac{1}{1+\epsilon})W[j] \cdot T = \frac{\epsilon}{1+\epsilon} \cdot W[j] \cdot T.$$

Therefore, the total integral flow-time in algorithm $\mathcal{A}_{int}$ is at most $1 + \frac{1}{\epsilon}$ times the total fractional flow-time in algorithm $\mathcal{A}_{frac}$. On the other hand, the total energy consumed in algorithm $\mathcal{A}_{int}$ is at most $(1+\epsilon)^\alpha$ times that in algorithm $\mathcal{A}_{frac}$. To complete the proof, we set

$$\Gamma_{int} = \max\left\{(1+\epsilon)^\alpha, 1 + \frac{1}{\epsilon}\right\}\Gamma_{frac}.$$

$\square$

The next theorem follows from the above lemma and our result for minimizing fractional flow-time plus energy.

THEOREM 16. *There is a deterministic algorithm for the non-clairvoyant scheduling problem with non-uniform density that has a constant competitive ratio, where the constant only depends on α, for the objective of integral flowtime plus energy.*

6. IDENTICAL PARALLEL MACHINES

Throughout this section we will consider only deterministic algorithms. Let there be a set of k identical machines. The goal is to minimize the sum of the energy and (fractional/integral) flow-time on all the machines. In the immediate dispatch model, on the release of a job, the algorithm must specify which machine it will be processed on. The actual processing might be done later but the selection of the machine has to be immediate. We show a lower bound of $\Omega(k^\beta)$ where $\beta = 1 - 1/\alpha$ in the immediate dispatch model, even for uniform densities and fractional flow-time. The main property we use is that the algorithm has no way of distinguishing jobs of different volumes. Due to this, the adversary can pick the job volumes in such a way that the algorithm cannot do any load balancing. Release k^2 jobs at time 0, of which k jobs will have high volumes and the rest will have low volumes. The algorithm dispatches all the jobs right away and there exists a machine which has been assigned at least k jobs. The adversary chooses these k jobs to be the ones with the high volumes. The optimum schedule is the one that assigns all the high volume jobs to different machines. The cost of the optimum is (dominated by) the cost of processing a single high volume job whereas the cost of the algorithm is (dominated by) the cost of processing k high volume jobs. The ratio of these two costs gives a lower bound of $\Omega(k^\beta)$.

Now, we focus on the model where jobs do not need to be assigned immediately on arrival. However, once a job has started processing on a machine, it cannot be moved to another machine. In this model, we give an algorithm with constant competitive ratio. Our algorithm (we call it NC-PAR) is defined as follows. It maintains a global queue of unassigned jobs $\mathcal{Q}$ in FIFO order. Whenever

a machine is available, i.e., all jobs previously assigned to the machine have been completed, we assign the first job in NC-PAR to the available machine. The instantaneous speed on a machine is determined exactly as in Algorithm NC, where the current instance is defined by the processed volume of all jobs assigned by Algorithm NC-PAR to this machine.

THEOREM 17. *For all $\alpha > 1$ and power functions $P(s) = s^\alpha$, Algorithm NC-PAR is $O(\alpha + \frac{1}{\alpha-1})$-competitive for the objective of integral/fractional flow-time plus energy on identical parallel machines.*

Similar to the single machine case, the analysis of Algorithm NC-PAR relies on comparing its flow-time and energy consumption with those of a known competitive (immediate dispatch) clairvoyant algorithm that we call C-PAR. Algorithm C-PAR behaves identical to Algorithm C on each individual machine, i.e., the instantaneous speed is set such that power equals fractional remaining weight. In assigning jobs to machines, Algorithm C-PAR embraces a greedy policy and assigns each arriving job immediately to a machine that minimizes the increase in the fractional objective.

THEOREM 18 ([12]). *Algorithm C-PAR is $O(\alpha)$-competitive for the objective of fractional flow-time plus energy.*

Next, we will show that the job assignment of algorithm NC-PAR is identical to that of algorithm C-PAR. This suffices since on an individual machine, Algorithms NC-PAR and C-PAR are identical to Algorithms NC and C respectively. The next lemma characterizes the job assignment rule of Algorithm C-PAR.

LEMMA 19. *For every job j, Algorithm C-PAR assigns j to a machine i that has the least remaining (fractional) weight when j is released.*

PROOF. Suppose the fractional remaining weight of jobs on some machine i is W when job j is released, i.e., at time $r[j]$. Then, using Lemma 2, the total energy for processing the remaining jobs is given by

$$\int_0^W \frac{\alpha}{\alpha-1} w^{1-\frac{1}{\alpha}} dw = \frac{\alpha}{\alpha-1} \cdot \frac{\alpha}{2\alpha-1} W^{2-\frac{1}{\alpha}}.$$

So, assigning job j to machine i would increase the energy by

$$\frac{\alpha}{\alpha-1} \cdot \frac{\alpha}{2\alpha-1} \left((W + W[j])^{2-\frac{1}{\alpha}} - W^{2-\frac{1}{\alpha}}\right),$$

which is monotonically increasing in W by the convexity of $x^{2-\frac{1}{\alpha}}$. To conclude the proof, we note that since the fractional flow-time equals energy for Algorithm C-PAR, it assigns job j to the machine that minimizes the increase in the energy consumption after time $r[j]$. $\square$

Next, for convenience of presentation, we will assume that there is an arbitrary total order of all machines and both algorithms C-PAR and NC-PAR break ties according to this total order. This assumption can be removed with more careful analysis using the same idea. We omit the details for the sake of brevity.

LEMMA 20. *Algorithm NC-PAR assigns job j to machine i if and only if algorithm C-PAR assigns job j to machine i.*

PROOF. We will use induction on the order of arrival of jobs. All machines have zero remaining weight when the first job arrives. So the first job will be assigned to the first machine with respect to the total order in both algorithms C-PAR and NC-PAR.

Now, suppose that the assignments of all jobs before job j are identical in the two algorithm. We will show that this is also the case for job j. By Lemma 19, Algorithm C-PAR assigns job j to the machine i that has the least remaining weight at time $r[j]$. Further, by property 2 of Lemma 2, the completion time of all jobs on an individual machine is a monotonically increasing function of its fractional remaining weight at time $r[j]$. Finally, given that the job assignment has been the same in algorithms C-PAR and NC-PAR so far, it follows from Lemma 6 that for any individual machine, the completion time for all jobs released before job j on the machine is identical for algorithms C-PAR and NC-PAR. It follows that Algorithm C-PAR assigns job j to the machine with the earliest completion time in Algorithm NC-PAR for all jobs released before job j (breaking ties according to the total order of the machines). By definition of Algorithm NC-PAR, this is the same machine that Algorithm NC-PAR would assign job j to. $\square$

Combining Lemma 20 with Lemma 3 and 4 respectively, we relate the energy and fractional flow-time of C-PAR with those of NC-PAR.

LEMMA 21. *Both algorithms* C-PAR *and* NC-PAR *consume the same amount of energy.*

LEMMA 22. *The fractional flow-time of Algorithm* NC-PAR *equals the fractional flow-time of Algorithm* C-PAR *divided by* $(1 - \frac{1}{\alpha})$.

Lemmas 21 and 22, and Theorem 18 immediately yield Theorem 17 for the fractional objective. Extending our proof to the integral objective is almost identical to the the analysis in Section 3.3; we omit the details for brevity.

7. OPEN PROBLEMS

The most natural open problem is to extend our results to the case of non-uniform density and identical parallel machines.

In terms of getting a positive result, it is no longer feasible for the non-clairvoyant algorithm to mimic the job assignment rule of the clairvoyant algorithm. When the clairvoyant algorithm dispatches a higher density job, it takes into account the lower density jobs to compute the increase in the cost for each machine. The non-clairvoyant algorithm, however, has to dispatch the higher density job without exploring the lower density jobs thoroughly. A natural policy for the non-calirvoyant algorithm is to follow HDF (probably with rounded densities) and dispatch only as needed to follow this rule. A candidate clairvoyant algorithm to compare this with is the one that considers only jobs of equal or higher density to calculate the increase in the cost. However the job assignments could still be different: for instance, jobs released later could affect the machine a job is assigned to in the non-clairvoyant algorithm whereas they do not in the clairvoyant algorithm.

In terms of showing a hardness result, one natural attempt is to use different densities to force the algorithm to do immediate dispatch and then apply the hardness result for immediate dispatch in Section 6. However, the following somewhat surprising fact rules this approach out. Suppose there are l jobs with densities $1, \rho, \rho^2, \ldots, \rho^{l-1}$ such that the cost of processing any one of them by itself on a single machine is c. Then the cost of processing all of them on l machines is lc. However, the cost of processing them all on a single machine is at most $4lc$ as long as $\rho \geq 4$. Thus, not load balancing jobs of different densities costs only a constant factor unlike the case of uniform densities where it costs a super-constant factor.

These issues indicate that this is an interesting open problem that needs some new ideas.

8. REFERENCES

[1] Barroso, L.A.: The price of performance. ACM Queue **3**(7) (2005) 48–53

[2] Albers, S., Fujiwara, H.: Energy-efficient algorithms for flow time minimization. ACM Transactions on Algorithms **3**(4) (2007)

[3] Yao, F.F., Demers, A.J., Shenker, S.: A scheduling model for reduced cpu energy. In: FOCS. (1995) 374–382

[4] Pruhs, K., Uthaisombut, P., Woeginger, G.J.: Getting the best response for your erg. ACM Transactions on Algorithms **4**(3) (2008)

[5] Bansal, N., Pruhs, K., Stein, C.: Speed scaling for weighted flow time. SIAM J. Comput. **39**(4) (2009) 1294–1308

[6] Bansal, N., Chan, H.L., Lam, T.W., Lee, L.K.: Scheduling for speed bounded processors. In: ICALP (1). (2008) 409–420

[7] Lam, T.W., Lee, L.K., To, I.K.K., Wong, P.W.H.: Speed scaling functions for flow time scheduling based on active job count. In: ESA. (2008) 647–659

[8] Bansal, N., Chan, H.L., Pruhs, K.: Speed scaling with an arbitrary power function. In: SODA. (2009) 693–701

[9] Andrew, L.L.H., Wierman, A., Tang, A.: Optimal speed scaling under arbitrary power functions. SIGMETRICS Performance Evaluation Review **37**(2) (2009) 39–41

[10] Motwani, R., Phillips, S., Torng, E.: Nonclairvoyant scheduling. Theoretical computer science **130**(1) (1994) 17–47

[11] Chan, H.L., Edmonds, J., Lam, T.W., Lee, L.K., Marchetti-Spaccamela, A., Pruhs, K.: Nonclairvoyant speed scaling for flow and energy. Algorithmica **61**(3) (2011) 507–517

[12] Anand, S., Garg, N., Kumar, A.: Resource augmentation for weighted flow-time explained by dual fitting. In: SODA. (2012) 1228–1241

[13] Devanur, N.R., Huang, Z.: Primal dual gives almost optimal energy efficient online algorithms. In: SODA. (2014)

[14] Gupta, A., Krishnaswamy, R., Pruhs, K.: Scalably scheduling power-heterogeneous processors. In: ICALP (1). (2010) 312–323

[15] Bansal, N., Kimbrel, T., Pruhs, K.: Speed scaling to manage energy and temperature. J. ACM **54**(1) (2007)

[16] Albers, S.: Energy-efficient algorithms. Commun. ACM **53**(5) (2010) 86–96

Cost-Oblivious Reallocation for Scheduling and Planning

Michael A. Bender
Stony Brook University
bender@cs.stonybrook.edu

Martín Farach-Colton
Rutgers University
farach@cs.rutgers.edu

Sándor P. Fekete
TU Braunschweig
s.fekete@tu-bs.de

Jeremy T. Fineman
Georgetown University
jfineman@cs.georgetown.edu

Seth Gilbert
NUS
seth.gilbert@comp.nus.edu.sg

ABSTRACT

In a reallocating-scheduler problem, jobs may be inserted and deleted from the system over time. Unlike in traditional online scheduling problems, where a job's placement is immutable, in reallocation problems the schedule may be adjusted, but at some cost. The goal is to maintain an approximately optimal schedule while also minimizing the *reallocation cost* for changing the schedule.

This paper gives a reallocating scheduler for the problem of assigning jobs to p (identical) servers so as to minimize the sum of completion times to within a constant factor of optimal, with an amortized reallocation cost for a length-w job of $O(f(w) \cdot \log^3 \log \Delta)$, where Δ is the length of the longest job and $f()$ is the reallocation-cost function. Our algorithm is *cost oblivious*, meaning that the algorithm is not parameterized by $f()$, yet it achieves this bound for any subadditive $f()$. Whenever $f()$ is strongly subadditive, the reallocation cost becomes $O(f(w))$.

To realize a reallocating scheduler with low reallocation cost, we design a *k-cursor sparse table*. This data structure stores a dynamic set of elements in an array, with insertions and deletions restricted to k "cursors" in the structure. The data structure achieves an amortized cost of $O(\log^3 k)$ for insertions and deletions, while also guaranteeing that any prefix of the array has constant density. Observe that this bound does not depend on n, the number of elements, and hence this data structure, restricted to $k \ll n$ cursors, beats the lower bound of $\Omega(\log^2 n)$ for general sparse tables.

Categories and Subject Descriptors

F.2.2 [**Analysis of Algorithms and Problem Complexity**]: Nonnumerical Algorithms and Problems—*Sequencing and scheduling*

Supported in part by NSF grants CNS 1408695, CCF 1439084, IIS 1247726, IIS 1251137, CCF 1217708, CCF 1114809, IIS 1247750, CCF 1114930, CCF 1218188, CCF 1314633, DFG Grant FE407/17-1, Tier 2 ARC MOE2014-T2-1-157, and Sandia National Laboratories.

Keywords

Resource allocation; reallocation; cost-oblivious problems

1. INTRODUCTION

Scheduling is a ubiquitous aspect of life, and an essential aspect of real scheduling is that *schedules change*. Consider train and plain schedules: both are examples of schedules prone to disruption, where weather patterns and mechanical failures affect the availability of crew and aircraft.

In many such cases, there is a cost when resource allocations change (e.g., people miss flights, airlines have to pay overtime, etc.), so the objective is to minimize the cost of schedule disruptions (or resource reallocation) without violating scheduling constraints.

Scheduling subject to changes/disruptions is a classic example of a reallocation problem. In a reallocation problem, an allocator assigns resources to jobs. Unlike in tradition online problems, the allocator may *revise prior decisions, at some cost*. A good reallocation algorithm maintains an approximately optimal allocation of resources, while simultaneously minimizing the reallocation cost. Reallocation is online in the sense that the schedule is modified immediately when a new request arrives, however no decision is irrevocable and resources may always be reallocated.

Perhaps the most-studied problem with a reallocation flavor is multi-machine load-balancing (e.g., [1,6,16,28,30,33,34]), where a solution should simultaneously minimize the maximum machine load and the number of migrations across machines. When load-balancing a web server, for example, it makes sense to optimize for migration cost. In other scheduling problems, such airline scheduling, changing the start time of a job may be expensive and the goal is to minimize schedule updates.

In our experience, we have seen reallocation problems underlying many aspects of parallel systems. In our own research, we have modelled FPGA reorganization as a reallocation problem, minimizing reconfiguration costs [17]. We have also explored reallocation problems in database resource management with respect to crash safety and transactional support [8]. One of our long-term goals is to understand which scheduling objectives are amenable to efficient reallocation, and which ones are brittle.

Reallocation and Scheduling

This paper addresses the problem of minimizing the sum of completion times with reallocation in a system of p (identical) servers. The input consists of an online sequence of job insertions or deletions, where each job has a size w_j and a (re)scheduling cost $f(w_j)$ that depends only on its size.

The goal is to maintain, after each insert/delete request, a schedule that (approximately) minimizes the sum of completion times of all jobs currently in the system. We abbreviate this problem as $p|f(w)$ *realloc* $|\sum_j C_j$ (generalizing standard notation [18]).

The optimal static solution for sum of completion times is achieved by sorting jobs by increasing length and assigning them greedily to servers, allocating each job in turn to the first available server. However, it is not hard to show that achieving this optimal solution could require a large number of reallocations after each insert/delete.

To achieve low reallocation cost, we allow solutions that approximately minimize the sum of completion times. A natural way to *approximate* the optimal sum of completion times is to sort jobs by approximate size, e.g., schedule all jobs with size at most 2^i before larger jobs with size at most 2^{i+1}. Our solution adopts this approximate-sorting approach, but the difficulty is in maintaining this order with low reallocation cost as insertions and deletions occur.

There is a special case worth noting. When $f(w) = 1$ for all w, i.e., moving a job has constant cost regardless of size, there is a straightforward algorithm with $O(1)$ amortized reallocation cost that maintains a sum of completion times no more than 4 times the optimal.[1]

A goal of this paper is to explore reallocating schedulers for general reallocation-cost functions f, not just constant f. If $f(w) = w$, i.e., the cost is linear in the size of a job, the simple solution degrades, giving a reallocation cost of $O(\log \Delta)$, where Δ is the size of the largest job.

One option is to design a suite of algorithms, each specifically tuned to achieve a better reallocation cost for a specific function f. However, for some functions, e.g., the linear cost function $f(w) = w$, we know of no better solution than the one presented in this paper.

Our more elegant alternative to optimizing for specific cost functions is to produce a single algorithm that simultaneously achieves the best known reallocation cost for a wide range of reallocation-cost functions.

Our main result is a *cost oblivious* reallocating scheduler that has low reallocation cost for any subadditive, monotonically nondecreasing cost function f. (A monotonically nondecreasing function $f(x)$ is *subadditive* if $f(x + y) \le f(x) + f(y)$ for any positive x and y. All monotonic concave functions are subadditive.) Being cost oblivious means that the scheduler does not use any knowledge of f. Cost obliviousness was introduced in [8], motivated by the practical problem of storage reallocation in database systems. Cost obliviousness is desirable, because the true cost of reallocation may be complex or even unknown.

Our algorithm achieves an $O(1)$ reallocation cost for constant f and an $O(\log^3 \log \Delta)$ reallocation cost for linear f.

---

[1] Consider the single-server case, where $p = 1$. Allocate a job-sized gap in the schedule between each group of jobs. To insert a size-2^i job, schedule it immediately after the last size 2^i job, possibly evicting an overlapping larger job which is rescheduled recursively. This process may cascade across all sizes, but it is not hard to show that the amortized reallocation cost is $O(1)$ if $f(w) = 1$ since large-job evictions leave large gaps that facilitate many future small-job insertions.

Formalization of the reallocating scheduler problem

An *online execution* consists of a sequence of requests of the form ⟨INSERTJOB, *name*, *length*⟩ and ⟨DELETEJOB, *name*⟩, with integral lengths. Between requests, we define the *active jobs* to be those that have been inserted but not yet deleted. We typically assume throughout that we are given in advance Δ, the size of the largest job; we discuss how to remove this restriction. There is no given bound on the total number of jobs or the total number of active jobs.

After each insert/delete request, the scheduler must output a schedule for each server. If $\mathcal{S}$ and $\mathcal{S}'$ are schedules before and after a request r, then the *reallocation cost of* r is the sum of the reallocation costs of all jobs whose scheduling has changed between $\mathcal{S}$ and $\mathcal{S}'$. The reallocation cost of a sequence of requests is the sum of the reallocation costs for each request.

There are two different types of reallocations that may occur. If a job's schedule is modified, but it remains scheduled on the same server, it is considered a *nonmigrating* reallocation. If the job is rescheduled on a new server, it is considered a *migrating* reallocation.

A reallocating scheduler A is (f, a, b)-*competitive* for cost function $f()$, if (1) the objective function is always within an a-factor of optimal, and (2) the reallocation cost is at most b times the sum of the allocation costs of every object inserted thus far (including those that have subsequently been deleted).

Let $\mathcal{C}$ be a set of cost functions. A reallocation algorithm A is *cost oblivious* if it does not depend on $f()$. (This means not only that $f()$ is not a parameter to algorithm A, but also A learns nothing about $f()$ as A executes.) A cost-oblivious reallocator A is $(\mathcal{C}, a, b)$-*competitive* if it is (f, a, b)-competitive for every $f \in \mathcal{C}$; we abbreviate to (a, b)-*competitive* if the set $\mathcal{C}$ is unambiguous.

Results

We develop a reallocating scheduler for p servers that achieves an $O(1)$ approximation for the sum of completion times. For subadditive cost functions, the scheduling algorithm is

$$(O(1), O(\log^3 \log \Delta))$$

competitive, where Δ denotes the length of the longest job. For strongly subadditive cost functions, the algorithm is $(O(1), O(1))$-competitive. (We define a subadditive function $f(x)$ to be *strongly subadditive* if $f(2x) \le (2-\gamma)f(x)$ where $2 > \gamma > 0$ is bounded above 0 by a constant.) This scheduling algorithm is cost oblivious, and the same algorithm achieves both bounds. All the reallocations associated with insertions are nonmigrating, and each deletion triggers at most one migrating reallocation.

The key technical tool is a single-server scheduler that achieves a $1 + \varepsilon$ approximation ($0 < \varepsilon \le 1/2$) for the sum of completion times. We then build the general multi-server scheduler by properly load balancing jobs across servers.

To achieve these results, we develop a *k-cursor sparse table* that maintains constant prefix density in an array with inserts/deletes restricted to k "cursors" in the array. This data structure has an amortized $O(\log^3 k)$ insertion and deletion cost, which (critically) is independent of the number n of elements. We employ the structure with $k = \Theta(\log \Delta)$, giving the $O(\log^3 \log \Delta)$ bound.

In contrast, general sparse tables have an amortized update cost of $\Theta(\log^2 n)$ [21, 35–37], which is tight [11]. Replacing the k-cursor sparse table with a general sparse table in the scheduling algorithm of Section 2 would yield a significantly worse reallocation cost of $O(\log^3 V)$, where $V \geq \Delta$ is the total length of all jobs. Our k-cursor structure has significant complexity beyond that of a standard sparse table, with many more structural constraints to guarantee the stronger bound for the special case of cursors.

Other related work

Reallocation-style problems have been studied in a variety of contexts, particularly in the last several years. In the context of scheduling, we previously studied a reallocation scheduler for unit-sized jobs with arrival times and deadlines [7]. Some aspects of that problem were much simpler: all jobs had an identical size of one. Some aspects were more complicated: jobs could not be scheduled arbitrarily, but had to respect arrival times and deadlines. The techniques from [7] do not apply to the problem addressed in the current paper.

Cost oblivious reallocation is a relatively new concept that we recently introduced [8]. In that paper, the goal was to minimize the total space footprint of the data being stored; this is analogous to minimizing the makespan (i.e., the maximum time that any job completes) in scheduling. In the current paper, we focus on minimizing the sum of completion times, which imposes different constraints on the ordering of jobs. The storage reallocator [8] relied on different tools, e.g., cascading buffers, that would not help for minimizing sum of completion times; by contrast, the main tool here is the k-cursor sparse table.

Shachnai et al. [29] explore a form of reallocation for combinatorial optimization. Given an input, an optimal solution for that input, and a modified version of the input, they develop algorithms that find the minimum-cost modification of the optimal solution to the modified input. A difference between their setting and ours is that we measure the ratio of reallocation cost to allocation cost, whereas they measure the ratio of the actual transition cost to the optimal transition cost resulting in a good solution. Also, we focus on a sequence of changes, meaning we amortize the expensive changes against a sequence of updates.

Davis et al. [14] study a reallocation problem, where an allocator divides resources among a set of users, updating the allocation as the users' constraints change. The goal is to minimize the number of changes to the allocation. Other papers that solve specific instances of reallocation problems include [15, 17, 19, 28, 32].

Robust scheduling is a related notion, which involves designing schedules that can tolerate some uncertainty [12, 13, 22, 25–27, 31]. The assumption is that the problem is approximately static, but there is some error or uncertainty. The schedule remains near optimal even if the underlying situation changes.

Reoptimization problems minimize the computational cost for incrementally updating the schedule [2–5, 10]. By contrast, we focus on the resource-allocation cost instead of the computation cost of finding an allocation.

One of the contributions of this paper is a new sparse table data structure; many sparse tables have appeared previously in the literature [9, 11, 20, 21, 24, 35–37]. Indeed, one distinction between our paper and most prior work on reallocation and rescheduling is that the technical results seem to meld data structures and combinatorial optimization.

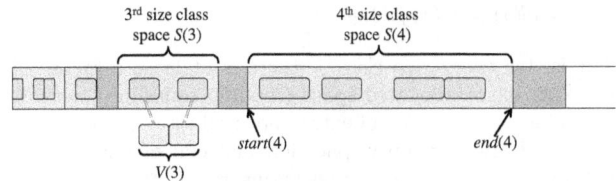

Figure 1: The layout of the schedule, viewed as an array, with $\delta = 0.5$. The light-gray rectangles are the regions assigned to each size class. The orange rounded rectangles are the jobs scheduled in each size class. The dark-gray rectangles are regions outside size classes and contain no jobs. Note that the 4th size class contains jobs of slightly different sizes in arbitrary order.

2. SINGLE SERVER SCHEDULING

This section presents a cost-oblivious reallocating scheduler for the problem of (approximately) minimizing the sum of completion times for the single-server case where $p = 1$. The algorithm achieves an efficient reallocation cost on job insertions and deletions, as stated by the following theorem, proved at the end of the section.

THEOREM 1. *For any constant ε with $0 < \varepsilon \leq 1$, there exists a cost-oblivious reallocating scheduler for $p = 1$ for minimizing the sum of completion times that is $(1 + \varepsilon, O((1/\varepsilon^5) \log^3 \log_{1+\varepsilon} \Delta))$-competitive over all subadditive cost functions, and $(1 + \varepsilon, O(1/\varepsilon^3))$-competitive over all strongly subadditive cost functions.*

On a single server, the optimal schedule for minimizing sum of completion times is to sort the jobs in order of increasing size; see [23]. The main goal of our algorithm is to maintain this order approximately by allowing jobs of roughly the same size to be in arbitrary order. Our algorithm organizes jobs into groups called *size classes*, containing jobs that differ in size by no more than a $1+\delta$ factor, for constant $\delta \leq 1$ with $\delta = \Theta(\varepsilon)$. (We shall specify δ more precisely in the analysis.) Precisely, a job of size w belongs to size class $j = \left\lfloor \log_{(1+\delta)}(w) \right\rfloor$, i.e., it belongs to size-class j if $(1+\delta)^{j-1} \leq w < (1+\delta)^j$.

Schedule-array layout

Think of the jobs as being placed in an array, as shown in Figure 1. The schedule array is divided into $\left\lceil \log_{(1+\delta)} \Delta \right\rceil$ segments, where the ith segment contains jobs from size class i. Let $V(i)$ denote the **volume**, or total length, of jobs in size class i, and let $S(i)$ denote the total space allocated in the array for size class i (possibly including empty space). We write $V(i, j) = \sum_{\ell=i}^{j} V(\ell)$ for the sum of the volumes of size classes i to j. Moreover, $start(i)$ and $end(i)$ are, respectively, the beginning and end of size class i.

The key challenge is managing the size-class boundaries in the array: each size class needs enough space to accommodate insertions, but sufficiently little to ensure that the sum of completions times is approximately optimal. The following property limits the amount of space:

PROPERTY 1. *For every $j \leq \log_{(1+\delta)} \Delta$:*
- $S(j) \geq \lfloor V(j)(1+\delta) \rfloor$,
- $start(j) \leq V(1, j-1)(1+\delta)^2$, *and*

- $end(j) \leq V(1, j)(1 + \delta)^2$.

That is, for every size class j, there is at least a factor of $(1 + \delta)$ of extra allocated space (modulo rounding), and at most a factor of $(1+\delta)^2$ of extra allocated space. Note there may be additional empty space left between size classes (to facilitate future growth and shrinking).

As insertions and deletions occur, the boundaries of size classes may change, but these movements must be limited to avoid expensive reallocations. Job movements within each size class must also be bounded, but these are easier to handle. We use the term **lost slots** to refer to any array slots that were part of a particular size class before an operation, but that are not part of that size class after. A second key property is that the algorithm supports the following "one directional" charging scheme for lost slots:

PROPERTY 2. *There exists a function g mapping lost slots to insert/delete operations subject to:*

- *The function g maps each slot lost by size class j to an insert/delete operation on a size class $\leq j$.*
- *There are $O(\log^3 \log_{1+\delta} \Delta/\delta^3)$ lost slots in total mapped to any particular insert/delete operation.*
- *There are $O(1)$ lost slots from each size class mapped to any particular insert/delete operation.*

To manage size-class boundaries dynamically, we employ a new data structure called a **k-cursor sparse table**. A k-cursor sparse table is a special case of a sparse table that contains k different regions called **cursor districts** (corresponding to size classes), each of which supports insertions and deletions of unit-size elements with amortized cost $O(\log^3 k)$. The k-cursor data structure has constant "prefix density," which implies Property 1, and it has "one directional rebalances" consistent with Property 2. Perhaps counterintuitively, we do not use the k-cursor table to reallocate jobs directly, but use it to indicate when size-class boundaries move and contained jobs should be reallocated.

We now describe the reallocation algorithm, ending with a proof of Theorem 1. The k-cursor data structure, hiding much of the technical complexity, is described in Section 4.

Reallocating scheduler algorithm

We now describe the basic algorithm. Every job is stored in array A, which is divided into $\left\lceil \log_{(1+\delta)} \Delta \right\rceil$ size-classes.[2] We use an auxiliary k-cursor data structure, where $k = \left\lceil \log_{(1+\delta)} \Delta \right\rceil$, to maintain the boundaries of job classes; each district boundary is interpreted as a size-class boundary.

Insertions: Consider a job of size w belonging to size class $j = \left\lfloor \log_{(1+\delta)}(w) \right\rfloor$. (Recall that w is an integer between 1 and Δ.) Let $\tilde{w}$ be the minimum size of a job in size class j. In order to insert the job:

1. Insert (roughly) $w(1+\delta)$ elements into district j of the k-cursor structure, more specifically, if $V(j)$ is the current volume of size class j, including the new job, insert until the number of elements in the district equals $\lfloor V(j)(1+\delta) \rfloor$.

2. Adjust the size classes in the array A to match the district boundaries indicated by the k-cursor structure. No jobs have moved yet.

3. Identify S, the set of jobs overlapping lost slots, i.e., those falling before the new starting point of their size class's segment. These jobs must be moved.

4. For each job in S from largest to smallest size class, remove it from its old location and re-**place** it in its size class, as described below.

5. Finally, place the newly inserted job in its size class.

To **(re)place** a job of length w in size class j, we identify a subinterval in the job class that has at least w empty space and is of size at most $O(w/\delta)$ (i.e., it contains at most $O(1/\delta)$ jobs). We then rearrange the jobs in this subinterval to make space, and (re)place the job.

One further restriction is that this subinterval should not include the first or last $\lfloor \tilde{w}\delta/4 \rfloor$ slots of the size class so as to avoid further changes should the size class boundary move again. (Recall that $\tilde{w}$ is the minimum size job for the size class.) We refer to the first and last $\lfloor \tilde{w}\delta/4 \rfloor$ slots as **boundary padding**, and the remaining slots as **non-boundary slots**. Whenever boundary movement causes jobs to shift, no job should be replaced within the first or last $\lfloor \tilde{w}\delta/4 \rfloor$ slots of the size class. This boundary padding prevents small changes in the boundary from causing jobs to move.

We now explain in more detail how a job is (re)placed. We begin with the case where $V(j) < 2/\delta$. Since there is at least one job in the size class, we know that $\tilde{w} \leq V(j) < 2/\delta$. Hence the boundary padding is of size $\lfloor \tilde{w}\delta/4 \rfloor = 0$. Thus, we simply rearrange all $< 2/\delta$ jobs to make room.

Next, we consider the case where $2/\delta < V(j) \leq 5w/\delta$. In this case, we have $\lfloor V(j)(1+\delta) \rfloor \geq V(j)(1+\delta/2)$. Consider the entire size class, excluding the boundary padding of size $\lfloor \tilde{w}\delta/4 \rfloor$. Since $V(j) \geq \tilde{w}$, we conclude that the excluded boundary padding contain at most $V(j)\delta/2$ slots, and hence there are at least $V(j)$ available non-boundary slots. Again, we move every job in the non-boundary portion of the size class to make room for the (re)placed one, moving at most $10/\delta$ jobs (as each job is of size at least $w/(1+\delta)$).

Lastly, assume $V(j) > 5w/\delta$. We identify a subinterval in size class j of length at most $10w/\delta$ that has at least w empty space and does not overlap the boundary padding.

First, we determine the percentage of empty slots in the non-boundary portion of the size class. Since (in this case) $V(j) > 5w/\delta \geq 4/\delta$, the total number of slots is at least $\lfloor V(j)(1+\delta) \rfloor \geq V(j)(1+3\delta/4)$. At most $\tilde{w}\delta/2 \leq V(j)\delta/2$ of these slots are boundary slots, and so the total number of non-boundary slots is at least $V(j)(1+\delta/4)$. Therefore, the fraction of free non-boundary slots in the size class is at least $1 - V(j)/V(j)(1+\delta/4) \geq \delta/(4+\delta)$.

Next, partition the non-boundary portion of the size class into (disjoint) subintervals of length between $5w/\delta$ and $10w/\delta$. (The total number of slots in the class is at least $5w/\delta$ in this case.) At least one of these intervals must have at least the average number of empty slots, i.e., for at least one interval, the fraction of free slots is at least $\delta/(4+\delta)$.

In this subinterval, the amount of free space is at least $(5w/\delta)(\delta/(4+\delta)) \geq w$. To make room, move all the jobs in the subinterval; there are at most $10/\delta$ jobs. We conclude:

CLAIM 2. *Given fixed size-class boundaries obeying Property 1, each job (re)placement causes at most $O(1/\delta)$ jobs within the same size class to move.* $\square$

---

[2]Due to interactions with the k-cursor structure, we assume here that Δ, the size of the largest job, is known in advance. This assumption can be removed as the k-cursor data structure allows addition and removal of the last district.

Deletions: Deletions differ only slightly from insertions. First, the size-w job is removed from the array. Then, roughly $(1 + \delta)w$ elements are removed from the k-cursor structure. Finally, adjust size-class boundaries and replace jobs as before, proceeding from smallest to largest size class.

Analysis

We now analyze the amortized reallocation cost of our algorithm. Combining the following lemma with a setting of $\delta = \Theta(\varepsilon)$ proves the reallocation-cost aspect of Theorem 1.

LEMMA 3. *Consider an execution of the reallocation scheduler. If the cost function f is subadditive, then the amortized reallocation cost per operation is at most $O\left((1/\delta^5) \log^3 \log_{1+\delta} \Delta\right)$ times the initial allocation cost. If f is strongly subadditive, then the amortized reallocation cost is at most $O(1/\delta^3)$ times the initial allocation.*

PROOF. Consider each job of size w as consisting of w unit-sized components. Our goal is to map the reallocation of each unit-sized component to some unit-sized component of an insertion or deletion in an earlier job class. More precisely, for an insertion/deletion of a size-w job, we will show that at most $O(w \log^3 k/\delta^5)$ unit-size components, all in the same or later size classes, are charged to the operation. The last step of the proof is to substitute $k = \log_{1+\delta} \Delta$.

Such a mapping implies the desired result for subadditive cost functions due to subadditivity and monotonicity. Subadditivity implies that the per-unit cost of reallocating larger jobs is less than that of smaller jobs. Monotonicity implies that all jobs in the same size class have a per-unit cost that varies by at most a constant factor.

Due to the boundary padding, there must be at least $\Omega(\lceil \delta w \rceil) = \Omega(\delta w)$ unit boundary movements to effect the reinsertion of a job in a size class having jobs of size at least w. (The ceiling arises because at least one slot must be lost to cause any job to move.) Due to Claim 2, the cost of this reinsertion is at most $O(1/\delta)$ times the initial allocation, or $O(1/\delta^2)$ per unit boundary slot lost.

Multiplying the lost slots of Property 2 with the $O(1/\delta^2)$ movements caused by each lost slot proves the lemma for subadditive functions. For strongly subadditive functions, observe that the per-unit cost of reallocating jobs geometrically decreases every $\log_{1+\delta} 2 = 1/\lg(1 + \delta) \approx 1/\delta$ size classes. Applying the other bound ($O(1)$ lost slots per district or size class) of Property 2 and multiplying by this additional $1/\delta$ factor completes the proof. □

We now bound the sum of completion times to complete the proof of Theorem 1. The analysis actually shows a $(1 + O(\delta))$ ratio; here is where we choose the constant in $\delta = \Theta(\varepsilon)$. The proof follows from the fact that the jobs are stored in order, and the empty space is limited by Property 1.

LEMMA 4. *At all times, the scheduled sum of completion times is at most $(1 + \varepsilon)$ times larger than optimal.*

PROOF. Fix a job class j containing jobs of size at least s and at most $s(1 + \delta)$. We show that the sum of completion times of the jobs in class j are within a $1 + O(\delta)$ factor of the sum of completion times for these same jobs in the optimal schedule. Let J be the set of jobs in job class j, and let $k = |J|$ be the number of jobs in J.

We divide the analysis into two parts, first examining the contribution of jobs in size classes $< j$, and then in size class j, to the sum of completion times of jobs in class j.

Recall that in an optimal schedule, the jobs are sorted in order from smallest to largest. Thus, every job that precedes job class j in the schedule also precedes every job in J in the optimal schedule. For each job in J, these earlier jobs contribute $V(1, j - 1)$ to the sum of completion times in the optimal schedule, i.e., at least $kV(1, j - 1)$ in total.

By Property 1, guaranteed by the k-cursor structure, job class j begins no later than $V(1, j - 1)(1 + \delta)^2$, and hence in the actual schedule these jobs contribute at most $kV(1, j - 1)(1 + \delta)^2$. The contribution of the jobs prior to job class j to the sum of completion times is within a $1 + 3\delta$ factor.

We now focus on the contribution of the jobs and empty space in job class j to the sum of completion times. Since there are k jobs of size at least s, the contribution of these jobs is at least $OPT_j = k(k + 1)s/2 \geq sk^2/2$.

We now consider the delay caused by the empty space that is part of job class j. Recall that job class j has size at most $V(j)(1 + \delta)^2$, and hence there is at most $3\delta V(j)$ empty space. Also, notice that since every job is of size at most $s(1 + \delta)$, we know that $V(j) \leq ks(1 + \delta) \leq 2ks$. Thus, the empty space contributes at most $k3\delta V(j) \leq 6\delta k^2 s$ to the sum of completion times, i.e., at most $12\delta OPT_j$.

Finally, we consider the delay caused by the jobs being out of order within job class j. Imagine beginning with the jobs in J in sorted order, and swapping jobs one at a time until the schedule matches that of the actual execution. This can be accomplished using at most k swaps, starting with the first job in the schedule and proceeding onwards. Since all the jobs have size at least s and at most $s(1 + \delta)$, each swap delays each later job by at most δs. This reordering adds $\delta k^2 s \leq 2\delta OPT_j$ to the sum of completion times.

In total, if OPT is the optimal schedule, then the schedule has a sum of completion times of at most $OPT(1 + 17\delta)$. □

3. PARALLEL SCHEDULING

This section generalizes the result from the previous section, showing how to design a reallocating scheduler for a parallel system consisting of p servers. The main result of this section is a scheduler where the sum of completion times is an $O(1)$ approximation of optimal, while the cost of insertions/deletions is $O(\log^3 \log \Delta)$ competitive with the total allocation costs (both bounds independent of p).

Algorithm

We consider a straightforward application of the previous scheduler. Each server executes an independent instance of the 1-processor reallocating scheduler.

As jobs are inserted and deleted, we use a simple balancing rule to ensure that within each size class, jobs are distributed evenly among the servers.

INVARIANT 5. *For any two servers s_k and s_ℓ, for every size class j, the number of jobs in size class j on the two servers differs by at most 1.*

In more detail, when an insertion happens: If the new job is in size class j, then we insert it on the server that has the smallest number of jobs in size class j (breaking ties by server id). That is, for each size class, we insert jobs in round-robin order. As such, there are no job migrations during an insertion. Thus each insertion has cost $O(\log^3 \log \Delta)$, i.e., the cost of scheduling one job on one server.

When a deletion happens, we may need to migrate a single job in order to maintain balance. Assume the job being deleted is in size class j and is deleted from server s_ℓ. If, after the deletion, Invariant 5 still holds, then we are done. Otherwise, we need to migrate one job to restore the invariant. Again, the cost is $O(\log^3 \log(\Delta))$: two deletions and one insertions yielding one migration.

Analysis

We show that this algorithm ensures that the sum of completion times is within a constant factor of optimal. For a given set of scheduled jobs, we consider the modified collection of jobs where the size of each job is rounded up to the nearest power of two. The real sum of completion times is bounded by the sum of completion times of the rounded set. We first observe the standard fact (see, e.g., [23]):

LEMMA 6. *Given a set of jobs in sorted order of size from smallest to largest, the sum of completion times is minimized by assigning jobs to servers round-robin.*

We next compare the schedule constructed by the optimal round-robin algorithm and the schedule constructed by our algorithm. The key difference is that when we start a new job class, we restart the round-robin scheduling with the first server. That is, within a job class, jobs are assigned round-robin across servers (in the order that they were added); but across job classes this is not true. We observe the following:

LEMMA 7. *For each job j, let S_j be the set of jobs that precede it on its server, as scheduled by the reallocating scheduler, and let S_j^{OPT} be the set of jobs that precede it on its server, as scheduled by the optimal round-robin schedule. The set difference $S_j \setminus S_j^{OPT}$ contains at most one job per size class.*

This immediately yields the following corollary:

COROLLARY 8. *The difference between the completion time of a job j when scheduled according to the reallocating scheduler and the optimal round-robin scheduler is at most $2size(j)$.*

Thus, the sum of completion times increases by at most a factor of two. This proves the following theorem:

THEOREM 9. *For a system with p servers, there exists a cost-oblivious reallocating scheduler for minimizing the sum of completion times that is $(O(1), O(\log^3 \log \Delta))$-competitive over all subadditive cost functions, and $(O(1), O(1/\varepsilon^3))$-competitive over all strongly subadditive cost functions. An insertion incurs only nonmigrating reallocations, and a deletion incurs at most one migrating reallocation.*

4. THE K-CURSOR DATA STRUCTURE

This section presents the *k-cursor sparse table*. A k-cursor table consists of k disjoint regions, called *cursor districts*, and supports insertion and deletion of the n unit-sized elements into a specified district. At any time, the districts must be stored in order in an (infinite) array, subject to *constant prefix density*. Specifically, given space parameter $\delta > 0$, the first x elements (i.e., those in the earliest districts) must be stored within the earliest $x + \lfloor \delta x \rfloor$ array slots.[3]

Each cursor district acts as a LIFO stack, where elements are inserted at the end of each district, and must be stored in each district in order of insertion. Similarly, elements must be deleted in reverse order of insertion. This is why we think of the data structure as consisting of *cursors*, e.g., editing at k locations within a single file. More precisely, the k-cursor sparse table supports:

- INSERT(x, j)—Insert the new element x at the end of the jth cursor district.
- DELETE(j)—Delete and return the last element from the jth cursor district, if the district is not empty.

Assume k is known *a priori*; we later relax this assumption.

Like standard sparse-tables [21], where elements may be inserted or deleted at arbitrary positions, we leave "empty space" in the array to support operations with a lower amortized cost. On insertion or deletion, an occasional "rebalance" may be triggered, where a (potentially large) region of the array is rebuilt, making room for future insertions or compacting the storage on deletion. Standard sparse tables are more general, but the amortized cost for insertion and deletion is $O(\log^2 n)$, which has a matching lower bound [11] in the worst case.

Our k-cursor sparse table supports insertions and deletions in amortized time $O(\log^3 k)$ per operation, with a constant that depends on the space parameter δ hidden in the big-O. Our k-cursor sparse table is also **one directional**: an insert or delete triggers a rebalance region that extends only to the right (for Property 2 of Section 2).

The remainder of this section is organized as follows. Section 4.1 provides an overview of the data structure, which includes most of the important ideas and intuition, with some details omitted. Section 4.2 fills-in the remaining details of the algorithm. Section 4.3 gives the space analysis and sketches the performance analysis, with more complete proofs deferred to the full version of the paper.

4.1 Overview

At a high level, the districts are stored in order in an array, with empty space carefully distributed to facilitate faster insertions and deletions. How this space is arranged and redistributed/rebalanced on insertions and deletions is the key to an efficient structure. The empty spaces in our data structure take two forms, which we call "buffers" and "gaps." The gaps add an additional complication, but they only arise in the data structure when districts have drastically different sizes. We describe a gapless version first, and later augment it to include gaps in Section 4.2.

We group cursor districts at $H + 1$ levels of granularity ($H = \lceil \lg k \rceil$) as follows. Without loss of generality, assume k is a power of 2, and make a complete binary tree of height $H = \lg k$ where the cursor districts are the leaves of the tree. A *level-0 chunk* corresponds to a single district and its buffer, stored sequentially in the array. A *level-$(i + 1)$ chunk*, for $0 \le i < H$, corresponds to a height-$(i + 1)$ subtree of districts, and thus includes the corresponding 2^{i+1} consecutive districts, as well as lower-level buffers and gaps. More precisely, a level-$(i + 1)$ chunk contains two level-i chunks plus a level-$(i + 1)$ buffer.[4] In the array, we

---

[3] For purposes of exposition, we allow $O(1)$ additional information per district to be stored outside the array, e.g., keeping pointers to the district's boundaries. In the scheduling reallocation problem, arbitrary bookkeeping is permitted.

[4] The binary tree can be represented implicitly because the chunks are "aligned," meaning that the 0th level-i chunk corresponds to districts $0, 1, \ldots, 2^i - 1$, and in general the rth level-i chunk consists of districts $r2^i, r2^i + 1, \ldots, (r+1)2^i - 1$.

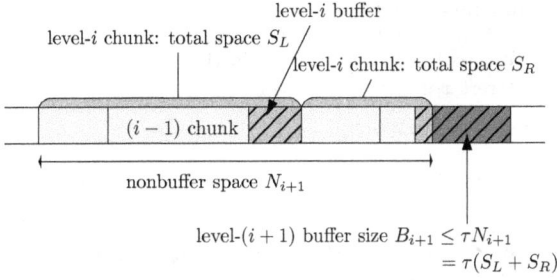

Figure 2: The recursive layout of a single level-$(i+1)$ chunk in the k-cursor sparse array, consisting of two level-i chunks and a level-$(i+1)$ buffer. An additional level of recursive layout is displayed.

store level-$(i+1)$ chunks recursively as its two child chunks, first the **left chunk** then the **right chunk**, followed by a **level-$(i+1)$ buffer**, as shown in Figure 2. Buffer slots are empty array slots that may be redistributed when insertions or deletions cause "rebalances" to occur. Every empty array slot (buffer and gap) is assigned to a particular chunk.

As a convention throughout this section, when referring to one chunk c_i we use the subscript i to denote its level. When referring to the left and right child chunks of a chunk, we use c_L and c_R, respectively.

The τ parameter: The data structure is parameterized by τ, which is set to $\tau = \Theta(\delta/H)$ for analysis. Since δ bounds the extra space, large δ only makes the problem easier; without loss of generality we assume $\delta \leq 1$ and thus $\tau \leq 1$. Due to rounding to integer indices within the array, it is convenient to restrict τ further. Specifically, we will choose τ such that $1/\tau \geq H$ is an integer.

Notation for space usage

For level-i chunk c_i, define space usage in the array as follows:

- **Buffer space**, denoted by $B(c_i)$, is the number of (empty) array slots assigned to c_i's buffer.
- **Gap space**, denoted by $G(c_i)$, is the number of (empty) array slots assigned to c_i as level-i gaps (see Section 4.2). A level-0 chunk has no gaps. For now, the reader should assume $G(c_i) = 0$.
- **Total space**, denoted by $S(c_i)$, includes all array slots assigned to c_i or its nested children. For $i \geq 1$, if c_i has children c_L and c_R, then $S(c_i) = S(c_L) + S(c_R) + B(c_i) + G(c_i)$. For a level-0 chunk, its total space is its buffer space plus the number of elements in the corresponding district.
- **Nonbuffer space**, denoted by $N(c_i)$, is defined as the total space excluding the buffer at that node but including its gaps, i.e., $N(c_i) + B(c_i) = S(c_i)$.

We maintain the following invariant over buffer/gap space, bounding the empty space with respect the total space of the children. This invariant alone is enough to bound the total space of the data structure, but it does not immediately imply prefix density, as we have not yet specified where the gaps are located.

INVARIANT 10. *(Space invariant) Except while processing an operation, for any chunk c_i we have:*

$$0 \leq B(c_i) \leq \tau N(c_i) .$$

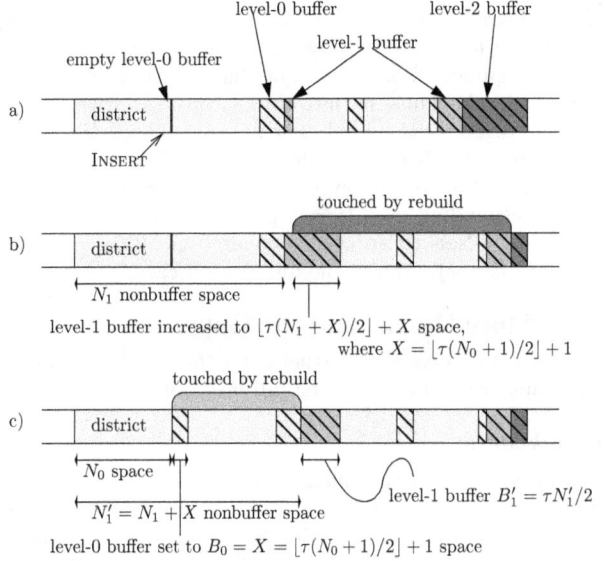

Figure 3: Example insertion into an empty buffer. (a) the initial layout of the structure. (b) the state after the level-1 buffer is rebuilt. (c) the state after the level-0 buffer is rebuilt. Finally (not shown), the element would be inserted into the newly rebuilt level-0 buffer, increasing and decreasing N_0 and B_0 by 1, respectively.

If c_i is a level-0 chunk, then $G(c_i) = 0$. Otherwise, let c_R be its right child, and we have:

$$0 \leq G(c_i) \leq \tau S(c_R) .$$

Insertion sketch

At a high level, ignoring gaps, insertions operate as described below. (See also Figure 3.) Section 4.2 gives more detail and pseudocode. To insert into a district, replace the leftmost buffer slot with the element being inserted. If no empty buffer slots remain, then the corresponding chunk must be "rebuilt." During a rebuild, the chunk increases its buffer space by taking slots from its parent chunk's buffer. "Taking slots" means scanning all slots between the current buffer and the parent buffer and sliding those elements to the right. If the parent does not have a large enough buffer to rebuild the child, the parent must first be rebuilt; this rebuild process may cascade up ancestors. When rebuilding a chunk c_i, it is rebuilt so that the *a posteriori* buffer size is $B'(c_i) = \lfloor \tau N'(c_i)/2 \rfloor$, where primed terms denote sizes after completion.

Analysis overview and why gaps occur

A main idea of the analysis (see Section 4.2) is that when rebuilding the buffer of a left level-i chunk c_L (the expensive case), the cost of the rebuild is proportional to the total space $S(c_R)$ of the right level-i chunk c_R that is moved out of the way. We amortize this cost against the $\geq \lfloor \tau N(c_L)/2 \rfloor$ slots moving into c_L's buffer. As long as the right level-i chunk satisfies $S(c_R) = O(N(c_L))$ slots, i.e., the right chunk is not much larger than the left chunk, then the amortized cost per buffer slot moved is $O(1/\tau)$. Summing across the

$H + 1$ levels yields an amortized insertion cost of $O(H/\tau)$, which is $O(\log^2 k/\delta)$ for $H = \lceil \lg k \rceil$ and $\tau = \Theta(\delta/H)$.

This argument fails if the right chunk is much larger than the left chunk. Thus, we introduce "gaps." As with buffers, gaps are tagged with a level. The purpose of level-$(i+1)$ gaps is similar to level-$(i + 1)$ buffers—when rebuilding a level-i chunk, take the nearest level-$(i+1)$ empty slots, either from the corresponding level-$(i + 1)$ gaps or buffer. Careful gap placements leads to an efficient operation (albeit increased by a $1/\tau$ factor), even in the unbalanced case.

4.2 More Details and the Gaps

This section describes further algorithmic details, notably how gaps are laid out and the full insertion algorithm.

Chunk states

The presence of small buffers poses a challenge in the analysis, primarily due to roundoff errors (floors and ceilings) aggregating across multiple levels. We avoid this issue by excluding small buffers using an additional chunk state, described next. This detail allows us to amortize the rounding error against more elements.

We associate with each chunk a state that is either BUFFERED or UNBUFFERED. As the name suggests, UN-BUFFERED chunks have no buffer; BUFFERED chunks may contain some buffer bounded by the buffer space invariant.[5] The states toggle as follows. An empty chunk is initially UN-BUFFERED. When the chunk's size grows to $N(c_i) \geq 2/\tau^2$, it becomes BUFFERED. When the chunk's nonbuffer space drops below $N(c_i) < 1/\tau^2$, it becomes UNBUFFERED.

In summary, a chunk with $N(c_i) < 1/\tau^2$ is always UN-BUFFERED, a chunk with $N(c_i) \geq 2/\tau^2$ is always BUFFERED, and a chunk with $1/\tau^2 \leq N(c_i) < 2/\tau^2$ may be either BUFFERED or UNBUFFERED depending on which threshold it crossed more recently.

Insertions and deletions

Insertions operate as follows; see Figure 4. This code includes handling of gaps, which we ignore for now in our discussion, i.e., ignore lines 10–16 and line 19, and assume $Z = Y$ in line 17. To insert an element into a district (level-0 chunk c_0), if the corresponding level-0 buffer has nonzero size $B(c_0) > 0$, replace the leftmost buffer slot with the element being inserted, thereby decreasing the buffer size.

If $B(c_0) = 0$, on the other hand, then a **rebalance** occurs, which consist of cascading chunk **rebuilds**, starting at the level-0 chunk c_0. In general, an (insertion-triggered) rebuild of a chunk c_i causes c_i to increase its total space by taking empty space from its parent's buffer, and moving that empty space to the right end of c_i's buffer. If the parent's buffer is not large enough to handle the child's space request, the parent must first be rebuilt. In this way, the rebuild may cascade through the nearest ancestor chunks of c_0, whose buffers are all located to the right of c_0. The rebalance ensures that after the insertion, all rebuilt BUFFERED ancestor chunks c_i have the **desired buffer size** $\lfloor \tau N'(c_i)/2 \rfloor$, where N' denotes the sizes after the operation completes.

More precisely, a rebuild (on insertion) takes as argument a level-i chunk c_i and some number X of additional slots to be given to a nested child, with $X = 1$ when rebuilding a

```
1:  procedure INSERT(x, j)      // add x to jth district
2:      Let c₀ be level-0 chunk containing the jth district.
3:      if B(c₀) = 0 then REBUILD(c₀,1)
4:      Insert x in first empty buffer slot.

5:  procedure REBUILD(cᵢ, X)
        // X ≥ 1 is the number of slots taken by a child
6:      if N(cᵢ) + X ≥ 2/τ² then mark cᵢ as BUFFERED
        // d is desired buffer size
7:      d = 0
8:      if cᵢ is BUFFERED then d = ⌊τ(N(cᵢ) + X)/2⌋
9:      Y = (d − B(cᵢ)) + X      // Y is increased to S(cᵢ)
10:     if cᵢ is a left chunk then
11:         gₚ = G(parent(cᵢ))
12:         TAKE leftmost min{gₚ, Y} level-(i + 1) gaps
            from parent(cᵢ).
13:         Z = Y − gₚ
            // Z is the number of level-(i + 1) buffer slots to take
14:     else // cᵢ is a right chunk
15:         Calculate g, the number of level-(i + 1) gaps
            distributed throughout the Y new space.
16:         Z = Y + g
17:     if Z > B(parent(cᵢ)) then REBUILD(parent(cᵢ), Z)
18:     TAKE leftmost Z slots from parent(cᵢ)'s buffer.
19:     Tag g of the slots as level-(i+1) gaps if cᵢ is a right chunk.
```

Figure 4: Pseudocode for insert and rebuild in the k-cursor data structure.

level-0 chunk (to accommodate the newly inserted element). Since the child is to add X slots to its total space, we have $N'(c_i) = N(c_i) + X$ after the operation; hence the desired buffer size is $d = \lfloor \tau(N(c_i) + X)/2 \rfloor$ as long as the chunk is BUFFERED. The rebuild of c_i takes $Y = d - B(c_i) + X$ slots from its parent, if available. If not, the parent is rebuilt first with requested space $Z = Y$. After taking space from the parent, $S(c_i)$ increases by Y slots, all of which are initially stored in the buffer. After this recursion, each chunk has collected all the space that it needs and rebuilds, leaving the final buffer size matching the desired buffer size.

We now consider how c_i takes Z space from its parent. Without gaps, all of the space in question belongs to the parent's buffer, which is located somewhere to the right of c_i. If c_i is the left child of its parent, then this space can be taken by sliding the entire intervening right level-i chunk to the right by Z slots. If c_i is a right child, then the parent's buffer is contiguous with it, and the empty buffer slots can simply be reassigned to c_i.

Figure 3 shows an example for insertion and rebalance, where all chunks are BUFFERED. An insert into the leftmost cursor district has insufficient space in the level-0 buffer (a). There is also insufficient space in the level-1 buffer to rebuild the level-0 buffer, so the rebalance propagates to the next level. First, the level-1 buffer is rebuilt by moving the sibling level-1 chunk (including 2 districts) to the right to move space from the level-2 buffer. Then the level-0 buffer is rebuilt by moving the sibling district to the right. In general, a rebalance may propagate through all H levels, requiring a buffer at each level to be rebuilt. At the end, the rebuilt buffers (in this case at levels 0 and 1) have buffer sizes equaling $\lfloor \tau N'(c)/2 \rfloor$.

Deletions are similar, but instead of taking slots from the parent's buffer, slots are returned to the parent's buffer.[6]

---

[5]Note that BUFFERED does not mean that $B(c_i) > 0$. A BUFFERED chunk may have $B(c_i) = 0$.

[6]In fact, deletions are more straightforward as the parent can be rebuilt *after* the slots are returned to it.

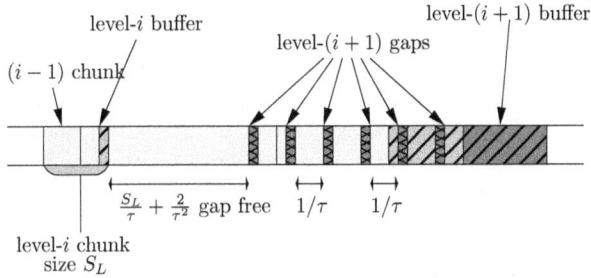

Figure 5: The recursive layout of a single level-$(i + 1)$ chunk with gaps present, including a left level-i chunk followed by a right level-i chunk followed by a level-$(i+1)$ buffer. As with Figure 2, a second level of the recursive layout is displayed. Level-$(i + 1)$ gaps are spread throughout the right level-i chunk, with $1/\tau$ slots between each gap. The leftmost S_L gaps (have been used and) are not present, where S_L is the total size of the left level-i chunk.

When deleting the last element in a district (level-0 chunk c_0), the slot it occupies is "returned" to the corresponding level-0 buffer. If the level-0 buffer size now violates the buffer space invariant, i.e., $B(c_0) > \tau N(c_0)$ where $N(c_0)$ is the number of postdeletion elements, then it is rebuilt to the same desired buffer size $d = \lfloor \tau N(c_0)/2 \rfloor$ by returning space to its parent. If the nonbuffer size is too small, i.e., $N(c_0) < 1/\tau^2$, then the chunk becomes UNBUFFERED and $d = 0$. In general, a level-i buffer is rebuilt to the desired buffer size by returning the excess elements to the nearest level-$(i+1)$ buffer to the right and sliding the entire intervening level-i sibling (if there is one) to the left. This process is analogous to the insertion rebuild. If the rebuild causes the level-$(i + 1)$ parent chunk c_{i+1}'s buffer to exceed its threshold (i.e., either $B(c_{i+1}) > \tau N(c_{i+1})$ or $N(c_{i+1}) < 1/\tau^2$), then it should also be rebuilt in a similar manner. After the rebalance completes, all rebuilt buffers of BUFFERED chunks have buffer space exactly $\lfloor \tau N(c_i)/2 \rfloor$, as with insertions.

Gap placement

Consider a level-$(i + 1)$ chunk c_{i+1}. The level-$(i + 1)$ gaps, each a single slot in the array, are incorporated into only the right level-i chunk c_R as shown in Figure 5 according to the following invariant. There are no level-$(i+1)$ gaps in the left level-i chunk. Here is where we require $1/\tau$ to be an integer, and we choose τ later to satisfy this integrality assumption.

INVARIANT 11. *(Gap invariant) Consider a level-$(i + 1)$ chunk c_{i+1} containing left and right level-i chunks c_L and c_R, respectively. The leftmost level-$(i + 1)$ gap appears after the first $2/\tau^2 + S(c_L)/\tau$ slots of the right level-i chunk c_R. Another gap appears after each of the next $1/\tau$ slots in c_R.*

The gap invariant is important from both directions. Specifically, the insert analysis requires that gaps not be too far from the left chunk so that a scan does not need to travel far to find empty space. The delete analysis, on the other hand, requires that gaps not be too near the left chunk so that gaps can be inserted into the right chunk without scanning very far. The gap invariant also implies the space invariant on gaps (i.e., $G(c_{i+1}) \leq \tau S(c_R)$). The additive $2/\tau^2$ term implies that UNBUFFERED chunks contain no gaps, which is convenient in the analysis.

Recall that each level-$(i + 1)$ gap is counted towards the nonbuffer space $N(c_{i+1})$ and the total space $S(c_{i+1})$ for the chunk c_{i+1}, but these gaps are not counted towards a child's space even though they interleave with the right chunk. When recursively considering the layout or rebuilding of the contained level-i chunks, think of the level-$(i + 1)$ or higher gaps as being elided—the position of level-$(i + 1)$ gaps are only manipulated when considering the level-$(i + 1)$ chunk. This elision is only for understanding the algorithm—the analysis must cope with the fact that "skipping" the gaps introduce additional cost.

How gaps affect updates in the k-cursor structure

We discuss how the insertion procedure copes with gaps; see Figure 4. The variable X should now be interpreted as the number of slots to add to the child's buffer plus the number of level-i gaps in c_i that this additional space requires. Since these gaps count towards c_i's nonbuffer space, it is still true that $N(c_i)$ is to increase by X, leaving the desired buffer space unaffected. Thus, Y denotes the total increase to $S(c_i)$ as before. We next consider two cases, depending on whether c_i is a left child or right child of its parent. Some handling of the cases is combined in the pseudocode, but we consider each case separately from start to finish here.

Suppose c_i is a left child, and let c_R be its right sibling. When rebuilding c_i, it should not contain any level-$(i+1)$ gaps. Hence, c_i need only take Y empty level-$(i + 1)$ slots from its parent. The difference is how it takes that space. Rather than drawing only from its parent's buffer, c_i first consumes the leftmost g_p level-$(i + 1)$ gaps that are spread throughout c_R. Taking these gaps means sliding some prefix of c_R to the right to fill in the appropriate previously empty spaces.[7] If there are not enough level-$(i + 1)$ gaps to handle c_i's space request, i.e., $Y > g_p$, then c_i takes the remaining $Z = Y - g_p$ level-$(i + 1)$ slots from its parent's buffer. If the parent does not have that many, it must first be rebuilt.

Suppose c_i is a right child, and let c_L be its left sibling. In this case, there are no level-$(i + 1)$ gaps to the right of c_i's buffer, and all the space c_i takes from its parent comes from the parent's buffer. But adding Y space to c_i may require introducing up to $\lceil \tau Y \rceil$ level-$(i + 1)$ gaps, according to the gap invariant. It is straightforward to calculate the number g of new gaps given the total space $S(c_i)$, the total space of its left neighbor $S(c_L)$, and the amount Y of increase to $S(c_i)$. These gaps would be counted towards the parent's nonbuffer space, so the space needed from the parent's level-$(i + 1)$ buffer is increased to $Z = Y + g$. Once appropriated, all of these empty slots appear at the end of c_i's buffer, but g of them (spread evenly, according to the gap invariant) belong to c_i's parent as level-$(i + 1)$ gaps and should be tagged appropriately (line 19).

Deletions may be similarly augmented to handle gaps. When rebuilding a left level-i chunk to return slots to its parent, return them as either level-$(i + 1)$ gaps or buffers according to the gap invariant. Gaps can be introduced to the right sibling by sliding the right sibling to the left to consume the returned space. When returning space from a right level-i chunk to its parent, also return any level-$(i + 1)$ gaps that are embedded in that space.

---

[7]Note that taking these gaps leaves the nonbuffer space of the parent unaffected, and hence this step does not risk violating the invariant on buffer space.

4.3 Analysis

This section analyzes the space usage and provides a sketch of the performance analysis.

Space analysis and prefix density

We now prove claims on the number of array slots used by regions of the k-cursor sparse array.[8] These claims are useful for proving both the desired prefix density and bounds on the cost of rebuilding buffers. We show that the data structure achieves constant prefix density. Throughout this section, we set $\tau = \frac{\delta'}{\lceil \lg k \rceil + 1}$, for some $0 < \delta'$ to be defined later in terms of τ so that $1/\tau$ is an integer greater than $\lceil \lg k \rceil + 1$.

The following bounds the space used by any chunk. Recall that slots counted towards a level-i chunk include those for all level-($\leq i$) buffers and gaps, but not higher-level gaps, so these slots are not necessarily contiguous.

LEMMA 12. *A level-i chunk c_i with a total of x elements in all descendent districts is assigned at most $S(c_i) \leq (1 + 3\tau)^{i+1} x$ array slots.*

PROOF. We proceed by induction on level i. For the base case, a level-0 chunk corresponds to a district with x elements and its size $\leq \tau x$ buffer, for at most $(1 + \tau)x$ slots. There are no level-0 gaps.

For the inductive step, consider a level-i chunk with $i > 0$. Let x_L and x_R be the number of elements in the left and right level-($i - 1$) chunks, respectively, and let S_L and S_R be the total number of slots used by these chunks. Then the space used by the level-i chunk is at most $(S_L + S_R)$ plus any level-i gaps plus the level-i buffer. By the gap-space invariant we have $G(c_i) \leq \tau S_R \leq \tau (S_L + S_R)$. The nonbuffer space is then upper bounded by $N(c_i) \leq (1 + \tau)(S_L + S_R)$, which implies the buffer space is at most $\tau(1 + \tau)(S_L + S_R)$ by the buffer-space invariant. Adding the nonbuffer space to the buffer space, we have $S(c_i) \leq (1 + \tau)^2(S_L + S_R) \leq (1 + 3\tau)(S_L + S_R)$ for $\tau \leq 1$. By inductive assumption, we have $S_L + S_R \leq (1 + 3\tau)^i x_L + (1 + 3\tau)^i x_R = (1 + 3\tau)^i x$. We thus conclude that the level-i chunk uses at most $(1 + 3\tau)(1 + 3\tau)^i x = (1 + 3\tau)^{i+1} x$ space. $\square$

We now extend the above lemma for a particular choice of τ:

COROLLARY 13. *Let $\tau = \frac{\delta'}{H+1}$ and $H = \lceil \lg k \rceil$, where δ' is chosen from the range $0 < \delta' \leq 1/6$. Then a chunk with x elements in all descendent districts is stored in at most $(1 + 6\delta')x$ array slots.*

PROOF. The worst case space usage occurs at the highest level (level H). According to Lemma 12, the space is at most $(1 + 3\tau)^{H+1} x = (1 + \frac{3\delta'}{H+1})^{H+1} x$ space. We then observe that $(1 + \frac{3\delta'}{H+1})^{H+1} \leq e^{3\delta'} = \sum_{j=0}^{\infty} \frac{(3\delta')^j}{j!} < \sum_{j=0}^{\infty} (3\delta')^j$. For $0 < \delta' \leq 1/6$, we have $\sum_{j=0}^{\infty} (3\delta')^j = \frac{1}{1-3\delta'} \leq 1 + 6\delta'$. Multiplying by x gives the corollary. $\square$

The preceding lemma and corollary ignore higher-level gaps within each chunk. The following lemma and corollary bound the number of gaps in a contiguous subarray.

LEMMA 14. *Any contiguous region of s slots in the array contains at most $\lceil \tau s \rceil$ level-i gaps, for any level i. Moreover, the first s slots in the array contain at most $\lfloor \tau s \rfloor$ level-i gaps.*

PROOF. By the gap invariant, there are $1/\tau$ slots allocated to a nested level-($i - 1$) chunk between each level-i gap. This fact is true even when the region spans different level-i chunks, as the first gap in the chunk does not appear until at after least $1/\tau$ slots. The addition of higher-level gaps can only cause the distance between two gaps in the array to increase. We conclude that there are at least $1/\tau$ array slots between any two level-i gaps, and hence the total number of level-i gaps in the region is at most $\lceil \tau s \rceil$.

When the region corresponds to a prefix of the array, the first gap begins after at least $2/\tau^2 \geq 1/\tau$ slots, which completes the proof. $\square$

COROLLARY 15. *Let $\tau = \frac{\delta'}{H+1}$ and $H = \lceil \lg k \rceil$, where $\delta' > 0$. Any contiguous region of s slots in the array contains at most $\delta' s + (H + 1)$ gaps across all levels. Moreover, the first s slots in the array contain at most $\delta' s$ gaps.*

PROOF. Sum Lemma 14 across all $H + 1$ levels with $\lceil \tau s \rceil$ rounded up to $\tau s + 1$. $\square$

The following theorem shows that our k-cursor sparse array guarantees constant prefix density. Setting $\delta' \leq \delta/9$ yields a space bound of $(1+\delta)x$ array slots to store the first x elements. To satisfy the integrality requirement on τ, we choose $\delta' = \frac{1}{\lceil 9/\delta \rceil}$.

THEOREM 16. *Let $\tau = \frac{\delta'}{H+1}$ and $H = \lceil \lg k \rceil$, where δ' is chosen from the range $0 < \delta' \leq 1/6$. Then the earliest x elements in the k-cursor sparse array are stored within the first $(1 + 9\delta')x$ array slots.*

PROOF. First, observe that any prefix of the array consists of a sequence of complete chunks of decreasing level, followed by at most one partial district.[9] Ignoring any higher-level gaps, a complete chunk with y elements uses $(1+6\delta')y$ space from Corollary 13. Ignoring higher-level gaps, a partial district contains only real elements, and thus uses y space to store y elements. Summing across all these chunks, we have $(1 + 6\delta')x$ space.

To incorporate higher-level gaps, we apply Corollary 15. Specifically, the first s slots in the array contains at most $\delta' s$ gaps. It follows that the first s slots include the first x elements as long as $s - \delta' s \geq (1+6\delta')x$, or $s \geq \frac{(1+6\delta')}{1-\delta'}x$. With $\delta' \leq 1/6$, we have $\frac{(1+6\delta')}{1-\delta'} < 1 + 9\delta'$, and hence $(1 + 9\delta')x$ slots must contain at least x elements. $\square$

Performance analysis

We now outline the analysis for the amortized cost of insertions and deletions. We focus on achieving an $O(\log^4 k/\delta^2)$ amortized cost per operation, with a brief discussion about removing a $\delta \log k$ factor. Proving the $O(\log^3 k/\delta^3)$ bound entails some additional complications (notably rounding error). The full details, including the $O(\log^3 k/\delta^3)$ analysis, are deferred to the full version.

Note that the reason for chunk states (BUFFERED and UNBUFFERED) is also to facilitate the better analysis. Throughout this section, instead consider a simplified version of the data structure where every chunk is always BUFFERED.

Our analysis is an accounting argument—we associate money with particular substructures, and we argue that

---

[8] All of these claims are implicitly intended to apply after fully processing some sequence of operations—the bounds may temporarily be violated during a rebalance event.

[9] E.g., the first 11 districts correspond to a level-3 chunk followed by a level-1 chunk followed by a level-0 chunk.

enough money is released to pay for the cost of any rebuild. Throughout this section, we implicitly adopt the terminology/variables (i.e., X, Y, Z) used in Figure 4.

We first consider the actual cost of each rebuild:

LEMMA 17. *Consider a* BUFFERED *chunk c_i that is being rebuilt to increase or decrease its space usage by $Y \geq 1$ slots. Then the cost of the rebuild is $O(Y/\tau^2)$.*

PROOF SKETCH. There are several cases to consider (insert or delete on a left or right chunk). Since the parent's buffer is contiguous, the most expensive case is when c_i is a left child and the Y slots taken (or returned) are gaps. From the gap invariant, these Y slots are located within the next $2/\tau^2 + S(c_i)/\tau + Y/\tau$ slots of the parent. From Corollary 15 and the fact that $H < 1/\tau$, the cost of scanning that many slots in the parent is at most a constant factor more.

To complete the proof sketch, we claim that whenever a BUFFERED chunk c_i is rebuilt, we must have $Y = \Omega(\tau S(c_i))$. Combining this claim with the above bound, the dominating term is $O(S(c_i)/\tau) = O(Y/\tau^2)$. Again, there are several cases. For an insert, the idea is that a chunk is only rebuilt if its buffer would be more than drained, and hence the number of slots Y it takes is at least $\lceil \tau S(c_i)/2 \rceil$. □

Our accounting argument pins a specific amount of money to each level-i chunk. More precisely, we define currencies $\$_i$ at each level in the data structure. For any chunk, we maintain the invariant that c_i has at least

$$\$_i \left| \widehat{B}(c_i) - B(c_i) \right| ,$$

where $B(c_i)$ is the current buffer space and $\widehat{B}(c_i)$ is the buffer just after the previous rebalance the rebuilt c_i.

The value of a level-i dollar $\$_i$ depends on i. Specifically, a level-i dollar is worth the following number of normal $\$$'s:

$$\$_i 1 = \$(H + 1 - i) \left(1 + \frac{4}{H+1} \right)^{H+1-i} , \quad (1)$$

where $H = \lceil \lg k \rceil$. We will charge $\Theta(1/\tau^2) = \Theta(\log^2 k/\delta^2)$ units of work to each dollar. Note that level-0 dollars are the most valuable, each worth $\$_0 1 \leq \$(H+1)e^4 = \$\Theta(\log k)$, or $\Theta(\log^3 k/\delta^2)$ units of work.

The main idea of the analysis is to leverage the difference in values across levels. In particular, consider when a level-i chunk c_i is rebuilt (on insert), requesting Y slots from its parent. During the rebuild, $\widehat{B}(c_i)$ changes and after the rebalance $\widehat{B}(c_i) = B(c_i)$. Thus, c_i's entire account can be used for the rebuild. The challenge is that slots are taken from c_i's parent's buffer, so the parent must be compensated. The key observation, following from Equation 1, is that currency can be converted across levels at the following rate:

$$\$_i 1 \geq \$1 + \$_{i+1} \left(1 + \frac{4}{H+1} \right) . \quad (2)$$

In this way, if c_i has $\$_i D$, then we can afford $\$D$ for the rebuild itself, and also pass $\$_{i+1}(1 + \frac{4}{H+1})D$ to the parent.

The remaining argument is to show that c_i has enough money stored to pay for its rebuild and to compensate its parent. The argument proceeds by induction over rebuilds from low to high: We assume inductively that c_i has $\$_i D$, where D is at least the number of buffer slots already consumed plus the number X of slots requested by the rebuilding child; we prove that c_i can afford to pass $\$_{i+1}Z$ to its parent. To do so, we argue that $Z \leq (1+O(\tau))D + O(1) \leq (1 +$

$\frac{4}{H+1})D + O(1)$, which entails applying relationships among different types of space. (The constant 4 in Equation 1 was specifically chosen to exceed the one in $O(\tau)$.) From the conversion rate, $\$_i D$ yields $\$_{i+1}(1+\frac{4}{H+1})D \geq \$_{i+1}Z - \$_{i+1}O(1)$, which almost fully pays the parent (except for $\$_{i+1}O(1)$). Moreover, $D = \Omega(Z)$ and hence $D = \Omega(Y)$, so by Lemma 17 the $\$D$ given off by the conversion are also enough to pay for the rebuild itself. We charge the $\$_{i+1}O(1)$ at each rebuilt level to the insertion itself, giving a total cost of at most $\$_0 O(H) = \$O(\log^2 k) = O(\log^2 k/\tau^2) = O(\log^4 k/\delta^2)$.

The preceding argument suffers from rounding errors that may occur at all H levels of granularity. A more sophisticated argument leveraging the chunk states allows us to amortize most of those $\$_{i+1}O(1)$'s against $\Theta(1/\tau^2)$ insertions, requiring each insert to pay at most $\$_0 O(1) = O(\log^3 k/\delta^2)$ work. (Our current analysis has a potentially unnecessary extra $1/\delta$ factor due to some extra boundary condition on chunk states.) To summarize the main result:

THEOREM 18. *The amortized cost of an insertion or deletion into the k-cursor sparse table is $O(\log^3 k/\delta^3)$.*

We next specialize the bound to the reallocation scheduler of Section 2 by considering the "charging pattern" and lost slots. Specifically, the next theorem directly implies Property 2. There are two main ideas to the proof, which is deferred to the full version. First, all money is passed only up to ancestors. Rebuilds of a chunk touch only space to the right of the chunk, so as money moves up it pays only for rebuilds that occur even further to the right. Second, to get an $O(1)$ bound on lost slots per district, let us consider what happens when rebuilding a left level-i chunk takes (or returns) Z slots from the parent. Essentially, Z empty space is moved to the left (or to the right), causing any district boundary in the right subtree to move rightward (or leftward) by up to Z slots; thus these districts lose at most $2Z$ slots. As we have $\$_i\Omega(Z)$ to work with, we need only charge $O(1)$ lost slots against each level-i dollar. Considering the path of money in the structure, a district can only charge to an insert when that insert's money is at a specific ancestor.

THEOREM 19. *A total of $O(\log^3 k/\delta^3)$ lost slots are charged to each insert or delete. Each lost slot is only charged to an operation occurring in a district to the left. There are at most $O(1)$ lost slots in each district charged to a particular insert or delete.*

Creating more cursors

If k is not known *a priori*, cursors can be added at the end of the structure without increasing the asymptotic costs. These additions must be at the end—the data structure does not support arbitrary cursor insertions. The one complication is that if k changes, then τ changes. Fortunately, we can modify the data structure to define τ locally—any chunk containing districts $\leq \ell$ uses $L = \lceil \lg \ell \rceil$ and hence $\tau' = \Theta(\delta/(\lceil \lg \ell \rceil + 1))$. None of the performance theorems are asymptotically affected by this change.

5. CONCLUSIONS

This paper has presented an efficient cost-oblivious reallocation algorithm for the sum of completion times. It remains open whether constant reallocation cost is possible; there are no nontrivial lower bounds. More generally, there exist a wealth of unexplored reallocation problems in combinatorial optimization and scheduling, problems that arise when online decisions can be changed at some cost.

6. REFERENCES

[1] M. Andrews, M. X. Goemans, and L. Zhang. Improved bounds for on-line load balancing. *Algorithmica*, 23(4):278–301, 1999.

[2] C. Archetti, L. Bertazzi, and M. G. Speranza. Reoptimizing the Traveling Salesman Problem. *Networks*, 42(3):154–159, 2003.

[3] C. Archetti, L. Bertazzi, and M. G. Speranza. Reoptimizing the 0-1 knapsack problem. *Disc. Appl. Math.*, 158(17):1879–1887, Oct. 2010.

[4] G. Ausiello, V. Bonifaci, and B. Escoffier. Complexity and approximation in reoptimization. In S. B. Cooper and A. Sorbi, editors, *Computability in Context: Computation and Logic in the Real World*, pages 101–129. World Scientific, 2011.

[5] G. Ausiello, B. Escoffier, J. Monnot, and V. T. Paschos. Reoptimization of minimum and maximum traveling salesman's tours. *J. Disc. Alg.*, 7(4):453–463, 2009.

[6] G. Baram and T. Tamir. Reoptimization of the minimum total flow-time scheduling problem. In G. Even and D. Rawitz, editors, *Proc. MedAlg*, volume 7659 of *LLNCS*, pages 52–66, 2012.

[7] M. A. Bender, M. Farach-Colton, S. P. Fekete, J. T. Fineman, and S. Gilbert. Reallocation problems in scheduling. In *Proc. SPAA*, pages 271–279, 2013.

[8] M. A. Bender, M. Farach-Colton, S. P. Fekete, J. T. Fineman, and S. Gilbert. Cost-oblivious storage reallocation. In *Proc. PODS*, pages 278–288, 2014.

[9] M. A. Bender and H. Hu. An adaptive packed-memory array. *Trans. Datab. Syst.*, 32(4), 2007.

[10] H.-J. Böckenhauer, L. Forlizzi, J. Hromkovic, J. Kneis, J. Kupke, G. Proietti, and P. Widmayer. Reusing optimal TSP solutions for locally modified input instances. In *Proc. TCS*, pages 251–270, 2006.

[11] J. Bulánek, M. Koucký, and M. Saks. Tight lower bounds for the online labeling problem. In *Proc. STOC*, pages 1185–1198, 2012.

[12] A. Caprara, L. Galli, L. Kroon, G. Maróti, and P. Toth. Robust train routing and online re-scheduling. In *Proc. ATMOS*, pages 24–33, 2010.

[13] V. Chiraphadhanakul and C. Barnhart. Robust flight schedules through slack re-allocation. *EURO Journal on Transportation and Logistics*, 2(4):277–306, 2013.

[14] S. Davis, J. Edmonds, and R. Impagliazzo. Online algorithms to minimize resource reallocations and network communication. In *Proc. APPROX-RANDOM*, pages 104–115, 2006.

[15] L. Epstein and A. Levin. A robust APTAS for the classical bin packing problem. In *Proc. ICALP*, pages 214–225, 2006.

[16] L. Epstein and A. Levin. Robust algorithms for preemptive scheduling. In *Proc. ESA*, pages 567–578, 2011.

[17] S. P. Fekete, T. Kamphans, N. Schweer, C. Tessars, J. C. van der Veen, J. Angermeier, D. Koch, and J. Teich. Dynamic defragmentation of reconfigurable devices. *ACM Trans. Reconf. Technol. Syst.*, 5(2):8:1–8:20, June 2012.

[18] R. Graham, E. Lawler, J. Lenstra, and A. Kan. Optimization and approximation in deterministic sequencing and scheduling: a survey. *Ann. Disc. Math.*, 5:287 – 326, 1979.

[19] N. G. Hall and C. N. Potts. Rescheduling for new orders. *Op. Res.*, 52(3), 2004.

[20] A. Itai and I. Katriel. Canonical density control. *IPL*, 104(6):200–204, 2007.

[21] A. Itai, A. G. Konheim, and M. Rodeh. A sparse table implementation of priority queues. In *Proc. ICALP*, pages 417–431, 1981.

[22] H. Jiang and C. Barnhart. Dynamic airline scheduling. *Transp. Sc.*, 43(3):336–354, 2009.

[23] D. Karger, C. Stein, and J. Wein. *Scheduling Algorithms*. CRC Press, 1998.

[24] I. Katriel. Implicit data structures based on local reorganizations. Master's thesis, Technion, May 2002.

[25] P. Kouvelis and G. Yu. *Robust Discrete Optimization and Its Applications*. Kluwer, 1997.

[26] S. Lan, J.-P. Clarke, and C. Barnhart. Planning for robust airline operations: Optimizing aircraft routings and flight departure times to minimize passenger disruptions. *Transp. Sc.*, 40(1):15–28, 2006.

[27] J. M. Mulvey, R. J. Vanderbei, and S. A. Zenios. Robust optimization of large-scale systems. *Op. Res.*, 43(2), 1995.

[28] P. Sanders, N. Sivadasan, and M. Skutella. Online scheduling with bounded migration. *Math. Oper. Res.*, 34(2):481–498, 2009.

[29] H. Shachnai, G. Tamir, and T. Tamir. A theory and algorithms for combinatorial reoptimization. In *Proc. LATIN*, pages 618–630, 2012.

[30] M. Skutella and J. Verschae. A robust PTAS for machine covering and packing. In *Proc. ESA*, pages 36–47, 2010.

[31] C. A. Tovey. Rescheduling to minimize makespan on a changing number of identical processors. *Nav. Res. Logist.*, 33:717–724, 1986.

[32] A. T. Unal, R. Uzsoy, and A. S. Kiran. Rescheduling on a single machine with part-type dependent setup times and deadlines. *Ann. Op. Res.*, 70, 1997.

[33] J. C. Verschae. *The Power of Recourse in Online Optimization Robust Solutions for Scheduling, Matroid and MST Problems*. PhD thesis, TU Berlin, June 2012.

[34] J. Westbrook. Load balancing for response time. *J. of Alg.*, 35(1):1 – 16, 2000.

[35] D. Willard. Maintaining dense sequential files in a dynamic environment (extended abstract). In *Proc. STOC*, pages 114–121, 1982.

[36] D. E. Willard. Good worst-case algorithms for inserting and deleting records in dense sequential files. In *Proc. SIGMOD*, pages 251–260, 1986.

[37] D. E. Willard. A density control algorithm for doing insertions and deletions in a sequentially ordered file in good worst-case time. *I&C*, 97(2):150–204, 1992.

Temporal Fairness of Round Robin: Competitive Analysis for Lk-norms of Flow Time

Sungjin Im
University of California, Merced
Merced, CA 95343
sim3@ucmerced.edu

Janardhan Kulkarni
Duke University
Durham, NC 27708
kulkarni@cs.duke.edu

Benjamin Moseley
Washington University in St. Louis.
St. Louis, MO 63130
bmoseley@wustl.edu

ABSTRACT

Fairness is an important criterion considered in scheduling together with overall job latency. Round Robin (RR) is a popular scheduling policy that distributes resources to jobs equally at any point in time guaranteeing instantaneous fairness of jobs. In this paper we give the *first* analysis of RR for the ℓ_2-norm of flow time and show that it is $O(1)$-speed $O(1)$-competitive on multiple machines. The ℓ_2-norm is a popular scheduling objective that makes a natural balance between temporal fairness and jobs latency. Prior to our work, RR has not been analyzed for the ℓ_2-norm even in the single machine setting. Our result establishes that RR is fair not only instantaneously but also *temporarily*.

Categories and Subject Descriptors

F.2.2 [**Nonnumerical Algorithms and Problem**]: Sequencing and scheduling

General Terms

Algorithms, Theory

Keywords

Online scheduling, Round Robin, Fairness.

1. INTRODUCTION

Most server-client scheduling settings can be characterized by a set of servers/machines/processors and clients who send their requests to the servers over time for service. Each request/job j typically has a processing time/size p_j and an arrival time r_j, which is the first time the scheduler is aware of the existence of the job and can start processing it. Commonly, each client wants her job j to be completed as early as possible, i.e. the job j's flow time to be minimized. A job j's response/flow time is defined as its completion time C_j minus its arrival time r_j, the amount of time the job waits in the system to be satisfied.

However, when multiple jobs compete for limited resources to get service earlier, the scheduler must prioritize between jobs. While there are many scheduling objectives that could be optimized, the most popular is the objective of minimizing the total (or equivalently average) flow time, i.e. $\sum_j (C_j - r_j)$. Indeed, algorithms have been analyzed in various setting for the total flow objective in the competitive analysis framework. An online scheduling policy is said to be c-competitive for a certain objective if its objective is at most a c factor more than the optimal scheduler's objective for any sequence of jobs. Competitive analysis is of fundamental importance since performance guarantees hold even in the worst scenarios.

Unfortunately, competitive analysis often yields pessimistic results. For example, it is folklore that Shortest Remaining Time Processing (SRPT) is optimal, i.e. 1-competitive, in the single machine setting for the average flow time objective. However, it is known that no online algorithm is $O(1)$-competitive when there are multiple machines [23]. To alleviate this pessimistic view, the resource augmentation model was proposed by [22]. In the resource augmentation model, if an online algorithm is given s times faster machine(s) and has an objective at most c times the optimal objective, then the algorithm is said to be s-speed c-competitive. In general, $O(1)$-speed $O(1)$-competitiveness is considered to be an indicator of "reasonably good" scheduling algorithms although $(1 + \epsilon)$-speed is $O(1)$-competitiveness for any fixed $\epsilon > 0$, a.k.a. scalability, is the most desirable. Resource augmentation has enabled the development and analysis of algorithms for various scheduling environments.

Another important scheduling criterion is *fairness* which is not captured by objectives focusing on the overall job latency such as the average flow time objective. There are largely two types of fairness typically considered, *instantaneous* and *global*. For instantaneous fairness, the main goal is to distribute resources to jobs evenly at each moment in time. While the notion of fairness can be somewhat subjective, there is a widely accepted fair algorithm when the resources are homogeneous/identical, Round Robin. Round Robin (RR) is an algorithm that achieves fairness by giving an equal share of the machine(s) to all jobs at all times. This fairness also coincides with maximizing the minimum fairness, which is the most widely accepted fairness notion in many disciplines.

The other type of fairness, which we call temporal fairness, is measured by global scheduling objectives. As mentioned before, average flow time only measures the average latency of job service times, thereby potentially allowing some jobs to starve for service for an unacceptably long time. However, Silberschatz, Galvin and Gagne's classic textbook on Operating Systems [26] states *"A system with reasonable and predictable response time may be considered more desirable than a system that is faster on the average, but is highly variable."* and *"... for interactive systems, it is more important to minimize the variance in the response time than it is to minimize the average response time."*

Motivated by temporal fairness, Bansal and Pruhs analyzed various scheduling policies such as SRPT and Shortest Job First (SJF) for minimizing the ℓ_2-norms of flow time (more generally ℓ_k-norms [1] of flow time, $(\sum_j (C_j - r_j)^k)^{1/k}$) in an influential paper [4], and showed they are $O(1)$-speed $O(1)$-competitive. Intuitively, the ℓ_2-norm of flow time objective attempts to minimize the variance of flow times of jobs as well as the average. However, the aforementioned algorithms do not provide instantaneous fairness since they may schedule only one job for a long time until the priorities change due to job processing or other jobs arrival.

A natural looming question is if there is an algorithm that achieves the instantaneous and global fairness simultaneously while optimizing the overall job latency. The RR algorithm is widely used in situations where fairness is an important criteria. For example, [8, 17, 25]. However, despite the algorithm being used for its fair properties, it is not known to be fair globally. It is known that RR is $O(1)$-speed $O(1)$-competitive for average flow time [11, 13]. However, RR has no known guarantees for the ℓ_2-norm of flow time and it has remained an open question if this algorithm, which is intuitively as fair as possible, is in fact temporally fair even in the single machine scheduling setting.

1.1 Our Results

In this paper we answer the above question in the affirmative by giving the first analysis of the instantaneously fair algorithm Round Robin (RR) for the ℓ_k-norms of flow time. We show that RR has provable guarantees for temporal fairness in the multiple identical machines setting. The algorithm RR has a natural interpretation in this setting: at any point in time when there are more jobs than machines, allocate machines to jobs equally. Otherwise, process each job on one machine exclusively. We show that this algorithm has the following guarantees.

Theorem 1 *The scheduling policy Round Robin (RR) is $2k(1 + 10\epsilon)$-speed $O(\frac{k}{\epsilon})$-competitive for the ℓ_k-norm of flow time for any $0 < \epsilon \leq 1/10$ and all $k \geq 1$. Furthermore, this result holds even when there are multiple identical machines.*

In particular, our analysis shows that RR is $(4 + \epsilon)$-speed $O(1)$-competitive for the ℓ_2-norm of flow time for any fixed $\epsilon > 0$. We emphasize that the same algorithm RR is $O(1)$-speed $O(1)$-competitive for both the ℓ_1 and ℓ_2-norms of flow time simultaneously. Prior to our work, it was unknown if RR is $O(1)$-speed $O(1)$-competitive for the ℓ_2-norm even in the simplest single machine setting.

We note that it is known that RR is $\Omega(n^{1-2\epsilon p})$-competitive when given $(1 + \epsilon)$-speed [4]. Particularly, this means that RR is not $O(1)$-competitive with speed less than $3/2$ for the ℓ_2-norm objective. On the positive side, our result shows RR is $O(1)$-competitive with speed $4 + \epsilon$.

1.2 Our Techniques and Backstory

Perhaps the reason why the temporal fairness of RR was not studied before is due to the underlying technical challenges arising in the analysis. The first analysis of RR for the ℓ_1-norm of flow time was algebraically very involved [11]. This was in a stark contrast to the fact that other simple scheduling policies such as SRPT and SJF have considerably simpler analysis. This is no surprise considering that the sharing aspect of RR does not result in an mathematically easy expression of total flow time unlike other scheduling policies.

A significantly simpler analysis of RR for the ℓ_1-norm was later given by Edmonds and Pruhs [13]. They gave a very elegant analysis using a novel potential function, and the analysis has been extremely useful for other various scheduling problems; for an overview of potential function based analysis of online scheduling algorithms, see [21]. However, the ℓ_2-norm is very different from the ℓ_1-norm since older jobs contribute more to the objective than young jobs and the analysis of RR for the ℓ_1-norm does not extend to the ℓ_2-norm. Another possible analysis approach to study RR for the ℓ_2-norm is linear programming and dual fitting, which was recently introduced for scheduling analysis [1, 16].

A potential issue with using potential functions or dual fitting is that the analysis seems to require a weighted version of RR. Let's focus on the total square of flow times of jobs, i.e. $\sum_j (C_j - r_j)^2$ by peeling out the square root of the ℓ_2-norm objective. As mentioned before, when jobs arrive over time, RR does not admit a closed form of mathematical expression of the square objective. Hence an alternative approach is to focus on the instantaneous increase of the square objective in the RR's schedule at each time. At any point in time each alive job j contributes by twice the job's current age to the instantaneous increase in the objective. Here if jobs are given machines in proportion to their ages (a 'weighted' version of RR), both the potential function and dual fitting approaches go through relatively easily. However, the analysis of RR is significantly more challenging since it is oblivious to jobs ages.

Even algorithmically, it was not clear if RR was a right algorithm for the ℓ_2-norm of flow time. In fact, in other scheduling environments such as the arbitrary speed-up curves and broadcast settings, RR was shown not to be $O(1)$-speed $O(1)$-competitive [15]. However, the weighted variant of RR that distributes machines to jobs in proportion to their ages was shown to be $O(1)$-speed $O(1)$-competitive for the ℓ_2-norm [12]. These results suggest that there was no strong reason to believe RR would perform well in the standard scheduling setting for the ℓ_2-norm.

Our analysis is based on linear programming and dual fitting. The challenge is how to set up dual variables. While our analysis inspired by the recent work [18,19], our setting of dual variables is very different from the previous work. Roughly speaking, there are two types of dual variables that one is required to set, how much each job is responsible for the objective, and how much a job contributes to each time t. A naive extension of the previous work fails. In particular, as alluded to before, we had to add "global" quantities to both variables not only just the instantaneous quantities such as jobs ages. This will be further discussed in Section 3.2.

---

[1]In practice, $k \in [1, 3] \cup \{\infty\}$ are considered.

1.3 Related Work

As mentioned before, it is well known that SRPT is optimal for the ℓ_1-norm of flow time in the single machine setting. The algorithms SJF and Shortest Elapsed Time First (SETF) are known to be $O(1+\epsilon)$-speed $O(1)$-competitive [7, 22]. The same objective was extensively studied in the multiple machines setting [2,3,6,9,10,14,23,27]. In particular, SRPT and SJF both are $O(1+\epsilon)$-speed $O(1)$-competitive on multiple machines [14,27]. However, only a "fractional" version of SETF was shown to be scalable [5] on multiple machines.

For ℓ_k-norms of flow time, [4] showed various algorithm are scalable $((1+\epsilon)$-speed $O(1)$-competitive), including SRPT, SJF, and SETF. It is known that SJF and SRPT are scalable for ℓ_k-norms of flow time even on multiple machines [14,27].

In [13], RR and its extension were analyzed. The setting was the arbitrary speed-up curves setting where each job can be sped up by being assigned more machines, and can have a different degree of parallelizability. In the closely related broadcast scheduling setting, jobs asking for the same data can be processed simultaneously. As mentioned, while RR is $O(1)$-speed $O(1)$-competitive for the ℓ_1-norm in both settings [12], it is not $O(1)$-competitive even with any $O(1)$-speed for the ℓ_2-norm [15].

For recent results for heterogeneous machines, see [1, 19, 20]. For a nice (but slightly outdated) survey on online scheduling, we refer the reader to [24].

2. PROBLEM DEFINITION AND NOTATION

In this section, we formally define the problem along with notation which will be used throughout this paper. There are m identical machines available. Each job j arrives at time r_j, and this is the first time when the online scheduler learns about job j. In a feasible schedule, each machine can schedule at most one job at each moment in time. Let $A(t)$ denote the set of jobs alive at time t in the schedule of the online algorithm we consider. A feasible schedule can alternatively be characterized by $\{m_j(t)\}_{j \in A(t)}$ at each time t such that $\sum_j m_j(t) \leq 1$, and $m_j(t) \in [0,1]$ for all jobs j and times $t \geq 0$. That is, any $\{m_j(t)\}$ satisfying these constraints can be easily translated into a feasible schedule that fits in the former definition, and vice versa. It is easy to see that in the RR's schedule,

$$m_j(t) = \min\{1, m/n_t\},$$

where $n_t := |A(t)|$ is the number of jobs alive at time t.

Job j completes at time t when it gets p_j amount of total processing since its arrival. Note that RR does not need to know job j's size, p_j, until its completion, and such an algorithm is called non-clairvoyant. In the ℓ_k norms of flow time, the goal is to minimize $\sqrt[k]{\sum_{j \in [n]} (C_j - r_j)^k}$.

We refine $A(t)$ by adding an extra constraint to refer to jobs that are alive at time t and satisfy the constraint. For example, $A(t, \leq r_j)$ refers to jobs alive at time t and arrive before job j. For notational simplicity, we may use RR to denote RR's objective. Likewise, OPT may denote the optimal scheduler's objective, not only the scheduling policy itself. The flow time of job j in RR's schedule will be denoted F_j.

3. ANALYSIS

3.1 LP relaxation

In this section we will prove Theorem 1. We assume throughout the analysis that RR is given $\eta := 2k(1 + 10\epsilon)$-speed where $0 < \epsilon \leq 1/10$. Note that every job $j \in A(t)$ is processed at a rate of $\eta \cdot \min\{1, m/n_t\}$ in RR's schedule at each time t where $n_t := |A(t)|$ denotes the number of jobs alive at time t. As mentioned earlier, our analysis will be based on dual fitting which was first used by [1,16] in online scheduling literature. It will be more convenient to compare RR's kth power of flow time to the analogous quantity of the optimal scheduler – the competitive analysis of ℓ_k norms of flow time will immediately follow by taking the kth root on the kth power of flow time objective.

A linear programming relaxation of the problem $\mathsf{LP}_{\text{primal}}$ is described as follows. The variables x_{jt} denote the rate at which job j is processed at time t. The first constraint says that every job must be completely processed. The second constraint says the total rate at which all jobs are processed at each time t is upper bounded by m, the number of machines available. (Alternatively, one can think of m machines as one super machine with speed m.) In this LP relaxation, a job is allowed to be processed simultaneously across different machines, but we assume a feasible algorithm can schedule a job on at most one machine at each point in time. In the LP, let $\gamma = k(k/\epsilon)^{k-1}$ be a constant that depends on ϵ and k. For technical reasons in the dual fitting analysis, we add a factor γ to the objective. We note that this simply increases the value of the primal by a factor γ.

$$\text{Min} \quad \sum_j \sum_{t \geq r_j} \gamma \left(\frac{(t - r_j)^k}{p_j} + \frac{p_j^k}{p_j} \right) \cdot x_{jt} \qquad (\mathsf{LP}_{\text{primal}})$$

$$\sum_{t \geq r_j} x_{jt} \geq p_j \qquad \forall j$$
$$\sum_{j : t \geq r_j} x_{jt} \leq m \qquad \forall t$$
$$x_{jt} \geq 0 \qquad \forall j, t : t \geq r_j$$

Observe that the above LP lower bounds the optimal flow time of a feasible schedule within factor 2γ. This is becuase $t - r_j \leq F_j$ if job j is alive at time t, and job j's flow time is at least p_j in any feasible schedule. Next we write the dual of $\mathsf{LP}_{\text{primal}}$.

$$\text{Max} \quad \sum_j \alpha_j - \sum_t \beta_t \qquad (\mathsf{LP}_{\text{dual}})$$

$$\frac{\alpha_j}{p_j} - \frac{\beta_t}{m} \leq \gamma \left(\frac{(t - r_j)^k}{p_j} + \frac{p_j^k}{p_j} \right) \qquad \forall j, t : t \geq r_j$$
$$\alpha_j \geq 0 \qquad \forall j$$
$$\beta_t \geq 0 \qquad \forall t$$

The dual has a variable α_j for every job j corresponding to the first constraint in the primal and a variable β_t corresponding to the second constraint. We will show that there is a setting of dual variables such that objective function of the dual is at least $\Omega(\epsilon)$ times RR's kth power of flow time. This will imply that RR's kth power of flow time is at most

$O(1/\epsilon)$ times the dual objective, hence $O(\gamma/\epsilon)$ times the optimal scheduler's kth power of flow time. By taking the kth root, we will have Theorem 1.

3.2 Setting of Dual Variables

Let $T_o := \{t \mid |A(t)| \geq m\}$ denote the set of *overloaded times* where all m machines are busy in RR's schedule (in other words, total number jobs available for processing is at least m), and T_u denote the other times which will be referred to as *underloaded times*. We set α_j as follows:

$$\alpha_j = \left(\sum_{t' \in [r_j, C_j] \cap T_o} \sum_{j' \in A(t', \leq r_j)} \frac{k(t' - r_{j'})^{k-1}}{n_{t'}} \right)$$
$$+ \left(\sum_{t' \in [r_j, C_j] \cap T_u} k(t - r_j)^{k-1} \right)$$
$$- \epsilon F_j^k \qquad \forall j$$

Recall that $A(t', \leq r_j)$ denotes the set of jobs that are alive at time t and have arrived no later than job j (including job j itself).

We continue to set β_t as follows. Below, for a fixed time t let $\mathbf{1}(t \in [r_j, C_j + \delta F_j])$ be 1 if $t \in [r_j, C_j + \delta F_j])$ and 0 otherwise; δ will be set to ϵ later.

$$\beta_{jt} = (1/2 - 3\epsilon) \cdot \mathbf{1}(t \in [r_j, C_j + \delta F_j]) \cdot F_j^{k-1} \qquad \forall j, t$$
$$\beta_t = \sum_j \beta_{jt} \qquad \forall t$$

Note that a job j can contribute to β_t not only during its lifespan $[r_j, C_j]$ but also even after it gets completed, for $\delta F_j = \delta(C_j - r_j)$ time steps. The amount j adds to β_t at time t (if it does) is F_j^{k-1}, the $(k-1)$th power of j's flow time.

We briefly discuss how our setting of dual variables differentiates from the previous work, starting with dual variables α_j. We had to distinguish between overloaded and underloaded time steps. This is because RR behaves on m machines as it does on 1 machine with speed m when machines are overloaded, and otherwise, it schedules each job on a separate machine exclusively. The summation over overloaded times is inspired by the work [13, 19] – in particular, this amortized accounting is exactly the same when $k = 1$. However, we had to subtract ϵF_j^k from α_j. Hence while the first two terms in α_j are derived from RR's instantaneous status, the last term is a global term which is derived from j's final flow time. Also we had to make job j contribute to β_j for a while even after it completes. This helps compare job j to job j' that is considered in α_j, and turns out to be very useful for our analysis.

3.3 Bounding The Dual Objective

We start with showing that the dual objective for the above setting of α_j and β_t is $\Omega(\epsilon)$ times RR's kth power of flow time. Throughout the analysis we will use the fact that for any job $j \in A(t)$ it is the case that $(t - r_j) \leq F_j$ because the job must be alive at time t to be in $A(t)$.

Lemma 1 $\sum_j \alpha_j \geq (\frac{1}{2} - \epsilon)\text{RR}$.

PROOF.

$$\sum_j \alpha_j = \sum_{t' \in T_o} \sum_{j \in A(t')} k(t' - r_j)^{k-1} \frac{|A(t', \geq r_j)|}{n_{t'}}$$
$$+ \sum_{t' \in T_u} \sum_{j' \in A(t')} k(t' - r_{j'})^{k-1} - \epsilon \text{RR}$$
$$\geq \frac{1}{2} \sum_{t' \in T_o} \sum_{j \in A(t')} k(t' - r_j)^{k-1}$$
$$+ \sum_{t' \in T_u} \sum_{j' \in A(t')} k(t' - r_{j'})^{k-1} - \epsilon \text{RR}$$
$$\geq (\frac{1}{2} - \epsilon)\text{RR}$$

Since verifying the above sequence of equations is straightforward for underloaded time steps, we will focus on overloaded time steps. The first equality follows by observing that the term $\frac{k(t' - r_{j'})^{k-1}}{n_{t'}}$ due to job j' is counted by all jobs in $A(t')$ that arrive no earlier than job j'. The second inequality holds for the following reason. Fix time t' and define j's rank as $|A(t', \geq r_j)|$, denoted as π_j. Note that the earliest arriving job in $A(t')$ has rank $n_{t'}$ and the latest arriving job has rank 1. Also observe $k(t - r_i)^{k-1} \geq k(t - r_j)^{k-1}$ if and only if $\pi_i \geq \pi_j$ since earlier arriving jobs have higher ranks. By pairing two jobs i and j such that $\pi_i + \pi_j = n+1$, we have

$$(k(t' - r_i)^{k-1}\pi_i + k(t' - r_j)^{k-1}\pi_j)/n_{t'}$$
$$\geq \frac{n_{t'} + 1}{2n_{t'}}(k(t' - r_i)^{k-1} + k(t' - r_j)^{k-1})$$
$$\geq \frac{1}{2}(k(t' - r_i)^{k-1} + k(t' - r_j)^{k-1})$$

Summing over all pairs yields the inequality. $\square$

Lemma 2 $\sum_t \beta_t \leq (\frac{1}{2} - 2\epsilon) \cdot \text{RR}$.

PROOF. From the definiton of β_t, we derive,

$$\sum_t \beta_t = \sum_{j,t} \beta_{jt} = \sum_j (1 + \delta)F_j \cdot (1/2 - 3\epsilon)F_j^{k-1}$$
$$= (1 + \delta)(1/2 - 3\epsilon) \sum_j F_j^k$$
$$\leq (1/2 - 2\epsilon) \cdot \text{RR}$$

The last inequality follows from the fact that $0 < \delta = \epsilon \leq 1/10$. $\square$

The previous two lemmas show the objective for our setting of the dual variables is $\Omega(\epsilon)$ times RR's kth power flow time. Thus, if we show that the dual constraints are satisfied, this will show that $\Omega(\epsilon)$ times RR's kth power flow time is less than the optimal dual objective. Knowing that the dual objective is at most 2γ times OPT's kth power flow time, we can derive Theorem 1.

3.4 Verifying The Dual Constraints

It now remains to show the dual constraints are satisfied. Clearly the last two sets of constraints are satisfied. Consider the first set of constraints for some fixed job j and time $t \geq r_j$. Define $B(t') := \{j' \mid t' \in [r_{j'}, C_{j'} + \delta F_{j'}]\}$ as the set of jobs j' that contribute to $\beta_{t'}$ by a positive quantity. Note that $A(t') \subseteq B(t')$, but not necessarily $A(t') = B(t')$. First we bound α_j/p_j.

$$\frac{\alpha_j}{p_j} = \frac{1}{p_j}\left(\sum_{t' \in [r_j, C_j] \cap T_u} k(t - r_j)^{k-1}\right) - \frac{1}{p_j}\epsilon F_j^k \qquad (1)$$

$$+ \frac{1}{p_j}\left(\sum_{t' \in [r_j, C_j] \cap T_o} \sum_{j' \in A(t', \leq r_j)} \frac{k(t' - r_{j'})^{k-1}}{n_{t'}}\right) \qquad (2)$$

It is easy to upper bound Equation (1) that concerns underloaded times:

$$\frac{1}{p_j}\left(\sum_{t' \in [r_j, C_j] \cap T_u} k(t - r_j)^{k-1}\right) - \frac{1}{p_j}\epsilon F_j^k$$

$$\leq \frac{1}{p_j}\frac{p_j}{\eta} \cdot k \cdot F_j^{k-1} - \frac{1}{p_j}\epsilon F_j^k$$

$$\leq \frac{1}{p_j}\left(\epsilon \cdot F_j^k + k\left(\frac{k}{\epsilon}\right)^{k-1} \cdot p_j^k\right) - \frac{1}{p_j}\epsilon F_j^k$$

$$\leq \frac{\gamma\, p_j^k}{p_j} \qquad (3)$$

The first inequality holds due to the fact that job j can be processed by at most p_j and, at each underloaded time, all alive jobs get processed at a rate of $\eta \geq 1$. The last inequality follows considering whether $k \cdot p_j \leq \epsilon F_j$ or not.

We shift our attention to upper bounding Equation (2).

$$(2) = \frac{1}{p_j}\left(\sum_{t' \in [r_j, C_j] \cap T_o} \sum_{j' \in A(t', \leq r_j) \setminus B(t)} \frac{k(t' - r_{j'})^{k-1}}{n_{t'}}\right) \qquad (4)$$

$$+ \frac{1}{p_j}\left(\sum_{t' \in [r_j, C_j] \cap T_o} \sum_{j' \in A(t', \leq r_j) \cap B(t)} \frac{k(t' - r_{j'})^{k-1}}{n_{t'}}\right) \qquad (5)$$

Note that the two Equations (4) and (5) come from jobs not in $B(t)$ and jobs in $B(t)$, respectively; it is important to note that this partition is based on $B(t)$, not $B(t')$.

We first upper bound Equation (4).

Lemma 3 *For all j and $t \geq r_j$, we have,*

$$\frac{1}{p_j}\sum_{t' \in [r_j, C_j] \cap T_o} \sum_{j' \in A(t', \leq r_j) \setminus B(t)} \frac{k(t' - r_{j'})^{k-1}}{n_{t'}} \leq \frac{\gamma(t - r_j)^k}{p_j}.$$

PROOF. Note that any job j' considered in the summation arrives before job j, is alive at time t', completes before time t, and is not in $B(t)$. Hence we have $r_{j'} \leq r_j \leq C_{j'} \leq C_{j'} + \delta F_{j'} \leq t$, which implies that $\delta F_{j'} \leq (t - r_j)$. This also implies that we can further restrict t' to the range $[r_j, \min\{t, C_j\}]$ because no job j' contributes to the second summation at time t or later. Thus, we derive,

$$(LHS)$$

$$\leq \frac{1}{p_j}\sum_{t' \in [r_j, \min\{t, C_j\}] \cap T_o} \sum_{j' \in A(t', \leq r_j) \setminus B(t)} \frac{k(t' - r_{j'})^{k-1}}{n_{t'}}$$

$$\leq \frac{1}{p_j}\sum_{t' \in [r_j, \min\{t, C_j\}] \cap T_o} \sum_{j' \in A(t', \leq r_j) \setminus B(t)} \frac{kF_{j'}^{k-1}}{n_{t'}}$$

$$\leq \frac{1}{p_j}\sum_{t' \in [r_j, \min\{t, C_j\}] \cap T_o} \sum_{j' \in A(t', \leq r_j) \setminus B(t)} \frac{k(1/\delta)^{k-1}(t - r_j)^{k-1}}{n_{t'}}$$

$$= \frac{1}{p_j} \cdot k(1/\delta)^{k-1}(t - r_j)^{k-1}$$

$$\cdot \sum_{t' \in [r_j, \min\{t, C_j\}] \cap T_o} \sum_{j' \in A(t', \leq r_j) \setminus B(t)} \frac{1}{n_{t'}}$$

$$\leq \frac{1}{p_j} \cdot k(1/\delta)^{k-1}(t - r_j)^k$$

$$\leq \frac{1}{p_j}\gamma(t - r_j)^k$$

The second to last inequality follows from the fact that $|A(t', \leq r_j)| \leq |A'(t)| \leq n_{t'}$. $\square$

We now upper bound Equation (5).

Lemma 4 *For all jobs j and $t \geq r_j$, we have,*

$$\frac{1}{p_j}\left(\sum_{t' \in [r_j, C_j] \cap T_o} \sum_{j' \in A(t', \leq r_j) \cap B(t)} \frac{k(t' - r_{j'})^{k-1}}{n_{t'}}\right) \leq \frac{\beta_t}{m}.$$

PROOF. Consider,

$$(LHS) \leq \frac{1}{p_j}\sum_{t' \in [r_j, C_j] \cap T_o} \sum_{j' \in A(t') \cap B(t)} \frac{kF_{j'}^{k-1}}{n_{t'}}$$

$$\leq \frac{1}{p_j}\sum_{j' \in B(t)} \sum_{t' \in [r_j, C_j] \cap [r_j, C_j] \cap T_o} \frac{kF_{j'}^{k-1}}{n_{t'}}$$

$$\leq \frac{1}{\eta m}\sum_{j' \in B(t)} kF_{j'}^{k-1} \cdot \frac{1}{p_j} \sum_{t' \in [r_{j'}, C_{j'}] \cap [r_j, C_j] \cap T_o} \frac{\eta m}{n_{t'}}$$

$$\leq \frac{1}{\eta m}\sum_{j' \in B(t)} kF_{j'}^{k-1}$$

$$= \frac{k}{(1/2 - 3\epsilon)\eta m}\sum_{j' \in B(t)} (1/2 - 3\epsilon)F_{j'}^{k-1}$$

$$= \frac{k}{(1/2 - 3\epsilon)\eta}\frac{\beta_t}{m}$$

$$\leq \frac{\beta_t}{m} \qquad [\text{Since } \eta := 2k(1 + 10\epsilon)]$$

The second inequality follows from the observation that job j' adds $kF_{j'}^{k-1}/n_{t'}$ to the summation only when jobs j and j' are both alive, and the time step is overloaded. The penultimate inequality follows since while both jobs j and j' are alive, they are processed at an equal rate of $\eta m/n_{t'}$ at each overloaded time t, hence the second summation is upper bounded by job j's size. $\square$

We are now ready to complete the analysis. By combining the previous equations, we have

$$\frac{\alpha_j}{p_j} \leq \frac{1}{p_j}\left(\sum_{t' \in [r_j, C_j] \cap T_u} k(t - r_j)^{k-1}\right) - \frac{1}{p_j}\epsilon F_j^k$$

$$+ \frac{1}{p_j}\left(\sum_{t' \in [r_j, C_j] \cap T_o} \sum_{j' \in A(t', \leq r_j)} \frac{k(t' - r_{j'})^{k-1}}{n_{t'}}\right)$$

$$\leq \frac{\gamma\, p_j^k}{p_j} + \frac{\gamma(t - r_j)^k}{p_j} + \frac{\beta_t}{m},$$

proving that the dual constraints are satisfied, as desired.

Acknowledgements. The first author's research was supported in part by NSF grant CCF-1409130. Kulkarni's research was supported by NSF awards CCF-0745761, CCF-1008065, and CCF-1348696.

4. REFERENCES

[1] S. Anand, Naveen Garg, and Amit Kumar. Resource augmentation for weighted flow-time explained by dual fitting. In *SODA*, pages 1228–1241, 2012.

[2] Nir Avrahami and Yossi Azar. Minimizing total flow time and total completion time with immediate dispatching. In *SPAA '03: Proceedings of the fifteenth annual ACM symposium on Parallel algorithms and architectures*, pages 11–18, 2003.

[3] Baruch Awerbuch, Yossi Azar, Stefano Leonardi, and Oded Regev. Minimizing the flow time without migration. *SIAM J. Comput.*, 31(5):1370–1382, 2002.

[4] Nikhil Bansal and Kirk Pruhs. Server scheduling to balance priorities, fairness, and average quality of service. *SIAM Journal on Computing*, 39(7):3311–3335, 2010.

[5] Neal Barcelo, Sungjin Im, Benjamin Moseley, and Kirk Pruhs. Shortest-elapsed-time-first on a multiprocessor. In *Design and Analysis of Algorithms - First Mediterranean Conference on Algorithms, MedAlg 2012, Kibbutz Ein Gedi, Israel, December 3-5, 2012. Proceedings*, pages 82–92, 2012.

[6] Luca Becchetti and Stefano Leonardi. Nonclairvoyant scheduling to minimize the total flow time on single and parallel machines. *J. ACM*, 51(4):517–539, 2004.

[7] Luca Becchetti, Stefano Leonardi, Alberto Marchetti-Spaccamela, and Kirk Pruhs. Online weighted flow time and deadline scheduling. *Journal of Discrete Algorithms*, 4(3):339–352, 2006.

[8] Hemant M. Chaskar and Upamanyu Madhow. Fair scheduling with tunable latency: a round-robin approach. *IEEE/ACM Trans. Netw.*, 11(4):592–601, 2003.

[9] Chandra Chekuri, Ashish Goel, Sanjeev Khanna, and Amit Kumar. Multi-processor scheduling to minimize flow time with epsilon resource augmentation. In *STOC*, pages 363–372, 2004.

[10] Chandra Chekuri, Sanjeev Khanna, and An Zhu. Algorithms for minimizing weighted flow time. In *STOC*, pages 84–93, 2001.

[11] Jeff Edmonds. Scheduling in the dark. *Theor. Comput. Sci.*, 235(1):109–141, 2000.

[12] Jeff Edmonds, Sungjin Im, and Benjamin Moseley. Online scalable scheduling for the ℓ_k-norms of flow time without conservation of work. In *A*, 2011.

[13] Jeff Edmonds and Kirk Pruhs. Scalably scheduling processes with arbitrary speedup curves. In *ACM-SIAM Symposium on Discrete Algorithms*, pages 685–692, 2009.

[14] Kyle Fox and Benjamin Moseley. Online scheduling on identical machines using srpt. In *SODA*, pages 120–128, 2011.

[15] Anupam Gupta, Sungjin Im, Ravishankar Krishnaswamy, Benjamin Moseley, and Kirk Pruhs. Scheduling jobs with varying parallelizability to reduce variance. In *Syposium on Parallel Algorithms and Architectures*, pages 11–20, 2010.

[16] Anupam Gupta, Ravishankar Krishnaswamy, and Kirk Pruhs. Online primal-dual for non-linear optimization with applications to speed scaling. In *WAOA*, 2012.

[17] Ellen L. Hahne. Round-robin scheduling for max-min fairness in data networks. *IEEE Journal on Selected Areas in Communications*, 9(7):1024–1039, 1991.

[18] Sungjin Im, Janardhan Kulkarni, and Kamesh Munagala. Competitive algorithms from competitive equilibria: non-clairvoyant scheduling under polyhedral constraints. In *Symposium on Theory of Computing, STOC 2014, New York, NY, USA, May 31 - June 03, 2014*, pages 313–322, 2014.

[19] Sungjin Im, Janardhan Kulkarni, Kamesh Munagala, and Kirk Pruhs. Selfishmigrate: A scalable algorithm for non-clairvoyantly scheduling heterogeneous processors. In *55th IEEE Annual Symposium on Foundations of Computer Science, FOCS 2014, Philadelphia, PA, USA, October 18-21, 2014*, pages 531–540, 2014.

[20] Sungjin Im and Benjamin Moseley. Online scalable algorithm for minimizing ℓ_k-norms of weighted flow time on unrelated machines. In *SODA '11: Proceedings of the Twenty-first Annual ACM -SIAM Symposium on Discrete Algorithms*, pages 95–108, 2011.

[21] Sungjin Im, Benjamin Moseley, and Kirk Pruhs. A tutorial on amortized local competitiveness in online scheduling. *SIGACT News*, 42:83–97, June 2011.

[22] Bala Kalyanasundaram and Kirk Pruhs. Speed is as powerful as clairvoyance. *Journal of the ACM*, 47(4):617–643, 2000.

[23] Stefano Leonardi and Danny Raz. Approximating total flow time on parallel machines. *J. Comput. Syst. Sci.*, 73(6):875–891, 2007.

[24] Kirk Pruhs, Jiri Sgall, and Eric Torng. *Handbook of Scheduling: Algorithms, Models, and Performance Analysis*, chapter Online Scheduling. 2004.

[25] M. Shreedhar and George Varghese. Efficient fair queueing using deficit round-robin. pages 375–385, 1996.

[26] Abraham Silberschatz, Peter B Galvin, and Greg Gagne. *Operating system concepts*, volume 8. Wiley, 2013.

[27] Eric Torng and Jason McCullough. Srpt optimally utilizes faster machines to minimize flow time. *ACM Transactions on Algorithms*, 5(1), 2008.

Scheduling Non-Unit Jobs to Minimize Calibrations

Jeremy T. Fineman
Georgetown University
jfineman@cs.georgetown.edu

Brendan Sheridan
Georgetown University
bss45@georgetown.edu

ABSTRACT

The recently proposed Integrated Stockpile Evaluation (ISE) problem extends a classic offline scheduling problem where n jobs, each with arrival times and deadlines, must be scheduled nonpreemptively on m machines. The additional constraint in the ISE problem is that a machine may only be used if it has been calibrated recently. The goal is to minimize the number of calibrations necessary to complete all the jobs before their deadlines.

This paper presents a good polynomial-time approximation algorithm for the ISE problem general case where each job may have a different processing time. (Prior work was restricted to unit processing times.) The ISE problem generalizes a classic interval-scheduling problem where the goal is to minimize the number of machines. We show constructively that the other direction is also true, i.e., that the interval-scheduling bounds are also achievable. Specifically, suppose we have a black-box interval scheduling algorithm that finds an s-speed αm-machine solution to the interval scheduling problem. Then our ISE algorithm finds an $O(\alpha)$-approximation for number of calibrations using $O(\alpha m)$ machines with s-speed augmentation.

Categories and Subject Descriptors

F.2.2 [**Analysis of Algorithms and Problem Complexity**]: Non-numerical Algorithms and Problems—*Sequencing and scheduling*

Keywords

Integrated Stockpile Evaluation; approximation algorithms; calibration; resource allocation; scheduling

1. INTRODUCTION

The *Integrated Stockpile Evaluation (ISE)* problem is an offline multi-machine scheduling problem, recently introduced by Bender et al. [5]. What distinguishes the ISE problem is that a machine is unusable unless it undergoes a calibration, and jobs may only be scheduled on a machine if that machine has been calibrated recently. Specifically, if a calibration is performed on a machine at

time t, then the machine remains usable or *calibrated* for the interval $[t, t+T)$, for fixed T. Each machine may be calibrated multiple times, but the machine must remain idle between its calibrated intervals. Calibrations are instantaneous, so it is feasible to calibrate the machine at times 0, T, $2T$, and so on. Although calibrations have no temporal cost, they are considered the expensive feature of a solution.

More precisely, the ISE problem (denoted $P|r_j, d_j|\text{\#calibrations}$ in standard scheduling notation [10]) is defined as follows [5]. The input consists of a set J of n jobs, an integer number m of identical machines, and an integer $T \geq 2$ specifying a *calibration length*. Each job j has a processing time $p_j \leq T$, a release time r_j, and a deadline $d_j \geq r_j + p_j$. A schedule is feasible if it schedules jobs nonpreemptively[1] on machines such that 1) every job completes before its deadline, and 2) every job is scheduled without preemption completely within a single calibrated interval. The goal is to find a feasible schedule that minimizes the number of calibrations performed.

The ISE problem formalizes scheduling issues that arise as part of a nuclear-weapons-testing program with the same name at Sandia National Laboratories [6]. The high-level goal is to perform tests on a set of nuclear weapons to verify their integrity, with the constraint that the testing devices be frequently re-calibrated to guarantee accurate results. See [5, 6] for more details.

Bender et al. [5] give the first algorithms for the ISE problem. They study the restricted case that for all jobs j, $p_j = 1$. Even in this special case of unit processing times, the problem is nontrivial. Bender et al. [5] give two greedy scheduling algorithms. Their first algorithm guarantees an optimal schedule (i.e., minimizing the number of calibrations) whenever a 1-machine schedule is feasible. Their second algorithm gives a 2-approximation for the multi-machine case.

This paper addresses the ISE problem for non-unit processing times, which Bender et al. [5] leave as an open problem. It is not hard to see that testing whether a feasible schedule exists is NP-hard by a reduction from Partition. (Use $m = 2$ machines, and assign all jobs the same release time $r_j = 0$ and deadline $d_j = T$.) Thus ignoring the goal of minimizing calibrations, obtaining a polynomial-time algorithm that finds any feasible schedule necessitates *resource augmentation* [12], where the algorithm is given more or faster machines than the optimal solution against which it is compared. While the notion of resource augmentation was introduced as a technique for producing online algorithms, it has also become commonplace in recent offline scheduling literature.

More precisely, we define resource augmentation as follows. Let $\text{OPT}(I)$ denote the best possible value of the objective function

---

[1]Nonpreemptive means that when job j is scheduled on a machine, it must be scheduled for p_j consecutive timesteps.

(i.e., number of calibrations) over feasible m-machine schedules of instance I. Adopting terminology introduced by Phillips et al. [13], we say that an algorithm is a *w-machine s-speed ρ-approximation algorithm* if it always achieves a feasible schedule with value at most $\rho \text{OPT}(I)$ given wm machines each operating s times faster.

To understand how good a solution we can expect for the ISE problem, observe that the ISE problem extends the classic machine-minimization (MM) problem: given a set of jobs with release times, deadlines, and processing times, find the minimum number of machines necessary to schedule all jobs by their deadlines. Specifically, given an instance to MM, construct an ISE instance by setting $T = \max_j \{d_j\} - \min_j \{r_j\}$. A w-machine s-speed solution to the ISE problem (with any approximation quality) would yield an s-speed w-approximation to the MM problem. Thus if the best s-speed approximation algorithm to the MM problem uses α times the optimum number of machines, then the ISE problem requires α-machine augmentation when limited to s-speed augmentation. Similarly, because the number of machines and the number of calibrations are identical in this construction, the best s-speed α-machine approximation we can expect for the ISE problem has an approximation ratio $\rho \geq \alpha$.

Contributions

Our main result is an algorithm that uses any MM algorithm as a black box, with only a constant factor overhead in terms of machine augmentation. Specifically, suppose we have an s-speed α-approximation algorithm for the MM problem. Then our algorithm results in an $O(\alpha)$-machine s-speed $O(\alpha)$-approximation to the ISE problem. As explained above, this is the best we can expect to within constant factors.

To understand this result concretely, let us consider the current best approximation algorithms for the MM problem. Chuzhoy et al. [8] give an $O(\text{OPT})$-approximation for the MM problem, meaning that the solution uses $O(\text{OPT}^2)$ machines. If $\text{OPT} = O(1)$, then their algorithm is a 1-speed $O(1)$-approximation algorithm. More generally, combining their solution with Raghavan and Thompson's previous best $O(\log n / \log \log n)$-approximation [14] yields an $O(\sqrt{\log n / \log \log n})$-approximation for the MM problem for arbitrary OPT. Both of these results use no speed augmentation and apply to the general case.

In more recent work, Bansal et al.[2] study the case that $\text{OPT} = 1$, giving an $O(1)$-speed 1-approximation (i.e., a one-machine solution) for this special case. Unfortunately, it is not clear how to generalize this result past 1 machine. Im et al. [11] give an algorithm guaranteeing either a $(1+\varepsilon)$-speed 2-approximation or a $(2+\varepsilon)$-speed 1-approximation for the MM problem for any OPT. But unlike the preceding results, their algorithm runs in *quasi-polynomial time*, i.e., $O(n^{O(\log^c n)})$ for some $c > 0$, not polynomial time.

Combining our algorithm with the above MM algorithms, we get the following concrete results:

- A polynomial-time $O(\sqrt{\log n / \log \log n})$-machine 1-speed algorithm giving an $O(\sqrt{\log n / \log \log n})$ approximation for the ISE problem. That is, given an ISE instance that is feasible using m machines and C calibrations, our algorithm produces a solution using $O(C\sqrt{\log n / \log \log n})$ calibrations on $O(m\sqrt{\log n / \log \log n})$ machines.

- Whenever the input instance is feasible on $O(1)$ machines, then we have a polynomial-time $O(1)$-machine 1-speed $O(1)$-approximation for the ISE problem. More generally, if the instance is feasible on m machines, then we get a 1-speed $O(m)$-machine $O(m)$-approximation, which is better than the first bound if $m = o(\sqrt{\log n / \log \log n})$.

- A quasi-polynomial-time $O(1)$-machine $O(1)$-speed $O(1)$-approximation for the ISE problem.

2. ALGORITHM OVERVIEW

This section gives our top-level algorithm for the ISE problem. The high-level algorithm is simple: partition the input jobs J into two subsets J_{long} and J_{short}, each containing the jobs with "long" and "short" windows respectively. Schedule those jobs independently, on disjoint machines, using the specialized algorithms described in Sections 3 and 4. The partitioning itself is trivial, and this process at most doubles the number of calibrations and machines beyond either of the algorithms.

More precisely, we define long and short jobs as follows. Note that the definition of long and short is based on the job's window (release time and deadline), not its processing time.

DEFINITION 1. *We say that job j is **long** or a **long-window job** if $d_j - r_j \geq 2T$. We say that a job j is **short** or a **short-window job** if $d_j - r_j < 2T$.*

Our algorithm for long-window jobs uses an integer-program relaxation followed by a greedy rounding procedure (Section 3). Assuming all jobs have long windows, our algorithm yields an $O(1)$-machine 1-speed $O(1)$-approximation to the ISE problem. The algorithm can also be modified to trade more speed for fewer machines, giving a 1-machine $O(1)$-speed $O(1)$-approximation. These bounds are better than those stated in the introduction with regard to the approximation ratio on number of calibrations and the amount of machine-augmentation employed. The higher overheads arise in scheduling short-window jobs (Section 4), where we apply an MM algorithm as a black box. The short-window algorithm also increases the number of machines and the approximation ratio by a constant factor. Unfortunately, for small-window jobs (as for the MM problem in general), it is not clear how to trade speed for machines.

Combining all of these results, we get our main theorem, whose proof follows directly from Theorems 12 and 20.

THEOREM 1. *Suppose there is an s-speed $O(\alpha)$-approximation algorithm $\mathcal{A}$ for the MM problem. Then using $\mathcal{A}$ as a black box, our algorithm is an $O(\alpha)$-machine s-speed $O(\alpha)$-approximation for the ISE problem. Moreover, the running time of our algorithm is a polynomial in the length of the input (i.e., polynomial in n and the precision of other numbers), multiplied by the running time of $\mathcal{A}$.*

3. SCHEDULING LONG-WINDOW JOBS

This section focuses on the special case of ISE where all jobs have long windows. For this special case, our main algorithm yields a 1-speed $O(1)$-machine $O(1)$-approximation, and we also show that this solution can be transformed into an $O(1)$-speed 1-machine $O(1)$-approximation. Intuitively, long jobs are easier to cope with than short jobs because they have more options on where to be scheduled, but capturing this intuition is not trivial.

We begin this section with one key insight: introducing an extra restriction to the long-window ISE problem makes it easier to solve, without significantly compromising the quality of solution. Specifically, we focus on what we call the ***trimmed ISE (TISE)*** problem. The TISE problem is exactly the same as the ISE problem, except that there is one additional restriction on the schedule: a job may be scheduled only inside a calibration that falls completely within the job's window. Said differently, consider a calibration starting at time t, spanning the time interval $[t, t+T]$. Job j, with window $[r_j, d_j)$, may only be scheduled in this calibration if

$r_j \leq t \leq d_j - T$. We call this extra restriction the ***TISE restriction*** or ***TISE constraint***. Note that the TISE constraint is specific to long jobs because jobs with windows shorter than T are infeasible in the TISE problem.

The main advantage of the TISE problem is that whenever a job is scheduled within a particular calibration, it would be feasible to schedule the job anywhere within that calibration, which gives us flexibility in the schedule. Moreover, because of this flexibility, given an assignment of jobs to calibrations we can infer a schedule. We thus need only focus on 1) finding a schedule of calibrations, and 2) finding an assignment of jobs to those calibrations.

The bulk of this section gives an algorithm for the TISE problem, which includes several steps. First, we construct a linear-programming (LP) relaxation of the TISE problem. The LP allows for both fractional calibrations and fractional job assignments. We then perform a greedy rounding step that yields an integer calibration schedule such that a fractional assignment of jobs to calibrations remains feasible. This rounding step increases the number of calibrations and machines by a constant factor. Note that fractional job assignments correspond to a preemptive schedule, whereas integer job assignments correspond to a nonpreemptive schedule. Finally, we convert the preemptive schedule to a nonpreemptive schedule, using a constant factor extra machines and calibrations, through a variant of earliest deadline first (EDF) scheduling. Earliest deadline first does not generally work for nonpreemptive scheduling with arbitrary release times, deadlines, and processing times, but the TISE restriction helps us here.

A TISE solution is good enough

Because the TISE problem is more restricted, any valid TISE schedule is also a valid ISE schedule. The question is what happens to the quality of the solution. We argue in the following lemma that the TISE solution is as good, to within constant factors. Specifically, the optimal TISE solution uses at most three times the number of machines and calibrations as the optimal ISE solution. It thus suffices to solve a TISE problem on $m' = 3m$ machines.

The proof of the following lemma leverages the definition of long-window jobs. In particular, in order for the presented construction to apply, the threshold for being long must be at least $2T$. This proof is the reason for the choice of constant in Definition 1. (Making the threshold larger is okay, but that would weaken the bounds for short-window jobs.)

LEMMA 2. *Consider any long-window ISE instance. Suppose that there exists a feasible ISE schedule using m machines and C calibrations. Then there exists a feasible TISE schedule using at most $m' = 3m$ machines and $3C$ calibrations.*

PROOF. The proof is by construction, which is illustrated by Figure 1. Consider any machine i in the ISE schedule. We shall use three machines, denoted i', i^+, and i^-, in the TISE schedule. For a calibration starting at time t on machine i in the ISE schedule, we create three calibrations in the TISE schedule: a calibration on machine i' at time t, a calibration on machine i^+ at time $t + T$, and a calibration on machine i^- at time $t - T$. Because the calibrations on machine i^+ and i^- are T-step translations of the calibrations on i, the calibrations themselves are feasible.

We next transform the schedule of jobs. Consider each job j in the ISE schedule. Let x_j be the job's start time in the ISE schedule. Let i be the machine on which the job is scheduled. Let t_j be the start time of the calibration containing the job, i.e., such that $x_j \in [t_j, t_j + T)$. If $r_j \leq t_j \leq d_j - T$, i.e., the job is already feasibly scheduled with regards to the TISE restriction, then schedule the job at time x_j on machine i'. If $r_j > t_j$, then delay the job, schedul-

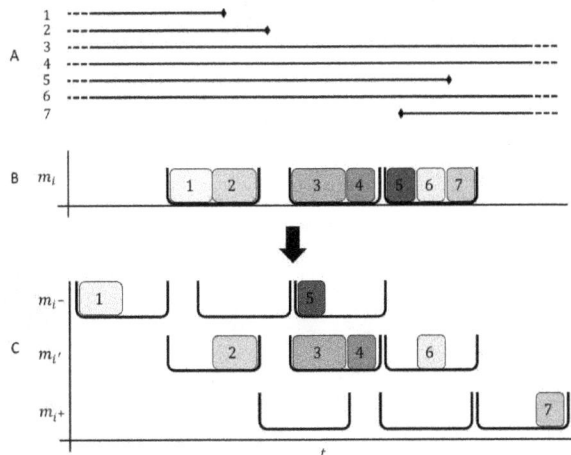

Figure 1: **Example of the transformation from a feasible ISE schedule on one machine to a feasible TISE schedule on 3 machines with $3\times$ the calibrations, as described in proof of Lemma 2. (A) indicates the job windows for the relevant long-window jobs, with the endpoints of line j corresponding to r_j and d_j. (B) shows the original feasible schedule on machine i, and (C) shows the constructed TISE schedule given by the proof, where the buckets are calibrations and the shaded rectangles are jobs—the width of rectangle j is its processing time p_j. Jobs 1 and 5 are moved to the advanced calibrations on i^- because their deadlines fall within the original calibration. Similarly, job 7 is moved to the delayed calibrations on i^+ because its release time falls within the original calibration.**

ing it at time $x_j + T$ on machine i^+. If $d_j < t_j + T$, then advance the job, scheduling it at time $x_j - T$ on machine i^-.

We must show that delaying or advancing a job enforces the TISE restriction. Consider a delayed job j, i.e., one with $r_j > t_j$ in the ISE schedule. Because the job is long, we have $d_j \geq r_j + 2T > t_j + 2T$. Thus the calibration $[t_j + T, t_j + 2T)$ is contained fully within j's window. Moreover, the job must complete by time $t_j + T$ in the ISE schedule, so it must also complete by time $t_j + 2T$ in the TISE schedule. A similar argument applies to advanced jobs.

Finally, because the ISE schedule is a nonpreemptive schedule such that no two jobs run at the same time on the same machine, and each of the machines i', i^+, and i^- only receives a subset of jobs from the ISE schedule on i (all translated by 0, $+T$, or $-T$ timesteps), the TISE schedule is also a valid nonpreemptive schedule. □

Polynomially many calibration points suffice

When constructing scheduling LPs, it is common practice to use variables indexed by each timestep and then argue after the fact that the LP can be transformed to one where the number of variables is polynomial in n. This approach, however, may require that time be discrete, whereas our TISE problem statement does not require that release times, processing times, or deadlines be integers. We thus determine what the important times are up front before constructing the LP. The following lemma states that there are only n^2 times that matter.

LEMMA 3. *There exists an optimal solution to the TISE problem such that the following holds for every calibration on every machine i. If a calibration is made at time t on machine i, then*

Algorithm 1: Rounding calibrations produced by the LP

```
carryover = 0 ;          // carried calibration fraction
C = ∅ ;                  // new calibration schedule
i = 0 ;                  // machine number
foreach t ∈ T in increasing order do
    carryover = carryover + Cₜ
    while carryover ≥ 1/2 do
        add a calibration at time t on machine i to C
        carryover = carryover − 1/2
        i = i + 1  mod 3m′
```

either t is equal to the release time of a job, or the calibration immediately follows the preceding calibration on that machine (i.e., there is a calibration at time $t - T$ on machine i).

PROOF. Consider an optimal schedule for the TISE problem. We can iteratively transform it to one that obeys the lemma as follows. Consider the calibrations on each machine in increasing order of time. If the kth calibration does not obey the lemma, then decrease its start time (and the corresponding start time of any jobs therein) until the calibration's start time hits a release time or the end of the $(k-1)$th calibration, whichever comes first. Because the calibration is not moved past any release times, all jobs in the calibration can be advanced without sacrificing feasibility. □

Because an optimal solution does not use any empty calibrations, the lemma implies that there are at most n^2 possible calibrations on each machine. Specifically, there may be a calibration at any release time. There may also be calibrations packed immediately after this one, but there can only be n such calibrations.

We define $T = \{r_j + kT \mid j \in J, k \in \{0, 1, 2, \ldots, n\}\}$ as the set of *potential calibration points*.

A linear-program for the TISE problem

The goal of our linear program (LP) is to determine a schedule of calibrations on machines and an assignment of jobs to those calibration points. (Recall that for the TISE problem, a full schedule can be inferred by an assignment of jobs to calibrations because the jobs can, by definition, be scheduled in any order.) An integer solution to the LP corresponds to a feasible TISE schedule. We will start from a fractional solution and round it.

Before stating the LP, let us mention two simplifying ideas. It should be clear that both of the simplifications can only improve the value of the optimal solution because feasible TISE schedules can be trivially transformed into LP solutions.[2] First, our LP ignores the mapping of calibrations to machines, instead only requiring that at most $m′$ calibrations overlap at any time. Second, our LP groups calibrations by time, ignoring how jobs are partitioned across same-time calibrations.

Leveraging these simplifications, our LP has two types of variables. The variable C_t denotes the number of calibrations made at time t. The variable X_{jt} indicates whether (or how much of) job j is assigned to the calibrations at time t. In both cases, following from Lemma 3, we use the restriction that $t \in T$ be one of the potential calibration points.

[2]In fact, one can argue that for the fractional solution, the value of the optimal solution is unchanged. For an integer solution, however, it may not be feasible to produce a TISE schedule from the integer solution.

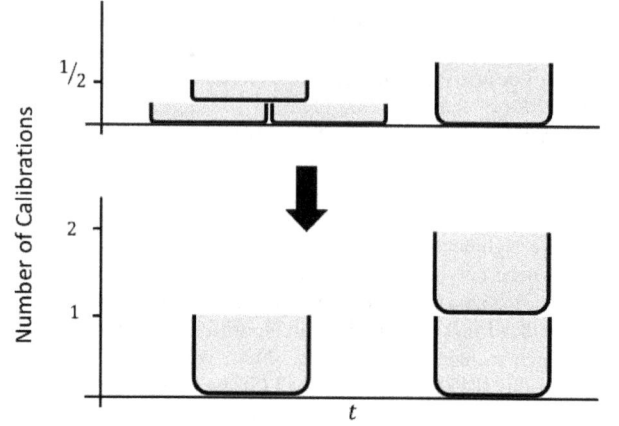

Figure 2: Example calibration rounding following Algorithm 1. Buckets indicate scheduled calibrations and their height represents the amount of calibration. Calibration points are reached after the second and fourth fractional calibrations, resulting in a full calibration and two full calibrations respectively.

We are left with the following LP relaxation of the TISE problem:

$$\text{minimize} \quad \sum_{t \in T} C_t$$

$$\text{subject to} \quad \sum_{t' \in T, t-T < t' \leq t} C_{t'} \leq m' \qquad \forall t \in T \quad (1)$$

$$X_{jt} \leq C_t \qquad \forall j \in J_{long}, t \in T \quad (2)$$

$$\sum_j X_{jt} p_j \leq C_t T \qquad \forall t \in T \quad (3)$$

$$\sum_{t \in T} X_{jt} = 1 \qquad \forall j \in J_{long} \quad (4)$$

$$X_{jt} = 0 \qquad \begin{array}{l} \forall j \in J, t \in T \\ \text{s.t. } t < r_j \text{ or } t+T > d_j \end{array} \quad (5)$$

$$X_{jt}, C_t \geq 0 \qquad \forall j \in J_{long}, t \in T \quad (6)$$

The first constraint guarantees that there are not more than m' calibrations at any timestep. The second constraint says that each job can only be assigned to each calibration once (or more accurately, the fraction of a job assigned to a calibration point cannot exceed the fraction of calibrations performed at that point). The third constraint enforces that the total work assigned to a calibration point (i.e., the fraction of jobs times their processing time) be at most the total processing power of the calibration point (i.e., the number of calibrations times T). The fourth constraint requires that every job be scheduled completely. The fifth constraint enforces the TISE restriction, that jobs only be assigned to calibrations that are contained in their windows. Finally, the last constraint is a nonnegativity constraint on job assignments and calibrations.

The TISE algorithm

As noted previously, our TISE algorithm has three steps. First, we solve the LP relaxation for $m' = 3m$ machines. The LP solution could have both fractional calibrations C_t and fractional job assignments X_{jt}. Second, we apply a simple greedy-rounding algorithm, given by Algorithm 1, to produce an integer calibration schedule on $3m'$ machines. The rounding algorithm scans calibrations C_t in order of time, keeping a running total. Whenever the total reaches the next multiple of $1/2$, the algorithm creates 1 new calibration at

Algorithm 2: Assign jobs J_{long} given calibration schedule C

---

mirror the calibration schedule C on twice as many machines
let C' be the resulting calibration schedule

foreach *calibration in C' in nondecreasing order of time* **do**
    let t be the start time of the calibration
    $used = 0$;   // work in calibration
    let $J' = \{ j \in J_{long} | j$ unscheduled and $r_j \leq t \leq d_j - T \}$
    let $j \in J'$ be a job with earliest deadline
    while $j \neq$ NULL *and $p_j + used \leq T$* **do**
        schedule job j at time $t + used$ in the calibration
        $used = used + p_j$
        remove j from J'
        let $j \in J'$ be a job with earliest deadline

Algorithm 3: Augmented calibration-rounding procedure used only for the proof of Lemma 5 and Corollary 6

$carryover = 0$;   // carried calibration fraction
set $y_j = 0$ for all j ;   // carried job fractions
$C = \emptyset$;   // new calibration schedule
foreach $t \in \mathcal{T}$ *in increasing order* **do**
    while *$carryover + C_t \geq 1/2$* **do**
        create a calibration at time t in C
        $frac = \frac{1/2 - carryover}{C_t}$;   // take part of C_t
        $carryover = carryover + frac \cdot C_t$
        foreach *job j* **do**
            $y_j = y_j + frac \cdot X_{jt}$
            $X_{jt} = X_{jt} - frac \cdot X_{jt}$
            if $r_j \leq t \leq d_j - T$ **then**
                schedule $2y_j$ fraction of job j in calibration
            reset $y_j = 0$
        $carryover = 0$
        $C_t = C_t - frac \cdot C_t$
    $carryover = carryover + C_t$
    foreach job j, $y_j = y_j + X_{jt}$

---

that time. Figure 2 shows an example of this process. The resulting calibrations are assigned to machines in round-robin fashion. We use C to denote the schedule of calibrations produced by the rounding step. Our third and final step is to assign jobs to calibrations, given by Algorithm 2. First we double the calibration schedule C using twice as many machines (for $6m'$ in total). Then we can scan the calibrations in increasing time order, and assign jobs using earliest-deadline-first scheduling. More precisely, we choose a job with earliest deadline from those unscheduled jobs obeying the TISE constraint, with ties broken arbitrarily. If there is still room in the calibration, schedule the job. Otherwise, finish this calibration and move on to the next one.

Note that the rounding step discards any of the job assignments X_{jt}, so it should not be obvious that our algorithm schedules all jobs. We shall show that a fractional assignment of jobs to calibrations is still feasible after the rounding step. Intuitively, this assignment shows that a preemptive schedule is possible on those calibrations. Our final EDF step transforms the preemptive schedule into a nonpreemptive one. This transformation does not work in general with EDF scheduling, so it should not be obvious that it works here.

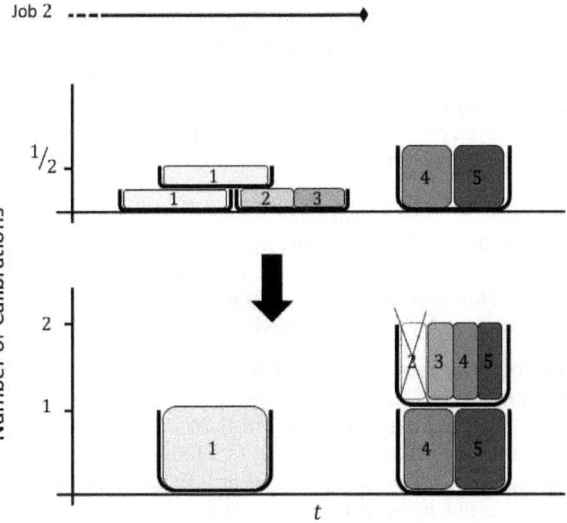

Figure 3: **Example of the fractional job assignment generated by Algorithm 3 on the calibration schedule shown in Figure 2. Buckets represent calibrations, and shaded rectangles represent job assignments. (The ordering of jobs within a bucket does not matter, but the width indicates the amount of the calibration consumed by the job assignment.) In this example, the rounding process delays job 2, whose window is indicated by the line at the top, past its deadline. Consequently, this assignment is discarded; the idea of Corollary 6 is to show that such discarding can only occur if the job is already sufficiently scheduled.**

Correctness and performance analysis

We begin by focusing on Algorithm 1. For correctness, we must show two things. First, we show that the rounded calibrations are valid (i.e., calibrations do not overlap on a machine). Second, we show that the calibration schedule has a feasible, fractional job assignment. Finally, we conclude that the rounding step has only a constant-factor overhead.

LEMMA 4. *The rounding process (Algorithm 1) produces a valid schedule C of calibrations on $3m'$ machines, where no two calibrations on the same machine overlap.*

PROOF. Due to constraint 1, slightly restated, the LP solution guarantees that for all t, we have $\sum_{t' \in \mathcal{T}, t \leq t' < t+T} C_t \leq m'$. That is, there are at most m (total fractional) calibrations started in any time-T period. The rounding process delays at most a $1/2$ calibration at a time. It follows that the number of integer calibrations output in the range $[t, t+T)$ can be at most $\lfloor 2 \cdot (1/2 + \sum_{t' \in \mathcal{T}, t \leq t' < t+T} C_t) \rfloor \leq 2(1/2 + m') = 2m' + 1 \leq 3m'$

Because we have at most $3m'$ integer calibrations started within a size-T window, the oldest calibration must end before the $(3m' + 1)$th calibration begins. Thus, round-robin scheduling suffices. $\square$

We next prove that the rounded calibration schedule permits a fractional assignment of all jobs. We do so constructively by using an augmented algorithm, Algorithm 3, that maps job assignments while creating rounded calibrations. Because this is an existential proof, the modified algorithm is only used for the proof. The idea of Algorithm 3 is similar to Algorithm 1. Namely, continue to accrue fractional calibrations *carryover* until reaching a total of exactly $1/2$ a calibration, then create a new full calibration. Logically, the fractional calibrations (and all their jobs) are simply delayed. The augmentation is that when accruing the fractional calibrations, also record the fractions y_j of jobs being delayed, and write them into the full calibration whenever they obey the TISE constraint. Figure 3 gives an example of this process. Because some of the job can be delayed past a TISE-feasible calibration, we overschedule a $2y_j$ fraction of the job.

LEMMA 5. *At any point when executing Algorithm 3, we have $y_j \leq carryover$. That is, the unscheduled fraction of job j being delayed is at most the unscheduled fraction of calibration being delayed. Moreover, the fraction of jobs fits within the fractional calibration, i.e., $\sum_j y_j p_j \leq carryover \cdot T$.*

PROOF. The proof is by induction over iterations. From the pseudocode, y_j only increases by $frac \cdot X_{jt}$ after $carryover$ increases by $frac \cdot C_t$. Similarly, at the end of the loop, y_j only increases by X_{jt} after $carryover$ increases by C_t. From LP constraint (2), $C_t \geq X_{jt}$, so $carryover$ increases by at least as much y_j. Using a similar argument with LP constraint (3), we also have $C_t T \geq \sum_j X_{jt} p_j$, so the increases to $y_j p_j$ cannot exceed the increases to $carryover \cdot T$ $\square$

COROLLARY 6. *For every job j, the fractional assignments of job j to calibrations produced by Algorithm 3 sum to at least 1. Moreover, the total work assigned to any calibration does not exceed T.*

PROOF. Consider a time t when deciding whether to schedule a $2y_j$ fraction of job j, i.e., determining whether the current calibration obeys the TISE constraint for the job. If $X_{jt'} > 0$ for any $t' \geq t$, then the current calibration is feasible, because the LP only assigns jobs to feasible calibrations. Thus, the only time the calibration can be infeasible for job j is the last time y_j is reset. By Lemma 5, $y_j \leq carryover \leq 1/2$ at this point. Thus, at least the first half of the job is scheduled. The extra factor of 2 when scheduling the job means that the job is (at least) fully scheduled. The bound on total work follows from Lemma 5 even if the $2y_j$ fraction of the job is always scheduled in the calibration. $\square$

LEMMA 7. *Assuming the TISE instance is feasible on m' machines, the calibration schedule C resulting from Algorithm 1 is a feasible set of calibrations such that all jobs can be (fractionally) assigned to calibrations without violating the TISE constraint. Moreover, C uses at most $3m'$ machines and $2C^*$ calibrations, where C^* is the minimum possible number of calibrations on m' machines.*

PROOF. The correctness of the calibrations and feasibility of the fractional assignment follow from Lemma 4 and Corollary 6. Moreover, C also uses $3m'$ machines by construction.

To get the bound on calibrations, observe that any feasible TISE schedule is feasible for the LP. Thus, the optimal solution to the LP has value at most C^*. The rounding process doubles the number of calibrations (creating a full calibration for every $1/2$ calibration produced by the LP), yielding a total of at most $2C^*$ calibrations. $\square$

We next turn to our earliest-deadline-first (EDF) variant (Algorithm 2) scheduling the jobs within the calibrations. We interpret an assignment of jobs to calibrations C as a preemptive schedule. We first show that whenever a preemptive schedule is possible on C, a preemptive version of EDF is feasible. Perhaps unsurprisingly, this proof is similar to the preemptive optimality of EDF when considering the classic problem without calibrations. Then we show that for a TISE instance, EDF can be transformed into a nonpreemptive schedule by doubling the number of machines.

For the purposes of the proof only, we define the ***fractional EDF*** algorithm as follows (similar to Algorithm 2). Consider the calibrations in nondecreasing order of start time. For the current calibration, let J' be the set of unscheduled fractional jobs whose windows contain the calibration (i.e., obeying the TISE constraint). Let $j \in J'$ be the job with the earliest deadline, with ties broken by job number. Assign as much of job j as possible to the calibration. When J' is empty or the calibration is full, continue to the next calibration.

LEMMA 8. *Consider a valid integer calibration schedule C. Suppose that a fractional TISE assignment of jobs to calibrations is feasible. Then the fractional EDF strategy produces a feasible fractional TISE job assignment to calibration schedule C.*

PROOF. Suppose for the sake of contradiction that the EDF schedule is not feasible. Let S be a feasible TISE schedule that shares the longest possible prefix with the EDF schedule. Consider the earliest point at which S and EDF differ, and let k be the rank of the calibration (in sorted order) during which that difference occurs. Then S schedules some job j during calibration k, whereas EDF schedules a different job j'. Because this is the first point of difference, S must schedule j' to some later calibration k'. Swap (as much as possible) of j with j'. If this swap is feasible, this contradicts the assumption that there is a longest matching prefix.

We must prove that this swap is feasible. Because j is not the EDF job, we know $d_j \geq d_{j'}$. Moreover, j' is the EDF job, so it must have release time before the start of calibration k and hence also before calibration k'. It follows that calibration k' is feasible for job j with respect to the TISE constraint. $\square$

LEMMA 9. *Suppose that EDF produces a valid fractional TISE assignment on calibration schedule C. Then there is a feasible integer schedule using twice as many machines and calibrations, specifically by duplicating C across another set of machines.*

PROOF. Let S be the fractional EDF schedule on C. Consider each calibration in turn. If the last job assigned to that calibration is fractional, instead assign the full job to the corresponding mirrored calibration. Remove any other fractional pieces of the job.

Because at most one new fractional job can be created at the end of each calibration, this process resolves all fractional assignments. $\square$

The following lemma states that Algorithm 2 is at least as good as the mapping in the preceding lemma. In some sense, this lemma is not necessary—we could instead use the algorithm of Lemma 9 in place of Algorithm 2. But we think Algorithm 2 is more natural, so we opt for a small increase to the analytical complexity.

LEMMA 10. *After the kth calibration, all jobs completed by the fractional EDF transformation of Lemma 9 are also completed by Algorithm 2.*

PROOF. The proof is by induction on k. For each job chosen by fractional EDF, either it has the earliest deadline and hence our algorithm would also choose it, or the job has already been executed. $\square$

Finally, we conclude by giving bounds on the full TISE algorithm as well as the ISE algorithm.

LEMMA 11. *Assuming the TISE instance is feasible on m' machines using at most C^* calibrations, our TISE algorithm produces a feasible schedule on $6m'$ machine using at most $4C^*$ calibrations.*

PROOF. From Lemma 7, the LP and calibration-rounding steps produces a feasible calibration schedule using at most $2C^*$ calibrations on $3m'$ machines. Lemma 10 states that our algorithm is at least as good as the fractional-EDF-to-integer transformation of Lemma 9. Combining this fact with Lemma 8, we conclude that our algorithm produces a feasible (integer) schedule using twice the number of machines and calibrations, i.e., $6m'$ machines and $4C^*$ calibrations. □

The following theorem states that using our TISE algorithm to solve an ISE instance gives an $O(1)$ approximation using $O(1)$ machine augmentation and no speed augmentation.

THEOREM 12. *Consider any feasible long-job ISE instance on m machines. Let C^* denote the minimum possible number of calibrations to feasibly solve the problem on m machines. Then running our TISE algorithm on that instance produces a feasible TISE schedule using at most 18m machines and $12C^*$ calibrations. Moreover, a TISE schedule is also a valid ISE schedule.*

PROOF. This follows directly from Combining the factor of 3 from Lemma 2 with Lemma 11. □

Trading speed augmentation for machine augmentation

Thus far we have shown how to construct an $O(1)$-machine 1-speed $O(1)$-approximation for the ISE problem (producing a more restricted TISE solution). We conclude this section by showing how to transform this TISE solution into a 1-machine $O(1)$-speed $O(1)$-approximation. The fact that we are working with long jobs and a TISE solution is pivotal here. It is not clear how to make this sort of transformation in general.

Suppose we have a TISE schedule on cm machines, for integer c. (Following from Theorem 12, we shall set $c = 18$.) Here is the algorithm. Group the machines arbitrarily into groups of c machines that will all map to one target speed-$2c$ machine. First, construct the calibration schedule on the target machine as follows. Start at time $t = 0$. Repeat the following steps. If any calibration on the source machine includes timestep t, calibrate the target machine at time t, advance to time $t = t + T$, and repeat. Otherwise, increase t to the next earliest calibration on any of the source machines. This calibration schedule guarantees that every calibrated timestep on any of the source machines is also a calibrated timestep on the target machine.

Next, consider each calibration interval $[t, t + T)$ on the target machine in any order. For any calibration ℓ on a source machine $i \in \{0, 1, \ldots, c-1\}$ that fully contains the first half of the target calibration, i.e., $[t, t + T/2)$, assign ℓ to the size-$T/(2c)$ time interval $[t + iT/2c, t + (i+1)T/2c)$. Keep the jobs in the same order within the interval; just scale the processing times by a factor of $1/2c$. Perform a similar process for each source calibration fulling containing the second half, $[t + T/2, T)$, of the target calibration.

LEMMA 13. *Given a TISE schedule on cm speed-1 machines with C calibrations, the above algorithm produces an ISE schedule on m speed-2c machines with at most C calibrations.*

PROOF. Consider a single group of c source machines. At most one source machine is mapped to each size-$T/(2c)$ subinterval of a target calibration. Moreover, because calibrations on each machine do not overlap, at most one calibration on each machine can be mapped there.

These mappings are feasible because a) the target interval is fully contained in the source calibration, and b) we start from a TISE instance, meaning that the jobs can be run at any time within their calibration.

To see that every source calibration is mapped somewhere, suppose that a source calibration only overlaps part of the end of $[t, t + T)$. Then there is another calibration on the target machine at time $[t + T, t + 2T)$. The source calibration must either overlap half of $[t, t + T)$ or half of $[t + T, T + 2T)$. A similar argument applies on the front end of target calibrations. Thus, every source calibration is mapped.

Finally, to count the number of calibrations, consider the calibration process. A calibration only occurs on the target machines if 1) there is a calibration on some source machine at the same time, or 2) there is a calibration on some source machine between the previous calibration and the current one. Thus, we can charge all target calibrations against source calibrations. □

Combining this speed transformation with Theorem 12, we get the following theorem, meaning a 1-machine $O(1)$-speed $O(1)$-approximation.

THEOREM 14. *Consider any feasible long-job ISE instance on m machines. Let C^* denote the minimum possible number of calibrations to feasibly solve the problem on m machines. Then running our TISE algorithm followed by the machine-to-speed transformation produces a feasible ISE schedule using at most m machines, each at 36 speed, with at most $12C^*$ calibrations.* □

4. STRATEGY FOR SHORT-WINDOW JOBS

This section presents an ISE algorithm for the special case that all jobs have short windows. Our algorithm exploits similarities between the ISE problem and the classic machine minimization (MM) problem, applying any MM algorithm as a black box while asymptotically preserving its approximation guarantees.

Our main idea stems from the following simplified case. Suppose that all jobs fall within a single size-T time interval, i.e., $\max_j\{d_j\} - \min_j\{r_j\} \leq T$. Then an optimal ISE solution uses either 0 or 1 calibration per machine. Thus, minimizing the number of machines and minimizing the number of calibrations are equivalent, and applying the MM algorithm as a black box yields a good solution to the ISE instance. With some manipulation, we generalize this relationship and use it to construct solutions for a short-window ISE input. Note that applying the MM algorithm globally does not work, because there may be long periods of time where we can use fewer machines (and hence fewer calibrations).

Throughout this section, to avoid confusion about where constants are being introduced we use γT to denote the maximum window length of a short job, i.e., $\gamma = 2$ according to Definition 1.

The algorithm

The rough idea of our algorithm is as follows. Partition time into size-$2\gamma T$ intervals. For each interval, consider the subset of jobs whose windows are contained inside the interval. Apply an MM algorithm to the interval. Transform the MM schedule to an ISE schedule by adding appropriate calibrations, but executing all jobs at the same time as before. The final schedule is the union of the schedules for each interval.

The simple partitioning strategy does not quite work because there may be arbitrarily many jobs whose windows span the boundaries separating intervals. Fortunately, there is a trivial fix for this issue: partition time again but at an offset of γT, and schedule any remaining jobs on a new set of machines as before. This revised partitioning step is given as pseudocode in Algorithm 4. For clarity, the partitioning pseudocode as presented is linear in the length of the schedule, but it is straightforward to transform the code to be polynomial in the number of jobs.

Algorithm 4: Partitioning short jobs into length-$2\gamma T$ intervals

Let J_{short} be the set of all short-window jobs
Allocate disjoint sets of machines M_1 and M_2

$t \leftarrow 0$
while $t \leq \max_j \{d_j\}$ **do**
    Let $J' \subseteq J_{short}$ be the jobs nested in $[t, t + 2\gamma T)$,
        i.e., with $t \leq r_j < d_j \leq t + 2\gamma T$.
    Schedule J' on machines M_1 using Algorithm 5
    $t \leftarrow t + 2\gamma T$

Remove from J_{short} any jobs scheduled above
$t \leftarrow \gamma T$
while $t \leq \max_j \{d_j\}$ **do**
    Let $J' \subset J_{short}$ be the jobs nested in $[t, t + 2\gamma T)$,
        i.e., with $t \leq r_j < d_j \leq t + 2\gamma T$.
    Schedule J' on machines M_2 using Algorithm 5
    $t \leftarrow t + 2\gamma T$

Algorithm 5: Scheduling each length-$2\gamma T$ interval

Let t be the start time of the interval
Let J' be the set of jobs assigned to this interval

Run an MM algorithm on J' to produce schedule S
Let w be the number of machines used by S

Use $3w$ machines for S'
for $i = 1$ to w **do**
    calibrate machine i at $t + kT$ for $k \in \{0, 1, 2, \ldots, 2\gamma - 1\}$
for *each job* $j \in J'$ **do**
    Let m_j be the machine to which j is assigned in S
    Let x_j be the start time of j in S
    if j is not a crossing job **then**
        assign j to machine m_j at time x_j in S'
    else
        if j is a k-th crossing job for even k **then**
            calibrate machine $w + m_j$ at time x_j in S'
            assign j to machines $w + m_j$ at time x_j in S'
        else
            calibrate machine $2w + m_j$ at time x_j in S'
            assign j to machine $2w + m_j$ at time x_j in S'

For each of the intervals $[t, t + 2\gamma T)$ produced by the partitioning step, we produce a subschedule for the jobs J' in that interval as follows (see Algorithm 5). First construct an MM schedule S for jobs J' using w machines. Note that the MM schedule S specifies a start time x_j for each job as well as a machine on which to run that job, but an ISE schedule S' must also specify a schedule of calibrations on each machine. Moreover, S' must ensure that each job's execution fall fully within a single calibration. We transform the MM schedule S to ISE schedule S' as follows. First calibrate each of the w machines 2γ times. Next, map S to S' by preserving the times at which the jobs are executed. The remaining question is how to assign jobs to machines. There are two cases. If a job is fully contained in a calibration, it is assigned to the same machine in S' as in S. The more challenging case arises when a job crosses calibration boundaries, an issue that we cope with by introducing more machines.[3] We call a job j a *k-th crossing job* if the start

---
[3]If a calibration is allowed to be performed before the previous calibration ends, then no extra machines are necessary, just ex-

time x_j of the job falls in the k-th calibration, i.e., $t + kT \leq x_j < t + (k+1)T$, but the completion time of the job falls in a different calibration, i.e., $x_j + p_j > t + (k+1)T$. For each machine used by S, introduce a new machine to handle crossing jobs for odd k, and another machine to handle crossing jobs for even k. For each crossing job, we create a new calibration dedicated specifically to the job. As we shall prove, all of the jobs in S' fall fully within a calibration, and no calibrations on a single machine overlap, so the schedule S' is a feasible schedule.

Correctness and performance analysis

To see that the algorithm produces a valid schedule, we first show that the subschedules produced for each interval are feasible. We then show that the main algorithm combines these interval schedules without introducing any conflicts.

LEMMA 15. *Consider any set of short jobs J' with windows nested inside a time interval $[t, t + 2\gamma T)$. Algorithm 5 produces a valid ISE schedule for these jobs.*

PROOF. A feasible MM schedule has two main properties. 1) Every job is scheduled nonpreemptively within its window, i.e., starting no earlier than its release time and finishing no later than its deadline. 2) Jobs on the same machine cannot have overlapping execution periods. An ISE schedule adds two additional restrictions, namely: 3) Every job's execution must be contained fully within a calibration on the machine to which it is assigned, and 4) for each machine, the calibrations on that machine must be nonoverlapping.

Algorithm 5 starts with a feasible MM schedule, preserving all execution times, so property (1) holds trivially. Moreover, for each machine in the MM schedule, the jobs assigned to that machine are spread across three machines in the ISE schedule, so (2) also holds trivially.

We next show properties (3) and (4). For the first w machines, where w is the number of machines used by the MM schedule, property (4) holds by construction—calibrations are performed exactly every T timesteps. Moreover, noncrossing jobs satisfy property (3) on those machines by definition. For each crossing job, Algorithm 5 creates a new calibration, thereby satisfying property (3). We need only argue that those calibrations do not overlap each other, and hence the schedule also observes property (4). Consider two crossing jobs assigned to the same machine in the ISE schedule. Because they are assigned to the same machine, they must have the same crossing parity (even or odd). Moreover, they must start from the same machine in the MM schedule, so those crossing numbers must differ by at least 2. Thus, the scheduled start times for the jobs must differ by at least T, meaning that the calibrations do not overlap. $\square$

LEMMA 16. *Our short-window algorithm (combining Algorithms 4 and 5) produces a valid schedule for an ISE instance of short-window jobs.*

PROOF. We first argue that all jobs are assigned to some interval in the partitioning step, and hence all jobs are part of some interval schedule. We then argue that the interval schedules do not interfere, and hence a final schedule can be formed by taking the union across intervals. Combining these two facts implies that the overall schedule is feasible.

Consider a particular job j in the partitioning step. If j is scheduled during the first loop of Algorithm 4, we are done. Suppose

---
tra calibrations. We focus here on the more difficult version of the ISE problem, where calibrations cannot be invoked less than T timesteps of each other.

instead that j is not scheduled during the first loop. Then j's window crosses a multiple of $2\gamma T$, say $2k\gamma T$ for integer k. Because j is short, its window has length at most γT, and hence $r_j \geq 2k\gamma T - \gamma T$ and $d_j \leq 2k\gamma T + \gamma T$. Thus, j's window is contained completely in the interval $[(2k-1)\gamma T, (2k+1)\gamma T)$, and j is assigned to an interval in the second loop.

We next argue that the interval schedule in Algorithm 5 only creates calibrations nested inside the interval $[t, 2\gamma T)$. The calibrations for noncrossing jobs fall inside $[t, 2\gamma T)$ by construction as long as γ is an integer. Crossing jobs, on the other hand, must have start times within the range $[t, (2\gamma - 1)T)$, so those calibrations are also inside the interval. Thus, taking the union of interval schedules is feasible as long as the intervals themselves are disjoint (which is true for the first or second loop of Algorithm 4). $\square$

Next we analyze the performance of our short-window algorithm. This analysis has a few components. First, we argue that for each interval instance, the MM solution serves as a lower bound for the number of calibrations for the ISE problem. Then we extend the lower bound across a set of disjoint intervals as produced by each pass of the partitioning phase. Finally, we conclude by arguing that our algorithm only loses a constant factor beyond the MM algorithm applied.

LEMMA 17. *Consider any set of short jobs J' with windows nested inside a time interval $[t, t+2\gamma T)$. Let w^* be the value of the optimal solution to the MM problem on J', i.e., the minimum number of machines. Then the ISE problem requires at least w^* calibrations and machines.*

PROOF. The lemma follows from the fact that all feasible solutions require at least w^* machines, and each machine must be calibrated at least once to schedule any jobs. $\square$

LEMMA 18. *For fixed offset time τ, suppose J_i is a set of short jobs with windows nested inside time interval $[\tau + 2i\gamma T, \tau + 2(i+1)\gamma T)$. Let w_i^* be the value of the optimal solution to the MM problem on J_i.*

Then any feasible solution to the ISE problem on the $r+1$ disjoint intervals $\cup_{i=0}^{r} J_i$ requires at least $\max_i w_i^*$ machines. Moreover, an optimal solution to the ISE problem on $\cup_{i=0}^{r} J_i$ requires at least $\sum_{i=0}^{r} w_i^*/2$ calibrations.

PROOF. From Lemma 17, each subset requires w_i^* machines. Adding more jobs only increases the number of machines. Thus $\max_i w_i^*$ is a lower bound.

Consider every other interval $J_0, J_2, J_4, \ldots$ or $J_1, J_3, J_5, \ldots$. Intervals J_i and J_{i+2} are separated by much more than T timesteps. So no calibration used for J_i can also be used for J_{i+2}. Thus, following from Lemma 17, $w_0^* + w_2^* + w_4^* + \cdots$ is a lower bound for the minimum possible number of calibrations. Similarly, $w_1^* + w_3^* + w_5^* + \cdots$ is also a lower bound. Taking the maximum of the two, we have a lower bound of $\sum_{i=0}^{r} w_i^*/2$ calibrations. $\square$

LEMMA 19. *Consider any set of short jobs J' with windows nested inside a time interval $[t, t+2\gamma T)$. Let w be the number of machines found by the black-box MM algorithm. Then our ISE solution on J' performs at most $4\gamma w$ calibrations on $3w$ machines.*

PROOF. Consider a single machine in the MM solution. Our algorithm constructs three machines for the ISE schedule. The first of these machines gets calibrated every T timesteps, for 2γ calibrations. Each of the crossing jobs is assigned to one of the other two machines, with one calibration per crossing job. Since there can be at most $2\gamma - 1$ crossing jobs, there are at most $4\gamma - 1$ calibrations arising from this machine. Multiplying by the number w of machines completes the proof. $\square$

Finally, we conclude that for constant γ, our algorithm asymptotically preserves the approximation guarantees of the MM algorithm applied.

THEOREM 20. *Consider any short-job instance J_{short}. Let w^* denote the minimum possible number of machines among feasible ISE schedules. Let C^* be the minimum possible number of calibrations among feasible ISE schedule.*

Suppose that we have a black-box α-approximation algorithm to the MM problem. Then our ISE algorithm produces a feasible ISE schedule on at most $6\alpha w^* = O(\alpha w^*)$ machines using at most $16\gamma\alpha C^* = O(\alpha C^*)$ calibrations.

PROOF. Consider a sequence of disjoint intervals as defined in Lemma 18. From Lemma 18, we have $C^* \geq \sum_i w_i^*/2$ and $w^* \geq \max_i w_i^*$, where w_i^* is the optimal number of machines for the ith interval. For the ith interval, the MM algorithm finds a solution using at most αw_i^* machines. Thus applying Lemma 19, Algorithm 5 makes at most $(4\gamma)\alpha w_i^*$ calibrations on $3w_i^*$ machines. Summing across all i, our ISE algorithm uses at most $4\gamma\alpha \sum_i w_i^* \leq 8\gamma\alpha C^*$ calibrations on $3\max_i \alpha w_i^* \leq 3\alpha w^*$ machines.

We lose a factor of 2 in both bounds because Algorithm 4 runs on two sets of disjoint intervals using disjoint machines. $\square$

5. OTHER RELATED WORK

Beyond its practical applications, ISE is an interesting interval scheduling variation because it is often optimal to delay the scheduling of a job. This property is unusual in more standard metrics like machine minimization and throughput maximization. However, it is certainly not unique.

Interval scheduling for power minimization is a popular [1] and ostensibly similar problem when the goal can be reduced to minimizing idle periods for a continuous interval schedule. Like ISE, this makes starting work on a machine expensive, which tends to discourage scheduling a job as early as possible and reward job clustering. It should be noted however that since calibrations last a discrete amount of time, the problems are subtly different. Baptiste et al. [3, 4] give an $O(n^5)$-time dynamic programming based algorithm for finding an optimal solution on a single processor with preemption, reducing to $O(n^4)$-time in the unit-job case. Demaine et al. [9] extend their work to a multi-processor environment, yielding a polynomial-time optimal algorithm for the unit-job case.

Chang et al. [7] propose a model for minimizing active processor time which is deceptively similar to ISE. Instead of calibrations length T, they consider timesteps of depth B. That is, up to B jobs can be scheduled in the same timestep at no additional cost and the goal is to minimize the active number of time-steps. However, they consider only preemptive scheduling and don't offer an approximation for the $B > 2$, NP-complete version.

6. CONCLUSIONS

In this paper, we showed how to reduce the ISE problem to the MM problem, producing approximation guarantees that are almost as good as those for the MM problem. To within constant factors, we have also argued that this is the best possible. In the case that all jobs have long windows, our algorithm is asymptotically optimal.

Because the best general approximation to the MM problem is an $O(\sqrt{\log n/\log\log n})$ approximation, we made little effort to minimize the constants in this paper. We think that some of the constants in the reduction could be reduced. That said, partitioning jobs into long and short jobs inherently has an overhead of at least 2 in terms of both machines and calibrations. It would be nice to achieve constants that look like $(1+\varepsilon)$, but that would require some new ideas.

Acknowledgments

This research was supported in part by National Science Foundation grants CCF-1218188 and CCF-1314633.

7. REFERENCES

[1] S. Albers. Energy-efficient algorithms. *Commun. ACM*, 53(5):86–96, May 2010.

[2] N. Bansal, H.-L. Chan, R. Khandekar, K. Pruhs, B. Schieber, and C. Stein. Non-preemptive min-sum scheduling with resource augmentation. In *Proceedings of the 48th Annual IEEE Symposium on Foundations of Computer Science*, pages 614–624, Oct 2007.

[3] P. Baptiste. Scheduling unit tasks to minimize the number of idle periods: A polynomial time algorithm for offline dynamic power management. In *Proceedings of the Seventeenth Annual ACM-SIAM Symposium on Discrete Algorithms*, pages 364–367, Philadelphia, PA, USA, 2006. Society for Industrial and Applied Mathematics.

[4] P. Baptiste, M. Chrobak, and C. Dürr. Polynomial-time algorithms for minimum energy scheduling. *ACM Trans. Algorithms*, 8(3):26:1–26:29, July 2012.

[5] M. A. Bender, D. P. Bunde, V. J. Leung, S. McCauley, and C. A. Phillips. Efficient scheduling to minimize calibrations. In *Proceedings of the Twenty-fifth Annual ACM Symposium on Parallelism in Algorithms and Architectures*, pages 280–287, New York, NY, USA, 2013.

[6] C. Burroughs. New integrated stockpile evaluation program to better ensure weapons stockpile safety, security, reliability. http://www.sandia.gov/LabNews/060331.html, march 2006.

[7] J. Chang, H. Gabow, and S. Khuller. A model for minimizing active processor time. In L. Epstein and P. Ferragina, editors, *Algorithms - ESA 2012*, volume 7501, pages 289–300. Springer Berlin Heidelberg, 2012.

[8] J. Chuzhoy, S. Guha, S. Khanna, and J. Naor. Machine minimization for scheduling jobs with interval constraints. In *Proceedings of the 45th Annual IEEE Symposium on Foundations of Computer Science*, pages 81–90, Oct 2004.

[9] E. D. Demaine, M. Ghodsi, M. T. Hajiaghayi, A. S. Sayedi-Roshkhar, and M. Zadimoghaddam. Scheduling to minimize gaps and power consumption. In *Proceedings of the 19th ACM Symposium on Parallelism in Algorithms and Architectures*, pages 46–54, New York, NY, USA, 2007.

[10] R. Graham, E. Lawler, J. Lenstra, and A. Kan. Optimization and approximation in deterministic sequencing and scheduling: a survey. *Ann. Disc. Math.*, 5:287–326, 1979.

[11] S. Im, S. Li, B. Moseley, and E. Torng. A dynamic programming framework for non-preemptive scheduling problems on multiple machines. In *Proceedings of the ACM-SIAM Symposium on Discrete Algorithms*, pages 1070–1086, 2015.

[12] B. Kalyanasundaram and K. Pruhs. Speed is as powerful as clairvoyance. *J. ACM*, 47(4):617–643, July 2000.

[13] C. A. Phillips, C. Stein, E. Torng, and J. Wein. Optimal time-critical scheduling via resource augmentation (extended abstract). In *Proceedings of the Twenty-ninth Annual ACM Symposium on Theory of Computing*, pages 140–149, New York, NY, USA, 1997.

[14] P. Raghavan and C. D. Thompson. Randomized rounding: A technique for provably good algorithms and algorithmic proofs. *Combinatorica*, 7(4):365–374, Dec. 1987.

Scheduling in Bandwidth Constrained Tree Networks
[Extended Abstract]

Sungjin Im
University of California, Merced
Merced, CA 95343
sim3@ucmerced.edu

Benjamin Moseley
Washington University in St. Louis
St. Louis, MO 63130
bmoseley@wustl.edu

ABSTRACT

In this paper we introduce a new network scheduling model. Here jobs need to be sent via routers on a tree to machines to be scheduled, and the communication is constrained by network bandwidth. The scheduler coordinates network communication and job machine scheduling. This type of scheduler is highly desirable in practice; yet few works have considered combing networking with job processing. We consider the popular objective of total flow time in the online setting. We give a $(1+\epsilon)$-speed $O(\frac{1}{\epsilon^7})$-competitive algorithm when all routers are identical and all machines are identical for any fixed $\epsilon > 0$. Then we go on to show a $(2 + \epsilon)$-speed $O(\frac{1}{\epsilon^7})$-competitive algorithm when the routers are identical and the machines are *unrelated*. To show these results we introduce an interesting combination of potential function and dual fitting techniques as well as a reduction of general tree scheduling to a special case of trees.

Categories and Subject Descriptors

F.2.2 [**Nonnumerical Algorithms and Problem**]: Sequencing and scheduling

General Terms

Algorithms, Theory

Keywords

Online scheduling, Flow time, Bandwidth, Tree network.

1. INTRODUCTION

Scheduling jobs online in a distributed computing environment is fundamental to a variety of applications in practice. Due to the essential nature of multiple machines scheduling, there has been a continual effort to design efficient scheduling algorithms for such systems. See [33] for pointers to previous work. In the most basic multiple machine environment there are n jobs which arrive over time online that are to be scheduled on a set of identical machines. In the *online* setting, the scheduler becomes aware of a job only when it arrives. Most systems require online schedulers because they typically do not know of a job until the client submits the job to the system. In the *identical* machines setting each job J_j requires processing time p_j and the processing time of a job is the same on any machine. The identical machine model is the most basic multiple machine model.

The identical machine setting, although widely studied and an important model, does not capture a variety of systems seen today in practice. Indeed, machines can have different processor speeds, amounts of memory, I/O devices, and even consume different amounts of energy. Due to this, a variety of generalized models have been addressed in scheduling theory. One such model is the related machine model. In the *related* machines setting each machine i runs at some fixed speed s_i and the processing requirement of a job J_j on a machine is p_j/s_i. This captures the case where machines have different processor speeds. However, some job's processing time may not only depend on processor speeds. Indeed, a job has multiple resources it requires (e.g. I/O devices, memory). Due to the multiple dimensions of resources a job requires, the *unrelated* machine model has been considered. In the unrelated machine model, a job J_j's processing requirement on machine i is $p_{j,i}$. The processing time of a job can be arbitrarily different between machines.

There has been an extensive study of scheduling jobs online in these machine environments. For example, see [3, 6, 12–14, 18, 19, 30]. It is fair to say that it has been challenging to develop algorithms with strong guarantees for the more general models. This line of work has had two goals. One is to understand the online complexity of each of these basic scheduling models and to find good algorithms which can be used in practice.

Unfortunately, these multiple machine models have made the unrealistic assumption that a job can be immediately sent to any machine and start being processed instantaneously on the machine. This is generally not the case in practice. Indeed, jobs typically require access to data before they can be started on a machine. The job requires its data to be moved from its current location to the machine that schedules the job. This can be a main performance bottleneck in practice because off-site memory accesses take several orders of magnitude more time than local memory accesses and computation. For a scheduler to be useful in practice, it would need to incorporate this time into its scheduling decisions. Indeed, many distributed systems today are used for large data analysis and, when data sets are

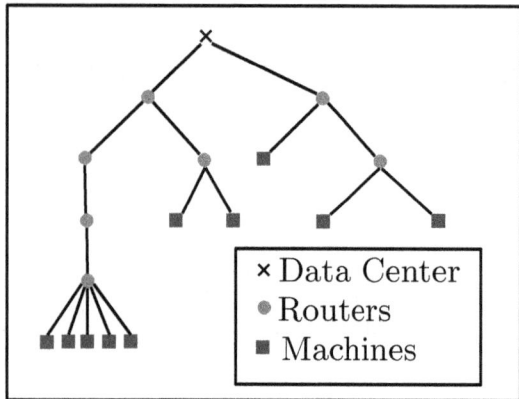

Figure 1: Tree network

large, the main time constraint for job processing is moving the massive data between the machines. For instance this is the case in MapReduce and Hadoop environments [27, 31]. Since this is a main bottleneck in systems, algorithms developed for multiple machine scheduling may not be used since they do not take this constraint into consideration.

This type of scheduling constraint has been referred to as a communication or networking constraint. Addressing these scheduling issues is not new. Besides a large amount of work being done in practical scheduling literature, there has been some theoretical work done offline with the goal of minimizing makespan [8, 9, 16, 17, 20, 21]. Additionally, over two decades ago Phillps, Stein and Wein [32] introduced an interesting model of network scheduling and argued its importance in practice. In their model, before a job can be started on a machine, the job and its data need to be moved to the machine. Here there is a graph that induces the time a job requires to be moved to a machine. When moving a job's data through the network, jobs do not conflict with each other. That is, jobs can freely share links in the network. In their model, this essentially results in jobs having different 'arrival' times depending on the machine they are scheduled on.

Since the work of [32], even in the offline setting, there has been essentially no work which takes networking constraints into consideration for flow objectives such as total flow time. Further there has been essentially no previous work in the online setting. No model has been introduced where there is *congestion* constraints in the network. That is, if a job's data is being moved through a network then a scheduler will need to prioritize which job's data is moved across a particular link or router at a moment in time. Perhaps the reason previous work has not considered networking constraints is because scheduling on multiple machines alone is quite challenging in itself and it is not clear that positive results can be shown for such settings or even what an algorithm might look like.

Tree Network Model: In this paper we consider a network scheduling problem with congestion constraints on tree networks. Trees are among the most popular network topologies [1, 15]. This is because trees scale well to large networks [2, 23]. In this problem we are given a rooted tree T. It is assumed that the root node of the tree is the job distribution center. The leaves of the tree are machines which perform the job processing. A job must be assigned to a leaf

for processing, which is decided by the scheduler. Each of the interior nodes of the tree network is a router. A job's data need to be routed from the root to the leaf machine it is to be scheduled on. A job J_j's data has some size p_j. If all of the nodes of the tree are identical, then J_j requires p_j time steps on a link to send its data to another router. Each link can only move one job at each time and cannot send a job until all of a job's data has been received from the previous router. Generally, the different nodes of the tree could run at different speeds to capture different router speeds. Finally, once a job's data has been moved to a leaf node, the job can be processed at this node. The machines at the leaves could be modeled using identical, related or unrelated machines. See Figure 1. This model captures the widely used tree network topologies seen in practice. Further, it can be seen that this model captures bus topologies where offsite data is routed along a bus to machines the job is to be scheduled on. A natural generalization of our models is to allow jobs to be created at different machines (leaves) in the tree. This extension seems challenging and we leave this to future work.

Results: In this paper we initiate the study of scheduling jobs online in the tree network model. One of the main contributions of this paper is initiating the study of schedulers that coordinate scheduling on a network and on machines online. The objective function we consider is minimizing total (average) flow time. The flow time of a job is the amount of time the job waits in the system until it is satisfied. By minimizing the total flow time, the scheduler focuses on optimizing the average quality of service. This is perhaps the most popular objective considered in scheduling theory. When scheduling jobs in multiple machine environments, it is known that strong lower bounds exist online and offline even in the most basic special cases of the problems we consider [30]. Due to this, we consider the popular resource augmentation model introduced in [26] where our algorithm is given extra speed over the adversary. We say an algorithm is s-speed c-competitive if each router or machine can run up to s times faster than that routers/machines in the adversary's schedule and the algorithm achieves a competitive ratio of c. For all of our results, we consider non-migratory algorithms that compare against a non-migratory adversary. A *non-migratory* algorithm processes a job only on one machine (one leaf machine in our model). Our algorithms will also be immediate-dispatch. An *immediate-dispatch* algorithm decides the leaf that will process a job as soon as the job arrives.

In the online setting we consider two cases. The first case we consider we call the identical endpoint case. Here each job J_j requires p_j time units to be completed on any leaf machine it is assigned to and further the job requires p_j time units to be sent to any router. We consider this model because it essentially captures just the networking aspect of the tree network model. Here we show the following theorem.

Theorem 1 *In the tree network model when all routers and machines are identical there exists a $(1 + \epsilon)$-speed $O(\frac{1}{\epsilon^7})$-competitive algorithm for any $\epsilon > 0$.*

It is known that any algorithm is $\omega(1)$-competitive even when scheduling on identical machines [30], a special case of

172

the identical endpoint model, thus this is essentially the best positive result one can hope for in this setting using worst case analysis. We then go on to consider a more general setting, which we call the unrelated endpoints setting. Here all the processing requirement on each of the routers for a job is identical. However, the processing times of each job on the leaf machines are *unrelated* (can be completely different). Thus, this is a combination of a network with identical routers and unrelated machines environment where processing times of a job (on the leaves) are unrelated between machines. Here we show the following.

Theorem 2 *In the tree network model when all routers are identical and machines are unrelated there exists a $(2 + \epsilon)$-speed $O(\frac{1}{\epsilon^7})$-competitive algorithm for any $\epsilon > 0$.*

Techniques: An overview of our algorithms and analysis is given in Section 3.1 and here we just remark on some techniques used. In the tree network setting, it is fairly difficult to adapt existing scheduling techniques. This is because we have a layered scheduling problem where scheduling decisions made on one router will later affect decisions on routers further down the tree. Due to this, we will not have the structure that is usually present when scheduling on multiple machines, such as having a simple expression for what a job's flow time will be assuming no more jobs arrive. This is usually very important to potential function or dual fitting analysis. See [24] for a survey on potential functions for scheduling analysis and [3,22] for recent developments on dual fitting for scheduling. Due to this, we need to develop new techniques. We introduce a new potential type analysis to determine an approximation of a job's waiting time at any point in time. Then we consider reducing a general tree to a simpler more structured tree *online*. We then combine these two ideas in conjunction with an online primal-dual analysis of our algorithm on the simpler tree. Then we show that if our algorithm works well on the simpler tree, we can generate *online* an algorithm which works well for any tree.

Related Work: Scheduling on multiple machine was first considered on identical machines. For this setting $O(\min\{\log P, \log(n/m)\})$-competitive algorithm is known for minimizing total flow time and there is a matching lower bound online [30]. Here P is the ratio of the maximum to minimum processing time of a job. Assuming resource augmentation a series of works [3,12–14,18] has culminated in a $(1 + \epsilon)$-speed $O(1/\epsilon)$-competitive algorithm for unrelated machines.

As stated, our model is related to packet routing. Most previous work on packet routing has focused on two models. The first model studies stability of a network where the goal is to keep the number of packets in the system bounded when the system runs for an arbitrary long period of time. See [4, 10,11] for example and pointers to relevant work. The other model is where routers have a fixed buffer size at each of the routers and packets can be dropped when the buffer becomes full. The goal is to maximize the total throughput, i.e. the number of packets sent [7,28,34]. These works differ from ours because we requires all job (packets) to be completely processed and we consider the flow time objective over all the packets. One recent work [5] has considered minimizing total flow time when routing in a *line* network. Here for total flow time, no positive results were shown, but it was shown that no algorithm can be $O(1)$-competitive, giving evidence that the problem is algorithmically challenging. For minimizing the maximum flow time of packets on a line they give a $(1+\epsilon)$-speed $O(1)$-competitive algorithm for any fixed $\epsilon > 0$. In the offline setting, packet routing was studied when each packet needs to be routed along its own path, but the goal was to route all packets as early as possible. For example, see the seminal work in [29].

2. PRELIMINARIES

In this section we introduce notation and the problem formally. We will be given a rooted tree T on m nodes and n jobs arrive over time. A job J_i arrives at time r_i. We will assume without loss of generality that all jobs arrive at distinct times. Each of these jobs needs to be processed by some leaf machine/node in T. The algorithm decides the leaf assignment. To be processed on a leaf machine, the job must have its data transferred from the root to the leaf machine before it can start being processed. A job's data must be transferred through links in the network. No more than one job can use a fixed edge/link at any moment in time. For simplicity of explanation, we can view this as a job requiring processing at each node in the tree on the path to the leaf it is assigned to. Thus, we no longer discuss jobs on edges. Further, a job cannot be processed by any node until it is processed by its parent and no job needs to be processed by the root node and no leaf is adjacent to the root. We assume congestion is at the links, thus a job need not be processed by the root node in this view. Note that the problem where congestion happens at the routers can be captured by our setting as well.

One may ask why we consider a model where a job cannot be processed on a router until it is fully processed by the parent router. The main reason this is presented in the paper is that this is a more challenging setting to analyze. The challenge is because extra congestion can happen at internal routers in the network and this effect is effectively negated when the jobs can be divided into unit sized packets when routing. In fact, all the results in this paper can be extended in a fairly straightforward manner to the case where jobs can be sent in small pieces on the routers to obtain similar results in both the identical and unrelated endpoint settings. The details of this are omitted and will appear in a full version of this paper. Also, we consider this case because it captures packet routing, one application of our model. In many packet routing settings packets must be sent completely to a router before it can be forwarded. To see how this fits in our setting, you can imagine packets of data originating at a data collection site that must be transferred to machines to be processed. We note that even in the simplest setting for packet forwarding of unit time packets there are no known results for flow time on tree networks.

We will consider two models for how the job can be processed in the tree. In the identical node setting, a job requires p_j units of processing on every node. In the unrelated endpoint setting, a job requires p_j units of processing on nodes which are not leaf nodes. On a leaf node v, a job requires $p_{j,v}$ units of processing which can be arbitrarily different depending on the leaf.

We will be considering algorithms in the resource augmentation setting, where the algorithm is given extra resources over the adversary. We will give our nodes extra speed over the adversary. In some case, we may only augment the speed of some nodes in the tree for technical reasons. We will assume that a job's processing time is a power of $(1 + \epsilon)^k$ for some integer k. This can be assumed while only loosing a $(1+\epsilon)$ extra factor in speed on each of the nodes. For jobs of size $(1 + \epsilon)^i$ on a node v, we say that these jobs are in class i on v. Our algorithm will utilize the Shortest-Job-First (SJF) algorithm. This algorithm on a node v just schedules the job with the shortest *original* processing time on v amongst the jobs available to process on v. In the case of ties, the algorithm processes the oldest job in the class.

We will require a fair bit of notation in the paper. For any job J_i and node v, $p_{i,v}$ denotes the processing time of J_i on v. This may be simplified to p_i in the identical node case. The set $\mathcal{L}$ and $\mathcal{R}$ are the set of leaf nodes and nodes adjacent to the root, respectively. For any non-root node v, let $R(v)$ be the node adjacent to the root such that v is in the subtree rooted at $R(v)$. Also let $L(v)$ be the set of leaf nodes in the subtree rooted at v. The value of d_v is the total number of nodes on the path from v to $R(v)$ including v and $R(v)$. Let $\rho(v)$ be the parent of v and $c(v)$ be the children of v. For a node $v \in \mathcal{L}$ and a job J_j let $P_{v,j}$ be the sum of the processing time of job J_j on all nodes from the root to v. Note this is a lower bound on job J_j's flow time if it is assigned to leaf v.

For a given algorithm A, let $Q_v^A(t)$ be the set of jobs that have arrived by time t, have not completed processing on v, and have v in the path from the root to the leaf node they are assigned to in A. If A uses SJF on v, let $S_{v,i}^A(t)$ denote the set of jobs in $Q_v^A(t)$ which have higher priority than J_i on v and it also includes J_i. That is, the set of jobs that have smaller processing time than p_i, or that have processing time p_i and have arrived earlier than r_i. Let $d_j^A(t)$ be the remaining number of nodes J_j still requires processing time on. Let $d_{v,j}^A(t)$, for a node v that J_j still needs to be processed on, be the total number of nodes J_j needs to be processed on to reach v. Finally $p_{j,v}^A(t)$ is the remaining processing time J_j requires on node v in A at time t.

The goal of the scheduler is to minimize the total flow time of the schedule. Say an algorithm A completes job J_j at time C_j^A (it is completely processed on a leaf node). The goal is to minimize $\sum_{J_j}(C_j^A - r_j)$. This is equivalent to $\int_{t=0}^{\infty} \sum_{J_j \in \bigcup_{v \in \mathcal{L}} Q_v^A(t)} 1 dt$. However, analyzing this objective seems challenging. Due to this, we will consider a variant of fractional flow time. Fractional flow time is a standard technique used in scheduling theory. See [13] for an overview. In our variant, say that job J_j is assigned to leaf node $v_j \in \mathcal{L}$. The goal is to minimize $\int_{t=0}^{\infty} \sum_{J_j \in \bigcup_{v \in \mathcal{L}} Q_v^A(t)} \frac{p_{j,v_j}^A(t)}{p_{j,v_j}} dt$. Note that this only depends on how must a job has been processed on its *leaf* node(s). In any valid schedule each job J_j must be scheduled on a unique leaf node v_j; however, in a linear programming relaxation the job could possibly be scheduled on multiple leaf nodes. The following theorem follows immediately from known techniques. For instance, a simple extension of the proof in [25] gives the following theorem.

Theorem 3 *If an (online) algorithm A is s-speed c-competitive for fractional flow time on trees then there exists a $(1+\epsilon)s$-speed $O(c/\epsilon)$-competitive (online) algorithm A' for minimizing total flow time on trees for any constant $\epsilon > 0$.*

Further, if SJF is used by A on the leaves of T then one can use A as A'.

Now we introduce the LP and the dual below which we will use throughout the paper. Let $x_{v,j,t}$ denote the amount which job J_j is scheduled on node v at time t. Let $\eta_{j,v}$ denote the total processing time job J_j requires on all nodes on the path from the root to node v. Note that for valid schedule x where each job J_j is assigned to a unique leaf node v_j, each of the two quantities, $\sum_{v \in \mathcal{L}} \sum_t x_{v,j,t} \cdot \frac{t - r_j}{p_{j,v}}$ and $\sum_{v \in \mathcal{L}} \sum_t x_{v,j,t} \cdot \eta_{j,v}/p_{j,v}$ is a lower bound to job J_j's flow time. The first quantity is a valid lower bound since $\sum_t \frac{x_{v_j,j,t}}{p_{j,v}} = 1$, and $x_{v,j,t} = 0$ for all $v \neq v_j$, and $(t - r_j)$ is at most J_j's flow time while J_j is being processed. The second quantity is a valid lower bound that incorporates the total processing time, P_{j,v_j}, J_j requires on the path to v_j if J_j is assigned to node v_j. Hence the sum of these two quantities is also a valid lower bound within a factor of two. In the objective, we also count the flow time of a job when it is finished on a root node. In general, it is sufficient to count when a job is finished on a leaf, but we will also count the root because it only increases the optimal solution by a constant factor. We use these lower bounds on the flow time of each job in the objective of the LP for technical reasons that will be useful in the dual fitting analysis. The first constraint (1) states node processes more than one job in a time step. The second constraint (2) states thata job is fully processed on the leaf nodes. Finally the last constraint (3) says that the amount a job is processed on the children of a node is at most that of the fraction it is processed on the node. Note that in an integral solution, a job cannot be processed on a child of a node until it is processed on the node.

$$\min \sum_{j \in [n]} \left(\sum_{v \in \mathcal{L} \cup \mathcal{R}} \sum_t x_{v,j,t} \left(\frac{t - r_j}{p_{j,v}} \right) + \sum_{v \in \mathcal{L}} x_{v,j,t} \eta_{j,v}/p_{j,v} \right)$$
$$\text{(LP} - \text{Primal)}$$

$$\text{s.t.} \quad \sum_{j=1}^n x_{v,j,t} \leq 1 \quad \forall v \in [m], t \tag{1}$$

$$\sum_{v \in \mathcal{L}} \sum_{t \geq r_j} \frac{x_{v,j,t}}{p_{j,v}} \geq 1 \quad \forall j \in [n] \tag{2}$$

$$\sum_{r_j \leq t' \leq t} \frac{x_{v,j,t'}}{p_{j,v}} \geq \sum_{r_j \leq t' \leq t} \sum_{v' \in c(v)} \frac{x_{v',j,t'}}{p_{j,v}} \quad \forall v \in [m], j \in [n], t \tag{3}$$

$$x_{v,j,t} \geq 0 \quad \forall v \in [m], j \in [n], t \geq r_j$$

$$\max \sum_{j=1}^n \beta_j - \sum_{i=1}^m \sum_t \alpha_{v,t} \quad \text{(LP} - \text{Dual)}$$

$$\text{s.t.} \quad -\alpha_{v,t} + \frac{\beta_j}{p_{j,v}} - \sum_{t' \geq t} \frac{\gamma_{\rho(v),j,t'}}{p_{j,v}} \leq \frac{t - r_j}{p_{j,v}} + \eta_{j,v}/p_{j,v}$$
$$\forall v \in \mathcal{L}, j \in [m], t \geq r_j \tag{4}$$

$$-\alpha_{v,t} + \sum_{t' \geq t} \frac{\gamma_{v,j,t'}}{p_{j,v}} \leq \frac{t - r_j}{p_{j,v}}$$
$$\forall v \in \mathcal{R}, j \in [m], t \geq r_j \tag{5}$$

$$-\alpha_{v,t} + \sum_{t' \geq t} \frac{\gamma_{v,j,t'}}{p_{j,v}} - \sum_{t' \geq t} \frac{\gamma_{\rho(v),j,t'}}{p_{j,v}} \leq 0$$

$$\forall v \notin \mathcal{L} \cup \mathcal{R}, j \in [n], t \geq r_j \qquad (6)$$

$$\alpha_{v,t} \geq 0 \quad \forall v \in [m], t \qquad \beta_j \geq 0 \quad \forall j \in [n]$$

$$\gamma_{v,i,t} \geq 0 \quad \forall v \in [m], j \in [n], t \geq r_j$$

3. ONLINE SCHEDULING ON TREES

In this section, we show a $(1+\epsilon)$-speed $O(\frac{1}{\epsilon^5})$-competitive algorithm for the identical node case and a $(2+\epsilon)$-speed $O(\frac{1}{\epsilon^6})$-competitive algorithm for the unrelated endpoint case. Both of the results will use fractional flow time as defined in Section 2. Using Theorem 3 these results will imply Theorems 1 and 2.

3.1 Overview of the Algorithm and Analysis

In this section we give an overview of the algorithm and analysis. Say that we are given a tree T to schedule our jobs on. Our algorithm will schedule using SJF on each of the nodes of T amongst jobs which are available to schedule on that node. To us, it is somewhat surprising that such a simple greedy scheduling policy can be used on all of the nodes of the tree without considering jobs on other nodes or a job's leaf assignment. With this policy in place, the only other decision made by the algorithm is assigning jobs to leaves of the tree.

Ideally, one would like to keep the policy simple by say assigning a job to its closest leaf. Unfortunately, this will not be suitable since it does not consider the congestion in the tree. Another reasonable scheduling policy to use would be to assign the job to the leaf such that it causes the minimum increase in the objective function (assuming no more jobs arrive). Here one takes into consideration how long the new job will take to complete and how much the new job will delay already assigned jobs. Unfortunately, making such an assignment is not trivial. The main challenge comes from being unable to determine an exact algebraic expression for the cost of assigning a job to a leaf.

To circumvent this hurdle, we will prove using a potential analysis (Lemma 3) an upper bound on how long a job will wait to be completed if it is assigned to a fixed leaf node assuming no more jobs arrive. Using this bound, we would like to assign a job to the leaf such that it minimizes the increase in cost. Unfortunately, there is another hurdle. In particular, it seems challenging to analyze the algorithm on general trees. The difficulty arises due to jobs that conflict on a node, but are assigned to different leaves. These jobs maybe cause congestion a particular node, but split in different directions in the tree. For such jobs, it is challenging to determine whether or not they will actually conflict at a node or if one will be processed quickly reaching a node not shared with the other job. This results in the two jobs never interacting with each other. This comes crucially into play in the dual fitting analysis.

To overcome this second hurdle, we simplify the problem. From T we construct a new tree T', which we call a *broomstick*. Our analysis begins by showing that the objective of the optimal scheduler on the broomstick is not much larger than that for T. Then we analyze the above algorithm on trees which are broomsticks where we assign a job to the leaf that minimizes the increase in the algorithm's cost. By the structure of the broomstick, jobs will share a common path until they reach their leaf node if the are both processed

by the same child of the root. This property greatly helps in setting the dual variables when determining which jobs conflict with each other.

Finally, once we have an algorithm which works well on broomsticks, we will show an algorithm for general trees. Recall that our only remaining task was to determine the leaf assignment policy for jobs. Our algorithm will construct the broomstick from T and simulate what an algorithm would have done on the broomstick. Then the algorithm will assign a job to a leaf node in T which corresponds to a leaf node on the broomstick. Finally, by construction of the broomstick, we will be able to show that the algorithm on T will have an objective smaller than that of the algorithm on the broomstick. Since we know that the broomstick algorithm has strong guarantees and that the optimal solution on T is similar to the optimal solution on the broomstick, we will have our final result. We believe that the dual fitting techniques we use for the network setting and the ideas we introduce in the reduction of the tree to broomsticks will prove useful in understanding the communication constrained scheduling problems on other network topologies.

3.2 Bounding the Waiting Time on Interior Nodes for SJF

The following lemma will prove useful throughout the analysis. The lemma essentially states that no job will be delayed by more than a constant factor multiplied by the processing it requires once it leaves the root node until it leaves its last identical node. This is a key structural property which only holds if the routers are identical; leaf nodes need not be identical. This lemma will allow us to use SJF on the nodes of the tree. It will also be useful when reducing general trees to broomstick trees and in bounding the algorithm's objective. The remainder of this section will be devoted to proving the lemma. One thing to note is that although we can bound the time on interior nodes, there is congestion at the root nodes and the endpoints if they are unrelated. Thus, we cannot simply say assign jobs to the closest leaf.

For the remainder of the section, fix any tree T in the unrelated endpoint or identical settings, a time t and any algorithm A which uses SJF amongst jobs assigned to each node. The assignment policy A uses to assign jobs to leaves can be arbitrary. Further, say that A is given s resource augmentation on all nodes except those adjacent to the root where $s \geq 1 + \epsilon$ for some constant ϵ – later we will scale up the speed all nodes get uniformly. Note that we are not speeding up the nodes adjacent to the root. In the identical setting, we call all nodes of T identical. In the unrelated endpoint setting, we call the routers identical nodes and the leafs unrelated nodes. The goal of this section is to prove the following lemma.

Lemma 1 *Say that J_j is assigned to leaf node $v \in \mathcal{L}$. The total time it takes for J_j to be completed on the last identical node on its path is at most $\frac{6}{\epsilon^2} p_j d_v$ after leaving node $R(v)$.*

First we bound the volume of work which remains for jobs which are available to schedule on some identical node that is not adjacent to the root.

Lemma 2 *Consider any time t, job J_j and any identical node v which is not adjacent to the root such that J_j*

still needs to use v at time t. Then it is the case that $\sum_{J_i \in S^A_{v,j}(t) \setminus Q^A_{\rho(v)}(t)} p^A_{i,v}(t) \le \frac{2}{\epsilon} p_j$.

PROOF. The quantity $\sum_{J_i \in S^A_{v,j}(t) \setminus Q^A_{\rho(v)}(t)} p^A_{i,v}(t)$ counts the remaining volume of work A has for jobs which have higher priority than J_j on v which are *currently* available to schedule on v. For the sake of contradiction, say the lemma is false at some time t. Let t_1 be the earliest time before time t such that node v is always processing a job that has higher priority than J_j during $(t_1, t]$. Knowing that at time t_1 A is not processing a job of higher priority than J_j on v it must be the case that $\sum_{J_i \in S^A_{v,j}(t_1) \setminus Q^A_{\rho(v)}(t_1)} p^A_{i,v}(t_1) = 0$.

Now consider the total volume of work of jobs with higher priority than J_j which can reach v during $(t_1, t]$. All of the work that arrives to v must come from jobs which pass through $\rho(v)$. Say that job J_j is of class k (e.g. $p_j = (1 + \epsilon)^k$). There can be at most one job of each class partially processed on $\rho(v)$ at any point in time by definition of SJF. Besides partially processed jobs on $\rho(v)$ at time t_1, every job which reaches v during $(t_1, t]$ requires its full processing to be done on $\rho(v)$ during $(t_1, t]$. This implies that the total volume of work which can reach v from $\rho(v)$ during $(t_1, t]$ which has higher priority than J_j is at most $s(t - t_1) + \frac{2}{\epsilon} p_j$ because $\rho(v)$ has speed at most s. Now we know that v is always busy doing work on jobs which have higher priority than J_j during $(t_1, t]$ by definition of t_1 and A. Thus, v does $s(t - t_1)$ volume of work on these jobs during $(t_1, t]$. However, this implies that $\sum_{J_i \in S^A_{v,j}(t) \setminus Q^A_{\rho(v)}(t)} p^A_{i,v}(t) \le \frac{2}{\epsilon} p_j$, a contradiction. $\square$

Recall that $d^A_{v,i}(t)$ denotes the number of nodes on the path from where J_i is currently available to schedule to a node v. Let $P^A_i(t)$ be the remaining nodes which job J_i needs to still be processed on at time t which are identical nodes (do not include an unrelated node). We now use a potential argument to give our first upper bound of how long it will take for a job to complete processing, after passing the first node, on all remaining identical nodes.

Lemma 3 *Say A is given speed s on all nodes except those adjacent to the root for any $s \ge 1 + \epsilon$. Consider job J_j which is available to schedule at time t on a node not adjacent to the root and which is not an unrelated node. Then the remaining time until either J_j is completed in the identical case, or reaches an unrelated node in the unrelated endpoint case, is a most the following assuming no jobs arrive after time t,*

$$\Phi_j(t) = \frac{1}{s} \max_{v \in P^A_j(t)} \left\{ \sum_{J_i \in S^A_{v,j}(t)} p^A_{i,v}(t) + \frac{2}{\epsilon} (d^A_j(t) - d^A_{v,j}(t)) p_j \right\}$$

PROOF. First we bound the continuous change in $\Phi_j(t)$. Let $v^* \in P_j(t)$ be the node which maximizes $\sum_{p_i \in S^A_{v,j}(t)} p^A_{i,v}(t) + \frac{2}{\epsilon} (d^A_j(t) - d^A_{v,j}(t)) p_j$. We begin by proving that there must exist a job available to schedule on v^* which is in $S^A_{v^*,j}(t)$. Indeed, say that this is not the case for the sake of contradiction. First, clearly v^* is not equal to the node job J_j is currently available on, because in this case J_j is in $S^A_{v,j}(t)$ and we get a contradiction. Now, it must be the case that $S^A_{v^*,j}(t) \subseteq S^A_{\rho(v^*),j}(t)$ because no job in $S^A_{v^*,j}(t)$ is available to schedule. Further, there can be at

most one job of each class partially processed on node $\rho(v)$ since SJF is used on node $\rho(v)$. Thus, it must be the case that $\sum_{p_i \in S^A_{v^*,j}(t)} p^A_{i,v^*}(t) \le \sum_{p_i \in S^A_{\rho(v^*),j}(t)} p^A_{i,\rho(v^*)}(t) + \frac{2}{\epsilon} p_j$. However, this contradicts the definition of v^* since $d^A_{v^*,j}(t) = d^A_{\rho(v^*),j}(t) + 1$. Now we know that there is a job in $S^A_{v^*,j}(t)$ which is available to schedule at time t on v^*. This implies that a job in $S^A_{v^*,j}(t)$ is worked on at time t on v^* and $\sum_{p_i \in S^A_{v^*,j}(t)} p^A_{i,v^*}(t)$ must decrease at a rate of s. Thus $\Phi_j(t)$ decreases at a rate of one.

Now we bound the discontinuous change in $\Phi_j(t)$. This occurs by job J_j moving to a new node at some time t. Say that J_j is on node v_c and moves to node v' at time t. Then $P^A_j(t)$ becomes $P^A_j(t) \setminus \{v_c\}$ and $d^A_j(t)$ decreases by one. Let v^* be the node that maximizes $\sum_{p_i \in S^A_{v,j}(t)} p^A_{i,v}(t) + \frac{2}{\epsilon} (d^A_j(t) - d^A_{v,j}(t)) p_j$ just before J_j moves to v'. If $v_c \ne v^*$ then it is easy to see that $\Phi_j(t)$ does not increase after J_j moves. Consider when $v^* = v_c$. In this case, any job in $S^A_{v',j}(t)$ that is not available to schedule at time t is also not available to schedule on v^* at time t since v^* was processing job J_j at t. These jobs contributed the same amount to $\sum_{p_i \in S^A_{v^*,j}(t)} p^A_{i,v^*}(t)$ and $\sum_{p_i \in S^A_{v',j}(t)} p^A_{i,v'}(t)$. Any other job in $S^A_{v',j}(t)$ that is available to schedule on v' at t can contribute at most $\frac{2}{\epsilon} p_j$ to $\sum_{p_i \in S^A_{v',j}(t)} p^A_{i,v'}(t)$ by Lemma 2. Thus, $\sum_{p_i \in S^A_{v^*,j}(t)} p^A_{i,v^*}(t) + \frac{2}{\epsilon} p_j \le \sum_{p_i \in S^A_{v',j}(t)} p^A_{i,v'}(t)$ after job J_j moves. Since, $d^A_j(t)$ decreases by one and $d^A_{v',j}(t)$ decreases by one it is the case that $\frac{2}{\epsilon} (d^A_j(t) - d^A_{v^*,j}(t)) p_j$ before J_j moves is $\frac{2}{\epsilon} p_j$ more than $\frac{2}{\epsilon} (d^A_j(t) - d^A_{v',j}(t)) p_j$ after J_j moves. Thus, $\Phi_j(t)$ cannot increase after J_j moves since the term for v' after J_j moves is no more than the term for v^* before J_j moves.

Thus, knowing that $\Phi_j(t)$ will never increase so long as jobs do not arrive and the expression decreases at a rate of one at each continuous time, it must be the case that $\Phi_j(t)$ is an upper bound on the remaining time job J_j waits to be satisfied so long as no jobs arrive after time t. $\square$

Finally we are ready to show Lemma 1.

Proof of [Lemma 1] Let r'_j be the first time when J_j is available to schedule on a node $v' \notin \mathcal{R}$. Let v_e be the last identical node on J_j's path. Let C'_j denote the time that job J_j finished on v_e. Consider Φ_j in Lemma 3. What we see is that $\Phi_j(r'_j) \le \frac{4}{s\epsilon} d_{v_e} p_j$ by Lemma 2. Further, we see that each job J_i can contribute at most $\frac{1}{s} p_i$ to the summation in $\Phi_j(t)$ at any time t by definition of $\Phi_j(t)$. For a time $t \in (r'_j, C'_j)$ the only jobs which can contribute to $\Phi_j(t)$ which were not contributing to $\Phi_j(r'_j)$ must come from $R(v')$. Now, we know that at time r'_j there can be at most one job partially processed on $R(v')$ for each class. All of the above implies that the total increase which can happen to Φ_j during (r'_j, C'_j) is $\frac{2}{s\epsilon} p_j + \frac{1}{s}(C'_j - r'_j)$ because $R(v')$ is assumed to have one speed.

Now we also know that at any point in time $t \in (r'_j, C'_j)$ it is the case that $\Phi(t)$ is non-negative and $\Phi(t)$ decreases at a rate of one. This implies that, $(C'_j - r'_j) \le \Phi_j(r'_j) + \frac{2}{s\epsilon} p_j + \frac{1}{s}(C'_j - r'_j) \le \frac{4}{s\epsilon} d_{v_e} p_j + \frac{2}{s\epsilon} p_j + \frac{1}{s}(C'_j - r'_j)$. The second inequality is due to the fact that $\Phi_j(r'_j) \le \frac{4}{s\epsilon} d_{v_e} p_j$. Since $s \ge 1 + \epsilon$, we derive $C'_j - r'_j \le \frac{6}{\epsilon^2} d_{v_e} p_j$. $\square$

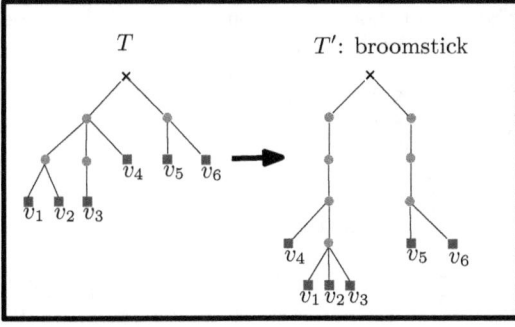

Figure 2: Tree reduction

3.3 Reduction to Broomsticks

In this section we show our reduction to broomsticks. Consider any rooted tree T in either the unrelated endpoint or identical settings and let r be the root vertex. From this tree we create a new tree T'. First add a root to T'. For every node adjacent to the root in T there is an identical node in T' adjacent to the root. Let v_0 denote some node which is a child of the root in T'. Let ℓ denote the length of the longest path from v_0 to a leaf in the subtree rooted at v_0 in T. We create a path P of length $\ell + 1$ from v_0 in T' consisting of nodes $v_0, v_1, \ldots, v_\ell$. All node on this path are identical nodes. Now consider any *leaf* v which is of distance ℓ' from v_0 in T and v is in the subtree rooted at v_0. For such a node we create a node adjacent to $v_{\ell'+1}$ in P. Note the distance in T' of v to v_0 is $\ell' + 2$ now, thus it has been increased by 2. In the identical setting this node is also an identical node, in the unrelated setting the processing time of a job on this node is the same as the processing time of a job on v in T. This is the reduction. See Figure 2 for a visual representation of the reduction. This theorem will let us focus on broomsticks in the dual fitting. The proof is deferred to the full version of this paper.

Theorem 4 *Let T be any tree in either the identical or unrelated endpoint settings and T' be it's corresponding broomstick. Fix any job sequence and let OPT_T denote the value of the optimal solution on T. Let $\text{OPT}_{T'}$ denote the value of the optimal solution on T' where all nodes, besides those connected to the root, are given $(1+\epsilon)^2$ resource augmentation and nodes adjacent to the root are given $(1+\epsilon)$ resource augmentation for some fixed constant $\epsilon > 0$. It is the case that $\text{OPT}_{T'} \leq O(\frac{1}{\epsilon^3})\text{OPT}_T$.*

3.4 Assignment Policy of the Algorithm on a Broomstick

In this section we define the algorithms which we will use in the case where the tree is a broomstick. Later in Section 3.7 we will show how this algorithm can be used to generate an algorithm for general trees. In our algorithm A all of the nodes of the tree will use SJF amongst the jobs which are available to schedule on each of the nodes. Thus, it only remains to define the machine assignment policy when a job arrives. Before we define this, first we will show some bounds on how long it will take a job to be completed assuming no more jobs arrive. This will then be used to greedily decide which machine to assign a job to.

Lemma 4 *Consider any algorithm A which uses SJF on each of the identical nodes of a tree T that is a broomstick. Further say that the nodes adjacent to the root are given resource augmentation s and the nodes not adjacent to the root are given resource augmentation at least $(1+\epsilon)s$ for any $s \geq 1$ and $\epsilon > 0$. Let $v \in \mathcal{L}$ be the leaf node J_j is assigned to. Then after time t, assuming no more jobs arrive, J_j waits at most $\frac{1}{s} \sum_{J_i \in S^A_{R(v),j}(t)} p^A_{i,R(v)}(t)$ while available on $R(v)$, $\frac{6}{\epsilon^2} p_j d_v$ time steps while available on identical nodes not in $\mathcal{R}$, and $\frac{1}{s(1+\epsilon)} \sum_{J_i \in S^A_{v,j}(t)} p^A_{i,v}(t)$ while available to schedule on v.*

PROOF. If J_j is available on $R(v)$ or v, then the term $\sum_{J_i \in S^A_{R(v)}(t)} p^A_{i,R(v)}(t)$ or $\sum_{J_i \in S^A_v(t)} p^A_{i,v}(t)$ decrease at a rate of at least s or $(1+\epsilon)s$, respectively. This is because the node would either process job J_j or a job of higher priority than job J_j. These terms can never increase because no job arrives. Thus, this bounds the time that job J_j can wait on while available on $R(v)$ or v. Finally, we know that J_j can wait at most $\frac{6}{\epsilon^2} p_j d_v$ time units in identical nodes which are not in $\mathcal{R}$ by Lemma 1 □

Now we are ready to define the assignment policy of our algorithm. Note that we simply need to specify the leaf node that a job should be processed on when a job arrives. Consider a job J_i which arrives at time $t = r_j$. The machine we assign a job to is the machine which minimizes the upper bound in the increase in the objective as predicted in Lemma 4. In the identical machines case we assign job J_i to the leaf node $v \in \mathcal{L}$ which minimizes the following.

$$\sum_{J_i \in S^A_{R(v),j}(t)} p^A_{i,R(v)}(t) + \frac{6}{\epsilon^2} d_v p_j + p_j \sum_{J_i \in Q^A_{R(v)}(t), p_i > p_j} 1$$

Now consider the case where endpoints are unrelated. In this case, we assign the jot to the node v such that the following is minimized.

$$\sum_{J_i \in S^A_{R(v),j}(t)} p^A_{i,R(v)}(t) + p_j \sum_{J_i \in Q^A_{R(v)}(t), p_i > p_j} 1$$
$$+ \sum_{J_i \in S^A_{v,j}(t)} p^A_{i,v}(t) + p_{j,v} \sum_{J_i \in Q^A_v(t), p_{i,v} > p_{j,v}} \frac{p^A_{i,v}(t)}{p_{i,v}} + \frac{6}{\epsilon^2} d_v p_j$$

3.5 Identical Endpoints on Broomsticks

In this section we show that our algorithm for the case of identical endpoints on a tree which is a broomstick is $O(\frac{1}{\epsilon^3})$ competitive for fractional flow time when the algorithm is given $(1+\epsilon)$ resource augmentation on nodes adjacent to the root and $(1+\epsilon)^2$ resource augmentation on the other nodes. To do this we consider a dual fitting argument. Let $F(j,v) = \sum_{J_i \in S^A_{R(v),j}(t)} p^A_{i,R(v)}(t) + \sum_{J_i \in Q^A_{R(v)}(t), p_i > p_j} p_j$ assuming $t = r_j$ and $v \in \mathcal{L}$. Note that we assign J_j to leaf node $\texttt{argmin}_{v \in \mathcal{L}} \{ F(j,v) + \frac{6}{\epsilon^2} d_v p_j \}$. Let $\beta_j = F(j,v) + \frac{6}{\epsilon^2} d_v p_j$ assuming J_j is assigned to v. Let $\gamma_{v,j,t} = 0$ for all v, j and $t \neq \infty$. Let $\gamma_{v,j,\infty} = F(j,v)$. Finally, set $\alpha_{v,t} = 0$ for all v not adjacent to the root and $\alpha_{v,t} = \sum_{v' \in L(v)} \sum_{J_i \in Q^A_{v'}(t)} \frac{p^A_{i,v'}(t)}{p_{i,v'}}$ for v adjacent to the root.

The first thing to notice is that $\sum_{v,t} \alpha_{v,t}$ is exactly the factional cost for the algorithm. Also, by Lemma 4 we have that $\sum_j \beta_j$ is more than $(1+\epsilon)$ times the algorithm's cost (here we assume without loss of generality that $0 < \epsilon \leq 1/4$

since this assumption can be easily removed by scaling ϵ appropriately). Thus, the dual objective in this case is at least ϵ times the algorithm's cost. Now we will show that we can divide all the dual variables by $\frac{10}{\epsilon^2}$ to obtain a feasible solution to the dual. This will give an $O(\frac{1}{\epsilon^3})$-competitive algorithm. Our goal will be to show the following theorem which follows by scaling ϵ appropriately.

Theorem 5 *There is a $(1+\epsilon)$-speed $O(1/\epsilon^3)$-competitive algorithm for minimizing total fractional flow time on broomsticks with all identical nodes.*

To show the theorem, we show that each of the constraints are satisfied.

Lemma 5 *Constraint (4) is satisfied.*

PROOF. Fix any job J_j, any node $v \in \mathcal{L}$ and any time t. Our goal is to show that

$$\frac{\epsilon^2}{10}\left(-\alpha_{v,t} + \frac{\beta_j}{p_j} - \sum_{t' \geq t} \frac{\gamma_{\rho(v),j,t'}}{p_j}\right) - \frac{t - r_j}{p_j} - \eta_{j,v}/p_j \leq 0$$

Say that job J_j is assigned to node v^*. In this case, we have that $\beta_j = F(j, v^*) + \frac{6}{\epsilon^2}d_{v^*}p_j$. We also know $F(j,v) + \frac{6}{\epsilon^2}d_v p_j \geq F(j, v^*) + \frac{6}{\epsilon^2}d_{v^*}p_j$ by definition of the algorithm. Thus it suffices to show that,

$$\frac{\epsilon^2}{10}\left(-\alpha_{v,t} + \frac{F(j,v) + \frac{6}{\epsilon^2}d_v p_j}{p_j} - \sum_{t' \geq t} \frac{\gamma_{\rho(v),j,t'}}{p_j}\right) - \frac{t - r_j}{p_j}$$
$$- \eta_{j,v}/p_j \leq 0,$$

which holds since $\sum_{t' > t} \gamma_{\rho(v),j,t'} = F(j, \rho(v)) = F(j,v)$ and $\eta_{j,v} = d_v p_j$. $\square$

The following lemma is the most challenging part of the dual fitting proof.

Lemma 6 *Constraint (5) is satisfied.*

PROOF. Fix any job J_j, any node $v \in \mathcal{R}$ and any time $t \geq r_j$. Our goal is to show that,

$$\frac{\epsilon^2}{10}\left(-\alpha_{v,t} + \sum_{t' \geq t} \frac{\gamma_{v,j,t'}}{p_j}\right) - \frac{t - r_j}{p_j} \leq 0$$

We know that $\alpha_{v,t} = \sum_{v' \in L(v)} \sum_{J_i \in Q_{v'}^A(t)} \frac{p_{i,v'}^A(t)}{p_{i,v'}}$. Also we have that $\sum_{t' \geq t} \gamma_{v,j,t'} = F(j,v) = \sum_{J_i \in S_{v,j}^A(r_j)} p_{i,v}^A(r_j) + \sum_{J_i \in Q_v^A(r_j), p_i > p_j} p_j$. Let V be the total volume of work that has been done on jobs in $S_{v,j}^A(r_j)$ between r_j and time t on v. Recall that since v is a node adjacent to the root, it is given $(1 + \epsilon)$ resource augmentation and this implies that $V \leq (1 + \epsilon)(t - r_j)$. Let V' be the total volume of jobs J_i in $Q_v^A(r_j)$ where $p_i > p_j$ that has been processed on the (only) child of v by time t. Let v_c be the child of v. This implies that $p_{i,v_c}(r_j) \geq p_j$ for $J_i \in Q_v^A(r_j)$ where $p_i > p_j$. Thus, it must be case that $V' \leq (1+\epsilon)^2(t-r_i)$. Indeed, this is the case because all jobs in $Q_v^A(r_j)$ must not have been scheduled on the node which is a child of v at all before time r_j (note there is only one child of v by definition of the broomstick). Further, all of these jobs must be eventually

scheduled on this node to be completed and this node has speed $(1 + \epsilon)^2$. We derive that,

$$\frac{\epsilon^2}{10}\left(-\alpha_{v,t} + \sum_{t' \geq t} \frac{\gamma_{v,j,t'}}{p_j}\right) - \frac{t - r_j}{p_j}$$

$$= \frac{\epsilon^2}{10}\left(-\sum_{v' \in L(v)} \sum_{J_i \in Q_{v'}^A(t)} \frac{p_{i,v'}^A(t)}{p_i} + \right.$$
$$\left. \frac{\sum_{J_i \in S_{v,j}^A(r_j)} p_{i,v}^A(r_j) + \sum_{J_i \in Q_v^A(r_j), p_i > p_j} p_j}{p_j}\right) - \frac{t - r_j}{p_j}$$

$$= \frac{\epsilon^2}{10}\left(-\sum_{v' \in L(v)} \sum_{J_i \in S_{v',j}^A(t)} \frac{p_{i,v'}^A(t)}{p_i}\right.$$
$$- \sum_{v' \in L(v)} \sum_{J_i \in Q_{v'}^A(t) \setminus S_{v',j}^A(t)} \frac{p_{i,v'}^A(t)}{p_i}$$
$$\left. + \frac{\sum_{J_i \in S_{v,j}^A(r_j)} p_{i,v}^A(r_j) + \sum_{J_i \in Q_v^A(r_j), p_i > p_j} p_i}{p_j}\right) - \frac{t - r_j}{p_j}$$

$$\leq \frac{\epsilon^2}{10}\left(\frac{V}{p_j} - \sum_{v' \in L(v)} \sum_{J_i \in Q_{v'}^A(t) \setminus S_{v',j}^A(t)} \frac{p_{i,v'}^A(t)}{p_i}\right.$$
$$\left. + \frac{\sum_{J_i \in Q_v^A(r_j), p_i > p_j} p_i}{p_j}\right) - \frac{t - r_j}{p_j} \tag{7}$$

The last inequality holds since $V = \sum_{J_i \in S_{v,j}^A(r_j)} p_{i,v}^A(r_j) - \sum_{J_i \in S_{v,j}^A(r_j)} p_{i,v}^A(t)$, and for any descendent v' of v in T, $p_{i,v'}^A(t) \geq p_{i,v}^A(t)$. Before we continue to upper bound (7), we show

$$V' = \sum_{J_i \in Q_v^A(r_j), p_i > p_j} p_{i,v_c}^A(r_j) - \sum_{J_i \in Q_v^A(t), p_i > p_j} p_{i,v_c}^A(t)$$

$$= \sum_{J_i \in Q_v^A(r_j), p_i > p_j} p_i - \sum_{J_i \in Q_v^A(t), p_i > p_j} p_{i,v_c}^A(t)$$

$$\geq \sum_{J_i \in Q_v^A(r_j), p_i > p_j} p_i - \sum_{v' \in L(v)} \sum_{J_i \in Q_{v'}^A(t) \setminus S_{v',j}^A(t)} p_{i,v'}^A(t)$$

The first equality comes from the definition of V'. The second equality holds since job J_i is not completed on node v at time r_j implies that J_i has not been processed at all on its unique child node v_c. The last inequality follows from that fact that for any descendent v' of v in T, $p_{i,v'}^A(t) \geq p_{i,v_c}^A(t)$ (also note that $Q_{v'}^A(t) \setminus S_{v',j}^A(t) = Q_v^A(t), p_i > p_j$ since the algorithm is SJF).

Hence we further derive that,

$$(7) = \frac{\epsilon^2}{10}\left(\frac{V}{p_j} - \sum_{v' \in L(v)} \sum_{J_i \in Q_{v'}^A(t) \setminus S_{v',j}^A(t)} \frac{p_{i,v'}^A(t)}{p_i}\right.$$
$$\left. + \sum_{J_i \in Q_v^A(r_j), p_i > p_j} \frac{p_i}{p_j}\right) - \frac{t - r_j}{p_j}$$

$$\leq \frac{\epsilon^2}{10}\left(\frac{V}{p_j} + \frac{V'}{p_j}\right) - \frac{t - r_j}{p_j}$$

The last inequality follows since $V \leq (1 + \epsilon)(t - r_j)$ and $V' \leq (1+\epsilon)^2(t-r_i)$, and $\epsilon \leq 1$. This completes the proof. $\square$

Lemma 7 *Constraint (6) is satisfied.*

PROOF. Fix any job J_j, any node $v \notin \mathcal{L} \cup \mathcal{R}$ and any time t. Our goal is to show that

$$\frac{\epsilon^2}{10} \left(-\alpha_{v,t} + \sum_{t' \geq t} \frac{\gamma_{v,j,t'}}{p_j} - \sum_{t' \geq t} \frac{\gamma_{\rho(v),j,t'}}{p_j} \right) \leq 0$$

We know that $\sum_{t' > t} \gamma_{\rho(v),j,t'} = F(j, \rho(v))$ and $\sum_{t' > t} \gamma_{v,j,t'} = F(j, v)$. By definition of F this implies that $\sum_{t' > t} \gamma_{\rho(v),j,t'} = \sum_{t' > t} \gamma_{v,j,t'}$. Since $\alpha_{v,t}$ is positive, the lemma follows. □

3.6 Unrelated Endpoints on Broomsticks

In this section we show that our algorithm for the case of unrelated endpoints on a tree which is a broomstick is $O(\frac{1}{\epsilon^3})$-competitive for fractional flow time when the algorithm is given $2(1 + \epsilon)$ resource augmentation on nodes adjacent to the root and $2(1 + \epsilon)^2$ resource augmentation on the other nodes. To do this we consider a dual fitting argument. Let $F(j, v) = \sum_{J_i \in S^A_{R(v),j}(t)} p^A_{i,R(v)}(t) + \sum_{J_i \in Q^A_{R(v)}(t), p_i > p_j} p_j$ and $F'(j, v) = \sum_{J_i \in S^A_{v,j}(t)} p^A_{i,v}(t) + p_{j,v} \sum_{J_i \in Q^A_v(t), p_i > p_j} \frac{p^A_{i,v}(t)}{p_{i,v}}$ assuming $t = r_j$ and $v \in \mathcal{L}$. We assign J_j to leaf node $\operatorname{argmin}_{v \in \mathcal{L}} \{F(j, v) + F'(j, v) + \frac{6}{\epsilon^2} p_j d_v\}$. Let $\beta_j = F(j, v) + F'(j, v) + \frac{6}{\epsilon^2} d_v p_j$ assuming J_j is assigned to v. Let $\gamma_{v,j,t} = 0$ for all v, j and $t \neq \infty$. Let $\gamma_{v,j,\infty} = F(j, v)$. Finally, set $\alpha_{v,t} = 0$ for all $v \notin \mathcal{L}$ which are not adjacent to the root, $\alpha_{v,t} = \sum_{v' \in L(v)} \sum_{J_i \in Q^A_{v'}(t)} \frac{p^A_{j,v'}(t)}{p_{j,v'}}$ for v adjacent to the root and $\alpha_{v,t} = \sum_{J_i \in Q^A_v(t)} \frac{p^A_{j,v}(t)}{p_{j,v}}$ for $v \in \mathcal{L}$.

The first thing to notice that that $\sum_{v,t} \alpha_{v,t}$ is exactly twice the factional cost for the algorithm. Also, by Lemma 4 we have that $\sum_j \beta_j$ is more than $2(1 + \epsilon)$ times the algorithm's cost. Thus, the dual objective in this case is at least 2ϵ times the algorithm's cost (here we without loss of generality assume that $\epsilon \leq 1/8$, and we can remove this assumption easily by scaling ϵ). Now we will show that we can divide all the dual variables by $\frac{20}{\epsilon^2}$ to obtain a feasible solution to the dual. This will give an $O(1/\epsilon^3)$ competitive algorithm. Our goal will be to show the following theorem which follows by scaling ϵ appropriately. The formal proof will appear in the full version of this paper.

Theorem 6 *There is a $(2 + \epsilon)$-speed $O(1/\epsilon^3)$-competitive algorithm for minimizing total fractional flow time on broomsticks with all identical routers and unrelated endpoints.*

3.7 Algorithm for General Trees

In this section, we put all of the pieces together and give an algorithm for general trees for fractional flow time. This and the conversion from fractional flow time will complete the proofs. Our algorithm works as follows. Let T be any arbitrary tree. We will define an algorithm A_T on T. The algorithm is given resource augmentation $(1 + \epsilon)$ on nodes besides those connected to the root for some constant $\epsilon > 0$. From T the algorithm creates a new tree T' which is a broomstick, preserving the resource augmentation for non-root nodes. On T' the algorithm simulates the algorithm from the previous section. Let this algorithm be denoted $A_{T'}$. Say that job J_j is assigned to node $v_j^{T'} \in \mathcal{L}$ in T' by $A_{T'}$. The algorithm A_T assigns job J_j to the node corresponding to $v_j^{T'}$

in T, which we denote by v_j^T. Then, in A_T the algorithm schedules jobs using SJF on all of the nodes.

Lemma 8 *The total flow time of A_T is at most that of $A_{T'}$.*

PROOF. To show the theorem, we will show that the flow time of each job in A_T is at most that the job waits in $A_{T'}$, which will imply the lemma. Fix any job J_j assigned to the leaf node v_j. Let d_{v_j} be the distance of v_j to a node adjacent to the root in T. First we will show that the time J_j completes on the ith identical node on its path is only sooner in A_T than in $A_{T'}$. We show this by induction on on the number of nodes which J_j has finished being processed on. For the base case, consider a node adjacent to the root. The schedule on this node is exactly the same in A_T as it is in $A_{T'}$, thus the claim holds. Now consider the ith identical node which J_j reaches. Let $v_{i,j}^T$ and $v_{i,j}^{T'}$ denote this node in T and T', respectively. By construction of T', any job that is processed on $v_{i,j}^T$ in A_T must also be processed by $v_{i,j}^{T'}$ in T (the opposite does not need to hold though). By definition of SJF and the fact that all jobs arrive to $v_{i,j}^T$ in A_T before they arrive to $v_{i,j}^{T'}$ in $A_{T'}$ by the inductive hypothesis it must be the case that J_j is complete on $v_{i,j}^T$ in A_T by the time it is completed on $v_{i,j}^{T'}$ in $A_{T'}$.

Finally, in the case that we have unrelated endpoints, we show that J_j completes on its leaf node in T by the time it completes on its leaf node in T'. From the above every job processed v_j^T in A_T is also processed on $v_j^{T'}$ in $A_{T'}$. Further, the above implies that any job assigned to v_j^T arrives to v_j^T in A_T by the time it arrives to $v_j^{T'}$ in $A_{T'}$. Thus the definition of SJF implies that J_j completes on v_j^T in A_T by the time it completes on $v_j^{T'}$ on $A_{T'}$. Thus the flow time of J_j in A_T is at most the flow time of J_j in $A_{T'}$ and we have the lemma. □

The previous lemma combined with Theorem 4 and Theorems 5 and 6 complete the proofs of Theorems 1 and 2.

4. CONCLUSION

In this paper, we initiate the study of scheduling online on a set of machines under networking constraints. As far as the authors know, this is the first time networking has been considered in conjunction with scheduling on machines in the online setting. There are many interesting open questions. One question is whether the speed required in the unrelated setting we consider can be reduced from $2 + \epsilon$ to $1 + \epsilon$. There appears to be a challenging hurdle in reducing the speed which arises from the processing times of jobs changing once they arrive to the machine that they are to be processed on. More broadly, it would be of interest to further address scheduling under networking constraints in general. In particular, what more general networks than those considered in this paper allow for provably good scheduling algorithms? What can be shown if jobs arrive at arbitrary nodes in the network? What can be shown for different objectives such as maximum flow time or the ℓ_k-norms of flow time? As mentioned, the work by Antoniadis et al. [5] has addressed this case when the graph is a line network in what corresponds to our identical setting when all jobs have unit size. They also showed that the objective of maximum flow time becomes hard in this setting if the network is a tree.

Acknowledgements. The first author's research was supported in part by NSF grant CCF-1409130.

5. REFERENCES

[1] M. Al-Fares, A. Loukissas, and A. Vahdat. A scalable, commodity data center network architecture. In *SIGCOMM*, pages 63–74, 2008.

[2] M. Al-Fares, S. Radhakrishnan, B. Raghavan, N. Huang, and A. Vahdat. Hedera: Dynamic flow scheduling for data center networks. In *NSDI*, pages 281–296, 2010.

[3] S. Anand, N. Garg, and A. Kumar. Resource augmentation for weighted flow-time explained by dual fitting. In *SODA*, pages 1228–1241, 2012.

[4] M. Andrews and L. Zhang. The effects of temporary sessions on network performance. *SIAM J. Comput.*, 33(3):659–673, 2004.

[5] A. Antoniadis, N. Barcelo, D. Cole, K. Fox, B. Moseley, M. Nugent, and K. Pruhs. Packet forwarding algorithms in a line network. In *LATIN*, 2014.

[6] N. Avrahami and Y. Azar. Minimizing total flow time and total completion time with immediate dispatching. In *SPAA '03*, pages 11–18, 2003.

[7] B. Awerbuch, Y. Azar, and S. A. Plotkin. Throughput-competitive on-line routing. In *FOCS*, pages 32–40, 1993.

[8] E. Bampis, R. Giroudeau, and A. Kononov. Scheduling tasks with small communication delays for clusters of processors. *Annals OR*, 129(1-4):47–63, 2004.

[9] D. Bernstein and I. Gertner. Scheduling expressions on a pipelined processor with a maximal delay of one cycle. *ACM Trans. Program. Lang. Syst.*, 11(1):57–66, 1989.

[10] A. Borodin, J. M. Kleinberg, P. Raghavan, M. Sudan, and D. P. Williamson. Adversarial queuing theory. *J. ACM*, 48(1):13–38, 2001.

[11] A. Z. Broder, A. M. Frieze, and E. Upfal. A general approach to dynamic packet routing with bounded buffers. *J. ACM*, 48(2):324–349, 2001.

[12] C. Bussema and E. Torng. Greedy multiprocessor server scheduling. *Oper. Res. Lett.*, 34(4):451–458, 2006.

[13] J. S. Chadha, N. Garg, A. Kumar, and V. N. Muralidhara. A competitive algorithm for minimizing weighted flow time on unrelated machines with speed augmentation. In *Symposium on Theory of Computing*, pages 679–684, 2009.

[14] C. Chekuri, A. Goel, S. Khanna, and A. Kumar. Multi-processor scheduling to minimize flow time with epsilon resource augmentation. In *STOC*, pages 363–372, 2004.

[15] Y.-C. Cheng and T. Robertazzi. Distributed Computation for a Tree-Network with Communication Delay. *IEEE transactions on aerospace and electronic systems*, 26(3), 1990.

[16] D. W. Engels, J. Feldman, D. R. Karger, and M. Ruhl. Parallel processor scheduling with delay constraints. In *SODA*, pages 577–585, 2001.

[17] L. Finta and Z. Liu. Single machine scheduling subject to precedence delays. *Discrete Applied Mathematics*, 70(3):247–266, 1996.

[18] K. Fox and B. Moseley. Online scheduling on identical machines using srpt. In *SODA*, pages 120–128, 2011.

[19] N. Garg and A. Kumar. Minimizing average flow-time : Upper and lower bounds. In *FOCS*, pages 603–613, 2007.

[20] R. Giroudeau and J.-C. König. General scheduling non-approximability results in presence of hierarchical communications. *European Journal of Operational Research*, 184(2):441–457, 2008.

[21] R. Giroudeau, J.-C. König, F.-K. Moulaï, and J. Palaysi. Complexity and approximation for the precedence constrained scheduling problem with large communication delays. In *Euro-Par*, pages 252–261, 2005.

[22] A. Gupta, R. Krishnaswamy, and K. Pruhs. Online primal-dual for non-linear optimization with applications to speed scaling. In *WAOA*, 2012.

[23] B. Heller, S. Seetharaman, P. Mahadevan, Y. Yiakoumis, P. Sharma, S. Banerjee, and N. McKeown. Elastictree: Saving energy in data center networks. In *NSDI*, pages 249–264, 2010.

[24] S. Im, B. Moseley, and K. Pruhs. A tutorial on amortized local competitiveness in online scheduling. *SIGACT News*, 42:83–97, June 2011.

[25] S. Im, B. Moseley, and K. Pruhs. Online scheduling with general cost functions. In *SODA*, pages 1254–1265, 2012.

[26] B. Kalyanasundaram and K. Pruhs. Speed is as powerful as clairvoyance. *Journal of the ACM*, 47(4):617–643, 2000.

[27] H. J. Karloff, S. Suri, and S. Vassilvitskii. A model of computation for MapReduce. In *SODA*, pages 938–948, 2010.

[28] A. Kesselman, Y. Mansour, and R. van Stee. Improved competitive guarantees for QoS buffering. *Algorithmica*, 43(1-2):63–80, 2005.

[29] F. T. Leighton, B. M. Maggs, and S. Rao. Packet routing and job-shop scheduling in o(congestion + dilation) steps. *Combinatorica*, 14(2):167–186, 1994.

[30] S. Leonardi and D. Raz. Approximating total flow time on parallel machines. *J. Comput. Syst. Sci.*, 73(6):875–891, 2007.

[31] B. Moseley, A. Dasgupta, R. Kumar, and T. Sarlós. On scheduling in map-reduce and flow-shops. In *SPAA*, pages 289–298, 2011.

[32] C. A. Phillips, C. Stein, and J. Wein. Task scheduling in networks. *SIAM J. Discrete Math.*, 10(4):573–598, 1997.

[33] K. Pruhs, J. Sgall, and E. Torng. *Handbook of Scheduling: Algorithms, Models, and Performance Analysis*, chapter Online Scheduling. 2004.

[34] A. Srinivasan and C.-P. Teo. A constant-factor approximation algorithm for packet routing and balancing local vs. global criteria. *SIAM J. Comput.*, 30(6):2051–2068, 2000.

The Revolution in Graph Theoretic Optimization Problems

Gary Miller

Professor of Computer Science, Carnegie Mellon University
Pittsburgh, PA, USA
glmiller@cs.cmu.edu

ABSTRACT

Over the last several years there have been major breakthroughs in the design of approximation algorithms for such classic problems as finding the maximum flow in a graph. Maximum flow for undirected graphs can now be approximately solved in almost linear time. This result by researchers at Berkeley and MIT, I claim, is only the beginning of a new era in efficient algorithm design.

Graph theoretic optimization problems, that have been dormant for fifty years are now seeing new and exciting algorithms. These advances have been made possible by Spectral Graph Theory, the interplay between linear algebra and combinatorial graph theory. One application of this interplay is a nearly linear time solver for Symmetric Diagonally Dominate systems (SDD). This seemingly restrictive class of linear systems has received substantial interest in the last 15 years. Both algorithm design theory and practical implementations have made major progress. Surprisingly, there is an ever growing list of problems that can be efficiently solved using SDD solvers including image segmentation, image denoising, finding solutions to elliptic equations, computing maximum flow in a graph, graph sparsification, and graphics. All these examples can be viewed as special cases of convex optimization problems that arise from graph problems. I can imagine a world where such optimization problems that seem to require at least quadratic work will all be solvable by practical algorithms guaranteed to run in near linear work and are very parallel.

Categories and Subject Descriptors

G.1.3 Mathematics of Computing, NUMERICAL ANALYSIS, Numerical Linear Algebra: Eigenvalues and eigenvectors (direct and iterative methods)

SPAA'15, June 13–15, 2015, Portland, OR, USA.
ACM 978-1-4503-3588-1/15/06.
http://dx.doi.org/10.1145/2755573.2764965

Space and Time Efficient Parallel Graph Decomposition, Clustering, and Diameter Approximation

Matteo Ceccarello
Department of Information
Engineering
University of Padova
Padova, Italy
ceccarel@dei.unipd.it

Andrea Pietracaprina
Department of Information
Engineering
University of Padova
Padova, Italy
capri@dei.unipd.it

Geppino Pucci
Department of Information
Engineering
University of Padova
Padova, Italy
geppo@dei.unipd.it

Eli Upfal
Department of Computer
Science
Brown University
Providence, RI, USA
eli_upfal@brown.edu

ABSTRACT

We develop a novel parallel decomposition strategy for un-weighted, undirected graphs, based on growing disjoint connected clusters from batches of centers progressively selected from yet uncovered nodes. With respect to similar previous decompositions, our strategy exercises a tighter control on both the number of clusters and their maximum radius.

We present two important applications of our parallel graph decomposition: (1) k-center clustering approximation; and (2) diameter approximation. In both cases, we obtain algorithms which feature a polylogarithmic approximation factor and are amenable to a distributed implementation that is geared for massive (long-diameter) graphs. The total space needed for the computation is linear in the problem size, and the parallel depth is substantially sublinear in the diameter for graphs with low doubling dimension. To the best of our knowledge, ours are the first parallel approximations for these problems which achieve sub-diameter parallel time, for a relevant class of graphs, using only linear space. Besides the theoretical guarantees, our algorithms allow for a very simple implementation on clustered architectures: we report on extensive experiments which demonstrate their effectiveness and efficiency on large graphs as compared to alternative known approaches.

Categories and Subject Descriptors: F.2 [Theory of Computation]: Analysis of Algorithms and Problem Complexity

Keywords: Parallel Graph Algorithms; Graph Decomposition; k-Center Problem; Diameter Approximation; MapReduce

SPAA '15, June 13 - 15, 2015, Portland, OR, USA
Copyright is held by the owner/author(s). Publication rights licensed to ACM.
ACM 978-1-4503-3588-1/15/06 ...$15.00.
DOI: http://dx.doi.org/10.1145/2755573.2755591 .

1. INTRODUCTION

Graph analytics is rapidly establishing itself as a major discovery tool in such diverse application domains as road systems, social networks, natural language processing, biological pattern discovery, cybersecurity, and more. Graph analytics tasks for big data networks are typically run on distributed architectures such as clusters of loosely-coupled commodity servers, where the challenge is to minimize communication overhead between processors, while each processor can store only a small fraction of the entire network. A number of computational models proposed in recent years [18, 14, 24] provide rigorous frameworks for studying algorithms for massive data, subject to these constraints. Under this new computational paradigm, state-of-the-art graph algorithms often do not scale up efficiently to process massive instances, since they either require superlinear memory or exhibit long critical paths resulting in a large number of communication rounds.

In this work we focus on *graph decomposition*, which is a fundamental primitive for graph analytics as well as for several other application contexts, especially in distributed settings, where decompositions are often at the base of efficient parallel solutions. We develop an efficient parallel decomposition algorithm for partitioning the nodes of an unweighted, undirected graph into disjoint, internally connected *clusters*, which is able to control the maximum radius of the clusters (the maximum distance of a node in a cluster to the cluster's center). Similarly to other known decomposition approaches, our algorithm grows clusters from several batches of centers which are progressively selected from the uncovered nodes. However, rather than fixing the radius of each grown cluster a priori, or randomly delaying the activation of the centers, as in previous works, we activate a new batch of centers every time that the number of uncovered nodes halves, while continuing growing the clusters of previously activated centers. The idea behind such a strategy is to force more clusters to grow in poorly connected regions of the graph while keeping both the total number of clusters and the maximum cluster radius under control.

We demonstrate the quality and utility of our decomposition strategy by applying it to the solution of two extensively studied problems, metric k-center clustering and diameter approximation, for which we obtain space and time efficient parallel algorithms.

In the *metric k-center* clustering problem [13, 15] the goal is to partition an undirected graph into k clusters so that the maximum radius of the clusters is minimized. The problem is NP-hard and we are therefore interested in efficient approximations. Given an n node unweighted undirected graph, building on our parallel graph decomposition method, we obtain a randomized $O\left(\log^3 n\right)$-approximation algorithm to the k-center problem. The algorithm can be implemented on the MapReduce (MR) model of [24] in a number of parallel rounds proportional to the maximum cluster radius using overall linear space, as long as each processing node is provided with $\Omega(n^\epsilon)$ local space, for any constant $\epsilon > 0$. In order to derive a more explicit bound on the parallel complexity, we analyze the maximum cluster radius, hence the number of rounds, as a function of the doubling dimension of the graph (see Definition 2), showing that for a graph of diameter Δ and doubling dimension $b > 0$ the algorithm can provide a decomposition into k clusters with maximum cluster radius $\tilde{O}(\lceil \Delta/k^{1/b}\rceil)$.

Next, we apply our graph decomposition strategy to a challenging problem in the context of graph analytics, namely, the approximation of the graph diameter, a global property of a graph, in a number of parallel rounds which is substantially less than the diameter itself, and using linear global space and local memory at each processor sufficient to store only a small fraction of the graph. We remark that known parallel approaches to estimating the diameter of a graph either require up to quadratic space (e.g., using transitive closure) or require a number of parallel rounds which is inherently linear in the diameter (e.g., using straightforward parallelization of breadth-first search or neighborhood function estimations).

To estimate the diameter of a graph G, we first compute a decomposition of G of suitable granularity with our novel algorithm, and then we estimate the diameter through the diameter of the *quotient graph*, that is, the graph whose nodes correspond to the clusters and whose edges connect clusters containing nodes which are adjacent in G. The granularity is chosen so that the size of the quotient graph is small enough so that its diameter can be computed using limited local memory and very few communication rounds.

We show that on any unweighted, undirected connected graph G with n nodes and m edges, our algorithm returns an upper bound to its diameter which is a factor $O\left(\log^3 n\right)$ away from the true value, with high probability. The algorithm can be implemented on the aforementioned MR model using overall linear space and $\Omega(n^\epsilon)$ local space, with $\epsilon > 0$, in a number of parallel rounds which is $\tilde{O}(\lceil \Delta/(\max\{m^{1/3}n^{\epsilon/6}, n^{\epsilon'}\})^{1/b}\rceil)$ where b is the doubling dimension of the graph and ϵ' is any constant less than ϵ. Observe that for graphs with small (e.g., constant) doubling dimension, which arise in important practical realms [17], the number of rounds can be made asymptotically much smaller than the diameter if sufficient yet sublinear local memory is available. While a similar approach for diameter estimation has been used in the past in the external-memory setting (see Section 2), the algorithm presented here, to the best of our knowledge, is the first linear-space distributed

algorithm for the problem requiring a number of parallel rounds which is sublinear in the diameter.

A very desirable feature of our algorithms is that they lend themselves to efficient practical implementations. We report on an extensive set of experiments conducted on a number of large graphs. A first batch of experiments shows the effectiveness of our decomposition strategy in minimizing the maximum cluster radius, compared against the recent parallel decomposition strategy of [22], while a second batch shows that the approximation obtained by our diameter approximation algorithm is in fact much smaller than the asymptotic bound, even for graphs of unknown doubling dimension (less than twice the diameter in all tested cases) and that the algorithm's performance compares very favorably to the one exhibited by direct competitors such as breadth-first search and the (almost exact) diameter estimation algorithm HADI [16]. For graphs of very large diameter, the speed-up of our algorithm can be of orders of magnitude.

The rest of the paper is organized as follows. Section 2 summarizes relevant previous work on graph decomposition, k-center clustering, and diameter estimation. Section 3 presents our novel decomposition and discusses how it can be employed to approximate the k-center problem. Section 4 presents our decomposition-based algorithm for diameter approximation. Section 5 analyzes our strategies in the MR model of [24]. Section 6 reports on the experimental results, and, finally, Section 7 offers some concluding remarks.

2. PREVIOUS WORK

Parallel clustering algorithms relevant to this work have been studied in [8, 5, 22]. In [8] the notion of (β, W)-cover for a weighted graph G is introduced, which is essentially a decomposition of the graph into nondisjoint clusters, where each node is allowed to belong to $O\left(\beta n^{1/\beta} \log n\right)$ distinct clusters and for any two nodes at weighted distance at most W in the graph, there is a cluster containing both. A (β, W)-cover is obtained by growing clusters of decreasing radii from successive batches of centers. The algorithm presented in [5] is similar but returns disjoint clusters and guarantees a bound on the average number of edges between clusters. In [22] an alternative clustering algorithm is proposed which assigns to each node $u \in V$ a random time shift δ_u, taken from an exponential distribution with parameter β, and grows a cluster centered at u starting at time $\delta_{\max} - \delta_u$, where $\delta_{\max}$ is the maximum shift, unless by that time node u has been already covered by some other cluster. The authors show that in this fashion the graph is partitioned into clusters of maximum radius $O\left((\log n)/\beta\right)$, with high probability, while the average number of edges between clusters, hence the size of the quotient graph, is at most $O\left(\beta m\right)$. None of the above clustering approaches guarantees that the maximum radius of the returned clusters is (close to) minimum with respect to all possible decompositions of the graph featuring the same number of clusters.

The related *metric k-center* optimization problem requires that given a set V of n points in a metric space, a subset $M \subset V$ of k points be found so to minimize the maximum distance between any $v \in V$ and M. The problem is NP-hard even if distances satisfy the triangle inequality [28], but polynomial-time 2-approximation sequential algorithms are known [13, 15]. Recently, a constant-approximation MapReduce algorithm was developed in [12] under the assumption that the distances among all $\Theta\left(n^2\right)$ pairs of points are given in input. The problem remains NP-hard even if V represents the set of nodes of an undirected connected graph G, and the distance between two nodes is the length of the shortest path between them. To the best of our knowledge, no low-depth linear-space parallel strategy that yields a provably good approximation for this important graph variant is known in the literature.

In recent years, efficient sequential algorithms for estimating the diameter of very large graphs have been devised, which avoid the costly computation of all-pairs shortest paths or the memory-inefficient transitive closure by performing a limited number of Breadth-First Searches (BFS) from suitably selected source nodes [10, 7]. Unfortunately, due to the inherent difficulty of parallelizing BFS [27, 19] these approaches do not appear amenable to efficient low-depth parallel implementations. External-memory algorithms for diameter estimation which employ a clustering-based strategy similar to ours have been recently proposed in [21, 3]. The algorithm by [21] basically selects k centers at random and grows disjoint clusters around the centers until the whole graph is covered. The author shows that the diameter of the original graph can be approximated within a multiplicative factor of $\Theta\left(\sqrt{k}\log n\right)$, with high probability, by computing the diameter on the quotient graph associated with the clustering with suitable edge weights. In [3] a recursive implementation of this strategy is evaluated experimentally. This approximation ratio is competitive with our result only for polylogarithmic values of k. However, observe that for such small values of k the radius of the k clusters must be within a small (polylogarithmic) factor of the graph diameter, and thus the parallel number of rounds cannot be substantially sublinear in the diameter itself.

Efficient PRAM algorithms for approximating shortest path distances between given pairs of nodes are given in [8, 9]. For sparse graphs with $m \in \Theta(n)$, these algorithms feature $O\left(n^\delta\right)$ depth, for any fixed constant $\delta \in (0,1)$, but incur a polylogarithmic space blow-up due to the use of the (β, W)-covers mentioned above. The algorithms are rather involved and communication intensive, hence, while theoretically efficient, in practice they may run slowly when implemented on distributed-memory clusters of loosely-coupled servers, where communication overhead is typically high. Moreover, their depth is not directly related to the graph diameter.

In [23], an efficient algorithm, called ANF, is devised to tightly approximate the *neighborhood function* of a graph G, which, for every $t \geq 0$, gives the number of pairs of nodes at distance at most t in G, and, therefore, it can be used to estimate the diameter. On a connected graph G of diameter Δ, ANF executes Δ iterations and maintains at each node v a suitable succinct data structure to approximate, at the end of each Iteration t, the number of nodes at distance at most t from v. A MapReduce implementation of ANF, called HADI, has been devised in [16] using Apache Hadoop. Little experimental evidence of HADI's performance on large benchmark graphs is available. However, as confirmed by our experiments (see Section 6), for large-diameter graphs HADI's strategy, even if implemented using faster engines than Hadoop, runs very slowly because of the large number of rounds and the high communication volume. A very fast,

multithreaded version of ANF, called HyperANF, has been devised in [6] for expensive tightly-coupled multiprocessors with large shared memories, which are not the architectures targeted by our work.

3. CLUSTERING ALGORITHM

Let $G = (V, E)$ be an undirected connected graph with $n = |V|$ nodes and $m = |E|$ edges. For any two nodes $u, v \in V$ let $\text{dist}(u, v)$ denote the number of edges in the shortest path between u and v in G. Also, for any $u \in V$ and $X \subseteq V$, let $\text{dist}(u, X)$ denote the minimum distance between u and a node of X. We now present an algorithm (CLUSTER) that partitions V into disjoint clusters around suitably selected nodes called *centers*, so that the radius of each cluster, defined as the maximum distance of a cluster node from the center, is small. As in [8, 5, 22], our algorithm activates batches of centers progressively, so to allow more clusters to cover sparser regions of the graph. However, unlike those previous works, we can show that our algorithm minimizes the maximum cluster radius, within a polylogarithmic factor, a property that later will turn out crucial for the efficiency of the diameter-approximation algorithm. A parameter $\tau > 0$ is used to control the size of each batch of activated centers. When two or more clusters attempt to cover a node concurrently, only one of them, arbitrarily chosen, succeeds, so to maintain clusters disjoint. The algorithm's pseudocode is given below[1].

Algorithm 1: CLUSTER(τ)

begin
    $C \leftarrow \emptyset$ // *(current set of clusters)*
    $V' \leftarrow \emptyset$ // *(nodes covered by current set of clusters)*
    while $|V - V'| > 8\tau \log n$ **do**
        Select each node of $V - V'$ as a new center
            independently with probability $4\tau \log n/|V - V'|$
        Add to C the set of singleton clusters centered at the
            selected nodes
        In parallel grow all clusters of C disjointly until
            $\geq |V - V'|/2$ new nodes are covered
        $V' \leftarrow$ nodes covered by the clusters in C
    end
    return
    $C \cup \{\text{singleton clusters centered at the nodes of } V - V'\}$
end

We define a crucial benchmark for analyzing each iteration of the algorithm.

DEFINITION 1. *Let k be an integer, with $1 \leq k \leq n$, and let $V' \subseteq V$ be a subset of at most $n - k$ nodes. We define*

$$r(G, V', k) = \min\{r : \exists U \subseteq V - V' \text{ s.t. } |U| = k$$
$$\wedge \forall w \in V - V' \ \text{dist}(w, V' \cup U) \leq r\}.$$

Suppose that we have partially grown some clusters covering a subset $V' \subset V$. We know that by continuing to grow these clusters plus k new clusters centered in uncovered nodes, $r = r(G, V', k)$ growing steps are necessary to cover the whole graph. We have:

THEOREM 1. *For any integer $\tau > 0$, with high probability, CLUSTER(τ) computes a partition of V into $O\left(\tau \cdot \log^2 n\right)$*

---

[1]Unless explicitly indicated, the base of all logarithms is 2.

disjoint clusters of maximum radius

$$R_{\mathrm{ALG}} = O\left(\sum_{i=1}^{\ell} R(i, \tau)\right)$$

where $\ell = \lceil \log(n/(8\tau \log n)) \rceil$ and,

$$R(i, \tau) = \max\{r(G, V', \tau) : V' \subset V \wedge |V - V'| = n/2^{i-1}\}.$$

for $1 \le i \le \ell$.

PROOF. The bound on the number of clusters follows by observing that the number of clusters added in each iteration is a binomial random variable with expectation $4\tau \log n$, and that at most $\ell = O(\log n)$ iterations are executed overall. As for the upper bound on R_{ALG}, it is sufficient to show that in the ith iteration, with $i \ge 1$, the radius of each cluster (new or old) grows by $O(R(i, \tau))$, with high probability. Let V_i be the set of nodes that at the beginning of Iteration i are already covered by the existing clusters. By construction, we have that $|V_1| = 0$ and, for $i > 1$, $|V_i| \ge \sum_{j=1}^{i-1} n/2^j$. Hence, $|V - V_i| \le n/2^{i-1}$. Let $R_i = r(G, V_i, \tau)$. It is easy to verify that

$$
\begin{aligned}
R_i &\le \max_{V' \subset V, |V-V'| = |V-V_i|} r(G, V', \tau) \\
&\le \max_{V' \subset V, |V-V'| = n/2^{i-1}} r(G, V', \tau) \\
&= R(i, \tau).
\end{aligned}
$$

By definition of $r(G, V_i, \tau)$ we know that there must exist τ nodes, say $u_1, u_2, \dots, u_\tau \in V - V_i$, such that each node of $V - V_i$ is at distance at most R_i from either V_i or one of these nodes. Let us consider the partition

$$V - V_i = B_0 \cup B_1 \cup \cdots \cup B_\tau$$

where B_0 is the set of nodes of $V - V_i$ which are closer to V_i than to any of the u_j's, while B_j is the set of nodes of $V - V_i$ which are closer to u_j than to V_i or to any other $u_{j'}$. Let

$$J = \{j \ge 1 : |B_j| \le |V - V_i|/(2\tau)\}$$

and note that

$$\sum_{j \in J} |B_j| \le \tau(|V - V_i|/(2\tau)) \le |V - V_i|/2$$

Therefore, we have that $\sum_{j \notin J} |B_j| \ge |V - V_i|/2$. Since $|V - V_i| \ge 8\tau \log n$, it is easy to see that for any $j \ge 1$ and $j \notin J$, in the ith iteration a new center will be chosen from B_j with probability at least $1 - 1/n^2$. Hence, by the union bound, we conclude that a new center will fall in every B_j with $j \ge 1$ and $j \notin J$, with probability at least $1 - \tau/n^2$. When this event occurs, $R_i \le R(i, \tau)$ cluster growing steps will be sufficient to reach half of the nodes of $V - V_i$ (namely, the nodes belonging to $B_0 \cup (\cup_{j \notin J} B_j)$). The theorem follows by applying the union bound over the $\ell \le \log n$ iterations. $\square$

An important issue, which is crucial to assess the efficiency of the diameter approximation algorithm discussed in the next section, is to establish how much smaller is the maximum radius R_{ALG} of the clusters returned by CLUSTER with respect to the graph diameter Δ, which is an obvious upper bound to R_{ALG}. Our analysis will express the relation between R_{ALG} and Δ as a function of the *doubling dimension* of the graph, a concept that a number of recent works have shown to be useful in relating algorithms' performance to graph properties [2].

DEFINITION 2. *Consider an undirected graph $G = (V, E)$. The ball of radius R centered at node v is the set of nodes at distance at most R from v. Also, the doubling dimension of G is the smallest integer $b > 0$ such that for any $R > 0$, any ball of radius $2R$ can be covered by at most 2^b balls of radius R.*

The following lemma provides an upper bound on R_{ALG} in terms of the doubling dimension and of the diameter of the graph G.

LEMMA 1. *Let G be a connected n-node graph with doubling dimension b and diameter Δ. For $\tau \in O(n/\log^2 n)$, with high probability, CLUSTER(τ) computes a partition of V into $O(\tau \cdot \log^2 n)$ disjoint clusters of maximum radius*

$$R_{\mathrm{ALG}} = O\left(\left\lceil \frac{\Delta}{\tau^{1/b}} \right\rceil \log n\right).$$

PROOF. Let $R_{\mathrm{OPT}}(\tau)$ be the smallest maximum radius achievable by any decomposition into τ clusters. It is easy to see that each $R(i, \tau)$ is a lower bound to $R_{\mathrm{OPT}}(\tau)$, whence $R_{\mathrm{ALG}} = O\left(\sum_{i=1}^{\ell} R(i, \tau)\right) = O(R_{\mathrm{OPT}}(\tau) \log n)$. By iterating the definition of doubling dimension starting from a single ball of radius Δ containing the whole graph, one can easily argue that G can be decomposed into (at most) τ disjoint clusters of radius $R = O\left(\lceil \Delta/\tau^{1/b} \rceil\right)$. The bound on R_{ALG} follows since $R = \Omega(R_{\mathrm{OPT}}(\tau))$. $\square$

Observe that for graphs with diameter $\Delta = \omega(\log n)$ and low (e.g., constant) doubling dimension, R_{ALG} becomes $o(\Delta)$ when τ is large enough. Indeed, some experimental work [17] reported that, in practice, big data networks of interest have low doubling dimension. Also, for applications such as the diameter estimation discussed in the next section, it is conceivable that parameter τ be made as large as n^ϵ, for some constant $\epsilon > 0$. In fact, the gap between the graph diameter and R_{ALG} can be even more substantial for irregular graphs where highly-connected regions and sparsely-connected ones coexist. For example, let G consist of a constant-degree expander of $n - \sqrt{n}$ nodes attached to a path of $\sqrt{n}$ nodes, and set $\tau = \sqrt{n}$. It is easy to see that $R(i, \tau) = O(\mathrm{poly}(\log n))$, for $i \ge 1$. Hence, CLUSTER(τ) returns $\sqrt{n} \log^2 n$ clusters of maximum radius $R_{\mathrm{ALG}} = O(\mathrm{poly}(\log n))$, which is exponentially smaller than the $\Omega(\sqrt{n})$ graph diameter.

3.1 Approximation to k-center

Algorithm CLUSTER can be employed to compute an approximate solution to the k-center problem, defined as follows. Given an undirected connected graph $G = (V, E)$ with unit edge weights, a set $M \subseteq V$ of k centers is sought which minimizes the maximum distance $R_{\mathrm{OPT}}(k)$ in G of any node $v \in V$ from M. As mentioned in Section 2 this problem is NP-hard. The theorem below states our approximation result.

THEOREM 2. *For $k = \Omega(\log^2 n)$, algorithm CLUSTER can be employed to yield a $O(\log^3 n)$-approximation to the k-center problem with unit edge weights, with high probability.*

PROOF. Fix $\tau = \Theta(k/\log^2 n)$ so that our algorithm returns at most k clusters with high probability, and let M be the set of centers of the returned clusters. Without loss of generality, we assume that M contains exactly k nodes (in case $|M| < k$, we can add $k - |M|$ arbitrary nodes to M, which will not increase the value of objective function). Let R_{ALG} be the maximum radius of the clusters returned by our algorithm. As proved in Lemma 1, we have that, with high probability $R_{\text{ALG}} = O(R_{\text{OPT}}(\tau) \log n)$. We conclude the proof by arguing that $R_{\text{OPT}}(\tau) = O(R_{\text{OPT}}(k) \log^2 n)$. Consider the optimal solution to the k-center problem on the graph, and the associated clustering of radius $R_{\text{OPT}}(k)$. Let T be a spanning tree of the quotient graph associated with this clustering. It is easy to see that T can be decomposed into τ subtrees of height $O(\log^2 n)$ each. Merge the clusters associated with the nodes of each such subtree into one cluster and pick any node as center of the merged cluster. It is easy to see that every node in the graph is at distance $D = O(R_{\text{OPT}}(k) \log^2 n)$ from one of the picked nodes. Since $D \geq R_{\text{OPT}}(\tau)$, we conclude that $R_{\text{OPT}}(\tau) = O(R_{\text{OPT}}(k) \log^2 n)$, and the theorem follows. $\square$

3.2 Extension to disconnected graphs

Let G be an n-node graph with $h > 1$ connected components. It is easy to see that for any $\tau \geq h$, algorithm CLUSTER(τ) works correctly with the same guarantees stated in Theorem 1. Also, observe that for $k \geq h$, the k-center problem still admits a solution with noninfinite radius. Given $k \geq h$, we can still get a $O(\log^3 n)$-approximation to k-center on G as follows. If $k = \Omega(h \log^2 n)$ we simply run CLUSTER(τ) with $\tau = \Theta(k/\log^2 n)$ as before. If instead $h \leq k = o(h \log^2 n)$ we run CLUSTER(h) and then reduce the number of clusters $W = O(h \log^2 n)$ returned by the algorithm to k by using the merging technique described in the proof of Theorem 2. It is easy to show that the approximation ratio is still $O(\log^3 n)$.

4. DIAMETER ESTIMATION

Let G be an n-node connected graph. As in [21], we approximate the diameter of G through the diameter of the quotient graph associated with a suitable clustering of G. For the distributed implementation discussed in the next section, the clustering will be made sufficiently coarse so that the diameter of the quotient graph can be computed on a single machine. In order to ensure a small approximation ratio, we need a refined clustering algorithm (CLUSTER2), whose pseudocode is given in Algorithm 2, which imposes a lower bound on the number of growing steps applied to each cluster, where such a number is precomputed using the clustering algorithm from Section 3.

Let $\tau > 0$ be an integral parameter. We have:

LEMMA 2. *For any integer* $\tau > 0$, *with high probability algorithm* CLUSTER2(τ) *computes a partition of* V *into* $O(\tau \log^4 n)$ *clusters of radius* $R_{\text{ALG2}} \leq 2R_{\text{ALG}} \log n$, *where* R_{ALG} *is the maximum radius of a cluster returned by* CLUSTER(τ).

PROOF. The bound on R_{ALG2} is immediate. Let W be the number of clusters returned by the execution of CLUSTER(τ) within CLUSTER2(τ). By Theorem 1, we have that $W = O(\tau \log^2 n)$, with high probability. In what follows, we condition on this event. For $\gamma = 4/\log_2 e$, define H as the smallest integer such that $2^H/n \geq (\gamma W \log n)/n$, and let $t = \log n - H$. For $0 \leq i < t$, define the event $E_i =$ "at the end of Iteration $H+i$ of the **for** loop, at most $n/2^i$ nodes

---

Algorithm 2: CLUSTER2(τ)

begin
    Run CLUSTER(τ) and let R_{ALG} be the maximum radius of the returned clusters
    $C \leftarrow \emptyset$ // *(current set of clusters)*
    $V' \leftarrow \emptyset$ // *(nodes covered by current set of clusters)*
    for $i \leftarrow 1$ **to** $\log n$ **do**
        Select each node of $V - V'$ as a new center independently with probability $2^i/n$
        Add to C the set of singleton clusters centered at the selected nodes
        In parallel grow all clusters of C disjointly for $2R_{\text{ALG}}$ steps
        $V' \leftarrow$ nodes covered by the clusters in C
    end
    return C
end

---

are still uncovered". We now prove that the event $\cap_{i=0}^{t-1} E_i$ occurs with high probability. Observe that

$$
\Pr\left(\cap_{i=0}^{t-1} E_i\right) = \Pr(E_0) \prod_{i=1}^{t-1} \Pr(E_i | E_0 \cap \cdots \cap E_{i-1})
$$

$$
= \prod_{i=1}^{t-1} \Pr(E_i | E_0 \cap \cdots \cap E_{i-1})
$$

since E_0 clearly holds with probability one. Consider an arbitrary i, with $0 < i < t$, and assume that $E_0 \cap \cdots \cap E_{i-1}$ holds. We prove that E_i holds with high probability. Let V_i be the set of nodes already covered at the beginning of Iteration $H + i$. Since E_{i-1} holds, we have that $|V - V_i| \leq n/2^{i-1}$. Clearly, if $|V - V_i| \leq n/2^i$ then E_i must hold with probability one. Thus, we consider only the case

$$
\frac{n}{2^i} < |V - V_i| \leq \frac{n}{2^{i-1}}
$$

Note that $n/2^i > 2^H \geq \gamma W \log n$. Let $R_i = r(G, V_i, W)$ and observe that since R_{ALG} is the maximum radius of a partition of G into W clusters, we have that $R_{\text{ALG}} \geq R_i$. By the definition of R_i, there exist W nodes, say $u_1, u_2, \ldots, u_W \in V - V_i$, such that each node of $V - V_i$ is at distance at most R_i from either V_i or one of these nodes. Let us consider the partition

$$
V - V_i = B_0 \cup B_1 \cup \cdots \cup B_W
$$

where B_0 is the set of nodes of $V - V_i$ which are closer to V_i than to any of the u_j's, while B_j is the set of nodes of $V - V_i$ which are closer to u_j than to V_i or to any other $u_{j'}$ (with ties broken arbitrarily). Let

$$
J = \{j \geq 1 : |B_j| \geq |V - V_i|/(2W)\}
$$

It is easy to see that $|B_0| + \sum_{j \in J} |B_j| \geq |V - V_i|/2$. Since we assumed that $|V - V_i| > n/2^i$, we have that for every B_j with $j \in J$,

$$
|B_j| \geq \frac{|V - V_i|}{2W} \geq \frac{n \gamma \log n}{2^{H+i+1}}
$$

As a consequence, since $\gamma = 4/\log_2 e$, a new center will be chosen from B_j in Iteration $H+i$ with probability at least $1 - 1/n^2$. By applying the union bound we conclude that in Iteration $H+i$ a new center will fall in every B_j with $j \in J$, and thus the number of uncovered nodes will at least halve, with probability at least $1 - W/n^2 \geq 1 - 1/n$.

By multiplying the probabilities of the $O(\log n)$ conditioned events, we conclude that event $\cap_{i=0}^{t-1} E_i$ occurs with high probability. Note that in the last iteration (Iteration $H+t$) all uncovered nodes are selected as centers, and, if $\cap_{i=0}^{t} E_i$ occurs, these are $O(W \log n)$. Now, one can easily show that, with high probability, in the first H iterations, $O(W \log^2 n)$ clusters are added and, by conditioning on $\cap_{i=0}^{t-1} E_i$, at the beginning of each Iteration $H+i$, $1 \leq i \leq t$, $O(W \log n)$ new clusters are added to C, for a total of $O(W \log^2 n) = O(\tau \log^4 n)$ clusters. $\square$

Suppose we run **CLUSTER2** on a graph G, for some $\tau \in O(n/\log^4 n)$, to obtain a set C of clusters of maximum radius R_{ALG2}. Let G_C denote the quotient graph associated with the clustering, where the nodes correspond to the clusters and there is an edge between two nodes if there is an edge of G whose endpoints belong to the two corresponding clusters. Let Δ_C be the diameter of G_C. We have:

THEOREM 3. *If Δ is the true diameter of G, then $\Delta_C = O((\Delta/R_{\text{ALG}}) \log^2 n)$, with high probability.*

PROOF. Let us fix an arbitrary pair of distinct nodes and an arbitrary shortest path π between them. We show that at most $O(\lceil |\pi|/R_{\text{ALG}}\rceil \log^2 n)$ clusters intersect π (i.e., contain nodes of π), with high probability. Divide π into $\lceil |\pi|/R_{\text{ALG}}\rceil$ *segments* of length at most R_{ALG}, and consider one such segment S. Clearly, all clusters containing nodes of S must have their centers at distance at most R_{ALG2} from S (i.e., distance at most R_{ALG2} from the closest node of S). Recall that $R_{\text{ALG2}} \leq 2R_{\text{ALG}} \log n$. For $1 \leq j \leq 2\log n$, let $C(S, j)$ be the set of nodes whose distance from S is between $(j-1)R_{\text{ALG}}$ and jR_{ALG}, and observe that any cluster intersecting S must be centered at a node belonging to one of the $C(S, j)$'s. We claim that, with high probability, for any j, there are $O(\log n)$ clusters centered at nodes of $C(S, j)$ which may intersect S. Fix an index j, with $1 \leq j \leq 2\log n$, and let i_j be the first iteration of the for loop of algorithm **CLUSTER2** in which some center is selected from $C(S, j)$. It is easy to see that, due to the smooth growth of the center selection probabilities, the number of centers selected from $C(S, j)$ in Iteration i_j and in Iteration $i_j + 1$ is $O(\log n)$, with high probability. Consider now a center v (if any) selected from $C(S, j)$ in some Iteration $i > i_j + 1$. In order to reach S, the cluster centered at v must grow for at least $(j-1)R_{\text{ALG}}$ steps. However, since in each iteration active clusters grow by $2R_{\text{ALG}}$ steps, by the time the cluster centered at v reaches S, the nodes of S have already been reached and totally covered by clusters whose centers have been selected from $C(S, j)$ in Iterations i_j and $i_j + 1$ or, possibly, by some other clusters centered outside $C(S, j)$. In conclusion, we have that the nodes of segment S will belong to $O(\log^2 n)$ clusters, with high probability. The theorem follows by applying the union bound over all segments of π, and over all pairs of nodes in G. $\square$

Let $\Delta' = 2R_{\text{ALG2}} \cdot (\Delta_C + 1) + \Delta_C$. It is easy to see that $\Delta_C \leq \Delta \leq \Delta'$. Moreover, since $R_{\text{ALG2}} \leq 2R_{\text{ALG}} \log n$ and $R_{\text{ALG2}} = O(\Delta)$, we have from Theorem 3 that $\Delta' = O(\Delta \log^3 n)$. The following corollary is immediate.

COROLLARY 1. *Let G be an n-node connected graph with diameter Δ. Then, the clustering returned by **CLUSTER2** can be used to compute two values Δ_C, Δ' such that $\Delta_C \leq \Delta \leq \Delta' = O(\Delta \log^3 n)$, with high probability.*

In order to get a tighter approximation, as in [21], after the clustering we can compute the diameter Δ'_C of the following weighted instance of the quotient graph $G_C = (V_C, E_C)$. Specifically, we assign to each edge $(u, v) \in E_C$ a weight equal to the length of the shortest path in G that connects the two clusters associated with u and v and comprises only nodes of these two clusters. It is easy to see that $\Delta'' = 2R_{\text{ALG2}} + \Delta'_C$ is an upper bound to the diameter Δ of G, and $\Delta'' \leq \Delta'$.

It is important to remark that while in [21] the approximation factor for the diameter is proportional to the square root of the number of clusters, with our improved clustering strategy the approximation factor becomes independent of this quantity, a fact that will also be confirmed by the experiments. As we will see in the next section, the number of clusters, hence the size of the quotient graph, can be suitably chosen to reduce the complexity of the algorithm, based on the memory resources.

As a final remark, we observe that the proof of Theorem 3 shows that for any two nodes u, v in G their distance $d(u, v)$ can be upper bounded by a value $d'(u, v) = O(d(u, v) \log^3 n + R_{\text{ALG2}})$. As a consequence, by running **CLUSTER2**(τ) with $\tau = O(\sqrt{n}/\log^4 n)$ and computing the $O(n)$-size all-pairs shortest-path matrix of the (weighted) quotient graph G_C we can obtain a linear-space distance oracle for G featuring the aforementioned approximation quality, which is polylogarithmic for farther away nodes (i.e., nodes at distance $\Omega(R_{\text{ALG2}})$).

5. DISTRIBUTED IMPLEMENTATION AND PERFORMANCE ANALYSIS

We now describe and analyze a distributed implementation of the clustering and diameter-approximation algorithms devised in the previous sections, using the MapReduce (MR) model introduced in [24]. The MR model provides a rigorous computational framework based on the popular MapReduce paradigm [11], which is suitable for large-scale data processing on clusters of loosely-coupled commodity servers. Similar models have been recently proposed in [18, 14]. An MR algorithm executes as a sequence of *rounds* where, in a round, a multiset X of key-value pairs is transformed into a new multiset Y of pairs by applying a given reducer function (simply called *reducer* in the rest of the paper) independently to each subset of pairs of X having the same key. The model features two parameters M_G and M_L, where M_G is the maximum amount of global memory available to the computation, and M_L is the maximum amount of local memory available to each reducer. We use $\text{MR}(M_G, M_L)$ to denote a given instance of the model. The complexity of an $\text{MR}(M_G, M_L)$ algorithm is defined as the number of rounds executed in the worst case, and it is expressed as a function of the input size and of M_G and M_L. Considering that for big input instances local and global space are premium resources, the main aim of algorithm design on the model is to provide strategies exhibiting good space-round tradeoffs for large ranges of the parameter values.

The following facts are proved in [14, 24].

FACT 1. *The sorting and (segmented) prefix-sum primitives for inputs of size n can be performed in $O(\log_{M_L} n)$ rounds in $\text{MR}(M_G, M_L)$ with $M_G = \Theta(n)$.*

FACT 2. *Two $\ell \times \ell$-matrices can be multiplied in $O\left(\log_{M_L} n + \ell^3/(M_G\sqrt{M_L})\right)$ rounds in $MR(M_G, M_L)$.*

We can implement the sequence of cluster-growing steps embodied in the main loops of CLUSTER and CLUSTER2 as a progressive shrinking of the original graph, by maintaining clusters coalesced into single nodes and updating the adjacencies accordingly. Each cluster-growing step requires a constant number of sorting and (segmented) prefix operations on the collection of edges. Moreover, the assignment of the original graph nodes to clusters can be easily maintained with constant extra overhead. By using Fact 1, we can easily derive the following result.

LEMMA 3. CLUSTER *(resp., CLUSTER2) can be implemented in the $MR(M_G, M_L)$ model so that, when invoked on a graph G with n nodes and m edges, it requires $O\left(R\log_{M_L} m\right)$ rounds, where R is the total number of cluster-growing steps performed by the algorithm. In particular, if $M_L = \Omega(n^\epsilon)$, for some constant $\epsilon > 0$, the number of rounds becomes $O(R)$.*

The diameter-approximation algorithm can be implemented in the $MR(M_G, M_L)$ model by running CLUSTER2(τ) for a value of τ suitably chosen to allow the diameter of the quotient graph to be computed efficiently. The following theorem shows the space-round tradeoffs attainable when M_L is large enough.

THEOREM 4. *Let G be a connected graph with n nodes, m edges, doubling dimension b and diameter Δ. Also, let $\epsilon' < \epsilon \in (0, 1)$ be two arbitrary constants. On the $MR(M_G, M_L)$ model, with $M_G = \Theta(m)$ and $M_L = \Theta(n^\epsilon)$, an upper bound $\Delta' = O(\Delta \log^3 n)$ to the diameter of G can be computed in*

$$O\left(\left\lceil \frac{\Delta \log^{4/b} n}{(\max\{m^{1/3}n^{\epsilon/6}, n^{\epsilon'}\})^{1/b}} \right\rceil \log^2 n\right)$$

rounds, with high probability.

PROOF. Fix $\tau = \Theta\left(n^{\epsilon'}/\log^4 n\right)$ so that CLUSTER2(τ) returns $O\left(n^{\epsilon'}\right)$ clusters with high probability. (In case the number of returned clusters is larger, we repeat the execution of CLUSTER2.) Let $G_C = (V_C, E_C)$ be quotient graph associated with the returned clustering. If $|E_C| \leq M_L$, we can compute the diameter of G_C in one round using a single reducer. Otherwise, by employing the sparsification technique presented in [4] we transform G_C into a new graph $G'_C = (V_C, E'_C)$ with $|E'_C| \leq M_L$, whose diameter is a factor at most $O(\epsilon'/(\epsilon - \epsilon')) = O(1)$ larger than the diameter of G_C. The sparsification technique requires a constant number of cluster growing steps similar in spirit to those described above, which can be realized through a constant number of prefix and sorting operations. Hence, the transformation can be implemented in $O(1)$ rounds in $MR(M_G, M_L)$. Once G'_C is obtained, its diameter and the resulting approximation Δ' to Δ can be computed in one round with a single reducer. Therefore, by combining the results of Lemmas 1, 2, and 3, we have that CLUSTER(τ) runs in $O\left(\lceil \Delta/\tau^{1/b}\rceil \log n\right)$ rounds, and CLUSTER2(τ) runs $O\left(\lceil \Delta/\tau^{1/b}\rceil \log^2 n\right)$ rounds. Hence, we have that the total number of rounds for computing Δ' is $O\left(\lceil \Delta \log^{4/b} n/n^{\epsilon'/b}\rceil \log^2 n\right)$. Alternatively,

we can set $\tau = O\left(\min\{n, m^{1/3}n^{\epsilon/6}/\log^4 n\}\right)$ so to obtain a quotient graph G_C with $|V_C| = \Theta\left(m^{1/3}n^{\epsilon/6}\right)$ nodes. We can compute the diameter of the quotient graph by repeated squaring of the adjacency matrix. By applying the result of Fact 2 with $\ell = |V_C|$ and observing that $|V_C|^3 = O\left(m \cdot n^{\epsilon/2}\right) = O\left(M_G\sqrt{M_L}\right)$, we conclude that the computation of the quotient graph diameter requires only an extra logarithmic number of rounds. In this fashion, the total number of rounds for computing Δ' becomes $O\left(\lceil \Delta \log^{4/b} n/(m^{1/3}n^{\epsilon/6})^{1/b}\rceil \log^2 n\right)$. The theorem follows by noting that for both the above implementations, the quality of the approximation is ensured by Corollary 1. □

We remark that while the upper bound on the approximation factor is independent of the doubling dimension of the graph, the round complexity is expressed as a function of it. This does not restrict the generality of the algorithm but allows us to show that for graphs with small doubling dimension, typically graphs with low expansion, the number of rounds can be made substantially smaller than the graph diameter and, in fact, this number decreases as more local memory is available for the reducers, still using linear global space. This feature represents the key computational advantage of our algorithm with respect to other linear-space algorithms, that, while yielding tighter approximations, require $\Omega(\Delta)$ rounds.

6. EXPERIMENTAL RESULTS

We tested our algorithms on a cluster of 16 hosts, each equipped with a 12 GB RAM and a 4-core I7 processor, connected by a 10 gigabit Ethernet network. The algorithms have been implemented using Apache Spark [26], a popular engine for distributed large-scale data processing. We performed tests on several large graphs whose main characteristics are reported in Table 1. The first graph is a symmetrization of a subgraph of the Twitter network obtained from the LAW website [20]. The next four graphs are from the Stanford Large Network Datasets Collection [25] and represent, respectively, the Livejournal social network and three road networks. The last graph is a synthetic 1000×1000 mesh, which has been included since its doubling dimension is known, unlike the other graphs, and constant ($b = 2$), hence it is an example of a graph where our algorithms are provably effective.

6.1 Experiments on the Clustering Algorithm

We compared the quality of the clustering returned by algorithm CLUSTER (see Section 3) against that of the clustering returned by the algorithm presented in [22] and reviewed in Section 2, which, for brevity, we call MPX. Recall that CLUSTER uses a parameter τ to control the number of clusters, while MPX uses (an exponential distribution of) parameter β to decide when nodes are possibly activated as cluster centers, hence indirectly controlling the number of clusters. Both algorithms aim at computing a decomposition of the graph into clusters of small radius, so we focused the experiments on comparing the maximum radius of the returned clusterings. However, since the minimum maximum radius attainable by any clustering is a nonincreasing function of the number of clusters, but neither algorithm is able to precisely fix such a number a priori, we structured the experiments as follows.

We aimed at decomposition granularities (i.e., number of clusters) which are roughly three orders of magnitude smaller than the number of nodes for small-diameter graphs, and roughly two orders of magnitude smaller than the number of nodes for large-diameter graphs. We ran MPX and CLUSTER setting their parameters β and τ so to obtain a granularity close enough to the desired one, and compared the maximum cluster radius obtained by the two algorithms. In order to be conservative, we gave MPX a slight advantage setting β so to always yield a comparable but larger number of clusters with respect to CLUSTER.

Table 2 shows the results of the experiments for the benchmark graphs. Each row reports the graph, and, for each algorithm, the number of nodes (n_C) and edges (m_C) of the quotient graph associated with the clustering, and the maximum cluster radius (r). The table provides a clear evidence that our algorithm is more effective in keeping the maximum cluster radius small, especially for graphs of large diameter. This is partly due to the fact that MPX starts growing only a few clusters, and before more cluster centers are activated the radius of the initial clusters is already grown large. On the other hand, MPX is often more effective in reducing the number of edges of the quotient graph, which is in fact the main objective of the MPX decomposition strategy. This is particularly evident for the first two graphs in the table, which represent social networks, hence feature low diameter and high expansion (thus, probably, high doubling dimension). In these cases, the few clusters initially grown by MPX are able to absorb entirely highly expanding components, thus resulting in a more drastic reduction of the edges.

6.2 Experiments on the Diameter-Approximation Algorithm

For the diameter approximation, we implemented a simplified version of the algorithm presented in Section 4, where, for efficiency, we used CLUSTER instead of CLUSTER2, thus avoiding repeating the clustering twice. Also, in order to get a tighter approximation, we computed the diameter of the weighted variant of the quotient graph as discussed at the end of Section 4. We performed three sets of experiments, which are discussed below.

The first set of experiments aimed at testing the quality of the diameter approximation provided by our algorithm. The results of the experiments are reported in Table 3. For each graph of Table 1 we estimated the diameter by running our algorithm with two clusterings of different granularities (dubbed *coarser* and *finer* clustering, respectively) reporting, in each case, the number of nodes (n_C) and edges (m_C) of the quotient graph G_C, the approximation Δ' and the true diameter Δ.[2] Since the quotient graphs turned out to be sufficiently sparse, the use of sparsification techniques mentioned in Section 5 was not needed. We observe that in all cases $\Delta'/\Delta < 2$ and, in fact, the approximation factor appears to decrease for sparse, long-diameter graphs. Also, we observe that, as implied by the theoretical results, the quality of the approximation does not seem to be influenced

by the granularity of the clustering. Therefore, for very large graphs, or distributed platforms where individual machines are provided with small local memory, one can resort to a very coarse clustering in order to fit the whole quotient graph in one machine, and still obtain a good approximation to the diameter, at the expense, however, of an increased number of rounds, which are needed to compute the clustering.

With the second set of experiments, we assessed the time performance of our algorithm against two competitors: HADI [16], which was reviewed in Section 2 and provides a rather tight diameter (under)estimation; and Breadth First Search (BFS), which, as well known, can be employed to obtain an upper bound to the diameter within a factor two. HADI's original code, available from [1], was written for the Hadoop framework. Because of Hadoop's known large overhead, for fairness, we reimplemented HADI in Spark, with a performance gain of at least one order of magnitude. As for BFS, we implemented a simple and efficient version in Spark. Table 4 reports the running times and the diameter estimates obtained with the three algorithms where, for our algorithm, we used the finer clustering granularity adopted in the experiments reported in Table 3. The figures in the table clearly show that HADI, while yielding a very accurate estimate of the diameter, is much slower than our algorithm, by orders of magnitude for large-diameter graphs. This is due to the fact that HADI requires $\Theta(\Delta)$ rounds and in each round the communication volume is linear in the number of edges of the input graph. On the other hand BFS, whose approximation guarantee is similar to ours in practice, outperforms HADI and, as expected, is considerably slower than our algorithm on large-diameter graphs. Indeed, BFS still requires $\Theta(\Delta)$ rounds as HADI, but its aggregate communication volume (rather than the per round communication volume) is linear in the number of edges of the input graph.

As remarked in the discussion following Lemma 1, a desirable feature of our strategy is its capability to adapt to irregularities of the graph topology, which may have a larger impact on the performance of the other strategies. In order to provide experimental evidence of this phenomenon, our third set of experiments reports the running times of our algorithm and BFS on three variants of the two small-diameter graphs (livejournal and twitter) obtained by appending a chain of $c \cdot \Delta$ extra nodes to a randomly chosen node, with $c = 1, 2, 4, 6, 8, 10$, thus increasing the diameter accordingly, without substantially altering the overall structure of the base graph. The plots in Figure 1 clearly show that while the running time of our algorithm is basically unaltered by the modification, that of BFS grows linearly with c, as expected due to the strict dependence of the BFS number of rounds from the diameter. A similar behaviour is to be expected with HADI because of the same reason.

Putting it all together, the experiments support the theoretical analysis since they provide evidence that the main competitive advantages of our algorithm, which are evident in large-diameter graphs, are the linear aggregate communication volume (as in BFS) coupled with its ability to run in a number of rounds which can be substantially smaller than Δ.

7. CONCLUSIONS

We developed a novel parallel decomposition strategy for unweighted, undirected graphs which ensures a tighter control on both the number of clusters and their maximum ra-

---

[2]In fact, in some cases the "true diameter" reported in the table has been computed through approximate yet very accurate algorithms and may exhibit some small discrepancies with the actual value.

dius, with respect to similar previous decompositions. We employed our decomposition to devise parallel polylogarithmic approximation algorithms for the k-center problem and for computing the graph diameter. The algorithms use only linear overall space and, for a relevant class of graphs (i.e., those of low doubling dimension), their parallel depth can be made substantially sublinear in the diameter as long as local memories at the processing nodes are sufficiently large but still asymptotically smaller than the graph size.

While the improvement of the approximation bounds and the parallel depth of our algorithms is a natural direction for further research, the extension of our findings to the realm of weighted graphs is a another challenging and relevant open problem. We are currently exploring this latter issue and have devised a preliminary decomposition strategy that, together with the number clusters and their weighted radius, also controls their hop radius, which governs the parallel depth of the computation.

Acknowledgements

This work was supported, in part, by NSF award IIS-124758, by MIUR of Italy under project AMANDA, and by the University of Padova under project CPDA121378/12. The authors wish to thank Babis Tsourakakis for helpful discussions in the early stages of this work, and the anonymous reviewers for their useful comments.

8. REFERENCES

[1] Project PEGASUS. www.cs.cmu.edu/ pegasus.

[2] I. Abraham, S. Chechik, C. Gavoille, and D. Peleg. Forbidden-set distance labels for graphs of bounded doubling dimension. In *ACM PODC*, pages 192–200, 2010.

[3] D. Ajwani, U. Meyer, and D. Veith. I/O-efficient hierarchical diameter approximation. In *ESA*, pages 72–83, 2012.

[4] S. Baswana and S. Sen. A simple and linear time randomized algorithm for computing sparse spanners in weighted graphs. *Random Structures & Algorithms*, 30(4):532–563, 2007.

[5] G. E. Blelloch, A. Gupta, I. Koutis, G. L. Miller, R. Peng, and K. Tangwongsan. Near linear-work parallel sdd solvers, low-diameter decomposition, and low-stretch subgraphs. In *SPAA*, pages 13–22, 2011.

[6] P. Boldi, M. Rosa, and S. Vigna. HyperANF: approximating the neighbourhood function of very large graphs on a budget. In *WWW*, pages 625–634, 2011.

[7] S. Chechik, D. Larkin, L. Roditty, G. Schoenebeck, R. E. Tarjan, and V. V. Williams. Better approximation algorithms for the graph diameter. In *SODA*, pages 1041–1052, 2014.

[8] E. Cohen. Fast algorithms for constructing t-spanners and paths with stretch t. *SIAM J. Comput.*, 28(1):210–236, 1998.

[9] E. Cohen. Polylog-time and near-linear work approximation scheme for undirected shortest paths. *J. ACM*, 47(1):132–166, 2000.

[10] P. Crescenzi, R. Grossi, M. Habib, L. Lanzi, and A. Marino. On computing the diameter of real-world undirected graphs. *Theor. Comput. Sci.*, 514:84–95, 2013.

[11] J. Dean and S. Ghemawat. Mapreduce: simplified data processing on large clusters. *Communications of the ACM*, 51(1):107–113, 2008.

[12] A. Ene, S. Im, and B. Moseley. Fast clustering using mapreduce. In *KDD*, pages 681–689, 2011.

[13] T. F. Gonzalez. Clustering to minimize the maximum intercluster distance. *Theor. Comput. Sci.*, 38:293–306, 1985.

[14] M. Goodrich, N. Sitchinava, and Q. Zhang. Sorting, searching, and simulation in the MapReduce framework. In *ISAAC*, pages 374–383, 2011.

[15] D. S. Hochbaum and D. B. Shmoys. A best possible parallel approximation algorithm to a graph theoretic problem. *Operational Research*, pages 933–938, 1987.

[16] U. Kang, C. E. Tsourakakis, A. P. Appel, C. Faloutsos, and J. Leskovec. Hadi: Mining radii of large graphs. *TKDD*, 5(2), 2011.

[17] D. R. Karger and M. Ruhl. Finding nearest-neighbors in growth-restricted metrics. In *STOC*, pages 741–750, 2002.

[18] H. Karloff, S. Suri, and S. Vassilvitskii. A model of computation for mapreduce. In *SODA*, pages 938–948, 2010.

[19] P. N. Klein and S. Sairam. A parallel randomized approximation scheme for shortest paths. In *STOC*, pages 750–758, 1992.

[20] Laboratory for Web Algorithmics, University of Milano. http://law.di.unimi.it

[21] U. Meyer. On trade-offs in external-memory diameter-approximation. In *SWAT*, pages 426–436, 2008.

[22] G. L. Miller, R. Peng, and S. C. Xu. Parallel graph decompositions using random shifts. In *SPAA*, pages 196–203, 2013.

[23] C. R. Palmer, P. B. Gibbons, and C. Faloutsos. Anf: a fast and scalable tool for data mining in massive graphs. In *KDD*, pages 81–90, 2002.

[24] A. Pietracaprina, G. Pucci, M. Riondato, F. Silvestri, and E. Upfal. Space-round tradeoffs for mapreduce computations. In *ICS*, pages 235–244, 2012.

[25] Stanford Large Network Dataset Collection http://snap.stanford.edu/data

[26] Spark: Lightning-fast cluster computing. http://spark.apache.org

[27] J. D. Ullman and M. Yannakakis. High-probability parallel transitive-closure algorithms. *SIAM J. Comput.*, 20(1):100–125, 1991.

[28] V. V. Vazirani. *Approximation algorithms*. Springer, 2001.

[29] M. Zaharia, M. Chowdhury, T. Das, A. Dave, J. Ma, M. McCauly, M. J. Franklin, S. Shenker, and I. Stoica. Resilient distributed datasets: A fault-tolerant abstraction for in-memory cluster computing. In *NSDI*, pages 15–28, 2012.

Table 1: Characteristics of the graphs used in our experiments

Dataset	nodes	edges	diameter
twitter	39,774,960	684,451,342	16
livejournal	3,997,962	34,681,189	21
roads-CA	1,965,206	2,766,607	849
roads-PA	1,088,092	1,541,898	786
roads-TX	1,379,917	1,921,660	1,054
mesh1000	1,000,000	1,998,000	1,998

Table 2: Comparison between the clusterings returned by CLUSTER and MPX. n_C is the number of clusters, m_C is the number of edges between clusters, and r is the maximum cluster radius.

Dataset	Algorithm CLUSTER			Algorithm MPX		
	n_C	m_C	r	n_C	m_C	r
twitter	40001	17216285	5	41431	109348	6
livejournal	4020	230326	7	5796	17098	9
roads-CA	15038	40597	31	16429	34021	61
roads-PA	7710	13300	30	8529	18446	58
roads-TX	10653	28582	30	11238	23308	55
mesh1000	7641	18476	34	9112	25885	56

Table 3: Diameter approximation returned by our algorithm on the benchmark graphs. Δ is the diameter of the graph, Δ' is the approximation given by the algorithm.

Dataset	Coarser clustering				Finer clustering			
	n_C	m_C	Δ'	Δ	n_C	m_C	Δ'	Δ
twitter	1835	18865	23	16	5276	895356	27	16
livejournal	1933	24442	29	21	7837	570608	29	21
roads-CA	1835	5888	1504	849	3863	10946	1477	849
roads-PA	1087	3261	1240	786	4286	12314	1245	786
roads-TX	1316	3625	1568	1054	3821	10880	1603	1054
mesh1000 t	880	3224	2128	1998	3588	14198	2014	1998

Table 4: Comparison of our approach (CLUSTER) with HADI and BFS. Numbers in parentheses are the estimated diameter Δ'. Column Δ reports the original diameter.

Dataset	Time (Δ')			Δ
	CLUSTER	BFS	HADI	
twitter	303 (27)	144 (22)	3697 (14)	16
livejournal	113 (29)	123 (26)	388 (26)	21
roads-CA	742 (1477)	5796 (1418)	11008 (838)	849
roads-PA	369 (1245)	5245 (1244)	10090 (770)	786
roads-TX	622 (1603)	5844 (1466)	12572 (998)	1054
mesh1000	373 (2014)	8627 (2224)	17287 (1998)	1998

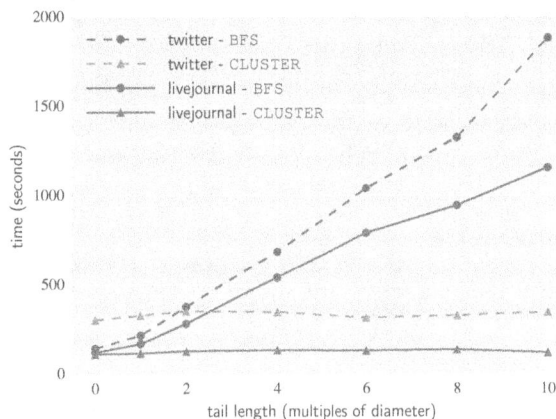

Figure 1: Performance of CLUSTER and BFS on graphs with small variations.

Improved Parallel Algorithms for Spanners and Hopsets

Gary L. Miller
Carnegie Mellon University
glmiller@cs.cmu.edu

Richard Peng
MIT
rpeng@mit.edu

Adrian Vladu
MIT
avladu@mit.edu

Shen Chen Xu
Carnegie Mellon University
shenchex@cs.cmu.edu

ABSTRACT

We use exponential start time clustering to design faster parallel graph algorithms involving distances. Previous algorithms usually rely on graph decomposition routines with strict restrictions on the diameters of the decomposed pieces. We weaken these bounds in favor of stronger local probabilistic guarantees. This allows more direct analyses of the overall process, giving:

- Linear work parallel algorithms that construct spanners with $O(k)$ stretch and size $O(n^{1+1/k})$ in unweighted graphs, and size $O(n^{1+1/k} \log k)$ in weighted graphs.

- Hopsets that lead to the first parallel algorithm for approximating shortest paths in undirected graphs with $O(m \operatorname{poly} \log n)$ work.

1. INTRODUCTION

Graph decompositions are widely used algorithmic routines. They partition the graph to enable divide-and-conquer algorithms. One form that has proven to be particularly useful is the low diameter decomposition: the decomposed pieces should have small diameter, while few edges have endpoints in different pieces. Variants of the low diameter decomposition are used in algorithms for spanners [Coh98], distance oracles [TZ05], and low stretch embeddings [AKPW95, Bar96, CMP+14].

Early applications of the low diameter decomposition include distributed algorithms by Awerbuch [Awe85], and low-stretch spanning trees by Alon et al. [AKPW95]. Further study of low stretch tree embeddings led to a probabilistic decomposition routine by Bartal [Bar96]. On an unweighted graph, this decomposition partitions the graph so that only a β fraction of the edges are cut, and the resulting pieces have diameter $O(\beta^{-1} \log n)$.

The development of parallel algorithms for finding tree embeddings [BGK+14] led to a parallel low diameter clustering routine using exponential start times [MPX13]. This

routine then led to algorithms that generate tree embeddings suitable for a variety of applications [CMP+14]. The clustering algorithm itself has properties suitable for reducing the communication required in parallel connectivity algorithms [SDB14]. This suggests that exponential start time clusterings have a variety of other applications in graph algorithms.

Graph decomposition routines are often invoked hierarchically, leading to many levels, each refining the output of the previous one. The $O(\log n)$ discrepancy between the probability of edges being cut and diameters of pieces in standard low diameter decomposition could then accumulate through the levels. To address this issue, recent algorithms using low diameter decompositions usually require stronger properties at intermediate steps.

In this paper, we give an alternate approach based on the probabilistic guarantees of the exponential start time clustering. We regard the multiple levels as independent events, and analyze the output probabilistically in each locality. This weakens the interactions between the levels, while still allowing us to analyze the final outcome using probabilistic methods. We apply this method to several classical graph problems involving distances.

Spanners are sparse subgraphs that approximate distances in the original graph. We show that one round of exponential start time clustering augmented with a few edges leads to spanners. This algorithm extends to the weighted setting by bucketing the edges by weights, and then clustering them hierarchically. This leads to an overhead of $O(\log k)$ in the size compared to the optimal construction where k is the stretch factor, and $O(\log U)$ in depth, where U is the ratio between the maximum and minimum edge weights.

THEOREM 1.1. *There exists an algorithm that given as input a graph G and parameter $k \geq 1$, finds with high probability a subgraph H in which shortest path distances are preserved up to a factor of $O(k)$ (i.e. H is a $O(k)$-spanner of G). If G is an unweighted graph, then H has expected size $O(n^{1+1/k})$ and is computed in $O(\log n \log^* n)$ depth with $O(m)$ work. If G is a weighted graph with ratio of maximum and minimum edge weights bounded by U, H has expected size $O(n^{1+1/k} \log k)$ and is computed in $O(\log U \log n \log^* n)$ depth with $O(m)$ work.*

Closely related to spanners are hopsets, which do not limit the edge count, but aim to reduce the number of edges in the shortest paths. These objects are crucial for speeding up parallel algorithms for (approximate) shortest paths [KS97,

Coh00]. Using the exponential start time clustering, we construct hopsets which lead to the first parallel algorithm for approximating shortest paths in undirected graphs with $O(m\,\mathrm{poly}\log n)$ work. Here, our key idea is to employ backward analysis and analyze the algorithm with respect to a single (unknown) optimal s-t path. We show that in expectation this path is not cut in too many places by the decomposition scheme, and use this to bound the overall distortion.

THEOREM 1.2. *There exists an algorithm that given as input an undirected, non-negatively weighted graph G, and parameters $\alpha, \epsilon \in (0, 1)$, preprocesses the graph in $O(m\epsilon^{-2-\alpha}\log^{3+\alpha} n)$ work and $O\left(n^{\frac{4+\alpha}{4+2\alpha}}\epsilon^{-1-\alpha}\log^2 n\log^* n\right)$ depth, so that for any vertices s and t one can return a $(1+\epsilon)$-approximation to the $s - t$ shortest in $O(m\epsilon^{-1-\alpha})$ work and $O\left(n^{\frac{4+\alpha}{4+2\alpha}}\epsilon^{-2-\alpha}\right)$ depth.*

The paper is organized as follows: Section 2 reviews some standard notions and compares our results with related works. In Section 3, we describe our spanner construction for both unweighted and weighted graphs. We then describe our hopset algorithm for unweighted graphs in Section 4, and extend it to the weighted setting in Section 5.

Although the probabilistic analysis allows us to decouple some of the levels, mild dependencies between the levels remain. Such dependencies result in terms of $O(\log k)$ and $O(\log^2 n)$ in our results for spanners and hopsets respectively. A promising direction for improvements is to construct the clusterings on different levels in a dependent manner. Picking the randomness across levels from the same source could allow more streamlined analysis of the overall process.

2. BACKGROUND AND RELATED WORKS

We consider a graph $G = (V, E, w)$ with $|V| = n$, $|E| = m$ and edge weights/lengths $w : E \to \mathbb{R}_+$. Throughout the paper we will only deal with undirected graphs with positive edge weights, so we can assume $w(e) \geq 1$ by normalizing and $w(u, v) = w(v, u)$. Furthermore, the graph is unweighted if $w(e) = 1$ for all $e \in E$. If X is a subset of V or E, we will use $G[X]$ to denote the induced subgraph of G on X. If H is a subgraph of G, we will use G/H to denote the quotient graph obtained from G after contracting the connected components of H into points, removing self-loops and merging parallel edges (by keeping the shortest edge).

The parallel performances of our algorithms are analyzed in the standard PRAM model. The longest sequence of dependent operations is known as depth, while the total number of operations performed is termed work. In practice, the abilities of algorithms to parallelize are often limited by the number of processors. For instance, a common assumption in the MapReduce model is that the number of processors is n^δ for some small δ [KSV10]. In such settings, an algorithm will fully parallelize as long as the depth is less than $n^{1-\delta}$. As a result, it is more important to reduce work in order to obtain speed-ups over sequential algorithms.

2.1 Exponential Start Time Clustering

We start by formalizing the key routine in this paper, a graph decomposition routine which we call Exponential Start Time Clustering. It generates a partition of V into subsets $X_1, \cdots, X_k$, and a center c_i for each X_i. It also outputs a spanning tree for each cluster rooted at its center. For convenience, if $v \in X_i$, we use $c(v)$ to denote c_i. We use a routine from [MPX13].

Algorithm 1 Exponential Start Time Clustering

ESTCLUSTER(G, β)

Input: Graph $G = (V, E, w)$, parameter $0 < \beta < 1$.

Output: Decomposition of G.

1: For each vertex u, pick δ_u independently from the exponential distribution $\exp(\beta)$.
2: Create clusters by assigning each $v \in V$ to $u = \arg\min_{u \in V}\{\mathrm{dist}(u, v) - \delta_u\}$, if $v = u$ we let it be the center its cluster.
3: Return the clusters along with a spanning tree on each cluster rooted at its center.

In this paper we extend the algorithm to efficiently run on weighted graphs and also extend the analysis bounding the number of inter-cluster edges to more general subgraphs. The following lemma gives bounds on the run time and cluster diameter for the weighted case.

LEMMA 2.1. *(Theorem 1.2 from [MPX13]) Given a weighted graph $G = (V, E, w)$ where $|V| = n$, $|E| = m$, $w : E \to \mathbb{Z}_+$ with $\min_{e \in E} w(e) = 1$, ESTCLUSTER(G, β) generates a set of disjoint clusters $\cup_i X_i = V$. The diameter of each X_i is certified by a spanning tree on X_i, which has diameter at most $\frac{k}{\beta}\log n$ with probability at least $1 - 1/n^{k-1}$, for any $k \geq 1$. This computation takes $O(\beta^{-1}\log n\log^* n)$ depth with high probability and $O(m)$ work.*

We discuss the efficient implementation of the ESTCLUSTER routine in Appendix A, as well as the effect different models of parallelism have on the depth. An analysis of the resulting decomposition in unweighted graphs is in Section 4 of [MPX13], and it extends immediately to weighted graphs. Our spanner algorithm requires a stronger variant of the edge cutting guarantee which we state below and prove in Appendix A.

Let G be a weighted graph, a ball centered at c of radius r is defined as $B(c, r) = \{v \in V \mid d(v, c) \leq r\}$. The center c may either be a vertex or the midpoint of an edge. We can show that balls with small radius do not intersect with too many clusters.

LEMMA 2.2. *The probability that a ball of radius r intersects at least k clusters from ESTCLUSTER is at most γ^{k-1} where $\gamma = 1 - \exp(-2r\beta)$.*

COROLLARY 2.3. *An edge e with weight $w(e)$ is cut in the clustering produced by ESTCLUSTER with probability at most $1 - \exp(-\beta \cdot w(e)) < \beta \cdot w(e)$.*

2.2 Spanners

A subgraph H of G is said to be a k-spanner, if for every $u, v \in V$, we have $\mathrm{dist}_H(u, v) \leq k \cdot \mathrm{dist}_G(u, v)$, where k is also called the stretch factor. Notice that it is sufficient to prove the stretch bound for endpoints of every edge. It is known that for any integer $k \geq 1$, any undirected graph with n vertices admits $(2k - 1)$-spanners with $O(n^{1+1/k})$ edges, and this is essentially the best tradeoff between sparsity and

weighted graphs				
multiplicative distortion	Size	Work	Parallel depth	Notes
$2k-1$	$\frac{1}{2}n^{1+1/k}$	$O(mn^{1+1/k})$	$O(n^{1+1/k})$	[ADD+93]
$2k-1$	$O(kn^{1+1/k})$	$O(km)$	$O(\log n)$	[BS07]
$2k-1$	$O(kn^{1+1/k})$	$O(km)$	$O(\log n)$	[RTZ05]
$O(k)$	$O(n^{1+1/k}\log k)$	$O(m)$	$O(\log U \log n \log^* n)$	new

unweighted graphs				
multiplicative distortion	Size	Work	Parallel depth	Notes
$2k-1$	$n^{1+1/k}$	$O(m)$	$O(\log^3 n)$	[Pel00]
$2k-1$	$O(kn^{1+1/k})$	$O(km)$	$O(\log n)$	[BKMP10]
$O(2^{\log^* n}\log n)$	$O(n)$	$O(m\log n)$	$O(\log n)$	[Pet08]
$O(k)$	$O(n^{1+1/k})$	$O(m)$	$O(\log n \log^* n)$	new

Figure 1: Known results for spanners, U represents the range of weights.

stretch [PS89, TZ05]. These notions have also been studied under additive error [DHZ00, BKMP05].

A summary of efficient algorithms for constructing spanners can be found in Figure 1. Our algorithms improve upon the $O(k)$ overhead in spanner sizes from previous parallel algorithms while losing constant factors in the stretch. On unweighted graphs, this improvement comes mainly from the ability to invoke exponential start time decomposition in the spanner construction by Peleg and Schaffer algorithm [PS89]. Our extension of this routine to the weighted case relies on the probabilistic aspects of the decomposition. This leads to improvements by factors of $\frac{k}{\log k}$ in spanner size and factors of k in work over the previous best [BS07]. Such routines are also directly applicable to the graph sparsification algorithm by Koutis [Kou14].

2.3 Hopsets

Hopsets were formalized by Cohen [Coh00] as a crucial component for parallel shortest path algorithms. The goal is to add a set of extra edges to the graph so that the h-hop distance in the new graph suffices for a good approximation. Let weight of a path p, denoted as $w(p)$, be the sum of weights of all edges on it, $w(p) = \sum_{e\in p} w(e)$. The distance between two vertices s and t, dist(s,t), is the weight of the shortest (lightest) s-t path. Furthermore, with a set of edges E', the h-hop distance between s and t in E', denoted by dist$_{E'}^h(u,v)$, is defined to be the weight of the minimum weight path with at most h edges between s and t, using only edges from E'. If h is omitted we assume $h = n$, if E' is omitted we assume $E' = E$. A probabilistic version of hopsets can be described as follows:

DEFINITION 2.4. *Given a graph $G = (V, E, w)$, a (ϵ, h, m')-hopset is a set of edges E' such that:*

1. $|E'| \le m'$.

2. *Each edge uv in E' corresponds to a uv-path p in G such that $w(uv) = w(p)$.*

3. *For any vertices u and v, with probability $1/2$ we have:*

$$dist_{E\cup E'}^h(u,v) \le (1+\epsilon)dist_E(u,v).$$

Given such a hopset, a result by Klein and and Subramanian [KS97] allows us to approximate the length of the

path efficiently. They showed that when given an (ϵ, h, m')-hopset, a shortest path can be found in $O(m\epsilon^{-1})$ work and $O(h^\alpha\epsilon^{-1})$ depth. As a result, the main work in parallel shortest path algorithms is to efficiently compute hopsets. A summary of previous algorithms, as well as ours, is below in Figure 2.

For Cohen's algorithm, n^α processors are needed for parallel speedups in both the construction and query stages [1]. In our case, if ϵ is a constant, $O(\log^{3+\alpha} n)$ processors are sufficient for parallel speedups. Furthermore, once a hopset is constructed, even a constant number of processors suffices for speedups.

3. SPANNERS

We first describe our spanner construction. Our spanner construction in unweighted graphs has the same structure as the sequential routine by Peleg and Schaffer [PS89]: after the decomposition step, we add in single edges between adjacent clusters. We formalize this algorithm for completeness here.

Algorithm 2 Spanner construction for unweighted graphs.

UNWEIGHTEDSPANNER(G, δ)

Input: An unweighted graph G and parameter $k \ge 1$.
Output: A $O(k)$-spanner of G.
1: Compute an exponential start time clustering with $\beta = \frac{\log n}{2k}$, let H be the forest produced.
2: From each boundary vertex, add to H one edge connecting to each adjacent cluster.
3: Return H.

The Peleg and Schaffer algorithm [PS89] relied on a bound introduced by Awerbuch [Awe85], which bounds the number of interacting clusters around a single vertex. The same bound can be obtained with exponential start time clusterings using Lemma 2.2.

COROLLARY 3.1. *In an exponential start time decomposition with parameter $\beta = \frac{\log n}{2k}$, for any vertex $v \in V$, the ball $B(v, 1) = \{u \in V \mid d(u, v) \le 1\}$ intersects $O(n^{1/k})$ clusters in expectation.*

---

[1]A more detailed analysis leads to a tighter bound of $\Omega(\exp(\sqrt{\log n}))$

Hop count	Size	Work	Depth	Notes
$O(n^{1/2})$	$O(n)$	$O(mn^{0.5})$	$O(n^{0.5}\log n)$	[KS97, SS99],exact
$O(\text{poly}\log n)$	$O(n^{1+\alpha}\text{poly}\log n)$	$\tilde{O}(mn^\alpha)$	$O(\text{poly}\log n)$	[Coh00]
$(\log n)^{O((\log\log n)^2)}$	$O\left(n^{O(\frac{1}{\log\log n})}\right)$	$\tilde{O}\left(mn^{O(\frac{1}{\log\log n})}\right)$	$(\log n)^{O((\log\log n)^2)}$	[Coh00]
$O(n^{\frac{4+\alpha}{4+2\alpha}})$	$O(n)$	$O(m\log^{3+\alpha}n)$	$O(n^{\frac{4+\alpha}{4+2\alpha}})$	new

Figure 2: **Performances of Hopset Constructions, omitting ϵ dependency.**

Proof By Lemma 2.2, $B(v,1)$ intersects k or more clusters with probability at most $(1-\exp(2\beta))^{k-1}$. Let K be the number of clusters intersecting $B(v,1)$, we then have

$$\mathbf{E}[K] = \sum_{k=1}^\infty \mathbf{Pr}[K \geq k] \leq \sum_{k=1}^\infty (1-\exp(-2\beta))^{k-1}$$
$$= \frac{1}{\exp(-2\beta)}$$
$$= \frac{1}{\exp(-\log n/k)}$$
$$= n^{1/k}.$$

■

LEMMA 3.2. *Given a connected unweighted graph and for any $k \geq 1$, UNWEIGHTEDSPANNER constructs a $O(k)$-spanner with high probability of expected size $O(n^{1+1/k})$. This takes $O(\log n \log^* n)$ depth with high probability and $O(m)$ work.*

Proof The algorithm starts by constructing an exponential start time decomposition with parameter $\beta = \frac{\log n}{2k}$. Let F be the forest obtained from the decomposition, notice that F has at most $n-1$ edges. Then for each boundary vertex v, (i.e. v is incident to an inter-cluster edge), we add one edge between v and each of the adjacent clusters to our spanner. Using Corollary 3.1 and considering the ball $B(v,1)$ for each $v \in V$, we see that $O(n^{1+1/k})$ edges are added this way in expectation.

For an edge e internal to a cluster, its stretch is certified by the spanning tree within the cluster, whose diameter is bounded by $O(k)$ with high probability by Lemma 2.1. If the edge e has its endpoints in two different clusters, our spanner must contain some edge between these two clusters. As with high probability both of these clusters has diameter $O(k)$, the stretch of e is agin bounded by $O(k)$ with high probability. The depth and work bounds also follow from Lemma 2.1. ■

This routine can be extended to the weighted setting by bucketing the edges by powers of 2. Given $G = (V, E, w)$ where $U = (\max_e w(e))/(\min_e w(e))$ is the ratio between maximum and minimum edge weights, we bucket the edges as

$$E_i = \{e \in E \mid w(e) \in [2^{i-1}, 2^i)\}.$$

This allows us to run the unweighted algorithm on essentially disjoint sets of edges, but leads to an overhead of $\log U$ in the total size. We reduce this overhead to $\log\log n$ using an approach introduced in [CMP$^+$14] that's closely related to the AKPW low-stretch spanning tree algorithm [AKPW95]. We build spanners on these buckets in order, but contract the low-diameter components with smaller weights. Lemma 3.2

then allows us to bound the expected rate at which vertices are contracted, and in turn the size of the spanner.

Our contraction scheme is significantly simpler than previous ones because we will be able to ensure that edge weights in different levels differ by factors of poly k, where k is the stretch factor. To this end, we first break up the input graph into $O(\log k)$ graphs where edge lengths are well separated. We define G_j to be the graph with vertex set V and edge set $\cup_{i\geq 0}E_{j+i\cdot c\lg k}$, where c is an appropriate constant[2]. It is clear that the union of $O(\log k)$ such G_js form the whole graph, and they all have $O(\log U)$ buckets of edges, where weights differ by at least $O(k^c)$ between different buckets. Thus if we can find a $O(n^{1+1/k})$-sized spanner for each of G_j, we obtain a $O(n^{1+1/k}\log k)$-sized spanner for G.

For each G_j, we use the fact that the weights are well-separated to form hierarchical contraction schemes. Pseudocode of this algorithm is given in Algorithm 3.

Algorithm 3 Spanner Construction on graphs with well separated edge weights.

WELLSEPARATEDSPANNER(G)

Input: A weighted graph G with well separated edge weight buckets as described above.

Output: A $O(n)$-sized spanner for G.

1: Relabel the edge buckets to be $A_1, A_2, \ldots, A_s$ in increasing order of weights, such that edges in A_i have weights in $[w_i, 2w_i]$ and $w_{i+1}/w_i \geq O(k)$.
2: Initialize $H_0 = \emptyset$ and $S = \emptyset$.
3: **for** $i = 1$ to s **do**
4:     Let $\Gamma_i = G[A_i]/H_{i-1}$ with uniform edge weights.
5:     Perform ESTCLUSTER with $\beta = \frac{\log n}{2k}$ on Γ_i.
6:     Let F be the forest produced in the previous step.
7:     $S = S \cup F$ and $H_i = H_{i-1} \cup F$.
8:     For each boundary vertex, add one edge connecting each of the adjacent clusters to S.
9: **return** S.

THEOREM 3.3. *Given a weighted graph G with n vertices, m edges and for any $k \geq 1$, we can compute with hight probability a $O(k)$-spanner for G of expected size $O(n^{1+1/k}\log k)$, using $O(\log n \log^* n \log U)$ depth and $O(m)$ work.*

Proof As discussed above, we break G into $O(\log k)$ edge-disjoint graphs in which edge weights are well separated. We run WELLSEPARATEDSPANNER on each of these graphs in parallel, each iterations of the loop performs an exponential start time decomposition on disjoint sets of edges, thus the

---
[2]The constant c should be chosen to achieve the desired succes probability from Lemma 2.1. We will hide c inside big-O notations from now on.

overall work is $O(m)$. As there are $O(\log U)$ iterations, the overall depth is $O(\log n \log^* n \log U)$ with high probability.

Now we show that WELLSEPARATEDSPANNER produces a spanner for each of these graphs. In each iteration of the for-loop, the unweighted algorithm is run on $\Gamma_i = G[A_i]/H_{i-1}$. This produces an unweighted spanner for edges in A_i by Lemma 3.2. Since the edge weights differ by at least $O(k)$ between levels, using Lemma 2.1 and induction on the loop index we see that vertices in the quotient graph Γ_i corresponds to pieces of diameter at most w_i in the spanner constructed so far, with high probability. Therefore the stretch bound for edges from A_i in Γ_i gets worse by at most a factor of 2 when translated in G.

We finish by bounding the size of our spanner. Using an argument similar to the proof of Lemma 2.1, we notice that any non-singleton vertex in one of Γ_i has probability at least $1/n^{1/k}$ of being contracted away. Thus in expectation each vertex participates in $O(n^{1/k})$ level of WELLSEPARATEDSPANNER, and in each level it contributes $O(n^{1/k})$ inter-cluster edges and $O(1)$ forest edges in expectation. Thus WELLSEPARATEDSPANNER produces a spanner of size $O(n^{1+2/k})$, where the exponent $1 + 2/k$ can be reduced to $1 + 1/k$ if we back down on the stretch bound by a factor of 2. Since the graph is decomposed into $O(\log k)$ well separated graphs, this gives us the $O(n^{1+1/k} \log k)$ overall bound on the expected size of our spanner. ∎

4. HOPSETS IN UNWEIGHTED GRAPHS

Our hop-set construction is based on recursive application of the exponential start time clustering from Section 2.1. We will designate some of the clusters produced, specifically the larger ones, as special. Since each vertex belongs to at most one cluster, there cannot be too many large clusters. As a result we can afford to compute distances from their centers to all other vertices, and keep a subset of them as hopset edges in the graph. There are two kinds of edges that we keep:

1. *star edges* between the center of a large cluster and all vertices in that cluster.

2. *clique edges* between the center of a large cluster and the centers of all other large clusters.

In other words, in building the hopset we put a star on top of each large cluster and connect their centers into a clique. Then if our optimal s-t path p^* encounters two or more of these large clusters, we can jump from the first to the last by going through their centers. One possible interaction between the decomposition scheme and a path p^* in one level of the algorithm is shown in Figure 3.

This allows us to replace what hopefully is a large part of p^* with only three edges: two star edges and one clique edge. However this replacement may increase the length of the path by the diameter of the large clusters. But as this distortion can only happen once, it is acceptable as long as the diameter of the clusters are less than $\epsilon w(p^*)$. Our algorithm then recursively builds hopsets on the small clusters. The probabilistic guarantees of an edge being cut gives that p^* does not interact with too many such clusters. So once again a reasonable distortion within these clusters can be incurred.

Formally, two parameters are crucial to our algorithm: the parameter β with which the decomposition routine is run,

and the threshold ρ by which a cluster is deemed large. The algorithm then has the following main steps:

1. Compute a exponential start time clustering with parameter β

2. Identify clusters with more than n/ρ vertices as large clusters.

3. Construct star and clique edges from the centers of each large cluster.

4. Recurse on the small clusters.

Our choice of β at each level of the recursion is constrained by the additive distortion that we can incur. Consider a cluster obtained at the ith level of the decomposition ran with β_i. Since the path has length d and each edge is cut with probability β_i, the path is expected to be broken into $\beta_i d$ pieces. Therefore on average, the length of each piece in a cluster is about β_i^{-1}. The diameter of a cluster in the next level on the other hand can be bounded by $k\beta_{i+1}^{-1} \log n$, where the constant $k \geq 1$ can be chosen with desired success probability using Lemma 2.1. Therefore, we need to set β_{i+1} so that:

$$k\beta_{i+1}^{-1} \log n \leq \epsilon \beta_i^{-1}$$
$$\beta_{i+1} \geq \left(k\epsilon^{-1} \log n\right) \beta_i.$$

In other words, the βs need to increase from one level to the next by a factor of $k\epsilon^{-1} \log n$ where $\epsilon < 1$ the distortion parameter. This means that the path p^* is cut with granularity that increases by a factor of $O(\epsilon^{-1} \log n)$ each time. Note that the number of edges cut in all level of the recursion serves as a rough estimate to the number of hops in our shortcut path. Therefore, a different termination condition is required to ensure that the path is not completely shattered by the decomposition scheme. As we only recurse on small clusters, if we require their size to decrease at a much faster rate than the increase in β, our recursion will terminate with most pieces of the path within large clusters. To do this, we introduce a parameter ρ to control this rate of decrease. Given a cluster with n vertices, we designate a cluster X_i to be small if $|X_i| \leq n/\rho$. As our goal is a faster rate of decrease, we will set $\rho = \left(k\epsilon^{-1} \log n\right)^{\delta}$ for some $\delta > 1$.

Pseudocode of our hopset construction algorithm is given in Algorithm 4. Two additional parameters are needed to control the first and last level of the recursion: $\beta = \beta_0$ is the decomposition parameter on the top level, and n_{final} is the base case size at which the recursion stops.

We start with the following simple claim about the β parameters in the recursion.

CLAIM 4.1. *If the top level of the recursion is called with $\beta = \beta_0$ as the input parameter. then the parameter β in i^{th} a level, denoted β_i, is given by $\beta_i = \left(k\epsilon^{-1} \log n\right)^i \beta_0$.*

We now describe how hopsets are used to speed up the parallel BFS. We prove the lemma in the generalized weighted setting as it will become useful in Section 5.

LEMMA 4.2. *Given a weighted graph $G = (V, E, w)$ with $|V| = n$ and $|E| = m$, let E' be the set of edges added by running HOPSET(V, E, β_0). Then for any $u, v \in V$, we have with probability at least $1/2$:*

$$dist_{E \cup E'}^h(u, v) \leq dist_E(u, v) + O(\epsilon \log_\rho n \cdot dist_E(u, v))$$

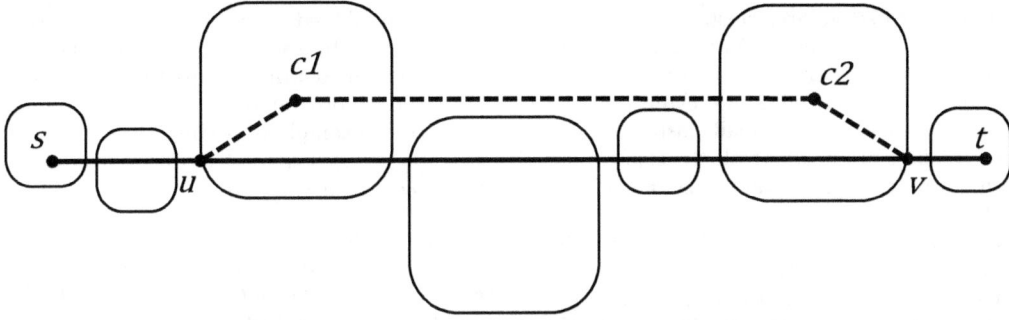

Figure 3: Interaction of an $s - t$ path with the decomposition scheme. Shortcut edges connecting the centers of large clusters allow us to 'jump' from the first vertex of p^* in a large cluster (u), to the last vertex of p^* in a large cluster (v). The edges uc_1, c_2v are star edges, while c_1c_2 is a clique edge.

Algorithm 4 Hop Set Construction on Unweighted Graphs

HopSet(V, E, β).

Input: Undirected, unweighted graph $G = (V, E)$ and decomposition parameter β.

Output: The input graph G augmented with a set of weighted edge E^*.

1: If $|V| \leq n_{final}$, exit.
2: Compute a exponential start time clustering of G with parameter β, $\mathcal{X}$.
3: **if** this is first call **then**
4:     For each cluster X and *in parallel*, recursively call HopSet($X, E(X), (k\epsilon^{-1} \log n)\beta$).
5: **else**
6:     Let $\mathcal{X}_b = \{X \in \mathcal{X} : |X| \geq |V|/\rho\}$ be the set of large clusters.
7:     Let $\mathcal{X}_s = \{X \in \mathcal{X} : |X| < |V|/\rho\}$ be the set of small clusters.
8:     For each large cluster $X \in \mathcal{X}_b$ with center c and $v \in X$, add a star edge (v, c) with weight $dist(v, c)$
9:     For all pairs of large clusters $X_1, X_2 \in \mathcal{X}_b$ with centers c_1, c_2 respectively, add a clique edge (c_1, c_2) with weight $dist(c_1, c_2)$.
10:     For each $X \in \mathcal{X}_s$, recursively call HopSet($X, E(X), (k\epsilon^{-1} \log n)\beta$) *in parallel*.

---

where $h = n_{final}^{1-1/\delta} n^{1/\delta} \beta_0 dist_E(u, v)$.

Proof Let p be any shortest path with endpoints u and v, we show how to transform it into a path p' satisfying the above requirements using edges in E'. In each level of the algorithm, the clustering routine breaks p up into smaller pieces by cutting some edges of p. Consider an input subgraph in the recursion that intersects the path p from vertex x to vertex y. The decomposition partitions this intersection into a number of segments, each contained in a cluster. Starting from x, we can identify the first segment that is contained in a large cluster, whose start point is denoted by x', and similarly we can find the last segment contained in a large cluster with its end point denoted by y'. We drop all edges on p between x' and y' and reconnect them using three edges $(x', c(x'))$, $(c(x'), c(y'))$ and $(c(y'), y')$. We will refer to this procedure as shortcutting. We then recursively build the shortcuts on each segment before u' and after v'. Note that these segments are all contained in small clusters, thus

they are also recursed on during the hopset construction. We stop at the base case of our hopset algorithm.

We first analyze the number of edges in the final path p', obtained by replacing some portion of p with shortcut edges. The path p' consists of edges cut by the decomposition, shortcut edges that we introduced, and segments that are contained in base case pieces. It suffices to bound the number of cut edges, as the segments in p' separated by the cut edges have size at most the size of the base case. Recall from Lemma 2.2 that any edge of weight $w(e)$ has probability $\beta w(e)$ of being cut in the clustering. Thus, the expected number of cut edges can be bounded by

$$\sum_{e \in p} \left(\sum_i \beta_i \right) w(e) = \left(\sum_i \beta_i \right) w(p).$$

Since β_is are geometrically increasing, we can use the approximation $\sum_i \beta_i \approx \beta_l$, where $l = \log_\rho n$ is the depth of recursion. Recalling that $\rho = (k\epsilon^{-1} \log n)^\delta$:

$$\beta_l d = (k\epsilon^{-1} \log n)^{\log_\rho \left(\frac{n}{n_{final}} \right)} \beta_0 d$$

$$= \left(\rho^{1/\delta} \right)^{\log_\rho \left(\frac{n}{n_{final}} \right)} \beta_0 d$$

$$= \left(\frac{n}{n_{final}} \right)^{1/\delta} \beta_0 d.$$

As the recursion terminates when clusters have fewer than n_{final} vertices, each path in such a cluster can have at most n_{final} hops. Multiplying in this factor gives $n^{1/\delta} n_{final}^{1-1/\delta} \beta_0 d$.

Next we analyze the distortion introduced by p' compared to the original path p. Shortcutting in level i introduces an additive distortion of at most $4c\beta_i^{-1} \log n$. The expected number of shortcut made in level i, in other words the expected number of cluster in $(i - 1)^{\text{th}}$ level intersecting the path p, is bounded by $\beta_{i-1}d$. Thus the amount of additive distortion introduced in level i is at most

$$(\beta_{i-1}d) \cdot \frac{4c \log n}{\beta_i} = O(\epsilon d).$$

This gives an overall additive distortion of $O(\epsilon d \log_\rho n)$. ∎

LEMMA 4.3. *If HopSet is run on a graph G with n vertices, it adds at most n star edges and $O\left((n/n_{final}) \log^{2\delta} n \right)$ clique edges to G.*

197

Proof As we do not recurse on large clusters, each vertex is part of a large cluster at most once. As a result, we add at most n edges as star edges in Line 8 of HOPSET.

To bound the number of clique edges, we claim that the worst case is when we always generate small clusters, except in the level above the base cases, where all the clusters are large. Suppose an adversary trying to maximize the number of clique edges decides which clusters are large. Since we do not recurse on large clusters, if on any level above the base case we have a large cluster, the adversary can always replace it with a small cluster, losing at most ρ clique edges doing so (since there are at most ρ large clusters), and gain ρ^2 edges in the next level by making the algorithm recurse on that cluster. Since the base case clusters have size at most n_{final}, there are at most n/n_{final} clusters in the level above, where each cluster adding at most ρ^2 edges. Therefore at most $(n/n_{final})\rho^2 = (n/n_{final})(\log n/\epsilon)^{2\delta}$ edges are added in total. ∎

THEOREM 4.4. *Given constants $\delta > 1$ and $\gamma_1 < \gamma_2 < 1$, we can construct a $(\epsilon \log n, h, O(n))$-hopset on a graph with n vertices and m edges in $O(n^{\gamma_2} \log^2 n \log^* n)$ depth and $O(m \log^{1+\delta} n \epsilon^{-\delta})$ work, where $h = n^{1+1/\delta+\gamma_1(1-1/\delta)-\gamma_2}$.*

Proof We claim that the theorem statement can be obtained by setting $\beta_0 = n^{-\gamma_2}$ and $n_{final} = n^{\gamma_1}$. The correctness of the constructed hopset follows directly from Lemma 4.2, Lemma 4.3, and the fact that any path in an unweighted graph has weight at most n. Specifically, for any vertices u and v with $\text{dist}(u,v) = d$, the expected hop-count is:

$$n^{1/\delta} n_{final}^{1-1/\delta} \beta_0 d \leq n^{1/\delta} n^{\gamma_1(1-1/\delta_2)} n^{-\gamma_2} n$$
$$= n^{1+1/\delta+\gamma_1(1-1/\delta)-\gamma_2}$$

and the expected distortion is $O(\epsilon \log n \cdot d)$. By Markov's inequality, the probability of both of these exceeding four times their expected value is at most $1/2$, and the result can be obtained by adjusting the constants.

So we focus on bounding the depth and work. As the size of each cluster decreases by a factor of ρ from one level to the next, the number of recursion levels is bounded by $\log_\rho(n/n_{final})$. As n/n_{final} is polynomial in n with our choice of parameters, we will treat this term as $\log n$.

The algorithm starts by calling HOPSET$(V, E, n^{-\gamma_2})$. Since the recursive calls are done in parallel, it suffices to bound the time spent in a single call on each level. Lemma 2.1 gives that the clustering takes $O(\beta^{-1} \log n \log^* n)$ depth and linear work. Since the value of β only increases in subsequent levels, all decompositions in each level of the recursion can be computed in $O(n^{\gamma_2} \log n \log^* n)$ depth and $O(m)$ work. This gives a total of $O(n^{\gamma_2} \log^2 n \log^* n)$ depth and $O(m \log n)$ work from Line 2. In addition, Line 8 can be easily incorporated into the decomposition routine at no extra cost.

To compute the all-pair shortest distances between the centers of the large clusters (Line 9), we perform the parallel BFS by [UY91] from each of the centers. By Lemma 2.1, the diameter of the input graphs to recursive calls after the top level is bounded by $O(n^{\gamma_2} \log n)$. Therefore the parallel BFS only need to be ran for $O(n^{\gamma_2} \log n)$ levels. This gives a total depth of $O(n^{\gamma_2} \log n \log^* n)$ and work of $O(\rho m)$ per level. Summing over $O(\log n)$ levels of recursion gives $O(n^{\gamma_2} \log^2 n \log^* n)$ depth and $O(\rho m \log n) = O(\epsilon^{-\delta} m \log^{1+\delta} n)$ work. ∎

The unweighted version of Theorem 1.2 then follows from Theorem 4.4 by setting $\delta = 1 + \alpha$, and solving $h = n^{\gamma_2}$ to balance the depth for hopset construction and the depth for finding approximate distances using hopsets [KS97]. For a concrete example of setting these parameters, $\delta = 1.1$, $\epsilon = \frac{\epsilon'}{\log n}$, $\gamma_2 = 0.96$, and setting γ_1 to some small constant leads to the following bound.

COROLLARY 4.5. *For any constant $\epsilon' > 0$, there exists an algorithm for finding $(1 + \epsilon')$-approximation to unweighted $s - t$ shortest path that runs in $O(n^{0.96} \log^2 n \log^* n)$ depth and $O(m \log^{3.2} n)$ work.*

5. HOPSETS IN WEIGHTED GRAPHS

In this section we show how to construct hopsets in weighted graphs with positive edge weights. We will assume that the ratio between the heaviest and the lightest edge weights is $O(n^3)$. This is due to a reduction similar to the one by Klein and Subramanian [KS97]. In that work, they partition the edges into categories with weights between powers of 2, and show that only considering edges from $O(\log n)$ consecutive categories suffices for approximate shortest path computation. This scheme can be modified by choosing categories with powers of n, and then considering a constant number of consecutive categories suffices for good approximations. This result is summarized in the following lemma, we refer the readers to the full version of this paper [MPVX14] for the full proof.

LEMMA 5.1. *Given a weighted graph $G = (V, E, w)$, we can efficiently construct a collection of graphs with $O(|V|)$ vertices and $O(|E|)$ edges in total, such that the edge weights in any one of these graphs are within $O(n^3)$ of each other. Furthermore, given a shortest path query, we can map it to a query on one of the graphs whose answer is a $(1 - \epsilon)$-approximation for the original query.*

Recall that the parallel BFS of [UY91] conducts the search level by level, and divides the work of each level between the processors. So a simple adaptation of parallel BFS to weighted graphs can lead to depth linear in path lengths, which can potentially be big even though the number of edge hops is small. To alleviate this we borrow a rounding technique from [KS97]. The main idea is to round up small edge weights and pay a small amount of distortion, so that the search advances much faster.

Suppose we are interested in a path p with at most k edges whose weight is between d and cd. We can perturb the weight of each edge additively by $\frac{\zeta d}{k}$ without distorting the final weight by more than ζd. This value serves as the "granularity" of our rounding, which we denote using $\hat{w}$:

$$\hat{w} = \frac{\zeta d}{k}$$

for some $0 < \zeta < 1$ and round the edge weights $w(e)$ to $\tilde{w}(e)$

$$\tilde{w}(e) = \left\lceil \frac{w(e)}{\hat{w}} \right\rceil.$$

Notice that this rounds edge weights to multiples of $\hat{w}$. The properties we need from this rounding scheme is summarized in the following lemma.

LEMMA 5.2 (KLEIN AND SUBRAMANIAN [KS97]). *Given a weighted graph and a number d. Under the above rounding*

198

scheme, any shortest path p with size at most k and weight $d \leq w(p) \leq cd$ for some c in the original graph now has weight $\tilde{w}(p) \leq \lceil ck/\zeta \rceil$ and $\hat{w} \cdot \tilde{w}(p) \leq (1+\zeta)w(p)$.

Thus we only need to run weighted parallel BFS for $O(ck\zeta^{-1})$ levels to recover p, giving a depth of $O(ck\zeta^{-1}\log n)$. Therefore, if we set $c = n^\eta$ for some $\eta < 1$, and since the edge weights are within $O(n^3)$ of each other, we can just try building hopsets using $O(3/\eta)$ estimates, incurring a factor of $O(3/\eta)$ in the work. As one of the values tried satisfies $d \leq w(p) \leq cd$, Lemma 5.2 gives that if ζ is set to $\epsilon/2$, an $(1+\epsilon/2)$-approximation of the shortest path in the rounded graph is in turn an $(1+\epsilon)$-approximation to the shortest path in the original graph. Therefore, from this point on we will focus on finding an $(1+\epsilon)$-approximation of the shortest path in the rounded graph with weights $\tilde{w}(e)$. In particular, we have that all edge weights are positive integers, and the shortest path between s and t has weight $O(n^{1+\eta}/\zeta) = O(n^{1+\eta}/\epsilon)$.

THEOREM 5.3. *For any constants $\delta > 1$ and $\gamma_1 < \gamma_2 < 1$, we can construct a $(\epsilon \log n, h, O(n))$-hopset on a graph with n vertices and m edges in expected $O((n/\epsilon)^{\gamma_2} \log^2 n \log^* n)$ depth and $O(m \log^{1+\delta} n \epsilon^{-\delta})$ work, where $h = n^{1+1/\delta+\eta+\gamma_1(1-1/\delta)-\gamma_2}/\epsilon^{1-\gamma_2}$.*

Proof Since the edge weights are within a polynomial of each other, we can build $O(1/\eta)$ hopsets in parallel for all values of d being powers of n^η. For any pair of vertices s and t, one of the value tried will satisfy $d \leq \text{dist}(s,t) \leq n^\eta d$. Given such an estimate, we first perform the rounding described above, then we run Algorithm 4 with $\beta = (n/\epsilon)^{-\gamma_2}$ and $n_{final} = n^{\gamma_1}$. The exponential start time clustering in Line 2 takes place in the weighted setting, and Line 9 becomes a weighted parallel BFS. The correctness of the hopset constructed follows from Lemma 4.2, Lemma 4.3, and the fact that $\text{dist}(s,t) = O(n^{1+\eta}/\epsilon)$ by the rounding. Specifically, the expected hop count is

$$n^{1/\delta} n_{final}^{1-1/\delta} \beta d \leq n^{1/\delta} n^{\gamma_1(1-1/\delta)} \left(\frac{n}{\epsilon}\right)^{-\gamma_2} \frac{n^{1+\eta}}{\epsilon}$$
$$= n^{1+1/\delta+\eta+\gamma_1(1-1/\delta)-\gamma_2}/\epsilon^{1-\gamma_2}$$

and the expected distortion is $O(\epsilon d)$. By Markov's inequality, the probability of both of these exceeding four times their expected values is at most $1/2$.

The number of recursion levels is still bounded by $\log_\rho n$. Since the βs only increase, according to Lemma 2.1 we spend $O((n/\epsilon)^{\gamma_2} \log n \log^* n)$ depth in each level of the recursion and $O((n/\epsilon)^{\gamma_2} \log^2 n \log^* n)$ overall in Line 2. Since our decomposition is laminar, we spend $O(m)$ work in each level and $O(m \log n)$ overall in Line 2. Again, Line 8 can be incorporated into the decomposition with no extra cost.

Since the diameter of the pieces below the top level is bounded by $\beta^{-1} \log n = (n/\epsilon)^{\gamma_2} \log n$ and the minimum edge weight is one, Line 9 can be implemented by weighted parallel BFS in depth $O((n/\epsilon)^{\gamma_2} \log n \log^* n)$ in one level and $O((n/\epsilon)^{\gamma_2} \log^2 n \log^* n)$ in total. The work done by the weighted parallel BFS is $O(\rho m)$ per level and $O(\rho m \log n) = O(m \log^{1+\delta} n \epsilon^{-\delta})$ in total. ∎

Theorem 1.2 then follows from Theorem 5.3 by adjusting the various parameters. Again, to give a concrete example, we can set $\delta = 1.1$, $\epsilon = \epsilon'/(\log n)$, $\gamma_2 = 0.96$, and set γ_1 and ζ to some small constants to obtain the following corollary

COROLLARY 5.4. *For any constant error factor ϵ', there exists an algorithm for finding $(1+\epsilon')$-approximation to weighted s-t shortest path that runs in $O(n^{0.96} \log^2 n \log^* n)$ depth and $O(m \log^{3.2} n)$ work in a graph with polynomial edge weight ratio.*

Notice that with our current scheme it is not possible to push the depth under $\tilde{O}(\sqrt{n})$ as the hop count becomes the bottle neck. A modification that allows us to obtain a depth of $\tilde{O}(n^\alpha)$ for arbitrary $\alpha > 0$ at the expense of incurring more work can be found in the full version of this paper [MPVX14].

Acknowledgements

Miller and Xu are supported by the National Science Foundation under grant number CCF-1018463 and CCF-1065106. Peng was partially supported by a Microsoft Research Ph.D. Fellowship.

We thank Timothy Chu and Yiannis Koutis for helpful discussions.

6. REFERENCES

[ADD+93] Ingo Althöfer, Gautam Das, David Dobkin, Deborah Joseph, and José Soares. On sparse spanners of weighted graphs. *Discrete Comput. Geom.*, 9(1):81–100, January 1993. 2.2

[AKPW95] N. Alon, R. Karp, D. Peleg, and D. West. A graph-theoretic game and its application to the k-server problem. *SIAM J. Comput.*, 24(1):78–100, 1995. 1, 3

[Awe85] Baruch Awerbuch. Complexity of network synchronization. *J. Assoc. Comput. Mach.*, 32(4):804–823, 1985. 1, 3

[Bar96] Yair Bartal. Probabilistic approximation of metric spaces and its algorithmic applications. In *Foundations of Computer Science, 1996. Proceedings., 37th Annual Symposium on*, pages 184–193. IEEE, 1996. 1

[BGK+14] Guy E. Blelloch, Anupam Gupta, Ioannis Koutis, Gary L. Miller, Richard Peng, and Kanat Tangwongsan. Nearly-linear work parallel SDD solvers, low-diameter decomposition, and low-stretch subgraphs. *Theory Comput. Syst.*, 55(3):521–554, 2014. 1

[BKMP05] Surender Baswana, Telikepalli Kavitha, Kurt Mehlhorn, and Seth Pettie. New constructions of (α, β)-spanners and purely additive spanners. In *Proceedings of the Sixteenth Annual ACM-SIAM Symposium on Discrete Algorithms*, SODA '05, pages 672–681, Philadelphia, PA, USA, 2005. Society for Industrial and Applied Mathematics. 2.2

[BKMP10] Surender Baswana, Telikepalli Kavitha, Kurt Mehlhorn, and Seth Pettie. Additive spanners and (α, β)-spanners. *ACM Transactions on Algorithms (TALG)*, 7(1):5, 2010. 2.2

[BS07] Surender Baswana and Sandeep Sen. A simple and linear time randomized algorithm for computing sparse spanners in weighted graphs. *Random Struct. Algorithms*, 30(4):532–563, July 2007. 2.2, 2.2

[CMP+14] Michael B. Cohen, Gary L. Miller, Jakub W. Pachocki, Richard Peng, and Shen Chen Xu. Stretching stretch. *CoRR*, abs/1401.2454, 2014. 1, 3

[Coh98] Edith Cohen. Fast algorithms for constructing t-spanners and paths with stretch t. *SIAM J. Comput.*, 28(1):210–236, 1998. 1

[Coh00] Edith Cohen. Polylog-time and near-linear work approximation scheme for undirected shortest paths. *J. ACM*, 47(1):132–166, 2000. 1, 2.3, 2.3

[DHZ00] Dorit Dor, Shay Halperin, and Uri Zwick. All-pairs almost shortest paths. *SIAM J. Comput.*, 29(5):1740–1759, March 2000. 2.2

[GMV91] Joseph Gil, Yossi Matias, and Uzi Vishkin. Towards a theory of nearly constant time parallel algorithms. In *FOCS*, pages 698–710. IEEE Computer Society, 1991. A

[Kou14] Ioannis Koutis. Simple parallel and distributed algorithms for spectral graph sparsification. In *Proceedings of the 26th ACM Symposium on Parallelism in Algorithms and Architectures*, SPAA '14, pages 61–66, New York, NY, USA, 2014. ACM. 2.2

[KS97] Philip N Klein and Sairam Subramanian. A randomized parallel algorithm for single-source shortest paths. *Journal of Algorithms*, 25(2):205–220, 1997. 1, 2.3, 4, 5, 5, 5.2, A

[KSV10] Howard Karloff, Siddharth Suri, and Sergei Vassilvitskii. A model of computation for mapreduce. In *Proceedings of the Twenty-first Annual ACM-SIAM Symposium on Discrete Algorithms*, SODA '10, pages 938–948, Philadelphia, PA, USA, 2010. Society for Industrial and Applied Mathematics. 2

[MPVX14] Gary L. Miller, Richard Peng, Adrian Vladu, and Shen Chen Xu. Improved parallel algorithms for spanners and hopsets. *CoRR*, abs/1309.3545, 2014. 5, 5

[MPX13] Gary L. Miller, Richard Peng, and Shen Chen Xu. Parallel graph decompositions using random shifts. In *Proceedings of the 25th ACM symposium on Parallelism in algorithms and architectures*, SPAA '13, pages 196–203, New York, NY, USA, 2013. ACM. 1, 2.1, 2.1

[Pel00] David Peleg. *Distributed Computing: A Locality-sensitive Approach*. Society for Industrial and Applied Mathematics, Philadelphia, PA, USA, 2000. 2.2

[Pet08] Seth Pettie. Distributed algorithms for ultrasparse spanners and linear size skeletons. In *Proceedings of the Twenty-seventh ACM Symposium on Principles of Distributed Computing*, PODC '08, pages 253–262, New York, NY, USA, 2008. ACM. 2.2

[PS89] David Peleg and Alejandro A. Schäffer. Graph spanners. *Journal of Graph Theory*, 13(1):99–116, 1989. 2.2, 2.2, 3, 3

[RTZ05] Liam Roditty, Mikkel Thorup, and Uri Zwick. Deterministic constructions of approximate distance oracles and spanners. In *Proceedings of the 32nd International Conference on Automata, Languages and Programming*, ICALP'05, pages 261–272, Berlin, Heidelberg, 2005. Springer-Verlag. 2.2

[SDB14] Julian Shun, Laxman Dhulipala, and Guy Blelloch. A simple and practical linear-work parallel algorithm for connectivity. In *Proceedings of the 26th ACM Symposium on Parallelism in Algorithms and Architectures*, SPAA '14, pages 143–153, New York, NY, USA, 2014. ACM. 1, A

[SS99] Hanmao Shi and Thomas H. Spencer. Timework tradeoffs of the single-source shortest paths problem. *J. Algorithms*, 30(1):19–32, January 1999. 2.3

[TZ05] Mikkel Thorup and Uri Zwick. Approximate distance oracles. *J. ACM*, 52(1):1–24, Jan 2005. 1, 2.2

[UY91] J. Ullman and M. Yannakakis. High-probability parallel transitive-closure algorithms. *SIAM Journal on Computing*, 20(1):100–125, 1991. 4, 5

APPENDIX

A. DEFERRED PROOFS

We now show the properties of the exponential start time clustering routine from Section 2.1 in more detail.

Proof of Lemma 2.1:

The bound on diameter of the clusters follows from taking a union bound on the maximum value of δ_u at vertices:

$$\Pr\left[\delta_{\max} > \frac{k \log n}{\beta}\right] \leq \sum_{v \in V} \Pr\left[\delta_v > \frac{k \log n}{\beta}\right]$$
$$= n \cdot \exp\left(-\beta \cdot \frac{k \log n}{\beta}\right)$$
$$= \frac{1}{n^{k-1}}.$$

To compute the output of EST CLUSTER efficiently, we can add a super-source and connect it to vertex u via an edge of length δ_u, then we build a shortest path tree in increasing order of distance. The clusters then correspond to the subtrees below the super-source. We can construct this shortest path tree level by level in $O(\frac{\log n}{\beta})$ steps, taking only the integer part of the δ_us into consideration with arbitrary tie breaking in the search. Since we assume the minimum edge weight is 1, this modification in implementation can be shown to have negligible effect on the probabilistic guarantee from Lemma 2.2 (see Theorem 2 from [SDB14]). The overhead of $O(\log^* n)$ per search level comes from the overhead of CRCW PRAM [GMV91]. We remark that this factor of $\log^* n$ depends on the model of parallelism, but is standard in parallel BFS algorithms [KS97]. It is $O(1)$ in the OR CRCW PRAM model, and can be bounded by $O(\log n)$ in most models of parallelism. ∎

Proof of Lemma 2.2:

Let B be a subgraph of G with center c and radius r. From c's point of view, the algorithm can be seen as a race between all the vertices to c: vertex v starts its race at time $\delta_{\max} - \delta_v$, and arrives at c at time $d(v, c) + \delta_{\max} - \delta_v$. In particular, the winner of this race will include c in its cluster. For B to intersect k or more clusters, the first k arrivals at c must be within $2r$ units of time of each other. Since $\delta_{\max}$ is a common term in everyone's arrival time, we can drop it and flip the sign to obtain a quantity $Y_v = \delta_v - d(v, x)$, for each vertex v. Notice that it is just an exponential random variable with some constant offset. The event we are interested in then becomes: the k largest Y_v's are within $2r$ of each other.

We will use the law of total probability for continuous random variables. Let S vary over subsets of V of size $k-1$, $u \in V \setminus S$, and α a fix real number. Let $E_{S,u,\alpha}$ be the event that $Y_u = \alpha$ and $Y_v \geq \alpha$ if $v \in S$ and $Y_v < \alpha$ if $v \notin S$. That is, set S represents the first $k-1$ arrivals, and u is the kth arrival at time α. Clearly, ranging over all possible S, u and α gives a paritition of the probability space. Thus it suffices to show

$$\Pr[Y_v \leq \alpha + 2r \text{ for all } v \in S \mid E_{S,u,\alpha}] \leq (1 - \exp(-2r\beta))^{k-1}$$

for any fixed S, u and α.

By independence of the Y_vs we have that

$$\Pr[Y_v \leq \alpha + 2r \text{ for all } v \in S \mid E_{S,u,\alpha}]$$
$$= \prod_{v \in S} \Pr[Y_v \leq \alpha + 2r \mid \alpha \leq Y_v].$$

For each $v \in S$,

$$\Pr[Y_v \leq \alpha + 2r \mid \alpha \leq Y_v]$$
$$= \Pr[\delta_v \leq \alpha + 2r + d(v, c) \mid \alpha + d(v, c) \leq X_v].$$

There are two cases to consider. If $\alpha + d(v, c) \leq 0$, then by the definition of the exponential distribution

$$\Pr[\delta_v \leq \alpha + 2r + d(v, c) \mid \alpha + d(v, c) \leq X_v]$$
$$\leq \Pr[\delta_v \leq 2r]$$
$$= 1 - \exp(1 - 2r\beta).$$

If $\alpha + d(v, c) > 0$, using the memoryless property of the exponential distribution, we have

$$\Pr[\delta_v \leq \alpha + 2r + d(v, c) \mid \alpha + d(v, c) \leq X_v]$$
$$= \Pr[\delta_v \leq 2r]$$
$$= 1 - \exp(1 - 2r\beta).$$

This finishes the proof. ∎

Access to Data and Number of Iterations: Dual Primal Algorithms for Maximum Matching under Resource Constraints [*]

Kook Jin Ahn[†]
Computer and Information Sciences
University of Pennsylvania
Philadelphia, PA 19104
kookjin@cis.upenn.edu

Sudipto Guha[‡]
Computer and Information Sciences
University of Pennsylvania
Philadelphia, PA 19104
sudipto@cis.upenn.edu

ABSTRACT

In this paper we consider graph algorithms in models of computation where the space usage (random accessible storage, in addition to the read only input) is sublinear in the number of edges m and the access to input data is constrained. These questions arises in many natural settings, and in particular in the analysis of MapReduce or similar algorithms that model constrained parallelism with sublinear central processing. In SPAA 2011, Lattanzi etal. provided a $O(1)$ approximation of maximum matching using $O(p)$ rounds of iterative filtering via mapreduce and $O(n^{1+1/p})$ space of central processing for a graph with n nodes and m edges.

We focus on weighted nonbipartite maximum matching in this paper. For any constant $p > 1$, we provide an iterative sampling based algorithm for computing a $(1 - \epsilon)$-approximation of the weighted nonbipartite maximum matching that uses $O(p/\epsilon)$ rounds of sampling, and $O(n^{1+1/p})$ space. The results extends to b-Matching with small changes. This paper combines adaptive sketching literature and fast primal-dual algorithms based on relaxed Dantzig-Wolfe decision procedures. Each round of sampling is implemented through linear sketches and executed in a single round of MapReduce. The paper also proves that nonstandard linear relaxations of a problem, in particular penalty based formulations, are helpful in mapreduce and similar settings in reducing the adaptive dependence of the iterations.

1. INTRODUCTION

In many practical settings, such as map-reduce and its many variants, the overall framework of an algorithm is constrained. To find a large maximum matching (the actual edges and not just an estimate), the natural algorithm is obvious: we iteratively sample edges, and show that the sampled edges contain a large matching. Often these iterative algorithms converge fast and provide a solution which is much better than the worst case guarantees. One such example is the problem of weighted maximum matching where Lattanzi et al. [24] showed that for a n node m edge graph, we can find a $O(1)$ approximation using $O(p)$ rounds of filtering and $O(n^{1+1/p})$ space (for any constant $p > 1$). However it was also shown that the approximation bound achieved was better than the worst case. This raises the natural question: is a $(1 - \epsilon)$-approximation achievable without storing the entire graph in central processing?

Unfortunately, there are few systematic techniques that allow us to analyze iterative algorithms. One well known example is linear (or convex) programming – and for maximum weighted matching there are LP relaxations which are exact. Therefore any algorithm that provides a $(1 - \epsilon)$ approximation must also (possibly implicitly) provide a bound for the underlying LP. This raises the question: Can we analyze iterative algorithms for maximum matching? Note that augmentation path based techniques either require random access or many (superconstant) iterations. However the exact relaxation of matching has m variables – y_{ij} indicating the presence of the edge (i, j) in the matching. Moreover, for the nonbipartite case the number of constraints is 2^n, corresponding to each odd set. The LP is given by LP1 below. Since we can address b–matching without much difficulty, we present that version. Let $||U||_b = \sum_{i \in U} b_i$ and $\mathcal{O} = \{U| \ ||U||_b \text{ is odd}\}$. For standard matching all $b_i = 1$. Let $B = \sum_i b_i$. For a graph $G = (V, E)$ consider:

$$\beta^* = \max \sum_{(i,j) \in E} w_{ij} y_{ij} \qquad \text{(LP1)}$$

$$\sum_{j:(i,j) \in E} y_{ij} \leq b_i \qquad \forall i \in V$$

$$\sum_{(i,j) \in E : i,j \in U} y_{ij} \leq \lfloor ||U||_b/2 \rfloor \qquad \forall U \in \mathcal{O}$$

$$y_{ij} \geq 0 \qquad \forall (i,j) \in E$$

To achieve a $(1 - \epsilon)$-approximation, the number of constraints in LP1 can be reduced to $n^{O(1/\epsilon)}$ by considering $\mathcal{O}_s = \{U \in \mathcal{O}| \ ||U||_b \leq 4/\epsilon\}$. However $n^{O(1/\epsilon)}$ is still large.

---

[*]Extended Abstract. Full version [2] at Arxiv:1307:4359.

[†]The author is currently affiliated with Google Inc., 1600 Amphitheatre Parkway Mountain View, CA 94043. Email kookjin@google.com

[‡]Research supported in part by NSF Award CCF-1117216.

There has been an enormous amount of research on solving LPs efficiently starting from Khachian's early result [22], for example, the multiplicative weight update framework ([25] and many others), positive linear programming [26], fractional packing and covering ([33] and subsequent results), matrix games [18], and many similar descriptions which exist in different literature across different subfields (see the surveys [6, 16]). None of the existing methods allow constant number of iterations.

Each of these methods maintain multipliers (often referred to as weights in the literature, we use a different term since we consider matching in weighted graphs) on the constraints and seek to optimize a linear combination (using the respective multipliers) of the constraints, thereby reducing multiple constraints to a single objective function. This is referred to as Dantzig-Wolfe type decomposition, since the resulting object is typically a simpler problem. Methods which only maintain dual multipliers typically require $\Omega(\rho\epsilon^{-2}\log M)$ iterations for M constraints, where ρ is the width parameter (a variant of conditioning, defined shortly in the sequel). In fact this is a lower bound for random constraint matrices shown in [23]; moreover the width parameter is a fundamental barrier. The width parameter of LP1 is at least n. Methods such as [10, 30, 31] which maintain both primal and dual multipliers, are dominated by storing all the edges in the graph (same as number of primal variables)! Moreover most of these methods [30, 31] provide additive feasibility guarantees over an unit ball, and conversion to multiplicative error makes the number of iterations depend on the (square root of the) number of variables [10], a detailed discussion is available in the full version[2].

Our Results: For any $\epsilon > 0, p > 1$ we provide a $(1-\epsilon)$ approximation scheme for the weighted nonbipartite matching problem using $O(p/\epsilon)$ rounds of adaptive sketching which can be implemented in MapReduce and $O(n^{1+1/p})$ centralized space. The space requirement increases to $O(n^{1+1/p}\log B)$ if $B = \sum_i b_i$ is super polynomial in n. The running time is $O(m\,\text{poly}(\epsilon^{-1}, \log n)\log B)$. From the perspective of techniques, we *partially* simulate multiple iterations of solving an LP in a single iteration – this can be also viewed as defining an less adaptive method of solving LPs. However such a method naturally works for a subclass of LPs which we discuss next. In particular we focus on the dual of the LP we wish to solve, which leads to *Dual Primal Algorithms*. In the context of matching the overall algorithm we get is very natural, given in Algorithm 1.

Algorithm 1 An algorithm for maximum matching

1: Start with an initial sampling distribution over the edges.
2: **while** we do not have a certificate of $(1-\epsilon)$ approximation **do**
3:     Sample $O(n^{1+1/p})$ edges, subdivided into $t = O(\frac{1}{p\epsilon}\log n)$ independent parts, say $S_1, S_2, \ldots S_t$.
4:     Use S_1 to simulate a step of solving a dual LP of matching. Then use S_1 to refine or adjust S_2 and then use S_2. In general, use $S_1, \ldots, S_q$ to refine S_{q+1} and use S_{q+1}.
5:     We prove that either we succeed in the refinement and use of S_{q+1} or produce an explicit dual (of the dual) certificate – which is a large explicit primal solution, in this case the desired matching.
6: **end while**

The while loop in Algorithm 1 is executed for at most $O(p/\epsilon)$ steps. Given the subdivision of each sample into $O(\frac{1}{p\epsilon}\log n)$ parts – we have an algorithm that uses $O(\epsilon^{-2}\log n)$ iterations, but the adaptivity *at the time of sampling* is only $O(p/\epsilon)$. However the adaptivity *at the time of use* is still $O(\epsilon^{-2}\log n)$. This differentiation is key and is likely to be use in many other settings. One such setting (albeit in retrospect) is the linear sketch based connectivity algorithm in [4, 5], where the linear sketches[1] were computed in parallel in 1 round *but used sequentially* in $O(\log n)$ steps of postprocessing to produce a spanning tree. In this paper we show that $S_1, \ldots, S_t$ are relatives of cut-sparsifiers. Cut sparsifiers, introduced by Benczur and Karger [8], are combinatorial objects that preserve every cut to within $1 \pm \epsilon$ factor. Use of cut sparsifiers is nontrivial since:

$$\sum_{(i,j)\in E: i,j\in U} y_{ij} \leq \lfloor \|U\|_b/2 \rfloor$$

is equivalent to sum and difference of cuts:

$$\frac{1}{2}\sum_{i\in U}\left(\sum_{(i,j)\in E} y_{ij}\right) - \left(\sum_{(i,j)\in E: i\in U, j\notin U} y_{ij}\right) \leq \lfloor \|U\|_b/2 \rfloor$$

and no sparsifier can preserve differences of cuts approximately (since that would answer the sign of the difference exactly). In fact, it it easy to observe that the size of the largest matching in a graph has no connection to large matchings in the sparsifier of that graph.

New Relaxations: The dual of the standard relaxation for matching is LP2, where the variables x_i corresponds to the vertex constraints and z_U correspond to the odd-sets. The dual multipliers (of this dual) corresponds to the edges.

$$\beta^* = \min \sum_i b_i x_i + \sum_{U\in\mathcal{O}} \lfloor \|U\|_b/2 \rfloor z_U$$
$$x_i + x_j + \sum_{U\in\mathcal{O}; i,j\in U} z_U \geq w_{ij} \quad \forall (i,j)\in E \qquad \text{(LP2)}$$
$$x_i, z_U \geq 0 \qquad\qquad \forall i\in V, U\in\mathcal{O}$$

The width of the formulation LP2 is 2^n or $O(n^{1/\epsilon})$ – there are no obvious ways of reducing the width. Consider now a different formulation of maximum matching ($w_{ij} = 1$):

$$\max \sum_{(i,j)\in E} y_{ij} - 3\sum_i \mu_i \qquad\qquad \text{(LP3)}$$
$$\sum_{j:(i,j)\in E} y_{ij} - 2\mu_i \leq b_i \qquad\qquad \forall i\in V$$
$$\sum_{(i,j)\in E: i,j\in U} y_{ij} - \sum_{i\in U} \mu_i \leq \lfloor \|U\|_b/2 \rfloor \qquad \forall U\in\mathcal{O}$$
$$y_{ij}, \mu_i \geq 0 \qquad\qquad \forall i\in V, \forall (i,j)\in E$$

The above formulation allows each vertex to be fractionally matched to $b_i + 2\mu_i$ edges, yet the overall objective is

---

[1] Linear Sketches are inner product of the input with suitable pseudorandom matrices, in this case the input is an oriented vertex-edge adjacency matrix. The sketch is computed first, and subsequently an adversary provides a cut. We then sample an edge across that cut (if one exists, or determine that no such edge exists) with high probability.

charged for this flexibility – this is a classic penalty based formulation. It can be shown (and we do, for the general weighted case, through ideas based on the proof of total dual integrality) the objective function has not increased from LP1 (for $w_{ij} = 1$). Use of LP3 is more obvious if we consider its dual LP4.

$$\min \sum_i b_i x_i + \sum_{U \in \mathcal{O}} \lfloor ||U||_b/2 \rfloor z_U$$

$$x_i + x_j + \sum_{U \in \mathcal{O}; i,j \in U} z_U \geq 1 \quad \forall (i,j) \in E$$

$$2x_i + \sum_{U:i \in U} z_U \leq 3 \qquad \forall i \in V \qquad \text{(LP4)}$$

$$x_i, z_U \geq 0 \qquad\qquad \forall i \in V, U \in \mathcal{O}$$

Note subject to $2x_i + \sum_{U:i \in U} z_U \leq 3$ and non-negativity

$$x_i + x_j + \sum_{U \in \mathcal{O}; i,j \in U} z_U \leq 6$$

or in other words, the width of the dual formulation is now independent of any problem parameters! Therefore penalty based formulations are a natural candidate to study if we wish to add constraints to the dual; and such constraints may have to be added if we want to solve the dual faster.

However the biggest difficulty in implementing Algorithm 1 arises from the step where we show that either we make large progress in the dual or we can construct a large approximate matching. Note that complementary slackness does not hold for approximate solutions, so lack of improvement in the dual does not typically imply anything for a primal solution. However, we prove that *when we cannot make progress on the dual* then the multipliers on the constraints (which are now assignment of values to primal variables, since we started with the dual) are such that a (weighted) cut-sparsifier, that treats the multiplier values on edges as weight/strength (this is not the edge weight in the basic matching problem) values, contains a large matching! This provides us an explicit sparse subgraph containing a large matching as well as fractional matching solution.

We modify the linear sketch based algorithm in [5] that constructs cut-sparsifiers in a single round to over sample the edges with probability by at most $(1 + \epsilon)^t$ which is the maximum amount by which the multiplier on an edge can change. For $t = O(\frac{1}{p\epsilon} \log n)$ that bound is $n^{1/(2p)}$, and since sparsification has $\tilde{O}(n)$ edges, the oversampled object would have size $n^{1+1/p}$ (absorbing the terms polynomial in $1/\epsilon$ and $\log n$). The modified algorithm allows us *deferred evaluation/refinement*, as was needed in Algorithm 1.

Weighted nonbipartite graphs: Finally, we show the new relaxation we need to consider for weighted non-bipartite graphs. Assume that the edge weights are at least 1 and rounded to integral powers of $(1+\epsilon)$. Let $\hat{w}_k = (1+\epsilon)^k$ and $\hat{E}_k$ the set of edges (i,j) with that weight. Then the (dual of the) maximum b-matching is given by LP5. Observe that LP5 is very similar to LP4, where we are considering a "layered" variant – $x_{i(k)}$ corresponds to the cost of vertex i in level k. $x_i = \max_k x_{i(k)}$ is the contribution of vertex i to the objective. However the cost of each set U in level ℓ is $z_{U,\ell}$ and the contribution of a set U is *additive*!

An Edge (i,j) is covered from the cost of the two vertices i, j (specifically their cost in level k) and the sum of the costs of all odd U (containing both i, j) of all layers *below or equal k*.

$$\beta^* = \min \sum_i b_i x_i + \sum_{U \in \mathcal{O}} \left\lfloor \frac{||U||_b}{2} \right\rfloor \sum_\ell z_{U,\ell} \qquad \text{(LP5)}$$

$$x_{i(k)} + x_{j(k)} + \sum_{\ell \leq k} \left(\sum_{U \in \mathcal{O}; i,j \in U} z_{U,\ell} \right) \geq \hat{w}_k$$

$$\forall (i,j) \in E_k$$

$$2x_{i(k)} + \sum_{\ell \leq k} \left(\sum_{U \in \mathcal{O}: i \in U} z_{U,\ell} \right) \leq 3\hat{w}_k \quad \forall i, k$$

$$x_i - x_{i(k)} \geq 0 \qquad\qquad \forall i, k$$

$$x_{i(k)}, x_i, z_{U,\ell} \geq 0 \qquad\qquad \forall i, k, U, \ell$$

It is not obvious why LP5 should express maximum matching – however as a consequence, again, the width of the dual formulation is independent of any problem parameters. The dual of LP5 is used in LP7 in Lemma 5, and the proof of LP5 follows from the proof of Lemma 5. It is interesting that vertices and odd-sets are treated differently in LP5 – LP5 is likely to be of interest independent of resource constraints.

Other Related Work: For weighted non-bipartite matching no previous result was known where the number of iterations is independent of the problem parameters. For unweighted cardinality matching McGregor [28] provided an algorithm with $2^{O(1/\epsilon)}$ iterations. Maximum matching is well studied in the context of **bipartite** graphs, see for instance [1, 7, 13–15, 21, 24, 35]. The best known results in that context are either a $O(1)$ approximation using a single round [13–15, 35], a $(1 - \epsilon)$-approximation in $O(\epsilon^{-2} \log \frac{1}{\epsilon})$ rounds [1], a $O(\epsilon^{-2})$ rounds in a vertex arrival model (assuming order on the list of input edges) [21]. The authors of [19] show that a space bound of $n^{1+\Omega(1/p)}/p^{O(1)}$ is necessary for a p round communication protocol to find the exact maximum even in a bipartite setting.

In the algorithm provided in this paper the probability of sampling each edge (i,j) depends on (along with i and j) the z_U values of different odd sets U of size at most $1/\epsilon$ (and containing both i, j). The number of such odd sets with $z_U > 0$ is at most $O(\epsilon^{-5}(\log B)(\log^2 n) \log^2 \frac{1}{\epsilon})$. This is useful to show that the full $O(n^{1+1/p})$ space is not needed to define the value of the multiplier for an edge, specially in distributed settings. The linear sketches can be viewed as requiring each vertex to sketch its neighborhood $n^{1/p}$ times. This has an obvious connections to distributed computing, and in particular to the Congested Clique model [11]. Our linear sketch based result shows that in that model we can compute a $(1 - \epsilon)$ approximation for the maximum weighted nonbipartite b-matching problem using $O(p/\epsilon)$ rounds and $O(n^{1/p})$ size message per vertex. See [27] for results in other distributed computation models.

Roadmap: We provide the main definition and the main theorem (Theorem 1) about the dual-primal framework in Section 2.1. We then show how these definitions and theorems are applied to matching in Section 2.2. The proofs and other algorithmic details are available in the full version [2].

2. DUAL-PRIMAL MATCHING

2.1 The Framework

DEFINITION 1. *The problem* PRIMAL *is defined to be*

$$\beta^* = \max \mathbf{c}^T \mathbf{y}; \mathbf{y} \in \{\mathcal{A}^T \mathbf{y} \leq \mathcal{b}, \mathbf{y} \geq 0\} \qquad \text{(PRIMAL)}$$

(ρ_0, ρ_i)-**Dual-Primal amenable** *if there exist* $\mathbf{A} \in \mathbb{R}_+^{m \times N}$, $\mathbf{b}, \mathbf{x} \in \mathbb{R}_+^N$ $\mathbf{P}_o \in \mathbb{R}_+^{\tilde{n}_o \times N}, \mathbf{q}_o \in \mathbb{R}_+^{\tilde{n}_o}, \mathbf{P}_i \in \mathbb{R}_+^{\tilde{n}_i \times N}, \mathbf{q}_i \in \mathbb{R}_+^{\tilde{n}_i}$, *convex polytope* $\mathbf{Q}$ *with* $\mathbf{0} \in \mathbf{Q}$ *and an absolute constant* a_1 *such that the following hold simultaneously:*

(d1) (PROOF OF DUAL FEASIBILITY.) *A feasible solution to* $\{\mathbf{b}^T \mathbf{x} \leq \beta, \mathbf{A}\mathbf{x} \geq (1 - 3\epsilon)\mathbf{c}, \mathbf{x} \in \mathbf{Q}, \mathbf{x} \geq 0\}$ *implies* $\beta^* \leq \beta/(1 - a_1 \epsilon)$.

(d2) (OUTER WIDTH.) $\{\mathbf{P}_o \mathbf{x} \leq 2\mathbf{q}_o, \mathbf{x} \in \mathbf{Q}, \mathbf{x} \geq 0\}$ *implies* $\mathbf{A}\mathbf{x} \leq \rho_o \mathbf{c}$.

(d3) (INNER WIDTH.) $\{\mathbf{P}_i \mathbf{x} \leq \mathbf{q}_i, \mathbf{x} \in \mathbf{Q}, \mathbf{x} \geq 0\}$ *implies* $\mathbf{P}_o \mathbf{x} \leq \rho_i \mathbf{q}_o$.

(d4) (A DEFERRED $\mathbf{u}$-SPARSIFIER.) *Given* $\mathbf{u}, \mathbf{v} \in \mathbb{R}_+^m$, *and the promise that all nonzero* $\mathbf{u}_\ell$ *satisfy* $1/\mathcal{L}_0 \leq \mathbf{v}_\ell/\gamma \leq \mathbf{u}_\ell \leq \gamma \mathbf{v}_\ell \leq \mathcal{L}_0$ *for each* $\ell \in [m]$ *given fixed* $\gamma, \mathcal{L}_0 \geq 1$, *we can construct a data structure* $\mathcal{D}$ *that samples a subset of indices in* $[m]$ *of size* $\tilde{n}_s$ *based on the* $\mathbf{v}$ *values and stores the indices. After* $\mathcal{D}$ *has been constructed, the exact values of those stored entries of* $\mathbf{u}$ *are revealed and the data structure constructs a nonnegative vector* $\mathbf{u}^s$ *such that for some property* $\mathbb{G}(\mathbf{u}^s, \mathbf{x})$ *which is convex in* $\mathbf{x}$ *and* $\mathbf{x} = \mathbf{0}$ *satisfies* $\mathbb{G}(\mathbf{u}^s, \mathbf{x})$, *we have:*

$$(\mathbf{u}^s)^T \mathbf{A}\mathbf{x} \geq \left(1 - \frac{\epsilon}{8}\right)(\mathbf{u}^s)^T \mathbf{c}, \quad \mathbb{G}(\mathbf{u}^s, \mathbf{x}) \text{ and } \mathbf{x} \geq 0$$

$$\implies \quad \mathbf{u}^T \mathbf{A}\mathbf{x} \geq \left(1 - \frac{\epsilon}{2}\right)\mathbf{u}^T \mathbf{c} \qquad \text{(SWITCH)}$$

(d5) (INITIAL SOLUTION.) *We can efficiently find a solution to* INITIAL *given below for some* $a_\epsilon \geq 2$:

$$\begin{cases} \mathbf{A}\mathbf{x}_0 \geq (1 - \epsilon_0)\mathbf{c} \\ \frac{\beta^*}{a_\epsilon} \leq \beta_0 = \mathbf{b}^T \mathbf{x}_0 < \frac{\beta^*}{2} \\ \mathbf{P}_o \mathbf{x}_0 \leq 2\mathbf{q}_o \\ \mathbf{P}_i \mathbf{x}_0 \leq \mathbf{q}_i \\ \mathbf{x}_0 \in \mathbf{Q}, \mathbf{x}_0 \geq 0 \end{cases} \qquad \text{(INITIAL)}$$

Observe that we can set $\rho_o = \rho_i = \infty$ but unbounded values of ρ_o, ρ_i will not have any algorithmic consequence. For bounded ρ_o, ρ_i the matrices $\mathbf{A}$ and $\mathcal{A}$ of course have to be related – but that relationship is not necessarily a simple representation (such as column sampling). The main consequence of (ρ_o, ρ_i)-dual primal amenability is as follows:

THEOREM 1. *Suppose for a* (ρ_o, ρ_i)-*dual-primal amenable system* PRIMAL *there exists a* MICROORACLE *which given: an absolute constant* $a_2 > 0$, ϵ *such that* $0 < \epsilon \leq 1$, $\mathbf{u}^s \in \mathbb{R}_+^m, \zeta \in \mathbb{R}_+^{\tilde{n}_o}$, *and* $\varrho > 0$, *provides either:*

(i) *A feasible solution for* PRIMAL *with* $\mathbf{c}^T \mathbf{y} \geq (1 - a_2 \epsilon)\beta$ *such that for all* $\ell \in [m]$, $\mathbf{y}_\ell > 0$ *implies* $\mathbf{u}_\ell^s > 0$, *i.e., a solution only involving the primal variables corresponding to the sampled constraints in the deferred sparsifier.*

(ii) *Or a solution* $\mathbf{x}$ *of* LAGINNER, *where the number of non-zero entries of* $\mathbf{x}$ *is at most* $\tilde{n}_x$.

$$(\mathbf{u}^s)^T \mathbf{A}\mathbf{x} - \varrho \zeta^T \mathbf{P}_o \mathbf{x} \geq \left(1 - \frac{1}{16}\right)(\mathbf{u}^s)^T \mathbf{c} - \varrho \zeta^T \mathbf{q}_o$$

$$\mathbb{G}(\mathbf{u}^s, \mathbf{x}) \qquad \text{(LAGINNER)}$$

$$\tilde{\mathbf{Q}}(\beta) = \{\mathbf{b}^T \mathbf{x} \leq \beta, \mathbf{P}_i \mathbf{x} \leq \mathbf{q}_i, \mathbf{x} \in \mathbf{Q}, \mathbf{x} \geq 0\}$$

Then we can find a $(1 - (1 + a_1 + a_2)\epsilon)$-*approximate solution to* PRIMAL *using* τ *rounds of deferred* $\mathbf{u}$-*sparsifier construction,* $\tau_o = O\left(\rho_o \left(\frac{1}{\epsilon} + \epsilon \log \frac{1}{1-\epsilon_0}\right) \frac{\log(m/\epsilon)}{\log \gamma} + \frac{\log a_\epsilon}{\log \gamma}\right)$. *In each round we construct* $O(\epsilon^{-1} \log \gamma)$ *deferred* $\mathbf{u}$-*sparsifiers. For a fixed deferred sparsifier* MICROORACLE *is invoked for at most* $\tau_i = O(\rho_i (\log \rho_i)(\log \tilde{n}_o) \log \frac{1}{\epsilon})$ *times and we use a simple exponential of a linear combination of the returned solutions (of part (ii)) to define the weights* $\mathbf{u}$.

Each nonzero $\mathbf{u}_\ell \in \left[(2m/\epsilon)^{-O\left(\frac{\rho_o}{\epsilon(1-\epsilon_0)}\right)}, 1\right]$ *and* $\log \mathcal{L}_0 = O\left(\frac{\rho_o}{\epsilon(1-\epsilon_0)} \log(m/\epsilon) + \log \gamma\right)$. *Moreover the algorithm computes (approximately)* $\max \lambda; \mathbf{A}\tilde{\mathbf{x}} \geq \lambda \mathbf{c}$ *for a* $\tilde{\mathbf{x}}$ *which is a weighted average of the* $\mathbf{x}$ *returned by successive applications of part (ii) – the algorithm can stop earlier than the stated number of* τ *rounds if it observes* $\lambda \geq (1 - 3\epsilon)$.

Algorithm 2 An algorithm for Theorem 1. This is an abstract version of Algorithm 1.

1: Start with $\mathbf{x} = \mathbf{x}_0$ and $\beta = \beta_0$, where $\mathbf{x}_0, \beta_0$ refer to the initial solution.
2: Consider the following **family** of decision problems:

$$\{\mathbf{A}\mathbf{x} \geq \mathbf{c}, \mathbf{x} \in \mathcal{P}(\beta)\} \quad \text{where}$$
$$\mathcal{P}(\beta) = \begin{cases} \mathbf{P}_o \mathbf{x} \leq 2\mathbf{q}_o \\ \tilde{\mathbf{Q}}(\beta) = \{\mathbf{b}^T \mathbf{x} \leq \beta; \mathbf{P}_i \mathbf{x} \leq \mathbf{q}_i; \mathbf{x} \in \mathbf{Q}; \mathbf{x} \geq 0\} \end{cases}$$
$$\text{(DUAL)}$$

3: **while** $\lambda < 1 - 3\epsilon$ (where $\lambda = \min_\ell (\mathbf{A}\mathbf{x})_\ell / \mathbf{c}_\ell$) **do**
4:     Define exponential weights $\mathbf{u}$. Compute $\frac{\ln \gamma}{\epsilon}$ deferred $\mathbf{u}$-sparsifiers denoted by $\{\mathcal{D}_q\}$.
5:     Consider the union of the constraints sampled in the previous step and compute a $(1 - a_3 \epsilon)$ approximation to PRIMAL restricted to these constraints. Say that value is β'.
6:     If $\beta' > \beta(1 - a_3 \epsilon)/(1 + \epsilon)$ remember the new solution and set $\beta = \beta'(1 + \epsilon)/(1 - a_3 \epsilon)$.
7:     Update $\mathbf{x}, \mathbf{u}(q)$ etc. as required by the proof of Theorem 1, we are guaranteed to not invoke condition (i) of MICROORACLE due to the Step (5). This provides a new sampling weight function for Step (4).
8: **end while**
9: Output the $\mathbf{y}$ corresponding to largest $\beta' \geq (1 - a_3 \epsilon)\beta/(1 + \epsilon)$. We prove that such a β' exists.

The running time of the algorithm in Theorem 1 is dominated by the time to construct the deferred sparsifiers (which includes the evaluation of $\mathbf{u}$) plus the invocations of MICROORACLE. The space used to maintain the current average $\mathbf{x}$ is $O(\tilde{n}_x \tau_o \tau_i \frac{1}{\epsilon} \log \gamma)$. The space to store a single deferred sparsifier is typically $O(n \gamma^2 \text{poly}(\epsilon^{-1}, \log n, \log \gamma))$ (this is application specific and depends on $\mathbf{u}, \mathcal{L}_0$). Therefore if ρ_o, ρ_i are $poly(\epsilon^{-1})$, $\gamma = n^{1/(2p)}$ and $\tilde{n}_x = O(n \epsilon^{-1} \log n)$, the overall asymptotic space complexity will typically be at most $n^{1+1/p}$ (absorbing the $poly(\epsilon^{-1}, \log n)$ terms), which is $o(m)$ if $m \gg n^{1+1/p}$. For b-matching $\tilde{n}_x = O(n \epsilon^{-1} \log B)$ where $B = \sum_i b_i$.

Algorithmic Interpretations and Integral Solutions:
The algorithm behind Theorem 1 can be expressed as a natural algorithm (relegating the details of how the $\mathbf{u}$ are defined) as described in Algorithm 2. That algorithm worsens the guarantee to $(1 - (1 + a_1 + a_2 + a_3)\epsilon)$-approximation; but also provides an integral solution (assuming such an approximation algorithm against the LP relaxation exists as in Step 5) or we can set $a_3 = 0$ and settle for a fractional solution. For weighted b–Matching, such approximation algorithms which provide integral solutions exist [3, 12]. Finally observe the following corollary of Theorem 1.

COROLLARY 2. *if we can construct (i) $\mathcal{D}$ used for the deferred $\mathbf{u}$–sparsifier using g rounds of sketching, and (ii) the initial solution using k rounds of sketching and n_{init} space, then the algorithm in Theorem 1 can be implemented in $(g\tau + k)$ rounds of adaptive sketching.*

The Intuition behind the Dual-Primal Setup: Suppose that the true dual weights at time t is $\mathbf{u}(t)$ then primal-dual algorithm can be thought of as progressing through the sequence $\mathbf{u}(1), \tilde{\mathbf{x}}(1), \mathbf{u}(2), \tilde{\mathbf{x}}(2), \mathbf{u}(3), \tilde{\mathbf{x}}(3), \ldots$. If we do not prove any further properties, we do not change the fundamental dependence between $\mathbf{u}(1), \mathbf{u}(2), \ldots$ and the overall process with sketching remains as adaptive as before, i.e., $\mathbf{u}(1) \to \mathbf{u}(2) \to \mathbf{u}(3)$ changes to $\mathbf{u}(1) \to \mathbf{u}^s(1) \to \mathbf{u}(2) \to \mathbf{u}^s(2) \to \mathbf{u}(3)$, which are identical from the perspective of the number of adaptive steps required to compute $\mathbf{u}(t)$ or $\mathbf{u}^s(t)$. This is shown in the top part of the Figure 1.

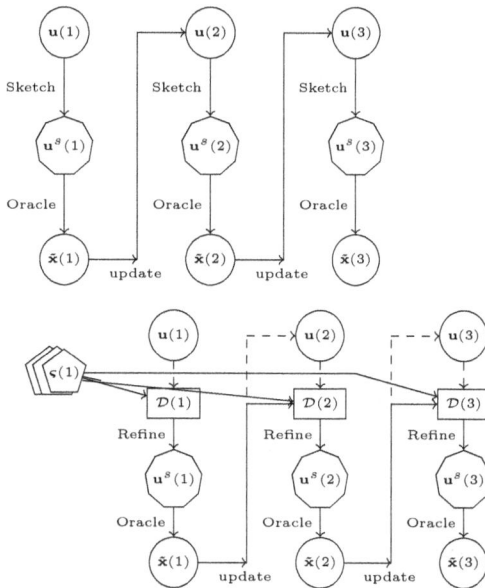

Figure 1: Adaptivity in a dual primal algorithm.

Deferred sparsifiers constructed via sampling allows us to bypass that dependency chain mentioned above. The sparsifier construction is broken into two parts – the first part of the construction can be made non-adaptive and in parallel. Then the second part can be performed sequentially, but over a small subset of edges stored in memory. We construct $\varsigma(1), \ldots, \varsigma(t)$ in parallel which eventually give us the deferred sparsifiers $\mathcal{D}(1), \ldots, \mathcal{D}(t)$. We derive the actual sparsifier $\mathbf{u}^s(1)$ and the update $\tilde{\mathbf{x}}(1)$. Instead of ex-

plicitly computing $\mathbf{u}(2)$, we refine the weights of $\mathcal{D}(2)$ and produce $\mathbf{u}^s(2)$ directly. Therefore we sequentially compute $\mathbf{u}^s(1) \to \mathbf{u}^s(2) \to \cdots \to \mathbf{u}^s(t)$ and are able to make t simultaneous steps without further access to data. This is shown in the bottom of Figure 1. However such a reduction of adaptivity is only feasible for specific linear programming relaxations and we should choose that relaxation with care.

2.2 Weighted Nonbipartite b–Matching.

In this section we show the application of Theorem 1 in the context of b–Matching. Ideally, that demonstration should have shown three separate examples – in the interest of space we provide a single proof. We start with:

DEFINITION 2. *Let $W^* = \max_{(i,j) \in E} w_{ij}$. For $k \geq 0$, let $\hat{w}_k = (1 + \epsilon)^k$. Using $O(p)$ rounds and $n^{1+1/p}$ space we can easily find an edge with the maximum weight W^* (using ℓ_0 sampling, which can be implemented using sketches).*

DEFINITION 3. *Given an edge $(i,j) \in E$ we can define an unique level $k \geq 0$ such that $\frac{\epsilon W^*}{B} \hat{w}_k \leq w_{ij} < \frac{\epsilon W^*}{B} \hat{w}_{k+1}$ and let $\hat{w}_{ij}$ be that $\hat{w}_k$. Let $\hat{E}_k = \left\{ (i,j) \big| (i,j) \in E, \hat{w}_{ij} = \hat{w}_k = (1+\epsilon)^k \right\}$ and let $\hat{E} = \bigcup_k \hat{E}_k$. Let $\hat{w}_L$ correspond to the largest weight class in $\hat{E}$. Observe that $L = O(\frac{1}{\epsilon} \ln B)$ and the number of levels is $L + 1$.*

Recall the system LP1 that defines the maximum weighted non-bipartite b–Matching. We will however consider the alternate rescaled system LP6.

OBSERVATION 1. *$\hat{\beta} \leq \frac{B}{\epsilon W^*} \beta^* \leq \frac{(1+\epsilon)}{(1-\epsilon)} \hat{\beta}$ where $\hat{\beta}$ is defined in LP6. Moreover any b–Matching in $\hat{E}$ corresponds to a b–Matching in E under rescaling of edge weights.*

$$\hat{\beta} = \max \sum_{(i,j) \in \hat{E}} \hat{w}_{ij} y_{ij}$$

$$\sum_{j:(i,j) \in \hat{E}} y_{ij} \leq b_i \qquad \forall i \qquad \text{(LP6)}$$

$$\sum_{(i,j) \in \hat{E}:i,j \in U} y_{ij} \leq \lfloor \|U\|_b / 2 \rfloor \qquad \forall U \in \mathcal{O}$$

$$y_{ij} \geq 0 \qquad \forall (i,j) \in \hat{E}$$

In the remainder of the discussion we find an integral $(1 - O(\epsilon))$-approximate solution of LP6 and use the observation to show that the same solution is an integral $(1 - O(\epsilon))$-approximate solution of LP1. Moreover the transformation of $w_{ij} \to \hat{w}_k$ in can be achieved efficiently. We define $\mathbf{A}, \mathbf{c}, \mathbf{P}_o, \mathbf{P}_i, \mathbf{q}_o, \mathbf{q}_i$ as follows, $\mathbf{Q} = \{x_i - x_{i(\ell)} \geq 0, \forall i, \ell\}$. We define $\{\mathbf{Ax} \geq \mathbf{c}\}$ as

$$x_{i(k)} + x_{j(k)} + \sum_{\ell \leq k} \left(\sum_{U \in \mathcal{O}_s, i,j \in U} z_{U,\ell} \right) \geq \hat{w}_k \qquad \forall (i,j) \in \hat{E}_k$$

and $\{\mathbf{P}_o \mathbf{x} \leq \mathbf{q}_o\}$ as

$$2x_{i(k)} + \sum_{\ell \leq k} \left(\sum_{U \in \mathcal{O}_s: i \in U} z_{U\ell} \right) \leq 3\hat{w}_k \qquad \forall i, k$$

We define $\{\mathbf{P}_i \mathbf{x} \le \mathbf{q}_i\}$ as

$$2x_{i(k)} + \sum_{\ell \le k}\left(\sum_{U \in \mathcal{O}_s : i, \in U} z_{U\ell}\right) \le \left(\frac{24}{\epsilon} + \frac{24}{\epsilon^2}\right)\hat{w}_k \qquad \forall i, k$$

And finally we define $\mathbb{G}(\mathbf{u}^s, \mathbf{x})$ as for all $U \in \mathcal{O}_s, \ell$

$$z_{U,\ell}\left(\sum_{k \ge \ell}\left(\sum_{(i,j) \in \hat{E}_k, i, j \in U} u^s_{ijk} - \sum_{i \in U}\left(\sum_{j \notin U,(i,j) \in \hat{E}_k} u^s_{ijk}\right)\right)\right) \ge 0$$

We show that LP6 is $\left(6, O(\epsilon^{-2})\right)$–dual-primal amenable with $a_1 = 3$, since a solution of $\mathbf{Ax} \ge (1 - 3\epsilon)\mathbf{c}$, setting $x_i = \frac{1}{1-3\epsilon}\max_\ell x_{i(\ell)}, z_U = \frac{1}{1-3\epsilon}\sum_\ell z_{U,\ell}$ will satisfy the dual of LP6. Therefore the conditions (d1)–(d3) in Definition 1 hold with $a_1 = 3$. Note that for $\mathbf{P}_o \mathbf{x} \le \mathbf{q}_o$ we do not need to have constraints for i, k if the vertex i has no edges of level k incident to it. The same holds for $\mathbf{P}_i \mathbf{x} \le \mathbf{q}_i$. Therefore $\tilde{n}_o = \tilde{n}_i = \min\{m, \frac{n}{\epsilon}\log B\}$. We focus on condition (d4) in Definition 1. Let $\mathbf{x} = \{x_{i(k)}, x_i, z_{U,\ell}\}$. Note u_{ijk} is:

$$\frac{1}{\hat{w}_k}\exp\left(-\alpha\left(x_{i(k)} + x_{j(k)} + \sum_{\ell \le k}\left(\sum_{U \in \mathcal{O}_s, i,j \in U} z_{U,\ell}\right)\right)/\hat{w}_k\right)$$

and with $\mathbf{u} = \{u_{ijk}\}$, we have:

$$\mathbf{u}^T \mathbf{Ax} = \sum_{i,k} x_{i(k)}\left(\sum_{j:(i,j) \in \hat{E}_k} u_{ijk}\right)$$
$$+ \sum_{U \in \mathcal{O}_s, \ell} z_{U,\ell}\left(\sum_{k \ge \ell}\left(\sum_{(i,j) \in \hat{E}_k, i, j \in U} u_{ijk}\right)\right)$$

The next lemma follows from sparsifiers. Note that the sparsifiers are computed separately for each class of edges, and union of sparsifiers constructed for each class is a sparsifier itself over the entire set of edges. For each weight class k we construct a "weighted" sparsifier where the "weight" of an edge (i,j) is given by u_{ijk}.

Lemma 3. *If for each $k \ge 0$ we have $H_k = (V, E'_k, \{u^s_{ijk}\})$ as a $(1\pm\epsilon/16)$-Cut-Sparsifier for $G^w_k = (V, \hat{E}_k, \{u_{ijk}\})$, then let their union be $\mathbf{u}^s = \{u^s_{ijk}\}$. Then,*

$$(\mathbf{u}^s)^T \mathbf{Ax} \ge \sum_k\left(\sum_{(i,j) \in \hat{E}_k} \hat{w}_k u^s_{ijk}\right), \; \mathbb{G}(\mathbf{u}^s, \mathbf{x}), \; \mathbf{x} \in \mathbf{Q}$$

$$\Rightarrow \mathbf{u}^T \mathbf{Ax} \ge \left(1 - \frac{\epsilon}{2}\right)\sum_k\left(\sum_{(i,j) \in \hat{E}_k} \hat{w}_k u_{ijk}\right)$$

which is the desired equation SWITCH *in Condition (d4) of Definition 1.*

For condition (d5) observe that setting all $z_{U,\ell} = 0$ corresponds to a bipartite relaxation. Let β^b be the optimum value of the bipartite relaxation, $\hat{\beta} \le \beta^b \le \frac{3}{2}\hat{\beta}$. We use:

Lemma 4. *(Initial Solution) Given $\{M_k\}$, where each M_k is a maximal b-Matching for $\hat{E}_k$, we construct an initial solution $\mathbf{x}_0 = \{x_i\}, \{x_{i(k)}\}$ satisfying $\mathbf{Q}, \mathbf{P}_o, \mathbf{Ax}_0 \ge (1 - \epsilon_0)\mathbf{c}$ and $\frac{\beta^b}{a_\epsilon} \le \beta_0 = \mathbf{b}^T\mathbf{x}_0 = \sum_i b_i x_i \le \frac{\beta^b}{2}$ where $a_\epsilon = 2048\epsilon^{-2}$ and $\epsilon_0 = 1 - \epsilon/256$. $\{M_k\}$ is computed using $n_{init} = O(n^{1+1/(2p)}L)$ space and $O(p)$ rounds of sketching.*

The MICROORACLE is provided by the next two lemmas:

Lemma 5. *(Part (i) of the MICROORACLE) For any $0 < \epsilon \le \frac{1}{16}$, suppose we are given a subgraph $G = (V, E')$ where $|V| = n$ and the weight $\hat{w}_{ij}$ of every edge $(i,j) \in E$ is of the form $\hat{w}_k = (1 + \epsilon)^k$ for $k \ge 0$, and thus $E'_k = \{(i,j) | \hat{w}_{ij} = \hat{w}_k\}$ and $E' = \cup_k E'_k$. If we are also given a feasible solution to the system LP7 then we find an integral solution of LP6 of weight $(1 - 2\epsilon)\beta$ using $O(|E'| \text{poly}(\epsilon^{-1}, \log n))$ time using edges of E'.*

$$\sum_k \hat{w}_k\left(\sum_{(i,j) \in E'_k} y_{ij} - 3\sum_i \mu_{ik}\right) \ge (1-\epsilon)\beta \qquad \text{(LP7)}$$

$$\sum_{j:(i,j) \in \hat{E}'_k}(y_{ij} - 2\mu_{ik}) \le y_{i(k)} \qquad \forall i, k$$

$$\sum_k y_{i(k)} \le b_i \qquad \forall i$$

$$\sum_{k \ge \ell}\left(\sum_{(i,j) \in \hat{E}_k : i, j \in U} y_{ij} - \sum_{i \in U}\mu_{ik}\right) \le \left\lfloor\frac{\|U\|_b}{2}\right\rfloor \qquad \forall U \in \mathcal{O}_s, \forall\ell$$

$$y_{ij}, y_{i(k)}, \mu_{ik} \ge 0 \qquad \forall(i,j) \in \hat{E}, i, k$$

Lemma 6. *(Part (ii) of The MICROORACLE.) Suppose we are given nonnegative $\{u^s_{ijk}\}, \{\zeta_{ik}\}, \beta$ and $\epsilon \in (0, \frac{1}{16})$, $\varrho > 0$, such that u^s_{ijk} corresponds to an edge (i,j) and $k \ge 0$. Suppose further that there exists at most one k such that $u^s_{ijk} \ne 0$. Let $E'_k = \{(i,j) | u^s_{ijk} \ne 0\}$ and $E' = \cup_k E'_k$. Then using time $O(|E'| \text{poly}(\epsilon^{-1}, \log n))$ we either provide (i) a solution to the system LP7 or (ii) a solution to the system LP8 along with $\mathbb{G}(\mathbf{u}^s, \mathbf{x})$ where $\hat{w}_k = (1 + \epsilon)^k$.*

$$\sum_{i,k} x_{i(k)}\left(\sum_{j:(i,j) \in E'_k} u^s_{ijk} - 2\varrho\zeta_{ik}\right) +$$

$$\sum_{U \in \mathcal{O}_s, \ell} z_{U,\ell}\left(\sum_{k \ge \ell}\left(\sum_{(i,j) \in E'_k, i, j \in U} u^s_{ijk} - \varrho\sum_{i \in U}\zeta_{ik}\right)\right)$$

$$\ge \left(1 - \frac{\epsilon}{16}\right)\sum_k \hat{w}_k\left(\sum_{(i,j) \in E'_k} u^s_{ijk} - 3\varrho\sum_i \zeta_{ik}\right)$$

$$\sum_{k \ge \ell}\left(\sum_{(i,j) \in \hat{E}_k, i, j \in U} u^s_{ijk} - \sum_{i \in U}\left(\sum_{j \notin U,(i,j) \in \hat{E}_k} u^s_{ijk}\right)\right) \ge 0$$
$$\forall U \in \mathcal{O}_s, \ell$$

$$\sum_i b_i x_i + \sum_{\ell, U \in \mathcal{O}_s} z_{U,\ell}\lfloor\|U\|_b/2\rfloor \le \beta \qquad \text{(LP8)}$$

$$x_{i(k)} + \sum_{U \in \mathcal{O}_s : i \in U}\sum_{\ell \le k} z_{U,\ell} \le \left(\frac{24}{\epsilon} + \frac{24}{\epsilon^2}\right)\hat{w}_k \qquad \forall i, k$$

$$x_i - x_{i(\ell)} \qquad \forall i, \ell$$

$$x_{i(k)}, x_i, z_{U,k} \ge 0 \qquad \forall i, U, k$$

Furthermore $\{U | z_{U,\ell} > 0\}$ are disjoint for any fixed ℓ which shows $\tilde{n}_x = O(nL)$.

The proof of Lemma 5 is based on showing that if we restrict ourselves to the edges $\{(i,j)|y_{ij} > 0\}$, then given an optimal dual solution of LP6 (where the first constraint expressed as a maximization), we can produce a feasible solution to the dual of LP7 which is less than $(1 + \epsilon)$ times the optimal dual solution of LP6. Thus we have a lower bound to the feasible solution of the dual of LP7, and in turn a lower bound to the optimal dual solution of LP6. But that lower bound implies that there exists a large primal solution restricted to those edges. Lemma 6 either provides a solution of LP7, which using Lemma 5 proves the existence of a large matching (as a factor of β), or Lemma 6 makes progress towards solving the dual (proving that the current bound of β is appropriate). Any offline $(1 - \epsilon)$ approximation to the maximum matching on the union of the edges stored by the t deferred sparsifiers (e.g., [3, 12]) can be used and we adjust β and the multipliers as in Algorithm 2. Summarizing:

THEOREM 7. *For any constant $0 < \epsilon \leq \frac{1}{16}$ and $p > 1$, we can find a $(1 - 14\epsilon)$ approximate integral weighted b–Matching for nonbipartite graphs in $O(m\operatorname{poly}(\epsilon^{-1}, \log n))$ time, $O(p/\epsilon)$ rounds and $O(n^{1+1/p}\log B)$ centralized space.*

2.3 New Relaxations and Oracles: Lemma 6

The micro-oracle is provided by Algorithm 3. Observe that if $\gamma \leq 0$ then the Lemma is trivially satisfied by setting $x_i = x_{i(\ell)} = z_{U,\ell} = 0$ for all i, U, ℓ. The overall idea of the algorithm is simple: *find the violated constraints of LP6* – either the contribution of those constraints are small in comparison to a rescaled value of β, in which case simply zeroing out the associated variables (carefully) will preserve a large solution and satisfy LP6 – or the contribution is large and thus giving small weights to each of them we satisfy LP8. The algorithm 3 uses the following lemma:

LEMMA 8. *In time $O(n\operatorname{poly}(\log n, \frac{1}{\epsilon}))$ time we can find a collection $\mathcal{K}(\ell)$ such that every pair of sets are mutually disjoint and Equations 1 and 2 hold in Step 12.*

Note that the algorithm runs in time $O(nL\operatorname{poly}(\log n, 1/\epsilon))$ for $L + 1$ levels of the discretized weights since we invoke Lemma 8 at most $L + 1$ times. For the **return** step in Step 7 in the algorithm, observe:

$$\sum_{i,k} x_{i(k)}\left(\sum_{j:(i,j)\in\hat{E}_k} u^s_{ijk} - 2\varrho\zeta_{ik}\right)$$

$$= \sum_{i\in\mathcal{V}iol(V)}\left(\sum_{k\leq k_i^*, k\in\mathcal{P}os(i)}\frac{\gamma\hat{w}_k}{\Gamma(V)}\left(\sum_{j:(i,j)\in\hat{E}_k} u^s_{ijk} - 2\varrho\zeta_{ik}\right)\right.$$

$$\left. + \sum_{k>k_i^*, k\in\mathcal{P}os(i)}\frac{\gamma\hat{w}_{k_i^*}}{\Gamma(V)}\left(\sum_{j:(i,j)\in\hat{E}_k} u^s_{ijk} - 2\varrho\zeta_{ik}\right)\right)$$

(Using Definitions of $x_{i(\ell)}, \Delta(i, \ell), \mathcal{V}iol(V)$ in Steps (6),(2) and (4) respectively.)

$$= \frac{\gamma}{\Gamma(V)}\sum_{i\in\mathcal{V}iol(V)}\Delta(i, k_i^*) = \gamma \quad \text{(Definition of } \Gamma(V) \text{ in Step (4))}$$

Algorithm 3 The part (ii) of MICROORACLE for matching

1: Let $\gamma = \sum_k \hat{w}_k\left(\sum_{(i,j)\in\hat{E}_k} u^s_{ijk} - 3\varrho\sum_i \zeta_{ik}\right)$. Note $\varrho > 0, 0 < \epsilon \leq \frac{1}{16}$. Also $\gamma > 0$ below.

2: Define for all i, $\mathcal{P}os(i) = \left\{k \,\middle|\, \sum_{j:(i,j)\in\hat{E}_k} u^s_{ijk} - 2\varrho\zeta_{ik} > 0\right\}$ and for all i, ℓ
$$\Delta(i, \ell) = \sum_{k\in\mathcal{P}os(i), \ell\geq k} \hat{w}_k\left(\sum_{j:(i,j)\in\hat{E}_k} u^s_{ijk} - 2\varrho\zeta_{ik}\right)$$
$$+ \sum_{k\in\mathcal{P}os(i), k>\ell} \hat{w}_\ell\left(\sum_{j:(i,j)\in\hat{E}_k} u^s_{ijk} - 2\varrho\zeta_{ik}\right)$$

3: Let $k_i^* = \operatorname{argmax}_\ell \Delta(i, \ell) > \frac{\gamma b_i \hat{w}_\ell}{\beta}$ and $k_i^* = -1$ if no ℓ exists.

4: $\mathcal{V}iol(V) = \{i|k_i^* \geq 0\}$ and $\Gamma(V) = \sum_{i\in\mathcal{V}iol(V)}\Delta(i, k_i^*)$

5: **if** $\Gamma(V) \geq \epsilon\gamma/24$ **then**

6:     **for** all $i \in \mathcal{V}iol(V)$, (implies $k_i^* \geq 0$) set
$$x_{i(\ell)} = \begin{cases} \gamma\hat{w}_{k_i^*}/\Gamma(V) & \ell \in \mathcal{P}os(i), \ell > k_i^* \\ \gamma\hat{w}_\ell/\Gamma(V) & \ell \in \mathcal{P}os(i), \ell \leq k_i^* \end{cases}$$

7:     Set $x_{i(\ell)} = 0$ for $i \notin \mathcal{V}iol(V)$ or $\ell \notin \mathcal{P}os(i)$, all $z_{U,\ell} = 0$ and **return**.

8: **end if**

9: $\bar{\zeta}_{ik} \leftarrow \begin{cases} \frac{1}{2\varrho}\sum_{j:(i,j)\in\hat{E}_k} u^s_{ijk} & \text{if } i \in \mathcal{V}iol(V), k \leq k_i^*, k \in \mathcal{P}os(i) \\ \zeta_{ik} & \text{otherwise} \end{cases}$

10: Let $\gamma' = \sum_k \hat{w}_k\left(\sum_{(i,j)\in\hat{E}_k} u^s_{ijk} - 3\varrho\sum_i \bar{\zeta}_{ik}\right)$.

11: **for** level $\ell = L$ downto 0 **do**

12:     Find a collection of sets $\mathcal{K}(\ell)$ using Lemma 8 such that any two sets in $\mathcal{K}(\ell)$ are disjoint and for all $U \in \mathcal{K}(\ell)$:
$$\sum_{k\geq\ell}\left(\sum_{(i,j)\in\hat{E}_k: i,j\in U} u^s_{ijk} - \sum_{i\in U} \varrho\bar{\zeta}_{ik}\right) \geq \frac{\gamma\lfloor\|U\|_b/2\rfloor}{(1-\epsilon/4)\beta} \tag{1}$$

And for all $U' \cap \left(\cup_{U\in\mathcal{K}(\ell)} U\right) = \emptyset$,
$$\sum_{k\geq\ell}\left(\sum_{(i,j)\in\hat{E}_k: i,j\in U'} u^s_{ijk} - \sum_{i\in U'} \varrho\bar{\zeta}_{ik}\right) \leq \gamma\frac{\lfloor\|U'\|_b/2\rfloor + \frac{\epsilon}{2}}{(1-\epsilon/4)\beta} \tag{2}$$

13:     For $U \in \mathcal{K}(\ell)$ define
$$\Delta(U, \ell) = \sum_{k\geq\ell}\left(\sum_{(i,j)\in\hat{E}_k, i,j,\in U} u^s_{ijk} - \varrho\sum_{i\in U} \bar{\zeta}_{ik}\right)$$

14: **end for**

15: Define $\Gamma(\mathcal{O}_s) = \sum_\ell \sum_{U\in\mathcal{K}(\ell)} \Delta(U, \ell)\hat{w}_\ell$.

16: **if** $\Gamma(\mathcal{O}_s) \geq \epsilon\gamma'/24$ (Note use of γ'.) **then**

17:     For $U \in \mathcal{K}(\ell)$ set $z_{U,\ell} = \gamma'\hat{w}_\ell/\Gamma(\mathcal{O}_s)$ otherwise $z_{U,\ell} = 0$. (Note use of γ'.)

18:     Set $z_U = \max_\ell z_{U,\ell}$ for all U. All $x_{i(\ell)}$ are set to 0 and **return**.

19: **end if**

20: For $i \in U \in \mathcal{K}(\ell)$, set $\hat{\zeta}_{i\ell} \leftarrow \bar{\zeta}_{i\ell} + \frac{b_i\gamma}{2\varrho\beta}\Delta(U, \ell)$, otherwise $\hat{\zeta}_{i\ell} \leftarrow \bar{\zeta}_{i\ell}$.

21: Set $y_{ij} \leftarrow \frac{(1-\epsilon/4)\beta}{(1+\epsilon/2)\gamma}u^s_{ijk}$. Set $\mu_{ik} = \frac{(1-\epsilon/4)\beta\varrho}{(1+\epsilon/2)\gamma}\hat{\zeta}_{ik}$. **return** $\{y_{ij}\}, \{\mu_{ik}\}$.

$$\sum_i x_i b_i = \sum_{i \in \mathcal{V}iol(V)} \frac{\gamma \hat{w}_{k_i^*}}{\Gamma(V)} b_i = \frac{\beta}{\Gamma(V)} \sum_{i \in \mathcal{V}iol(V)} \frac{\gamma b_i \hat{w}_{k_i^*}}{\beta}$$

$$\leq \sum_{i \in \mathcal{V}iol(V)} \Delta(i, k_i^*) \quad \text{(Definition of } k_i^*\text{)}$$

$$= \frac{\beta}{\Gamma(V)} \Gamma(V) = \beta \quad \text{(Definition of } \Gamma(V)\text{)}$$

Observe that each $x_{i(\ell)} \leq \frac{24}{\epsilon} \hat{w}_\ell$. Therefore we satisfy Lemma 6 in this case. In the remainder of the the proof we assume $\Gamma(V) \leq \epsilon \gamma / 24$. Observe that:

$$\gamma' = \sum_k \hat{w}_k \left(\sum_{(i,j) \in \hat{E}_k} u_{ijk}^s - 3\varrho \sum_i \bar{\zeta}_{ik} \right)$$

$$= \gamma - 3 \sum_{i \in \mathcal{V}iol(i)} \left(\sum_{k \in \mathcal{P}os(i), k \leq k_i^*} \hat{w}_k \left(\bar{\zeta}_{ik} - \zeta_{ik} \right) \right)$$

$$= \gamma - \frac{3}{2} \sum_{i \in \mathcal{V}iol(i)} \sum_{k \in \mathcal{P}os(i), k \leq k_i^*} \hat{w}_k \left(\sum_{j:(i,j) \in \hat{E}_k} u_{ijk}^s - 2\varrho \zeta_{ik} \right)$$

$$\geq \gamma - \frac{3}{2} \sum_{i \in \mathcal{V}iol(i)} \Delta(i, k_i^*) \geq \gamma - \frac{3}{2} \Gamma(V) \geq \gamma - \epsilon \gamma / 16$$

and therefore as a consequence $\gamma' \geq (1 - \epsilon/16)\gamma$ as stated in Step (10) in Algorithm 3. Further, for every i,

$$\frac{\gamma b_i \hat{w}_{k_i^*+1}}{\beta} \geq \sum_{k \in \mathcal{P}os(i), k > k_i^*} \hat{w}_{k_i^*+1} \left(\sum_{j:(i,j) \in \hat{E}_k} u_{ijk}^s - 2\varrho \zeta_{ik} \right)$$

$$\Longrightarrow \frac{\gamma b_i}{\beta} \geq \sum_{k \in \mathcal{P}os(i), k > k_i^*} \left(\sum_{j:(i,j) \in \hat{E}_k} u_{ijk}^s - 2\varrho \zeta_{ik} \right)$$

Which further implies that for any set S of indices (adding nonpositive quantities to the RHS):

$$\frac{\gamma b_i}{\beta} \geq \sum_{k \in S, k > k_i^*} \left(\sum_{j:(i,j) \in \hat{E}_k} u_{ijk}^s - 2\varrho \zeta_{ik} \right)$$

Now $\bar{\zeta}_{ik} = \zeta_{ik}$ for all $i \notin \mathcal{V}iol(V)$, $k > k_i^*$ or $k \notin \mathcal{P}os(i)$. Otherwise we increase ζ_{ik} to $\bar{\zeta}_{ik} = \frac{1}{2\varrho} \sum_{j:(i,j) \in \hat{E}_k} u_{ijk}^s$ and those terms occur with a negative sign. Therefore for any i and any set S of indices

$$\frac{\gamma b_i}{\beta} \geq \sum_{k \in S} \left(\sum_{j:(i,j) \in \hat{E}_k} u_{ijk}^s - 2\varrho \bar{\zeta}_{ik} \right) \tag{3}$$

Observe that we have already proven the lemma for bipartite graphs! We now observe that the **return** statement in Step (18) in Algorithm 3 satisfies:

$$\sum_\ell \sum_{U \in \mathcal{O}_s} z_{U,\ell} \left(\sum_{k \geq \ell} \left(\sum_{(i,j) \in \hat{E}_k, i,j \in U} u_{ijk}^s - \varrho \sum_{i \in U} \zeta_{ik} \right) \right)$$

$$\geq \sum_\ell \sum_{U \in \mathcal{O}_s} z_{U,\ell} \left(\sum_{k \geq \ell} \left(\sum_{(i,j) \in \hat{E}_k, i,j \in U} u_{ijk}^s - \varrho \sum_{i \in U} \bar{\zeta}_{ik} \right) \right)$$

(since $\zeta_{ik} \leq \bar{\zeta}_{ik}$ for all i, k.)

$$= \sum_\ell \sum_{U \in \mathcal{K}(\ell)} \frac{\hat{w}_\ell \gamma'}{\Gamma(\mathcal{O}_s)} \left(\sum_{k \geq \ell} \left(\sum_{(i,j) \in \hat{E}_k, i,j \in U} u_{ijk}^s - \varrho \sum_{i \in U} \bar{\zeta}_{ik} \right) \right)$$

(Definition of $z_{U,\ell}$ in Step (17).)

$$= \frac{\gamma'}{\Gamma(\mathcal{O}_s)} \sum_\ell \hat{w}_\ell \sum_{U \in \mathcal{K}(\ell)} \Delta(U, \ell) = \frac{\gamma'}{\Gamma(\mathcal{O}_s)} \Gamma(\mathcal{O}_s) \geq \left(1 - \frac{\epsilon}{16} \right) \gamma$$

(Using Steps (10), (15).)

$$\sum_{\ell, U \in \mathcal{O}_s} z_{U,\ell} \lfloor \|U\|_b/2 \rfloor = \sum_\ell \sum_{U \in \mathcal{K}(\ell)} \frac{\hat{w}_\ell \gamma'}{\Gamma} \lfloor \|U\|_b/2 \rfloor$$

$$\leq \sum_\ell \sum_{U \in \mathcal{K}(\ell)} \frac{\hat{w}_\ell \gamma'}{\Gamma(\mathcal{O}_s)} \frac{\beta}{\gamma} \sum_{k \geq \ell} \left(\sum_{(i,j) \in \hat{E}_k : i,j \in U} u_{ijk}^s - \varrho \bar{\zeta}_{ik} \right)$$

(Due to Equation 1.)

$$\leq \frac{\beta}{\Gamma(\mathcal{O}_s)} \sum_\ell \hat{w}_\ell \sum_{U \in \mathcal{K}(\ell)} \Delta(U, \ell) = \frac{\beta}{\Gamma(\mathcal{O}_s)} \Gamma(\mathcal{O}_s) = \beta$$

($\gamma' \leq \gamma$ and Definition of $\Delta(U, \ell), \Gamma(\mathcal{O}_s)$)

Again observe that $z_{U,\ell} \leq 24\hat{w}_\ell/\epsilon$, and that the $\mathcal{K}(\ell)$ are mutually disjoint. Therefore for any fixed i, $\sum_{U:i \in U} z_{U,\ell} \leq 24\hat{w}_\ell/\epsilon$ as well. Thus for any i,

$$\sum_{\ell \leq k} \left(\sum_{U:i \in U} z_{U,\ell} \right) \leq \frac{24}{\epsilon} \hat{w}_k \left(1 + \frac{1}{1+\epsilon} + \frac{1}{(1+\epsilon)^2} \cdots \right) \leq \frac{24}{\epsilon^2} \hat{w}_k$$

Finally, based on simple accounting of the edges in a cut, if U, ℓ were to violate $\mathbb{G}(\mathbf{u}^s, \mathbf{x})$ then,

$$3 \sum_{k \geq \ell} \left(\sum_{(i,j) \in \hat{E}_k, i,j \in U} u_{ijk}^s \right) < \sum_{k \geq \ell} \left(\sum_{i \in U} \left(\sum_{j:(i,j) \in \hat{E}_k} u_{ijk}^s \right) \right) \tag{4}$$

But from Equation 1, if $U \in \mathcal{K}(\ell)$ (which must happen if $z_{U,\ell} > 0$) then since $\|U\|_b \geq 3$,

$$\sum_{k \geq \ell} \left(\sum_{(i,j) \in \hat{E}_k : i,j \in U} u_{ijk}^s - \sum_{i \in U} \varrho \bar{\zeta}_{ik} \right) \geq \frac{\gamma}{\beta} \left\lfloor \frac{\|U\|_b}{2} \right\rfloor$$

$$\geq \frac{\gamma}{\beta} \frac{\|U\|_b}{3} = \frac{1}{3} \sum_{i \in U} \frac{\gamma b_i}{\beta}$$

$$\geq \frac{1}{3} \sum_{i \in U} \sum_{k \geq \ell} \left(\sum_{j:(i,j) \in \hat{E}_k} u_{ijk}^s - 2\varrho \bar{\zeta}_{ik} \right)$$

(Using Equation 3.) $\tag{5}$

But since $\bar{\zeta}_{ik} \geq 0$ we have

$$3\sum_{k \geq \ell}\left(\sum_{(i,j)\in \hat{E}_k : i,j \in U} u^s_{ijk}\right) - 2\sum_{k \geq \ell}\left(\sum_{i \in U} \varrho\bar{\zeta}_{ik}\right)$$
$$\geq 3\sum_{k \geq \ell}\left(\sum_{(i,j)\in \hat{E}_k : i,j \in U} u^s_{ijk} - \sum_{i \in U}\varrho\bar{\zeta}_{ik}\right)$$
$$\geq \sum_{i \in U}\sum_{k \geq \ell}\left(\sum_{j:(i,j)\in \hat{E}_k} u^s_{ijk} - 2\varrho\bar{\zeta}_{ik}\right)$$

(Using Equation 5.)

which contradicts Equation 4. Therefore for all $z_{U,\ell} > 0$, the constraints $\mathbb{G}(\mathbf{u}^s, \mathbf{x})$ hold. We satisfy Lemma 6 in this case as well.

In the remainder of the the proof we assume $\Gamma(\mathcal{O}_s) \leq \epsilon^2\gamma/64$. and show that the constraints of LP7 are satisfied. Observe that a consequence of Equation 3, even if we increase $\bar{\zeta}_{ik}$ to $\hat{\zeta}_{ik}$, we continue to satisfy:

$$\sum_{k \in S}\left(\sum_{j:(i,j)\in \hat{E}_k} y_{ij} - 2\mu_{ik}\right) \leq b_i \qquad (6)$$

We set $y_{(k)} = \max\{0, \sum_{j:(i,j)\in \hat{E}_k} u^s_{ijk} - 2\varrho\hat{\zeta}_{ik}\}$. Setting $S = \{k : y_{i(k)} > 0\}$ in Equation 6 satisfies the constraint $\sum_k y_{i(k)} \leq b_i$ for vertex i in LP7.

Moreover for $i \in \left(\cup_{U \in \mathcal{K}(\ell)} U\right)$, $\hat{\zeta}_{i\ell}$ increased from $\bar{\zeta}_{i\ell}$ by $\frac{\gamma b_i}{2\varrho\beta}$ – thus using the observation in Step (9) for $i \in \left(\cup_{U \in \mathcal{K}(\ell)} U\right)$ we have:

$$\sum_{k \geq \ell}\left(\sum_{j:(i,j)\in \hat{E}_k} u^s_{ijk} - 2\varrho\hat{\zeta}_{ik}\right) \leq 0$$

which implies

$$\sum_{k \geq \ell}\left(\sum_{j:(i,j)\in \hat{E}_k} y_{ij} - 2\mu_{ik}\right) \leq 0 \qquad (7)$$

which as we will shortly see, corresponds to the vertices having no effect on feasibility of LP7. For an $U' \in \mathcal{O}_s$ and ℓ, if $U' \cap \left(\cup_{U \in \mathcal{K}(\ell)} U\right) = \emptyset$ then from Equation 2:

$$(1+\epsilon/2)\left(\sum_{k \geq \ell}\left(\sum_{(i,j)\in \hat{E}_k : i,j \in U'} y_{ij} - \sum_{i \in U}\mu_{ik}\right)\right) \leq \lfloor\|U'\|_b/2\rfloor + \frac{\epsilon}{2}$$

which implies that the constraint corresponding to U', ℓ is satisfied in LP7. If on the other hand, $U' \cap \left(\cup_{U \in \mathcal{K}(\ell)} U\right) = U'' \neq \emptyset$ then

$$\sum_{k \geq \ell}\left(\sum_{(i,j)\in \hat{E}_k : i,j \in U'} y_{ij} - \sum_{i \in U'}\mu_{ik}\right)$$
$$= \frac{1}{2}\sum_{i \in U'}\left(\sum_{k \geq \ell}\left(\sum_{j \in U',(i,j)\in \hat{E}_k} y_{ij} - 2\mu_{ik}\right)\right)$$
$$\leq \frac{1}{2}\sum_{i \in U'}\left(\sum_{k \geq \ell}\left(\sum_{j:(i,j)\in \hat{E}_k} y_{ij} - 2\mu_{ik}\right)\right)$$

which using Equations 7 and 6 implies that

$$\sum_{k \geq \ell}\left(\sum_{(i,j)\in \hat{E}_k : i,j \in U'} y_{ij} - \sum_{i \in U'}\mu_{ik}\right) \leq \frac{1}{2}\sum_{i \in U'-U''} b_i$$
$$= \frac{\|U\|_b - \|U''\|_b}{2} \leq \frac{\|U\|_b - 1}{2} = \left\lfloor\frac{\|U\|_b}{2}\right\rfloor$$

which implies that the constraint corresponding to U', ℓ is also satisfied in LP7. We now focus on the last remaining constraint of LP7:

$$\sum_k \hat{w}_k\left(\sum_{(i,j)\in \hat{E}_k} u^s_{ijk} - 3\varrho\sum_i \hat{\zeta}_{ik}\right)$$
$$= \gamma' - 3\sum_\ell \hat{w}_\ell \sum_{U \in \mathcal{K}(\ell)}\sum_{i \in U}\frac{\gamma b_i}{2\beta}$$
$$\geq \gamma' - 3\sum_\ell \hat{w}_\ell \sum_{U \in \mathcal{K}(\ell)}\frac{3\gamma\lfloor\|U\|_b/2\rfloor}{2\beta}$$

(Using $\lfloor\|U\|_b/2\rfloor \geq \frac{1}{3}\|U\|_b$.)

$$\geq \gamma' - 3\sum_\ell \hat{w}_\ell \sum_{U \in \mathcal{K}(\ell)}\frac{3}{2}\left(\sum_{k \geq \ell}\left(\sum_{(i,j)\in \hat{E}_k : i,j \in U} u^s_{ijk} - \sum_{i \in U}\varrho\bar{\zeta}_{ik}\right)\right)$$

(Using Eqn. 1.)

$$= \gamma' - 3\sum_\ell \hat{w}_\ell \sum_{U \in \mathcal{K}(\ell)}\frac{3}{2}\Delta(U,\ell)$$

(Using Definition of $\Delta(U, \ell)$.)

$$\geq \gamma' - \frac{9}{2}\Gamma(\mathcal{O}_s) \geq \gamma' - 3\epsilon\gamma/16 \geq (1 - \epsilon/4)\gamma$$

Therefore

$$\sum_k \hat{w}_k\left(\sum_{(i,j)\in \hat{E}_k} y_{ij} - 3\sum_i \mu_{ik}\right) \geq (1-\epsilon/4)\gamma\frac{(1-\epsilon/4)\beta}{(1+\epsilon/2)\gamma}$$
$$\geq (1-\epsilon)\beta$$

The lemma follows. Observe that the proof was not very involved, which is the benefit of having a good relaxation LP7 to prove the existence of a large matching.

References

[1] K. J. Ahn and S. Guha. Linear programming in the semi-streaming model with application to the maximum matching problem. *Inf. Comput., ICALP 2011 Issue*, 222:59–79, 2013.

[2] K. J. Ahn and S. Guha. This paper. *CORR, 1307.4359*, 2013.

[3] K. J. Ahn and S. Guha. Near linear time approximation schemes for uncapacitated and capacitated *b*–matching problems in nonbipartite graphs. *Proc. of SODA, also at Arxiv 1307.4355*, 2014.

[4] K. J. Ahn, S. Guha, and A. McGregor. Analyzing graph structure via linear measurements. In *SODA*, 2012.

[5] K. J. Ahn, S. Guha, and A. McGregor. Graph sketches: Sparsification, spanners and subgraphs. *PODS*, 2012.

[6] S. Arora, E. Hazan, and S. Kale. The multiplicative weights update method: a meta algorithm and applications. *Theor. of Comput.*, 8(6):121–164, 2012.

[7] B. Bahmani, A. Goel, and K. Munagala. Efficient primal dual algorithms for mapreduce. *Manuscript*, 2012.

[8] A. A. Benczúr and D. R. Karger. Approximating *s-t* minimum cuts in $\tilde{O}(n^2)$ time. In *STOC*, pages 47–55, 1996.

[9] A. Bhalgat, R. Hariharan, T. Kavitha, and D. Panigrahi. An $\tilde{O}(mn)$ Gomory-Hu tree construction algorithm for unweighted graphs. *STOC*, 2007.

[10] D. Bienstock and G. Iyengar. Solving fractional packing problems in $O^*(1/\epsilon)$ iterations. *Proc. of STOC*, pages 146–155, 2004.

[11] A. Drucker, F. Kuhn, and R. Oshman. On the power of the congested clique model. In *Proceedings of PODC*, pages 367–376, 2014.

[12] R. Duan and S. Pettie. Approximating maximum weight matching in near-linear time. In *Proc. FOCS*, pages 673–682, 2010.

[13] S. Eggert, L. Kliemann, and A. Srivastav. Bipartite graph matchings in the semi-streaming model. In *ESA*, pages 492–503, 2009.

[14] L. Epstein, A. Levin, J. Mestre, and D. Segev. Improved approximation guarantees for weighted matching in the semi-streaming model. *STACS*, pages 347–358, 2010.

[15] J. Feigenbaum, S. Kannan, A. McGregor, S. Suri, and J. Zhang. On graph problems in a semi-streaming model. *Theor. Comput. Sci.*, 348(2-3):207–216, 2005.

[16] D. Foster and R. Vohra. Regret in the on-line decision problem. *Games and Economic Behavior*, 29:7–35, 1999.

[17] W. S. Fung, R. Hariharan, N. J. A. Harvey, and D. Panigrahi. A general framework for graph sparsification. In *Proc. of STOC*, pages 71–80, 2011.

[18] M. D. Grigoriadis and L. G. Khachiyan. A sublinear time randomized approximation algorithm for matrix games. *Operations Research Letters*, 18:53–58, 1995.

[19] V. Guruswami and K. Onak. Superlinear lower bounds for multipass graph processing. *Electronic Colloquium on Computational Complexity (ECCC)*, 20(2), 2013.

[20] R. Hariharan, T. Kavitha, and D. Panigrahi. Efficient algorithms for computing all low s-t edge connectivities and related problems. *Proceedings of SODA*, 2007.

[21] M. Kapralov. Better bounds for matchings in the streaming model. *SODA*, 2013.

[22] L. G. Khachiyan. Convergence rate of the game processes for solving matrix games. *Zh. Vychisl. Mat. and Mat. Fiz. ,17:1421–1431,1977. Eng. translation in USSR Comput. Math and Math. Phys.*, 17:78–88, 1978.

[23] P. N. Klein and N. E. Young. On the number of iterations for dantzig-wolfe optimization and packing covering approximation algorithms. *Proc. of IPCO*, pages 320–327, 1999.

[24] S. Lattanzi, B. Moseley, S. Suri, and S. Vassilvitskii. Filtering: a method for solving graph problems in mapreduce. In *SPAA*, pages 85–94, 2011.

[25] N. Littlestone and M. M. Warmuth. The weighted majority algorithm. *Information and Computation*, 108:212–261, 1994.

[26] M. Luby and N. Nisan. A parallel approximation algorithm for positive linear programming. *Proc. of STOC*, pages 448–457, 1993.

[27] Y. Mansour and S. Vardi. A local computation approximation scheme to maximum matching. *APPROX-RANDOM*, pages 260–273, 2013.

[28] A. McGregor. Finding graph matchings in data streams. In *APPROX RANDOM*, pages 170–181, 2005.

[29] H. Nagamochi and T. Ibaraki. A linear-time algorithm for finding a sparse *k*-connected spanning subgraph of a *k*-connected graph. *Algorithmica*, 7(1-6):583–596, 1992.

[30] A. Nemirovski. Prox-method with rate of convergence $O(1/t)$ for variational inequalities with lipschitz continuous monotone operators and smooth convex concave saddle point problems. *SIAM J. on Opt.*, 15(1):229–251, 2005.

[31] Y. Nesterov. Smooth minimization of non-smooth functions. *Math. Program., Ser. A*, 103:127–152, 2005.

[32] M. W. Padberg and M. R. Rao. Odd minimum cut-sets and b-matchings. *Mathematics of Operations Research*, 7(1):67–80, 1982.

[33] S. A. Plotkin, D. B. Shmoys, and É. Tardos. Fast approximation algorithms for fractional packing and covering problems. *Math. of OR*, 20:257–301, 1995.

[34] A. Schrijver. *Combinatorial Optimization - Polyhedra and Efficiency*, volume 24 of *Algorithms and Combinatorics*. Springer, 2003.

[35] M. Zelke. Weighted matching in the semi-streaming model. *STACS*, pages 669–680, 2008.

Branch-Avoiding Graph Algorithms

Oded Green
Georgia Institute of
Technology
College of Computing
Atlanta, Georgia, USA

Marat Dukhan
Georgia Institute of
Technology
College of Computing
Atlanta, Georgia, USA

Richard Vuduc
Georgia Institute of
Technology
College of Computing
Atlanta, Georgia, USA

ABSTRACT

This paper quantifies the impact of branches and branch mispredictions on the single-core performance of certain graph problems, specifically for computing connected components. We show that branch mispredictions are costly and can reduce performance by as much as 30%-50%. This insight suggests that one should seek graph algorithms and implementations that *avoid branches*.

As a proof-of-concept, we devise such branch-avoiding implementations of the Shiloach-Vishkin algorithm for computing connected components. We evaluate these implementations on current x86 and ARM-based processors to show the efficacy of the approach. Our results suggest how both compiler writers and architects might exploit this insight to improve graph processing systems more broadly and create better systems for such problems.

Categories and Subject Descriptors

D.2.8 [**Software**]: Software EngineeringMetrics[Performance measures]
; C.4 [**Computer Systems Organization**]: Performance of Systems—*Performance attributes*

Keywords

Branch prediction; predication; connected components; performance engineering; code generation

1. INTRODUCTION

This paper concerns computations on a graph $G = (V, E)$, where V is a set of vertices and $E = \{(u,v)|u, v \in V\}$ is a set of edges.[1] Traditionally, the key challenges associated with creating high-performance graph implementations are computational demand, irregular memory access, difficulty

[1]In general, the graph may be directed or undirected, weighted or unweighted. These issues do not matter for this study.

of load balancing, storage, and optimization criteria that cause the problem to be intractable, among others. In this work, we consider an additional challenge, which is critical to practical implementation but largely unstudied: *branch prediction*, which is an important factor in single-core performance on essentially all modern multi- and emerging many-core processors. We show subtle and sometimes unexpected performance phenomena that suggest incorrectly predicted branches can reduce single-core efficiency. These observations suggest that a simple algorithmic redesign, in which branches are avoided, can improve performance and can even make it more consistent.

We study branches because exploiting instruction-level parallelism is critical to achieving high single-core throughput, which is the building block for all higher levels of parallelization, such as shared memory or distributed memory parallelism. The presence of a conditional branch interrupts the flow of instructions; if it is not known whether the branch will be taken, the processor cannot know which instruction to fetch next, creating stalls in the processor pipeline. To address this problem, a modern processor core tracks the history of a branch, and uses this state to speculatively fetch the next instruction in what it estimates is the most likely outcome. If it guesses incorrectly, any speculatively executed instructions must be cancelled, causing slowdowns in time and potential reductions in energy-efficiency.

We have analyzed two different graph algorithms with respect to their branching behavior: connected components, based on the classic Shiloach-Vishkin (SV) algorithm [46], and the classical form of breadth-first search (BFS) [18], sometimes referred to as the "top-down" algorithm [8]. SV is a propagation-based algorithm and BFS is a shortest-path algorithm. Our results can in principle be extended to other algorithms in both families, including all-pairs shortest-paths, betweenness centrality, and depth-first search, among numerous others [10, 24, 26, 32, 50].

This paper focuses primarily on our findings for connected components. Our complete set of results appear in an accompanying technical report, which includes BFS [28].[2] We occasionally summarize and allude to the BFS results herein as needed.

Our analysis quantifies the effect of branch mispredictions, both analytically and empirically. Our empirical studies rely on our own highly-tuned assembly language implementations of the target algorithms. We show that SV, which performs an equal amount of work in every iteration, suffers a performance penalty in its early iterations

[2]See: http://arxiv.org/abs/1411.1460

due in part to an increase in the number of branch mispredictions, which are also called *branch misses*. In SV's later iterations, when the branch prediction accuracy increases, the performance increases as well. This observation motivates a *branch-avoiding* algorithm that reduces the number of branches and branch mispredictions that the algorithm incurs. This change yields overall speedups over the highly tuned branch-based assembly implementation. The variations in per-iteration performance and number of executed instructions of SV essentially go away in the branch-avoiding version as well, bringing with it more consistent and predictable performance.

BFS also exhibits branch mispredictions, and we develop a branch-avoiding algorithm for it, too. However, our specific algorithm significantly increases the number of store operations by more than an order of magnitude. Consequently, there is no performance win for BFS [28]. Nevertheless, taken together we believe these two cases, SV and BFS, raise a number of intriguing new questions, both about the role of branch-avoidance in algorithm design, whether compilers can produce our hand-generated transformations, and whether additional architectural support could exploit the branching behavior we observe and mitigate cases of performance loss.

2. RELATED WORK

Our work focuses on connected components (CC) and breadth-first search (BFS), in part because they are primitive building blocks of higher-level graph analytics. Such analytics include connected components itself [38, 45], computing modularity [42], detecting communities [42, 43], partitioning graphs [33], computing clustering coefficients [51], computing betweenness centrality [10, 26, 29], computing closeness centrality [44]), as well as computing a wide variety of distance-based analytics. A variety of packages implement these analytics, including STINGER [4, 22], GraphCT [1, 21], Ligra [47], Pregel [37], and the Combinatorial BLAS [13]. However, these packages focus on shared memory multicore, manycore, distributed memory parallelism [9, 12, 15, 30, 54], and massively multithreaded systems [5, 7]. Thus, our study of low-level single-core behavior and instruction-level parallelism complements this other work, and should also apply broadly thereto.

Branch predictors.

A significant number of prior works on branch predictors has focused on their design and implementation in hardware; see Smith's survey of strategies [48], among other seminal references [20, 34, 35, 49, 52, 53]. Little is known publicly about the actual implementation of the branch predictors in modern processors, since these are vendor-specific and proprietary. As such, there is some ongoing empirical research that tries to demystify these implementations using synthetic benchmarks [25, 40]. However, with few exceptions, most of the other work on branch prediction evaluates against general benchmark suites, such as SPECint2006 and SPECfp2006.[3] Therefore, they do not provide the additional level of understanding possible with a focus on more specific and application-oriented kernels, as in our study.

It has been shown that the impact of branch predictors on merging two sorted arrays can in fact increase the total

execution time by up to $5\times$ [27]. These results are relevant to both sorting algorithms and to triangle-counting in graphs, the latter of which is a building-block for clustering coefficients when list intersection is used for finding the triangles [51]. Thus, these studies corroborate one another with respect to the affects of branch misprediction.

Performance engineering of graph computations.

There is some work on low-level performance engineering of graph computations. Green-Marl is domain specific language, which targets shared-memory platforms [31]. It emits back-end code that manages shared variables using, for instance, atomic instructions; from published code samples, its implementations are branch-based. Cong and Makarychev describe techniques to implement graph algorithms that are more cache-friendly [17]. They also show how to use software prefetching to improve spatial locality on IBM Power7 and Sun Niagara2 platforms. Both platforms support multiple threads per core, which can help in memory latency hiding.

For BFS specifically, there are additional studies. Chhugani et al. present a shared-memory parallel BFS [16]. They focus on reducing cross-socket communication, and use lock-free techniques. Merrill and Garland have developed a highly-tuned GPU implementation [39]. Beamer et al. have proposed algorithmic changes, which they refer to as being direction- optimizing [8]. None of these studies considers the impact of branching per se, and so largely complements our study.

Graph property characterizations.

Many researchers have characterized high-level properties of real-world graphs, like the existence of power-law degree distributions and small-world algorithmic effects [3, 6, 11, 23, 36, 41, 51]. Our analysis is justified in part by some of these findings, such as the existence of a large connected component [11], which has implications for how our target graph computations will behave.

At a lower-level, Burtscher et al. develop metrics to quantify irregularity, with respect to both memory accesses and control-flow [14]. They use these metrics to compare different computations, including graph computations, confirming some aspects of conventional wisdom about what we consider "regular" versus "irregular." However, it is not clear (to us) how to translate these metrics into actionable transformations of code that improve performance.

3. BRANCH PREDICTION

Given a particular (static) *conditional*[4] branch in a graph algorithm, our analysis goal is to estimate how many times the branch predictor will mispredict it. We base our analysis on a simple *2-bit branch predictor* [48]. The empirical evaluation of § 5 will justify this choice. Like most branch prediction techniques, it uses the history of previous executions of a given branch to predict the next outcome;[5] as such, one may formalize the analysis of predictors mathematically using Markov chains and reason about expected

---

[3] See: https://www.spec.org/benchmarks.html

[4] As opposed to an unconditional branch, which always jumps and therefore does not need to be predicted.

[5] For instance, a simple *1-bit* predictor predicts that if the last occurrence of a given branch was taken, then so will the next one.

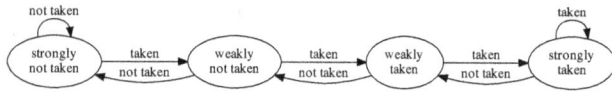

Figure 1: A 2-bit branch predictor behaves as shown in this finite-state automaton. Each node is a state representing the next prediction, e.g., the strongly and weakly taken states predict "taken," the others, "not taken." Each edge shows how the state changes once the actual branch condition is resolved.

branch misses, which we have done. However, for concerns of readability and space, this paper omits the details of such analysis, instead stating the key results and offering more intuitive high-level explanations.

3.1 A model of 2-bit predictors

For each (static) conditional branch in the program, a 2-bit predictor maintains a 2-bit state value, which encodes four possible states. Each state value is a prediction for the next occurrence of this branch; once the true branch condition is known, this state is updated. The precise states and transitions appear in the finite-state automaton (FSA) of figure 1. In particular, there are four possible states, named STRONGLY-TAKEN, WEAKLY-TAKEN, WEAKLY-NOT-TAKEN, and STRONGLY-NOT-TAKEN. The "strong" states reflect that the last few branches were all the same, i.e., all "taken" or all "not taken," and so it is likely the next branch will be the same. The weak states allow for the predictor's bias to change if a new pattern emerges.

We will further assume that the processor has enough branch state storage to track, for each conditional branch of interest, its 2-bit state for the duration of the program. That is, we will not consider the case when the processor runs out of branch state storage and must "evict" (and therefore lose or reset) the branch state. Our target programs are sufficiently compact that this assumption is reasonable.

Algorithm 1: A simple sequential while-loop, which executes its body exactly n times

---

Let $n \geq 0$;
$i \leftarrow 0$;
while $i < n$ **do**
 | // ... i, n unmodified; no early exits ...
 | $i \leftarrow i + 1$;

3.2 Analysis of simple loops

A common programming pattern in graph algorithms is a *simple sequential loop*. Such loops iterate over, for example, the set of vertices, edges, or neighbors of a vertex (the *adjacency list*).

Consider, for example, the *simple sequential while-loop* of algorithm 1. By "simple," we mean that (a) the iteration variable i increases monotonically by 1 at each iteration; (b) the loop bound n is constant as the loop executes; and (c) there are no early exits. Thus, this loop executes its body exactly n times. The conditional branch in this case depends on the condition, $i < n$. We will assume the convention, for this loop, that the branch is taken when the condition is true, and not taken when the condition is false.[6] There will be exactly $n + 1$ evaluations of this branch, only the last of which is *not* taken, namely, when exiting the loop.[7] We can state a number of facts about such loops, assuming the 2-bit branch predictor.

LEMMA 1. *When $n \geq 3$, the final state of the 2-bit predictor is* WEAKLY-TAKEN.

PROOF. The conditional branch is taken n times. In the worst case, we begin the loop in the STRONGLY-NOT-TAKEN state. According to the FSA of figure 1, after three taken state transitions, the predictor will be in the STRONGLY-TAKEN state. Since the final branch is *not* taken, the predictor must move into the WEAKLY-TAKEN state. □

LEMMA 2. *When $n \geq 3$, the maximum number of branch mispredictions incurred by the loop's conditional test (ignoring conditional branches in the body) is 3.*

PROOF. As with lemma 1, the the initial state of the predictor may be STRONGLY-NOT-TAKEN, which will cause 2 mispredictions before reaching either of the TAKEN states. For the last loop iteration, when $i = n \geq 3$, the predictor will be in the STRONGLY-TAKEN state but the branch will be taken, incurring one more branch miss. Thus, there could be up to 3 misses. Furthermore, there must be at least 1 branch miss, which occurs on the last (not taken) branch; the reason is that the predictor must be in the STRONGLY-TAKEN state by iteration $i = n-1$, independent of the initial state. □

LEMMA 3. *Suppose we execute the same loop $k \geq 2$ times, where $n \geq 3$ on the first execution, and $n \geq 1$ on every subsequent execution. An example is a nested loop, where k designates the outer-loop iteration count and n the inner-loop count. Then there may be up to $k + 2$ mispredictions for the inner loop—that is, up to 3 misses during the first execution and 1 additional miss on each of the $k-1$ remaining executions.*

PROOF. Based on lemma 1 the branch predictor is in the WEAKLY-TAKEN state at the end of the first execution of the loop and may see up to 3 mispredictions. This state becomes the initial state for the next execution. If $n \geq 1$ on every execution after the first, then the predictor will move to the STRONGLY-TAKEN state; on the last iteration, it will return to the WEAKLY-TAKEN state, incurring 1 misprediction. That is, we will bounce back-and-forth between STRONGLY-TAKEN and WEAKLY-TAKEN. □

COROLLARY 1. *If $k \gg 2$, we should expect approximately k branch misses.*

LEMMA 4. *Suppose $n = 0$. Then the predictor will move toward the STRONGLY-NOT-TAKEN state and cannot be in the STRONGLY-TAKEN state; furthermore, it will incur either 0 or 1 branch misses.*

---

[6]This choice is arbitrary and depends on the specific code generated. There is an equivalent argument if one assumes code such that the branch is taken only when the condition is false.

[7]There is an additional branch at the bottom of the loop. However, this branch is *unconditional*, since it *must* jump back to the top of the loop.

Algorithm 2: Branch-based Shiloach-Vishkin algorithm for finding connect components.

```
// Algorithm initialization
for v ∈ V do
  └ CC_id[v] ← v
change ← 1
// Connected component labeling
while change ≠ 0 do
    change ← 0
    for v ∈ V do
        c_v ← CC_id[v]
        for u ∈ Neighbors[v] do
            c_u ← CC_id[u]
            if c_u ≤ c_v then
                └ CC_id[v] ← c_u
                  change ← 1
```

Algorithm 3: Branch-avoiding Shiloach-Vishkin algorithm for finding connect components.

```
// Algorithm initialization
for v ∈ V do
  └ CC_id[v] ← v
change ← 1
// Connected component labeling
while change ≠ 0 do
    change ← 0
    for v ∈ V do
        c_v^init ← CC_id[v]
        c_v ← c_v^init
        for u ∈ Neighbors[v] do
            c_u ← CC_id[u]
            CMPLEQ(c_u, c_v) // replaces the branch
            CMOV(c_v, c_u) // analogue of CC_id[v] ← c_u
        CC_id[v] ← c_v
        change ← change ∨ c_v ⊕ c_v^init
```

LEMMA 5. *Suppose $n = 1$. Then the predictor will return to its initial state, incurring either 1 or 2 branch misses.*

LEMMA 6. *Suppose $n = 2$. Then the branch predictor must end in either the WEAKLY-TAKEN or WEAKLY-NOT-TAKEN states, and will incur between 1 and 3 branch misses.*

4. CONNECTED COMPONENTS

For the problem of finding connected components, we assume the Shiloach and Vishkin (SV) algorithm [46]. It has been implemented on numerous multiprocessor systems, including the massively threaded Cray XMT [1, 21] and a variety of x86 systems [38].

SV is based on a propagation technique, and its pseudocode appears in algorithm 2. It maintains for each vertex v a component label, $CC_{id}[v]$, and updates this label to place adjacent vertices into the same connected component. Initially, each vertex v is placed into a connected component by itself, which by convention is a label equal to the vertex number. As such, there are a total of $|V|$ connected components at this stage. In the first iteration, each vertex v compares its own label with each of its neighbors, $u \in \text{adj}(v)$. Again by convention, the vertex replaces its own label with the minimum label among itself and its neighbors. The algorithm is iterative and stops when no further label changes occur, maintained by a flag.

Each iteration requires $O(|V| + |E|)$ computations, since the algorithm accesses all vertices and their respective adjacencies. The maximal length of propagation is limited by

Table 1: Graphs from the 10th DIMACS Implementation Challenge used in our experiments.

Name	Graph Type	$|V|$	$|E|$
audikw1	Matrix	943,695	38,354,076
auto	Partitioning	448,695,	3,314,611
coAuthorsDBLP	Collaboration	299,067	977,676
cond-mat-2005	Clustering	40,421	175,691
ldoor	Matrix	952,203	22,785,136

the graph diameter d. As such, the total time complexity of the algorithm is $O(d \cdot (|V| + |E|))$. Relative to algorithm 2, there is a shortcut that can reduce the number of iterations to $d/2$ [46]. However, this shortcut does not change our analysis, and we do not consider it further.

Conceptually, the component labels propagate as figure 2 depicts. Initially (a), four of the components have minimal labels locally; these labels propagate gradually, and the label of a given node may change several times, (b)-(e), possibly even within the same iteration. Eventually, the algorithm reaches a final state (e) where for a fully-connected graph there will be a single connected component.

4.1 Branch (Mis)predictions in SV

The standard version of the SV algorithm (algorithm 2) has four static conditional branches. To analyze the branch mispredictions, we assume the 2-bit branch predictor model of §3.

The first conditional branch is the termination test of the *while* statement. This condition is evaluated $d + 1$ times, where d is the diameter of the graph. Per §3, assuming $d \geq 3$, it should incur at most 3 mispredictions, ignoring mispredictions in the body of the loop.

Next, consider the two conditional branches associated with the two for-loops. The first for-loop iterates over all vertices; the second for-loop iterates over all neighbors of each vertex, thereby effectively visiting all edges. From the facts of §3.2, the first for-loop will incur up to 3 branch misses in total, assuming sufficiently large $|V|$. The second for-loop is an instance of a repeated loop (see lemma 3), which is executed $|V|$ times. Though the exact behavior of the inner loop depends on the degree distribution, we can estimate the misses by applying corollary 1, which implies approximately $|V|$ branch misses.

Finally, the if-statement is the hardest to analyze offline. The actual number of branch mispredictions will depend on the input graph. To get a qualitative idea of what to expect, consider the example in figure 2. In the first iterations, vertices are likely to "swap" their connected components multiple times, which complicates branch prediction as there may not be a regular pattern. As iterations proceed, labels begin to stabilize, making this condition more predictable. Thus, we should expect to see many mispredictions initially, gradually decreasing as iterations proceed.

4.2 Branch-avoiding SV

Algorithm 3 shows the pseudocode for a branch-avoiding SV algorithm. This algorithm compares the values of the connected component labels; however, it does not branch based on the value of the comparison. Instead, this approach uses a conditional move that copies the value into the variable c_v if and only if the label of u is smaller than the value

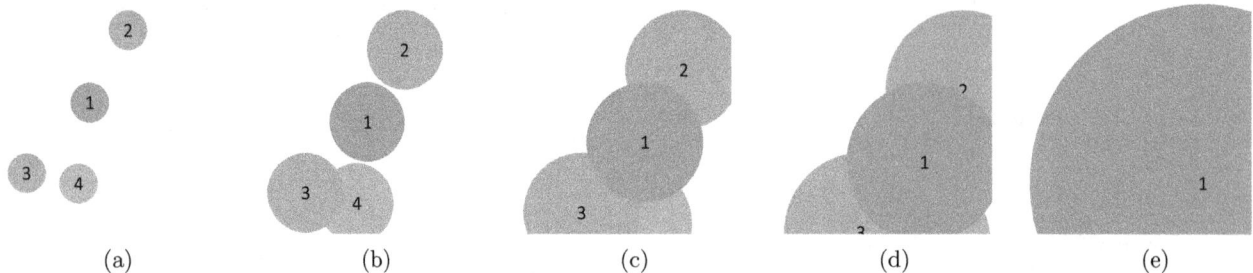

Figure 2: These sub-figures conceptually show how the connected component id propagates through the graph as time evolves - each subfigure is for a different iteration of the algorithm. This example assumes that all vertices are connected and for simplicity shows only the connected components are 1 through 4. Initially the number of connected components is equal to the number vertices. (a) Depicts the initial state in which each vertex is in its own component. (b)-(d) depict that some vertices belong to the same connected component yet may require multiple label updates (in either the same iteration or a separate iteration). (e) is the final state in which there is a single connected component.

in c_v. For the SV algorithm the value of the connected component of v is stored in c_v which is a register, meaning that the number of writebacks (stores) is $|V|$. To ensure the correctness of the algorithm and that the algorithm will stop at some point, the variable *change* is updated using a bitwise OR of bitwise XOR between the initial c_v^{init} and the updated c_v. If the value of the connected component changed for the current vertex, then c_v is not equal to c_v^{init} and their XOR value is non-zero. Accordingly, if any connected component changed, then *change* will be non-zero.

5. EMPIRICAL RESULTS

5.1 Implementation Details

To carry out a carefully controlled experiment that would allow us to isolate the effect of branches, it was ultimately necessary to hand-code the implementations of the SV algorithm in assembly language.

Prior to doing so, we tried several implementations of the SV algorithm for both the x86-64 and ARM architectures. Unfortunately, compilers do not provide explicit control over the use of branches or conditional moves in the generated code, which complicated our analysis. The compilers on our x86-64 systems tended to generate conditional branches when conditional moves could be used. While we found two ways to make these compilers avoid branches, both of them involved unnecessary inefficiencies. The first was to use inline assembly, which allowed manual selection of instructions. However, the compilers generated suboptimal code around the inlined assembly. The second was to force the compiler to use **SETcc** instructions by storing the result of the comparison into a byte variable followed by extending the bit mask for conditional selection. This approach caused the compiler to generate multiple instructions where a single **CMOVcc** instruction sufficed. On the ARM system we had the reverse problem: instead of a conditional branch or move, compilers preferred to use conditional store instructions, which impose an especially big performance penalty on our *Cortex-A15* platform.

Thus, we resorted to hand-coded *x86-64* and ARM assembly. We used an in-house (but open-source) tool, called

PeachPy [19]. We used the PeachPy framework for improved productivity over using conventional assemblers; the assembly code generated by PeachPy is nearly equal to handwritten assembly code.

We performed our experiments on the seven systems, which vary by microarchitecture, shown in table 2. On all systems the assembly implementations performed at least as well as C implementations - typically the assembly implementations significantly outperformed the C implementations. The algorithms were tested on graphs taken from the DIMACS 10 Graph Challenge [2], detailed in table 1.

5.2 Connected Components

Figure 3 plots execution time (y-axis) as a function of the iteration number (x-axis) during execution of the SV algorithm, for all of the systems in table 2. These times are normalized by the the fastest iteration time of the branch-based algorithm. The branch-based algorithm is shown as a red curve and the branch-avoiding algorithm as a blue curve. In each subplot, the total speedup of the branch-avoiding algorithm over the branch-based algorithm is shown as a text annotation (e.g., "1.20×" in the top-left subplot). For several of the iterations, the difference between the branch-based algorithm and the branch-avoiding is as high as $30\% - 50\%$, with the branch-avoiding algorithm being the faster of these. In a handful of cases, specifically on the Bonnell system, the branch-based algorithm is 20% faster than the branch-avoiding algorithm.

Recall that as the connected component labels propagate, fewer vertices change their connected component. This fact makes the branch predictor's job easier. Figures 4 and 5 show the ratio of branches and number of branch mispredictions as a function of the iteration, respectively, which confirms this behavior.

On some systems, such as the Cortex-A15, the branch-avoiding algorithm offers better performance for all iterations of the algorithm over all the graphs. On other systems, in the initial iterations the branch-avoiding algorithms offers better performance and in the later iterations the branch-based algorithm gives better performance. This behavior appears to be both system- and input graph-dependent. When a performance crossover point exists, it is a single crossover

Shiloach–Vishkin Connected Components: Time
[Normalized to branch-based minimum]

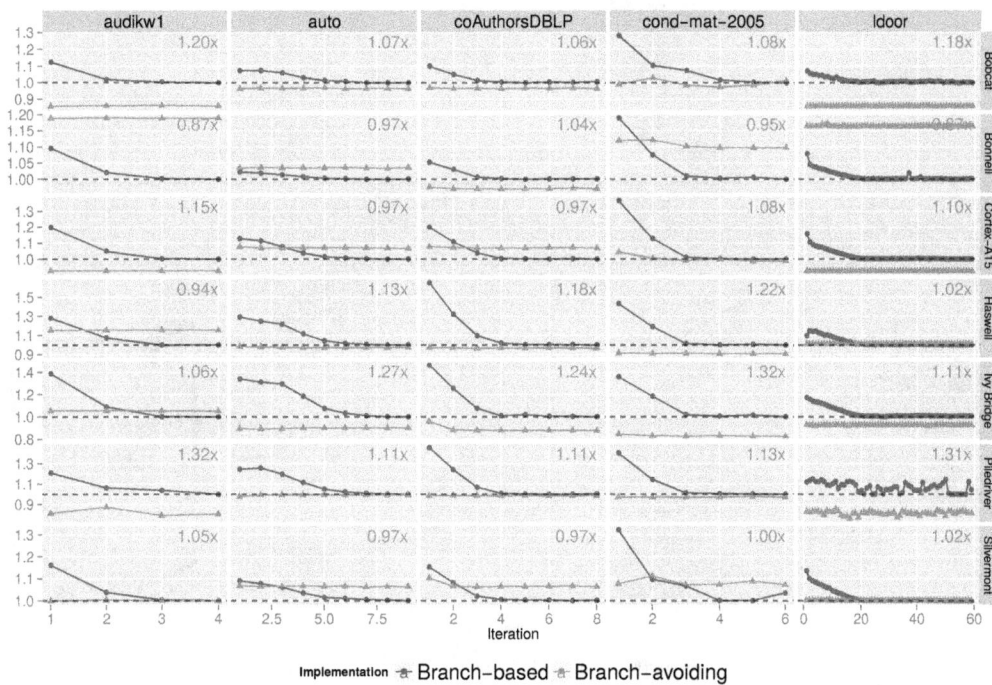

Figure 3: Time as a function of the iteration for the Shiloach-Vishkin algorithm.

Shiloach–Vishkin Connected Components: Branches
[Normalized to branch-based minimum]

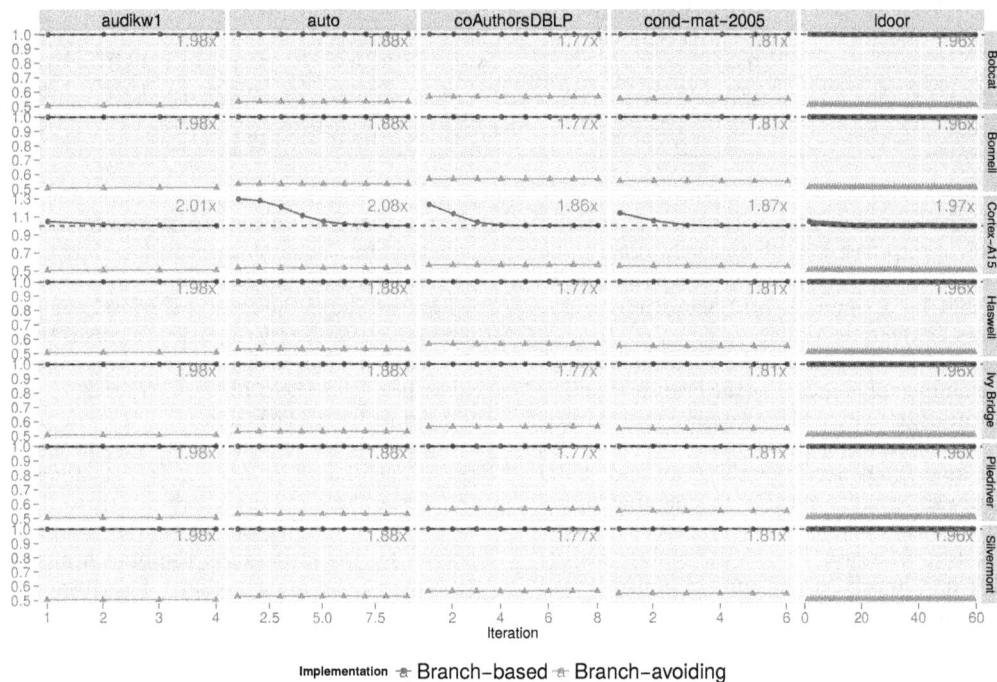

Figure 4: Branches as a function of the iteration for the Shiloach-Vishkin algorithm.

Shiloach–Vishkin Connected Components: Mispredictions
[Normalized to branch-based minimum]

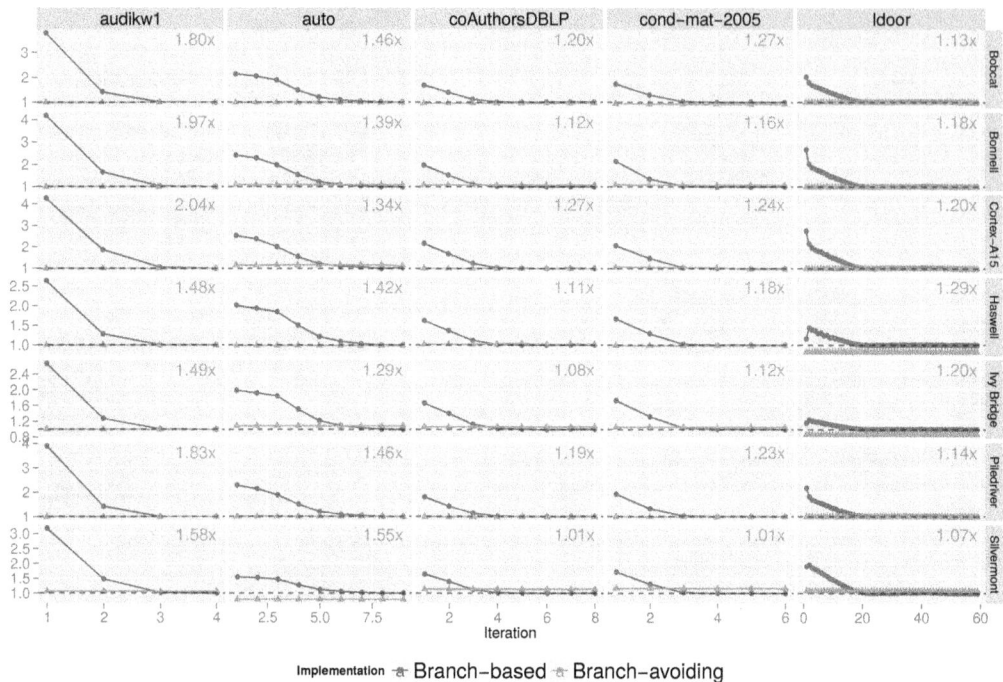

Figure 5: Branch mispredictions as a function of the iteration for the Shiloach-Vishkin algorithm.

Table 2: Systems used in experiments.

Architecture	Microarchitecture	Processor	Frequency	L1 Cache	L2 Cache	L3 Cache	DRAM Type
ARM v7-A	Cortex-A15 [arn]	Samsung Exynos 5250	1.7 GHz	32 KB	1 MB		SC DDR3-800
x86-64	Piledriver [pld]	AMD FX-6300	3.5 GHz	16 KB	2 MB	8 MB	DC DDR3-1600
x86-64	Bobcat	AMD E2-1800	1.7 GHz	32 KB	512 KB		SC DDR3-1333
x86-64	Haswell [hsw]	Intel Core i7-4770K	3.5 GHz	32 KB	256 KB	8 MB	DC DDR3-2133
x86-64	Ivy-Bridge [ivb]	Intel Core i3-3217U	1.8 GHz	32 KB	256 KB	3 MB	DC DDR3-1600
x86-64	Silvermont [slv]	Intel Atom C2750	2.4 GHz	24 KB	1 MB		DC DDR3-1600
x86-64	Bonnell	Intel Atom 330	1.6 GHz	24 KB	512 KB		SC DDR3-800

point from which the branch-avoiding algorithm is initially faster to where the branch-based is subsequently faster. The significance of a single crossover point is that it naturally suggests there could be a simple hybrid algorithm to run the right algorithm at the right time.

Figure 4 shows that the branch-based algorithm executes nearly double the number of branches as the branch-avoiding algorithm. For the Intel and AMD systems, the number of branches is constant throughout the iterations, while for the Cortex-A15 system, it is not. For the Intel and AMD systems, the hardware counter returns the number of retired branch instructions, while the ARM system returns the number of dispatched branches. Due to the higher misprediction rate in the first iterations, the number of dispatched branches is also higher as these are flushed instructions.

The branch-based algorithm can potentially have as many as 4× the number of branch mispredictions as that of the branch-avoiding algorithm, as shown in figure 5. In all cases, the branch-avoiding algorithm has fewer branches and branch mispredictions. For most graphs, the ratio between the total number of mispredictions for the two algorithms, indicated by the number at the top-right corner of each subplot, is for a given graph within a small region for all systems.

Figure 6 shows the ratio of the total number of branch mispredictions for the two algorithms versus the lower-bound on the number of branch mispredictions. The lower-bound is given in § 4 for the 2-bit branch-predictor, and is shown in the figure by a black line at y=1. For most systems, the branch-avoiding algorithm is near the lower-bound, while the branch-based algorithm is well above this line. For the Cortex-A15 system, there are three different graphs in which the branch misprediction rate is well above the lower-bound, for the *auto* graph the branch misprediction rate is 50% above the lower-bound. This means that the implemented branch-predictor in fact increases the misprediction rate. Both the Bonnell and the Silvermont systems also have higher than lower-bound miss rate for several of the graphs. However, these are lower than the miss rate of the Cortex-A15 system. While we are not able to show an upper-bound miss rate for the connected components algorithm, we are able to do so for the classic top-down algorithm for BFS. Those details can be found in our extended technical report [28].

5.3 The effects of misprediction

To get an idea of how strongly mispredictions influence performance, we show pairwise correlations among the *a priori* most likely predictors of execution time: instructions, loads, stores, and based on the subject of this paper, branches and branch mispredictions. Figure 7 shows this data for the branch-based versions of the algorithms. The 6×6 grid of subplots shows the correlations among time, instructions, branches, mispredictions, loads, and stores, measured per edge traversal. For example, (row 1, column 2) subplot in each half is a scatter plot comparing time ("T") on the y-axis with instructions ("I") on the x-axis. The points are color-coded by platform, on the subset of platforms that supported all necessary hardware performance counters. For each (R, C) plot in the upper-triangle, the computed correlation coefficients appear in the transposed (C, R) position of the lower-triangle.

In the case of SV, mispredictions more strongly correlate with time than instructions, branches, loads, and stores. Though not a strict proof-of-cause, this observation is nevertheless somewhat surprising, as it implies mispredictions may be nearly or even more important than memory behavior. By contrast, in the case of BFS (not shown), the correlations with stores and mispredictions is roughly equal, with stores being slightly more strongly correlated than time; refer to our technical report for details [28].

6. CONCLUSIONS

On the one hand, our study is a positive result for the branch-avoiding technique in the case of SV, where mispredictions are more strongly correlated to time than even memory traffic, much to our surprise. This raises the question of whether branch-avoidance might be important in other computations, and whether increased microarchitectural support for predicated instructions might have more significant benefits.

For BFS, our study did not show significant speedups for the branch avoiding algorithms [28]. Stores are as critical as branch mispredictions, so the tradeoff that reduces branches at the cost of significantly increasing stores cannot pay off. One question is why: although total stores increased by much as $100\times$, the actual slowdown was always $2\times$ or less. Indeed, the extra stores are purely "local" in that they should mostly hit in cache, by design of the implementation. Thus, there is a potential in the microarchitecture to address whatever resource constraints the additional stores impose, such as buffers for more outstanding operations. We will look into these in future work. We also hope to explore the impact of the branch predictor on additional graph building blocks.

An additional question is how compilers and programming languages could expose the choice between branch-based and branch-avoiding implementations to the programmer. Presently, programmers have no control over this aspect of code generation. In addition, the compilers we used relied on heuristics that, for our graph algorithms, we found to be sub-optimal and inconsistent across architectures. In our view, explicit control could elevate branch behavior from an implementation detail to a part of algorithm design and analysis.

Acknowledgments

We thank Anita Zakrzewska for useful discussions of this work. This material is based upon work supported by the U.S. National Science Foundation (NSF) Award Number 1339745, Award Number 1337177, and CAREER Award Number 0953100. Any opinions, findings and conclusions or recommendations expressed in this material are those of the authors and do not necessarily reflect those of NSF.

7. REFERENCES

[1] *GraphCT: A Graph Characterization Toolkit.*

[2] 10th dimacs implementation challenge - graph partitioning and graph clustering, 2013.

[3] R. Albert, H. Jeong, and A. Barabãasi. Internet: Diameter of the world-wide web. *Nature*, 401(6749):130–131, Sep 09 1999.

[4] D. A. Bader, J. Berry, A. Amos-Binks, D. Chavarría-Miranda, C. Hastings, K. Madduri, and S. C. Poulos. STINGER: Spatio-Temporal Interaction Networks and Graphs (STING) Extensible Representation. Technical report, Georgia Institute of Technology, 2009.

[5] D. A. Bader and K. Madduri. Designing multithreaded algorithms for breadth-first search and st-connectivity on the Cray MTA-2. In *Parallel Processing, 2006. ICPP 2006. International Conference on*, pages 523–530. IEEE, 2006.

[6] A.-L. Barabãasi and R. Albert. Emergence of scaling in random networks. *Science*, 286(5439):509–512, 1999.

[7] B. W. Barrett, J. W. Berry, R. C. Murphy, and K. B. Wheeler. Implementing a portable multi-threaded graph library: The MTGL on Qthreads. In *Parallel & Distributed Processing, 2009. IPDPS 2009. IEEE International Symposium on*, pages 1–8. IEEE, 2009.

[8] S. Beamer, K. Asanovic, and D. Patterson. Direction-optimizing breadth-first search. In *High Performance Computing, Networking, Storage and Analysis (SC), 2012 International Conference for*, pages 1–10. IEEE, 2012.

[9] S. Beamer, A. Buluç, K. Asanovic, and D. Patterson. Distributed memory breadth-first search revisited: Enabling bottom-up search. In *Proceedings of the 2013 IEEE 27th International Symposium on Parallel and Distributed Processing Workshops and PhD Forum*, pages 1618–1627. IEEE Computer Society, 2013.

[10] U. Brandes. A faster algorithm for betweenness centrality. *Journal of Mathematical Sociology*, 25(2):163–177, 2001.

[11] A. Broder, R. Kumar, F. Maghoul, P. Raghavan, S. Rajagopalan, R. Stata, A. Tomkins, and J. Wiener. Graph structure in the Web. *Computer Networks*, 33:309 – 320, 2000.

[12] A. Buluç and K. Madduri. Parallel breadth-first search on distributed memory systems. In *Proceedings of 2011 International Conference for High Performance Computing, Networking, Storage and Analysis*, page 65. ACM, 2011.

[13] A. BuluÃğ and J. R. Gilbert. The Combinatorial BLAS: design, implementation, and applications. *International Journal of High Performance Computing Applications*, 25(4):496–509, 2011.

[14] M. Burtscher, R. Nasre, and K. Pingali. A quantitative study of irregular programs on GPUs. In *Workload Characterization (IISWC), 2012 IEEE International Symposium on*, pages 141–151. IEEE, 2012.

[15] F. Checconi, F. Petrini, J. Willcock, A. Lumsdaine, A. R. Choudhury, and Y. Sabharwal. Breaking the speed and scalability barriers for graph exploration on distributed-memory machines. In *High Performance Computing, Networking, Storage and Analysis (SC), 2012 International Conference for*, pages 1–12. IEEE, 2012.

[16] J. Chhugani, N. Satish, C. Kim, J. Sewall, and P. Dubey. Fast and efficient graph traversal algorithm for CPUs: Maximizing single-node efficiency. In *Parallel & Distributed Processing Symposium (IPDPS), 2012 IEEE 26th International*, pages 378–389. IEEE, 2012.

[17] G. Cong and K. Makarychev. Optimizing large-scale graph analysis on multithreaded, multicore platforms. In *Parallel & Distributed Processing Symposium (IPDPS), 2012 IEEE 26th International*, pages 414–425. IEEE, 2012.

[18] T. H. Cormen, C. E. Leiserson, R. L. Rivest, and C. Stein. *Introduction to Algorithms*. The MIT Press, New York, 2001.

[19] M. Dukhan. PeachPy: A python framework for developing high-performance assembly kernels, PyHPC 2013.

[20] A. N. Eden and T. Mudge. The YAGS branch prediction scheme. In *Proceedings of the 31st annual ACM/IEEE international symposium on Microarchitecture*, pages 69–77. IEEE Computer Society Press, 1998.

[21] D. Ediger, K. Jiang, J. Riedy, and D. Bader. Graphct: Multithreaded algorithms for massive graph analysis. *Parallel and Distributed Systems, IEEE Transactions on*, PP(99):1–1, 2012.

[22] D. Ediger, R. McColl, J. Riedy, and D. Bader. Stinger: High performance data structure for streaming graphs. In *Proc. High Performace Embedded Computing Workshop (HPEC 2012)*, Waltham, MA, Sept. 2012.

[23] M. Faloutsos, P. Faloutsos, and C. Faloutsos. On Power-Law Relationships of The Internet Topology. In *ACM SIGCOMM Computer Communication Review*, pages 251–262. ACM, 1999.

[24] R. W. Floyd. Algorithm 97: Shortest path. *Commun. ACM*, 5:345–345, June 1962.

[25] A. Fog. The microarchitecture of Intel, AMD and VIA CPUs. *An optimization guide for assembly programmers and compiler makers. Copenhagen University College of Engineering*, 2013.

[26] L. C. Freeman. A set of measures of centrality based on betweenness. *Sociometry*, 40(1):pp. 35–41, 1977.

[27] O. Green. When merging and branch predictors collide. In *Proceedings of the Fourth Workshop on Irregular Applications: Architectures and Algorithms*, pages 33–40. IEEE Press, 2014.

[28] O. Green, M. Dukhan, and R. W. Vuduc. Branch-avoiding graph algorithms. *CoRR*, abs/1411.1460, 2014.

[29] O. Green, R. McColl, and D. A. Bader. A Fast Algorithm For Streaming Betweenness Centrality. In *Proceedings of the 4th ASE/IEEE International Conference on Social Computing*, SocialCom '12, 2012.

[30] D. Gregor and A. Lumsdaine. The parallel BGL: A generic library for distributed graph computations. *Parallel Object-Oriented Scientific Computing (POOSC)*, page 2, 2005.

[31] S. Hong, H. Chafi, E. Sedlar, and K. Olukotun. Green-Marl: a DSL for easy and efficient graph analysis. In *ACM SIGARCH Computer Architecture News*, volume 40, pages 349–362. ACM, 2012.

[32] J. Hopcroft and R. Tarjan. Algorithm 447: efficient algorithms for graph manipulation. *Commun. ACM*, 16(6):372–378, June 1973.

[33] G. Karypis and V. Kumar. Metis-unstructured graph partitioning and sparse matrix ordering system, version 2.0. 1995.

[34] C.-C. Lee, I.-C. Chen, and T. N. Mudge. The bi-mode branch predictor. In *Microarchitecture, 1997. Proceedings., Thirtieth Annual IEEE/ACM International Symposium on*, pages 4–13. IEEE, 1997.

[35] J. K. Lee and A. J. Smith. Branch prediction strategies and branch target buffer design. *Computer*, 17(1):6–22, 1984.

[36] J. Leskovec, J. Kleinberg, and C. Faloutsos. Graph evolution: Densification and shrinking diameters. *ACM Trans. Knowl. Discov. Data*, 1(1), 2007.

[37] G. Malewicz, M. H. Austern, A. J. Bik, J. C. Dehnert, I. Horn, N. Leiser, and G. Czajkowski. Pregel: a system for large-scale graph processing. In *Proceedings of the 2010 ACM SIGMOD International Conference on Management of data*, pages 135–146. ACM, 2010.

[38] R. McColl, O. Green, and D. Bader. Parallel streaming connected components using "parent-neighbor" subgraphs. In *IEEE International Conference on High Performance Computing*, 2013.

[39] D. Merrill, M. Garland, and A. Grimshaw. Scalable gpu graph traversal. In *ACM SIGPLAN symposium on Principles and Practice of Parallel Programming*, PPoPP '12, pages 117–128, New York, NY, USA, 2012. ACM.

[40] M. Milenkovic, A. Milenkovic, and J. Kulick. Demystifying intel branch predictors. In *Workshop on Duplicating, Deconstructing and Debunking*, 2002.

[41] S. Milgram. The Small World Problem. *Psychology Today*, 2(1):60–67, 1967.

[42] M. Newman and M. Girvan. Finding and evaluating community structure in networks. *Physical review E*, 69(2):026113, 2004.

[43] E. J. Riedy, H. Meyerhenke, D. Ediger, and D. A. Bader. Parallel community detection for massive graphs. In *Parallel Processing and Applied Mathematics*, pages 286–296. Springer, 2012.

[44] G. Sabidussi. The centrality index of a graph. *Psychometrika*, 31(4):581–603, 1966.

[45] Y. Shiloach and S. Even. An on-line edge-deletion problem. *J. ACM*, 28:1–4, January 1981.

[46] Y. Shiloach and U. Vishkin. An O(logn) parallel connectivity algorithm. *Journal of Algorithms*, 3(1):57 – 67, 1982.

[47] J. Shun and G. E. Blelloch. Ligra: a lightweight graph processing framework for shared memory. In *Proceedings of the 18th ACM SIGPLAN symposium on Principles and practice of parallel programming*, pages 135–146. ACM, 2013.

[48] J. E. Smith. A study of branch prediction strategies. In *Proceedings of the 8th annual symposium on Computer Architecture*, pages 135–148. IEEE Computer Society Press, 1981.

[49] E. Sprangle, R. S. Chappell, M. Alsup, and Y. N. Patt. The agree predictor: A mechanism for reducing negative branch history interference. In *ACM SIGARCH Computer Architecture News*, volume 25, pages 284–291. ACM, 1997.

[50] S. Warshall. A theorem on boolean matrices. *J. ACM*, 9:11–12, Jan. 1962.

[51] D. J. Watts and S. H. Strogatz. Collective Dynamics of "Small-World" Networks. *Nature*, 393(6684):440–442, 1998.

[52] T.-Y. Yeh and Y. N. Patt. Two-level adaptive training branch prediction. In *Proceedings of the 24th annual international symposium on Microarchitecture*, pages 51–61. ACM, 1991.

[53] T.-Y. Yeh and Y. N. Patt. Alternative implementations of two-level adaptive branch prediction. In *ACM SIGARCH Computer Architecture News*, volume 20, pages 124–134. ACM, 1992.

[54] A. Yoo, E. Chow, K. Henderson, W. McLendon, B. Hendrickson, and U. Catalyurek. A scalable distributed parallel breadth-first search algorithm on BlueGene/L. In *Supercomputing, 2005. Proceedings of the ACM/IEEE SC 2005 Conference*, pages 25–25. IEEE, 2005.

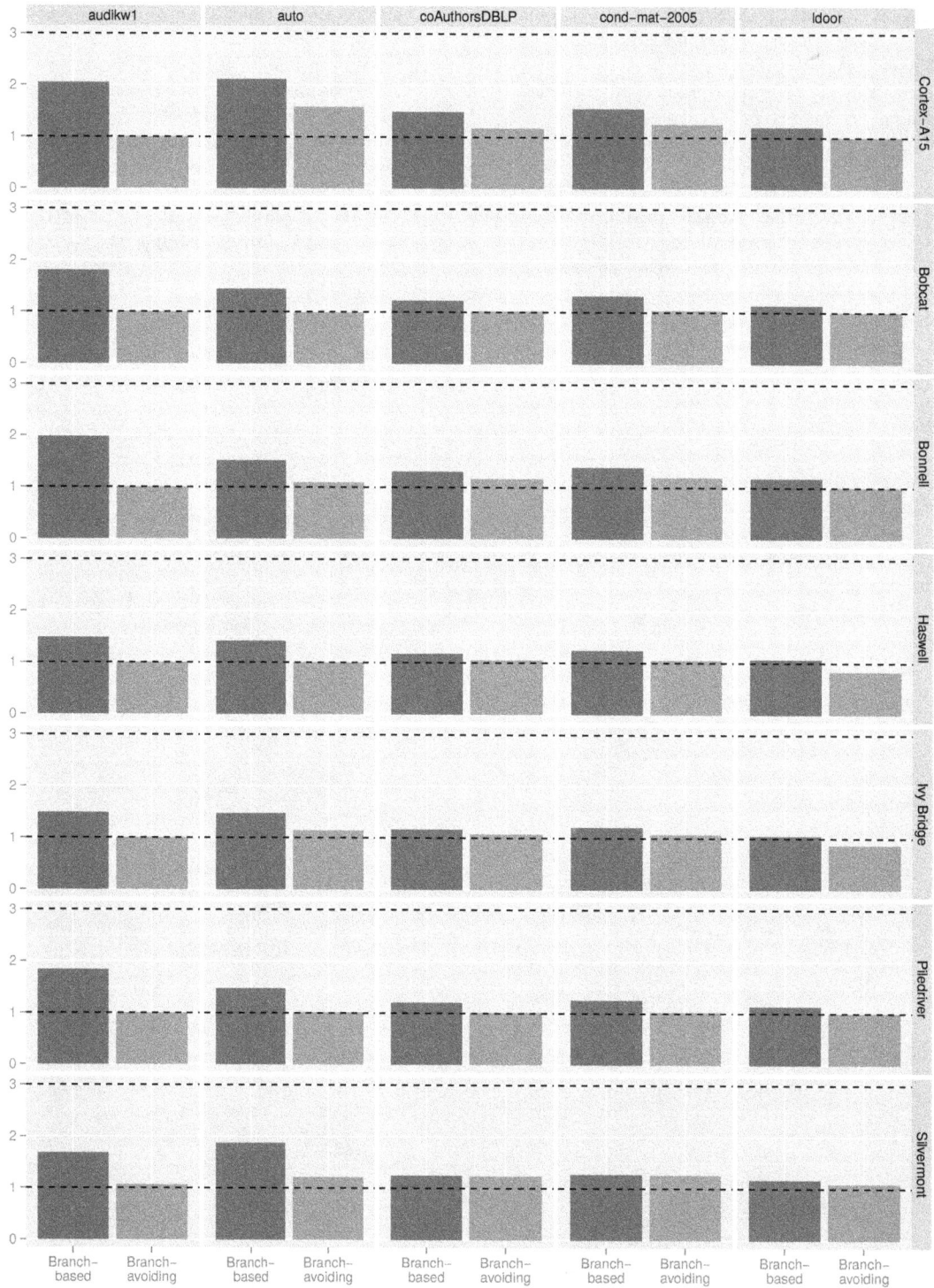

Shiloach–Vishkin Connected Components Branch Mispredictions
(relative to lower–bound, at y=1)

Figure 6: Lower bounds on the number of branch mispredictions for SV, based on the model of § 4. The bars for each algorithm show the ratio of branch mispredictions over the lower bound.

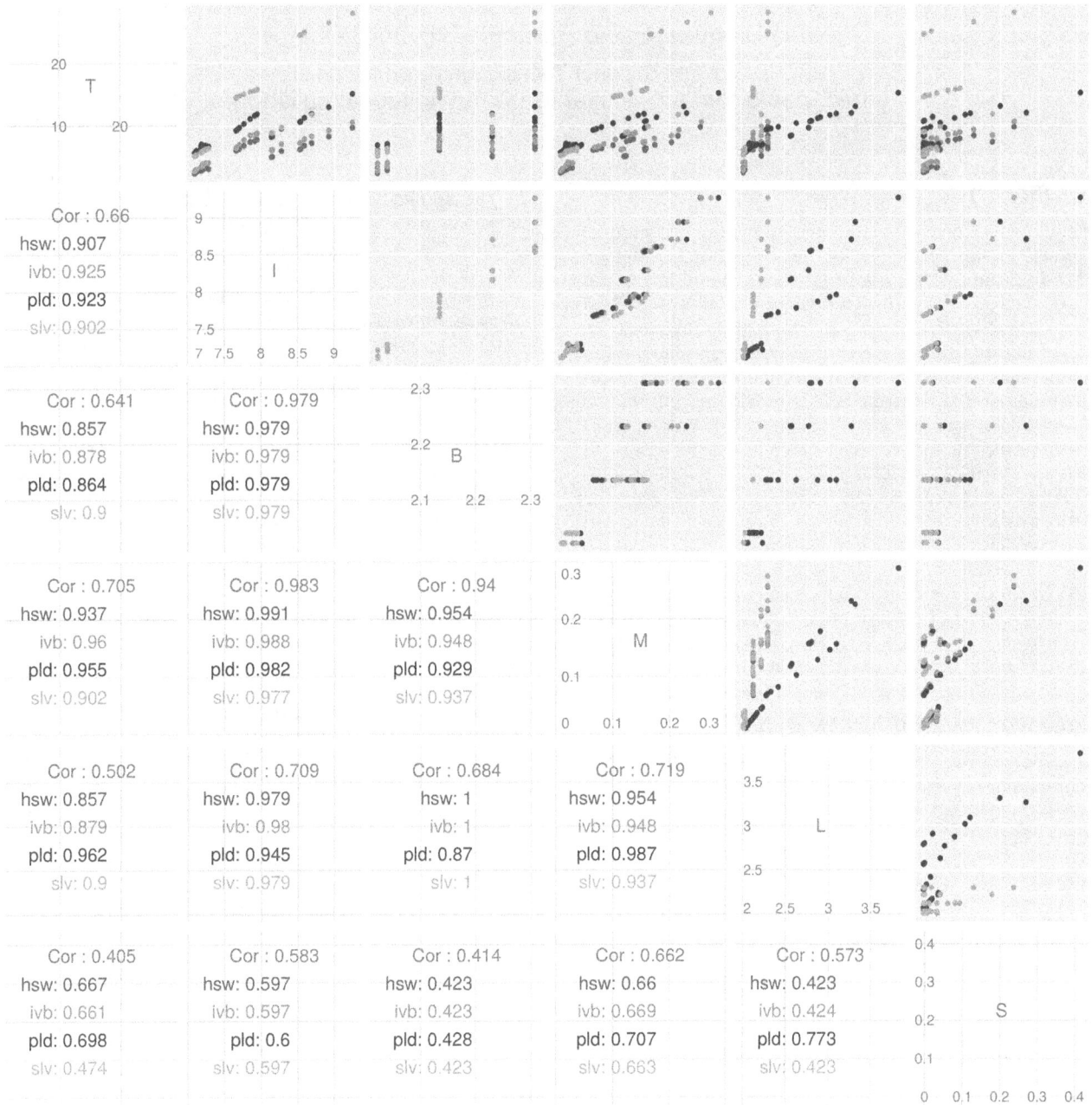

Figure 7: Correlations among time (T), instructions (I), branches (B), mispredictions (M), load operations (L), and store operations (S) per edge, both for (a) SV, and (b) BFS. Each sample is a different iteration/level for one of the graph.

Seer: Probabilistic Scheduling for Hardware Transactional Memory

Nuno Diegues, Paolo Romano, Stoyan Garbatov

INESC-ID, Instituto Superior Técnico, Universidade de Lisboa
{nmld, paolo.romano, stoyan.garbatov}@tecnico.ulisboa.pt

ABSTRACT

Scheduling concurrent transactions to minimize contention is a well known technique in the Transactional Memory (TM) literature, which was largely investigated in the context of software TMs. However, the recent advent of Hardware Transactional Memory (HTM), and its inherently restricted nature, pose new technical challenges that prevent the adoption of existing schedulers: unlike software implementations of TM, existing HTMs provide no information on which data item or contending transaction caused abort.

We propose SEER, a scheduler that addresses precisely this restriction of HTM by leveraging on an on-line probabilistic inference technique that identifies the most likely conflict relations, and establishes a dynamic locking scheme to serialize transactions in a fine-grained manner. Our evaluation shows that SEER improves the performance of the Intel TSX HTM by up to 2.5×, and by 62% on average, in TM benchmarks with 8 threads. These performance gains are not only a consequence of the reduced aborts, but also of the reduced activation of the HTM's pessimistic fall-back path.

Categories and Subject Descriptors

D.1.3 [**Software**]: Programming Techniques - Concurrent Programming

Keywords

Hardware Transactional Memory; Best-Effort; Scheduling

1. INTRODUCTION

Context. Transactional Memory (TM) [16] emerged over the last decade as an attractive alternative to lock-based synchronization. Contrarily to lock-based approaches, in which programmers identify shared data and specify how to synchronize concurrent accesses to it, the TM paradigm requires only to identify which portions of the code have to execute atomically, and not *how* atomicity should be achieved.

The simplicity and potential of TM has motivated many advances in software prototypes (STMs both in shared memory, e.g. [14, 12, 7, 9] and distributed systems, e.g. [17, 22]) as well as in hardware. Our focus is on Hardware implementations of Transactional Memory (HTM), which have recently entered the realm of mainstream computing since Intel shipped its first HTM — Transactional Synchronization Extensions (TSX) [27] — in its commodity processors.

Problem. Due to the speculative nature of TM, transactions are likely to be restarted and aborted multiple times in conflict prone workloads. This has motivated a large body of research on scheduling techniques, whose key idea is to serialize the execution of transactions that are known to generate frequent aborts. However, most of existing scheduling techniques were designed to operate with software implementations of TM (STM), and rely on specific support provided by the STM to gather knowledge on the conflicts that occurred between transactions. Typically, upon a transaction abort, the STM library can report back to the scheduler which specific memory access and concurrent transaction dictated the abort. This is illustrated in Figure 1, where we depict transaction T_1 aborting due to a read-write conflict with a concurrent transaction T_2. An STM library is able to report this precise information back to a TM scheduler.

With the adoption of HTMs such as Intel TSX, however, we lose much of this ability. When a hardware transaction is aborted, the feedback is limited and insufficient to pinpoint which transaction caused the abort. As shown in [10], and exemplified in Figure 1, these HTMs merely distinguish between a conflict and other abort causes (e.g., exceeding hardware buffers). For this reason, schedulers for STMs

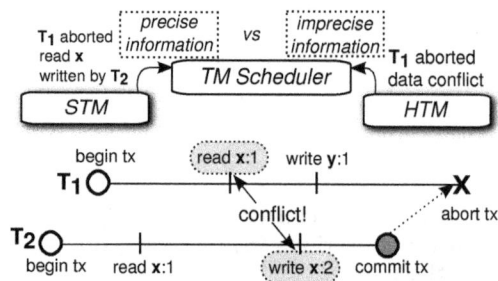

Figure 1: Two transactions causing a conflict. The information returned by the TM varies depending on its nature: STMs are able to precisely identify the source of the abort, whereas commodity HTMs provide only a coarse categorization of the abort.

fall short because they rely on precise information, whereas HTMs are only capable of providing *imprecise information.*

Contributions. In this work we introduce SEER, the first scheduler (to the best of our knowledge) to address the HTM restrictions discussed above. The key idea of our proposal is to gather statistics to detect, in a lightweight but possibly imprecise way, the set of concurrently active transactions upon abort and commit events. This information is used as input for an on-line inference technique that uses probabilistic arguments to identify conflict patterns between different atomic blocks of the program in a reliable way, despite the imprecise nature of the input statistics. The final step consists in exploiting probabilistic knowledge on the existence of conflict relations to synthesize a fine-grained, dynamic (i.e., possibly varying over time) locking scheme that serializes "sufficiently" conflict-prone transactions.

A noteworthy feature of SEER is that it relies on reinforcement learning techniques to self-tune the parameters of the probabilistic inference model. To this end, SEER relies on a stochastic hill-climbing technique that explores the configuration space of the model's parameter, while gathering feedback at run-time about the application running and accordingly adjusting the granularity of the locking scheme. Indeed, an appealing characteristic of this dynamically inferred locking scheme is that it does not need to be perfect (e.g., it can suffer of false negatives) in capturing conflicts between atomic blocks of the application, since correctness for transactions is still enforced by the underlying HTM.

SEER includes also an additional novel mechanism that is designed to address another performance pathology of existing HTM systems: when multiple hardware threads are concurrently active on the same physical core, the likelihood of incurring in aborts due to capacity exceptions can grow to such an extent that it cripples performance. This is a direct consequence of the fact that the information used by the HTM concurrency control algorithm is entirely stored in the CPU caches, which may be shared by hardware threads running on the same core. SEER copes with this issue by introducing a simple, yet effective abstraction, the *core lock*, which serializes the execution of hardware threads that share the same core when capacity exceptions are detected.

Besides reducing aborts due to conflicts on data items, SEER achieves also a drastic reduction of the frequency of activation of the pessimistic software fall-back path of the HTM system. In fact, in order to ensure the eventual success of transactions that may fail deterministically using HTM, after a limited number of attempts using hardware transactions, transactions are executed pessimistically using a fall-back path that uses a software-based synchronization mechanism — typically, a single-global lock [27, 18]. By reducing the number of retries necessary to commit a transaction, our proposal also contributes to reducing the frequency of activation of the software fall-back, whose sequential nature is known to hamper HTM performance [27, 18, 15]. Overall, our experimental study shows that, by applying SEER to standard TM benchmarks, one can obtain gains up to 2.5× and average speed-ups of 62% at 8 threads.

This paper is organized as follows. Section 2 surveys the state of the art in TM schedulers and identifies the key factors that make our proposal novel. Then, in Section 3, we provide an overview of our solution. We present the details of our SEER implementation in Section 4. Finally, we evaluate our proposal in Section 5 and conclude in Section 6.

2. RELATED WORK

Roughly speaking, the objective of a TM scheduler is to decide when it is best to execute a transaction, possibly deciding to serialize concurrent transactions based on their likelihood of contending with each other, with the ultimate goal of maximizing performance (typically throughput).

Most of the existing schedulers target STM systems, which are assumed to be able to provide precise information on the conflicts that caused the abort of a transaction. This is the case for CAR-STM [11] and Steal-On-Abort [3], where there are N serialization queues (one for each thread), and an aborting transaction T_i is placed in the queue of T_j that caused its abort. The idea is that T_i is serialized after T_j because it shall be executed by the thread currently running T_j, with which it conflicted. Both these schedulers were proposed in the scope of STMs, which were extended to obtain the required precise information on aborts.

Steal-On-Abort, although initially implemented in software, was later also proposed for an HTM simulator [2]. However, this work assumed hardware extensions to support enqueuing the serialized transactions in each core of the processor. The current expectation is that manufacturers, such as Intel and IBM, will be quite resistant to changes in the hardware due to its complexity [18]. Hence, it is particularly relevant to devise a scheduling solution for *current* HTMs: one that operates in absence of accurate information on the conflict patterns among transactions, like SEER does.

More recently, ProPS [24] followed a similar approach to the ones above but, instead, focused on long running transactions: each abort event is used to accumulate a contention probability between every pair of transaction types (i.e., atomic blocks); whenever a transaction T is about to start, it may have to wait in case there is an atomic block being executed in a concurrent transaction that is expected to conflict with T with high probability. This approach also requires precise information to guide the scheduling decision, which is not the case for HTMs such as Intel's TSX. Shrink [13] acts in a similar way to ProPS, but it is additionally fed with past history of transactions' read- and write-sets: assuming there is some data accesses locality between transactions' restarts, the scheduler uses this information to predict conflicts that would happen if the transaction were allowed to run against current concurrent transactions. Such fine-grained information is not available in HTMs, and could only be made available via additional software instrumentation, yielding considerable overheads.

TxLinux [25] and SER [19] both changed the Linux scheduler to be transaction-aware, the difference being that the former was integrated in a simulated HTM called MetaTM and the latter was fully in software. Similarly to the other works, these proposals also require precise information.

Contrarily the schedulers above, ATS [26] is the only solution that works with imprecise information, i.e., coping with the lack of knowledge on which pairs of transactions conflict during their execution. ATS maintains a contention factor in each thread, updated when transactions abort and commit, such that a single lock is acquired when contention exceeds a specified threshold. This simple approach is agnostic of the atomic blocks being executed, as the whole problem is subsumed by a single contention factor. The positive side is that it works with currently available HTMs. In fact, this is the *de facto* technique used with commodity HTMs due to their best-effort nature: because no transaction is guar-

Scheduler	SW	HW	Imprecise Information	Fine-Grained
ATS [26]	✓	✓	✓	χ
CAR-STM [11]	✓	χ	χ	✓
Shrink [13]	✓	χ	χ	✓
ProPS [24]	✓	χ	χ	✓
SER [19]	✓	χ	χ	✓
TxLinux [25]	χ	✓	χ	✓
SOA [3, 2]	✓	✓	χ	✓
Seer	χ	✔	✔	✔

Table 1: Comparison of TM schedulers in terms of: regulating an STM and/or HTM, working without precise information on which transaction caused the abort, and whether it uses multiple fine-grained locks to schedule transactions' execution. Seer, our proposal, is the only scheduler that provides all the following properties: 1) works with HTM; 2) does not require precise feedback on aborts; and 3) and adopts a fine-grained serialization mechanism.

anteed to commit, a software fall-back must be provided to ensure progress; the single lock fall-back that is typically used [27, 18, 20, 15] is, in essence, akin to ATS. Since ATS relies on a single contention factor and one lock for serialization, it alternates between serializing all transactions or letting them all execute concurrently; hence, that is why we characterize it as a a coarse-grained scheduler.

We summarize the above state of the art in Table 1. We can see that our contribution SEER is unique by being applicable to commodity HTMs (i.e., it works with imprecise input) and allowing to serialize multiple transactions concurrently in a fine-grained manner (i.e., it does not have a single lock for serialization, as ATS does).

Finally, recent works [8, 4] have investigated the use of online profiling and optimization techniques in a similar spirit to what SEER does, but for a different, complementary purpose: decide the best software fall-back and retry policies.

3. OVERVIEW OF THE SOLUTION

Schedulers for TM systems, independently of their software or hardware nature, benefit particularly from the availability of fine-grained precise information about what causes the abort of a transaction. This means that if we are running a transaction for an atomic block of our program, and we know that it aborted due to a concurrent transaction executing another specific atomic block, then it is best to schedule them in a way that prevents their concurrent execution.

Having access to such information is typically trivial in STMs. However, mainstream HTMs provide little to no feedback with respect to this matter. In particular for Intel TSX (and also for IBM's HTMs), upon the abort of a hardware transaction, it is possible to know only a rough categorization: for instance, whether it was a data conflict; or whether the space available for the read- or write-set buffers in the hardware caches was exhausted; or whether there was an interrupt that caused a context switch or a ring transition. As such, no information is given about which transaction was the cause for the abort. This is the challenge that prevents existing schedulers from being effectively applicable to existing HTMs.

The high level idea of our solution is to take a probabilistic approach. While we do not know what exactly causes a transaction T_i to abort, because the HTM provides no such information, we can try to infer the answer by observing enough times which transactions were active when T_i aborted. By repeating this observation over time, we can gather probabilistic knowledge on the likelihood of conflicts between pairs of transactions. This knowledge can then be exploited to decide, when a transaction starts, whether to schedule it or not depending on the conflict probabilities with the currently active transactions.

The probabilistic inference mechanism of SEER is based on three key ideas: (1) we continuously collect on-line information about the transactions concurrently active upon commit and abort events, by means of a lightweight, synchronization-free monitoring mechanism; (2) we periodically analyze this information and estimate probabilities of aborting/committing in the presence of other specific transactions; and (3) this information is used to periodically devise a fine-grained locking-scheme, whose locks are acquired upon the start of a transaction and allow for serializing the execution of conflict prone-pairs of transactions (without blocking other transactions not likely to incur any conflict).

Figure 2 portrays the life-cycle of transactions within our scheduler. The objective of this life-cycle is to populate a global table that reifies the automatically inferred locking scheme. SEER uses one lock for each transaction in the target application (identified in the columns). Each row i of the table specifies the locks that transaction T_i should acquire, indicating that T_i conflicts often with the transactions associated with these locks, and that these transactions should not be executed concurrently. We associate each atomic block in the application source code to a different transaction T_i: this way, we seek to serialize transactions with a fine granularity, contrarily to other approaches that work with HTM and that use a single lock for serialization [26].

To understand how to reach that objective, we begin by describing the life-cycle of SEER. In step ①, a transaction T_3 is about to be executed on core C_1. Before doing so, it acquires the locks defined by SEER in a global table: in this case, lock L_1. Then, it announces that C_1 is executing T_3 in the list of active transactions in step ②. Step ⑦ shows that transactions are removed from that list when they are finished.

By acquiring lock L_1 in the lock table, this means that transaction T_3 was deemed to contend with T_1. Although instances of T_1 do not acquire lock L_1, because they do not contend with 'themselves', they do co-operate with contending transactions (such as T_2 and T_3) by waiting for their completion, before starting executing, if lock L_1 is found to be taken. In general:

1. A transaction T_x **waits** for its lock L_x to be free before proceeding, which serves to respect our scheduling policy.
2. It **locks** L_y if it contends with T_y (we allow $x = y$, in which case T_x contends with instances of itself).

We are left with describing how the locking scheme is generated. Step ③ illustrates that, upon a commit or abort of a transaction T_n running on core C_n, the active transactions list is scanned and the transactions found there are incremented in two per-thread matrices, namely commitStats and abortStats, which are stored as thread-local variables (step ④). An entry x, y in commitStats (resp. abortStats) tracks

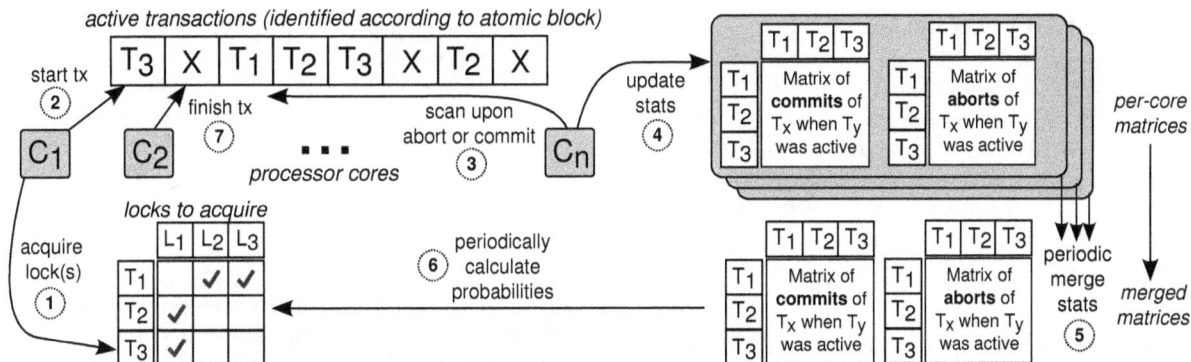

Figure 2: Overview of Seer. The idea is to assess the probability of conflicts between transactions, without requiring precise information by the HTM. To do so, transactions are announced right before they are executed on a given core, and then this information is scanned upon commits and aborts, to compensate for the lack of feedback from the HTM. While not totally accurate, this information allows to probabilistically infer the relevant conflict patterns among transactions over time, and then to produce a dynamic locking scheme that serves to schedule transactions (by preventing some transactions from running concurrently).

the frequency of commit (resp. abort) events for transaction T_x, in which T_y was found to be running (in the active transactions list), after the commit (resp. abort) of T_x. Consider for instance that T_1 only conflicts often with T_3. Such fact is unknown beforehand and our approach aims to infer it in run-time: as we gather statistics, over time, recurrent events emerge and become identifiable using probabilistic inference.

Periodically, these statistics are merged, across all per-core's matrices, into two global matrices in step (5). These are used to calculate and update the locking scheme to reduce aborts of transactions. The intuition is to use the information about how often T_x committed and aborted in the presence of each different transaction. The challenge in doing so is to identify, among all captured conflicts, which ones occur frequently enough to benefit from throttling down concurrency. The ability to extract these decisions using solely the imprecise information provided by commodity HTMs is what makes SEER novel with respect to other schedulers.

As a result, we are able to periodically generate a dynamic locking scheme, as depicted in step (6). As explained above, these locks are used to serialize transactions with

a fine granularity. This is a key feature that allows SEER to yield substantial performance improvements as we later show in Section 5. Another noteworthy feature of SEER is that it works in a completely transparent fashion to the programmer. We require only minimalist compiler support, by enumerating the atomic blocks in the program, and passing their unique identifier (one per source code atomic block) into the TM library calls. The scheduler itself is implemented in the TM library that regulates the software fallback management. Further, SEER fully automates the tuning of internal parameters in the probabilistic inference, via a self-optimization mechanism that is driven by the feedback gathered at run-time on the throughput of the TM system.

Finally, SEER introduces the abstraction of *core locks*, i.e., locks that prevent the concurrent execution of multiple hardware threads on the same physical core. The idea of core locks is based on the observation that, in workloads characterized by frequent transactions with non-minimal memory footprints, the likelihood of capacity aborts in the HTM is exacerbated when multiple threads are allowed to execute freely, as they contend for the shared caches of the core.

Variable	Description
thread	Per-thread structure to hold metadata during the execution of a transaction.
sgl	Single-global lock used in the software fall-back path of the HTM.
activeTxs	Global array where threads announce the transactions they are executing.
commitStats	Global matrix where, each line for transaction T_i, reports the transactions that were concurrently running whenever T_i committed. This matrix is periodically built by summing the per-core equivalent matrices kept in each thread variable.
abortStats	Similar to commitStats, but for abort statistics.
executions	Array with total number of executions (commits and aborts) of each transaction.
locksToAcquire	Global matrix where each line corresponds to a transaction and the columns define the locks that should be acquired for the transaction according to SEER.
txLocks	Global array of locks, one per transaction (i.e., atomic block) of the program.
coreLocks	Global array of locks, one per core of the processor.

Table 2: Characterization of the data-structures used in Seer. Some of these are visible in the high-level overview in Figure 2, whereas the rest is used in Algorithms 1-5.

4. DETAILED ALGORITHM

We now present the detailed description of SEER. We report the data-structures used by SEER in Table 2, most of which were already presented in the overview.

Conventional HTM usage. We start by describing the basic software mechanisms that govern HTM transactions and the fall-back path, in which SEER is implanted. We highlight lines associated with the conventional HTM mechanisms with a △ (other lines belong to SEER). We begin with the START procedure, in Alg. 1, where a transaction *txId* is initiated by a given *thread*.

The START procedure implements a retry loop to try to execute a hardware transaction, up to some threshold (`MAX_ATTEMPTS`), resorting to a fall-back path in case the threshold is reached (in line 20). Note that the function to begin a hardware transaction, *_xbegin()* (in line 9), returns a status that normally represents that the transaction has started, i.e., the predicate in line 10 evaluates to true. Otherwise, this status indicates a coarse categorization of the abort. Note that an aborted hardware transaction transparently jumps back, and returns from this function, akin to the *setjmp/longjmp* mechanism used in C/C++.

Seer Algorithm. We now discuss the various mechanisms that augment this conventional procedure: i) transactions are announced to other cores (see line 5), ii) aborts are registered in the per-core statistics (see line 16), and iii) locks are used to induce fine-grained serialization between contending transactions (see lines 8 and 23). We present each part next.

The END procedure is presented in Alg. 2 where we finish the hardware transaction, or release the global lock, depending on the path taken in START. In case the transaction was successfully committed via a hardware transaction, we add this information to our per-core statistics in line 28, and possibly release locks acquired by our scheduler in line 29. Finally, we remove the transaction from the activeTxs list.

The procedures for registering aborts and commits are shown in Alg. 3. The idea is to scan the activeTxs list and to increase the frequency of the transactions found there, in the row corresponding to the transaction that has aborted/committed (identified by txId). This is the mechanism that we use to infer information about conflicts, and to compensate for the lack of feedback from the HTM about the pairs of conflicting transactions. In general, this collection of statistics may not be completely accurate, and could suffer of both false positives and false negatives. SEER copes with this uncertainty using probabilistic inference techniques, whose details we shall discuss shortly.

Notice that the aforementioned statistics are maintained per-core, i.e., in a private fashion. Furthermore, the activeTxs list ends up being a set of single-writer multi-reader registers; we do not place any synchronization when accessing the list, with the intent of keeping it lightweight.

The procedures for lock management, according to our scheduler, are defined in Alg. 4. We use two types of locks:

1. **txLocks:** one per transaction of the application, to serialize contending transactions according to the probabilities (line 48) that we describe later (in Alg. 5). Our scheduler may dictate that a transaction acquires some of these locks only when the transaction has spent most of its attempts in hardware transactions — it has one left — as a last resort measure to obtain progress before triggering the global lock in the fall-back.

2. **coreLocks:** one per physical core of the processor, to reduce capacity aborts, which are amplified due to hardware threads that share the private caches of a physical core. These caches are small and limit the size of hardware transactions, more so if shared among several. Hence, we acquire the coreLock when a capacity abort is detected (line 45).

Furthermore, we also introduce a contention avoidance technique, which imposes waiting before starting a transac-

---

Algorithm 1 SEER algorithm.

1: **START(thread, txId)**
2:   thread.core ← current-core() ▷ *thread is bound to core*
3:   thread.acquiredTxLocks ← false
4:   thread.acquiredCoreLock ← false
5:   activeTxs[thread.core] ← txId
6△:   attempts ← MAX_ATTEMPTS
7△:   *begin:* ▷ *used to jump to and re-attempt with HTM*
8:   WAIT-SEER-LOCKS(thread, txId)
9△:   htmStatus ← *_xbegin()*
10△:   **if** htmStatus = _XBEGIN_STARTED
11△:   **if** is-locked(sgl) ▷ *ensure correctness with fall-back*
12△:   *_xabort()*
13△:   **else**
14△:   **return** ▷ *hw transaction enabled, proceed to tx*
15△:   ▷ *hw transaction aborted, handle before restarting*
16:   REGISTER-ABORT(thread, txId)
17△:   attempts ← attempts - 1
18△:   **if** attempts = 0 ▷ *give up on HTM, fall-back to lock*
19:     RELEASE-SEER-LOCKS(thread, txId)
20△:   acquire-lock(sgl) ▷ *SW fall-back with a single lock*
21△:   **return** ▷ *SW fall-back path taken, proceed to tx*
22△:   ▷ *before re-attempting, trigger our scheduler* SEER
23:   ACQUIRE-SEER-LOCKS(thread, txId, htmStatus)
24△:   **goto** *begin*

Algorithm 2 SEER algorithm.

25: **END(thread, txId)**
26△:   **if** _xtest() ▷ *returns true if inside a HW transaction*
27△:   _xend() ▷ *tries to commit the HW transaction*
28:     REGISTER-COMMIT(thread, txId)
29:     RELEASE-SEER-LOCKS(thread, txId)
30△:   **else**
31△:   release-lock(sgl) ▷ *executed with lock-based fall-back*
32:   activeTxs[thread.core] ← ⊥

Algorithm 3 SEER algorithm.

33: **REGISTER-ABORT(thread, txId)**
34:   thread.executions[txId]++
35:   **for all** i = 0 **until** activeTxs.length
36:     **if** i ≠ thread.core ∧ activeTxs[i] ≠ ⊥
37:       thread.abortStats[txId][activeTxs[i]]++

38: **REGISTER-COMMIT(thread, txId)**
39:   thread.executions[txId]++
40:   **for all** i = 0 **until** activeTxs.length
41:     **if** i ≠ thread.core ∧ activeTxs[i] ≠ ⊥
42:       thread.commitStats[txId][activeTxs[i]]++

Algorithm 4 SEER algorithm.

43: **ACQUIRE-**SEER**-LOCKS(thread, txId, htmStatus)**
44:   **if** htmStatus & `_XABORT_CAPACITY` $\wedge$ ¬thread.acquiredCoreLock
45:     acquire-lock(coreLocks[thread.core % `PHYSICAL_CORES`]) ▷ *adapted to the topology of hyper-threads in Intel processors*
46:     thread.acquiredCoreLock $\leftarrow$ true
47:   **if** attempts = 1
48:     ACQUIRE-TX-LOCKS(txId)   ▷ *acquire locks specified in row locksToAcquire[txId]*
49:     thread.acquiredTxLocks $\leftarrow$ true

50: **WAIT-**SEER**-LOCKS(thread, txId)**
51:   **if** is-locked(sgl)   ▷ *avoid starting hardware transactions if the fall-back is in use*
52:     **if** thread.core = 0   ▷ *only one thread updates the serialization locks*
53:     UPDATE-SEER-LOCKS()   ▷ *exploit the wait time to run* SEER
54:       **if** *enough-samples()* **then** *stochastic-hill-climbing*($\mathcal{T}h_1$, $\mathcal{T}h_2$)   ▷ *periodically adapt the parameters used in Alg 5*
55:     **wait while** is-locked(sgl)   ▷ *wait here instead of aborting in line 12*
56:   ▷ *if some other thread is owning these* SEER *locks, cooperate with it and wait*
57:   **wait while** ¬thread.acquiredTxLocks $\wedge$ is-locked(txLocks[txId])
58:   **wait while** ¬thread.acquiredCoreLock $\wedge$ is-locked(coreLocks[thread.core])

59: **RELEASE-**SEER**-LOCKS(thread, txId)**
60:   **if** thread.acquiredTxLocks
61:     RELEASE-TX-LOCKS(txId)
62:   **if** thread.acquiredCoreLock
63:     release-lock(coreLocks[thread.core])

Algorithm 5 SEER algorithm.

65: **UPDATE-**SEER**-LOCKS()**
66:   **for all** x $\in$ A   ▷ *A is the set of txs in the application source code*
67:     $\eta \leftarrow$ avg$\left(\{P(x \text{ aborts } | x\|y), \forall y \in A\}\right)$
68:     $\sigma^2 \leftarrow$ var$\left(\{P(x \text{ aborts } | x\|y), \forall y \in A\}\right)$
69:     **for all** y $\in$ A   ▷ *determine if y is likely to contend with x*
70:       ▷ 1st *condition checks whether abort events of x, in which y is seen running concurrently, are common enough*
71:       ▷ 2nd *condition checks if y is among the txs that, when executed concurrently with x, most likely contend with x*
72:       **if** (P(x aborts $\cap$ x$\|$y) $> \mathcal{T}h_1 \wedge$ P(x aborts $| $ x$\|$y)$> \mathcal{T}h_2$-th percentile of a Gaussian $\mathcal{N}(\eta,\sigma^2)$)
73:         locksToAcquire[x] $\leftarrow$ y   ▷ *contending txs take each other's locks when they abort*
74:         locksToAcquire[y] $\leftarrow$ x   ▷ *recall that a tx also waits for its own tx-lock to be free (line 57)*
75:   ▷ *sort all locks in each row of locksToAcquire, and swap the old matrix by the new one (using an indirection pointer)*

---

tion (in line 8). This is presented in WAIT-SEER-LOCKS, in Alg. 4, where there are two main ideas. First, we use a known technique to avoid the lemming effect [6]. The problem is that hardware transactions quickly exhaust their budget of attempts when the fall-back lock is taken and tend to execute mostly in the fall-back as a consequence. To reduce this chance, a transaction waits if the global lock is taken, as otherwise it would likely abort in line 12.

The second idea behind WAIT-SEER-LOCKS is to also wait in case the txLock and/or coreLock are taken by another thread (lines 57 and 58). The intuition is that, even though this thread may not have had aborts that lead it to acquire locks, it is beneficial if it co-operates with concurrent threads that have taken the locks, giving them a chance to complete without conflicting. Doing so is instrumental for the meaningfulness of the locking scheme that we present next while avoiding a transaction to having to pessimistically always acquire the lock of its transaction.

We also opportunistically take the chance to update the locking scheme of SEER in line 53, instead of having the thread waiting idle for the global lock to be released. We specifically do this in one designated thread to avoid syn-

chronization. Furthermore, we have an active transactions list with as many slots as threads in the program, making each entry of the list a single-writer multi-reader register.

The procedure to acquire the transaction locks simply goes over the row *locksToAcquire[txId]* and acquires each lock. All rows are sorted consistently by the periodic update, hence this procedure acquires them in that order to avoid deadlocks. We also optimize this procedure to acquire the locks with a hardware transaction when there are two or more locks, instead of performing multiple compare-and-swap operations (CAS) to acquire all locks. The rationale of this optimization is to batch the synchronization of two or more CASes into a single TSX hardware transaction. If the transaction is not successful, we fall-back to the normal acquisition. Note that this is not lock elision [23]; we are effectively using TSX as a multi-CAS, not eliding the locks acquired.

Devising the Locking Scheme. We are left with the logic for updating the locking scheme for fine-grained serialization of transactions in SEER, which we present in Alg. 5. This procedure, opportunistically invoked by one thread, starts by summing the commit and abort per-core statistics.

For all transactions in the application, we consider a pair x, y at a time, and calculate the conditional probability of x aborting, *given* that y was running concurrently with it, $P(\text{x aborts} \mid x \parallel y)$, and the conjunctive probability of x aborting *and* y running concurrently, $P(\text{x aborts} \cap x \parallel y)$:

$$P(\text{x aborts} \mid x \parallel y) = \frac{a_{x,y}}{c_{x,y} + a_{x,y}}$$

$$P(\text{x aborts} \cap x \parallel y) = P(\text{x aborts} \mid x \parallel y) \times P(x \parallel y))$$
$$= \frac{a_{x,y}}{c_{x,y} + a_{x,y}} \times \frac{c_{x,y} + a_{x,y}}{e_x} = \frac{a_{x,y}}{e_x}$$

where we abbreviated commitStats$[x][y]$ to $c_{x,y}$, abortStats$[x][y]$ to $a_{x,y}$ and executions$[x]$ to e_x. These two probabilities can be efficiently calculated with the statistics that are at our disposal, and are used to define two thresholds, $\mathcal{T}h_1$ and $\mathcal{T}h_2$, aimed at pursuing different goals.

The threshold $\mathcal{T}h_1$ establishes a lower bound on the probability $P(\text{x aborts} \cap x \parallel y)$, below whose value SEER avoids serializing transactions x and y. Low values of this probability imply that the frequency of aborts events of x, in which y was found to run concurrently with it, are rare. It is hence beneficial to avoid the cost of restricting concurrency and sparing the costs of additional lock acquisitions.

The threshold $\mathcal{T}h_2$ is instead used to establish a cut-off on the probability distribution of $P(\text{x aborts} \mid x \parallel y)$ (henceforth abbreviated as $\mathcal{P}_{x,y}$), which aims at determining which subset $\mathcal{S}$, of the set of transactions y, suspected to conflict x, should be prevented from running in parallel with x.

More in detail, SEER includes in $\mathcal{S}$ only the transactions y whose probability $\mathcal{P}_{x,y}$ is larger than $\mathcal{T}h_2$-th percentile of a Gaussian distribution $\mathcal{N}(\eta, \sigma^2)$ with mean η and variance σ equal, respectively, to the mean and variance of the values of $\mathcal{P}_{x,y}$ (for all possible values of y). The rationale here is that a transaction y' that is wrongly suspected of conflicting with x (due to false positives while probing the active transactions) will have significantly lower values of $\mathcal{P}_{x,y'}$, with respect to a transaction y'' that conflicts with x often. Hence, for such transactions y'', $\mathcal{P}_{x,y''}$ will fall in the tail of the cumulative distribution function of probabilities, which we fit with a Gaussian distribution having equivalent mean and variance.

Using the conditional probability $P(\text{x aborts} \mid x \parallel y)$ (differently from the case of $\mathcal{T}h_1$, in which we rely on the conjunctive probability $P(\text{x aborts} \cap x \parallel y)$) is aimed at factoring out, in the inference process, the cases in which x and y are not concurrent. This allows for focusing the analysis solely on the available evidences that support the hypothesis of a cause-effect relation between the concurrent execution of x with y and the abort of x, and for separating falsely suspected pairs of transactions from actually conflicting ones more reliably than if one used the conjunctive probability.

Summarizing: if both conditions in line 72 are met, meaning that x is deemed to abort too often because of y, SEER requires that transactions x and y have to acquire each other's lock (recall that we associate on lock per transaction).

Finally, SEER relies on an on-line self-tuning mechanism that automates the identification of the values of the thresholds $\mathcal{T}h_1$ and $\mathcal{T}h_2$, hence sparing users from the burden of identifying statically defined values that may be suboptimal in heterogeneous, or time varying, workloads. To this end, SEER uses a simple and lightweight bi-dimensional stochastic hill-climbing search, which exploits the feedback of the TM performance (throughput obtained via RTDSC-based measurements) to guide the search in the parameter's space $[0,1] \times [0,1]$ for the thresholds $\mathcal{T}h_1$ and $\mathcal{T}h_2$. Our hill-climbing is stochastic in the sense that, with a small probability p, it performs random jumps in the parameters' space to avoid getting stuck in local minima. We configured this self-tuning mechanism with standard values that were applied to irregular concurrent applications such as those used with TM [8]. Specifically, we set p to 0.1% and the initial values of $\mathcal{T}h_1 = 0.3$ and $\mathcal{T}h_2 = 0.8$.

5. EVALUATION

To evaluate our proposal, we formulate several questions and experiments. First, in Section 5.1, we compare SEER with the available alternatives for HTM. Next, in Section 5.2, we assess how often hardware transactions are successful and to what extent locks are acquired. Finally, in Section 5.3, we seek to understand the merit of each design choice of SEER and its overheads.

All the experimental results were obtained using a TSX-enabled Intel Haswell Xeon E3-1275 processor with 32GB RAM and 8 virtual cores (4 physical, each one running up to 2 hardware threads). We ran our experiments in a dedicated machine running Ubuntu 12.04, and the results reported are the average of 20 runs. Our evaluation uses the standard STAMP suite, a popular set of benchmarks for TM [21], encompassing applications representative of various domains that generate heterogeneous workload. We excluded Bayes given its non-deterministic executions, and Labyrinth as most of its transactions exceed TSX capacity.

5.1 How much can we gain with Seer?

To assess the benefits of SEER we consider 3 alternatives:

1. **HLE** where transactions may be retried a small number of times (processor implementation-dependent), but without any scheduling or contention management, which may cause the lemming effect [6] on the elided lock[1].

2. **RTM** where the retry logic is controlled in software and hence we retry a given number of attempts in HTM and always wait before doing so if the single-global lock is taken. As already discussed in Section 2, the usage of a single lock in the fall-back path of these two baseline mechanisms makes them analogous in spirit to the ATS scheduler [26].

3. **SCM** where we implemented the Software-assisted Conflict Management [1] technique. SCM uses an auxiliary lock to serialize transactions that are aborted, thus decreasing the chance of having the lemming effect, where failed hardware transactions keep exhausting the attempts and fall-back to the single-global lock.

We used a budget of 5 attempts for hardware transactions in all approaches (as used by Intel for this set of benchmarks [27]). We present the results for these approaches together with SEER in Figure 3. The speedups are relative to a sequential non-instrumented execution. In general we can see that SEER performs similarly to the best solution up to 3 threads, and better with 4 or more threads. This is a consequence of having more opportunity for our fine-grained scheduling to shine when there is more concurrency.

Figure 3i shows the geometric mean speedup across all the benchmarks, where we can see that SEER yields 62% improvement over RTM and SCM with 8 threads, with peak

---

[1]STAMP benchmarks are executed as having 1 lock to elide.

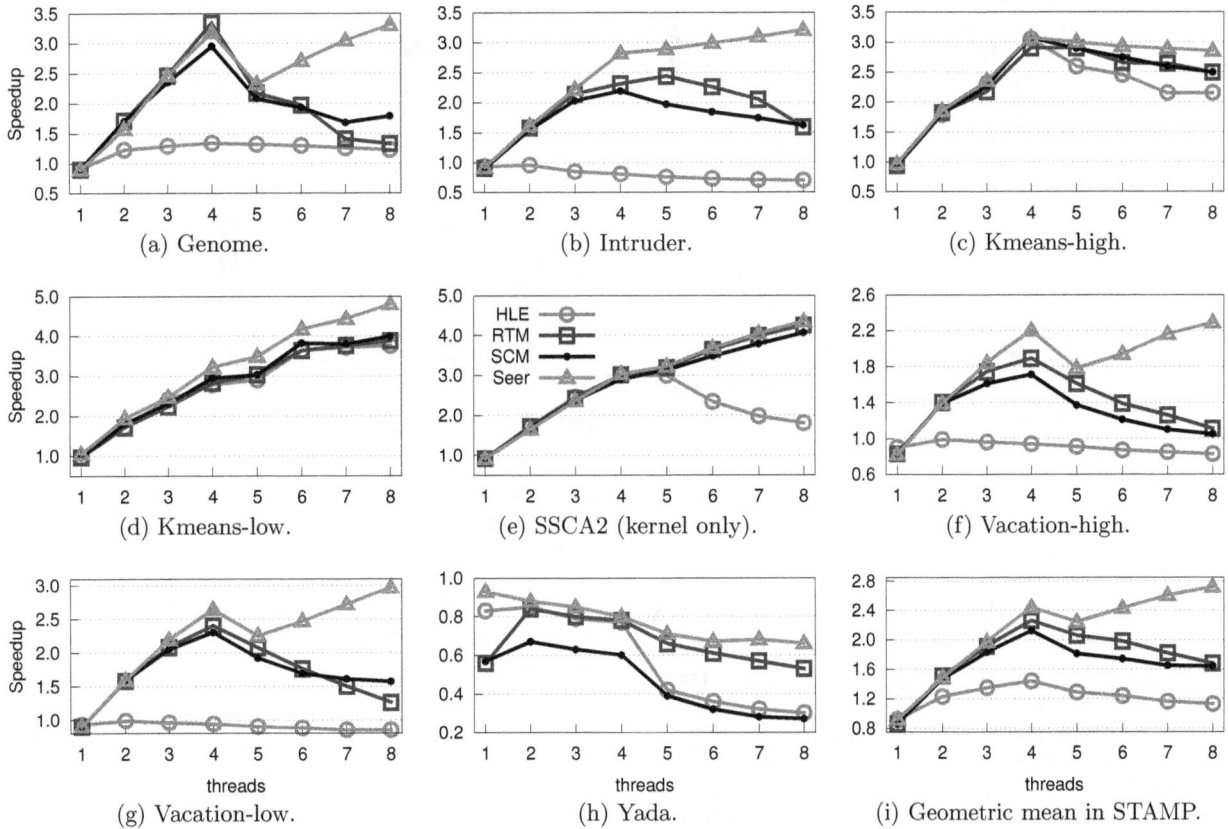

Figure 3: Speedup of different HTM based approaches across STAMP benchmarks.

gains of approximately $2-2.5\times$ over the best performing alternative baseline in benchmarks such as Genome, Intruder and Vacation.

5.2 Where are the gains of Seer coming from?

HTM performance is known to be strongly affected by the likelihood with which transactions resort to acquiring the global lock [10]. Furthermore, even in cases in which hardware transactions are used successfully, parallelism may be overly restricted by the usage of the auxiliary lock in the case of SCM, or of fine-grained locks in the case of SEER.

Table 3 provides a breakdown of the usage of locks for each considered approach, shedding lights on the reasons underlying the performance gains achieved by SEER. The reported results are averaged across all benchmarks.

As expected, HLE drastically loses its ability to execute transactions in hardware, as threads increase, because it suffers from the lemming effect and at higher concurrency degrees most transactions use the single-global lock. RTM improves over this scenario but still uses hardware transactions only in 63% of the executions at 8 threads. The SCM approach has significantly lower usage of the fall-back path (up to 5%). However, there are up to 29% hardware transactions that execute under the auxiliary lock. We highlight that this is a single lock, which prevents parallelism among all restarting transactions. This is why SCM is unable to provide noticeable speedups over RTM in practice, as shown in the previous section.

Table 3: Breakdown of percentage (%) of types of transactions used in average across STAMP.

Variant	Transaction Mode	2t	4t	6t	8t
HLE	HTM no locks	75	52	39	23
	SGL fall-back	25	48	61	77
RTM	HTM no locks	94	82	76	63
	SGL fall-back	6	18	24	37
SCM	HTM no locks	90	83	77	66
	HTM + Aux lock	8	15	20	29
	SGL fall-back	2	2	3	5
SEER	HTM no locks	94	94	85	80
	HTM + Tx Locks	2	2	2	3
	HTM + Core Locks	3	1	4	4
	HTM + Tx + Core Locks	1	2	8	12
	SGL fall-back	0	1	1	1

Finally, SEER is able to improve over all previously described alternatives, exactly because the frequency with which it uses a single-global lock is drastically lower (around 1%), and the other locks that it exploits have a much finer granularity — one per transaction and one per core — that allow to cope with conflict dependencies and cache capacity exceptions (in case multiple hardware threads share the same cache) without serializing *every* active transaction. In fact, in 50% of the cases in which *some* transaction lock is acquired by SEER, the fraction of transaction locks that are actually acquired is lower than 23% of the globally avail-

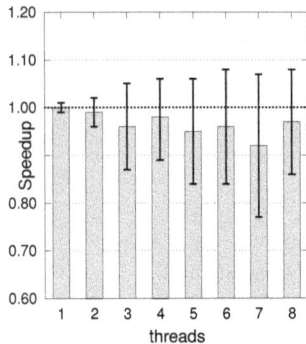

Figure 4: Overhead of SEER when profiling and calculating locks to acquire.

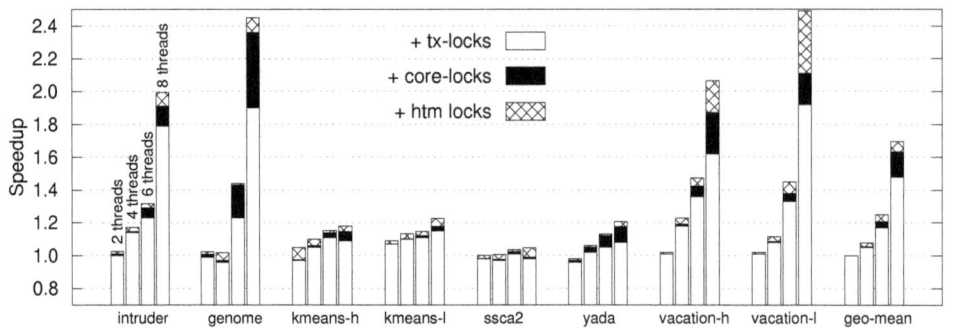

Figure 5: Cumulative contribution of each technique employed in SEER: speedups are shown relatively to SEER without any lock acquisition (but with all the profiling enabled) and the three variants are incrementally added.

able transaction locks. This experimental result confirms the ability of the proposed lock inference mechanism to synthesize effective fine-grained locking schemes.

5.3 How much does each design choice contribute to Seer?

The design of SEER encompassed: 1) capturing statistics about commits, aborts, and concurrent transactions; 2) acquiring transaction locks when aborts occur; 3) acquire a core lock when a capacity abort happens; 4) acquire transaction locks with a hardware transaction to reduce the overheads of multiple compare-and-swaps; and 5) adapt the thresholds Th_1, Th_2 via a stochastic hill-climbing algorithm.

We first assess the overhead of the monitoring, lock-inference and self-tuning mechanisms of SEER. For this, we ran a variant of SEER that incurs the overheads of all its mechanisms, without however acquiring any lock. In Figure 4, we show the average speed-up of this SEER's variant relatively to RTM (that consistently performed second best in our evaluation in Section 5.1). These results are the geometric mean across the STAMP benchmarks, and we can see that the mean slowdown is less than 5% and varies from negligible to at most 8%. Even challenging scenarios, such as a low contention small hash-map (4k elements and 1k buckets) yielded a maximum of 4% overhead.

In fact, these overheads could be made even lower by reducing the frequency with which SEER samples statistics and updates the locking scheme, at the cost of increasing the latency for identifying an adequate scheduling strategy. Our choice of using relatively aggressive monitoring/optimizations rates is motivated by the need to ensure quick convergence times given that STAMP benchmarks have very short runs (on the order of a few seconds); yet in long running services, where convergence speed is a less critical issue, SEER may be configured to use less frequent sampling/optimization strategies in order to further reduce its overheads.

To quantify the relative relevance of each of the mechanisms integrated in SEER, we conducted a series of experiments, whose results, shown in Figure 5, evaluate the speedup of different variants of SEER. We consider as baseline, the SEER variant previously considered for the plots in Figure 4, which incurs the costs of collecting statistics and updating the locking strategy, without ever acquiring any lock. Then, we consider four improving variants where

we cumulatively add the transaction locks acquisition, the core locks acquisition, the hardware transaction acquisition of locks, and the adaptation of the thresholds used.

In general the transaction locks provide the largest boost in performance as they capture the conflicts inherent to each benchmark. Unsurprisingly, the core locks are only beneficial when using 6 or 8 threads, i.e., when we start executing multiple hardware threads on the same core. The hardware lock acquisition also shows improvements with larger concurrency degrees, since these scenarios are the ones that more often trigger the necessity of acquiring locks (and, which hence trigger this optimization more frequently). Also, a similar gain is provided by adapting on-line the thresholds used in the transaction locks probabilities calculations. Finally, we experimented also by enabling only the core-locks and obtained geometric mean speedups of 9% and 22% at 6 and 8 threads. This corroborates the need for both transaction and core locks.

6. CONCLUSIONS AND FUTURE WORK

In this work we presented SEER, the first *fine-grained* scheduler designed to cope with specific challenges arising with HTMs. The most innovative feature of our proposal is that it can probabilistically infer conflict patterns among pairs of transactions of a TM program, without relying on the availability of precise information from the underlying TM system. Conversely, SEER relies on lightweight, yet inherently imprecise techniques, to gather information on the set of concurrently active transactions upon the commit and abort events of transactions. Probabilistic techniques are then used to filter out false positives and infer an effective dynamic locking scheme that is used to serialize contention-prone transactions in a fine-grained fashion. We evaluated our solution, SEER, against several alternatives using a mainstream HTM (Intel TSX). As a result, we obtained 62% performance improvements on average in standard benchmarks with 8 threads, with speed-ups peaking up to $2 - 2.5\times$ in complex benchmarks like Genome, Intruder and Vacation.

In the future we plan to extend SEER in several directions. This includes experimenting with probabilistic sampling techniques [5], as well as adopting even more fine-grained locking schemes, which associate locks depending on both the atomic block *and* the identifier of the data structure being manipulated in that atomic block.

Acknowledgements: This work was supported by national funds through Fundação para a Ciência e Tecnologia (FCT), via the projects UID/CEC/50021/2013 and EXPL/EEI-ESS/0361/2013. We are grateful to the anonymous reviewers for their insightful feedback.

7. REFERENCES

[1] Y. Afek, A. Levy, and A. Morrison. Software-improved Hardware Lock Elision. In *Proc. Symposium on Principles of Distributed Computing*, PODC, pages 212–221, 2014.

[2] M. Ansari, et al. Improving Performance by Reducing Aborts in Hardware Transactional Memory. In *Proc. High Performance Embedded Architectures and Compilers*, HiPEAC, pages 35–49, 2010.

[3] M. Ansari et al. Steal-on-Abort: Improving Transactional Memory Performance Through Dynamic Transaction Reordering. In *Proc. High Performance Embedded Architectures and Compilers*, HiPEAC, pages 4–18, 2009.

[4] D. Dice, A. Kogan, Y. Lev, T. Merrifield, and M. Moir. Adaptive Integration of Hardware and Software Lock Elision Techniques. In *Proc. Symposium on Parallelism in Algorithms and Architectures*, SPAA, pages 188–197, 2014.

[5] D. Dice, Y. Lev, and M. Moir. Scalable statistics counters. In *Proc. Symposium on Parallelism in Algorithms and Architectures*, SPAA, pages 43–52, 2013.

[6] D. Dice et al. Early Experience with a Commercial Hardware Transactional Memory Implementation. In *Proc. Conference on Architectural Support for Programming Languages and Operating Systems*, ASPLOS, pages 157–168, 2009.

[7] N. Diegues and J. Cachopo. Practical Parallel Nesting for Software Transactional Memory. In *Proc. of Symposium on Distributed Computing*, DISC, pages 149–163, 2013.

[8] N. Diegues and P. Romano. Self-Tuning Intel Transactional Synchronization Extensions. In *Proc. Conference on Autonomic Computing*, ICAC, pages 209–219, 2014.

[9] N. Diegues and P. Romano. Time-warp: lightweight abort minimization in transactional memory. In *Proc. of Principles and Practice of Parallel Programming*, PPoPP, pages 167–178, 2014.

[10] N. Diegues, P. Romano, and L. Rodrigues. Virtues and limitations of commodity hardware transactional memory. In *Proc. Conference on Parallel Architectures and Compilation Techniques*, PACT, pages 3–14, 2014.

[11] S. Dolev, D. Hendler, and A. Suissa. CAR-STM: Scheduling-based Collision Avoidance and Resolution for Software Transactional Memory. In *Proc. Symposium on Principles of Distributed Computing*, PODC, pages 125–134, 2008.

[12] A. Dragojević, R. Guerraoui, and M. Kapalka. Stretching transactional memory. In *Proc. of Conference on Programming Language Design and Implementation*, PLDI, pages 155–165, 2009.

[13] A. Dragojević, R. Guerraoui, A. V. Singh, and V. Singh. Preventing Versus Curing: Avoiding Conflicts in Transactional Memories. In *Proc.*

[14] P. Felber, C. Fetzer, and T. Riegel. Dynamic performance tuning of word-based software transactional memory. In *Proc. Principles and Practice of Parallel Programming*, PPoPP, pages 237–246, 2008.

[15] T. Heber, D. Hendler, and A. Suissa. On the Impact of Serializing Contention Management on STM Performance. *Journal of Parallel and Distributed Computing*, 72(6):739–750, June 2012.

[16] M. Herlihy and J. E. B. Moss. Transactional Memory: Architectural Support for Lock-free Data Structures. In *Proc. Symposium on Computer Architecture*, ISCA, pages 289–300, 1993.

[17] S. Hirve, R. Palmieri, and B. Ravindran. HiperTM: High Performance, Fault-Tolerant Transactional Memory. In *Proc. Confenrece on Distributed Computing and Networking*, ICDCN, pages 181–196, 2014.

[18] C. Jacobi, T. Slegel, and D. Greiner. Transactional Memory Architecture and Implementation for IBM System Z. In *Proc. Symposium on Microarchitecture*, MICRO, pages 25–36, 2012.

[19] W. Maldonado, et al. Scheduling Support for Transactional Memory Contention Management. In *Proc. Principles and Practice of Parallel Programming*, PPoPP, pages 79–90, 2010.

[20] A. Matveev and N. Shavit. Reduced Hardware Transactions: A New Approach to Hybrid Transactional Memory. In *Proc. Symposium on Parallelism in Algorithms and Architectures*, SPAA, pages 11–22, 2013.

[21] C. Minh et al. STAMP: Stanford Transactional Applications for Multi-Processing. In *Proc. Symposium on Workload Characterization*, IISWC, pages 35–46, 2008.

[22] S. Peluso, P. Romano, and F. Quaglia. SCORe: A Scalable One-Copy Serializable Partial Replication Protocol. In *Proc. of Middleware*, pages 456–475, 2012.

[23] R. Rajwar and J. R. Goodman. Speculative Lock Elision: Enabling Highly Concurrent Multithreaded Execution. In *Proc. Symposium on Microarchitecture*, MICRO, pages 294–305, 2001.

[24] H. Rito and J. Cachopo. ProPS: A Progressively Pessimistic Scheduler for Software Transactional Memory. In *Proc. European Conference on Parallel Processing*, Euro-Par, pages 150–161, 2014.

[25] C. Rossbach et al. TxLinux: Using and Managing Hardware Transactional Memory in an Operating System. In *Proc. Symposium on Operating Systems Principles*, SOSP, pages 87–102, 2007.

[26] R. Yoo and H. Lee. Adaptive Transaction Scheduling for Transactional Memory Systems. In *Proc. Symposium on Parallelism in Algorithms and Architectures*, SPAA, pages 169–178, 2008.

[27] R. Yoo et al. Performance Evaluation of Intel; Transactional Synchronization Extensions for High-performance Computing. In *Proc. Conference on High Performance Computing, Networking, Storage and Analysis*, SC, pages 1–11, 2013.

Conflict Reduction in Hardware Transactions Using Advisory Locks*

Lingxiang Xiang and Michael L. Scott
Computer Science Department, University of Rochester
{lxiang, scott}@cs.rochester.edu

ABSTRACT

Preliminary experience with hardware transactional memory suggests that aborts due to data conflicts are one of the principal obstacles to scale-up. To reduce the incidence of conflict, we propose an automatic, high-level mechanism that uses advisory locks to serialize (just) the portions of the transactions in which conflicting accesses occur. We demonstrate the feasibility of this mechanism, which we refer to as *staggered transactions*, with fully developed compiler and runtime support, running on simulated hardware.

Our compiler identifies and instruments a small subset of the accesses in each transaction, which it determines, statically, are likely to constitute initial accesses to shared locations. At run time, the instrumentation acquires an advisory lock on the accessed datum, if (and only if) prior execution history suggests that the datum—or locations "downstream" of it—are indeed a likely source of conflict. Policy to drive the decision requires one hardware feature not generally found in current commercial offerings: nontransactional loads and stores within transactions. It can also benefit from a mechanism to record the program counter at which a cache line was first accessed in a transaction. Simulation results show that staggered transactions can significantly reduce the frequency of conflict aborts and increase program performance.

Categories and Subject Descriptors

D.1.3 [**Programming Techniques**]: Concurrent Programming—*Parallel Programming*; D.3.4 [**Programming Languages**]: Processors—*Code generation*

General Terms

Algorithms, Design, Performance

---

*This work was supported in part by grants from the National Science Foundation (CCF-0963759, CCF-1116055, CNS-1116109, CNS-1319417, CCF-1337224, and CCF-1422649) and by the IBM Canada Centres for Advanced Studies (CAS).

Benchmark	S	%I	W/U	Contention Source	LA	LP
list-hi	1.0	27%	4.92	linked-list	N	Y
tsp	3.6	10%	1.53	priority queue	Y	Y
memcached	2.6	25%	3.11	statistics information	Y	Y
intruder	3.2	32%	4.02	task queue	Y	Y
kmeans	4.6	35%	3.57	arrays	N	Y
vacation	9.7	1%	0.34	red-black trees	N	Y

Table 1: HTM contention in representative benchmarks. S: speedup with 16 threads over sequential run. %I: % of txns forced into irrevocable mode. W/U: ratio of wasted to useful cycles in transactions. LA: locality of contention addresses. LP: locality of contention PCs.

Keywords

Hardware Transactional Memory, Advisory Lock

1. INTRODUCTION

Transactional Memory combines the convenience of atomic blocks as a programming idiom with the potential performance gains of speculation as an implementation. With the recent deployment of hardware support (HTM) on Intel's Haswell [33], IBM's zEC12 [13] and IBM's POWER 8 [4], we anticipate a "virtuous cycle" in which more and more multi-threaded programs employ TM, and the performance of the hardware becomes increasingly important.

Preliminary experience with HTM suggests that the raw performance, scalability, and energy consumption of transactional programs—especially those with medium- or large-scale transactions—are all limited by the hardware transaction abort rate [33]. Aborts happen for two main reasons: hardware overflow and conflicts with other transactions. We have addressed the overflow case in prior work [31]; we focus here on conflicts.

Conflicts among transactions lead to poor scalability and energy waste. Table 1 shows several representative TM programs running on a typical 16-core eager HTM system (the experimental methodology is described in Section 6). Repeated aborts limit speedup (column "S") and force many transactions to acquire a global lock and revert to irrevocable mode (column "%I") in order to make forward progress. A high ratio of cycles spent in aborted transactions relative to committed transactions ("W/U" column) correlates strongly with energy waste. As shown in the final, vacation row, wasted work can still be significant even in programs with reasonable speedup.

Several previous projects have proposed hardware mechanisms to reduce the incidence of conflict aborts. Examples include DATM [21], RETCON [3], Wait-n-GoTM [14], and

OmniOrder [20]. While these proposals achieve nontrivial improvements in abort rates and system throughput, they suffer from several limitations. First, most entail significant new hardware complexity—e.g., for the transactional-cycle detector of Wait-n-GoTM or the 8 new coherence protocol states of DATM. Second, they tend to target specific patterns of contention—e.g., the simple conflicting code slices of RETCON or the circular dependences of DATM and Wait-n-GOTM; they may miss other opportunities. Third, they are often specific to particular styles of HTM—e.g., lazy for RETCON, eager for others—and may not apply across the rest of the HTM design spectrum.

As an alternative to all-hardware mechanisms, we introduce the notion of *Staggered Transactions*, an automatic technique to reduce the frequency of aborts. Staggered Transactions serialize the execution of conflict-heavy portions of transactions by means of advisory (optional) locks, implemented using nontransactional loads and stores. Nonconflicting code continues to execute speculatively in parallel, thereby maintaining scalability. Because correctness remains the responsibility of the underlying TM system, Staggered Transactions function correctly even if some transactions neglect to obey the locking protocol. Moreover, the contention reduction achieved is largely independent of other HTM implementation details; in particular, it should be compatible with most conflict resolution techniques.

Effective implementation of Staggered Transactions requires a combination of compile-time and run-time mechanisms to choose *whether* to acquire a lock and, if so, *which* lock to acquire and *where* to acquire it. In our (fully automated) system, the compiler uses Data Structure Analysis [15] to identify and instrument a small subset of the accesses in each transaction, which it determines, statically, are likely to constitute initial accesses to shared locations. These accesses constitute *advisory locking points*. At run time, a locking policy decides which of these locking points to activate, and which lock to acquire at each, based on prior execution history. As we will shown in Section 6, a careful fusion of compile-time and run-time information allows us to avoid not only simple, repetitive contention but also more complex cyclic dependences, in which each transaction in the cycle accesses a (typically dynamically chosen) location on which the next transaction has already performed a conflicting access.

To escape isolation when acquiring locks, Staggered Transactions require nontransactional loads and stores within transactions. They also benefit from a hardware mechanism to identify the PC at which a conflicting location was first accessed. Neither of these features is common on existing machines, but both appear orthogonal to most other HTM features, and neither seems prohibitively difficult to add.

Our principal contributions, discussed in the following sections, include

- A hybrid optimistic / pessimistic execution model for hardware transactions, in which the most commonly conflicting portions of transactions are serialized by advisory locks, built with nontransactional loads and stores.

- Compiler techniques to insert required instrumentation with negligible impact on run-time overhead.

- Run-time techniques to detect contention and enable advisory locks that avoid it, using high-level program knowledge learned by the compiler.

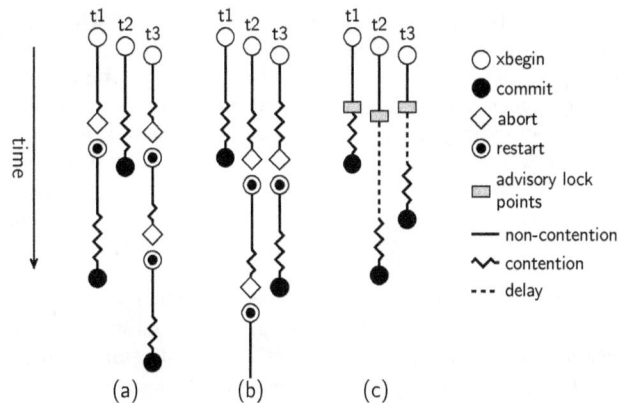

Figure 1: Execution of 3 transactions (t1–t3) (a) on an eager HTM, (b) on a lazy HTM, and (c) with Staggered Transactions optimization.

2. OVERVIEW

Unlike conventional TM, Staggered Transactions force portions of transactions to serialize; the remaining portions run concurrently. Specifically, when conflicts tend to arise in the middle of a given atomic block, our compiler and runtime arrange to acquire an advisory lock at the end of the contention-free prefix, and to hold it until commit time.

Figure 1 illustrates the execution of three transactions with mutually conflicting accesses, shown with a diamond symbol. On a typical eager (Figure 1a) or lazy (Figure 1b) HTM system, only one of the transactions will be able to commit if all three execute concurrently. In a Staggered Transactions system (Figure 1c), execution of the portion of a transaction beginning with the conflicting access is preceded by an *advisory locking point* (ALP). In the diagram, t1, t2, and t3 all attempt to acquire the same advisory lock. Transaction t1 acquires it first; the others wait their turn, and all are able to commit. We say that the conflicting portions of the transactions have been *staggered*. While a transaction could, in principle, acquire multiple advisory locks, we acquire only one per transaction in this paper.

Accurate identification of all and only the contention-prone portions of transactions requires careful coordination of compile-time and run-time techniques. Figure 2 illustrates how the pieces fit together in our system.

The main goal of the compile-time steps (①–③) is to statically insert ALPs in the source code, so that once a frequently conflicting access is found during execution, the runtime can activate the nearest ALP ahead of that access, preventing concurrent accesses to the same object in other transactions. A dedicated compiler pass inspects the IR (intermediate representation) of all atomic blocks (①) and considers load and store instructions as *anchors*—accesses in front of which to insert an ALP (②). To minimize the number of ALPs (and thus the run-time overhead of instrumentation), the compiler uses Data Structure Analysis [15] to select as anchors only those instructions that are likely to be initial accesses to shared objects (data structure nodes) inside a transaction. To help the runtime locate ALPs quickly, the compiler builds an *anchor table* that maps PC ranges to the closest prior ALP in each atomic block (③).

The run-time steps (④–⑧) focus on two decisions concerning advisory locks: (1) whether the runtime should acquire an advisory lock for the current transaction, and if so,

(2) which advisory lock to acquire, at which ALP. The first decision is made by tracking abort history for every atomic block. When an atomic block runs on HTM (④) and a contention abort occurs (⑤), the hardware-triggered handler receives an indication of the conflicting address and (ideally) the program counter at which that address was first accessed (⑥). The runtime appends this information to a per-thread *abort history table* for the current atomic block. Based on the frequency of contention aborts, a software *locking policy* makes decision (1).

Decision (2) is harder. As shown in Table 1 ("LA" and "LP" columns), the program counters associated with initial accesses to conflicting locations are often the same across dynamic transactions, but the accessed data locations often differ: sometimes a common datum is responsible for most aborts; other times, it differs from one transaction instance to another.

The locking policy augments its understanding of the conflict pattern each time a contention abort occurs (⑦). Once a pattern is found, the runtime consults the anchor table to identify an ALP and activate it for future instances of the transaction (⑧). For simplicity, we currently allow only one active ALP for a given atomic block. We also employ a fairly simple policy (more complex possibilities are a subject of future work). Specifically, we activate an ALP only if it corresponds to a PC that has frequently performed the initial access to data that subsequently proved to be the source of conflict. If the addresses of the data in these conflicts were usually the same, the ALP is activated in *precise mode*: it acquires a lock only if the data address in the current transaction instance matches the address of past conflicts. If data addresses have varied in past conflicts, the ALP is activated in *coarse-grain* mode: it acquires a lock regardless of the current data address. In either case, the choice of which lock to acquire is based on the current data address: this will always be the same in precise mode; it may vary in coarse-grain mode.

If conflicts continue to be common despite the activation of a coarse-grain ALP, the runtime uses information gathered by the compiler to activate the *parent* of the ALP instead. The notion of parents again leverages Data Structure Analysis. In a linked data structure, if node B is reached via a pointer from node A, we say that the ALP associated with the initial access to A is the parent of the ALP associated with the initial access to B. In code that traverses a linked list, for example, each node other than the first is accessed through its predecessor; the first is accessed through the head node. In typical traversal code, nodes within the list will share an ALP (embedded in a loop). The parent of that ALP will be the ALP of the head node. Interested readers may consult Lattner's thesis for details [15].

As a simple example, suppose in Figure 2 that q→head is a frequent source of conflicts. After a few aborts, the locking policy will realize that most conflicts happen on the data address q→head, whose initial access in the transaction is usually at the same instruction address, say Addr. The policy categorizes the conflict pattern as *precise* and the runtime activates the ALP right before Addr.

Like the advisory locks of database and file systems, Staggered Transaction advisory locks are purely a performance optimization. Correctness is ensured by the underlying TM system. If the runtime fails to instrument a transaction that participates in a conflict, the only consequence is continued

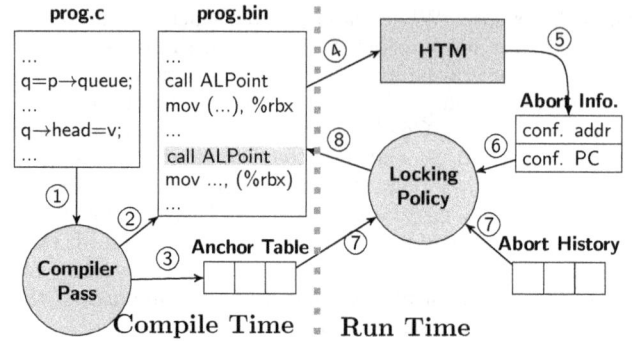

Figure 2: An overview of Staggered Transactions, including compile-time steps ①–③ and run-time steps ④–⑧.

aborts. Likewise, when a transaction *does* attempt to acquire a lock, it need not wait forever—to avoid blocking on a very long transaction (or, on hardware that supports it, a transaction that has been preempted), an ALP can specify a timeout for its acquire operation, and simply proceed when the timeout expires.

3. COMPILER SUPPORT

Our Staggered Transactions system uses a compiler pass for static insertion of advisory locking points (ALPs). Using Data Structure Analysis [15], the compiler identifies and instruments only those loads and stores (anchors) that are likely to constitute initial accesses to shared locations. It also generates an *anchor table* for each atomic block to describe the anchors and non-anchors (uninstrumented loads and stores) and the relationships among them. Anchor tables are subsequently consulted by the runtime to make locking decisions and to locate desired advisory locking points.

Compared to naive instrumentation of every load and store, our technique significantly reduces the number of ALPs, thereby minimizing execution overhead. Moreover, by capturing information about the hierarchical structure of program data, the generated anchor tables allow the runtime to make better locking decisions.

3.1 A Data Structure Approach

We consider program-level objects (data structure nodes) to be an appropriate granularity for the insertion of advisory locking points, based on two observations: First, fields of the same object frequently fit together in just a few cache lines. Since HTM systems typically detect conflict at cache-line granularity, if there is contention on the object, the contended code region will usually start at the first instruction that accesses the data structure node. Second, assuming modular program structure, instructions that access the same object are often concentrated in a short code segment. This implies that the initial access to an object in a given function or a method is likely to be a good anchor candidate. Once these candidates are instrumented, we can skip a number of following loads and stores that access the same objects, without losing the ability to trace back from an abort to an appropriate ALP.

A field-sensitive Data Structure Analysis can be used to identify the objects associated with loads and stores and their alias relationships. We base our compiler pass on Lattner's DSA [15], which we use essentially as a black box. DSA distinguishes pointer-to sets according to the data structure type and field to which they point. It has previously been used for improved heap allocation [16] and type safety checking. A complete DSA pass has three stages: (1) A *local* stage creates a data structure node (DSNode) for each unique pointer target in a function, and links each pointer access to a DSNode. All pointers linked to the same DSNode may point to the same instance of a data structure. If a pointer field in a data structure points to another data structure (or itself), there will be an outgoing edge from this DSNode to the target DSNode. All DSNodes of a function are organized together as a data structure graph (DSGraph). (2) A *bottom-up* stage merges callees' local DSGraphs into those of their callers. (3) A *top-down* stage merges callers' DSGraphs into those of their callees. We utilize only the result from stage 2, which is more context sensitive than that of stage 3 (to get more accurate alias results, which we do not need, the latter may collapse too many DSNodes).

Given DSA results, our algorithm works in three stages of its own, which we describe in Sections 3.2–3.4.

3.2 Building Local Anchor Tables

A local anchor table keeps information for all loads and stores of a function directly or indirectly called in an atomic block (static transaction). Each load/store is described by a table entry, ATEntry, a 4-field tuple: (instr, isAnchor, parent, pioneer). Field instr indicates the location of the load/store instruction. Field isAnchor is a Boolean flag. We call a load-/store an *anchor* if it is the initial access to a DSNode in a possible execution path. (ALPs are placed before anchors in a later stage.) Field parent points to another anchor though which a pointer to the current node was loaded. For example, in the code sequence {B = A→child; ... = B→size;}, if the loads of A→child and B→size are anchors, then the first one is the second one's parent. For a non-anchor access, field pioneer points to the anchor that accesses the same DSNode. For example, in {n = queuePtr→head; ...; queuePtr→tail = m;}, the pioneer of the store to queuePtr→tail is the load of queuePtr→head (assuming that load is an anchor).

Algorithm 1 shows how the compiler constructs an anchor table for a given function. The first stage (lines 3–14) categorizes load and store instructions as anchors or non-anchors through a depth-first traversal of the function's dominator tree. The second stage (lines 15–19) sets up the parent relationship among anchors, using the result of DSA's field-sensitive analysis.

3.3 Building Unified Anchor Tables

Walking from callers to callees, a top-down stage creates one unified anchor table for each atomic block. This stage doesn't change the local tables. Instead, it clones and merges them, taking account of the DSNode mapping from caller to callee at function call sites. Missing parent information for certain anchors, if passed via function arguments, is filled in at this stage. From the construction procedure, we can see that unified anchor tables are context-sensitive: anchors originating from the same instruction may have different parents in different unified anchor tables.

3.4 Instrumentation

Once per-function local anchor tables and per-atomic-block unified anchor tables are available, the insertion of advisory locking points is straightforward: the compiler iterates over all local tables and inserts calls to ALPoint right before each

---

Algorithm 1: BuildLocalAnchorTable(func)

Input: a function *func*
Output: a local anchor table *aTable*

```
1   aTable ← ∅;
2   domTree ← GetDominateTree (func);
3   foreach BasicBlock b in DepthFirstVisit (domTree) do
4       foreach LoadStoreInst inst in b do
5           dsNode ← GetDSNode (inst.pointerOperand);
6           entry ← new ATEntry;
7           entry.inst ← inst;
8           if ∃ m ∈ aTable[dsNode]: m.inst dominates inst
            then
9               entry.isAnchor ← false;
10              entry.pioneer ← m.inst;
11          else
12              entry.isAnchor ← true;
13              entry.parent ← nil;
14          aTable[dsNode].push (entry);
15  foreach DSNode n in aTable do
16      foreach Edge e in n.edges do
17          foreach ATEntry m in aTable[e.toNode] do
18              if m.isAnchor then
19                  m.parent ← n;
```

```
TM_BEGIN(); // genome/sequencer.c:292
...
for (ii = i; ii < ii_stop; ii++) {
    void* segment = vector_at(segmentsContentsPtr, ii);
    TMhashtable_insert(uniqueSegmentsPtr, segment, segment);
}
TM_END();
void* vector_at (vector_t* vectorPtr, long i){ //lib/vector.c:164
    if ((i < 0) || (i ≥vectorPtr→size))        ▶ A 51: Parent 0
        return NULL;
    return (vectorPtr→elements[i]);            ▶ 53: Pioneer 51
// lib/hashtable.c:171
bool_t TMhashtable_insert (hashtable_t* hashtablePtr, ...) {
    long numBucket = hashtablePtr→numBucket;  ▶ A 42: Parent 0
    ...
    ... = TMlist_find(hashtablePtr→buckets[i],
                      &findPair);              ▶ 46: Pioneer 42
void* TMlist_find (list_t* listPtr, ...) { // lib/list.c:588
    list_node_t* nodePtr;
    list_node_t* prevPtr = &(listPtr→head);
    for (nodePtr=(list_node_t*)prevPtr→nextPtr;  ▶ A 35: Parent 42
        nodePtr != NULL;
        nodePtr = (list_node_t*)nodePtr→nextPtr) ▶ 38: Pioneer 35
```

Figure 3: An atomic block in genome. ▶ marks an entry with its ID and parent/pioneer field in the unified anchor table.

---

anchor. Every ALP is assigned a unique ID so that the run-time locking policy can locate and activate it. After the binary code has been generated, the compiler knows the real PC of each instruction. It makes the unified anchor tables indexable by PC address, and then emits all unified tables.

3.5 Example

Figure 3 presents a portion of the generated anchor table for an atomic block in the STAMP genome benchmark. The compiler pass first runs DSA for functions called inside the atomic block (vector_at, TMhashtable_insert, and TMlist_find). Function TMlist_find, for example, contains a single DSNode (for nodePtr and prevPtr) with two loads on it. The first load is marked as an anchor (A 35), according to

Algorithm 1; the second is a non-anchor (38) whose pioneer is A 35. A 35's parent field is not filled in until the unified anchor table is constructed.

As we can see, the parent chain between anchors (from hashtablePtr to listPtr) is preserved in the unified anchor table, through which the runtime can make advanced locking decisions. For this code snippet, the compiler will finally instrument three loads (vectorPtr→size, hashtablePtr→num-Bucket, and prePtr→nextPtr) as advisory locking points.

4. HARDWARE REQUIREMENTS

Staggered Transactions require—or can benefit from—several hardware features. First, they must be able to acquire an advisory lock from within an active hardware transaction. This operation violates the usual isolation requirement, but is compatible with several real and proposed HTM architectures. Second, they must be able to identify the data address that has been the source of a conflict leading to abort. This capability is supported by all current HTM designs. Third, they can benefit from a mechanism to identify the address of the instruction that first accessed an address that was the source of a data conflict. While no such mechanism is available on current hardware, it seems relatively straightforward to provide. Moreover, unlike the hardware features required by systems like DATM [21] and Wait-n-GoTM [14], both intra-transaction lock acquisition and initial access recording appear to be independent of other details of HTM design.

Advisory lock acquisition is most easily performed using *nontransactional loads and (immediate) stores*. Nontransactional loads have appeared in Sun's Rock processor [6] and AMD's ASF proposal [8]. They allow a transaction to see writes that have been performed (by other threads) since the beginning of the current transaction. They do not modify the transaction's speculative state: that is, a store by another thread to a nontransactionally-read location will not cause the transaction to abort (unless the location has also been accessed transactionally). Nontransactional stores similarly allow a transaction to update locations even in the event of an abort, and (in the absence of transactional loads or stores to the same location) will not lead to aborts due to conflicting accesses in other threads. To be of use in acquiring an advisory lock, a nontransactional store must (as in ASF) take place immediately; it cannot (as in Rock or IBM's z series machines [13]) be delayed until the end of the transaction.

On ASF, Rock, and z, nontransactional accesses are performed by special load and store instructions. On IBM's POWER 8 [4], a transaction can *suspend* and *resume* execution. While suspended, its loads and stores are nontransactional, and its stores immediately visible. Significantly, nontransactional accesses have a variety of other uses, including hybrid TM [9, 25]; debugging, diagnostics, and statistics gathering [11]; and ordered speculation (e.g., for speculative parallelization of loops).

Conflict information of some sort is provided on abort by all current HTM designs. All, in particular, provide the address of the location (or cache line) on which a conflict has occurred. For Staggered Transactions, a machine would also, ideally, provide the address of the instruction at which the conflicting datum was *initially* accessed in the transaction. We call this address the *conflicting PC*. Note that it

```
struct ABContext { // per thread, per atomic block
    int activeAnchor; // ID of the currently active anchor
    int blockAddress; // probable conflicting memory address
    AbortInfo abtHistory[NUM_HISTORY]; // abort history
    const AnchorTable *anchorTable; // pointer to anchor table
};
```

Figure 4: ABContext structure.

is generally *not* the current PC at the time the conflict is discovered.

In an HTM system implemented in the L1 cache, conflicting PC information could be maintained by adding a PC tag to each cache line, in addition to transaction status bits. This tag would be set whenever a line transitions into speculative mode. Because the tag is inspected only when the line is the source of a data conflict, it need not ever be cleared. As we shall see in Section 6, one can in fact get by with just a subset of the PC (e.g., the 12 low-order bits). This suffices to keep the space overhead under 2.4%.

Software Alternatives to Conflicting PC.

While commercial HTMs have begun to support nontransactional loads and stores, hardware recording of the conflicting PC is still a missing feature. Without it, we need a software alternative to map a conflicting data address to the appropriate anchor in instruction space. A relatively cheap solution is to keep a map M for each thread, indexed by cache line address. At every ALP (with anchor ID I, preceding a load/store of some data address A), the runtime can use nontransactional loads and stores to set $M(A)$ to I, if A was previously absent. If a conflict subsequently occurs on address A, $M(A)$ can be used to identify the ALP that should, perhaps, be activated. While the overhead of this method is nontrivial, it can sometimes be acceptable. Section 6.2 compares this method with hardware-supported conflicting PC tracking.

5. RUNTIME SUPPORT

Our compiler assigns a unique ID to each source code atomic block. For each of these, the runtime maintains an ABContext data structure, as shown in Figure 4, for each executing thread. A pointer to the ABContext for the current atomic block and thread is loaded into a local variable at the beginning of each transaction, and accessed at each ALP. If the transaction aborts, the ABContext may also be accessed by the policy for ALP activation.

5.1 Instrumentation

In our current implementation, each ALP comprises a call to the ALPoint function, shown in Figure 5. The function takes three arguments—a pointer to the appropriate ABContext, the ID of the anchor, and the data address accessed in the following load or store instruction.

The ALPoint function acquires an advisory lock if the current anchor is active (line 2) and either the cache line of the data address matches that of the address in the AB-Context, or the ALP is in coarse-grain mode (indicated by c→blockAddress == 0). This disjunction is checked by function IsAddressMatched (line 3). When a lock is acquired, c→activeAnchor is cleared to avoid additional locking attempts within the current transaction (line 4). The advisory lock is released when the transaction commits or aborts. The activeAnchor field is restored the next time the thread begins a transaction for the same atomic block.

```
1   void ALPoint (ABContext *c, int myID, void* addr) {
2       if (c→activeAnchor == myID &&
3           IsAddressMatched(c→blockAddress, addr) {
4               c→activeAnchor = 0;
5               AcquireLockFor(addr);
6       }
7   }
```

Figure 5: ALPoint instrumentation function.

The actual blocking/waiting is performed in function AcquireLockFor. In our implementation, this function uses a hash of the data address to choose one of a static set of pre-allocated locks, which it then accesses using nontransactional loads and stores. In a system that allows a transaction to remain active when its thread is preempted or blocked, it is important not to force all other transactions to wait if the stalled one holds a lock. With appropriate OS support, the runtime could register the location of any advisory lock it acquires, and the kernel could free this lock when descheduling the thread. Alternatively, a transaction that waits "too long" for an advisory lock could simply time out and proceed without it.

5.2 Locking Policy

The locking policy serves to predict, based on past behavior, which instructions are likely to constitute the first access within a transaction to a location that is likely to be the source of a conflict. Based on this prediction, the runtime activates an appropriate ALP. Many policies are possible. We describe our current choice, which is simple and seems to perform well in practice.

Table 1 suggests that the conflicting data address alone may not be a predictor of contention, due to its poor locality in certain access patterns. Likewise, PC alone is an overpredictor: while the same instruction is very often the initial access to a conflicting location, there are often cases in which that instruction accesses a location that is *not* a source of conflict. These observations suggest that the combination of PC and data address might make an effective predictor. A policy based on this idea appears in Figure 6. The policy works on a per-thread, per-atomic block basis. Function ActivateALPoint is called on an abort. Depending on the frequency with which the current conflicting data address (line 6) and initially-accessing PC (line 7) have appeared in the recent past, the policy chooses one of four behaviors:

Precise Mode. Both the conflicting PC and the data address appear multiple times in the history. This is typical of statistics and bookkeeping information, or of cyclic dependences. In this mode, the appropriate anchor is activated (line 9) with the conflicting address as the target (line 10).

Coarse-grain Mode. In this case the conflicting PC is recurrent, but the data address keeps changing. This is typical of pointer-based structures like lists (Figure 3) and trees, whose nodes are scattered across cache lines. In this mode we activate the anchor with a "wild card" data address (line 14). In the next instance of the transaction, the first accessed DSNode of the structure (usually the root or head node—i.e., the whole data structure) will be locked.

Locking Promotion. If contention persists in coarse-grain mode, the lock is promoted to the parent anchor (line 16) in the hope of avoiding contention there.

```
1   void ActivateALPoint(ABContext *c, AbortInfo *abt) {
2       AEntry *en=SearchByPC(c→anchorTable, abt→confPC);
3       if (!en→isAnchor) // always begin with an anchor
4           en = en→pioneer;
5       AbortInfo *history = c→abtHistory;
6       bool a=CountAddr(history,abt→confAddr)>ADDR_THR;
7       bool p = CountPC(history, en→PC) > PC_THR;
8       if (p && a) {                    ▶ case 1: precise mode
9           c→activeAnchor = en→ID;
10          c→blockAddress = abt→confAddr;
11      } else if (p && !a) {
12          if (retries < PROM_THR) {    ▶ case 2: coarse grain
13              c→activeID = en→ID;
14              c→blockAddr = 0;
15          } else {                     ▶ case 3: locking promotion
16              c→activeID = en→parent;
17              c→blockAddr = 0;
18          }
19      } else { // !p                   ▶ case 4: training mode
20          c→activeID = 0;
21          c→blockAddr = 0;
22      }
23      AppendToHistory(history, en→PC, abt→confAddr);
24  }
```

Figure 6: Pseudocode of a simple locking policy.

Training Mode. When no pattern has (yet) emerged, the policy simply continues to gather statistics.

When a transaction commits while holding an advisory lock, but there was no contention on that lock, an empty entry can be appended to the abort history to shift out the previous records, avoiding over-locking in the case of low contention.

Coarse-grain locking and locking promotion serve to break cycles of conflict among transactions that occur on separate locations. In pointer-based data structures in particular, conflicting addresses may vary across both time and threads. Location-based hardware techniques for conflict avoidance (e.g., Wait-n-GoTM [14]) are generally unable to avoid such conflicts. With the advantage of information from the compiler's Data Structure Analysis, Staggered Transactions handle these conflicts by acquiring locks at a coarser granularity or a higher (more abstract) level of the data structure. Consider, for example, the transaction in Figure 3, which consumes significant time in genome. The transaction inserts segments into several lists in a shared table. A cycle of conflict may easily arise among threads—thread 1 inserts segments to lists A, B, and D; thread 2 to D and C; thread 3 to C and A. With a frequently conflicting PC (Anchor 35) and unstable conflicting addresses, the locking policy will eventually reach the advisory lock for the whole table (Anchor 42), breaking the conflict cycle.

6. EXPERIMENTAL RESULTS

Hardware. Since no existing HTM provides all the hardware features required by Staggered Transactions, we conducted our experiments on MARSSx86 [19], a full-system cycle-accurate x86 simulator with high fidelity HTM support [7]. The HTM simulation is based on a variant of AMD's Advanced Synchronization Facility (ASF) proposal [7, 10]. The ISA uses speculate/commit instructions to mark a transaction region. Read and write sets are maintained in the L1 cache by adding two bits (tx read and tx write) to each cache line. An eager requester-wins conflict resolution policy is implemented on top of a modified MOESI coherence

CPU cores	2.5GHz, 4-wide out-of-order issue/commit
L1 cache	private, 64K D + 64K I, 8-way, write-back, 64-byte line, 2-cycle
L2 cache	private, 1M, 8-way, write-back, 10-cycle
L3 cache	shared, 8M, 8-way, write-back, 30-cycle
Coherence	MOESI
Memory	4 GB, 50ns, 2 memory channels
HTM	2-bit (r/w) per L1 cache line eager requester-wins policy
Stag. Trans.	12-bit PC tag per L1 cache line

Table 2: Configuration of the HTM simulator.

Program	Static Stats		Dynamic Stats (1 thread)			Accuracy (16 thds)
	ld/st instrs	anchs	u-ops per txn	anchs per txn	exec. time inc	
genome	82	19	957	17.6	<1%	100%
intruder	410	56	351	8.5	<1%	97.2%
kmeans	13	6	261	4.5	1.6%	99.1%
labyrinth	418	18	16968	89.4	<1%	100%
ssca2	33	7	86	3.1	<1%	97.9%
vacation	442	76	4621	63.9	<1%	95.3%
list-hi	43	5	391	32.9	5.1%	98.7%
tsp	737	75	2348	9.7	<1%	97.0%
memcached	405	54	2520	80.9	<1%	98.3%

Table 3: Static and dynamic statistics of instrumentation.

protocol. This HTM, designed to "incur the fewest modifications to the existing cache coherence and core designs" [33], is similar to those employed in Intel's Haswell [33] and IBM's zEC12 [13], with the notable addition of nontransactional loads and stores within transactions. We made the following modifications to the simulator:

- The original ASF proposal treated only annotated load/store instructions (lock mov) as transactional operations, and normal load/store as nontransactional. In keeping with later changes in the proposal, we reversed this behavior to match that of other HTM systems.

- As described in Section 4, we added a 12-bit PC tag to every L1 cache line to record bits of the conflicting PC. The space overhead in the L1 cache is less than 2.4%.

- On a contention abort, the hardware places the low 12 bits of the conflicting PC and the low 52 bits of the conflicting data address into the %rbx register.

We model a 16-core machine with the configuration shown in Table 2.

Compiler and HTM Runtime. Our compiler support is realized in LLVM 3.4 as an optimization pass, using an existing DSA implementation.

The locking policy keeps 8 recent abort records in each ABContext, with PC_THR=2 and ADDR_THR=2. The HTM runtime tries each hardware transaction up to 10 times; it then enters irrevocable mode by acquiring a global lock. Hardware transactions add the global lock to their read set immediately before attempting to commit. Prior to a retry, the runtime spins for an amount of time whose mean value is proportional to the number of retries (as in the "Polite" policy of Scherer & Scott [26]).

Benchmarks. We use the STAMP suite [18] and three other representative TM programs as benchmarks, as sum-

marized in Table 4. STAMP's yada and bayes are excluded because yada has overflow issues and bayes has unstable execution time. The list-hi microbenchmark is drawn from the RSTM test suite [22]. It comprises a set of threads that search and update a single shared, sorted list. The tsp benchmark is our own C++ implementation of a branch-and-bound TSP solver. All candidate tasks are kept in a B+ tree-based [1] priority queue, which supports $O(1)$ pop and $O(n \log n)$ push operations. We eliminated the tree's size field, which tends to be highly contended. The memcached benchmark is a modified version of memcached 1.4.9. The network code is elided in order to speed up simulation and to increase the number of working threads. We obtain the input data from memslap and inject them directly into the application's command processing functions.

All binaries were compiled with -O2 optimizations, running on Debian 7.0 with a Linux 3.2 kernel. To avoid the potential contention bottleneck in the default glibc memory allocator, we use the Lockless Memory Allocator [12] instead. To reduce the impact of the OS scheduler, we pin every worker thread to a specific CPU core during program initialization. Each run was repeated 5 times; the average number is reported.

6.1 Instrumentation Overhead and Accuracy

The "Static Stats" section of Table 3 shows the number of loads and stores analyzed by the compiler and the number of these that were instrumented as anchors ("anchs") at compile time. On average, 13% of loads and stores are instrumented.

The "Dynamic Stats" section reflects the behavior of instrumented code in single-threaded runs. Since the number of anchors executed in each transaction is small compared to the total number of μ-ops, and an inactive ALP is simply a test and a non-taken branch, the execution time change is negligible in most benchmarks. The principal exception

Program	Source	Description and input	ABs	%TM	S	Abts/C	Contention
genome	STAMP	-g1024 -s16 -n16384	5	61%	6.0	0.25	low
intruder		-a10 -l4 -n2038 -s1	3	98%	3.2	5.28	high
kmeans		-m15 -n15 -t0.05 -i random-n2048-d16-c16	3	42%	4.6	4.74	high
labyrinth		-i random-x16-y16-z3-n64, w/ early release	3	91%	1.9	3.47	high
ssca2		-s13 -i1.0 -u1.0 -l3 -p3	10	16%	4.8	0.02	low
vacation		-n4 -q40 -u90 -r16387 -t4096	3	87%	9.7	0.49	med
list-lo	IntSet[22]	64 nodes, 90%/5%/5% lookup/insert/delete	4	86%	3.6	1.11	med
list-hi		64 nodes, 60%/20%/20% lookup/insert/delete	4	83%	1.0	4.05	high
tsp	[1]	travel salesman problem solver, 17 cities	3	90%	3.6	1.74	med
memcached	[17]	in-memory key-value storage	17	85%	2.6	4.77	high

Table 4: Benchmark characteristics. ABs: number of atomic blocks in the source code. %TM: percentage of execution time spent in transactional mode. S: speedup with 16 threads over sequential run on the baseline HTM. Abts/C: aborts per commit on the baseline with 16 threads.

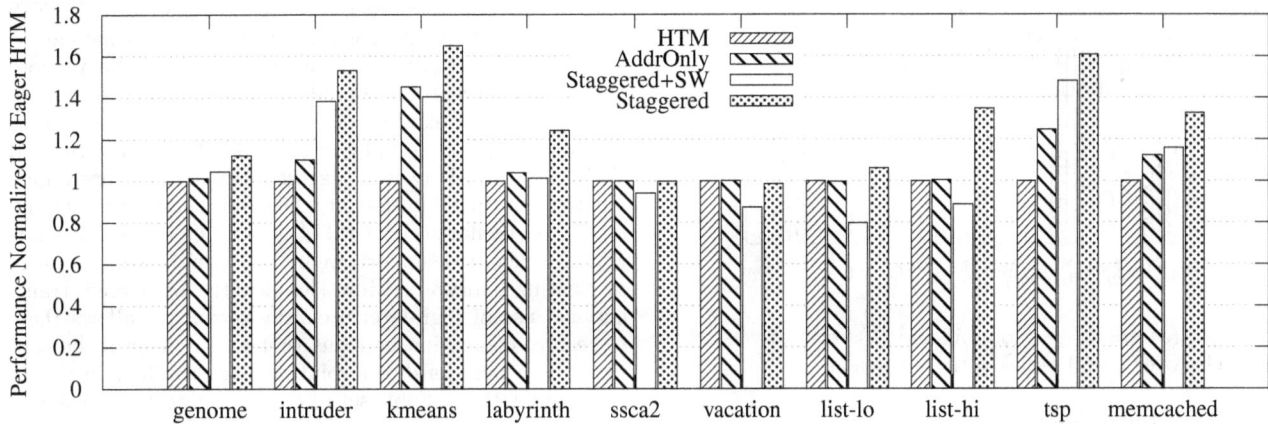

Figure 7: Performance comparison with 16 threads.

is the list microbenchmark, in which the anchors appear in tight loops. Further optimization of such loops may be a fruitful direction for future work.

For comparison, we also constructed a naive implementation in which every load and store was instrumented. This lead to slowdowns in excess of 10% for six of the benchmark programs (labyrinth, kmeans, vacation, list, tsp, and memcached).

The "Accuracy" section of the table shows the percentage of dynamic aborts for which our runtime was able to correctly identify the anchor associated with the initial access of the contended datum. All are above 95%; six out of nine are above 98%.

6.2 Parallel Performance

In the "S" column of Table 4, we list the speedup of benchmarks running on the baseline eager HTM at 16 threads. These benchmarks show low to high contention, as indicated in the final column. The worst is list-hi, which stops scaling after 4 threads.

Comparative performance on 16 threads appears in Figure 7, which plots speedup relative to the baseline ("HTM") for "StaggeredTM" (with hardware Conflict PC support) and "StaggerTM w/o CPC" (with software-based anchor tracking, as described in Section 4). Also plotted is a much simpler scheme, "AddrOnly," which places one fixed ALP at the beginning of each atomic block and uses only precise mode to trigger lock acquisition.

Result 1: *Staggered Transactions improve the performance of high-contention applications without slowing down application with low contention.*

We see substantial performance improvement (>30%) in intruder, kmeans, list-hi, tsp, and memcached. The improvement in intruder comes from serializing the modifications to a global queue, especially an enqueue that occurs near the end of a long transaction (TMdecoder_process). In kmeans, most conflicts take place when updating an array of pointers representing the centers of data clusters. Due to the good locality of conflicting PC and data addresses, Staggered Transactions are able to acquire advisory locks on a per-cluster basis (close to what fine-grain locking could achieve). In list-hi, Staggered Transactions avoid repetitive aborts among several conflicting transactions by locking the entire list (case 2 in Figure 6). Note that locking is triggered only when contention actually arises, and transactions that

do not contribute to that contention are not blocked. In tsp, Staggered Transactions successfully discover that the head of the priority queue (left-most node of the tree) is the most contended object. Transactions that perform insertions on the same leaf node are also serialized if they repeatedly abort each other. Most conflicts in memcached are due to access to global shared statistics, accessed in the middle of transactions. Staggered Transactions introduce significant serialization, but still allow more concurrency than the baseline with fallback to a global lock.

Moderate performance improvements (6–24%) are obtained in genome, list-lo, and labyrinth. In genome, the most time-consuming transaction inserts a few elements into a fixed-sized hash table, which ends up overloaded and prone to contention, particularly when a conflict chain is established among several transactions. Although the conflicting PC is associated with the list-traversal code used to access buckets of the table, the Staggered Transactions policy can serialize at the level of the table as a whole via locking promotion (Section 5.2), thereby avoiding aborts even in the presence of conflict chains. Two benchmarks (ssca2 and vacation) see no significant improvement in execution time. Even in these, however, Staggered Transactions reduce the frequency of aborts, as shown in Section 6.3.

The harmonic mean of performance improvements across all benchmarks is 24%.

Result 2: *Staggered Transactions benefit from both partial overlap and a flexible blocking policy.*

In intruder, tsp, and memcached, conflicting data addresses are stable across transaction instances. Here the performance improvements stem simply from serializing the conflicting portions of those transactions, and allowing the remainder to execute in parallel. In the other benchmarks, conflicting data addresses vary greatly; for these, coarse-grain locking and locking promotion are essential to conflict reduction.

6.3 Reduced Aborts and Wasted Cycles

Result 3: *Staggered Transactions reduce contention and wasted CPU cycles for most applications.*

For each of our benchmark applications, we compare Staggered Transactions to the baseline HTM with regard to (1) the ratio of aborted to committed transactions and (2) the ratio of wasted to committed *work* (cycles) (Figure 8). Stag-

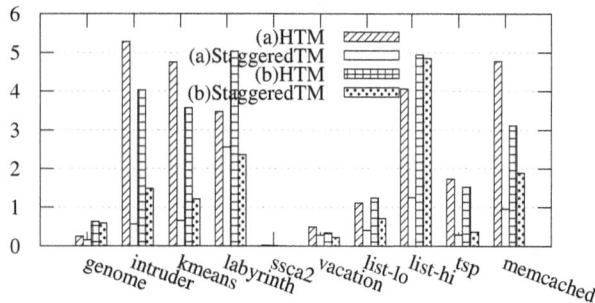

Figure 8: (a) aborts per commit and (b) ratio of wasted CPU cycles over useful cycles with 16 threads.

gered Transactions eliminate up to 89% of the aborts (in intruder) and an average of 64% across the benchmark set (excluding ssca2, which has too few aborts for the numbers to be meaningful). This results in an average savings of 43% of the wasted CPU cycles (a lower number than the savings in abort rate, because aborted transactions typically stop when only part-way through). Assuming that cycles that would have been wasted on aborted transactions are instead devoted either to useful work or to waiting (at relatively low power consumption) for advisory locks, it seems reasonable to expect Staggered Transactions to achieve a significant reduction in energy as well.

7. RELATED WORK

HTM systems can be broadly categorized as *eager* or *lazy*, depending on whether conflicts are discovered "as they occur" or only at commit time. A few systems, such as FlexTM [28] and EazyHTM [30], support mixed policies. Most current commercial systems employ a "requester wins" policy in order to avoid changes to the coherence protocol (IBM's z series machines leverage existing NAK messages to delay aborts, in an attempt to give the victim a chance to commit [13]). A few designs are more sophisticated: LogTM-SE [32], for example, will stall some transactions on conflict; potential deadlock is detected using timestamps in coherence messages. Even a simple conflict manager, however, introduces significant implementation challenges because of the necessary protocol extensions and validation cost [27].

Nonetheless, several ambitious solutions have been proposed for eager HTM. In the dependence-aware transactions (DATM) of Ramadan et al. [21], speculative data may be forwarded from transaction A to transaction B if prior accesses have already dictated that A must commit before B, and B attempts to read something A has written. In the Wait-n-GoTM of Jafri et al. [14], hardware may generate an exception that prompts the runtime to delay a transaction, if prior experience indicates that upcoming instructions are likely to introduce a circular dependence with some other active transaction. Most recently, Qian et al. proposed Omni-Order [20] to support cycle detection and conflict serialization in a directory-based coherence protocol. RETCON [3], which targets lazy HTMs, tries to "rescue" conflicting transactions by re-executing the conflicting code slice at commit time.

While these hardware proposals may achieve significant reductions in conflict rate, most are specific to a particular class of HTM (e.g., eager or lazy), or are applicable only to certain conflict patterns. FlexTM and DATM, for example,

require changes to the cache coherence protocol. RETCON can resolve only simple conflicts such as counter increment. Wait-n-GoTM requires the underlying TM to be version-based, and the centralized predictor tends to be a bottleneck.

Staggered Transactions share the "stall before encountering contention" philosophy of systems like LogTM-SE and Wait-n-GoTM. Because Staggered Transactions are implemented principally in software, however, they are not bound to any particular style of HTM or conflict resolution strategy. The required support, we believe, could be added easily to existing hardware. More significantly, Staggered Transactions' use of high-level program knowledge allows them to resolve contention patterns that are unlikely to be captured by a pure hardware solution (e.g., conflicts in a data structure with no stable set of conflicting data addresses).

Contention management has also been a subject of active research in STM systems, where the flexibility of software and the high baseline overhead of instrumentation can justify even very complex policies. While much early work (including our own [26, 29]) served mainly to recover from contention once it happened, several projects have aimed to avoid contention proactively. Multi-version STM, pioneered by Riegel et al. [23], significantly reduces contention by allowing a transaction to "commit in the past" if it has not written any location that was read by a subsequent transaction. Later work by the same authors [24] uses Data Structure Analysis [16] to partition shared data and choose a potentially different STM algorithm or locking policy for each partition. Chakrabarti et al. [5] use a profiling-based *abort information graph* to identify data dependences and optimize STM policy. Given their reliance on software instrumentation, none of these techniques are compatible with existing HTM, and all would be difficult to integrate into future hardware designs.

In a manner less dependent on TM system details, contention can sometimes be avoided by carefully scheduling the threads that run conflicting transactions. Proactive Transaction Scheduling [2] learns from repeated aborts and predicts future contention. The scheduler uses the prediction to serialize entire transactions when they are likely to conflict with one another. In comparison to such techniques, Staggered Transactions avoid the overhead of scheduling decisions, thereby avoiding any negative impact on the performance of short transactions. Also, by serializing only the conflicting portions of transactions, Staggered Transactions can achieve more parallelism.

8. CONCLUSIONS

We have presented an automatic mechanism, Staggered Transactions, to serialize the conflicting portions of hardware transactions, thereby reducing aborts. Our technique employs compile-time Data Structure Analysis to understand program data, allowing us to accommodate a wide variety of conflict patterns. While the choice of which lock to acquire is always based on the address of the data being accessed, the decision as to *whether* to acquire a lock, and at what instruction address, is made adaptively at run time.

From the hardware, Staggered Transactions require the ability to acquire an advisory lock from within an active transaction; they also benefit from a mechanism to recall the program counter of the initial speculative access to a given conflicting location. Experiments on the MARSSx86 ASF simulator demonstrate speedups averaging 24% on a collection of 9 TM applications. In future work we hope to experiment with a wider range of run-time policies and with compatible physical hardware (e.g., the POWER 8). We also plan to extend our simulations to lazy TM protocols.

References

[1] T. Bingmann. *STX B+ Tree C++ Template Classes*. URL http://panthema.net/2007/stx-btree.

[2] G. Blake, R. G. Dreslinski, and T. Mudge. Proactive transaction scheduling for contention management. In *42nd IEEE/ACM Intl. Symp. on Microarchitecture*, MICRO 42, New York, NY, 2009.

[3] C. Blundell, A. Raghavan, and M. M. Martin. RETCON: Transactional repair without replay. In *37th Intl. Symp. on Computer Architecture*, ISCA '10, Saint-Malo, France, 2010.

[4] H. W. Cain, M. M. Michael, B. Frey, C. May, D. Williams, and H. Le. Robust architectural support for transactional memory in the Power architecture. In *40th Intl. Symp. on Computer Architecture*, ISCA '13, Tel-Aviv, Israel, 2013.

[5] D. R. Chakrabarti, P. Banerjee, H.-J. Boehm, P. G. Joisha, and R. S. Schreiber. The runtime abort graph and its application to software transactional memory optimization. In *9th IEEE/ACM Intl. Symp. on Code Generation and Optimization*, CGO '11, 2011.

[6] S. Chaudhry, R. Cypher, M. Ekman, M. Karlsson, A. Landin, and S. Yip. Rock: A high-performance Sparc CMT processor. *IEEE Micro*, 29(2):6–16, Mar.–Apr. 2009.

[7] D. Christie, J.-W. Chung, S. Diestelhorst, M. Hohmuth, M. Pohlack, C. Fetzer, M. Nowack, T. Riegel, P. Felber, P. Marlier, and E. Rivière. Evaluation of AMD's Advanced Synchronization Facility within a complete transactional memory stack. In *5th European Conf. on Computer Systems*, EuroSys '10, 2010.

[8] J. Chung, L. Yen, S. Diestelhorst, M. Pohlack, M. Hohmuth, D. Christie, and D. Grossman. ASF: AMD64 extension for lock-free data structures and transactional memory. In *2010 43rd IEEE/ACM Intl. Symp. on Microarchitecture*, MICRO 43, 2010.

[9] L. Dalessandro, F. Carouge, S. White, Y. Lev, M. Moir, M. L. Scott, and M. F. Spear. Hybrid NOrec: A case study in the effectiveness of best effort hardware transactional memory. In *16th Intl. Conf. on Architectural Support for Programming Languages and Operating Systems*, ASPLOS '11, Newport Beach, CA, 2011.

[10] S. Diestelhorst. *Marss86-ASF*, 2013. URL http://bitbucket.org/stephand/marss86-asf.

[11] V. Gajinov, F. Zyulkyarov, O. S. Unsal, A. Cristal, E. Ayguade, T. Harris, and M. Valero. QuakeTM: Parallelizing a complex sequential application using transactional memory. In *23rd Intl. Conf. on Supercomputing*, ICS '09, 2009.

[12] L. Inc. *The Lockless Memory Allocator*. URL http://locklessinc.com.

[13] C. Jacobi, T. Slegel, and D. Greiner. Transactional memory architecture and implementation for IBM System z. In *2012 45th IEEE/ACM Intl. Symp. on Microarchitecture*, MICRO '12, Vancouver, B.C., Canada, 2012.

[14] S. A. R. Jafri, G. Voskuilen, and T. N. Vijaykumar. Wait-n-GoTM: Improving HTM performance by serializing cyclic dependencies. In *18th Intl. Conf. on Architectural Support for Programming Languages and Operating Systems*, ASPLOS '13, Houston, Texas, 2013.

[15] C. Lattner. *Macroscopic Data Structure Analysis and Optimization*. PhD thesis, Computer Science Dept., University of Illinois at Urbana-Champaign, May 2005.

[16] C. Lattner and V. Adve. Automatic pool allocation: Improving performance by controlling data structure layout in the heap. In *2005 ACM SIGPLAN Conf. on Programming Language Design and Implementation*, PLDI '05, Chicago, IL, 2005.

[17] Memcached. URL http://memcached.org.

[18] C. C. Minh, J. Chung, C. Kozyrakis, and K. Olukotun. STAMP: Stanford transactional applications for multi-processing. In *IEEE Intl. Symp. on Workload Characterization, 2008.*, IISWC '08, 2008.

[19] A. Patel, F. Afram, S. Chen, and K. Ghose. MARSSx86: A Full System Simulator for x86 CPUs. In *Design Automation Conf. 2011 (DAC'11)*, 2011.

[20] X. Qian, B. Sahelices, and J. Torrellas. Omniorder: Directory-based conflict serialization of transactions. In *41st Intl. Symp. on Computer Architecture*, ISCA '14, June 2014.

[21] H. E. Ramadan, C. J. Rossbach, and E. Witchel. Dependence-aware transactional memory for increased concurrency. In *41st IEEE/ACM Intl. Symp. on Microarchitecture*, MICRO 41, Como, Italy, 2008.

[22] Reconfigurable Software Transactional Memory Runtime. URL http://code.google.com/p/rstm.

[23] T. Riegel, P. Felber, and C. Fetzer. A lazy snapshot algorithm with eager validation. In *20th Intl. Symp. on Distributed Computing*, DISC '06, Stockholm, Sweden, Sept. 2006.

[24] T. Riegel, C. Fetzer, and P. Felber. Automatic data partitioning in software transactional memories. In *20th Symp. on Parallelism in Algorithms and Architectures*, SPAA '08, Munich, Germany, 2008.

[25] T. Riegel, P. Marlier, M. Nowack, P. Felber, and C. Fetzer. Optimizing hybrid transactional memory: The importance of nonspeculative operations. In *23rd ACM Symp. on Parallelism in Algorithms and Architectures*, SPAA '11, 2011.

[26] W. N. Scherer, III and M. L. Scott. Advanced contention management for dynamic software transactional memory. In *24th ACM Symp. on Principles of Distributed Computing*, PODC '05, Las Vegas, NV, 2005.

[27] A. Shriraman and S. Dwarkadas. Refereeing conflicts in hardware transactional memory. In *23rd Intl. Conf. on Supercomputing*, ICS '09, Yorktown Heights, NY, 2009.

[28] A. Shriraman, S. Dwarkadas, and M. L. Scott. Flexible decoupled transactional memory support. In *35th Intl. Symp. on Computer Architecture*, ISCA '08, Beijing, China, 2008.

[29] M. F. Spear, L. Dalessandro, V. J. Marathe, and M. L. Scott. A comprehensive strategy for contention management in software transactional memory. In *14th ACM SIGPLAN Symp. on Principles and Practice of Parallel Programming*, PPoPP '09, Raleigh, NC, 2009.

[30] S. Tomić, C. Perfumo, C. Kulkarni, A. Armejach, A. Cristal, O. Unsal, T. Harris, and M. Valero. EazyHTM: Eager-lazy hardware transactional memory. In *42nd IEEE/ACM Intl. Symp. on Microarchitecture*, MICRO 42, New York, NY, 2009.

[31] L. Xiang and M. L. Scott. Software partitioning of hardware transactions. In *20th ACM SIGPLAN Symp. on Principles and Practice of Parallel Programming (PPoPP)*, San Francisco, CA, Feb. 2015.

[32] L. Yen, J. Bobba, M. R. Marty, K. E. Moore, H. Volos, M. D. Hill, M. M. Swift, and D. A. Wood. LogTM-SE: Decoupling hardware transactional memory from caches. In *2007 IEEE 13th Intl. Symp. on High Performance Computer Architecture*, HPCA '07, Phoenix, AZ, 2007.

[33] R. M. Yoo, C. J. Hughes, K. Lai, and R. Rajwar. Performance evaluation of Intel transactional synchronization extensions for high-performance computing. In *Intl. Conf. for High Performance Computing, Networking, Storage and Analysis*, SC '13, Denver, CO, 2013.

Transactional Acceleration of Concurrent Data Structures

Yujie Liu
Lehigh University
yul510@lehigh.edu

Tingzhe Zhou
Lehigh University
tiz214@lehigh.edu

Michael Spear
Lehigh University
spear@cse.lehigh.edu

ABSTRACT

Concurrent data structures are a fundamental building block for scalable multi-threaded programs. While Transactional Memory (TM) was originally conceived as a mechanism for simplifying the creation of concurrent data structures, modern hardware TM systems lack the progress properties needed to completely obviate traditional techniques for designing concurrent data structures, especially those requiring nonblocking progress guarantees.

In this paper, we introduce the Prefix Transaction Optimization (PTO) technique for employing hardware TM to accelerate existing concurrent data structures. Our technique consists of three stages: the creation of a prefix transaction, the mechanical optimization of the prefix transaction, and then algorithm-specific optimizations to further improve performance. We apply PTO to five nonblocking data structures, and observe speedups of up to 1.5x at one thread, and up to 3x at 8 threads.

Categories and Subject Descriptors

D.1.3 [**Programming Techniques**]: Concurrent Programming— *Parallel Programming*

Keywords

Lock-Freedom, Transactional Memory, Concurrency, Synchronization

1 Introduction

Modern parallel programs rely on concurrent data structures (CDS) to achieve scalable synchronization. Over the past two decades, dozens of concurrent data structures have been proposed, providing highly scalable stacks, queues, lists, trees, hash tables, skiplists, heaps, and many other data structures.

The design of concurrent data structures is challenging, for a number of reasons. First, they must achieve good performance across a variety of workloads. An implementation ought to have low latency when accessed by a single thread. This property is valuable for applications whose threads rarely access the data structure at the same time: if latency is too high, then the programmer

may instead opt to protect a sequential data structure with a coarse-grained lock. However, an implementation should also exhibit high scalability. That is, in highly concurrent workloads, threads should not impede each others' progress when they access disjoint parts of the data structure. There is typically a tension between these goals: to ensure good scalability, a greater amount of metadata manipulation is required to coordinate potential concurrent accesses to the data structure; however, the injection of metadata introduces overhead to the streamlined sequential implementations, and moreover, metadata accesses often require the use of expensive atomic synchronization primitives, such as compare-and-swap (CAS). Introducing fine-grained metadata can result in more atomic primitives per operation, and thus more latency.

Secondly, many programs expect progress guarantees from concurrent data structures. Wait-freedom [19], the strongest progress guarantee, ensures that at any point in an execution, regardless of the states of other threads, there exists a finite bound on the number of steps for any thread to complete its operation. Wait-free algorithms often require expensive synchronization among threads. The weaker guarantee of lock-freedom [20], where at any point in a program's execution there exists *some* thread that can complete its operation in a finite number of steps, has been achieved in many practical data structures. However, even in lock-free data structures, there is often significant overhead to make concurrent updates to multiple locations appear atomic (e.g., by simulating a multi-word compare-and-swap [15, 32]).

Hardware Transactional Memory (HTM) [21] was originally designed to simplify the task of creating concurrent data structures. The idea behind HTM is simple: programmers mark regions of code that ought to execute as a single, indivisible operation, and then the hardware runs these "transactions" concurrently, while tracking their memory accesses. By tracking accesses, the hardware can identify conflicting memory accesses among transactions. By also providing a buffering mechanism, the hardware can abort, roll-back, and retry some of the transactions involved in a conflict, so that each transaction appears to execute in isolation.

Unlike research HTM proposals, the first-generation HTM systems from IBM [23, 44] and Intel [22] expose significant limitations, which limit their suitability to lock-free programming. These "best effort" HTMs [7, 27] do not guarantee progress for arbitrary transactions: a transaction attempt will fail if it (a) attempts to access too many distinct locations; (b) executes for longer than a scheduler quantum of the operating system; or (c) attempts to perform an unsupported operation, such as a system call. Transaction attempts can also fail due to memory accesses that conflict with concurrent operations from transactions, or accesses that conflict with concurrent nontransactional code. This property, called "strong atomicity" [2], is a natural outcome of implementing HTM through the cache coherence protocol. It also allows for clever composition of transactional and nontransactional code [7,8,46].

Even if these limitations did not exist, it is unlikely that HTM could ever fully replace the best concurrent data structure implementations. As recently reported by Gramoli [13], concurrent data structures implemented directly from atomic primitives (i.e. CAS) tend to provide the best performance in comparison to those implemented by using locks or transactions.

This paper explores how HTM might still benefit the design and implementation of concurrent data structures. Specifically, we propose a methodology, called Prefix Transaction Optimization (PTO), by which HTM can be used to accelerate an existing implementation. There are three components of PTO, which vary in terms of the degree to which they can be automated, the amount of implementation-specific knowledge needed, and the potential gain. In the first step, we create a prefix transaction to execute a sequence of steps in the existing implementation, which uses HTM but may fail. In the second step, we mechanically optimize this prefix through strength reduction and elimination of corner cases [38], and other classic compiler optimizations. In the third step, we modify the original algorithm so as to introduce minimal "overhead" while affording more aggressive optimization of the prefix transaction.

PTO offers many compelling properties. It preserves the progress guarantees of the original algorithm, which is an improvement over many approaches to transactional acceleration of concurrent programs. It is also a composable technique, which can be applied at multiple levels of granularity. PTO optimizations can be linked together, and the benefits of doing so are (more or less) additive. Lastly, and most significantly, PTO can dramatically improve performance. We observe speedups of up to 1.5x at one thread, and up to 3x at 8 threads, on state-of-the-art nonblocking data structures.

2 Prefix Transaction Optimization

In this section, we present the algorithm-agnostic aspects of the Prefix Transaction Optimization (PTO) technique. Enhancements and modifications specific to a single data structure or class of data structures are discussed in Section 3.

2.1 Model

The PTO technique is applicable to concurrent objects implemented in shared memory using read/write registers and common synchronization primitives (e.g. compare-and-swap, fetch-and-add, etc). The object interface defines a set of invocable operations.

We adopt the *control flow graph* representation [37] for each operation (and its sub-operations), where a node represents a step in the algorithm and an edge represents a transition in the control flow. We assume each operation has a single *start* node. For two nodes a and b in a control flow graph, a *dominates* b if any code path from start to b includes a. A *superblock* is a connected sub-graph where all nodes are dominated by a single *entry* node. An edge from a node within a superblock to one outside is called an *exit* edge.

We assume that HTM is supported by the architecture via three instructions: TxBegin starts a transaction, TxEnd commits the transaction, and TxAbort causes the transaction to abort. The TxBegin instruction can return more than once: if a transaction cannot commit for any reason, then the effects of the transaction are undone, and control returns to the point of TxBegin with a return value indicating the cause of the inability to commit. A return value of OK indicates that the code is running as a transaction.

HTM is assumed to provide strong atomicity [2]. When a hardware transaction is running, none of its effects are visible to any concurrent code; all effects become visible atomically at TxEnd.

During the execution of the transaction, if any concurrent transaction performs a conflicting access, the HTM will choose (at least) one transaction to abort. If any nontransactional code performs a conflicting access, the transaction will immediately abort. Upon any abort, control will return to TxBegin, where the program can decide whether to attempt the transaction again.

2.2 The Prefix Transaction Transformation

Given a superblock B in a control flow graph G, the Prefix Transaction Transformation (illustrated in Figure 1) is constructed by attempting to execute the superblock using a hardware transaction. If that attempt fails, then the original version of code is invoked, without the use of a transaction. More precisely:

DEFINITION 1. *Let B be a superblock of a control flow graph G. The Prefix Transaction Transformation is a function $\mathcal{T}_B(G)$ that maps G to G', a copy of G with B replaced by B', such that:*

- *T_B is a copy of T where a TxEnd instruction is inserted at each exit edge, and zero or more TxAbort instructions are inserted at any edges of T except the exit edges;*
- *S is a TxBegin instruction with a branch to the dominator of T_B if the return value is OK and a branch to the dominator of B otherwise;*
- *Let B' be the superblock dominated by S with all nodes of T_B and B included.*

Given a transformation $\mathcal{T}_B(G)$ defined in Definition 1, we say B' is the *optimized superblock*. Inside B', we say T_B is the *prefix transaction* of B, and B is the *fallback*.

The following theorems capture basic properties of the Prefix Transaction Transformation. We first prove the correctness of our transformation, by constructing a refinement mapping [1] from the transformed implementation to the original (Theorem 2). We then prove the progress guarantee of the original implementation is preserved by the transformation (Theorem 3). Finally, implied by the theorems, we observe that the program may choose to explicitly abort a transaction at any point (within the transaction) without compromising correctness or progress conditions.

THEOREM 2 (REFINEMENT). *Let G be the control flow graph of some operation of an implementation I, and let I' be the implementation with $\mathcal{T}_B(G)$ applied to I. I' refines I.*

PROOF SKETCH. The mapping of states is simply an identical function that maps the states of I' to the states of I. For a process p taking a step in I', if the step is not a transactional instruction or access, we let p take a corresponding step in I. For a TxBegin, TxAbort, or a transactional access step in I', p takes no step in I. For a TxEnd step in I', let k be the number of steps p has taken in-between the TxEnd the last TxBegin step, we let process p take k steps in I. □

THEOREM 3 (PROGRESS PRESERVATION). *Let G be the control flow graph of some operation of a lock-free (or wait-free) implementation I, and let I' be the implementation with $\mathcal{T}_B(G)$ applied to I. I' provides lock-free (or wait-free) progress.*

PROOF SKETCH. Suppose I is lock-free. Then some operation in I completes if process p takes a bounded number of steps. For a given configuration c of I, let k be this bound. Then at most k steps are spent in superblock B before some operation completes, and since B contains at least one step, it can be executed no more than k times before some operation completes.

Let f be the refinement mapping constructed in Theorem 2. For a configuration c' in I' where $c = f(c')$, process p can spend at

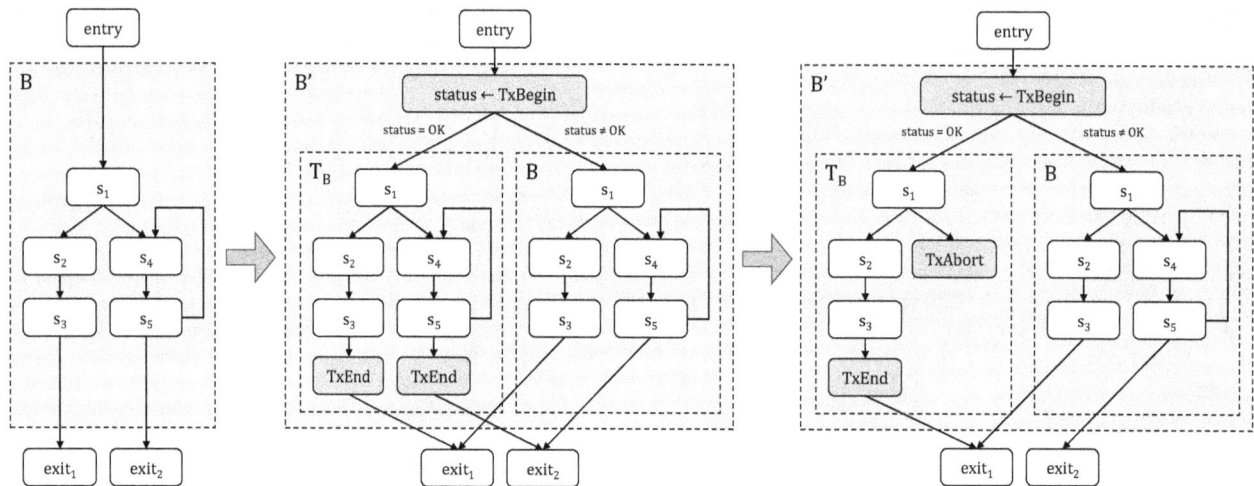

Figure 1: Prefix Transaction Transformation

most k steps in a transaction (excluding the `TxBegin`, `TxAbort` and `TxEnd` steps) before some operation completes. A committed or aborted transaction takes at most $(k + 3)$ steps including the `TxBegin`, `TxAbort` and `TxEnd` steps. In case the transaction aborts, at most $(2k + 3)$ steps are spent to execute the optimized superblock. Hence, we know in configuration c', some operation completes within $k \cdot (2k + 3)$ steps taken by process p.

Proving the preservation of wait-free progress employs the similar technique. □

2.3 Optimizing Prefix Transactions

We now turn our discussion to how to optimize the prefix transaction. We first present optimizations that can be easily identified and performed by a compiler using canonical static analyses.

Eliminating Synchronization: Correctness proofs of concurrent data structures often assume sequential consistency [26]. Implementations, in turn, must entail memory fences to enforce explicit ordering on architectures with weaker memory models.

Within a prefix transaction, memory fences can be elided, since they are subsumed by the implicit memory fences of `TxBegin` and `TxEnd` instructions, and atomic synchronization primitives, such as compare-and-swap and read-modify-write operations, can be replaced with their corresponding loads, stores, and branches.

Eliminating Redundant Loads: Double-checking is a technique used in many concurrent data structures [9,35]. Implementations employ double-checking to ensure a consistent view of multiple memory locations. In the prefix transaction, a single read to a shared location suffices, since the second read will always return the same value (given the transaction does not perform a write to the location in-between the reads); any conflicting write to the location will cause the transaction to abort.

For implementations that use the atomic compare-and-swap primitive, the compare-and-swap is usually attempted after a preceding read to the location. Since in a transaction we convert the compare-and-swap to a read followed by a conditional write, the read (produced by the conversion) can coalesce with the former read.

We also observe that many search data structures [9,45] employ a *search phase*, followed by an *update phase* that performs its writes after validating selected locations accessed in the search phase. These implementations are likely to benefit from the elimination of redundant loads enabled by our transformation.

Eliminating Redundant Stores: Nonblocking data structures often exploit *intermediate states* during an update operation to allow helping from concurrent threads. The size of intermediate states may vary from unused bits embedded in the data fields [14, 28] to complex, dynamically-allocated auxiliary structures [9, 39]. Fundamentally, these intermediate states are introduced to overcome the difficulty that traditional synchronization primitives can update only a single word at a time.

It is commonly seen in nonblocking algorithms [9,29,39,41] that operations first attempt to change several locations from a clean state to some intermediate state, and then restore them back to a clean state. Given that an update is performed within a transaction, and all stores to a location appear atomically, the temporary change to intermediate states can be eliminated. Furthermore, if dynamic memory allocations are involved to create intermediate objects, these allocations can be eliminated together with the silent stores, mitigating pressure on the shared allocator object.

In CDSs using hazard pointers [34] or reference counts [42] to manage dynamic memory, intermediate updates to the hazard lists (i.e., insertion followed by removal) or to the reference counters (i.e., increment followed by decrement) can be safely eliminated as redundant stores in the prefix transaction.

2.4 Avoiding Helping in Prefix Transactions

Although helping is the key idea behind many nonblocking concurrent data structures, it tends to increase contention among threads in some cases [16,25,29,36].

When a prefix transaction observes states in which it must perform helping to make progress, it may be preferable to simply abort the transaction and switch to executing the lock-free fallback. The rationale governing such decision is twofold: First, when a prefix transaction determines to help, the situation suggests a concurrent operation is accessing locations touched by the transaction (and vice versa) and is likely to create a conflict that causes the transaction to abort. Thus, the explicit abort can serve as an ad-hoc backoff mechanism to avoid the contention in the first place. Second, if the prefix transaction is optimized (as discussed in Section 2.3) so that it does not introduce intermediate states, it can be desirable to maximally avoid helping (which introduces intermediate states) in the prefix transaction for the sake of improving total throughput.

From a pragmatic perspective, we argue that it is fairly straightforward for a concurrent data structure designer to identify the helping code paths in the algorithm, and decide whether to replace them with explicit aborts in the prefix transactions. Examples of how to make such choices are discussed in subsequent sections of the paper. On the other hand, we found that in most nonblocking algorithms, a helping code path can be defined as an unreachable sub-path in the control flow graph of a single-threaded executions. A trivial example is the code to handle a failed compare-and-swap operation. Using this definition as a heuristic, an optimizing compiler can collect information from a single-threaded profile run, and (approximately) identify the helping paths for making optimization decisions.

2.5 Recursive Optimizations

Prefix Transaction Transformation is a *local* optimization, which means it can be applied to a whole operation or to individual components (superblocks) of the operation. More importantly, the optimization can be repeatedly applied on optimized code until achieving the best performance.

The simplest example of an recursive optimization is to allow an aborted prefix transaction to retry before attempting the fallback. For instance, the following transformation attempts the same prefix transaction T_B twice before switching to the fallback:

$$\mathcal{T_B}(\mathcal{T_B}(G))$$

A more powerful use of recursive optimization is to compose optimizations in a hierarchical structure. Suppose that in the control flow graph G of some operation, superblock B is a sub-graph of superblock A. The following transformation:

$$\mathcal{T_B}(\mathcal{T_A}(G)) \text{ where } B \subset A$$

first attempts the prefix transaction T_A, and in the fallback path of T_A, the program can still benefit from the optimizations of $\mathcal{T_B}(G)$.

Hierarchical composition has an important impact in practice: Applying the transformation on larger superblocks maximizes the opportunity for eliminating redundancy (i.e. loads, stores, and fences), but makes it harder for transactions to make progress under contention, and thus, hurts scalability. Applying the transformation on smaller superblocks facilitates making progress, but reduces the opportunity to reduce latency. Composing optimizations makes it possible to achieve low latency and high scalability at the same time. We also notice that, by Theorem 3, applying the transformation for a bounded number of times preserves the progress guarantees of the original implementation.

3 Applying Prefix Transaction Optimization

The PTO technique presented in Section 2 does not require much algorithm-specific knowledge, though a programmer with knowledge about expected common paths may insert explicit aborts to increase optimization opportunities. We now turn our attention to the technical details of applying PTO to specific concurrent data structures, including additional algorithm-specific optimizations.

3.1 Data Structures with Simple Applications

Mindicators We first consider the Mindicator data structure [28]. Like SNZI [10] and the f-array [24], the Mindicator is a static-sized tree that computes a function over a set of values, where each thread offers at most one value as an input to the function. The original Mindicator algorithm uses a marking phase to traverse from a per-thread leaf up to some point in the tree, and unmarks nodes as it traverses back to the leaf. Unlike f-Array, not all operations must traverse to the root; unlike SNZI, additional functions (min, max) are supported in addition to 0/1 saturating addition.

The application of PTO to the Mindicator did not make use of any algorithm-specific optimizations, primarily because the tree is static and hence there is no memory allocation. By applying PTO, the marking and unmarking steps could be coalesced: marking and unmarking were previously both implemented as increments to a per-node counter; with PTO, the counter is incremented once, by two. This, in turn, eliminated the downward traversal entirely. After applying PTO, we tuned the threshold for retries before PTO falls back to the lock-free slow path. A choice of three attempts yielded the best performance.

Mounds We also applied PTO to the Mound [29], a heap-like data structure that implements a priority queue. Like the Mindicator, the Mound is a tree-shaped data structure. However, it is a tree of sorted lists, where each list is only modified at its head. We did not choose the Mound because it is the best nonblocking heap or priority queue. We chose it instead for the value it adds when evaluating PTO. Specifically, the Mound employs double-compare-and-swap (DCAS) and double-compare-single-swap (DCSS) operations throughout its implementation, to perform atomic updates on up to two locations. This afforded an opportunity to evaluate the impact of applying PTO locally, e.g., to individual DCAS and DCSS operations.

In the Mound, insertion consists of a search, followed by a double-compare-single-swap (DCSS), which is implemented in software through a sequence of CAS instructions. Removal entails performing a CAS to remove the top of the heap, and then several DCAS operations to restore invariants at the root and then on its children, recursively. Insertions can barely benefit from PTO, because they are streamlined and contention-free already: the heap itself is a static tree, obviating memory management overheads, and the insertion entails a log-log-depth traversal and just one simulated DCSS. Similarly, employing PTO on the entire removal operation is not effective at any level of concurrency, since all concurrent removals contend at the top of the heap. However, it is profitable to use PTO on a sub-operation of insert and removal, namely the DCAS/DCSS operations.

Skip Lists Lock-free skip lists [12] are a widely used search data structure to implement concurrent maps and sets. In the skip list algorithm, an update operation first locates the predecessor and successor nodes of a given key value, and then uses a sequence of compare-and-swap operations to link/unlink the nodes into the hierarchy of lists.

We experimentally determined that local application of PTO was the only promising technique. We proceeded to apply PTO only to the insert and remove operations. In an insert operation, we use a prefix transaction to update the next pointers of the predecessors. Similarly, in a remove operation, we attempt to mark the deleted node's next pointers using a single transaction, instead of performing individual compare-and-swap operations.

3.2 Nonblocking Binary Search Trees

We now discuss our experience with applying PTO to the nonblocking binary search tree (BST) algorithm created by Ellen et al. [9]. The algorithm implements a set object with insert, remove, and lookup operations. To achieve lock-freedom, the algorithm employs a "marking" technique to coordinate concurrent updates to the BST. During an insert or a remove operation, the thread first traverses down the tree (the search phase) to locate an appropriate position to perform the update. Then in the update phase, the thread allocates an operation descriptor (Info record) that contains sufficient information to allow helping from other threads. The descriptor is installed at nodes involved in the update, using compare-and-swap operations: one node is marked in an insertion and two are marked in a removal. An operation linearizes if it successfully marks all nodes involved in the update. Upon completion, some of the nodes are restored to a clean state.

We identify two opportunities to apply PTO in the binary search tree algorithm. The first is to put the entire update operation inside a transaction. The second is to use a prefix transaction to execute the update phase, leaving the search phase out of the transaction. In both choices, we can eliminate the allocation of the descriptor for an insert operation, because the node is restored to a clean state at the end of the transaction. For a remove operation, since the algorithm does *not* restore one of the updated nodes to a clean state, we cannot safely eliminate its descriptor. However, we can use a unique, statically-allocated dummy descriptor in place of a dynamically allocated one: When all updates are performed in a transaction, there is no need for helping if the transaction commits, and the dummy descriptor is simply ignored by subsequent operations.

3.3 Dynamic-Sized Hash Tables

The final data structure we studied is a nonblocking resizable hash table [30]. The algorithm employs a "freezable set" abstraction to achieve nonblocking size adjustments. In the hash table, each bucket is a pointer to a freezable set object, which is implemented as an unsorted array of elements. All updates to the array are performed via copy-on-write, that is, by creating an updated version of the array to replace the old one, and then using a compare-and-swap on the bucket pointer.

A straightforward application of PTO on the hash table appears barely helpful, since the algorithm is streamlined: In the common case, an insert or a remove operation on the hash table consists of a single allocation and an uncontended compare-and-swap on the bucket pointer. To improve performance, we changed the algorithm by removing the copy-on-write within transactions.

The idea of our optimization is to perform *speculative in-place writes* to the array objects, so that allocations could be avoided in the common case. When making this change, we attached a counter to the bucket pointers, so that a transactional update could increment the counter and modify the bucket in place. Unfortunately, this can affect the correctness of a concurrent lookup to the bucket. To prevent errors, we degrade the progress of lookups from wait-free to lock-free, by requiring lookups to double-check the bucket pointer counter after they search the bucket.

4 Evaluation

In this section, we evaluate the effectiveness of PTO in accelerating concurrent data structures. We consider five data structures as discussed in Section 3, which affords us the ability to look at the various aspects of PTO in detail.

4.1 Microbenchmarks

We use three microbenchmarks in our experiments:

setbench evaluates of set implementations which support insert, remove, and lookup operations. Each thread repeatedly invokes a lookup or an update operation (with equal chance of being an insert or a remove) with some random value within range.

pqbench evaluates priority queue implementations where each thread repeatedly invokes a push with some random value or a pop; the pop returns a null value if the queue is empty.

mbench evaluates Mindicator objects where each thread repeatedly invokes an arrive operation with some random value, followed by a depart operation.

All experiments were conducted on an machine equipped with an Intel Core i7-4770 CPU running at 3.40GHz, with 8 GB of RAM. The i7-4770 supports Intel's Restricted Transactional Memory (rtm) interface. There are 4 cores, each 2-way multi-threaded, for a total of 8 hardware threads. The software stack included Ubuntu 14.04.1 and GCC 4.8.2. All experiments were run in 32-bit mode, and data points are the average of 5 trials.

4.2 Latency and Scalability Improvement

Figure 2(a) contrasts the performance of the PTO Mindicator with the original lock-free implementation. We also compare to a version in which the Mindicator is protected by a coarse-grained lock, and the transactional lock elision (TLE) [40] is employed to allow concurrency. In the experiment, threads repeatedly insert and then remove a randomly-chosen value; this ensures that some operations must traverse to the top of the tree. We configured the Mindicator as a binary tree with 64 leaves, and used the default mapping, where threads were assigned to leaves from left to right.

There are two important trends: First, we see that at a single thread, PTO provides latency that is nearly as good as TLE, which does not have marking, unmarking, or helping phases. Thus we can conclude that PTO can provide near-optimal single-thread performance. Second, we see that whereas TLE scales poorly, due to its locking fallback, PTO scales comparably to the original lock-free code. Thus in all cases, PTO is on par with the best performing algorithm. Furthermore, beyond 4 threads we see that PTO scales better than the lock-free code. This is a natural consequence of the workload: when using random keys, as the number of threads increases, the likelihood that any thread must traverse to the root decreases. As fewer threads traverse to the root, the likelihood of conflicts for any thread also decreases, and the prefix transaction becomes more likely to succeed.

Figure 2(b) shows performance for a workload with an even mix of insert and removeMin operations on the Mound, using random keys. Using PTO, we were able to replace up to five CAS operations with a single transaction for each of the DCAS and DCSS operations. We encapsulated the DCAS in a function, and tuned the retry parameter once, ultimately settling on a value of four. This value was used for all DCASes, whether at the (high contention) root of the Mound, or at leaves.

The main benefit of PTO for the Mound was in removing latency from each DCAS. This result is similar to the finding of Yoo et al. [46], that coarsening atomic regions via hardware transactions can amortize some of the costs of atomicity. In terms of concurrent data structure design, the lesson is that thinking in terms of DCAS and other simpler primitives remains useful: assuming the availability of DCAS allowed the Mound designers to split removeMin into multiple atomic operations, thereby limiting the duration of contention on the Mound root.

4.3 Impacts on Relative Performance

We next turn our attention to skiplists. We evaluate skiplists in two settings: as a search data structure (Figure 3) and as a priority queue (Figure 2(b)).

We began with Gramoli's skiplist implementation [13]. To create a skiplist priority queue, we employed a modified version of the

(a) Mindicators

(b) Priority Queues

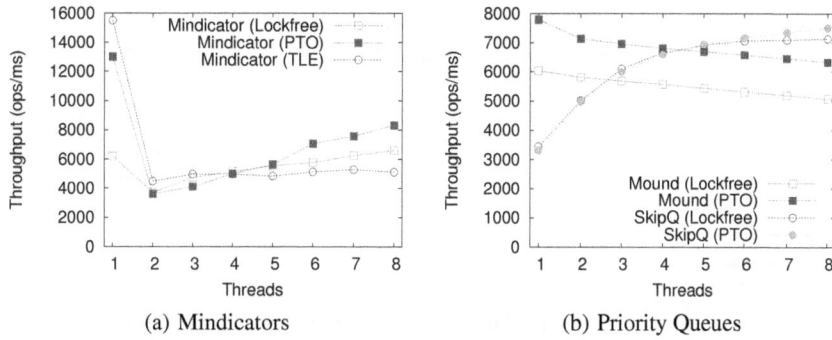

Figure 2: Mindicator and Priority Queue Microbenchmarks

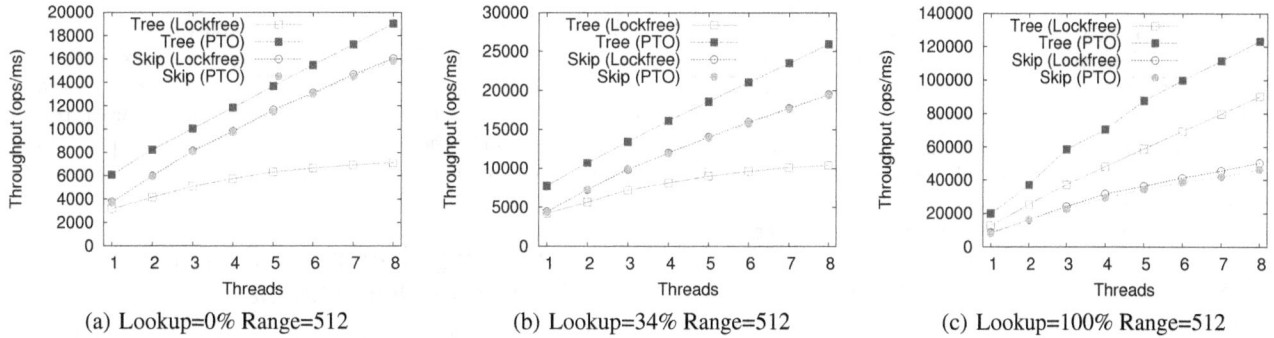

(a) Lookup=0% Range=512

(b) Lookup=34% Range=512

(c) Lookup=100% Range=512

Figure 3: Logarithmic Search Data Structure Microbenchmark

Lotan-Shavit technique [31], and made it linearizable by disallowing a pop operation from traversing through an marked node.

While we expected to observe a similar decrease in latency to the Mound, due to the reduced latency for coarsened atomic operations, such benefit did not manifest. There are two drivers of this result. First, the main source of latency is not silo maintenance, but accessing locations that are not in the cache, during the traversal stage. According to the criteria in [5], the skiplist implementation is already close to optimal with respect to concurrency. Thus at one thread, there was little to gain. The second impediment to speedup at higher thread counts is that as a silo maintenance operation traverses the silo, it becomes increasingly prone to conflicts with concurrent readers. Intel TSX employs a requester-wins [3] conflict detection strategy, and thus any read to the write set of an PTO operation causes the PTO operation to fail.

4.4 Additive Benefits in Recursive PTO

PTO is a compositional technique, and can be used to optimize an entire operation, as well as a portion of its fallback path. To assess this property, we evaluated the nonblocking BST created by Ellen et al. [9]. We transliterated the code from Java to C++, replacing `volatile` variables with sequentially consistent `std::atomic` variables. We also employed an epoch-based memory reclamation policy, to ensure that locations were not reclaimed while a concurrent thread held a reference to them.

We identified two applications of PTO to the BST, which we refer to as PTO1 and PTO2. In PTO1, the entire insert, remove, and lookup operations are transformed using PTO. By optimizing the lookup phase, we are able to remove code that double-checks the values of reads. We were also able to replace sequentially consistent `std::atomic` accesses with relaxed accesses, which may avoid processor and compiler fences on some architectures.

As Figure 5(a) shows, PTO1 results in more than 75% higher throughput at low thread counts. In contrast, PTO2 only optimizes the update phase of the insert and remove operations. While it also offers an improvement at all thread counts, the effect is much less at low levels of concurrency, where search overhead dominates, but much higher as concurrency increases. The improvement at higher thread counts is a consequence of a smaller contention window: since the traversal is not part of the hardware transaction, there are fewer opportunities to conflict with concurrent transactions. However, the lookup phase no longer runs in a hardware transaction, and thus must incur the overheads of double-checking and fences.

In PTO1+PTO2, we employ PTO1, and then use PTO2 within the fallback path. To fall back all the way to the original lock-free algorithm, an operation must first fail 2 times in PTO1, and then 16 times in PTO2. This composition achieves close to the best of both approaches. Even more remarkably, the composition of PTO+PTO2 boosts the BST performance to a constant factor higher than the skiplist set. As Figure 3 shows, the optimized BST provides the same scalability as the skiplist, but with lower latency.

4.5 Fast Speculative Inplace Updates

We ported the hash table from Java to C++, again using an epoch-based memory reclamation policy. We applied PTO to each of the insert, lookup, and remove operations, and then performed algorithm-specific optimizations to eliminate copy-on-write.

The simple application of PTO does little to benefit updates, since their overhead is dominated by the cost of allocating a new bucket, copying the old bucket's values, and applying the corresponding insert or removal. However, lookup operations show a

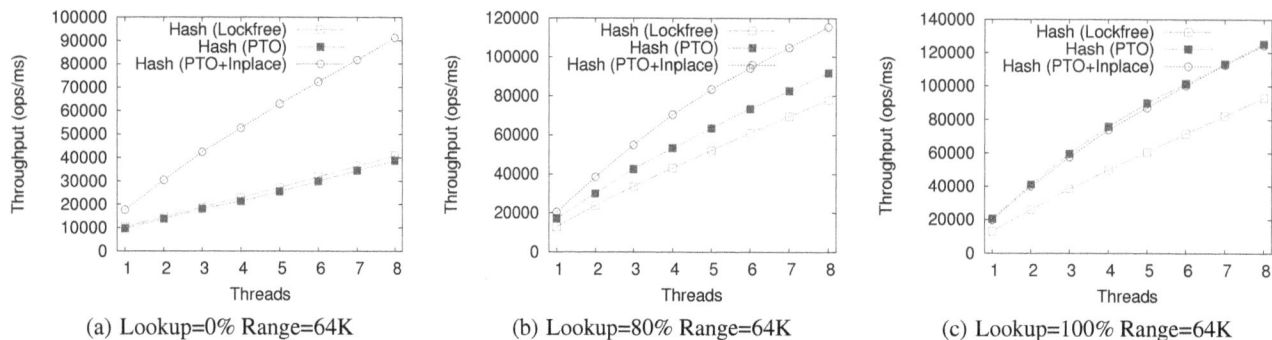

(a) Lookup=0% Range=64K   (b) Lookup=80% Range=64K   (c) Lookup=100% Range=64K

Figure 4: Hash Table Microbenchmark

decrease in latency. When PTO is applied to the lookup, all interaction with the epoch-based reclaimer can be elided. This eliminates two memory fences and two stores. Given the streamlined code path, there is a noticeable impact on latency.

Figure 4 presents the performance improvement for this optimization. In a write-only workload, we observe more than 2x speedup at 8 threads, and 1.8x speedup at one thread. The improvement is a consequence of the elimination of copying, and reduced interaction with the allocator. Since the allocator can require system calls, and its metadata can present a bottleneck, the benefits increase at higher thread counts.

4.6   What Makes PTO Fast?

Our evaluation shows some dramatic improvements in performance, particularly for the BST and hash table. However, it also shows some more modest gains, and fails to improve the skiplist at all. While the methodology does simplify the task of accelerating a concurrent data structure, it is still beneficial to be able to analyze an algorithm and predict whether it will benefit from PTO.

Generalizing our above experiments, we believe that there are four principal sources of latency that PTO can eliminate:

Memory Fences: Figure 5(b) and (c) present additional results for the Mound and BST, showing the impact when we did not elide memory fences within hardware transactions. For both the Mound, where the placement of fences was hand-optimized, and the BST, where the placement of fences mirrored their placement in the equivalent (and necessarily conservative) Java code, we see that the elimination of fences contributed significantly to savings in latency. For the Mound, the impact of removing fences was the sole source of improvement. For the BST, fences were a component of a suite of techniques that decreased latency.

Double-Checking Reads: Double-checked reads introduce two costs: not only do they add more instructions to the operation, but they also introduce branches, for when the check fails. In Figure 5(c), we break down sources of reduced latency for the BST write-only experiment. While fence removal plays a significant role, the baseline improvement comes without it. At low thread counts, where the entire operation is enclosed in a transaction, the credit is largely due to eliminating double-checking of reads.

Redundant Stores: In the Mindicator and Mound, the process of marking and unmarking nodes during an update or DCAS creates unnecessary work. Eliminating this work was the primary driver of improved latency in the Mound.

Allocation: The ability to replace copy-on-write in the hash table was single-handedly responsible for more than 2x speedup on the write-dominated workload. This improvement directly followed from the reduced interaction with the allocator. A similar benefit arose in the BST, where we were able to avoid allocating descriptors, but did not affect the Mound, where descriptors are reused from one operation to the next.

5   Rethinking Concurrent Data Structure Design and Implementation

We highlight two implications of PTO on concurrent data structure design.

Optimization on Strengthened Invariants: We first observe that the use of a hardware transaction can strengthen some of the invariants of the original data structure. The most straightforward example is that within a hardware transaction, the intermediate states of an operation are not visible to other threads. In many nonblocking data structures, operation descriptors are installed by the operation to indicate that a certain objects are involved in an operation, and those descriptors are removed during the clean-up phase of the operation, after its linearization point. In many algorithms, it will be possible to avoid not only the installation and removal of descriptors, but also their allocation and deallocation.

Similarly, some algorithms employ hazard pointers to prevent objects from being made unreachable during critical periods in a method's execution. When the method is executed within a hardware transaction, there is an invariant that memory accessed by the transaction will not change due to external events. Thus it is not possible for an object accessed by a transaction T to become unreachable before T commits. While T must respect the hazard pointers reserved by concurrent (non-transactional) threads, T need not guard locations via hazard pointers during its own operation. In an analogous manner, hardware transactions do not need to update memory management epochs [12, 33]. This latter case clearly cannot be handled by the compiler, since epochs are represented with monotonically increasing counters. For short operations, such as those on hash tables, epoch operations and their corresponding memory fences can be a significant contributor to latency; for read-only operations, epochs can again be a significant cost, due to their introduction of memory fences.

Progress vs. Optimization Trade-off: A more aggressive opportunity lies in weakening the progress guarantees of the original algorithm to increase the opportunity for fast-path optimization. There exist algorithms [16, 30] in which read-only lookup operations are wait-free. Reducing the progress of lookups to lock-free

250

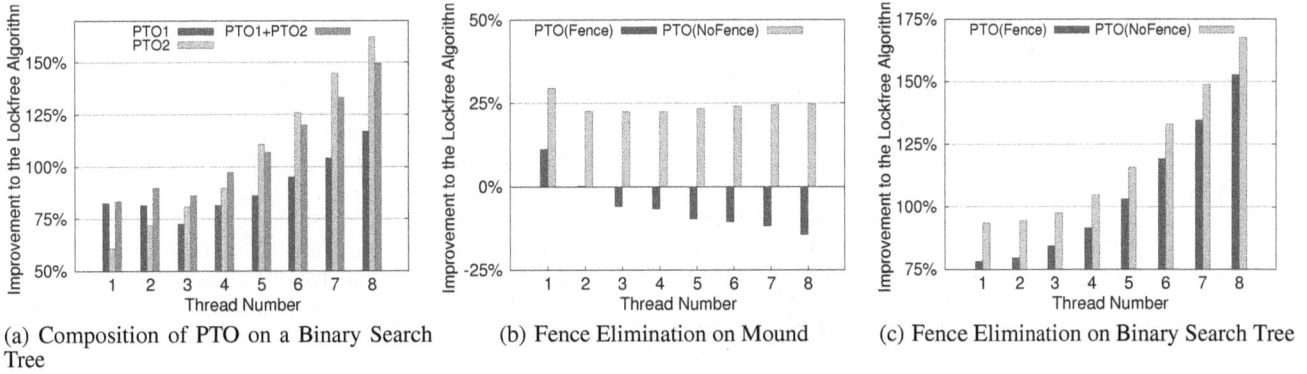

(a) Composition of PTO on a Binary Search Tree

(b) Fence Elimination on Mound

(c) Fence Elimination on Binary Search Tree

Figure 5: Effectiveness of Specific Factors in PTO

can have non-local benefits by increasing the opportunity to optimize the PTO fastpath of inserts and removals.

In the hash table case, we see a PTO insertion or removal can modify the array in-place, as long as it increments the counter within its hardware transaction. Doing so ensures that concurrent lookups will not miss a value concurrently removed and inserted, at the cost of the operation retrying when there is concurrency. If concurrency between modifications and lookups is rare, or if modifications are, themselves, frequent, the optimization may outweigh the added overhead (and reduced progress guarantees) of the modified set. Modifications of this technique can be applied to algorithms that use copy-on-write, marking, descriptors, simulated DCAS, and indirection-based versioning of data.

In summary, we see significant potential to (re)design concurrent data structures to be PTO-friendly. If the prefix succeeds with high probability, then common costs, especially those related to memory management (reference counts, hazard pointers, epochs, indirection), become less significant. A slow-path that bears these costs, coupled with an unencumbered fast-path, may provide a "sweet spot" for algorithm designers. When these techniques cease to be performance bottlenecks, they may be employed to more rapidly develop novel concurrent data structures.

6 Related Work

While there are a number of high-performance nonblocking data structures, there are few methodologies for creating or accelerating them. Herlihy presented a universal construction for creating nonblocking data structures [18], but its emphasis was progress, not performance. Subsequent improvements [11] have increased the practicality of universal constructions, particularly for wait-free data structures. However, these techniques were designed before HTM became available in commodity microprocessors, and their focus on progress still results in overhead relative to the best ad-hoc nonblocking data structure designs. Similarly, Petrank et al. [25, 43] have created methodologies for making lock-free data structures wait-free, but without eliminating the overheads of the baseline lock-free data structure.

A variety of combining techniques have gained prominence for their ability to accelerate concurrent data structures [17]. Unfortunately, these techniques do not perform well on search data structures [17], and they sacrifice nonblocking progress. In contrast, our technique can perform well on search structures, and it preserves the original progress guarantees.

Neelakantam et al. were among the first to use HTM to optimize existing software [38]. Their focus was not on concurrency, but rather on speculative optimization of a program trace. As in our work, their system replaced unlikely code paths with explicit transactional aborts. Our work builds upon these ideas by introducing the notions of progress and composition to their transformation, and by extending it to concurrent code. We also add the option of algorithm-specific optimizations, instead of limiting to automatic compiler transformations.

Dice et al. were the first to analyze the impact of a real HTM system on concurrent data structures [7]. In their work, they showed that many concurrent applications could be simplified by attempting to execute operations in HTM, and then falling back to a single global lock if the HTM operation did not succeed.

Perhaps most notably, our work demonstrates that the fallback path is a significant design consideration. Early work on hardware lock elision [40] suggested that a locking fallback would suffice. Calciu et al. showed that optimizations to the lock-based fallback path could have significant impact on throughput [4]. Similarly, hybrid TM researchers have embraced the need for an intermediate point between HTM execution and serialized fallback. Our work does the same for concurrent data structures, demonstrating that the progress guarantees of the fallback path can play a significant role in overall system throughput.

Recently, Dice et al. pointed out several subtle pitfalls [6] in the lazy subscription technique [4]. We believe these issues do not apply to the PTO-accelerated data structures investigated in this paper. The intuition is that in TLE, the execution of fallback code assumes mutual exclusion. Speculative transactions inherit this assumption, since they run the same code as the fallback. Any violation of the mutual exclusion condition (even when observed by a speculative transaction) may lead the program to reach a state that would not be reachable in the original implementation. In PTO, the situation is nuanced. A prefix transaction coalesces multiple steps of the original implementation into a single super-step. Given that the original implementation is nonblocking, no step assumes mutual exclusion, and hence PTO will never cause the implementation to reach a state that was not reachable in the original code. However, this situation can lead to more aborts.

Yoo et al. studied the same Intel HTM implementation as us, applying it to high-performance-computing applications [46]. Like Dice et al., they employed HTM in a more ad-hoc fashion to a number of applications. They identified certain techniques, like transactional coarsening, that are captured by PTO. They also presented valuable guidelines for users of Intel's HTM, such as the importance of tuning retry parameters, and the possibility of different behavior for read-only and writing hardware transactions. As we saw in Section 4, this latter difference plays a significant role in the PTO BST and hash table algorithms.

Our techniques bear a complex relationship with the concept of asynchronized concurrency [5]. Certainly ASCY explains why it is so difficult to accelerate the skiplist. ASCY also provides insight into the PTO-accelerated BST: we essentially remove from the transactional fast-path those operations that are in opposition to the ASCY principles. However, in the case of the hash table, we see that sometimes it is beneficial to reduce the ASCY compliance of the original data structure in order to accelerate the transactional prefix. A weak reduction in ASCY (double-checking lookups) was able to deliver substantial improvement by obviating copy-on-write.

7 Conclusions and Future Work

In this paper, we introduced a methodology for accelerating concurrent data structures by using transactional memory. Our technique involves creating a fast-path transaction that succeeds or fails in bounded time, and a set of optimizations that can be applied to that fast-path to eliminate latency. In evaluation on five data structures[1], we saw performance benefits ranging from 50% to 3x for the hash table and binary search tree. Even when the methodology did not improve performance, we did not observe any significant slowdowns.

Apart from performance, our methodology offers many other benefits: It relies upon, and hence confirms the value of, strongly atomic hardware transactions. It preserves nonblocking progress, despite the absence of progress guarantees for current hardware transactional memory. Our technique is oblivious to the capacity of the underlying HTM. Lastly, it is both local and compositional. This last point is crucial, as it allows data structure designers to use existing mechanisms, such as lock-free DCAS, and then transactionally accelerate them.

Among the many future directions this work encourages, we highlight two. The first is for hardware designers, who we hope will see this work as an encouragement to reduce the latency of HTM boundary operations. As HTM becomes cheaper, we believe that PTO will become even more profitable, especially for DCAS replacement and other small transactions.

Secondly, we believe that the concurrent data structure community may want to re-think its approach to data structure design. For example, the accelerated BST dramatically outperforms the skiplist, even though the un-accelerated skiplist has been shown, repeatedly, to be among the most efficient and scalable lock-free ordered sets. PTO makes costly operations, such as copy-on-write, descriptor allocation, helping, and marking, inexpensive. This, in turn, encourages the design of nonblocking data structures with slower slow-paths, as long as they afford faster fast-paths.

Acknowledgments

This material is based upon work supported by the National Science Foundation under Grants CAREER-1253362 and CCF-1218530. Any opinions, findings, and conclusions or recommendations expressed in this material are those of the authors and do not necessarily reflect the views of the National Science Foundation.

8 References

[1] M. Abadi and L. Lamport. The Existence of Refinement Mappings. *Theoretical Computer Science*, pages 253–284, May 1991.

[2] C. Blundell, E. C. Lewis, and M. M. K. Martin. Subtleties of Transactional Memory Atomicity Semantics. *Computer Architecture Letters*, 5(2), Nov. 2006.

[3] J. Bobba, K. E. Moore, H. Volos, L. Yen, M. D. Hill, M. M. Swift, and D. A. Wood. Performance Pathologies in Hardware Transactional Memory. In *Proceedings of the 34th International Symposium on Computer Architecture*, San Diego, CA, June 2007.

[4] I. Calciu, J. Gottschlich, T. Shpeisman, G. Pokam, and M. Herlihy. Invyswell: A Hybrid Transactional Memory for Haswell's Restricted Transactional Memory. In *Proceedings of the 23rd International Conference on Parallel Architectures and Compilation Techniques*, Edmonton, AB, Canada, Aug. 2014.

[5] T. David, R. Guerraoui, T. Che, and V. Trigonakis. Designing ASCY-compliant Concurrent Search Data Structures. Technical Report EPFL-REPORT-203822, Ecole Polytechnique Federale de Lausanne, 2014.

[6] D. Dice, T. Harris, A. Kogan, Y. Lev, and M. Moir. Pitfalls of Lazy Subscription. In *Proceedings of the 6th Workshop on the Theory of Transactional Memory*, Paris, France, July 2014.

[7] D. Dice, Y. Lev, V. Marathe, M. Moir, M. Olszewski, and D. Nussbaum. Simplifying Concurrent Algorithms by Exploiting Hardware TM. In *Proceedings of the 22nd ACM Symposium on Parallelism in Algorithms and Architectures*, Santorini, Greece, June 2010.

[8] A. Dragojevic, M. Herlihy, Y. Lev, and M. Moir. On The Power of Hardware Transactional Memory to Simplify Memory Management. In *Proceedings of the 30th ACM Symposium on Principles of Distributed Computing*, San Jose, CA, June 2011.

[9] F. Ellen, P. Fatourou, E. Ruppert, and F. van Breugel. Non-blocking Binary Search Trees. In *Proceedings of the 29th ACM Symposium on Principles of Distributed Computing*, Zurich, Switzerland, July 2010.

[10] F. Ellen, Y. Lev, V. Luchangco, and M. Moir. SNZI: Scalable NonZero Indicators. In *Proceedings of the Twenty-Sixth ACM Symposium on Principles of Distributed Computing*, Portland, OR, Aug. 2007.

[11] P. Fatourou and N. D. Kallimanis. A Highly-Efficient Wait-Free Universal Construction. In *Proceedings of the 23rd ACM Symposium on Parallelism in Algorithms and Architectures*, San Jose, CA, June 2011.

[12] K. Fraser. *Practical Lock-Freedom*. PhD thesis, King's College, University of Cambridge, Sept. 2003.

[13] V. Gramoli. More Than You Ever Wanted to Know about Synchronization. In *Proceedings of the 20th ACM Symposium on Principles and Practice of Parallel Programming*, San Francisco, CA, Feb. 2015.

[14] T. Harris. A Pragmatic Implementation of Non-Blocking Linked Lists. In *Proceedings of the 15th International Symposium on Distributed Computing*, Lisbon, Portugal, Oct. 2001.

[15] T. Harris, K. Fraser, and I. Pratt. A Practical Multi-word Compare-and-Swap Operation. In *Proceedings of the 16th International Conference on Distributed Computing*, Toulouse, France, Oct. 2002.

[16] S. Heller, M. Herlihy, V. Luchangco, M. Moir, W. Scherer, and N. Shavit. A Lazy Concurrent List-Based Set Algorithm. In *Proceedings of the 9th international conference on Principles of Distributed Systems*, Pisa, Italy, Dec. 2006.

---

[1]The source code from this evaluation is available on Github at mfs409/nonblocking.

[17] D. Hendler, I. Incze, N. Shavit, and M. Tzafrir. Flat Combining and the Synchronization-Parallelism Tradeoff. In *Proceedings of the 22nd ACM Symposium on Parallelism in Algorithms and Architectures*, Santorini, Greece, June 2010.

[18] M. Herlihy. A Methodology for Implementing Highly Concurrent Data Structures. In *Proceedings of the Second ACM Symposium on Principles and Practice of Parallel Programming*, Seattle, WA, Mar. 1990.

[19] M. Herlihy. Wait-Free Synchronization. *ACM Transactions on Programming Languages and Systems*, 13(1):124–149, 1991.

[20] M. Herlihy. A Methodology for Implementing Highly Concurrent Data Objects. *ACM Transactions on Programming Languages and Systems*, 15(5):745–770, 1993.

[21] M. P. Herlihy and J. E. B. Moss. Transactional Memory: Architectural Support for Lock-Free Data Structures. In *Proceedings of the 20th International Symposium on Computer Architecture*, San Diego, CA, May 1993.

[22] Intel Corporation. Intel Architecture Instruction Set Extensions Programming (Chapter 8: Transactional Synchronization Extensions). Feb. 2012.

[23] C. Jacobi, T. Slegel, and D. Greiner. Transactional Memory Architecture and Implementation for IBM System Z. In *Proceedings of the 45th International Symposium On Microarchitecture*, Vancouver, BC, Canada, Dec. 2012.

[24] P. Jayanti. f-arrays: Implementation and applications. In *Proceedings of the 21st ACM Symposium on Principles of Distributed Computing*, Monterey, California, July 2002.

[25] A. Kogan and E. Petrank. A Methodology for Creating Fast Wait-Free Data Structures. In *Proceedings of the 16th ACM Symposium on Principles and Practice of Parallel Programming*, New Orleans, LA, Feb. 2012.

[26] L. Lamport. How to Make a Multiprocessor Computer that Correctly Executes Multiprocess Programs. *IEEE Transactions on Computers*, C-28(9):241–248, Sept. 1979.

[27] Y. Lev and J.-W. Maessen. Split Hardware Transactions: True Nesting of Transactions Using Best-Effort Hardware Transactional Memory. In *Proceedings of the 13th ACM Symposium on Principles and Practice of Parallel Programming*, Salt Lake City, UT, Feb. 2008.

[28] Y. Liu, V. Luchangco, and M. Spear. Mindicators: A Scalable Approach to Quiescence. In *Proceedings of 33rd International Conference on Distributed Computing Systems*, Philadelphia, PA, July 2013.

[29] Y. Liu and M. Spear. Mounds: Array-Based Concurrent Priority Queues. In *Proceedings of the 41st International Conference on Parallel Processing*, Pittsburgh, PA, Sept. 2012.

[30] Y. Liu, K. Zhang, and M. Spear. Dynamic-Sized Nonblocking Hash Tables. In *Proceedings of the 33rd ACM Symposium on Principles of Distributed Computing*, Paris, France, July 2014.

[31] I. Lotan and N. Shavit. Skiplist-Based Concurrent Priority Queues. In *Proceedings of the 14th International Parallel and Distributed Processing Symposium*, Cancun, Mexico, May 2000.

[32] V. Luchangco, M. Moir, and N. Shavit. Nonblocking k-compare-single-swap. In *Proceedings of the 15th ACM Symposium on Parallel Algorithms and Architectures*, San Diego, CA, June 2003.

[33] P. E. McKenney. *Exploiting Deferred Destruction: An Analysis of Read-Copy-Update Techniques in Operating System Kernels*. PhD thesis, OGI School of Science and Engineering at Oregon Health and Sciences University, 2004.

[34] M. Michael. Hazard Pointers: Safe Memory Reclamation for Lock-Free Objects. *IEEE Transactions on Parallel and Distributed Systems*, 15(6):491–504, June 2004.

[35] M. M. Michael and M. L. Scott. Simple, Fast, and Practical Non-Blocking and Blocking Concurrent Queue Algorithms. In *Proceedings of the 15th ACM Symposium on Principles of Distributed Computing*, May 1996.

[36] A. Morrison and Y. Afek. Fast Concurrent Queues for x86 Processors. In *Proceedings of the 18th ACM Symposium on Principles and Practice of Parallel Programming*, Shenzhen, China, Feb. 2013.

[37] S. S. Muchnick. *Advanced Compiler Design Implementation*. Morgan Kaufmann, 1997.

[38] N. Neelakantam, R. Rajwar, S. Srinivas, U. Srinivasan, and C. Zilles. Hardware Atomicity for Reliable Software Speculation. In *Proceedings of the 34th International Symposium on Computer Architecture*, San Diego, CA, June 2007.

[39] A. Prokopec, N. Bronson, P. Bagwell, and M. Odersky. Concurrent Tries with Efficient Non-Blocking Snapshots. In *Proceedings of the 17th ACM Symposium on Principles and Practice of Parallel Programming*, Feb. 2012.

[40] R. Rajwar and J. R. Goodman. Speculative Lock Elision: Enabling Highly Concurrent Multithreaded Execution. In *Proceedings of the 34th IEEE/ACM International Symposium on Microarchitecture*, Austin, TX, Dec. 2001.

[41] N. Shafiei. Non-blocking Patricia Tries with Replace Operations. In *Proceedings of 33rd International Conference on Distributed Computing Systems*, Philadelphia, PA, July 2013.

[42] H. Sundell and P. Tsigas. Fast and Lock-Free Concurrent Priority Queues for Multi-Thread Systems. *Journal of Parallel and Distributed Computing*, 65:609–627, May 2005.

[43] S. Timnat, A. Braginsky, A. Kogan, and E. Petrank. Wait-Free Linked-Lists. In *Proceedings of the 16th International Conference on Principles of Distributed Systems*, Rome, Italy, Dec. 2012.

[44] A. Wang, M. Gaudet, P. Wu, J. N. Amaral, M. Ohmacht, C. Barton, R. Silvera, and M. Michael. Evaluation of Blue Gene/Q Hardware Support for Transactional Memories. In *Proceedings of the 21st International Conference on Parallel Architectures and Compilation Techniques*, Minneapolis, MN, Sept. 2012.

[45] L. Xiang and M. L. Scott. Compiler Aided Manual Speculation for High Performance Concurrent Data Structures. In *Proceedings of the 18th ACM Symposium on Principles and Practice of Parallel Programming*, Shenzhen, China, Feb. 2013.

[46] R. Yoo, C. Hughes, K. Lai, and R. Rajwar. Performance Evaluation of Intel Transactional Synchronization Extensions for High Performance Computing. In *Proceedings of the International Conference for High Performance Computing, Networking, Storage and Analysis*, Denver, CO, Nov. 2013.

Efficient Memory Management for Lock-Free Data Structures with Optimistic Access*

Nachshon Cohen
Technion Institute of Technology, Israel
nachshonc@gmail.com

Erez Petrank
Technion Institute of Technology, Israel
erez@cs.technion.ac.il

ABSTRACT

Lock-free data structures achieve high responsiveness, aid scalability, and avoid deadlocks and livelocks. But providing memory management support for such data structures without foiling their progress guarantees is difficult. Often, designers employ the hazard pointers technique, which may impose a high performance overhead.

In this work we propose a novel memory management scheme for lock-free data structures called *optimistic access*. This scheme provides efficient support for lock-free data structures that can be presented in the normalized form of [24]. Our novel memory manager breaks the traditional memory management invariant which never lets a program touch reclaimed memory. In other words, it allows the memory manager to reclaim objects that may still be accessed later by concurrently running threads. This broken invariant provides an opportunity to obtain high parallelism with excellent performance, but it also requires a careful design. The optimistic access memory management scheme is easy to employ and we implemented it for a linked list, a hash table, and a skip list. Measurements show that it dramatically outperforms known memory reclamation methods.

Categories and Subject Descriptors

D.4.2 [**Storage Management**]: Allocation/deallocation strategies; D.1.3 [**Programming Technique**]: Parallel Programming

General Terms

Algorithms, Design, Theory.

Keywords

Memory Management, Concurrent Data Structures, Non-blocking, Lock-free, Hazard Pointers

---

*This work was supported by the Israeli Science Foundation grant No. 274/14.

1. INTRODUCTION

The rapid deployment of highly parallel machines has resulted in the acute need for parallel algorithms and their supporting parallel data structures. *Lock-free* data structures (a.k.a. *non-blocking*) [11, 13] are immune to deadlocks and livelocks, fast, scalable and widely used in practice. However, when designing a dynamic non-blocking data structure, one must also address the challenge of memory reclamation. The problem arises when one thread attempts to reclaim an object while another thread is still using it. Accounting for all accesses of all threads before reclaiming an object is difficult and costly, especially when threads may be delayed for a while while still holding pointers to nodes in the shared memory.

One easy approach to this problem is to not reclaim memory at all during the execution. But this solution is only applicable to short-running programs. Another approach to reclaiming memory is to assume automatic garbage collection, which guarantees that an object is never reclaimed while it is being used. However, this only delegates the problem to the garbage collector. There has been much work on garbage collectors that obtain some partial guarantee for progress [14, 15, 20, 21, 2, 22], but current literature offers no garbage collection that supports lock-free execution [19].

A different approach is to coordinate the accessing threads with the threads that attempt reclamations. The programmer uses a memory management interface to allocate and reclaim objects and the reclamation scheme coordinates the memory recycling of reclaimed objects with the accessing threads. The most popular schemes of this type are *hazard pointers* and *pass the buck* [17, 12]. These (similar) methods require that each thread announces each and every object it accesses. To properly announce the accessed objects, a memory fence must be used for each shared memory read, which is costly. Employing one of these schemes for a linked list may slow its execution down by a factor of 5 [3]. To ameliorate this high cost, a recent extension by Braginsky et al. [3] proposed the *anchors* scheme, which is a more complex method that requires a fence only once per several accesses. The *anchors* scheme reduces the overhead substantially, but the cost still remains non negligible. Furthermore, the *anchors* scheme is difficult to design and it is currently available for the Harris-Maged linked list [16] only.

All known memory management techniques, including garbage collection and the above ad-hoc reclamation methods, provide a guarantee that a thread never accesses a reclaimed object. Loosely speaking, supporting this guarantee causes a significant overhead, because whenever a thread reads a pointer to an object, the other threads must become aware of this read and not reclaim the object. For an arbitrary program, this might mean a memory fence per each read, which is very costly. For more specialized programs or for specific lock-free data structures, better handling is possible, but a substantial performance penalty seems to always exist.

In this paper we propose to deviate from traditional methods in a novel manner by letting the program execute optimistically, allowing the threads to sometimes access an object that has been previously reclaimed. Various forms of optimistic execution have become common in the computing world (both hardware and software) as a mean to achieve higher performance. But optimistic access has never been proposed in the memory management literature due to the complications that arise in this setting. Optimistically accessing memory that might have been reclaimed requires careful checks that must be executed at adequate locations; and then, proper measures must be taken when the accessing of a reclaimed object has been detected. When a thread realizes that it has been working with stale values, we let it drop the stale values and return to a point where the execution is safe to restart.

Achieving such timely checks and a safe restart in this setting is quite difficult for arbitrary lock-free programs. Therefore, we chose to work only with lock-free data structures that can be presented in a *normalized form*. We used the normalized form proposed in [24]. This normalized form is on the one hand very general: it covers all concurrent data structure that we are aware of. On the other hand, it is very structured and it allows handling the checks and restarts in a prudent manner. As with other optimistic approaches, we found that the design requires care, but when done correctly, it lets the executing threads run fast with low overhead. We denote the obtained memory reclamation scheme *optimistic access*.

Measurements show that the overhead of applying the optimistic access scheme is never more than 19% compared to no reclamation, and it consistently outperform the hazard pointers and anchors schemes. Moreover, the application of the optimistic access method to a normalized lock-free data structure is almost automatic and can easily be applied to a given data structure. The optimistic access mechanism is lock-free and it may reclaim nodes even in the presence of stuck threads that do not cooperate with the memory reclamation process.

In order for the optimistic access to be possible at all, the underlying operating system and runtime are required to behave "reasonably". The specific required assumptions are detailed in Section 3. Loosely speaking, the assumption is that reading or writing a field in a previously allocated object does not trigger a trap, even if the object has been reclaimed. For example, a system in which a reclaimed object is returned to the operating system and the operating system unmaps its memory thereafter, is not good for us since reading a field of that object would create a segmentation fault and an application crash.[1] It is easy to satisfy an adequate assumption by using a user-level allocator. This may be a good idea in general, because a user-level allocator can be constructed to provide a better progress guarantee. For example, using an object pooling mechanism for the nodes of the data structure would be appropriate.

The main contribution of this paper is an efficient memory reclamation scheme that supports lock-freedom for normalized lock-free data structures. The proposed scheme is much faster than existing schemes and is easy to employ. We exemplify the use of the optimistic access scheme on a linked list, a hash table, and a skip list. The obtained memory recycling scheme for the **skip list** incurred an overhead below 12%, whereas the overhead of the hazard pointers scheme always exceeded a factor of 2. For the **hash** table, the optimistic access scheme incurred an overhead below 12%, whereas the overhead of the hazard pointers method was $16\% - 40\%$ for $1 - 32$

threads (and negligible for 64 threads). For **linked list**, the optimistic access method always outperforms the hazard pointers and the anchors mechanisms. The optimistic access method typically incurs an overhead of a few percents and at a worst setting it incurs an overhead of 19%. The hazard pointers mechanism typically incurs a large overhead of up to 5x. The anchors mechanism improves performance significantly over the hazard pointers but with short lists and high contention it incurs a significant overhead as well.

This paper is organized as follows. In Section 2 we present an overview of the optimistic access mechanism. In Section 3 we specify the assumption we make of the underlying system. Section 4 presents the optimistic access mechanism. In Section 5 we present the implementation and an evaluation. We discuss related work in Section 6 and conclude in Section 7.

2. OVERVIEW

Let us start with an intuitive overview of the optimistic access scheme. The main target of this scheme is to provide fast reads, as reads are most common. In particular, we would like to execute reads without writing to the shared memory. On the other hand, a lock-free memory reclamation scheme must be able to reclaim memory, even if some thread is stuck just before a read of an object that is about to be reclaimed. Thus, we achieve fast reads by allowing a thread to sometimes read an object after it was reclaim (and allocated to other uses).

The optimistic access scheme maintains correctness in spite of reading reclaimed objects using three key properties. First, a read *must not fault*, even when accessing a reclaimed memory. Second, the scheme *identifies* a read that accesses a reclaimed object immediately after the read. Third, when a read of such stale value is detected, the scheme allows a *rollback* of the optimistic read. We follow by describing how these three properties can be satisfied.

The first requirement is obtained by the underlying memory management system. We will require that accessing previously allocated memory will never cause a fault. This can be supported by using user-level allocators that allocate and de-allocate without returning pages to the system. Such allocators can be designed to support lock-free algorithms. (Typically, returning pages to the system foils lock freedom.)

Jumping to the third property, i.e., the roll back, we first note that the ability to roll back is (informally) made possible in most lock-free data structures. Such data structures handle races by simply restarting the operation from scratch. The same restarting mechanism can be used to handle races between data-structure operations and memory reclamation; indeed, such a roll-back mechanism is assumed and used in previous work (e.g., [17]). However, to formally define a roll-back (or restart) mechanism, we simply adopt the normalized form for lock-free data structures [24]. This normalized form is on one hand very general - it covers all data structure we are aware of. On the other hand, its strict structure provides a well-defined restart mechanism, which can be used for rolling back the execution when a stale value has been read.

Next we discuss how to satisfy the second property, i.e., noting that a stale read has occurred due to a race between the read and memory reclamation. The optimistic access scheme divides the memory reclamation into phases, which may be thought of as epochs, and poses the following restrictions. First, an object is never reclaimed at the same phase in which it is unlinked from the data structure. It can only be reclaimed at the next phase or later. Second, a thread that acknowledges a new phase does not access objects that were unlinked in previous phases. These two restrictions provide a lightweight mechanism to identify a potential read

---

[1] As an aside, we note that the implementation of unmap is typically not lock-free and it is not to be used with lock-free data structures. For example, in the Linux operating system, an unmap instruction both acquires a lock and communicates with other processes via an interprocess interrupt.

of a stale value. If a thread is not aware that a phase has changed, then his read may potentially be of a stale value. Otherwise, i.e., if the thread is aware of the current reclamation phase, then his read is safe.

To make the (frequent) read operation even lighter, we move some of the related computation work to the (infrequent) reclaiming mechanism. To this end, each thread is assigned with an associated warning flag that a phase has changed. This flag is called the *warning-bit*. This bit is set if a new phase had started without the thread noticing, and clear otherwise. During a phase change the warning bits of all threads are set. When a thread acknowledges a phase change it resets its bit. This way, checking whether a read might have read a stale value due to reclamation, is as simple as checking whether the flag is non-zero.

To summarize, reading of shared memory is executed as follows. First the shared memory is read. Next, the thread's warning-bit is checked. Finally, if the warning bit is set, a restart mechanism is used to roll back the execution to a safe point.

We now deal with program writes. We cannot allow an event in which a thread writes to an object that has previously been reclaimed. Such an event may imply a corruption of objects in use by other threads. Therefore, for writes we adopt a simplified version of the hazard pointers scheme that prevents writes to reclaimed objects. A thread declares a location it is about to write to in a hazard pointer. Reclamation is avoided for such objects. Since writes are less frequent, the overhead of hazard pointers for writes is not high. The warning flag allows a quick implementation, as explained in Section 4 below.

Finally, it remains to describe the the memory reclamation scheme itself. A simplified version of such an algorithm may work as follows. It starts by incrementing the phase number, so that it can identify objects that were unlinked before the reclamation started. It can then reclaim all objects that were unlinked in previous phases and are not pointed by hazard pointers.

The problem with the simple solution is that each thread that starts reclamation will increment the phase number and trigger restarts by all other threads. This should not happen too frequently. To reduce this overhead, we accumulate retired objects in a global buffer and let a reclaiming thread process objects unlinked by *all* threads. This reduces the number of phase changes and hence also the number of restarts. Even when using global pools, the optimistic access scheme naturally benefits from using temporary local pools that are used to reduce the contention on the global pools. Performance is somewhat reduced when space is limited and measurements of the tradeoff between space overhead and time overhead are provided in Section 5.

Advantage of the optimistic access scheme. Hazard pointers and anchors require an involved and costly read barrier that runs a verification process and a memory fence. In contrast, ours scheme works with a light-weight read barrier (that checks the warning bit). Hazard pointers are used for writes in a ways that is easy to install (practically, automatic), and being used for writes only, hazard pointers also incur a low overhead, as shown by the measurements.

3. ASSUMPTIONS AND SETTINGS

In this section we specify the assumption required for our mechanism to work and define the normalized representation of data structures. Finally, in Subsection 3.4 we present a running example: the delete operation of Harris-Maged linked list.

3.1 System Model

We use the standard computation model of Herlihy [11]. A shared memory is accessible by all threads. The threads communicate through memory access instructions on the shared memory; and a thread makes no assumptions about the status of any other thread, nor about the speed of its execution. We also assume the TSO memory model, used by the common x86 architecture [18].

Finally, as discussed in Section 2, we assume that accessing previously allocated memory does not trigger traps. Formally, we assume the following of the underlying system.

ASSUMPTION 3.1. *Suppose a memory address p is allocated at time t. Then, if the program at time $t' > t$ executes an instruction that reads from p, then the executing of this instruction does not trigger a runtime-system trap.*

3.2 Normalized Data Structures

The optimistic access scheme assumes that the data structure implementation is given in a normalized form. In this subsection we provide a motivating discussion and an overview over normalized representation. The formal definition following [24] is provided in the full version of this paper [4]. The memory management scheme proposed in this paper lets threads infrequently access reclaimed space. When this happens, the acting thread will notice the problem thereafter and it will restart the currently executing routine. The strict structure of the normalized algorithm provides safe and easily identifiable points of restart. Let us now informally explain how a normalized implementation looks like.

Loosely speaking, a normalized implementation of a data structure partitions each operation implementation into three parts. The first part, denoted the *CAS generator*, prepares a list of CASes that need to be executed for the operation. It may modify the shared data structure during this process, but only in a way that can be ignored and restarted at any point, typically these modifications improve the underlying representation of the data structure without changing its semantics[2]. The second part, denoted the *CAS executor*, attempts to execute the CASes produced by the CAS generator one by one. It stops when a CAS fails or after all have completed successfully. The third part, denoted the *wrap-up*, examines how many CASes completed successfully and decides whether the operation was completed or whether we should start again from the CAS generator. A particular interesting property of the CAS generator and the wrap-up methods, is that they can be restarted at any time with no harm done to the data structure.

Very loosely speaking, think, for example, of a search executed before a node is inserted into a linked list. This search would be done in a CAS generator method, which would then specify the CAS required for the insertion. For reasonable implementations, the search can be stopped at any time and restarted. Also, when the wrap-up method inspects the results of the (single) CAS execution and decides whether to start from scratch or terminate, it seems intuitive that we can stop and restart this examination at any point in time. The normalized implementation ensures that the CAS generator and the wrap-up methods can be easily restarted any time with no noticeable effects.

In contrast, the actual execution of the CASes prepared by the CAS generator is not something we can stop and restart because they have a noticeable effect on the shared data structure. Therefore, the optimistic access scheme must make sure that the CAS executor method never needs to restart, i.e., that it does not access reclaimed space. Here, again, thanks to the very structured nature of the executed CASes (given in a list), we can design the protection automatically and at a low cost.

---

[2]A typical example is the physical delete of nodes that were previously logically deleted in Harris-Maged linked list implementation.

One additional requirement of a normalized data structure is that all modifications of the structure are done in a CAS operation (and not a simple write). Efficient normalized representations exist for all lock-free data structures that we are aware of.

The formal definition of the normalized method is required for a proof of correctness. These details appear in the full version of this paper [4] and also in the original paper that defined this notion, but the informal details suffice to understand the optimistic access scheme as described below.

3.3 Assumptions on the Data Structure

Here, we specify assumptions that we make about the data structure to which memory management is added. Most of these assumptions are assumed also by all previous memory reclamation schemes.

Many lock-free algorithms mark pointers by modifying a few bits of the address. The programmer that applies the optimistic access scheme should be able to clear these bits to obtain an unmarked pointer to the object. Given a pointer O, the notation $unmark(O)$ denotes this unmarked pointer. This is one issue that makes our scheme not fully automatic.

Second, we assume that the data structure operations do not return a pointer to a reclaimable node in the data structure. Accessing a node can only happen by use of the data structure interface, and a node can be reclaimed by the memory manager if there is no possibility for the data structure interface functions to access it.

The data structure's functions may invoke the memory management interface. Following the (standard) interface proposed for the hazard pointers technique of [17], two instructions are used: *alloc* and *retire*. Allocation returns immediately, but a *retire* request does not immediately reclaim the object. Instead, the retire request is buffered and the object is reclaimed when it is safe. Deciding where to put the (manual) *retire* instructions (by the programmer) is far from trivial. It sometimes require an algorithmic modification [16] and this is the main reason why the optimistic access scheme is not an automatic transformation.

The third assumption is a proper usage of *retire*. We assume that retire is operated on a node in the data structure only after this node is unlinked from the data structure, and is no longer accessible by other threads that traverse the data structure. For example, we can properly retire a node in a linked list only after it has been disconnected from the list. We further assume that only a single thread may attempt to retire a node.

We emphasize that an object can be accessed after it has been properly retired. But it can only be accessed by a method that started before the object was retired. Nevertheless, because of this belated access, an object cannot be simply recycled after being retired.

3.4 A Running Example: Harris-Michael delete operation

We exemplify the optimistic access scheme throughout the paper by presenting the required modifications for the delete operation of Harris-Maged linked list. In Listing 1 we present the delete operation in its normalized form and including a retire instruction for a node that is removed from the list. In its basic form (and ignoring the constraints of the normalized representation), Harris-Michael delete operation consists of three steps: (1) *search*: find the node to be deleted and the node before it, (2) *logical delete*: mark the node's next pointer to logically delete it, and (3) *physical delete*: update the previous node's next pointer to skip the deleted node. During the search of the first stage, a thread also attempts to physically delete any node that is marked as logically deleted.

The normalized form of the operation is written in the three standard methods. The first method is the CAS generator method which performs the search and specifies the CAS that will logically delete the node by marking its next pointer. If the key is not found in the linked list then a list of length zero is returned from the CAS generator. The CAS executor method (not depicted in Listing 1) simply executes the CAS output by the CAS generator, and thus performs the logical deletion. The wrap-up method checks how many CASes were on the CAS list and how many of them were executed to determine if we need to return to the CAS generator, or the operation is done. The wrap-up interprets an empty CAS list as an indication that the key is not in the structure and then FALSE can be returned. Otherwise, if the CAS succeeded, then a TRUE is returned. If the CAS failed, the wrap-up determines a restart.

Note that the third step of the basic algorithm, physical delete, is not executed at all in the normalized form. The reason is that in its strict structure the wrap-up method does not have access to the pointer to the previous node and so it cannot execute the physical delete. However, this is not a problem because future searches will physically delete this node from the list and the logical delete (that has already been executed) means that the key in this node is not visible to the contains operation of the linked list. Another difference between the original implementation and the normalized one is that the original implementation may simply return FALSE upon failing to find the key in the structure. The normalized implementation creates an empty CAS list that the wrap-up method properly interprets and returns FALSE.

Finally, we added a retire instruction to Listing 1 after any physical delete. This is proper reclamation because new operations will not be able to traverse it anymore. Using a retire after the logical deletion is not proper because it is still accessible for new list traversals.

Listing 1: Harris-Michael linked list delete operation: normalized form with retire instructions

```
1   bool delete(int sKey, Node *head, *tail);
2   descList CAS_Generator(int sKey, Node *head, *tail){
3       descList ret;
4   start:
5       while(true) {/*Attempt to delete the node*/
6           Node *prev = head, *cur = head->next, *next;
7           while(true) { /*search for sKey position*/
8               if(cur==NULL){
9                   ret.len=0;
10                  return ret;
11              }
12              next = cur->next;
13              cKey = cur->key
14              if(prev->next != cur)
15                  goto start;
16              if(!is_marked(next)){
17                  if(cKey>=sKey)
18                      break;
19                  prev=cur;
20              }
21              else{
22                  if( CAS(&prev->next, cur, unmark(next)) )
23                      retire(cur);
24                  else
25                      goto start;
26              }
27              cur=unmark(next);
28          }
29          if(cKey!=sKey){
30              ret.len=0;
31              return ret;
32          }
```

```
33      ret.len=1;
34      ret.desc[0].address=&cur−>next;
35      ret.desc[0].expectedval=next;
36      ret.desc[0].newval=mark(next);
37      return ret; /*Return to CAS executor*/
38    }
39  }
40  int WRAP_UP(descList exec, int exec_res,
41                    int sKey, Node *head, *tail){
42    if(exec.len==0) return FALSE;
43    if(exec_res==1) /*CAS failed*/
44        return RESTART_GENERATOR;
45    else return TRUE;
46  }
```

4. THE MECHANISM

In this section we present the optimistic access mechanism, which adds lock-free memory recycling support to a given data structure implementation with a memory management interface (i.e., alloc and proper retire instructions).

The mechanism uses a single bit per thread, denoted *thread.warning*. The warning bit is used to warn a thread that a concurrent recycling had started. If a thread reads *true* of its warning bit, then its state may contain a stale value. It therefore starts the CAS generator or wrap-up methods from scratch. On the other hand, if the thread reads *false* from its warning bit, then it knows that no recycling had started, and the thread's state does not contain any stale values. We assume that a thread can read its warning bit, clear its warning bit, and also set the warning bits of all other threads (non-atomically).

Modification of the shared memory is visible by other threads, and modifying an object that has been recycled is disastrous to program semantics. Therefore, during any modification of the shared data structure we use the hazard pointers mechanism [17] to mark objects that cannot be recycled. Each thread has a set of three pointers denoted $thread.HP_1$, $thread.HP_2$, $thread.HP_3$ that are used to protect all parameters of any CAS operation in the CAS generator or the wrap-up methods.

In addition, the CAS executor method and the wrap-up method can access all the objects mentioned in the CASes list that is produced by the CAS generator. The optimistic access scheme prevents these objects from being recycled by an additional set of hazard pointers. Let C be the maximum number of CASes executed by the CAS executor method in any of the operations of the given data structure. Each thread keeps an additional set of $3 \cdot C$ pointers denoted $thread.HP_1^{owner}, \ldots, thread.HP_{3C}^{owner}$. These hazard pointers are installed in the end of the CAS generator method and are cleared in the end of the wrap-up method. A thread may read the hazard pointers of all threads but it writes only its own hazard pointers.

Modifications to the Data Structure Code.

In Algorithm 1 we present the code for reading from shared memory (the read-barrier for shared memory). This code is used in the CAS generator and wrap-up methods. (There are no reads in the CAS executor method.)

As a read from the shared memory may return a stale value, when using the optimistic access memory recycling scheme, checking the warning bit lets the reading thread identify such an incident. If the warning bit is false, then we know that the read object was not recycled, and the read value is not stale. If, on the other hand, the warning bit is true, the read value may be arbitrary. Furthermore, pointers previously read into the thread's local variables may point to stale objects. Thus, the thread discards its local state, and restarts

---

ALGORITHM 1: Read shared memory (var = *ptr)

```
1:  temp = *ptr
2:  if thread.warning == true then
3:      thread.warning:= false
4:      restart
5:  end if
6:  var = temp
```

from a safe location: the start of the CAS generator or wrap-up method.

The code in Algorithm 1 resets the warning bit before restarting. This can be done because the recycler will only recycle objects that appear in the recycling candidates list when it starts. This means that the warning bit is set after the data structure issued a retire instruction on the objects in the list. Since the retire instruction is *proper* in the data structure implementation, we know that all these objects are no longer accessible from the data structure and we will not encounter any such object after we restart the method from scratch. Therefore, upon restarting, we can clear the warning bit.

In order to exemplify such a read on our running example, consider, for example, Line 12 from Listing 1. It should be translated into the following code (COMPILER-FENCE tells the compiler to not change the order during compilation).

Listing 2: Algorithm 1 for Listing 1 Line 12

```
1  next = cur−>next;
2  COMPILER−FENCE;
3  if(thread−>warning){thread−>warning=0;goto start;}
```

Next we define the write-barrier for all instructions that modify the shared memory. By the properties of normalized representation, this only happens with a CAS instruction. Algorithm 2 is applied to all modifications, except for the execution of the CASes list in the CAS executor, which are discussed in Algorithm 3. A simplified version of the hazard pointer mechanism [17] is used to protect the objects whose address or body is accessed in this instruction. If a CAS modifies a non-pointer field then only one hazard pointer is required for the object being modified. Recall that *unmark* stands for removing marks embedded in a pointer to get the pointer itself.

ALGORITHM 2: An observable instruction $res=CAS(\&O.field, A_2, A_3)$

```
1:   thread.HP_1 = unmark(O)
2:   if A_2 is a pointer then thread.HP_2 = unmark(A_2)
3:   if A_3 is a pointer then thread.HP_3 = unmark(A_3)
4:   memoryFence (ensure HP are visible to all threads)
5:   if thread.warning == true then
6:       thread.warning:= false
7:       thread.HP_1=thread.HP_2=thread.HP_3 = NULL
8:       restart
9:   end if
10:  res=CAS(\&O.field, A_2, A_3)
11:  thread.HP_1=thread.HP_2=thread.HP_3 = NULL
```

Running Example. The only case where Algorithm 2 is used in the running example is in Line 22 of Listing 1, which is translated to the following code in Listing 3.

Listing 3: Algorithm 2 for Line 22 of Listing 1

```
1  HP[0]=prev;
2  HP[1]=cur;
3  HP[2]=unmark(next);
4  __memory_fence();
5  if(thread−>warning){thread−>warning=0;goto start;}
6  if( CAS(&prev−>next, cur, unmark(next)) ){
7      HP[0]=HP[1]=HP[2]=NULL;
8      ...
9  else{
10     HP[0]=HP[1]=HP[2]=NULL;
11     ...
```

We stress that *prev* and *cur* are unmarked. If, for example, *prev* was possibly marked, Line 1 would contain HP[0]=unmark(prev);.

Finally, the optimistic access scheme also protects all the objects that are accessed during the execution of the CASes list. Recall that this list is generated by the CAS generator method and executed thereafter by the CAS executor method. We need to protect all these objects so that no CAS is executed on reclaimed memory. To that end, we protect the relevant objects by hazard pointers at the end of the CAS generator method. The protection is kept until the end of the wrap-up method, because these objects are available to the wrap-up method and can be written by it. All these hazard pointers are nullified before the wrap-up method completes. The code for this protection is presented in Algorithm 3.

ALGORITHM 3: End of CAS Generator.

Input: A list of ℓ CASes $S=$ CAS($\&O_1$.field, $A_{1,2}, A_{1,3}$),...,CAS($\&O_C$.field, $A_{C,2}, A_{C,3}$).

```
1:  for i ∈ 1...ℓ do
2:      thread.HP^owner_{3·i+1} = unmark(O_i)
3:      if A_{i,2} is a pointer then thread.HP^owner_{3·i+2} = unmark(A_{i,2})
4:      if A_{i,3} is a pointer then thread.HP^owner_{3·i+2} = unmark(A_{i,3})
5:  end for
6:  memoryFence (ensure HP are visible to all threads)
7:  if thread.warning == true then
8:      thread.warning:= false
9:      for i ∈ 1...ℓ, j ∈ 1,2,3 do thread.HP^owner_{i,j}=NULL
10:     restart
11: end if
12: return S (finish the CAS generator method)
```

A basic optimization. A trivial optimization that we have applied in our implementation is to not let two hazard pointers point to the same object. Algorithm 3 guards objects until the end of the wrap-up method. So all these objects need not be guarded (again) during this interval of execution. Moreover, in case this optimization eliminates all assignment of hazard pointers in Algorithm 3 or 2, then the memory fence and the warning check can be elided as well.

Running Example. There are three places where the CAS generator method finishes: Line 10, Line 31, and Line 37. For Lines 10 and 31 there is no need to add any code because, in this case, the CAS generator method returns a CAS list of length zero and there is no object to protect. Thus there is no need to execute the memory fence or the warning check. For Line 37 we add the following code:

Listing 4: Algorithm 3 for Listing 1 Line 37

```
1  //Original code before the return (Lines 34 − 36).
2  ret.desc[0].address=&cur−>next;
3  ret.desc[0].expectedval=next;
4  ret.desc[0].newval=mark(next);
```

```
5   //Algorithm 3 added instructions
6   HP[3]=cur;
7   HP[4]=next;
8   //No need to set HP[5] (equal to HP[4])
9   __memory_fence();
10  if(thread−>warning)
11      {thread−>warning=0; HP[3]=HP[4]=NULL;goto start;}
12  //End of Algorithm 3
13  return ret;
```

The Recycling Mechanism.

Having presented code modifications of data structure operations, we proceed with describing the recycling algorithm itself: Algorithms 4-6.

The recycling is done in *phases*. A phase starts when there are no objects available for allocation. During a phase, the algorithm attempts to recycle objects that were retired by the data structure until the phase started. The allocator can then use the recycled objects until exhaustion, and then a new phase starts.

The optimistic access scheme uses three shared objects pools, denoted *readyPool*, *retirePool*, and *processingPool*. The readyPool is a pool of ready-to-be-allocated objects from which the allocator allocates objects for the data structure. The retirePool contains objects on which the retire instruction was invoked by the data structure. These objects are waiting to be recycled in the next phase. In the beginning of the phase, the recycler moves all objects from the retirePool to the processingPool. The processingPool is used during the recycling process to hold objects that were retired before the current phase began and can therefore be processed in the current phase. Note that while the recycling is being executed on objects in the processingPool, the data structure may add newly retired objects to the retirePool. But these objects will not be processed in the current phase. They will wait for the subsequent phase to be recycled. During the execution of recycling, each object of the processingPool is examined and the algorithm determines whether the object can be recycled or not. If it can, it is moved to the readyPool, and if not, it is moved back to the retirePool and is processed again at the next phase.

Since we are working with lock-free algorithms, we cannot wait for all threads to acknowledge a start of a phase (as is common with concurrent garbage collectors). Since no blocking is allowed and we cannot wait for acknowledgements, it is possible that a thread is delayed in the middle of executing a recycling phase r and then it wakes up while other threads are already executing a subsequent recycling phase $r' > r$. The optimistic access scheme must ensure that threads processing previous phases cannot interfere with the execution of the current phase. To achieve this protection, we let a modification of the pools only succeed if the phase number of the local thread matches the phase number of the shared pool. In fact, we only need to protect modifications of the retirePool and the processingPool. Allocations from the readyPool do not depend on the phase and also once a thread discovers that an object can be added to the readyPool, this discovery remains true even if the thread adds the object to the readyPool much later.

There are various ways to implement such phase protection, but let us specify the specific way we implemented the pools and the matching of local to global phase numbers. Each pool is implemented as a lock-free stack with a version (phase) field adjacent to the head pointer. The head pointer is modified only by a wide CAS instruction that modifies (and verifies) the version as well. When adding an object or popping an object from the pool fails due to version mismatch, a special return code VER-MISMATCH is returned. This signifies that a new phase started, and the thread should update its phase number. Each thread maintains a local variable denoted *localVer* that contains the phase that the thread thinks it is helping. The thread uses this variable whenever it adds or removes objects to or from the pool.

A phase starts by moving the content of the retirePool to the processingPool (which also empties the retirePool), and increasing the version of both pools. This operation should be executed in an atomic (or at least linearizable) manner, to prevent a race condition where an object resides in both the retirePool and the processingPool. We use a standard trick of lock-free algorithms to accomplish this without locking (in a lock-free manner). The versions (localVer and the versions of the pools) are kept even (i.e., they represent the phase number multiplied by 2) at all times except for the short times in which we want to move the items from the retirePool to the processingPool. Swapping the pools starts by incrementing the retirePool version by 1. At this point, any thread attempting to insert an object to the retirePool will fail and upon discovering the reason for the failure, it will help swapping the pools before attempting to modify the retirePool again. Then the thread attempting to recycle copies the content of the retirePool into the processingPool while incrementing its version by 2. This can be done atomically by a single modification of the head and version. Finally, the retirePool version is incremented by 1 (to an even number), and the pool content is emptied. Again, these two operations can also be executed atomically.

When the data structure calls the retire routine, the code in Algorithm 4 is executed. It attempts to add the retired object to the retirePool (and it typically succeeds). If the attempt to add fails due to unequal versions (VER-MISMATCH), the thread proceeds to the next phase by calling Recycling (Algorithm 6), and then retries the operation.

ALGORITHM 4: Reclaim(obj)

1: **repeat**
2:    res=MM.retirePool.add(obj,localVer)
3:    **if** res==VER-MISMATCH **then**
4:       Call Recycling (Algorithm 6)
5:    **end if**
6: **until** res!=VER-MISMATCH

The allocation procedure appears in Algorithm 5. It attempts to pop an object from the readyPool. If unsuccessful, the thread calls Recycling (Algorithm 6), which attempts to recycle objects. Then it restarts the operation.

ALGORITHM 5: Allocate

1: **repeat**
2:    obj = MM.readyPool.pop()
3:    **if** obj==EMPTY **then**
4:       Call Recycling (Algorithm 6)
5:    **end if**
6: **until** obj!=EMPTY
7: memset(obj, 0); //Zero obj
8: **return** obj

The recycling procedure of the optimistic access scheme is presented in Algorithm 6. It starts by moving the content of the retirePool into the processingPool in a linearizable lock-free manner as described above, and it then increments the local phase counter. In Line 10, the thread checks if the (new) retirePool version matches the thread version. If not, the current phase was completed by other

threads and the thread returns immediately. Note that the thread is unable to access the retirePool or the processingPool until it calls the recycling procedure again. The thread then sets the warning bits of all threads at Line 12. This tells the threads that objects for which the retire procedure was invoked before the current phase are candidates for recycling, and accessing them may return stale values. Finally, the thread collects the hazard pointer records of all threads. Objects that are pointed to by an hazard pointer are potentially modified, and should not be recycled in the current phase.

ALGORITHM 6: Recycling

1: //Start a new phase
2: localRetire=MM.retirePool
3: localProcessingPool=MM.processingPool
4: **if** localRetire.ver==localVer **or**
         localRetire.ver==localVer+1 **then**
5:    MM.retirePool.CAS(<localRetire, localVer>,
         <localRetire, localVer+1>)
6:    MM.processingPool.CAS(<localProcessingPool,
         localVer>, <localRetire, localVer+2>)
7:    MM.retirePool.CAS(<localRetire, localVer+1>,
         <Empty, localVer+2>)
8: **end if**
9: localVer=localVer+2
10: **if** MM.retirePool.ver > localVer **then return**
11:                    //Phase already finished
12: **for** each thread *T* **do**
13:    Set *T.warning = true*
14: **end for**
15: memoryFence (ensure warning bits are visible)
16: **for** each HP record *R* **do**
17:    Save *R* in a *LocalHParray*.
18: **end for**
19: //Processing the objects
20: **while** res = MM.processingPool.pop(localVer) is not empty **do**
21:    **if** res!=VER-MISMATCH **then**
22:       **if** *res* does not exist in *LocalHParray* **then**
23:          MM.readyPool.add(n)
24:       **else**
25:          res=MM.retirePool.add(res, localVer)
26:       **end if**
27:    **end if**
28:    **if** res==VER-MISMATCH **then return**
29:                    //Phase already finished
30: **end while**

Next, the processingPool is processed. For each candidate object in the processingPool, if it is not referenced by a hazard pointer, then it is eligible for recycling and therefore it is moved to the readyPool. Otherwise, the object cannot be recycled and it is returned to the retirePool, where it will be processed again in the next phase. Accesses to the processingPool and to the retirePool are successful only if the phase number is correct.

In order to determine if a given object is protected by a hazard pointer it is advisable to sort the hazard pointers to make the search faster or to insert the hazard pointers into a hash table (which is what we did).

5. METHODOLOGY AND RESULTS

To evaluate the performance of the optimistic access reclamation scheme with lock-free data structures, we have implemented it with three widely used data structures: Harris-Maged linked list and hash table [16], and Herlihy and Shavit's skip list [13]. The optimistic access memory management scheme (and additional schemes as well) were applied to the baseline algorithm in a normalized form, which performs no memory recycling. The baseline algorithm, denoted *NoRecl*, serves as a base for performance comparison. The proposed optimistic access method is denoted *OA* in the measurements.

To obtain an allocator that does not unmap pages that were previously allocated (as specified in Assumption 3.1), we use object pooling for allocation. The pool is implemented using a lock-free stack, where each item in the stack is an array of 126 objects. To allocate, a thread obtains an array from the stack (using the lock-free stack pop operation) and then it can allocates 126 times locally with no synchronization. To fairly compare the memory management techniques and not just the underlying allocator, we converted all implementations to use the same object pool allocation for all allocations of objects of the data structure (except for the EBP method, discussed below, which uses its own allocator). As a sanity check, we verified that the object pooling method performed similarly (or better) than malloc on all measured configurations.

Additional Memory Management Schemes compared. We discuss related memory management techniques for lock-free data structures that are available in the literature in Section 6. Let us now specify which methods were compared per data structure.

For Harris-Maged linked list [16], a comprehensive comparison of memory management techniques was done by [3]. We used their baseline implementation (*NoRecl*), their hazard pointers implementation (*HP*), and their *anchors* implementation[3]. We also compare the Epoch Base Reclamation (*EBR*), proposed by Harris [9]; we took an implementation of this method by Fraser [8], which uses its integrated allocator. Namely, We did not replace the allocator. The latter method is not lock-free, but is sometimes used in practice to implement lock-free algorithms (to reduce the overhead associated with lock-free reclamation methods). Its disadvantage is that it does not deal well with threads failures, which is a major concerns for the lock-free methods. Finally, we implemented the optimistic access technique proposed in this paper. All implementations were coded in C.

For the hash table, each bucket was implemented as a linked list of items and the above linked-list implementations were used to support each of the buckets. For the hash table size, we used a load factor of 0.75. While both the linked list test and the hash table test use Harris-Maged linked list, the list length differed greatly for the two tests. In the linked list test all items reside on a single (relatively long) linked list, while in the hash table test the average length of a linked list is below one item. A hash table is probably a better example of a widely used data structure. We did not implement the *anchors* version of a hash table because the anchors improve accesses to paths of pointer dereferencing, while the lists in the hash table implementation are mostly of size 1, i.e, contain only a single entry.

For Herlihy and Shavit's skip list [13], we ported the Java implementation of [13] into C, and then converted it into a normalized form. We implemented the hazard pointers scheme for the skip list; the implementation uses $2 \cdot MAXLEN + 3$ hazard pointers. Finally, we implemented the optimistic access technique. The CAS generator method of the delete operation generates at most $MAXLEN + 1$ CASes to mark the next fields of the deleted node. This implies that $3 \cdot MAXLEN + 6$ hazard pointers are needed by the *OA* implemen-

tation. However, many of the protected objects are the same, and so the actual number of hazard pointers required is $MAXLEN + 5$: all CASes executed by the CAS executor method share one single modified object, and for each level the expected and new object pointers are the same. An *anchor* version for the skip list was not used because it is complex to design and no such design appears in the literature.

Methodology. It is customary to evaluate data structures by running a stressful workload that runs the data structure operations repeatedly on many threads. Similarly to Alistarh et al. [1], in all our tests, 80% of the operations were read-only. Additional test configurations are reported in the full version of this paper [4]. The hash table and the skip list were initialized to 10,000 nodes before the measurement began. The linked list was initialized to 5,000 nodes (thus denoted LinkedList5K). We also measure a short linked list which is initialized to 128 nodes (thus denoted LinkedList128), which creates reasonable high contention. Each micro-benchmark was executed with a varied number of threads being power-of-2 numbers between from 1 and 64 to check the behavior in different parallel settings. Each execution was measured for 1 seconds, which captures the steady-state behavior. We ensure that a 10-seconds test behave similarly to a 1-second test.

The code was compiled using the GCC compiler version 4.8.2 with the -O3 optimization flag. We ran the experiments on two platforms. The first platform featured 4 AMD Opteron(TM) 6272 2.1GHz processors, each with 16 cores (64 threads overall). The second platform featured 2 Intel Xeon(R) CPU E5-2690 2.90GHz processors, each with 8 cores with each core running 2 hyper-threads (32 threads overall). Measurements for the Intel Xeon platform are provided in the full version of this paper [4].

For each micro-benchmark we tested, we depict the ratio of the throughput between the evaluated memory management mechanism and the baseline algorithm (*NoRecl*), across different numbers of threads. A high number is better, meaning that the scheme has higher throughput. E.g., a result of 90% means the throughput was 0.9 of the baseline's throughput. A figure depicting the actual throughput is provided in the full version of this paper [4]. Each test was repeated 20 times and the ratio of the average throughput is reported with error bars that represent 95% confidence level. The x-axis denotes the number of threads, and the y-axis denotes the average throughput for the evaluated method divided by the average throughput for the *NoRecl* method.

Results. In Figure 1 we compare the running time of the measured data structures with the various memory management methods. In this test, reclamation is triggered infrequently, once every 50,000 allocations, to capture the base overhead of the reclamation schemes. For the LinkedList5K micro-benchmark, operations have long execution time that is mostly spent on traversals. The *OA* has a very low overhead in most configurations and at max it reaches 4%. The EBR also has very low overhead, and in some cases it even ran slightly faster (recall that it uses a different allocator). However, for 64 threads its overhead was 12%. The HP overhead always exceeds $3x$. The Anchors has an overhead of $3\% - 52\%$, and the overhead increases as the number of threads increases.

For the LinkedList128 micro-benchmark, operations are shorter, and traversals do not take over the execution. Also, the baseline reaches maximum throughput at 16 threads, and then throughput decreases due to contention. For higher numbers of threads, memory reclamation methods behave better and even slightly improve performance of over no-reclamation by reducing contention. (This was previously reported by [6, 1].) The *OA* has an overhead of $-1\% - 19\%$ and the overhead is lower for a high number of threads. The EBR has an overhead of $-2\% - 26\%$, again lower for high

---

[3]Loosely speaking, the *anchors* implementation installs a hazard pointer once every every K reads. We picked $K = 1000$ for best performance results, as thread failures are rare.

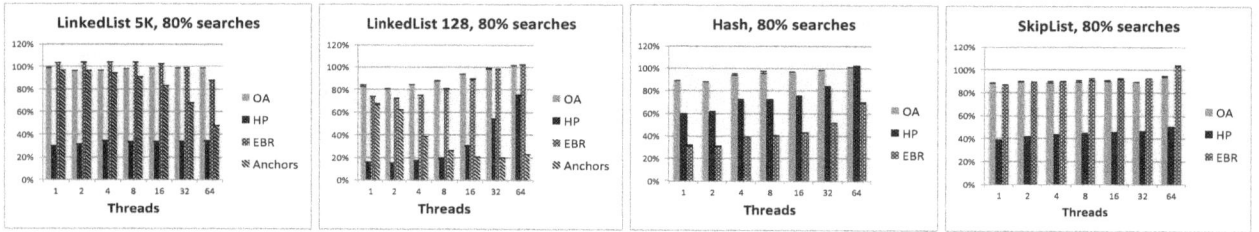

Figure 1: Throughput ratios for the various memory management techniques and various data structures. The *x*-axis is the number of participating threads. The *y*-axis is the ratio between the throughput of the presented scheme and the throughput of NoRecl.

number of threads. The overhead of the HP method is above $3x$ for up to 16 threads. For $32 - 64$ threads it behaves better with an overhead of $25\% - 46\%$. The Anchors responds poorly to the shorter linked-list length, and incurs an overhead of $2x - 5x$. For a large number of threads (and higher contention), it became even slower than the hazard pointers method.

For the hash micro-benchmark, operations are extremely short, and modifications have a large impact on insert and delete operations. Contention has noticeable effect for 64 threads, letting executions with memory reclamation demonstrate low overheads and sometimes even slightly improved performance. The *OA* has an overhead of $-1\% - 12\%$. EBR responds poorly to the short operation execution times, and it demonstrates an overhead of $2x - 3x$ for $1 - 32$ threads. For 64 threads it slightly improves with an overhead of 30%. HP has an overhead of $16\% - 40\%$ for $1 - 32$ thread and -2% for 64 threads.

For the skip list micro-benchmark, operations take approximately the same time as LinkedList128, but face less contention. Moreover, operations are significantly more complex (executes more instructions). The *OA* has an overhead of $8\% - 12\%$. the EBR has overhead of $8\% - 13\%$ for $1 - 32$ threads, but slightly improved performance for 64 threads. The HP has overhead of $2x - 2.5x$.

To summarize, the *OA* overhead is at most 19% in all measured configurations, which is significantly faster than currently state-of-the-art lock-free reclamation methods. The optimistic access method has comparable performance to the EBR method (which is not lock-free), and is significantly better than EBR for the hash micro-benchmark.

Next, we study how the various choice of parameters affects performance. The impact of choosing the size of the local pools is depicted in Figure 2. Measurements for the LinkedList5K and the Hash micro benchmarks are depicted, showing the behavior with long and short operations time. All tests were executed with 32 threads. We started a new reclamation phase approximately every 16,000 allocations. We later show that this choice is immaterial. It can be seen that the choice of local pool size has minor effect on the LinkedList5K micro-benchmark. For the hash micro-benchmark, all methods suffer a penalty for small local pools, but the *OA* scheme suffers a penalty also for a medium sized local pool. Using the *perf* Linux tool, we found that Algorithm 6 was the source of this slow-down. The reason is that local pools are popped from the *processingPool* and pushed into the *readyPool* in a tight loop, so contention becomes noticeable for medium sizes. Reasonably sized pools of 126 objects are sufficiently large to obtain excellent performance for *OA*.

Next, we study how the frequency of reclamation phases affects performance; the results are depicted in Figure 3. All tests were executed with 32 threads. The *OA* triggers a new phase when no object is available for allocation. We initialized the number of entries available for allocation to be the data structure size plus an

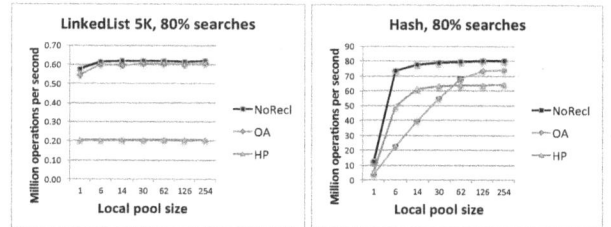

Figure 2: Throughput as a function of the size of the local pools.

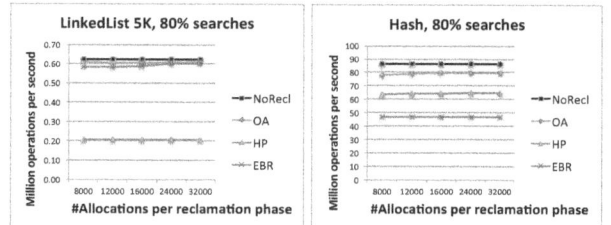

Figure 3: Throughput as a function of collection phases frequency.

additional δ, for δ equals 8000, 12000, 16000, 24000, or 32000. Thus a new phase is triggered approximately every δ allocations. We started with $\delta = 8000$ because allocations are counted system-wide. For example, $\delta = 32000$ means that each thread allocated approximately $32000/32 = 1000$ objects before a phase begin. Each thread has two local pools: one for allocation and one for retired objects. The local pool size is 126. Thus $\delta = 8000 \approx 32 \cdot 126 \cdot 2$ is the minimum size where threads do not starve. With $\delta < 7600$ performance indeed drops drastically, due to thread starvation. In Figure 3 it is possible to see that different frequencies have a low impact on the performance of *OA*.

The other schemes do not use a global counting mechanisms. Therefore, measuring same effect for other schemes might mean a significant change in their triggering. Instead, we made an effort to compare the reclamation schemes without changing the algorithmic behavior. In the HP scheme we picked $k = \delta/32$, where each thread starts a reclamation phase *locally* after it retired k objects. In the EBR scheme, a reclamation starts *locally* after q operations started. We picked $q = (\delta/32) \cdot 10$ since deletions are about 10% of the total operations. We also made sure that threads do not starve in the other schemes for these settings of δ.

6. RELATED WORK

The basic and most popular lock-free reclamation schemes are the *hazard pointers* and *pass the buck* mechanisms of [17] and

[12]. In these schemes every thread has a set of *hazard pointers* or *guards*, which mark objects the thread is accessing. Before accessing a data structure node, the object's address is saved in a thread's hazard pointer. A validation check is executed to verify that the object was not reclaimed just before it became guarded by a hazard pointer. If the validation fails, the thread must restart its operation. A node can be reclaimed only if it is not guarded by any thread's hazard pointers. The main disadvantage of these schemes is their cost. Each access (even a read) of a node requires a write (to the hazard pointer), a memory fence (to make sure that the hazard pointer value is visible to all other threads), and some additional reads for computing the validation test. Fence elision techniques [7] can be used to ameliorate this overhead, but such methods foil lock-freedom.

Braginsky et al. [3] proposed the *anchor* scheme as an improvement to the hazard pointer scheme. The anchor scheme allows a hazard pointer to be registered only once per each k reads of the data structure. The anchor method significantly reduces the overhead, but not to a negligible level (see measurements in Section 5). Moreover, the complexity of designing an anchor reclamation scheme for a given data structure is high, and the authors only provided an example implementation for the linked list.

Alistarh et al. [1] have recently proposed the StackTrack method, which utilizes hardware transactional memory to solve the memory reclamation problem. This method breaks each operation to a series to transactions, such that a successfully committed transaction cannot be interfered with a memory reclamation.

Another method for manual object reclamation that supports lock-freedom is reference counting. Each object is associated with a count of threads that access it and a node can be reclaimed if its reference count is dropped to 0. Correctness requires either a type persistence assumption [25, 23] or the use of the double compare-and-swap (DCAS) primitive [5] which is not always available. The performance overhead is high as these methods require (at least) two atomic operations per object read [10].

If lock-freedom is not required, then in most cases the epoch-based reclamation method is a high performant solution [9, 16]. Before an operation starts, the executing thread reports the timestamp it reads, and upon operation completion it clears the published timestamp. An object A can be reclaimed when every thread that started an operation before A was retired completes its operation.

7. CONCLUSIONS

This paper presents the *optimistic access* lock-free memory management mechanism. Unlike previous memory managers, this algorithm allows threads (infrequent) access to reclaimed objects. This optimistic mechanism obtains a drastic reduction in the reclamation overheads compared to other schemes available in the literature. It is also simpler to implement. In order to preserve correctness in spite of potentially reading stale values, the algorithm implements a low-overhead cooperation mechanism, where a thread that reclaims objects warns other threads that a reclamation has taken place, and accessing threads check for this warning at appropriate locations. As far as we know this is the first memory management scheme that allows accessing reclaimed objects in order to obtain (considerable) performance improvement.

8. REFERENCES

[1] D. Alistarh, P. Eugster, M. Herlihy, A. Matveev, and N. Shavit. Stacktrack: An automated transactional approach to concurrent memory reclamation. In *EuroSys*. ACM, 2014.

[2] J. Auerbach, D. F. Bacon, P. Cheng, D. Grove, B. Biron, C. Gracie, B. McCloskey, A. Micic, and R. Sciampacone. Tax-and-spend: Democratic scheduling for real-time garbage collection. In *EMSOFT*, pages 245–254, 2008.

[3] A. Braginsky, A. Kogan, and E. Petrank. Drop the anchor: lightweight memory management for non-blocking data structures. In *SPAA*, pages 33–42. ACM, 2013.

[4] N. Cohen and E. Petrank. Efficient memory management for lock-free data structures with optimistic access. http://www.cs.technion.ac.il/~erez/papers.html.

[5] D. L. Detlefs, P. A. Martin, M. Moir, and G. L. Steele Jr. Lock-free reference counting. *DISC*, pages 255–271, 2002.

[6] D. Dice, M. Herlihy, Y. Lev, and M. Moir. Lightweight contention management for efficient compare-and-swap operations. In *EuroPar*. ACM, 2013.

[7] D. Dice, H. Huang, and M. Yang. Techniques for accessing a shared resource using an improved synchronization mechanism, 2010. Patent US 7644409 B2.

[8] K. Fraser. http://www.cl.cam.ac.uk/research/srg/netos/lock-free/src/temp/lockfree-lib/.

[9] T. L. Harris. A pragmatic implementation of non-blocking linked-lists. In *DISC*, pages 300–314. Springer, 2001.

[10] T. E. Hart, P. E. McKenney, A. D. Brown, and J. Walpole. Performance of memory reclamation for lockless synchronization. *JPDC*, pages 1270–1285, 2007.

[11] M. Herlihy. Wait-free synchronization. *TOPLAS*, pages 124–149, 1991.

[12] M. Herlihy, V. Luchangco, P. Martin, and M. Moir. Nonblocking memory management support for dynamic-sized data structures. *TOCS*, 23(2):146–196, 2005.

[13] M. Herlihy and N. Shavit. *The Art of Multiprocessor Programming, Revised Reprint*. Elsevier, 2012.

[14] M. P. Herlihy and J. E. B. Moss. Lock-free garbage collection for multiprocessors. *TPDS*, pages 304–311, 1992.

[15] R. L. Hudson and J. E. B. Moss. Sapphire: Copying GC without stopping the world. In *Joint ACM-ISCOPE Conference on Java Grande*, pages 48–57, 2001.

[16] M. M. Michael. High performance dynamic lock-free hash tables and list-based sets. In *SPAA*, pages 73–82. ACM, 2002.

[17] M. M. Michael. Hazard pointers: Safe memory reclamation for lock-free objects. *TPDS*, 15(6):491–504, 2004.

[18] S. Owens, S. Sarkar, and P. Sewell. A better x86 memory model: x86-tso. In *Theorem Proving in Higher Order Logics*, pages 391–407. Springer, 2009.

[19] E. Petrank. Can parallel data structures rely on automatic memory managers? In *MSPC*, pages 1–1. ACM, 2012.

[20] F. Pizlo, D. Frampton, E. Petrank, and B. Steensgard. Stopless: A real-time garbage collector for multiprocessors. In *ISMM*, pages 159–172, 2007.

[21] F. Pizlo, E. Petrank, and B. Steensgaard. A study of concurrent real-time garbage collectors. In *PLDI*, pages 33–44, 2008.

[22] F. Pizlo, L. Ziarek, P. Maj, A. L. Hosking, E. Blanton, and J. Vitek. Schism: Fragmentation-tolerant real-time garbage collection. In *PLDI*, pages 146–159, 2010.

[23] H. Sundell. Wait-free reference counting and memory management. In *IPDPS*, pages 24b–24b. IEEE, 2005.

[24] S. Timnat and E. Petrank. A practical wait-free simulation for lock-free data structures. In *PPoPP*, pages 357–368. ACM, 2014.

[25] J. D. Valois. Lock-free linked lists using compare-and-swap. In *PODC*, pages 214–222. ACM, 1995.

Fault Tolerant BFS Structures:
A Reinforcement-Backup Tradeoff

Merav Parter [*]
Dept. of Computer Science and Applied Math
The Weizmann Institute
Rehovot, Israel
merav.parter@weizmann.ac.il

David Peleg [†]
Dept. of Computer Science and Applied Math
The Weizmann Institute
Rehovot, Israel
david.peleg@weizmann.ac.il

ABSTRACT

This paper initiates the study of fault resilient network structures that mix two orthogonal protection mechanisms: (a) *backup*, namely, augmenting the structure with many (redundant) low-cost but fault-prone components, and (b) *reinforcement*, namely, acquiring high-cost but fault-resistant components. To study the trade-off between these two mechanisms in a concrete setting, we address the problem of designing a (b, r) *fault-tolerant* BFS (or (b, r) FT-BFS for short) structure, namely, a subgraph H of the network G consisting of two types of edges: a set $E' \subseteq E$ of $r(n)$ fault-resistant *reinforcement* edges, which are assumed to never fail, and a (larger) set $E(H) \setminus E'$ of $b(n)$ fault-prone *backup* edges, such that subsequent to the failure of a single fault-prone backup edge $e \in E \setminus E'$, the surviving part of H still contains a BFS spanning tree for (the surviving part of) G, satisfying $\text{dist}(s, v, H \setminus \{e\}) \leq \text{dist}(s, v, G \setminus \{e\})$ for every $v \in V$ and $e \in E \setminus E'$. We establish the following tradeoff: For every real $\epsilon \in (0, 1]$, if $r(n) = \tilde{\Theta}(n^{1-\epsilon})$, then $b(n) = \tilde{\Theta}(n^{1+\epsilon})$ is necessary and sufficient. More specifically, as shown in [14], for $\epsilon = 1$, FT-BFS structures (with no reinforced edges) require $\Theta(n^{3/2})$ edges, and this is sufficient. At the other extreme, if $\epsilon = 0$, then $n - 1$ reinforced edges suffice (with no need for backup). Here, we present a polynomial time algorithm that given an undirected graph $G = (V, E)$, a source vertex s and a real $\epsilon \in (0, 1]$, constructs a $(b(n), r(n))$ FT-BFS with $r(n) = O(n^{1-\epsilon})$ and $b(n) = O(\min\{1/\epsilon \cdot n^{1+\epsilon} \cdot \log n, n^{3/2}\})$. We complement this result by providing a nearly matching lower bound, showing that there are n-vertex graphs for which any $(b(n), r(n))$ FT-BFS structure requires $\Omega(\min\{n^{1+\epsilon}, n^{3/2}\})$ backup edges when $r(n) = \Omega(n^{1-\epsilon})$ edges are reinforced.

[*]Recipient of the Google European Fellowship in distributed computing; research is supported in part by this Fellowship.

[†]Supported in part by the Israel Science Foundation (grant 894/09), and the I-CORE program of the Israel PBC and ISF (grant 1549/13).

SPAA'15, June 13–15, 2015, Portland, OR, USA.
Copyright © 2015 ACM 978-1-4503-3588-1/15/06 ...$15.00.
DOI: http://dx.doi.org/10.1145/2755573.2755590.

Categories and Subject Descriptors

F.2.3 [**Theory of Computation**]: Analysis of Algorithms and Problem Complexity—*Tradeoffs among Complexity Measures*

General Terms

Algorithms, Reliability, Theory

Keywords

Fault-tolerance, replacement-paths, tree-decomposition

1. INTRODUCTION

Background and Motivation. Modern day communication networks support a variety of logical structures and services, and depend on their undisrupted operation. Following the immense recent advances in telecommunication networks, the explosive growth of the Internet, and our increased dependence on these infrastructures, guaranteeing the survivability of communication networks has become a major objective in both practice and theory. An important aspect of this objective is *survivable network design*, namely, the design of low cost high resilience networks that satisfy certain desirable *performance requirements* concerning, e.g., their connectivity, distance or capacity. Our focus here, however, is not on planning survivable networks "from scratch", but rather on settings where an initially existing infrastructure needs to be improved and optimized.

Our interest in this paper is in exploring a natural "quality vs. quantity" tradeoff in survivable network design. Designers and manufactures often face the following design choice when dealing with ensuring product reliability. One option is to invest heavily in the quality and resilience of the various components of the product, making them essentially failure-free. An alternative option is to use unreliable but cheap components, and ensure the reliability of the whole product by employing redundancy, namely, including several "copies" of each component in the design, so that the failure of one component will not disable the operation.

In the context of survivable network design, where the goal is to overcome link disconnections, the "quantity-based" approach to survivability relies on adding to the network many inexpensive (but failure-prone) *backup* links, counting on redundancy to provide resilience and guarantee the desired performance requirements in the presence of failures. In contrast, a "quality-based" approach may rely on *reinforcing* some of the network links, and thus making them failure-resistant (but expensive), counting on these links to ensure the performance requirements. Clearly, these two approaches address two different and *orthogonal* factors affecting the survivability of a network: the *topology*, e.g., the presence of redundant alternate paths, and the *reliability* of individual network components. We would like to study the tradeoff betwen these two factors in various survivable network design problems.

Towards exploring this tradeoff, we consider the following "mixed" model. Assume that the existing infrastructure consists of a given fixed set V of vertices and a collection E of existing links, and it is required to decide, for each link, among the following three choices: (a) discard the link (in which case it will cost us nothing), (b) purchase it as is (at some low cost B), or (c) "reinforce" it (at some high cost R), making it failure-resilient. The existing initial graph $G(V, E)$ provides a baseline for comparison, in the sense that if we decide on the conservative approach of making no changes, namely, purchasing all the links of the existing network G "as is" (at a cost of $B \cdot |E|$), then the performance properties that can be guaranteed in the presence of failures are those of the existing G. An alternative baseline is obtained by the opposite extreme, namely, basing the design on selecting the smallest subgraph $H \subseteq G$ that satisfies the desired requirements in the absence of failures, and reinforcing all its links, thus ensuring this performance level.

Unfortunately, both of these two extremes might be too costly. Hence, constructing a survivable subnetwork with a *limited* budget introduces a tradeoff between backup and reinforcement and the system designer is faced with a choice: reinforcing just a few of the links may potentially lead to considerable savings, by allowing one to discard many of the ordinary backup edges and still obtain the same performance properties. To illustrate this point, consider an n-vertex network consisting of a single vertex s connected via a single edge e to an $n - 1$-vertex clique. The edge connectivity of this network is 1, as the removal of e disconnects the graph. Hence the conservative approach of keeping all existing edges leaves this network with a low level of survivability. In contrast, in a mixed model allowing also reinforcements, it is sufficient to reinforce a single edge, namely, e, in order to obtain a high level of survivability, even by purchasing only a fraction of the edges of the clique.

Our Contributions. To initiate the study of the tradeoff between reinforcement and backup in survivable network design, we consider in this paper the concrete problem of designing (in the mixed model) a *fault-tolerant Breadth-First structure* (or **FT-BFS** for short), namely, a subnetwork that preserves distances with respect to a given source vertex s in the presence of an edge failure. Formally, given a network $G(V, E)$ and a source vertex s in G, a $(b(n), r(n))$-**FT-BFS** is a subgraph H of G consisting of two types of edges: a set $E' \subseteq E$ of $r(n)$ fault-resistant *reinforcement* edges, which are assumed to never fail, and a (larger) set $E(H) \setminus E'$ of $b(n)$ fault-prone *backup* edges, such that subsequent to the failure of a single fault-prone backup edge $e \in E \setminus E'$, the surviving part of H still contains a BFS spanning tree for (the surviving part of) G, satisfying $\text{dist}(s, v, H \setminus \{e\}) \leq \text{dist}(s, v, G \setminus \{e\})$ for every $v \in V$ and $e \in E \setminus E'$. We establish the following tradeoff between $b(n)$ and $r(n)$: For every real $\epsilon \in [0, 1]$, if $r(n) = \tilde{\Theta}(n^{1-\epsilon})$, then $b(n) = \tilde{\Theta}(\min\{n^{1+\epsilon}, n^{3/2}\})$ is necessary and sufficient. It was shown in [14], that for $\epsilon = 1$, **FT-BFS** structure requires $\Theta(n^{3/2})$ edges. In the other extreme case of $\epsilon = 0$, by reinforcing all the edges of the BFS tree, no backup is needed.

We complement the upper bound construction of (r, b) **FT-BFS** structures by presenting a nearly matching lower bound. We show that there are n-vertex graphs for which any $(b(n), r(n))$ **FT-BFS** structure for $r(n) = \Omega(n^{1-\epsilon})$ requires $\Omega(\min\{n^{1+\epsilon}, n^{3/2}\})$ backup edges. In our lower bound constructions, we also consider a generalized structure referred to as a (b, r) *fault-tolerant multi-source BFS tree*, or **FT-MBFS** *tree* for short, aiming to provide a (b, r) **FT-BFS** structure at each source vertex $s \in S$ for some subset of sources $S \subseteq V$. We show that a (b, r) **FT-MBFS** structure for $r(n) = \Omega(|S|^\epsilon \cdot n^{1-\epsilon})$ requires $b(n) = \Omega(\min\{\sqrt{|S|} \cdot n^{3/2}, |S|^{1-\epsilon} \cdot n^{1+\epsilon}\})$ edges for every $\epsilon \in (0, 1]$.

Techniques and proof outline. Studying (b, r) **FT-BFS** structures significantly differs from their standard **FT-BFS** counterparts (for $r(n) = 0$) in both the upper and lower bounds. Let $\pi(s, v)$ be an $s - v$ shortest-path in G. The initial structure consists of the BFS tree $T_0 = \bigcup_{v \in V} \pi(s, v)$. It is then augmented by adding to it the last edges of some carefully chosen replacement-paths. For an edge $e \in \pi(s, v)$, a replacement path $P_{v,e}$ is *new-ending* path if its last edge was not present in the structure when the path was selected by the algorithm. A new-ending replacement path $P_{v,e}$ has the following structure. It consists of a prefix of $\pi(s, v)$ followed by a detour D avoiding the failing edge e and joining the $\pi(s, v)$ path at the terminal v. An essential component in our analysis deals with the detour segment of the single failure replacement paths. The analysis of **FT-BFS** structure [14] focused on a *single* terminal v and showed that it has $O(\sqrt{n})$ new-ending replacement-paths (with distinct last edges). The current setting of (b, r) **FT-BFS** structures is more involved and requires studying the interactions between detours of *different* vertices. In particular, the current construction has two simultaneous objectives: minimizing the number of backup edges in the structure as well as selecting at most $r(n)$ reinforced edges. In other words, when constructing a (b, r) **FT-BFS** structure with $o(n^{3/2})$ edges, one has the privilege of discarding the protection against the failure of $r(n)$ edges, which are reinforced.

The upper bound of [14] relied on analyzing the interactions between the detours of $s - v$ new-ending replacement-paths P_{v,e_i} and P_{v,e_j} for some $e_i, e_j \in \pi(s, v)$. It was shown that upon a proper construction of the replacement-paths, these detours are vertex disjoint[1], except for the common endpoint v, and hence these detours are vertex-consuming, which enables bounding their number. In contrast, studying (b, r) structures requires understanding the interaction between detours of *distinct* terminals. These detours may overlap and are not necessarily vertex disjoint, hence bounding their number calls for new techniques.

Our key observation is that the interactions (referred hereafter as *interference*) between detours can be roughly classified into two types depending on the relation between the edges protected by the corresponding detours. Each of these interference types gives raise to unique structural characterization and volume constraints that enable us to bound the cardinality of their corresponding paths. The first type of interference concerns paths $P_{v,e}$ and $P_{t,e'}$ both whose failing edges e and e' occur below $\text{LCA}(v, t)$, the least common ancestor of v and t in the BFS tree T_0. We show that adding

---

[1] if their last edge is distinct

the last edges of $O(n^\epsilon)$ such replacement-paths protecting against the failure of the deepest edges of each $s - v$ path is sufficient, i.e., it leaves no unprotected edge in the structure (among those protected by a replacement-path of this type). We then turn to consider the second type of interference, where at least one of the faulty edges, say e, occurs *above* LCA(v, t). Analyzing the interaction between detours that protect edges on the *same* shortest-path turns out to be more involved. Our technique is based on the *heavy-path-decomposition* procedure of Sleator and Tarjan [20] (slightly adapted by Baswana and Khanna [2]), applied on T_0. This decomposition is obtained by $O(\log n)$ recursive calls on partial trees $T' \subseteq T_0$, where each recursive call results with a collection of paths in T_0 whose edges appear in the $s - v$ shortest-paths of a *distinct* set of vertices. The advantage of this approach is that equipped with our interference classification, the analysis is reduced to solving the subproblem (i.e., designing the (b, r) structure) for the case where the failing events are restricted to a given path $\psi \subseteq T_0$ in the tree-decomposition (a similar approach is taken in [2] for a different problem). In other words, when handling the second type of interference, there is an *independence* between the tree-decomposition paths $\psi_i, \psi_j \subseteq T_0$ that were generated at the same level of the recursion. Since there are $O(\log n)$ recursion levels, summing over all levels increases our bounds by a logarithmic factor. The final structure H is then given by the union of the substructures for each of the paths in the tree-decomposition[2]. By collecting the last edges of carefully selected replacement-paths protecting the failures on ψ, for every path ψ in the tree-decomposition, it is then shown that there are $\widetilde{O}(n^{1-\epsilon})$ unprotected edges in the structure.

Turning to the lower bound, (b, r) FT-BFS structures for large $b(n)$ and $r(n)$ values require a more delicate construction when compared to standard FT-BFS structures. The design of the lower bound graph is governed by two opposing forces whose balance is to be found. Specifically, since detours are vertex consuming, to end up with a dense structure with many backup edges, the detours (and as a result also the shortest-paths) of many vertices should *collide*. For instance, in the lower bound construction of FT-BFS structures, the $s - v$ shortest-path of $\Theta(n)$ vertices is the *same*. In other words, a large number of backup edges implies packing many shortest-paths and detours efficiently. Since the lower bound construction of [14] involved only $\Theta(\sqrt{n})$ edges on the $s - v$ shortest-paths, a new approach is needed when trying to maximize the number of reinforced edges in the structure to $O(n^{1-\epsilon})$ for $\epsilon \in (0, 1/2)$. In particular, large reinforcement forces the construction to distribute the vertices on *distinct* shortest-paths so as to increase the number of edges that have large cost and hence should be reinforced. Our construction then finds the fine balance between these forces, matching our upper bounds up to logarithmic factors.

Related Works. To the best of our knowledge, this paper is the first to study the backup - reinforcement tradeoff in survivable nework design for (b, r) FT-BFS structures.

The question of designing sparse FT-BFS structures (without link reinforcement) has been studied in [14], using the notion of *replacement paths*. For a source node s, a target

node v and an edge $e \in G$, a *replacement path* is the shortest $s - v$ path $P_{v,e}$ that does not go through e. An FT-BFS structure consists of the collection of all $P_{v,e}$ replacement paths for every target $v \in V$ and edge $e \in E$. It is shown in [14] that for every graph G and source node s there exists a (polynomial time constructible) FT-BFS structure H with $O(n^{3/2})$ edges. This result was complemented by a matching lower bound showing that for every sufficiently large integer n, there exist an n-vertex graph G and a source node $s \in V$, for which every FT-BFS structure is of size $\Omega(n^{3/2})$. Hence the insistence on *exact* distances makes FT-BFS structures significantly denser (hence expensive) compared their fault-prone counterparts (namely, BFS trees). This last observation motivates the idea of studying the mixed model and makes FT-BFS structures an attractive platform for studying the backup-reinforcement tradeoff.

The notion of FT-BFS trees is also closely related to the *single-source replacement paths* problem [9], which requires to compute the collection $\mathcal{P}(s)$ of all $s - t$ replacement paths $P_{t,e}$ for every $t \in V$ and every failed edge e that appears on the $s - t$ shortest-path in G. The vast literature on *replacement paths* (cf. [3, 9, 18, 21, 22]) focuses on *time-efficient* computation of these paths as well as on their efficient maintenance in data structures (a.k.a *distance oracles*).

Constructions of sparse fault tolerant *spanners* for $\mathbb{R}^d$ Euclidean space were studied in [7, 12, 13]. Algorithms for constructing sparse edge and vertex fault tolerant spanners for arbitrary undirected weighted graphs were presented in [5, 8]. Note, however, that the use of costly link reinforcements for attaining fault-tolerance in spanners is less attractive than for FT-BFS structures, since the cost of adding fault-tolerance via backup edges (in the relevant complexity measure) is often low (e.g., merely polylogarithmic in the graph size n), hence the gains expected from using reinforcement are relatively small. Constructions of edge fault-tolerant spanners with *additive* stretch are given in [4], and the case of single vertex fault has been recently studied in [17].

The current setting reflects the notion of *economy of scale*. These scenarios are known in the literature as *buy-at-bulk* problems [1, 19, 6] in which capacity is sold with a "volume discount". In the full version [16] we describe the relation between buy-at-bulk problems and (b, r) FT-BFS structures.

This paper aims at establishing universal lower and upper bounds for (b, r) FT-BFS structures. In particular, although the universal upper bound is nearly tight (upto logarithmic factors), our upper bound constructions might be far from optimal in some instances (see the example of Fig. 5 in [15]). This motivates the study of (b, r) FT-BFS structures from the combinatorial optimization point of view, in [16]. Aside from optimization tasks for (r, b) FT-BFS structures, the presented reinforcement-backup tradeoff can be studied in a more generalized setting. In fact, it can be integrated into a large collection of survivability network design tasks. We hope that this work will pave the way for studying this setting, leading to new theoretical tools and techniques as well as to a better understanding of fault resilient structures.

2. PRELIMINARIES AND NOTATION

Let $E(v, G) = \{(u, v) \in E(G) \mid u \in V\}$ be the set of edges incident to the vertex v in the graph G and let $\deg(v, G) = |E(v, G)|$ denote the degree of v in G. When the graph G is clear from the context, we may simply write

---

[2]The paths of the tree-decomposition do not cover all the edges in the BFS tree, however, the remaining uncovered edges can be handled directly by adding the last edges of the corresponding replacement-paths.

$\deg(v)$ and $E(v)$. For a subgraph $G' = (V', E') \subseteq G$ (where $V' \subseteq V$ and $E' \subseteq E$) and a pair of vertices $u, v \in V$, let $\text{dist}(u, v, G')$ denote the shortest-path distance in edges between u and v in G'. For a path $P = [u_1, \ldots, u_k]$, let $\text{LastE}(P)$ denote the last edge of P, let $|P|$ be the length of P in edges, i.e., $k - 1$, and let $P[u_i, u_j]$ be the subpath of P from u_i to u_j. For paths P_1 and P_2 where the last vertex of P_1 equals the first vertex of P_2, let $P_1 \circ P_2$ denote the path obtained by concatenating P_2 to P_1. Throughout, the edges of these paths are considered to be directed away from the source s. Given an $s - t$ path P and an edge $e = (u, v) \in P$, let $\text{dist}(s, e, P)$ be the distance (in edges) between s and e on P. For an edge $e = (u, v) \in T_0$, define $\text{dist}(s, e) = i$ if $\text{dist}(s, u, G) = i - 1$ and $\text{dist}(s, v, G) = i$. For a subset $V' \subseteq V$, let $G(V')$ be the subgraph of G induced by V'. Let $\text{LCA}(u, v)$ be the least common ancestor of u and v in T_0.

For vertices $u, v \in V$ and subgraph $G' \subseteq G$, let $SP(u, v, G')$ be the collection of all $s - v$ shortest-path in G', i.e, $|P| = \text{dist}(s, v, G')$ for every $P \in SP(s, v, G')$. For a positive weight assignment $W : E(G) \to \mathbb{R}_{>0}$, let $SP(s, v, G', W)$ be the collection of $s - v$ shortest-paths in G' according to the weights of W. In this paper, the weight assignment W is chosen as to guarantee the uniqueness the shortest-paths in every $G' \subseteq G$. That is W is used to break to shortest-path ties in G' in a consistent manner. In such a case, we override notation and let $SP(s, v, G', W) \in SP(s, v, G')$ be the unique $s - v$ shortest-path in G' with the weights of W. Given a source vertex s and target vertex v, let $\pi(s, v) = SP(s, v, G, W)$ be the unique $s - v$ path in G according to W. Define $T_0(s) = \bigcup_{v \in V} \pi(s, v)$ as the BFS tree rooted at s. When the source s is clear from the context, we simply write T_0.

For a vertex v and an edge e, each path in $SP(s, v, G \setminus \{e\})$ is called a *replacement-path*. Note that if $e \notin \pi(s, v)$, then $\pi(s, v)$ is a replacement path as it appears in $SP(s, v, G \setminus \{e\})$. A vertex w is a *divergence point* of the $s - v$ paths P_1 and P_2 if $w \in P_1 \cap P_2$ but the next vertex u after w (i.e., such that u is closer to v) in the path P_1 is not in P_2.

ϵ FT-BFS *and protected edges.* For a subgraph $H \subseteq G$ and and a source vertex s, an edge e is *protected* in H if $\text{dist}(s, v, H \setminus \{e\}) = \text{dist}(s, v, G \setminus \{e\})$ for every $v \in V$ and otherwise it is *unprotected*. In other words, the edge e is protected if for every vertex v, H contains at least one replacement path $P_{v,e} \in SP(s, v, G \setminus \{e\})$.

DEFINITION 3 (ϵ FT-BFS). *For every real $\epsilon \in [0, 1]$, a subgraph $H \subseteq G$ is an ϵ FT-BFS with respect to s, if it contains $O(n^{1-\epsilon})$ unprotected edges. That is, there exists a subset of $O(n^{1-\epsilon})$ edges E' such that $\text{dist}(s, v, H \setminus \{e\}) = \text{dist}(s, v, G \setminus \{e\})$ for every $v \in V$ and $e \in E(G) \setminus E'$. Alternately, an ϵ FT-BFS H can be thought of as a (b, r) FT-BFS taking E' to be the set of $r(n) = O(n^{1-\epsilon})$ reinforcement edges and $E(H) \setminus E' == O(b(n))$ to be the backup edges.*

Note that in the context of the reinforcement-backup model, unprotected edges are viewed as edges that should be reinforced in the structure, since by definition, in the (b, r) FT-BFS structure, all backup edge are *protected*, and unprotected edges are not allowed to exist.

We now define a more refined notion of protected edges that is determined by the existence of the *last edges* of the replacement-paths in the subgraph H (instead of requiring the existence of the entire replacement path in H). Given a subgraph $H \subseteq G$, we say that the edge e is *v-last-unprotected*

in H if there exists no replacement path $P_{v,e} \in SP(s, v, G \setminus \{e\})$ whose last edge $\text{LastE}(P_{v,e})$ is in H, otherwise the edge is *v-last-protected*. An edge e is *last-unprotected* in H, if there exists at least one vertex $v \in V$ for which e is v-last-unprotected, otherwise it is *last-protected*. Note that the notion of protected edge refers to the case where every vertex v has at least one $s - v$ replacement-path protecting against the failing of e in H. In contrast, the notion of last-protected edges refers to the existence of the last edge of these replacement-path (and not the entire path) in the subgraph H. The next observation relates the properties of "last-protected" and "protected".

FACT 3.1. *If e is last-protected in H, then e is protected, i.e., $\text{dist}(s, v, H \setminus \{e\}) = \text{dist}(s, v, G \setminus \{e\})$, $\forall\ v \in V$.*

4. ALGORITHM

In this section, we describe a construction of an ϵ FT-BFS subgraph H containing $O(1/\epsilon' \cdot \log n \cdot n^{1+\epsilon'})$ edges where $\epsilon' = \epsilon + \log(\log n / \epsilon) / \log n$ for every $\epsilon \in (0, 1]$. In the next section we prove the following.

THEOREM 4.1. *For every input n-vertex graph G, source vertex s and real $\epsilon \in (0, 1]$, there exists an ϵ FT-BFS $H \subseteq G$ with $O(\min\{1/\epsilon' \cdot \log n \cdot n^{1+\epsilon'}, n^{3/2}\})$ edges. Hence one can construct a (b, r) FT-BFS structure with $b(n) = O(\min\{1/\epsilon \cdot n^{1+\epsilon} \cdot \log n, n^{3/2}\})$ and $r(n) = O(1/\epsilon \cdot n^{1-\epsilon} \cdot \log n)$.*

By [14], there exists a polynomial time algorithm for constructing FT-BFS structures with $O(n^{3/2})$ edges, hence the claim holds trivially for $\epsilon \geq 1/2$, and to establish the theorem, it remains to consider the case where $\epsilon \in (0, 1/2)$. To deal with this case, we next describe an explicit construction for an ϵ FT-BFS H, analyzed in the following section.

4.1 Phase S0: Preprocessing

Algorithm Pcons *for constructing the replacement-paths.* The goal of the preprocessing phase S0 is to define a function $\mathcal{RP} : (V \times E) \to E$ that maps each vertex-edge pair $\langle v, e \rangle$ to a replacement path $P_{v,e} \subseteq E$. These paths will be used in the main construction. Let T_0 be a BFS tree rooted at s in G. Algorithm Pcons iterates over every vertex $v \in V$ and every edge $e \in \pi(s, v)$. For a given pair $\langle v, e \rangle$, the algorithm first tests if there exists an $s - v$ replacement path whose last edge is already in T_0. Let $G'(v) = (G \setminus E(v, G)) \cup E(v, T_0)$. Now, if $\text{dist}(s, v, G'(v) \setminus \{e\}) = \text{dist}(s, v, G \setminus \{e\})$, then let $\mathcal{RP}(\langle v, e \rangle) = P_{v,e} = SP(s, v, G'(v) \setminus \{e\}, W)$. Else, (i.e., the replacement-path $P_{v,e}$ must include a new last edge that is not in T_0), the algorithm attempts to select the $s - v$ replacement-path whose divergence point from $\pi(s, v)$ is as close to s as possible. Specifically, let $\pi(s, v) = [u_0 = s, u_1, \ldots, u_k = v]$ and $e = (u_i, u_{i+1})$. For every $j \in \{0, \ldots, i\}$, define $G_j(v) = G \setminus V(\pi(u_j, u_k)) \cup \{u_j, u_k\}$. Note that $e \notin G_j(v)$. Define j^* as the minimal index j satisfying that $\text{dist}(s, v, G_j(v)) = \text{dist}(s, v, G \setminus \{e\})$ and let $P_{v,e} = SP(s, v, G_{j^*}(v) \setminus \{e\}, W)$.

Replacement-path classification. A replacement-path $P = P_{v,e}$ is *new-ending* if its last edge is not in T_0. A vertex-edge pair $\langle v, e \rangle$ is *uncovered* if its replacement path $P_{v,e}$ is new-ending. The following observation follows immediately by the construction of Alg. Pcons.

OBSERVATION 4.2. *Consider a new-ending path $P = P_{v,e}$. Let $d(P)$ be the first divergence point of P and $\pi(s, v)$. Then*

P can be decomposed into $P = \pi(s, d(P)) \circ D(P)$ where $D(P) = P \setminus E(\pi(s, v))$, referred to as the detour segment, departs from $\pi(s, v)$ at $d(P)$ and returns only at v, i.e., $D(P) = P[d(P), v]$ and $\pi(s, v)$ are vertex disjoint besides the common endpoints $d(P)$ and v.

Let $\mathcal{UP} = \{\langle v, e \rangle \mid \text{LastE}(P_{v,e}) \notin T_0\}$ be the collection of all uncovered vertex-edge pairs. Let $\mathcal{UP}(v) = \{\langle w, e \rangle \in \mathcal{UP} \mid w = v\}$ be the uncovered pairs of v (hence, $\mathcal{UP} = \bigcup_{v \in V} \mathcal{UP}(v)$). Throughout, we consider the edges of T_0 to be directed away from s, hence referring to the edge $e = (x, y) \in T_0$ implies that $\text{dist}(s, x, G) < \text{dist}(s, y, G)$.

The following definitions are key to in our construction and the subsequent analysis. For two tree edges $e = (a, b), e' = (c, d) \in T_0$, we say that $e \sim e'$ if $\text{LCA}(b, d) \in \{b, d\}$, i.e., $e, e' \in \pi(s, v)$ for $v = \{b, d\} \setminus \{\text{LCA}(b, d)\}$, otherwise $e \nsim e'$. In our construction, we may impose an ordering on a subset of v's uncovered pairs. For a given subset of v's pairs $\text{Add}(\mathcal{P}, v) = \{\langle v, e_1 \rangle, \ldots, \langle v, e_k \rangle\} \subseteq \mathcal{UP}(v)$, let $\overrightarrow{\mathcal{P}}(v)$ be ordered in increasing distance of e_i from v, i.e.,

$$\overrightarrow{\mathcal{P}}(v) = \{\langle v, e_{i_1} \rangle, \ldots, \langle v, e_{i_k} \rangle\}$$

where $\text{dist}(v, e_{i_1}, \pi(s, v)) < \ldots < \text{dist}(v, e_{i_k}, \pi(s, v))$.

$(\sim)$-interference and $(\nsim)$-interference.
The paths $P = P_{v,e}, P' = P_{t,e'}$ for $\langle v, e \rangle, \langle t, e' \rangle \in \mathcal{UP}$ and $v \neq t$ interfere with each other if their detours intersect at some vertex z internal to both, i.e.,

$$V(D(P)) \cap V(D(P')) \nsubseteq \{d(P), d(P'), v, t\} . \quad (1)$$

Note that according to this definition, interference is symmetric, i.e., if P interferes with P' then P' interferes with P as well. For every uncovered pair $\langle v, e \rangle \in \mathcal{UP}$, denote the set of pairs $\langle t, e' \rangle$ whose corresponding path $P' = P_{t,e'}$ interferes with $P = P_{v,e}$ by

$$\mathcal{I}(\langle v, e \rangle) = \{\langle t, e' \rangle \in \mathcal{UP} \mid t \neq v, P_{t,e'} \text{ and } P_{v,e} \quad (2)$$
$$\text{satisfy Eq. (1)}\} .$$

Our construction is heavily based on distinguishing between two types of interference, depending on the relation of the two failing edges protected by the interfered paths. In particular, if the interfering paths $P_{v,e}$ and $P_{t,e'}$ satisfy that $e \nsim e'$, then we call it $(\nsim)$-interference, and if $e \sim e'$, then it is $(\sim)$-interference. For an illustration, see Fig. 1. Let $\mathcal{I}^{\nsim}(\langle v, e \rangle) = \{\langle t, e' \rangle \in \mathcal{I}(P) \mid e \nsim e'\}$ be the set of pairs whose corresponding paths $(\nsim)$-interfere with $P_{v,e}$.

A given subset of uncovered pairs $\mathcal{P}' \subseteq \mathcal{UP}$ is called a $(\sim)$-set if $\mathcal{I}^{\nsim}(\langle v, e \rangle) \cap \mathcal{P}' = \emptyset$ for every $\langle v, e \rangle \in \mathcal{P}'$. Otherwise, it is called $(\nsim)$-set. In other words, in a $(\sim)$-set there is no $(\nsim)$-interference between any pair of paths.

4.2 The main construction

Let us start with an overview of the main construction phases. The initial structure H contains T_0. In phases S1 and S2, we add backup edges to H corresponding to last edge of the new ending replacement paths $P_{v,e}$ so that eventually the set of T_0 edges unprotected by H is bounded by $O(1/\epsilon \cdot n^{1-\epsilon} \cdot \log n)$. (These edges will have to be reinforced; all other edges of H will be taken as backup edges.) The high level idea of our main construction is as follows. First, we divide the uncovered pairs $\mathcal{UP}$ into two sub-sets $(\nsim)$-set $\mathcal{I}_1$ and a $(\sim)$-set $\mathcal{I}_2$, by letting

$$\mathcal{I}_1 = \{\langle v, e \rangle \in \mathcal{UP} \mid \mathcal{I}^{\nsim}(\langle v, e \rangle) \neq \emptyset\} \text{ and } \mathcal{I}_2 = \mathcal{UP} \setminus \mathcal{I}_1.$$

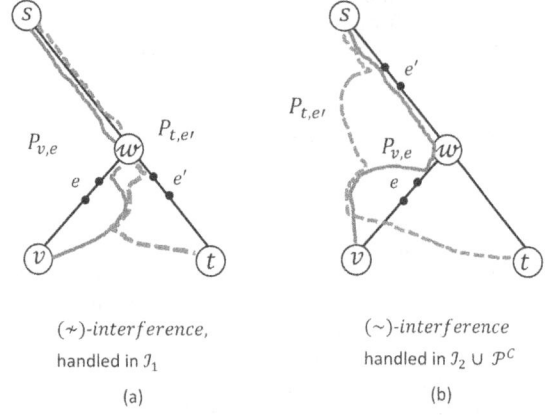

Figure 1: Illustration of the two types of interference. The replacement paths $P_{v,e}$ (solid) and $P_{t,e'}$ are (a) $(\nsim)$ interfering as $e \nsim e'$, and (b) $(\sim)$ interfering as $e \sim e'$.

Phase S1 starts by setting the first $(\sim)$-set to be $\mathcal{P}_0^C = \mathcal{I}_2$. Then, Phase S1 employs an iterative process of $K_\epsilon = O(1/\epsilon)$ iterations. Each of these iterations does the following. For every vertex $v \in V$, the algorithm repeatedly adds the $\lceil n^{1/\epsilon} \rceil$ distinct last edges of the remaining $s - v$ replacement-paths of the uncovered pairs in $\mathcal{I}_1$ protecting the deepest edges on $\pi(s, v)$. In addition, each such iteration i may yield an additional $(\sim)$-set, $\mathcal{P}_i^C$, which would be handled in Phase S2. Thus, at the end of Phase S1, we have at most $O(1/\epsilon)$ such $(\sim)$-sets $\mathcal{P}_i^C$ that partially cover the pairs of $\mathcal{I}_1$. The last edges of the replacement-paths of the pairs in $\mathcal{I}_1$ that are not covered by the $(\sim)$-sets are added to H. Phase S2 of the algorithm is then devoted for considering the $(\sim)$-sets (i.e., $\mathcal{I}_2$ and the $O(1/\epsilon)$ additional $(\sim)$-sets that were created in Phase S1). For each such $(\sim)$-set $\mathcal{P}'$ and for every vertex v, the algorithm adds a collection of $O(n^\epsilon \cdot \log n)$ backup edges corresponding to the last edges of $s - v$ replacement-paths of the pairs in $\mathcal{P}'$. The analysis shows that after Phase S2, for each of the $O(1/\epsilon)$ $(\sim)$-sets $\mathcal{P}_i^C$ the number of edges protected by replacement paths corresponding to the pairs collection $\mathcal{P}_i^C$ that are still unprotected by H is $O(n^{1-\epsilon} \cdot \log n)$. Hence, overall there are at most $O(1/\epsilon \cdot n^{1-\epsilon} \cdot \log n)$ edges that are still unprotected by H. Those edges will have to be reinforced.

We now describe the algorithm in detail.

Phase S1: Handling the $(\nsim)$-set $\mathcal{I}_1$. The next definition is important in this context. For $v \neq t$, a path $P_{v,e}$ π-intersects with path $P_{t,e'} \in \mathcal{I}^{\nsim}(P_{v,e})$ if the detour of $P_{v,e}$ intersects at least one of the vertices of $\pi(\text{LCA}(v, t), t)) \setminus \{\text{LCA}(t, v)\}$. Note that this property may *not* be symmetric (unlike interference). That is, it might be the case that $P_{v,e}$ π-intersects $P_{t,e'}$ but not vice-versa.

The replacement paths of the uncovered pairs in some subset $\mathcal{P}_\ell \subseteq \mathcal{I}_1$ can be roughly classified into three types, termed A,B, and C with respect to $\mathcal{P}_\ell$. A replacement-path $P_{v,e}$ for $\langle v, e \rangle \in \mathcal{P}_\ell$ is of *type A with respect to* $\mathcal{P}_\ell$ if it π-intersects at least one path in $\mathcal{I}^{\nsim}(\langle v, e \rangle) \cap \mathcal{P}_\ell$. Let $\mathcal{P}_\ell^A \subseteq \mathcal{P}_\ell$

be the subset of all pairs whose paths is of type A, i.e.,

$$\mathcal{P}_\ell^A = \{\langle v, e\rangle \in \mathcal{P}_\ell \mid \exists \langle t, e'\rangle \in \mathcal{I}^{\not\sim}(\langle v, e\rangle) \cap \mathcal{P}_\ell, \tag{3}$$
$$P_{v,e} \ \pi\text{-intersects} \ P_{t,e'}\} \ .$$

A replacement-path $P_{v,e}$ for $\langle v, e\rangle \in \mathcal{P}_\ell$ is of *type B with respect* to $\mathcal{P}_\ell$, if it is not of type A and it $(\not\sim)$-interferes with at least one path $P_{t,e'}$ for $\langle t, e'\rangle \in \mathcal{P}_\ell$ that is not of type A as well, i.e., $\langle t, e'\rangle \in \mathcal{P}_\ell \setminus \mathcal{P}_\ell^A$. In such a case, both $\langle v, e\rangle$ and $\langle t, e'\rangle$ are not in $\mathcal{P}_\ell^A$, and hence $P_{v,e}$ does not π-intersect $P_{t,e'}$ and vice-versa, implying that $P_{t,e'}$ is of type B as well. Let $\mathcal{P}_\ell^B$ be the collection of the pairs whose corresponding path is of type B; formally

$$\mathcal{P}_\ell^B = \{\langle v, e\rangle \in \mathcal{P}_\ell \setminus \mathcal{P}_\ell^A \mid \mathcal{I}^{\not\sim}(\langle v, e\rangle) \cap \left(\mathcal{P}_\ell \setminus \mathcal{P}_\ell^A\right) \neq \emptyset\} \ . \tag{4}$$

Finally, a replacement-path $P_{v,e} \in \mathcal{P}_\ell$ is of *type C with respect* to $\mathcal{P}_\ell$ if it is not of type A or B. Note that such a path $P_{v,e}$ satisfies that the intersection $\mathcal{I}^{\not\sim}(\langle v, e\rangle) \cap (\mathcal{P}_\ell \setminus \mathcal{P}_\ell^A)$ is empty. (This can happen either because $\mathcal{I}^{\not\sim}(\langle v, e\rangle) \cap \mathcal{P}_\ell = \emptyset$ or because $\left(\mathcal{I}^{\not\sim}(\langle v, e\rangle) \cap \mathcal{P}_\ell\right) \subseteq \mathcal{P}_\ell^A$.) Let $\mathcal{P}_\ell^C = \mathcal{P}_\ell \setminus \left(\mathcal{P}_\ell^A \cup \mathcal{P}_\ell^B\right)$ be the set of pairs whose path is of type C. Let

$$K_\epsilon = \lceil 1/\epsilon\rceil + 2 \ . \tag{5}$$

The uncovered pairs of $\mathcal{I}_1$ are now partitioned into $K_\epsilon + 1$ subsets: K_ϵ $(\sim)$-sets $\mathcal{P}_1^C, \ldots, \mathcal{P}_{K_\epsilon}^C$ and a subset containing all the remaining pairs $\mathcal{I}_1' = \mathcal{I}_1 \setminus \bigcup_{i=1}^{K_\epsilon} \mathcal{P}_i^C$. Essentially, the subset $\mathcal{I}_1'$ is "implicit" and is not actually constructed by the algorithm; it consists of all $\mathcal{I}_1$ pairs $\langle v, e\rangle$ whose last edge of their path $P_{v,e}$ was added to H during one of the K_ϵ iterations of Phase S1. The analysis shows that the number of distinct last edges of the replacement paths of $\mathcal{I}_1'$ that were added into H is bounded by $O(1/\epsilon \cdot n^{1+\epsilon})$.

The partition of $\mathcal{I}_1$ is conducted in K_ϵ iterations. At the end of each iteration, $O(n^{1+\epsilon})$ distinct last edges of the paths that correspond to the first $\langle v, e\rangle$ pairs from $\mathcal{I}_1$ (the paths protecting the deepest edges on $\pi(s, v)$) are added to H (and intuitively, the pairs of these replacement paths join $\mathcal{I}_1'$). Initially, let $\mathcal{P}_1 = \mathcal{I}_1$. For every $i = \{1, \ldots, K_\epsilon\}$, the next steps are performed:

- Divide $\mathcal{P}_i$ into the subsets $\mathcal{P}_i^A$, $\mathcal{P}_i^B$ and $\mathcal{P}_i^C$ (according to Eq. (3,4)).   (* Handling the paths of $\mathcal{P}_i^C$ is deferred to Phase S2. The following steps attempt to handle the paths of $\mathcal{P}_i^A \cup \mathcal{P}_i^B$. *)

- Let $\overrightarrow{\mathcal{P}}_i^J(v) = \{\langle v, e_{i_1}\rangle, \ldots, \langle v, e_{i_{k_{J_v}}}\rangle\}$ be the ordered $\langle v, e\rangle$ uncovered pairs of v in $\mathcal{P}_i^J$ for every $v \in V$ and $J \in \{A, B\}$ (in increasing distance of the failing edge e_{i_j} from v).

- Add to H, the $\lceil n^\epsilon\rceil$ distinct last edges of the *first* replacement-paths of the pairs in the ordering $\overrightarrow{\mathcal{P}}_i^J(v)$.

- Set $\mathcal{P}_{i+1} = \{\langle v, e\rangle \in \mathcal{P}_i^A \cup \mathcal{P}_i^B \mid \text{LastE}(P_{v,e}) \notin H\}$.

This completes Phase S1. Observe that a pair $\langle v, e\rangle \in \mathcal{P}_i$ that was classified as, say, type A in iteration i, but was not handled (i.e., its last edge was not added to H), joins $\mathcal{P}_{i+1}$ and is re-classified in iteration $i+1$, where it may be classified differently. In particular, if it gets classified into $\mathcal{P}_{i+1}^C$, then its handling will be deferred to Phase S2.

Phase S2: Handling the remaining $(\sim)$-sets. The input for this step is a collection of $(\sim)$ multi-sets

$$\mathcal{S} = \{\mathcal{P}_0^C, \mathcal{P}_1^C, \ldots, \mathcal{P}_{K_\epsilon}^C\}.$$

Preprocessing Sub-Phase S2.0: Building tree-decomposition for T_0. As a preprocessing step for handling the $(\sim)$-sets, the algorithm begins applying to the BFS tree T_0 the *heavy-path-decomposition* technique presented by Sleator and Tarjan [20] and slightly adapted by Baswana and Khanna [2]. Using this technique, the tree T_0 is broken into vertex disjoint paths $\mathcal{TD} = \{\psi_1, \ldots, \psi_t\}$ that satisfy some desired properties.

FACT 4.3. *[2] There exists an $O(n)$ time algorithm for computing a path ψ in T_0 whose removal splits T_0 into disjoint subtrees $T_0(v_1), \ldots, T_0(v_j)$ s.t. for every $1 \leq i \leq j$, (1) $|T_0(v_i)| \leq n/2$ and $\psi \cap T_0(v_i) = \emptyset$, and (2) $T_0(v_i)$ is connected to ψ through an edge hereafter denoted $e(\psi, i)$.*

The algorithm of Fact 4.3 is applied recursively on T_0. The output of this recursive procedure is a collection $\mathcal{TD}$ of paths $\psi \subseteq T_0$ plus a set of T_0 edges $e(\psi, i)$ that glue the paths ψ to the tree T_0. Let $E^+(\mathcal{TD}) = \bigcup_{\psi \in \mathcal{TD}} E(\psi)$ be the set of tree edges occurring on the paths of the decomposition and let $E^-(\mathcal{TD}) = T_0 \setminus E^+(\mathcal{TD})$ be the collection of "glue" edges. In the next Sub-Phase, the algorithm iterates over all the vertices v and add to the structure H a collection of last edges of the replacement-paths protecting against the failing of the glue edges. (In the analysis it is shown that at most $O(n \log n)$ edges are added due to this step.)

Sub-Phase S2.1: Edge addition based on tree-decomposition [for fixed v]. Add to H the set of last edges of the new-ending replacement paths protecting the glue edges $E^-(\mathcal{TD}) \cap \psi(s, v)$,

$$\widehat{E}(\mathcal{TD}, v) = \{\text{LastE}(P_{v,e}) \mid \langle v, e\rangle \in \mathcal{UP} \text{ and } e \in E^-(\mathcal{TD})\}.$$

We now turn to the main part of Phase S2. The algorithm treats each $(\sim)$-set $\mathcal{P} \in \mathcal{S}$ separately, by adding to H $O(n^{1+\epsilon} \cdot \log n)$ distinct last edges of replacement paths carefully selected from the uncovered pairs of $\mathcal{P}$. The analysis shows that the total number of edges e with a pair $\langle v, e\rangle$ in $\mathcal{P}$ that are unprotected by H is bounded by $O(n^{1-\epsilon} \cdot \log n)$, and since there are $K_\epsilon + 1 = O(1/\epsilon)$ sets in $\mathcal{S}$ (see Eq. (5)), overall there are $O(1/\epsilon \cdot n^{1-\epsilon} \cdot \log n)$ edges in T_0 that are unprotected by H (and will have to be reinforced).

The selection of the uncovered pairs $\langle v, e\rangle$ whose last edge of their replacement path $P_{v,e}$ is to be added into H is performed in the following manner. The algorithm iterates over every $(\sim)$-set $\mathcal{P} \in \mathcal{S}$ and every vertex $v \in V$, and selects a subset $\text{Add}(\mathcal{P}, v)$ of v's uncovered pairs from $\mathcal{P}$, where the total number of last edges of their corresponding replacement paths in bounded by $O(n^\epsilon \cdot \log n)$, and then adds these last edges to H. The selection, for $\mathcal{P}$ and v, of pairs to be included in $\text{Add}(\mathcal{P}, v)$ is done in two main phases.

Sub-Phase S2.2 [for fixed $\mathcal{P}$, v]: Covering pairs based on shortest-path decomposition. The $s-v$ shortest-path $\pi(s, v) = [s = u_0, \ldots, u_k = v]$ is decomposed into $k' = \lfloor \log|\pi(s, v)|\rfloor$ subsegments of exponentially decreasing length, i.e., where each subsegment consists of the first half of the remaining $\pi(s, v)$ path. Formally, letting u_{i_j} be the vertex at distance $\left\lceil \sum_{\ell=1}^{j} \left(|\pi(s, v)|/2^\ell\right)\right\rceil$ from s on $\pi(s, v)$ for $j \in \{1, \ldots, k'\}$, and $u_{i_0} = u_0$, the j'th subsegment is given by $\pi_j(s, v) = \pi(u_{i_{j-1}}, u_{i_j})$ for every $j \in \{1, \ldots, k'\}$. It then holds that

$$|\pi_j(s, v)| \geq \left\lfloor |\pi(s, v)|/2^{j-1}|\right\rfloor \text{ and} \tag{6}$$
$$\sum_{j' > j} |\pi_j(s, v)| \geq |\pi_j(s, v)|/2$$

269

For each of the k' subsegments $\pi_j(s,v)$, let $\mathcal{P}_j(v) = \{\langle v, e \rangle \in \mathcal{P} \mid e \in \pi_j(s,v)\}$ be the set of v's uncovered pairs from $\mathcal{P}$ whose paths protect the edges in $\pi_j(s,v)$; let $\mathcal{LE}_j(\mathcal{P},v) = \{\text{LastE}(P_{v,e}) \mid \langle v, e \rangle \in \mathcal{P}_j(v)\}$ be the corresponding last edges of these replacement paths.

A subsegment $\pi_j(s,v)$ is *heavy* with respect to $\mathcal{P}$ if $|\mathcal{LE}_j(\mathcal{P},v)| \geq \lceil n^\epsilon \rceil$, otherwise it is *light*. For every light subsegment $\pi_j(s,v)$, add $\mathcal{P}_j(v)$ to the collection of selected pairs $\text{Add}(\mathcal{P},v)$ whose last edges (of their corresponding replacement paths) are later added to H. I.e., add to $\text{Add}(\mathcal{P},v)$ the pairs $\bigcup \mathcal{P}_j(v)$, where the union is over all $j \in \{1, \ldots, k'\}$ s.t. $\pi_j(s,v)$ is light. In addition, we move to $\text{Add}(\mathcal{P},v)$ some additional pairs $\langle v, e_j^* \rangle$ as follows. For every $j \in \{1, \ldots, k'\}$, let e_j^* be the first edge on $\pi_j(s,v)$ (closest to s) such that $\langle v, e_j^* \rangle$ is in $\mathcal{P}_j(v)$.

The algorithm adds $\bigcup_{j=1}^{k'} \langle v, e_j^* \rangle$ to $\text{Add}(\mathcal{P},v)$. (This addition would ensure that the divergence point $d(P_{v,e})$ of the replacement paths $P_{v,e}$ protecting edges e on the segment $\pi_j(s,v)$ and whose last edge was not added to the output structure H, is located inside the segment $\pi_j(s,v)$.)

Sub-Phase S2.3: Covering pairs depending on both the tree-decomposition and $\pi(s,v)$ decomposition [for fixed $\mathcal{P}, \psi, v$].

Define $E(\psi, \mathcal{P}, v) = \{e \mid \langle v, e \rangle \in \mathcal{P} \text{ and } e \in \psi \cap \pi(s,v)\}$. Let e^* be the upmost edge in $E(\psi, \mathcal{P}, v)$ (i.e., closest to s). Add $\langle v, e^* \rangle$ to $\text{Add}(\mathcal{P},v)$.

Next, consider the intersection of ψ with $\pi(s,v)$. Recall that in Sub-Phase S2.1, the $s-v$ path $\pi(s,v)$ was decomposed into $k' = \lfloor \log |\pi(s,v)| \rfloor$ segments $\pi_1(s,v), \ldots, \pi_{k'}(s,v)$. Let $\pi_U(\psi, v)$ be the first, i.e., closest to s, subsegment of $\pi(s,v)$ that intersects ψ such that $\pi_U(\psi, v) \not\subseteq \psi$ and $\pi_U(\psi, v) \cap \psi \neq \emptyset$ (if such exists). Similarly, let $\pi_L(\psi, v)$ be the last, i.e., closest to v, subsegment of $\pi(s,v)$ that intersects ψ such that $\pi_L(\psi, v) \not\subseteq \psi$ and $\pi_L(\psi, v) \cap \psi \neq \emptyset$.

Let $\mathcal{P}_U(\psi, v) = \{\langle v, e \rangle \in \mathcal{P} \mid e \in \pi_U(\psi, v) \cap \psi\}$ be the pairs in $\mathcal{P}$ whose replacement paths protect against the failing of the edges in the intersection $\pi_U(s,v) \cap \psi$ and let $\mathcal{LE}_U(\mathcal{P}, \psi, v) = \{\text{LastE}(P_{v,e}) \mid \langle v, e \rangle \in \mathcal{P}_U(\psi, v)\}$ be the last edges of the corresponding replacement paths. If $|\mathcal{LE}_U(\mathcal{P}, \psi, v)| \leq \lceil n^\epsilon \rceil$, then add $\mathcal{P}_U(\psi, v)$ to $\text{Add}(\mathcal{P},v)$. Finally, let e_U^* be the upmost edge on $\pi(s,v)$ with a pair $\langle v, e_U^* \rangle \in \mathcal{P}_U(\psi, v)$. Then, add $\langle v, e_U^* \rangle$ to $\text{Add}(\mathcal{P},v)$. The set $\mathcal{P}_L(\psi, v)$ is handled in the same manner as $\mathcal{P}_U(\psi, v)$. Finally, for every $\mathcal{P}$ and v and for every edge e such that $\langle v, e \rangle \in \text{Add}(\mathcal{P},v)$ add the last edge of $P_{v,e}$ to H. This completes the description of the algorithm.

5. ANALYSIS

5.1 Size Bound

We start with size analysis and use the following fact.

FACT 5.1 ([2]). *For every node $v \in V$, (a) $\pi(s,v) \cap E^-(\mathcal{TD}) = O(\log n)$, and (b) $\pi(s,v)$ intersects at most $O(\log n)$ paths in $\mathcal{TD}$ [Lemma 3.6 of [2]].*

LEMMA 5.2. $|E(H)| = O(\min\{1/\epsilon \cdot n^{1+\epsilon} \cdot \log n, On^{3/2}\})$.

Proof: For $\epsilon \geq 1/2$, the claim trivially holds by [14]. From now on, consider $\epsilon \in (0, 1/2)$. By Fact 5.1(a), the set of edges $\widehat{E}(\mathcal{TD}, v)$ that was added in Sub-Phase S2.1 contains $O(\log n)$ edges. We now focus on a specific vertex v and $(\sim)$-set $\mathcal{P}$ and bound the number of new edges corresponding

to the pairs of $\text{Add}(\mathcal{P}, v)$ that were collected in Sub-Phases S2.2-S2.3.

In Sub-Phase S2.2, the algorithm adds the pairs of the light subsegments $\pi_j(s,v)$. Since there are $O(\log n)$ subsegments and as the number of last edges of replacement paths protecting the edges of a light subsegment is bounded by $O(n^\epsilon)$ edges, overall $O(\log n \cdot n^\epsilon)$ edges are added due to these pairs.

In Sub-Phase S2.3 we restrict attention to a specific path $\psi \in \mathcal{TD}$ and consider the intersection of $\pi(s,v)$ and ψ. By Fact 5.1(b), every path $\pi(s,v)$ intersects with $O(\log n)$ paths ψ in $\mathcal{TD}$. Since the algorithm adds the last edges of replacement paths protecting edges on $\pi_U(s,v)$ and $\pi_L(s,v)$ only if their number is bounded by $O(n^\epsilon)$, overall $O(\log n \cdot n^\epsilon)$ edges are added due to this sub-phase. Finally, the total number of pairs $\langle v, e_j^* \rangle$ and $\langle v, e_U^* \rangle, \langle v, e_L^* \rangle$ that are added in Sub-Phases S2.2-S2.3 is bounded by $O(\log n)$. Altogether, we get that the pairs of $\text{Add}(\mathcal{P}, v)$ contributes $O(\log n \cdot n^\epsilon)$ edges to H. The lemma follows by summing over all n vertices and the $O(1/\epsilon)$ ($\sim$) sets. ∎

We proceed by presenting some useful properties of the paths constructed by Alg. Pcons. Missing profs are deferred to the full version [16].

5.2 Basic Replacement Path Properties

LEMMA 5.3. *For every $v \in V$, $e \in \pi(s,v)$, it holds that $P_{v,e} \in SP(s,v,G \setminus \{e\})$.*

Recall that for a new-ending path $P_{v,e}$ (i.e., $\langle v, e \rangle \in \mathcal{UP}$), $d(P_{v,e})$ is the first divergence point of $P_{v,e}$ from $\pi(s,v)$. By the construction of the new-ending paths, we have the following.

CLAIM 5.4. *For every new-ending path $P_{v,e}$: (1) the divergence point $d(P_{v,e})$ is unique; (2) there exists no $s-v$ replacement path in $G \setminus \{e\}$ whose unique divergence point is above $d(P_{v,e})$ on $\pi(s,v)$ (i.e., closer to s).*

CLAIM 5.5. *Consider two new-ending $s-v$ replacement paths $P_{v,e_{i_1}}, P_{v,e_{i_2}}$ such that $\text{LastE}(P_{v,e_{i_1}}) \neq \text{LastE}(P_{v,e_{i_2}})$ where without loss of generality $e_{i_1} = (x_{i_1}, y_{i_1})$ is above (closer to s) $e_{i_2} = (x_{i_2}, y_{i_2})$ on $\pi(s,v)$. Then, $d(P_{v,e_{i_2}}) \in \pi(y_{i_1}, x_{i_2})$.*

CLAIM 5.6. *For every $P = P_{v,e}$ such that $\langle v, e \rangle \in \mathcal{UP}(v)$, (1) $|D(P)| = \Omega(dist(e, v, \pi(s,v)))$. (2) For every $P' = P_{v,e'} \langle v, e \rangle \in \mathcal{UP}(v)$ satisfying that $\text{LastE}(P) \neq \text{LastE}(P')$ it holds that $D(P') \cap D(P) = \{v\}$.*

5.3 Bounding the number of T_0 edges unprotected by H

Throughout, we consider the final structure H (obtained by the end of Phase S2) and denote the path $P_{v,e}$ as *H-new-ending* if $\text{LastE}(P_{v,e}) \notin H$. Let

$$\mathcal{UP}(H) = \{\langle v, e \rangle \mid \text{LastE}(P_{v,e}) \notin H\}$$

be the uncovered pairs in the final structure H.

For every $(\sim)$-set $\mathcal{P} \in \mathcal{S}$, let $\mathcal{P}_{miss} = \{\langle v, e \rangle \in \mathcal{P} \cap \mathcal{UP}(H)\}$ be the pairs of $\mathcal{P}$ that are uncovered by H. Let $E_{miss}(\mathcal{P}, v) = \{e \mid \langle v, e \rangle \in \mathcal{P}_{miss}\}$ be the set of edges on $\pi(s,v)$ such that the last edge of the replacement paths of $\mathcal{P}$ pairs were not added to H. Let

$$E_{miss}(\mathcal{P}) = \bigcup_{v \in V} E_{miss}(\mathcal{P}, v) \qquad (7)$$

be the collection of T_0 edges unprotected by H, corresponding to the paths of $\mathcal{P}$ and let $E_{miss}(H) = \{e \mid \exists v \text{ s.t } \langle v, e \rangle \in \mathcal{UP}(H)\}$ be the set of T_0 edges that are unprotected by H. Toward the end of this section, we show that

LEMMA 5.7. $|E_{miss}(H)| = O(1/\epsilon \cdot n^{1-\epsilon} \cdot \log n)$.

The analysis proceeds in two steps. Let $\mathcal{P}^C = \bigcup_{i=1}^{K_\epsilon} \mathcal{P}_i^C$ be the collection of pairs whose corresponding paths are of type C defined in Phase S1. First, we show that due to Phase S1, $\mathcal{I}_1 \setminus \mathcal{P}^C$ contains *no* uncovered pair in H, i.e., there is no pair $\langle v, e \rangle \in \mathcal{I}_1 \setminus \mathcal{P}^C$ such that $P_{v,e}$ is H-new-ending path. This implies that it suffices to consider the uncovered pairs of $\mathcal{P}_i^C$, since $\mathcal{UP}(H) = \bigcup_{\mathcal{P} \in \mathcal{S}} \mathcal{P}_{miss}$. In the second step, we complete the argument by showing that for each of the $O(1/\epsilon)$ $(\sim)$-sets $\mathcal{P}$, the cardinality of $E_{miss}(\mathcal{P})$, the set of T_0 edges that are unprotected by H, is bounded by $O(n^{1-\epsilon} \cdot \log n)$. Since there are $O(1/\epsilon)$ such sets, overall we get that $|E_{miss}(H)| = |\bigcup_{\mathcal{P} \in \mathcal{S}} E_{miss}(\mathcal{P})| = O(1/\epsilon \cdot n^{1-\epsilon} \cdot \log n)$ as desired. We now describe the analysis in detail.

Analysis of Phase S1. We begin by establishing a property that holds for every two pairs $\langle v, e_1 \rangle, \langle v, e_2 \rangle \in \mathcal{P}_i^J$ for $J \in \{A, B\}$ such that $\mathsf{LastE}(P_{v,e_1}) \neq \mathsf{LastE}(P_{v,e_2})$. This property plays a key role in our analysis and justifies the classification of the paths of $\mathcal{P}_i$ pairs into the three types.

LEMMA 5.8. *Let* $P_1 = P_{v,e_1}, P_2 = P_{v,e_2}$ *be such that* $e_1 = (x_1, y_1)$ *is above* $e_2 = (x_2, y_2)$ *on* $\pi(s, v)$, $\mathsf{LastE}(P_1) \neq \mathsf{LastE}(P_2)$, $\langle v, e_2 \rangle \in \mathcal{P}_i^J$ *for some* $J \in \{A, B\}$ *and* $i \in \{2, \ldots, K_\epsilon\}$. *Then there exist a vertex* t *and an edge* $e' \in \pi(s, t)$ *satisfying (see Fig. 2)*

(a) $\langle t, e' \rangle \in \mathcal{P}_i$ *and hence also* $\langle t, e' \rangle \in \mathcal{P}_{i-1}^A \cup \mathcal{P}_{i-1}^B$,

(b) $\mathsf{LCA}(t, v) \in \pi(y_1, x_2)$.

Proof: Let $\mathcal{I}_i(\langle v, e_2 \rangle) = \mathcal{I}^{\nsucc}(\langle v, e_2 \rangle) \cap \mathcal{P}_i$. Since $\langle v, e_2 \rangle \in \mathcal{P}_i^A \cup \mathcal{P}_i^B$, by Eq. (3) and (4), we get that $\mathcal{I}_i(\langle v, e_2 \rangle) \neq \emptyset$ and $\mathcal{I}_i(\langle v, e_2 \rangle) \subseteq \mathcal{P}_{i-1}^A \cup \mathcal{P}_{i-1}^B$.

To identify the path $P' = P_{t,e'}$ where $\langle t, e' \rangle \in \mathcal{I}_i(\langle v, e_2 \rangle)$, consider two cases depending on the type of the path P_2 with respect to $\mathcal{P}_i$. *Case 1:* $\langle v, e_2 \rangle \in \mathcal{P}_i^A$ (i.e., P_2 is of type A). Let $\langle t, e' \rangle \in \mathcal{I}_i(\langle v, e_2 \rangle)$ be such that P π-intersects $P' = P_{t,e'}$. By Eq. (3) such $\langle t, e' \rangle$ exists. *Case 2:* $\langle v, e_2 \rangle \in \mathcal{P}_i^B$ (i.e., P_2 is of type B). Let $P' = P_{t,e'}$ be some type B path for $\langle t, e' \rangle \in \mathcal{I}_i(\langle v, e_2 \rangle) \setminus \mathcal{P}_i^A$. By Eq. (4) such a pair $\langle t, e' \rangle$ exists. By the definition of type B, P_2 does not π-intersect P' and vice-versa. Note that in either case, P' satisfies part (a) of the lemma. To prove part (b), let $w = \mathsf{LCA}(v, t)$. Since $\langle t, e' \rangle \in \mathcal{I}^{\nsucc}(\langle v, e_2 \rangle)$ (i.e., $e' \nsucc e_2$), it holds that w is not below x_2. In addition, since P_1 and P_2 are new-ending $s - v$ paths ending with a distinct edge, by Cl. 5.5, it holds that d_2, the unique divergence point of P_2 and $\pi(s, v)$, occurs on the segment $\pi(y_1, x_2)$.

CLAIM 5.9. *There exists an* $s - v$ *replacement-path protecting against* e_2, $P_3 \subseteq G \setminus \{e_2\}$, *whose unique divergence point from* $\pi(s, v)$ *is not below* w *(see Fig. 2).*

Proof: First consider the case where $\langle v, e_2 \rangle \in \mathcal{P}_i^A$, see Fig. 2(a). In this case, by the selection of P', it holds that P_2 π-intersects P'. Let $w' \in (V(\pi(w, t)) \setminus \{w\}) \cap V(P_2)$ and define $P_3 = \pi(s, w') \circ P_2[w', v]$. First, observe that w is the unique divergence point of P_3 and $\pi(s, v)$ since $P_2[w', v] \subseteq D(P_2)$. Next, observe that $e_2 \notin P_3$. This holds since $\pi(s, w') = \pi(s, w) \circ \pi(w, w')$. Since $e_2 \in \pi(w, v)$ and $E(\pi(w, w')) \cap$

$E(\pi(w, v)) = \emptyset$, indeed the failing edge is not on P_3. Finally, by the optimality of the BFS tree T_0, $|P_3| = |P_2|$. Hence, the path P_3 satisfies the desired property as it diverges from $\pi(s, v)$ at w.

It remains to consider the case where $\langle v, e_2 \rangle \in \mathcal{P}_i^B$. See Fig. 2(b). Since both P_2 and P' are of type B, P_2 does not π-intersect P' and vice-versa, and hence

$$V(\pi(w, v) \cap P') \setminus \{w\} = \emptyset \quad \text{and} \quad (8)$$
$$V((\pi(w, t) \cap P_2)) \setminus \{w\} = \emptyset.$$

Let $w' \notin \{d(P_2), d(P'), v, t\}$ be a common point of the detours $D(P_2)$ and $D(P')$. Since $\langle t, e' \rangle \in \mathcal{I}^{\nsucc}(P_2)$, by Eq. (1), such vertex w' exists. Let $P_3 = P'[s, w'] \circ P_2[w', v]$. We first claim that P_3 has a unique divergence point from $\pi(s, v)$ which is not below w. Let $d(P')$ be the unique divergence point of P' from $\pi(s, t)$ (which exists by Cl. 5.4(1)). Clearly, $P'[s, w'] = \pi(s, d(P')) \circ P'[d(P'), w']$. Since $P'[d(P'), w'] \subseteq D(P')$, it holds that $(P'[d(P'), w'] \cap \pi(s, w)) \setminus \{d(P')\} = \emptyset$. Since P' does not π-intersect with P_2, by Eq. (8), it also holds that $(P'[d(P'), w'] \cap \pi(w, v)) \setminus \{d(P'), w\} = \emptyset$, and since $P_2[w', v] \subseteq D(P_2)$, overall it holds that $V(P_3[d(P'), v]) \cap V(\pi(s, v)) \setminus \{d(P'), v\} = \emptyset$.

Note that the last point common to P' and $\pi(s, v)$ is not below w and hence the unique divergence point of P_3 and $\pi(s, v)$ is not below w. Also note that $P_3 \subseteq G \setminus \{e_2\}$ since $e_2 \in \pi(w, v)$ and P' does not intersect $\pi(w, v) \setminus \{w\}$. It remains to bound the length of P_3. By Eq. (8), $P'[s, w']$, $P_2[s, w'] \subseteq G \setminus \{e', e_2\}$, and the optimality of P' and P_2 implies $|P'[s, w']| = |P_2[s, w']|$. The claim follows. ∎

Since Algorithm Pcons attempt to select the replacement-path whose divergence point is as close to s as possible, (see Cl. 5.4(2)), it holds that d_2 is not below w. Altogether, w is above e_2 but not above d_2, implying that $w \in \pi(y_1, x_2)$ as well, thus proving part (b) of the lemma. ∎

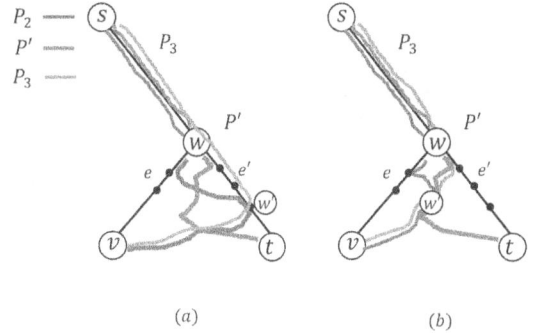

(a)   (b)

Figure 2: Schematic Illustration for Lemma 5.8: (a) P_2 of type A. (b) P_2 of type B that does not intersect $\pi(w, t)$.

We conclude the analysis of Phase S1 by showing that $\mathsf{LastE}(P_{v,e}) \in H$ for every $\langle v, e \rangle \in \mathcal{I}_1 \setminus \mathcal{P}^C$. The high level idea of the proof is to use Lemma 5.8 to show that the existence of at least one H-new-ending path $P_{v,e}$ where $\langle v, e \rangle \in \mathcal{I}_1 \setminus \mathcal{P}^C$ implies that T_0 has expansion at least n^ϵ, so after $O(1/\epsilon)$ steps of expansion, it covers more than n vertices, leading to contradiction.

LEMMA 5.10. $(\mathcal{I}_1 \setminus \mathcal{P}^C) \cap \mathcal{UP}(H) = \emptyset$.

Analysis of Phase S2. We begin by showing the following.

OBSERVATION 5.11. *Every $\mathcal{P}_i^C \in \mathcal{S}$, $i \in \{1, \ldots, K_\epsilon\}$, is a $(\sim)$-set.*

Recall that $E^-(\mathcal{TD})$ is the collection of glue edges, namely, T_0 edges that do not appear by the paths ψ of the tree-decomposition $\mathcal{TD}$. Sub-Phase S2.2 and Fact 3.1 imply:

CLAIM 5.12. *Every edge $e \in E^-(\mathcal{TD})$ is protected by H.*

Hence, it remains to bound the number of unprotected edges on the paths of $\mathcal{TD}$. The following definitions are useful in our reasoning. For a vertex v and an $s_\psi - t_\psi$ path $\psi \in \mathcal{TD}$, define

$$\mathcal{P}_{miss}(\psi, v) = \{\langle v, e \rangle \in \mathcal{P}_{miss} \mid e \in \pi(s, v) \cap \psi\},$$

as the set of uncovered pairs in H that belong to $\mathcal{P}$ and whose corresponding replacement paths protect against the failure of the edges on $\pi(s, v) \cap \psi$. Let $E_{miss}(\mathcal{P}, \psi, v) = \{e \mid \langle v, e \rangle \in \mathcal{P}_{miss}(\psi, v)\}$ be the corresponding last-unprotected edges by H on $\pi(s, v) \cap \psi$. Let $E_{miss}(\mathcal{P}, \psi) = \bigcup_{v \in V} E_{miss}(\mathcal{P}, \psi, v)$. By Cl. 5.12,

$$E_{miss}(\mathcal{P}) = \bigcup_{\psi \in \mathcal{TD}} E_{miss}(\mathcal{P}, \psi).$$

Note that the replacement paths of the pairs of $\mathcal{P}_{miss}(\psi, v)$ may end with the same last edge. We now identify a set $\mathcal{P}_{miss}^{UN}(\mathcal{P}, \psi, v)$ of unique representatives for each last edge as follows. For every edge e' that has several replacement paths $P_{v,e}$ for $\langle v, e \rangle \in \mathcal{P}_{miss}(\psi, v)$ whose last edge $\mathtt{LastE}(P_{v,e}) = e'$, we pick one representative pair $\langle v, e^* \rangle$ corresponding to the path P_{v,e^*} whose failing edge e^* is closest to s among all other candidates. Formally, let

$$\mathcal{LE}_{miss}(\mathcal{P}, \psi, v) = \{\mathtt{LastE}(P_{v,e}) \mid \langle v, e \rangle \in \mathcal{P}_{miss}(\psi, v)\}$$

be the last edges of the replacement paths of the pairs in $\mathcal{P}_{miss}(\psi, v)$. For every $e' \in \mathcal{LE}_{miss}(\mathcal{P}, \psi, v)$, let $\mathcal{P}(e', \mathcal{P}, \psi, v) = \{\langle v, e \rangle \in \mathcal{P}_{miss}(\psi, v) \mid \mathtt{LastE}(P_{v,e}) = e'\}$. The representative pair for the last edge e', denoted by $\widehat{P}(e') = \langle v, e^* \rangle$ for $\langle v, e^* \rangle \in \mathcal{P}(e', \mathcal{P}, \psi, v)$, satisfies that $\mathrm{dist}(s, e^*, \pi(s,v)) < \mathrm{dist}(s, e'', \pi(s,v))$ for every $e'' \neq e^*$ and $\langle v, e'' \rangle \in \mathcal{P}(e', \mathcal{P}, \psi, v)$. Finally, define $\mathcal{P}_{miss}^{UN}(\mathcal{P}, \psi, v) = \{\widehat{P}(e') \mid e' \in \mathcal{LE}_{miss}(\mathcal{P}, \psi, v)\}$ and

$$E_{miss}^{UN}(\mathcal{P}, \psi, v) = \{e_j \mid \langle v, e_j \rangle \in \mathcal{P}_{miss}^{UN}(\mathcal{P}, \psi, v)\}.$$

We proceed by showing that $E_{miss}^{UN}(\mathcal{P}, \psi, v)$ is either *empty* or sufficiently *large*.

LEMMA 5.13. *For every $v \in V$ and every $\psi \in \mathcal{TD}$, if $E_{miss}^{UN}(\mathcal{P}, \psi, v) \neq \emptyset$, then (a) $|E_{miss}^{UN}(\mathcal{P}, \psi, v)| \geq \lceil n^\epsilon \rceil$, and (b) the first $\lceil n^\epsilon \rceil$ edges in $E_{miss}^{UN}(\mathcal{P}, \psi, v)$ are contained in $\pi_{j^*}(s, v) \subseteq \pi(s, v)$, which is the highest heavy subsegment that intersects ψ with respect to $\mathcal{P}$.*

Note that if $E_{miss}^{UN}(\mathcal{P}, \psi, v) = \emptyset$, then also $E_{miss}(\mathcal{P}, \psi, v) = \emptyset$, so this set needs not concern us anymore. Hence hereafter we concentrate on vertices v with a large set $E_{miss}^{UN}(\mathcal{P}, \psi, v)$. For such a vertex v, let

$$\overrightarrow{E}_{miss}^{UN}(\mathcal{P}, \psi, v) = \{e_{i_1}, \ldots, e_{i_\ell}\}$$

be the edges of $E_{miss}^{UN}(\mathcal{P}, \psi, v)$ ordered in *increasing* distance from s. By Lemma 5.13, $\ell \geq \lceil n^\epsilon \rceil$. Define $\mathcal{D}(\mathcal{P}, \psi, v) = \{D(P_{v,e_{i_j}}) \mid j \in \{1, \ldots, \lceil n^\epsilon \rceil\}\}$ as the collection of the detours protecting against the failure of the first $\lceil n^\epsilon \rceil$ ordered edges in the ordering $\overrightarrow{E}_{miss}^{UN}(\mathcal{P}, \psi, v)$. Note that by the definition of $E_{miss}^{UN}(\mathcal{P}, \psi, v)$, each of the detours in $\mathcal{D}(\mathcal{P}, \psi, v)$ ends with a distinct last edge (in particular, by Cl. 5.6, these detours are vertex disjoint, except for the terminal v).

We next claim that each of the detours of $\mathcal{D}(\mathcal{P}, \psi, v)$ is sufficiently long.

LEMMA 5.14.
$$|D_i| \geq |\sigma(\mathcal{P}, \psi, v)|/4 \text{ for every } D_i \in \mathcal{D}(\mathcal{P}, \psi, v).$$

For a vertex v with a large set $E_{miss}^{UN}(\mathcal{P}, \psi, v)$, let $e^*(\mathcal{P}, \psi, v) \in E_{miss}(\mathcal{P}, \psi, v)$ be the closest edge to s on $\pi(s, v) \cap \psi$ among all edges in $E_{miss}(\mathcal{P}, \psi, v)$. Hence, $e^*(\mathcal{P}, \psi, v) \in E_{miss}^{UN}(\mathcal{P}, \psi, v)$. Note that by the end of the Sub-Phases S2.2 - S2.3 and by Cl. 5.5, the divergence point of $P_{v,e^*(\mathcal{P}, \psi, v)}$ from $\pi(s, v)$ must occur on ψ. (This is because the last edges of the new ending paths protecting the first failing edges on each subsegment $\pi_j(s, v)$ and the intersected segments $\pi_U(s, v), \pi_L(s, v)$ were added into H, the divergence point of the H-new-ending paths protecting the other edges on these segments are internal to their segments.) Define the segments

$$\sigma(\mathcal{P}, \psi, v) = \pi(d(P_{v,e^*(\mathcal{P}, \psi, v)}), \mathtt{LCA}(v, t_\psi)),$$

and the segment collection

$$\mathcal{SG}(\mathcal{P}, v) = \{\sigma(\mathcal{P}, \psi, v) \mid E_{miss}(\mathcal{P}, \psi, v) \neq \emptyset\}, \quad (9)$$

where ψ is an $s_\psi - t_\psi$ path.

OBSERVATION 5.15. $E_{miss}(\mathcal{P}, \psi) \subseteq \bigcup_{\sigma \in \mathcal{SG}(\mathcal{P}, \psi)} \sigma$.

From now on, we focus on a particular path ψ in the tree decomposition $\mathcal{TD}$. We proceed by defining a notion of independence between two segments $\sigma_i = \sigma(\mathcal{P}, \psi, v_i)$ and $\sigma_j = \sigma(\mathcal{P}, \psi, v_j)$ in $\mathcal{SG}(\mathcal{P}, \psi)$ (see Eq. (9) for the definition of $\mathcal{SG}(\mathcal{P}, \psi)$). Let x_i (resp. x_j) be the first vertex of σ_i (resp., σ_j) and let $y_i = \mathtt{LCA}(v_i, t_\psi)$ (resp., $y_j = \mathtt{LCA}(v_j, t_\psi)$) be the last vertex of σ_i, σ_j.

DEFINITION 6 (INDEPENDENT SEGMENTS). *Let $\sigma_i = \pi(x_i, y_i), \sigma_j = \pi(x_j, y_j) \in \mathcal{SG}(\mathcal{P}, \psi)$ be such that $\mathrm{dist}(s, x_i, G) \leq \mathrm{dist}(s, x_j, G)$ and let $\ell = \max\{|\sigma_i|, |\sigma_j|\}$. Then, σ_i and σ_j are independent if*
$$\mathrm{dist}(s, x_j, G) - \mathrm{dist}(s, y_i, G) \geq \ell,$$
otherwise they are dependent.

By Lemma 5.13, we have the following.

OBSERVATION 6.1. *For a vertex v, if $E_{miss}^{UN}(\mathcal{P}, \psi, v) \neq \emptyset$, then $|\sigma(\mathcal{P}, \psi, v)| = \Omega(n^\epsilon)$.*

Set $\mathcal{SG}'(\mathcal{P}, \psi) \leftarrow \mathcal{SG}(\mathcal{P}, \psi)$. We now compute a collection of maximal weighted independent set $\mathcal{SG}_{IS}(\mathcal{P}, \psi)$ greedily by adding to $\mathcal{SG}_{IS}(\mathcal{P}, \psi)$ at each step the segment $\sigma(\mathcal{P}, \psi, v) \in \mathcal{SG}'(\mathcal{P}, \psi)$ whose length is maximal among all remaining segments $\mathcal{SG}'(\mathcal{P}, \psi)$ and removing from it the segments $\sigma(\mathcal{P}, \psi, v'')$ that are *dependent* with $\sigma(\mathcal{P}, \psi, v)$. The next observation shows that the total length of the independent set $\mathcal{SG}_{IS}(\mathcal{P}, \psi)$ is of the same order as the original set $\mathcal{SG}(\mathcal{P}, \psi)$.

CLAIM 6.2. $\sum_{\sigma \in \mathcal{SG}_{IS}(\mathcal{P}, \psi)} |\sigma| \geq |E_{miss}(\mathcal{P}, \psi)|/5$.

We next show the following (for the given ψ and $\mathcal{P}$).

LEMMA 6.3.

$$n^\epsilon \cdot \sum_{\sigma \in \mathcal{SG}_{IS}(\mathcal{P},\psi)} |\sigma| \leq \left| \bigcup_{P \in \mathcal{P}_{miss}(\mathcal{P},\psi)} V(D(P)) \right| .$$

To prove the lemma, we consider an iterative process on the set $VS = \{v \mid \sigma(\mathcal{P},\psi,v) \in \mathcal{SG}_{IS}(\mathcal{P},\psi)\}$, the set of vertices whose segment is in the independent set $\mathcal{SG}_{IS}(\mathcal{P},\psi)$. In this process, the detours of these vertices v' are added in decreasing distance of $\mathtt{LCA}(v',t_\psi)$ and s. (Note that the order is strictly decreasing since the segments are independent and hence also vertex disjoint.) Formally, let $\overrightarrow{VS} = \{v_{i_1}, \ldots, v_{i_k}\}$ be the collection of VS vertices sorted in decreasing distance of $\mathtt{LCA}(v_{i_j}, t_\psi)$ and s, i.e.,
$\mathrm{dist}(s, \mathtt{LCA}(v_{i_1}, t_\psi)) > \ldots > \mathrm{dist}(s, \mathtt{LCA}(v_{i_k}, t_\psi))$.
Starting with $G'_1 = \emptyset$, at step $\tau \geq 1$, let

$$G'_{\tau+1} = G'_\tau \cup \bigcup_{D' \in \mathcal{D}(\mathcal{P},\psi,v_{i_\tau})} D' .$$

Let $\widehat{G} = G'_k$ be the final subgraph. Hence,

$$\widehat{G} \subseteq \bigcup_{\langle v,e \rangle \in \mathcal{P}} D(P_{v,e}) . \tag{10}$$

LEMMA 6.4. *For every $\tau \in \{1, \ldots, k\}$,*
$|V(G'_\tau) \setminus V(G'_{\tau-1})| \geq n^\epsilon \cdot |\sigma(\mathcal{P},\psi,v_{i_\tau}))|/4.$

By the last two lemmas we get that

$$\left| \bigcup_{P \in \mathcal{P}_{miss}(\mathcal{P},\psi)} V(D(P)) \right| = \Omega(n^\epsilon \cdot |E_{miss}(\mathcal{P},\psi)|).$$

In the full version [16] we combine these lemmas and establish Thm. 4.1.

7. LOWER BOUND

Finally, we establish lower bounds on the size of the ϵ FT-BFS structures. These bounds match the upper bound of Sec. 4 up to logarithmic factors in both the number of reinforced edges and the size of the construct. The proof appears in the full version [16].

THEOREM 7.1. *For every $\epsilon \in (0, 1/2)$, there exists an n-vertex graph $G(V,E)$ and a source node $s \in V$ such that any ϵ FT-BFS tree rooted at s with at most $\lfloor n^{1-\epsilon}/6 \rfloor$ reinforced edges has $\Omega(n^{1+\epsilon})$ edges. In other words, there exists a graph for which any $(b(n), r(n))$ FT-BFS structure for $r(n) = \Omega(n^{1-\epsilon})$ requires $\Omega(\min\{n^{1+\epsilon}, n^{3/2}\})$ backup edges.*

The single source lower bound is extended in [16] to the generalized setting of multiple source $S \subseteq V$. Finding a (nearly) matching upper bound for the latter case is a remaining open problem.

8. REFERENCES

[1] B. Awerbuch and Y. Azar. Buy-at-bulk network design. In Proc. *FOCS*, 1997.

[2] S. Baswana and N. Khanna. Approximate shortest paths avoiding a failed vertex: near optimal data structures for undirected unweighted graphs. *Algorithmica*, 66(1):18–50, 2013.

[3] A. Bernstein and D. Karger. A nearly optimal oracle for avoiding failed vertices and edges. In Proc. *STOC*, 101–110, 2009.

[4] G. Braunschvig, S. Chechik and D. Peleg. Fault tolerant additive spanners. In Proc. *WG*, 206–214, 2012.

[5] S. Chechik, M. Langberg, D. Peleg, and L. Roditty. Fault-tolerant spanners for general graphs. In Proc. *STOC*, 435–444, 2009.

[6] C. Chekuri, M. T. Hajiaghayi, G. Kortsarz, and M.R. Salavatipour. Approximation algorithms for nonuniform buy-at-bulk network design. *SIAM J. Computing*, 39(5), 1772-1798, 2010.

[7] A. Czumaj and H. Zhao. Fault-tolerant geometric spanners. *Discrete & Computational Geometry* **32**, (2003).

[8] M. Dinitz and R. Krauthgamer. Fault-tolerant spanners: better and simpler. In Proc. *PODC*, 2011, 169-178.

[9] F. Grandoni and V.V Williams. Improved Distance Sensitivity Oracles via Fast Single-Source Replacement Paths. In Proc. *FOCS*, 2012.

[10] F. Grandoni and G.F. Italiano. Improved approximation for single-sink buy-at-bulk. In Proc. *ISAAC*, 111–120, 2006.

[11] A. Gupta and A. Kumar and T. Roughgarden. Approximation via cost sharing: Simpler and better approximation algorithms for network design. *J. ACM*, 54(3), 2007.

[12] C. Levcopoulos, G. Narasimhan, and M. Smid. Efficient algorithms for constructing fault-tolerant geometric spanners. In Proc. *STOC*, 186–195, 1998.

[13] T. Lukovszki. New results of fault tolerant geometric spanners. In Proc. *WADS*, 193–204, 1999.

[14] M. Parter and D. Peleg. Sparse Fault-Tolerant BFS Trees. In Proc. *ESA*, 2013.

[15] M. Parter and D. Peleg. Sparse Fault-Tolerant BFS Trees. arxiv.org/pdf/1302.5401v1.pdf.

[16] M. Parter and D. Peleg. Fault Tolerant BFS Structures: A Reinforcement-Backup Tradeoff arxiv.org/pdf/1504.04169v1.pdf.

[17] M. Parter. Vertex Fault Tolerant Additive Spanners. In Proc. *DISC*, 2014.

[18] L. Roditty and U. Zwick. Replacement paths and k simple shortest paths in unweighted directed graphs. *ACM Trans. Algorithms* ,2012.

[19] F.S. Salman, J. Cheriyan, R. Ravi, S. Subramanian Buy-at-bulk network design: Approximating the single-sink edge installation problem. In Proc. *SODA*, 1997.

[20] D.D Sleator and R.E. Tarjan. A data structure for dynamic trees. In Proc. *STOC*, 1981.

[21] M. Thorup and U. Zwick. Approximate distance oracles. *J. ACM*, 52:1–24, 2005.

[22] O. Weimann and R. Yuster. Replacement paths via fast matrix multiplication. In Proc. *FOCS*, 2010.

Distributed Backup Placement in Networks

Magnús M. Halldórsson[*]
Reykjavik University, Iceland
mmh@ru.is

Sven Köhler
Tel Aviv University, Israel
sven@eng.tau.ac.il

Boaz Patt-Shamir[†‡]
Tel Aviv University, Israel
boaz@eng.tau.ac.il

Dror Rawitz[§‡]
Bar Ilan University, Israel
dror.rawitz@biu.ac.il

ABSTRACT

We consider the *backup placement* problem, defined as follows. Some nodes (processors) in a given network have objects (e.g., files, tasks) whose backups should be stored in additional nodes for increased fault resilience. To minimize the disturbance in case of a failure, it is required that a backup copy should be located at a neighbor of the primary node. The goal is to find an assignment of backup copies to nodes which minimizes the maximum load (number or total size of copies) over all nodes in the network. It is known that a natural selfish local improvement policy has approximation ratio $\Omega(\log n / \log \log n)$; we show that it may take this policy $\Omega(\sqrt{n})$ time to reach equilibrium in the distributed setting. Our main result in this paper is a distributed algorithm which finds a placement in polylogarithmic time and achieves approximation ratio $O(\frac{\log n}{\log \log n})$. We obtain this result using a distributed approximation algorithm for f-matching in bipartite graphs that may be of independent interest.

1. INTRODUCTION

There are many scenarios in networks, e.g., in the context of cloud computing, where an object, such as a file or a task, resides in an unreliable processor. It is common practice in such cases to store a *backup copy* of the object at a nearby location (say, an adjacent node), so that in case of a failure in the primary location, the required service can be quickly switched over to the backup, thus minimizing unavailability time.

[*]Supported in part by Icelandic Research Fund (grants No. 120032011 and 152679-051)

[†]Supported in part by the Israel Science Foundation (grant No. 1444/14).

[‡]Supported in part by a grant from the Ministry of Science, Technology and Space, Israel (French-Israeli project Maimonide 31768XL).

[§]Supported in part by the Israel Science Foundation (grant No. 497/14).

Clearly, not all backup placements are equal: consider, as the simplest example, an n-node fully connected network. If all nodes choose to place their backup copies at node 0 (except node 0, of course), then a fault at node 0 will make all backup copies unavailable. A much preferable placement would be for each node i to place its backup at node $(i+1) \bmod n$: this way, each node stores exactly one copy, which is the minimum possible in any case. To quantify this preference, one can measure the quality of a placement by the *maximum load*, i.e., the maximum, over all nodes, of the number (or total size) of copies they store, and the optimization goal is to minimize the maximum load.

Observe that there are cases which do not admit a good solution: if the network topology is a star, then all leaves must store their backup copies at the center node (in this case, all solutions are isomorphic). Therefore it makes sense to measure not the absolute maximum load of a given placement, but rather the *approximation ratio*, i.e., the ratio between the maximum load of a given placement and the smallest possible maximum load in the given topology, i.e., the maximum load of an optimal placement.

In this paper we study distributed solutions to the backup placement problem. To the best of our knowledge, the only known distributed algorithm for this problem is the very simple (and hence attractive) *local improvement* rule, which says that nodes act selfishly to decrease the load their backup copy sees [21]. For example, if the backup copy of node v resides in a neighbor u which stores 7 backup copies, and if v learns that its other neighbor w stores only 3 copies, then v will move its copy from u to w (assuming that moving an object is an atomic operation). It is known that the approximation ratio (called *price of anarchy* in this context) for this rule is $\Theta(\frac{\log n}{\log \log n})$, where n is the number of nodes in the system [12]. While the upper bound on the approximation ratio may be acceptable, it turns out that the *dynamics* of the local improvement rule is problematic: as we show in this paper, the number of rounds required to reach equilibrium may be as large as $\Omega(\sqrt{n})$ in the worst case, even under the most optimistic assumptions on concurrency.

Our main result is a polylogarithmic-time distributed algorithm for backup placement, an exponential improvement over the running time over the selfish rule. The algorithm runs in the CONGEST model, i.e., execution proceeds in synchronous rounds in which nodes send small messages (see details in Section 2). The algorithm can be used in two ways: in one mode of operation, the algorithm guarantees approximation ratio $O(\frac{\log n}{\log \log n})$. In the other mode of operation, the algorithm is fed a load bound L and a parameter

$\epsilon > 0$, and it finds a placement with maximum load L which places at least a $(1 - \epsilon)$-fraction of the maximum possible number of backups that can be placed under the given constraint of maximum load L (the running time in this case is also polynomial in ϵ^{-1}). In both cases, the algorithm can deal with the following generalizations of the problem:

- The primary locations may be any subset of nodes.
- The backup locations for each primary location may be any subset of nodes, assuming that each primary location can communicate with all its possible backup locations in $O(1)$ rounds.
- Objects may have different sizes, and the load of a node is the sum of the sizes of the copies it stores.
- Each object must have k backup copies in different locations, where $k \in \mathbb{N}$ is a given parameter.

Our algorithm is based on a distributed approximation algorithm for f-matching in bipartite graphs that may be of independent interest. We provide hardness results and both minimum load and maximum coverage versions of the problem, and we also compare maximal solutions to maximum solutions in the maximum coverage case.

Paper organization. The remainder of this paper is organized as follows. In Section 2 we formalize the problem. Related work is given in Section 3. Section 4 discusses the sequential complexity of the problems. In Section 5 we analyze a few simple distributed algorithms and present our polylog-time algorithm. Section 6 relates maximal solutions to maximum solutions. We conclude in Section 7.

2. MODEL

Throughout this paper, we consider a simple undirected graph $G = (V, E)$, where V is the set of nodes and E is the set of edges. We use n to denote $|V|$ and Δ to denote the maximum node degree of G. We use $N(u) \stackrel{\text{def}}{=} \{v \mid (u, v) \in E\}$ to denote the set of neighbors of a node u. The set of all positive integers is denoted by $\mathbb{N}$ and $\mathbb{N}_0$ is used to denote the set of all non-negative integers.

Problem Statement. In the *backup placement problem* the input is as follows. We are given a set $C \subseteq V$ of *client* nodes and a set $S \subseteq V$ of *server* nodes. The sets may overlap, and their union need not be V. For each client $c \in C$ we are given a *size* (or *length*) $\ell(c) \in \mathbb{N}$. Let $\ell_{\max} \stackrel{\text{def}}{=} \max_{c \in C} \ell(c)$ denote the maximum size. We refer to an instance as *uniform* if all sizes are 1. In the non-uniform case, we assume that $\ell_{\max} = n^{O(1)}$. In addition, we are given a parameter $k \in \mathbb{N}$ called the *replication factor*. Without loss of generality, we assume that $|S \cap N(c)| \geq k$ for every client $c \in C$.

The required output is a mapping $\beta : C \to 2^S$ which satisfies, for all $c \in C$, that $\beta(c) \subseteq S \cap N(c)$ and $|\beta(c)| \in \{0, k\}$. We say that a *backup copy* (a.k.a. *file*) of c is stored at s if $s \in \beta(c)$. A client $c \in C$ is said to be *satisfied* if $|\beta(c)| = k$, and *unsatisfied* otherwise. Let $\beta^{-1}(s) \stackrel{\text{def}}{=} \{c \in C \mid s \in \beta(c)\}$, i.e., $\beta^{-1}(s)$ is the set of clients whose files are stored at s. Define the *load* of a server $s \in S$ by $L(s) \stackrel{\text{def}}{=} \sum_{c \in \beta^{-1}(s)} \ell(c)$, i.e., $L(s)$ is the total size of backups stored at s. We call $\max\{L(s) \mid s \in S\}$ the *maximum load* of β.

We consider the following optimization goals for backup placement:

Min Load (MINLOAD): Minimize the maximum load under the constraint that all clients must be satisfied.

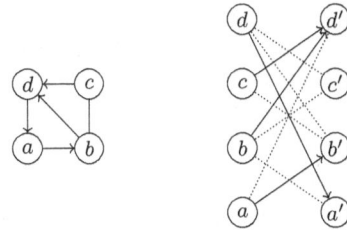

Figure 1: Left: A backup placement in a graph. All nodes are servers and clients, and $k = 1$. Placement is indicated by arrows from clients to servers. Right: the corresponding bipartite graph.

Max Coverage (MAXCOV): Maximize the number of satisfied clients, under the constraint that the maximum load is no more than a certain L (L is an additional input parameter).

We mainly focus on the former, while the latter is mainly used as an intermediate goal.

It is sometimes convenient to formalize the backup problem using a corresponding bipartite graph $G' = (C, S, E')$, where C is the set of clients, S is the set of servers (a node of G may be represented twice in G'), and E' connects a client c to a server s if and only if $(c, s) \in E$. See Figure 1 for an example. Note that the definitions of backup placement and server load apply to the bipartite graph without change.

Execution Model. We use the CONGEST model [28], which is a network model with small messages. Briefly, in this model nodes are processors with unique IDs, connected by links that can carry $O(\log n)$-bit messages in a time unit. Processors are not restricted computationally (all computations required by our algorithms are polynomial, though). As usual, for our upper bounds, we implicitly assume that the α synchronizer [2] is employed in the system, so that the algorithms operate in a synchronous manner in the following sense. Execution proceeds in global *rounds*, where in each round each processor: Receives messages sent by its neighbors in the previous round, performs a local computation, and sends (possibly distinct) messages to its neighbors.

3. RELATED WORK

MINLOAD with a replication factor of 1 is a special case of the problem of *load balancing with restricted assignment*. In the centralized offline setting, the problem is optimally solvable in polynomial time using flow techniques (see Section 4). Most work on this problem concerns either online algorithms (see, e.g., [3]), or selfish agents (see, e.g., [23]). It is known that the simple (and centralized) on-line greedy algorithm where each job is assigned to the least loaded server is $(\lceil \log n \rceil + 1)$-competitive [4].

In the centralized setting, a special case of the backup placement problem, called "assigning papers to referees," was studied by Garg et al. [14]. In this problem it is assumed that each client ranks its available servers, and the goal of an algorithm is to find an assignment which maximizes a certain fairness measure defined in terms of the ranking (feasibility of load and coverage constraints is assumed to be trivial).

The "degree constrained subgraph" framework is a generalization of the backup placement problem considered in the centralized setting. In this family of problems the goal is to find a subgraph optimizing a certain measure (e.g., minimize number of edges) while conforming to given degree constraints (e.g., minimum degree at least some d). See [1] for relatively recent results and survey. *Semi-matchings*, introduced in [16], is more closely related to backup placement. Given a bipartite graph $G = (C, S, E)$, a semi-matching is a subset $E' \subseteq E$ of edges such that each client $c \in C$ is the endpoint of exactly one edge in E'. The cost of a semi-matching is defined by the L_p norm of the server load vector (the vector in which each node in S is assigned the number of E' edges it is incident with). In [16], a polynomial time algorithm to find an optimal semi-matching is presented, under any L_p norm, including L_∞ (i.e., minimizing the maximal load). A faster deterministic algorithm is provided in [11], and a randomized algorithm is presented in [13]. Low [25] considers weighted semi-matchings, where each client has a non-negative weight, and the load of a server is the sum of weights of clients assigned to it: under the L_∞ norm, it is shown that the weighted version is NP-hard, and a $\frac{3}{2}$-approximation algorithm is presented. All these algorithms are centralized.

Bokal et al. [6] introduce "(f, g)-quasi-matchings" and "(f, g)-semi-matchings." An (f, g)-quasi-matching of $G = (C, S, E)$ is a set $M \subseteq E$, such that each $c \in C$ is an endpoint of at least $f(c)$ edges and each $s \in S$ is end endpoint of at most $g(s)$ edges of M. In (f, g)-semi-matchings, also called f-matchings in general graphs [8], both functions f and g define an upper bound on the number of edges each node is an endpoint of. In the sequential setting, a maximum (f, g)-semi-matching of a bipartite graphs can be found in polynomial time [20].

In the distributed setting, the basic building block used is fast approximate maximum matching algorithms. The best known algorithms are [24, 5], both randomized (for deterministic algorithms, see [15, 26]). Using a matching algorithm, [27] presents a polylogarithmic time algorithm for MaxCov with $k = 1$ which guarantees, for any $\epsilon > 0$ and with high probability, a $(1 + \epsilon)\frac{2-r}{1-r}$-approximation, where r is the maximum ratio between a client demand and a server capacity. A 2-approximation of MaxCov with $k = 1$ and uniform file sizes can be computed using the matching algorithm of [22]. Regarding MinLoad, we are only aware of distributed algorithms which use large messages (i.e., they run in the LOCAL model [28]): in [7] it is shown how to find an approximation of optimal semi-matchings in $O(\Delta^5)$ rounds under the L_2 norm. The approximation ratio is $\min(2, \frac{2s+n}{n})$, where s is the number of servers and n is the number of all nodes. In [7] they also provided a constant approximation LOCAL algorithm that runs in $O(\min\{\Delta^2, \Delta \log^4 n\})$ rounds.

4. SEQUENTIAL COMPLEXITY

In this section we study the complexity of the backup placement problem. It is easy to see that MaxCov is polynomial for $k = 1$ and uniform file sizes, as it can be reduced to a maximum flow problem: Given the bipartite representation of the MaxCov instance, add a source s with links of capacity $k = 1$ connecting it to all clients, a sink t with links of capacity L connecting it to all servers, and assign capacity 1 to each edge in the original bipartite graph (see example in Figure 2). Since we can find an integral solution, each client with incoming flow 1 can be unambiguously assigned to the unique server to which this unit flow is directed.

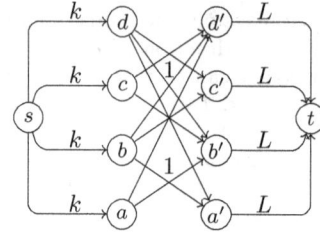

Figure 2: The flow problem corresponding to the backup placement problem of Figure 1.

However, if $k > 1$, this reduction does not work, since it maximizes the number of placed backups instead of maximizing the number of satisfied clients. Even worse, in the case of non-uniform sizes, the maximum flow may split a single backup copy between servers, which is not feasible in our setting. The following theorem shows that the failure of the reduction in these cases is no accident.

THEOREM 4.1. MaxCov *with uniform file sizes is APX-complete for $k \geq 3$ and cannot be approximated to within* $\Omega(\frac{\log k}{k})$, *unless* P $=$ NP.

The proof is by reduction from 3- and k-Dimensional Matching [19, 17].

MinLoad can be solved using the following reduction of MinLoad to MaxCov.

LEMMA 4.2. *If an optimal solution to* MaxCov *can be found in T_{MaxCov} time, then an optimal solution to* MinLoad *can be found in $O(T_{\text{MaxCov}} \log n)$ time.*

PROOF. Given a MinLoad instance, do a binary search over the value of L to find the minimal value which allows to cover all clients. To bound the number of times the MaxCov algorithm is called, note that the largest L to consider is $n \cdot \ell_{\max} = n^{O(1)}$ by our assumption that sizes are polynomial in n. $\square$

Using a reduction to max-flow, wrapped by a binary search as in the proof of Lemma 4.2, we get that MinLoad is polynomial for uniform file sizes even for general replication factor.[1] However, for non-uniform file sizes, MinLoad is strongly NP-hard, as stated next.

THEOREM 4.3. MinLoad *with non-uniform file sizes is strongly NP-hard, even for replication factor 1.*

The proof is by reduction from 3-Partition. It follows from Theorem 4.3 and Lemma 4.2 that MaxCov is strongly NP-hard, but Theorem 4.1 provides a stronger result.

5. DISTRIBUTED ALGORITHMS

In this section we consider distributed algorithms solving MinLoad. First we show that simple solutions do not work well: simple randomized assignments may produce solutions with $\Omega(n)$ approximation ratio, and a simple selfish rule may yield $\Omega(\sqrt{n})$ running time for approximation ratio $\Omega(\frac{\log n}{\log \log n})$. By contrast, we present a polylog-complexity algorithm for MinLoad, derived by a series of reductions culminating in an algorithm for bipartite f-matching which may be of independent interest.

---

[1] The reduction works for general k because the target flow value is known in advance (it is nk). The proof of Theorem 4.1 uses instances that are not fully covered.

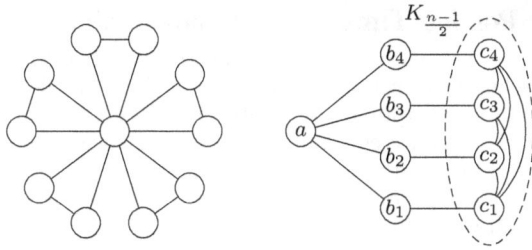

Figure 3: Graphs used in the proofs of Theorem 5.1 (left) and Theorem 5.2 (right).

5.1 Random placements

It may be tempting to consider random placement as a solution to MINLOAD. While this method is extremely fast, we show that its approximation ratio is quite bad, even for replication factor 1. Let R_1 be the algorithm where each client selects a neighbor server uniformly at random.

THEOREM 5.1. R_1 has approximation ratio $\Omega(n)$.

PROOF. We show that for every odd n there exists an instance where the expected maximum load generated by R_1 is $(n-1)/2$ whereas the optimal maximum load is 1. Consider a graph with a center node v_0 connected to $n-1$ nodes, such that nodes v_{2i-1} and v_{2i} are connected (see Figure 3-left). Since each of the $n-1$ nodes chooses the center node with probability $1/2$, the expected load on the center is $\frac{n-1}{2}$. However, an optimal solution with a maximum load of 1 exists: nodes v_{2i-1} and v_{2i}, for $i > 1$, select each other, while v_0, v_1, and v_2 select v_1, v_2, and v_0, resp. $\square$

One may be further tempted to fix the problem of R_1 by extending the range which nodes consider. Specifically, let R_2 denote the algorithm where each client selects a neighbor server with probability inversely proportional to the neighbor's degree. While R_2 is not fooled by the simplistic example in the proof of Theorem 5.1, its approximation ratio is still linear, as we show next.

THEOREM 5.2. R_2 has approximation ratio $\Omega(n)$.

PROOF. Assume w.l.o.g. that n is odd, and let $n' = \frac{n-1}{2}$. Define a graph with n nodes $\{a\} \cup \bigcup_{i=1}^{n'} \{b_i, c_i\}$, and edges $\{(c_i, c_j) \mid i \neq j\} \cup \bigcup_{i=1}^{n'} \{(a, b_i), (b_i, c_i)\}$ (see Figure 3-right for an example). The c_i nodes induce a complete graph with n' nodes. Since a and each c_i have degree exactly n', in R_2 node b_i selects node a with probability $\frac{1}{2}$, resulting in $n'/2 = \Omega(n)$ expected load on a. However, optimal backup placements on this graph have maximum load 2, for example: nodes b_i and c_i exchange copies, and node a selects an arbitrary neighbor. $\square$

5.2 The Local Improvement Rule

We now turn our attention to the much-studied *local improvement* rule, defined as follows. Starting with an arbitrary placement, clients move their copy at will: a client moves one of its copies to another neighbor server if the resulting load at the target server is smaller than the load at the current server. Such a move is called a *local improvement step*. An assignment in which no such move is possible is called (Nash) equilibrium. A self-stabilizing distributed implementation of the local improve rule is given in [21].

For a distributed implementation, we assume that the local improvement steps are done *atomically* and in *adversarial* order. We require atomicity to make sure that each step is indeed an improvement (otherwise non-termination may occur [21]). The adversarial order is for the sake of studying the worst case. It is easy to see that the local improvement rule converges to a Nash equilibrium, in which no client wants to move its copy: the vector of sorted loads decreases lexicographically in each move. However, we now prove the following stronger result.

THEOREM 5.3. *Starting at any initial backup placement, Nash equilibrium is reached in $O(\ell_{\max}^2 kn\Delta_S)$ local improvement steps, where Δ_S is the maximum server degree.*

PROOF. We generalize the proof of [21] to backups of arbitrary size. Define a potential function $\sum_{c \in C} L(c)^2$. A client that moves a backup of size ℓ from server s to t decreases the potential by $L(s)^2 + L(t)^2 - (L(s) - \ell)^2 - (L(t) + \ell)^2 = 2\ell(L(s) - L(t) - \ell)$. Since this is a local improvement step, it must hold that $L(s) > L(t) + \ell$ beforehand. Moreover, all file sizes and thus the server loads are integers. Thus the potential function decreases by at least $2\ell \geq 2$ with each local improvement step. The potential function attains its worst-case value if there are n clients and the backups are concentrated on as few servers as possible. In our case, a server can store at most Δ_S backups. So assume that $\lfloor kn/\Delta_S \rfloor$ servers store Δ_S backups each. Since backup sizes are at most $\ell_{\max}$, each of the $\lfloor kn/\Delta_S \rfloor$ servers has a load of at most $\ell_{\max}\Delta_S$. The $O(\ell_{\max}^2 kn\Delta_S)$ upper bound follows. $\square$

Moreover, the following result is known regarding the price of anarchy for the local improvement rule.

THEOREM 5.4 ([12]). *A Nash-equilibrium of the local improvement rule is a $\Theta(\frac{\log n}{\log \log n})$-approximate backup placement for the case of replication factor 1.*

We complement the above results with some bad news, namely that there are scenarios in which a large number of steps is required to reach equilibrium.

THEOREM 5.5. *Fix a replication factor k. For any given integers n and $\Delta < n$, there exists a graph with n nodes and max degree Δ and an initial backup placement such that $\Omega(kn\sqrt{\Delta})$ local improvement steps can be performed before an equilibrium is reached.*

PROOF. We first show a $\Omega(kn^{3/2})$ lower bound for a complete graph with n nodes. This is used as a building block to obtain the desired $\Omega(kn\sqrt{\Delta})$ lower bound.

Let G be a complete graph with n nodes, where all nodes are both clients and servers. Then for the corresponding bipartite graph $G' = (C, S, E')$ we have $|C| = |S| = n$, where C and S are the client and server sets. Let all backups have size 1. The initial placement is as follows. Partition the servers into three sets S_h, S_c, and S_p with $|S_h| = k$, $|S_c| = c \stackrel{\text{def}}{=} \lceil \sqrt{n} \rceil$, and $|S_p| = n - k - c$. Let $s_1, s_2, \ldots, s_c$ denote servers in S_c. We place backups on these servers so that the load of each $s_i \in S_c$ is equal to $k + i - 1$. We place the backups of as few clients as possible on servers in S_c. It may happen that not all backups of these clients can be placed on servers of S_c, for example if $c < k$. The remaining backups of these clients are evenly distributed among the servers of S_h. Note that no server of S_h has a load of $k + c$

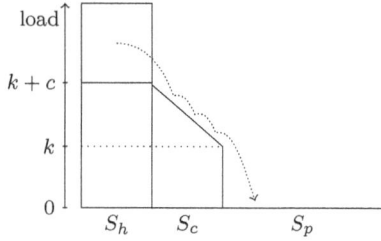

Figure 4: Initial server load distribution used in the proof of Theorem 5.5

or higher. If $c \geq k$, then backups can be placed such that the maximum load in S_h is 1. On the other hand, if $c < k$, then $k + c$ clients may be placed such that the maximum load in S_h is $k + c$. More backups are placed on the servers of S_h until all of them have a load equal to $k + c$. None of the backups that have been placed so far will be moved by a local improvement step in our example.

We are now left with $h \stackrel{\text{def}}{=} kn - k(k + c) - kc - \frac{c(c-1)}{2}$ unplaced backups. We distribute these backups evenly among the servers of S_h. No backup is placed on any server in S_p. The resulting sever load distribution should look similar to what is shown in Figure 4. Starting at this initial placement, as many of the S_h backups as possible are moved to servers of S_p. For each backup we use a sequence of local improvement steps such that the backup visits the servers s_c to s_1 exactly once. Since s_1 has a load of k, at most $k(n - k - c)$ backups can be moved from s_1 to servers in S_p as their load grows over time.

Summing up, at most $b \stackrel{\text{def}}{=} \min(h, k(n - k - c))$ backups can be moved from the servers in S_h to servers in S_p. Since each backup visits each server of S_c once, we have c local improvement steps per backup yielding $b \cdot c = \Omega(kn\sqrt{n} - k^2\sqrt{n})$ improvement steps in total. Since $n - k = \Omega(n)$, it holds $b \cdot c = \Omega(kn\sqrt{n})$.

To create a graph with n' nodes and degree $\Delta < n'$, we use the complete graph described above with Δ nodes as a building block and create $\lfloor n'/\Delta \rfloor$ copies of it. Summing up the number of local improvement steps that can be done in all building blocks, we then obtain the claimed lower bound of $\Omega(kn'\sqrt{\Delta})$. □

We note that Theorem 5.5 is an improvement over the previously known lower bound, which cannot exceed $\Omega(n\frac{\log^2 n}{\log \log n})$ in an n-node graph [10]. A construction similar to Figure 4 is used in [9] to prove a $\Omega(n\sqrt{n})$ lower bound for the problem inverse to ours with $k = 1$.

Consider now a distributed implementation of the local improvement rule. Since even under the most optimistic assumption about concurrency, only $O(n)$ local improvement steps can be performed in a single parallel round, Theorem 5.5 yields the following immediate corollary.

COROLLARY 5.6. *For any given n, k, and Δ there are instances of graphs with n nodes, maximal degree Δ and replication factor k such that the worst-case distributed running time of the local rule is $\Omega(k\sqrt{\Delta})$.*

We note that the self-stabilizing algorithm of [21] meets the lower bound of Corollary 5.6.

5.3 Polylog-Time Approximation Algorithm

We now present our main result, namely an algorithm for the backup placement problem in the CONGEST model.

We start with a standard classify-and-select reduction that allows us to reduce non-uniform file sizes to the case of uniform file sizes, and whose cost is an additional $O(\log n)$ factor in both the running time and approximation ratio. The reduction works for general k.

LEMMA 5.7. *Let Δ_S denote the maximum server degree in an instance. If MINLOAD can be solved for uniform file size and replication factor k in time T_k and approximation ratio α_k, then MINLOAD can be solved for non-uniform file size and replication factor k in time $O(T_k \log \Delta_S)$ and approximation ratio $O(\alpha_k \log \Delta_S)$.*

In the following proof we assume that $\ell_{\max}$ is known to each node. A proof that does not rely on this assumption is omitted due to space constraints.

PROOF. We classify all clients according to their file size: class i contains all clients with file sizes in $(2^{i-1}, 2^i]$. We first consider the top $\lceil \log \Delta_S \rceil$ classes and solve MINLOAD for each class independently, pretending that file sizes are uniform. Thus, the approximation ratio for each class is $2\alpha_k$. It follows that the total load on a server is $2\alpha_k \log \Delta_S \cdot \text{OPT}$, where OPT is the optimal load. The remaining small files have sizes less than $\frac{2}{\Delta_S}\ell_{\max}$ and are placed arbitrarily. This adds at most load $2\ell_{\max}$ per server as a single server has at most Δ_S adjacent clients. The result follows. □

Let us consider now the problem of minimizing the maximum load with uniform sizes and replication factor k. Fix the instance graph. Given a value L, let MAXCOV(L) denote the number of clients that can be satisfied when the instance is viewed as an instance of MAXCOV with server load cap L. We say that an algorithm A α-*solves* MAXCOV, for some parameter $\alpha \geq 1$, if for any given $L \geq 0$, A finds a placement which places at least $k \cdot \text{MAXCOV}(L)$ files, but with relaxed maximum load αL.

LEMMA 5.8. *If MAXCOV with uniform file size and replication factor k can be α-solved in time T_c for any L, then MINLOAD with uniform file size and replication factor k can be solved in time $O(T_c \log n)$ and approximation ratio 4α.*

PROOF. Let A be an algorithm which α-solves the instance in time T_c. We use the following algorithm:

- For $i = 0$ to $\log n$ do
  1. Run A with parameter $L = 2^i$. Obtain solution β_i which places at least $k \cdot \text{MAXCOV}(2^i)$ files.
  2. Add β_i to the output, and remove all edges used by β_i from further consideration.

Let OPT be the optimal load for the given MINLOAD instance. Clearly, when $L \geq \text{OPT}$, the algorithms can place all remaining files. Thus all files are placed by some β_i for some $i \leq \lceil \log \text{OPT} \rceil$. Hence the algorithm produces all its output by time $O(T_c \log \text{OPT}) = O(T_c \log n)$. Since each β_i with $i \leq \lceil \log \text{OPT} \rceil$ is a backup placement with maximum server load at most $\alpha 2^i$, the load of the union of all placements is at most $\sum_{i=0}^{\lceil \log \text{OPT} \rceil} \alpha 2^i \leq 4\alpha\text{OPT}$. □

Finally, we reduce the problem of α-solving MAXCOV to finding approximate f-matchings. Given a graph $G = (V, E)$ and a mapping $f : V \to \mathbb{N}_0$, an f-*matching* is a subset

$M \subseteq E$ such that each node $v \in V$ is incident to at most $f(v)$ edges of M. The goal is to find such a set M of maximum size. In the remainder of this section, ordinary matchings, where $f(v) = 1$ for all nodes $v \in V$, will be called 1-*matchings*.

LEMMA 5.9. *If f-matching can be approximated to within $(1 - \frac{1}{x})$ on bipartite graphs in time T_m for some $x > 1$, then* MAXCOV *with uniform file size, replication factor k, and maximum load L can be $O(\log_x n)$-solved in time $O(T_m \log_x n)$.*

PROOF. Let A be an algorithm obtaining, in T_m time, $(1 - \frac{1}{x})$-approximate f-matchings. For each client c we set $f(c) := k$ and for each server s we set $f(s) = L$. We set $t = \lfloor \log_x kn \rfloor + 1$ and use the following algorithm:

- For $i = 1$ to t do
  1. Run A. Obtain matching M_i which places at least a $(1 - \frac{1}{x})$-fraction of the remaining files.
  2. Add M_i to the output, remove all edges used by M_i, and for each client c, decrease $f(c)$ by the number of edges of M_i incident to c.

Let OPT denote the number of replicas placed in an optimal solution, and let ALG(i) denote the number of replicas placed by our algorithm after iteration i. Then OPT − ALG($i+1$) ≤ (OPT − ALG(i))/x. The value of t is chosen such that OPT − ALG(t) < 1. This is true for any $t > \log_x kn$ since OPT ≤ kn. This immediately proves the claimed time bound. Regarding the approximation ratio, note that each M_i increases the max load by at most L. $\square$

By the chain of reductions above, it suffices to focus on f-matching alone. We present an approach for computing approximate f-matchings based on the algorithm of [24] and a reduction of f- to 1-matchings by Shiloach [29].

The basic idea in the algorithm of [24] is to eliminate all augmenting paths up to a certain length: Hopcroft and Karp [18] show how to translate a lower bound on the length of augmenting paths to a lower bound on the approximation ratio in 1-matching. Using Shiloach's reduction, we generalize the result of [18] to f-matchings.

We start by generalizing the notions of augmenting paths and of independent set of augmenting paths to the context of f-matchings. Let M be an f-matching in a graph $G = (V, E)$. Let $\deg_M(v)$ denote the number of edges of M incident with $v \in V$. A node v is called *saturated* if $\deg_M(v) = f(v)$ and *unsaturated* if $\deg_M(v) < f(v)$. An *augmenting path* of M is a non-simple path of odd length that starts and ends at unsaturated nodes and alternates between edges of $E \setminus M$ and M. (A *non-simple path* may visit nodes multiple times but its edges are distinct.) An augmenting path of M may start and end in the same node v, but only if $\deg_M(v) \leq f(v) - 2$.

When augmenting an f-matching M with an augmenting path p, the edges of p with an odd index are added to M and the edges with an even index are removed from M. Observe that $\deg_M(v)$ of a node v increases by exactly $gain(v, p)$ defined as follows:

$$gain(v, p) \overset{\text{def}}{=} \begin{cases} 2 & \text{if } v \text{ is both start- and end-node of } p \\ 1 & \text{if } v \text{ is either start or end-node of } p \\ 0 & \text{otherwise} \end{cases}$$

Using this function, we now give a definition of independent sets of augmenting paths.

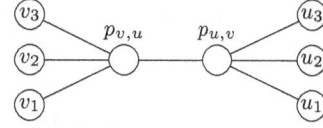

Figure 5: Subgraph of the f-replicated graph corresponding to an edge (v, u), where $f(v) = f(u) = 3$.

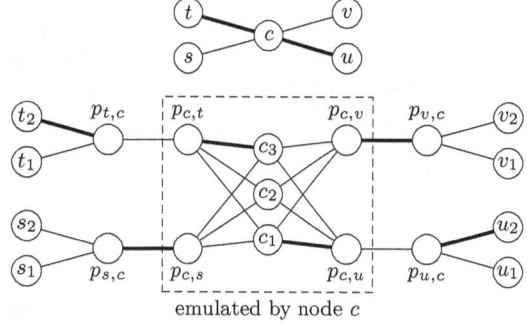

emulated by node c

Figure 6: An f-matching (top) and a corresponding matching in the replicated graph (bottom) with $f(c) = 3$ and $f(s) = f(t) = f(u) = f(v) = 2$.

DEFINITION 5.1. *A set P of augmenting paths of an f-matching M is called* independent *if the augmenting paths in P are pairwise edge-disjoint and for all nodes v,*

$$\sum_{p \in P} gain(v, p) \leq f(v) - \deg_M(v) .$$

If P is an independent set of augmenting paths, then a node v can occur as an internal node of the non-simple paths of P at most $\deg_M(v) \leq f(v)$ times. This is due to the edge-disjointness requirement, since there are exactly $\deg_M(v)$ edges of M incident to a node v. This means, for example, that in the case of 1-matchings (but not in general), all paths in an independent set are node-disjoint.

Shiloach [29] showed that every maximum f-matching in a graph $G = (V_G, E_G)$ has a corresponding maximum 1-matching in a graph $H = (V_H, E_H)$ which is obtained by replacing every edge of G with the subgraph shown in Figure 5. We call H the f-*replicated graph*. It is formally defined as follows:

$$V_H \overset{\text{def}}{=} \{v_i \mid v \in V_G \wedge i \in [1, f(v)]\} \cup \{p_{v,u} \mid (v, u) \in E_G\}$$

$$\begin{aligned} E_H \overset{\text{def}}{=}\ & \{(v_i, p_{v,u}) \mid (v, u) \in E_G \wedge i \in [1, f(v)]\} \\ & \cup \{(p_{v,u}, p_{u,v}) \mid (v, u) \in E_G\} \end{aligned}$$

The nodes v_i with $v \in V_G$ and $i \in [1, f(v)]$ are called *virtual copies* of v. A node $p_{v,u}$ with $(v, u) \in E_G$ is called a *port node*. An edge between two port nodes is called *physical edge*. If f is clear from the context, then f is omitted and H is just called the replicated graph of G.

As we will show, any f-matching M_G has a corresponding 1-matching M_H in the replicated graph such that if M_H has an independent set of augmenting paths, then M_G has an independent set of augmenting paths of the same size. This holds true even if we require M_H to be a *normalized* 1-matching, where a 1-matching is called normalized if it saturates all port nodes. An f-matching M_G of a graph $G = (V_G, E_G)$ and a normalized 1-matching M_H in the replicated graph H are called *corresponding* if $(c, s) \in M_G$ if and only if $(p_{c,s}, p_{s,c}) \notin M_H$. An example of an f-matching and the corresponding 1-matching is shown in Figure 6.

LEMMA 5.10. *Let M_G be an f-matching of a graph $G = (V_G, E_G)$. Then M_G has a corresponding 1-matching M_H in the replicated graph H with $|M_H| = |E_G| + |M_G|$.*

PROOF. Start with the normalized 1-matching $M_H = \{(p_{v,u}, p_{u,v}) \mid (v, u) \in E_G\}$. For each edge $(v, u) \in M_G$, augment M_H with a path $v_i, p_{v,u}, p_{u,v}, u_j$ where i and j are chosen such that v_i and u_j are unsaturated. Clearly, the result is a normalized matching and it contains exactly $|E_G| + |M_G|$ edges. Note that H contains enough unsaturated virtual copies of each node of G for this procedure to complete. □

LEMMA 5.11. *Every augmenting path of a normalized 1-matching M in a replicated graph $H = (V_H, E_H)$ contains an odd number of physical edges and these edges alternate between M and $E_H \setminus M$.*

PROOF. Fix an augmenting path p of M. Recall that p must start at an unsaturated node. Since H is normalized, all unsaturated nodes are virtual copies. Also, any non-simple path of H of odd length that starts at a virtual copy and does not include a physical edge ends at a port node. Hence, p must contain a physical edge.

Also note that any non-simple path of H that starts at a virtual copy and ends with its first physical edge is of even length. Thus, the first physical edge of p must be in M. By symmetry, the last edge of p must also be in M. Furthermore, any non-simple path of H that starts with a physical edge and ends with its second physical edge is of even length. Thus, the physical edges of p must alternate between M and $E_H \setminus M$. □

LEMMA 5.12. *Let M_G be an f-matching in a graph G and let M_H be a corresponding 1-matching in the replicated graph H. If there is an independent set P_H of augmenting paths of M_H, then there is an independent set P_G of augmenting paths of M_G such that $|P_G| = |P_H|$.*

PROOF. The set P_G contains one augmenting path p_G for each $p_H \in P_H$. In the remainder of the proof, we describe how to construct p_G from p_H and show that P_G is indeed independent.

Let p'_H be the subsequence of p_H that contains all physical edges of p_H. Each physical edges $(p_{v,u}, p_{u,v})$ of p'_H corresponds to the edge $(v, u) \in E_G$. We set p_G to the sequence obtained by replacing each edge of p'_H with the corresponding edge of E_G.

By Lemma 5.11, the subsequence of physical edges of p_H alternates between M_H and $E_H \setminus M_H$ and is of odd length. Thus, p_G is of odd length and alternates between $E_G \setminus M_G$ and M_G since M_G and M_H are corresponding. Also, as p_H contains each physical edge at most once, p_G contains each edge at most once. Thus p_G is a valid augmenting path.

The paths in P_G are edge-disjoint as the paths in P_H are edge-disjoint and each physical edge of H corresponds to a different edge of G. It remains to show that for all $v \in V_G$, $\sum_{p \in P_G} gain(v, p) \leq f(v) - \deg_{M_G}(v)$. Fix a node $v \in V_G$. The matching M_H saturates exactly $\deg_{M_G}(v)$ virtual copies of v. The remaining $f(v) - \deg_{M_G}(v)$ virtual copies are unsaturated. We proceed by mapping $gain(v, p_G)$ unsaturated virtual copies of v to each $p_G \in P_G$ which proves the claim.

By construction, p_G with $gain(v, p_G) = 2$ was derived from an augmenting path p_H that starts at v_i and ends at v_j, both distinct unsaturated virtual copies of v. We map v_i and v_j to p_G. If $gain(v, p_G) = 1$, then p_G was derived from an augmenting path p_H that either starts or ends at a virtual copy v_i. We map v_i to p_G. Note that since M_H is a 1-matching, the paths in P_H are vertex-disjoint and thus no virtual copy of v is mapped twice. □

With the above results in place, we now proceed to prove the following generalizations of results in [18].

LEMMA 5.13. *Let M_G and N_G be f-matchings of a graph G. If $|M| = r$, $|N| = s$, and $r > s$, then there is an independent set of at least $s - r$ augmenting paths of M.*

PROOF. Let H be the replicated graph of G. Lemma 5.10 implies that there are two 1-matchings M_H and N_H that correspond to M_G and N_G, resp., and it holds $|N_H| - |M_H| = s - r$. As this lemma is known to hold for 1-matchings [18], we have that M_H has an independent set of at least $s - r$ augmenting paths. Hence, M_G has an independent set of at least $s - r$ augmenting paths by Lemma 5.12. □

THEOREM 5.14. *Let M be an f-matching of a graph G and let s be the cardinality of a maximum f-matching of G. Then M has an augmenting path of length at most $2 \lfloor r/(s-r) \rfloor + 1$ with $r = |M|$.*

PROOF. By Lemma 5.13 there is an independent set P of at least $s - r$ augmenting paths of M. Since the augmenting paths of P are pairwise edge-disjoint, P contains at most r edges from M. On average, an augmenting paths in P contains at most $r/(s-r)$ edges of M. Thus there is at least one augmenting path p of P that contains at most $\lfloor r/(s-r) \rfloor$ edges of M. As the edges of p alternate between $V \setminus M$ and M, the length of p is at most $2 \lfloor r/(s-r) \rfloor + 1$. □

Theorem 5.14 yields the following relation between the approximation ratio and the length of the shortest augmenting path of an f-matching.

COROLLARY 5.15. *If the shortest augmenting path of an f-matching M has length $2x - 1$ for some $x \in \mathbb{N}$, then the approximation ratio of M is at least $(1 - \frac{1}{x})$.*

PROOF. Let $r = |M|$ and let s be the size of a maximum f-matching. By Theorem 5.14 we have $2x - 1 \leq 2 \lfloor r/(s-r) \rfloor + 1$. It follows that $x - 1 \leq r/(s-r)$ and that $r \geq \left(1 - \frac{1}{x}\right) s$ which proves the claim. □

So as in the case of 1-matchings, the approximation ratio of f-matchings is related to the length of the shortest augmenting path. We now show that this relation carries over to the length of the shortest augmenting path of the corresponding 1-matching in the replicated graph.

LEMMA 5.16. *If an f-matching M_G of a graph G has an augmenting path of length x, $x \in \mathbb{N}$, then any corresponding matching M_H of the replicated graph H has an augmenting path of length $3x$.*

PROOF. Let p_G be the augmenting path of M_G. We construct the augmenting path p_H of M_H as follows. The augmenting path p_H consists of x segments of length 3, one per each edge of p_G. Let s_i denote the i-th segment of p_H and

e_i denote the i-the edge of p_G. The second edge of segment s_i is the physical edge $(p_{v,u}, p_{u,v})$ where $e_i = (v, u)$. We continue by specifying the first and last edge of segments s_i with even index (i.e., $e_i \in M_G$) as well as the start-node and end-node of p_H. The first and last edges of all segments s_i with odd index (i.e., $e \notin M_G$) are implied as the $(i+1)$-th segment of p_H starts with the node that the i-th segment ends with.

Let i be even and $e_i = (v, u)$. The first edge of s_i is the edge of M_H that connects a virtual copy of v to $p_{v,u}$. Similarly, the last edge of s_i is the edge of M_H that connects $p_{u,v}$ to a virtual copy of u. It remains to specify the start-node and end-node of p_H.

Let v be the start-node and u the end-node of p_G. Since M_H is corresponding to M_G, there must be at least one unsaturated virtual copy of each v and u. They are chosen as start-node and end-node of p_H. Note that if $v = u$, then at least two virtual copies of v are unsaturated and p_H starts and ends at distinct virtual copies of v. $\square$

COROLLARY 5.17. *Let M_G be an f-matching. If the corresponding 1-matching M_H in the replicated graph does not have augmenting paths of length less than $3(2x - 1)$, $x \in \mathbb{N}$, then the approximation ratio of M_G is at least $(1 - \frac{1}{x})$.*

PROOF. Assume that M_H has no augmenting path of length less than $3(2x - 1)$. Also assume that M_G has an augmenting path of length less than $2x - 1$. Then M_H has an augmenting path of length less than $3(2x - 1)$ by Lemma 5.16 which is a contradiction to the first assumption. Thus the shortest augmenting path of M_G has length at least $2x - 1$ and thus M_G is a $(1 - \frac{1}{x})$-approximation by Corollary 5.15. $\square$

In addition, computations on the replicated graph can be efficiently emulated on the original graph as the following result shows.

LEMMA 5.18. *Let $G = (V, E)$ be a graph, and let $f : V \to \mathbb{N}_0$ be such that $f(v) \leq |V|$ for every $v \in V$. Let A be an algorithm in the CONGEST model. An execution of x rounds of A on the f-replicated graph of G can be emulated by an algorithm running on G in $O(x)$ rounds in the CONGEST model.*

PROOF. Let H be the f-replicated graph of G and $n = |V|$. Then H has $n' = 2m + \sum_{v \in V} f(v) \leq 3n^2$ nodes, namely $f(v)$ virtual copies per node $v \in V$ and 2 port nodes per edge of G.

The emulation of a computation of A on H sends all messages exchanged over a physical edge $(p_{v,u}, p_{u,v})$ over the corresponding edge (v, u) of G. All other communication of A is over an edge $(v_i, p_{v,u})$ which is emulated internally by node v. This is depicted in Figure 6.

Since A is designed for the CONGEST model, each node of the replicated graph transmits at most $O(\log n')$ bits over a physical edge of H per round. Thus the emulation transmits at most $O(\log n') = O(\log n)$ bits per emulated round and edge of G. Hence, it takes $O(1)$ rounds to emulate one round of A running on H. $\square$

The above results on f-matchings hold for general graphs. However, we now shift the focus back to bipartite graphs $G = (C, S, E)$, where C is the set of clients and S the set of servers. Note that if G is bipartite, then a replicated graph

of G is also bipartite. The authors of [24] provide an algorithm for bipartite graphs that computes 1-matchings such that the shortest augmenting path has a length of at least $2x - 1$, where $x \in \mathbb{N}$ is an input parameter of the algorithm. Note that the matching algorithm for general graphs does not have this property. Starting at a matching $M_0 = \emptyset$, the algorithm for bipartite graphs operates in phases. In phase i, the algorithm finds a maximal independent set P_i of augmenting paths of M_{i-1}, where all augmenting paths of P_i are of length $2i - 1$. The matching M_i is then obtained by augmenting M_{i-1} with P_i. In [24] it is shown by induction on i that M_i does not have augmenting paths shorter than length $2i - 1$. Hence, M_x is the desired output of the algorithm. The construction of a maximal independent set of augmenting paths in each phase is randomized. However, with high probability, the independent sets found in all phases are maximal. As shown in [24], the algorithm completes x phases within $O(x^3 \log n)$ rounds in the CONGEST model.

We modify the algorithm to find normalized 1-matchings of the replicated graph. The modified algorithm skips the first phase and starts with the 1-matching M_1 which consists of all physical edges of the replicated graph. Note that M_1 does not have augmenting paths of length 1. Thus, the proofs of [24] apply and by induction on i, M_i does not have augmenting paths shorter than length $2i - 1$. Furthermore, we show that M_i is normalized if M_{i-1} is normalized. Thus, by induction on i, the algorithm computes a normalized matching.

LEMMA 5.19. *If the 1-matching M' is the result of augmenting a normalized 1-matching M of a replicated graph, then M' is also normalized.*

PROOF. Since M' is the result of augmenting M, it holds that $\deg_{M'}(v) \geq \deg_M(v)$ for all nodes v. In particular, this holds for all port nodes. Thus, since M saturates all port nodes, so does M'. $\square$

We summarize our results on the modified bipartite 1-matching algorithm as follows:

LEMMA 5.20. *A normalized 1-matching M of a bipartite replicated graph such that its shortest augmenting path has a length of at least $2x - 1$, $x \in \mathbb{N}$, can be computed within $O(x^3 \log n)$ rounds with messages of $O(\log n)$ bits, where n denotes the number of nodes in the replicated graph.*

We conclude our results on bipartite f-matching with the following result:

THEOREM 5.21. *For any $x > 1$, a $(1 - \frac{1}{x})$-approximate f-matching of a bipartite graph G can be computed in time $O(x^3 \log n)$ in the CONGEST model, where n is the number of nodes of G.*

PROOF. By Lemma 5.20, a normalized 1-matching without any augmenting paths shorter than length $6x - 3$ can be computed in time $O(x^3 \log n')$, where n' is the number of nodes of the replicated graph. Since $n' \leq 3n^2$, we have that $O(x^3 \log n') = O(x^3 \log n)$. By Corollary 5.17, the corresponding f-matching is a $(1 - \frac{1}{x})$-approximation. $\square$

Combining the above result with the reductions of Lemmas 5.8 and 5.9, we obtain

COROLLARY 5.22. *Given a* MINLOAD *instance with uniform sizes and replication factor k and some $x > 1$, an $O(\frac{\log n}{\log x})$-approximate solution can be found w.h.p. in the* CONGEST *model within $O(\frac{x^3 \log^3 n}{\log x})$ rounds.*

If we set $x = 2$, our algorithm computes an $O(\log n)$-approximation of MINLOAD in $O(\log^3 n)$ rounds. We optimize slightly by choosing $x = \frac{\log n}{\log \log n}$ to get an $O(\frac{\log n}{\log \log n})$-approximate solution of MINLOAD in $O(\frac{\log^6 n}{(\log \log n)^4})$ rounds. Another possible choice for our algorithm is $x = n^{1/c}$, for any positive constant c. It then computes an $O(1)$-approximation in $O(n^{3/c} \log^2 n)$ rounds.

By combining Corollary 5.22 with Lemma 5.7, we obtain:

COROLLARY 5.23. *Given a* MINLOAD *instance with non-uniform sizes and replication factor k and some $x>1$, an $O(\frac{\log^2 n}{\log x})$-approximation can be found w.h.p. in the* CONGEST *model within $O(\frac{x^3 \log^4 n}{\log x})$ rounds.*

6. MAXIMAL VS. MAXIMUM COVERAGE

An alternative approach to approximate MINLOAD is via reduction to maximal MAXCOV. If the replication factor is k and file sizes are uniform, then this approach leads to a $O(k \log n)$-approximation of MINLOAD. A central ingredient in the proof is the fact that a maximal solution to MAXCOV is a $\frac{1}{k+1}$-approximation to the optimal solution. In the remainder of this section we prove this algorithm-independent bound and show that it is tight.

Let us first define maximal and maximum solutions to MAXCOV. Given an instance I of MAXCOV, an assignment β which satisfies a client set C is called *maximum* if for every other solution β' for I, the set of satisfied clients C' is such that $|C'| \le |C|$. The solution β is called *maximal* if there is no solution β' for I that strictly extends β, i.e., there is no β' such that $\beta(c) \subseteq \beta'(c)$ for all clients c and $\beta(c) \ne \beta'(c)$ for some client c.

Note that all maximum solutions satisfy the same number of clients, which is the optimum. Regarding maximal solutions, we have the following results. First, we show that the number of satisfied clients in a maximal solution to MAXCOV is at least a $(\frac{1}{k+1})$-fraction of the number of satisfied clients in any maximum solution.

THEOREM 6.1. *Let $I = (G, k, L)$ be a* MAXCOV *instance with uniform file sizes. Let* OPT *be the set of clients satisfied by some optimal solution and* ALG *be the set of clients satisfied by some maximal solution to I. Then $|\text{ALG}| \ge \frac{|\text{OPT}|}{k+1}$.*

PROOF. We shall define a mapping $f : \text{OPT} \to \text{ALG}$, and the claim will follow from showing that $|f^{-1}(c)| \le k+1$ for any $c \in \text{ALG}$. We first define an auxiliary function $g : (\text{OPT} \setminus \text{ALG}) \to S_{\text{ALG}}$, where S_{ALG} is the set of servers with load L in ALG. For a client c, we define $g(c)$ to be an arbitrary server which is used for c under OPT and is fully loaded under ALG. Such a server always exists because otherwise c could be added to ALG, contradicting its maximality. Note that $|g^{-1}(s)| \le |\beta_{\text{OPT}}^{-1}(s)| \le L$ for all $s \in S_{\text{ALG}}$, because under OPT, at most L clients are mapped to s.

We now define f. Let $c \in \text{OPT}$. If $c \in \text{ALG}$, define $f(c) := c$. Suppose now that $c \in \text{OPT} \setminus \text{ALG}$. For this part, we construct f using the following procedure. For any node c', we record whether c' was assigned to c via $g(c)$. Initially

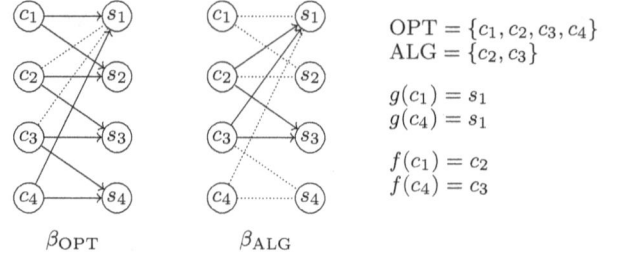

Figure 7: **Example of the construction of the mapping f used in the proof of Theorem 6.1.**

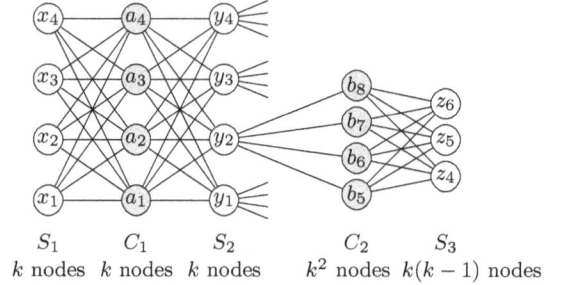

Figure 8: **The graph used in the proof of Theorem 6.2 for $k = 4$. Each node of S_2 is attached to a distinct complete bipartite graph (only one shown) with k clients of C_2 and $k - 1$ servers of S_3.**

no node is assigned this way. To define $f(c)$, we choose any node $c' \in \beta_{\text{ALG}}^{-1}(g(c))$ that was not assigned yet by f via $g(c)$. We set $f(c) := c'$ and we say that c' is assigned to c via $g(c)$. This is possible, because $|\beta_{\text{ALG}}^{-1}(g(c))| = L$, and the number of times we assign f via $g(c)$ is at most $|g^{-1}(g(c))| \le L$. This concludes the construction of f. An example is depicted in Figure 7.

To complete the proof, observe that for all $c \in \text{ALG}$, $|f^{-1}(c)| \le k+1$: it could be that $c \in f^{-1}(c)$, and on top of that, there are k servers s such that $c \in \beta_{\text{ALG}}^{-1}(s)$, and by construction, f assigns a client to c at most once via each of these servers. □

The $\frac{1}{k+1}$ ratio from Theorem 6.1 cannot be improved in general, as made precise in the following result.

THEOREM 6.2. *For any replication factor k and uniform file sizes, there exists a* MAXCOV *instance I_k and a maximal solution ALG_k such that $|\text{ALG}_k| = \frac{|\text{OPT}_k|}{k+1}$, where OPT_k is the set of clients satisfied by an optimal solutions of I_k.*

PROOF. We construct I_k as follows (see Figure 8). There are two sets of clients: $C_1 = \{a_i\}_{i=1}^k$ and $C_2 = \{b_i\}_{i=1}^{k^2}$. There are three sets of servers: $S_1 = \{x_i\}_{i=1}^k$, $S_2 = \{y_i\}_{i=1}^k$, and $S_3 = \{z_i\}_{i=1}^{k(k-1)}$. The edges are defined as follows.
- Each $a_i \in C_1$ is connected to every server from $S_1 \cup S_2$,
- Each $b_i \in C_2$ is connected to $y_{\lceil i/k \rceil} \in S_2$, and
- Each $b_i \in C_2$ is also connected to every $z_j \in S_3$ with $\lceil j/(k-1) \rceil = \lceil i/k \rceil$.

Let all servers have capacity k, i.e., $L := k$. This concludes the description of the instance I_k. (This graph of $2(k^2 + k)$ nodes can be replicated any desired number of times.)

Now, in an optimal solution to I_k, each client in C_1 is assigned all servers in S_1, and each client in C_2 is assigned

$k-1$ servers from S_3 and a single server from S_2. Thus, all $k^2 + k$ clients can be satisfied. On the other hand, consider the solution in which each client in C_1 is assigned all servers in S_2. This is a maximal solution since clearly no other client (namely, from C_2) can be added to this assignment, since all servers in S_2 are fully loaded. Hence, there is a maximal solution with k satisfied clients. The claim follows. $\square$

7. CONCLUSION

This paper considered the backup placement problem which we view as a central problem in network algorithms. We showed that simple random placements perform very badly in terms of placement quality, and that selfish local improvement may run a very long time until stabilization is reached. Our algorithm uses at its core a distributed matching procedure, and thus it can guarantee, with high probability, both polylog running time and a good approximation ratio. Several open problems remain, including

- The sequential complexity of MaxCov with replication factor $k = 2$ remains open: it is solvable in polynomial time with $k = 1$ while it is NP-hard with $k \geq 3$.
- Can MinLoad be approximated distributively to within $(1 + \epsilon)$ in polylogarithmic time?
- Is there an improvement over the classify-and-select technique used in the non-uniform case?

A collateral result of our paper is a distributed approximation algorithm for f-matching in bipartite graphs. It remains open whether it can be extended to general graphs.

8. REFERENCES

[1] O. Amini, D. Peleg, S. Pérennes, I. Sau, and S. Saurabh. On the approximability of some degree-constrained subgraph problems. *Discrete Applied Mathematics*, 160(12):1661–1679, 2012.

[2] B. Awerbuch. Complexity of network synchronization. *J. ACM*, 32(4):804–823, 1985.

[3] Y. Azar. *Online Algorithms: The State of the Art*, volume 1442 of *LNCS*, chapter On-line load balancing, pages 178–195. Springer, 1998.

[4] Y. Azar, J. Naor, and R. Rom. The competitiveness of on-line assignments. *J. Algorithms*, 18(2):221–237, 1995.

[5] L. Barenboim, M. Elkin, S. Pettie, and J. Schneider. The locality of distributed symmetry breaking. In *53rd FOCS*, pages 321–330, 2012.

[6] D. Bokal, B. Brešar, and J. Jerebic. A generalization of hungarian method and Hall's theorem with applications in wireless sensor networks. *Discrete Applied Mathematics*, 160(4-5):460–470, 2012.

[7] A. Czygrinow, M. Hańćkowiak, E. Szymańska, and W. Wawrzyniak. Distributed 2-approximation algorithm for the semi-matching problem. In *26th DISC*, pages 210–222, 2012.

[8] A. Dessmark, O. Garrido, and A. Lingas. A note on parallel complexity of maximum f-matching. *Inform. Process. Lett.*, 65(2):107–109, 1998.

[9] G. Dósa and L. Epstein. The convergence time for selfish bin packing. In *7th SAGT*, pages 37–48, 2014.

[10] E. Even-Dar, A. Kesselman, and Y. Mansour. Convergence time to Nash equilibrium in load balancing. *ACM T. Algorithms*, 3(3), 2007.

[11] J. Fakcharoenphol, B. Laekhanukit, and D. Nanongkai. Faster algorithms for semi-matching problems. In *37th ICALP*, pages 176–187, 2010.

[12] M. Gairing, T. Lücking, M. Mavronicolas, and B. Monien. The price of anarchy for restricted parallel links. *Parallel Processing Letters*, 16(1):117–131, 2006.

[13] F. Galčík, J. Katrenič, and G. Semanišin. On computing an optimal semi-matching. In *37th WG*, pages 250–261, 2011.

[14] N. Garg, T. Kavitha, A. Kumar, K. Mehlhorn, and J. Mestre. Assigning papers to referees. *Algorithmica*, 58(1):119–136, 2010.

[15] M. Hańćkowiak, M. Karoński, and A. Panconesi. A faster distributed algorithm for computing maximal matchings deterministically. In *18th PODC*, pages 219–228, 1999.

[16] N. J. A. Harvey, R. E. Ladner, L. Lovász, and T. Tamir. Semi-matchings for bipartite graphs and load balancing. *J. Algorithms*, 59(1):53–78, 2006.

[17] E. Hazan, S. Safra, and O. Schwartz. On the complexity of approximating k-set packing. *Computational Complexity*, 15(1):20–39, 2006.

[18] J. E. Hopcroft and R. M. Karp. An $n^{5/2}$ algorithm for maximum matchings in bipartite graphs. *SIAM J. Comput.*, 2(4):225–231, 1973.

[19] V. Kann. Maximum bounded 3-dimensional matching is MAX SNP-complete. *Inform. Process. Lett.*, 37(1):27–35, 1991.

[20] J. Katrenič and G. Semanišin. Maximum semi-matching problem in bipartite graphs. *Discussiones Mathematicae Graph Theory*, 33(3):559–569, 2013.

[21] S. Köhler, V. Turau, and G. Mentges. Self-stabilizing local k-placement of replicas with minimal variance. In *14th SSS*, pages 16–30, 2012.

[22] C. Koufogiannakis and N. E. Young. Distributed algorithms for covering, packing and maximum weighted matching. *Distributed Computing*, 24(1):45–63, 2011.

[23] S. Lahaie, D. M. Pennock, A. Saberi, and R. V. Vohra. *Algorithmic Game Theory*, chapter Selfish Load Balancing, pages 699–716. Cambridge University Press, 2007.

[24] Z. Lotker, B. Patt-Shamir, and S. Pettie. Improved distributed approximate matching. In *20th SPAA*, pages 129–136, 2008.

[25] C. P. Low. An approximation algorithm for the load-balanced semi-matching problem in weighted bipartite graphs. *Inform. Process. Lett.*, 100(4):154–161, 2006.

[26] A. Panconesi and R. Rizzi. Some simple distributed algorithms for sparse networks. *Distributed Computing*, 14(2):97–100, 2001.

[27] B. Patt-Shamir, D. Rawitz, and G. Scalosub. Distributed approximation of cellular coverage. *J. Parallel Distr. Com.*, 72(3):402–408, 2012.

[28] D. Peleg. *Distributed Computing: A Locality-sensitive Approach*. SIAM, 2000.

[29] Y. Shiloach. Another look at the degree constrained subgraph problem. *Inform. Process. Lett.*, 12(2):89–92, 1981.

Better Deterministic Online Packet Routing on Grids

Guy Even
School of Electrical
Engineering
Tel Aviv University
Tel Aviv 6997801, Israel
guy@eng.tau.ac.il

Moti Medina
LIAFA
Université Paris Diderot
75205 Paris Cedex 13, France
moti.medina@liafa.univ-
paris-diderot.fr

Boaz Patt-Shamir*
School of Electrical
Engineering
Tel Aviv University
Tel Aviv 6997801, Israel
boaz@tau.ac.il

ABSTRACT

We consider the following fundamental routing problem. An adversary inputs packets arbitrarily at sources, each packet with an arbitrary destination. Traffic is constrained by link capacities and buffer sizes, and packets may be dropped at any time. The goal of the routing algorithm is to maximize throughput, i.e., route as many packets as possible to their destination. Our main result is an $O(\log n)$-competitive deterministic algorithm for an n-node uni-directional line network (i.e., 1-dimensional grid), requiring only that buffers can store at least 5 packets, and that links can deliver at least 5 packets per step. We note that $O(\log n)$ is the best ratio known, even for randomized algorithms, even when allowed large buffers and wide links. The best previous deterministic algorithm for this problem with constant-size buffers and constant-capacity links was $O(\log^5 n)$-competitive. Our algorithm works like admission-control algorithms in the sense that if a packet is not dropped immediately upon arrival, then it is "accepted" and guaranteed to be delivered. We also show how to extend our algorithm to a polylog-competitive algorithm for any constant-dimension uni-directional grid.

Categories and Subject Descriptors

C.2.1 [**Computer-Communication Networks**]: Network Architecture and Design—*Packet-switching networks, Store and forward networks*; F.2.2 [**Analysis of Algorithms and Problem Complexity**]: Nonnumerical Algorithms and Problems—*Routing and layout, Sequencing and scheduling*; G.2.2 [**Discrete-Mathematics**]: Graph Theory—*Network problems*

Keywords

Online Algorithms; Packet Routing; Bounded Buffers; Admission Control; Grid Networks

*Supported in part by the Israel Science Foundation (grant No. 1444/14) and by the Israel Ministry of Science and Technology.

1. INTRODUCTION

The core function of any packet-switching network is to route packets from their origins to their destinations, but many fundamental questions about packet routing are far from being well understood. In this paper we consider one of these questions, namely the *competitive throughput network model*, introduced by [3].

Briefly, the model is as follows. The network consists of n nodes (switches) connected by point-to-point unidirectional communication links, and we are given two positive integer parameters, B and c, called the buffer size and link capacity, respectively. Executions proceed as follows. Packets are input by an adversary over time. Each packet is input at its *source* node with a given *destination* node. At each step, each packet is either forwarded over an incident link, stored in its current location buffer, or dropped (i.e., removed from the system). Storing and forwarding are subject to the constraints that a buffer can store at most B packets simultaneously and that a link can carry at most c packets in a time step. These constraints can be met for all input sequences since the model allows for packets to be dropped at any time. The *routing algorithm* selects, at each step, which packets are forwarded, which are stored, and which are dropped. The goal of the algorithm is to maximize the number of packets delivered at their destination. Since we consider on-line algorithms, we evaluate algorithms by their competitive ratio, i.e., the minimum ratio, over all finite packet input sequences, between the number of packets delivered by the on-line algorithm and the maximum number of packets that can be delivered by any (off-line) constraint-respecting schedule.

It is nearly an embarrassment to find that very little is known about this problem, even in the simplest case, where the network topology is the trivial n-node unidirectional line. In this work we provide an improved deterministic algorithm for networks whose topology is a d-dimensional grid.

1.1 Our Results

Our main result is a centralized *deterministic* $O(\log n)$-competitive packet routing algorithm for unidirectional lines with n nodes. The algorithm requires buffer size $B \geq 5$ and link capacity $c \geq 5$. In addition, both B and c must be $O(\log n)$. We show how to extend the algorithm to d dimensions, where the competitive ratio is $O(\log n)^d$, assuming that $B, c \geq 2^{d+1} + 1$. Our algorithm is *nonpreemptive*, namely, packets are dropped only at the time of their arrival (similarly to admission control policies, which "accept" or "reject" requests upon arrival). By contrast, preemptive

Ref.	Dim.	Comp. Ratio	Deterministic?	Range of B, c	Remarks
[11, 12, 13]	1	$O(\log n)$	✓	$B, c > \log n,\ B/c = n^{O(1)}$	immediate from s-t reduction
[4]	1	$O(\log^3 n)$	—	$B \geq 2, c = 1$	
[7]	1	$O(\log^2 n)$	—	$B \geq 2, c = 1$	FIFO buffers
[11, 13]	1	$O(\log n)$	—	$B \in [1, \log n], c \geq 1$	also for $\log n \leq B/c \leq n^{O(1)}$
[12, 13]	1	$O(\log^5 n)$	✓	$[3, O(\log n)]$	preemptive
[12, 13]	d	$O(\log^{d+4} n)$	✓	$[3, O(\log n)]$	preemptive
Theorem 11	1	$O(\log n)$	✓	$[5, O(\log n)]$	
Theorem 19	d	$O(\log n)^d$	✓	$[2^{d+1} + 1, O(\log n)]$	

Table 1: *Some results for centralized online algorithms for packet routing. The networks are uni-directional grids. In the special case of $B = 0$ and $c \geq 3$, the algorithm in [12, 13] is $O(\log^{d+2} n)$-competitive.*

algorithms may drop packets at any time, i.e., packets are not guaranteed to reach the destination even after they start traversing the network. The best previous deterministic algorithm [12, 13] is preemptive.

Table 1 provides a summary of our results and a comparison of our algorithm with some previous results along various aspects.

1.2 Overview of Techniques

We first explain our approach for the 1-dimensional case.

The high-level idea is to reduce packet routing in a graph G to circuit switching (or path packing, see [15, 6]) in the *space-time graph* $G \times T$, where T denotes the set of time steps. This so-called space-time transformation has been used extensively in this context [5, 2, 7, 16, 11, 12, 13]. To be effective, the space-time transformation requires an upper bound on path lengths which does not result in losing too much throughput. We use the bound of [12, 13] (which extends [7]), that ensures that the loss is at most some constant fraction. After the transformation, we have an instance of *online path packing* [6, 9]. It is known that if the capacities are large enough, i.e., $\log n \leq B, c \leq n^{O(1)}$, then online path packing is solvable with logarithmic competitive ratio [6, 11, 12, 13]. We overcome the difficulty that B and c are $O(\log n)$ by employing a technique called *tiling*, i.e., partitioning the network nodes into large enough subgrids. Tiling has been used in the past [15, 8, 11, 12, 13]; in our algorithm, we use 4 distinct tilings, and work on each of them independently. Each tiling induces a new graph called the *sketch graph* whose nodes are the tiles. The capacity of the edges in the space-time graph between adjacent tiles is $O(\log n)$ to allow for applying $O(\log n)$-competitive path packing algorithms. Path packing algorithms over the sketch graph produce sketch paths for accepted packets. Thus, after these preliminary simplifications, we arrive at the subtask of *detailed routing*, in which coarse sketch paths must be expanded to paths in the original space-time graph.

Fractional Optimum. Key to our application of the path-packing algorithm is the analysis of Buchbinder and Naor [9, 10], which bounds the performance of the algorithm w.r.t. the *fractional* optimum, which may deliver packet fractions. This result allows us to scale buffer sizes and link capacities up and down while keeping the competitive ratio under control.

Combining algorithms. Another central component in the analysis of our algorithm is the combination technique introduced by Kleinberg and Tardos [15]. Loosely speaking, this technique deals with an admission control algorithm that is the conjunction of two competitive algorithms, the state of which depends only on the requests accepted by both. The technique enables one to prove that the competitive ratio of the combined algorithm is the sum (rather than the product) of the competitive ratios of the constituent algorithms.

1.3 Previous Work

Algorithms for dynamic routing on networks with bounded buffers have been studied extensively both in theory and in practice (see, e.g., [1] and references therein). Let us first focus on centralized algorithms for d-dimensional grids. We note that while centralized algorithms for packet routing were always relevant for switch scheduling, recently the idea of centralization of network functions, including route computation, gained substantial additional traction due to the concept of software-defined networks (SDN). See, e.g., [14]. The special case of 2-dimensional grids (with or without buffers) is of particular interest as this is the underlying topology of crossbars in switches [17].

Online Algorithms for Unidirectional Lines. There is a series of papers on uni-directional line networks, starting with [3], which introduced the model. In [3], a lower bound of $\Omega(\sqrt{n})$ was proved for the greedy algorithm on unidirectional lines if the buffer size $B \geq 2$. For the case $B = 1$ (in a slightly different model), an $\Omega(n)$ lower bound for any deterministic algorithm was proved by [7, 4]. Both [7] and [4] developed, among other things, online randomized centralized algorithms for uni-directional lines with $B \geq 2$. In [4] an $O(\log^3 n)$-competitive randomized centralized algorithm was presented for $B \geq 2$. In addition, it is proved in [4] that nearest-to-go[1] is $\tilde{O}(\sqrt{n})$-competitive for $B \geq 2$. For the case $B = 1$, [4] presented a randomized $\tilde{O}(\sqrt{n})$-competitive distributed algorithm. (This algorithm also applies to rooted trees when all packet are destined at the root.) In [7], an $O(\log^2 n)$-competitive randomized algorithm was presented for the case $B \geq 2$. (This algorithm also applies to rings and trees.) In [11], an $O(\log n)$-competitive, nonpreemptive, randomized algorithm was presented. The algorithm in [11] is applicable to a wide range of buffer sizes and link capac-

---

[1]The policy that gives priority to packets according to the remaining distance to the destination.

ities, including the case $B = c = 1$. In [12], an $O(\log^5 n)$-competitive deterministic algorithm was presented. The algorithm in [12] is applicable for $B, c \in [3, \log n]$.

Online Algorithms for Unidirectional Grids. Angelov et al. [4] showed that the competitive ratio of greedy algorithms in unidirectional 2-dimensional grids is $\Omega(\sqrt{n})$ and that nearest-to-go policy achieves a competitive ratio of $\tilde{\Theta}(n^{2/3})$. In [12], an $O(\log^6 n)$-competitive deterministic algorithm was presented. An extension of this algorithm to d-dimensional unidirectional grids, with competitive ratio $O(\log^{d+4} n)$, is presented in [12].

For more related results, refer to [13].

Organization.

The problem is formalized in Section 2. In Section 3 we explain the reduction of packet-routing to path packing, and the construction of sketch graph. In Section 4 we describe the overall algorithm, and in Section 5 we analyze it. Sections 3–5 deal with the 1-dimensional grid (line); extension to the d dimensional case is also discussed in Section 6.

2. MODEL AND PROBLEM STATEMENT

We consider the standard model of synchronous store-and-forward packet routing networks [3, 4, 7]. The network is modeled by a directed graph $G = (V, E)$, and by two integer parameters $B, c > 0$. For the most part of this paper, we consider a network whose topology is a *directed line* of n vertices, i.e., $V = \{v_0, \ldots, v_{n-1}\}$, $E = \{(v_{i-1}, v_i) \mid 0 < i < n\}$.

Execution proceeds in discrete steps. In step t, an arbitrary set of *requests* is input to the algorithm. Each request represents a packet, and we will use both terms interchangeably. A request is specified by a 3-tuple $r_i = (a_i, b_i, t_i)$, where $a_i \in V$ is the *source node* of the packet, $b_i \in V$ is its *destination node*, and $t_i \in \mathbb{N}$ is the time step in which the request is input.

In each time step, the *routing algorithm* removes packets that reached their destination, and decides, for each packet currently in the network, including packets input in the current step, whether (i) to drop the packet, or (ii) to send it over an incident link, or (iii) to store it in the current node. The selection of the action is done subject to the following considerations.

- If a packet is dropped, it is lost forever.
- A packet sent from node u over link (u, v) at time t will be located at node v at time $t + 1$. The *link capacity constraint* asserts that at any step, at most c packets can be sent over each link.
- A packet stored at node u at time t will be located at node u at time $t + 1$. The *buffer capacity constraint* asserts that at any step, at most B packets can be stored in each buffer.

We use the following terminology. A packet $r_i = (a_i, b_i, t_i)$ is said to be *input* (or arrive) at a_i at time t_i. We say that r_i is *rejected* if it is dropped at time t_i, otherwise it is *accepted*. (Our algorithm will guarantee that all accepted packets arrive at their destination.)

Given a set of requests, the *throughput* of a packet routing algorithm is the number of packets that are delivered to their destination. We consider the problem of maximizing the throughput of an online centralized deterministic packet-routing algorithm. By *online* we mean that by time t, the algorithm received as input only requests that have been input by time t. By *centralized* we mean that the algorithm

receives all requests and controls all packets currently in the system without delay. By *nonpreemptive* we mean that every accepted packet reaches its destination.

Competitive Ratio. Let σ denote an input sequence. Let ALG denote a packet-routing algorithm. Let ALG(σ) denote the throughput obtained by ALG on input σ. Let OPT(σ) denote the largest possible subset of requests in σ that can be delivered without violating the capacity constraints. We say that an online deterministic ALG is ρ-*competitive*, if for every input sequence σ, $|\text{ALG}(\sigma)| \geq \frac{1}{\rho} \cdot |\text{OPT}(\sigma)|$. Our goal is to design an algorithm with the smallest possible competitive ratio.

3. FIRST STEPS

In this section we present preliminary simplifications we apply to the problem. They include reducing the packet routing on a line problem to path packing on grids, and then path packing on sketch graphs.

3.1 From Packet-Routing on a Line to Path Packing in a Grid

Let $G = (V, E)$ denote a directed line with link capacities c and buffer sizes B. The space-time grid of $G = (V, E)$ is a directed acyclic infinite graph $G^{st} = (V^{st}, E^{st})$ with edge capacities $c^{st}(e)$, where (i) $V^{st} \triangleq V \times \mathbb{N}$. Each vertex $v \in V$ has infinitely many copies in the space-time grid G^{st}; namely, vertex $(v, t) \in V^{st}$ is the copy of v that corresponds to time t. (ii) $E^{st} \triangleq E_0 \cup E_1$ where E_0 denotes forward edges and E_1 denotes the store edges. Formally, $E_0 \triangleq \{(u, t) \to (v, t+1) : (u, v) \in E, t \in \mathbb{N}\}$ and $E_1 \triangleq \{(u, t) \to (u, t+1) : u \in V, t \in \mathbb{N}\}$. (iii) The capacity of all edges in E_0 is c, and all edges in E_1 have capacity B.

The transformation. We transform a request $r_i = (a_i, b_i, t_i)$ for routing a packet in the directed line G to a path request $r_i^{st} = ((a_i, t_i), \text{row}(b_i))$ in the grid G^{st}. The correctness of the reduction is based on a one-to-one correspondence between paths in G^{st} and a routing of a packet in G. Each vertical edge $(v_i, t) \to (v_{i+1}, t+1)$ in G^{st} corresponds to forwarding a packet from v_i to v_{i+1} in step t, and each horizontal edge $(v_i, t) \to (v_i, t+1)$ in G^{st} corresponds to storing a packet in v_i in step t.

Embedding in the plane. The naïve depiction of G^{st} maps vertex (v_i, t) to the point (t, i) in the plane (i.e., the x-axis is the time axis and the y-axis is the "vertex-index" axis). This embedding of G^{st} results with a lattice of vertices in which edges are either horizontal or diagonal. We prefer the embedding in which the edges are axis parallel, which means that vertex (v_i, t) is mapped to the point $(t - i, i)$. In the axis-parallel depiction, all the copies of a vertex $v_i \in V$ still reside in the ith row. However, column j corresponds to a traversal of the complete line, starting at v_0 at time j and ending at v_{n-1} at time $j + n - 1$.

3.2 From One Grid to Four Sketch Graphs

Given a grid generated by the transformation above, we apply another transformation to produce a coarsened version, called the *sketch graph*. Specifically, we use *tiling*. Tiling is a partition of the grid nodes into $\ell_h \times \ell_v$ subgrids, where ℓ_h and ℓ_v are parameters to be determined later. We also add dummy nodes to the space-time grid G^{st} to complete all tiles. This augmentation has no effect on routing because a dummy vertex does not belong to any route between real vertices.

The tiling is specified by two additional parameters ϕ_x and ϕ_y called *offsets*. The offsets determine the positions of the corners of the tiles; namely, the left bottom corner of the tiles are located in the points $(\phi_x + i \cdot \ell_h, \phi_y + j \cdot \ell_v)$, for $i, j \in \mathbb{N}$. The algorithm uses four offsets $(\phi_x, \phi_y) \in \{-\ell_h/2, 0\} \times \{-\ell_v/2, 0\}$. We denote these four tilings by $T_1, \ldots, T_4$.

PROPOSITION 1. *For every vertex (v, t) of the space-time grid G^{st}, there exists exactly one tiling T_j such that (v, t) is in the south-west quadrant of a tile of T_j.*

Proposition 1 suggests a partitioning of the requests.

DEFINITION 2. *A request $r_i = (a_i, b_i, t_i)$ is in SW$_j$ if the source vertex (a_i, t_i) of request r_i belongs to the south-west quadrant of a tile in the tiling T_j.*

The Sketch Graphs. Each tiling T_j induces a grid, called the sketch graph, each vertex of which corresponds to a tile. The sketch graph induced by T_j is denoted by $S_j \triangleq (V(S_j), E(S_j))$, where $V(S_j)$ is the set of tiles in T_j. There is a directed edge $(s_1, s_2) \in E(S_j)$ if $s_1 \neq s_2$ and $E^{st} \cap (s_1 \times s_2) \neq \emptyset$. All edges in the sketch graph are assigned unit capacity.

3.3 Online Packing of Paths

We use the sketch graphs to solve *path packing* problems. Intuitively, the path packing model resembles the packet routing model, except that there are no buffers, and that each link e may have a different capacity $c(e)$. In addition, we generalize the notion of a request to allow for a set of destinations (similar to "anycast") as follows. Usually, the destination of a request consists of a single vertex. If G is a directed graph, then it is easy to reduce the case in which the destination is a subset to the case in which the destination is a specific vertex. The reduction simply adds a sink node that is connected to every vertex in the destination subset. In our setting of space-time grid, the destination subset is a row. Thus it suffices to add a sink node for each row (as in [7]).

Formally, a *path request* r_i in G is a pair (a_i, D_i), where $a_i \in V$ is the source vertex and $D_i \subseteq V$ is the destination subset. Let $P(r_i)$ denote the set of paths that can be used to serve request r_i; namely, every path $p \in P(r_i)$ begins in a_i, ends in a vertex in D_i, and satisfies some additional constraint (e.g., bounded length, bounded number of turns, etc.). Given a sequence $R = \{r_i\}_{i \in I}$ of path requests, we call a sequence $P = \{p_i\}_{i \in J}$ a *partial routing* of R if $J \subseteq I$ and $p_i \in P(r_i)$ for every $i \in J$. The *load* of an edge $e \in E$ induced by P is the ratio $\frac{|\{p_j \in P : e \in p_j\}|}{c(e)}$. A partial routing of a set of path requests is called a β-*packing* if the load induced on each edge is at most β. The *throughput* of P is simply the number $|J|$ of paths in P.

Integral and Fractional Partial Routings.

In the integral scenario, a path request is either served by a single path or is not served. In *fractional routing*, a request r_i can be (partially) served by a combination of paths $p_1, \ldots, p_k$. Namely, each path p_j serves a fraction λ_j of the request, where $\lambda_j \geq 0$ for all j and $\sum_j \lambda_j \leq 1$. We refer to $\sum_j \lambda_j$ as the *flow amount* of request r_i. The *load* of an edge

$e \in E$ induced by request r_i is the ratio $\sum_{j : e \in p_j} \lambda_j / c(e)$. A fractional solution is β-packing if the total load on in each edge, from all requests, is at most β. The *throughput* of a fractional routing is the sum of the flow amounts of all requests. Given a fractional routing g, we use $|g|$ to denote its throughput. Trivially, the maximum throughput attainable by a fractional β-packing is an upper bound on the maximum throughput attainable by an integral β-packing. An optimal-throughput fractional β-packing can be computed off-line by solving a linear program.

Online Path Packing: Problem and Solution.

In the online path packing problem, the input is a sequence of path requests $R = \{r_i\}_{i \in I}$. Upon arrival of a request r_i, the algorithm must either allocate a path $p \in P(r_i)$ to r_i or reject r_i. An online path packing algorithm is said to be (α, β)-*competitive* if it computes a β-packing whose throughput is at least $1/\alpha$ times the maximum throughput over all 1-packings. Note that for online path packing, we assume that all edges have capacity at least 1.

The online path packing algorithm in [6] (analyzed also by [9]) assigns weights to the edges that are exponential in the load of the edges. This load is the load incurred by the paths allocated to the requests that have been accepted so far. The algorithm is based on an oracle that is input r_i and the edge weights, and outputs a lightest path p_i in $P(r_i)$. If the weight of p_i is large, then request r_i is rejected; otherwise, request r_i is routed along p_i. We refer to the online algorithm for online integral path packing by IPP. The competitive ratio of the IPP algorithm is summarized in the following theorem.

THEOREM 3 ([13], FOLLOWING [6, 9]). *Consider an online path packing problem on an infinite graph with edge capacities such that $\inf_e c(e) \geq 1$. Assume that, for every request r_i, the length of every legal path in $P(r_i)$ is bounded by $p_{\max}$. Then algorithm IPP is $(2, \log(1 + 3 \cdot p_{\max}))$-competitive online integral path packing algorithm. Moreover, the throughput of IPP for any request sequence is at least $1/2$ the throughput of any fractional packing for that sequence.*

Bounded Path Lengths.

The load obtained by the IPP algorithm is logarithmic in the maximum path length $p_{\max}$. This suggests that $p_{\max}$ should be polynomial in n. Lemma 4 states that limiting the number of store steps per packet by a polynomial in n decreases the fractional throughput only by a constant factor.

We use the following notation. Given a request sequence $R = \{r_i\}_i$, let $f^*(R)$ denote a maximum throughput fractional 1-packing of R, and let $f^*(R|p_{\max})$ denote a maximum throughput fractional 1-packing with respect to R under the constraint that each path is of length at most $p_{\max}$.

LEMMA 4 (AFTER [7]). *Let $p_{\max} \triangleq 2n \cdot (1 + \frac{B}{c})$. Then $|f^*(R|p_{\max})| > 0.31 \cdot |f^*(R)|$.*

3.4 Routing paths across 2-d Grids

Consider the following special case of routing in grids. Suppose that each path request has a specific source vertex which resides on either the south or the west side, and the

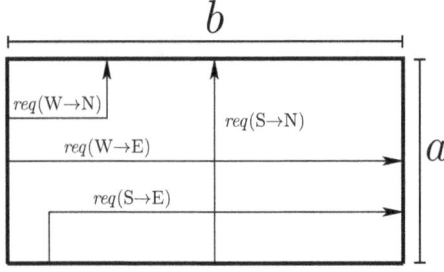

Figure 1: *An $a \times b$ grid. The four types of requests (i.e., $req(W\to N), req(S\to N), req(W\to E), req(S\to E)$) are depicted by the four arrows.*

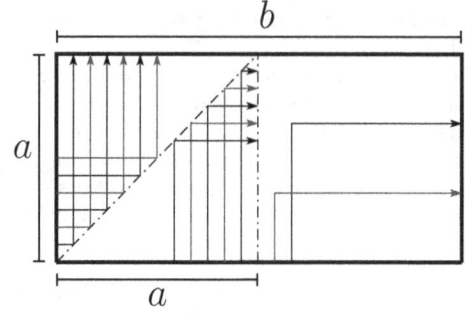

Figure 2: *Satisfying the path requests in the $a \times b$ two dimensional directed grid, where $a \le b$.*

destination is either the north or the east side (i.e., we can route to any vertex on the requested side). For $X \in \{S, W\}$ and $Y \in \{N, E\}$, let $req(X \to Y)$ denote the set of path requests whose source is in the X side and whose destination is the Y side (see Figure 1). The following claim establishes sufficient and necessary conditions for satisfying such path requests. We refer to the routing algorithm used in this case as *crossbar routing*.

PROPOSITION 5 (CROSSBAR ROUTING). *The path requests can be packed in the 2-dimensional $a \times b$ directed grid if and only if $|req(W \to E)| + |req(S \to E)| \le a$ and $|req(W\to N)| + |req(S\to N)| \le b$.*

PROOF. The "only if" part is obvious. We now present a distributed algorithm that proves the "if" part. Without loss of generality, we may assume that $req(S\to N)$ and $req(W \to E)$ are empty. This assumption is satisfied by routing such requests along straight paths and giving them precedence over other requests. Thus we may ignore these lines henceforth, and we are left with the task of routing $req(S \to E)$ and $req(W \to N)$ under the assumption that $|req(S\to E)| \le a$ and $|req(W\to N)| \le b$.

These requests are served as follows. Order the rows from bottom to top and the columns from left to right. Assume, w.l.o.g., that $a \le b$ (the case that $a > b$ is solved analogously). Requests whose source vertex is in the first a rows or columns turn in the vertex along the diagonal emanating from the SW corner. For example, a request in $req(W\to N)$ whose source is in row i is routed eastward for i hops, and then north for $a - i$ hops (i.e., to the north side of the grid). See Figure 2.

The requests whose source vertex is in the last $b - a$ columns are routed northward until they reach a vertex that does not receive an east-bound path from its west neighbor. Once such a vertex is found, the path turns east and continues straight until it reaches the east side of the grid. Indeed, such a right turn is always possible because $a \ge |req(S\to E)|$ and hence a "vacant row" is always found. $\square$

REMARK 6. *Proposition 5 extends to the case of capacitated edges assuming all horizontal edges have the same capacity and all vertical edges have the same capacity. In this case, the requests can be routed iff the number of requests for each destination side is bounded by total capacity of edges crossing that side.*

Algorithm 1 Top-level algorithm for packet routing in the 1-dimensional grid. Code for step t.

1: Let R_t be a list of new requests, sorted by source-destination distance.
2: For each vertex v, let $R'_t(v)$ the first $B' + c'$ requests in R_t whose source is v. ▷ filter requests
3: **for** each request $r_i \in \bigcup_v R'_t(v)$ **do**
4:     **if** $r_i \in Near$ **then** ROUTE-NEAR(r_i)
5:     **else**
6:         Let $j \in \{1, \ldots, 4\}$ be s.t. $r_i \in SW_j$ ▷ classify r_i
7:         $sketch_i \leftarrow$ IPP$(S_j, accepted_j, r_i)$ ▷ path lengths bounded by p_{max}
8:         $init_i \leftarrow$ INITIAL-ROUTE$(accepted_j, r_i)$
9:         **if** $sketch_i \ne$ REJECT and $init_i \ne$ REJECT **then**
10:             add r_i to $accepted_j$
11:             DETAILED-ROUTE$(r_i, init_i, sketch_i)$▷ update routes
12:         **else** Reject r_i
13:         **end if**
14:     **end if**
15: **end for**

---

4. THE PACKET ROUTING ALGORITHM

We now present the routing algorithm. Pseudo-code is provided in Algorithm 1. The algorithm works as follows. First, in lines 1-3, an initial filtering of the requests removes requests if too many requests originate in the same space-time vertex (see Definition 9). Then each remaining new request is processed. In lines 4-6, it is classified as either *Near* or *Far*, based on its source-destination distance (see paragraph on packet classification). *Near* requests are routed by the ROUTE-NEAR algorithm, described in Section 4.4. Each *Far* request is associated with the tiling T_j in which its source vertex belongs to a south-west quadrant of a tile. Each tiling is processed separately by three procedures: (i) The IPP algorithm, which performs online path packing over the sketch graph S_j (line 7). The outcome $sketch_i$ is either "REJECT" or a path in a sketch graph S_j, i.e., a sequence of tiles from the initial tile to the destination tile. (ii) The INITIAL-ROUTE procedure looks for a routing within the SW-quadrant of the first tile of r_i: its outcome is either such a path denoted $init_i$ or "REJECT". Only IPP and INITIAL-ROUTE may reject a far request. If both procedures are successful, then DETAILED-ROUTE is called (line 8). Detailed routing computes a path in the space-time graph, i.e., a complete schedule for each packet. In our algorithm, the sketch path for each accepted request is computed once and it is fixed, but the future part of a detailed route of a request may change due to the insertion of new packets. Therefore, the procedure DETAILED-ROUTE not only computes a path for r_i in G^{st}, but may also alter the detailed routes of other requests (without changing the high-level sketch-graph routes).

An important property of IPP and INITIAL-ROUTE is that their state is determined by the requests that are actually in the system, i.e., accepted by both. (Rejected requests by either do not affect the state of the system.) This property enables us to employ the combination technique of [15]. The listing emphasizes this property by explicitly managing the sets of accepted requests for each class (denoted by $accepted_j$). These sets are arguments of IPP and INITIAL-ROUTE and determine their states. We now proceed to explain the algorithm in detail.

Packet classification.

A request $r_i = (a_i, b_i, t_i)$ is called *near* if $b_i - a_i \leq \ell_v$, and *far* otherwise. We denote the sets of near and far requests by *Near* and *Far*, respectively. The far requests are further classified into four classes denoted by Far_j, where $Far_j \triangleq Far \cap \text{sw}_j$. Namely, Far_j is the set of far requests whose source node is in the SW-quadrant of a tile s in the tiling T_j.

Link Multiplexing.

After classification, there are five classes of requests: one for *Near* and one for each tiling. Routes for each class are computed independently and the final result is the union of routes over all classes. This is made possible by partitioning the capacity of each edge in the space-time grid into virtual *tracks*, one track per class. The capacity of each track is $\frac{1}{5}$ of the capacity of the edge, rounded down, i.e., track capacities are $B' \triangleq \lfloor B/5 \rfloor$ and $c' \triangleq \lfloor c/5 \rfloor$. (This explains why we require that $B, c \geq 5$.)

Tiling Parameters.

Tile side lengths are set so that the trivial greedy routing algorithm is $O(\log n)$-competitive for requests that can be satisfied within a tile. Each tile has length ℓ_h and height ℓ_v, defined as follows. Recall that the maximum path length $p_{\max} = 2n \cdot (1 + \frac{B}{c})$ (cf. Lemma 4).

DEFINITION 7. *We use the following parameters.*
- $k \triangleq \log(1 + 3 \cdot p_{\max})$
- $\ell_h = 30 \cdot \lceil \frac{k}{5c'} \rceil$ *and* $\ell_v = 30 \cdot \lceil \frac{k}{5B'} \rceil$

We summarize with the following claim.

PROPOSITION 8. *If B/c is bounded by a polynomial in n, then the tiling parameters satisfy the following properties.*
1. *$\ell_h + \ell_v = O(\log n)$.*
2. *The sum of the edge capacities along each tile side is $\Theta(k)$.*
3. *For each track type, the sum of the track capacities of this type along a tile side is at least $6k$.*

PROOF. Clearly $\ell_h + \ell_v = O(k)$. If B/c is polynomial in n, then $k = O(\log n)$. The sum of the edge capacities along a vertical side is $\ell_v \cdot B = \Theta(k)$. The sum of the track capacities crossing a vertical side of a tile is at least $\ell_v \cdot B' \geq 6k$. The capacities along a horizontal edge is bounded similarly. □

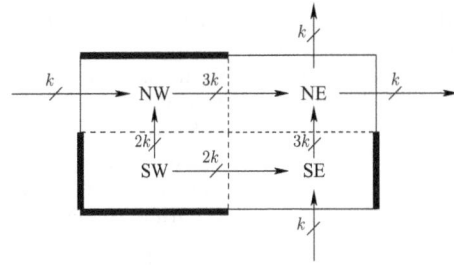

Figure 3: The quadrants of a tile. Traversing requests may not cross the thick border lines. Upper bounds on the number of paths in each class that traverse the quadrant sides follow from the path packing algorithm IPP.

Filtering superfluous simultaneous requests with identical sources.

Since we do not impose any restriction on the requests, it could well be that many requests arrive at the same source vertex in a single time step. To deal with that, we use that fact that for each node v and step t, no more than $c + B$ requests can leave (v, t) in *any* routing. The partition of link capacities for tracks imposes a stricter limitation in the sense that within each class, no more than $c' + B'$ paths can have the same source vertex.

DEFINITION 9. *Given a sequence R of requests, let R' denote the subsequence of R defined as follows. For each source vertex (a_i, t_i), choose $c' + B'$ packets whose destination is closest to the source node. (If at most $B' + c'$ requests originate at the same node, then all of them are kept in R'.)*

Proposition 14 shows that rejecting the requests in $R \setminus R'$ reduces the fractional optimal throughput only by a constant factor.

4.1 Routing Rules

The routing at the high level (sketch path) is determined by the IPP algorithm. We now explain the ideas behind refining these rough paths (in the sketch graph) into actual paths (in the space-time grid). Throughout this section we consider, w.l.o.g., a single tiling T_j.

Fix a tile s in T_j. We distinguish between the following three types of requests in Far_j (we deal with *Near* requests in Section 4.4).
- *Initial requests:* requests whose source vertex is in the south-west quadrant of the tile s.
- *Traversing requests:* these are requests that enter s from a specific vertex on one side (either west or south) and must leave through any vertex of another side (either east or north). The entry vertex is determined by a previously-invoked detailed routing, and the exit side is determined by the sketch path.
- *Final requests:* these are requests whose sketch path ends in tile s. The destination of a final request is the north side of s.[2]

Each tile is partitioned into 4 quadrants, denoted NE, SE, SW and NW. We constrain the way requests are routed

---

[2] The detailed path for r_i should end in a copy of the destination vertex b_i in s. As any path that reaches the north side of s also reaches a copy of b_i, we use the pessimistic assumption that $row(b_i)$ is the northmost row of tile s.

within a tile using the following rules (see Figure 3; no request may cross a thick line).

1. Initial requests always start in the SW-quadrant and are routed to the north or east side of the SW-quadrant along a straight path. The SW-quadrant of each tile is reserved for routing of initial requests.
2. Traversing requests whose source and destination sides are opposite (e.g., from the south to the north side) are routed along a straight path.
3. Paths enter the tile either in the east half of the south side or the north half of the west side.
4. Paths exit the tile through either the east half of the north side or the north half of the east side.

4.2 Procedure INITIAL-ROUTE

Initial routing takes place in the SW-quadrant of the first tile of a *Far* request. The goal of INITIAL-ROUTE is modest: route the request to the boundary of the SW-quadrant. This is done greedily along straight paths if possible: it may be the case that some of the edges are already reserved for another request (also routed by INITIAL-ROUTE of the same tile). If no straight path is available, INITIAL-ROUTE returns REJECT. This means that incoming traffic (of earlier requests) continues uninterrupted along a straight path. Only remaining capacity along edges that emanate from a vertex (i, j), if any, is used for routing the requests that originate in (i, j).

4.3 Procedure DETAILED-ROUTE

The goal in detailed routing is to compute a detailed path p_i in the space-time graph G^{st} given a sketch path $sketch_i$ in the sketch graph S_j and the initial part of the route $init_i$. The sketch path specifies the sequence of tiles to be traversed by the detailed path. In addition, the sketch path specifies the tile sides through which the detailed path should enter and exit each tile. Requests that have been assigned a sketch path and an initial route must be successfully routed by detailed routing.

Detailed routing is computed by applying crossbar routing (cf. Proposition 5) to the NW, SE and NE quadrants. This routing is computed based on the present requests. As new requests arrive, the future portions of the detailed routes may change dynamically so that all requests which are "in progress" will reach their destination. Below we argue that crossbar routing indeed succeeds.

CLAIM 10. *Detailed routing successfully completes the route of each accepted far request.*

PROOF. By Proposition 5, to ensure successful routing it is sufficient to bound the number of paths that need to traverse a quadrant by the capacity of the quadrant side. By Proposition 8, the track capacity of each quadrant side is at least $3k$. We now prove upper bounds on the number of paths that traverse each quadrant side (see Figure 3). The IPP path packing algorithm is a k-packing over the sketch graph (whose edges have unit capacity). It follows that at most k paths traverse each side of the tile. As every request that originates in the SW-quadrant of a tile must exit the tile, there are at most $2k$ paths that traverse each side of the SW-quadrant (although their sum is also bounded by $2k$). Hence the upper bounds depicted in Figure 3 follow. We need to elaborate more on the NE-quadrant because it is also used for routing final requests (i.e., requests that do not

exit the tile, but do want to reach its top row). Consider the north side of the NE-quadrant. There are at most k traversing requests that wish to exit the tile. In addition, there are at most $2k$ final requests that wish to reach to top row (as each final far request must have entered the tile). Thus, in total there are at most $3k$ paths that wish to reach the top side of the NE-quadrant. To summarize, the number of paths that wish to reach any quadrant side is bounded by the side's capacity, and hence by Proposition 5, detailed routing succeeds. $\square$

Finally, we note that in order for DETAILED-ROUTE to be well defined, we compute it in tiles in column-major order, i.e., we start with the bottom tile of the leftmost column and go up, then the bottom tile of the second-from left column and go up etc. This ensures that when we reach a tile, all input vertices are fixed. We remark that detailed routing can be executed in a local distributed manner; in each time step, each vertex needs only to know the initial paths and the sketch paths of the incoming packets.

4.4 Procedure ROUTE-NEAR

Finally, we describe the algorithm for the near requests. The ROUTE-NEAR Algorithm is extremely simple: it never stores a packet (i.e., it uses only vertical edges in G^{st}, and gives precedence to older requests). In more detail, upon arrival of a request $r_i \in Near$, the algorithm checks the number of requests already routed along the outgoing vertical edge (from (a_i, t) to $(a_i + 1, t + 1)$). If this number is less than c', then the algorithm routes r_i along the vertical path in G^{st} from (a_i, t) to $(b_i, t + (b_i - a_i))$. Note that these edges occur in the future, and hence cannot have been saturated by ROUTE-NEAR if the edge outgoing from (a_i, t) is not saturated. If there is no free capacity in the outgoing vertical edge, r_i is rejected. Note that if r_j is accepted, then it guaranteed to reach its destination.

5. ANALYSIS OF COMPETITIVE RATIO OF THE ROUTING ALGORITHM

In this section we prove the following theorem for a directed line G of n vertices with buffer sizes B and link capacities c, where $B, c \in [5, \log n]$.

THEOREM 11. *Algorithm 1 is $O(\log n)$-competitive with respect to the throughput of a maximum fractional routing.*

We translate the problem to a path packing problem over the space-time graph G^{st}. Let $f^*_{G^{st}}(R)$ denote a maximum throughput fractional routing, and let $|f^*_{G^{st}}(R)|$ denote its throughput. Let $|\text{ALG}(R)|$ denote the throughput of Algorithm 1. Theorem 11 follows directly from the following lemma.

LEMMA 12. *For every sequence of requests R, $|f^*_{G^{st}}(R)| \leq O(\log n) \cdot |\text{ALG}(R)|$.*

We outline the proof of Lemma 12. We scale the capacities down by a factor of $\Theta(k) = \Theta(\log n)$ in the sketch graph. By linearity, this reduces the optimal fractional throughput by the same factor (see Proposition 13). We show that the filtering stage in Line 2 incurs only a constant factor reduction to the optimal fractional throughput (see Proposition 14). The filtered request set R' are partitioned into near requests and far requests (which are further partitioned into 4 classes, one per tiling). The far and near requests are analyzed separately. The analysis of the throughput for far requests builds on the competitive ratio of the IPP algorithm and the INITIAL-ROUTE algorithm (see Claim 15 and Claim 16). By applying the combining analysis of Kleinberg and Tardos [15], we show that the competitive ratio for the combined algorithm is the sum of the two algorithms (see Claim 17). In Theorem 18, we show that the ROUTE-NEAR algorithm succeeds in routing a logarithmic fraction of the filtered near requests. In Section 5.4, the parts of the proof are combined together to prove Lemma 12.

5.1 Scaling and Filtering

One advantage of working with fractional routings is that, by linearity, the throughput scales exactly with the capacities. Let $f^*_{S_j}(R)$ denote a maximum throughput fractional routing in the sketch graph S_j. Recall that the sketch graph has unit capacities. Coalescing of vertices of G^{st} in each tile results with edge capacities that are $\Theta(k) = \Theta(\log n)$. Hence, we obtain the following proposition.

PROPOSITION 13. $|f^*_{S_j}(R)| = \frac{1}{\Theta(k)} \cdot |f^*_{G^{st}}(R)|$.

Recall that by Definition 9, in the input sequence R', at most $B' + c'$ requests originate in each space-time vertex.

PROPOSITION 14. $|f^*_{G^{st}}(R)| \leq 9 \cdot |f^*_{G^{st}}(R')|$.

PROOF. Fix a space-time vertex $v = (a_i, t_i)$. Let R_v (reps. R'_v) denote requests in R (reps. R') that originate in v. Let $f = f^*_{G^{st}}(R)$. Consider the flow $f/9$. For every vertex v, the amount of flow that originates in v is bounded by $(B+c)/9 \leq B' + c'$. Divert flow from in $f/9$ from $R_v \setminus R'_v$ to R'_v along shorter paths, to obtain a flow g with respect to R' such that $|g| = |f|/9$. Since $|f^*_{G^{st}}(R')| \geq |g|$, the proposition follows. □

5.2 Far Requests

Two algorithms determine whether a far request is rejected: (i) the IPP path packing algorithm over the sketch graph, and (ii) the INITIAL-ROUTE algorithm that deals with routing in the initial SW-quadrant of the source tile. We begin by showing that, if invoked separately, each of these algorithms accepts at least a constant fraction of the maximum fractional throughout over the sketch graph.

Let R'_j denote the subsequence of requests in R' that are in the class Far_j. Suppose we invoke the IPP algorithm in isolation over the sketch graph S_j with the input sequence R'_j. By isolation we mean that the accepted requests are determined solely by IPP. Let $|\text{IPP}_{S_j}(R'_j)|$ denote the number of requests that are accepted by this invocation.

CLAIM 15. $|f^*_{S_j}(R'_j)| \leq \frac{2}{0.31} \cdot |\text{IPP}_{S_j}(R'_j)|$.

PROOF. By Lemma 4, the restriction of the path lengths by $p_{\max}$ only reduces the fractional throughput by a factor less than 0.31. By Theorem 3, the IPP algorithm is $(2, k)$-competitive, and hence its throughput is half the optimal fractional throughput with bounded path lengths. □

Let $|\text{INITIAL-ROUTE}(R'_j)|$ denote the number of requests that are accepted by INITIAL-ROUTE if invoked in isolation with the input sequence R'_j.

CLAIM 16. $|f^*_{S_j}(R'_j)| \leq 2 \cdot |\text{INITIAL-ROUTE}(R'_j)|$.

PROOF. A far request must exit the tile in which it begins. The edge capacities in the sketch graph are unit. Hence, the amount of flow in $f^*_{S_j}(R'_j)$ that originates in each tile is at most 2. On the other hand, if a positive amount of flow originates in a tile s, then at least one request starts in the SW-quadrant of s. Hence INITIAL-ROUTE(R'_j) accepts at least one request that begins in s. □

A naïve analysis of the requests accepted by the conjunction of the IPP and INITIAL-ROUTE algorithms implies that the accepted requests are in the intersection, which might be empty. However, in our algorithm the subsequence of accepted requests is determined by both algorithms, and this set of accepted requests determines the state of both algorithms. Hence, by applying the combining analysis of Kleinberg and Tardos [15], the combined competitive ratio is shown to be the sum of the isolated competitive ratios.

CLAIM 17. $f^*_{S_j}(R'_j) \leq \left(2 + \frac{2}{0.31}\right) \cdot |\text{ALG}(R'_j)|$.

PROOF. To simplify notation, let A_1 denote the IPP algorithm in isolation, A_2 denote the INITIAL-ROUTE algorithm in isolation, and ALG denote the combined algorithm. Let I denote the input sequence R'_j.

Consider the execution of ALG with the input sequence I. Let X denote the subsequence of requests accepted by the combined algorithm A on input I (i.e., $X = A(I)$). Let X_ℓ denote the subsequence of requests accepted by algorithm A_ℓ during this same execution. Note that $X = X_1 \cap X_2$. Let us rewrite $f^*_{S_j}(I)$ as a function $f^* : I \to [0, 1]$ in which $f^*(i)$ equals the amount of flow assigned to request $i \in I$ by $f^*_{S_j}(I)$. We abuse notation and view X also as its characteristic function (i.e., $X(i) = 1$ if and only if $i \in X$).

Consider the packet routing version in which requests have demands in $[0, 1]$. A demand of 1 corresponds to the situation till now. A demand of zero means that the request does not appear (the input skips over this request). A fractional demand means that (i) at most this fraction can be routed by the fractional routing, and (ii) the request only occupies this fraction of the capacity of an edge. Fractional demand functions can be added and multiplied. If both functions are integral, then addition corresponds to the union, and multiplication corresponds to the intersection.

Consider the demand function $Z_\ell \triangleq X + f^* \cdot (1 - A_\ell)$, for $\ell \in \{1, 2\}$. First, note that it attains values in $[0, 1]$ because (i) an accepted request $i \in X$ satisfies $A_\ell(i) = 1$, and (ii) a rejected request $i \notin X$ satisfies $X(i) = 0$. Note also that $f^* \cdot (X + 1 - A_\ell)$ is a feasible fractional flow with respect to the demand Z_ℓ, hence

$$|f^*_{S_j}(Z_\ell)| \geq \|f^* \cdot (X + 1 - A_\ell)\|_1. \tag{1}$$

We claim that the isolated algorithm A_ℓ on input Z_ℓ accepts exactly X. To prove this consider the sequence of states of $A_\ell(Z_\ell)$ and $A(X)$. Let S^i_ℓ denote the prefix of accepted requests by $A_\ell(Z_\ell)$ till but not including the arrival of request i. Similarly, let X^i denote the prefix of accepted requests by $A(X)$ till but not including the arrival of request i. If $S^i_\ell = X^i$, for every i, then $A_\ell(Z_\ell) = X$. Now we prove that $S^i_\ell = X^i$ by induction on i. Before the first request, both sets are empty. The induction step for $i \in X$ is easy because A_ℓ accepts i when the state is X^i. On the other hand, if $i \notin X$ and $Z_\ell(i) > 0$, then $A_\ell(i) = 0$.

Let CR_ℓ denote the competitive ratio of A_ℓ. Then

$$|f^*_{S_j}(Z_\ell)| \leq CR_\ell \cdot A_\ell(Z_\ell) = CR_\ell \cdot |X| \tag{2}$$

By Equations 1 and 2

$$\|f^* \cdot (X + 1 - A_\ell)\|_1 \leq CR_\ell \cdot |X|. \qquad (3)$$

Observe that $1 \leq (X + 1 - A_1) + (X + 1 - A_2)$. Indeed, if $i \in X$, then $A_1(i) = A_2(i) = 1$, so both sides equal 1. If $i \notin X$, then $A_1(i)$ or $A_i(2)$ equals zero (perhaps both), and hence the right hand side is at least 1. Hence,

$$\|f^*\|_1 \leq \|f^* \cdot (X + 1 - A_1)\|_1 + \|f^* \cdot (X + 1 - A_2)\|_1$$
$$\leq CR_1 \cdot |X| + CR_2 \cdot |X|,$$

and the claim follows. $\square$

5.3 Near Requests

In this section we analyze the competitive ratio of the ROUTE-NEAR algorithm with respect to near requests. Recall that: (1) A request is a near request if the distance from the source to the destination is at most ℓ_v. Note that $\ell_v = \Theta(\frac{\log n}{B})$ and $B < \log(1 + 3p_{\max}) = O(\log n)$. (2) The incoming requests are filtered so that at most $B' + c'$ requests originate in every space-time vertex.

The following theorem states that ROUTE-NEAR succeeds in routing at least a logarithmic fraction of the filtered near requests. This theorem implies that the throughput is at least a logarithmic fraction of the optimal fractional routing of the filtered near requests.

THEOREM 18. $|\text{ALG}(Near)| \geq \Omega(\frac{1}{\log n}) \cdot |Near|$.

PROOF. It suffices to prove that $|\text{ALG}(Near)| \geq \Omega\left(\frac{1}{\log n}\right) \cdot |Near \setminus \text{ALG}(Near)|$. Consider the following bipartite conflict graph. Nodes on side L are the requests of $\text{ALG}(Near)$, and nodes on side R are the requests of $Near \setminus \text{ALG}(Near)$. There is an edge $(r_i, r_j) \in L \times R$ if r_j is rejected by the ROUTE-NEAR Algorithm and the vertical route of r_i traverses the source vertex (a_j, t_j) of r_j. A request $r_i \in L$ conflicts with at most $B' + c'$ requests in each vertex. Hence, the degree of r_i in the conflict graph is at most $(B' + c') \cdot \ell_v$. On the other hand, the degree of $r_j \in R$ equals c' (where c' is the capacity of the track reserved for the near requests). By counting edges on each side we conclude that

$$\sum_{r_i \in L} \deg(r_i) = \sum_{r_j \in R} \deg(r_j).$$

Hence,

$$(B' + c') \cdot \ell_v \cdot |L| \geq c' \cdot |R|.$$

We conclude that

$$|L| \geq \frac{c'}{(B' + c')\ell_v} \cdot |R|.$$

As $\frac{(B'+c')\ell_v}{c'} = \Theta(\frac{\log n}{c'} + \frac{\log n}{B'}) = O(\log n)$, and the theorem follows. $\square$

5.4 Putting Things Together

In this section we prove Lemma 12. We partition the input sequence R' into $Near$ and R'_j, for $j \in \{1, 2, 3, 4\}$ (recall that $R'_j = R' \cap Far_j$). By subadditivity,

$$|f^*_{G^{st}}(R')| \leq |f^*_{G^{st}}(Near)| + \sum_{j=1}^{4} |f^*_{G^{st}}(R'_j)|, \qquad (4)$$

$$|\text{ALG}(R')| = |\text{ALG}(Near)| + \sum_{j=1}^{4} |\text{ALG}(R'_j)|. \qquad (5)$$

In order to bound the ratio $|f^*_{G^{st}}(R')|/|\text{ALG}(R')|$, it suffices to separately bound the ratios of the terms. Indeed, by Theorem 18

$$|f^*_{G^{st}}(Near)| \leq O(\log n) \cdot |\text{ALG}(Near)|.$$

By Proposition 13 and Claim 17,

$$|f^*_{G^{st}}(R'_j)| \leq O(\log n) \cdot |\text{ALG}(R'_j)|.$$

Finally, by Proposition 14, $|f^*_{G^{st}}(R)| \leq 9 \cdot |f^*_{G^{st}}(R')|$. Since $\text{ALG}(R) = \text{ALG}(R')$, the lemma follows.

6. EXTENSION TO D-DIMENSIONAL GRIDS

The following theorem is proved by extending Algorithm 1 for a line network to d-dimensional grid.

THEOREM 19. For $B, c \in [2^{d+1} + 1, \log n]$, there is a deterministic $O(\log n)^d$-competitive online algorithm for the throughput maximization problem.

PROOF (SKETCH). As in the one-dimensional case, perform a space-time transformation on the d-dimensional n-node grid G to obtain the $(d + 1)$-dimensional space-time grid G^{st}. Partition G^{st} to $\ell_1 \times \ldots \times \ell_{d+1}$ subgrids (or subcubes). The side length of a subgrid equals ℓ_v for directions that correspond to forward steps and ℓ_h in the direction that corresponds to store steps. There are two offsets per dimension, resulting with 2^{d+1} tilings. The number of tracks equals the number of offsets plus one (the extra one is for the near requests), hence we require that $B, c \geq 2^{d+1} + 1$. Similarly to the 1-dimensional case, a request is classified as a near request if the distance from the source to the destination is at most $d \cdot \ell_v$.

Detailed routing within a tile is successful by the following observation. Every time a packet cannot turn to the direction that is dictated by its sketch path, there is a packet that did turn to its desired direction. Consider a packet whose sketch path exits a tile via an edge parallel to the time axis (an analogous argument holds for the edges in other directions). The number of paths emanating the tile along edges parallel to the time axis is bounded by $k = O(\log n)$. On the other hand, the track capacity of the edges parallel to the time axis in a quadrant's side is $B' \cdot \ell_h/2$. Since $B' \cdot \ell_h/2 \geq k$, it follows that every packet will eventually turn, if needed, within its quadrant, thus respecting its sketch path.

Since the link capacity to track capacity ratio is $O(2^d)$, this scaling of capacities incurs an $O(2^d)$ factor to the competitive ratio. The sketch graph is obtained in the same way (the number of paths that IPP routes out of a $(d + 1)$-dimensional tile is at most $(d + 1) \cdot O(\log n)$). The ratio of edge capacities in G^{st} between adjacent faces of tiles and the capacity of the edge in the sketch graph is $O(\log n)^d$. This incurs an additional factor of $O(\log n)^d$ for routing far requests due to capacity scaling. The routing of near requests succeeds in routing at least a fraction of $d \cdot O(\log n)$ of the near requests. We conclude that the competitive ratio is determined by the far requests, and hence the theorem follows. $\square$

7. CONCLUSION

In this paper we presented an online deterministic packet routing algorithm. For the one dimensional grid (with constant-size buffers and constant-capacity links), this algorithm closes the gap with the best throughput achieved by a randomized algorithm. This closes a problem which was open for more than a decade, but still leaves open quite a few problems. The most urgent one is to reduce the gap between the upper and lower bounds on the competitive ratio. Currently the best upper bound is $O(\log n)$ for the line, and we are not aware of any no non-trivial lower bound. We note that reducing the upper bound to $o(\log n)$ seems to require new techniques, as the reduction to online path packing introduces a logarithmic factor in the competitive ratio.

Another important question is to come up with reasonable distributed algorithms. Even though, as mentioned above, the SDN model shifts many network operation tasks to the centralized setting, it is very interesting to find out what can be done without a central coordinator.

8. REFERENCES

[1] M. Adler, S. Khanna, R. Rajaraman, and A. Rosén. Time-constrained scheduling of weighted packets on trees and meshes. *Algorithmica*, 36(2):123–152, 2003.

[2] M. Adler, A. L. Rosenberg, R. K. Sitaraman, and W. Unger. Scheduling time-constrained communication in linear networks. *Theory Comput. Syst.*, 35(6):599–623, 2002.

[3] W. Aiello, E. Kushilevitz, R. Ostrovsky, and A. Rosén. Dynamic routing on networks with fixed-size buffers. In *SODA*, pages 771–780, 2003.

[4] S. Angelov, S. Khanna, and K. Kunal. The network as a storage device: Dynamic routing with bounded buffers. *Algorithmica*, 55(1):71–94, 2009. (Appeared in APPROX-05).

[5] B. Awerbuch, Y. Azar, and A. Fiat. Packet routing via min-cost circuit routing. In *ISTCS*, pages 37–42, 1996.

[6] B. Awerbuch, Y. Azar, and S. Plotkin. Throughput-competitive on-line routing. In *FOCS '93: Proceedings of the 1993 IEEE 34th Annual Foundations of Computer Science*, pages 32–40, Washington, DC, USA, 1993. IEEE Computer Society.

[7] Y. Azar and R. Zachut. Packet routing and information gathering in lines, rings and trees. In *ESA*, pages 484–495, 2005. (See also manuscript in http://www.cs.tau.ac.il/~azar/).

[8] Y. Bartal and S. Leonardi. On-line routing in all-optical networks. In *ICALP*, pages 516–526, 1997.

[9] N. Buchbinder and J. S. Naor. Improved bounds for online routing and packing via a primal-dual approach. *Foundations of Computer Science, Annual IEEE Symposium on*, 0:293–304, 2006.

[10] N. Buchbinder and J. S. Naor. The design of competitive online algorithms via a primal-dual approach. *Foundations and Trends in Theoretical Computer Science*, 3(2-3):99–263, 2009.

[11] G. Even and M. Medina. An $O(\log n)$-Competitive Online Centralized Randomized Packet-Routing Algorithm for Lines. In *ICALP (2)*, pages 139–150, 2010.

[12] G. Even and M. Medina. Online packet-routing in grids with bounded buffers. In *Proc. 23rd Ann. ACM Symp. on Parallelism in Algorithms and Architectures (SPAA)*, pages 215–224, 2011.

[13] G. Even and M. Medina. Online packet-routing in grids with bounded buffers. *CoRR*, abs/1407.4498, 2014.

[14] N. Gude, T. Koponen, J. Pettit, B. Pfaff, M. Casado, N. McKeown, and S. Shenker. Nox: Towards an operating system for networks. *SIGCOMM Comput. Commun. Rev.*, 38(3):105–110, July 2008.

[15] J. M. Kleinberg and É. Tardos. Disjoint paths in densely embedded graphs. In *FOCS*, pages 52–61, 1995. (See also manuscript in http://www.cs.cornell.edu/home/kleinber/).

[16] H. Räcke and A. Rosén. Approximation algorithms for time-constrained scheduling on line networks. In *SPAA*, pages 337–346, 2009.

[17] J. S. Turner. Strong performance guarantees for asynchronous buffered crossbar scheduler. *IEEE/ACM Trans. Netw.*, 17(4):1017–1028, 2009.

APPENDIX

A. $O(\sqrt{\log n})$-COMPETITIVENESS OF INITIAL ROUTING

LEMMA 20. *Fix a tile s and let q denote its SW quadrant. Suppose that the sources of m path requests are in q. Then $\Omega(\sqrt{m})$ path requests are served by the initial routing in q.*

PROOF. We restrict attention to rows of q which contain at least B' sources and columns of q which contain at least c' sources of requests which cannot be routed horizontally. Since all other packets are trivially routed by the algorithm, we may assume w.l.o.g. that there are no other packets with sources in q.

Let y denote the number of rows that contain a source vertex of an initial request, and let x denote the number of columns that contain a source vertex of an initial request that is not routed horizontally. Clearly, $m \leq xy(B' + c')$. On the other hand, detailed routing in q serves $yB' + xc'$ requests. We now prove that $yB' + xc' = \Omega(\sqrt{xy(B' + c')})$.

Without loss of generality, assume that $c' \geq B'$. Thus it suffices to prove that

$$\sqrt{\frac{y}{x}} \cdot B' + \sqrt{\frac{x}{y}} \cdot c' = \Omega(\sqrt{c'}).$$

We proceed with case analysis. If $y \leq x$, then $\sqrt{\frac{y}{x}} \cdot B' + \sqrt{\frac{x}{y}} \cdot c' \geq c'$, as required. Otherwise $y > x$. We further distinguish between two cases:

1. If $y/x \geq c'/B'$, then $\sqrt{\frac{y}{x}} \cdot B' + \sqrt{\frac{x}{y}} \cdot c' \geq \sqrt{\frac{c'}{B'}} \cdot B' \geq \sqrt{c'}$, as required.

2. If $x/y > B'/c'$, then $\sqrt{\frac{y}{x}} \cdot B' + \sqrt{\frac{x}{y}} \cdot c' \geq \sqrt{\frac{B'}{c'}} \cdot c' \geq \sqrt{c'}$, as required.

$\square$

Note that, if a single requested is input to a SW-quadrant, then initial routing accepts it.

Minimizing the Total Weighted Completion Time of Coflows in Datacenter Networks

Zhen Qiu, Cliff Stein and Yuan Zhong

Dept. of Industrial Engineering and Operations Research, Columbia University
New York, NY 10027, USA
zq2110@columbia.edu, cs2035@columbia.edu, yz2561@columbia.edu

ABSTRACT

Communications in datacenter jobs (such as the shuffle operations in MapReduce applications) often involve many parallel flows, which may be processed simultaneously. This highly parallel structure presents new scheduling challenges in optimizing job-level performance objectives in data centers.

Chowdhury and Stoica [11] introduced the coflow abstraction to capture these communication patterns, and recently Chowdhury et al. [13] developed effective heuristics to schedule coflows. In this paper, we consider the problem of efficiently scheduling coflows with release dates so as to minimize the total weighted completion time, which has been shown to be strongly NP-hard [13]. Our main result is the first polynomial-time deterministic approximation algorithm for this problem, with an approximation ratio of $67/3$, and a randomized version of the algorithm, with a ratio of $9 + 16\sqrt{2}/3$. Our results use techniques from both combinatorial scheduling and matching theory, and rely on a clever grouping of coflows. We also run experiments on a Facebook trace to test the practical performance of several algorithms, including our deterministic algorithm. Our experiments suggest that simple algorithms provide effective approximations of the optimal, and that our deterministic algorithm has near-optimal performance.

1. INTRODUCTION

With the explosive growth of data-parallel computation frameworks such as MapReduce [14], Hadoop [1, 8, 32], Spark [36], Google Dataflow [2], etc., modern data centers are able to process large-scale data sets at an unprecedented speed. A key factor in materializing this efficiency is parallelism: many applications written in these frameworks alternate between computation and communication stages, where a typical computation stage produces many pieces of intermediate data for further processing, which are transferred between groups of servers across the network. Data transfer within a communication stage involves a large col-

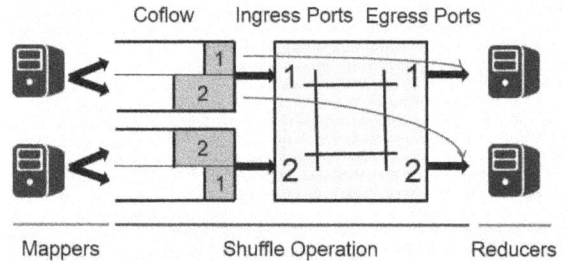

Figure 1: A MapReduce application in a 2×2 network

lection of parallel flows, and a computation stage often cannot start until all flows within a preceding communication stage have finished [12, 15].

While the aforementioned parallelism creates opportunities for faster data processing, it also presents challenges for network scheduling. In particular, traditional networking techniques focus on optimizing flow-level performance such as minimizing flow completion times, and ignore application-level performance metrics. For example, the time that a communication stage completes is the time that the last flow within that stage finishes, so it does not matter if other flows of the same stage complete much earlier than the last.

To faithfully capture application-level communication requirements, Chowdhury and Stoica [11] introduced the *coflow* abstraction, defined to be a collection of parallel flows with a common performance goal. Effective scheduling heuristics were proposed in [13] to optimize coflow completion times. In this paper, we are interested in developing scheduling algorithms with provable performance guarantees, and our main contribution is a deterministic polynomial-time $67/3$-approximation algorithm and a randomized polynomial-time $(9 + 16\sqrt{2}/3)$-approximation algorithm, for the problem of minimizing the total weighted completion time of coflows with release dates. These are the first $O(1)$-approximation algorithms for this problem. We also conduct experiments on real data gathered from Facebook, in which we compare our deterministic algorithm and its modifications to several other algorithms, evaluate their relative performances, and compare our solutions to an LP-based lower bound. Our algorithm performs well, and is much closer to the lower bound than the worst-case analysis predicts.

1.1 System Model

The network.

In order to describe the coflow scheduling problem, we first need to specify the conceptual model of the datacenter network. Similar to [13], we abstract out the network as one giant *non-blocking* switch [4, 6, 19, 29] with m *ingress ports* and m *egress ports* – which we call an $m \times m$ network switch – where m specifies the network size. Ingress ports represent physical or virtual links (e.g., Network Interface Cards) where data is transferred from servers to the network, and egress ports represent links through which servers receive data. We assume that the transfer of data within the network switch is *instantaneous*, so that any data that is transferred out of an ingress port is immediately available at the corresponding egress port. There are capacity constraints on the ingress and egress ports. For simplicity, we assume that all ports have unit capacity, i.e., one unit of data can be transferred through an ingress/egress port per unit time. See Figure 1 for an example of a 2×2 datacenter network switch. In the sequel, we sometimes use the terms *inputs* and *outputs* to mean ingress and egress ports respectively.

Coflows.

A *coflow* is defined as a collection of parallel flows with a common performance goal. We assume that all flows within a coflow arrive to the system at the same time, the *release date* of the coflow. To illustrate, consider the shuffling stage of a MapReduce application with 2 mappers and 2 reducers that arrives to a 2×2 network at time 0, as shown in Figure 1. Both mappers need to transfer intermediate data to both reducers. Therefore, the shuffling stage consists of $2 \times 2 = 4$ parallel flows, each one corresponding to a pair of ingress and egress ports. For example, the size of the flow that needs to be transferred from input 1 to output 2 is 2. In general, we use an $m \times m$ matrix $D = (d_{ij})_{i,j=1}^m$ to represent a coflow, in a $m \times m$ network. d_{ij} denotes the size of the flow to be transferred from input i to output j. We also assume that flows consist of discrete data units, so their sizes are integers.

Scheduling constraints.

Since each input can transmit at most one data unit and each output can receive at most one data unit per time slot, a *feasible* schedule for a single time slot can be described by a *matching* between the inputs and outputs. When an input is matched to an output, a corresponding data unit (if available) is transferred across the network. To illustrate, consider again the coflow in Figure 1, given by the matrix $\begin{pmatrix} 1 & 2 \\ 2 & 1 \end{pmatrix}$. When this coflow is the only one present, it can be completed in 3 time slots, using matching schedules described by $\begin{pmatrix} 1 & 0 \\ 0 & 1 \end{pmatrix}$, $\begin{pmatrix} 0 & 1 \\ 1 & 0 \end{pmatrix}$ and $\begin{pmatrix} 0 & 1 \\ 1 & 0 \end{pmatrix}$. Here entry 1 indicates a connection between the corresponding input and output, so for example, the first matching connects input 1 with output 1, and input 2 with output 2. When multiple coflows are present, it is also possible for a matching to involve data units from different coflows.

An alternative approach toward modeling the scheduling constraints is to allow the feasible schedules to consist of *rate allocations*, so that *fractional* data units can be processed in each time slot. This approach corresponds to finding fractional matchings, and is used in most of the networking literature. We do *not* adopt this approach. When rate allocations can vary continuously over time, there is a much larger (infinite) set of allowable schedules. Furthermore, unless the time horizon is exceptionally short, restricting decision making to integral time units results in a provably negligible degradation of performance. Integral matchings will give rise to a much cleaner problem formulation, as we see below, without sacrificing the richness of the problem.

Problem statement.

We consider the following offline coflow scheduling problem with release dates. There are n coflows, indexed by $k = 1, 2, \ldots, n$. Coflow k is released to the system at time r_k, $k = 1, 2, \ldots, n$. Let the matrix of flow sizes of coflow k be denoted by $D^{(k)} = \left(d_{ij}^{(k)} \right)_{i,j=1}^m$, where $d_{ij}^{(k)}$ is the size of the flow to be transferred from input i to output j, of coflow k. The completion time of coflow k, denoted by C_k, is the time when all flows from coflow k have finished processing. Data units can be transferred across the network subject to the scheduling constraints described earlier. Let $y(i, j, k, t)$ be the number of data units being served in time slot t, which belong to coflow k and which require transfer from input i to output j. Then, in each time slot t, the following $2m$ *matching* constraints must be satisfied. For $i = 1, 2, \ldots, m$, $\sum_{k=1}^n \sum_{j'=1}^m y(i, j', k, t) \leq 1$, ensuring that input i processes at most one data unit at a time, and similarly, $\sum_{k=1}^n \sum_{i'=1}^m y(i', j, k, t) \leq 1$, for each output $j = 1, 2, \ldots, m$.

For given positive weight parameters w_k, $k = 1, 2, \ldots, n$, we are interested in minimizing $\sum_{k=1}^m w_k C_k$, the total weighted completion time of coflows with release dates. In a data center, coflows often come from different applications, so the total weighted completion time of coflows is a reasonable user/application oriented performance objective. A larger weight indicates higher priority, i.e., the corresponding coflow needs to be completed more quickly.

To summarize, we can formulate our problem as the following mathematical program.

$$(O) \quad \text{Minimize} \sum_{k=1}^n w_k C_k \quad \text{subject to}$$

$$\sum_{t=1}^{C_k} y(i, j, k, t) \geq d_{ij}^{(k)}, \text{ for } i, j = 1, \ldots, m, k = 1, \ldots, n; \quad (1)$$

$$\sum_{k=1}^n \sum_{j'=1}^m y(i, j', k, t) \leq 1, \text{ for } i = 1, \ldots, m, \ \forall t; \quad (2)$$

$$\sum_{k=1}^n \sum_{i'=1}^m y(i', j, k, t) \leq 1, \text{ for } j = 1, \ldots, m, \ \forall t; \quad (3)$$

$$y(i, j, k, t) = 0 \text{ if } t < r_k, \text{ for } i, j = 1, \ldots, m, \ \forall t, k; \quad (4)$$

$$y(i, j, k, t) \text{ binary}, \ \forall i, j, t, k. \quad (5)$$

The load constraints (1) state that all processing requirements of flows need to be met upon the completion of each coflow. (2) and (3) are the matching constraints. The release date constraints (4) guarantee that coflows are being served only after they are released in the system. Note that this mathematical program is not an integer linear programming formulation because variables C_k are in the limit of the summation.

The coflow scheduling problem (O) generalizes some well-known scheduling problems. First, when $m = 1$, it is easy to see that coflow scheduling is equivalent to single-machine scheduling with release dates with the objective of minimizing the total weighted completion time, where preemption is allowed. The latter problem is strongly NP-hard [22], which immediately implies the NP-hardness of problem (O) in general. When all coflow matrices are diagonal, coflow scheduling is equivalent to a concurrent open shop scheduling problem [3, 30]. This connection has been observed in [13], and is described in more detail in the full paper on arXiv for completeness. Utilizing this connection, it can be shown that the problem (O) is strongly NP-hard, even in the special case where $r_k = 0$ and $w_k = 1$ for all k. A major difference between concurrent open shop scheduling and coflow scheduling is that for concurrent open shop, there exists an optimal *permutation* schedule in which jobs can be processed in the same order on all machines [3], whereas permutation schedules need not be optimal for coflow scheduling [13].

1.2 Main Results

Theoretical results.

Since the coflow scheduling problem (O) is NP-hard, we focus on finding approximation algorithms, that is, algorithms which run in polynomial time and return a solution whose value is guaranteed to be close to optimal. Let $C_k(OPT)$ and $C_k(A)$ be the completion times of coflow k under an optimal and an approximation scheduling algorithm respectively. Our main results are:

THEOREM 1. *There exists a deterministic polynomial time $67/3$-approximation algorithm, i.e.*

$$\frac{\sum_{k=1}^{n} w_k C_k(A)}{\sum_{k=1}^{n} w_k C_k(OPT)} \leq \frac{67}{3}.$$

THEOREM 2. *There exists a randomized polynomial time $(9 + 16\sqrt{2}/3)$-approximation algorithm, i.e.*

$$\frac{\mathbb{E}\left[\sum_{k=1}^{n} w_k C_k(A)\right]}{\sum_{k=1}^{n} w_k C_k(OPT)} \leq 9 + \frac{16\sqrt{2}}{3}.$$

When all coflows have release dates 0, i.e., $r_k = 0$ for all k, we can improve the approximation ratios.

COROLLARY 1. *If all coflows are released into the system at time 0, then there exists a deterministic polynomial time $64/3$-approximation algorithm.*

COROLLARY 2. *If all coflows are released into the system at time 0, then there exists a randomized polynomial time $(8 + 16\sqrt{2}/3)$-approximation algorithm.*

Our deterministic (described in Algorithm 2) and randomized algorithms combine ideas from combinatorial scheduling and matching theory along with some new insights. First, as with many other scheduling problems (see e.g. [17]), particularly for average completion time, we relax the problem formulation (O) to a polynomial-sized interval-indexed linear program (LP). The relaxation involves both dropping the matching constraints (2) and (3), and using intervals to make the LP polynomial sized. We then solve this LP, and use an optimal solution to the LP to obtain an ordered list of coflows. Then, we use this list to derive an actual schedule. To do so, we partition coflows into a polynomial number of groups, based on the minimum required completion times of the ordered coflows, and schedule the coflows in the same group as a single coflow using matchings obtained from an integer version of the Birkhoff-von Neumann decomposition theorem (Lemma 4 and Algorithm 1).

The analysis of the algorithm couples techniques from the two areas in interesting ways. We analyze the interval-indexed linear program using tools similar to those used

for other average completion time problems, especially concurrent open shop. The interval-indexed rather than time-indexed formulation is necessary to obtain a polynomial time algorithm, and we use a lower bound based on a priority-based load calculation (see Lemma 3). We also show how each coflow can be completed by a time bounded by a constant times the optimal completion time, via a clever grouping and decomposition of the coflow matrices. Here a challenge is to decompose the not necessarily polynomial length schedule into a polynomial number of matchings.

Experimental findings.

We evaluate our algorithm as well as the impact of several additional algorithmic and heuristic decisions, including coflow ordering, coflow grouping and backfilling. Our evaluation uses a Hive/MapReduce trace collected from a large production cluster at Facebook [12, 13]. The main findings are as follows, with a more detailed discussion in Section 4 and in Appendix D in the full version.

- Algorithms with coflow grouping consistently outperform those without grouping. Similarly, algorithms that use backfilling consistently outperform those that do not use backfilling.

- The performance of algorithms that use the LP-based ordering (15) is similar to those that order coflows according to their loads (see (18)). When combined with grouping and backfilling, these algorithms are nearly optimal. Note that the ordering of coflows according to load is used in [13].

- Our LP-based deterministic algorithm has near-optimal performance.

1.3 Related work

The coflow abstraction was first proposed in [11], although the idea was present in a previous paper [12]. Chowdhury et al. [12] observed that the optimal processing time of a coflow is exactly equal to its *load*, when the network is scheduling only a single coflow, and built upon this observation to schedule data transfer in a datacenter network. Chowdhury et al. [13] introduced the coflow scheduling problem without release dates, and provided effective scheduling heuristics. They also observed the connection of coflow scheduling with concurrent open shop, established the NP-hardness of the coflow scheduling problem, and showed via a simple counter-example how permutation schedules need not be optimal for coflow scheduling.

There is a great deal of success over the past 20 years on combinatorial scheduling to minimize average completion time, see e.g. [17, 27, 28, 33]. This line of works typically uses a linear programming relaxation to obtain an ordering of jobs and then uses that ordering in some other polynomial-time algorithm. There has also been much work on shop scheduling, which we do not survey here, but note that traditional shop scheduling is not "concurrent". In the language of our problem, that would mean that traditionally, two flows in the same coflow could *not* be processed simultaneously. The recently studied concurrent open shop problem removes this restriction and models flows that can be processed in parallel. There have been several results showing that even restrictive special cases are NP-hard [3, 10, 16, 34]. There were several algorithms with super-constant (actually at least m, the number of machines) approximation ratios, e.g., [3, 23, 34, 35]. Recently there have been several constant factor approximation algorithms using LP-relaxations. Wang and Cheng [35] used an interval-indexed formulation. Several authors have observed that a relaxation in completion time variables is possible [10, 16, 23], and Mastrolilli et al. [25] gave a primal-dual 2-approximation algorithm and showed stronger hardness results. Relaxations in completion time variables presume the optimality of permutation schedules, which does not hold for the coflow scheduling problem. Thus, our work builds on the formulation in Wang and Cheng [35], even though their approach does not yield the strongest approximation ratio.

The design of our scheduling algorithms relies crucially on a fundamental result (Lemma 4 in this paper) concerning the decomposition of nonnegative integer-valued matrices into permutation matrices, which states that such a matrix can be written as a sum of ρ permutation matrices, where ρ is the maximum column and row sum. This result is closely related to the classical Birkhoff-von Neumann theorem [7], and has been stated in different forms and applied in different contexts. For an application in scheduling theory, see e.g., [21]. For applications in communication networks, see e.g., [9, 24, 31, 26].

2. LINEAR PROGRAM (LP) RELAXATION

In this section, we present an interval-indexed linear program relaxation of the scheduling problem (O), which produces a lower bound on $\sum_{k=1}^{n} w_k C_k(OPT)$, the optimal value of the total weighted completion time, as well as an ordering of coflows for our approximation algorithms (§2.1). We then define and analyze the concepts of *maximum total input/output loads*, which respect the ordering produced by the LP, and relate these concepts to $C_k(OPT)$ (§2.2). These relations will be used in the proofs of our main results in §3.3.

2.1 Two Linear Program Relaxations

From the discussion in §1.1, we know that problem (O) is NP-hard. Furthermore, the formulation in (1) - (5) is not immediately of use, since it is at least as hard as an integer linear program. We can, however, formulate an *interval-indexed linear program* (LP) by relaxing the following components from the original formulation. (i) First, we develop new load constraints (see (8) and (9)), by relaxing the matching constraints (2) and (3) and the load constraints (1), and formulate a *time-indexed linear program*. (The matching constraints will be enforced in the actual scheduling algorithm.) The time-indexed LP has been used many times (e.g. [5, 17]) but typically for non-shop scheduling problems. Note that in order to use it for our problem, we drop the explicit matching constraints. We call this (LP-EXP) below. (ii) Second, in order to get a polynomial sized formulation, we divide time (which may not be polynomially bounded) into a set of geometrically increasing intervals. We call this an *interval-indexed integer program*, and it is also commonly used in combinatorial scheduling. In doing so, we have a weaker relaxation than the time-indexed one, but one that can be solved in polynomial time. We then relax the interval-indexed integer program to a linear program and solve the linear program.

To implement relaxation (i), let us examine the load and matching constraints (1) – (3). Constraints (2) and (3) imply that in each time slot t, each input/output can process

at most one data unit. Thus, the total amount of work that can be processed by an input/output by time t is at most t. For each time slot t and each $k = 1, 2, \ldots, n$, let $z_t^{(k)} \in \{0, 1\}$ be an indicator variable of the event that coflow k completes in time slot t. Then

$$\sum_{s=1}^{t} \sum_{k=1}^{n} \sum_{j'=1}^{m} d_{ij'}^{(k)} z_s^{(k)} \quad \text{and} \quad \sum_{s=1}^{t} \sum_{k=1}^{n} \sum_{i'=1}^{m} d_{i'j}^{(k)} z_s^{(k)}$$

are, respectively, the total amount of work on input i and output j, from all coflows that complete before time t. Therefore, for each t, we must have

$$\sum_{s=1}^{t} \sum_{k=1}^{n} \sum_{j'=1}^{m} d_{ij'}^{(k)} z_s^{(k)} \leq t, \quad \text{for all } i = 1, 2, \ldots, m, \quad (6)$$

$$\sum_{s=1}^{t} \sum_{k=1}^{n} \sum_{i'=1}^{m} d_{i'j}^{(k)} z_s^{(k)} \leq t, \quad \text{for all } j = 1, 2, \ldots, m, \quad (7)$$

which are the load constraints on the inputs and outputs.

To complete relaxation (i), we require an upper bound on the time needed to complete all coflows in an optimal scheduling algorithm. To this end, note that the naive algorithm which schedules one data unit in each time slot can complete processing all the coflows in $T = \max_k\{r_k\} + \sum_{k=1}^{n} \sum_{i,j=1}^{m} d_{ij}^{(k)}$ units of time, and it is clear that an optimal scheduling algorithm can finish processing all coflows by time T. Taking into account constraints (6) and (7), and relaxing the integer constraints $z_t^{(k)} \in \{0, 1\}$ into the corresponding linear constraints, we can formulate the following linear programming relaxation (LP-EXP) of the coflow scheduling problem (O).

(LP-EXP) Minimize $\sum_{k=1}^{n} w_k \sum_{t=1}^{T} t z_t^{(k)}$ subject to

$$\sum_{s=1}^{t} \sum_{k=1}^{n} \sum_{j'=1}^{m} d_{ij'}^{(k)} z_s^{(k)} \leq t, \text{ for } i = 1, \ldots, m, \ t = 1, \ldots, T; \quad (8)$$

$$\sum_{s=1}^{t} \sum_{k=1}^{n} \sum_{i'=1}^{m} d_{i'j}^{(k)} z_s^{(k)} \leq t, \text{ for } j = 1, \ldots, m, \ t = 1, \ldots, T; \quad (9)$$

$$z_t^{(k)} = 0 \text{ if } r_k + \sum_{j'=1}^{m} d_{ij'}^{(k)} > t \text{ or } r_k + \sum_{i'=1}^{m} d_{i'j}^{(k)} > t; \quad (10)$$

$$\sum_{t=1}^{T} z_t^{(k)} = 1, \text{ for } k = 1, \ldots, n;$$

$$z_t^{(k)} \geq 0, \text{ for } k = 1, \ldots, n, \ t = 1, 2, \ldots, T.$$

Since the time T can be exponentially large in the sizes of the problem inputs, it is not *a priori* clear that the relaxation LP-EXP can be solved in polynomial time. In order to reduce the running time and find a polynomial time algorithm, we divide the time horizon into increasing time intervals: $[0, 1], (1, 2], (2, 4], \ldots, (2^{L-2}, 2^{L-1}]$, where L is chosen to be the smallest integer such that $2^{L-1} \geq T$. The inequality guarantees that 2^{L-1} is a sufficiently large time horizon to complete all the coflows, even under a naive schedule. We also define the following notation for time points: $\tau_0 = 0$, and $\tau_l = 2^{l-1}$, for $l = 1, \ldots, L$. Thus, the lth time interval runs from time τ_{l-1} to τ_l.

For $k = 1, \ldots, n$ and $l = 1, \ldots, L$, let $x_l^{(k)}$ be the binary decision variable which indicates whether coflow k is scheduled to complete within the interval $(\tau_{l-1}, \tau_l]$. We approximate the completion time variable C_k by $\sum_{l=1}^{L} \tau_{l-1} x_l^{(k)}$, the left end point of the time interval in which coflow k finishes, and consider the following linear program relaxation (LP).

$$(LP) \quad \text{Minimize} \sum_{k=1}^{n} w_k \sum_{l=1}^{L} \tau_{l-1} x_l^{(k)} \quad \text{subject to}$$

$$\sum_{u=1}^{l} \sum_{k=1}^{n} \sum_{j'=1}^{m} d_{ij'}^{(k)} x_u^{(k)} \le \tau_l, \text{ for } i = 1, \ldots, m, \ l = 1, \ldots, L; \quad (11)$$

$$\sum_{u=1}^{l} \sum_{k=1}^{n} \sum_{i'=1}^{m} d_{i'j}^{(k)} x_u^{(k)} \le \tau_l, \text{ for } j = 1, \ldots, m, \ l = 1, \ldots, L; \quad (12)$$

$$x_l^{(k)} = 0 \text{ if } r_k + \sum_{j'=1}^{m} d_{ij'}^{(k)} > \tau_l \text{ or } r_k + \sum_{i'=1}^{m} d_{i'j}^{(k)} > \tau_l; \quad (13)$$

$$\sum_{l=1}^{L} x_l^{(k)} = 1, \text{ for } k = 1, \ldots, n;$$

$$x_l^{(k)} \ge 0, \text{ for } k = 1, \ldots, n, \ l = 1, \ldots, L.$$

The relaxations (LP-EXP) and (LP) are similar, except that the time-indexed variables $z_t^{(k)}$ are replaced by interval-index variables $x_l^{(k)}$. The following lemma is immediate.

LEMMA 1. *The optimal value of the linear program (LP) is a lower bound on the optimal total weighted completion time $\sum_{k=1}^{n} w_k C_k(OPT)$ of coflow scheduling problem (O).*

PROOF. Consider an optimal schedule of problem (O) and set $x_u^{(k)} = 1$ if coflow k completes within the uth time interval. This is a feasible solution to problem (LP) with the load and capacity constraints (11) and (12) and the feasibility constraint (13) all satisfied. Moreover, since coflow k completes within the uth interval, the coflow completion time is at least τ_{u-1}. Hence, the objective value of the feasible solution constructed is no more than the optimal total weighted completion time $\sum_{k=1}^{n} w_k C_k(OPT)$. □

Since the constraint matrix in problem (LP) is of size $O((n+m)\log T)$ by $O(n \log T)$ and the maximum size of the coefficients is $O(\log T)$, the number of bits of input to the problem is $O(n(m+n)(\log T)^3)$. The interior point method can solve problem (LP) in polynomial time [20].

From an optimal solution to (LP), we can obtain an ordering of coflows, and use this order in our scheduling algorithms (see e.g., Algorithm 2). To do so, let an optimal solution to problem (LP) be $\bar{x}_l^{(k)}$ for $k = 1, \ldots, n$ and $l = 1, \ldots, L$. The relaxed problem (LP) computes an approximated completion time

$$\bar{C}_k = \sum_{l=1}^{L} \tau_{l-1} \bar{x}_l^{(k)} \quad (14)$$

for coflow k, $k = 1, 2, \ldots, n$, based on which we reorder coflows. More specifically, we re-order and index the coflows in a nondecreasing order of the approximated completion times $\bar{C}_k$, i.e.,

$$\bar{C}_1 \le \bar{C}_2 \le \ldots \le \bar{C}_n. \quad (15)$$

For the rest of the paper, we will stick to this ordering and indexing of the coflows.

Wang and Cheng [35] gave a 16/3-approximation algorithm for the concurrent open shop problem using a similar interval-indexed linear program. Our algorithms are more involved because we also have to address the matching constraints, which do not appear in the concurrent open shop problem.

2.2 Maximum Total Input / Output Loads

Here we define the *maximum total input/output loads*, respecting the ordering and indexing of (15). For each k, $k = 1, 2, \ldots n$, define the *maximum total input load I_k*, the *maximum total output load J_k* and the *maximum total load V_k* by

$$I_k = \max_{i=1,\ldots,m} \left\{ \sum_{j'=1}^{m} \sum_{g=1}^{k} d_{ij'}^{(g)} \right\}, \ J_k = \max_{j=1,\ldots,m} \left\{ \sum_{i'=1}^{m} \sum_{g=1}^{k} d_{i'j}^{(g)} \right\}$$

$$\text{and} \quad V_k = \max\{I_k, J_k\} \quad (16)$$

respectively. For each i (each j, respectively), $\sum_{j'=1}^{m} \sum_{g=1}^{k} d_{ij'}^{(g)}$ $\left(\sum_{i'=1}^{m} \sum_{g=1}^{k} d_{i'j}^{(g)}, \text{ respectively} \right)$ is the total processing requirement on input i (output j) from coflows $1, 2, \ldots, k$. That is, the *total load* is the sum of the loads of the lower numbered coflows. By the load constraints, V_k is a universal lower bound on the time required to finish processing coflows $1, 2, \ldots, k$, under any scheduling algorithm. We state this fact formally as a lemma.

LEMMA 2. *For $k = 1, 2, \ldots, n$, let $\tilde{C}^{(k)}$ be the time that all coflows $1, \ldots, k$ complete, where the indexing respects the order (15). Then, under any scheduling algorithm,*

$$V_k \le \tilde{C}^{(k)} \quad (17)$$

for all k simultaneously.

The following lemma, which states that with a proper ordering of the coflows, V_k is a 16/3-approximation of the optimal $C_k(OPT)$ for all k simultaneously, is crucial for the proof of our main results in the next section. The proof of the lemma is similar to that of Theorem 1 in [35]. We defer this proof to Appendix C in the full version.

LEMMA 3. *Let $\bar{C}_k$ be computed from problem (LP) by Eq. (14) and be indexed such that (15) is satisfied. Then $V_k \le (16/3)C_k(OPT)$, $k = 1, \ldots, n$.*

3. APPROXIMATION ALGORITHMS

In this section, we describe a deterministic and a randomized polynomial time scheduling algorithm, with approximation ratios of $67/3$ and $9 + 16\sqrt{2}/3$ respectively, in the presence of arbitrary release dates. The same algorithms have approximation ratios $64/3$ and $8 + 16\sqrt{2}/3$, respectively, when all coflows are released at time 0. Both algorithms are based on the idea of efficiently scheduling coflows according to the ordering (15) produced by (LP). To fully describe the scheduling algorithms, we first present some preliminaries on the minimal amount of time to finish processing an arbitrary coflow using only matching schedules (Algorithm 1 and §3.1). Algorithm 1 will be used crucially in the design of the approximation algorithms, and, as we will see, it is effectively an integer version of the famous Birkhoff-von Neumann theorem [7], and hence the name *Birkhoff-von Neumann decomposition*. Details of the main algorithms are provided in §3.2, and we supply proofs of the complexities and approximation ratios in §3.3.

3.1 Birkhoff-von Neumann Decomposition

For an arbitrary coflow matrix $D = (d_{ij})_{i,j=1}^m$, where $d_{ij} \in \mathbb{Z}_+$ for all i and j, we define $\rho(D)$, the *load* of coflow D, as follows.

$$\rho(D) = \max\left\{ \max_{i=1,\ldots,m}\left\{ \sum_{j'=1}^m d_{ij'} \right\}, \max_{j=1,\ldots,m}\left\{ \sum_{i'=1}^m d_{i'j} \right\} \right\}. \tag{18}$$

Note that for each i, $\sum_{j'=1}^m d_{ij'}$ is the total processing requirement of coflow D on input i, and for each j, $\sum_{i'=1}^m d_{i'j}$ is that on output j. By the matching constraints, $\rho(D)$ is a universal lower bound on the completion time of coflow D, were it to be scheduled alone.

LEMMA 4. *There exists a polynomial time algorithm which finishes processing coflow D in $\rho(D)$ time slots (using the matching schedules), were it to be scheduled alone.*

Algorithm 1 describes a polynomial-time scheduling algorithm that can be used to prove Lemma 4. The idea of the algorithm is as follows. For a given coflow matrix $D = (d_{ij})_{i,j=1}^m$, we first augment it to a "larger" matrix $\tilde{D}$, whose row and column sums are all equal to $\rho(D)$ (Step 1). In each iteration of Step 1, we increase one entry of D such that at least one more row or column sums to ρ. Therefore, at most $2m - 1$ iterations are required to get $\tilde{D}$. We then decompose $\tilde{D}$ into *permutation matrices* that correspond to the matching schedules (Step 2). More specifically, at the end of Step 2, we can write $\tilde{D} = \sum_{u=1}^U q_u \Pi_u$, so that Π_u are permutation matrices, $q_u \in \mathbb{N}$ are such that $\sum_{u=1}^U q_u = \rho(D)$, and $U \leq m^2$. The key to this decomposition is Step 2 (ii), where the existence of a perfect matching M can be proved by a simple application of Hall's matching theorem [18]. We now consider the complexity of Step 2. In each iteration of Step 2, we can set at least one entry of $\tilde{D}$ to zero, so that the algorithm ends in m^2 iterations. The complexity of finding a perfect matching in Step 2 (ii) is $O(m^3)$, e.g., by using the maximum bipartite matching algorithm. Since both Steps 1 and 2 of Algorithm 1 has polynomial-time complexity, the algorithm itself has polynomial-time complexity.

If we divide both sides of the identity $\tilde{D} = \sum_{u=1}^U q_u \Pi_u$ by $\rho(D)$, then $\tilde{D}/\rho(D)$ is a doubly stochastic matrix, and the coefficients $q_u/\rho(D)$ sum up to 1. Therefore, $\tilde{D}/\rho(D)$ is a convex combination of the permutation matrices Π_u. Because of this natural connection of Algorithm 1 with the Birkhoff-von Neumann theorem [7], we call the algorithm the Birkhoff-von Neumann decomposition. Lemma 4 has been stated in slightly different forms, see e.g., Theorem 1 in [21], Theorem 4.3 in [31], and Fact 2 in [26].

3.2 Approximation Algorithms

Here we present our deterministic and randomized scheduling algorithms. The deterministic algorithm is summarized in Algorithm 2, which consists of 2 steps. In Step 1, we solve (LP) to get the approximated completion time $\bar{C}_k$ for coflow ordering. Then, in Step 2, for each $k = 1, 2, \ldots, n$, we compute the maximum total load V_k of coflow k, and identify the time interval $(\tau_{r(k)-1}, \tau_{r(k)}]$ that it belongs to, where τ_l are defined in §2.1. All the coflows that fall into the same time interval are combined into and treated as a single coflow, and processed using Algorithm 1 in §3.1.

The randomized scheduling algorithm follows the same steps as the deterministic one, except for the choice of the

---

Algorithm 1: Birkhoff-von Neumann Decomposition

Data: A single coflow $D = (d_{ij})_{i,j=1}^m$.

Result: A scheduling algorithm that uses at most a polynomial number of different matchings.

- Step 1: Augment D to a matrix $\tilde{D} = \left(\tilde{d}_{ij} \right)_{i,j=1}^m$, where $\tilde{d}_{ij} \geq d_{ij}$ for all i and j, and all row and column sums of $\tilde{D}$ are equal to $\rho(D)$.

  Let $\eta = \min\left\{ \min_i\left\{ \sum_{j'=1}^m d_{ij'} \right\}, \min_j\left\{ \sum_{i'=1}^m d_{i'j} \right\} \right\}$ be the minimum of row sums and column sums, and let $\rho(D)$ be defined according to Equation (18).

  $\tilde{D} \leftarrow D$.

  while $(\eta < \rho)$ **do**

  $\quad i^* \leftarrow \arg\min_i \sum_{j'=1}^m \tilde{D}_{ij'}; \; j^* \leftarrow \arg\min_j \sum_{i'=1}^m \tilde{D}_{i'j}.$

  $$\tilde{D} \leftarrow \tilde{D} + pE,$$

  $\quad$ where $p = \min\{\rho - \sum_{j'=1}^m \tilde{D}_{i^*j'}, \rho - \sum_{i'=1}^m \tilde{D}_{i'j^*}\}$, $E_{ij} = 1$ if $i = i^*$ and $j = j^*$, and $E_{ij} = 0$ otherwise.

  $\quad \eta \leftarrow \min\left\{ \min_i\left\{ \sum_{j'=1}^m \tilde{D}_{ij'} \right\}, \min_j\left\{ \sum_{i'=1}^m \tilde{D}_{i'j} \right\} \right\}$

  end

- Step 2: Decompose $\tilde{D}$ into permutation matrices Π.

  while $(\tilde{D} \neq 0)$ **do**

  (i) Define an $m \times m$ binary matrix G where $G_{ij} = 1$ if $\tilde{D}_{ij} > 0$, and $G_{ij} = 0$ otherwise, for $i, j = 1, \ldots, m$.

  (ii) Interpret G as a bipartite graph, where an (undirected) edge (i, j) is present if and only if $G_{ij} = 1$. Find a perfect matching M on G and define an $m \times m$ binary matrix Π for the matching by $\Pi_{ij} = 1$ if $(i, j) \in M$, and $\Pi_{ij} = 0$ otherwise, for $i, j = 1, \ldots, m$.

  (iii) $\tilde{D} \leftarrow \tilde{D} - q\Pi$, where $q = \min\{\tilde{D}_{ij} : \Pi_{ij} > 0\}$. Process coflow D using the matching M for q time slots. More specifically, process dataflow from input i to output j for q time slots, if $(i, j) \in M$ and there is processing requirement remaining, for $i, j = 1, \ldots, m$.

  end

---

time intervals in Step 2 of Algorithm 2. Define the *random time points* τ_l' by $\tau_0' = 0$, and $\tau_l' = T_0 a^{l-1}$, where $a = 1 + \sqrt{2}$, and $T_0 \sim Unif[1, a]$ is uniformly distributed between 1 and a. Having picked the random time points τ_l', we then proceed to process the coflows in a similar fashion to the deterministic algorithm. Namely, for each $k = 1, 2, \ldots, n$, we identify the (random) time interval $(\tau_{r'(k)-1}', \tau_{r'(k)}']$ that coflow k belongs to, and for all coflows that belong to the same time interval, they are combined into a single coflow and processed using Algorithm 1.

3.3 Proofs of Main Results

We now establish the complexity and performance properties of our algorithms. We first provide the proof of Theorem 1 in detail. By a slight modification of the proof of Theorem 1, we can establish Corollary 1. We then provide the proofs of Theorem 2 and Corollary 2.

Algorithm 2: Deterministic LP-based Approximation

Data: Coflows $\left(d_{ij}^{(k)}\right)_{i,j=1}^m$, for $k = 1, \ldots, n$.

Result: A scheduling algorithm that uses at most a polynomial number of different matchings.

- Step 1: Given n coflows, solve the linear program (LP). Let an optimal solution be given by $\bar{x}_l^{(k)}$, for $l = 1, 2, \ldots, L$ and $k = 1, 2, \ldots, n$. Compute the approximated completion time $\bar{C}_k$ by Eq. (14). Order and index the coflows according to (15).

- Step 2: Compute the maximum total load V_k for each k by (16). Suppose that $V_k \in (\tau_{r(k)-1}, \tau_{r(k)}]$ for some function $r(\cdot)$ of k. Let the range of function $r(\cdot)$ consist of values $s_1 < s_2 < \ldots < s_P$, and define the sets $S_u = \{k : \tau_{s_{u-1}} < V_k \leq \tau_{s_u}\}$, $u = 1, 2, \ldots, P$.

  $u \leftarrow 1$.

  while $u \leq P$ **do**

  After all the coflows in set S_u are released, schedule them as a single coflow with transfer requirement $\sum_{k \in S_u} d_{ij}^{(k)}$ from input i to output j and finish processing the coflow using Algorithm 1.

  $u \leftarrow u + 1$;

  end

Proofs of Theorem 1 and Corollary 1.

Let $C_k(A)$ be the completion time of coflow k under the deterministic scheduling algorithm (Algorithm 2). The following proposition will be used to prove Theorem 1.

PROPOSITION 1. *For all $k = 1, 2, \ldots, n$, the coflow completion time $C_k(A)$ satisfies*

$$C_k(A) \leq \max_{1 \leq g \leq k}\{r_g\} + 4V_k, \qquad (19)$$

where we recall that r_g is the release time of coflow g, and the total loads V_k are defined in Eq. (16).

PROOF. Recall the notation used in Algorithm 2. For any coflow $k \in S_u$, $V_k \leq \tau_{s_u}$. By Lemma 4, we know that all coflows in the set S_u can be finished processing within τ_{s_u} units of time. Define $\bar{\tau}_0 = 0$ and $\bar{\tau}_u = \bar{\tau}_{u-1} + \tau_{s_u}$, $u = 1, 2, \ldots, P$. A simple induction argument shows that under Algorithm 2, $C_k(A)$, the completion time of coflow k, satisfies $C_k(A) \leq \max_{1 \leq g \leq k}\{r_g\} + \bar{\tau}_u$, if $k \in S_u$.

We now prove by induction on u that $\bar{\tau}_u \leq 2\tau_{r(k)}$, if $k \in S_u$, $u = 1, 2, \ldots, P$. Suppose that this holds for $k \in S_u$. Let $k^* = \max\{k : k \in S_u\}$ such that $k^* + 1 \in S_{u+1}$. Then,

$$\bar{\tau}_{u+1} = \bar{\tau}_u + \tau_{s_{u+1}} \leq 2\tau_{r(k^*)} + \tau_{r(k^*+1)}.$$

Since the time interval increases geometrically and satisfies $\tau_{l+1} = 2\tau_l$ for $l = 1, 2, \ldots, L$, $\bar{\tau}_{u+1} \leq 2\tau_{r(k^*+1)} = 2\tau_{r(k)}$, if $k \in S_{u+1}$. This completes the induction. Furthermore, if $\tau_{r(k)-1} < V_k \leq \tau_{r(k)}$, $\tau_{r(k)} = 2\tau_{r(k-1)} < 2V_k$. Thus,

$$C_k(A) \leq \max_{1 \leq g \leq k}\{r_g\} + 2\tau_{r(k)} \leq \max_{1 \leq g \leq k}\{r_g\} + 4V_k.$$

□

The proof of Theorem 1 is now a simple consequence of Lemmas 1 and 3 and Proposition 1.

Proof of Theorem 1. For all k, $\max_{1 \leq g \leq k}\{r_g\} \leq \bar{C}_k$, where $\bar{C}_k$ (cf. (15)) are the approximated completion times computed from (LP), follows immediately from the feasibility constraints (13), and the ordering of $\bar{C}_k$ in (15). By Proposition 1 and Lemma 3, we have

$$C_k(A) \leq \max_{1 \leq g \leq k}\{r_g\} + 4V_k \leq \bar{C}_k + \frac{64}{3}C_k(OPT).$$

It follows that

$$\begin{aligned}
\sum_{k=1}^n w_k C_k(A) &\leq \sum_{k=1}^n w_k\left(\bar{C}_k + \frac{64}{3}C_k(OPT)\right) \\
&\leq \sum_{k=1}^n w_k C_k(OPT) + \frac{64}{3}\sum_{k=1}^n w_k C_k(OPT) \\
&= \frac{67}{3}\sum_{k=1}^n w_k C_k(OPT),
\end{aligned}$$

where the second inequality follows from Lemma 1.

We now consider the running time of Algorithm 2. The program (LP) in Step 1 can be solved in polynomial time, as discussed in §2.1. Thus, it suffices to show that Step 2 runs in polynomial time. Since there are only $O(\log T)$, a polynomial number of intervals of the form $(\tau_{l-1}, \tau_l]$, it now suffices to show that for each $u = 1, 2, \ldots, P$, Algorithm 1 completes processing all coflows in the set S_u in polynomial time, where we recall the definition of S_u in Step 2 of Algorithm 2. But this follows from Lemma 4. Thus, Algorithm 2 runs in polynomial time. □

Proof of Corollary 1. Consider Algorithm 2 and suppose that all coflows are released at time 0, i.e., $r_k = 0$ for all k. By Proposition 1, $C_k(A) \leq 4V_k$ for all $k = 1, 2, \ldots, n$. By inspection of the proof of Theorem 1, we have,

$$\sum_{k=1}^n w_k C_k(A) \leq \frac{64}{3}\sum_{k=1}^n w_k C_k(OPT).$$

The fact that Algorithm 2 has a polynomial running time was established in the proof of Theorem 1. □

Before proceeding to the proofs of Theorem 2 and Corollary 2, let us provide some remarks on the upper bounds (19) in Proposition 1. Recall that Ineq. (19) hold simultaneously for all k. Then, a natural question is whether the upper bounds in (19) are tight. We leave this question as future work, but provide the following observation for now. Suppose that all coflows are released at time 0, then the upper bounds in (19) become $C_k(A) \leq 4V_k$ for all k. By inspecting the proof of Proposition 1, it is easy to see that in fact, $\tilde{C}^{(k)}(A) \leq 4V_k$ for all k, where $\tilde{C}^{(k)}(A)$ is the completion time of coflows $1, 2, \ldots, k$ under our algorithm. Compared this with the lower bounds (17) in Lemma 2, we see that the upper bounds are off by a factor of at most 4. The lower bounds (17) cannot be achieved simultaneously for all k; this fact can be demonstrated through a simple counter-example. See Appendix B in the full version for details.

Proofs of Theorem 2 and Corollary 2.

Similar to the proof of Theorem 1, the proof of Theorem 2 relies on the following proposition, the randomized counterpart of Proposition 1.

PROPOSITION 2. *Let $C_k(A')$ be the random completion time of coflow k under the randomized scheduling algorithm* *described in §3.2. Then, for all $k = 1, 2, \ldots, n$,*

$$\mathbb{E}[C_k(A')] \le \max_{1 \le g \le k} \{r_g\} + \left(\frac{3}{2} + \sqrt{2}\right) V_k. \quad (20)$$

PROOF. Recall the random time points τ_l' defined by $\tau_0' = 0$, and $\tau_l' = T_0 a^{l-1}$, where $a = 1 + \sqrt{2}$, and $T_0 \sim Unif[1, a]$. Suppose that $V_k \in (\tau_{r'(k)-1}', \tau_{r'(k)}']$ and let $T_k = \tau_{r'(k)}' - \tau_{r'(k)-1}'$ for all k. Then,

$$\frac{\tau_{r'(k)}'}{T_k} = \frac{T_0 a^{r'(k)-1}}{T_0 a^{r'(k)-1} - T_0 a^{r'(k)-2}} = \frac{a}{a-1}.$$

Since $T_0 \sim Unif[1, a]$, T_k is uniformly distributed on the interval $((a-1)V_k/a, (a-1)V_k)$. Thus,

$$\mathbb{E}\left[\tau_{r'(k)}'\right] = \frac{a}{a-1}\mathbb{E}[T_k]$$
$$= \frac{a}{a-1} \times \frac{1}{2}\left(\frac{a-1}{a} + a - 1\right) V_k = \frac{1+a}{2} V_k.$$

Similar to $\bar{\tau}_u$ used in the proof of Proposition 1, define $\bar{\tau}_u'$ inductively by $\bar{\tau}_0' = 0$ and $\bar{\tau}_u' = \bar{\tau}_{u-1}' + \tau_{s_u}'$, $u = 1, 2, \ldots P$. If $k \in S_u$, then

$$\bar{\tau}_u' \le \sum_{l=1}^{r'(k)} \tau_l' = \tau_{r'(k)}' + \frac{\tau_{r'(k)}'}{a} + \frac{\tau_{r'(k)}'}{a^2} + \ldots + T_0 \le \frac{a}{a-1}\tau_{r'(k)}'.$$

Similar to the proof of Proposition 1, we can establish that if $k \in S_u$, then $C_k(A') \le \max_{1 \le g \le k}\{r_g\} + \bar{\tau}_u'$. Thus, with $a = 1 + \sqrt{2}$,

$$\mathbb{E}[C_k(A')] \le \mathbb{E}\left[\max_{1 \le g \le k}\{r_g\} + \bar{\tau}_u'\right] \le \max_{1 \le g \le k}\{r_g\} + \frac{a}{a-1}\mathbb{E}[\tau_{r'(k)}']$$
$$\le \max_{1 \le g \le k}\{r_g\} + \frac{a^2 + a}{2(a-1)} V_k = \max_{1 \le g \le k}\{r_g\} + \left(\frac{3}{2} + \sqrt{2}\right) V_k.$$

□

Proof of Theorem 2. By Proposition 2 and Lemma 3, we have $\mathbb{E}[C_k(A')] \le \max_{1 \le g \le k}\{r_g\} + (3/2 + \sqrt{2}) V_k < \bar{C}_k + (8 + 16\sqrt{2}/3) C_k(OPT)$. It follows that

$$\mathbb{E}\left[\sum_{k=1}^{n} w_k C_k(A')\right] \le \sum_{k=1}^{n} w_k \left(\bar{C}_k + \left(8 + \frac{16\sqrt{2}}{3}\right) C_k(OPT)\right)$$
$$\le \sum_{k=1}^{n} w_k C_k(OPT)$$
$$+ \left(8 + \frac{16\sqrt{2}}{3}\right) \sum_{k=1}^{n} w_k C_k(OPT)$$
$$= \left(9 + \frac{16\sqrt{2}}{3}\right) \sum_{k=1}^{n} w_k C_k(OPT),$$

where the second inequality follows from Lemma 1. □

Proof of Corollary 2. Consider the randomized algorithm and suppose that all coflows are released at time 0, i.e., $r_k = 0$ for all k. By Proposition 2, for all $k = 1, 2, \ldots, n$, $\mathbb{E}[C_k(A')] \le (3/2 + \sqrt{2}) V_k$. From the proof of Theorem 2, we have $\mathbb{E}\left[\sum_{k=1}^{n} w_k C_k(A')\right] \le \left(8 + \frac{16\sqrt{2}}{3}\right) \sum_{k=1}^{n} w_k C_k(OPT)$. □

4. EXPERIMENTS

In previous sections, we presented deterministic and randomized approximation algorithms with provable performance guarantees. In this section, we conduct some preliminary experiments to evaluate the practical performance of several algorithms, including our deterministic algorithm described in §3.2.

At a high level, both of our algorithms consist of two related stages. The *ordering stage* computes an ordering of coflows, and the *scheduling stage* produces a sequence of feasible schedules that respects this ordering. It is intuitively clear that an intelligent ordering of coflows in the ordering stage can substantially reduce coflow completion times. As a result, we consider three different coflow orderings, including the LP-based ordering (15), and study how they affect algorithm performance. See §4.1 for more details.

The derivation of the actual sequence of schedules in the scheduling stage relies on two key ideas: scheduling according to an optimal (Birkhoff-von Neumann) decomposition, and a suitable grouping of the coflows. We note that to some extent, grouping can be thought of as a *dovetailing* procedure, where skewed coflow matrices are consolidated to form more uniform ones, which can be efficiently cleared by matching schedules. It is then reasonable to expect that grouping can improve performance, so we compare algorithms with grouping and those without grouping to understand its effect. The particular grouping procedure that we consider here is the one described in Algorithm 2.

Backfilling is a common strategy used in scheduling for computer systems to increase utilization of system resources (see, e.g. [13]). Therefore, we will also investigate the performance gain of using backfilling in the scheduling stage. We focus on one natural backfilling technique, described in detailed in §4.1.

In summary, we will evaluate the performance impact of coflow ordering, coflow grouping and backfilling. Our evaluation uses a Hive/MapReduce trace collected from a large production cluster at Facebook [12, 13]. The main findings are as follows.

- Algorithms with coflow grouping consistently outperform those without grouping. Similarly, algorithms that use backfilling consistently outperform those that do not use backfilling.

- The performance of algorithms that use the LP-based ordering (15) is similar to those that order coflows according to their loads (see (18)). When combined with grouping and backfilling, these algorithms are nearly optimal. Furthermore, our LP-based deterministic algorithm has near-optimal performance.

4.1 Methodology

Workload.

We use the same workload as described in [13]. The workload is based on a Hive/MapReduce trace at Facebook that was collected on a 3000-machine cluster with 150 racks, so the datacenter in the experiments can be modeled as 150×150 network switch (and each coflow represented by a 150×150 matrix). The cluster has a 10:1 core-to-rack oversubscription ratio with a total bisection bandwidth of 300Gbps. Therefore, each ingress/egress port has a capacity of 1Gbps, or equivalently 128MBps. We select the time unit to be $1/128$ second accordingly so that each port has the capacity of 1MB per time unit. We filter the coflows based on the number of non-zero flows, which we denote by M', and we consider three collections of coflows, filtered by the conditions $M' \geq 50$, $M' \geq 40$ and $M' \geq 30$, respectively. As pointed out in [13], coflow scheduling algorithms may be ineffective for very sparse coflows in real datacenters, due to communication overhead, so we investigate the performance of our algorithms for these three collections. We also assume that all coflows arrive at time 0, so we do not consider the effect of release dates.

Algorithms and Metrics.

We consider 12 different scheduling algorithms, which are specified by the ordering used in the ordering stage, and the actual sequence of schedules used in the scheduling stage. We consider three different orderings, which we describe in detail below, and the following 4 cases in the scheduling stage: (a) without grouping or backfilling, which we refer to as the base case, (b) without grouping but with backfilling, (c) with grouping and without backfilling, and (d) with both grouping and backfilling. Algorithm 2 corresponds to the combination of LP-based ordering and case (c).

For ordering, three different possibilities are considered. We use H_A to denote the naive ordering of coflows by coflow IDs from the production trace, H_ρ to denote the ordering of coflows by the ratios between the maximum load ρ (defined in (18)) and weight w, which is also considered in [13], and H_{LP} to denote the LP-based coflow ordering given in (15).

Given an ordering of the coflows, it is possible to partition them into groups using the procedure described in Step 2 of Algorithm 2. As discussed, we will consider algorithms with and without such grouping. When we do group the coflows, we treat all coflows within a group as a whole and say that they are *consolidated* into an *aggregated* coflow. Scheduling of coflows within a group makes use of the Birkhoff-von Neumann decomposition described in Algorithm 1, respecting the coflow order. Namely, if two data units from coflows k and k' within the same group use the same pair of input and output, and k is ordered before k', then we always process the data unit from coflow k first.

For backfilling, given a sequence of coflows with a given order, for coflow k with a coflow matrix $D^{(k)}$, $k = 1, \ldots, n$, we compute the augmented coflow matrix $\tilde{D}^{(k)}$ and schedule the coflow by the Birkhoff-von Neumann decomposition in Algorithm 1. This decomposition may introduce unforced idle time, whenever $D^{(k)} \neq \tilde{D}^{(k)}$. When we use a schedule that matches input i to output j to serve coflow k with $D_{ij}^{(k)} < \tilde{D}_{ij}^{(k)}$, and if there is no more service requirement on the pair of input i and output j for coflow k, we backfill in order from the flows on the same pair of ports in the subsequent coflows. When grouping is used, backfilling is applied to the aggregated coflows.

We compare the performances of different algorithms, by considering ratios of the total weighted completion times. For the choice of coflow weights, we consider both the case of uniform weights, as well as the case where weights are given by a random permutation of the set $\{1, 2, \ldots, n\}$.

4.2 Performance

We compute the total weighted completion times for all 3 orders in the 4 different cases (a) – (d) described in §4.1, through a set of experiments on filtered coflow data. The complete results can be found in the full version, and we present representative comparisons of the algorithms here.

Figure 2a, plots the total weighted completion times as percentages of the base case (a), for the case of random

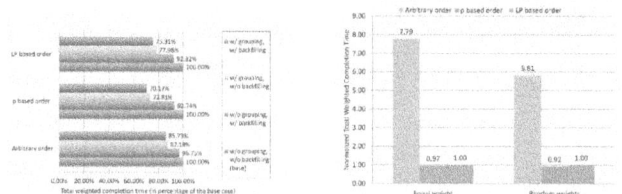

(a) Comparison of total weighted completion times with respect to the base case for each order. Data are filtered by $M' \geq 50$. Weights are random.

(b) Comparison of total weighted completion times evaluated on data filtered by $M' \geq 50$ in case (d) with both grouping and backfilling.

Figure 2: Comparisons of total weighted completion times

weights. Grouping and backfilling both improve the total weighted completion time with respect to the base case for all 3 orders. The reduction in the total weighted completion time from grouping is up to 27.19%, and is consistently higher than the reduction from backfilling, which is up to 8.68%. For all 3 orders, scheduling with both grouping and backfilling (i.e., case (d)) gives the smallest total weighted completion time, but the improvement from case (c) (only grouping) to case (d) is marginal.

We then compare the performances of different coflow orderings. Figure 2b shows the comparison of total weighted completion times evaluated on filtered coflow data for both equal weight and random weights in case (d) where the scheduling stage uses both grouping and backfilling. Compared with H_A, both H_ρ and H_{LP} reduce the total weighted completion times of coflows by a ratio up to 8.05 and 7.79, respectively, with H_ρ performing consistently better than H_{LP}. A natural question to ask is how close H_ρ and H_{LP} are to the optimal. In order to get a tight lower bound of the scheduling problem (O), we solve (LP-EXP) for the case of random weights and when the number of non-zero flows $M' \geq 50$. The ratio of the lower bound over the weighted completion time under H_{LP} is 0.9447, which implies that both H_ρ and H_{LP} in the ordering stage provide a good approximation of the optimal in practice. Due to time constraint, we did not compute the lower bounds for all cases, because (LP-EXP) is exponential in the size of the input and is extremely time consuming to solve.

Our experiments are only preliminary and leave open many questions. For example, we should systematically measure the benefit of the time-indexed versus the interval-indexed linear program. We should also compare the performance of the randomized algorithm, include varying release dates, and think of other heuristics to improve the solutions obtained. We leave this work, and testing on other data sets, to the full paper.

5. CONCLUSION AND OPEN PROBLEMS

We have given the first $O(1)$-approximation algorithms for minimizing the total weighted completion time of coflows in a datacenter network, in the presence of release dates, and have performed preliminary experiments to evaluate the algorithm and several additional heuristics. Beyond the obvious question of improving the approximation ratio, this work opens up several additional interesting directions in coflow scheduling, such as the consideration of other metrics and the addition of other realistic constraints, such as precedence constraints. We are particularly interested in minimizing weighted coflow *processing* time (usually called *flow time* in the literature), which is harder to approximate (the various hardness results from single machine schedule will clearly carry over), but may lead to the development and understanding of better algorithms, possibly by considering resource augmentation.

Perhaps the most interesting questions involve making the algorithms and models more practical for them to work in real-time in a real system. While we consider release dates, our algorithms are not *on-line*, as they require the solution of an LP to compute a global ordering. We would also like to remove the centralized control and develop distributed algorithms, more suitable for implementation in a data center. To do so would require the development of a much simpler algorithm than the one here, possibly a primal-dual based algorithm. Finally, we observe that in applications the D matrices may have uncertainty, and it would be interesting to design algorithms to deal with this uncertainty, via robust or stochastic optimization.

Acknowledgement.

Yuan Zhong would like to thank Mosharaf Chowdhury and Ion Stoica for numerous discussions on the coflow scheduling problem, and for sharing the Facebook data.

6. REFERENCES

[1] Apache hadoop. http://hadoop.apache.org.
[2] Google dataflow. https://www.google.com/events/io.
[3] Reza Ahmadi, Uttarayan Bagchi, and Thomas Roemer. Coordinated scheduling of customer orders for quick response. *Naval Research Logistics*, 52(6):493–512, 2005.
[4] Mohammad Alizadeh, Shuang Yang, Milad Sharif, Sachin Katti, Nick McKeown, Balaji Prabhakar, and Scott Shenker. pfabric: Minimal near-optimal datacenter transport. *SIGCOMM Computer Communication Review*, 43(4):435–446, 2013.
[5] E. Balas. On the facial structure of scheduling polyhedra. *Mathematical Programming Studies*, 24:179–218, 1985.
[6] Hitesh Ballani, Paolo Costa, Thomas Karagiannis, and Ant Rowstron. Towards predictable datacenter networks. *SIGCOMM Computer Communication Review*, 41(4):242–253, 2011.
[7] Garrett Birkhoff. Tres observaciones sobre el algebra lineal. *Univ. Nac. Tkcumán. Rev. A*, 5:147–151, 1946.
[8] Dhruba Borthakur. The hadoop distributed file system: Architecture and design. Hadoop Project Website, 2007.
[9] Cheng-Shang Chang, Wen-Jyh Chen, and Hsiang-Yi Huang. Birkhoff-von neumann input buffered crossbar switches. In *INFOCOM*, volume 3, pages 1614–1623, 2000.
[10] Zhi-Long Chen and Nicholas G. Hall. Supply chain scheduling: Conflict and cooperation in assembly systems. *Operations Research*, 55(6):1072–1089, 2007.
[11] Mosharaf Chowdhury and Ion Stoica. Coflow: A networking abstraction for cluster applications. In *HotNets-XI*, pages 31–36, 2012.
[12] Mosharaf Chowdhury, Matei Zaharia, Justin Ma, Michael I. Jordan, and Ion Stoica. Managing data transfers in computer clusters with orchestra. *SIGCOMM Computer Communication Review*, 41(4):98–109, 2011.
[13] Mosharaf Chowdhury, Yuan Zhong, and Ion Stoica. Efficient coflow scheduling with Varys. In *SIGCOMM*, 2014.
[14] Jeffrey Dean and Sanjay Ghemawat. Mapreduce: Simplified data processing on large clusters. In *OSDI*, pages 10–10, 2004.
[15] Fahad Dogar, Thomas Karagiannis, Hitesh Ballani, and Ant Rowstron. Decentralized task-aware scheduling for data center networks. Technical Report MSR-TR-2013-96, 2013.
[16] Naveen Garg, Amit Kumar, and Vinayaka Pandit. Order scheduling models: Hardness and algorithms. In *FSTTCS*, pages 96–107, 2007.
[17] Leslie A Hall, Andreas S. Schulz, David B. Shmoys, and Joel Wein. Scheduling to minimize average completion time: Off-line and on-line approximation algorithms. *Mathematics of Operations Research*, 22(3):513–544, 1997.
[18] Marshall Hall. *Combinatorial Theory*. Addison-Wesley, 2nd edition, 1998.
[19] Nanxi Kang, Zhenming Liu, Jennifer Rexford, and David Walker. Optimizing the "one big switch" abstraction in software-defined networks. In *CoNEXT*, pages 13–24, 2013.
[20] Narendra Karmarkar. A new polynomial-time algorithm for linear programming. *Combinatorica*, 4(4):373–395, 1984.
[21] E. L. Lawler and J. Labetoulle. On preemptive scheduling of unrelated parallel processors by linear programming. *Journal of the ACM*, 25(4):612–619, 1978.
[22] J. K. Lenstra, A. H. G. Rinnooy Kan, and P. Brucker. Complexity of machine scheduling problems. *Annals of Discrete Mathematics*, 1:343–362, 1977.
[23] Joseph Y. T. Leung, Haibing Li, and Michael Pinedo. Scheduling orders for multiple product types to minimize total weighted completion time. *Discrete Applied Mathematics*, 155(8):945–970, 2007.
[24] J. Li and N. Ansari. Enhanced birkhoff-von neumann decomposition algorithm for input queued switches. *IEE Proceedings - Communications*, 148(6):339–342, 2001.
[25] Monaldo Mastrolilli, Maurice Queyranne, Andreas S. Schulz, Ola Svensson, and Nelson A. Uhan. Minimizing the sum of weighted completion times in a concurrent open shop. *Operations Research Letters*, 38(5):390–395, 2010.
[26] Michael J. Neely, Eytan Modiano, and Yuan-Sheng Cheng. Logarithmic delay for $N \times N$ packet switches under the crossbar constraint. *IEEE/ACM Transactions on Networking*, 15(3):657–668, 2007.
[27] Cynthia A. Phillips, Cliff Stein, and Joel Wein. Minimizing average completion time in the presence of release dates. *Mathematical Programming*, 82(1-2):199–223, 1998.
[28] Michael Pinedo. *Scheduling: Theory, Algorithms, and Systems*. Springer, New York, NY, USA, 3rd edition, 2008.
[29] Lucian Popa, Arvind Krishnamurthy, Sylvia Ratnasamy, and Ion Stoica. Faircloud: Sharing the network in cloud computing. In *HotNets-X*, pages 22:1–22:6, 2011.
[30] Thomas A. Roemer. A note on the complexity of the concurrent open shop problem. In *Integer Programming and Combinatorial Optimization*, pages 301–315, 2006.
[31] Devavrat Shah, John. N. Tsitsiklis, and Yuan Zhong. On queue-size scaling for input-queued switches. preprint, 2014.
[32] Konstantin Shvachko, Hairong Kuang, Sanjay Radia, and Robert Chansler. The hadoop distributed file system. In *MSST*, pages 1–10, 2010.
[33] Martin Skutella. *List Scheduling in Order of α-Points on a Single Machine*, volume 3484 of *Lecture Notes in Computer Science*, pages 250–291. Springer, Berlin, Heidelberg, 2006.
[34] Chang Sup Sung and Sang Hum Yoon. Minimizing total weighted completion time at a pre-assembly stage composed of two feeding machines. *International Journal of Production Economics*, 54(3):247–255, 1998.
[35] Guoqing Wang and T.C. Edwin Cheng. Customer order scheduling to minimize total weighted completion time. *Omega*, 35(5):623–626, 2007.
[36] Matei Zaharia, Mosharaf Chowdhury, Tathagata Das, Ankur Dave, Justin Ma, Murphy McCauley, Michael J. Franklin, Scott Shenker, and Ion Stoica. Resilient distributed datasets: A fault-tolerant abstraction for in-memory cluster computing. In *NSDI*, pages 2–2, 2012.

Electing a Leader in Wireless Networks Quickly Despite Jamming*

Marek Klonowski
Department of Computer Science at the Faculty
of Fundamental Problems of Technology
Wrocław, Poland
marek.klonowski@pwr.wroc.pl

Dominik Pająk
Computer Laboratory
University of Cambridge
Cambridge, UK
dsp39@cl.cam.ac.uk

ABSTRACT

In this paper we present a fast leader election protocol for single-hop wireless networks, provably robust against jamming by an external and powerful adversary. A $(T, 1 - \varepsilon)$-bounded adversary can jam at most $(1 - \varepsilon)w$ out of any $w \geq T$ contiguous time slots, for $0 < \varepsilon < 1$. The network consists of n stations that do not have knowledge of **any** global parameter n, T, ε. Each station can transmit or listen to the common communication channel. In each slot, all listeners are notified in which of the three states the communication channel is in the current slot: no transmitters, exactly one transmitter or at least two transmitters. To the listening stations, a jammed slot is indistinguishable from the case of at least two transmitters.

Our protocol elects a leader, with high probability, in the presence of an arbitrary, adaptive $(T, 1 - \varepsilon)$-adversary. For any constant ε and $T = \mathcal{O}(\log n)$, the protocol works in optimal time $\mathcal{O}(\log n)$. The protocol also works for general T and ε in $\mathcal{O}\left(\frac{\log \log(1/\varepsilon)}{\varepsilon^3} \log n\right)$ slots if $T \leq \frac{\log n}{\varepsilon^3 \log(1/\varepsilon)}$ and $\mathcal{O}\left(\max\left\{\log \log\left(\frac{T}{\varepsilon \log n}\right), \log(1/\varepsilon) \log \log(1/\varepsilon)\right\} T\right)$ otherwise.

Categories and Subject Descriptors

C.2.5 [**Computer-Communication Networks**]: Local and Wide-Area Networks—Access schemes; F.2.2 [**Analysis of Algorithms and Problem Complexity**]: Nonnumerical Algorithms and Problems—Sequencing and scheduling

General Terms

Algorithms; Reliability; Theory

Keywords

Wireless Network; Leader Election; Jamming

*This paper is supported by Polish National Science Center - decision number 2013/09/B/ST6/02258.

1. INTRODUCTION

A wireless network is a set of stations working without any central control and communicating wirelessly using a common medium. Due to the lack of a central arbiter, electing a leader in such a distributed system is a challenging task. Despite dozens of protocols devoted to this problem have been presented, some particular yet important from practitioners' point of view, issues are left unaddressed. In this paper we present and analyze a leader election protocol immune against a powerful adversary that is capable of jamming the common communication channel used by all the stations of the wireless network. Despite similarities to numerous previous results, to the best of our knowledge, our contribution cannot be realized by any of them by any straightforward manner mainly due to a very restricted model - on the one hand we assume a presence of a very strong, adaptive adversary, and on the other hand the stations have only local knowledge. In particular, they do not know the size of the network (or even its bound) nor parameters governing the strength of the adversary.

The assumed model of the adversary covers a significant number of threats spanning from random faults generated by incidental transmissions of coexisting networks to a powerful malicious adversary capable of jamming the network unpredictable number of times in an adaptive manner in order to perform a DoS-like attack. Note that such type of attacks can be launched without any special hardware by listening to the open channel and broadcasting at the same frequency band as the network.

1.1 Our Model

We consider a wireless network consisting of a set of n honest and reliable stations. Each station is placed within transmission (and interference) range of each other - that is, we assume a *single-hop* network. Time is divided into discrete steps called *slots* and nodes are synchronized as if they had an access to a global clock. Stations communicate via a single channel as the only medium. In a single slot each station can transmit a message or sense (listen to) the channel. For simplicity, we assume that each station that is not transmitting in a given slot, is listening. If a single station transmits all listening stations receive the message (and the state of the channel is described as **Single**). If two or more stations transmit, the state of the channel is described as **Collision**. The third state is **Null**, while the channel is idle in a given slot (i.e. none of stations is transmitting). We assume that when a station is listening to the channel it receives the state of the channel in the current slot.

The ability of the stations to distinguish between Null and Collision is sometimes called *collision detection*. We will consider two variants of collision detection: *weak collision detection* (weak-CD) and *strong collision detection* (strong-CD). In strong-CD stations are assumed to be capable of transmitting and listening at the same time. In each slot all stations receive the current state of the channel. On the other hand, in weak-CD simultaneous listening and transmitting is not possible and only stations which are not transmitting are notified about the state of the channel. Clearly, even in weak-CD, the transmitters have partial knowledge about the state of the channel because they know that there is either Single or Collision. Let us stress however that the main result of our paper holds for the more demanding weak-CD.

In literature also a model without collision detection (no-CD) is considered. There, the channel can be only in two states: Single in which there is exactly one transmitter or no-Single in which there is either zero or at least two transmitters.

The disruptions of the communication are made by an adversary who knows the entire history of the channel and the protocol executed by honest stations. Additionally, the real number of stations, which is unknown to the stations in advance, may be known to the adversary. All this knowledge can be used by the adversary to jam particular slots so that his disruptions will inflict the largest possible damage to the algorithm executed by the honest stations. Moreover we do **not** assume that the stations share any secret unknown to the adversary as we would like to avoid special initialization of the system required for distribution of such a secret.

The adversary can jam at most $(1-\varepsilon)w$ out of any $w \geq T$ contiguous slots. Note that the adversary can block even all slots in short windows of less than T slots. Such a model of adversary is known in literature as $(T, 1-\varepsilon)$-bounded (e.g., [3]). We assume that the stations cannot distinguish between the adversarial jamming or a collision of two or more messages that are sent at the same time by honest stations. The adversary is adaptive - the decision whether to jam a given slot may depend on the state of the channel in previous slots. Note however that it has to make a jamming decision before it knows the actions of the nodes in the current slot.

We consider a leader election problem that consist in assigning *leader* or *non-leader* status to each station in such way that exactly one station is a leader and all stations know their status after completing the protocol. This goal is always realized in a such way that a single station has to transmit and is later notified that it has successfully transmitted.

A specific class of algorithms widely studied in literature are so-called *uniform algorithms* ([27]). In each slot of such an algorithm, each station of the network transmits with the same probability independently of other stations. The probability for each slot may depend on the history of the channel.

1.2 Our Results and Organization of the Paper

In the subsection below we present previous work in leader election and other related problems.

Section 2 is devoted to a basic leader election protocol called LESK in a simplified model, wherein we assume strong-CD model and the global knowledge of the parameter ε. LESK works in time $O(\max\{T, (\log(1/\varepsilon)/\varepsilon^3) \log n\})$ with high

probability and is immune against any $(T, 1-\varepsilon)$-bounded adversary. We also show a lower bound of $\Omega(\max\{T, (\log n)/\varepsilon\})$ for leader election algorithms working with high probability. This shows that LESK is optimal for any T and any constant ε. In Section 2.3 we show that LESK can be modified to work with unknown ε for the price of a small overhead. We introduce algorithm LESU which works for any unknown ε and T in time $\mathcal{O}\left(\frac{\log\log(1/\varepsilon)}{\varepsilon^3}\log n\right)$, if $T \leq \frac{\log n}{\varepsilon^3 \log(1/\varepsilon)}$ and $\mathcal{O}\left(\max\left\{\log\log\left(\frac{T}{\varepsilon \log n}\right), \log\left(1/\varepsilon\right)\log\log\left(1/\varepsilon\right)\right\}T\right)$ otherwise.

In Section 3 we show a method of translating our results from previous section into a weak-CD model with only a constant-factor overhead. Both algorithms LESK with known ε and LESU with unknown ε can be applied to weak-CD using this method.

In Section 4 we conclude the paper and present some open problems in the area of robust algorithms in wireless networks.

1.3 Related and Previous Work

There is a well developed body of literature devoted to jamming and leader election. Our model of the network and adversary is the same as the one in [3, 33]. Authors of [3] present a general Medium Access Control (MAC) protocol achieving a constant throughput in single-hop wireless networks under $(T, 1 - \varepsilon)$-bounded adaptive adversary jamming the communication channel. Leader election is one of the applications of their general framework. The algorithm from [3] was the first evidence that it is feasible to solve classical problems in wireless networks even when the fraction of non-jammed slots can be arbitrarily close to 0. In [33] authors present a self-stabilizing leader election algorithm robust against a more powerful reactive adversary who can jam slots based on the information whether the slot is idle or not (but the adversary cannot distinguish between Single and Collision prior to making his decision). The algorithm from [3] has a proven runtime of $O(\log^4 n)$. No upper bound on the runtime of the algorithm from [33] is known. In our paper we would like to focus more on time efficient solution to leader election in the presence of a jammer. Our solution will not be self-stabilizing and will work only for the leader election but we expect that our approach can be extended. For an arbitrary constant $\varepsilon < 1$ and $T = O(\log n)$ our protocol needs only $O(\log n)$ slots to elect a leader with high probability. For constant ε and very large T our protocol needs time $O(T \log \log T)$ improving the known bound of $O(T \log T)$ [3]. More importantly, our protocol does not need any information about global parameters, while in the previous papers the parameter $\gamma = O(1/(\log\log n + \log T)$ is explicitly used by the stations. On the other hand, we do not present the energy-efficiency analysis of the presented methods - we expect, however that the energetic efficiency of our protocol should be similar to the leader election from [3].

Leader election is a fundamental problem of distributed systems. For wireless radio networks (or equivalent/similar models) it has been described in many notable papers including [2, 25, 24, 27, 36, 20]. In [17] authors discuss leader election in the context of energy consumption. A survey of classic leader election protocols for radio networks can be found in [26] or in Chapter 8 of [15]. The leader election is closely linked to problem of *selection resolution* in wireless networks. In this problem, the goal of the stations is to obtain the first Single in the channel. In the CD model, the selection resolution can be solved in expected time $O(\log \log n)$ [36] and this time is optimal [29]. With probability at least $1 - 1/f$, time $O(\log \log n + \log f)$ is necessary and sufficient [24]. In the no-CD model, the problem can be solved with high probability in time $O(\log^2 n)$ [25] and a lower bound $\Omega(\log n \log f)$ holds for any algorithm working with probability at least $1 - 1/f$ [11]. The selection resolution in strong-CD model is equivalent to leader election, as the station that transmits successfully can be chosen to be a leader. Also without an adversary, any algorithm working in the strong-CD can be simulated using weak-CD by executing the algorithm in odd time slots and using the even time slots to notify about each **Single**. However in the presence of an adversary, an algorithm for selection resolution in weak-CD does not immediately translate to an algorithm for leader election.

The problem of leader election is considered under various adversarial models. In [14, 19] authors consider an *inner* adversary controlling some stations. The aim of the adversary is to force the network to elect one of the adversarial stations as the leader. Authors present an algorithm with execution time $\Theta(n^3)$ that partially protects against such adversary, where n is the size of the network. One can also point to some other papers about leader election or some wider class of protocols in wireless network under adversary jamming the communication. Some theoretical and experimental results can be found in [32, 1, 7]. In all those papers the assumed model is different than in our paper (or in [3]) or the analysis is based on experimental results. In [21] authors demonstrate that in practice it is very hard to detect a jamming adversary. Moreover in [4] authors present how standard IEEE 802.11 protocols can be efficiently attacked by an adaptive adversary with moderately limited energy and without any special hardware. Some general countermeasures against jamming based on physical methods can be found in [28, 22, 5]. However it turned out that such approach cannot be efficiently combined with popular technologies like 802.11 protocols. In [8] one can find some more theoretical approach to this issue. The leader election problem has been also considered from self-stability perspective (i.e., [1, 6]). It turned out however that the described approach does not provide immunity against adversarial jamming.

There are many other papers dealing with adversary capable of jamming the communication channel in similar models. None of them however focuses on leader election problem. In [31] authors discuss maximal throughput for a multihop unit-disc model of the network without collision-detection assuming that jammer can transmit in a constant fraction of slots. In [30] authors consider similar settings for SINR model. Paper [34] is devoted to the case, wherein several co-existing networks have to operate in the same area (and can interfere each other). In [35] authors consider throughput and fairness in a single-hop network with a jamming adversary. Some of the mentioned protocols can be adopted for our model and used for choosing a leader, however such approach would require significantly greater time comparing to the method presented in our paper.

Some other significant paper assuming acting of an adversary jamming the communication channel (or spontaneous interferences) for substantially different models and considered problems include [12, 18, 23, 13, 10, 9].

Some further references can be found in [37, 3].

2. LEADER ELECTION IN STRONG-CD

In this section we present an algorithm for $(T, 1 - \varepsilon)$-bounded adversary for the (easier) strong-CD model.

In [3], the authors present a solution that is immune against any (T, ε)-bounded adversary. Stations in their algorithm ignore all **Collisions** and the decisions are made based only on **Nulls** and **Singles**. Such an approach is immune against an adversary since we can be certain that slots with **Nulls** and **Singles** were not influenced. We would like to propose a different approach. We will make use of the **Collisions** but we will value **Nulls** much more than **Collisions**. Informally speaking, each **Collision** will be "worth" 1 and each **Null** will be "worth" $1/\varepsilon$. Clearly, to use this intuition, our protocol needs to initially know the value of ε. Moreover we assume that stations successfully transmitting immediately receive feedback from the channel (i.e. we assume the strong *collision detection* model). In the next sections both assumptions can be relaxed for the price of a small overhead.

2.1 Protocol Description

In this section we present an algorithm **LESK** for Leader Election in Strong-CD with Known ε. The following procedure **Broadcast** is a basic primitive in our algorithm.

Function 1 Broadcast(u)

---

transmit with probability 2^{-u}
$state \leftarrow$ status of the channel
if transmitted **then**
    return $(state, true)$
else
    return $(state, false)$

Algorithm 1 LESK (ε)

$a \leftarrow 8/\varepsilon$
$u \leftarrow 0$
$state \leftarrow$ Collision
repeat
    $(state, transmitted) \leftarrow$ Broadcast(u)
    if $status =$ Null **then**
        $u \leftarrow \max(u - 1, 0)$
    else if $status =$ Collision **then**
        $u \leftarrow u + 1/a$
until $state \neq$ Single
if transmitted **then**
    $leader \leftarrow true$
else
    $leader \leftarrow false$

In **LESK** we maintain a variable u which serves as an estimate of $\log_2 n$. In each slot each station transmits independently with probability 2^{-u}. Our objective is to make the value of u close to $\log_2 n$ as the transmission with probability $1/n$ results in **Single** with highest probability. Intuitively, when each station transmits with probability 2^{-u} and the state of the channel is **Null** then one can suspect that the estimate is too big and it should be decreased to increase the probability of **Single**. Conversely, each **Collision** should yield the increase of estimate u. However a $(T, 1 - \varepsilon)$-bounded adversary with $\varepsilon < 1/2$ can jam more than a half of the slots. Thus to make the protocol robust even against such a powerful adversary we cannot use symmetric changes or the adversary could force the estimate u to diverge to infinity. Instead, knowing that roughly at most ε fraction of all slots is not-jammed, our algorithm increases the estimate of u by only $\varepsilon/8$ upon each Collision. Then, each Null that decreases the estimate by 1 is sufficient to "neutralize" around $8/\varepsilon$ jammed slots. Indeed, we take advantage of the fact that the adversary cannot induce a Null to the channel and only "one-side errors" are possible.

Observe that algorithm LESK is a *uniform* one as in each slot each station transmits with the same probability 2^{-u}.

2.2 Analysis

Let us note that the variable u in consecutive slots is performing a form of a biased random walk on a discrete subset of real numbers. The walk (and the algorithm) is completed if finally a single station transmits and becomes the leader. In our analysis we would like to show that with high probability, the value of u is in a close proximity of $\log_2 n$ for a significant number of slots, independent on how the adversary acts.

Let us consider an execution of the algorithm such that the leader is not chosen in the first t slots. We divide the t slots of the execution into several groups depending on the value of u at the beginning of each slot and the state of the channel. Let us define the groups and respective *counters* of the slots belonging to each group. Let $u_0 = \log_2 n$ denote the exact value of the estimator.

IS - is the number of *irregular silences*, i.e. slots, such that $u \leq u_0 - \log_2(2\ln a)$ and the state of the channel is Null.

IC - is the number of *irregular collisions*, i.e. slots such that $u \geq u_0 + \frac{1}{2}\log_2 a$ and the state of the channel is Collision and the adversary does **not** jam the channel.

CS - is the number of *correcting silences*, i.e. slots, such that $u \geq u_0 + \frac{1}{2}\log_2 a + 1$ and the state of the channel is Null.

CC - is the number of *correcting collisions*, i.e. slots, such that $u \leq u_0 - \log_2(2\ln a)$ and the state of the channel is Collision and the adversary does **not** jam the channel.

E - number of slots jammed by the adversary.

R - all other, called **regular** slots.

Note that the value of u at the beginning of each regular slot satisfies $u_0 - \log_2(2\ln a) \leq u \leq u_0 + \frac{1}{2}\log_2 a + 1$.

In the following auxiliary lemma we prove several relations between the probability of Null, Single and Collision in a slot and the probability p of transmission by each station. Recall that in a fixed time slot, each station transmits on the channel independently with the same probability p.

LEMMA 2.1. *Let $p = \frac{1}{xn}$ be the probability of transmission in a single slot by each station for some $n > 1$ and $x > 0$.*

1. $\mathbb{P}[\text{Null}] \leq e^{-\frac{1}{x}}$.

2. $\mathbb{P}[\text{Collision}] \leq \frac{1}{x^2}$.

3. $\mathbb{P}[\text{Single}] \geq \frac{1}{x}e^{-\frac{1}{x}}$.

4. $\mathbb{P}[\text{Single}] \geq \frac{1}{x} - \frac{1}{x^2}$.

PROOF. Knowing that $\mathbb{P}[\text{Null}] = (1-p)^n$, $\mathbb{P}[\text{Single}] = np(1-p)^{n-1}$, $\mathbb{P}[\text{Collision}] = 1 - \mathbb{P}[\text{Null}] - \mathbb{P}[\text{Single}]$, all above statements can be derived using the following two double inequalities:

$$\left(1 - \frac{1}{k}\right)^k \leq \frac{1}{e} \leq \left(1 - \frac{1}{k}\right)^{k-1},$$

$$1 + ky \leq (1+y)^k \leq 1 + ky + \frac{ky^2}{2},$$

which are true for $k \geq 1$ and $y > -1$. The latter double inequality can be shown by a straightforward induction. □

Using the previous lemma we can show an upper bound on the probability of a slot being an irregular silence or an irregular collision.

LEMMA 2.2. *For any number of stations n and any slot of algorithm LESK:*

1. *the slot is an irregular silence with probability at most $1/a^2$, independently of the state of the channel in previous rounds,*

2. *the slot is an irregular collision with probability at most $1/a$, independently of the state of the channel in previous rounds .*

PROOF. Observe that a slot is an irregular silence if $u \leq u_0 - \log_2(2\ln a)$ thus the transmission probability p of each station satisfies $p \geq 2\ln a/n$. The first point now follows from Lemma 2.1 (p.1). A slot is an irregular collision if $u \geq u_0 + \frac{1}{2}\log_2 a$. The probability of transmission satisfies in this case $p \leq 1/(n\sqrt{a})$ and the second point follows from Lemma 2.1 (p.2). □

In the following lemma we show relations between the counters of slots of each type.

LEMMA 2.3. *Following observations hold*

1. $t = IS + IC + CS + CC + E + R$,

2. IS *is stochastically dominated by* $Bin(t, 1/a^2)$,

3. IC *is stochastically dominated by* $Bin(t, 1/a)$,

4. $CS \leq \frac{IC+E}{a}$,

5. $CC \leq IS \cdot a + u_0 \cdot a$.

PROOF. The first point is implied by the fact that each slot before the leader is chosen falls into exactly one category. Points 2 and 3 follow from Lemma 2.2.

To prove 4 observe that a slot s is a correcting silence if the initial estimate u at the beginning of s satisfies $u \geq u_0 + \log_2\sqrt{a} + 1$ and the result of the slot is Null. Recall that a slot is an irregular collision if $u \geq u_0 + \log_2\sqrt{a}$ and the transmissions result in Collision. In a correcting silence the estimate is decreased from u to $u-1$. Consider steps before step s in which the estimate was increased from $u-1$ to u. Since $u - 1 \geq u_0 + \log_2\sqrt{a}$ then each such slot was either an irregular collision or was a slot jammed by the adversary. Since each Collision causes the estimate to increase by $1/a$ we can exclusively assign exactly a irregular collision or slots with adversarial jamming to each correcting silence.

Similarly we can justify point 5. The total number of correcting collisions cannot be greater then a times the number of steps caused by irregular silence plus slots necessary to reach $u_0 - \log_2(2\ln a)$ from 0 (note that the initial value of u is 0). Clearly each irregular silence can cause decrementing u by at most 1. $\square$

At the beginning of each regular slot, the estimate u is close to u_0 thus each such slot yields a significant probability of **Single**.

LEMMA 2.4. *In each regular slot, the probability of* **Single** *is at least* $C = \frac{\ln a}{a^2}$.

PROOF. By definition, in each regular slot the variable u satisfies the following double inequality

$$u_0 - \log_2(2\ln a) \le u \le u_0 + \log_2(\sqrt{a}).$$

Thus the probability of transmitting of each station is $\frac{2\ln(a)}{n} \ge p \ge \frac{1}{n\sqrt{a}}$. Let us recall that the probability of **Single** in a slot in which all n stations transmit independently with probability p is $f(p) = n \cdot p(1-p)^{n-1}$. Since f has a single local maximum for $p \in [0,1]$ then the minimal value of $f(p)$ for $p \in \left[\frac{2\ln(a)}{n}, \frac{1}{n\sqrt{a}}\right]$ is $\min\{f(\frac{2\ln(a)}{n}), f(\frac{1}{n\sqrt{a}})\}$.

By Lemma 2.1 (p.3) we have that $f(\frac{2\ln(a)}{n}) > \frac{2\ln a}{a^2}$ and from (p.4) we get that $f(\frac{1}{n\sqrt{a}}) > \frac{1}{\sqrt{a}} - \frac{1}{a}$. Let us observe that $\frac{2\ln a}{a^2} < \frac{1}{\sqrt{a}} - \frac{1}{a}$ for all $a \ge 8$. $\square$

To prove the next lemma we need following version of the Chernoff bound.

FACT 1. *Let* $X \sim Bin(n,p)$, *then for any* $0 \le \delta < 3/2$

$$Pr[X > (\delta+1)np] \le exp\left(-\frac{\delta^2 np}{3}\right).$$

PROOF. This inequality is obtained by substituting $t = \delta np$ to Thm. 2.1, formula 2.5 in [16]. $\square$

In the following lemma we show upper bounds, that hold with high probability, on the numbers of irregular silences and irregular collisions.

LEMMA 2.5. *For any* $\beta \ge 1$

$$\mathbb{P}\left[IS(1+a) > \frac{2t}{a^2}(1+a)\right] \le \frac{1}{3n^\beta},$$

$$\mathbb{P}\left[\frac{9}{8}IC > \frac{9}{4}\frac{t}{a}\right] \le \frac{1}{3n^\beta}.$$

for $t > 3a^2\log(3n^\beta)$.

PROOF. Since IS, IC are bounded by a binomially distributed random variable (Lemma 2.3 points 2 and 3) we can apply a standard Chernoff bound. The proof follows directly from Fact 1 for $\delta = 1$. $\square$

Finally, using all the previous lemmas we can show a bound on the runtime of **LESK** algorithm.

THEOREM 2.6. *For any* $0 < \varepsilon < 1$ *and any constant* $\beta \ge 1$ **LESK** *chooses a leader in strong-CD model with knowledge of* ε, *in time*

$$t = \mathcal{O}\left(\max\left\{T, \frac{\log n}{\varepsilon^3 \log(1/\varepsilon)}\right\}\right)$$

with probability at least $1 - 1/n^\beta$ *in the presence of any* $(T, 1-\varepsilon)$-*adversary with known* ε *and unknown* T.

PROOF. From Lemma 2.4 we have that in each regular slot we have probability of **Single** at least $C = \frac{2\ln a}{a^2}$ independently of other slots. One can easily prove that it suffices to have at least $\frac{\ln(3n^\beta)}{C}$ regular slots to get at least one **Single** with probability at least $1 - 1/(3n^\beta)$.

We will demonstrate that the number of regular slots is big with high probability independently on the way the adversary acts.

From Lemma 2.3 and since $a \ge 8$ we have

$$
\begin{aligned}
R &= t - IS - IC - CS - CC - E \\
&\ge t - IS - IC - \frac{IC + E}{a} - IS \cdot a - u_0 \cdot a - E \\
&\ge t - IS(1+a) - \frac{9}{8}IC - u_0 \cdot a - (1 + \frac{1}{a})E = (\star)
\end{aligned}
$$

Let us assume that $> T$. Since, by the definition of the adversary $E < (1-\varepsilon)t$, then $(1 + \frac{1}{a})E < (1-\varepsilon)(1 + \frac{\varepsilon}{8})t \le (1 - \frac{7}{8}\varepsilon)t$.

Applying this observation and a bound for u_0 to $(\star)$ we get

$$R > \frac{7}{8}\varepsilon t - IS(1+a) - \frac{9}{8}IC - a \cdot \log n - 1. \tag{1}$$

From Lemma 2.5 we have that

$$
\begin{aligned}
R &> \frac{7}{8}\varepsilon t - \frac{2t}{a^2}(1+a) - \frac{9t}{4a} - a \cdot \log n - 1 \\
&= \frac{7}{8}\varepsilon t - \frac{17t}{4a} - \frac{2t}{a^2} - a \cdot \log n - 1
\end{aligned}
$$

for $t > 3a^2\log(3n)$ with probability at least $1 - 2/3n^\beta$. Since $a \ge 8$

$$
\begin{aligned}
R &> \frac{7}{8}\varepsilon t - \frac{9t}{2a} - a \cdot \log n - 1 \\
&\ge \frac{7}{8}\varepsilon t - \frac{9}{16}\varepsilon t - a \cdot \log n - 1 = \frac{5}{16}\varepsilon t - a \cdot \log n - 1.
\end{aligned}
$$

Finally, it is enough to take t such that

$$
\begin{aligned}
R &> \frac{5}{16}\varepsilon t - a \cdot \log n - 1 > \frac{a^2 \ln(3n^\beta)}{2\ln a} \\
&\text{or equivalently,} \\
t &> \frac{16}{5\varepsilon}\left(\frac{a^2 \ln(3n^\beta)}{2\ln a} + a \cdot \log n + 1\right) = \\
&\mathcal{O}\left(\frac{\log(n^\beta)}{\varepsilon^3 \log(1/\varepsilon)}\right)
\end{aligned}
$$

to complete **LESK** with probability at least $1 - 1/n^\beta$. $\square$

LEMMA 2.7. *Any leader election algorithm working with probability at least* $1 - 1/n$ *in presence of a* $(T, 1-\varepsilon)$-*bounded adversary requires time* $\Omega(\max\{T, 1/\varepsilon \log n\})$, *for any* T, n, ε, *where* $0 < \varepsilon < 1$.

PROOF. To choose a leader in the considered model, even without an adversary with probability at least $1 - 1/n$, one needs $\Omega(\log n)$ slots [24]. The adversary can simply jam the first $\lfloor(1-\varepsilon)T\rfloor$ slots out of each T consecutive time steps ensuring that in order to have $c \log n$ non-jammed slots, for any constant c, the algorithm needs to work for $\Omega(\max\{T, 1/\varepsilon \log n\})$ slots. $\quad\square$

2.3 Extension for Unknown ε

In the previous section we presented the algorithm LESK (ε), which is immune against any $(T, 1 - \varepsilon)$-bounded adversary, but needs the knowledge of parameter ε. In this section we will propose an algorithm that estimates ε and therefore works without the knowledge of this parameter. In order to perform leader election without knowledge of ε we would like to execute LESK $(\hat{\varepsilon})$ multiple times with different values of $\hat{\varepsilon}$, for example $\hat{\varepsilon} = 1/2, 1/4, 1/8, \ldots$. But to do so we need to know the estimate of the runtime of LESK $(\hat{\varepsilon})$ to stop its execution if $\hat{\varepsilon}$ is not the correct estimate of ε. Thus we are looking for an estimate of value $\max\{\log n, T\}$. We will show that using the following function Estimation we can obtain a value that is between $\log\log n - 1$ and $\max\{\log\log n, \log T\} + 1$ w.h.p.

Function 2 Estimation
$\quad$ **for** $round \leftarrow 1, 2, \ldots$ **do**
$\quad\quad$ Repeat 2^{round} times $\mathsf{Broadcast}(2^{round})$
$\quad\quad$ $nulls \leftarrow$ number of Nulls in this round
$\quad\quad$ **if** $nulls \geq 2$ **then**
$\quad\quad\quad$ **return** $round$

LEMMA 2.8. *For any $\varepsilon > 0$, if $n \geq 115$ then with probability at least $1 - 2/n^2$ function Estimation in the presence of $(T, 1 - \varepsilon)$-adversary obtains Single or returns value i satisfying $\log\log n - 1 \leq i \leq \max\{\log\log n, \log T\} + 1$ in time $\mathcal{O}(\max\{\log n, T\})$*

PROOF. Assume that Single did not occur in any of the slots of procedure Estimation. Denote by p, the transmission probability in a given round r. Observe that the following facts are true by Lemma 2.1:

$$\mathbb{P}\left[\mathsf{Null \ in} \ r | p \geq \frac{1}{\sqrt{n}}\right] \leq e^{-\sqrt{n}}, \qquad (2)$$

$$\mathbb{P}\left[\mathsf{Collision \ in} \ r | p \leq \frac{1}{n^2}\right] \leq \frac{1}{n^2}. \qquad (3)$$

To show that $\log\log n - 1 \leq i$ observe that in rounds $1, 2, \ldots \lfloor \log\log n \rfloor - 1$ there is a total number of at most $\log n$ time slots. And in each of these time slots, the probability of transmission is at least $2^{-2^{\lfloor \log\log n \rfloor - 1}} \geq \frac{1}{\sqrt{n}}$. Thus by (2) and the Union Bound we obtain that the probability that in any of these slots there was a Null is at most $\log n \cdot e^{-\sqrt{n}}$. Starting with $n \geq 115$ we have $\log n \cdot e^{-\sqrt{n}} \leq 2/n^2$, thus with probability at least $1 - 2/n^2$ we have $i \geq \log\log n - 1$.

Now we want to show that

$$i \leq \max\{\lceil \log\log n \rceil + 1, \lceil \log T \rceil + 1\}.$$

In the i-th round there are at least $2^{\lceil \log T \rceil + 1} \geq 2T$ slots. Among T slots at most $(1 - \varepsilon)T$ slots can be jammed, thus, since $\varepsilon > 1$, then at least 1 slot is not-jammed. Thus in i-th round we have at least 2 not-jammed slots. By (3), and using the Union Bound we obtain that with probability at least $1 - 2/n^2$ in both of these rounds we obtain Null. Thus with probability at least $1 - 2/n^2$ the returned value is at most $\max\{\lceil \log\log n \rceil + 1, \lceil \log T \rceil + 1\}$. $\quad\square$

Now let us denote by LESK $(\hat{\varepsilon}, t)$ the execution of procedure LESK $(\hat{\varepsilon})$ terminated after exactly t steps. Let c be such a constant that execution LESK $(\hat{\varepsilon}, c \max\{T, \frac{\log n}{\varepsilon^3 \log(1/\varepsilon)}\})$ results in a Single with probability at least $1 - 1/n^2$ in the presence of any $(T, 1 - \varepsilon)$-bounded adversary, where $\varepsilon/2 \leq \hat{\varepsilon} \leq \varepsilon$. Such a constant exists by Theorem 2.6. The following algorithm LESU solves Leader Election in Strong-CD with Unknown ε.

Algorithm 2 LESU
$\quad$ $\varepsilon_i \leftarrow 2^{-i/3}$
$\quad$ $t_0 \leftarrow c \cdot 2^{1 + \mathsf{Estimation}}$
$\quad$ $t_i \leftarrow \frac{t_0}{\varepsilon_i^3 \log(1/(\varepsilon_i))}$
$\quad$ **for** $i \leftarrow 1, 2, \ldots$ **do**
$\quad\quad$ **for** $j \leftarrow 1, 2, \ldots, i$ **do**
$\quad\quad\quad$ LESK $\left(\varepsilon_j, t_i \cdot \frac{i}{j}\right)$

THEOREM 2.9. *If $n \geq 115$, then algorithm LESU elects a leader in strong-CD model in time:*

1. *$\mathcal{O}\left(\frac{\log\log(1/\varepsilon)}{\varepsilon^3} \log n\right)$, if $T \leq \frac{\log n}{\varepsilon^3 \log(1/\varepsilon)}$,*

2. *$\mathcal{O}\left(\max\left\{\log\log\left(\frac{T}{\varepsilon \log n}\right), \log(1/\varepsilon) \log\log(1/\varepsilon)\right\} T\right)$, if $T > \frac{\log n}{\varepsilon^3 \log(1/\varepsilon)}$,*

with probability at least $1 - 1/(3n)$ in the presence of any $(T, 1 - \varepsilon)$-bounded adversary with unknown ε and T.

PROOF. First assume that the value returned by function Estimation is between $\log\log n - 1$ and $\max\{\log\log n, \log T\} + 1$. This happens with probability at least $1 - 2/n^2$ by Lemma 2.8. Thus variable t_0 satisfies $4c \max\{\log n, T\} \geq t_0 \geq c \log n$.

Observe that for a fixed i we execute procedures LESK $(\varepsilon_1, t_i \cdot i)$, LESK $(\varepsilon_2, t_i \cdot i/2)$, ..., LESK (ε_i, t_i), where $t_i = 2^i t_0/(i/3 - 1) = 3 \cdot 2^i t_0/i$. Thus the total time of all procedures executed for a fixed i equals

$$\sum_{j=1}^{i} t_i \frac{i}{j} \leq 3 \cdot 2^i c t_0 \cdot \sum_{j=1}^{i} \frac{1}{j} \leq 3 \cdot 2^i (\ln i + 1) t_0.$$

Consequently, I is the largest value of variable i in algorithm LESU then the total time of the algorithm is

$$\sum_{i=1}^{I} 3 \cdot 2^i (\ln i + 1) t_0 \leq 3 \cdot 2^{I+1} (\ln I + 1) t_0 \qquad (4)$$

We will consider two cases:
First assume that $T \leq \frac{\log n}{\varepsilon^3 \log(1/\varepsilon)}$. Take $i^* = \lceil 3 \log_2(1/\varepsilon) \rceil$ and consider procedure LESK $(\varepsilon_{i^*}, t_{i^*})$. Observe that $\varepsilon/2 \leq \varepsilon_{i^*} \leq \varepsilon$. We have $t_{i^*} = \frac{1}{\varepsilon_{i^*}^3 \log(1/(\varepsilon_{i^*}))} \cdot t_0$ and

$$t_{i^*} \geq \frac{c \log n}{\varepsilon^3 \log(1/\varepsilon)},$$

thus by the choice of constant c, with probability at least $1 - 1/n^2$ procedure LESK $(\varepsilon_{i^*}, t_{i^*})$ results in a Single. The total time in this case is by Equation (4) at most:

$$2^{i^*+1} (\ln i^* + 1) t_0 = \mathcal{O}\left(\frac{\log\log(1/\varepsilon)}{\varepsilon^3} \log n\right).$$

309

Consider the second case of $T > \frac{\log n}{\varepsilon^3 \log(1/\varepsilon)}$. Take $i^* = \lceil \log(cT/t_0) \rceil + \lceil \log_2(\log_2(1/\varepsilon)) \rceil$ and $j^* = \lceil 3 \log_2(1/\varepsilon) \rceil$. Assume that $j^* \leq i^*$. Consider procedure LESK $(\varepsilon_{j^*}, t_{i^*} \frac{i^*}{j^*})$. Observe that, similarly as in the previous case, $\varepsilon/2 \leq \varepsilon_{j^*} \leq \varepsilon$, and

$$t_{i^*} \frac{i^*}{j^*} = \frac{2^{\lceil \log(cT/t_0) \rceil} \cdot 2^{\lceil \log_2(\log_2(1/\varepsilon)) \rceil} 3 \cdot t_0}{\lceil 3 \log_2(1/\varepsilon) \rceil} \geq cT.$$

It follows that procedure LESK $(\varepsilon_{j^*}, t_{i^*} \frac{i^*}{j^*})$ results in **Single** with probability at least $1 - 1/n^2$. The total time in this case by Equation (4) is at most:

$$2^{i^*+1}(\ln i^* + 1)t_0 = \mathcal{O}\left(\log \log \left(\frac{T}{\varepsilon \log n} \right) T \right).$$

On the other hand if $j^* > i^*$, we consider procedure LESK (j^*, j^*). We have

$$t_{j^*} = \frac{2^{j^*} 3 t_0}{j^*} \geq \frac{2^{i^*} 3 t_0}{j^*} \geq cT.$$

Since $\varepsilon/2 \leq \varepsilon_{j^*} \leq \varepsilon$, then LESK $(\varepsilon_{j^*}, t_{j^*} \frac{i^*}{j^*})$ results in **Single** with probability at least $1 - 1/n^2$, and the total time is in this case

$$2^{j^*+1}(\ln j^* + 1)t_0 = \mathcal{O}\left(\frac{\log \log(1/\varepsilon)}{\varepsilon^3} t_0 \right) =$$
$$= \mathcal{O}\left(\log(1/\varepsilon) \log \log(1/\varepsilon) T \right),$$

because since $j^* > i^*$, then $1/\varepsilon^3 \geq cT \log(1/\varepsilon)/(4t_0)$.

The probability of failure of **Estimation** is at most $2/n^2$ and the probability of failure of the selected LESK procedure is at most $1/n^2$. By the Union Bound, algorithm LESU successfully elects a leader in the correct time with probability at least $1 - 3/n^2 \geq 1 - 1/(3n)$. $\square$

3. LEADER ELECTION IN WEAK-CD

In the previous section we presented an algorithm that succeeds with high probably in electing a leader in strong-CD model by obtaining a **Single** in the channel. It is usually unrealistic in practice to assume that a station can simultaneously transmit and listen so we would like to propose a solution working in the weak-CD model.

In our solution, each station that transmits assumes that the transmission results in a **Collision**. The pseudocode of function **Broadcast** in weak-CD is as follows:

Function 3 Broadcast(u)
---
transmit with probability 2^{-u}
if transmitted **then**
    return $(\text{Collision}, true)$
else
    return (status of the channel, $false$)

Using such a modified **Broadcast** function we can deploy our algorithms for strong-CD from previous sections in weak-CD and they will give the same result until the first **Single**. It means any leader election in strong-CD can be immediately used as a selection resolution algorithm in weak-CD. After the first **Single** all the stations, except the

transmitter, are aware that the leader is elected. But the transmitter itself does not know that it became the leader and the procedure should be finished. Thus we need a procedure to notify the transmitter. With no adversary, a simple notification mechanism is sufficient: one can perform the algorithm only in odd time slots and whenever a successful transmission occurs, the stations that heard the transmission, broadcast in the corresponding even time slot. Using this mechanism, the leader can realize that it had become a leader and therefore ensuring the termination of the algorithm. However even a simple adversary can disrupt such algorithm by jamming some even time slot. In this section we will propose a new mechanism that will allow us to notify the leader and terminate the algorithm with only a constant factor overhead in the presence of any $(T, 1-\varepsilon)$-bounded adversary.

Instead of dividing the slots into sets of odd and even we will use a partition into three sets $\mathcal{C}_1, \mathcal{C}_2, \mathcal{C}_3$. The partition is defined as follows:

$$\mathcal{C}_1^i = \{3 \cdot 2^i - 3, 3 \cdot 2^i - 2, \ldots, 4 \cdot 2^i - 5, 4 \cdot 2^i - 4\}$$

$$\mathcal{C}_2^i = \{4 \cdot 2^i - 3, 4 \cdot 2^i - 2, \ldots, 5 \cdot 2^i - 5, 5 \cdot 2^i - 4\}$$

$$\mathcal{C}_3^i = \{5 \cdot 2^i - 3, 5 \cdot 2^i - 2, \ldots, 6 \cdot 2^i - 4, 6 \cdot 2^i - 4\}$$

$$\mathcal{C}_1 = \bigcup_{i=1}^{\infty} \mathcal{C}_1^i, \ \mathcal{C}_2 = \bigcup_{i=1}^{\infty} \mathcal{C}_2^i, \ \mathcal{C}_3 = \bigcup_{i=1}^{\infty} \mathcal{C}_3^i$$

Sets $\mathcal{C}_j^i$ will be called intervals because they are composed of consecutive time steps. For a fixed i, each interval $\mathcal{C}_j^i$, for $j \in \{1, 2, 3\}$ has size 2^i, thus for $i \geq \log_2 T$, the adversary cannot jam the entire interval.

Take any algorithm $\mathcal{A}$ which obtains the first **Single** in the channel in time $t(n)$ with probability at least $1 - 1/(3n)$ in the presence of a $(T, 1-\varepsilon)$-bounded adversary. Algorithm **Notification** will transform any such algorithm $\mathcal{A}$ into a leader election algorithm working in time $O(t(n))$ with probability at least $1 - 1/n$ immune against the same adversary.

In algorithm **Notification** we will execute algorithm $\mathcal{A}$ twice, once in slots from $\mathcal{C}_1$ and once in slots from $\mathcal{C}_2$. We use a specific way of executing the algorithm in these sets. Assume that we want to execute $\mathcal{A}$ in $\mathcal{C}_1$. Then we will perform 2^i first steps of the algorithm in interval $\mathcal{C}_1^i$, then all stations will revert all variables associated with algorithm $\mathcal{A}$ to their initial state and will perform 2^{i+1} first steps in interval $\mathcal{C}_1^{i+1}$. For randomized algorithms $\mathcal{A}$ we perform new random choices after the restart. Thus the first 2^i steps of $\mathcal{A}$ in $\mathcal{C}_1^{i+1}$ might produce different result than 2^i steps in $\mathcal{C}_1^i$.

Such execution can last for example until **Single** in $\mathcal{C}_1$ (however we need to remember that such **Single** will not be heard by the transmitter) or until **Single** in $\mathcal{C}_2$.

In the pseudocode we write "perform algorithm $\mathcal{A}$ in $\mathcal{C}_1$ until a **Single** in $\mathcal{C}_1$ or $\mathcal{C}_2$". This means that all stations that are executing this line of pseudocode are performing algorithm $\mathcal{A}$ using slots from $\mathcal{C}_1$. The stations proceed to the next line if they hear **Single** in one of the slots from $\mathcal{C}_1$ or $\mathcal{C}_2$. Observe that the stations execute different parts of the pseudocode depending on whether the **Single** was in $\mathcal{C}_1$ or $\mathcal{C}_2$.

LEMMA 3.1. *If $n \geq 3$ and algorithm $\mathcal{A}$ obtains the first* **Single** *in the channel in weak-CD in time $t(n)$ with probability at least $1 - 1/(3n)$ and $t(n)$ is non-decreasing, then*

Function 4 Notification

$leader \leftarrow undefined$
perform algorithm $\mathcal{A}$ in $\mathcal{C}_1$ until a **Single** in $\mathcal{C}_1$ or $\mathcal{C}_2$
if $status(\mathcal{C}_1) =$ **Single then**
   $leader \leftarrow false$
   stop the algorithm in $\mathcal{C}_1$
perform algorithm $\mathcal{A}$ in $\mathcal{C}_2$ until a **Single** in $\mathcal{C}_2$ or $\mathcal{C}_3$
if $status(\mathcal{C}_2) =$ **Single then**
   if $leader = false$ **then**
      transmit in each step in $\mathcal{C}_1$ until a **Single** in $\mathcal{C}_3$
      return
   else if $leader = undefined$ **then**
      $leader \leftarrow true$
      transmit in each step in $\mathcal{C}_3$ until a **Null** in $\mathcal{C}_1$
      return

---

1. algorithm Notification *elects a leader in weak-CD in time* $\mathcal{O}\left(t(n)\right)$ *with probability at least* $1 - 1/n$,

2. *if* $\mathcal{A}$ *is immune against any* $(T, 1 - \epsilon)$-*bounded adversary for any* T *and any* ϵ *then* Notification *is also immune against any* $(T, 1 - \epsilon)$-*bounded adversary.*

PROOF. Take $i = \lceil \log_2 t(n) \rceil$ and observe that, based on the definition of Notification set $\mathcal{C}_1^i$ contains $2^i \geq t(n)$ consecutive time slots. Thus algorithm $\mathcal{A}$ succeeds in obtaining the first single in $\mathcal{C}_1^i$ with probability at least $1 - 1/(3n)$.

Assume that it happens and the **Single** is obtained in a time slot from $\mathcal{C}_1^i$. Then all stations, except the transmitter, will stop performing the algorithm in $\mathcal{C}_1$ and start a new execution of $\mathcal{A}$ in $\mathcal{C}_2$. Only the successfull transmitter from $\mathcal{C}_1$ will continue performing algorithm $\mathcal{A}$ in $\mathcal{C}_1$. Since $t(n)$ is non-decreasing then $t(n-1) \leq t(n)$ and with probability at least $1 - 1/(3n - 3)$, the second **Single** is obtained in a time slot from $\mathcal{C}_2^i \subset \mathcal{C}_2$. Now, the transmitter from $\mathcal{C}_1$ will notice this **Single**, set its leader value to $true$ and will start transmitting in $\mathcal{C}_3$. Now observe that the adversary cannot jam all slots from $\mathcal{C}_3^i$, or otherwise algorithm $\mathcal{A}$ with time complexity $t(n)$ could not exist. Thus conditioned that **Single** was obtained in $\mathcal{C}_1^i$ and in $\mathcal{C}_2^i$, we will also obtain **Single** in $\mathcal{C}_3^i$.

Let us denote by l the station that transmitted in $\mathcal{C}_1^i$, by s the station that transmitted in $\mathcal{C}_2^i$ and by R the rest of the stations. After the first **Single**, all stations from $R \cup \{s\}$ set their values of variable $leader$ to false. The only station that does not hear the first **Single** is l. Notice that l does not participate in algorithm $\mathcal{A}$ in $\mathcal{C}_2^i$ and thus will hear the second **Single**. Thus l will be the only station with variable $leader$ set to $true$. After the successful transmission in $\mathcal{C}_3^i$, all stations from $R \cup \{s\}$ will terminate the algorithm. Clearly in $\mathcal{C}_1^{i+1}$ there will be at least one **Null** since the adversary cannot jam 2^{i+1} consecutive slots. After the first **Null** in $\mathcal{C}_1^{i+1}$, station l will also terminate. Thus algorithm Notification is a correct leader election algorithm and it works in time at most $8t(n)$ with probability at least $(1 - 1/(3n)) \cdot (1 - 1/(3n - 3)) \geq 1 - 1/n$ in the presence of a $(1 - \epsilon, T)$-bounded adversary.

Observe that if $\mathcal{A}$ executed in $\mathcal{C}_1$ or $\mathcal{C}_2$ will take longer than $t(n)$ to obtain the **Single**, the algorithm Notification will still obtain the correct result and terminate. $\square$

By applying the procedure Notification to LESK we obtain an algorithm LEWK solving Leader Election in weak-CD with

Known ε. Lemma 3.1 immediately implies bound on the time complexity of such an algorithm.

THEOREM 3.2. *There exists an algorithm electing a leader in a wireless network of n stations in weak-CD model in time $O(\max\{T, \log(1/\varepsilon)/\varepsilon^3\})$ with probability at least $1 - 1/n$ in in the presence of any $(T, 1 - \varepsilon)$-bounded adversary for any known ε, unknown T and unknown $n \geq 3$.*

Finally, we apply Notification to LESU to obtain an algorithm LEWU in weak-CD without the knowledge of any global parameter. By Lemma 3.1 we immediately obtain the following theorem.

THEOREM 3.3. *There exists an algorithm electing a leader in a wireless network of n stations in weak-CD in time*

1. $\mathcal{O}\left(\frac{\log\log(1/\varepsilon)}{\varepsilon^3} \log n\right)$, *if* $T \leq \frac{\log n}{\varepsilon^3 \log(1/\varepsilon)}$,

2. $\mathcal{O}\left(\max\left\{\log\log\left(\frac{T}{\varepsilon \log n}\right), \log(1/\varepsilon)\log\log(1/\varepsilon)\right\} T\right)$, *if* $T > \frac{\log n}{\varepsilon^3 \log(1/\varepsilon)}$,

with probability at least $1 - 1/n$ in the presence of any $(T, 1 - \varepsilon)$-bounded adversary for any unknown T, ε and unknown $n \geq 115$.

Observe that for unknown constant ε and $T = \omega(\log n)$ our algorithm has complexity $O(T \log\log(T))$.

4. CONCLUSIONS

In this paper we presented a fast leader election protocol robust against a very intensive jamming caused by an adaptive adversary. The presented protocol offers an optimal (with respect to size of the network n) execution time for a practical combination of parameters. Moreover it is also close to optimal with respect to parameter T. However the problem of obtaining an algorithm that for unknown constant ε and very large $T \gg \log n$ works in time $O(T)$ is left open.

The most important is, however, that our protocol does not need any knowledge about global parameters of the model - including T, ε that describe the adversary. That is - our protocol has a purely **local** character. We believe that some of the presented procedures can be also used as building blocks in constructions of other protocols including size approximation, k-selection or fair use of the wireless channel.

Despite a well developed body of literature many vital questions are left unanswered. In particular it is not clear what countermeasures against a jammer can be constructed for the communication model without collision detection.

5. ACKNOWLEDGMENTS

This paper is supported by Polish National Science Center - decision number 2013/09/B/ST6/02258. We would like to thank anonymous reviewers for very important observations and remarks that significantly improved this paper. We also would like to thank Marcin Kardas for many inspiring discussions.

6. REFERENCES

[1] G. Antonoiu and P. K. Srimani. A self-stabilizing leader election algorithm for tree graphs. *J. Parallel Distrib. Comput.*, 34(2):227–232, 1996.

[2] B. Awerbuch. Optimal distributed algorithms for minimum weight spanning tree, counting, leader election and related problems (detailed summary). In A. V. Aho, editor, *STOC*, pages 230–240. ACM, 1987.

[3] B. Awerbuch, A. W. Richa, C. Scheideler, S. Schmid, and J. Zhang. Principles of robust medium access and an application to leader election. *ACM Transactions on Algorithms*, 10(4):24, 2014.

[4] E. Bayraktaroglu, C. King, X. Liu, G. Noubir, R. Rajaraman, and B. Thapa. On the performance of IEEE 802.11 under jamming. In *INFOCOM*, pages 1265–1273, 2008.

[5] T. X. Brown, J. E. James, and A. Sethi. Jamming and sensing of encrypted wireless ad hoc networks. In S. Palazzo, M. Conti, and R. Sivakumar, editors, *MobiHoc*, pages 120–130. ACM, 2006.

[6] S. Cai, T. Izumi, and K. Wada. Space complexity of self-stabilizing leader election in passively-mobile anonymous agents. In *SIROCCO*, volume 5869 of *LNCS*, pages 113–125. Springer, 2009.

[7] J. T. Chiang and Y. Hu. Cross-layer jamming detection and mitigation in wireless broadcast networks. In *MOBICOM*, pages 346–349, 2007.

[8] S. Dolev, S. Gilbert, R. Guerraoui, D. Kowalski, C. Newport, F. Kuhn, and N. Lynch. Reliable distributed computing on unreliable radio channels. *Proc. 2009 MobiHoc S3 Workshop*, 2009.

[9] S. Dolev, S. Gilbert, R. Guerraoui, and C. C. Newport. Gossiping in a multi-channel radio network. In *DISC*, volume 4731 of *LNCS*, pages 208–222. Springer, 2007.

[10] S. Dolev, S. Gilbert, R. Guerraoui, and C. C. Newport. Secure communication over radio channels. In *PODC*, pages 105–114. ACM, 2008.

[11] M. Farach-Colton, R. J. Fernandes, and M. A. Mosteiro. Bootstrapping a hop-optimal network in the weak sensor model. In *ESA*, pages 827–838, 2005.

[12] S. Gilbert, R. Guerraoui, D. R. Kowalski, and C. C. Newport. Interference-resilient information exchange. In *INFOCOM*, pages 2249–2257. IEEE, 2009.

[13] S. Gilbert, V. King, S. Pettie, E. Porat, J. Saia, and M. Young. (near) optimal resource-competitive broadcast with jamming. In *SPAA*, pages 257–266. ACM, 2014.

[14] Z. Golebiewski, M. Klonowski, M. Koza, and M. Kutylowski. Towards fair leader election in wireless networks. In *ADHOC-NOW*, pages 166–179, 2009.

[15] J. Hromkovic, R. Klasing, A. Pelc, P. Ruzicka, and W. Unger. *Dissemination of Information in Communication Networks - Broadcasting, Gossiping, Leader Election, and Fault-Tolerance*. Texts in Theoretical Computer Science. An EATCS Series. Springer, 2005.

[16] S. Janson, T. Luczak, and A. Rucinski. *Random Graphs*. Addison-Wesley, 2000.

[17] M. Kardas, M. Klonowski, and D. Pajak. Energy-efficient leader election protocols for single-hop radio networks. In *ICPP*, pages 399–408, 2013.

[18] V. King, J. Saia, and M. Young. Conflict on a communication channel. In *PODC*, pages 277–286. ACM, 2011.

[19] M. Klonowski, M. Koza, and M. Kutylowski. Repelling sybil-type attacks in wireless ad hoc systems. In *ACISP*, pages 391–402, 2010.

[20] E. Korach, S. Kutten, and S. Moran. A modular technique for the design of efficient distributed leader finding algorithms. *ACM Trans. Program. Lang. Syst.*, 12(1):84–101, 1990.

[21] M. Li, I. Koutsopoulos, and R. Poovendran. Optimal jamming attacks and network defense policies in wireless sensor networks. In *INFOCOM*, pages 1307–1315, 2007.

[22] X. Liu, G. Noubir, R. Sundaram, and S. Tan. SPREAD: foiling smart jammers using multi-layer agility. In *INFOCOM*, pages 2536–2540, 2007.

[23] D. Meier, Y. A. Pignolet, S. Schmid, and R. Wattenhofer. Speed dating despite jammers. In *DCOSS*, volume 5516 of *LNCS*, pages 1–14. Springer, 2009.

[24] K. Nakano and S. Olariu. A randomized leader election protocol for ad-hoc networks. In *SIROCCO*, pages 253–267, 2000.

[25] K. Nakano and S. Olariu. Randomized leader election protocols in radio networks with no collision detection. In *ISAAC*, pages 362–373, 2000.

[26] K. Nakano and S. Olariu. A survey on leader election protocols for radio networks. In *ISPAN*, page 71, 2002.

[27] K. Nakano and S. Olariu. Uniform leader election protocols for radio networks. *IEEE Trans. Parallel Distrib. Syst.*, 13(5):516–526, 2002.

[28] V. Navda, A. Bohra, S. Ganguly, and D. Rubenstein. Using channel hopping to increase 802.11 resilience to jamming attacks. In *INFOCOM*, pages 2526–2530, 2007.

[29] C. C. Newport. Radio network lower bounds made easy. In *DISC*, pages 258–272, 2014.

[30] A. Ogierman, A. W. Richa, C. Scheideler, S. Schmid, and J. Zhang. Competitive MAC under adversarial SINR. In *INFOCOM*, pages 2751–2759. IEEE, 2014.

[31] A. W. Richa, C. Scheideler, S. Schmid, and J. Zhang. A jamming-resistant MAC protocol for multi-hop wireless networks. In *DISC*, volume 6343 of *LNCS*, pages 179–193. Springer, 2010.

[32] A. W. Richa, C. Scheideler, S. Schmid, and J. Zhang. Competitive and fair medium access despite reactive jamming. In *ICDCS*, pages 507–516, 2011.

[33] A. W. Richa, C. Scheideler, S. Schmid, and J. Zhang. Self-stabilizing leader election for single-hop wireless networks despite jamming. In *MobiHoc 2011*, page 15, 2011.

[34] A. W. Richa, C. Scheideler, S. Schmid, and J. Zhang. Competitive and fair throughput for co-existing networks under adversarial interference. In *PODC*, pages 291–300. ACM, 2012.

[35] A. W. Richa, C. Scheideler, S. Schmid, and J. Zhang. An efficient and fair MAC protocol robust to reactive interference. *IEEE/ACM Trans. Netw.*, 21(3):760–771, 2013.

[36] D. E. Willard. Log-logarithmic selection resolution protocols in a multiple access channel. *SIAM J. Comput.*, 15(2):468–477, 1986.

[37] J. Zhang. Robust and efficient medium access despite jamming. *PhD. Thesis*, 2012.

Communication-Efficient Computation on Distributed Noisy Datasets

Qin Zhang[*]
Indiana University Bloomington
qzhangcs@indiana.edu

ABSTRACT

This paper gives a first attempt to answer the following general question: Given a set of machines connected by a point-to-point communication network, each having a *noisy* dataset, how can we perform communication-efficient statistical estimations on the union of these datasets? Here 'noisy' means that a real-world entity may appear in different forms in different datasets, but those variants should be considered as the same universe element when performing statistical estimations. We give a first set of communication-efficient solutions for statistical estimations on distributed noisy datasets, including algorithms for distinct elements, L_0-sampling, heavy hitters, frequency moments and empirical entropy.

1. INTRODUCTION

In many of today's applications, data is distributed in different machines/sites which are connected by a network. The sites need to answer queries defined on the union of their datasets. Different from the traditional centralized data processing where the primary goal is to minimize the number of cells/blocks probed in the RAM/disk, in the distributed setting we are mainly interested in minimizing the total bits of communication between sites and the total number of rounds of the computation, since they directly link to the network bandwidth and energy consumption, and typically dominate the total running time of the computation. These two measurements are captured by various distributed/parallel computational models, such as the BSP model [43], the $\mathcal{MRC}$ MapReduce [31], the generic MapReduce model [22] and the Massively Parallel model [34].

In this paper we consider statistical estimations in the distributed model, including computing distinct elements, heavy hitters, frequency moments and entropy, all of which are fundamental problems in data analytics. A natural way to communication-efficiently compute these statistics in the distributed model is to use linear sketches developed in the data stream literature, such as AMS-sketch [4] for frequency moments and Count-Min sketch [13] / Count-Sketch [11] for point queries. We can designate an arbi-trary site as the *coordinator*, and every other site simply computes a linear sketch of its local data and sends it to the coordinator. The coordinator adds up all local linear sketches to obtain a sketch for the global data, and then extracts the answer from the global sketch. In this paper we consider a more challenging question:

> *What if data objects in different sites are* noisy, *that is, the same real-world entity may appear in different forms in different datasets?*

We list a few scenarios where noisy data is generated.

- People may upload the same video/image to YouTube/Flickr with different sizes, formats and compression ratios.

- Queries of the same meaning may be sent to Google using different keywords combinations.

- Customers may use different spellings of their shipping addresses in their online purchases from different merchants.

Note that these types of noise, if not treated properly, will cause incorrect results in data analytics. For example, if we do not treat 100 images of the same object but compressed in different rates as the same entity, then the distinct elements of this dataset changes from 1 to 100, and the entropy changes from 0 to log 100, which is clearly unacceptable in practice.

Noisy data is universal and has caused significant obstruction to business practices [17, 19]. How to manage noisy datasets has been studied for several decades under different names, e.g., "entity resolution", "de-duplication", "reference reconciliation", "record linkage", etc. See surveys and book chapters [15, 18, 24, 33] for introductions. However, most of the proposed methods are designed for centralized computations, and focus on detecting items representing the same entity and unifying their representations, and/or outputting all distinct entities. The de-duplication procedure usually involves complicated inference models, such as relational approaches [5, 28] and collective approaches [9, 42]. In other words, those approaches target a comprehensive de-duplication, and thus have a time/space complexity at least linear (often much larger) in terms of the input size. While in this paper we consider the "big data" setting, where we assume it is relatively easy to determine whether two given items are duplicates or not (by a pairwise comparison using some distance measure), the sizes of the datasets and the number of duplicates are huge. We are interested in algorithms for statistical queries with *sublinear* communication cost and *constant or logarithmic* rounds at a modest cost of accuracy, and thus we cannot afford a comprehensive de-duplication. Therefore our setting is very different from the traditional ones for entity resolution.

This work is largely motivated by noticing that the aforementioned linear sketching approach can not be used directly for noisy

---

[*]This project was funded by IU's Office of the Vice Provost for Research through the Faculty Research Support Program.

datasets, simply because frequencies of items representing the same entity may *not* be mapped into the same bucket in the sketch and added together if sites do not communicate with each other before performing linear sketching individually. On the other hand, as mentioned above, converting noisy datasets to noise-free ones before sketching is communication expensive. Thus new approach is needed to obtain communication efficient algorithms for distributed noisy datasets.

Robust Statistics on Distributed Noisy Datasets. Now we formally define our model. We have k sites, each holding a multiset of items S_i. Let multiset $S = \bigcup_{i \in [k]} S_i$. The premise is that items in S can be partitioned into a set of groups (multisets) $\mathcal{G} = \{G_1, \ldots, G_n\}$ (for an unknown n) such that items in the same group represent the same real-world entity. The k sites would like to jointly compute some statistical function f defined on S by treating items from the same group as the same item. For example, the distinct elements function is defined to be $F_0(S) = |\mathcal{G}| = n$. We always allow a $(1 + \epsilon)$-approximation since for exact computation, in the worst case, there is often no better way than shipping all items to one site (for many statistical problems, this holds even in the noise-free case, see [45]). The precise meaning of the $(1 + \epsilon)$-approximation depends on specific problems.

We assume that each site is quipped with a *comparison metric* which, given two items, can determine whether they belong to the same group. We also assume transitivity, that is, if u, v represent the same entity (write $u \sim v$) and $v \sim w$, then $u \sim w$. This assumption guarantees a unique partition of $\mathcal{G} = \{G_1, \ldots, G_n\}$, and was used in literature [23, 39].

In fact, using a local comparison metric we can interpret a "real-world entity" in a broader sense: it can be a topic, a class, etc. In other words, we can perform statistical analysis directly on groups for arbitrary similarity-based clusterings of the dataset. For example, our algorithms can also be used for queries such as how many search topics over the union of the k datasets each of which consists of a bag of search keywords.

Justifying the Model and Assumptions. Since the model studied in this paper is new, we would like to put a few remarks trying to answer the questions readers may have, including why do we use a local comparison model with a transitivity assumption? Whether there exist some "magic" hash functions that can map all items in the same group to the same entity and make our problems easy? Can the parties resolve locally their own entity-resolution problem by considering a shared vocabulary/ontology? Due to the space constraints, we leave the discussions on these questions to the full version of this paper [47].

The Coordinator Model. For the convenience of presenting our algorithms, we introduce an extra party called the *coordinator* whose input is an empty set (we can also designate an arbitrary site as the coordinator). We divide the whole computation into *rounds*. In each round the coordinator sends a message of arbitrary length to each site, and then each site who has been contacted may send a message of arbitrary length to the coordinator. A round is completed when the coordinator has received a message from each site from whom it is expecting to get a response. We call this model the coordinator model. Our goal is to minimize the total bits of communication between all parties and the total number of rounds of the computation. Note that the underlying communication topology of the coordinator model is in fact a clique, up to a factor of 2 (the k sites can use the coordinator as the router), thus the coordinator model is essentially equivalent to the case when we allow sites to have direct point-to-point communication with each other.

The coordinator model has attracted a lot of attentions in recent years [1, 25, 41, 45]. In the high level, it is similar to the congested clique model [16, 35, 36, 40] and the k-machine model [32]. The main difference is that in the coordinator model there is no bandwidth limit on each coordinator-site communication channel. However, in our algorithms the amount of communication at each communication channel are similar since sites' positions are *symmetric*. Moreover, in all of our algorithms the total bits of communication is sublinear (low polynomials in k and $1/\epsilon$, see Table 1), thus the number of rounds will be sublinear even when in each round only 1 bit can be communicated through each coordinator-site channel.

Our Contributions. This work aims to initiate the study of designing communication-efficient algorithms for distributed noisy data objects *without* a comprehensive but still resource-consuming data de-duplication step, which is critical to queries in scenarios where data is massive, distributed and constantly evolving. We will focus on statistical estimations on the datasets. In particular, we consider distinct elements, frequency moments, L_0-sampling, heavy hitters and empirical entropy, all of which are basic measurements for understanding the distribution of a dataset, and are well-studied (on noise-free datasets) in the streaming model (e.g. [4, 7, 10, 20, 29]), the coordinator model (e.g., using linear sketches mentioned before, or mergeable summaries [1]) and the distributed monitoring model[1] [6, 14, 26, 44].

We first give the precise definitions of these problems, and then state our results. Denote $[t] = \{1, 2, \ldots, t\}$. Let $[N]$ be the item universe. Let $m = |S|$ be the total number of items in the union of the k datasets, and let n be the number of groups in S (i.e., $|\mathcal{G}|$).

1. *p-th frequency moment* of S: $F_p(S) = \sum_{i \in [n]} |G_i|^p$. When $p = 0$, F_0 simply counts the number of groups (distinct universe elements) of S (i.e., $|\mathcal{G}|$). In general, F_p can be used to measure how skew a dataset is. By allowing a $(1 + \epsilon)$-approximation we mean that the algorithm can return any value in $[(1 - \epsilon)F_p(S), (1 + \epsilon)F_p(S)]$.

2. *L_0-sampling* on S: return a group G_i (or an arbitrary item in G_i) uniformly at random from $\mathcal{G}$. Besides being used to perform *duplicate-free* sampling, L_0-sampling is the key tool for designing graph sketches [2, 3].

3. *ϕ-heavy-hitter* $(0 < \phi \leq 1)$ of S: return those "heavy" groups whose frequency is larger than ϕm. If we allow an ϵ-approximation $(0 < \epsilon \leq \phi)$, then we can return a set $\mathcal{G}' \subseteq \mathcal{G}$ containing all groups G (or an arbitrary item from each group G) such that $|G| \geq \phi m$, and no group G such that $|G| \leq (\phi - \epsilon)m$. Decisions for groups G with $(\phi - \epsilon)m \leq |G| \leq \phi m$ can be made arbitrarily. We call the relaxed version (ϕ, ϵ)-heavy-hitter of S.

4. *Empirical entropy*: $\text{Entropy}(S) = \sum_{i \in [n]} \frac{|G_i|}{m} \log \frac{m}{|G_i|}$. Empirical entropy is very effective to detect subtle changes of the data distribution.

We summarize our results in Table 1. For simplicity, we use $\tilde{O}(f)$ to denote $f \cdot \text{poly} \log(f \cdot kmN)$, and for technical convenience, we assume that $m \geq n \gg \{k, 1/\epsilon\} \gg \log(mN)$. We usually think k is larger than $1/\epsilon$ since one of the main goals of

	noisy datasets		noise-free datasets	
	(comm.) bits UB	rounds UB	bits UB	bits LB
F_0	$\tilde{O}(\min\{k/\epsilon^3, k^2/\epsilon^2\})$	$\tilde{O}(1)$	$\tilde{O}(k/\epsilon^2)$ * [14]	$\Omega(k/\epsilon^2)$ [44, 46]
L_0-sampling	$\tilde{O}(k)$	$\tilde{O}(1)$	$\tilde{O}(k)$	$\Omega(k)$
F_p $(p \geq 1)$	$\tilde{O}((k^{p-1} + k^3)/\epsilon^3)$	$O(1)$	$\tilde{O}((k^{p-1}/\text{poly}(\epsilon))$ * [44]	$\Omega(k^{p-1}/\epsilon^2)$ [44]
(ϕ, ϵ)-HH	$\tilde{O}(\min\{k/\epsilon, 1/\epsilon^2\})$	1	$\tilde{O}(\min\{\frac{\sqrt{k}}{\epsilon}, \frac{1}{\epsilon^2}\})$ * [26]	$\Omega(\min\{\frac{\sqrt{k}}{\epsilon}, \frac{1}{\epsilon^2}\})$ [44]
Entropy	$\tilde{O}(k/\epsilon^2)$	$O(1)$	$\tilde{O}(k/\epsilon^2)$ * [12]	$\Omega(k/\epsilon^2)$ ** [44]

Table 1: Our results. HH denotes heavy-hitter. UB and LB denote upper bound and lower bound respectively. We compare our communication costs with the upper and lower bounds of that for noise-free datasets. *These upper bounds hold even in the (continuous) distributed monitoring model. **This lower bound requires item deletions.

distributed/parallel computation is to scale to a large number of sites, while ϵ often can be thought as a constant. In this sense k/ϵ^3 is better than k^2/ϵ^2 for F_0. Moreover, in our algorithm for L_0-sampling we use an algorithm for F_0 with ϵ setting to be a constant as a subroutine, thus using the first bound $O(k/\epsilon^3)$ for F_0 will help to save a factor of k for L_0-sampling, which is significant.

We also compare our results with the corresponding bounds for the noise-free datasets in the coordinator model. Somewhat surprisingly, our upper bounds for the noisy datasets match or almost match the corresponding lower bounds for the noise-free datasets.

A Brief Technical Overview. As mentioned, some popular techniques such as hashing and linear sketching in literature cannot be used for handling noisy datasets. We thus need new approaches.

Our main results are algorithms for F_0 and an algorithm for L_0-sampling, presented in Section 3 and Section 4 respectively. For F_0 we give two algorithms. The first algorithm (Section 3.1) is an adaptation of the BJKST algorithm [7] by explicitly resolving item duplications in a final clean up step. This gives an $\tilde{O}(k^2/\epsilon^2)$ bound on communication and $O(1)$ rounds.

Our main technical contribution is the second algorithm for F_0 presented in Section 3.2.2, which achieves an $\tilde{O}(k/\epsilon^3)$ bound on communication. We proceed in two steps. We first observe a simple sampling approach using the fact that the variance can be bounded if we can reduce the maximum duplication of items to k by an initial local de-duplication step. We next further reduce the variance of the second algorithm (Section 3.2.1) by partitioning items to classes based on their duplication factors. However, it is impossible to perform a complete classification in the distributed setting without a signification amount of communication, since we have to spend some bits on each of the items. To bypass this difficulty, we first perform a local hierarchical sampling, and then use a rejection sampling process to classify items *on the fly*. In this way we only need to classify those *sampled* items, but how to bound the number of sampled items involves quite some subtleties.

For those who are familiar with sampling algorithms, we would like to comment that our distributed hierarchical sampling algorithm is very different from the now standard sub-sampling methods by Indyk and Woodruff [27] in the streaming model, and the hierarchical sampling algorithm by Gibbons and Tirthapura [21] in the distributed streaming model. The main difference is that in our setting, hierarchical sampling at each site is performed *independently*, and items reference to the same entity may be sampled at different levels at different sites because there does *not* exist a global magic hash function to assign levels to items of the same group consistently. This difference makes our hierarchical sampling algorithm and the corresponding analysis more complicated than that in [21].

In our L_0-sampling algorithm, we make use of a random shuffling step plus a synchronization step to efficiently "eliminate" noise.

The algorithms for heavy hitters, frequency moments and entropy, presented in Section 5, are straightforward adaptations of existing algorithms for the noise-free data setting. However, one needs to pick the right algorithms (for noise-free datasets) to extend. We note that most algorithms for F_p in the literature (e.g., [27]), cannot be used for noisy datasets.

2. PRELIMINARIES

We write $u \sim v$ if u and v belong to a same group G, and $u \not\sim v$ otherwise. Given $u \in S$, let $G_{(u)}$ be the group containing u. Let $a \in_R A$ denote a sample a chosen uniformly at random from A.

We need the following versions of the Chernoff bound.

Lemma 1 (Standard Chernoff Bound) *Let $X_1, \ldots, X_n$ be independent Bernoulli random variables such that $\mathbf{Pr}[X_i = 1] = p_i$. Let $X = \sum_{i \in [n]} X_i$. Let $\mu = \mathbf{E}[X]$. It holds that $\mathbf{Pr}[X \geq (1 + \delta)\mu] \leq e^{-\delta^2 \mu/3}$ and $\mathbf{Pr}[X \leq (1 - \delta)\mu] \leq e^{-\delta^2 \mu/2}$ for any $\delta \in (0, 1)$.*

Lemma 2 *Let $X_1, \ldots, X_n$ be independent scalar random variables with $|X_i| \leq M$ almost surely, with mean μ_i and variance σ_i^2. Let $X = \sum_{i \in [n]} X_i$. Then for any $\mu > 0$,*

$$\mathbf{Pr}(|X - \mu| \geq \lambda\sigma) \leq C \max\{e^{-c\lambda^2}, e^{-c\lambda\sigma/M}\}$$

for some absolute constants $C, c > 0$, where $\mu = \sum_{i=1}^n \mu_i$ and $\sigma^2 = \sum_{i=1}^n \sigma_i^2$.

Lemma 3 *Let $Y_1, \ldots, Y_n$ be n independent random variables such that $Y_i \in [0, T]$ for some $T > 0$. Let $\mu = \mathbf{E}[\sum_i Y_i]$. Then for any $a > 0$, we have $\mathbf{Pr}\left[\sum_{i \in [n]} Y_i > a\right] \leq e^{-(a-2\mu)/T}$.*

We also need the following observation.

Observation 1 *The coordinator can sample s items from S uniformly at random with replacement using $\tilde{O}(k + s)$ bits of communication and $O(1)$ rounds.*

PROOF. First each site i sends $|S_i|$ to the coordinator and the coordinator computes $|S| = \sum_{i \in [k]} |S_i|$. Next, the coordinator samples s sites from the k sites with replacement such that the probability that site i is sampled each time is $|S_i| / |S|$, and then each sampled site i samples an item uniformly at random from S_i and sends to the coordinator. $\square$

3. THE DISTINCT ELEMENTS PROBLEM

In this section we give algorithms for distinct elements (F_0). W.l.o.g., we assume that for any S_i, for any $u, v \in S_i$, we have

---

Algorithm 1: Estimating F_0 for Distributed Noisy Datasets by Extending BJKST

1 the coordinator picks a random hash function $h : [N] \to [N]$ from a 2-universal family, and sends it to each of the k sites;

2 each site i individually runs the BJKST algorithm with $\lambda = ck$ for a large enough constant c, and sends z_i and the set B_i to the coordinator;

3 the coordinator computes $z = \max\{z_i \mid i \in [k]\}$;

4 for each $i \in [k]$, the coordinator removes all pairs $(u, \text{zero}(h(u)))$ in B_i with $\text{zero}(h(u)) < z$, getting set $B_i' \subseteq B_i$;

5 (*synchronization*) the coordinator checks for each $i \in [k]$, for each $u \in B_i'$, if there exists a $j < i$ such that $v \in S_j$ and $u \sim v$, by communicating u with sites $1, \ldots, i-1$ in order. If yes, coordinator deletes u from B_i'. Let $B_1'', \ldots, B_k''$ be the sets of $B_1', \ldots, B_k'$ after the synchronization;

6 the coordinator computes set $B'' = \bigcup_{i \in [k]} B_i''$, and outputs $|B''| 2^z$.

Algorithm 2: Estimating F_0 for Distributed Noisy Datasets by Sampling

1 the coordinator computes $m = \sum_{i \in [k]} |S_i|$ by contacting each site;

2 **for** $i = 1, \ldots, \eta_k$ **do**

3   the coordinator samples a random item $u_i \in S$ using Observation 1;

4   the coordinator computes $|G_{(u_i)}|$ by contacting k sites, and sets $X_i = 1/|G_{(u_i)}|$;

5 the coordinator outputs $\left(\frac{1}{\eta_k} \sum_{i \in [\eta_k]} X_i\right) m$.

$u \not\sim v$, that is, we only keep one item in the same group for each S_i. We can assume this because removing local duplicates will not affect the value of F_0 (or performing L_0-sampling in Section 4), and each site can remove local duplicates without any communication.

3.1 Warm Up: Extending BJKST

We first briefly sketch the BJKST algorithm for the noise-free data setting (slightly modified for our purpose). We choose a random hashing function $h : [N] \to [N]$ from a 2-universal hash family. For each item $u \in S$, we apply the hash function h on u and compute $\text{zeros}(h(u))$, which is the number of tailing zeros in the binary representation of $h(u)$. At the end we compute the largest number z such that there are at least λ/ϵ^2 (for a parameter λ specified later) items with $\text{zeros}(h(u)) \geq z$. We call z the *threshold* of the set S. We also maintain a set of pairs $B = \{(u, \text{zeros}(h(u))) \mid \text{zeros}(h(u)) \geq z\}$ during the run of the algorithm.

Lemma 4 ([7]) *For a large enough constant λ, the quantity $|B| 2^z$ is a $(1 + \epsilon)$-approximation of the distinct elements of the set S in the noise-free setting with probability at least 0.99.*

Remark 1 The BJKST algorithm [7] is originally designed to work in the streaming model, thus we want to choose the *largest z* which will guarantee that $|\{u \in S \mid \text{zeros}(h(u)) \geq z\}| \in [\lambda/\epsilon^2, 4\lambda/\epsilon^2]$ with high probability, thus also the space usage. However, picking any z satisfying $|\{u \in S \mid \text{zeros}(h(u)) \geq z\}| \geq \lambda/\epsilon^2$ for a large enough constant λ is sufficient to make $|B| 2^z$ a $(1 + \epsilon)$-approximation of $F_0(S)$ with probability at least 0.99. This hashing idea can be traced back to Flajolet-Martin [20] and Alon et al. [4] who gave constant approximations.

Our algorithm for noisy datasets is presented in Algorithm 1, where $c, z_i, B_i, B_i', B_i'', B''$ are defined. Line 1 to 4 is basically a run of the BJKST in the distributed setting, but we need to sample $\Theta(k/\epsilon^2)$ items even after the item removals at Line 4. The reason is that at Line 5 we need to perform a synchronization step to make sure that only one item in each group (the first one counting from site 1 to site k) is considered, so as to make the decisions (i.e., sampled or not) for items in a single group consistent. In other words, we are sampling groups, not individual items.

Correctness. Let $B' = \bigcup_{i \in [k]} B_i'$. First, it is easy to see that $|B'| \geq ck/\epsilon^2$, since there is at least one $i \in [k]$ such that $z_i = z$, thus $B_i' = B_i$ and $|B_i'| \geq ck/\epsilon^2$. The synchronization step guarantees that only one item (the one appears in the site with the smallest index) in each group is considered in the "global" BJKST algorithm. Since $|B'| \geq ck/\epsilon^2$, and each group only has at most one item in each site (see the discussion at the beginning of Section 3), we have $|B''| \geq |B'|/k \geq c/\epsilon^2$. Thus Lemma 4 and Remark 1 give the correctness.

Complexities. Lines 1, 3 cost $\tilde{O}(k)$ bits of communication. Lines 2, 4, 5 cost $\tilde{O}(k^2/\epsilon^2)$ bits of communication. Line 6 is entirely local, and can be done by the coordinator without any communication. It is easy to see that this algorithm can be implemented in $O(1)$ rounds.

Theorem 1 *Algorithm 1 computes a $(1+\epsilon)$-approximation of $F_0(S)$ correctly with probability at least 0.99 in the distributed noisy data setting, using $\tilde{O}(k^2/\epsilon^2)$ bits of communication and $O(1)$ rounds.*

3.2 An Improved Algorithm (for Large k)

In this section we give an improved algorithm for robust F_0 when $k = \omega(1/\epsilon)$.

3.2.1 A Sampling Algorithm

We first introduce a simple sampling algorithm, which will be used in our improved algorithm as a subroutine. The sampling algorithm is presented in Algorithm 2, where u_i, X_i's are defined. Let $\eta_q = c_\eta \cdot q/\epsilon^2 \cdot \log(1/\delta)$ for a sufficiently large constant c_η.

Correctness. We will show that $\left(\frac{1}{\eta_k} \sum_{i \in [\eta_k]} X_i\right) m$ is a $(1 + \epsilon)$-approximation of n with probability at least $1 - \delta$.

Let $\rho = n/m$. We have $1/k \leq \rho \leq 1$ since we can assume that each group only has at most one item in each site. Our goal is to show that $\left(\frac{1}{\eta_k} \sum_{i \in [\eta_k]} X_i\right)$ is a $(1 + \epsilon)$-approximation of ρ, and consequently ρm will be a $(1 + \epsilon)$-approximation of $n = F_0(S)$.

For each $i \in [\eta_k]$, we have

$$\mu_i = \mathbf{E}[X_i] = \sum_{j \in [n]} \left(\mathbf{Pr}[u_i \in G_j] \cdot \frac{1}{|G_j|}\right)$$
$$= \sum_{j \in [n]} \left(\frac{|G_j|}{m} \cdot \frac{1}{|G_j|}\right)$$
$$= \frac{n}{m} = \rho.$$

$$
\begin{aligned}
\sigma_i^2 = \mathbf{Var}[X_i] &= \mathbf{E}[X_i^2] - (\mathbf{E}[X_i])^2 \\
&= \sum_{j \in [n]} \left(\mathbf{Pr}[u_i \in G_j] \cdot \frac{1}{|G_j|^2} \right) - \left(\frac{n}{m} \right)^2 \\
&\le \frac{n}{m} - \left(\frac{n}{m} \right)^2 \qquad (|G_j| \ge 1) \\
&\le \rho.
\end{aligned}
$$

Let $X = \sum_{i \in [\eta_k]} X_i$. Then $\mu = \mathbf{E}[X] = \sum_{i \in [\eta_k]} \mu_i = \eta_k \rho$, and $\sigma^2 = \mathbf{Var}[X] = \sum_{i \in [\eta_k]} \sigma_i^2 \le \eta_k \rho$. Setting $\lambda = \epsilon\mu/\sigma$ in Lemma 2, noting that $X_i \le 1$ for all $i \in [\eta_k]$, by Lemma 2 we have

$$
\begin{aligned}
\mathbf{Pr}[|X - \mu| \ge \epsilon\mu] &\le C \max\{ e^{-c(\epsilon\mu/\sigma)^2}, e^{-c(\epsilon\mu/\sigma)\sigma} \} \\
&\le C \max\{ e^{-c\epsilon^2(\eta_k\rho)^2/(\eta_k\rho)}, e^{-c\epsilon(\eta_k\rho)} \} \\
&\le C \cdot e^{-c\epsilon^2/k \cdot \eta_k},
\end{aligned}
$$

which is at most δ if $\eta_k = c_\eta \cdot k/\epsilon^2 \cdot \log(1/\delta)$ for a sufficient large constant c_η. Therefore $\frac{1}{\eta_k} X = \left(\frac{1}{\eta_k} \sum_{i \in [\eta_k]} X_i \right)$ is a $(1 + \epsilon)$-approximation of ρ with probability at least $1 - \delta$.

Complexities. Set $\delta = 0.01$. Line 1 costs $\tilde{O}(k)$ bits of communication. Both Line 3 and 4 cost $\tilde{O}(k)$ bits of communication. Thus the total communication cost is $\tilde{O}(\eta_k \cdot k) = \tilde{O}(k^2/\epsilon^2)$. The number of rounds is $O(1)$ since we can run the algorithm for each sample in parallel.

Theorem 2 *Algorithm 2 computes a $(1+\epsilon)$-approximation of $F_0(S)$ correctly with probability at least 0.99 in the distributed noisy data setting, using $\tilde{O}(k^2/\epsilon^2)$ bits of communication and $O(1)$ rounds.*

Note that this sampling algorithm achieves the same complexity as Algorithm 1. We would like to include both since the idea in Algorithm 1 will be shared by the algorithm for L_0-sampling in Section 4, and this sampling algorithm will be used as a subroutine in our improved algorithm in the next subsection.

3.2.2 The Improved Algorithm

We now present our improved algorithm (when $k = \omega(1/\epsilon)$) for estimating robust F_0. The main idea is to reduce the variance of each X_i in Algorithm 2. Imagine that in the special case when the frequency of each group is either 1 or 2, the variance of each X_i in Algorithm 2 will be reduced by a factor of $\Theta(k)$ (in the worst case). Thus if we can partition all groups in $\mathcal{G}$ into classes $\mathcal{G}_0, \mathcal{G}_1, \ldots, \mathcal{G}_{\log k}$ such that $\mathcal{G}_j = \{ G \in \mathcal{G} \mid |G| \in (2^{j-1}, 2^j] \}$, and apply Algorithm 2 on each class individually, then we can shave a factor of k in the number of X_i needed (i.e., reduce the number of samples from η_k to η_2), thus also the communication cost. However, we cannot afford to partition the groups into classes in the distributed setting, because to do so we basically need to estimate the cardinality of each group up to a factor of 2, which needs $\Omega(F_0)$ bits communication.

In our new approach we do the following: Each site independently subsamples its items with probability $p_\ell = 1/2^\ell$ for $\ell = 0, 1, \ldots, L$ ($L = \log k$), which we call the *sample levels*. This naturally partitions all items (*not* groups) in S into a hierarchy of classes. As mentioned in the introduction, due to the lack of a global magic hash function, items in the same group may be sampled into different levels in different sites, which is very different from previous distributed/streaming sampling algorithms [21, 27], and is one of the major difficulties in our algorithm design and analysis.

More precisely, site i sets $V_i^0 = S_i$, and then for $\ell = 1, \ldots, L$, it constructs V_i^ℓ by subsampling each item in $V_i^{\ell-1}$ with probability $1/2$. Finally, site i sets $W_i^L = V_i^L$, and for $\ell = L - 1, \ldots, 1, 0$, it sets $W_i^\ell = V_i^\ell \setminus V_i^{\ell+1}$. Let multiset $W^\ell = \bigcup_{i \in [k]} W_i^\ell$. Note that $\{W^0, \ldots, W^L\}$ is a partition of S. For a group $G \in \mathcal{G}$, let $G^\ell = G \cap W^\ell$ be the multiset of items in G whose maximum sample levels are ℓ.

The first natural idea is to estimate $F_0(S)$ as $\sum_{i=0}^L F_0(W^i)$, but there are two issues: First, we will have the problem of double-counting, that is, we may have $u \in W^\ell$ and $v \in W^{\ell'}$ ($\ell' \ne \ell$) such that $u \sim v$. In other words, two items in the same group may belong to two different W^ℓ's, and consequently this group will be counted at least twice. Second, for a level ℓ and an item $u \in W^\ell$, it may still be the case that $|G_{(u)}^\ell|$ is large, and then if we run Algorithm 2, the variance of the estimator X_i will again be high. To handle these two issues, we define $\tilde{W}^\ell \subseteq W^\ell$ for each $\ell = 0, 1, \ldots, L$ as follows.

Definition 1 Let $\tilde{W}^\ell$ be the multiset containing all items u satisfying the following.

1. $u \in W^\ell$.

2. There does not exists $v \in W^{\ell'}$ such that $u \sim v$ and $\ell' > \ell$. In other words, $\ell = \max\{\ell' \mid |G_{(u)}^{\ell'}| > 0\}$.

3. $|G_{(u)}^\ell| \le \tau$, where $\tau = 16 \log m$.

The second constraint is used to avoid double-counting: each group G will only be counted at most once at the level $\max\{\ell \mid |G^\ell| > 0\}$. The third constraint is used to force the frequency of each group at each level to be no more than τ, for the purpose of reducing the variance when running Algorithm 2. However, by doing this it is possible that some groups are not counted at any level. Denote Q to be the set of such groups, then

$$
F_0(S) = \sum_{\ell=0}^L F_0(\tilde{W}^\ell) + |Q|.
$$

The following lemma shows that $|Q| = 0$ with high probability.

Lemma 5 *Let Q consist of all groups $G \in \mathcal{G}$ such that there exists an $\ell \in \{0, 1, \ldots, L\}$ with $|G^\ell| > \tau$, and there does not exist a $u \in G$ such that $u \in W^{\ell'}$ for an $\ell' > \ell$. We have that $|Q| = 0$ with probability at least $1 - 1/m$.*

PROOF. First, at level $\ell = L$, for each group G, by Lemma 3, noting that $\mu \le k \cdot 1/k = 1$, we have,

$$
\mathbf{Pr}[|G^L| > \tau] \le e^{-(\tau-2)} \le 1/m^3.
$$

By a union bound, with error probability at most $\delta_L = 1/m^3 \cdot n \le 1/m^2$, $|G^L| \le \tau$ holds for each group $G \in \mathcal{G}$.

We next consider any fixed level $\ell \in \{0, 1, \ldots, L-1\}$. For each group G, if $|G^\ell| > \tau$, then by a Chernoff bound we have

$$
\begin{aligned}
\mathbf{Pr}[|G^{\ell+1}| = 0] &\le \mathbf{Pr}\left[|G^{\ell+1}| < (1 - 99/100) \cdot |G^\ell|/2 \right] \\
&\le e^{-\frac{(99/100)^2 \cdot |G^\ell|/2}{2}} \le e^{-\tau/5} \le 1/m^3.
\end{aligned}
$$

By a union bound, with error probability at most $\delta_{<L} = 1/m^3 \cdot L \cdot n$, for any group $G \in \mathcal{G}$ and any level $\ell \in \{0, 1, \ldots, L-1\}$, if $|G^\ell| \ge \tau$, then $|G^{\ell+1}| \ge 1$, which means that G should be counted in $\tilde{W}^{\ell'}$ for some $\ell' > \ell$.

Combining the two cases, the probability that $|Q| = 0$ is at least $1 - \delta_L - \delta_{<L} \ge 1 - 1/m^2 - 1/m^3 \cdot L \cdot n \ge 1 - 1/m$. $\square$

We say a level ℓ is *contributing* if $F_0(\tilde{W}^\ell) \geq (\epsilon/L) \cdot F_0(S)$, otherwise non-contributing. Then,

$$F_0(S) \geq \sum_{\text{contributing } \ell} F_0(\tilde{W}^\ell) \tag{1}$$

$$= F_0(S) - |Q| - \sum_{\text{non-contributing } \ell} F_0(\tilde{W}^\ell)$$

$$\geq (1 - \epsilon/L \cdot L)F_0(S) \quad \text{(w. pr. } 1 - 1/m \text{ by Lemma 5)}$$

$$= (1 - \epsilon)F_0(S). \tag{2}$$

Therefore to get a $(1 + O(\epsilon))$-approximation of $F_0(S)$, it suffices to estimate $F_0(\tilde{W}^\ell)$ for each contributing ℓ up to a $(1 + \epsilon)$-approximation.

The difficulty of estimating $F_0(\tilde{W}^\ell)$ is that the k sites cannot compute $\tilde{W}^\ell$ exactly or even approximately without spending $\Omega(k)$ bits of communication to check if an item u is in $\tilde{W}^\ell$, which is communication prohibitive. We therefore have to check whether $u \in \tilde{W}^\ell$ when running Algorithm 2 on W^ℓ (from which sites can sample items easily, since site i knows W_i^ℓ exactly), and then reject those samples in $W^\ell \backslash \tilde{W}^\ell$.

Our algorithm is presented in Algorithm 3. We will show that for a contributing level ℓ, with high probability Algorithm 3 will reach Line 22, thus obtaining a $(1 + \epsilon)$-approximation of $F_0(\tilde{W}^\ell)$.

One may observe that items from groups with large cardinalities will be sampled with a higher probability at Line 5, but those items are more likely in $W^\ell \backslash \tilde{W}^\ell$, thus we may waste communication on items that will be rejected eventually. Fortunately, we can show in the following lemma that such items can be rejected quickly, thus will not affect the efficiency of the rejection-sampling (to get a sample from $\tilde{W}^\ell$).

Lemma 6 *For a sample $u \in U$ at level ℓ, with probability at least $1 - 1/m^4$, we will contact at most $2\tau k/|G_{(u)}^\ell|$ (random) sites at Line 9 in Algorithm 3 before existing the while loop.*

PROOF. If $|G_{(u)}^\ell| \leq \tau$, then $2\tau k/|G_{(u)}^\ell| \geq k$. We thus only need to prove that the number of sites contacted at Line 9 is bounded by $2\tau k/|G_{(u)}^\ell|$ when $|G_{(u)}^\ell| > \tau$.

Let $\gamma = 2\tau k/|G_{(u)}^\ell|$. Let i_j $(j = 1, \ldots, \gamma)$ be the site sampled in the j-th trial (without replacement). Let $Y_j = 1$ if there exists a $v \in W_{i_j}^\ell$ such that $u \sim v$, and $Y_j = 0$ otherwise. Let $Y = \sum_{j \in [\gamma]} Y_j$. Let $\mu = |G_{(u)}^\ell|/k$. By a Chernoff bound (Chernoff bound also holds for sample without replacement, cf. [8]),

$$\mathbf{Pr}[Y \leq \tau] = \mathbf{Pr}[Y \leq \gamma\mu/2]] \leq e^{-\frac{(1/2)^2 \gamma\mu}{2}} = e^{-\tau/4} = 1/m^4.$$

We thus can detect $|G_{(u)}^\ell| \geq Y > \tau$ with probability $1 - 1/m^4$. $\square$

We now present our key lemma.

Lemma 7 *For a contributing level ℓ, with probability $1 - 1/m^3$, we will reach Line 22 in Algorithm 3, or, we will have $|U| \geq \eta_\tau$.*

PROOF. It is easy to observe that in the worst case (w.r.t. the total communication cost), $\forall u \in \tilde{W}^\ell$ has $|G_{(u)}^\ell| = 1$. This is because (1) the sample probability for each item u is proportional to $|G_{(u)}^\ell|$; and (2) the communication spent on sampling sites and checking at Line $9 - 18$ for items in $\tilde{W}^\ell$ is negligible compared with the total budget t (defined at Line 3 of Algorithm 3):

$$|U| \cdot k \cdot c_u \log N$$
$$\leq \eta_\tau \cdot c_u k \log N$$
$$= c_\eta \cdot 16 \log^2 m/\epsilon^2 \cdot \log(200(L+1)) \cdot c_u k \log N$$
$$= o(t),$$

Algorithm 3: Estimating $F_0(\tilde{W}^\ell)$ for an $\ell \in \{0, 1, \ldots, L\}$

```
1  cost ← 0, U ← ∅;
2  η_τ ← c_η · 16 log² m/ε² · log(200(L + 1))      /* set
      δ = 1/(200(L + 1)) */;
3  t ← c_t · k/ε³ · log³ k log² m log N      /* c_t is a
      sufficiently large constant */;
4  while (cost ≤ t) ∧ (|U| < η_τ) do
5  |  the coordinator and sites generate a new sample (with
   |    replacement) u ∈ W^ℓ;
6  |  s ← 0  /* number of sites contacted */;
7  |  z ← 0 /* number of items in G_(u)^ℓ found in
   |    sampled sites */;
8  |  while s < k do      /* test whether u ∈ W̃^ℓ */
9  |  |  the coordinator samples (without replacement) a
   |  |    random site I ∈ [k], and sends u to site I ;
10 |  |  s ← s + 1, cost ← cost + 1 ;
11 |  |  if ∃v ∈ W_I^ℓ such that u ~ v then
12 |  |  |  z ← z + 1;
13 |  |  |  if z > τ then
14 |  |  |  |  mark u bad;
15 |  |  |  |  break /* do not satisfy item 3 in
   |  |  |  |    Definition 1 */;
16 |  |  if ∃v ∈ W_I^{ℓ'} such that ℓ' > ℓ and u ~ v then
17 |  |  |  mark u bad;
18 |  |  |  break      /* do not satisfy item 2 in
   |  |  |    Definition 1 */;
19 |  if u is not marked bad then
20 |  |  U ← U ∪ {u};
21 if |U| ≥ η_τ then
22 |  run Algorithm 2 on U and output whatever Algorithm 2
   |    outputs      /* Since U can be kept at the
   |    coordinator locally, Algorithm 2 can be
   |    run on U without any communication */;
23 else output 0;
```

---

where $c_u \log N$ (for a small constant c_u) is the communication cost between Line $9 - 18$ (the coordinator sends u to the sampled site, and site gives feedback). We thus consider this worst case for simplicity.

Let $C_j^\ell = \{u \in S \mid |G_{(u)}^\ell| \in (2^{j-1}, 2^j]\}$ $(j = 0, 1, \ldots, \log k)$. Let $W_j^\ell = W^\ell \cap C_j^\ell$. In words, W_j^ℓ contains all items u in W^ℓ such that the corresponding group $G_{(u)}$ satisfies $|G_{(u)}^\ell| \in (2^{j-1}, 2^j]$. According to our worst case assumption, we have $\tilde{W}^\ell \subseteq W_0^\ell$.

Let $D^\ell \subseteq W^\ell$ be the set of sampled items at Line 5. Then $U = \tilde{W}^\ell \cap D^\ell$. Let $D_j^\ell = W_j^\ell \cap D^\ell$. We prove by contradiction. Suppose $|U| < \eta_\tau$, we will show that the total communication spent should be less than t with high probability. We need the following technical claim, which says that if the cardinality of U (useful samples from $\tilde{W}^\ell$) is small, then the cardinalities of all D_j are also small.

Claim 1 *If $|U| < \eta_\tau$, then $|D_j^\ell| < 2 \cdot 2^j \cdot L/\epsilon \cdot \eta_\tau$ with probability $1 - 1/m^4$ for each $j = 0, 1, \ldots, \log k$.*

PROOF. (for Claim 1) For each $j \in \{0, 1, \ldots, \log k\}$, we can assume that there are only two sets of items (overlap when $j = 0$), $\tilde{W}^\ell$ and W_j^ℓ, in W^ℓ, since a sample outside $\tilde{W}^\ell$ and W_j^ℓ will

---

Algorithm 4: Estimating F_0 for Distributed Noisy Datasets by Hierarchical Sampling

---

1 for $\ell = 0, 1, \ldots, L$ **do**

2 $\quad$ run Algorithm 3, and let z_ℓ be the output (i.e., an estimation of $F_0(\tilde{W}^\ell)$).

3 output $\sum_{\ell=0}^{L} z_\ell$.

---

not contribute to either U or D_j^ℓ. By the fact that the sampling probability for each item u is proportional to $|G_{(u)}^\ell|$, and $|\tilde{W}^\ell| \geq \epsilon/L \cdot n$ (definition of a contributing level ℓ), and the worst case assumption that $|G_{(u)}^\ell| = 1$ for each $u \in \tilde{W}^\ell$, we have that for each sample u,

$$\mathbf{Pr}\left[u \in \tilde{W}^\ell\right] = \frac{|\tilde{W}^\ell|}{|\tilde{W}^\ell \cup W_j^\ell|} \geq \frac{1 \cdot (\epsilon/L \cdot n)}{2^j \cdot n} = \frac{1}{2^j L/\epsilon}. \quad (3)$$

Let s be the total number of items we have sampled from $\tilde{W}^\ell \cup W_j^\ell$. Let $X_i = 1$ if the i-th sample in $|U \cup D_j^\ell|$ is in $\tilde{W}^\ell$, and $X_i = 0$ otherwise. Thus $\mathbf{E}[X_i] \geq 1/(2^j L/\epsilon)$ by Inequality (3) for each $i \in [s]$. Note that $U = \sum_{i \in [s]} X_i$, thus $\mathbf{E}[U] \geq s/(2^j L/\epsilon)$. By a Chernoff bound,

$$\mathbf{Pr}\left[|U| \geq \frac{\mathbf{E}[U]}{2}\right] \geq \mathbf{Pr}\left[|U| \geq \frac{s}{2 \cdot 2^j L/\epsilon}\right] \geq 1 - e^{-\frac{s}{8 \cdot 2 \cdot 2^j L/\epsilon}}.$$

Thus given $|U| < \eta_\tau$, we have $|U \cup D_j^\ell| = s < 2 \cdot 2^j L/\epsilon \cdot \eta_\tau$ with probability $(1 - e^{-\eta_\tau/8}) \geq (1 - 1/m^4)$. Therefore $|D_j^\ell| \leq |U \cup D_j^\ell| < 2 \cdot 2^j L/\epsilon \cdot \eta_\tau$ with probability at least $1 - 1/m^4$. $\quad\square$

By Lemma 6, Claim 1, and union bounds, with probability $1 - 1/m^4 \cdot t - 1/m^4 \cdot (\log k + 1) \geq 1 - 1/m^3$, the communication cost spent on Line $9 - 18$ (which is the asymptotically dominating cost) is bounded by

$$\sum_{j=0}^{\log k} \left(|D_j^\ell| \cdot 2\tau k/2^{j-1} \cdot c_u \log N\right) \quad \text{(Lemma 6)}$$

$$\leq \sum_{j=0}^{\log k} \left((2 \cdot 2^j \cdot L/\epsilon \cdot \eta_\tau) \cdot 2\tau k/2^{j-1} \cdot c_u \log N\right) \quad \text{(Claim 1)}$$

$$\leq 8c_u c_\eta \cdot k/\epsilon^3 \cdot \tau^2 \cdot L \log(200(L+1)) \cdot \log N \cdot (\log k + 1)$$

$$\leq 10000 c_u c_\eta \cdot k/\epsilon^3 \cdot \log^3 k \log^2 m \log N.$$

We get a contradiction by choosing a large enough constant c_t in the total communication budget t.

We run Algorithm 3 for each level $\ell = 0, 1, \ldots, L$, and the final output is the sum of outputs of the $L + 1$ runs. Our final algorithm is presented in Algorithm 4.

Theorem 3 *Algorithm 4 computes a $(1+\epsilon)$-approximation of $F_0(S)$ correctly with probability at least 0.99 in the distributed noisy data setting, using $\tilde{O}(k/\epsilon^3)$ bits of communication and $\tilde{O}(1)$ rounds.*

PROOF. For the correctness, by Lemma 7 and Theorem 2 (setting the error parameter $\delta = 1/(200(L+1))$), we know that the run of Algorithm 3 at a contributing level ℓ correctly computes a $(1 + \epsilon)$-approximation of $F_0(\tilde{W}^\ell)$ with probability at least $1 - 1/m^3 - 1/(200(L+1)) \geq 1 - 1/(150(L+1))$. By a union bound over all (at most $L + 1$) contributing levels, with probability at least $1 - 1/150$, we can compute a $(1 + \epsilon)$-approximation

---

Algorithm 5: L_0-Sampling for Distributed Noise-free Datasets

---

1 the coordinator and sites compute $\tilde{n}$, a $(1 + 0.1)$-approximation to n, using Algorithm 4;

2 the coordinator picks a random hash function $h : [N] \to [0, 2^{2+\log \tilde{n}} - 1]$ and sends to k sites;

3 each site i hashes all items in S_i using h, and sends $B_i = \{u \in S_i \mid h(u) = 0\}$ to the coordinator. Let $B = \bigcup_{i \in [k]} B_i$.

4 the coordinator outputs B if $|B| = 1$.

---

of $\tilde{W}^\ell$ for all contributing ℓ. By Lemma 5, $|Q| = 0$ with probability at least $1 - 1/m$. Plugging inequality (2), with probability $1 - 1/150 - 1/m \geq 0.99$, we correctly compute a $(1 + O(\epsilon))$-approximation of $F_0(S)$.

For the communication cost, we run Algorithm 3 for $L + 1 = \tilde{O}(1)$ levels. The cost of each run is bounded by

$$\tilde{O}(k + k/\epsilon^3) + \tilde{O}(k/\epsilon^3) + \tilde{O}(\eta_\tau \cdot k) = \tilde{O}(k/\epsilon^3),$$

where the first term in LHS counts the cost of sampling items at Line 5; by Observation 1, the coordinator can sample s items with replacement using $\tilde{O}(k + s)$ bits of communication. The second term in LHS counts the cost of sampling the sites and performing the test if a sample $u \in \tilde{W}^\ell$ at Lines $8 - 18$, which is essentially bounded by t up to some $\tilde{O}(1)$ factor. The third term in LHS counts the cost of running Algorithm 2 where the cardinality of each group is upper bounded by τ. Summing up, the cost of $L + 1$ runs is bounded by $\tilde{O}(k/\epsilon^3)$.

For communication rounds, for each level ℓ, at Line 5, we can first sample $x_1 = t/k$ samples from W^ℓ, and find y_1 of them are in $\tilde{W}^\ell$. If $y_1 \geq \eta_\tau$ we stop, otherwise we sample another set of $x_2 = 2x_1$ samples from W^ℓ, and find y_2 of them are in $\tilde{W}^\ell$. If $y_1 + y_2 \geq \eta_\tau$ we stop, otherwise we keep doubling the sample size. For Line 9, we again use the doubling method to sample sites, that is, we start with sampling 1 site, and then keep testing and doubling the sample size if necessary. In this way the number of rounds spent on each sample level ℓ can be bounded by $\tilde{O}(1)$, thus also $\tilde{O}(1)$ for all $L + 1$ levels. Using the doubling method instead of sampling items and sites one by one will increase the total communication cost by at most a constant factor. $\quad\square$

4. L_0-SAMPLING

An algorithm for F_0 can be used to design an algorithm for L_0-sampling. Let's first recall an algorithm, presented in Algorithm 5, for L_0-sampling in the noise-free setting (cf. [37]). This algorithm was originally designed for the data stream model, and we have modified/simplified it for our distributed setting when an approximation of the distinct elements n is known.

Lemma 8 (cf. [37]) *In Algorithm 5, $|B| = 1$ with probability at least $1/24$.*

In the noise-free setting, we run Algorithm 5 for C times in parallel for a sufficiently large constant C, pick the first instance that has a unique item u such that $h(u) = 0$, and output u as the outcome of the L_0-sampling. While in the noisy data setting, we again run Algorithm 5 for C times in parallel for a sufficiently large constant C, but with the following modifications:

1. Add Line 0: the coordinator (locally) randomly shuffles the order of the sites.

2. Replace Line 4 by Line 4': (*synchronization*, similar to the one in Algorithm 1) the coordinator checks for each $i \in [k]$, for each $u \in B_i$, if there exists a $j < i$ such that $v \in S_j$ and $v \sim u$. If yes, the coordinator deletes u from B_i. The check can be done by communicating u with site 1 to $i-1$ in order. Let $B'_1, \ldots, B'_k$ be the sets of $B_1, \ldots, B_k$ after the synchronization. The coordinator outputs $B' = \bigcup_{i \in [k]} B'_i$ if $|B'| = 1$.

The first random shuffling step is critical to bound the communication cost in the analysis.

Theorem 4 *There is an L_0-sampler that succeeds with probability at least 0.99 in the distributed noisy data setting, using $\tilde{O}(k)$ bits of communication and $\tilde{O}(1)$ rounds.*

PROOF. Our new algorithm is formed by adding Line 0 and replacing Line 4 with Line 4' in Algorithm 5, as described above. The correctness just inherits the one for the noise-free setting (Lemma 8), since in our algorithm we only consider a random but fixed item for each group G (the rest items in G will be deleted in the synchronization step at Line 4').

For the communication cost, Line 0 can be done locally at the coordinator. Line 1 needs $\tilde{O}(k)$ bits of communication by Theorem 3. Line 2 also needs $\tilde{O}(k)$ bits. For the cost at Line 3, we bound the size of $\sum_{i \in [k]} |B_i|$. Observe that for each $u \in S$, $\mathbf{Pr}[u \in B] = \mathbf{Pr}[h(u) = 0] = 1/2^{2+\log \tilde{n}} < 1/(2n)$, and we have $|S| = \sum_{i \in [k]} |S_i| \leq kn$ (recall that each site can eliminate local duplicates at the beginning), thus $\mathbf{E}[\sum_{i \in [k]} |B_i|] \leq 1/(2n) \cdot kn = k/2$. By a Chernoff bound, with probability at least $1 - 2^{-\Omega(k)}$, we have $\sum_{i \in [k]} |B_i| \leq k$.

Now we bound the cost at Line 4'. For each $u \in B$, let $I(u)$ be the smallest index (after the random shuffling in the newly added Line 0) such that there exists $v \in B_{I(u)}$ with $u \sim v$. This is well defined since $u \sim u$ (itself). The cost of Line 4' can be bounded $\sum_{u \in B} I(u)$.

For $j = 0, 1, \ldots, \log k$, let $C_j = \{u \in S \mid |G_{(u)}| \in (2^{j-1}, 2^j]\}$. Let $D_j = C_j \cap B$. We try to bound $\sum_{u \in D_j} I(u)$ for each j. First, since we have shuffled the sites randomly at the beginning, for a $u \in C_j$, $\mathbf{E}[I(u)] \leq k/2^{j-1}$. On the other hand, $\mathbf{E}[D_j] \leq 1/(2n) \cdot 2^j n = 2^{j-1}$, thus by Lemma 3, with probability at least $1 - 1/m^{10}$, $|D_j| \leq 2 \cdot 2^{j-1} + C \log m$ for a sufficiently large constant C. Thus with probability $(1 - 1/m^{10} \cdot m) \geq (1 - 1/m^9)$, we have

$$\mathbf{E}\left[\sum_{u \in D_j} I(u)\right] = \sum_{u \in D_j} \mathbf{E}[I(u)]$$
$$\leq (2 \cdot 2^{j-1} + C \log m) \cdot k/2^{j-1}$$
$$\leq 4Ck \log m.$$

Summing over all classes $j = 0, 1, \ldots, \log k$, we have that with probability $1 - 1/m^8$,

$$\mathbf{E}\left[\sum_{j=0}^{\log k} \sum_{u \in D_j} I(u)\right] \leq 8Ck \log m \log k.$$

By a Markov inequality and a union bound, we have $\sum_{u \in B} I(u) = \sum_{j=0}^{\log k} \sum_{u \in D_j} I(u) \leq \tilde{O}(k)$ with probability at least 0.999.

Summing up all lines, the total communication cost is bounded by $\tilde{O}(k)$ with probability 0.99 (need to properly adjust the constant success probability of Algorithm 4 at Line 1).

Algorithm 6: Finding Heavy Hitters for Distributed Noisy Datasets

1 each site i computes a Misra-Gries sketch of size $\theta = c_\theta/\epsilon$ (for some sufficiently large constant c_θ), denoted by $\mathsf{MG}_i = \{(u_1, ct_1), \ldots, (u_\theta, ct_\theta)\}$, and sends MG_i to the coordinator;

2 the coordinator merges $\mathsf{MG}_1, \ldots, \mathsf{MG}_\theta$, by treating items belonging to the same group as one item, and adding up their ct's. At the end the coordinator outputs all items whose frequencies are more than $(\phi - \epsilon)m$ as (ϕ, ϵ)-heavy-hitter.

The number of rounds can be bounded by $\tilde{O}(1)$, by Theorem 3 and the fact that Line 4' can be done in $\tilde{O}(1)$ rounds using the doubling method when communicating u with site 1 to $i-1$ in order. $\square$

5. HEAVY HITTERS, ENTROPY AND FREQUENCY MOMENTS

In this section we consider several statistical functions for which we can easily adopt existing algorithms designed for noise-free datasets, but one needs to find the right algorithms to extend.

5.1 Heavy Hitters

We note that the heavy-hitter problem is easy in the noisy data setting: Each site simply computes a Misra-Gries sketch [38] and sends it to the coordinator, and then the coordinator merges the k sketches and computes the set of heavy-hitters. See Algorithm 6 for details. The key feature here is that the Misra-Gries sketch simply consists of a list of (item ID, count) pairs, thus the coordinator can recognize if two items belong to the same group, and add up their counts.

Another algorithm that computes (ϕ, ϵ)-heavy-hitter is the simple sampling: The coordinator and sites sample $C \log N/\epsilon^2$ (for some large enough constant C) items from S, which is enough to estimate the cardinalities of all groups in $\mathcal{G}$ up to an additive error ϵm with success probability 0.99 (by a union bound).

Theorem 5 *There is an algorithm that correctly computes (ϕ, ϵ)-heavy-hitter with probability 0.99 in the distributed noisy data setting, using $\tilde{O}(\min\{k/\epsilon, 1/\epsilon^2\})$ bits of communication and 1 round.*

5.2 F_p $(p \geq 1)$

We observe that a very recent algorithm by Kannan et al. [30] for F_p in the coordinator model for noise-free datasets can be adapted for computing F_p in the noisy data setting. We comment that most F_p algorithms proposed in the streaming literature, e.g., [27], cannot be used here.

Denote $f(x) = x^p$ $(p \geq 1)$. In the noise-free setting, let a_{iu} be the frequency of u in S_i, and in the noisy data setting, let $a_{iu} = |G_{(u)} \cap S_i|$. Let $[N]$ be the item universe. Let $C_i = \sum_{u \in [N]} f(a_{iu})$; $B_u = \sum_{i \in [k]} f(a_{iu})$; $A_u = f\left(\sum_{i \in [k]} a_{iu}\right)$. Let $A = \sum_{u \in [N]} A_u, B = \sum_{u \in [N]} B_u, C = \sum_{i \in [k]} C_i$.

For completeness, we first present the algorithm in [30] in Algorithm 7 (adapted to our notations), and then explain how to implement it in the noisy data setting.

Lemma 9 ([30]) *Algorithm 7 computes F_p $(p \geq 1)$ correctly with probability at least 0.99 in the distributed noise-free setting, using $\tilde{O}((k^{p-1} + k^3)/\epsilon^3)$ bits of communication and $O(1)$ rounds.*

Algorithm 7: [30] Estimating F_p ($p \geq 1$) for Distributed Noise-free Datasets

1 the coordinator picks an i.i.d. sample Z_0 of $z_0 = k^{p-2}/\epsilon^3$ items $u \in S$, where each u is picked according to the probability $\frac{B_u}{B}$. More precisely, the coordinator first picks a site $i \in [k]$ according to the probability $\frac{C_i}{B}$, and then site i picks an item $u \in S_i$ according to the probability $\frac{f(a_{iu})}{C_i}$;

2 **foreach** $u \in Z_0$ **do**
3 $\quad$ the coordinator computes A_u and B_u by contacting k sites;

4 the coordinator computes $\rho = \frac{1}{z_0} \sum_{u \in Z_0} \frac{A_u}{B_u}$, and $\tilde{A} = \rho B$;

5 **if** $\tilde{A} \geq kB$ **then** output $\tilde{A}$ and terminate;

6 the coordinator picks an i.i.d. sample Z of $z = O(k^{p-1}(\log k)^2/\epsilon^3)$ items $u \in S$, each according to the probability B_u/B (same as Line 1);

7 let $\Gamma = \{k^{p-1}, e^{-\epsilon}k^{p-1}, e^{-2\epsilon}k^{p-1} \ldots, 1\}$;

8 **foreach** $\gamma \in \Gamma$ **do** (by the coordinator)
9 $\quad$ pick a subset $Y \subseteq Z$ of size $y = \Theta(\gamma(\log k)^2/\epsilon^3)$ uniformly at random;
10 $\quad$ **foreach** $u \in Y$ **do**
11 $\quad\quad$ **for** $j = 1, \ldots, \kappa = \Theta(p\log k + \log(1/\epsilon))$ **do**
12 $\quad\quad\quad$ pick a set I of $q = \frac{k^{p-1}}{\gamma}$ of sites uniformly at random;
13 $\quad\quad\quad$ find all a_{iu} ($i \in I$) and compute $x_j = \frac{k^p}{q^p}(\sum_{i \in I} a_{iu})^p$;
14 $\quad\quad$ set $\tilde{A}_i$ to be the median of $x_1, \ldots, x_\kappa$;
15 $\quad$ **foreach** $u \in Y$ **do**
16 $\quad\quad$ set $\tilde{B}_u = a_{i(u),u}$, where $i(u)$ denotes the index of the site where u is sampled in Line 6;
17 $\quad$ **foreach** $u \in Y$ such that $\tilde{A}_u/\tilde{B}_u \in [\gamma e^{-\epsilon}, 10k\log k \cdot \gamma)$ **do**
18 $\quad\quad$ do an exact computation of A_u and B_u by contacting each site. Let $\phi_\gamma = \left| \{u \mid A_u/B_u \in [\gamma e^{-\epsilon}, \gamma)\} \right|$;
19 $\quad$ set $\varphi_\gamma = \phi_\gamma y/z$.

20 output $B \sum_{\gamma \in \Gamma} \varphi_\gamma \gamma$.

Algorithm 8: Estimating the Empirical Entropy for Distributed Noisy Datasets

1 let $\gamma = c_\gamma \cdot 1/\epsilon^2 \log m$ for some large enough constant c_γ;
2 **for** $i = 1, \ldots, \gamma$ **do**
3 $\quad$ sample an item $u_i \in_R S$, and sample $r_{u_i} \in_R |G_{(u_i)}|$, by contacting the k sites;
4 $\quad$ compute $X_i = f(r_{u_i}) - f(r_{u_i} - 1)$;
5 $\quad$ sample an item $v_i \in_R S \setminus \{x \in S \mid x \sim u_i\}$, and sample $r_{v_i} \in_R |G_{(v_i)}|$, by contacting the k sites;
6 $\quad$ compute $Y_i = f(r_{v_i}) - f(r_{v_i} - 1)$;

7 use the Algorithm 6 (setting $\phi = 0.6, \epsilon = 0.01$) to test if there is a group $G \in \mathcal{G}$ s.t. $|G| \geq 0.6m$;

8 **if** *such a group G exists* **then**
9 $\quad$ compute $p_{\max} = |G|/m$ exactly;
10 $\quad$ **foreach** *sample u_i ($i \in [\gamma]$)* **do**
11 $\quad\quad$ **if** $G = G_{(u_i)}$ **then** $Z_i \leftarrow Y_i$;
12 $\quad\quad$ **else** $Z_i \leftarrow X_i$;
13 $\quad$ output $(1 - p_{\max})\frac{1}{\gamma} \sum_{i \in [\gamma]} Z_i + p_{\max} \log(1/p_{\max})$;

14 **else**
15 $\quad$ output $\frac{1}{\gamma} \sum_{i \in [\gamma]} X_i$;

5.3 Entropy

We can simply implement the AMS-sampling based algorithm in [10] for the streaming model in our distributed noisy data setting. We present our algorithm in Algorithm 8, which is basically a simplified version of the one in [10]. The main difference is that we always work on groups.

Theorem 7 *Algorithm 8 computes a $(1 + \epsilon)$-approximation of the empirical entropy correctly with probability 0.99 in the distributed noisy data setting using $\tilde{O}(k/\epsilon^2)$ bits of communication and $O(1)$ rounds.*

PROOF. The correctness of Algorithm 8 directly follows from that in [10]. For the communication cost, the sampling part (Line 2-6) needs $\tilde{O}(k/\epsilon^2)$ bits of the communication, which is the dominating cost. $\square$

Acknowledgments: The author would like to thank Funda Ergun, Dirk Van Gucht and Ke Yi for helpful discussions.

6. REFERENCES

[1] P. K. Agarwal, G. Cormode, Z. Huang, J. M. Phillips, Z. Wei, and K. Yi. Mergeable summaries. *ACM Trans. Database Syst.*, 38(4):26, 2013.

[2] K. J. Ahn, S. Guha, and A. McGregor. Analyzing graph structure via linear measurements. In *SODA*, pages 459–467, 2012.

[3] K. J. Ahn, S. Guha, and A. McGregor. Graph sketches: sparsification, spanners, and subgraphs. In *PODS*, pages 5–14, 2012.

[4] N. Alon, Y. Matias, and M. Szegedy. The space complexity of approximating the frequency moments. *J. Comput. Syst. Sci.*, 58(1):137–147, 1999.

[5] R. Ananthakrishna, S. Chaudhuri, and V. Ganti. Eliminating fuzzy duplicates in data warehouses. In *VLDB*, pages 586–597, 2002.

[6] C. Arackaparambil, J. Brody, and A. Chakrabarti. Functional monitoring without monotonicity. In *ICALP (1)*, pages 95–106, 2009.

Algorithm 7 can be easily adapted to the noisy data setting. The general idea of the adaptation is that when we sample an item u or compute A_u, B_u for item u in Algorithm 7, we should sample or compute for the corresponding group $G_{(u)}$. We observe that in Algorithm 7:

1. When we want to compute A_u or B_u, we contact all sites.

2. When we need to sample an item with probability proportional to B_u/B, we first sample a site and then the site samples the item (Line 1). We can do this *without* knowing the frequency of that item.

These features enable us to run Algorithm 7 directly for groups instead of items. One can check that all steps in Algorithm 7 go through in the noisy data setting.

Theorem 6 *There is an algorithm that computes F_p ($p \geq 1$) correctly with probability 0.99 in the distributed noisy data setting, using $\tilde{O}((k^{p-1} + k^3)/\epsilon^3)$ bits of communication and $O(1)$ rounds.*

[7] Z. Bar-Yossef, T. S. Jayram, R. Kumar, D. Sivakumar, and L. Trevisan. Counting distinct elements in a data stream. In *RANDOM*, pages 1–10, 2002.

[8] R. Bardenet and O.-A. Maillard. Concentration inequalities for sampling without replacement. *arXiv preprint arXiv:1309.4029*, 2013.

[9] I. Bhattacharya and L. Getoor. A latent dirichlet model for unsupervised entity resolution. In *ICDM*, pages 47–58, 2006.

[10] A. Chakrabarti, G. Cormode, and A. McGregor. A near-optimal algorithm for estimating the entropy of a stream. *ACM Transactions on Algorithms*, 6(3), 2010.

[11] M. Charikar, K. Chen, and M. Farach-Colton. Finding frequent items in data streams. *Theor. Comput. Sci.*, 312(1):3–15, 2004.

[12] J. Chen and Q. Zhang. AMS-Sampling in Distributed Monitoring, with Application to Tracking Entropy. *Manuscript*, 2014.

[13] G. Cormode and S. Muthukrishnan. An improved data stream summary: the count-min sketch and its applications. *J. Algorithms*, 55(1):58–75, 2005.

[14] G. Cormode, S. Muthukrishnan, and K. Yi. Algorithms for distributed functional monitoring. *ACM Transactions on Algorithms*, 7(2):21, 2011.

[15] X. L. Dong and F. Naumann. Data fusion: resolving data conflicts for integration. *Proceedings of the VLDB Endowment*, 2(2):1654–1655, 2009.

[16] A. Drucker, F. Kuhn, and R. Oshman. On the power of the congested clique model. In *PODC*, pages 367–376. ACM, 2014.

[17] W. W. Eckerson. Data quality and the bottom line. *TDWI Report, The Data Warehouse Institute*, 2002.

[18] A. K. Elmagarmid, P. G. Ipeirotis, and V. S. Verykios. Duplicate record detection: A survey. *IEEE Trans. Knowl. Data Eng.*, 19(1):1–16, 2007.

[19] L. English. Plain English on data quality: Information quality management: The next frontier. *DM Review Magazine*, Apr. 2000.

[20] P. Flajolet and G. Nigel Martin. Probabilistic counting algorithms for data base applications. *Journal of computer and system sciences*, 31(2):182–209, 1985.

[21] P. B. Gibbons and S. Tirthapura. Estimating simple functions on the union of data streams. In *SPAA*, pages 281–291, 2001.

[22] M. T. Goodrich, N. Sitchinava, and Q. Zhang. Sorting, searching, and simulation in the mapreduce framework. In *ISAAC*, pages 374–383, 2011.

[23] M. A. Hernández and S. J. Stolfo. The merge/purge problem for large databases. In *SIGMOD*, pages 127–138, 1995.

[24] T. N. Herzog, F. J. Scheuren, and W. E. Winkler. *Data quality and record linkage techniques*, volume 1. Springer, 2007.

[25] Z. Huang, K. Yi, Y. Liu, and G. Chen. Optimal sampling algorithms for frequency estimation in distributed data. In *INFOCOM*, pages 1997–2005, 2011.

[26] Z. Huang, K. Yi, and Q. Zhang. Randomized algorithms for tracking distributed count, frequencies, and ranks. In *PODS*, pages 295–306, 2012.

[27] P. Indyk and D. P. Woodruff. Optimal approximations of the frequency moments of data streams. In *STOC*, pages 202–208, 2005.

[28] D. V. Kalashnikov, S. Mehrotra, and Z. Chen. Exploiting relationships for domain-independent data cleaning. In *SDM*, 2005.

[29] D. M. Kane, J. Nelson, and D. P. Woodruff. An optimal algorithm for the distinct elements problem. In *PODS*, pages 41–52, 2010.

[30] R. Kannan, S. Vempala, and D. P. Woodruff. Principal component analysis and higher correlations for distributed data. In *COLT*, pages 1040–1057, 2014.

[31] H. J. Karloff, S. Suri, and S. Vassilvitskii. A model of computation for mapreduce. In *SODA*, pages 938–948, 2010.

[32] H. Klauck, D. Nanongkai, G. Pandurangan, and P. Robinson. The distributed complexity of large-scale graph processing. 2015.

[33] N. Koudas, S. Sarawagi, and D. Srivastava. Record linkage: similarity measures and algorithms. In *SIGMOD*, pages 802–803. ACM, 2006.

[34] P. Koutris and D. Suciu. Parallel evaluation of conjunctive queries. In *PODS*, pages 223–234, 2011.

[35] C. Lenzen. Optimal deterministic routing and sorting on the congested clique. In *PODC*, pages 42–50. ACM, 2013.

[36] Z. Lotker, E. Pavlov, B. Patt-Shamir, and D. Peleg. Mst construction in o (log log n) communication rounds. In *SPAA*, pages 94–100. ACM, 2003.

[37] A. McGregor. Lecture notes. Available at `http://people.cs.umass.edu/~mcgregor/courses/CS711S12/index.html`, 2012.

[38] J. Misra and D. Gries. Finding repeated elements. *Sci. Comput. Program.*, 2(2):143–152, 1982.

[39] A. E. Monge and C. Elkan. An efficient domain-independent algorithm for detecting approximately duplicate database records. In *DMKD*, pages 23–29, 1997.

[40] B. Patt-Shamir and M. Teplitsky. The round complexity of distributed sorting. In *PODC*, pages 249–256. ACM, 2011.

[41] J. M. Phillips, E. Verbin, and Q. Zhang. Lower bounds for number-in-hand multiparty communication complexity, made easy. In *SODA*, pages 486–501, 2012.

[42] P. Singla and P. Domingos. Entity resolution with markov logic. In *ICDM*, pages 572–582, 2006.

[43] L. G. Valiant. A bridging model for parallel computation. *Commun. ACM*, 33(8):103–111, 1990.

[44] D. P. Woodruff and Q. Zhang. Tight bounds for distributed functional monitoring. In *STOC*, pages 941–960, 2012.

[45] D. P. Woodruff and Q. Zhang. When distributed computation is communication expensive. In *DISC*, pages 16–30, 2013.

[46] D. P. Woodruff and Q. Zhang. An optimal lower bound for distinct elements in the message passing model. In *SODA*, pages 718–733, 2014.

[47] Q. Zhang. Communication-efficient computation on distributed noisy datasets. In `http://homes.soic.indiana.edu/qzhangcs/papers/robust-stat-full.pdf`, 2015.

Parallel Computation of Persistent Homology using the Blowup Complex

Ryan Lewis
Stanford University
Stanford, CA
me@ryanlewis.net

Dmitriy Morozov
Lawrence Berkeley National Laboratory
Berkeley, CA
dmitriy@mrzv.org

ABSTRACT

We describe a parallel algorithm that computes persistent homology, an algebraic descriptor of a filtered topological space. Our algorithm is distinguished by operating on a spatial decomposition of the domain, as opposed to a decomposition with respect to the filtration. We rely on a classical construction, called the Mayer–Vietoris blowup complex, to glue global topological information about a space from its disjoint subsets. We introduce an efficient algorithm to perform this gluing operation, which may be of independent interest, and describe how to process the domain hierarchically. We report on a set of experiments that help assess the strengths and identify the limitations of our method.

Categories and Subject Descriptors

F.1.2 [**Computation by Abstract Devices**]: Modes of Computation—*Parallelism and concurrency*; F.2.2 [**Analysis of Algorithms and Problem Complexity**]: Nonnumerical Algorithms and Problems

Keywords

persistent homology; Mayer–Vietoris blowup complex

1. INTRODUCTION

Persistent homology was introduced fifteen years ago by Edelsbrunner, Letscher, and Zomorodian [1] and later placed on a firm algebraic footing by Carlsson and Zomorodian [2]. From its roots as a method to measure shape across scales, it has evolved into a rich mathematical theory with applications to clustering [3] and dimensionality reduction [4], to materials science [5] and cosmology [6], to integral geometry [7] and image analysis [8], to name just a few. We refer the reader to the several excellent surveys [9, 10, 11, 12, 13] for a more detailed look at what makes persistence so exciting both to mathematicians and practitioners.

Without losing too much generality, we can think of persistence as operating on scalar functions, $f : X \to \mathbb{R}$. It tracks

Publication rights licensed to ACM. ACM acknowledges that this contribution was authored or co-authored by an employee, contractor or affiliate of the United States government. As such, the United States Government retains a nonexclusive, royalty-free right to publish or reproduce this article, or to allow others to do so, for Government purposes only.

SPAA'15, June 13–15, 2015, Portland, OR, USA.

Copyright is held by the owner/author(s). Publication rights licensed to ACM.

ACM 978-1-4503-3588-1/15/06 ..$15.00.

DOI: http://dx.doi.org/10.1145/2755573.2755587

evolution of homology classes (an algebraic formalization of "holes") in the sublevel sets, $f^{-1}(-\infty, a]$, of these functions for varying values of threshold a. Specifically, it pairs those values of a where new homology classes appear and where they die. Such birth–death information is valuable for inference (e.g., when the domain X is high-dimensional and cannot be seen directly) and as a statistical descriptor of the function that can be used, for example, to compare different measurements of a physical phenomenon.

One ingredient in the success of persistent homology has been the development of efficient algorithms for its computation. The original paper [1] introduced a cubic-time algorithm that computes persistence by reducing a boundary matrix via a constrained Gaussian elimination. A different, output-sensitive analysis in the same paper hints at why the algorithm performs so much more efficiently in practice than the worst-case analysis would suggest. Since then an algorithm for computing persistence in matrix multiplication time has appeared [14], with a matching lower bound [15]. Other notable theoretical results include an output-sensitive algorithm that computes persistence in a top-down manner [16], the connection between different variations of the original algorithm and algebraic dualities [17], including an algorithm to compute persistent cohomology [4] and a data structure that improves its performance [18].

Another important direction in understanding computational aspects of persistence is the work on various optimizations of the algorithms. Already the original paper [1] observed that one can get rid of the so-called negative simplices during the computation. Another notable result is the *clearing* optimization [19], which zeroes out entire columns of the matrix without processing them. It's also possible to combine the two optimizations together [20], although doing so requires a different algorithm.

Despite significant successes, there is still a large gap between the sizes of data sets that persistent homology algorithms can process and what's needed in practice. One way to close this gap is to develop parallel algorithms and take advantage of the modern massively parallel computers. But any such attempt faces a fundamental difficulty: topology tracks global information, while parallel computation thrives on locality. In this paper we explore one approach to computing persistent homology in parallel. It's distinguished by dividing the work with respect to a spatial decomposition of the domain of the function, a feature important, for example, for integrating with existing decompositions used in simulation codes.

Related work. Ours is not the first attempt to design a parallel algorithm for persistent homology. Broadly, such algorithms can be split into two categories based on how they partition the computation between processors. Algorithms in the first category divide the data by function value, grouping ranges of function values together. Edelsbrunner and Harer [28] introduced the "spectral sequence algorithm," which divides the input matrix into blocks and processes them along diagonals. The algorithm is naturally parallel: blocks within a diagonal can be processed independently. Bauer, Kerber, and Reininghaus [20, 21] have examined the practical aspects of this algorithm. Notably they found clever ways to combine seemingly incompatible optimizations and implemented the algorithm, both in shared and distributed memory.

Another way to parallelize persistence, when dividing the data by function value, is using zigzag persistent homology [22]. The approach, suggested at the end of that paper, has not yet been tried in practice, as far as we know.

The second way to break up the computation between processors is to partition the domain of the function, assigning different regions to different processors. Although the approach sounds simple — it is probably the most common way to divide data for independent processing — for persistence such a partition presents a distinct challenge. Homology captures global properties of a topological space; persistent homology does so for a large collection of topological spaces at once. Gluing information from different subsets of the domain requires resolving certain algebraic issues. Translating any such resolution into a practical algorithm is a challenge of its own.

Although formulated in a different language (of spectral sequences), the work of Lipsky et al. [23] is close to ours, at least in spirit. They describe an algebraic construction that prescribes how to combine information from different subsets of the domain into a coherent whole. There are two problems with that paper. First, there is a serious technical error[1], which the authors are aware of and have a possible correction (according to a personal communication). The second problem is that, even if we restrict attention to ordinary homology (where the mentioned algebraic problem does not exist), the algorithm is not sufficiently detailed. It does not actually consider which information is available locally to any given processor, or what exactly is required to compute a particular algebraic object in parallel. There are also subtler differences between our approaches (for example, Lipsky et al. propose to collect information in the order of increasing dimension of the nerve, whereas we pursue a hierarchical decomposition of the domain), but they are less important. In this paper, we replace the algebraic construction with a geometric construction of Mayer–Vietoris blowup complex, which contains the same information, but is much more transparent computationally.

Mayer–Vietoris blowup complex was introduced to the computational topology community by Zomorodian and Carlsson [24], who used it to compute, what they called, localized homology. Although there is some overlap between the keywords of our papers, the details diverge significantly. They use persistent homology as a tool to localize homology classes to the individual sets of the cover. (And, accordingly, take a filtration with respect to the second factor of the blowup.) We are concerned with using the blowup complex as a tool to compute persistent homology of the base space. (And, therefore, filter by the first factor.)

Lewis and Zomorodian [25] use the Mayer–Vietoris blowup complex to compute ordinary homology in parallel, in shared memory. The basic ideas overlap between our papers, but persistent homology imposes more constraints on the operations one may perform during the matrix reduction. In the context of [25], Sections 3 and 4 of our paper can be seen as a way to adapt their results to persistent homology. Our work also finds more parallelism (afforded by the row operations) than exploited by Lewis and Zomorodian. As such it can be seen as an improved way to compute ordinary homology (over a field), which comes out as a byproduct of persistent homology. Also notably, Lewis and Zomorodian consider the complexity of cover construction, an important question that we ignore entirely in this paper.

To conclude our review of related work, we also note the work on distributed computation and representation of merge trees [26]. Merge trees can be used to recover 0-dimensional persistent homology, which is a very special case computationally (with different complexity characteristics than the general case). In the present paper, we are interested in the general problem in all dimensions.

Contributions. Our contributions are three-fold:

- we present the first parallel algorithm that computes persistent homology from a spatial decomposition of the domain;

- we present an efficient procedure, **Cascade** in Section 4, that combines persistence pairs from different subspaces of the domain into persistence pairs for the entire domain; that algorithm operates on matrices with a particular structure and may be of independent interest in other contexts;

- we present experiments and describe practical limitations of our results.

2. BACKGROUND

We briefly review the necessary background, but encourage the reader to consult a textbook on algebraic topology (e.g., by Hatcher [29]) or on computational topology (e.g., by Edelsbrunner and Harer [28]) for a thorough introduction to the subject.

Homology. Given a universal vertex set V, an (abstract) *simplex* is a subset of V, $\sigma \subseteq V$. The dimension of a simplex is one less than its cardinality, $\dim \sigma = \operatorname{card} \sigma - 1$. A subset of a simplex is called its *face*. A *simplicial complex* K is a collection of simplices closed under the face relation, i.e., if $\sigma \in K$ and $\tau \subseteq \sigma$, then $\tau \in K$.

In applications, simplicial complexes often arise from geometric constructions. For example, given a point set P with a metric $d : P \times P \to \mathbb{R}$, one can build a Vietoris–Rips complex for a parameter r by recording every subset $\sigma \subseteq P$,

---

[1]Briefly, the paper assumes that given a map between two persistent homology modules, the target module decomposes as the direct sum of the image module and the cokernel module, which is not the case. Recovering the former decomposition from the latter requires a certain amount of "repair." In effect, Sections 3 and 4 of our paper are dedicated to performing such a repair efficiently.

with $d(x, y) \leq r \; \forall x, y \in \sigma$. It's easy to verify that this construction is closed under the face relation.

A k-*chain* is a formal sum of k-dimensional simplices, $c = \sum a_i \sigma_i$. Throughout the paper, for ease of exposition, we assume the coefficients a_i are elements of the field $\mathbb{Z}/2\mathbb{Z}$, so a chain can be thought of as a set of simplices. The k-chains form an abelian group under addition, which we denote by C_k. The *boundary map* ∂_k takes a k-simplex σ into the sum of its $(k-1)$-dimensional faces. It extends linearly to the chain groups C_k, giving an operator $\partial_k : C_k \to C_{k-1}$.

The kernel of this operator, $\mathsf{Z}_k = \ker \partial_k$, is called the *cycle group*; by definition, it consists of all the chains with an empty boundary. The image of the operator, $\mathsf{B}_k = \operatorname{im} \partial_{k+1}$, is called the *boundary group*. A *homology group* is the quotient, $\mathsf{H}_k = \mathsf{Z}_k/\mathsf{B}_k$; it's the group of non-bounding cycles. It is convenient to suppress the dimensions by taking the direct sum of chain groups across all dimensions, $C(K) = \oplus C_k(K)$, with $\partial : C(K) \to C(K)$, and $\mathsf{H}(K) = \ker \partial / \operatorname{im} \partial$.

Persistent homology. A nested sequence of simplicial complexes, $K_0 \subseteq K_1 \subseteq \ldots \subseteq K_n = K$, is called a *filtration* of K. Passing to homology, we get a sequence of homology groups (one for each complex in the filtration), connected by linear maps induced by the inclusions.

$$\mathsf{H}(K_0) \to \ldots \to \mathsf{H}(K_i) \to \ldots \to \mathsf{H}(K_n) \qquad (1)$$

We denote the maps induced by inclusions of the simplicial complexes by $\mathbf{f}_i^j : \mathsf{H}(K_i) \to \mathsf{H}(K_j)$. Persistent homology tracks how elements appear and disappear in this sequence. We say that an element $\alpha \in \mathsf{H}(K_i)$ is born in $\mathsf{H}(K_i)$ if it's not in the image of the map $\mathbf{f}_{i-1}^i$. We say that α dies at $\mathsf{H}(K_j)$ if $\mathbf{f}_i^j(\alpha) \in \operatorname{im} \mathbf{f}_{i-1}^j$, but $\mathbf{f}_i^{j-1}(\alpha) \notin \operatorname{im} \mathbf{f}_{i-1}^{j-1}$. If there is an element α born in $\mathsf{H}(K_i)$ that dies in $\mathsf{H}(K_j)$, we record this as a pair (i, j). The goal of algorithms for computing persistent homology is to compute all such pairs (i, j) for a given filtration.

The following theorem characterizes when two sequences of homology groups produce the same persistence pairing.

PERSISTENCE EQUIVALENCE THEOREM [28]. *Given two filtrations $L_0 \subseteq \ldots \subseteq L_n$ and $K_0 \subseteq \ldots \subseteq K_n$, the induced sequences of homology groups produce the same persistence pairs, if there are isomorphisms $\mathsf{H}(L_i) \to \mathsf{H}(K_i)$ that commute with inclusions. In other words, if the vertical maps in the following diagrams are isomorphisms, and the diagram commutes.*

$$
\begin{array}{ccccccccc}
\mathsf{H}(K_1) & \longrightarrow & \cdots & \longrightarrow & \mathsf{H}(K_i) & \longrightarrow & \cdots & \longrightarrow & \mathsf{H}(K_n) \\
\uparrow & & & & \uparrow & & & & \uparrow \\
\mathsf{H}(L_1) & \longrightarrow & \cdots & \longrightarrow & \mathsf{H}(L_i) & \longrightarrow & \cdots & \longrightarrow & \mathsf{H}(L_n)
\end{array}
$$

Algorithms. Assume that we are given a filtration $K_0 \subseteq \ldots \subseteq K_i \subseteq \ldots \subseteq K_n = K$, where $K_{i+1} = K_i \cup \sigma_{i+1}$. We represent the boundary map, $\partial : C(K) \to C(K)$, as a matrix D, where $D[i, j] = 1$ if $(k-1)$-simplex σ_i is a face of k-simplex σ_j; $D[i, j] = 0$ otherwise. Notice that given such a representation, every upper-left square sub-matrix of D, sub-matrix consisting of rows and columns $[0 \ldots i]$, represents the boundary map of the subcomplex K_i, $\partial_i : C(K_i) \to C(K_i)$.

Given such a matrix, we can compute the persistence pairing in the sequence of homology groups (1) using algorithm

ELZ(D), Algorithm 1, introduced by Edelsbrunner et al. [1]. Let "low $R[\cdot, i]$" denote the lowest non-zero entry in the column $R[\cdot, i]$ (the map is undefined if the column is zero). We say that the matrix R is *reduced* if the lowest non-zero entry in every column falls in a unique row; in other words, if the map low is injective. The original algorithm [1] computes only the matrix R by greedily subtracting columns from left to right until no two columns have the lowest non-zero entry in the same row. When this happens, the lowest non-zero entries of the reduced matrix R record the sought after persistence pairing, i.e., we have a pair (i, j) in the sequence $\mathsf{H}(K_0) \to \ldots \to \mathsf{H}(K_n)$ if and only if low $R[\cdot, j] = i$.

An additional matrix U was introduced in a later work [27], which reinterpreted persistence computation as finding a decomposition $D = RU$, where the matrix R is reduced and the matrix U is invertible upper triangular. The crucial insight of that paper was that for any such decomposition, we get the same lowest non-zero entries in the columns of R (i.e., the same map low R). In particular, this means that one can subtract columns of R in any order, as long as such operations always happen from left to right. If in the end the matrix R is reduced, then we recover the correct pairing. We denote by $r_D(i, j)$ the following inclusion-exclusion of ranks of lower-left sub-matrices of D,

$$r_D(i, j) = \operatorname{rk} D_i^j - \operatorname{rk} D_{i+1}^j + \operatorname{rk} D_{i+1}^{j-1} - \operatorname{rk} D_i^{j-1},$$

where $\operatorname{rk} D_i^j$ denotes the rank of the lower-left sub-matrix of D, namely the sub-matrix that retains rows $[i..n]$ in columns $[0..j]$.

LEMMA 1 (PAIRING UNIQUENESS LEMMA [27]). *Letting $D = RU$, we have low $R[\cdot, j] = i$ iff $r_D(i, j) = 1$. In particular, the pairing function does not depend on the matrix R in the RU-decomposition.*

We do not repeat the proof of the lemma here, but briefly recall that it depends on the fact that if R is reduced then low $R[\cdot, j] = i$ iff $r_R(i, j) = 1$. Then it's easy to see that left-to-right column operations will not change the ranks of lower-left sub-matrices and, therefore, $r_R(i, j) = r_D(i, j)$.

For the present work, we need to extend this lemma to allow row operations on the matrix R.

LEMMA 2. *Letting $D = SRU$, where S and U are invertible upper-triangular and R is reduced, we have low $R[\cdot, j] = i$ iff $r_D(i, j) = 1$.*

The proof is the same as before. Neither the left-to-right column operations, expressed by the matrix U, nor the bottom-up row operations, expressed by matrix S, change the ranks of lower-left sub-matrices. Therefore, $r_R(i, j) = r_D(i, j)$.

As an immediate consequence of the amended lemma, we can choose the matrix S to be such that we get a decomposition $D = SPU$, where P is not only reduced, but it has at most one non-zero entry per column. To achieve this, we first perform the reduction prescribed by the **ELZ**(D) algorithm to get the decomposition $D = RU$. Then we go through the rows of the matrix R from the bottom up and, whenever we encounter a (unique, by induction) non-zero in a row, we subtract it from the rest of the entries in its column. This operation is formalized in the algorithm **Sparsify**(R), Algorithm 2. For clarity, we prove its correctness.

PROOF (CORRECTNESS OF ALGORITHM 2). We want to show by induction that after the outer loop processes row

Algorithm 1 Persistence reduction algorithm.

ELZ(D):
   $R = D, U = I$
   for all columns $R[\cdot, i]$ **do**
      while $R[\cdot, i] \neq 0$ and $\exists j < i$ with low $R[\cdot, i] =$ low $R[\cdot, j]$ **do**
         $R[\cdot, i] = R[\cdot, i] - R[\cdot, j]$
         $U[j, i] = 1$

Algorithm 2 Column sparsification algorithm.

Sparsify(R):
   $P = R, S = I$
   for all rows $P[i, \cdot]$ of P from bottom up **do**
      if $P[i, j]$ is not zero **then**
         for all non-zero entries $P[i', j]$ in $P[\cdot, j]$, with $i' \neq i$ **do**
            $P[i', \cdot] = P[i', \cdot] - P[i, \cdot]$ # zero out the entry $P[i', j]$
            $S[\cdot, i] = S[\cdot, i] + S[\cdot, i']$

---

i, the columns with the lowest non-zero entries in rows i and below have a unique non-zero entry, and the matrix P remains reduced. The base case is trivially true: either the lowest row of the matrix P is zero, or it has a unique non-zero entry since the input matrix R is reduced. Suppose the statement is true after the outer loop completes processing row $i + 1$. When processing row i, either the row is empty, and we are done, or again it has a unique non-zero entry. Why? Suppose there is more than one non-zero entry in the row. Then either all of them are the lowest entries in their columns, which would violate the assumption that the matrix P is reduced, or some of them have lower entries in their columns, which would violate the inductive hypothesis. Since the non-zero entry $P[i, j]$ is unique, after the inner loop of the algorithm, the column above it is zero, matrix P remains reduced, and the statement is true for all the rows up to i. By induction, at termination, the algorithm produces matrix P that is reduced and each of whose columns has at most one non-zero entry. $\square$

Blowup complex. We recall a classical construction used for gluing topological information from multiple disjoint subsets of a space. Its features relevant to our work are explained perspicuously by Zomorodian and Carlsson [24]; the original description of the structure was given by Segal [30]. Given a cover $\mathcal{C} = \{K^i\}_{i \in I}$ of a complex K by simplicial subcomplexes $K^i \subseteq K$, we denote the intersection of subcomplexes indexed by $J \subseteq I$ by $K^J = \cap_{j \in J} K^j$.

DEFINITION 3. *The* Mayer–Vietoris blowup complex *of simplicial complex K and cover $\mathcal{C}$, $K^{\mathcal{C}} \subseteq K \times I$, is defined by*

$$K^{\mathcal{C}} = \bigcup_{J \subseteq I} \bigcup_{\sigma \in K^J} \sigma \times J.$$

Figure 1 illustrates a simplicial complex, covered by three subcomplexes, and the resulting blowup complex.

Chain complex of the blowup. A basis for the chain complex may be prescribed via tensor products $C_*(K^{\mathcal{C}}) = \langle \sigma \times J \mid \sigma \times J \in K^{\mathcal{C}} \rangle$ [24, Section 4.3]. The tensor product structure endows the boundary operator of the blowup complex with a useful structure. The boundary of a cell $\sigma \times J \in K^{\mathcal{C}}$ is given by [24, Lemma 4],

$$\partial(\sigma \otimes J) = \partial\sigma \otimes J + (-1)^{\dim \sigma}\sigma \otimes \partial J. \tag{2}$$

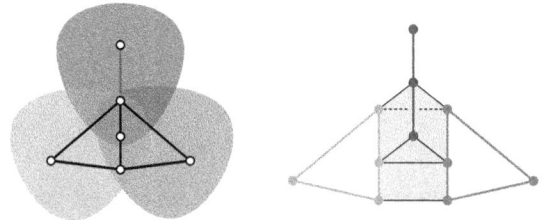

Figure 1: Left: Simplicial complex K. The subcomplexes of the cover are highlighted with three shaded regions. Right: The resulting blowup complex $K^{\mathcal{C}}$, with the disjoint subcomplexes of the cover shown in red, green, and blue.

With a boundary operator defined we may now consider the homology of the blowup complex $\mathsf{H}(K^{\mathcal{C}})$. Let $\pi : K^{\mathcal{C}} \to K$ denote the projection of the blowup complex onto the first factor. This map is a homotopy equivalence [24]. We do not define this technical term, but note that it implies that the map $\pi^* : \mathsf{H}(K^{\mathcal{C}}) \to \mathsf{H}(K)$, induced on homology, is an isomorphism.

In moving to persistent homology, we need only specify a partial order on the $K^{\mathcal{C}}$. Given a subcomplex $L \subseteq K$, its blowup complex (where the cover is the restriction of the original cover, $L^i = K^i \cap L$),

$$L^{\mathcal{C}} = \bigcup_{J \subseteq I} \bigcup_{\sigma \in (K^J \cap L)} \sigma \times J,$$

is a subcomplex of the blowup complex of $K^{\mathcal{C}}$, $L^{\mathcal{C}} \subseteq K^{\mathcal{C}}$. The projection map, $\pi_L : L^{\mathcal{C}} \to L$, is also a homotopy equivalence, so the map $\pi_L^* : \mathsf{H}(L^{\mathcal{C}}) \to \mathsf{H}(L)$, induced on homology groups, is an isomorphism. We arrive at the main reason for using the Mayer–Vietoris blowup complex.

THEOREM 4. *A filtration $K_1 \subseteq \ldots \subseteq K_i \subseteq \ldots \subseteq K$ of the base complex K induces a filtration $K_1^{\mathcal{C}} \subseteq \ldots \subseteq K_i^{\mathcal{C}} \subseteq \ldots \subseteq K^{\mathcal{C}}$ of the blowup complex. Passing to homology, we get two*

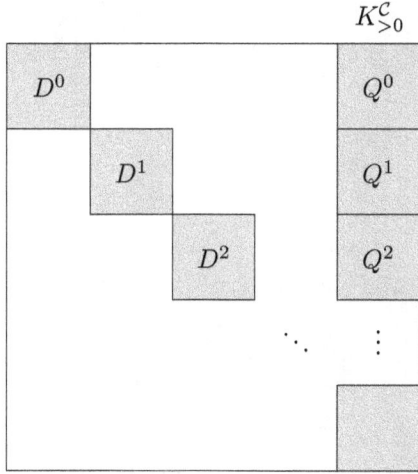

Figure 2: Schematic structure of the boundary matrix of the blowup complex. Only shaded regions may be non-zero.

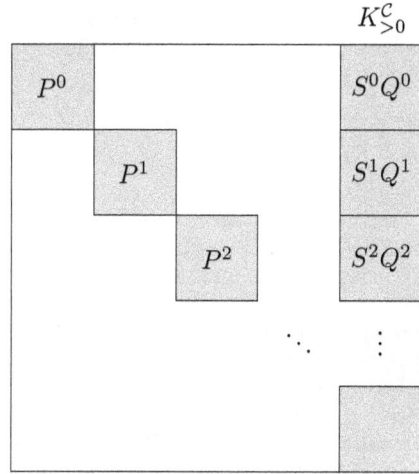

Figure 3: The matrix T', formed out of the boundary matrix of the blowup complex after the initial column and row reductions.

sequences of homology groups connected by isomorphisms,

$$\mathsf{H}(K_1) \longrightarrow \cdots \longrightarrow \mathsf{H}(K_i) \longrightarrow \cdots \longrightarrow \mathsf{H}(K_n)$$
$$\uparrow \pi_1^* \qquad\qquad \uparrow \pi_i^* \qquad\qquad \uparrow \pi_n^*$$
$$\mathsf{H}(K_1^{\mathcal{C}}) \longrightarrow \cdots \longrightarrow \mathsf{H}(K_i^{\mathcal{C}}) \longrightarrow \cdots \longrightarrow \mathsf{H}(K_n^{\mathcal{C}})$$

The persistence pairs in the two sequences are the same.

PROOF. The vertical maps are isomorphisms. The projections π_i commute with the inclusions, so the entire diagram commutes. Persistence Equivalence Theorem implies that the persistence pairs in the top and bottom sequences are the same. $\square$

In other words, we can compute the persistence pairing of the filtration of K from the filtration of $K^{\mathcal{C}}$.

We end this section by noting that in the filtration of $K^{\mathcal{C}}$, the complex is not constructed one cell at a time, i.e., the difference between $K_{i+1}^{\mathcal{C}}$ and $K_i^{\mathcal{C}}$ may consist of multiple cells. Within an algorithm we may break these ties in the partial order arbitrarily, as long as we respect the dimension of the cells. So we order the cells in $K_{i+1}^{\mathcal{C}} - K_i^{\mathcal{C}}$ by the dimension of their second factor.

3. ALGORITHM

It is helpful to understand the special structure of the boundary map (2) in the blowup complex. Over $\mathbb{Z}/2\mathbb{Z}$ coefficients, the boundary of a cell $\sigma \times J \in K^{\mathcal{C}}$ becomes

$$\partial(\sigma \otimes J) = \partial\sigma \otimes J + \sigma \otimes \partial J.$$

Let the matrix $D^{\mathcal{C}}$ represent this boundary map, with columns and rows ordered to respect the given filtration of $K^{\mathcal{C}}$. In other words, if we were to reduce $D^{\mathcal{C}}$ using the **ELZ**$(D^{\mathcal{C}})$ algorithm, we would get the correct persistence pairing.

Suppose we reorder the columns and the rows of $D^{\mathcal{C}}$ as follows. We group together the rows and the columns $\sigma \times \{i\}$ that belong to the individual disjoint sets of the cover (ordering them by filtration within these sets), and we group together columns that correspond to the cells $\sigma \times J$, where

the second factor J has dimension higher than 0, again ordering by filtration within those columns. Figure 2 shows this structure schematically: D^0, D^1, D^2 denote the submatrices of the disjoint sets, i.e., the columns of D^i record the boundaries of the cells $\sigma \times \{i\}$, where $\sigma \in K^i$. The right-most block of shaded columns represents the cells with higher-dimensional second factor, i.e., the cells $\sigma \times J$, where $\dim J > 0$. We denote by Q^i their sub-blocks that fall into the rows $\sigma \times \{i\}$ that correspond to the cells of the disjoint union. Notice that outside the shaded regions in Figure 2, the matrix is necessarily zero.

We observe that because we've ordered the cells within the blocks by filtration, we may carry out operations within the blocks — column operations from left to right, row operations from bottom up — without violating the column and row order within the original matrix $D^{\mathcal{C}}$.

Accordingly, we may column-reduce individual matrix blocks independently, decomposing $D^i = R^i U^i$ using **ELZ**(D^i) algorithm. We may further row-reduce matrices R^i, getting decomposition $D^i = S^i P^i U^i$ using **Sparsify**(R^i) algorithm. (The matrix P^i has an immediate interpretation: it records the persistence pairs in the restriction of the input filtration to the cover set K^i.) To be consistent in the full boundary matrix $D^{\mathcal{C}}$, we must perform the row operations on the full rows, thus replacing blocks Q^i with blocks $S^i Q^i$. We call the resulting matrix T', see Figure 3.

It is helpful to note the structure of the blocks Q_i. Which blowup cells have the base cells of the disjoint union, $\sigma \times \{i\}$, in their boundary? First of all, these are the cells $\tau \times \{i\}$, with $\sigma \in \partial\tau$; the first factor of their boundary map (2) consists of the cells $\sigma \times \{i\}$. Their boundaries define the columns of the sub-matrices D^i. The second type of a cell that has $\sigma \times \{i\}$ in its boundary are the cells $\sigma \times \{i, j\}$, where cover set K^j intersects cover set K^i. The part of the row of cell $\sigma \times \{i\}$ that falls into the block Q^i has non-zero entries in the columns of such cells. These are the only two possibilities allowed by the boundary formula (2). Most rows of matrices Q^i are zero, since only cells that fall into more than one cover set have non-zero entries in the columns of Q^i.

Now, if we reorder the columns and the rows of the matrix T' back into the original filtration order, call the resulting matrix T, and reduce it using algorithm $\mathbf{ELZ}(T)$, the low map on the resulting matrix R_T will produce the correct persistence pairing.

THEOREM 5. (i, j) is a pair in $\mathsf{H}(K_0^{\mathcal{C}}) \to \ldots \to \mathsf{H}(K_n^{\mathcal{C}})$ if and only if low $R_T[j] = i$.

PROOF. We pad and reorder the rows and columns of matrices S^i and U^i so that they match the original blowup boundary matrix $D^{\mathcal{C}}$. (The padding is to identity, i.e., the newly added rows and columns have 1s on the diagonal, so the padded matrices remain invertible upper-triangular.) Since the operations in matrices D^i respected the filtration order, the padded matrices S^i and U^i remain invertible upper-triangular. Therefore, so are their products $S = S^0 \cdot S^1 \cdot \ldots$ and $U = U^0 \cdot U^1 \cdot \ldots$. Therefore, the first set of independent reductions results in the decomposition $D^{\mathcal{C}} = STU$, with T appropriately reordered. Now reducing the matrix T using $\mathbf{ELZ}(T)$ algorithm produces decomposition $T = R_T U_T$, where R_T is reduced and U_T is invertible upper-triangular. Therefore, the complete decomposition is $D^{\mathcal{C}} = SR_T(U_T U)$, and Lemma 2 implies the claim. $\square$

Parallel setup. If we have p cover sets, i.e., $p = \operatorname{card} I$, then we can split the initial operations $\mathbf{ELZ}(D^i)$ and $\mathbf{Sparsify}(R^i)$ between p processors. The final reduction $\mathbf{ELZ}(T)$ can be performed by either one of them. If all the processors share the same memory, we may be satisfied with this solution, although we can perform a little more work in parallel, as explained in Section 5.

If the memory is distributed, the separate bits of information P^i and $S^i Q^i$, necessary for the final reduction, need to be brought to a single processor. In Section 5 we explain how this operation can be performed using a binary reduction. Meanwhile, we mention a simple, but important optimization: it suffices to send only those rows of P^i that are not zero in $S^i Q^i$; the rows that are zero in $S^i Q^i$ record the pairs that will not change.

4. CASCADE

So far it is unclear why we performed the seemingly unnecessary sparsification step, converting matrices R^i into matrices P^i. The sparsification is advantageous since it reduces the potentially quadratic size of matrices R^i down to the linear size of matrices P^i. In the distributed setting, this means less data to send to the processor responsible for the final reduction. But there is another advantage. The combined matrix T has a special sparsity pattern. This structure allows for a faster reduction even using the standard $\mathbf{ELZ}(T)$ algorithm. In addition, with a little extra work, presented in algorithm $\mathbf{Cascade}(T)$, Algorithm 3, we can preserve this structure throughout the computation and thus gain efficiency both in time and in space.

Suppose there are $n = \sum_{i \in I} \operatorname{card} K^i$ cells in the blowup complex that fall into the disjoint union, and there are m cells with higher-dimensional second factor, $m = \operatorname{card}\{\sigma \times J \mid \sigma \times J \in K^{\mathcal{C}}, \dim J > 0\}$. We assume $m < n$. Then reducing the matrix T using $\mathbf{ELZ}(T)$ algorithm takes, in the worst case, $\mathrm{O}(n^2 m)$ time and $\mathrm{O}(n^2)$ space. (The reason why the time complexity is tighter than $\mathrm{O}(n^3)$ is similar to the analysis in the proof of Theorem 7 below.)

The matrix T has special structure, see Figure 4. The n columns of the disjoint union are formed by matrices P^i,

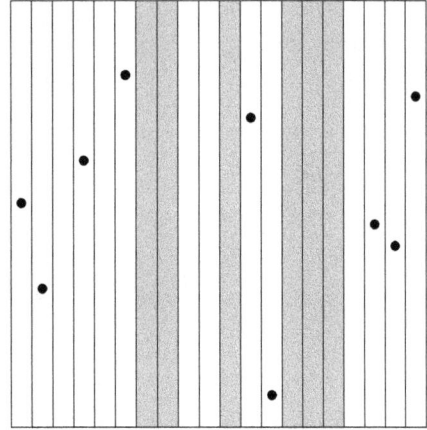

Figure 4: Structure of the matrix T prior to the reduction. Shaded columns are dense. The rest of the columns are ultra-sparse, they have at most one non-zero entry.

which have at most one non-zero entry per column. We call such columns *ultra-sparse*. The remaining m columns are *dense*. Given such a matrix, with n ultra-sparse columns and m dense columns, we can reduce it as follows.

We iterate over the rows of the matrix T from the bottom up, and consider the columns whose lowest ones fall into a given row. Let J be the set of their indices. At most one such column can be ultra-sparse because the matrices P^i are reduced. Let j denote the first column in the set J. We can subtract it from every other column in J. If one of those columns is ultra-sparse and column j is dense, then the ultra-sparse column becomes dense. To keep the number of dense columns constant, we subtract the current row (which after the column operations has a single non-zero in column j) from every other row with a non-zero entry in column j. In other words, we zero out column j, making it ultra-sparse. Algorithm 3 performs the described operations.

Since $\mathbf{Cascade}(T)$ performs operations from left to right and from bottom up, Lemma 2 immediately implies its correctness.

THEOREM 6. *Lowest ones of the matrix T reduced using $\mathbf{Cascade}(T)$ algorithm produce the correct pairing of the sequence of homology groups, $\mathsf{H}(K_0^{\mathcal{C}}) \to \ldots \mathsf{H}(K_n^{\mathcal{C}})$.*

What is the worst case complexity of $\mathbf{Cascade}(T)$?

THEOREM 7. $\mathbf{Cascade}(T)$ *algorithm reduces the matrix T with n ultra-sparse and m dense columns in time $\mathrm{O}(n^2 m)$, while keeping its size $\mathrm{O}(nm)$.*

PROOF. The initial number of nonzero elements in the matrix T is in $\mathrm{O}((n + m)m + n) = \mathrm{O}(nm)$. Since the number of dense columns is kept constant (or, more accurately, it never increases) thanks to the row operations that clear out column j, the space used during the cascade remains in $\mathrm{O}(nm)$.

It takes $\mathrm{O}(n + m)$ time to add two dense columns, or to add a dense column to a sparse column. How many such operations are there? At most m per row. There are $n + m$ rows, for a total of $\mathrm{O}((n + m)^2 m) = \mathrm{O}(n^2 m)$ operations. $\square$

Algorithm 3 Cascade algorithm for the reduction of the matrix T with ultra-sparse columns.

$\mathbf{Cascade}(T)$:

    for all rows $T[i, \cdot]$, from bottom up **do**

        J = columns with the lowest non-zero entry in row $T[i, \cdot]$

        $j = \min J$

        for all $j' \in J, j' > j$ **do**

            subtract $T[\cdot, j]$ from $T[\cdot, j']$

        for all $i' < i$ with $T[i, j] \neq 0$ **do**

            subtract $T[i, \cdot]$ from $T[i', \cdot]$ # zero out all but the lowest entry of column $T[\cdot, j]$

---

5. HIERARCHY

So far we have considered the case of a single cover of the domain, a collection of simplicial complexes $\mathcal{C} = \{K^i\}_I$ with domain $K = \bigcup \mathcal{C}$. But in many applications, it is natural to build a hierarchy of such covers. For example, if the domain K triangulates a cube or a flat torus (a cube with periodic boundary conditions), both exceedingly common scenarios for simulation data, one can build a refinement of covers following an oct-tree partition of the cube. The cubes at each level of the oct-tree become the cover sets. (Technically, the cover sets are the closures of the subcomplexes of K that intersect those cubes.)

Given such a hierarchy, it becomes possible to follow the standard reduction pattern and merge sets together in pairs (or, more generally, in small groups) and thus to extend the amount of useful work a processor can do. It also limits how many dense columns m a single processor has to handle at once. Consider the prototypical oct-tree example. If we have $p = 8^k$ processors and descend down to the k-th level in the tree, we end up with p cubes and $m = 3 \cdot 2^k \cdot c$ shared simplices, where c is the number of simplices in a side of the cube. On the other hand, if we merge the cubes in pairs (proceeding to a higher level in the oct-tree after each merge), m never exceeds c, the size of the initial cut that splits the domain into two.

We can abstract the hierarchical partition of an oct-tree as a nested collection of covers $\mathcal{C}_0, \mathcal{C}_1, \ldots$, such that $K = \bigcup \mathcal{C}_0 = \bigcup \mathcal{C}_1 = \ldots$ and every cover set $L^i \in \mathcal{C}_a$ is contained in exactly one cover set $K^j \in \mathcal{C}_{a-1}$, $L^i \subseteq K^j$.

Consider the structure of the boundary matrix for two consecutive levels in the cover, illustrated in Figure 5. Suppose at level $i + 1$ the cover consists of four sets, $\mathcal{C}_{i+1} = \{K^1, K^2, K^3, K^4\}$, and at level i the cover consists of two sets $\mathcal{C}_i = \{K^1 \cup K^2, K^3 \cup K^4\}$. The procedure outlined in Sections 3 and 4 would operate independently on the matrices D^1, D^2, D^3, and D^4 (on four different processors). The first two results would then be combined by first performing row updates on the matrices Q^1 and Q^2, then reordering the matrix and reducing it using the **Cascade** algorithm. The second pair of results would be combined similarly. The two combined matrices contain the same information as the reduced boundary matrices R^{12} and R^{34} for the cover sets $K^1 \cup K^2$ and $K^3 \cup K^4$ at level i. We could proceed with the algorithm at level i, with one caveat: the higher rows (the second to last column in the figure) involved in the combination did not get updated during the execution of **Sparsify** and **Cascade** algorithms. The fix is straight-forward: when processing any given level of the cover, we perform the row operations on the full rows, rather than on their restriction to the given level. The only information necessary to construct

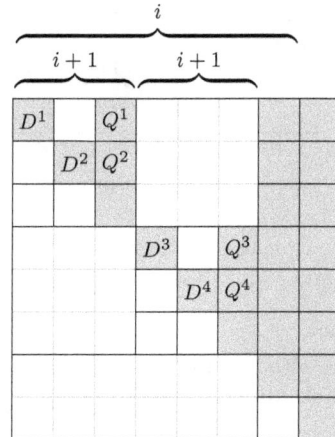

Figure 5: The structure of the boundary matrix for three consecutive levels of the hierarchy.

such rows is knowing which sets of the cover contain any given simplex.

6. EXPERIMENTS

We have implemented the described algorithm on top of MPI, and ran a strong scaling experiment on Edison supercomputer at the National Energy Research Scientific Computing Center (NERSC). Edison is a Cray XC30 system; its individual compute nodes have 24 Intel 'Ivy Bridge' processor cores, at 2.4 GHz, with 64KB and 256KB of L1 and L2 cache, respectively; the 24 cores share 64GB of RAM.

Our input is a snapshot of a combustion simulation, a $256^2 \times 512$ scalar field. The input simplicial complex is a Freudenthal triangulation of the grid, with $\sim 870 \cdot 10^6$ simplices. It is covered hierarchically via an oct-tree.

Figure 6 summarizes the running times (wallclock as reported by the PBS job resource manager). Going from 8 to 32 processes we see a near perfect scaling, with another improvement by a factor of ~ 1.5 going from 32 to 64 processes. But then the returns diminish rapidly. The behavior is not surprising: past 64 processes the binary reduction used to merge different cover sets is top-heavy, i.e., it's dominated by the merge of the information from the final two sets. As a result, adding more processes only speeds up the initial computation, which is already plenty fast.

What is worse is what the figure does not show. We have tried our code on larger data sets, but ran out of memory because the merge reduction is dominated by its final stages. Although the $(n + m)$ term in the space analysis of the **Cascade** algorithm is a gross worst-case overestimate, the

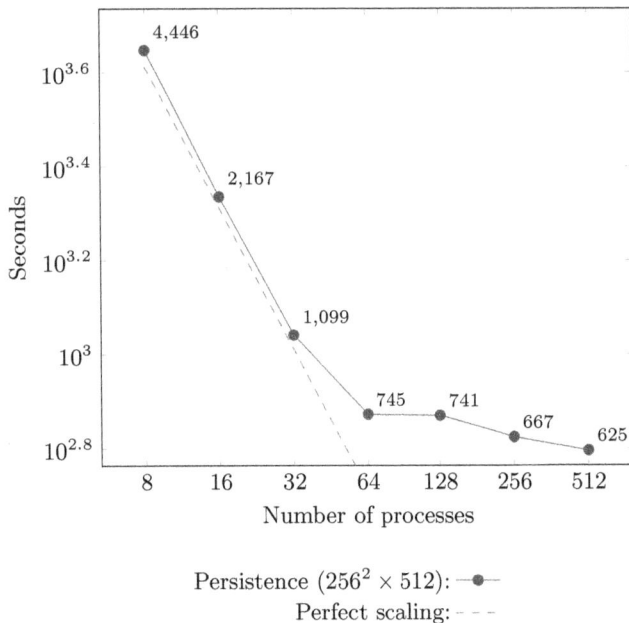

Figure 6: Times to compute persistence diagram for the $256^2 \times 512$ combustion data set.

growth of this term does follow the growth of n, the size of the domain, in many practical examples. So our technique does not solve the memory limitations of the persistence algorithm for the large data sets. We address this issue in the next section.

7. CONCLUSION

Despite the evident limitation of a merge reduction, we believe our theoretical results have a place as building blocks of a practical parallel persistence algorithm. In particular, an interesting (and, we believe, promising) research direction is combining the domain decomposition approach of our paper with the spectral sequence algorithm [28, 21]. One could initially distribute the data with respect to a domain decomposition: often such a distribution is either very cheap to compute, or entirely free in the cases when the data is supplied already decomposed directly from a simulation code, or it is stored decomposed (for I/O-efficiency). In this case, much processing could be performed on the individual chunks of the data; this part of our algorithm scales perfectly. Then, when combining the individual results, one could redistribute the remaining matrix (the input to the **Cascade** algorithm) with respect to the diagonal block partition of the spectral sequence algorithm. This way we could limit the space needed on any given processor.

Another important research topic is adapting our algorithm to the computation of persistent cohomology. Although the resulting pairing is the same, algorithms that keep track of cocycles rather than cycles have been reported to perform significantly better in practice [17, 18]. On the other hand, they are built around tracking the matrix U^{-1} in the $D = RU$ decomposition, while the algorithm that we've presented depends on manipulating the matrix R.

Similarly, it would be fruitful to understand the relationship of our algorithm to various practical optimizations [20].

Unexpectedly to us, the original optimization [1] that removes negative simplices from the columns of the matrix R cannot be used in our context. The reason is that a simplex that is negative in the filtration of a cover subcomplex K^i may be positive in the filtration of the entire space K. On the other hand, if a simplex creates a cycle in the filtration of K^i (i.e., it is positive), it must be positive in the filtration of the entire K. Thus the clearing optimization of Chen and Kerber [19] is readily applicable.

Acknowledgements

We gratefully acknowledge the use of the resources of the National Energy Research Scientific Computing Center (NERSC). The authors wish to thank Wes Bethel for his support. This work was supported by Advanced Scientific Computing Research, Office of Science, U.S. Department of Energy, under Contract DE-AC02-05CH11231.

8. REFERENCES

[1] HERBERT EDELSBRUNNER, DAVID LETSCHER, AND AFRA ZOMORODIAN. Topological Persistence and Simplification. *Proceedings of the Annual Symposium on Foundations of Computer Science*, pages 454–463, 2000. *Discrete and Computational Geometry*, **28**:511–533, 2002.

[2] AFRA ZOMORODIAN AND GUNNAR CARLSSON. Computing Persistent Homology. *Discrete and Computational Geometry*, **33**:249–274, 2005.

[3] FRÉDÉRIC CHAZAL, LEONIDAS J. GUIBAS, STEVE Y. OUDOT, PRIMOŽ ŠKRABA. Persistence-Based Clustering in Riemannian Manifolds. *Journal of the ACM*, **60**, 2013.

[4] VIN DE SILVA, DMITRIY MOROZOV, MIKAEL VEJDEMO-JOHANSSON. Persistent Cohomology and Circular Coordinates. *Discrete and Computational Geometry*, **45**:737–759, 2011.

[5] ROBERT D. MACPHERSON AND BENJAMIN SCHWEINHART. Measuring Shape with Topology. *Journal of Mathematical Physics*, **53**, 2012.

[6] RIEN VAN DE WEYGAERT ET AL. Alpha, Betti and the megaparsec Universe: on the topology of the cosmic web. *Trans. Comput. Sci. XIV*, pages 60–101, 2011.

[7] DAVID COHEN-STEINER AND HERBERT EDELSBRUNNER. Inequalities for the curvature of curves and surfaces. *Foundations of Computational Mathematics*, **7**:391–404, 2007.

[8] GUNNAR CARLSSON, TIGRAN ISHKHANOV, VIN DE SILVA, AFRA ZOMORODIAN. On the Local Behavior of Spaces of Natural Images. *International Journal of Computer Vision*, **76**:1–12, 2008.

[9] HERBERT EDELSBRUNNER AND JOHN HARER. Persistent homology — a survey. *Surveys on Discrete and Computational Geometry. Twenty Years Later.*, pages 257–282, 2008.

[10] HERBERT EDELSBRUNNER AND DMITRIY MOROZOV. Persistent homology: theory and practice. *Proceedings of European Congress of Mathematics*, pages 31–50, 2012.

[11] ROBERT GHRIST. Barcodes: The persistent topology of data. *Bulletin of the American Mathematical Society*, **45**:61–75, 2007.

[12] SHMUEL WEINBERGER. What is... Persistent Homology? *Notices of the American Mathematical Society*, **58**:36–39, 2011.

[13] GUNNAR CARLSSON. Topology and data. *Bulletin of the American Mathematical Society*, **46**:255–308, 2009.

[14] NIKOLA MILOSAVLJEVIĆ, DMITRIY MOROZOV, AND PRIMOŽ ŠKRABA. Zigzag persistent homology in matrix multiplication time. *Proceedings of the Annual Symposium on Computational Geometry*, pages 216–225, 2011.

[15] HERBERT EDELSBRUNNER AND SALMAN PARSA. On the computational complexity of Betti numbers: reductions from matrix rank. *Proceedings of the Annual Symposium on Discrete Algorithms*, pages 152–160, 2014.

[16] CHAO CHEN AND MICHAEL KERBER. An output-sensitive algorithm for persistent homology. *Computational Geometry: Theory and Applications*, **46**:435–447, 2013.

[17] VIN DE SILVA, DMITRIY MOROZOV, MIKAEL VEJDEMO-JOHANSSON. Dualities in Persistent (Co)Homology. *Inverse Problems*, **27**, 2011.

[18] JEAN-DANIEL BOISSONNAT, TAMAL K. DEY, CLÉMENT MARIA. The Compressed Annotation Matrix: An Efficient Data Structure for Computing Persistent Cohomology. *Proceedings of European Symposium on Algorithms*, pages 695–706, 2013.

[19] CHAO CHEN AND MICHAEL KERBER. Persistent Homology Computation With a Twist. *Proceedings of the European Workshop on Computational Geometry*, 2011.

[20] ULRICH BAUER, MICHAEL KERBER, JAN REININGHAUS. Clear and Compress: Computing Persistent Homology in Chunks. *Topological Methods in Data Analysis and Visualization III*, pages 103-117, 2014.

[21] ULRICH BAUER, MICHAEL KERBER, JAN REININGHAUS. Distributed Computation of Persistent Homology. *Proceedings of Algorithm Engineering and Experiments (ALENEX)*, 2014.

[22] GUNNAR CARLSSON, VIN DE SILVA, DMITRIY MOROZOV. Zigzag Persistent Homology and Real-valued Functions. *Proceedings of the Annual Symposium on Computational Geometry*, pages 247–256, 2009.

[23] DAVID LIPSKY, PRIMOŽ ŠKRABA, MIKAEL VEJDEMO-JOHANSSON. A spectral sequence for parallelized persistence. arXiv:1112.1245, 2011.

[24] AFRA ZOMORODIAN AND GUNNAR CARLSSON. Localized Homology. *Computational Geometry: Theory and Applications*, **41**:126–148, 2008.

[25] RYAN H. LEWIS AND AFRA ZOMORODIAN. Multicore Homology via Mayer Vietoris. arXiv:1407.2275, submitted to *Computational Geometry: Theory and Applications*, 2014.

[26] DMITRIY MOROZOV AND GUNTHER WEBER. Distributed Merge Trees. *Proceedings of the Annual Symposium on Principles and Practice of Parallel Programming*, pages 93–102, 2013.

[27] DAVID COHEN-STEINER, HERBERT EDELSBRUNNER, AND DMITRIY MOROZOV. Vines and Vineyards by Updating Persistence in Linear Time. *Proceedings of the Annual Symposium on Computational Geometry*, pages 119–126, 2006.

[28] HERBERT EDELSBRUNNER AND JOHN HARER. *Computational Topology: an Introduction*. AMS Press, 2010.

[29] ALLEN HATCHER. *Algebraic Topology*. Cambridge University Press, 2002.

[30] GRAEME SEGAL. Classifying spaces and spectral sequences *Publications Mathématiques de l'Institut des Hautes Études Scientifiques*, **34**:105–112, 1968.

Self-Stabilizing Repeated Balls-into-Bins [*]

Luca Becchetti
"Sapienza" Università di Roma
becchetti@dis.uniroma1.it

Andrea Clementi
Università di Roma "Tor Vergata"
clementi@mat.uniroma2.it

Emanuele Natale
"Sapienza" Università di Roma
natale@di.uniroma1.it

Francesco Pasquale
Università di Roma "Tor Vergata"
pasquale@mat.uniroma2.it

Gustavo Posta
"Sapienza" Università di Roma
gustavo.posta@mat.uniroma1.it

ABSTRACT

We study the following synchronous process that we call *repeated balls-into-bins*. The process is started by assigning n balls to n bins in an arbitrary way. Then, in every subsequent round, one ball is chosen according to some fixed strategy (random, FIFO, etc) from each non-empty bin, and re-assigned to one of the n bins uniformly at random. This process corresponds to a non-reversible Markov chain and our aim is to study its *self-stabilization* properties with respect to the *maximum (bin) load* and some related performance measures.

We define a configuration (i.e., a state) *legitimate* if its maximum load is $O(\log n)$. We first prove that, starting from any legitimate configuration, the process will only take on legitimate configurations over a period of length bounded by *any* polynomial in n, *with high probability* (w.h.p.). Further we prove that, starting from *any* configuration, the process converges to a legitimate configuration in linear time, w.h.p. This implies that the process is self-stabilizing w.h.p. and, moreover, that every ball traverses all bins in $O(n \log^2 n)$ rounds, w.h.p.

The latter result can also be interpreted as an almost tight bound on the *cover time* for the problem of *parallel resource assignment* in the complete graph.

Categories and Subject Descriptors

F.2 [**Theory of Computation**]: Analysis of Algorithms and Problem Complexity.

General Terms

Theory, Algorithms.

---

[*]Partially supported by Italian MIUR-PRIN 2010-11 Project *ARS TechnoMedia* prot. *2010N5K7EB* and the EU FET Project *MULTIPLEX* 317532.

SPAA'15, June 13–15, 2015, Portland, OR, USA.
Copyright © 2015 ACM 978-1-4503-3588-1/15/06 ...$15.00.
DOI: http://dx.doi.org/10.1145/2755573.2755584.

Keywords

Balls into Bins, Self-Stabilizing Systems, Markov Chains, Parallel Resource Assignment.

1. INTRODUCTION

We study the following *repeated balls-into-bins* process. Given any $n \geqslant 2$, we initially assign n balls to n bins in an arbitrary way. Then, at every round, from each non-empty bin one ball is chosen according to some strategy (random, FIFO, etc) and re-assigned to one of the n bins uniformly at random. Every ball thus performs a sort of *delayed* random walk over the bins and the delays of such random walks depend on the size of the bin queues encountered during their paths. It thus follows that these random walks are correlated. We study the impact of such correlation on the maximum load.

Inspired by previous concepts of (load) stability [1,8], we study the *maximum load* $M^{(t)}$, i.e., the maximum number of balls inside one bin at round t and we are interested in the largest $M^{(t)}$ achieved by the process over a period of *any polynomial* length. We say that a configuration is *legitimate* if its maximum load is $O(\log n)$ and a process is *stable* if, starting from any legitimate configuration, it only takes on legitimate configurations over a period of poly(n) length, w.h.p. We also investigate a probabilistic version of self-stabilization [14]: we say that a process is *self-stabilizing*[1] if it is stable and if, moreover, starting from *any* configuration, it converges to a legitimate configuration, w.h.p. The *convergence time* of a self-stabilizing process is the maximum number of rounds required to reach a legitimate configuration starting from any configuration. This natural notion of (probabilistic) self-stabilization has also been inspired by that in [21] for other distributed processes.

Stability has consequences for other important aspects of this process. For instance, if the process is stable, we can get good upper bounds on the *progress* of a ball, namely the number of rounds the ball is selected from its current bin queue, along a sequence of $t \geqslant 1$ rounds. Furthermore, we can eventually bound the *parallel* cover time, i.e., the time required for every ball to visit *all* bins. Self-stabilization has also important consequences when the system is prone to some transient faults [14,15,24].

---

[1]We observe that the probabilistic version of self-stabilization adopted here is different from the one introduced in [15], the latter being unsuitable in our context.

To the best of our knowledge, the repeated balls-into-bins process was first studied in [7] where it is used there as a crucial sub-procedure to optimize the message complexity of a gossip algorithm in the complete graph. The previous analysis in [7,17] (only) holds for very-short (i.e. logarithmic) periods, while the analysis in [5] considers periods of arbitrary length but it (only) allows to achieve a bound on the maximum load that rapidly increases with time: after t rounds, the maximum load is w.h.p. bounded by $O(\sqrt{t})$. By adopting the FIFO strategy at every bin queue, the latter result easily implies that the progress of any ball is w.h.p. $\Omega(\sqrt{t})$. Moreover, it is well known that the cover time for the single-ball process is w.h.p. $\Theta(n \log n)$ (it is in fact equivalent to the *coupon's collector* process [28]). These two facts easily imply an upper bound $O(n^2 \log^2 n)$ for the parallel cover time of the repeated balls-into-bins process.

Previous results are thus not helpful to establish whether this process is stable (or, even more, self-stabilizing) or not. Moreover, the previous analyses of the maximum load in [5,7,17] are far from tight, since they rely on some rough approximations of the studied process via other, much simpler Markov chains: for instance, in [5], the authors consider the process - which clearly dominates the original one - where, at every round, a new ball is inserted in every empty bin. Clearly, that analysis does not exploit the global invariant (a fixed number n of balls) of the original process.

Our Results. We provide a new, tight analysis of the repeated balls-into-bins process that significantly departs from previous ones and show that the system is self-stabilizing. These results are summarized in the following

THEOREM 1. *Let c be an arbitrarily-large constant, and let the process start from any legitimate configuration. The maximum load $M^{(t)}$ is $O(\log n)$ for all $t = O(n^c)$, w.h.p. Moreover, starting from any configuration, the system reaches a legitimate configuration within $O(n)$ rounds, w.h.p.*

Our result above strongly improves over the best previous bounds [5,7,17] and it is almost tight (since we know that maximum load is $\Omega(\log n / \log \log n)$ at least during the first rounds [29]). Moreover, the progress of any ball (by adopting the FIFO strategy) over a sequence of $t = \mathrm{poly}(n)$ rounds is $\Omega(t / \log n)$ w.h.p. and, thus, the parallel cover time is $O(n \log^2 n)$ which is only a $\log n$ factor away from the lower bound arising from the single-ball process.

Besides having *per-se* interest, balls-into-bins processes are used to model and analyze several important randomized protocols in parallel and distributed computing [4,6,31]. In particular, the process we study models a natural randomized solution to the problem of *(parallel) resource (or task) assignment* in distributed systems (this problem is also known as *traversal*) [26,30]. In the basic case, the goal is to assign one resource in mutual exclusion to *all* processors (i.e. nodes) of a distributed system. This is typically described as a *traversal* process performed by a *token* (representing the resource or task) over the network. The process terminates when the token has visited all nodes of the system. Randomized protocols for this problem [11] are efficient approaches when, for instance, the network is prone to faults/changes and/or when there is no global labeling of the nodes.

A simple randomized protocol is the one based on *random walks* [11,20,21]: starting from any node, the token performs a random walk over the network until all nodes are visited,

w.h.p. The first round in which all nodes have been visited by the token is called the *cover time* of the random walk [11,25]. The expected cover time for general graphs is $O(|V| \cdot |E|)$ (see for example [28]).

In distributed systems, we often are in the presence of *several* resources or tasks that must be processed by every node *in parallel*. This naturally leads to consider the parallel version of the basic problem in which n different tokens (resources) are initially distributed over the set of nodes and every token must visit all nodes of the network. Similarly to the basic case, an efficient randomized solution is the one based on (parallel) random walks. In order to visit the nodes, every token performs a random walk under the constraint that every node can process and release at most one token per round. Again, maximum load is a critical complexity measure: for instance, it can determine the required buffer size at every node, bounds on the token progress and, thus, on the parallel cover time.

It is easy to see that, when the graph is complete, the above protocol - based on parallel random walks - is in fact equivalent to the repeated balls-into-bins process analyzed in this paper. For this case, Theorem 1 implies that, every token visits all nodes of the system with at most a logarithmic delay w.r.t. the case of a single token: so, we can derive an upper bound $O(n \log^2 n)$ for the parallel cover time, starting from *any* initial configuration.

We can also consider the adversarial model in which, in some *faulty* rounds, an adversary can re-assign the tokens to the nodes in an arbitrary way. The self-stabilization and the linear convergence time shown in Theorem 1 imply that the $O(n \log^2 n)$ bound on the cover time still holds provided the faulty rounds happen with a frequency not higher than cn, for a sufficiently large constant c.

Related Work.

- *Random Walks on Graphs.* As mentioned earlier, the repeated balls-into-bins process was first considered in [5,7,17], since it describes the process of performing parallel random walks in the (uniform) gossip model (also known as random phone-call model [12,22]) when every message can contain at most one token. Maximum load (i.e. node congestion), token delays, mixing and cover times are here the most crucial aspects. We remark that the flavor of these studies is different from ours: indeed, their main goal is to keep maximum load and token delays logarithmic over some *polylogarithmic period*. Their aim is to achieve a fast mixing time for every random walk in the case of good expander graphs. In particular, in [7], a logarithmic bound is shown for the complete graph when $m = O(n / \log n)$ token random walks are performed over a logarithmic time interval. A similar bound is also given for some families of almost-regular random graphs in [17]. Finally, a new analysis is given in [5] for regular graphs yielding the bound $O(\sqrt{t})$.

- *Parallel Computing.* Balls-into-bins processes have been extensively studied in the area of parallel and distributed computing, mainly to address balanced-allocation problems [6,27,29], PRAM simulation [23] and hashing [13]. The most studied performance measure is the *maximum load*. In order to optimize the total number of random bin choices used for the allocation, further allocation strategies have been proposed and analyzed (see for instance [9,27,31]). As previously mentioned, our concept of stability is inspired by those studied in [1,8]. In such works, load balancing algorithms are analyzed in scenarios where new tasks arrive during the run of the system, and existing jobs are executed by the processors and leave the system. Another adversarial model for a sequential balls-into-bins process has been studied in [3]. We remark that, in the above previous works, the goal is different from ours: each ball/task must be allocated to *one, arbitrary* bin/processor. This crucial difference makes such previous analyses of little use to the purpose of our study.

- *Queuing Theory*. To the best of our knowledge, the closest model to our setting in classical queuing theory is the *closed Jackson network* [2]. In this model, time is continuous and each node processes a single token among those in its queue; processing each token takes an exponentially distributed interval of time. As soon as its processing is completed, each token leaves the current node and enters the queue of a neighbor chosen uniformly at random. Notice that, since time is continuous, the process' events are sequential, so that the associated Markov chain is much simpler than the one describing our parallel process. In particular, the stationary distribution of a closed Jackson network can be expressed as a product-form distribution. It is noted in [19] that "[...] virtually all of the models that have been successfully analyzed in classical queuing network theory are models having a so-called product form stationary distribution". Because of the above considerations regarding the difficulty of our process (especially the non-reversibility of its Markov chain), the stationary distribution is instead very likely not to exhibit a product-form distribution, thus laying outside the domain where the techniques of classical queuing theory seem effective. We finally cite the seminal work [10] on *adversarial queuing systems*: here, new tokens (having specified source and destination nodes) are inserted in the nodes according to some adversarial strategy and a notion of *edge-congestion* stability is investigated.

2. SELF-STABILIZATION

Overview of the analysis

In the repeated balls-into-bins process, every bin can release at most one ball per round. As a consequence, the random walks performed by the balls delay each other and are thus correlated in a way that can make the bin queues larger than in the independent case. Indeed, intuitively speaking, a large load observed in a bin in some round makes "any" ball more likely to spend several future rounds in that bin, because if the ball ends up in that bin in one of the next few rounds, it will undergo a large delay. This is essentially the major technical issue to cope with.

The previous approach in [5] relies on the fact that, in every round, the expected balance between the number of incoming and outgoing balls is always non-positive for every non-empty bin (notice that the expected number of incoming balls is always at most one). This may suggest viewing the process as a sort of parallel *birth-death* process [25]. Using this approach and with some further arguments, one can (only) get the "standard-deviation" bound $O(\sqrt{t})$ in [5]. Our new analysis proving Theorem 1 proceeds along three main steps.

i) We first show that, after the first round, the aforementioned expected balance is always negative, namely, not larger than $-1/4$. Indeed, the number of empty bins remains at least $n/4$ with (very) high probability, which is extremely

useful since a bin can receive tokens only from non-empty bins. This fact is shown to hold starting from *any* configuration and over any period of polynomial length.

ii) In order to exploit the above negative balance to bound the load of the bins, we need some strong concentration bound on the number of balls entering a specific bin u along any period of polynomial size. However, it is easy to see that, for any fixed u, the random variables $\{Z_u^{(t)}\}_{t \geqslant 0}$ counting the number of balls entering bin u are not mutually independent, neither are they negatively associated, so that we cannot apply standard tools to prove concentration. To address this issue, we consider a simpler repeated balls-into-bins process defined as follows.

THE TETRIS PROCESS. Starting from any configuration with at least $n/4$ empty bins, in each round
- from every non-empty bin we pick one ball and we throw it away, and
- we pick exactly $(3/4)n$ *new balls* and we put each of them independently and u.a.r. in one of the n bins.

Using a coupling argument and our previous upper bound on the number of empty bins, we prove that the maximum number of balls accumulating in a bin in the original process is not larger than the maximum number of balls accumulating in a bin in the TETRIS process, w.h.p.

iii) The TETRIS process is simpler than the original one since, at every round, the number of balls assigned to the bins does not depend on the system's state in the previous round. Hence, random variables $\{\hat{Z}_u^{(t)}\}_{t \geqslant 0}$ counting the number of balls arriving at bin u in the TETRIS process are mutually independent. We can thus apply standard concentration bounds. On the other hand, differently from the approximating process considered in [5], in the TETRIS process, the negative balance of incoming and outgoing balls proved in Step i) still holds, thus yielding a much smaller bound on the maximum load than that in [5].

In the remainder of this section, we formally describe the above three steps.

Preliminaries and notations

We always use capital letters for random variables, lower case for quantities, and bold for vectors. For each bin $u \in [n]$ let $\mathcal{Q}_u^{(t)}$ be the r.v. indicating the number of balls, i.e. the *load*, in u at round t. We write $\mathbf{Q}^{(t)}$ for the vector of these random variables, i.e., $\mathbf{Q}^{(t)} = \left(\mathcal{Q}_u^{(t)} : u \in [n] \right)$. We write $\mathbf{q} = (q_1, \ldots, q_n)$ for a *(load) configuration*, i.e., $q_u \in \{0, 1, \ldots, n\}$ for every $u \in [n]$ and $\sum_{u=1}^n q_u = n$. In order to enhance readability, in what follows we omit the indication of the round, when it is clear from context, e.g., we write $\mathbf{E}[\mathcal{Q}_u \mid \mathbf{q}]$ for $\mathbf{E}\left[\mathcal{Q}_u^{(t+1)} \mid \mathbf{Q}^{(t)} = \mathbf{q} \right]$.

On the number of empty bins

We next show that the number of *empty* bins is a constant fraction of n for a very large time-window, w.h.p.

LEMMA 2. *Let* $\mathbf{q} = (q_1, \ldots, q_n)$ *be a configuration in a given round and let* X *be the random variable indicating the number of empty bins in the next round. For any large enough* n, *it holds that*

$$\mathbf{P}\left(X \leqslant \frac{n}{4} \right) \leqslant e^{-\alpha n},$$

where α *is a suitable positive constant.*